FUNDAMENTAL
ACCOUNTING
PRINCIPLES

FOURTEENTH EDITION

FUNDAMENTAL
ACCOUNTING
PRINCIPLES

FOURTEENTH EDITION

KERMIT D. LARSON
University of Texas–Austin

Contributing Author

BARBARA CHIAPPETTA
Nassau Community College

IRWIN

Chicago • Bogotá • Boston • Buenos Aires • Caracas
London • Madrid • Mexico City • Sydney • Toronto

*D*edicated to
Nancy, Julie, Tim, Cindy, Albrecht, and Megan

Cover image: Stuart Simons
© Richard D. Irwin, a Times Mirror Higher Education Group, Inc. company, 1955, 1959, 1963, 1966, 1969, 1972, 1975, 1978, 1981, 1984, 1987, 1990, 1993, and 1996

Irwin Book Team

Executive editor:	Jeff Shelstad
Developmental editors:	Margaret Haywood, Jackie Scruggs, Stephen Isaacs
Marketing manager:	Cindy L. Ledwith
Production supervisor:	Bob Lange
Assistant manager, desktop services:	Jon Christopher
Assistant manager, graphics	Charlene R. Breeden
Photo researcher:	Keri Kunst
Project editor:	Denise Santor-Mitzit
Designer:	Heidi J. Baughman
Graphics supervisor:	Heather D. Burbridge
Compositor:	York Graphic Services, Inc.
Typeface:	10/12 Times Roman
Printer:	Von Hoffmann Press, Inc.

Times Mirror
Higher Education Group

Library of Congress Cataloging-in-Publication Data

Larson, Kermit D.
    Fundamental accounting principles/Kermit D. Larson,
    with contributions by Barbara Chiappetta.—14th ed.
       p.   cm.
    Includes index.
    ISBN 0-256-19645-1 0-256-17842-9 (F.A.S.T. edition)
    1. Accounting. I. II. Chiappetta, Barbara.
  III. Title.
  HF5635.P975   1996
  657—dc20   95–20806

Printed in the United States of America
2 3 4 5 6 7 8 9 0 VH 2 1 0 9 8 7 6

About the Author

Kermit D. Larson is the Arthur Andersen & Co. Alumni Professor of Accounting Emeritus at The University of Texas at Austin. He served as chairman of the U.T. Department of Accounting and was Visiting Associate Professor at Tulane University. His scholarly articles have been published in a variety of journals, including *The Accounting Review, Journal of Accountancy,* and *Abacus.* He is the author of several books, including *Financial Accounting* and *Fundamentals of Financial and Managerial Accounting,* both published by Richard D. Irwin, Inc.

Professor Larson is a member of The American Accounting Association, the Texas Society of CPAs, and the American Institute of CPAs. His activities with the AAA have involved serving as Vice President, as Southwest Regional Vice President, and as chairperson of several committees, including the Committee on Concepts and Standards. He was a member of the committee that planned the first AAA Doctoral Consortium and served as its Director.

Professor Larson currently is President of the Richard D. Irwin Foundation. His other activities have included serving on the Accounting Accreditation Committee and on the Accounting Standards Committee of the AACSB. He was a member of the Constitutional Drafting Committee of the Federation of Schools of Accountancy and a member of the Commission on Professional Accounting Education. He has been an expert witness on cases involving mergers, antitrust litigation, consolidation criteria, franchise taxes, and expropriation of assets by foreign governments. Professor Larson served on the Board of Directors and Executive Committee of Tekcon, Inc., and on the National Accountants Advisory Board of Safe-Guard Business Systems. In his leisure time, he enjoys skiing and is an avid sailor and golfer.

About the Contributing Author

Barbara Chiappetta received her BBA in Accounting and MS in Education from Hofstra University and is a tenured full professor at Nassau Community College. For the past 14 years she has been an active Executive Board member of the Teachers of Accounting at Two-Year Colleges (TACTYC), serving ten years as Vice President and currently as the President since the fall of 1993. As an active member of the American Accounting Association, she has served as a Northeast Regional Representative of the Two-Year Section, is currently a member of the Northeast Region Steering Committee, and continues to chair (for the third year) the Curriculum Revision Committee for the Two-Year Section. Chiappetta co-chaired the Curriculum Revision Project at Nassau Community College. She received the Dean of Instruction's Faculty Distinguished Achievement Award in the spring of 1995.

Ms. Chiappetta has two sons, Michael and David, and both will be celebrating graduations in 1996. Michael, a Colgate University graduate, will receive his law degree from USC, and David will graduate from Syracuse University. Her husband, Robert, is an entrepreneur in the leisure sport industry. Barbara enjoys downhill skiing; she is also an avid tennis player and plays on a USTA team. Barbara also enjoys the challenge of duplicate and tournament bridge.

Contents in Brief

Preface

The 14th edition has changed *Fundamental Accounting Principles* in many important ways. Extensive input obtained through surveys, focus groups, reviewers, and personal correspondence has driven the revision plan. Instructors confirm several trends that are affecting the world of accounting. The trends most prevalent in accounting education today include the demand for change, the visual orientation of students, the need for flexibility and innovation in the classroom, new pedagogy, and the impact of technology. The many changes that have been integrated throughout this revision are in response to these trends.

To emphasize the business orientation of this edition, the text incorporates a variety of features that expose students to real-world situations and show the relevance of the material to real decisions. These features include the following:

EXTENSIVE INTEGRATION OF COMPANY EXAMPLES

- Several actual company references in each chapter describe how the companies have applied the concepts being discussed. Typically, each reference is accompanied by a photo that draws attention to the nature of the business or the specific company.

If **TYCO Toys, Inc.'s** management made the preceding comparison, the resulting figures might motivate them to investigate how this compares to last year and how they could improve this ratio. Continuation of a financially sound business requires continuous monitoring of the liquidity of the firm's assets.

- End-of-chapter questions relate to the financial statements of Apple Computer, Inc.; Ben & Jerry's Homemade, Inc.; and Federal Express Corporation. These statements are provided in appendixes to the book. Apple Computer, Inc., serves as the basis for a Financial Statement Analysis Case in most chapters. Other chapters draw on the Apple Computer annual report for a managerial decision case or managerial analysis problem.

- An actual company scenario at the beginning of each chapter implicitly or explicitly raises questions related to the material covered in the chapter. Later in the chapter, one or more references show how the ideas being explained at that point apply to the company described in the chapter opening. Even before students read a chapter, they realize from the opening scenarios that what they will be learning is useful in solving real problems.

- The financial statements of Microsoft Corporation are used throughout Chapter 17 as a basis for discussing financial statement analysis. In this way, we emphasize the relevance of the discussion to actual decision situations.
- This edition continues the practice of having several chapters incorporate boxed quotations and biographical sketches of persons in business, accounting, and public service. In addition to providing role models for students, these individuals explain how the information in the chapter is relevant to their decision-making situations. This feature is called "As a Matter of Opinion."

As a Matter of Opinion

Diana Scott is a graduate of Wittenberg University. She worked for Price Waterhouse in its national office in New York before joining the FASB staff as a project manager in 1985. After leaving that position in 1991, she joined the management consulting firm of Towers Perrin in Chicago, where she is an accounting and financial consultant in the Technical Services Group.

Over the past several years, accountants have begun to pay much more attention to the potential future payments that businesses may be obligated to make as a result of current operations.

The standard requires them to provide information about their obligations and to recognize the expenses for probable future payments.

Are there other obligations that we presently ignore but someday may have to recognize as liabilities? I would not be surprised. One that comes to mind is potential claims from injuries to product users. Some juries have given large awards many years after a product was sold. Another possible liability is the cost of cleaning up toxic wastes discarded before anyone was aware of the danger.

Diana J. Scott, CPA

Instructors and reviewers have uniformly called for a new commitment to show students the relevance of accounting information and to teach them how to use the information. The Accounting Education Change Commission also has emphasized the importance of this approach. In response, this revision places much greater emphasis on the use of accounting information by managers, business owners, lenders, and other interested parties.

This shift in focus has been accomplished while maintaining the appropriate goal of showing students how the information is developed. Too often, the importance of this understanding to managers and other nonaccountant decision makers has been overlooked or dismissed. By gaining an introductory understanding of the processes by which accounting information and reports are generated, future decision makers learn the limits of accounting information. They learn to avoid overstating or misinterpreting the information. Thus, they are less apt to confuse such things as book values and market values, accumulated depreciation and spendable funds, or product costs and variable costs.

In every chapter, students learn and practice how to use accounting information in evaluating companies and making decisions. For example, "Using the Information" sections in the financial accounting chapters gradually expand students' understanding of financial ratios and other forms of analysis. Some of the Using the Information topics are:

Debt ratio—Chapter 2

Business segment information—Chapter 6

Return on total assets—Chapter 11

Price-earnings ratio—Chapter 14

Cash flow analyses—Chapter 16

INCREASED FOCUS ON USING ACCOUNTING INFORMATION

After studying this and the previous chapters, you have learned about all of the important classes of assets that businesses own. Recall from Chapter 10 that in evaluating the efficiency of a company in using its assets, a ratio that is often calculated and reviewed is total asset turnover. Another ratio that provides information about a company's efficiency in using its assets is **return on total assets.** You can calculate the return on total assets with this formula:

$$\text{Return on total assets} = \frac{\text{Net income}}{\text{Average total assets}}$$

For example, **Reebok International,** a worldwide distributor of sports and fitness products, earned a net income of $222.4 million during 1993. At the beginning of 1993, Reebok had total assets of $1,345.3 million, and at the end of the year total assets were $1,391.7 million. If the average total assets owned during the year is approximated by averaging the beginning and ending asset balances, Reebok's return on total assets for 1993 was:

USING THE INFORMATION— RETURN ON TOTAL ASSETS

LO 5

Explain the use of return on total assets in evaluating a company's efficiency in using its assets.

In Chapter 17, we review and discuss the relationships between all of the ratios using the annual report from Microsoft Corporation as a basis for discussion. We also discuss vertical and horizontal analyses and the use of other financial disclosures. The cost and managerial chapters continue this increased emphasis on using accounting information in decision making.

Several changes in this edition are intended to motivate students and help them study more effectively.

CHANGES TO PROMOTE STUDENT MOTIVATION AND STUDY TIME EFFECTIVENESS

A Shorter, Less Imposing Book

Perhaps the most obvious improvement in the new edition is that it is a more stream-lined book. This was accomplished by new restrictions on topical coverage, a renewed emphasis on concise writing, a new design, and the publication of the alternate problems in a separate booklet available at no extra charge. We believe *Fundamental Accounting Principles* is a text students will look forward to reading and be happy to carry—to class and to study groups.

Integrated Progress Checks with Answers

Progress Check

(Answers to Progress Checks are provided at the end of the chapter.)

2-1   **Which of the following are examples of accounting source documents?** *(a)* **Journals and ledgers;** *(b)* **Income statements and balance sheets;** *(c)* **External transactions and internal transactions;** *(d)* **Bank statements and sales tickets;** *(e)* **All of the above.**

2-2   **What kinds of economic events affect a company's accounting equation?**

2-3   **Why are business papers called source documents?**

A new feature in this edition is a series of Progress Checks integrated in each chapter. These review questions generally follow the discussion related to a learning objective. Occasionally, Progress Checks are presented more frequently. The goal is to have students stop momentarily and reflect on whether they should spend more time studying a given section of the text before moving on. Answers to the Progress Check questions are provided at the end of each chapter.

Pervasive Demonstration of Real-World Relevance

Motivation is typically stimulated by a reminder that the matter under study is truly relevant to life. *Fundamental Accounting Principles* brings these reminders in a variety of ways. For example, marginal notes in several chapters describe how an accounting principle being explained at that point is applied by a widely recognized company. The integration of the opening chapter scenarios with later portions of the chapters serves a similar purpose, as does the extensive use of actual company examples.

PRINCIPLE APPLICATION
Matching Principle, p. 108
In 1993, J.C. Penney Company had retail sales of $18,983 million. In addition to bad debt expenses, the credit costs the company matched with these revenues included operating expenses and third-party credit costs of $260 million.

In the last two entries, notice that the credit card expense was not recorded until cash was received from the credit card company. This practice is merely a matter of convenience. By following this procedure, the business avoids having to calculate and record the credit card expense each time sales are recorded. Instead, the expense related to many sales can be calculated once and recorded when cash is received. However, the *matching principle* requires reporting credit card expense in the same period as the sale. Therefore, if the sale and the cash receipt occur in different periods, you must accrue and report the credit card expense in the period of the sale by using an adjusting entry at the end of the year. For example, this year-end adjustment accrues $24 of credit card expense on a $600 receivable that the Credit Card Company has not yet paid.

Concept Testers

To encourage additional study of important glossary terms, selected chapters conclude the assignment material with a *concept tester* in the form of a short crossword puzzle. These puzzles are supported by the Working Papers.

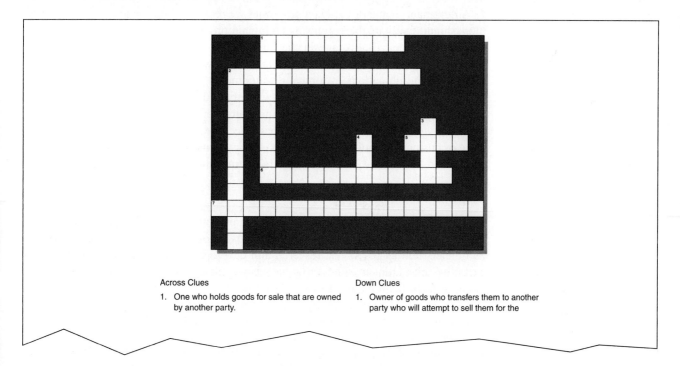

Across Clues
1. One who holds goods for sale that are owned by another party.

Down Clues
1. Owner of goods who transfers them to another party who will attempt to sell them for the

Some instructors have described today's students as the MTV generation. Increased exposure to television, computer screens, and movies has honed a visual orientation that influences how students learn most effectively. This edition has been designed with this visual orientation in mind. The design is intended to capture and hold the students' attention.

VISUAL ORIENTATION

Use of Color

Conscious, deliberate thought and effort have gone into the use of color to add more interest and appeal to the book. More importantly, color is used as a code to aid in learning. Blue indicates financial statements and reports that provide accounting information to be used in decision making. The primary documents that accountants generate for themselves as they develop informative statements and reports are green. Finally, documents that serve as sources of the data that go into accounting reports are yellow.

Other Visual Tools

Several other elements will also capture the students' interest via visual concepts. Crossword puzzles at the end of several chapters serve as an excellent method to reinforce verbal learning with a visual tool. Photographs of events and companies help show students how accounting fits into the real world. Supplementary videos make it possible for students to study accounting using television. PowerPoint software programs combine words and illustrations on one computer screen that students will enjoy being exposed to in a classroom environment.

FLEXIBILITY FOR INNOVATION

A common topic of discussion among introductory accounting instructors is the conflict between the extensive nature of traditional topical content and the need for new emphases on using accounting information in decision making, developing critical thinking, enhancing communication skills, and working in groups. Instructors clearly need more flexibility to innovate and develop an appropriate integration of these goals.

A dominant theme of the extensive input we received from instructors was that authors should facilitate these goals by taking a more proactive role in limiting the depth and range of topical coverage in the introductory accounting course. The clear imperative is that the text should reverse the trend toward being a complete resource for all possible combinations of topical development.

As a result, in close contact with reviewers and other instructors, we have taken numerous steps to avoid technical matters better left to intermediate level courses. In addition, we have deleted topics that have become less relevant in the changing climate of business practices. Instead, this edition focuses on the relevant topics that students need to know to be effective users of financial information.

Expanded Prologue

An important change in this direction was to prepare an expanded Prologue that now describes the accounting function in the context of other organizational functions such as finance, human resources, research and development, production, marketing, and executive management. The Prologue also explains the work accountants do, accounting certifications, the fields in which accountants work, and the pervasive importance of ethics in accounting. This accomplishes two basic improvements: First, as a separate learning unit, the Prologue emphasizes the overall importance of these topics to an understanding of the role accounting plays in providing information to a variety of decision makers. Instructors who want to give more attention to these topics, as suggested by the AECC, will find the Prologue especially appealing.

Financial Statement Orientation of Chapter 1

Second, as a result of the Prologue revision, Chapter 1 is now a much shorter and more manageable learning unit with a clear focus on financial statements. This includes the information contained in the statements, the basic concepts that guide the development and use of accounting information, and the relationship of the statements to the transactions and events in the life of a business.

Deletions in Chapters 4 and 5

Reviewers and adopters have overwhelmingly encouraged limiting the early examples in the book to proprietorships. As a result, the discussion of corporations has been deleted from Chapter 4 and from the illustrations in Chapter 5. Corporations are considered in the early chapters only as necessary to support student interaction with the financial statements at the back of the book and to recognize the existence of alternative forms of business organization.

Work sheets now are presented as an *optional* step in the accounting cycle. However, we also describe several reasons why an understanding of work sheets is useful. In addition, a more concise discussion of the adjusting entry method of accounting for inventories has eliminated the need for a separate appendix at the end of Chapter 5.

Discounting Notes Receivable

The revision of Chapter 8 recognizes the fact that an increasing number of companies routinely convert their receivables into cash without waiting to receive customer payments. In dealing with this modern business practice, the discussion of discounting notes receivable has been replaced with a more general examination of the various ways receivables may be converted into cash.

Topics Related to Inventories

Because perpetual inventory records are rarely maintained on a LIFO basis, LIFO has been deleted from the discussion of perpetual inventories in Chapter 9. Also, the discussion of lower of cost or market has been simplified to avoid the details of considering ceiling and floor limits on market value. Finally, the treatment of markups and markdowns has been eliminated from the discussion of the retail inventory method. Reviewers agree that all of these topics are better left to intermediate level courses.

Topics Related to Property, Plant, and Equipment

Sum-of-the-years' digits has been deleted from the discussion of accelerated depreciation, as has the apportioning of accelerated depreciation between accounting periods. To help students appreciate the differences between financial accounting and tax accounting, we continue to discuss MACRS. However, the discussion has been condensed to exclude the calculations that underlie MACRS tax rate tables. We also eliminated the discussions of plant asset subsidiary records and tax rules that govern plant asset exchanges.

Consolidated Financial Statements

Adopters indicate that the consolidated statements chapter in prior editions was the one they most frequently omitted. Nevertheless, long-term investments are an important financial consideration in evaluating many companies. The answer was to eliminate the consolidated statements chapter and to develop a more balanced set of asset chapters. As a result, Chapter 11 completes the asset coverage by discussing natural resources, intangible assets, and long-term investments. The long-term investments portion naturally concludes with a discussion of investments in international operations.

Leases and Deferred Income Tax Liabilities

In Chapter 12, the discussion of leases has been significantly shortened. Students learn the differences between capital and operating leases without having to journalize the entries related to capital leases. Also, the appendix on deferred income taxes has been deleted as a technical issue better left to intermediate level courses. The appendix on payroll records has been moved to the back of the book.

Streamlined Coverage of Partnerships

Reviewers and focus group participants suggested that we compress the coverage of partnerships. In response, we have streamlined the discussion and combined it with the introductory discussion of corporations in Chapter 13. This eliminated the separate chapter on partnerships.

Deletion of Cash Flows Appendix and Direct Method Worksheet

In explaining cash flows from operating activities in Chapter 16, we first explain the direct method, which is most relevant to managerial evaluations and predictions. However, the direct method work sheet has been deleted. We then explain the indirect method as the dominant method used in financial reporting. This approach eliminates the need for a separate appendix dealing with the indirect method.

Segmental Reporting

The illustration and discussion of segmental reporting has been eliminated from Chapter 17. However, a short section at the close of Chapter 6 recognizes that operating in several business segments complicates the design of the accounting system. Then, the use of business segment information by decision makers is briefly discussed.

Integrated Coverage of Mark-to-Market Accounting (*SFAS 115*)

The issuance of *SFAS 115* represents an accounting milestone in its break from the traditional cost and lower-of-cost-or-market bases of reporting. As a result, we incorporate this new development in several sections of the book. These include short-term investments in Chapter 8, long-term investments in Chapter 11, and alternative valuation methods in Appendix D.

Expanded Coverage of Activity-Based Costing

The practice of managerial accounting in United States industry continues to undergo a wide range of significant changes. Among these, the increasing implementation of activity-based costing systems is particularly noticeable. Accordingly, the introductory coverage of activity-based costing in Chapter 21 has been expanded in this new edition.

Emphasis on New Teaching Methods

The instructor's Fully Annotated Support for Teaching (F.A.S.T.) Edition of the text contains suggested ways of using selected problem assignments as the basis for group projects. Each chapter includes at least one group project suggestion. The group projects help students learn the skill of working effectively in teams and also encourage more active student participation in the classroom.

In addition to the hardcover version of the text, the first 12 chapters and the last 13 chapters are available in separate softcover versions that include Working Papers. A variety of special packaging and/or custom publishing options also is available depending on the unique needs of each school. Consult your Irwin representative for details.

A new supplement, *Student Learning Tools* (with an accompanying instructor's manual), is designed to facilitate both the development of interpersonal skills and a conceptual approach with a user emphasis. The introduction is aimed at motivating the student to participate by developing an understanding of the need for and the value of active learning. Tips for writing and recommended research/writing projects are also included.

END-OF-CHAPTER MATERIAL

The 14th edition includes several improvements in the end-of-chapter material. Many of these improvements have been added in response to calls for change from the AECC.

Enhanced Emphasis on Critical Thinking, Analysis, and Communication Skills

The assignment material in the book has been completely revised. Many assignments have been reoriented to increase the emphasis on critical thinking and communication skills. For example, the requirements for selected problems in each chapter now include a *Preparation Component* and a separate *Analysis Component.*

The Analysis Component generally requires students to think about the financial statement consequences of alternative situations. Students learn to consider the consequences of alternatives and the resulting effects on their interpretation of the results. This complements the more usual preparation component of end-of-chapter assignments.

Analysis component:

2. In comparing the results of the three alternatives, how would they change if MDI had been experiencing declining prices in the acquisition of additional inventory?

3. What specific advantages and disadvantages are offered by using LIFO and by using FIFO assuming the cost trends given at the beginning of this problem?

In addition, a new category of assignments is described as Critical Thinking: Essays, Problems, and Cases. Typical assignments in this category are:

Analytical Essays—Students evaluate a situation such as alternative facts related to another problem assignment and express their findings in writing.

Business Communication Cases—Students prepare a variety of correspondence items such as letters to customers, memoranda of record, or internal letters of explanation.

Financial Reporting Problems—Students examine the factual situation of a company and determine the financial statement consequences of alternative procedures.

Managerial Analysis Problems—Students analyze accounting information from the perspective of nonaccountant managers.

Financial Statement Analysis Cases—Students extract and interpret information from the financial information contained in Apple Computer Inc.'s annual report.

Management Decision Cases—Students assume the role of nonaccountant managers and use accounting information to reach various business decisions.

Ethical Issues Essays—Students are asked to consider the ethical implications of the "As A Matter of Ethics" cases presented in the chapters and express their personal conclusions regarding the appropriate actions that should be taken.

CRITICAL THINKING: ESSAYS, PROBLEMS, AND CASES

On March 26, Summerfield Office Supply received Miles Brokaw's check number 629, dated March 24, in the amount of $1,420. The check was to pay for merchandise Brokaw had purchased on February 25. The merchandise was shipped from Summerfield's office at 1715 Westgate Boulevard, Austin, Texas, 78704 to Brokaw's home at 823 Congress, Austin, Texas, 78701. On March 27, Summerfield's cashier deposited the check in the company's bank account. The bank returned the check to Summerfield with the March 31 bank statement. Also included was a debit memorandum indicating that Brokaw's check was returned for nonsufficient funds and the bank was charging Summerfield a $25 NSF processing fee. Immediately after reconciling

Business Communications Case

(LO 5)

Also, a number of the exercises and problems require students to think analytically by working "backward" from outputs to inputs or by analyzing the consequences of errors or omissions.

Instructors indicate an increasing reliance on shorter problem material for use as in-class illustrations and as homework assignments. Undoubtedly, the prospect of solving problems in a short time and the rapid feedback of having done so successfully are motivating factors that lead students to extend their study efforts. Accordingly, this edition contains a new category of very short exercises that are identified as Quick Study. At least one quick study is provided for each learning objective.

QUICK STUDY (Five-Minute Exercises)

QS 10–1
(LO 1)

Explain the difference between *(a)* plant assets and long-term investments; *(b)* plant assets and inventory; and *(c)* plant assets and current assets.

QS 10–2
(LO 1)

Mattituck Lanes installed automatic score-keeping equipment. The electrical work required to prepare for the installation was $12,000. The invoice price of the equipment was $120,000. Additional costs were $2,000 for delivery and $8,400, sales tax. During the installation, a component of the equipment was damaged because it was carelessly left on a lane and hit by the automatic lane cleaning machine during a daily maintenance run. The cost of repairing the component was $1,500. What is the cost of the automatic scorekeeping equipment?

THE IMPACT OF TECHNOLOGY

An increasing number of schools are moving toward multimedia education and a more interactive learning environment. Inevitably, this is a gradual process that requires a great deal of evaluation and reassessment along the way. Initial attempts to incorporate new technologies nearly always require modification and readjustment before the most effective applications are discovered. In light of these facts, the goal of our author-publisher team has been, and continues to be, to facilitate and encourage but not dictate the nature of the changes implemented by our adopters.

Given this objective, we have attempted to lead with technological innovations during the last two editions of *Fundamental Accounting Principles.* In 1990, for example, we began to offer the Telecourse option, teaming with Kirkwood Community College in Cedar Rapids, Iowa, to promote distance learning and interactive, telecommunicating options. In 1993, we offered the first CD-ROM version of an accounting principles package. This included the full text and all supporting supplemental material.

Further innovation is scheduled for this new edition. New *multimedia practice sets* will give the students a portable, exciting learning environment. Our new PowerPoint *Ready Slides, Ready Shows,* and *Ready Notes* give the instructor and student increased flexibility for classroom instruction and student retention. We also offer *computerized practice sets* covering a variety of companies and situations. Our *GLAS* and *SPATS* software provide unusually flexible general ledger and spreadsheet applications in both a DOS and Windows format.

Acknowledgments

We are grateful for the encouragement, suggestions, reviews, and counsel provided by students, colleagues, and instructors from across the nation. A tremendous amount of useful information was gained from the participants in the nationwide *Fundamental Accounting Principles* focus groups organized by the publisher. They include:

Ron Beckman
Sam Houston State University

Frank Beil
Lincoln University

Clifford Bellers
Washtenaw Community College

Kathy Bent
Cape Cod Community College

Lucille Berry
Webster University

Rick Bowden
Oakland Community College,
Auburn Hills

Sheila Bradford
Tulsa Junior College, Metro

Stewart Brown
Bristol Community College

Carol Buchl
Northern Michigan University

Robert Carpenter
Eastfield College

Janet Cassagio
Nassau Community College

Bruce Cassel
Dutchess Community College

Barbara Chiappetta
Nassau Community College

Sue Cook
Tulsa Junior College, S.E.

Jim Cosby
John Tyler Community College

Doris deLespinasse
Adrian College

Pam Dinville
Bellevue College

Irene Douma
Montclair State College

Bill Engel
Longview Community College

Mike Foland
Belleville Community College

Linda Frye
NW Missouri State University

Kathy Gardner
Johnson & Wales University

Mike Garms
Henry Ford Community College

John Godfrey
Springfield Technical Community College

Glenn Goodale
Castleton State College

Robert Gronstal
Metro Community College

Margie Hamilton
Lewis and Clark Community College

Robert Hardin
Henry Ford Community College

Linda Herrington
Community College of Alleghany County

Bob Hildenbrand
Albuquerque TVI, Main

Bob Holman
Longview Community College, Blue Springs Campus

Patty Holmes
Des Moines Area Community College

Zach Holmes
Oakland Community College

Susan Honig
Herbert Lehman College

Gloria Jackson
San Antonio College

Doug Johnson
Southeast Community College

George Katz
San Antonio College

Randy Kidd
Penn Valley Community College

Tom Knoll
DeVry Institute of Technology

Frank Korman
Mountain View College

Robert Landry
Massasoit Community College

Cathy Larson
Middlesex Community College

Douglas Larson
Salem State College

Paul Lospennato
Northshore Community College

Nancy Lynch
West Virginia University

Andrea Murowski
Brookdale Community College

Paul Nieman
Sanford Brown College

Vincent Osaghae
Chicago State University

Reed Peoples
Austin Community College, Rio Grande

Pat Prugh
East Central College

Allan Rabinowitz
Pace University, NYC

Michael Raff
Prince Georges Community College

Alan Rainford
Greenfield Community College

George Ritchey
Harrisburg Community College

Nancy Ruhe
West Virginia University

Helena Ruhl
Three Rivers Community College

Marilyn Scheiner
Montgomery College, Rockville

James Skidmore
Grand Rapids Community College

Dan Small
J. Sargeant Reynolds Community College

Charles Spector
SUNY, Oswego

Linda Spotts-Michael
Maple Woods Community College

Mary Ston
Oakland Community College

Kathy Tam
Tulsa Junior College, N.E.

Leslie Thysell
John Tyler Community College

John Vaccaro
Bunker Hill Community College

Cynthia Vest
Tarrant County Junior College

Joe Webster
TVI-Montoya

Kathleen Wessman
Montgomery College, Rockville

Jeff Wright
Johnson County Community College

Marilyn Young
Tulsa Junior College, S.E.

Those who reviewed various portions of the manuscript or participated in our in-depth survey were especially helpful. They include:

John Aheto
Pace University

Rodger Brannan
University of Minnesota, Duluth

Harvey J. Cooke
Penn Valley Community College

S.T. Desai
Cedar Valley College

Kayla Fessler
Oklahoma City Community College

George Gardner
Bemidji St. College

Bonnie Givens
Avila College

Frank Korman
Mountain View College

Linda Lessing
SUNY College of Technology, Farmingdale

Noel McKeon
Florida Community College, Jacksonville

Linda Spotts-Michael
Maple Woods Community College

Dick Schneider
Winona State

Sara Sadon
Evergreen College

Mary Ston
Oakland Community College

Al Taccone
Dean Junior College

Dick Wasson
Southwestern College, Chula Vista

Jane Wiese
Valencia Community College

I particularly want to thank Barbara Chiappetta of Nassau Community College for her participation in *Fundamental Accounting Principles.* Thanks also to Debra Smith of the University of Puget Sound and to Barbara Schnathorst for their important contributions. I am especially indebted to Paul Miller of the University of Colorado, Colorado Springs, whose previous work and continued counsel have helped shape this and future editions. Finally, I will always be grateful for Betsey Jones and Sue Ann Meyer, whose talents and dedication were essential to this project.

SUPPLEMENTS THAT SUPPORT THE TEXT

Fundamental Accounting Principles is supported by a full range of supplements. They include:

FAST HINT
Alternative Example:
If the fair values of these investments on December 31 was $70,000, what entry would be made?
Answer:
Unrealized Holding
  Gain (Loss)   3,000
    Long-Term Invest.,
    Fair Value
    Adjustments   3,000

	Book Value	Fair (Market) Value
Candice Corp. bonds payable	$30,000	$29,050
Intex Corp. common stock, 500 shares	43,000	45,500
Total	$73,000	$74,550

- *Fully Annotated Support for Teaching Edition.* Marginal annotations labeled Fast Hints have been expanded. We continue to include Important Points to Remember, Critical Thought Questions, and Alternative Examples. New to this edition are Additional Insights, Class Discussion Issues, Relevant Exercises, Group Projects, and Relevant Quick Studies.

- *Solutions Manuals.* The solutions manuals contain completely revised solutions for all assignment material. The solutions manuals are available in a new electronic format in both Lotus and Excel.
- *Working Papers.* These volumes include papers for the Exercises, the Problems or Alternate Problems, the Comprehensive Problems, the Serial Problem, and the Concept Testers.
- *Study Guides.* For each chapter and appendix, these guides review the learning objectives and the summaries, outline the topical coverage, and provide a variety of practice problems with solutions.
- *Student Learning Tools.* Written by Barbara Chiappetta, this supplement contains material for students' use in an active learning environment. The materials coordinate with the active learning applications or lessons described in the accompanying instructor's manual. For instructors who additionally address preparation/procedural issues, accounting forms (journal paper, 2 and 3 column paper, and T accounts) are provided for reproduction. Working papers for selected problems from *Fundamental Accounting Principles* are also provided.
- *Instructor's Manual for Student Learning Tools.* This manual illustrates how to use a traditional text and meet the objectives set forth by the Accounting Education Change Commission. The approach employs a concept and user focus. Specific applications using active learning techniques, coordinated with *Student Learning Tools,* are provided. The manual was designed to provide instructors with the materials necessary to create an active learning environment to facilitate the development of interpersonal skills. Active learning strategies and structures, group formation, and assessment techniques are discussed. Visuals coordinated with the applications are available in the form of PowerPoint displays or acetate teaching transparencies.
- *Alternate Problems.* A booklet containing alternate problems is available. Updated yearly, this booklet is free of charge for adopters.
- *Practice Sets.* These give the student practice with the procedures presented in the text. There are several practice sets accompanying this book:

    Fast Mart, Inc. Provides a narrative of transactions and features a retail corporation.

    Cog Hill Camping Equipment Company. A practice set involving a sole proprietorship that includes business papers for a retailing company.

    Republic Lighting Company. A narrative of transactions for a sole proprietorship; it illustrates special journals and includes a work sheet for a retailing company.

    Republic Lighting Company: Extended Version. This is similar to Republic Lighting Company above, but covering two accounting periods.

    KJC Manufacturers, Inc. A narrative of transactions featuring a manufacturing company.

    Freewheel Corporation. A narrative of transactions for a corporate practice set with special journals.

- *Computerized Practice Sets.* From Leland Mansuetti and Keith Weidkamp, both of Sierra College, these computerized practice sets are available in DOS and Windows versions; they offer an alternative to manual sets.

    Granite Bay Jet Ski, Level One. This package simulates a single proprietorship involved in the sales, service, and storage of Kawasaki Jet Ski personal watercraft and other watercraft equipment. It is intended for use after coverage of the accounting cycle and accounting for cash.

    Granite Bay Jet Ski, Level Two. This adds a corporate level to the business presented in Level One. It is intended for use after coverage of depreciation of plant and equipment, current and long-term liabilities, and corporations.

    Thunder Mountain Snowmobile. Comparable to Granite Bay Jet Ski, Level One; the two sets may be alternated to provide variety each semester.

Gold Run Snowmobile, Inc. Comparable to Granite Bay Jet Ski, Level Two; the two sets may be alternated to provide variety each semester.

Wild Goose Marina, Inc. This offers a complete corporate simulation using a business that generates revenue through new and used houseboat sales, accessory sales, service sales, and moorage fees. It is intended for use after coverage of stocks, bonds, and cash flows.

Ramblewood Manufacturing, Inc. This package introduces students to job order cost accounting with a company that specializes in customized fencing. This full corporation simulation is intended for use after coverage of job order cost accounting.

- *Multimedia Practice Sets.* These incorporate sound and video into our best-selling Mansuetti and Weidkamp sets. These new alternatives could provide a more dynamic learning environment for your students.

- *Real World Accounting Series.* These practice sets from Timothy Louwers and William Pasewark offer students hands-on experience in analyzing and understanding corporate annual reports. They show the big picture at the end of the accounting process, emphasizing interpretation and analysis rather than preparation of financial statements.

  Athletronics, Inc. This practice set emphasizes the effect of generally accepted accounting principles on decisions based on accounting data. The student is required to perform financial analysis on the data contained in the manual.

  Shoe Business, Inc. This humorous yet realistic practice set focuses on the frequent overemphasis of bottom-line net income by investors. The student is led through extensive analysis of footnote disclosures, financial ratios, and bankruptcy prediction models.

  Understanding Corporate Annual Reports. This practice set contains instructions for obtaining an annual report from a publicly traded corporation.

- *Testbank.* The testbank contains a wide variety of test questions, including true-false, multiple-choice, quantitative, matching, and essay questions of varying levels of difficulty.

- *Computest.* A computerized version of the manual testbank for more efficient use is available in Macintosh, Windows, or DOS versions. The extensive features of this test generator program include random question selection based on the user's specification of learning objectives, type of question, and level of difficulty.

- *Teletest.* By calling a toll free number, users can specify the content of exams and have laser printed copies of the exams mailed to them.

- *Achievement Tests.* These are available in quantity to adopters. A solutions guide is included with each packet.

- *GLAS (General Ledger Applications Software).* This revised package contains most of the features of commercial accounting software, yet is easily used by students with little or no computer background. A large number of problem assignments are preloaded on the package, and it can be used to solve any problem that calls for journal entries. Both DOS and Windows versions are available.

- *SPATS (Spreadsheet Applications Template Software).* This includes Lotus 1–2–3 (or the equivalent) templates for selected problems and exercises from the text. The templates gradually become more complex, requiring students to build a variety of formulas. What-if questions are added to show the power of spreadsheets and a simple tutorial is included. Instructors may request a free master template for students to use or copy, or students can buy shrinkwrapped versions for a nominal fee. Both DOS and Windows versions are available.

- *Tutorial Software.* Multiple-choice, true-false, journal entry review, and glossary review questions are randomly accessed by students. Explanations of right and wrong answers are provided and scores are tallied. Instructors may request a free master template for students to use or copy, or students can buy shrinkwrapped versions for a nominal fee. Both DOS and Windows versions are available.

- *Solutions Transparencies.* These transparencies are set in large, boldface type to maximize their effectiveness in large classrooms.

- *Ready Shows, Ready Slides, Ready Notes.* These teaching enhancement packages were prepared by Jon A. Booker, Charles W. Caldwell, Susan C. Galbreath, and Richard S. Rand, all of Tennessee Technological University.

   Ready Shows. This is a package of multimedia lecture enhancement aids that uses PowerPoint software to illustrate chapter concepts.

   Ready Slides. These selected four-color teaching transparencies are printed from the PowerPoint Ready Shows.

   Ready Notes. This booklet of Ready Show screen printouts enables students to take notes during Ready Show or Ready Slide presentations.

- *Lecture Enhancement Video Series.* These short, action-oriented videos provide the impetus for lively classroom discussion. The *Financial Accounting Video Library* includes videos with the Financial Accounting Standards Board, Ben & Jerry's, and a video with Art Wyatt discussing the impact of the International Accounting Standards Committee. The *Managerial Accounting Video Library* includes videos featuring George Bush at the Baldrige Award ceremony, on-site footage from manufacturers such as Ford, and service corporations such as First National Bank of Chicago.

- *Lecture Review Videos.* This completely updated video series, produced in conjunction with Kirkwood Community College, provides a complete review by topic for those students who may miss a class or struggle with a topic. Sixty-five tapes, each one approximately 15 minutes in length, provide a complete review of *Fundamental Accounting Principles,* 14th edition.

Kermit D. Larson

Contents

Appendixes

To the Student

Fundamental Accounting Principles is designed to get you actively involved in the learning process so you will learn quickly and more thoroughly. The more time you spend expressing what you are learning, the more effectively you will learn. In accounting, you do this primarily by answering questions and solving problems. But this is not the only way to learn. You also can express your ideas by using the book's wide margins for taking notes, summarizing a phrase, or writing down a question that remains unanswered in your mind. Ideas that pop into your head can lead to fruitful exploration. These notes will assist in your later review of the material, and the simple process of writing them will help you learn.

To guide your study, *learning objectives* are listed near the beginning of each chapter. Read these objectives to form some expectations about what you will learn from studying the chapter. Think of them as your goals while you study. Each learning objective is repeated in the margin at the point the chapter begins to provide material related to that objective. You will find each objective repeated at the end of each chapter in the summary. The exercises and problem assignments following each chapter also are coded to these objectives.

As you progress in your study of each chapter, you will periodically encounter Progress Check questions relating to the material you have just studied. Answer the questions and compare your answers with the correct answers at the end of each chapter. If you are not able to answer the questions correctly, review the preceding section of the chapter before going on.

Several features of the text emphasize the real-world usefulness of the material in the book. For example, the *opening paragraphs* of each chapter raise questions about a real business. As you progress through the chapter, keep a sharp eye out for points in the discussion that apply to the scenario in the opening paragraphs. Also be aware of *photographs* in the text that locate instances where the material under discussion is applied to a real company. You also will find brief inserts entitled "As a Matter of Opinion" in which business and community leaders tell how they use accounting in making decisions.

The use of color in the book has been carefully planned to facilitate your learning. For example, the **financial statements** and **reports** that accounting provides as information to be used in decision making are blue. The **primary documents that accountants generate for their own use** as they develop informative statements and reports are green. **Documents that serve as sources of the data** that go into an accounting system are yellow.

As you read the text, you will learn many important new terms. These **key terms** are printed in **black boldface** the first time they appear, and they are listed again in a *glossary* after each chapter. In addition, you can find these key terms in the index at the end of the book. As a reinforcement to learning, but also as a light break from regular study, several chapters close with a *crossword puzzle* that involves some of the glossary terms.

Computer technology is changing the way businesses operate and will continue to be a driving force in the 21st century. To reflect this change and to give you practice with software, some of the assignments in the book are preloaded on a general ledger software package called *GLAS*. The following logo identifies these assignments:

In addition, some of the problem assignments are preloaded on a set of computer spreadsheet templates called *SPATS*. These assignments are identified with the following logo:

Ask your instructor or check your school's bookstore for information about other supplemental items that are available to assist your study. The *tutorial software* contains multiple-choice, true-false, journal entry review, and glossary review questions to help you prepare for exams. The *study guide* reviews learning objectives and provides practice problems for each chapter. *Working papers* provide familiarity with the actual framework used in creating accounting information.

Accounting can be an informative, relevant, and engaging field of inquiry. *Fundamental Accounting Principles* offers many tools to lead you into an understanding of the importance of accounting. Read, discuss, and enjoy! What you learn in this course will be useful in your personal and professional affairs for the rest of your life.

Your Introduction to Business, Accounting, and Ethics

Lisa Jarrett and Brad Wilson are recent graduates of Johnson Community College in Kansas City. Shortly before they graduated, Jarrett approached Wilson with a proposal to start a new business together. Jarrett's idea was to seek contracts with companies in the Kansas City area to provide a shuttle service for employees to and from the Kansas City airport. Jarrett already had received tentative commitments from three companies and had discussed financing the purchase of a van with a local bank. Wilson agreed with the plan and they soon began operations using the business name JW Shuttle.

Jarrett and Wilson agreed that since Jarrett had the original idea and had done a substantial amount of the work to get started, Jarrett should receive 75% and Wilson 25% of any income the business earned during its first year of operations. After the first year, each would receive 50%. The business expanded more rapidly than expected and, near the end of the first year, they sought the advice of an accountant to determine how much income had been earned.

The accountant, who is Wilson's close relative, understands that the amount of income reported in the first year depends on the methods used to measure the income. More precisely, the total income for the first two years will include $30,000 that will either be recognized in the first year or the second year, depending on accounting method used. Based on projections through the end of the second year, the following table shows the results of the two alternatives:

	First Year	Second Year	Total
Using Method A:			
Reported income	$40,000	$40,000	$80,000
Allocation to Jarrett and Wilson:			
Jarrett (75% and 50%)	30,000	20,000	50,000
Wilson (25% and 50%)	10,000	20,000	30,000
Using Method B:			
Reported income	$10,000	$70,000	$80,000
Allocation to Jarrett and Wilson:			
Jarrett (75% and 50%)	7,500	35,000	42,500
Wilson (25% and 50%)	2,500	35,000	37,500

LEARNING OBJECTIVES

After studying the Prologue, you should be able to:

1. **Describe the main purpose of accounting and its role in organizations.**
2. **Describe the external role of accounting for organizations.**
3. **List the main fields of accounting and the activities carried on in each field.**
4. **State several reasons for the importance of ethics in accounting.**
5. **Define or explain the words and phrases listed in the prologue glossary.**

What goes on in business and other organizations? How are their activities carried out? Who is responsible for them? And, what part does accounting play? This prologue answers these questions and explains why your study of accounting is important even if you are not planning to be an accountant. You also learn about different kinds of accountants and the work they do. Finally, we consider the great importance of ethics in business and accounting.

ACCOUNTING AND ITS ROLE IN ORGANIZATIONS

LO 1

Describe the main purpose of accounting and its role in organizations.

The main purpose of **accounting** is to provide useful information to people who make rational investment, credit, and similar decisions.[1] Because accountants serve decision makers by providing them with financial information that helps them make better decisions, accounting is often described as a service activity. Decision makers who use accounting information include present and potential investors, lenders, managers, suppliers, customers, and other users.

Accounting is used to provide information about all profit-oriented businesses. Accountants also provide information about nonprofit organizations such as churches, hospitals, museums, schools, and various government agencies. The people who use accounting information about nonprofit organizations include their managers and people who donate to or pay taxes to them, who use their services, or who otherwise work with them. Whether you are planning to be an accountant, an employee, a manager within an organization, or an external user of the information, your knowledge of accounting will help you achieve more success in your career.

WHAT GOES ON IN ORGANIZATIONS?

Illustration PR–1 shows the major activities of businesses that manufacture and sell products. Businesses such as airlines and express delivery companies that sell services have similar activities. So do governmental and nonprofit organizations. The following paragraphs describe these functions in more detail.

Finance. Every organization needs money to operate and grow. Organizations use money to acquire equipment, buildings, vehicles, and financial holdings. The finance function has the task of planning how to obtain money from such sources as payments from customers, loans from banks, and new investments from owners. Government organizations acquire cash by collecting taxes and fees, while nonprofit organizations acquire most of their cash from contributions by donors. In preparing plans, the finance department identifies and evaluates alternative sources of funds. In addition, finance analyzes alternative investment opportunities to identify which to take and which to reject.

Human Resources. All organizations require efforts from people. As a result, employees must be located, screened, hired, trained, compensated, promoted, and counseled. And, they may be released from employment by being retired or laid off. The human resources function is responsible for handling these tasks. In large companies, literally hundreds of employees may be engaged in looking after the other employees.

---

[1]Financial Accounting Standards Board, *Statement of Financial Accounting Concepts No. 1,* "Objectives of Financial Reporting by Business Enterprises" (Norwalk, CT, 1978), par. 34.

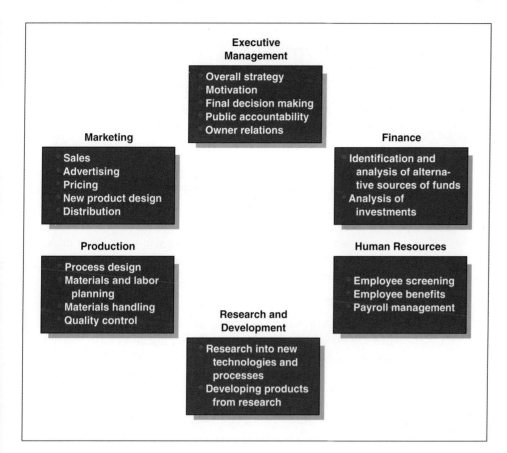

Illustration PR-1
Activities within an Organization

Research and Development. All organizations need to find new ways to meet the needs of their customers and others. Thus, research into new technologies and products or services is essential. This may be as simple as testing a new recipe for pizza or as complex as creating a more powerful computer. Once research is completed, the development process uses the new knowledge to design or modify specific products or services. If organizations are to survive, this function is essential.

Production. Many companies produce and then sell goods to their customers. Producing these goods requires planning and coordinating many specific activities. These activities include designing the production process, acquiring materials used in production, and selecting the workers' skills to be applied. In addition, materials handling systems must be in place to ensure that raw materials and finished goods are delivered on time. Production management also requires paying a great deal of attention to the quality of the goods. Similar activities in retail and service organizations ensure that quality merchandise and services are delivered to consumers.

Marketing. Companies can sell goods and services only if customers are willing to buy them. Marketing provides customers information about goods and services and encourages their purchase. This includes sales efforts that involve contacting customers directly. Marketing also includes advertising that provides information to large numbers of potential customers. Another activity is to set prices that are low enough to encourage sales and high enough to earn profits. Marketing also involves identifying new products that might meet customers' needs. It includes developing systems that distribute products to customers when and where they need them. These activities are sometimes summed up as the four P's of marketing—product, promotion, price, and place.

Executive Management. All organizations must have leadership, vision, and coordination. Long-term strategies need to be established and employees must be motivated to do their best. In addition, major decisions have to be made. These tasks are

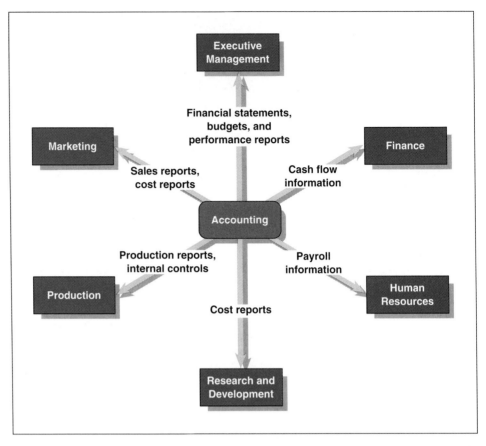

the duty of the company's executive managers, who also represent the company in dealing with the public. In some companies, the owner or owners carry out the executive management functions. In others, key employees take on these responsibilities. They may be called the president, the chief executive officer, or the chairman of the board of directors. In nonprofit organizations, the top managers often are called executive directors.

USING ACCOUNTING TO SERVE INTERNAL NEEDS

The internal role of accounting is to serve the organization's various functions by providing information that helps them complete their tasks. By providing this information, accounting helps the organization reach its overall goals. Illustration PR–2 shows some of the information accounting provides within an organization.

The finance function uses information about actual cash flows as a basis for projecting future cash flows and evaluating past decisions. Human resources can carry out its work more effectively if it has information about the company's employees, including payroll costs. Research and development managers need information about the costs they already have incurred so they can decide whether to continue their projects. Marketing managers also use accounting information, especially reports about the company's sales and its marketing costs.

The production division of a company depends heavily on accounting information to determine whether its operating costs are occurring as expected. In carrying out its work, the production department operates within a set of *internal controls* designed by the accounting department. To promote efficiency and prevent unauthorized use of the company's resources, these controls specify procedures that must be followed before certain actions can take place. For example, internal controls may require a manager's approval before any materials are moved to the production line. Internal controls also dictate procedures that are necessary to ensure that accounting reports about production activities are dependable and useful. You will learn more about internal control procedures in Chapter 6.

Because executive management has overall responsibility for the organization, it depends heavily on accounting information to understand what is happening. One important set of reports includes the *financial statements*. We explain the contents, usefulness, and limits of these statements throughout this book. (Chapter 1 introduces you to the four primary financial statements.) Executive management also receives and uses budget reports that describe future plans. After events have unfolded, accounting provides performance reports that help the managers to understand what was done well and to identify where improvements might be made.

Perhaps the most important point to learn at this stage is that accounting activities are not important by themselves. They are important only because they provide information that is useful to other parts of the organization.

Progress Check

(Answers to Progress Checks are provided at the end of the Prologue.)

PR-1   **The primary function of accounting is to provide financial information: (a) To an organization's managers; (b) To an organization's creditors; (c) That is useful in making rational investment, credit, and similar decisions.**

PR-2   **Identify six different categories of activities carried on within most organizations.**

In addition to using accounting information to meet internal needs, organizations use it for reporting to various external groups. These external decision makers include owners not actively involved in managing the business. For example, owners can use information about the company's performance and financial strength to help them determine whether to hold their investments.

In making decisions about an organization, internal and external decision makers generally begin by asking questions. The answers are often based on accounting information. For example, owners and managers use accounting information to help them answer questions like these:

*   What resources does the organization own?
*   What debts does it owe?
*   How much income is it earning?
*   Are the expenses appropriate for the amount of sales?
*   Are customers' accounts being collected promptly?

Other decision makers include people who loan money to the organization. These lenders, also called creditors, need information to decide whether the company has enough financial strength and profits to pay its debts. For example, they look for answers to questions like these:

*   Has the organization promptly paid its debts in the past?
*   Does it have the ability to pay its current debts?
*   Does it have good prospects for future earnings?
*   Should it be granted additional credit now?

Accounting information is used by voters, legislators, and officials who are concerned about a government agency's receipts and expenditures. Contributors to a nonprofit organization also use accounting information to understand what happens to their donations.

A company's employees have a special interest in knowing whether an organization represents a stable source of employment. They can use accounting information to help them understand their employer's financial health and performance.

USING ACCOUNTING TO SERVE EXTERNAL NEEDS

LO 2
Describe the external role of accounting for organizations.

Some government agencies are charged with regulating business activities. They often need financial information to carry out that responsibility. Other government agencies are responsible for collecting income taxes. As you know from personal experience, taxpayers use accounting information to determine how much income they have and how much tax they owe.

Recall that executive management is responsible for an organization's relationships with external decision makers. As the diagram on the preceding page shows, accounting provides most of the financial information that executive management presents to external decision makers. An objective of this book is to explain the contents and usefulness of the financial statements created for these reporting activities.

Some accounting information is designed to satisfy the needs of a particular external party. For example, information provided to the government for tax calculations may differ significantly from the information in the financial statements. We describe the work of tax accountants later in the Prologue.

THE DIFFERENCE BETWEEN ACCOUNTING AND BOOKKEEPING

Because accounting and bookkeeping both are concerned with financial information and records, some people mistakenly think that they are the same thing. In fact, accounting involves much more than bookkeeping. Although bookkeeping is critical to developing useful accounting information, it is only the clerical part of accounting. That is, **bookkeeping** is the part of accounting that records transactions and other events, either manually or with computers. In contrast, accounting involves analyzing transactions and events, deciding how to report them in financial statements, and interpreting the results. Accounting also involves designing and implementing systems to produce useful reports and to control the operations of an organization. Accounting involves more professional expertise and judgment than bookkeeping because accountants must analyze complex and unusual events.

Whether you want to be an accountant, plan to hold some other position in an organization, or expect to be an investor or creditor, you will benefit by understanding how accounting information is developed. To gain this understanding, initially you will study some basic bookkeeping practices. Later in the book, you use this knowledge to learn how accountants present financial data in useful reports. Eventually, you will be able to use the reports more effectively because you will understand how the information has been processed.

ACCOUNTING AND COMPUTERS

Since computers first became available in the 1950s, they have spread throughout our everyday lives and the business world. Computers are widely used in accounting because they efficiently store, process, and summarize large quantities of financial data. Furthermore, computers perform these functions quickly with limited operator involvement. Thus, computers reduce the time, effort, and cost of processing data while improving clerical accuracy. As a result of these advantages, most accounting systems are now computerized. Even so, manual accounting systems are still used by a surprisingly large number of small businesses.

To prepare, analyze, and use accounting information in today's world, you need to understand the important role computers play in most accounting systems. In essence, computers are tools that help accountants provide useful information for decision makers. The huge growth in the number and power of computers has greatly changed how accountants and other people work. However, computers have not eliminated the need for people to learn about accounting. A strong demand exists for people who can design accounting systems, supervise their operation, analyze complex transactions, and interpret reports. A strong demand also exists for people who can make good decisions because they clearly understand how accounting information relates to business activities. While computers have taken over many routine tasks, they are not substitutes for qualified people with abilities to generate and use accounting information.

Progress Check

PR-3 Accounting's external function is to provide: *(a)* Assurance that management has complied with all laws; *(b)* Information to users who are not involved in the organization's daily activities; *(c)* Information that managers use to control business operations.

PR-4 What is the relationship between accounting and bookkeeping?

WHY STUDY ACCOUNTING?

Because of the wide range of questions that are answered with accounting information, you will almost certainly use accounting in your future career. (In fact, you probably already use some accounting information as a result of having a credit card or checking account.) To use accounting effectively, you need to understand the unique accounting words and terms widely used in business.

You should also understand the concepts and procedures that are followed in generating accounting information. One important benefit of this understanding is that it will make you aware of the limitations of accounting information. For example, much of it is based on estimates instead of precise measurements. By understanding how these estimates are made, you will be able to avoid misinterpreting the information.

Another very good reason for studying accounting is to make it the basis for an interesting and rewarding career. The next section of this prologue describes what accountants do.

THE TYPES OF ACCOUNTANTS

LO 3
List the main fields of accounting and the activities carried on in each field.

One way to classify accountants is to identify the kinds of work they perform. In general, accountants work in these three broad fields:

- Financial accounting.
- Managerial accounting.
- Tax accounting.

These fields provide a variety of information to different users. We describe the activities of accountants in these fields later in this prologue.

Another way to classify accountants is to identify the kinds of organizations in which they work. Most accountants are **private accountants.** A private accountant works for a single employer, which is often a business. A large business might employ a hundred or more private accountants, but most companies have fewer.

Many other accountants are **public accountants.** Public accountants provide their services to many different clients. They are called *public accountants* because their services are available to the public. Some public accountants are self-employed. Many others work for public accounting firms that may have thousands of employees or only a few.

Government accountants work for local, state, and federal government agencies. Some government accountants perform accounting services for their own agencies. Other government accountants are involved with business regulation. Still others investigate violations of laws.

Accounting is a profession like law and medicine because accountants have special abilities and responsibilities. The professional status of an accountant is often indicated by one or more certificates.

The CPA Certificate

Each state in the United States, as well as the District of Columbia, Guam, Puerto Rico, and the Virgin Islands, has an agency that licenses Certified Public Accountants **(CPAs).** The licensing process helps ensure that a high standard of professional service is available to the public. Individuals can legally identify themselves as CPAs only if they hold this license.

To become a licensed CPA, an individual must meet education and experience requirements and must pass the CPA examination. In general, states require an applicant to be a citizen of the United States, to be at least 21 years of age, to have good ethical character, and to hold a college degree with a major in accounting.

The CPA examination covers topics in financial and managerial accounting, as well as income taxes, auditing, and business law. The uniform two-day examination is given in all states and other jurisdictions every May and November. Although the exam is administered by individual state boards, it is prepared and graded by the American Institute of Certified Public Accountants **(AICPA),** the largest and most influential national professional organization of CPAs.

In addition, many states issue a certificate only after the applicant has one or more years of experience working under the supervision of a CPA. Nearly all states reduce the amount of experience if an applicant has completed a specified amount of coursework beyond the undergraduate degree. Some states do not require any work experience. A few states allow applicants to substitute work experience for part of the formal education requirements.

As early as 1969, the AICPA's governing council took the position that CPAs need at least five years of college education (150 semester hours). This position was supported in 1983 by the National Association of State Boards of Accountancy **(NASBA).** In 1988, the members of the AICPA voted to require all CPAs admitted to the institute after 2000 to have 150 semester hours of college education. More than 30 states have changed their laws to eventually require new CPAs to complete at least 150 semester hours. We expect many more to adopt this requirement before 2000.

Other Professional Certificates

Many private accountants hold CPA certificates because they were public accountants earlier in their careers. Some private accountants hold other certificates in addition to or instead of the CPA license. For example, you may want to obtain a Certificate in Management Accounting **(CMA)** or become a Certified Internal Auditor **(CIA).** Holders of these certificates must meet examination, education, and experience requirements similar to those applied to CPAs. Unlike the CPA license, the CMA and CIA certificates are not issued by the government and do not give their holders any legal authority. The CMA is awarded by the Institute of Management Accountants and the CIA is granted by the Institute of Internal Auditors.

THE FIELDS OF ACCOUNTING

Accountants practice in three fields—financial, managerial, and tax accounting. The actual work done by an accountant depends on the field and whether the person is employed in private, public, or government accounting. Illustration PR–3 identifies the specific activities of the three types of accountants within these fields.

Financial Accounting

Financial accounting provides information to decision makers who are not involved in the day-to-day operations of an organization. As we described earlier, these external decision makers include investors, creditors, and others. The information is distributed primarily through general purpose financial statements. Financial statements describe the condition of the organization and the events that happened during the year. Chapter 1 explains the form and contents of financial statements.

The Financial Accounting column of Illustration PR–3 shows that financial statements are prepared by a company's private accountants. However, many companies issue their financial statements only after an **audit.** An audit is a thorough check of an organization's accounting systems and records; it is performed to add credibility

Illustration PR-3   Activities of Accountants

Types of Accountants	Fields of Accounting		
	Financial Accounting	Managerial Accounting	Tax Accounting
Private accountants	Preparing financial statements	General accounting Cost accounting Budgeting Internal auditing	Preparing tax returns Planning
Public accountants	Auditing financial statements	Providing management advisory services	Preparing tax returns Planning
Government accountants	Preparing financial statements Reviewing financial reports Writing regulations Assisting companies Investigating violations	General accounting Cost accounting Budgeting Internal auditing	Reviewing tax returns Assisting taxpayers Writing regulations Investigating violations

to the financial statements.[2] For example, banks require audits of the financial statements of companies applying for large loans. Also, federal and state laws require companies to have audits before their securities (stocks and bonds) can be sold to the public. Thereafter, their financial statements must be audited as long as the securities are traded.

To perform an audit, auditors examine the financial statements and the accounting system. Their objective is to decide whether the statements reflect the company's financial position and operating results in agreement with **generally accepted accounting principles (GAAP).** These principles are rules adopted by the accounting profession as guides for measuring and reporting the financial condition and activities of a business. You learn more about GAAP in Chapter 1 and in many of the following chapters.

When an audit is completed, the auditors prepare a report that expresses their professional opinion about the financial statements. The auditors' report must accompany the statements when they are distributed.

As the first column of Illustration PR–3 shows, some government accountants prepare financial statements. These statements describe the financial status of government agencies and results of events occurring during the year. The financial statements of governmental bodies are usually audited by independent CPAs.

Other government accountants are involved with regulating financial accounting practices used by businesses. For example, some accountants work for the Securities and Exchange Commission **(SEC).** Congress created the SEC in 1934 to regulate securities markets, including the flow of information from companies to the public. SEC accountants review companies' financial reports before they are distributed to the public. The purpose of the review is to be sure that the reports comply with the SEC's regulations.

Accountants who work for other regulatory agencies, such as the Federal Trade Commission, may review reports filed by businesses subject to the agencies' authority.

---

[2]To achieve this result, audits are performed by independent CPAs who are public accountants. Little or no credibility would be added to the statements if they were audited by a company's own employees.

Government accountants help write regulations concerning financial accounting. They also help companies understand and comply with them.

As we mentioned briefly, some government accountants investigate possible violations of laws and regulations. For example, accountants who work for the SEC investigate crimes related to securities. Other accountants investigate financial frauds and white-collar crimes in their capacity as agents of the Federal Bureau of Investigation.

Managerial Accounting

The field of managerial accounting involves providing information to an organization's managers. Managerial accounting reports often include much of the same information used in financial accounting. However, managerial accounting reports also include a great deal of information that is not reported outside the company.

Look at the upper and lower sections of the Managerial Accounting column in Illustration PR–3. Notice that private and government accountants have the same four major activities. The middle section of the column shows that public accountants also perform activities related to managerial accounting. These activities are described next.

General Accounting. The task of recording transactions, processing the recorded data, and preparing reports for managers is called **general accounting.** General accounting also includes preparing the financial statements that executive management presents to external users. An organization's own accountants usually design the accounting information system, often with help from public accountants. The general accounting staff is supervised by a chief accounting officer, who is called the **controller.** This title stems from the fact that accounting information is used to control the organization's operations.

Cost Accounting. To plan and control operations, managers need information about the nature of costs incurred. **Cost accounting** is a process of accumulating the information managers need about operating costs. It helps managers identify, measure, and control these costs. Cost accounting may involve accounting for the costs of products, services, or specific activities. Cost accounting information is also useful for evaluating each manager's performance. Large companies usually employ many cost accountants because cost accounting information is so important.

Budgeting. Budgeting is the process of developing formal plans for an organization's future activities. A primary goal of budgeting is to give managers from different areas in the organization a clear understanding of how their activities affect the entire organization. After the budget has been put into effect, it provides a basis for evaluating actual performance.

Internal Auditing. Just as independent auditing adds credibility to financial statements, **internal auditing** adds credibility to reports produced and used within an organization. Internal auditors not only examine record-keeping processes but also assess whether managers are following established operating procedures. In addition, internal auditors evaluate the efficiency of operating procedures. Almost all large companies and government agencies employ internal auditors.

Management Advisory Services. Public accountants participate in managerial accounting by providing **management advisory services** to their clients. Independent auditors gain an intimate knowledge of a client's accounting and operating procedures when they conduct their examinations. As a result, auditors are in an excellent position to offer suggestions for improving the company's procedures. Most clients expect these suggestions as a useful by-product of the audit. For example, public accountants often help companies design and install new accounting and internal control systems. This effort includes offering advice on selecting new computer systems. Other advice might relate to budgeting procedures or employee benefit plans.

Tax Accounting

Many taxes raised by federal, state, and city governments are based on the income earned by taxpayers. These taxpayers include both individuals and corporate businesses. The amount of taxes is based on what the laws define to be income. Tax accountants help taxpayers comply with these laws by preparing their tax returns. Another **tax accounting** activity involves planning future transactions to minimize the amount of tax to be paid. The Tax Accounting column of Illustration PR–3 identifies the activities of accountants in this field.

Large companies usually have their own private accountants who are responsible for preparing tax returns and doing tax planning. However, large companies may consult with public accountants when they need special tax expertise. Most small companies rely on public accountants for their tax work.

Many accountants are employed on the government side of the tax process. For example, the Internal Revenue Service (**IRS**) employs numerous tax accountants. The IRS has the duty of collecting federal taxes and otherwise enforcing tax laws. Most IRS accountants review tax returns filed by taxpayers. Other IRS accountants offer assistance to taxpayers and help write regulations. Still other IRS accountants investigate possible violations of tax laws.

Summary

The preceding discussion shows how important accounting is for most organizations. Regardless of your career goals, you will surely use accounting information and work with accountants. The discussion also shows the variety of opportunities available if you find accounting to be enjoyable and challenging. Next we consider the important role of ethics in business and accounting.

Progress Check

PR–5   The services performed by public accountants generally include: (a) Income tax services, management advisory services, and independent auditing; (b) General accounting, independent auditing, and budgeting; (c) Government accounting, private accounting, and independent auditing.

PR–6   What are the three broad fields of accounting?

PR–7   What is the purpose of an audit? Describe what Certified Public Accountants do when they perform an audit.

As a student, you realize that ethics and ethical behavior are important features of any society. Disappointing stories in the media often remind us how much ethics affect our society. These stories tell us about attempts to defraud the elderly and other vulnerable people, missed child support payments, harassment, misconduct by public figures, bribery of government officials, and the use of insider information for personal gain in the stock market. Events like these make it difficult for people to trust each other. If trust is lacking, our commercial and personal lives are much more complicated, inefficient, and unpleasant.

In this section of the Prologue, we introduce the meaning of ethics in general and describe how ethics affect business and accounting in particular. Because the purpose of accounting is to provide useful information that can be trusted, it is essential that

THE IMPORTANCE OF ETHICS IN ACCOUNTING

LO 4

State several reasons for the importance of ethics in accounting.

accountants be ethical. How could the users of accounting information rely on it if they could not trust accountants? The need to avoid this difficult situation has prompted the development of special ethics for accountants.

The Meaning of Ethics

Ethics are the "principles that determine the rightness or wrongness of particular acts or activities." Ethics are also "accepted standards of good behavior . . . in a profession or trade."[3] Ethics and laws often coincide, with the result that many unethical actions (such as theft and physical violence) are also illegal. Other actions may not be against the law but are generally recognized as unethical. For example, the crime of perjury (not telling the truth) occurs only if the liar has been put under an oath. However, not telling the truth is nearly always unethical.[4] Because of differences between laws and ethics, we cannot count on laws to keep people ethical.

In some cases, a person may face difficulty in deciding whether an action is right or wrong. In these situations, the most ethical choice may be to take a course of action that avoids any doubt about the ethical correctness of the action. For example, financial statement readers would not trust a CPA's report on the statements if the CPA's financial success depended on the success of the reporting company.

Should this prevent an auditor from investing in a client if the investment is only a small part of the auditor's personal wealth? To avoid the question of how much would be too much, ethics rules for auditors simply forbid any direct investment in their clients' securities, regardless of the amount.[5] Also, auditors cannot accept contingent fees that depend on amounts reported in a client's financial statements.[6] These rules are designed to prevent conflicts of interest or even the possibility that the CPA might appear to lack independence.

Many controversial issues that we face in school, the workplace, or elsewhere have ethical implications. These ethical issues are an unavoidable part of life. However, a commitment to being ethical requires us to think carefully before we act to be certain that we are making ethical choices. Our success in making those choices affects how we feel about ourselves and how others feel about us. In fact, our combined individual choices greatly affect the quality of our entire society and the individual experience that each of us enjoys.

Beyond these general ideas, how do ethics relate to business, and more specifically, how do they relate to accounting?

Ethics in Business

We discuss ethics at the beginning of this book because business activity is so central to everyone's life and because useful accounting information is so important for business. Recent history shows that many people have been concerned about what they see as low ethical standards in business. For example, a survey of more than 1,100 executives, deans of business schools, and members of Congress, showed that 94% of the respondents agreed with the statement that "the business community is troubled by ethical problems."[7] However, we can be encouraged because the survey also showed that the vast majority of the respondents believed high ethical standards are followed by companies that are successful over the long run. This second finding

---

[3]*The New Lexicon Webster's Dictionary of the English Language* (New York: Lexington Publications, 1989), p. 324.

[4]The usual exceptions to this rule involve protecting another person against harm.

[5]*AICPA Code of Professional Conduct,* Rule 101.

[6]*AICPA Code of Professional Conduct,* Rule 301.

[7]Touche Ross & Co., *Ethics in American Business* (New York, 1988), pp. 1-2.

As a Matter of Opinion

Mr. Finkston received his B.A. in accounting from Brooklyn College and his J.D. from Brooklyn Law School. He is a member of the New York State Bar and was a public accountant early in his career. Since 1979, he has been the Director of the Division of Professional Ethics of the American Institute of CPAs.

The accounting profession has earned high regard because of its ethical standards. Our standards require ethical behavior in our relationships with our clients and our employers. They also require ethical behavior in our dealings with the public and its interests.

And, our standards require us to render high-quality professional services. By adhering to the concepts of objectivity, integrity, and independence, and by continued striving for quality, the profession has won a respected place in the entire business community and among the other professions.

As a student of accounting, be aware of the ethical implications of all that you study. As a member of the accounting profession, or any other profession, practice ethics in all that you do. By doing so, you will bring honor to yourself and your profession.

Herbert A. Finkston, CPA

confirms an old saying: "Good ethics is good business." Ethical business practices build trust, which in turn promotes loyalty and productive relationships with customers, suppliers, and employees. As a result, good ethics contribute to a company's reputation and eventually its success.

Because of the important public interest in business ethics, many companies have adopted their own codes of ethics. These codes establish standards for internal activities and for relationships with customers, suppliers, regulators, the public, and even competitors. Companies often use their codes as public statements of their commitment to ethical business practices. More importantly, they serve as guides for employees to follow.

Ethics in Accounting

As we mentioned earlier, ethics are important in accounting because accountants are expected to provide useful information for decision makers. These decisions can have a profound effect on many individuals, businesses, and other institutions. As a result, accountants often face ethical issues as they consider what information should be provided to decision makers. Accountants' choices can affect such things as the amount of money a company pays in taxes or distributes to its stockholders. The information can affect the price that a buyer pays for a business or the amount of compensation paid to a company's managers. Internal information can affect judgments about the success of a company's specific products or divisions. If inadequate accounting information would cause a successful division to be closed, its employees, customers, and suppliers would be significantly harmed. Accountants need to consider all these effects in deciding what information will be most useful for these important decisions.

In response to the need for guidance for accountants, ethics codes have been adopted and enforced by professional accounting organizations. These include the American Institute of Certified Public Accountants and the Institute of Management Accountants. To keep their codes up to date, these organizations continually monitor their effectiveness and applicability to new ways of operating. The As a Matter of Opinion box presents the views of Herbert Finkston, the director of the AICPA's division of professional ethics, on the importance of ethical behavior for accountants and others.

As an example of an ethical accounting issue, recall the JW Shuttle business described at the beginning of the Prologue. This case shows how accounting can affect the allocation of wealth between people. Wilson receives $7,500 more and Jarrett receives $7,500 less if Method B is used instead of Method A.

More information is needed in this case to help Jarrett and Wilson decide which method should be used. However, in explaining the appropriate uses of Method A and

Method B, the accountant has an ethical responsibility to be fair to both parties. Knowing that Method B is more favorable to Wilson, the accountant must be careful to avoid giving a biased argument in favor of Method B.

Accountants and managers often face situations that are similar to the JW Shuttle case. For example, many companies pay their managers bonuses based on amount of income reported. Generally, the managers benefit from the use of accounting alternatives that accelerate the reporting of income. However, those alternatives reduce the money available to invest for the benefit of the owners.

Another ethics issue in accounting involves the confidential nature of the information that accountants deal with in their work. For example, auditors have access to salary records and plans for the future. Their clients could be damaged if the auditors released this information to others. To prevent this, auditors' ethics require them to keep information confidential.[8] In addition, internal accountants are not supposed to use confidential information for personal advantage.[9]

These examples show why accountants, their clients, and the public need ethical guidance and commitment. Guidance provides a basis for knowing which actions to take and commitment provides the courage to do what needs to be done. Guidance also tells clients what they can rightfully expect from their accountants and gives the public a basis for having confidence in financial statements. In fact, the performance of the entire economy depends to a considerable extent on having financial information that is trustworthy.

The Ethical Challenge

As you proceed in your study of accounting, you will encounter many other situations in which ethical issues are raised. We encourage you to explore these issues. We also urge you to remember that accounting must be done ethically if it is to be an effective tool in the service of society. Of all the principles of accounting that you learn from this book, the need for ethics is certainly the most fundamental.

In your own approach to life, you are in control of your ethical standards and the ethical decisions that you make. Each of us is individually free to shape our personal morals. To paraphrase former Supreme Court Chief Justice Earl Warren, it can be said that civilized society "floats on a sea of ethics." It is your choice how you elect to navigate this sea. Do not be misled into thinking that your choice does not matter. Eventually, your choice affects everyone, and that is the ethical challenge each of us faces.

Progress Check

PR-8   Both the American Institute of Certified Public Accountants and the Institute of Management Accountants have adopted codes of ethics. Is this true or false?

PR-9   Ethical rules prevent CPAs from accepting certain kinds of contingent fees. Is this true of false?

SUMMARY OF THE PROLOGUE IN TERMS OF LEARNING OBJECTIVES

LO 1. Describe the main purpose of accounting and its role in organizations. The main purpose of accounting is to provide useful information to people who make rational investment, credit, and similar decisions. These decision makers include present and potential investors, lenders, and other users. The other users include managers of organizations, suppliers who sell to them, and customers who buy from them.

---

[8]*AICPA Code of Professional Conduct*, Rule 301.

[9]*Institute of Management Accountants Standards of Ethical Conduct.*

Internally, accounting provides information that managers use in the following areas of activity: finance, human resources, research and development, production, marketing, and executive management.

LO 2. Describe the external role of accounting for organizations. In addition to using accounting information to meet internal needs, organizations also report accounting information to various external parties. These external decision makers include people who invest in the organizations and people who loan money to them. Lenders need information to assess whether the company has enough financial strength and profitability to pay its debts.

LO 3. List the main fields of accounting and the activities carried on in each field. Accountants work in private, public, and government accounting. All three have members who work in financial, managerial, and tax accounting. Financial accountants prepare or audit financial statements that are distributed to people who are not involved in day-to-day management. Managerial accountants provide information to people who are involved in day-to-day management. Managerial accounting activities include general accounting, cost accounting, budgeting, internal auditing, and management advisory services. Tax accounting includes preparing tax returns and tax planning.

LO 4. State several reasons for the importance of ethics in accounting. Ethics are principles that determine the rightness or wrongness of particular acts or activities. Ethics are also principles of conduct that govern an individual or a profession. The foundation for trust in business activities is the expectation that people are trustworthy. Ethics are especially important for accounting because users of the information have to trust that it has not been manipulated. Without ethics, accounting information could not be trusted, and economic activity would be much more difficult to accomplish.

GLOSSARY

Accounting a service activity that provides useful information to people who make rational investment, credit, and similar decisions to help them make better decisions. p. 2

AICPA American Institute of Certified Public Accountants, the largest and most influential national professional organization of Certified Public Accountants in the United States. p. 8

Audit a thorough check of an organization's accounting systems and records that adds credibility to financial statements; the specific goal is to determine whether the statements reflect the company's financial position and operating results in agreement with generally accepted accounting principles. p. 8

Bookkeeping the part of accounting that records transactions and other events, either manually or with computers. p. 6

Budgeting the process of developing formal plans for future activities, which then serve as a basis for evaluating actual performance. p. 10

CIA Certified Internal Auditor; a certification that an individual is professionally competent in internal auditing; granted by the Institute of Internal Auditors. p. 8

CMA Certificate in Management Accounting; a certification that an individual is professionally competent in managerial accounting; awarded by the Institute of Management Accountants. p. 8

Controller the chief accounting officer of an organization. p. 10

Cost accounting a managerial accounting activity designed to help managers identify, measure, and control operating costs. p. 10

CPA Certified Public Accountant; an accountant who has passed an examination and has met education and experience requirements; CPAs are licensed by state boards to practice public accounting. p. 7

Ethics principles that determine the rightness or wrongness of particular acts or activities; also accepted standards of good behavior in a profession or trade. p. 12

GAAP the abbreviation for *generally accepted accounting principles*. p. 9

General accounting the task of recording transactions, processing the recorded data, and preparing reports for managers; also includes preparing the financial statements that executive management presents to external users. p. 10

Generally accepted accounting principles   rules adopted by the accounting profession as guides for measuring and reporting the financial condition and activities of a business. p. 9

Government accountants   accountants employed by local, state, and federal government agencies. p. 7

Internal auditing   an activity that adds credibility to reports produced and used within an organization; internal auditors not only examine record-keeping processes but also assess whether managers are following established operating procedures; internal auditors also evaluate the efficiency of operating procedures. p. 10

IRS   Internal Revenue Service; the federal agency that has the duty of collecting federal taxes and otherwise enforcing tax laws. p. 11

Management advisory services   the public accounting activity in which suggestions are offered for improving a company's procedures; the suggestions may concern new ac-counting and internal control systems, new computer systems, budgeting, and employee benefit plans. p. 10

NASBA   National Association of State Boards of Accountancy. p. 8

Private accountant   an accountant who works for a single employer, which is often a business. p. 7

Public accountants   accountants who provide their services to many different clients. p. 7

SEC   Securities and Exchange Commission; the federal agency created by Congress in 1934 to regulate securities markets, including the flow of information from companies to the public. p. 9

Tax accounting   the field of accounting that includes preparing tax returns and planning future transactions to minimize the amount of tax; involves private, public, and government accountants. p. 11

QUESTIONS

1. What is the main purpose of accounting?
2. Describe the internal role of accounting for organizations.
3. What are three or four questions that business owners might try to answer by looking to accounting information?
4. Why should people study accounting since computers are used to process accounting data?
5. Why do states license Certified Public Accountants?
6. According to the laws in at least 30 states, how many years of college education will a person need to enter the public accounting profession in the future?
7. Identify the three types of services typically offered by public accountants.

8. What title is frequently used for an organization's chief accounting officer? Why?
9. Identify four managerial accounting activities performed by private and government accountants.
10. Identify two management advisory services typically provided by public accountants.
11. Identify several examples of the types of work performed by government accountants.
12. What do tax accountants do in addition to preparing tax returns?
13. Identify the CPA firm that audited the financial statements of Apple Computer, Inc., in Appendix F at the end of this book.

CONCEPT TESTER

Test your understanding of the concepts introduced in this chapter by completing the following crossword puzzle.

Across Clues

1. The largest and most influential national professional association of CPAs in the United States.
4. The part of accounting that records transactions and other events.
5. A certification of professional competence in managerial accounting.
6. Rules adopted as guides for reporting the financial condition and activities of a business.

Down Clues

1. Providing useful information to people who make investment, credit, and similar decisions.
2. Federal agency that regulates securities markets and the flow information to the public.
3. A certification of professional competence in internal auditing.
4. The process of developing formal plans for future activities.
5. Accountants who are licensed by state boards to practice public accounting.

ANSWERS TO PROGRESS CHECKS

PR–1　*c*

PR–2　The activities are finance, human resources, research and development, production, marketing, and executive management.

PR–3　*b*

PR–4　Bookkeeping is the part of accounting that records transactions and other events, either manually or with computers. Accounting activities are concerned with identifying how transactions and events should be described in financial statements. Accounting activities also involve designing and implementing systems that make it possible to produce useful reports and to control the operations of an organization. Accounting involves more professional expertise and judgment than bookkeeping because accountants must analyze complex and unusual

events. Also, accountants must be able to interpret and explain the information in the financial reports.

PR–5　*a*

PR–6　The three broad fields of accounting are financial, managerial, and tax accounting.

PR–7　The purpose of an audit is to add credibility to financial statements. When performing an audit, CPAs examine financial statements and the accounting records used to prepare them. During the audit, they decide whether the statements reflect the company's financial position and operating results in agreement with generally accepted accounting principles.

PR–8　True

PR–9　True

CHAPTER 1

Financial Statements and Accounting Principles

Karen and Mark Smith recently graduated from Notre Dame University and have accepted employment with different companies in Chicago. Already committed to a long-term savings program, they have been seeking advice about alternative investments. One investment that has been suggested to them is H & R Block, Inc. As customers of H & R Block, the Smiths have used the company's services related to the preparation and filing of income tax returns. After receiving the company's annual report, however, they have learned that H & R Block also owns CompuServe Information Services, which provides communications and information services to personal computer owners. In addition, it owns Interim Services, Inc., which provides temporary personnel, health care workers, and other employment services.

Currently, the Smiths are trying to understand the financial information contained in H & R Block's annual report. In fact, they have become so fascinated by the process that they recently enrolled in Accounting Principles I, a course they are taking in the evening at South Suburban College near Chicago.

H & R Block, Inc. (In thousands)	Year Ended April 30	
	1993	1992
For the year:		
Total revenues	$1,525,330	$1,370,698
Net earnings	180,705	162,253
At year-end:		
Total assets	$1,005,834	$ 962,664
Stockholders' equity	650,488	613,713

LEARNING OBJECTIVES

After studying Chapter 1, you should be able to:

1. **Describe the information presented in financial statements, be able to prepare simple financial statements, and analyze a company's performance with the return on equity ratio.**
2. **Explain the accounting principles introduced in the chapter and describe the process by which generally accepted accounting principles are established.**
3. **Describe single proprietorships, partnerships, and corporations, including any differences in the owners' responsibilities for the debts of the organizations.**
4. **Analyze business transactions to determine their effects on the accounting equation.**
5. **Define or explain the words and phrases listed in the chapter glossary.**

In this chapter, you start to learn about the information accountants provide to decision makers in financial statements. Next, you study some general principles that guide accountants in developing these statements. This discussion also describes some of the organizations that regulate and influence financial accounting. To continue your introduction to business, this chapter explains several ways a business can be organized. The chapter also shows you how accountants analyze business transactions to generate useful information. This is important for understanding why financial statements are useful. Finally, the chapter explains the return on equity ratio, which you can use in evaluating a company's operating success during a reporting period.

FINANCIAL STATEMENTS

LO 1

Describe the information presented in financial statements, be able to prepare simple financial statements, and analyze a company's performance with the return on equity ratio.

Accounting exists for the purpose of providing useful information to people who make rational investment, credit, and similar decisions.[1] These decision makers include investors, lenders, managers, suppliers, customers, and other interested people. Be sure to read the As a Matter of Opinion box to learn how one decision maker uses accounting information to help him fulfill his responsibilities as a member of a city council.

Many organizations provide accounting information to managers and other decision makers in the form of financial statements. The statements are useful because they describe the organization's financial health and performance in a condensed and highly informative format. Because they give an overall view of the entire organization, financial statements are a good place to start your study of accounting. We begin by looking at the income statement and the balance sheet. This diagram represents the relationship between these two statements:

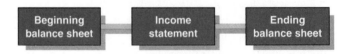

In effect, the income statement for the reporting period links the balance sheets as of the beginning and end of the reporting period.

---

[1]Financial Accounting Standards Board, *Statement of Financial Accounting Concepts No. 1,* "Objectives of Financial Reporting by Business Enterprises" (Norwalk, CT, 1978), par. 34.

CLEAR COPY CO.
Income Statement
For Month Ended December 31, 19X1

Revenues:		
Copy services revenue		$3,900
Operating expenses:		
Rent expense	$1,000	
Salaries expense	700	
Total operating expenses		1,700
Net income		$2,200

Illustration 1–1
Income Statement for
Clear Copy Co.

The Income Statement

Look at the **income statement** in Illustration 1–1. The income statement shows whether the business earned a profit (also called *net income.*) A company earns a **net income** if its revenues exceed its expenses. A company incurs a **net loss** if its expenses exceed its revenues. In Illustration 1–1, observe that the income statement does not simply report the amount of net income or net loss. Instead, it lists the types and amounts of the revenues and expenses. As another example, **The Walt Disney**

Company classifies the revenues and expenses on its income statement into the following categories: theme parks, filmed entertainment, and consumer products. This detailed information is more useful for decision making than just a simple profit or loss number.

Revenues are inflows of assets received in exchange for goods or services provided to customers as part of the major or central operations of the business.

Revenues also may occur as decreases in liabilities.[2] For now, think of assets as economic resources owned by a business and liabilities as the debts owed by a business. Later, we define these terms more completely.

The income statement in Illustration 1–1 shows that the business of Clear Copy Co. earned revenues of $3,900 by providing copy services to customers during the month of December. Examples of revenues for other businesses include sales of products, rent, commissions, and interest.

Expenses are outflows or the using up of assets as a result of the major or central operations of a business. Expenses also may occur as increases in liabilities.[3] The income statement in Illustration 1–1 shows that Clear Copy used up some of its assets by paying for rented office space. The $1,000 cost of the space is reported in Illustration 1–1 as rent expense. The business also paid for an employee's services at a cost of $700. This is reported on the income statement as salaries expense.

Notice that the heading in Illustration 1–1 names the business, states that the report is an income statement, and shows the time period covered by the statement. Information about the time period is important for evaluating the company's performance. For example, you need to know that Clear Copy earned the $2,200 net income during a one-month period to judge whether that amount is satisfactory.

The Balance Sheet

The purpose of the **balance sheet** is to provide information that helps users understand a company's financial status as of a given date. As a result, the balance sheet often is called the **statement of financial position.** The balance sheet describes financial position by listing the types and dollar amounts of assets, liabilities, and equity of the business. (Equity is the difference between a company's assets and its liabilities.)

Illustration 1–2 presents the balance sheet for Clear Copy as of December 31, 19X1. Unlike the income statement that refers to a period of time, the balance sheet describes conditions that exist at a point in time. Thus, the heading shows the specific date on which the assets and liabilities are identified and measured. The amounts in the balance sheet are stated as of the close of business on that date.

Illustration 1-2
Balance Sheet for Clear Copy Co.

CLEAR COPY CO.
Balance Sheet
December 31, 19X1

Assets		Liabilities	
Cash	$ 8,400	Accounts payable	$ 6,200
Store supplies	3,600	**Owner's Equity**	
Copy equipment	26,000	Terry Dow, capital	31,800
		Total liabilities and	
Total assets	$38,000	owner's equity	$38,000

The balance sheet in Illustration 1–2 reports that the company owned three different assets at the close of business on December 31, 19X1. The assets were cash, store supplies, and copy equipment. The total dollar amount for these assets was $38,000. The balance sheet also shows that there were liabilities of $6,200. Owner's equity was $31,800. This amount is the difference between the assets and the liabilities.

---

[2]Financial Accounting Standards Board, *Statement of Financial Accounting Concepts No. 6, "Elements of Financial Statements"* (Norwalk, CT, 1985), par. 78.

[3]Ibid., par. 80.

Notice that the total amounts on the two sides of the balance sheet are equal. This equality is why the statement is called a *balance sheet.* The name also reflects the fact that the statement reports the balances of the assets, liabilities, and equity on a given date.

In general, the **assets** of a business are the properties or economic resources owned by the business. More precisely, assets are defined as "probable future economic benefits obtained or controlled by a particular entity as a result of past transactions or events."[4] One familiar asset is cash. Another asset consists of amounts owed to the business by its customers for goods and services sold to them on credit. This asset is called **accounts receivable.** In general, individuals who owe amounts to the business are called its **debtors.** Other assets owned by businesses include merchandise held for sale, supplies, equipment, buildings, and land. Assets also can be intangible rights, such as those granted by a patent or copyright.

The **liabilities** of a business are its debts to others. Liabilities are defined more precisely as "probable future sacrifices of economic benefits arising from present obligations of a particular entity to transfer assets or provide services to other entities in the future as a result of past transactions or events."[5] One common liability consists of amounts owed for goods and services bought on credit. This liability is called **accounts payable.** Other liabilities are salaries and wages owed to employees, taxes payable, notes payable, and interest payable.

A liability represents a claim against a business. In general, those who have the right to receive payments from a company are called its **creditors.** From the creditor's viewpoint, a liability is the right to be paid by a business. (In effect, one company's payable is another company's receivable.) If a business fails to pay its debts, the law gives creditors the right to force the sale of its assets to obtain the money to meet their claims. When the assets are sold under these conditions, the creditors are paid first, up to the full amount of their claims, with the remainder (the residual) going to the owner of the business.

Creditors often use a balance sheet to help them decide whether to loan money to a business. They can use the balance sheet to compare the amounts of existing liabilities and assets. A loan is less risky if the liabilities are small in comparison to the assets. There is less risk because there is a larger cushion if the assets are sold for less than the amounts shown on the balance sheet. On the other hand, a loan is more risky if the liabilities are large compared to the assets. The risk is greater because it is more likely that the assets cannot be sold for enough cash to pay all the debts.

Equity is defined as "the residual interest in the assets of an entity that remains after deducting its liabilities."[6] Equity is also called **net assets.** If a business is organized as a corporation (which we describe later), the owners of the business are called stockholders and the equity is called *stockholders' equity.* Because Clear Copy is owned by one person and is not a corporation, the equity section in Illustration 1–2 is simply called *owner's equity.*

Earlier we defined net income as the difference between revenue and expense for a time period. Net income is also the change in owner's equity that occurred during the period as a result of the company's major or central operations. By describing this change, the income statement links the company's balance sheets from the beginning and end of the reporting period.

ASSETS, LIABILITIES, AND EQUITY

---

[4]Financial Accounting Standards Board, *Statement of Financial Accounting Concepts No. 6,* "Elements of Financial Statements" (Norwalk, CT, 1985), par. 25.

[5]Ibid., par. 35.

[6]Ibid., par. 49.

We use this background on the balance sheet and income statement to explain more about financial accounting. The next sections of the chapter describe the principles that guide the practice of financial accounting.

Progress Check

(Answers to Progress Checks are provided at the end of the chapter.)

1-1   Which set of information is reported on an income statement? *(a)* Assets, liabilities, and owner's equity; *(b)* Revenues, expenses, and owner's equity; *(c)* Assets, liabilities, and net income; *(d)* Revenues, expenses, and net income.

1-2   What do accountants mean by the term *expense?*

GENERALLY ACCEPTED ACCOUNTING PRINCIPLES (GAAP)

LO 2

Explain the accounting principles introduced in the chapter and describe the process by which generally accepted accounting principles are established.

In the Prologue, we explained that financial accounting practice is governed by a set of rules called *generally accepted accounting principles,* or *GAAP.* To use and interpret financial statements effectively, you need to have a basic understanding of these principles.

A primary purpose of GAAP is to make the information in financial reports relevant, reliable, and comparable. Information that is relevant has the capacity to affect the decisions made by financial statement users. Reliable information is necessary if decision makers are to depend on it. In addition, the information should allow statement users to compare companies. These comparisons are more likely to be useful if all companies use similar practices. GAAP impose limits on the variety of accounting practices that companies can use, thereby making the financial statements more useful.

The Development of GAAP

Prior to the 1930s, GAAP were developed through common usage. In effect, a practice was considered suitable if it was acceptable to most accountants. This history is still reflected in the phrase *generally accepted.* However, as the accounting profession grew and the world of business became more complex, many people were not satisfied with the profession's progress in providing useful information.

The desire for improvement caused many accountants, managers, and government regulators to want more uniformity in practice. Thus, in the 1930s, they began to give authority for defining accepted principles to small groups of experienced professional accountants. Since then, a series of committees or boards have had authority to establish GAAP. In general, the authority of these groups has increased over time. We describe the present arrangement for establishing GAAP later in this chapter.

Broad and Specific Accounting Principles

GAAP include both broad and specific principles. The broad principles describe the basic assumptions and general guidelines that accountants follow in preparing financial statements. The specific principles provide more detailed rules that accountants follow in reporting the results of various business activities. The broad principles stem from observing long-used accounting practices. In contrast, the specific principles are established more often by the rulings of authoritative bodies.

As a user of financial statements, an understanding of both broad and specific principles will give you insight as to what the information means. It will also help you know what the information does not mean, and thereby avoid using it incorrectly. Because the broad principles are especially helpful for learning about accounting, we emphasize them in the early chapters of the book. The broad principles include the following:[7]

---

[7]In describing these accounting principles, some writers have used different words to mean the same thing. For example, broad principles also have been called *concepts, theories, assumptions,* and *postulates.* We call them *principles,* but don't be confused if you see them called by other names in other books.

Specific principles are especially important for understanding individual items in the financial statements. They are described throughout the book as we come to them.

Accounting Principles, Auditing Standards, and Financial Accounting

Generally accepted accounting principles are not natural laws like the laws of physics or other sciences. Instead, GAAP are identified in response to the needs of users and others affected by accounting. Thus, GAAP are subject to change as needs change.

Three groups of people are most directly affected by financial reporting: preparers, auditors, and users. The following diagram shows the relationship between the financial statements and these groups.

Private accountants prepare the financial statements. To give users more confidence in the statements, independent auditors (CPAs) usually examine the financial statements and develop an audit report. The statements and the audit report are then distributed to the users.

Illustration 1–3 expands this diagram to show how accounting principles and auditing standards relate to the financial reporting process. First, in Illustration 1–3, we show that GAAP are applied in preparing the financial statements. Preparers use GAAP to decide what procedures to follow as they account for business transactions and put the statements together.

Second, in Illustration 1–3, we show that audits are performed in accordance with **generally accepted auditing standards (GAAS).** GAAS are the rules adopted by the accounting profession as guides for conducting audits of financial statements. GAAS tell auditors what they must do in their audits to determine whether the financial statements comply with GAAP.

Applying both GAAP and GAAS assures users that financial statements include relevant, reliable, and comparable information. The audit does not, however, ensure that they can safely invest in or loan to the company. The audit does not reduce the risk that the company's products and services will not be successfully marketed or that other factors could cause it to fail.

Illustration 1–3

Generally Accepted Accounting Principles (GAAP), Generally Accepted Auditing Standards (GAAS), and the Groups that Participate in Financial Accounting

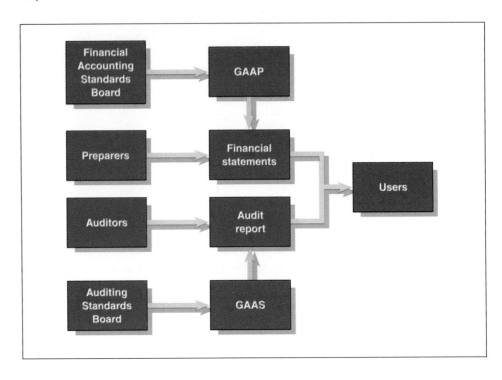

HOW ACCOUNTING PRINCIPLES ARE ESTABLISHED

In Illustration 1–3, we also identify the two organizations that are the primary authoritative sources of GAAP and GAAS. The primary authoritative source of GAAP is the Financial Accounting Standards Board **(FASB).** The FASB is a nonprofit organization with seven board members who serve full time. (In 1994, a board member's annual salary was $305,000.) The FASB is located in Norwalk, Connecticut, approximately 50 miles from New York City, and has a 40-member research staff to help identify problems in financial accounting and to find ways to solve them. The board seeks advice from groups affected by GAAP and often holds public hearings for this purpose. In summary, the FASB's job is to improve financial reporting while balancing the interests of the affected groups.[8]

The FASB announces its findings in several different publications. The most important are **Statements of Financial Accounting Standards (SFAS).** These statements establish generally accepted accounting principles in the United States and may affect practice in other countries.

The FASB gains its authority from a variety of sources. The most significant source is the Securities and Exchange Commission (SEC). Congress created the SEC in 1934 to regulate securities markets, including the flow of information from companies to the public. When the FASB began operating in 1973, the SEC designated it as the primary authority for establishing GAAP. However, the SEC may overrule the FASB if the SEC thinks doing so will protect the public interest. To date, this authority has been exercised only one time.[9]

The FASB also has authority because it has been endorsed by each of the state boards that license certified public accountants. In auditing financial statements, CPAs confirm that the statements comply with the FASB's rules. The state ethics codes require the CPAs' audit report to disclose any areas in which the statements fail to comply. If the CPAs fail to report these problems, they may lose their licenses to practice. The AICPA's Code of Professional Conduct includes a similar provision. Also,

---

[8]For more detailed information about the board, see Paul B. W. Miller, Rodney J. Redding, and Paul R. Bahnson, *The FASB—The People, the Process, and the Politics,* 3rd ed. (Burr Ridge, IL: Richard D. Irwin, 1994).

[9]The SEC overruled the FASB's *Statement of Financial Accounting Standards No. 19* in 1978. This standard concerned accounting for oil and gas producing companies.

a member of the AICPA may be expelled from the institute for not objecting to financial statements that fail to comply with FASB rules.

Many other professional organizations support the FASB's process by providing input and by giving financial support through the Financial Accounting Foundation.[10] They include:

- American Accounting Association **(AAA)**—a professional association of individuals, primarily college and university accounting faculty.
- Financial Executives Institute **(FEI)**—a professional association of private accountants.
- Institute of Management Accountants **(IMA)**—a professional association of private accountants, formerly called the National Association of Accountants.
- Association for Investment Management and Research **(AIMR)**—a professional association of people who use financial statements in the process of evaluating companies' financial performance.
- Securities Industry Association **(SIA)**—an association of individuals involved with issuing and marketing securities.

These groups boost the Board's credibility by participating in its process for identifying GAAP.

Prior to the FASB, the accounting profession depended on the Accounting Principles Board **(APB)** to identify GAAP. The APB was a special committee of the AICPA, and its members served as unpaid volunteers. The APB issued 31 *Opinions* from 1959 to 1973. These *Opinions* created GAAP, just like the FASB's standards. Many APB *Opinions* remain in effect, and we describe their requirements throughout this book.

Prior to the APB, the accounting profession depended on the Committee on Accounting Procedure **(CAP)** for identifying GAAP. Like the APB, the CAP was a committee of the AICPA with unpaid members. The CAP issued 51 *Accounting Research Bulletins* during its life from 1936 to 1959. Only a few bulletins remain in effect.

The authority for identifying generally accepted auditing standards (GAAS) presently belongs to the Auditing Standards Board **(ASB).** The ASB is a special committee of the AICPA with unpaid volunteer members. The SEC is an important source of the ASB's authority.

Pronouncements issued by the FASB, APB, CAP, and ASB define specific GAAP and GAAS. They are available for accountants and users of financial statements in publications issued by the FASB and the AICPA. Many of these principles are described in this book.

In today's world, people in different countries engage in business with each other more easily than in the past. A company in the United States might sell its products all over the world. Another company in Singapore might raise cash by selling stock to American and Japanese investors. At the same time, it might borrow from creditors in Saudi Arabia and Germany.

An increasing number of companies have international operations. For example, **Marriott International, Inc.,** is a United States company with operations in lodging and contract services. Most of the company's operations are in the United States. However, in 1993

INTERNATIONAL ACCOUNTING STANDARDS

---

[10]Working alongside the FASB is the Governmental Accounting Standards Board (GASB), which identifies special accounting principles to be applied in preparing financial statements for state and local governments. Both the FASB and the GASB operate under the Financial Accounting Foundation.

alone, the company added managed properties in Budapest, Hungary; Colombo, Sri Lanka; Dubai, United Arab Emirates; and a franchised hotel in Leeds, England. It also began construction on Marriott hotels in Hurghada Beach, Egypt; Aruba; Bangkok, Thailand; Kuala Lumpur, Malaysia; and Jakarta, Indonesia.

Despite this trend toward global business, a major problem exists because each country has its own unique set of acceptable accounting practices. Consider, for example, the Singapore company we described earlier. Should it prepare financial statements that comply with Singapore accounting standards, or with the standards used in the United States, Japan, Saudi Arabia, or Germany? Should it have to prepare five different sets of reports to gain access to financial markets in all five countries?

Accounting organizations from around the world responded to this problem by creating the International Accounting Standards Committee (**IASC**) in 1973. With headquarters in London, the IASC issues *International Accounting Standards* that identify preferred accounting practices and then encourages their worldwide acceptance. By narrowing the range of alternative practices, the IASC hopes to create more harmony among the accounting practices of different countries. If standards could be harmonized, a single set of financial statements could be used by one company in all financial markets.

In many countries, the bodies that set accounting standards have encouraged the IASC to reduce the differences. Both the FASB and the SEC have provided this encouragement and technical assistance. However, the IASC does not have the authority to impose its standards on companies. Although progress has been slow, interest is growing in moving United States GAAP toward the IASC's preferred practices. The authority to make such changes rests with the FASB and the SEC.

Progress Check

1-3 **Which body currently establishes generally accepted accounting principles in the United States?** *(a)* **The SEC;** *(b)* **The U.S. Congress;** *(c)* **The FASB;** *(d)* **The AICPA;** *(e)* **The IASC.**

1-4 **What is the difference between GAAP and GAAS?**

1-5 **Is it true that United States companies with operations in foreign countries are required to prepare their financial statements according to the rules established by the IASC?**

UNDERSTANDING GENERALLY ACCEPTED ACCOUNTING PRINCIPLES

LO 2

Explain the accounting principles introduced in the chapter and describe the process by which generally accepted accounting principles are established.

At the beginning of this chapter, we said that the purpose of accounting is to provide useful information to people who make rational investment, credit, and similar decisions. In fact, this description of the purpose of accounting comes from a major FASB project called the *conceptual framework*. This framework defines several accounting terms that should be understood by financial statement users as well as accountants. For example, we relied on the conceptual framework in preceding discussions when we defined revenues, expenses, assets, liabilities, and equity.

Another purpose of the conceptual framework is to describe the characteristics that make accounting information useful for decisions. Earlier, we referred to the conceptual framework's commonsense ideas that information is useful only if it has both *relevance* and *reliability*.

Now that you have some background on how accounting principles are developed, we can begin to describe some of the broad principles listed on page 25. These broad principles will help you understand financial statements and the procedures used to prepare them.

Business Entity Principle

The **business entity principle** requires every business to be accounted for separately and distinctly from its owner or owners. This principle also requires us to account separately for other entities that might be controlled by the same owners. The reason behind this principle is that separate information for each business is relevant to decisions that its users make.

To illustrate, suppose that the owner of a business wants to see how well it is doing. To be useful, the financial statements for the business should not mix the owner's personal transactions with the business's transactions. For example, the owner's personal expenses should not be subtracted from the company's revenues on its income statement because they do not contribute to the company's success. Thus, the income statement should not report such things as the owner's personal entertainment and transportation expenses. Otherwise, the company's reported net income would be understated and the business would appear less profitable than it really is.

In summary, a company's reports should not include its owner's personal transactions, assets, and liabilities or the transactions, assets, and liabilities of another business. If this principle is not carefully followed, the reported information about the company's financial position and net income is not useful for rational investment and credit decisions.

PRINCIPLE APPLICATION
Business Entity Principle
Dole Food Company, Inc., owns 82% of Castle & Cooke Homes, Inc.'s equity. Nevertheless, Castle & Cooke Homes accounts for its operations as a separate entity and prepares its own financial statements.

Objectivity Principle

The **objectivity principle** requires financial statement information to be supported by evidence other than someone's opinion or imagination. Information would not be reliable if it were based only on what the statement preparer thinks might be true. The preparer might be too optimistic or too pessimistic. In the worst case, an unethical preparer might try to mislead financial statement users by deliberately misrepresenting the truth. The objectivity principle is intended to make financial statements useful by ensuring that they present reliable information.

Cost Principle

The **cost principle** requires financial statement information to be based on costs incurred in business transactions. Sales and purchases are examples of **business transactions.** Business transactions are exchanges of economic consideration between two parties. The consideration may include such things as goods, services, money, or rights to collect money. In applying the cost principle, cost is measured on a cash or cash equivalent basis. If cash is given for an asset or service, the cost of the asset or service is measured as the entire amount of cash paid. If something other than cash is exchanged (such as an old vehicle traded in for a new one), cost is measured as the cash equivalent value of what was given up or of the item received, whichever is more clearly evident.[11]

The *cost principle* is accepted because it puts relevant information in the financial statements. Cost is the amount initially sacrificed to purchase an asset or service. Cost also approximates the market value of the asset or service when it was acquired. Information about the amount sacrificed and the initial market value of what was received is generally thought to be relevant to decisions. Complying with the cost principle provides this information.

In addition, the cost principle is consistent with the *objectivity principle.* Most accountants believe that information based on actual costs is more likely to be

---

[11]FASB, *Accounting Standards—Current Text* (Norwalk, CT, 1994), sec. N35.105. First published as *APB Opinion No. 29,* par. 18.

objective than information based on estimates of values. For example, reporting purchases of assets and services at cost is more objective than reporting the manager's estimate of their value. Thus, financial statements based on costs are believed to be more reliable because the information is more objective.

To illustrate, suppose that a business pays $50,000 for land used in its operations. The cost principle tells us to record the purchase at $50,000. It would make no difference if the buyer thinks that the land is worth at least $60,000. The cost principle requires the purchase to be recorded at the cost of $50,000. However, you learn in later chapters that, to provide more useful information, objective estimates of value are sometimes reported instead of costs.

Going-Concern Principle

The **going-concern principle** (also called the **continuing-concern principle**) requires financial statements to reflect the assumption that the business will continue operating instead of being closed or sold. Thus, a company's balance sheet does not report the liquidation values of operating assets that are being held for long-term use. Instead, these assets are reported at amounts based on their cost. Many accountants have argued that the going-concern principle leads to reporting relevant information because many decisions about a business are made with the expectation that it will continue to exist in the future.

As a result of applying the cost and going-concern principles, a company's balance sheet seldom describes what the company is worth. Thus, if a company is to be bought or sold, the buyer and seller are well advised to obtain additional information from other sources.[12]

The going-concern principle must be ignored if the company is expected to fail or be liquidated. In these cases, the going-concern principle and the cost principle do not apply. Instead, estimated market values are relevant and costs are not relevant.

Progress Check

1-6   **Name and describe two qualities of useful information identified by the FASB's conceptual framework.**

1-7   **Why are the personal activities of a business owner excluded from the financial statements of the owner's business?**

1-8   **If a company finds a bargain on some equipment worth $40,000 to the company and is able to buy the equipment for $25,000, what amount should be reported for the equipment on the company's balance sheet prepared immediately after the purchase? Which principle governs your answer?**

LEGAL FORMS OF BUSINESS ORGANIZATIONS

LO 3

Describe single proprietorships, partnerships, and corporations, including any differences in the owners' responsibilities for the debts of the organizations.

This section of the chapter describes three legal forms for business organizations. The forms are *single proprietorships, partnerships,* and *corporations.* The particular form chosen for a company creates some differences in its financial statements.

Single Proprietorships and Partnerships

A **single proprietorship** (or **sole proprietorship**) is owned by one person and is not organized under state or federal laws as a corporation. Small retail stores and service enterprises are often operated as single proprietorships. No special legal requirements must be met to start this kind of business. As a result, single proprietorships are the most numerous of all types of businesses.

---

[12]In *SFAS 107,* the FASB established a requirement for supplemental disclosures (in the notes to the financial statements) of the current market values of many assets and liabilities.

A **partnership** is owned by two or more people, called partners, and is not organized as a corporation. Like a single proprietorship, no special legal requirements must be met in starting a partnership. All that is required is an agreement between the partners to operate a business together. The agreement can be either oral or written. However, a written partnership agreement may help the partners avoid or resolve later disputes.

In a strict legal sense, single proprietorships and partnerships are not separate from their owners. Thus, for example, a court can order an owner to sell personal assets to pay the debts of a proprietorship or partnership. In fact, an owner's personal assets may have to be sold to satisfy *all* the debts of a proprietorship or a partnership, even if this amount exceeds the owner's equity in the company. This unlimited liability feature of proprietorships and partnerships is an important disadvantage.

Despite the lack of separate legal existence from their owners, the *business entity principle* applies to the financial statements of single proprietorships and partnerships. That is, relevant information for ordinary investment and credit decisions is more likely to be reported in the financial statements if each business is treated as being separate from its owner or owners.

Corporations

A **corporation** is a separate legal entity chartered (or *incorporated*) under state or federal laws. Unlike proprietorships or partnerships, corporations are legally separate and distinct from their owners.

A corporation's equity is divided into units called shares of **stock** and its owners are called **shareholders** or **stockholders.** For example, **Pier 1 Imports, Inc.,** is a corporation that had issued 37,617,000 shares of stock at the close of its 1994 business year. In other words, Pier 1's equity was divided into 37,617,000 units. A stockholder who owned 376,617 shares would own 1% of the company.

When a corporation issues only one class of stock, it is called **common stock** or *capital stock.* We discuss other classes of stock in Chapter 13.

A very important characteristic of a corporation is its status as a separate legal entity. This characteristic means that the corporation is responsible for its own acts and its own debts. As a result, the corporation's stockholders are not personally liable for these acts and debts. This limited liability feature is a major advantage of corporations over proprietorships and partnerships.

The separate legal status of a corporation also means that it can enter into its own contracts. For example, a corporation can buy, own, and sell property in its own name. It also can sue and be sued in its own name. In short, the separate legal status enables a corporation to conduct its business affairs with all the rights, duties, and responsibilities of a person. Of course, a corporation lacks a physical body and must act through its managers, who are its legal agents.

In addition, the separate legal status of a corporation means that its life is not limited by its owners' lives or by a need for them to remain owners. Thus, a stockholder can sell or transfer shares to another person without affecting the operations of the corporation.

There are fewer corporations in the United States than proprietorships and partnerships. However, the corporate form of business offers advantages for accumulating and managing capital resources. As a result, corporations control the most economic wealth.

Differences in Financial Statements

Despite the major legal differences among the three forms of businesses, there are only a few differences in their financial statements.

One difference is in the equity section of the balance sheet. A proprietorship's balance sheet lists the capital balance beside the single owner's name. Partnership balance sheets use the same approach, unless there are too many owners for their names to fit in the available space. The names of a corporation's stockholders are not listed in the balance sheet. Instead, the total stockholders' equity is divided into **contributed capital** (also called **paid-in capital**) and **retained earnings.** Contributed capital is created by the stockholders' investments. Retained earnings are created by the corporation's profitable activities.

Another difference exists in the term used to describe payments by a company to its owners. When an owner of a proprietorship or a partnership receives cash from the company, the payments are called **withdrawals.** When owners of a corporation receive cash from the company, the payments are called **dividends.** Withdrawals and dividends are not reported on a company's income statement because they are not expenses incurred to generate revenues.

Another difference involves reporting of payments to a company's managers when the managers are also owners. Because a corporation is a separate legal entity, salaries paid to its managers are reported as expenses on its income statement. In contrast, if the owner of a single proprietorship is also its manager, no salary expense is reported on the income statement for these services. The same is true for a partnership. This different treatment requires special consideration when analyzing the income statement. Our discussion at the end of this chapter describes this analysis in more detail.

To keep things simple while you are beginning to learn accounting, the examples in the first portion of this book are all based on single proprietorships. Chapters 13 and 14 provide additional information about the financial statements of partnerships and corporations.

Progress Check

1-9   A single proprietorship: *(a)* Divides its equity into shares of stock; *(b)* is a separate legal entity; *(c)* is owned by one person who is personally responsible for all its debts.

1-10   Why are a proprietor's withdrawals not reported on the company's income statement?

USING THE BALANCE SHEET EQUATION TO PROVIDE USEFUL INFORMATION

LO 4

Analyze business transactions to determine their effects on the accounting equation.

Up to this stage, you have learned that financial statements describe the financial activities of a business. You also know that many of these activities (for example, purchases and sales) involve business transactions. To clearly understand the information in the statements, you need to see how an accounting system captures relevant data from the transactions, classifies and saves it, and then organizes it on the financial statements. We begin to explain this in the next section of the chapter. Our explanation continues through Chapter 4. We start with a simple example.

The beginning point for accounting systems is the definition of *owner's equity* as the difference between an organization's assets and liabilities. This definition can be stated as the following equation for a single proprietorship:

$$\text{Assets} - \text{Liabilities} = \text{Owner's Equity}$$

Like any equation, this one can be modified by rearranging the terms. The following modified form of the equation is called the **balance sheet equation:**

$$\text{Assets} = \text{Liabilities} + \text{Owner's Equity}$$

		Assets				=	Owner's Equity	
	Cash	+	Store Supplies	+	Copy Equipment	=	Terry Dow, Capital	Explanation of Change
(1)	$30,000						$30,000	Investment
(2)	− 2,500		+$2,500					
Bal.	$27,500		$2,500				$30,000	
(3)	−20,000				+$20,000			
Bal.	$ 7,500	+	$2,500	+	$20,000	=	$30,000	

Illustration 1-4
Changes in the Balance Sheet Equation Caused by Asset Purchases for Cash

Because it serves as the basis for financial accounting information, the balance sheet equation also is called the **accounting equation.** The next section shows you how to use this equation to keep track of changes in a company's assets, liabilities, and owner's equity in a way that provides useful information.

THE EFFECTS OF TRANSACTIONS ON THE ACCOUNTING EQUATION

A transaction is an exchange between two parties of such things as goods, services, money, or rights to collect money. Because the two parties exchange assets and liabilities, transactions affect the components of the accounting equation. Importantly, each and every transaction always leaves the equation in balance. That is, the total assets always equal the sum of the liabilities and the equity regardless of what happens in a transaction. We show how this equality is preserved by looking at the transactions of a new small business called Clear Copy Co.

Transaction 1. On December 1, 19X1, Terry Dow formed a new photocopying store that was organized as a single proprietorship. Dow planned to be the manager of the store as well as its owner. The marketing plan for the store is to focus primarily on serving business customers who place relatively large orders. Dow invested $30,000 cash in the new company and deposited it in a bank account opened under the name of Clear Copy Co. After this event, the cash (an asset) and the owner's equity each equal $30,000; as you can see, the accounting equation is in balance:

Assets	=	Owner's Equity
Cash, $30,000		Terry Dow, Capital, $30,000

The equation shows that the business has one asset, cash, equal to $30,000. It has no liabilities, and the owner's equity is $30,000.

Transactions 2 and 3. In its second business transaction, Clear Copy used $2,500 of its cash to purchase store supplies. In a third transaction, Clear Copy spent $20,000 to buy photocopying equipment. These events, which we call transactions 2 and 3, were both exchanges of cash for other assets. Neither transaction produced an expense because no value was lost to the company. The purchases merely changed the form of the assets from cash to supplies and equipment.

The effects of these transactions are shown in color in the equations in Illustration 1–4. Observe that the decreases in cash are exactly equal to the increases in the store supplies and the copy equipment. As a result, the equation remains in balance after each transaction.

Transaction 4. Next, Dow decided that the business needed more store supplies and additional copy equipment. The items to be purchased would have a total cost of $7,100. However, as shown on the last line of the first column in Illustration 1–4, the business had only $7,500 in cash after transaction 3. Because these purchases would use almost all of Clear Copy's cash, Dow arranged to purchase them on credit from Handy Supply Company. That is, Clear Copy took delivery of the items in exchange for a promise to pay for them later. The supplies cost $1,100, the copy equipment cost $6,000, and the total liability to Handy Supply is $7,100.

Illustration 1-5 Changes in the Balance Sheet Equation Caused by Asset Purchases on Credit,
Revenues Received in Cash, and Expenses Paid in Cash

	Assets				Liabilities	Owner's Equity	
	Cash +	Store + Supplies	Copy Equipment	=	Accounts + Payable	Terry Dow, Capital	Explanation of Change
Bal.	$7,500	$2,500	$20,000			$30,000	
(4)		+1,100	+ 6,000		+$7,100		
Bal.	$7,500	$3,600	$26,000		$7,100	$30,000	
(5)	+2,200					+ 2,200	Revenue
Bal.	$9,700	$3,600	$26,000		$7,100	$32,200	
(6)	−1,000					− 1,000	Expense
Bal.	$8,700	$3,600	$26,000		$7,100	$31,200	
(7)	− 700					− 700	Expense
Bal.	$8,000 +	$3,600 +	$26,000	=	$7,100 +	$30,500	

The effects of this purchase are shown in Illustration 1–5 as transaction 4. Notice that the purchase increased total assets by $7,100 while the company's liabilities (called *accounts payable*) increased by the same amount. The transaction did not create an expense, so the amount of equity remained unchanged from the original $30,000 balance.

Transaction 5. A primary objective of a business is to increase its owner's wealth. This goal is met when the business produces a profit (also called *net income*). A net income is reflected in the accounting equation as a net increase in owner's equity. Clear Copy's method of generating revenues is to sell photocopying services to its customers. The business produces a net income only if its revenues are greater than the expenses incurred in earning them. As you should expect, the process of earning copy services revenues and incurring expenses creates changes in the accounting equation.

We can see how the accounting equation is affected by earning revenues in transaction 5. In this transaction, Clear Copy provided copying services to a customer on December 10 and immediately collected $2,200 cash. Illustration 1–5 shows that this event increased cash by $2,200 and increased owner's equity by $2,200. This increase in equity is identified in the last column as a revenue because it was earned by providing services. This information can be used later to prepare the income statement.

Transactions 6 and 7. Also on December 10, Clear Copy paid $1,000 rent to the owner of the building in which its store is located. Paying this amount allowed Clear Copy to occupy the space for the entire month of December. The effects of this event are shown in Illustration 1–5 as transaction 6. On December 12, Clear Copy paid the $700 salary of the company's only employee. This event is reflected in Illustration 1–5 as transaction 7.

Both transactions 6 and 7 produced expenses for the business. That is, they used up cash for the purpose of providing services to customers. Unlike the asset purchases in transactions 2 and 3, the cash payments in transactions 6 and 7 acquired services. The benefits of these services do not last beyond the end of the month. The equations in Illustration 1–5 show that both transactions reduced cash and Terry Dow's equity. Thus, the accounting equation remains in balance after each event. The last column in Illustration 1–5 shows that these decreases were expenses. This information is useful when the income statement is prepared.

Summary. We said before that a business produces a net income when its revenues exceed its expenses. Net income increases owner's equity. If the expenses exceed the revenues, a net loss occurs and equity is decreased. Remember that the amount of net income or loss is not affected by transactions completed between a business and its owner. Thus, Terry Dow's initial investment of $30,000 is not income to the business, even though it increased the equity.

To keep things simple, and to emphasize the fact that revenues and expenses produce changes in equity, the illustrations in this first chapter add the revenues directly to owner's equity and subtract the expenses directly from owner's equity. In actual practice, however, information about the revenues and expenses is accumulated separately and the amounts are added to or subtracted from owner's equity. We describe more details about this process in Chapters 2, 3, and 4.

Because of the importance of earning revenues for a company's success, we briefly interrupt the description of Clear Copy's transactions to describe the *revenue recognition principle*. This principle guides us in knowing when to record a company's revenue so that it can be usefully reported in the income statement.

REVENUE RECOGNITION PRINCIPLE

LO 2

Explain the accounting principles introduced in the chapter and describe the process by which generally accepted accounting principles are established.

Managers need guidance in deciding when to recognize revenue. (*Recognize* means to record an event for the purpose of reporting its effects in the financial statements.) For example, if revenue is recognized too early, the income statement reports net income sooner than it should and the business looks more profitable than it really is. On the other hand, if the revenue is not recognized on time, the income statement shows lower amounts of revenue and net income than it should and the business looks less profitable than it really is. In either case, the income statement does not provide decision makers with useful information about the company's success.

The question of when revenue should be recognized on the income statement is addressed by the **revenue recognition principle** (also called the **realization principle**). This principle includes three important guidelines:

1. *Revenue should be recognized at the time it is earned.* The whole process of getting ready to provide services, finding customers, convincing them to buy, and providing a service contributes to the earning of revenue. However, the amount of revenue earned at any point in the process usually cannot be determined reliably until the entire process is complete. This does not occur until the business acquires the right to collect the selling price. Therefore, in most cases, revenue should not be recognized on the income statement until the earnings process is essentially complete. For most businesses, the earnings process is completed only when services are rendered or when the seller transfers ownership of goods sold to the buyer. For example, suppose that a customer pays in advance of taking delivery of a good or service. Because the earnings process is not completed, the seller should not recognize any revenue. Instead, the seller must actually complete the earnings process before recognizing the revenue.[13] This practice is known as the *sales basis of* revenue recognition.

2. *The inflow of assets associated with revenue does not have to be in the form of cash.* The most common noncash asset acquired by the seller in a revenue transaction is an account receivable from a customer. These transactions, called *credit sales,* occur because it is convenient for the customer to get the goods or services now and pay for them later. (Remember that Clear Copy took advantage of this convenience in transaction 4 when it bought supplies and equipment on credit.) If objective evidence shows that the seller has the right to collect the account receivable, the seller

PRINCIPLE APPLICATION
Revenue Recognition Principle
MCI Communications Corporation records as revenue the amount of communications services rendered, as measured by the minutes of traffic processed, after deducting an estimate of the traffic which will be neither billed nor collected.

---

[13]FASB, *Accounting Standards—Current Text* (Norwalk, CT, 1994), sec. R75.101. First published as *APB Opinion No. 10, par. 12.*

Illustration 1-6 Changes in the Balance Sheet Equation Caused by Noncash Revenues, the Later Receipt of Cash, the Payment of Payables, and Withdrawals by the Owner

	Cash	+	Accounts Receivable	+	Store Supplies	+	Copy Equipment	=	Accounts Payable	+	Terry Dow, Capital	Explanation of Change
					Assets				**Liabilities**		**Owner's Equity**	
Bal.	$8,000				$3,600		$26,000		$7,100		$30,500	
(8)			+$1,700								+ 1,700	Revenue
Bal.	$8,000		$1,700		$3,600		$26,000		$7,100		$32,200	
(9)	+1,700		−1,700									
Bal.	$9,700		$ 0		$3,600		$26,000		$7,100		$32,200	
(10)	− 900								− 900			
Bal.	$8,800		$ 0		$3,600		$26,000		$6,200		$32,200	
(11)	− 400										− 400	Withdrawal
Bal.	$8,400	+	$ 0	+	$3,600	+	$26,000	=	$6,200	+	$31,800	

should recognize the revenue. When the cash is collected later, no additional revenue is recognized. Instead, collecting the cash simply changes the form of the asset from a receivable to cash.

3. *The amount of recognized revenue should be measured as the cash received plus the cash equivalent value (fair market value) of any other asset or assets received.* For example, if the transaction creates an account receivable, the seller should recognize revenue equal to the value of the receivable, which is usually equivalent to the amount of cash to be collected.

The footnotes to a company's financial statements should include an explanation of the specific approach to revenue recognition used by the company. For example, **General Motors Corporation** states in its 1993 annual report that "Sales are generally recorded by the Corporation when products are shipped to independent dealers."

THE EFFECTS OF ADDITIONAL TRANSACTIONS ON THE ACCOUNTING EQUATION

To show how the revenue recognition principle works, we return to the example of Clear Copy Co.

Transactions 8 and 9. Assume that Clear Copy provided copy services for a customer and billed that customer $1,700. This event is identified as transaction 8 in Illustration 1–6. Ten days later, the customer paid Clear Copy the full $1,700 in transaction 9.

Illustration 1–6 shows that transaction 8 created a new asset, the account receivable from the customer. The $1,700 increase in assets produces an equal increase in owner's equity. Notice that this increase in equity is identified as a revenue in the last column of Illustration 1–6.

Transaction 9 occurred when the customer in transaction 8 paid the account receivable. This event merely converted the receivable to cash. Because transaction 9 did not increase total assets and did not affect liabilities, equity did not change. Thus, this transaction did not create any new revenue. The revenue was generated when Clear Copy rendered the services, not when the cash was collected. This emphasis on the earning process instead of cash flows reflects the goal of providing useful information in the income statement by applying the *revenue recognition principle.*

Illustration 1-7 Changes in the Balance Sheet Equation Caused by Noncash Revenues, the Later Receipt of Cash, the Payment of Payables, and Withdrawals by the Owner

	Cash	+ Accounts + Receivable	Store Supplies	+ Copy Equipment	= Accounts + Payable	Terry Dow, Capital	Explanation of Change
			Assets		**Liabilities**	**Owner's Equity**	
(1)	$30,000					$30,000	Investment
(2)	− 2,500		+$2,500				
Bal.	$27,500		$2,500			$30,000	
(3)	−20,000			+$20,000			
Bal.	$ 7,500		$2,500	$20,000		$30,000	
(4)			+1,100	+ 6,000	+$7,100		
Bal.	$7,500		$3,600	$26,000	$7,100	$30,000	
(5)	+2,200					+2,200	Revenue
Bal.	$9,700		$3,600	$26,000	$7,100	$32,200	
(6)	−1,000					−1,000	Expense
Bal.	$8,700		$3,600	$26,000	$7,100	$31,200	
(7)	− 700					− 700	Expense
Bal.	$8,000		$3,600	$26,000	$7,100	$30,500	
(8)		+$1,700				+1,700	Revenue
Bal.	$8,000	$1,700	$3,600	$26,000	$7,100	$32,200	
(9)	+1,700	−1,700					
Bal.	$9,700	$ 0	$3,600	$26,000	$7,100	$32,200	
(10)	− 900				− 900		
Bal.	$8,800	$ 0	$3,600	$26,000	$6,200	$32,200	
(11)	− 400					− 400	Withdrawal
Bal.	$8,400 +	$ 0 +	$3,600 +	$26,000 =	$6,200 +	$31,800	

Transaction 10. In transaction 10, Clear Copy paid $900 to Handy Supply Company on December 24. The $900 payment relates to the earlier purchase of equipment from Handy. (The amount due Handy for the supplies purchase remains unpaid.) Illustration 1–6 shows that this transaction decreased Clear Copy's cash by $900 and decreased its liability to Handy Supply by the same amount. As a result, there was no reduction in owner's equity. This event did not create an expense, even though cash flowed out of the company.

Transaction 11. Another type of event, the payment of cash to the company's owner, is identified in Illustration 1–6 as transaction 11. In this case, Clear Copy paid $400 to Terry Dow to use for personal living expenses. Traditionally, a company's payments of cash (or other assets) to its owner are called *withdrawals*. Notice that this decrease in owner's equity is not called an expense in Illustration 1–6. Withdrawals are not expenses because they do not create revenues for the company. And, because withdrawals are not expenses, they are not used to calculate net income.

Summary. Illustration 1–7 presents the effects of the entire series of 11 transactions for Clear Copy. Take time now to see that the equation remains in balance after each transaction. This is because the effects of each transaction are always in balance. In transactions 1, 5, and 8, total assets and equity increased by equal amounts. In transactions 2, 3, and 9, one asset increased while another decreased by an equal amount. Transaction 4 increased total assets and a liability by equal amounts. In transactions 6, 7, and 11, assets and equity decreased by equal amounts. Finally, transaction 10 decreased an asset and a liability by the same amount. The equality of these effects is central to the working of double entry accounting. You learn more about double entry accounting in the next chapter.

Progress Check

1-11   A new business has the following transactions: (1) the owner invested $3,600 cash; (2) supplies were purchased for $2,600 cash; (3) services were provided to a customer for $2,300 cash; (4) a salary of $1,000 was paid to an employee; and (5) $3,000 cash was borrowed from the bank. After these transactions, total assets, total liabilities, and total owner's equity are: (a) $7,900, $5,300, $2,600;   (b) $7,900, $3,000, $4,900;   (c) $7,900, $3,000, $3,600.

1-12   Is it possible for a transaction to increase a liability without affecting any other asset, liability, or owner's equity? Explain.

UNDERSTANDING MORE ABOUT THE FINANCIAL STATEMENTS

LO 1

Describe the information presented in financial statements, be able to prepare simple financial statements, and analyze a company's performance with the return on equity ratio.

Up to this point, you have learned about only two financial statements: the income statement and the balance sheet. GAAP also require companies to include two other statements in their reports. They are the statement of changes in owner's equity and the statement of cash flows.

The following diagram shows how all four financial statements are linked:

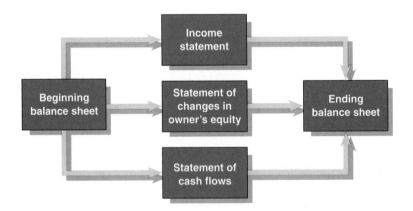

The income statement describes how owner's equity changed during the period through the company's income earning activities. The statement of changes in owner's equity describes all changes in equity, including net income, new investments by the owner, and withdrawals by the owner. The statement of cash flows describes how the amount of cash changed between the beginning and ending balance sheets. The statement of cash flows also describes many of the changes in the company's other assets and liabilities. Thus, most of the company's activities are described by the three statements in the middle, while the balance sheets describe the company's financial position before and after those activities occurred.

The Income Statement

The top section of Illustration 1–8 shows Clear Copy's income statement as it appeared in Illustration 1–1. Now you can see that it is based on the information about revenues and expenses recorded in the owner's equity column in Illustration 1–7.

In the income statement, the copy services revenue of $3,900 resulted from transactions 5 and 8. If the business had earned other kinds of revenues, they would have been listed separately to help users understand more about the company's activities.

Illustration 1-8   Financial Statements for Clear Copy Co.

CLEAR COPY CO.
Income Statement
For Month Ended December 31, 19X1

Revenues:		
Copy services revenue		$3,900
Operating expenses:		
Rent expense	$1,000	
Salaries expense	700	
Total operating expenses		1,700
Net income		$2,200

CLEAR COPY CO.
Statement of Changes in Owner's Equity
For Month Ended December 31, 19X1

Terry Dow, capital, November 30, 19X1		$ –0–
Plus: Investments by owner	$30,000	
Net income	2,200	32,200
Total		$32,200
Less withdrawals by owner		400
Terry Dow, capital, December 31, 19X1		$31,800

CLEAR COPY, INC.
Balance Sheet
December 31, 19X1

Assets		Liabilities	
Cash	$ 8,400	Accounts payable . . .	$ 6,200
Store supplies	3,600	**Owner's Equity**	
Copy equipment	26,000	Terry Dow, capital . . .	31,800
		Total liabilities and	
Total assets	$38,000	owner's equity	$38,000

The income statement then lists the rent and salaries expenses incurred in transactions 6 and 7. The types of expenses are identified to help users form a more complete picture of the events of the time period. Finally, the income statement presents the amount of net income earned during the month.

The Statement of Changes in Owner's Equity

The **statement of changes in owner's equity** presents information about everything that happened to equity during the reporting period. The statement shows the beginning equity, the events that increased it (new investments by the owner and net income), and the events that decreased it (a net loss and withdrawals).

The middle section of Illustration 1–8 shows the statement of changes in owner's equity for Clear Copy Co. The heading refers to December 19X1 because the statement describes events that happened during that month. The beginning balance of equity is stated as of the close of business on November 30. It is zero because the business did not exist before then. An existing business would report the balance as of the end of the prior reporting period. The Clear Copy statement shows that $30,000 of equity was created by Dow's initial investment. It also shows the $2,200 net income earned during the month. This item links the income statement to the statement of changes in owner's equity. The statement also reports Dow's $400 withdrawal and the $31,800 equity balance at the end of the month.

Illustration 1-9 Statement of Cash Flows for Clear Copy Co.

CLEAR COPY CO. Statement of Cash Flows For Month Ended December 31, 19X1		
Cash flows from operating activities:		
Cash received from customers	$ 3,900	
Cash paid for store supplies	(2,500)	
Cash paid for rent	(1,000)	
Cash paid to employee	(700)	
Net cash provided by operating activities . .		$ (300)
Cash flows from investing activities:		
Purchase of copy equipment	$(20,000)	
Net cash used by investing activities		(20,000)
Cash flows from financing activities:		
Investments by owner	$ 30,000	
Repayment of debt	(900)	
Withdrawals by owner	(400)	
Net cash provided by financing activities . .		28,700
Net increase in cash		$ 8,400
Cash balance, November 30, 19X1		–0–
Cash balance, December 31, 19X1		$ 8,400

The Balance Sheet

The lower section of Illustration 1–8 presents Clear Copy's balance sheet (the same statement appeared in Illustration 1–2). The heading shows that the statement describes the company's financial condition at the close of business on December 31, 19X1.

The left side of the balance sheet lists the company's assets: cash, store supplies, and copy equipment. The right side of the balance sheet shows that the company owes $6,200 on accounts payable. If any other liabilities had existed (such as bank loans), they would have been listed in this section. The equity section shows an ending balance of $31,800. Note the link between the statement of changes in owner's equity and the balance sheet.

The Statement of Cash Flows

The fourth financial statement is the **statement of cash flows,** which describes where a company's cash came from and where it went during the period. The statement also shows how much cash was on hand at the beginning of the period, and how much was left at the end. This information is important for both internal and external decision makers because a company must manage its cash well if it is going to survive and prosper. For example, **Delta Air Lines, Inc.,** had net losses totaling more than $1.8 billion during the three-year period ended June 30, 1993. Nevertheless, Delta avoided bankruptcy by carefully managing its cash through delayed capital spending, borrowing, and issuing additional stock.

Cash Flows from Operating Activities. Illustration 1–9 shows Clear Copy's statement of cash flows for December. The first section of the statement shows the amount of cash used by the company's *operating activities*. The $3,900 of cash received from customers equals the total revenues on the income statement only because Clear Copy collected all of its revenues in cash. If some credit sales are not collected, or if credit sales from a prior reporting period are collected, the amount of cash received from customers does not equal the revenues reported on the income statement for the same period.

This first section also lists cash payments for store supplies, rent, and salaries. These cash flows occurred in transactions 2, 6, and 7. Notice that the amounts are in parentheses to indicate that they are subtracted. The amounts for rent and salaries equal the expenses reported on Clear Copy's income statement only because Clear Copy paid cash for the expenses.

The payment for supplies is reported as an operating activity because supplies are expected to be consumed in short-term operations. (We explain this more completely in Chapter 16.) The net outflow from operating activities for December was $300. Decision makers are especially interested in this section of the statement of cash flows because companies must generate cash from their operating activities to stay in existence.

Cash Flows from Investing Activities. The second section of the statement of cash flows describes the cash flows from *investing activities*. In general, investing activities involve buying or selling assets such as land or equipment that are held for long-term use in the business. Clear Copy's only investing activity was the $20,000 purchase of equipment in transaction 3. Notice that no cash flows are reported for transaction 4, which was a credit purchase.

Decision makers are interested in this section of the statement of cash flows because it describes how a company is preparing for the future. If the company is spending cash for productive assets, it should be able to grow. On the other hand, the company might be spending too much on productive assets for its size. The information in the investing section helps decision makers understand what the company has done.

Cash Flows from Financing Activities. The third section of the statement shows the cash flows related to *financing activities*. Financing activities include borrowing cash from creditors and receiving cash investments from the owner. Financing activities also include loan repayments and cash withdrawals by the owner. The statement of cash flows in Illustration 1–9 shows that Clear Copy obtained $30,000 from Terry Dow's initial investment in transaction 1. If the business had borrowed cash, the amount would appear here as an increase in cash. Decision makers also are interested in the financing section. The sources of cash used by a company can affect the future. For example, excessive borrowing can burden the company with too much debt and reduce its potential for growth.

The financing activities section of Illustration 1–9 also shows the $900 paid to Handy Supply in transaction 10 and the $400 withdrawal from transaction 11. The overall effect of the financing activities was a $28,700 net inflow of cash. The information in this section explains why the business did not run out of cash even though it spent $20,000 on assets and used $300 in its operating activities.

The last section of the statement of cash flows shows that the company increased its cash balance by $8,400. Because the company started out with no cash, the ending balance is also $8,400. This final amount links the statement of cash flows to the balance sheet. We present a more detailed explanation of the statement of cash flows in Chapter 16.

USING THE INFORMATION— RETURN ON EQUITY

LO 1

Describe the information presented in financial statements, be able to prepare simple financial statements, and analyze a company's performance with the return on equity ratio.

An important reason for recording and reporting information about a company's assets, liabilities, equity, and net income is to help the owner judge the business venture's relative success compared to other activities or investments. One way to describe this success is to calculate the **return on equity ratio,** which equals the amount of income achieved in a period divided by the amount of owner's equity. The formula for this ratio is as follows:

$$\text{Return on equity} = \frac{\text{Net income}}{\text{Beginning owner's equity}}$$

Recall from the beginning of this chapter the story of Karen and Mark Smith, who are considering an investment in **H & R Block, Inc.** In starting to analyze that company, they could use the financial information presented on page 19 to calculate H & R Block's 1993 return on equity, as follows:

$$\frac{\text{Net earnings}}{\text{Beginning stockholders' equity}} = \frac{\$180,705}{\$613,713} = 29.4\%$$

Interpreting the rate of return achieved by a company requires an understanding of several factors. For example, the rate should be compared with the rates that could be earned on other kinds of investments.

In the example of Clear Copy Co., the financial statements show that Terry Dow earned a return on equity at the rate of 7.3% for the month of December. To find this rate, we divide $2,200 of net income by the $30,000 beginning balance of owner's equity.

Dow's rate for December is high compared to most investments, and may appear very appealing. Recall, however, that the income reported for a single proprietorship does not reflect any expense for the effort exerted by the owner in managing its operations. Thus, it is advisable to reduce the reported income by a fair value for the owner's efforts before calculating the return on equity. Thus, the formula can be restated as follows for a single proprietorship:

$$\text{Modified return on equity} = \frac{\text{Net income} - \text{Value of owner's efforts}}{\text{Beginning owner's equity}}$$

For example, suppose that other employment opportunities show that Dow's efforts are valued at $1,600 per month. If so, the numerator would be only $600 ($2,200 minus $1,600). As a result, the modified return would be $1,000/$30,000, which is only 2.0% for the month instead of the 7.3% just shown.

Dow should compare this rate with other investment alternatives to determine whether Clear Copy is producing an adequate return on equity. Because 2.0% per month is 24% per year, it is likely that Dow will be encouraged to stay in the business. However, we have not completely measured the income for the month. Chapters 2 and 3 introduce additional revenues and expenses, the net effect of which will be to reduce the net income amount shown here.

Progress Check

1-13   Which of the following is one of the three categories of cash flows that appear on the statement of cash flows? *(a)* Cash receipts from owner's investments. *(b)* Cash payments for operating expenses. *(c)* Cash provided or used by investing activities.

1-14   What financial statement item appears on both the income statement and the statement of changes in owner's equity?

1-15 What financial statement item appears on both the statement of changes in owner's equity and the balance sheet?

1-16 Why might a business owner calculate the return on equity ratio?

LO 1. Describe the information presented in financial statements, be able to prepare simple financial statements, and analyze a company's performance with the return on equity ratio. The income statement shows a company's revenues, expenses, and net income or loss. The balance sheet lists a company's assets, liabilities, and owner's equity. The statement of changes in owner's equity shows the effects on owner's equity from investments by the owner, withdrawals, and net income or net loss. The statement of cash flows shows the changes in cash that resulted from operating, investing, and financing activities. The financial statements are prepared with information about the effects of each transaction on the accounting equation. The company's performance can be analyzed by comparing the company's return on equity with rates on other investments available to the owner.

LO 2. Explain the accounting principles introduced in the chapter and describe the process by which generally accepted accounting principles are established. Accounting principles help accountants produce relevant and reliable information. Among others, broad accounting principles include the business entity principle, the objectivity principle, the cost principle, the going-concern principle, and the revenue recognition principle. Specific accounting principles for financial accounting are established in the United States primarily by the Financial Accounting Standards Board (FASB), with oversight by the Securities and Exchange Commission (SEC). Auditing standards are established by the Auditing Standards Board (ASB), a committee of the American Institute of CPAs (AICPA). The International Accounting Standards Committee (IASC) identifies preferred practices and encourages their adoption throughout the world.

LO 3. Describe single proprietorships, partnerships, and corporations, including any differences in the owners' responsibilities for the debts of the organizations. A single (or sole) proprietorship is an unincorporated business owned by one individual. A partnership differs from a single proprietorship in that it has more than one owner. Proprietors and partners are personally responsible for the debts of their businesses. A corporation is a separate legal entity. As such, its owners are not personally responsible for its debts.

LO 4. Analyze business transactions to determine their effects on the accounting equation. The accounting equation states that Assets = Liabilities + Owner's Equity. Business transactions always have at least two effects on the elements in the accounting equation. The equation is always in balance when business transactions are properly recorded.

SUMMARY OF THE CHAPTER IN TERMS OF LEARNING OBJECTIVES

DEMONSTRATION PROBLEM

After several months of planning, Barbara Schmidt started a haircutting business called The Cutlery. The following events occurred during its first month:

a. On August 1, Schmidt put $3,000 cash into a checking account in the name of The Cutlery. She also invested $15,000 of equipment that she already owned.

b. On August 2, she paid $600 cash for furniture for the shop.

c. On August 3, she paid $500 cash to rent space in a strip mall for August.

d. On August 4, she furnished the shop by installing the old equipment and some new equipment that she bought on credit for $1,200. This amount is to be repaid in three equal payments at the end of August, September, and October.

e. On August 5, The Cutlery opened for business. Receipts from cash sales in the first week and a half of business (ended August 15) were $825.

f. On August 17, Schmidt paid $125 to an assistant for working during the grand opening.

g. Cash receipts from sales during the second half of August were $930.

h. On August 31, Schmidt paid an installment on the account payable.

i. On August 31, she withdrew $900 cash for her personal use.

Required

1. Arrange the following asset, liability, and owner's equity titles in a table similar to the one in Illustration 1–7: Cash, Furniture, Store Equipment, Accounts Payable, and Barbara Schmidt, Capital. Show the effects of each transaction on the equation. Explain each of the changes in owner's equity.

2. Prepare an income statement for August.

3. Prepare a statement of changes in owner's equity for August.

4. Prepare a balance sheet as of August 31.

5. Prepare a statement of cash flows for August.

6. Determine the return on equity ratio for August.

7. Determine the modified return on equity ratio for August, assuming that Schmidt's management efforts were worth $1,000.

Planning the Solution

- Set up a table with the appropriate columns, including a final column for describing the events that affect owner's equity.

- Analyze each transaction and show its effects as increases or decreases in the appropriate columns. Be sure that the accounting equation remains in balance after each event.

- To prepare the income statement, find the revenues and expenses in the last column. List those items on the statement, calculate the difference, and label the result as *net income* or *net loss*.

- Use the information in the Explanation of Change column to prepare the statement of changes in owner's equity.

- Use the information on the last row of the table to prepare the balance sheet.

- To prepare the statement of cash flows, include all events listed in the Cash column of the table. Classify each cash flow as operating, investing, or financing. Follow the example in Illustration 1–9.

- Calculate the return on equity by dividing net income by the beginning equity. Calculate the modified return by subtracting the $1,000 value of Schmidt's efforts from the net income, and then dividing the difference by the beginning equity.

Solution to Demonstration Problem

1.

	Assets			= Liabilities +	Owner's Equity	
	Cash	+ Furniture +	Store Equipment	= Accounts Payable	+ Barbara Schmidt, Capital	Explanation of Change
a.	$3,000		$15,000		$18,000	Investment
b.	− 600	$600				
Bal.	$2,400	$600	$15,000		$18,000	
c.	− 500				− 500	Expense
Bal.	$1,900	$600	$15,000		$17,500	
d.			+1,200	+$1,200		
Bal.	$1,900	$600	$16,200	$1,200	$17,500	
e.	+ 825				+ 825	Revenue
Bal.	$2,725	$600	$16,200	$1,200	$18,325	
f.	− 125				− 125	Expense
Bal.	$2,600	$600	$16,200	$1,200	$18,200	
g.	+ 930				+ 930	Revenue
Bal.	$3,530	$600	$16,200	$1,200	$19,130	
h.	− 400			− 400		
Bal.	$3,130	$600	$16,200	$ 800	$19,130	
i.	− 900				− 900	Withdrawal
Bal.	$2,230 +	$600 +	$16,200 =	$ 800 +	$18,230	

2.

THE CUTLERY
Income Statement
For Month Ended August 31

Revenues:		
Sales		$1,755
Operating expenses:		
Rent expense	$500	
Salaries expense	125	
Total operating expenses		625
Net income		$1,130

3.

THE CUTLERY
Statement of Changes in Owner's Equity
For Month Ended August 31

Barbara Schmidt, capital, July 31		$ 0
Plus: Investments by owner	$18,000	
Net income	1,130	19,130
Total		$19,130
Less withdrawals by owner		(900)
Barbara Schmidt, capital, August 31		$18,230

4.

THE CUTLERY
Balance Sheet
August 31

Assets		Liabilities	
Cash.................	$ 2,230	Accounts payable	$ 800
Furniture..............	600	**Owner's Equity**	
Store equipment	16,200	Barbara Schmidt, capital ...	18,230
		Total liabilities and	
Total assets	$19,030	owner's equity	$19,030

5.

THE CUTLERY
Statement of Cash Flows
For Month Ended August 31

Cash flows from operating activities:		
Cash received from customers	$1,755	
Cash paid for rent	(500)	
Cash paid for wages	(125)	
Net cash provided by operating activities ...		$1,130
Cash flows from investing activities:		
Cash paid for furniture		(600)
Cash flows from financing activities:		
Cash received from owner	$3,000	
Cash paid to owner	(900)	
Repayment of debt	(400)	
Net cash provided by financing activities ...		1,700
Net increase in cash		$2,230
Cash balance, July 31		0
Cash balance, August 31		$2,230

6. $$\textbf{Return on equity} = \frac{\textbf{Net income}}{\textbf{Beginning owner's equity}} = \frac{\$1,130}{\$18,000} = 6.3\%$$

7. $$\textbf{Modified return on equity} = \frac{\textbf{Net income} - \textbf{Owner's efforts}}{\textbf{Beginning owner's equity}} = \frac{\$130}{\$18,000} = 0.7\%$$

GLOSSARY

AAA the American Accounting Association, a professional association of college and university accounting faculty. p. 27

Accounting equation a description of the relationship between a company's assets, liabilities, and equity; expressed as Assets = Liabilities + Owner's Equity; also called the *balance sheet equation*. p. 33

Accounts payable liabilities created by buying goods and services on credit. p. 23

Accounts receivable assets created by selling goods and services on credit. p. 23

AIMR Association for Investment Management and Research; a professional association of people who use financial statements in the process of evaluating companies' financial performance. p. 27

APB Accounting Principles Board, a former authoritative committee of the AICPA that was responsible for identifying generally accepted accounting principles from 1959 to 1973; predecessor to the FASB. p. 27

ASB the Auditing Standards Board; the authoritative committee of the AICPA that identifies generally accepted auditing standards. p. 27

Assets properties or economic resources owned by the business; more precisely, probable future economic benefits obtained or controlled by a particular entity as a result of past transactions or events. p. 23

Balance sheet a financial statement providing information that helps users understand a company's financial status; lists the types and dollar amounts of assets, liabilities, and equity as of a specific date; also called the *statement of financial position*. p. 22

Balance sheet equation another name for the *accounting equation*. p. 32

Business entity principle the principle that requires every business to be accounted for separately and distinctly from its owner or owners; based on the goal of providing relevant information about the business. p. 29

Business transaction an exchange between two parties of economic consideration, such as goods, services, money, or rights to collect money. p. 29

CAP the Committee on Accounting Procedure; the authoritative body for identifying generally accepted accounting principles from 1936 to 1959. p. 27

Common stock the name given to a corporation's stock when it issues only one kind or class of stock. p. 31

Continuing-concern principle another name for the *going-concern principle*. p. 30

Contributed capital the category of stockholders' equity created by the stockholders' investments. p. 32

Corporation a business chartered, or incorporated, as a separate legal entity under state or federal laws. p. 31

Cost principle the accounting principle that requires financial statement information to be based on costs incurred in business transactions; it requires assets and services to be recorded initially at the cash or cash-equivalent amount given in exchange. p. 29

Creditors individuals or organizations entitled to receive payments from a company. p. 23

Debtors individuals or organizations that owe amounts to a business. p. 23

Dividends payments of cash by a corporation to its stockholders. p. 32

Equity the difference between a company's assets and its liabilities; more precisely, the residual interest in the assets of an entity that remains after deducting its liabilities; also called *net assets*. p. 23

Expenses outflows or the using up of assets as a result of the major or central operations of a business; also, liabilities may be increased. p. 22

FASB Financial Accounting Standards Board, the seven-member nonprofit board that currently has the authority to identify generally accepted accounting principles. p. 26

FEI Financial Executives Institute, a professional association of private accountants. p. 27

GAAS the abbreviation for *generally accepted auditing standards*. p. 25

Generally accepted auditing standards rules adopted by the accounting profession as guides for conducting audits of financial statements. p. 25

Going-concern principle the rule that requires financial statements to reflect the assumption that the business will continue operating instead of being closed or sold, unless evidence shows that it will not continue. p. 30

IASC International Accounting Standards Committee; a committee that attempts to create more harmony among the accounting practices of different countries by identifying preferred practices and encouraging their worldwide acceptance. p. 28

IMA Institute of Management Accountants, a professional association of private accountants, formerly called the National Association of Accountants. p. 27

Income statement   the financial statement that shows whether the business earned a profit; it lists the types and amounts of the revenues and expenses. p. 21

Liabilities   debts owed by a business or organization; probable future sacrifices of economic benefits arising from present obligations of a particular entity to transfer assets or provide services to other entities in the future as a result of past transactions or events. p. 23

Net assets   another name for *equity*. p. 23

Net income   the excess of revenues over expenses for a period. p. 21

Net loss   the excess of expenses over revenues for a period. p. 21

Objectivity principle   the accounting guideline that requires financial statement information to be supported by evidence other than someone's opinion or imagination; objectivity adds to the reliability and usefulness of accounting information. p. 29

Paid-in capital   another name for *contributed capital*. p. 32

Partnership   a business that is owned by two or more people and that is not organized as a corporation. p. 31

Realization principle   another name for the *revenue recognition principle*. p. 35

Retained earnings   the category of stockholders' equity created by a corporation's profitable activities. p. 32

Return on equity ratio   the ratio of net income to beginning owner's equity; used to judge a business's success compared to other activities or investments; may be modified for proprietorships or partnerships by subtracting the value of the owner's efforts in managing the business from the reported income. p. 42

Revenue recognition principle   the rule that (1) requires revenue to be recognized at the time it is earned, (2) allows the inflow of assets associated with revenue to be in a form other than cash, and (3) measures the amount of revenue as the cash plus

the cash equivalent value of any noncash assets received from customers in exchange for goods or services. p. 35

Revenues   inflows of assets received in exchange for goods or services provided to customers as part of the major or central operations of the business; may occur as inflows of assets or decreases in liabilities. p. 21

Shareholders   another name for *stockholders*. p. 31

SIA   Securities Industry Association; an association of individuals involved with issuing and marketing securities. p. 27

Single proprietorship   a business owned by one individual that is not organized as a corporation. p. 30

Sole proprietorship   another name for a *single proprietorship*. p. 30

Statement of cash flows   a financial statement that describes where a company's cash came from and where it went during the period; the cash flows are classified as being caused by operating, investing, and financing activities. p. 40

Statement of changes in owner's equity   a financial statement that shows the beginning balance of owner's equity, the changes in equity that resulted from new investments by the owner, net income (or net loss), and withdrawals, and the ending balance. p. 39

Statement of financial position   another name for the *balance sheet*. p. 22

Statements of Financial Accounting Standards (SFAS)   the publications of the FASB that establish new generally accepted accounting principles in the United States. p. 26

Stock   equity of a corporation divided into units called shares. p. 31

Stockholders   the owners of a corporation; also called *shareholders*. p. 31

Withdrawal   a payment from a proprietorship or partnership to its owner or owners. p. 32

QUESTIONS

1. What information is presented in an income statement?

2. What do accountants mean by the term *revenue?*

3. Why does the user of an income statement need to know the time period that it covers?

4. What information is presented in a balance sheet?

5. Define (a) assets, (b) liabilities, (c) equity, and (d) net assets.

6. Identify two categories of generally accepted accounting principles.

7. What FASB pronouncements identify generally accepted accounting principles?

8. What does the objectivity principle require for information presented in financial statements? Why?

9. A business shows office stationery on the balance sheet at its $430 cost, although it cannot be sold for more than $10 as scrap paper. Which accounting principles require this treatment?

10. Why is the revenue recognition principle needed? What does it require?

11. What events or activities change owner's equity?

12. Identify four financial statements that a business presents to its owners and other users.

13. What should a company's return on equity ratio be compared with to determine whether the owner has made a good investment?

14. Find the financial statements of Federal Express Corporation in Appendix G. To what level of significance are the dollar amounts rounded? What time period does the income statement cover?

15. Review the financial statements of Ben & Jerry's Homemade, Inc., in Appendix G. What is the amount of total assets reported at December 26, 1992? How much net cash was provided by operating activities during the 1992 year?

QUICK STUDY (Five-Minute Exercises)

QS 1–1
(LO 1)

Name the financial statement on which each of the following items appears:

a. Rent expense.   e. Service fees earned.

b. Store equipment.   f. Accounts payable.

c. Cash received from customers.   g. Repayment of bank loan.

d. Owner, withdrawals.   h. Supplies.

QS 1–2
(LO 2)

Identify which broad accounting principle describes most directly each of the following practices:

a. If $15,000 cash is paid to buy land, the land should be reported on the purchaser's balance sheet at $15,000.

b. Jan Jacobson owns Freeland Bakery and also owns Westside Supplies, both of which are sole proprietorships. In having financial statements prepared for the bakery, Jacobson should be sure that the expense transactions of Westside Supplies are excluded from the statements.

c. In December, 19X1, Bartel Great Outdoors received a customer's order to provide two experienced guides for a June 19X2 fishing trip in Alaska. Bartel should record the revenue for the service in June 19X2, not in December 19X1.

QS 1–3
(LO 3)

For each of the following situations, determine whether the business is a sole proprietorship, partnership, or corporation.

a. The equity of Foster Company is divided into 10,000 shares of stock.

b. Metal Roofing Company is owned by Chris Fisher, who is personally liable for the debts of the business.

c. Jerry Forrentes and Susan Montgomery own Money Services, a company that cashes payroll checks for individuals and provides a variety of personal services. Neither Forrentes nor Montgomery has personal responsibility for the debts of Money Services.

d. Nancy Kerr and Frank Maples own Downtown Runners, a courier service. Both Kerr and Maples are personally liable for the any debts of the business.

QS 1–4
(LO 4)

Determine the missing amount for each of the following equations:

	Assets	=	Liabilities	+	Owner's Equity
a.	$ 25,000		$13,500		?
b.	$100,000		?		$28,500
c.	?		$62,500		$31,800

QS 1–5
(LO 4)

Use the accounting equation to determine:

a. The owner's equity in a business that has $249,800 of assets and $168,300 of liabilities.

b. The liabilities of a business having $100,600 of assets and $84,000 of owner's equity.

c. The assets of a business having $25,100 of liabilities and $75,000 of owner's equity.

QS 1–6
(LO 1)

In its 1993 financial statements, the Boeing Company, which is the largest aerospace company in the United States, reported the following:

Sales and other operating revenues	$25,438 million
Net earnings (net income)	1,244 million
Total assets	20,450 million
Total beginning-of-year shareholders' equity . .	8,056 million
Total end-of-year shareholders' equity	8,983 million

Calculate the return on beginning equity.

EXERCISES

The following equation shows the effects of five transactions on the assets, liabilities, and owner's equity of Dr. Kirby's dental practice. Write short descriptions of the probable nature of each transaction.

Exercise 1–1
Effects of transactions on the accounting equation
(LO 4)

			Assets			=	Liabil-ities	Owner's Equity
	Cash	+	Accounts Receivable	+	Office Supplies	+ Land =	Accounts Payable	+ M. Kirby, Capital
	$15,000				$5,000	$29,000		$49,000
a.	− 6,000					+ 6,000		
	$ 9,000				$5,000	$35,000		$49,000
b.					+ 800		$ 800	
	$ 9,000				$5,800	$35,000	$ 800	$49,000
c.			$2,100					+ 2,100
	$ 9,000		$2,100		$5,800	$35,000	$ 800	$51,100
d.	− 800						− 800	
	$ 8,200		$2,100		$5,800	$35,000	$ 0	$51,100
e.	+ 2,100		−2,100					
	$10,300	+	$ 0	+	$5,800 +	$35,000 =	$ 0	+ $51,100

Chris Bevit began operating a new consulting firm on January 15. The accounting equation showed the following balances after each of the company's first five transactions. Analyze the equations and describe each of the five transactions with their amounts.

Exercise 1–2
Analyzing the accounting equation
(LO 4)

After Transaction	Cash	+ Accounts Receivable	+ Office Supplies	+ Office Furniture	= Accounts Payable	+ C. Bevit, Capital
a.	$60,000	$ 0	$ 0	$ 0	$ 0	$60,000
b.	58,000	0	3,500	0	1,500	60,000
c.	42,000	0	3,500	16,000	1,500	60,000
d.	42,000	4,000	3,500	16,000	1,500	64,000
e.	35,000	4,000	3,500	16,000	1,500	57,000

A business had the following amounts of assets and liabilities at the beginning and end of a recent year:

Exercise 1–3
Determining net income
(LO 1, 4)

	Assets	Liabilities
Beginning of the year	$150,000	$60,000
End of the year	240,000	92,000

Determine the net income earned or net loss incurred by the business during the year under each of the following unrelated assumptions:

a. The owner made no additional investments in the business and withdrew no assets during the year.

b. The owner made no additional investments in the business during the year but withdrew $3,500 per month to pay personal living expenses.

c. The owner withdrew no assets during the year but invested an additional $65,000 cash in the business.

d. The owner withdrew $4,500 per month to pay personal living expenses and invested an additional $20,000 cash in the business at the end of the year.

Cathy Egan began a professional practice on July 1 and plans to prepare financial statements at the end of each month. During July, Egan completed these transactions:

Exercise 1–4
The effects of transactions on the accounting equation
(LO 1, 4)

a. Invested $25,000 cash and equipment that had a $5,000 fair market (cash equivalent) value.

b. Paid $800 rent for office space for the month.

c.   Purchased $6,000 of additional equipment on credit.

d.   Completed work for a client and immediately collected $1,000 cash.

e.   Completed work for a client and sent a bill for $3,500 to be paid within 30 days.

f.   Purchased $4,000 of additional equipment for cash.

g.   Paid an assistant $1,200 as wages for the month.

h.   Collected $2,500 of the amount owed by the client described in transaction e.

i.   Paid for the equipment purchased in transaction c.

Required

Create a table like the one in Illustration 1–7, using the following headings for the columns: Cash; Accounts Receivable; Equipment; Accounts Payable; and Cathy Egan, Capital. Then, use additions and subtractions to show the effects of the transactions on the elements of the equation. Show new totals after each transaction. Once you have completed the table, determine Egan's income for July. Determine the modified return on Egan's initial investment, assuming that her management efforts during the month have a value of $1,500.

Exercise 1–5
The effects of transactions on the accounting equation
(LO 4)

Following are seven pairs of changes in elements of the accounting equation. Provide an example of a transaction that creates the described effects:

a.   Decreases an asset and decreases equity.

b.   Decreases an asset and decreases a liability.

c.   Decreases a liability and increases a liability.

d.   Increases an asset and decreases an asset.

e.   Increases an asset and increases a liability.

f.   Increases an asset and increases equity.

g.   Increases a liability and decreases equity.

Exercise 1–6
Income statement
(LO 1)

On July 1, Maia Mears began the practice of tax accounting under the name of Maia Mears, CPA. On July 31, the company's records showed the following items. Use this information to prepare a July income statement for the business.

Cash	$ 4,000	Owner's withdrawals	$1,500
Accounts receivable	5,000	Tax fees earned	5,000
Office supplies	750	Miscellaneous expenses	180
Tax library	12,000	Rent expense	850
Office equipment	9,000	Salaries expense	2,000
Accounts payable	2,500	Telephone expense	220
Owner's investments . . .	28,000		

Exercise 1–7
Statement of changes in owner's equity
(LO 1)

Use the facts in Exercise 1–6 to prepare a July statement of changes in owner's equity for the business of Maia Mears, CPA.

Exercise 1–8
Balance sheet
(LO 1)

Use the facts in Exercise 1–6 to prepare a July 31 balance sheet for the business of Maia Mears, CPA.

Exercise 1–9
Information in financial statements
(LO 1)

Match each of these numbered items with the financial statement or statements on which it should be presented. Indicate your answer by writing the letter or letters for the correct statement in the blank space next to each item.

A. Income statement   C. Balance sheet
B. Statement of changes   D. Statement of cash flows
   in owner's equity

___ 1. Cash received from customers.

___ 2. Office supplies.

___ 3. Rent expense paid in cash.

___ 4. Consulting fees earned and received as cash.

___ 5. Accounts payable.

___ 6. Investments of cash by owner.

___ 7. Accounts receivable.

___ 8. Cash withdrawals by owner.

Calculate the amount of the missing item in each of the following independent cases:

Exercise 1–10
Missing information
(LO 4)

	a	b	c	d
Owner's equity, January 1	$ 0	$ 0	$ 0	$ 0
Owner's investments during the year	80,000	?	42,000	50,000
Owner's withdrawals during the year	?	(36,000)	(20,000)	(21,000)
Net income (loss) for the year	21,000	54,000	(6,000)	?
Owner's equity, December 31	68,000	66,000	?	57,000

Match each of these numbered descriptions with the term it best describes. Indicate your answer by writing the letter for the correct principle in the blank space next to each description.

Exercise 1–11
Accounting principles
(LO 2)

A. Broad principle
B. Cost principle
C. Business entity principle
D. Revenue recognition principle

E. Specific principle
F. Objectivity principle
G. Going-concern principle

___ 1. Requires every business to be accounted for separately from its owner or owners.

___ 2. Requires financial statement information to be supported by evidence other than someone's opinion or imagination.

___ 3. Usually created by a pronouncement from an authoritative body.

___ 4. Requires financial statement information to be based on costs incurred in transactions.

___ 5. Derived from long-used accounting practices.

___ 6. Requires financial statements to reflect the assumption that the business will continue operating instead of being closed or sold.

___ 7. Requires revenue to be recorded only when the earnings process is complete.

Use the information for each of the following independent cases to calculate the company's return on equity and its modified return on equity:

Exercise 1–12
Return on equity
(LO 1)

	a	b	c	d
Beginning equity	$25,000	$400,000	$150,000	$286,400
Net income	5,400	108,000	45,750	88,965
Value of owner's efforts	2,200	50,000	33,000	75,000

PROBLEMS

Ranca Carr secured her license and opened an architect's office. During its first year, the following transactions affected Carr's business:

Problem 1–1
Analyzing the effects of transactions on the accounting equation
(LO 4)

a.   Carr sold a personal investment in Apple Computer stock for $44,000, and deposited $30,000 of the proceeds in a bank account opened in the name of the business.

b.   Carr invested $15,000 of her own personal office equipment in the business.

c.   The business paid $150,000 for a small building to be used as an office. It paid $25,000 in cash and signed a note payable promising to pay the balance over several years.

d.   Purchased $2,000 of office supplies for cash.

e. Purchased $18,000 of office equipment on credit.

f. Completed a project design on credit and billed the client $2,000 for the work.

g. Paid a local newspaper $500 for an announcement that the office had opened.

h. Designed a house for a client and collected a $9,000 cash commission on completion of the construction.

i. Made a $1,000 payment on the equipment purchased in transaction *e.*

j. Received $1,500 from the client described in transaction *f.*

k. Paid $1,250 cash for the office secretary's wages.

l. Carr withdrew $4,000 from the company bank account to pay personal living expenses.

Required

Preparation component:

1. Create a table like the one in Illustration 1–7, using the following headings for the columns: Cash; Accounts Receivable; Office Supplies; Office Equipment; Building; Accounts Payable; Notes Payable; and Ranca Carr, Capital. Leave space for an Explanation column to the right of the Capital column.

2. Use additions and subtractions to show the transactions' effects on the elements of the equation. Show new totals after each transaction. Also, indicate next to each change in the owner's equity whether it was caused by an investment, a revenue, an expense, or a withdrawal.

CHECK FIGURE:
Net income, $9,250

3. Once you have completed the table, determine the company's net income.

4. Determine the return on the beginning-of-period equity, which consisted of the two amounts invested by Carr in transactions *a* and *b*. Next, assume that Carr could have earned $3,000 for the period from another job and determine the modified return on equity for the period.

Analysis component:

5. State whether you think the practice is a good use of Carr's money, if an investment in low-risk bonds would have returned 6% for the same period.

Problem 1–2
Balance sheet and income
statement
(LO 1, 3)

Benny Gates graduated from college in May with a degree in photographic arts. On June 1, Gates invested $30,000 in a new business under the name Benny Gates, Photographer. Gates plans on preparing financial statements for the business at the end of each month. The following transactions occurred during the first month:

June 1 Rented the furnished office and darkroom equipment of a photographer who was retiring. Gates paid $1,600 cash for the rent.

2 Purchased photography supplies for $840 cash.

4 Paid $400 cash for the month's cleaning services.

7 Completed work for a client and immediately collected $300 cash.

13 Completed work for Carl Simone on credit, $1,500.

15 Paid $425 cash for an assistant's salary for the first half of the month.

20 Received payment in full for the work completed for Carl Simone on June 13.

20 Completed work for Wendy Nation on credit, $1,400

21 Purchased additional photography supplies on credit, $500.

25 Completed work for Billie Carr on credit, $950.

26 Picked up brochures to be used right away to advertise the studio. Gates purchased them from a printer at a cost of $180, which he is to pay within 30 days.

28 Received full payment from Wendy Nation for the work completed on June 20.

June   29   Paid for the photography supplies purchased on June 21.

       30   Paid $100 cash for the month's telephone bill.

       30   Paid $240 cash for the month's utilities.

       30   Paid $425 cash for an assistant's salary for the second half of the month.

       30   Purchased insurance protection for the next 12 months (beginning July 1) by paying a $1,500 premium. Because none of this insurance protection had been used up, it was considered to be an asset called Prepaid Insurance.

       30   Gates withdrew $560 from the business for personal use.

Required

1. Arrange the following asset, liability, and owner's equity titles in an equation like Illustration 1–7: Cash; Accounts Receivable; Prepaid Insurance; Photography Supplies; Accounts Payable; and Benny Gates, Capital. Include an Explanation column for changes in owner's equity.

2. Show the effects of the transactions on the elements of the equation by recording increases and decreases in the appropriate columns. Indicate an increase with a + and a decrease with a − before the amount. Do not determine new totals for the items of the equation after each transaction. Next to each change in Benny Gates, Capital, state whether it was caused by an investment, a revenue, an expense, or a withdrawal. Determine the final total for each item and verify that the equation is in balance.

3. Prepare an income statement for June, a statement of changes in owner's equity for June, and a June 30 balance sheet.

CHECK FIGURE:
Ending capital balance, $30,220

The accounting records of Carmen King's dental practice show the following assets and liabilities as of the end of 19X1 and 19X2:

Problem 1–3
Calculating and interpreting net income and preparing a balance sheet
(LO 1, 3)

	December 31	
	19X1	**19X2**
Cash	$35,000	$ 12,500
Accounts receivable	19,000	14,900
Dental supplies	3,000	2,200
Dental equipment	92,000	98,000
Office equipment	36,000	36,000
Land		30,000
Building		120,000
Accounts payable	5,000	25,000
Note payable		70,000

Late in December 19X2 (just before the amounts in the second column were calculated), King purchased a small office building in the name of the practice, Carmen King, D.D.S., and moved the practice from rented quarters to the new building. The building and the land it occupies cost $150,000. The practice paid $80,000 in cash and a note payable was signed for the balance. King had to invest an additional $35,000 cash in the practice to enable it to pay the $80,000. The practice earned a satisfactory net income during 19X2, which enabled King to withdraw $3,000 per month from the practice for personal living expenses.

Required

Preparation component:

1. Prepare balance sheets for the business as of the end of 19X1 and the end of 19X2. (Remember that owner's equity equals the difference between the assets and the liabilities.)

2. By comparing the owner's equity amounts from the balance sheets and using the additional information presented in the problem, prepare a calculation to show how much net income was earned by the business during 19X2.

3. Calculate the return on equity for the dental practice, using the beginning balance of owner's equity for the year. Calculate the modified return on equity, assuming that the owner's efforts were worth $25,000 for the year.

Analysis component:

4. Consider the possibility that King might have organized the business as a corporation which would have paid King a salary of $25,000. Would organizing the business as a corporation instead of as a proprietorship affect your evaluation of return on equity? Explain why.

Problem 1–4
Analyzing transactions and preparing financial statements
(LO 1, 3)

Thom Stone began a new financial planning practice and completed these transactions during April:

April 1 Transferred $28,000 from a personal savings account to a checking account opened in the name of the business, Thom Stone, C.F.P.

1 Rented the furnished office of a planner who was retiring, and paid cash for the month's rent of $400.

2 Purchased the retiring person's professional library for $7,000 by paying $1,600 in cash and agreeing to pay the balance in six months.

4 Purchased office supplies by paying $450 cash.

6 Completed planning work for Karl Hubbell and immediately collected $500 for doing the work.

9 Purchased $1,900 of office equipment on credit.

15 Completed planning work for Carol Banks on credit in the amount of $2,000.

19 Purchased $250 of office supplies on credit.

21 Paid for the office equipment purchased on April 9.

25 Billed Sy Young $300 for planning work; the balance is due in 30 days.

29 Received $2,000 from Carol Banks for the work completed on April 15.

30 Paid the office assistant's salary of $1,600.

30 Paid the monthly utility bills of $220.

30 Withdrew $500 from the business for personal living expenses.

Required

Preparation component:

1. Arrange the following asset, liability, and owner's equity titles in an equation like Illustration 1–7: Cash; Accounts Receivable; Office Supplies; Professional Library; Office Equipment; Accounts Payable; and Thom Stone, Capital. Leave space for an Explanation column to the right of Thom Stone, Capital.

2. Use additions and subtractions to show the effects of each transaction on the items in the equation. Show new totals after each transaction. Next to each change in owner's equity, state whether the change was caused by an investment, a revenue, an expense, or a withdrawal.

3. Use the increases and decreases in the last column of the equation to prepare an income statement and a statement of changes in owner's equity for the month. Also prepare a balance sheet as of the end of the month.

4. Calculate the return on equity for the month, using the initial investment as the beginning balance of equity.

Analysis component:

5. Assume that the investment transaction on April 1 had been for $20,000 instead of $28,000 and the $8,000 difference had been borrowed from a bank. Explain the effect of this change on total assets, total liabilities, owner's equity, and return on equity.

The following financial statement information is known about five unrelated companies:

Problem 1–5
Missing information
(LO 1)

	Company A	Company B	Company C	Company D	Company E
December 31, 19X1:					
Assets	$90,000	$70,000	$58,000	$40,000	$82,000
Liabilities	47,000	45,000	28,000	19,000	?
December 31, 19X2:					
Assets	96,000	82,000	?	62,500	75,000
Liabilities	?	55,000	38,000	32,000	50,000
During 19X2:					
Owner investments ..	10,000	3,000	15,500	?	3,000
Net income	15,000	?	9,000	6,000	12,000
Owner withdrawals ..	5,000	7,000	6,500	0	6,000

Required

1. Answer the following questions about Company A:

    a. What was the owner's equity on December 31, 19X1?

    b. What was the owner's equity on December 31, 19X2?

    c. What was the amount of liabilities owed on December 31, 19X2?

2. Answer the following questions about Company B:

    a. What was the owner's equity on December 31, 19X1?

    b. What was the owner's equity on December 31, 19X2?

    c. What was the net income for 19X2?

3. Calculate the amount of assets owned by Company C on December 31, 19X2.

4. Calculate the amount of owner investments in Company D made during 19X2.

5. Calculate the amount of liabilities owed by Company E on December 31, 19X1.

CHECK FIGURE:
Company C, 12/31/X2 assets,
$86,000

Identify how each of the following transactions affects the company's financial statements. For the balance sheet, identify how each transaction affects total assets, total liabilities, and owner's equity. For the income statement, identify how each transaction affects Net Income. For the statement of cash flows, identify how each transaction affects cash flows from operating activities, cash flows from financing activities, and cash flows from investing activities. If there is an increase, place a + in the column or columns. If there is a decrease, place a − in the column or columns. If there is both an increase and a decrease, place + / − in the column or columns. The line for the first transaction is completed as an example.

Problem 1–6
Identifying the effects of
transactions on the financial
statements
(LO 1, 3)

Transaction	Balance Sheet			Income Statement	Statement of Cash Flows		
	Total Assets	Total Liabilities	Equity	Net Income	Operating	Financing	Investing
1 Owner invests cash	+		+			+	
2 Sell services for cash							
3 Acquire services on credit							
4 Pay wages with cash							
5 Owner withdraws cash							
6 Borrow cash with note payable							
7 Sell services on credit							
8 Buy office equipment for cash							
9 Collect receivable from (7)							
10 Buy asset with note payable							

CRITICAL THINKING: ESSAYS, PROBLEMS, AND CASES

Analytical Essays

AE 1–1
(LO 4)

Review the facts presented in Problem 1–2. Now assume that all of the company's revenue transactions generated cash (that is, none had been made on credit). Also assume that all of the expense and purchase transactions used cash and none were on credit. Describe the differences, if any, these alternate assumptions would create for the income statement, the statement of changes in owner's equity, and the balance sheet. Construct your answer in general terms without stating the actual dollar amounts of each difference. Be certain to explain why each statement would or would not be affected by the changes in the assumtions.

AE 1–2
(LO 2, 4)

Review the facts presented in Problem 1–1 for transactions *f* and *j*. Identify the transaction that creates a revenue and explain your answer. Then explain why the other transaction did not create a revenue. Next, review the facts for transactions *d* and *k*. Identify the transaction that creates an expense for the current reporting period and explain your answer. Finally, explain why the other transaction did not create an expense.

On Friday, September 3, Ann Walker invested $1,000 cash in a small enterprise to participate in a local flea market set up in her neighborhood for the Labor Day weekend. In the name of her business, Ann's Bangles and Baubles, she paid $250 rent for space in the market to sell various kinds of costume jewelry. She also paid $50 cash for plastic jewelry boxes, and paid her teenage children $130 to build a booth just for the market. Because she wasn't going to do this again until the next year, she planned to abandon the booth after the market closed. Walker purchased her jewelry from a local wholesaler at a total cost of $900, but could not pay the full price in cash because she had only $570 in cash. However, the wholesaler knew that Walker's credit was good, and agreed to accept $500 in cash and her promise that she would pay the $400 balance the day after the market closed. Over the weekend, she sold most of the jewelry for $2,000 cash and paid an assistant $90 cash for helping her. When the market closed, Walker estimated that her unsold goods could be returned to the wholesaler for their original cost of $60. Because of the large number of sales, none of the jewelry boxes was left.

Walker cannot decide whether this venture might be a good thing to repeat in the future. She needs to know whether she earned a satisfactory profit for the time and money that she put into it. Use the methods described in the chapter to develop the information. Prepare an income statement and a statement of changes in owner's equity for the four-day period ending on Monday, September 6. Also prepare a balance sheet as of the close of business on September 6. Then, evaluate whether you think her effort was suitably rewarded by the results, assuming that she could have earned $540 in wages on another job.

Financial Reporting Problem

(LO 1, 3)

Apple Computer, Inc., is in the business of manufacturing and marketing personal computer systems as well as software and other related products and services. The financial statements and other information from Apple's 1993 annual report are included in Appendix F at the end of the book. Use information from that report to answer the following questions:

1. Examine Apple's consolidated balance sheet. To what level of significance are the dollar amounts rounded?
2. What is the closing date of Apple's most recent annual reporting period?
3. What amount of net income did Apple have during the 1993 year?
4. How much cash (and cash equivalents) did the company hold at the end of the 1993 reporting period?
5. What was the net amount of cash used by the company's operating activities during the 1993 year?
6. Did the company's investing activities for 1992 create a net cash inflow or outflow? What was the amount of the net flow?
7. Compare 1993's results to 1992's results to determine whether the company's total revenues increased or decreased. If so, what was the amount of the increase or decrease?
8. What was the change in the company's net income between 1992 and 1993?
9. What amount was reported as total assets at the end of the 1993 reporting period?
10. Calculate the return on beginning shareholders' equity that Apple achieved in 1993.

Financial Statement Analysis Case

(LO 1)

Ben & Jerry's Homemade, Inc., is a well-known manufacturer and marketer of super-premium ice cream and frozen yogurt, specializing in unusually flavored products. The company is still managed by its founders, Ben Cohen and Jerry Greenfield, from its headquarters in Waterbury, Vermont. The company's annual filing with the Securities and Exchange Commission for 1992 showed annual sales of nearly $132 million and net income of $6.7 million. The report also included the following information about another company operated by Ben Cohen and Jeffrey Furman, a former officer of the ice cream company:

Item 13. Certain relationships and related transactions

During the year ended December 26, 1992, the Company purchased Rainforest Crunch cashew-brazilnut buttercrunch candy to be included in Ben & Jerry's Rainforest Crunch flavor ice cream for an aggregate purchase price of approximately $1,500,000 from Community Products, Inc., a company of which Messrs. Cohen and Furman are the

Principles Application Problem

(LO 2)

VERMONT'S FINEST • ICE CREAM & FROZEN YOGURT.

principal stockholders and of which Mr. Cohen is also president. The candy was purchased from Community Products, Inc., at competitive prices and on standard terms and conditions. Although the Company expects to purchase additional quantities of candy from Community Products, Inc., and had purchase commitments of approximately $1,500,000 as of March 1993, severance of Ben & Jerry's relationship with this supplier would not have a material effect on the Company's business.

Explain why Ben & Jerry's Homemade, Inc., might have included these comments in its report. What accounting principle might be compromised by related-party transactions like the purchases of Rainforest Crunch candy?

CONCEPT TESTER

Test your understanding of the concepts introduced in this chapter by completing the following crossword puzzle.

Across Clues

2. Debts owed by a business organization.
7. Generally accepted auditing standards.
9. Inflows of assets received in exchange for goods or services provided to customers.
10. Equity of a corporation divided into units.

Down Clues

1. The owners of a corporation.
3. Properties or economic resources owned by the business.
4. The difference between a company's assets and it liabilities.
5. Outflows or the using up of assets as a result of the major operations of a business.
6. Generally accepted accounting principles.
8. Financial Executives Institute.

ANSWERS TO PROGRESS CHECKS

1-1 *d*

1-2 An expense is an outflow or using up of assets as a result of the major or central operations of a business. An expense also may occur as an increase in liabilities.

1-3 *c*

1-4 GAAP are the principles that govern the reporting of information in the financial statements. GAAS, on the other hand, are the standards that guide auditors in performing an audit.

1-5 No. The IASC does not have the authority to impose standards. The United States company must comply with the GAAP established by the FASB.

1-6 The FASB's conceptual framework identifies relevance and reliability as two qualities of useful information.

1-7 A company's financial statements present its activities separate from its owner's activities because separate information is necessary for evaluating the company.

1-8 The equipment should be reported at its $25,000 cost, according to the cost principle.

1-9 *c*

1-10 A proprietor's withdrawals are not reported on the company's income statement because they are not expenses incurred to generate revenues.

1-11 *b*

1-12 No. If a liability increases, one or more of three other things must happen: an asset increases, or equity decreases, or another liability decreases.

1-13 *c*

1-14 Net income appears on both the income statement and the statement of changes in owner's equity.

1-15 The owner's capital account balance at the end of the period appears on both the statement of changes in owner's equity and the balance sheet.

1-16 Owners use the return on equity ratio to describe the success of the business in a way that can be compared to other investment opportunities.

CHAPTER 2

Recording Transactions

To prepare for her business communications class, Karen White spent an afternoon looking through the annual reports section of her school library. She was interested in learning about the information companies present in their annual reports.

One report that caught White's attention was the 1993 Annual Report of Chiquita Brands International, Inc. Chiquita is the largest producer and distributor of bananas in the world. It distributes a wide variety of fresh fruit and vegetables, and also markets a variety of processed foods.

As is true in most annual reports, Chiquita's 1993 report includes a letter from the executive officers. White found this Message from the Chairman and President interesting and informative. However, since White had not yet taken an accounting course, she found some of the statements in it hard to understand.

For example, under a Looking Forward heading, one sentence states that "our financing strategy is to de-leverage the balance sheet and lower Chiquita's overall cost of capital." The executive officers indicate that this strategy has been adopted as a future goal because the company had a large investment spending program during the previous several years. White concluded that the investment spending program apparently had caused the company's balance sheet to reflect too much leverage. However, White did not understand exactly what that meant and therefore was unclear as to why it might be desirable to de-leverage the balance sheet.

Chiquita Brands International, Inc.
(In thousands)

December 31	Total Assets	Total Liabilities	Shareholders' Equity
1993	$2,740,753	$2,138,755	$601,998
1992	2,880,624	2,205,737	674,887
1991	2,937,344	1,969,419	967,925
1990	1,913,674	1,225,965	687,709
1989	1,373,480	909,526	463,954

After studying Chapter 2, you should be able to:

1. Describe the events recorded in accounting systems and the importance of source documents and business papers in those systems.

2. Describe how accounts are used to record information about the effects of transactions, how code numbers are used to identify each account, and the meaning of the words *debit* and *credit.*

3. Describe how debits and credits are used to analyze transactions and record their effects in the accounts.

4. Record transactions in a General Journal, describe balance column accounts, and post entries from the journal to the ledger.

5. Prepare a trial balance, explain its usefulness, and calculate a company's debt ratio.

6. Define or explain the words and phrases listed in the chapter glossary.

In Chapter 1, you learned how the accounting equation (Assets = Liabilities + Owner's Equity) is affected by business transactions. In this chapter, you learn how the effects of transactions are recorded in accounts. All accounting systems, small or large, manual or computerized, use procedures similar to those described in this chapter. No matter how unusual or complicated a business might be, these procedures are the first steps in a process that leads to financial statements.

We begin by describing how source documents provide useful information about transactions. Then, we describe accounts and explain how they are used. Next, we explain debits and credits and use them to show how transactions affect the accounts. With this background in place, we describe the process of recording events in the journal and ledger. The chapter concludes by describing how to use a company's debt ratio to assess risk.

THE ACCOUNTING PROCESS

LO 1

Describe the events recorded in accounting systems and the importance of source documents and business papers in those systems.

Chapter 1 explains that accounting provides useful financial information to decision makers. To generate this information, a company uses an accounting process that analyzes economic events, records the results, and classifies and summarizes the information in reports and financial statements. These reports and statements are provided to individuals who find the information to be useful for making investment, credit, and other decisions about the entity. You can see the overall steps in this process in the flowchart in Illustration 2–1.

Business Transactions and Other Events

Notice that the economic events in Illustration 2–1 consist of business transactions and other events. Recall from Chapter 1 that business transactions are exchanges of economic consideration between two parties. Also, remember that a company's accounting equation is affected by transactions. The accounting process begins by analyzing transactions to determine how they affect the equation. Then, those effects are recorded in accounting records, informally referred to as *the books.* Additional processing steps summarize and classify the effects of all transactions. The process is not complete until it provides useful information to decision makers in financial statements or other reports.

Because business transactions are exchanges between the entity and some other person or organization, they are sometimes called **external transactions.** Other economic events, called **internal transactions,** can affect the accounting equation. These events are not transactions with outside parties. For example, suppose that a company uses a machine in its operations. As the machine is used, its total remaining useful-

Illustration 2-1 The Accounting Process

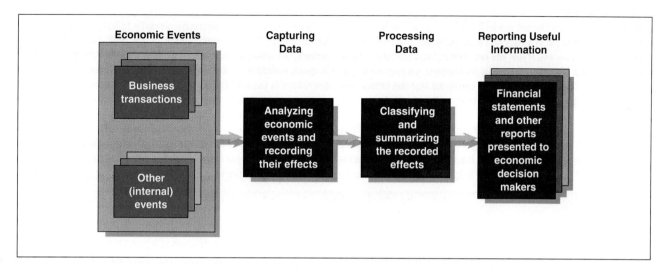

ness decreases. This using up of the machine's economic benefit is an economic event that decreases assets and decreases owner's equity.

Other events that can affect a company's accounting equation include natural events such as floods that destroy assets and create losses. In a few circumstances, changes in the market values of certain assets are also recorded. Economic events like these are not transactions between the company and other parties. We explain the analysis and recording of these economic events in Chapter 3.

Companies use various documents and other papers when they conduct business. These **business papers** include sales tickets, checks, purchase orders, bills to customers, bills from suppliers, employee earnings records, and bank statements. Business papers are also called **source documents** because they are the source of the information recorded with accounting entries. Source documents may be printed on paper or they may exist only in computer records.

SOURCE DOCUMENTS AND BUSINESS PAPERS

For example, when you buy a pocket calculator on credit, the store prepares at least two copies of a sales ticket. One copy is given to you. Another is sent to the store's accounting department and triggers an entry in the system to record the sale. (In many systems, this copy is sent electronically without a physical document.) Or, if you pay cash for the calculator, the sale is rung up on a cash register that records and stores the amount of each sale.

Some cash registers print the amount of each sale on a paper tape locked inside the register. Most newer registers store the data electronically. In either case, the proper keyboard commands at the end of the day cause the cash register to determine the total cash sales for that day. This total is then used to record the day's sales in the accounting records. These systems are designed to ensure that the accounting records include all transactions. They also help prevent mistakes and theft. The As a Matter of Ethics case on page 64 describes a challenge created by an instruction to overlook these accounting procedures. Read the case and think about what you would do if you were Karen Muñoz.

Both buyers and sellers use sales tickets (also called *invoices*) as source documents. For example, if the new calculator is going to be used in your business, your copy of the invoice is a source document. It provides information to record the purchase in accounting records for your business.

To summarize, business papers are the starting point in the accounting process. These source documents, especially if they are created outside the business, provide

As a Matter of Ethics

While taking classes toward her business degree, Karen Muñoz accepted a part-time job at a busy fast food restaurant in a large downtown mall. As a new employee, she received training from the restaurant's assistant manager, including instructions on operating the cash register. The assistant manager explained that the formal policy is to ring up each sale when an order is placed and the cash is received.

The assistant manager also told Muñoz that the pressure of the noon-hour rush makes it easier to just accept the customers' cash and make change without ringing up the sales. The assistant manager explained that the formal policy is ignored because it is more important to serve the customers promptly to keep them from going to any of the other restaurants in the mall. Then, after two o'clock, the assistant manager adds up the cash in the drawer and rings up sufficient sales to equal the collected amount. This way, the record in the register always comes out right and there are no problems to explain when the manager arrives at four o'clock to handle the dinner traffic.

Muñoz sees the advantages in this shortcut but wonders whether something is wrong with it. She also wonders what will happen if the manager comes in early some day and finds out that she isn't following the formal policy.

PRINCIPLE APPLICATION
Objectivity Principle p. 29
The need for credible source documents is created by the *objectivity principle*. For example, at the end of its 1993 business year, Mr. Coffee, inc., reported a Cash balance of $373,000. The company's auditors were able to confirm this amount primarily by analyzing the company's bank statements.

objective evidence about transactions and the amounts to be recorded for them. As you learned in Chapter 1, this type of evidence is important because it makes the reported information more reliable and useful.

Years ago, most accounting systems required pen and ink to manually record and process data about transactions. Today, only very small companies use manual systems. Now, large and small companies use computers to record and process the data. However, you will find it easier to understand the steps in the accounting process by learning to prepare accounting data manually. Despite the differences, the general concepts you learn by studying manual methods apply equally well to computerized accounting systems. More importantly, these concepts help you use financial statements because you understand the source of their information.

Progress Check
(Answers to Progress Checks are provided at the end of the chapter.)

2–1   Which of the following are examples of accounting source documents? *(a)* Journals and ledgers; *(b)* Income statements and balance sheets; *(c)* External transactions and internal transactions; *(d)* Bank statements and sales tickets; *(e)* All of the above.

2–2   What kinds of economic events affect a company's accounting equation?

2–3   Why are business papers called source documents?

RECORDING INFORMATION IN THE ACCOUNTS

LO 2

Describe how accounts are used to record information about the effects of transactions, how code numbers are used to identify each account, and the meaning of the words *debit* and *credit*.

An **account** is a place or location within an accounting system in which the increases and decreases in a specific asset, liability, owner's equity, revenue, or expense are recorded and stored. The diagram in Illustration 2–2 shows how the information about the company's events flows into the accounts and from the accounts into the financial statements.

When financial statements (or other reports) are needed, the information is taken from the accounts, summarized, and presented in helpful formats. To display information about a specific item in the statements, a separate account must be maintained for that item. Thus, a company's accounting system includes a separate account for each revenue and expense on the income statement. The system also includes a separate account for each asset, liability, and owner's equity item on the balance sheet. In addition, important changes such as withdrawals by the owner are captured in separate accounts. Because each company is different from all others, each has its own unique set of accounts. However, most companies use many accounts that are similar. The following paragraphs describe some commonly used accounts.

Asset Accounts

Because most companies own the following kinds of assets, their accounting systems include accounts for them.

Illustration 2-2 The Flow of Information through the Accounts into the Financial Statements

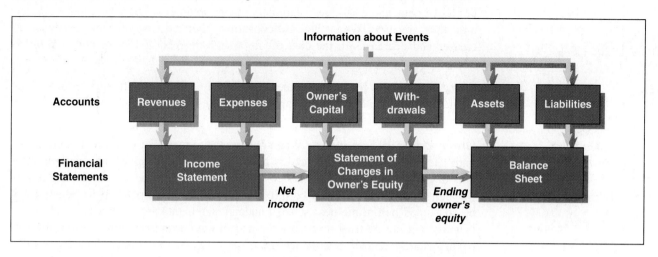

Cash. Increases and decreases in the amount of cash are recorded in a *Cash* account. A company's cash consists of money, balances in checking accounts, or any document that a bank accepts for deposit. Thus, cash includes coins, currency, checks, and money orders.

Accounts Receivable. Goods and services are often sold to customers in return for promises to pay in the future. These transactions are called *credit sales* or *sales on account.* The promises from the buyers are called the seller's *accounts receivable.* Accounts receivable are increased by new credit sales and are decreased by customer payments. Because a company sends bills to its credit customers, it needs to know the amount currently due from each of them. Therefore, it creates a separate record of each customer's purchases and payments. We describe the system for maintaining these separate records in Chapter 6. For now, however, we can use the simpler practice of recording all increases and decreases in receivables in a single account called *Accounts Receivable.*

The importance of accounts receivable depends on the nature of a company's operations. For example, at the end of its 1993 business year, **Showbiz Pizza Time, Inc.'s** accounts receivable amounted to less than 2% of its total assets. By comparison, **Nike, Inc.'s** accounts receivable amounted to more than 30% of its total assets.

Notes Receivable. A **promissory note** is an unconditional written promise to pay a definite sum of money on demand or on a defined future date (or dates). If a company holds one of these notes signed by another party, it owns a valuable asset. These assets called notes receivable are recorded in a *Notes Receivable* account.

Prepaid Insurance. Insurance contracts provide protection against losses caused by fire, thefts, accidents, or other events. Normally, an insurance policy requires the fee (called a *premium*) to be paid in advance, and the protection usually lasts for a year or even as much as three years. As a result, the unused portion of the coverage may be an asset for a substantial time after the premium is paid.

When an insurance premium is paid in advance, the cost is typically recorded in an asset account called *Prepaid Insurance.* When financial statements are prepared later, the expired portion of the insurance cost is removed from the asset account and reported as an expense on the income statement. The unexpired portion remains in the Prepaid Insurance account and is reported on the balance sheet as an asset.

Office Supplies. All companies use office supplies such as computer diskettes, printer ribbons and cartridges, stationery, paper, and pens. These supplies are assets until they are used. When they are consumed, their cost becomes an expense. Increases and decreases in the cost of the assets are recorded in an *Office Supplies* account.

Store Supplies. Many stores keep plastic and paper bags, gift boxes, cartons, and similar items on hand to use in wrapping purchases for their customers. Increases and decreases in the cost of the assets are recorded in a *Store Supplies* account.

Other Prepaid Expenses. When payments are made for assets that are not used until later, the assets are often called **prepaid expenses.** Then, as the economic benefits of the assets are used up, the costs of the assets become expenses. As a practical matter, an asset's cost can be initially recorded as an expense if its benefits will be consumed before the next set of financial statements are prepared. If the asset's benefits will not be used up before the end of the current reporting period, the prepayments are recorded in asset accounts.

Office supplies and store supplies are usually described as prepaid expenses. Other examples of prepaid expenses include prepaid insurance, prepaid rent, and legal or accounting fees paid in advance of receiving the services. To provide useful information, each prepaid expense is typically accounted for in a separate asset account.

Equipment. Virtually all companies own computers, printers, typewriters, desks, chairs, and other equipment that they use in their business. The costs incurred to buy the equipment are recorded in an *Office Equipment* account. The costs of assets used in a store, such as counters, showcases, and cash registers, are recorded in a separate *Store Equipment* account.

Buildings. A building owned by a business provides space for a store, an office, a warehouse, or a factory. Because they produce future benefits, buildings are assets, and their costs are recorded in a *Buildings* account. If several buildings are owned, separate accounts may record the cost incurred in buying each of them.

Land. A *Land* account is used to record the cost of land owned by a business. The cost of land is separated from the cost of buildings located on the land to provide more useful information in the financial statements. Although the land and the buildings may appear to be inseparable and a single asset, the buildings wear out, or *depreciate,* and their costs become expenses. Land does not depreciate, and its cost does not become an expense. Therefore, the costs of the land and the buildings are recorded in separate accounts to simplify accounting for depreciation.

Liability Accounts

Chapter 1 explained that liabilities are present obligations to transfer assets or provide services to other entities in the future. A business may have several different types of liabilities. Therefore, each type is represented by a separate account. The following liability accounts are widely used.

Accounts Payable. When purchases of merchandise, supplies, equipment, or services are made by an oral or implied promise to pay later, the resulting debts are called *accounts payable.* Because it is useful to know the amount owed to each creditor, accounting systems keep separate records about purchases from and the payments to each of them. We describe these individual records in Chapter 6. For now, however, we can use the simpler practice of recording all increases and decreases in payables in a single account called *Accounts Payable.*

Notes Payable. When an entity's promise to pay is formally recognized by having the entity sign a promissory note, the resulting liability is called a note payable.

Depending on how soon the liability must be repaid, its amount may be recorded in a *Short-Term Notes Payable* account or a *Long-Term Notes Payable* account.

Unearned Revenues. As you learned in Chapter 1, the *revenue recognition principle* requires accountants to report revenues on the income statement only after they are earned. This principle demands careful treatment of transactions in which customers pay in advance for products or services. Because the cash from these transactions is received before the revenues are earned, the seller considers them to be **unearned revenues.** An unearned revenue is a liability that is satisfied by delivering the product or service in the future. Unearned revenues include subscriptions collected in advance by a magazine publisher. For example, **The Reader's Digest Association, Inc.,** reported unearned revenues of $371,100,000 as of June 30, 1993. Other unearned revenues include rent collected in advance by a building owner, and professional or other service fees collected in advance.

When cash is received in advance, the seller records the amount in a liability account such as *Unearned Subscriptions, Unearned Rent,* or *Unearned Professional Fees.* When the products or services are delivered, the earned revenues are transferred to revenue accounts such as *Subscription Fees Earned, Rent Earned,* or *Professional Fees Earned.*

Other Short-Term Liabilities. Other short-term liabilities include wages payable, taxes payable, and interest payable. Each of these debts is normally recorded in a separate liability account. However, if they are not large in amount, one or more of them may be added together and reported as a single amount on the balance sheet. For example, the liabilities section of **La-Z-Boy Chair Company's** balance sheet at the end of its 1993 year included an item called Other current liabilities, which amounted to $17,046,000.

Owner's Equity, Withdrawals, Revenue, and Expense Accounts

In Chapter 1, we described four types of transactions that affected the owner's equity of a proprietorship. They are (1) investments by the owner, (2) withdrawals of assets by the owner, (3) revenues, and (4) expenses. Recall that in Chapter 1 we entered all equity transactions in a single column under the owner's name. We did this to help you understand how transactions affect the accounting equation. However, this simple approach caused a problem later when we needed to prepare an income statement and the statement of changes in owner's equity. The problem was that we had to analyze the items in the single column to see which ones belonged on which statement.

A better approach is to use separate accounts for the owner's capital, the owner's withdrawals, each revenue, and each expense. This allows us to record the effects of each kind of change in owner's equity in its own account. Then, the information in these accounts can be taken directly to the financial statements without further analysis. The following paragraphs describe these equity accounts.

Capital Account. When a person invests in a proprietorship, the invested amount is recorded in an account identified by the owner's name and the word **Capital.** For example, an account called *Terry Dow, Capital* can be used to record Dow's original investment in Clear Copy Co. If the owner makes additional investments, they also are recorded in the owner's capital account.

Withdrawals Account.   When a business earns income, the owner's equity increases. The owner may choose to leave this equity intact or may withdraw assets from the business as needed. Whenever the owner withdraws assets, perhaps to pay personal living expenses, the withdrawal reduces the company's assets and the owner's equity.

In many situations, owners of unincorporated businesses plan to withdraw regular weekly or monthly amounts of cash. The owners may even think of these withdrawals as salaries. However, the owners of unincorporated businesses cannot receive salaries because they are not legally separate from their companies. As a result, they cannot enter into salary (or any other) contracts with themselves. Therefore, withdrawals are neither income to the owners nor expenses of the businesses. They are simply the opposite of investments by the owners.

To record the owner's withdrawals, most accounting systems use an account that has the name of the owner and the word *Withdrawals.* For example, an account called *Terry Dow, Withdrawals* would be used to record Dow's withdrawals from Clear Copy Co. The owner's withdrawals account also may be called the owner's *personal* account or *drawing* account.

Revenue and Expense Accounts.   Decision makers often want information about the amounts of revenue earned and expenses incurred during the reporting period. A business uses a variety of revenue and expense accounts to provide this information on its income statement. As you might expect, various companies have different kinds of revenues and expenses. Examples of possible revenue accounts are *Sales, Commissions Earned, Professional Fees Earned, Rent Earned,* and *Interest Earned.* Examples of expense accounts are *Advertising Expense, Store Supplies Expense, Office Salaries Expense, Office Supplies Expense, Rent Expense, Utilities Expense,* and *Insurance Expense.*

You can get an idea of the variety of accounts that a company might use by looking at the list of accounts inside the covers of this text. It lists the accounts you need to solve the exercises and problems in this book.[1]

THE LEDGER AND THE CHART OF ACCOUNTS

Accounts may have different physical forms, depending on the system. In computerized systems, accounts are stored in files on floppy or hard disks. In manual systems, each account may be a separate page in a loose-leaf book or a separate card in a tray of cards. Regardless of their physical form, the collection of all accounts is called the **ledger.** If the accounts are in files on a hard disk, those files are the ledger. If the accounts are pages in a book or cards in a file, the book or file is the ledger. In other words, a ledger is simply a group of accounts.

A company's size affects the number of accounts needed in its accounting system. A small company may get by with as few as 20 or 30 accounts, while a large company may use several thousand. The **chart of accounts** is a list of all accounts used by a company. The chart also includes an identification number assigned to each account. To be efficient, companies assign their account identification numbers in a systematic manner. For example, a small business might use this numbering system for its accounts:

101–199	Asset accounts
201–299	Liability accounts
301–399	Owner's equity accounts
401–499	Revenue accounts
501–699	Operating expense accounts

[1]Remember that different companies may use different account titles than the titles in the list. For example, a company might use Interest Revenue instead of Interest Earned or Rental Expense instead of Rent Expense. All that is required is that an account title describe the item it represents.

Although this system provides for 99 asset accounts, a company may not use all of them. The numbers create a three-digit code that conveys information to the company's accountants and bookkeepers. For example, the first digit of the code numbers assigned to the asset accounts is a 1, while the first digit assigned to the liability accounts is a 2, and so on. In each case, the first digit of an account's number reveals whether the account appears on the balance sheet or the income statement. The second and third digits may also relate to the accounts' categories. We describe account numbering systems more completely in the next chapter.

In its simplest form, an account looks like the letter T:

USING T-ACCOUNTS

	(Name)
(Left side)	(Right side)

Because of its shape, this simple form is called a **T-account.** Notice that the T format gives the account a left side, a right side, and a convenient place for its name.

The shape of a T-account provides one side for recording increases in the item while the decreases are recorded on the other side. For example, the following T-account represents Clear Copy's cash account after the transaction. in Chapter 1:

		Cash	
Investment by owner	30,000	Purchase of store supplies	2,500
Copy services revenue earned	2,200	Purchase of copy equipment	20,000
Collection of account receivable	1,700	Payment of rent	1,000
		Payment of salary	700
		Payment of account payable	900
		Withdrawal by owner	400

Calculating the Balance of an Account

An **account balance** is simply the difference between the increases and decreases recorded in the account. Thus, for example, the balance of an asset account is the cost of that asset on the date the balance is calculated. The balance of a liability account is the amount owed on the date of the balance. Putting the increases on one side of the account and the decreases on the other makes it easy to find an account's balance. To determine the balance, simply find the total increases shown on one side (including the beginning balance), find the total decreases shown on the other side, and then subtract the sum of the decreases from the sum of the increases.

For example, the total increases in Clear Copy's Cash account were $33,900, the total decreases were $25,500, and the account balance is $8,400. This T-account shows how to calculate the $8,400 balance:

		Cash	
Investment by owner	30,000	Purchase of store supplies	2,500
Copy services revenue earned	2,200	Purchase of copy equipment	20,000
Collection of account receivable	1,700	Payment of rent	1,000
		Payment of salary	700
		Payment of account payable	900
		Withdrawal by owner	400
Total increases	**33,900**	Total decreases	**25,500**
Less decreases	**−25,500**		
Balance	**8,400**		

Debits and Credits

In accounting terms, the left side of a T-account is called the **debit** side, often abbreviated Dr. The right side is called the **credit** side, abbreviated Cr.[2] To enter amounts on the left side of an account is to *debit* the account. To enter amounts on the right side is to *credit* the account. The difference between the total debits and the total credits in an account is the account balance. When the sum of the debits exceeds the sum of the credits, the account has a debit balance. It has a credit balance when the sum of the credits exceeds the sum of the debits.

From looking at the Cash account, you might think that the terms *debit* and *credit* mean *increase* and *decrease.* That is not correct. Whether a debit is an increase or decrease depends on the type of account. Similarly, whether a credit increases or decreases an account depends on the type of account. In any account, however, a debit and a credit have opposite effects. That is, in an account where a debit is an increase, a credit is a decrease. And, if a debit is a decrease in a particular account, a credit is an increase.

When we work with T-accounts, a debit simply means an entry on the left side and a credit simply means an entry on the right side. For example, notice how Terry Dow's initial investment in Clear Copy Co. is recorded in the Cash and capital accounts:

Cash		Terry Dow, Capital	
Investment 30,000			Investment 30,000

Notice that the cash increase is recorded on the left side of the Cash account with a $30,000 debit entry; the corresponding increase in owner's equity is recorded on the right side of the capital account with a $30,000 credit entry. This method of recording the transaction is an essential feature of *double-entry accounting,* which we explain in the next section.

Progress Check

2-4   Which of the following answers properly classifies these commonly used accounts?
      (1) Prepaid Rent, (2) Unearned Fees, (3) Buildings, (4) Owner's Capital, (5) Wages
      Payable, (6) Office Supplies.

	Assets	Liabilities	Owner's Equity
a.	1,6	2,5	3,4
b.	1,3,6	2,5	4
c.	1,3,6	5	2,4

2-5   What are accounts? What is a ledger?

2-6   What determines the quantity and types of accounts used by a company?

2-7   Does debit always mean increase and credit always mean decrease?

USING DEBITS AND CREDITS IN DOUBLE-ENTRY ACCOUNTING

LO 3

Describe how debits and credits are used to analyze transactions and record their effects in the accounts.

In **double-entry accounting,** every transaction affects and is recorded in at least two accounts. When recording each transaction, *the total amount debited must equal the total amount credited.* Because each transaction is recorded with total debits equal to total credits, the sum of the debits for all entries must equal the sum of the credits for all entries. Furthermore, the sum of the debit account balances in the ledger must equal the sum of the credit account balances. The only reason the sum of the debit balances would not equal the sum of the credit balances would be that an error has

---

[2]These abbreviations are remnants of 18th-century English bookkeeping practices that used the terms *Debitor* and *Creditor* instead of *debit* and *credit.* These abbreviations use the first and last letters from the words, just as we still do for *Saint* (St.) and *Doctor* (Dr.).

occurred. Thus, an important result of double-entry accounting is that many errors are avoided by being sure that the debits and credits for each transaction are equal.

According to traditional double-entry accounting, increases in assets are recorded on the debit side of asset accounts.[3] Why are asset accounts given debit balances? There is no specific reason. The choice is simply a convention that makes it easier for accountants by having all accounting systems work the same way. Then, because asset accounts have debit balances, increases in those balances are recorded with debits and decreases are recorded with credits.

Because asset accounts have debit balances and because debits must equal credits, liability accounts and owner's equity accounts must have credit balances. This follows from the logic of the accounting equation (Assets = Liabilities + Owner's Equity). Therefore, increases in liability and owner's equity accounts are recorded with credit entries. In other words, if asset increases are recorded with debit entries, equal debits and credits for a transaction are possible only if increases in liabilities and owner's equity are recorded as credits. To summarize, double-entry accounting systems record increases and decreases in balance sheet accounts as follows:

Assets		=	Liabilities		+	Owner's Equity	
Debit for increases	Credit for decreases		Debit for decreases	Credit for increases		Debit for decreases	Credit for increases

The practices shown in these T-accounts can be expressed as the following rules for recording transactions in a double-entry accounting system:

1. Increases in assets are debited to asset accounts; therefore, decreases in assets are recorded with credit entries to asset accounts.

2. Increases in liabilities are credited to liability accounts; therefore, decreases in liabilities are recorded with debit entries to liability accounts.

3. Increases in owner's equity are credited to owner's equity accounts; therefore, decreases in owner's equity are recorded with debit entries to owner's equity accounts.

Chapter 1 taught you that owner's equity is increased by owner's investments and by revenues. You also learned that owner's equity is decreased by expenses and by withdrawals. Therefore, the following rules also apply:

4. The owner's investments are credited to the owner's capital account because they increase equity.

5. The owner's withdrawals of assets are debited to the owner's withdrawals account because they decrease equity.

6. Revenues are credited to revenue accounts because they increase equity. The system should include a separate account for each type of revenue.

7. Expenses are debited to expense accounts because they decrease equity. The system should include a separate account for each type of expense.

At this stage, you may find it helpful to memorize these rules. You will use them over and over in the course of your study. Before long, the rules will become second nature to you.

The following transactions for Clear Copy Co. will help you learn how to apply these debit and credit rules. Study each transaction carefully to be sure that you understand it before you go on to the next one.

EXAMPLES OF DEBITS AND CREDITS

---

[3]These double-entry practices originated in 15th-century Italy and have stood the test of more than 500 years of change and progress in business.

Each transaction is numbered so you can identify the transaction's effects on the accounts. You should recognize the first 11 transactions because they were used in Chapter 1 to show how transactions affect the accounting equation. In this chapter, we add five more transactions (numbers 12 through 16) to illustrate different kinds of events.

Before recording a transaction, the bookkeeper first analyzes it to determine what was increased or decreased. Then, the debit and credit rules are applied to decide how to record the increases or decreases. The bookkeeper's analysis for each of the example transactions appears next to the T-accounts. Study each analysis carefully to be sure that you understand the process.

1. On December 1, Terry Dow invested $30,000 in Clear Copy Co.

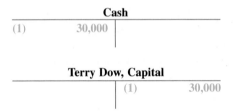

Cash

(1)	30,000		

Terry Dow, Capital

		(1)	30,000

Analysis of the transaction: The transaction increased the company's cash. At the same time, it increased Dow's equity. Increases in assets are debited and increases in owner's equity are credited. Therefore, record the transaction with a debit to Cash and a credit to Terry Dow, Capital, for $30,000.

2. Purchased store supplies by paying $2,500 cash.

Store Supplies

(2)	2,500		

Cash

(1)	30,000	(2)	2,500

Analysis of the transaction: The cost of the store supplies is increased by the purchase and cash is decreased. Increases in assets are debited and decreases are credited. Therefore, record the transaction with a debit to Store Supplies and a credit to Cash for $2,500.

3. Purchased copying equipment by paying $20,000 cash.

Copy Equipment

(3)	20,000		

Cash

(1)	30,000	(2)	2,500
		(3)	20,000

Analysis of the transaction: The cost of the copying equipment is increased and cash is decreased. Increases in assets are debited and decreases are credited. Debit Copy Equipment and credit Cash for $20,000.

4. Purchased $1,100 of store supplies and $6,000 of copying equipment on credit from Handy Supply Company.

Store Supplies

(2)	2,500		
(4)	1,100		

Copy Equipment

(3)	20,000		
(4)	6,000		

Accounts Payable

		(4)	7,100

Analysis of the transaction: This transaction increased two assets, store supplies and copy equipment. It also created a new liability. Increases in assets are debits and increases in liabilities are credits. Therefore, debit Store Supplies for $1,100, debit Copy Equipment for $6,000, and credit Accounts Payable for $7,100.

5. Provided copying services to a customer and immediately collected $2,200 cash.

Cash			
(1)	30,000	(2)	2,500
(5)	2,200	(3)	20,000

Copy Services Revenue	
(5)	2,200

Analysis of the transaction: This revenue transaction increased both assets and owner's equity. Increases in assets are debits and increases in owner's equity are credits. Revenue accounts are increased with credits because revenues increase owner's equity. Therefore, debit Cash $2,200 to record the increase in assets. Credit Copy Services Revenue $2,200 to increase owner's equity and to accumulate information for the income statement.

6. Paid $1,000 cash for rent for December.

Rent Expense	
(6)	1,000

Cash			
(1)	30,000	(2)	2,500
(5)	2,200	(3)	20,000
		(6)	1,000

Analysis of the transaction: The cost of renting the store during December is an expense, which decreases owner's equity. Because decreases in owner's equity are debits, expenses are recorded as debits. Therefore, debit Rent Expense $1,000 to decrease owner's equity and to accumulate information for the income statement. Also, credit Cash $1,000 to record the decrease in assets.

7. Paid $700 cash for the employee's salary for the pay period ended on December 12.

Salaries Expense	
(7)	700

Cash			
(1)	30,000	(2)	2,500
(5)	2,200	(3)	20,000
		(6)	1,000
		(7)	700

Analysis of the transaction: The employee's salary is an expense that decreased owner's equity. Debit Salaries Expense $700 to decrease owner's equity and to accumulate information for the income statement. Also, credit Cash $700 to record the decrease in assets.

8. Completed copying work on credit and billed the customer $1,700 for the services.

Accounts Receivable	
(8)	1,700

Copy Services Revenue		
	(5)	2,200
	(8)	1,700

Analysis of the transaction: This revenue transaction gave Clear Copy the right to collect $1,700 from the customer. Thus, it increased both assets and owner's equity. Therefore, debit Accounts Receivable $1,700 for the increase in assets and credit Copy Services Revenue $1,700 to increase owner's equity and to accumulate information for the income statement.

9. The customer paid the $1,700 account receivable created in transaction 8.

Cash			
(1)	30,000	(2)	2,500
(5)	2,200	(3)	20,000
(9)	1,700	(6)	1,000
		(7)	700

Accounts Receivable			
(8)	1,700	(9)	1,700

Analysis of the transaction: One asset was increased and another decreased. Debit Cash $1,700 to record the increase in cash, and credit Accounts Receivable $1,700 to record the decrease in the account receivable.

10. Paid Handy Supply Company $900 cash on the $7,100 owed for the supplies and equipment purchased on credit in transaction 4.

Accounts Payable		
(10)	900	(4) 7,100

Cash		
(1)	30,000	(2) 2,500
(5)	2,200	(3) 20,000
(9)	1,700	(6) 1,000
		(7) 700
		(10) 900

Analysis of the transaction: A payment to a creditor decreases an asset and a liability by the same amount. Decreases in liabilities are debited, and decreases in assets are credited. Debit Accounts Payable $900 and credit Cash $900.

11. Terry Dow withdrew $400 from Clear Copy Co. for personal living expenses.

Terry Dow, Withdrawals	
(11)	400

Cash		
(1)	30,000	(2) 2,500
(5)	2,200	(3) 20,000
(9)	1,700	(6) 1,000
		(7) 700
		(10) 900
		(11) 400

Analysis of the transaction: This event reduced owner's equity and assets by the same amount. The Terry Dow, Withdrawals account is debited $400 to decrease owner's equity and to accumulate information for the statement of changes in owner's equity. Cash is credited $400 to record the asset reduction.

12. Signed a contract with a customer and accepted $3,000 cash in advance of providing any services.

Cash		
(1)	30,000	(2) 2,500
(5)	2,200	(3) 20,000
(9)	1,700	(6) 1,000
(12)	3,000	(7) 700
		(10) 900
		(11) 400

Unearned Copy Services Revenue	
	(12) 3,000

Analysis of the transaction: The $3,000 inflow of cash increased assets but a revenue was not earned. Instead, the transaction creates a liability that will be satisfied by doing the client's copying work in the future. Record the asset increase by debiting Cash for $3,000 and record the liability increase by crediting Unearned Copy Services Revenue for $3,000.

13. Paid $2,400 cash for the premium on a two-year insurance policy.

Prepaid Insurance	
(13)	2,400

Cash		
(1)	30,000	(2) 2,500
(5)	2,200	(3) 20,000
(9)	1,700	(6) 1,000
(12)	3,000	(7) 700
		(10) 900
		(11) 400
		(13) 2,400

Analysis of the transaction: The advance payment of the insurance premium creates an asset (a prepaid expense) by decreasing another asset. The new asset is recorded with a $2,400 debit to Prepaid Insurance and the payment is recorded with a $2,400 credit to Cash.

14. Paid $120 cash for additional store supplies.

15. Paid $230 cash for the December utilities bill.

16. Paid $700 cash for the employee's salary for two weeks ended December 26.

Store Supplies

(2)	2,500
(4)	1,100
(14)	120

Analysis of the transactions: These transactions are similar because each of them decreased cash. They are different from each other because the store supplies are assets while the utilities and employee's salary are expenses. The $120 cost of the supplies should be debited to the Store Supplies asset account, while the $230 for utilities and the $700 salary should be debited to separate expense accounts. Each transaction requires its own credit to Cash.

Utilities Expense

(15)	230

Salaries Expense

(7)	700
(16)	700

Cash

(1)	30,000	(2)	2,500
(5)	2,200	(3)	20,000
(9)	1,700	(6)	1,000
(12)	3,000	(7)	700
		(10)	900
		(11)	400
		(13)	2,400
		(14)	120
		(15)	230
		(16)	700

Illustration 2–3 shows the accounts of Clear Copy Co. after the 16 transactions have been recorded and the balances computed. The three columns in the illustration relate the accounts to the assets, liabilities, and owner's equity elements of the accounting equation. When we take the totals of the balance in each of the three columns, we find that total assets are $40,070 ($7,950 + $0 + $2,400 + $3,720 + $26,000). The total liabilities are $9,200 ($6,200 + $3,000), and the total of the equity accounts is $30,870 ($30,000 − $400 + $3,900 − $1,000 − $1,400 − $230). Thus, the total assets of $40,070 equals the $40,070 sum of the liabilities and the owner's equity ($9,200 + $30,870). The withdrawals, revenue, and expense accounts in the box record the events that change equity; their balances are reported as events on the income statement and statement of changes in owner's equity. Their balances are eventually combined with the balance of the capital account to produce the amount of equity reported on the balance sheet. Chapter 4 describes the bookkeeping (closing) process for combining these balances.

ACCOUNTS AND THE ACCOUNTING EQUATION

Progress Check

2-8 Double-entry accounting requires that:
  a. All transactions that create debits to asset accounts must create credits to liability or owner's equity accounts.
  b. A transaction that requires a debit to a liability account must require a credit to an asset account.
  c. Every transaction must be recorded with total debits equal to total credits.

2-9 What kinds of transactions increase owner's equity? What kinds decrease owner's equity?

2-10 Why are most accounting systems called *double-entry?*

Illustration 2-3 The Ledger for Clear Copy Co.

	Assets			=	Liabilities			+	Owner's Equity	

Assets = **Liabilities** + **Owner's Equity**

Cash

(1)	30,000	(2)	2,500
(5)	2,200	(3)	20,000
(9)	1,700	(6)	1,000
(12)	3,000	(7)	700
		(10)	900
		(11)	400
		(13)	2,400
		(14)	120
		(15)	230
		(16)	700
Total	36,900	Total	28,950
	−28,950		
Balance	7,950		

Accounts Receivable

(8)	1,700	(9)	1,700

Prepaid Insurance

(13)	2,400	

Store Supplies

(2)	2,500	
(4)	1,100	
(14)	120	
Balance	3,720	

Copy Equipment

(3)	20,000	
(4)	6,000	
Balance	26,000	

Accounts Payable

(10)	900	(4)	7,100
Total	900	Total	7,100
			−900
		Balance	6,200

Unearned Copy Services Revenue

		(12)	3,000

Terry Dow, Capital

		(1)	30,000

Terry Dow, Withdrawals

(11)	1,500	

Copy Services Revenue

		(5)	2,200
		(8)	1,700
		Balance	3,900

Rent Expense

(6)	1,000	

Salaries Expense

(7)	700	
(16)	700	
Balance	1,400	

Utilities Expense

(15)	230	

The accounts in this box record increases and decreases in owner's equity. Their balances are reported on the income statement or the statement of changes in owner's equity.

$$\$40,070 = \$9,200 + \$30,870$$

TRANSACTIONS ARE FIRST RECORDED IN THE JOURNAL

LO 4

Record transactions in a General Journal, describe balance column accounts, and post entries from the journal to the ledger.

In the preceding pages, we used debits and credits to show how transactions affect accounts. This process of analyzing transactions and recording their effects directly in the accounts is helpful as a learning exercise. However, real accounting systems do not record transactions directly in the accounts. If the bookkeeper recorded the effects directly in the accounts, errors would be easily made and difficult to track down and correct.

To help avoid errors, accounting systems record transactions in a **journal** before recording them in the accounts. This practice provides a complete record of each transaction in one place and links the debits and credits for each transaction. After the debits and credits for each transaction are entered in the journal, they are transferred to the ledger accounts. This two-step process produces useful records for the auditor about a company's transactions. At the same time, the process helps the bookkeeper avoid errors. And, if errors are made, the process makes it easier to find and correct them.

Illustration 2-4 The Sequence of Steps in Recording Transactions

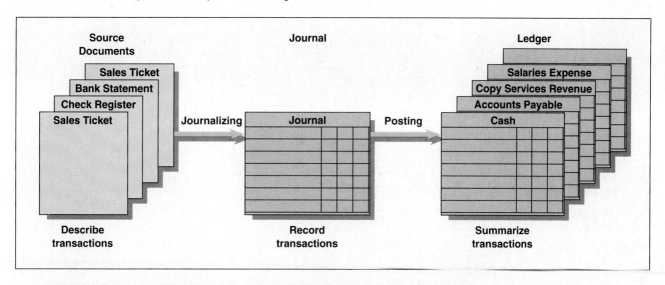

The process of recording transactions in a journal is called *journalizing.* The process of transferring journal entry information to the ledger is called **posting.** This sequence of steps is represented in Illustration 2–4. Various source documents provide the evidence that transactions have occurred. Next, these transactions are recorded in the journal. Finally, the journal entries are posted to the ledger. This sequence causes the journal to be called the **book of original entry** while the ledger is sometimes called the **book of final entry.**

The General Journal

The most flexible type of journal is the **General Journal.** The General Journal can be used to record any kind of transaction. A journal entry records this information about each transaction:

1. The transaction's date.
2. The names of the affected accounts.
3. The amount of each debit and credit.
4. An explanation of the transaction.
5. The identifying numbers of the accounts.

Illustration 2–5 shows how the first four transactions for Clear Copy would be recorded in a typical General Journal in a manual system. The General Journals used in computerized systems may look like the manual journal page, or they may differ. Regardless of their form or appearance, journals serve the same purpose in every system.

Notice that the fourth entry in Illustration 2–5 uses three accounts to record the credit purchase of store supplies and additional copying equipment. A transaction that affects at least three accounts is recorded in the General Journal with a **compound journal entry.**

Recording Transactions in a General Journal

A bookkeeper follows routine procedures when recording entries in the General Journal. The following steps were used to record the entries in Illustration 2–5. As you read these steps, compare them to the illustration to see how they produced the journal entries:

1. Enter the year at the top of the first column of the first line on the page.

Illustration 2-5　A General Journal Showing Transactions for Clear Copy Co.

								GENERAL JOURNAL							Page 1		

Date			Account Titles and Explanation	PR	Debit		Credit	
19X1 Dec.	1	Cash			30,000	00		
			Terry Dow, Capital				30,000	00
			Investment by owner.					
	2	Store Supplies			2,500	00		
			Cash				2,500	00
			Purchased store supplies for cash.					
	3	Copy Equipment			20,000	00		
			Cash				20,000	00
			Purchased copy equipment for cash.					
	6	Store Supplies			1,100	00		
			Copy Equipment			6,000	00		
			Accounts Payable				7,100	00
			Purchased supplies and equipment on credit.					

2. Enter the month on the first line of the journal entry in the first column. (Successive entries in the same month on the same page of the journal would not show the month again.)

3. Enter the day's date for the transaction in the second column on the first line of each entry.

4. Enter the names of the accounts to be debited. The account titles are taken from the chart of accounts and are aligned with the left margin of the Account Titles and Explanation column.

5. Enter the amount debited to each account in the Debit column of the journal on the same line as the account title.

6. Enter the names of the accounts to be credited. The account titles are taken from the chart of accounts and are indented far enough from the left margin of the column to distinguish them from the debited accounts (perhaps as much as an inch).

7. Enter the amount credited to each account in the Credit column of the journal on the same line as the account title.

8. Provide a brief explanation of the transaction to help an auditor or other person understand what happened. The explanation is indented about half as far as the credited account titles to avoid confusing the explanation with either a debit or credit entry. (For clarity, this book italicizes the explanations.)

9. Skip a single line between each journal entry to keep them separate.

Once the journalizing process is completed, the journal entry provides a complete and useful description of the event's effects on the organization.

Illustration 2-6 The Cash Account for Clear Copy Co. in the Balance Column Format

			Cash						Account No. 101	
Date		Explanation	PR	Debit		Credit		Balance	
19X1 Dec.	1		G1	30,000	00			30,000	00
	2		G1			2,500	00	27,500	00
	3		G1			20,000	00	7,500	00
	10		G1	2,200	00			9,700	00

In a manual system, nothing is entered in the **Posting Reference (PR) column** when a transaction is initially recorded in the journal. As a control over the posting process, the account numbers are not entered until the entries are posted to the ledger. (Because the old word for page was *folio,* and because each account used to be a separate page in a book, the Posting Reference column in the journal is occasionally called the *folio column.*)

Computerized Journals. Journals in computerized accounting systems serve the same purpose of providing a complete record of each transaction. In some systems, they even look like the manual journal page in Illustration 2–5. In addition, they may include error-checking routines that ensure the debits in the entry equal the credits. They often provide shortcuts that allow the computer operator to enter account numbers instead of names, or to enter the account names and numbers with pull-down menus or other easy-to-use techniques.

BALANCE COLUMN ACCOUNTS

T-accounts are used in textbooks and accounting classes to show how accounts work. T-accounts are helpful because they allow you to disregard some details and concentrate on the main ideas. Actual accounting systems, however, use **balance column accounts** like the one in Illustration 2–6.

The balance column account format is similar to a T-account because it has columns for entering each debit and credit. It is different because it provides space for the entry's date and any explanation that might be needed. It also has a third column for showing the balance of the account after each entry is posted. As a result, the amount on the last line in this column is the account's current balance. For example, Clear Copy's Cash account in Illustration 2–6 was debited on December 1 for the $30,000 investment by Terry Dow. As a result, the account had a $30,000 debit balance. The account was then credited on December 2 for $2,500, and its new $27,500 balance was entered in the third column. On December 3, it was credited again, this time for $20,000, and its balance was reduced to $7,500. Finally, the Cash account was debited for $2,200 on December 10, and its balance was increased to $9,700.

When the balance column format is used, the heading of the Balance column does not indicate whether the account has a debit or credit balance. However, this omission should not create any problems because every account has a *normal balance.* The normal balance of each type of account (asset, liability, owner's equity, revenue, or expense) is the same as the debit or credit entry used to record an increase in the account. The table on page 80 shows the normal balances for accounts.

Type of Account	Increases Are Recorded as	Normal Balance
Asset	Debits	Debit
Liability	Credits	Credit
Owner's equity:		
Capital	Credits	Credit
Withdrawals . . .	Debits	Debit
Revenue	Credits	Credit
Expense	Debits	Debit

Abnormal Balances. Some unusual events may cause an account to have an abnormal balance. For example, a credit customer might accidentally pay its balance twice, which would give the account receivable a credit balance instead of a zero balance. If an abnormal balance is created, the bookkeeper can identify it by circling the amount or by entering the balance in red or some other nonstandard color. Many computerized systems automatically provide a code beside the balance, such as *dr* or *cr* to identify the kind of balance.

Zero Balances. If an account has a zero balance, it is customary to indicate that fact by writing zeros or a dash in the Balance column. This practice avoids confusion between a zero balance and an accidentally omitted balance.

POSTING JOURNAL ENTRIES

Illustration 2–4 on page 77 shows that journal entries are posted to the accounts in the ledger. To ensure that the ledger is up to date, journal entries are posted as promptly as possible, which may be daily, weekly, or as time permits. All entries need to be posted before the end of the reporting period to provide the accounts with updated balances when the financial statements are prepared.

When posting the entries to the ledger, the bookkeeper copies the debits in the journal entries into the accounts as debits, and copies the journal entries' credits into the accounts as credits. The diagram in Illustration 2–7 identifies the six steps used in a manual system to post each debit and credit from the journal entry. Use the diagram to see how these six steps are completed:

For the debit:

1.   Find the account that was debited in the journal entry.
2.   Enter the date of the journal entry in the account on the next available line for the debit.
3.   Write the amount debited in the journal entry in the debit column of the account.
4.   To show where the debit came from, enter the letter *G* and the journal page number in the Posting Reference (PR) column for the account. (The letter *G* shows that the posted entry came from the General Journal. Other journals are identified by their own letters. We discuss other journals in Appendix E at the end of the book.)
5.   Calculate and enter the account's new balance in the third column.
6.   To show that the posting process is complete, enter the account number in the Posting Reference column on the entry's line in the journal. (If posting is interrupted, the bookkeeper can use the journal's Posting Reference column to take up the process where it was stopped.)

For the credit:

Repeat the six steps. However, the credit amount is entered in the Credit column and has a credit effect on the account balance.

Illustration 2-7 Six Steps for Posting a General Journal Entry to the Ledger

1. Find the account
2. Enter the date
3. Post the entered amount
4. Enter the journal page
5. Enter the account balance
6. Enter the account number

GENERAL JOURNAL Page 1

Date	Account Titles and Explanation	PR	Debit	Credit
19X1 Dec. 1	Cash	101	30,000 00	
	Terry Dow, Capital	301		30,000 00
	Investment by owner.			

LEDGER

Cash Account No. 101

Date	Explanation	PR	Debit	Credit	Balance
19X1 Dec. 1		G1	30,000 00		30,000 00

Terry Dow, Capital Account No. 301

Date	Explanation	PR	Debit	Credit	Balance
19X1 Dec. 1		G1		30,000 00	30,000 00

Notice that step 6 in the posting procedure for either the debit or the credit of an entry inserts the account number in the journal's Posting Reference column. This creates a link between the ledger and the journal entry. This link provides a cross-reference that helps the bookkeeper and the auditor trace an amount from one record to the other.

Posting in Computerized Systems. Computerized accounting systems do not require any additional effort by the operator to post the journal entries to the ledger. The programs in the systems are designed to automatically transfer the debit and credit entries from the journal into the database. In effect, the journal entries are posted directly into the accounts in the ledger without any additional steps. Many systems include error-detection routines that test the reasonableness of the journal entry and the account balance when the new entry is recorded.

Illustration 2-8

CLEAR COPY CO.
Trial Balance
December 31, 19X1

	Debit	Credit
Cash	$ 7,950	
Accounts receivable	0	
Prepaid insurance	2,400	
Store supplies	3,720	
Copy equipment	26,000	
Accounts payable		$ 6,200
Unearned copy services revenue		3,000
Terry Dow, capital		30,000
Terry Dow, withdrawals	400	
Copy services revenue		3,900
Rent expense	1,000	
Salaries expense	1,400	
Utilities expense	230	
Total	$43,100	$43,100

Progress Check

2-11   The owner of Davis Company invested $15,000 cash and land with a fair market value of $23,000 in the business. The company also assumed responsibility for an $18,000 note payable originally issued to finance the purchase of the land. The journal entry to record this investment consists of: *(a)* One debit and one credit; *(b)* Two debits and one credit; *(c)* Two debits and two credits; or *(d)* Debits that total $38,000 and credits that total $33,000.

2-12   What is a compound journal entry?

2-13   Why are posting reference numbers entered in the journal when entries are posted to the accounts?

PREPARING AND USING THE TRIAL BALANCE

LO 5

Prepare a trial balance, explain its usefulness, and calculate a company's debt ratio.

Recall that a double-entry accounting system records every transaction with equal debits and credits. As a result, the bookkeeper can tell that an error has occurred if the sum of the debit entries in the ledger does not equal the sum of the credit entries. The bookkeeper also knows that an error has occurred if the sum of the debit account balances does not equal the sum of the credit balances.

One purpose for preparing a **trial balance** is to find out if the debit and credit account balances are equal. A trial balance is a summary of the ledger that is a list of the accounts and their balances. The account balances are placed in either the debit or credit column of the trial balance. Illustration 2–8 presents the trial balance for Clear Copy Co. after the 16 entries described earlier in the chapter have been posted to the ledger.

The trial balance also serves as a helpful internal document for preparing the financial statements. The task of preparing the statements is simplified if the accountant can take the account balances from the trial balance instead of looking them up in the ledger. (Chapter 3 describes the statement preparation process in more detail.)

The bookkeeper uses these five steps to prepare a trial balance:

1.   Find the balance of each account in the ledger.

2.   List each account and place its balance beside it. Debit balances are entered in the Debit column and credit balances are entered in the Credit column. (If an

account has a zero balance, it may be included in the trial balance with a zero in the column for its normal balance.)
3. Compute the total of the debit balances.
4. Compute the total of the credit balances.
5. Verify that the sum of the debit balances equals the sum of the credit balances.

The trial balance for Clear Copy Co. in Illustration 2–8 is presented in a typical format. Notice that the total of the debit balances equals the total of the credit balances. If the two totals were not equal, we would know that at least one error had occurred. However, the fact that the two totals are equal does not prove that all errors were avoided.

The Information Provided by a Trial Balance

When a trial balance does not balance (that is, the columns are not equal), we know that at least one error has occurred. The error (or errors) may have occurred during these steps in the accounting process: (1) preparing journal entries, (2) posting journal entries to the ledger, (3) calculating account balances, (4) copying account balances to the trial balance, or (5) totaling the trial balance columns.

If the trial balance does balance, the accounts are likely to be free from errors that create unequal debits and credits. However, bookkeeping accuracy is not assured if the column totals are equal because some errors do not create unequal debits and credits. For example, the bookkeeper may debit a correct amount to the wrong account in preparing the journal entry or in posting a journal entry to the ledger. This error would cause two accounts to have incorrect balances but the trial balance would not be out of balance. Another error would be to record equal debits and credits of an incorrect amount. This error would give the two accounts incorrect balances but would not create unequal debits and credits. As a result, the fact that the trial balance column totals are equal does not prove that all journal entries have been recorded and posted correctly. However, equal totals do suggest that several types of errors probably have not occurred.

Searching for and Correcting Errors

If the trial balance does not balance, at least one error has occurred. The error (or errors) need to be found and corrected before going on to prepare the financial statements. The search for the error is more efficient if the bookkeeper checks the journalizing, posting, and trial balance preparation steps in reverse order.

First, the bookkeeper should verify that the trial balance columns were correctly added. Second, if that step does not find the error, the bookkeeper should verify that account balances were accurately copied from the ledger. Third, the bookkeeper should check to see if a debit or credit balance was mistakenly listed in the trial balance as a credit or debit. (A clue to this kind of error would be that the difference between the total debits and total credits in the trial balance would equal twice the amount of the incorrectly listed account balance.)

If the error remains undiscovered, the bookkeeper's fourth step is to recalculate each account balance. Then, if the error is not found, it is necessary to verify that each journal entry was properly posted to the accounts. Finally, the only remaining (and least likely) source of the error would be an original journal entry that did not have equal debits and credits.

One frequent error is called a *transposition*. This error occurs when two digits are switched or transposed within a number. For example, a $691 debit in a journal entry may be posted to the ledger as $619. If this happens and it is the only error, the difference between the two trial balance columns is evenly divisible by nine. For example, suppose that a posting error places a $619 debit in an account instead of the journal's correct amount of $691. As a result, the total credits in the trial balance would be larger than the total debits by $72 ($691 – $619). This number is evenly divisible by 9 ($72/9 = 8). Furthermore, the quotient (8) equals the difference between the two transposed numbers. The number of digits in the quotient also signals the location of the transposition. In this example, the fact that the quotient (8) has only one digit tells us that the transposition occurred in the first digit of the transposed numbers, starting from the right.[4]

Correcting Errors

If errors are discovered in either the journal or the ledger, they need to be corrected to ensure that the financial statements provide useful information. The approach to correcting the records depends on the nature of the errors and when they are discovered.

If an error in a journal entry is discovered before the error is posted, it can be corrected in a manual system by drawing a line through the incorrect information. Then, the correct information can be written above it to create a record of the change for the auditor. (Most computerized systems allow the operator to simply replace the incorrect information.) If a correct amount in the journal was posted incorrectly in the ledger, the bookkeeper can correct it the same way.

If an error in a journal entry is not discovered before it is posted, the correction may have to be done differently. For example, suppose that a journal entry incorrectly debited (or credited) the wrong account. If the journal entry has already been posted to that incorrect account, the bookkeeper generally does not strike through both erroneous entries in the journal and ledger. Instead, the usual practice is to correct the error in the original journal entry by creating another journal entry. This *correcting entry* removes the amount from the wrong account and moves it to the right account. For example, suppose that the bookkeeper recorded a purchase of office supplies with this incorrect debit in the journal entry to the Office Equipment account and then posted it to the accounts in the ledger:

Oct.	14	Office Equipment	1,600.00	
		Cash		1,600.00
		To record the purchase of office supplies.		

As a result of posting this incorrect entry, the Office Supplies account balance is too small (understated) by $1,600 and the Office Equipment account balance is too large (overstated) by the same amount. Three days later, the error is discovered and the following entry is made to correct both account balances:

Oct.	17	Office Supplies	1,600.00	
		Office Equipment		1,600.00
		To correct the entry of October 14 that incorrectly debited Office Equipment instead of Office Supplies.		

The credit in the correcting entry cancels the error from the first entry, and the debit correctly records the supplies. The explanation in the correcting entry allows the auditor to know exactly what happened.

Similar correcting entries may be needed in computerized accounting systems. The exact procedure depends on the particular program being used.

---

[4]If the transposition error had posted $961 instead of the correct $691, the difference would have been $270, and the quotient would have been $30 ($270/9). The fact that the quotient has two digits tells us to carefully examine the second digits from the right for a transposition of two numbers with a difference of 3.

When amounts are entered manually on ruled accounting paper in a journal, ledger, or trial balance, commas are not needed to indicate thousands and decimal points are not needed to separate dollars and cents. However, commas and decimal points are used in financial statements and other reports.

OTHER FORMATTING CONVENTIONS

As a matter of convenience, dollar signs are not used in journals and ledgers. However, they do appear in financial statements and other reports, including trial balances. This book follows the practice of putting a dollar sign beside the first amount in each column of numbers and the first amount appearing after a ruled line indicating that an addition or subtraction has been performed. The financial statements in Illustrations 1–8 and 1–9 on pages 39 and 40 demonstrate how dollar signs are used in this book. Different companies use various conventions for dollar signs. For example, dollar signs are used beside only the first and last numbers in the columns in the financial statements for Apple Computer, Inc., in Appendix F.

If an amount entered manually in a ledger or a journal consists of even dollars without cents, a convenient shortcut uses a dash in the cents column instead of two zeros. To simplify the illustrations, this book usually shows exact dollar amounts.

Even small companies seldom show decimal points or cents in their financial statements. Normally, the amounts are rounded, perhaps to the nearest dollar but often to a higher level. Exxon Corporation is typical of many very large companies in that it rounds its financial statement amounts to the nearest million dollars.

USING THE INFORMATION— THE DEBT RATIO

With so much emphasis in this chapter on bookkeeping activities, it might be easy to temporarily overlook the fact that accounting records are created for the purpose of providing useful information in financial statements. This chapter closes by describing a ratio that users apply to assess a company's risk of failing to pay its debts when they are due.

Almost all companies finance some portion of their assets with liabilities and the remaining portion with owner's equity. A company that finances a relatively large portion of its assets with liabilities is said to have a high degree of financial leverage.

You learn more about financial leverage in Chapter 13. However, you should understand that financial leverage involves risk. Because liabilities must be repaid and also require a company to pay interest, the risk of liabilities is that the company may not be able to make the required payments. In general, the risk is higher if a company is highly leveraged.

One way to evaluate the risk associated with a company's use of liabilities to finance its assets is to calculate and evaluate the **debt ratio.** This ratio describes the relationship between the amounts of the company's liabilities and assets, as follows:

$$\text{Debt ratio} = \frac{\text{Total liabilities}}{\text{Total assets}}$$

To see how the debt ratio is applied, consider the example of Chiquita Brands International, Inc. discussed at the beginning of the chapter. Using the data that was presented on page 61, the company's debt ratios at the end of each year from 1989 through 1993 are as follows:

	1993	1992	1991	1990	1989
a. Total liabilities	$2,138,755	$2,205,737	$1,969,419	$1,225,965	$ 909,526
b. Total assets	2,740,753	2,880,624	2,937,344	1,913,674	1,373,480
c. Debt ratio ($a \div b$) . . .	.780	.766	.670	.641	.662

Evaluating a company's debt ratio depends on several factors such as the nature of its operations, its ability to generate cash flows, the economic conditions at the time, and the industry in which it operates. Thus, it is not possible to say that a specific debt ratio is good for all companies.

However, notice that Chiquita's debt ratio increased each year since 1990. In the company's 1993 annual report, Chiquita's executives said they had adopted a strategy of de-leveraging the company's balance sheet in the future. In other words, they decided that the company's debt ratio had become too high.

To reduce the ratio in the future, they might use the cash provided by profitable operations to repay debt. Also, they might obtain additional money from the owners and use it to repay debt. A third possibility would be to sell some assets and use the proceeds to repay debt.

Progress Check

2-14   Which of the following terms describes a list of all of a company's accounts and their identifying numbers? *(a)* A journal; *(b)* A ledger; *(c)* A trial balance; *(d)* A source document; or *(e)* A chart of accounts.

2-15   When are dollar signs used in accounting reports?

2-16   A $4,000 debit to Store Equipment in a journal entry was incorrectly posted to the ledger as a $4,000 credit, and the account had a resulting debit balance of $20,000. What is the effect of the error on the trial balance column totals?

2-17   Which debt ratio implies more risk, ignoring other factors? *(a)* 6.6; *(b)* 5.0.

SUMMARY OF THE CHAPTER IN TERMS OF LEARNING OBJECTIVES

LO 1. Describe the events recorded in accounting systems and the importance of source documents and business papers in those systems. Accounting systems record transactions and other events that affect a company's assets, liabilities, and equity. The other events include internal transactions that use up assets or external events that cause the company's assets or liabilities to change. Source documents describe information that is recorded with accounting entries.

LO 2. Describe how accounts are used to record information about the effects of transactions, how code numbers are used to identify each account, and the meaning of the words *debit* and *credit*. Accounts are the basic building blocks of accounting systems. In one sense, accounts are symbols of the company's assets, liabilities, owner's equity, revenues, and expenses. In another sense, accounts are special records used to store information about transactions. The ledger is the collection of accounts used by an organization. Each account is assigned an identification number based on a code that indicates what kind of account it is. Debits record increases in assets, withdrawals, and expenses. Credits record decreases in these same accounts. Credits also record increases in liabilities, the owner's capital account, and revenues, while debits record decreases in these accounts.

LO 3. Describe how debits and credits are used to analyze transactions and record their effects in the accounts. To understand how a transaction affects a business, determine what accounts were increased or decreased. Every transaction affects at least two accounts, and the sum of the debits for each transaction equals the sum of the credits. As a result, the effects of business transactions never create an imbalance in the accounting equation (Assets = Liabilities + Owner's Equity).

LO 4. Record transactions in a General Journal, describe balance column accounts, and post entries from the journal to the ledger. Transactions are first recorded in a journal that provides a record of all their effects in one location. Second, each entry in the journal is posted to the accounts in the ledger. This process places information in the accounts that is used to produce the company's financial statements. Balance column accounts are widely used in accounting systems. These accounts include columns for debit entries, credit entries, and the balance after each entry.

LO 5. Prepare a trial balance, explain its usefulness, and calculate a company's debt ratio. A trial balance is a list of the accounts in the ledger that shows their debit and credit balances in separate columns. The trial balance is a convenient summary of the ledger's contents. It also reveals the existence of some kinds of errors if the sum of the debit account balances does not equal the sum of the credit account balances. A company's debt ratio is the ratio between its total liabilities and total assets. It provides information about the risk a company faces by using liabilities to finance its assets.

DEMONSTRATION PROBLEM

This demonstration problem is based on the same facts as the demonstration problem at the end of Chapter 1. The following events occurred during the first month of Barbara Schmidt's new haircutting business called The Cutlery:

a. On August 1, Schmidt put $3,000 cash into a checking account in the name of The Cutlery. She also invested $15,000 of equipment that she already owned.

b. On August 2, she paid $600 cash for furniture for the shop.

c. On August 3, she paid $500 cash to rent space in a strip mall for August.

d. On August 4, she furnished the shop by installing the old equipment and some new equipment that she bought on credit for $1,200. This amount is to be repaid in three equal payments at the end of August, September, and October.

e. On August 5, The Cutlery opened for business. Receipts from cash sales in the first week and a half of business (ended August 15) were $825.

f. On August 17, Schmidt paid $125 to an assistant for working during the grand opening.

g. Cash receipts from sales during the second half of August were $930.

h. On August 31, Schmidt paid an installment on the accounts payable.

i. On August 31, she withdrew $900 cash for her personal use.

Required

1. Prepare general journal entries for the preceding transactions.

2. Open the following accounts: Cash, 101; Furniture, 161; Store Equipment, 165; Accounts Payable, 201; Barbara Schmidt, Capital, 301; Barbara Schmidt, Withdrawals, 302; Haircutting Services Revenue, 403; Wages Expense, 623; and Rent Expense, 640.

3. Post the journal entries to the ledger accounts.

4. Prepare a trial balance as of August 31.

Planning the Solution

• Analyze each transaction to identify the accounts affected by the transaction and the amount of each effect.

• Use the debit and credit rules to prepare a journal entry for each transaction.

• Post each debit and each credit in the journal entries to the appropriate ledger accounts and cross-reference each amount in the Posting Reference columns in the journal and account.

• Calculate each account balance and list the accounts with their balances on a trial balance.

• Verify that the total debits in the trial balance equal total credits.

1. General journal entries:

Page 1

Date		Account Titles and Explanations	PR	Debit	Credit
Aug.	1	Cash	101	3,000.00	
		Store Equipment	165	15,000.00	
		Barbara Schmidt, Capital	301		18,000.00
		Owner's initial investment.			
	2	Furniture	161	600.00	
		Cash	101		600.00
		Purchased furniture for cash.			
	3	Rent Expense	640	500.00	
		Cash	101		500.00
		Paid rent for August.			
	4	Store Equipment	165	1,200.00	
		Accounts Payable	201		1,200.00
		Purchased additional equipment on credit.			
	15	Cash	101	825.00	
		Haircutting Services Revenue	403		825.00
		Cash receipts from ten days of operations.			
	17	Wages Expense	623	125.00	
		Cash	101		125.00
		Paid wages to assistant.			
	31	Cash	101	930.00	
		Haircutting Services Revenue	403		930.00
		Cash receipts from second half of August.			
	31	Accounts Payable	201	400.00	
		Cash	101		400.00
		Paid an installment on accounts payable.			
	31	Barbara Schmidt, Withdrawals	302	900.00	
		Cash	101		900.00
		Owner withdrew cash from the business.			

2. 3. Accounts in the ledger:

Cash   Account No. 101

Date		Explanation	PR	Debit	Credit	Balance
Aug.	1		G1	3,000.00		3,000.00
	2		G1		600.00	2,400.00
	3		G1		500.00	1,900.00
	15		G1	825.00		2,725.00
	17		G1		125.00	2,600.00
	31		G1	930.00		3,530.00
	31		G1		400.00	3,130.00
	31		G1		900.00	2,230.00

Furniture   Account No. 161

Date		Explanation	PR	Debit	Credit	Balance
Aug.	2		G1	600.00		600.00

Store Equipment   Account No. 165

Date		Explanation	PR	Debit	Credit	Balance
Aug.	1		G1	15,000.00		15,000.00
	4		G1	1,200.00		16,200.00

Accounts Payable   Account No. 201

Date		Explanation	PR	Debit	Credit	Balance
Aug.	4		G1		1,200.00	1,200.00
	31		G1	400.00		800.00

Barbara Schmidt, Capital   Account No. 301

Date		Explanation	PR	Debit	Credit	Balance
Aug.	1		G1		18,000.00	18,000.00

Barbara Schmidt, Withdrawals   Account No. 302

Date		Explanation	PR	Debit	Credit	Balance
Aug.	31		G1	900.00		900.00

Haircutting Services Revenue   Account No. 403

Date		Explanation	PR	Debit	Credit	Balance
Aug.	15		G1		825.00	825.00
	31		G1		930.00	1,755.00

Wages Expense   Account No. 623

Date		Explanation	PR	Debit	Credit	Balance
Aug.	17		G1	125.00		125.00

Rent Expense   Account No. 640

Date		Explanation	PR	Debit	Credit	Balance
Aug.	3		G1	500.00		500.00

4.

THE CUTLERY
Trial Balance
August 31, 19X1

	Debit	Credit
Cash	$ 2,230	
Furniture	600	
Store equipment	16,200	
Accounts payable		$ 800
Barbara Schmidt, capital		18,000
Barbara Schmidt, withdrawals	900	
Haircutting services revenue		1,755
Wages expense	125	
Rent expense	500	
Totals	$20,555	$20,555

GLOSSARY

Account a place or location within an accounting system in which the increases and decreases in a specific asset, liability, owner's equity, revenue, or expense are recorded and stored. p. 64

Account balance the difference between the increases (including the beginning balance) and decreases recorded in an account. p. 69

Balance column account an account with debit and credit columns for recording entries and a third column for showing the balance of the account after each entry is posted. p. 79

Book of final entry another name for a ledger. p. 77

Book of original entry another name for a journal. p. 77

Business papers various kinds of documents and other papers that companies use when they conduct their business; sometimes called *source documents*. p. 63

Chart of accounts a list of all accounts used by a company; includes the identification number assigned to each account. p. 68

Compound journal entry a journal entry that affects at least three accounts. p. 77

Credit an entry that decreases asset and expense accounts, or increases liability, owner's equity, and revenue accounts; recorded on the right side of a T-account. p. 70

Debit an entry that increases asset and expense accounts, or decreases liability, owner's equity, and revenue accounts; recorded on the left side of a T-account. p. 70

Debt ratio the ratio between a company's liabilities and assets; used to describe the risk associated with the company's debts. p. 85

Double-entry accounting an accounting system that records the effects of transactions and other events in at least two accounts with equal debits and credits. p. 70

External transactions exchanges between the entity and some other person or organization. p. 62

General Journal the most flexible type of journal; can be used to record any kind of transaction. p. 77

Internal transactions a term occasionally used to describe economic events that affect an entity's accounting equation but that are not transactions between two parties. p. 62

Journal a record in which the effects of transactions are first recorded; amounts are posted from the journal to the ledger; also called the *book of original entry*. p. 76

Ledger the collection of all accounts used by a business. p. 68

Posting the process of copying journal entry information to the ledger. p. 77

Posting Reference (PR) column a column in journals and accounts used to cross-reference journal and ledger entries. p. 79

Prepaid expenses assets created by payments for economic benefits that are not used until later; as the benefits are used up, the cost of the assets becomes an expense. p. 66

Promissory note an unconditional written promise to pay a definite sum of money on demand or on a defined future date (or dates). p. 65

Source documents another name for *business papers*; these documents are the source of information recorded with accounting entries. p. 63

T-account a simple account form widely used in accounting education to illustrate how debits and credits work. p. 69

Trial balance a summary of the ledger that lists the accounts and their balances; the total debit balances should equal the total credit balances. p. 82

Unearned revenues liabilities created by advance cash payments from customers for products or services; satisfied by delivering the products or services in the future. p. 67

QUESTIONS

1. What are the three fundamental steps in the accounting process?

2. What is the difference between a note receivable and an account receivable?

3. If assets are valuable resources and asset accounts have debit balances, why do expense accounts have debit balances?

4. Why does the bookkeeper prepare a trial balance?

5. Should a transaction be recorded first in a journal or the ledger? Why?

6. Are debits or credits listed first in general journal entries? Are the debits or the credits indented?

7. What kinds of transactions can be recorded in a General Journal?

8. If a wrong amount was journalized and posted to the accounts, how should the error be corrected?

9. Review the 1992 consolidated statement of cash flows for Ben & Jerry's Homemade, Inc., in Appendix G. What was the total effect on the company's Cash account of the sales of property, plant, and equipment? Were these transactions recorded with debits or credits to the Cash account?

10. Review the 1993 consolidated statement of cash flows for Federal Express Corporation in Appendix G. What was the total effect on the company's Cash account of the purchases of property and equipment? Were these transactions recorded with debits or credits to the Cash account?

QUICK STUDY (Five-Minute Exercises)

Select the items from the following list that are likely to serve as source documents:

a. Sales ticket.
b. Trial balance.
c. Bank statement.
d. Income statement.

e. Invoice from supplier.
f. Balance sheet.
g. Utility bill.
h. Owner's withdrawals account.

**QS 2–1
(LO 1)**

Indicate the financial statement on which each of the following accounts appears, using IS for income statement, SCOE for the statement of changes in owner's equity, and BS for balance sheet:

a. Accounts Receivable.
b. Consulting Services Revenue.
c. Owner, Withdrawals.
d. Land.
e. Unearned Rent.

f. Salaries Expense.
g. Owner, Capital.
h. Interest Payable.
i. Office Supplies.
j. Interest Earned.

**QS 2–2
(LO 2)**

Indicate whether a debit or credit is necessary to decrease the normal balance of each of the following accounts:

a. Accounts Receivable.
b. Consulting Services Revenue.
c. Owner, Withdrawals.
d. Land.
e. Unearned Rent.

f. Salaries Expense.
g. Owner, Capital.
h. Interest Payable.
i. Office Supplies.
j. Interest Earned.

**QS 2–3
(LO 3)**

Identify whether a debit or credit entry would be made to record the indicated change in each of the following accounts:

a. To increase Rent Earned.
b. To increase Owner, Withdrawals.
c. To decrease Owner, Capital.
d. To decrease Cash.
e. To decrease Prepaid Insurance.

f. To decrease Unearned Fees.
g. To increase Rent Expense.
h. To increase Accounts Payable.
i. To increase Office Equipment.
j. To decrease Accounts Receivable.

**QS 2–4
(LO 2, 3)**

Prepare journal entries for the following transactions:

a. On January 3, Jan Davis opened a new consulting business by investing $5,000 cash.
b. On January 5, Davis purchased office supplies on credit for $250.
c. On January 14, Davis received $1,600 in return for providing consulting services to a customer.

**QS 2–5
(LO 4)**

A trial balance has total debits of $14,000 and total credits of $17,000. Which one of the following errors would create this imbalance? Explain.

a. A $1,500 debit to Wages Expense in a journal entry was incorrectly posted to the ledger as a $1,500 credit, leaving the Wages Expense account with a $2,000 debit balance.

**QS 2–6
(LO 5)**

b.   A $3,000 debit to Wages Expense in a journal entry was incorrectly posted to the ledger as a $3,000 credit, leaving the Wages Expense account with a $500 debit balance.

c.   A $1,500 credit to Fees Earned in a journal entry was incorrectly posted to the ledger as a $1,500 debit, leaving the Fees Earned account with a $4,200 credit balance.

EXERCISES

Exercise 2–1
Increases, decreases, and normal balances of accounts
(LO 2, 3)

Complete the following table by (1) identifying the type of account listed on each line, (2) entering debit or credit in the blank spaces to identify the kind of entry that would increase or decrease the account balance, and (3) identifying the normal balance of the account.

	Account	Type of Account	Increase	Decrease	Normal Balance
a.	Accounts payable				
b.	Accounts receivable				
c.	B. Baxter, capital				
d.	B. Baxter, withdrawals				
e.	Cash				
f.	Equipment				
g.	Fees earned				
h.	Land				
i.	Postage expense				
j.	Prepaid insurance				
k.	Rent expense				
l.	Unearned revenue				

Exercise 2–2
Analyzing the effects of a transaction on the accounts
(LO 3)

Franklin Consulting Company recently notified a client that it would have to pay a $32,000 fee for consulting services. Unfortunately, the client did not have enough cash to pay the entire bill. Fran Franklin, the owner of the company, agreed to accept the following items in full payment: $5,000 cash and computer equipment worth $50,000. Franklin also had to assume responsibility for a $23,000 note payable related to the equipment. Which of the following effects would be recorded by Franklin for this transaction? (Your answer may include more than one of the listed effects. Some of the effects of the transaction may not be listed.)

a. $23,000 increase in a liability account.

b. $5,000 increase in the cash account.

c. $5,000 increase in a revenue account.

d. $32,000 increase in the F. Franklin, Capital account.

e. $32,000 increase in a revenue account.

Exercise 2–3
Recording the effects of transactions directly in T-accounts
(LO 3)

Open the following T-accounts: Cash; Accounts Receivable; Office Supplies; Office Equipment; Accounts Payable; R. J. Wainwright, Capital; Services Revenue; and Utilities Expense. Next, record these transactions of the Wainwright Company by recording the debit and credit entries directly in the T-accounts. Use the letters beside each transaction to identify the entries. Finally, determine the balance of each account.

a.   R. J. Wainwright invested $8,500 cash in the business.

b.   Purchased $250 of office supplies for cash.

c.   Purchased $4,700 of office equipment on credit.

d.   Received $1,000 cash as fees for services provided to a customer.

e.   Paid for the office equipment purchased in transaction c.

f.   Billed a customer $1,800 as fees for services.

g.   Paid the monthly utility bills with $350 cash.

h.   Collected $750 of the account receivable created in transaction f.

After recording the transactions of Exercise 2–3 in T-accounts and calculating the balance of each account, prepare the trial balance for the ledger. Use November 30, 19X1, as the date.

Exercise 2–4
Preparing a trial balance
(LO 5)

Complete the following table by filling in the blanks. For each of the listed posting errors, enter in column (1) the amount of the difference that the error would create between the two trial balance columns (show a zero if the columns would balance). If there would be a difference between the two columns, identify in column (2) the trial balance column that would be larger. The answer for the first error is provided as an example.

Exercise 2–5
Effects of posting errors on the trial balance
(LO 5)

	Description	(1) Difference between Debit and Credit Columns	(2) Column with the Larger Total
a.	A $1,600 debit to Utilities Expense was posted as a $1,060 debit.	$540	credit
b.	A $28,000 debit to Automobiles was posted as a debit to Accounts Payable.		
c.	A $3,300 credit to Fees Earned was posted as a $330 credit.		
d.	A $960 debit to Office Supplies was not posted at all.		
e.	A $1,500 debit to Prepaid Rent was posted as a debit to Rent Expense.		
f.	A $2,700 credit to Cash was posted twice as two credits to the Cash account.		
g.	A $6,600 debit to the owner's withdrawals account was debited to the owner's capital account.		

As the bookkeeper for a company, you are disappointed to learn that the column totals in your new trial balance are not equal. After going through a careful analysis, you have discovered only one error. Specifically, the balance of the Office Equipment account has a debit balance of $15,600 on the trial balance. However, you have figured out that a correctly recorded credit purchase of a computer for $3,500 was posted from the journal to the ledger with a $3,500 debit to Office Equipment and another $3,500 debit to Accounts Payable. Answer each of the following questions and present the dollar amount of any misstatement.

Exercise 2–6
Analyzing a trial balance error
(LO 5)

a. Is the balance of the Office Equipment account overstated, understated, or correctly stated in the trial balance?

b. Is the balance of the Accounts Payable account overstated, understated, or correctly stated in the trial balance?

c. Is the debit column total of the trial balance overstated, understated, or correctly stated?

d. Is the credit column total of the trial balance overstated, understated, or correctly stated?

e. If the debit column total of the trial balance is $240,000 before correcting the error, what is the total of the credit column?

On January 1, Rob Gregory created a new business called RG Public Relations Consulting. Near the end of the year, he hired a new bookkeeper without making a careful reference check. As a result, a number of mistakes have been made in preparing the following trial balance:

Exercise 2–7
Preparing a corrected trial balance
(LO 5)

RG PUBLIC RELATIONS CONSULTING
Trial Balance
December 31

	Debit	Credit
Cash	$ 11,000	
Accounts receivable		$ 15,800
Office supplies	5,300	
Office equipment	41,000	
Accounts payable		18,930
R. Gregory, capital	51,490	
R. Gregory, withdrawals	18,000	
Services revenue		45,600
Wages expense		12,000
Rent expense		9,600
Advertising expense		2,500
Totals	$126,790	$104,680

Gregory's analysis of the situation has uncovered these errors:

a. The sum of the debits in the Cash account is $74,350 and the sum of the credits is $61,080.

b. A $550 payment from a credit customer was posted to Cash but was not posted to Accounts Receivable.

c. A credit purchase of office supplies for $800 was completely unrecorded.

d. A transposition error occurred in copying the balance of the Services Revenue account to the trial balance. The correct amount was $46,500.

Other errors were made in placing account balances in the trial balance columns and in taking the totals of the columns. Use all this information to prepare a correct trial balance.

Exercise 2–8
Analyzing account entries and balances
(LO 2, 3)

Use the information in each of the following situations to calculate the unknown amount:

1. During June, Sunnyside Company had $65,000 of cash receipts and $67,500 of cash disbursements. The June 30 Cash balance was $11,200. Determine how much cash the company had on hand at the close of business on May 31.

2. On May 31, Sunnyside Company had a $65,000 balance in Accounts Receivable. During June, the company collected $59,300 from its credit customers. The June 30 balance in Accounts Receivable was $67,000. Determine the amount of sales on account that occurred in June.

3. Sunnyside Company had $98,000 of accounts payable on May 31 and $91,000 on June 30. Total purchases on account during June were $180,000. Determine how much cash was paid on accounts payable during June.

Exercise 2–9
Analyzing transactions from T-accounts
(LO 2, 3)

Seven transactions were posted to these T-accounts. Provide a short description of each transaction. Include the amounts in your descriptions.

Cash			
(a)	3,500	(b)	1,800
(e)	1,250	(c)	300
		(f)	1,200
		(g)	350

Truck		
(a)	5,500	

Accounts Payable			
(f)	1,200	(d)	4,800

Plumbing Supplies		
(c)	300	
(d)	100	

Vinnie Doran, Capital			
		(a)	11,800

Prepaid Insurance		
(b)	1,800	

Plumbing Fees Earned			
		(e)	1,250

	Plumbing Equipment			Gas and Oil Expense	
(a)	2,800		(g)	350	
(d)	4,700				

Use the information in the T-accounts in Exercise 2–9 to prepare general journal entries for the seven transactions. (Omit the account numbers.)

Exercise 2–10
General journal entries
(LO 4)

Prepare general journal entries to record the following transactions of Wayne's Water-Taxi Service.

Exercise 2–11
General journal entries
(LO 4)

May 1 Wayne Oldham invested $15,000 cash and a boat with a $65,000 fair value in a new company that will operate a water-taxi service in the harbor.

1 Rented space in a marina by paying $6,000 for the next three months in advance.

2 Purchased a two-way radio for the boat for $2,800 cash.

15 Collected $5,300 in fares over the preceding two weeks.

31 Paid $1,750 cash for gas and oil used by the boat during May.

Use the information provided in Exercise 2–11 to prepare a May 31 trial balance for Wayne's Water-Taxi Service. First, open these T-accounts: Cash; Prepaid Rent; Boat; Equipment; Wayne Oldham, Capital; Fares Earned; and Gas and Oil Expense. Then post the general journal entries to the T-accounts. Finally, prepare the trial balance.

Exercise 2–12
T-accounts and the trial balance
(LO 3, 5)

Examine the following transactions and identify those that created revenues for the business. Prepare general journal entries to record those transactions and explain why the other transactions did not create revenues.

Exercise 2–13
Analyzing and journalizing revenue transactions
(LO 4)

a. Received $25,500 cash from Dr. J. Runner, the owner of the medical practice.

b. Provided $900 of medical services to a patient on credit.

c. Received $1,050 cash for medical services provided to patient.

d. Received $6,100 from a patient in payment for medical services to be provided next year.

e. Received $3,000 from a patient in partial payment of an account receivable.

f. Borrowed $100,000 from the bank by signing a promissory note.

Examine the following transactions and identify those that created expenses for the business. Prepare general journal entries to record those transactions and explain why the other transactions did not create expenses.

Exercise 2–14
Analyzing and journalizing expense transactions
(LO 4)

a. Paid $9,400 cash for medical supplies purchased 30 days previously.

b. Paid the $750 salary of the doctor's assistant.

c. Paid $30,000 cash for medical equipment.

d. Paid utility bill with $620 cash.

e. Paid $700 to the owner of the medical practice as a withdrawal.

Calculate the debt ratio for each of the following cases:

Exercise 2–15
Calculating the debt ratio
(LO 5)

Case	Assets	Liabilities	Owner's Equity
1	$290,000	$110,000	$180,000
2	61,000	51,000	10,000
3	205,000	101,000	104,000
4	177,000	22,000	155,000
5	124,000	92,000	32,000
6	180,000	60,000	120,000

PROBLEMS

Problem 2–1
Recording transactions in
T-accounts; preparing a trial
balance
(LO 2, 3, 5)

Bobbie Benson opened a consulting firm and completed these transactions during June.

a. Invested $40,000 cash and office equipment with a $15,000 fair value in a business called Benson Consulting.

b. Purchased land and a small office building. The land was worth $15,000, and the building was worth $85,000. The purchase price was paid with $20,000 cash and a long-term note payable for $80,000.

c. Purchased $1,200 of office supplies on credit.

d. Bobbie Benson transferred title of an automobile to the business. The car was worth $9,000.

e. Purchased $3,000 of additional office equipment on credit.

f. Paid $750 salary to an assistant.

g. Provided services to a client and collected $3,000 cash.

h. Paid $400 for the month's utilities.

i. Paid account payable created in transaction c.

j. Purchased $10,000 of new office equipment by paying $9,300 cash and trading in old equipment with a recorded cost of $700.

k. Completed $2,600 of services for a client. This amount is to be paid within 30 days.

l. Paid $750 salary to an assistant.

m. Received $1,900 payment on the receivable created in transaction k.

n. The owner withdrew $2,000 cash from the business.

Required

1. Open the following T-accounts: Cash; Accounts Receivable; Office Supplies; Automobiles; Office Equipment; Building; Land; Accounts Payable; Long-Term Notes Payable; Bobbie Benson, Capital; Bobbie Benson, Withdrawals; Fees Earned; Salaries Expense; and Utilities Expense.

CHECK FIGURE:
Total debits in trial balance,
$152,600

2. Record the effects of the listed transactions by entering debits and credits directly in the T-accounts. Use the transaction letters to identify each debit and credit entry.

3. Determine the balance of each account and prepare a trial balance as of June 30.

Problem 2–2
Recording transactions in
T-accounts; preparing a trial
balance
(LO 2, 3, 5)

At the beginning of March, Avery Wilson created a custom computer programming company called Softouch. The following transactions occurred during the month:

a. Created the business by investing $35,000 cash, office equipment with a value of $2,000, and $15,000 of computer equipment.

b. Purchased land for an office. The land was worth $18,000, which was paid with $1,800 cash and a long-term note payable for $16,200.

c. Purchased a portable building with $25,000 cash and moved it onto the land.

d. Paid $2,000 cash for the premiums on two one-year insurance policies.

e. Provided services to a client and collected $1,900 cash.

f. Purchased additional computer equipment for $7,500. Paid $3,500 cash and signed a long-term note payable for the $4,000 balance.

g. Completed $4,000 of services for a client. This amount is to be paid within 30 days.

h. Purchased $750 of additional office equipment on credit.

i. Completed another software job for $6,000 on credit.

j. Received a bill for rent on a computer that was used on the completed job. The $400 rent must be paid within 30 days.

k. Collected $2,400 from the client described in transaction *g*.

l. Paid $500 wages to an assistant.

m. Paid the account payable created in transaction *h*.

n. Paid $225 cash for some repairs to an item of computer equipment.

o. The owner wrote a $3,200 check on the company's bank account to pay some personal expenses.

p. Paid $500 wages to an assistant.

q. Paid $1,000 cash to advertise in the local newspaper.

Required

1. Open the following T-accounts: Cash; Accounts Receivable; Prepaid Insurance; Office Equipment; Computer Equipment; Building; Land; Accounts Payable; Long-Term Notes Payable; Avery Wilson, Capital; Avery Wilson, Withdrawals; Fees Earned; Wages Expense; Computer Rental Expense; Advertising Expense; and Repairs Expense.

2. Record the transactions by entering debits and credits directly in the accounts. Use the transaction letters to identify each debit and credit. Prepare a trial balance as of March 31.

3. Calculate the company's debt ratio. Use $78,675 as the ending total assets.

CHECK FIGURE:
Total debits in trial balance, $84,500

Carrie Ford opened a new accounting practice called Carrie Ford, CPA, and completed these transactions during March:

Problem 2–3
Preparing and posting general journal entries; preparing a trial balance
(LO 4, 5)

Mar. 1	Invested $25,000 in cash and office equipment that had a fair value of $6,000.
1	Prepaid $1,800 cash for three months' rent for an office.
3	Made credit purchases of office equipment for $3,000 and office supplies for $600.
5	Completed work for a client and immediately received $500 cash.
9	Completed a $2,000 project for a client, who will pay within 30 days.
11	Paid the account payable created on March 3.
15	Paid $1,500 cash as the annual premium on an insurance policy.
20	Received $1,600 as partial payment for the work completed on March 9.
23	Completed work for another client for $660 on credit.
27	Carrie Ford withdrew $1,800 cash from the business to pay some personal expenses.
30	Purchased $200 of additional office supplies on credit.
31	Paid $175 for the month's utility bill.

Required

1. Prepare general journal entries to record the transactions.

2. Open the following accounts (use the balance column format): Cash (101); Accounts Receivable (106); Office Supplies (124); Prepaid Insurance (128); Prepaid Rent (131); Office Equipment (163); Accounts Payable (201); Carrie Ford, Capital (301); Carrie Ford, Withdrawals (302); Accounting Fees Earned (401); and Utilities Expense (690).

3. Post the entries to the accounts and enter the balance after each posting.

4. Prepare a trial balance as of the end of the month.

CHECK FIGURE:
Cash account balance, $18,225

Ada Evans started a business called The Pine Bough on August 1 and completed several transactions during the month. Her accounting and bookkeeping skills are not well-polished, and she needs some help gathering information at the end of the month. She recorded the following journal entries during the month:

Problem 2–4
Interpreting journals, posting, and analyzing trial balance errors
(LO 4, 5)

Aug.	1	Cash	15,000.00	
		Automobiles	11,000.00	
		Ada Evans, Capital		26,000.00
	3	Store Supplies	323.00	
		Cash		323.00
	7	Cash	500.00	
		Accounts Receivable	2,500.00	
		Fees Earned		3,000.00
	8	Store Equipment	3,200.00	
		Accounts Payable		3,200.00
	15	Cash	400.00	
		Fees Earned		400.00
	17	Prepaid Insurance	625.00	
		Cash		625.00
	23	Cash	2,500.00	
		Accounts Receivable		2,500.00
	25	Accounts Payable	3,200.00	
		Cash		3,200.00
	27	Office Equipment	4,700.00	
		Ada Evans, Capital		4,700.00
	28	Ada Evans, Withdrawals	1,230.00	
		Cash		1,230.00
	29	Store Supplies	727.00	
		Accounts Payable		727.00
	31	Salaries Expense	1,570.00	
		Cash		1,570.00

Based on these entries, Evans prepared the following trial balance:

THE PINE BOUGH
Trial Balance
For Month Ended August 31

Cash	$11,452	
Accounts receivable	0	
Store supplies	1,500	
Prepaid insurance	625	
Automobiles	11,000	
Office equipment	7,400	
Store equipment		$ 3,200
Accounts payable		7,270
Ada Evans, capital		30,700
Ada Evans, withdrawals	123	
Fees earned		3,400
Salaries expense	1,750	
Totals	$33,850	$44,570

Required

Preparation component:

Evans remembers something about trial balances and realizes that the preceding one has at least one error. To help her find the mistakes, set up the following balance column accounts and post the entries to them: Cash (101); Accounts Receivable (106); Store Supplies (125); Prepaid Insurance (128); Automobiles (151); Office Equipment (163); Store Equipment (165); Accounts Payable (201); Ada Evans, Capital (301); Ada Evans, Withdrawals (302); Fees Earned (401); and Salaries Expense (622).

Analysis component:

Although Evans's journal entries are correct, she forgot to provide explanations of the events. Analyze each entry and present a reasonable explanation of what happened. Then, prepare a correct trial balance and describe the errors that Evans made.

Jan Dell started a new business, Dimple Dell Day Care, and completed these transactions during October of the current year:

Oct. 1 Invested $35,000 in cash, $2,500 in teaching supplies, and school equipment worth $9,000.

2 Paid $750 cash for one month's rent for suitable space in a shopping center.

3 Paid a liability insurance policy premium of $1,400 for the first month.

4 Purchased a van for picking up the kids by paying $14,000 cash.

10 Purchased $800 of additional teaching supplies on credit.

21 Paid $4,000 cash for helpers' salaries.

23 Paid one-half of the account payable created on October 10.

28 Collected $9,000 cash from customers.

29 Paid $1,150 for the month's utility bills.

31 Withdrew $1,200 cash from the business to pay some personal expenses.

Required

1. Open the following accounts: Cash (101); Teaching Supplies (126); Automobiles (151); School Equipment (167); Accounts Payable (201); Jan Dell, Capital (301); Jan Dell, Withdrawals (302); Day Care Fees Earned (401); Salaries Expense (622); Insurance Expense (637); Rent Expense (640); and Utilities Expense (690).

2. Prepare general journal entries to record the transactions, post them to the accounts, and prepare a trial balance as of October 31.

3. Prepare an income statement for the month ended October 31.

4. Prepare a statement of changes in owner's equity for the month ended October 31.

5. Prepare a balance sheet dated October 31.

Lester Fenwick started a real estate agency and completed seven transactions, including Fenwick's initial investment of $8,500 cash. After these transactions, the ledger included the following accounts with their normal balances:

Cash	$11,300
Office supplies	330
Prepaid insurance	1,600
Office equipment	8,250
Accounts payable	8,250
Lester Fenwick, capital	8,500
Lester Fenwick, withdrawals	3,900
Commissions earned	12,000
Advertising expense	3,370

Required

Preparation component:

Prepare a trial balance for the business.

Analysis component:

Analyze the accounts and balances and prepare a list that describes each of the seven transactions and its amount. Also, present a schedule that shows how the transactions resulted in the $11,300 Cash balance.

SERIAL PROBLEM

Emerald Computer Services

(This comprehensive problem starts in this chapter and continues in Chapters 3, 4, and 5. Because of its length, this problem is most easily solved if you use the Working Papers that accompany this text.)

On October 1, 19X1, Tracy Green created a single proprietorship called Emerald Computer Services. Emerald will provide consulting services, including computer system installations and custom program development. Green has adopted the calendar year for reporting, and expects to prepare the company's first set of financial statements as of December 31, 19X1. The initial chart of accounts for the accounting system includes these items:

Account	No.	Account	No.
Cash	101	Tracy Green, Capital	301
Accounts Receivable	106	Tracy Green, Withdrawals	302
Computer Supplies	126	Computer Services Revenue	403
Prepaid Insurance	128	Wages Expense	623
Prepaid Rent	131	Advertising Expense	655
Office Equipment	163	Mileage Expense	676
Computer Equipment	167	Miscellaneous Expenses	677
Accounts Payable	201	Repairs Expense, Computer	684

Required

1. Prepare journal entries to record each of the following transactions for Emerald Computer Services.

2. Open balance column accounts for the company and post the journal entries to them.

Transactions:

Oct.   1   Tracy Green invested $30,000 cash in the business, along with a $12,000 computer system and $6,000 of office equipment.

     2   Rented office space for $750 per month and paid the first four months' rent in advance.

     3   Purchased computer supplies on credit for $880 from AAA Supply Co.

     4   Paid $1,440 cash for one year's premium on a property and liability insurance policy.

     5   Billed Bravo Productions $2,200 for installing a new computer.

     7   Paid for the computer supplies purchased from AAA Supply Co.

     9   Hired Fran Sims as a part-time assistant for $125 per day, as needed. These wages will be paid once each month.

   11   Billed Bravo Productions another $800 for services.

   14   Received $2,200 from Bravo Productions on their account.

   16   Paid $470 to repair computer equipment damaged when moving into the new office.

   18   Paid $1,240 for an advertisement in the local newspaper.

   21   Received $800 from Bravo Productions on their account.

   24   Paid Fran Sims for seven days' work.

   27   Billed Charles Company $2,150 for services.

   31   Paid $2,000 to Tracy Green for personal use.

Nov.   1   Reimbursed Tracy Green's business automobile mileage for 700 miles at $0.25 per mile.

     4   Received $3,100 cash from Delta Fixtures, Inc., for computer services.

     6   Purchased $640 of computer supplies from AAA Supply Co.

     7   Billed Fox Run Estates $2,900 for services.

   10   Notified by Alpha Printing Co. that Emerald's bid of $2,500 for an upcoming project was accepted.

   17   Paid $150 for Tracy Green's home utilities bill.

   19   Received $1,250 from Charles Company against the bill dated October 27.

Nov. 21   Donated $500 to the United Way in the company's name.

    24   Completed work for Alpha Printing Co. and sent them a bill for $2,500.

    26   Sent another bill to Charles Company for the past due amount of $900.

    27   Paid $2,000 to Tracy Green as a withdrawal.

    28   Reimbursed Tracy Green's business automobile mileage for 800 miles at $0.25 per mile.

    30   Paid Fran Sims for 14 days' work.

CRITICAL THINKING: ESSAYS, PROBLEMS, AND CASES

Consider the facts in Problem 2–2 and focus on transactions *h* and *o*. Explain how transaction *h* affects the balance sheet, income statement, and statement of changes in owner's equity differently from transaction *o*. Describe how the effects of transaction *o* would differ if the company's owner had written the check to pay the company's property taxes instead of the described purpose.

Analytical Essays

AE 2–1
(LO 3)

Consider the facts in Problem 2–3 and assume that the following mistakes were made in journalizing and posting the transactions. Explain how each mistake would affect the account balances and the column totals in the trial balance.

AE 2–2
(LO 3, 5)

a.   The March 1 investment by Ford was recorded correctly in the journal but the debit to Cash was incorrectly posted to the Cash account as $52,000.

b.   The March 5 transaction was incorrectly recorded in the journal as a collection of an account receivable.

c.   In recording the March 15 transaction in the journal, the account that should have been debited was credited and the account that should have been credited was debited.

d.   The March 30 transaction was recorded correctly in the journal, and the debit was correctly posted, but the credit was not posted at all.

e.   The $175 payment on March 31 was recorded incorrectly in both accounts in the journal as a $715 payment.

Ella Fant operates an interior decorating business. For the first few months of the company's life (through May), the accounting records were maintained by an outside bookkeeping service. According to those records, Fant's capital balance was $40,000 as of May 31. To save on expenses, Fant decided to keep the records herself. She managed to record June's transactions properly, but was a bit rusty when the time came to prepare the financial statements. Her first versions of the balance sheet and income statement follow; Fant is bothered that the company operated at a loss during the month, even though she had been very busy. Use the account balances included in the original financial statements to prepare revised statements (except for the capital account), including a statement of changes in owner's equity for the month.

Financial Reporting Problems

FRP 2–1
(LO 2)

ELLA FANT INTERIORS
Income Statement
June 30

Revenue:		
Investments by owner		$ 725
Unearned professional fees		10,575
Total		$11,300
Operating expenses:		
Prepaid insurance	$ 750	
Rent expense	450	
Telephone expense	300	
Professional library	8,000	
Travel and entertainment expense	3,100	
Utilities expense	400	
Withdrawals by owner	325	
Total operating expenses		13,325
Net income (loss)		$(2,025)

ELLA FANT INTERIORS
Balance Sheet
For Month Ended June 30

Assets		Liabilities	
Cash	$13,000	Accounts payable	$ 2,725
Accounts receivable	2,900	Professional fees earned	8,400
Insurance expense	250	Total liabilities	$11,125
Prepaid rent	900		
Office supplies	250	**Owner's Equity**	
Buildings	30,000	Ella Fant, capital	64,975
Land	12,000		
Salaries expense	3,300		
Short-term notes payable	13,500	Total liabilities and	
Total assets	$76,100	owner's equity	$76,100

FRP 2–2
(LO 4, 5)

At the end of the summer, Pat Hand closed down a small business that operated in Paradise Park. The business rented out two-passenger bicycles and sold shirts, sunglasses, and hats. Hand started the summer with $9,000 in cash and an agreement to rent a small building in the park for up to five years. The $2,400 annual rent must be paid every year, even though the business is open from only June 1 through August 31. At the beginning of the summer, Hand paid cash for the first year's rent and nine bicycles at the price of $250 each.

Over the summer, Hand also purchased shirts, sunglasses, and hats on credit for the total cost of $6,000. By August 31, all but $125 of the payables were paid. Over the summer, cash had been paid for $650 of utility bills and $3,000 of wages to several part-time workers. The owner had also withdrawn $250 of cash from the business each week for 13 weeks.

The summer's revenues included $7,500 in bicycle rentals and $13,500 for shirts, sunglasses, and hats. All revenue was collected in cash, except for $80 owed by a local day care center for some shirts.

Upon closing on August 31, Hand returned the unsold inventory of sunglasses to the distributor for a full cash refund of their $50 original cost. The owner took home the unsold inventory of shirts and hats as gifts for friends and family. Their original cost was $135. Finally, each of the nine used bicycles was sold for $110 cash.

Use the information to prepare an income statement describing the summer's business activities for the three months ended August 31. Also prepare a statement of changes in owner's equity for the same three months and a balance sheet as of August 31. The company's name is Paradise Pedals. As a first step in gathering the data, develop a list of brief explanations of the transactions. Next, post the amounts directly to T-accounts without using a general journal. Then use the T-account balances to prepare the statements. (Record the shirts, hats, and sunglasses in an account called Cost of Goods Sold and then reduce the balance for the unsold merchandise. Also record the difference between the original cost and the selling price of the bicycles in an account called Depreciation Expense.)

Financial Statement Analysis Case

(LO 2)

Refer to the financial statements and related information for Apple Computer, Inc., in Appendix F. Find the answers to the following questions by analyzing the information in the report:

1. What four broad categories of expenses are reported on Apple's income statement?
2. What six current assets are reported on Apple's balance sheet?
3. What seven current liabilities are reported on Apple's balance sheet?
4. What dollar amounts of provisions for income taxes are reported by Apple on its income statements for the annual reporting periods ending in 1993 and 1992?
5. During the annual reporting period ending in 1993, how much cash did Apple spend on new short-term investments? How much cash did Apple receive upon selling short-term investments during the same year? Use information in the cash flow statement to explain the change between the beginning and ending balances of short-term investments for the 1993 year.
6. Using the sum of the company's current liabilities and deferred income taxes as the total liabilities, what is Apple's debt ratio at the end of the 1993 year? How does this compare to the ratio at the end of the 1992 year?

Review the As a Matter of Ethics case on page 64. Discuss the nature of the dilemma faced by Karen Muñoz and evaluate the alternative courses of action that she should consider. **Ethical Issues Essay**

CONCEPT TESTER

Test your understanding of the concepts introduced in this chapter by completing the following crossword puzzle:

Across Clues

3. Two words; exchanges between the entity and some other person or organization.
6. An entry that decreases assets and expenses but increases other financial statement items.
9. Two words; total liabilities divided by total assets.
10. Three words; a list of the accounts used by a company, with identifying numbers.

Down Clues

1. Two words; an unconditional written promise to pay a definite sum on demand or a given future date.
2. Two words; documents that are the source of information recorded with accounting entries.
4. The collection of all accounts used by a business.
5. An entry that increases assets and expenses or decreases other financial statement items.
7. A record in which the effects of transactions are first recorded.
8. The process of copying journal entry information to the ledger.

ANSWERS TO PROGRESS CHECKS

2–1   *d*

2–2   A company's accounting equation is affected by external transactions and other economic events sometimes called internal transactions.

2–3   Business papers are called source documents because they are the source of information that is recorded with accounting entries.

2–4   *b*

2–5   Accounts are the basic building blocks of accounting systems used to develop a company's financial statements. Accounts are also symbols of items presented in the statements. They are special records used to store information about the effects of transactions on assets, liabilities, owner's equity, revenues, and expenses. A ledger is a collection of all accounts used by a business.

2–6   The quantity and types of accounts used by a business depend on the information the business needs to present in its financial statements.

2–7   No—debit and credit both mean increase and decrease; the particular meaning in a circumstance depends on the type of account. For example, a debit increases the balance of an expense account but decreases the balance in a revenue account.

2–8   *c*

2–9   Owner's equity is increased by revenues and new investments in the business by the owner. Owner's equity is decreased by expenses and withdrawals paid to the owner.

2–10 The name "double-entry" is used because all transactions are recorded in at least two accounts. There must be at least one debit in one account and at least one credit in another.

2–11 *c*

2–12 A compound entry affects at least three accounts.

2–13 Posting reference numbers are entered in the journal when posting to allow the bookkeeper or auditor to trace debits and credits in the journal to the specific accounts to which they were posted. This practice also creates a place marker in case the posting process is interrupted.

2–14 *e*

2–15 Dollar signs are used to identify the kind of currency being used in the reports. At the minimum, they are placed beside the first and last numbers in each column. Some companies prefer to also place dollar signs beside any amounts that appear after a ruled line that indicates that an addition or subtraction has taken place.

2–16 The effect of the error is to understate the trial balance's debit column total by $8,000. The credit column total would not be affected.

2–17 *a*

Adjusting the Accounts and Preparing the Statements

Jay Cochren has been a loyal owner of a Harley-Davidson motorcycle for years and has often thought an investment in the company might be a good thing. To learn more, he obtained a copy of the company's 1993 annual report. From the report, Cochren learned that the company shipped 81,696 motorcycle units to dealers during 1993. This represented a 6.8% increase over unit shipments in 1992.

The company also has a transportation vehicles segment that produces motor homes, other recreational vehicles, and commercial vehicles such as delivery vans and truck bodies. The transportation vehicles segment accounts for about 23% of Harley-Davidson's total dollar sales.

Cochren is not very familiar with financial statements but observed that one of the statements lists a variety of assets under Current Assets. It also lists several items under Current Liabilities. Cochren wonders why these items are separated from the other items on the statement and why they are described as being *current*. Perhaps they are related to each other in some important way.

HARLEY-DAVIDSON, INC.
(In thousands)

	Year Ended December 31	
	1993	**1992**
Total current assets	$333,758	$265,465
Total current liabilities	190,762	169,233

LEARNING OBJECTIVES

After studying Chapter 3, you should be able to:

1. **Explain why financial statements are prepared at the end of regular accounting periods, why the accounts must be adjusted at the end of each period, and why the accrual basis of accounting produces more useful income statements and balance sheets than the cash basis.**

2. **Prepare adjusting entries for prepaid expenses, depreciation, unearned revenues, accrued expenses, and accrued revenues.**

3. **Prepare a schedule that includes the unadjusted trial balance, the adjustments, and the adjusted trial balance; use the adjusted trial balance to prepare financial statements; and prepare entries to record cash receipts and cash disbursements related to accrued assets and liabilities.**

4. **Define each asset and liability category for the balance sheet, prepare a classified balance sheet, and calculate the current ratio.**

5. **Define or explain the words and phrases listed in the chapter glossary.**

After studying Appendix A at the end of Chapter 3, you should be able to:

6. **Explain why some companies record prepaid and unearned items in income statement accounts and prepare adjusting entries when this procedure is used.**

In business since 1903, Harley-Davidson, Inc., realizes the importance of communicating its position through its annual reports. For example, the company used its 1993 annual report to point out the 6.8% increase in motorcycle units shipped to dealers, its record sales and earnings, and the success of its operations overseas. To accurately present this financial picture, a company must have an effective accounting system in place.

You learned in Chapter 2 that companies use accounting systems to collect information about transactions and other economic events. That chapter showed you how journals and ledgers are used to capture information about external transactions. This chapter explains how the accounting system gathers information about economic events that are not transactions with outside parties. The process involves adjusting the account balances at the end of the reporting period to reflect the economic events that are sometimes called internal transactions. As a result, the adjusted accounts contain the amounts to be reported on the financial statements according to generally accepted accounting principles. The chapter ends with a description of the current ratio, which is used by decision makers to assess the company's ability to pay its liabilities in the near future.

ACCOUNTING PERIODS AND FISCAL YEARS

LO 1

Explain why financial statements are prepared at the end of regular accounting periods, why the accounts must be adjusted at the end of each period, and why the accrual basis of accounting produces more useful income statements and balance sheets than the cash basis.

To be useful, information must reach decision makers frequently and promptly. To provide this timely information, accounting systems are designed to produce periodic reports at regular intervals. As a result, the accounting process is based on the **time period principle.** According to this principle, an organization's activities are identified with specific time periods, such as a month, a three-month quarter, or a year. Then, financial statements are prepared for each reporting period. The time periods covered by the reports are called **accounting periods.** Most organizations use one year as their primary accounting period. As a result, they prepare annual financial statements. However, nearly all organizations also prepare **interim financial reports** that cover one or three months of activity.

The annual reporting period is not always the same as the calendar year ending December 31. In fact, an organization can adopt a **fiscal year** consisting of any 12 consecutive months.[1] An acceptable variation of this is to adopt an annual reporting period of 52 weeks. For example, look at the consolidated balance sheets of **Apple Computer, Inc.,** in Appendix F. The company's 1993 year ended on September 24, while the 1992 year ended on September 25.

Companies that do not experience much seasonal variation in sales volume within the year often choose the calendar year as their fiscal year. On the other hand, companies that experience major seasonal variations in sales often choose a fiscal year that corresponds to their **natural business year.** The natural business year ends when sales activities are at their lowest point during the year. For example, the natural business year for retail stores ends around January 31, after the Christmas and January selling seasons. As a result, they often start their annual accounting periods on February 1. The financial statements of the **Federal Express Corporation** in Appendix G reflect a fiscal year that ends on May 31.

WHY ARE THE ACCOUNTS ADJUSTED AT THE END OF AN ACCOUNTING PERIOD?

During an accounting period, the normal process is to record the economic events that occur in the form of external transactions (with outside parties). After all external transactions are recorded, several accounts in the ledger need to be updated before their balances appear in the financial statements. This need arises from the fact that some economic events remain unrecorded because they did not occur as external transactions.

For example, the costs of some assets expire as time passes. Notice that the third item in the trial balance of Clear Copy Co. in Illustration 3–1 is Prepaid insurance and that it has a balance of $2,400. This amount is the original cost of the premium for two years of insurance protection beginning on December 1, 19X1. By December 31, 19X1, one month's coverage has been used up, and $2,400 is no longer the cost of the remaining prepaid insurance. Because the coverage costs an average of $100 per month ($2,400/24 months), the Prepaid Insurance account balance should be reduced by that amount. In addition, the income statement should report $100 as insurance expense.

Similarly, the $3,720 balance in the Store Supplies account includes the cost of some supplies that were consumed during December. The cost of these supplies should be reported as an expense of the month. Because of these unrecorded events, the balances of the Prepaid Insurance and Store Supplies accounts should be *adjusted* before they are presented on the December 31 balance sheet.

Another adjustment is necessary because one month of the copy equipment's useful life has expired. In addition, the balances of the Unearned Copy Services Revenue, Copy Services Revenue, and Salaries Expense accounts should be adjusted before they appear on the December income statement.

The next section of the chapter explains how the adjusting process is accomplished. As you study the material, remember that our goal is to provide useful information in the financial statements.

---

[1]Some companies actually choose a 52-week fiscal year, with the result that their annual reports end on a different date each year. For example, this practice is reflected in the annual report for Apple Computer, Inc., in Appendix F and Ben & Jerry's Homemade, Inc., in Appendix G.

Illustration 3–1

CLEAR COPY CO.
Trial Balance
December 31, 19X1

	Debit	Credit
Cash	$ 7,950	
Accounts receivable	0	
Prepaid insurance	2,400	
Store supplies	3,720	
Copy equipment	26,000	
Accounts payable		$ 6,200
Unearned copy services revenue		3,000
Terry Dow, capital		30,000
Terry Dow, withdrawals	400	
Copy services revenue		3,900
Rent expense	1,000	
Salaries expense	1,400	
Utilities expense	230	
Total	$43,100	$43,100

THE ADJUSTING PROCESS

PRINCIPLE APPLICATION
Revenue Recognition
Principle, p. 35
One way IBM Corporation earns revenue is by providing maintenance and services to its customers. It reports those revenues as the services are performed. Revenues on the products it sells are reported when the products are shipped.

The adjusting process is consistent with two accounting principles, the *revenue recognition principle* and the *matching principle.* Chapter 1 explained that the *revenue recognition principle* requires revenue to be reported on the income statement only when it is earned, not before and not after. For most firms, revenue is earned when a service or a product is delivered to the customer. For example, if Clear Copy Co. provides copy services to a customer during December, the revenue is earned during December. As a result, it should be reported on the December income statement, even if the customer paid for the services in November or will pay for them in January. One major goal for the adjusting process is to ensure that revenue is reported, or recognized, in the time period when it is earned.

The goal of the **matching principle** is to report expenses on the income statement in the same accounting period as the revenues that were earned as a result of the expenses. For example, assume that a business earns revenues during December while it operates out of rented store space. According to the *revenue recognition principle,* the business should report its revenues on the December income statement. In earning those revenues, the business incurs rent expense. The *matching principle* tells us that the rent should be reported on the income statement for December, even if the rent was paid in November or will be paid in January. As a result, the rent expense for December is matched with December's revenues. This matching of expenses with revenues is a major goal of the adjusting process.

Matching expenses with revenues often requires a company to predict future events. To use financial statements wisely, you need to understand that they are based on predictions and therefore include measurements that are not precise. For example, **The Walt Disney Company's** 1993 annual report explains that the company allocates film production costs among years based on a ratio of actual revenues to date from the film divided by its predicted total gross revenues.

Illustration 3-2 Allocating the $2,400 Cost of Insurance Protection for 24 Months Beginning December 1, 19X1

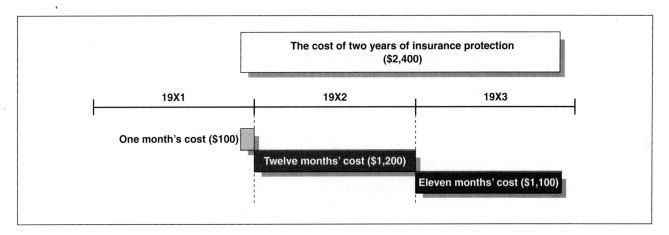

When the adjusting process assigns revenues to the periods in which they are earned and matches expenses with the revenues, the company is using **accrual basis accounting.** The objective of the accrual basis is to report the economic effects of revenues and expenses when they are earned or incurred, not when cash is received or paid.

The alternative to accrual accounting is **cash basis accounting.** Under the cash basis, revenues are recognized when cash is received and expenses are reported when cash is paid. For example, if revenue is earned in December but cash is not received from the customer until January, the cash basis reports the revenue in January. Because revenues are reported when cash is received and expenses are deducted when cash is paid, cash basis net income for a period is the difference between revenues received in cash (called *receipts*) and expenses paid with cash (called *expenditures* or *disbursements*).

Although some small companies use a cash basis for preparing their internal statements and reports, cash-basis income statements and balance sheets are not consistent with generally accepted accounting principles. "Accrual accounting generally provides a better indication of enterprise performance than information about current cash receipts and payments."[2] Accrual accounting increases the *comparability* of income statements and balance sheets from one period with those of another period.

For example, Clear Copy paid $2,400 for two years of insurance coverage beginning on December 1. Under accrual accounting, $100 of insurance expense is reported on the December 19X1 income statement. During 19X2, $1,200 of expense will be reported (the average monthly cost is $100). During 19X3, $1,100 expense will be reported for the first 11 months of the year. This allocation of the insurance cost among the three fiscal years is represented graphically in Illustration 3-2.

In contrast, a cash basis income statement for December 19X1 would report insurance expense of $2,400. The income statements for 19X2 and 19X3 would not report any insurance expense from this policy. To provide useful information about the company's activities and assets, the accrual basis shows that each of the 24 months had $100 of insurance expense. The balance sheet also reports the remaining unexpired premium as the cost of the prepaid insurance asset. However, the cash basis would never report an asset. In summary, the cash basis information would be less

ACCRUAL BASIS COMPARED WITH CASH BASIS ACCOUNTING

---

[2]*Statement of Financial Accounting Concepts No. 1,* "Objectives of Financial Reporting by Business Enterprises" (Norwalk, CT, 1978), par. 44.

useful for decisions because the reported income for 19X1, 19X2, and 19X3 would not reflect comparable measures of the cost of having insurance in those years.

The accrual basis is generally accepted for external reporting because it produces more useful information. The cash basis is not acceptable for a balance sheet or income statement because it provides incomplete information about assets, liabilities, revenues, and expenses. However, information about cash flows is also useful. That's why GAAP requires companies to report a statement of cash flows.

Progress Check
(Answers to Progress Checks are provided at the end of the chapter.)

3-1   A company's annual reporting period: *(a)* Is called the fiscal year; *(b)* Always ends at the close of the natural business year; *(c)* Always ends at the close of the calendar business year; *(d)* Cannot be divided into shorter interim periods.

3-2   Why do companies prepare interim financial statements?

3-3   Which accounting principles lead most directly to the adjustment process?

3-4   Is the cash basis of accounting consistent with the matching principle?

3-5   On April 1, 19X1, Collins Company paid a $4,800 premium for two years of insurance coverage. Under the cash basis, how much insurance expense will be reported in 19X2?

ADJUSTING SPECIFIC ACCOUNTS

LO 2

Prepare adjusting entries for prepaid expenses, depreciation, unearned revenues, accrued expenses, and accrued revenues.

The process of adjusting the accounts is similar to the process used to analyze and record transactions. Each account balance and the economic events that affect it are analyzed to determine whether an adjustment is needed. If an adjustment is needed, an **adjusting entry** is recorded to bring the asset or liability account balance up to date. The adjustment also updates the related expense or revenue account. Like other journal entries, adjusting entries are posted to the accounts. The following paragraphs explain why adjusting entries are needed to provide useful information.

Adjusting entries for prepaid expenses, depreciation, and unearned revenues involve previously recorded assets and liabilities. These entries are made to record the effects of economic events (including the passing of time) that have changed these assets and liabilities. On the other hand, adjusting entries for accrued expenses and accrued revenues involve liabilities and assets that have not yet been recorded. Adjusting entries record the effects of economic events that created these liabilities and assets as well as the related expenses and revenues.

Prepaid Expenses

A prepaid expense is an economic benefit paid for in advance of its use. When it is paid for, the company acquires an asset that will expire or be used up. As the asset is used, its cost becomes an expense.

Prepaid Insurance. For example, recall that Clear Copy paid $2,400 for two years of insurance protection that went into effect on December 1, 19X1. (The allocation of this cost to 19X1, 19X2, and 19X3 is described in Illustration 3–2.) As each day of December went by, some of the benefit of the insurance protection expired, and a portion of the asset's cost became an expense. By December 31, one month's insurance coverage had expired. This expense is measured as $100, which is 1/24 of $2,400. The following adjusting entry records the expense with a debit, and reduces the cost of the asset with a credit to the asset account:

Adjustment a

Dec.	31	Insurance Expense	100.00	
		Prepaid Insurance		100.00
		To record the expense created by expired insurance.		

Posting the adjusting entry has the following effect on the accounts:

Prepaid Insurance				**Insurance Expense**	
Dec. 26	2,400	Dec. 31	100	Dec. 31	100
	− 100				
Balance	2,300				

After the entry is posted, the $100 balance in Insurance Expense and the $2,300 balance in Prepaid Insurance are ready to be presented on the financial statements.

The allocation process in Illustration 3–2 shows that another adjusting entry in 19X2 transfers $1,200 from Prepaid Insurance to Insurance Expense. A third adjusting entry in 19X3 transfers the remaining $1,100 to the expense account.

Store Supplies. Store supplies are another prepaid expense that is adjusted. For example, Clear Copy purchased $3,720 of store supplies in December and used some of them up during the month. Consuming these supplies created an expense equal to their cost. However, the daily consumption of the supplies was not recorded in the accounts because the information was not needed. Due to the fact that the account balances are not presented in financial statements until the end of the month, bookkeeping effort can be reduced by making only one adjusting entry to record the total cost of all supplies consumed in the month.

Because an income statement is to be prepared for December, the cost of the store supplies used during the month needs to be recognized as an expense. To learn the amount used, Terry Dow counts (or, takes an inventory of) the remaining unused supplies. Then, the cost of the remaining supplies is deducted from the cost of the purchased supplies. For example, suppose that Dow finds that $2,670 of supplies remain out of the $3,720 purchased in December. The $1,050 difference between these two amounts is the cost of the consumed supplies. This amount is the month's store supplies expense. This adjusting entry records the expense with a debit and reduces the asset account balance with an equal credit:

Adjustment b

Dec.	31	Store Supplies Expense	1,050.00	
		Store Supplies		1,050.00
		To record the expense created by using store supplies.		

Posting the adjusting entry has the following effect on the accounts:

Store Supplies				**Store Supplies Expense**	
Dec. 2	2,500	Dec. 31	1,050	Dec. 31	1,050
6	1,100				
26	120				
Total	3,720	Total	1,050		
	− 1,050				
Balance	2,670				

As a result, the balance of the store supplies account now equals the $2,670 cost revealed by the manager's inventory.

Other Prepaid Expenses. Unlike the two previous examples, some prepaid expenses are both acquired and fully used up within a single accounting period. For example, a company usually pays monthly rent on the first day of each month. Every month, the payment creates a prepaid expense that fully expires by the end of the month. In these cases, the bookkeeper can ignore the fact that the payment creates an asset and record the payment with a debit to the expense account instead of the asset account. (These practices are described more completely in Appendix A at the end of this chapter.)

Depreciation

In accounting, the term **plant and equipment** describes tangible long-lived assets that are used to produce or sell goods and services. Examples of plant and equipment are land, buildings, machines, vehicles, and professional libraries. Except for land, plant and equipment assets eventually wear out or otherwise lose their usefulness and value. Therefore, income statements should report the cost of using these assets as expenses during their useful lives. The expense created by allocating the original cost of assets is called **depreciation.** Depreciation expense is recorded with an adjusting entry similar to the entries to record the using up of prepaid expenses. However, the entry is slightly more complicated because a special account is used to record the reduced asset balance.

For example, Clear Copy uses copy equipment to earn revenue. This equipment's cost should be depreciated to provide a complete income statement. Early in December, Clear Copy made two purchases of equipment for $20,000 and $6,000. Using information received from the manufacturer and other sources, Terry Dow predicts that the equipment will have a four-year useful life. Dow also predicts that the company will be able to sell the equipment for $8,000 at the end of the four years. Therefore, the net cost expected to expire over the useful life is $18,000 ($26,000 − $8,000). When this net cost is divided by the 48 months in the asset's predicted life, the result is an average monthly cost of $375 ($18,000/48). This average cost is recorded as depreciation expense for each month with this adjusting entry:

		Adjustment c		
Dec.	31	Depreciation Expense	375.00	
		Accumulated Depreciation, Copy Equipment		375.00
		To record the expense created by using the copying equipment.		

Posting the adjusting entry has the following effect on the accounts:

Copy Equipment			Depreciation Expense, Copy Equipment		
Dec. 3	20,000		**Dec. 31**	**375**	
6	6,000				
Total	26,000				

Accumulated Depreciation, Copy Equipment		
	Dec. 31	375

After the entry is posted, the Copy Equipment account and its related Accumulated Depreciation, Copy Equipment account together show the December 31 balance sheet amounts for this asset. The Depreciation Expense, Copy Equipment account shows the amount of expense that will appear on the December income statement.

In most cases, a decrease in an asset account is recorded by entering a credit directly in the account. However, note in the illustrated accounts that this procedure is not followed in recording depreciation. Instead, depreciation is recorded in a **contra account.** A contra account's balance is subtracted from a related account's balance to provide more information than simply the net amount. In this example, the contra account is Accumulated Depreciation, Copy Equipment.

Why are contra accounts used to record depreciation? Contra accounts allow balance sheet readers to observe both the original cost of the assets and the estimated amount of depreciation that has been charged to expense in the past. By knowing both the original cost and the accumulated depreciation, decision makers can more completely assess the company's productive capacity and the potential need to replace the assets. For example, Clear Copy's balance sheet shows both the $26,000 original cost of the equipment and the $375 balance in the accumulated depreciation contra account. This information lets statement users see that the equipment is almost new. In contrast, if Clear Copy simply reported the net remaining cost of $25,625, the users would not know whether the equipment is new or so old that it needs immediate replacement.

Note the words *accumulated depreciation* in the title of the contra account. This reflects the fact that this account reports the total amount of depreciation expense recognized in all prior periods since the assets were put into service. For example, the Copy Equipment and the Accumulated Depreciation accounts would look like this on February 28, 19X2, after three monthly adjusting entries:

	Copy Equipment			Accumulated Depreciation, Copy Equipment	
Dec. 3	20,000			Dec. 31	375
6	6,000			Jan. 31	375
Total	26,000			Feb. 28	375
				Total	1,125

These account balances would be presented on the February 28 balance sheet as follows:

Copy equipment	$26,000
Less accumulated depreciation	1,125
Net	$24,875

Later chapters describe how other contra accounts are used in other situations.

Unearned Revenues

An unearned revenue is a liability created when a customer's payment is received in advance of delivering the goods or services. For example, a recent balance sheet of the New York Times Company reported a $130 million liability for subscriptions. This amount was more than 30% of the company's total current liabilities.

Clear Copy Co. also has unearned revenue. On December 26, Terry Dow agreed to provide copying services for a customer for the fixed fee of $1,500 per month. On that day, the customer paid the first two months' fees in advance to cover the period from December 27 to February 26. This entry records the cash receipt:

Dec.	26	Cash	3,000.00	
		Unearned Copy Services Revenue		3,000.00
		Received advanced payment for copying services to be provided over two months.		

This advance payment increased cash and created an obligation to do copying work over the next two months. By December 31, the business provided five days' service and earned one-sixth of the $1,500 revenue for the first month. This amount is $250 ($1,500/6). The company also discharged one-twelfth of the total $3,000 liability because five days is one-twelfth of two months. According to the *revenue recognition principle,* the $250 of revenue should appear on the December income statement. Notice that the event that caused the earning of revenue was simply the passage of time. There was no external transaction. The following adjusting entry updates the accounts by reducing the liability and recognizing the earned revenue:

		Adjustment d		
Dec.	31	Unearned Copy Services Revenue	250.00	
		Copy Services Revenue ($1,500/6)		250.00
		Earned revenue that was received in advance.		

The accounts look like this after the entry is posted:

Unearned Copy Services Revenue				Copy Services Revenue	
Dec. 31	**250**	Dec. 26	3,000	Dec. 10	2,200
				12	1,700
				31	250

In effect, the adjusting entry transfers $250 of earned revenue from the liability account to the revenue account.

Accrued Expenses

Most expenses are recorded when they are paid with cash. In making the journal entry to record the transaction, the credit to the Cash account is accompanied by a debit to the expense account. However, because some expenses incurred during the period have not been paid for, they may remain unrecorded at the end of an accounting period. These incurred but unpaid expenses are called **accrued expenses.** One typical example of an accrued expense is the unpaid wages earned by employees for work they have already completed.

Accrued Salaries. For example, Clear Copy's only employee earns $70 per day or $350 for a five-day workweek that begins on Monday and ends on Friday. The employee's salary is paid every two weeks on Friday. On the 12th and the 26th of December, these wages were paid, recorded in the journal, and posted to the ledger. The Salaries Expense and Cash accounts show these entries:

December 19X1						
S	M	T	W	T	F	S
	1	2	3	4	5	6
7	8	9	10	11	12	13
14	15	16	17	18	19	20
21	22	23	24	25	26	27
28	29	30	31			

Cash				Salaries Expense	
Dec. 12	700		Dec. 12	700	
26	700		26	700	

The calendar for December 19X1 in the margin shows us that three working days (December 29, 30, and 31) come after the December 26 payday. Thus, the employee earned three days' salary at the close of business on Wednesday, December 31. Because this salary had not been paid, the expense was not recorded. But, the financial statements would be incomplete if they failed to report this additional expense and the liability to the employee for the unpaid salary. Therefore, this adjusting entry should be recorded on December 31 to produce a complete record of the company's expenses and liabilities:

		Adjustment e		
Dec.	31	Salaries Expense	210.00	
		Salaries Payable		210.00
		To record three days' accrued salary.		

After this entry is posted, the Salaries Expense and liability accounts appear as follows:

Salaries Expense			**Salaries Payable**	
Dec. 12	700		Dec. 31	210
26	700			
31	210			
Total	1,610			

As a result of this entry, $1,610 of salaries expense is reported on the income statement. In addition, the balance sheet reports a $210 liability to the employee.

Accrued Interest Expense. Another typical accrued expense is interest incurred on accounts and notes payable. Interest expense is incurred simply with the passage of time. Therefore, unless interest is paid on the last day of the accounting period, some additional amount will have accrued since the previous payment. A company's financial statements will be incomplete unless this expense and additional liability are recorded. The adjusting entry for interest is similar to the one used to accrue the unpaid salary.

Accrued Revenues

Many revenues are recorded when cash is received from the customer. Other revenues are recorded when goods and services are sold on credit. However, some earned revenues may remain unrecorded at the end of the accounting period. Although these **accrued revenues** are earned, they are unrecorded because the customer has not yet paid for them or the seller has not yet billed the customer. For example, suppose that Clear Copy agreed to provide copying services for a bank at a fixed fee of $2,700 per month. The terms of the agreement call for Clear Copy to provide services from the 12th of December, 19X1, through the 11th of the following month. The bank will pay $2,700 cash to Clear Copy on January 11, 19X2, when the service period is over.

As of December 31, 19X1, 20 days of services have been provided to the bank. However, because Clear Copy has not yet been paid, it has not recorded the earning of the revenue. Because 20 days equal two-thirds of a month, Clear Copy has earned two-thirds of one month's fee, or $1,800 ($2,700 × 2/3). According to the *revenue recognition principle,* this revenue should be reported on the December income statement because it was earned in that month. In addition, the balance sheet should report that the bank owes the company $1,800. Clear Copy makes this adjusting entry to record the effects of the agreement:

		Adjustment f		
Dec.	31	Accounts Receivable	1,800.00	
		Copy Services Revenue		1,800.00
		To record 20 days' accrued revenue.		

The debit to the receivable reflects the fact that the bank owes Clear Copy for the provided services. After this entry is posted, the affected accounts look like this:

Accounts Receivable				Copy Services Revenue		
Dec. 12	1,700	Dec. 22	1,700		Dec. 10	2,200
31	1,800				12	1,700
Total	3,500	Total	1,700		31	250
	-1,700				31	1,800
Balance	1,800				Balance	5,950

Accounts receivable are reported on the balance sheet at $1,800, and $5,950 of revenues are reported on the income statement.

Accrued Interest Income. We mentioned earlier that interest is an accrued expense recorded with an adjusting entry. Interest is also an accrued revenue when a company is entitled to receive it from a debtor. If a company has notes or accounts receivable that produce interest income, the bookkeeper records an adjusting entry to recognize any accrued but uncollected interest revenue. The entry also records the interest receivable from the debtor as an asset.

Take time to read the As a Matter of Ethics case. It tells about pressure being applied to an accountant to omit some adjusting entries that are needed to present complete financial statements. Consider the situation and determine what you would do if you were in this accountant's place.

Progress Check

3–6   At the end of its 19X1 fiscal year, Corona Company omitted an adjustment to record $200 of accrued service revenues. The effect of the error is to: (a) Overstate 19X1 net income by $200;   (b) Overstate 19X1 revenues by $200;   (c) Understate total assets by $200;   (d) Overstate total assets by $200.

3–7   What is a contra account?

3–8   What is an accrued expense? Give an example.

3–9   How does an unearned revenue arise? Give an example of an unearned revenue.

Illustration 3-3 The Unadjusted Trial Balance, Adjustments, and Adjusted Trial Balance for Clear Copy Co. as of December 31, 19X1

	Unadjusted Trial Balance		Adjustments		Adjusted Trial Balance	
Cash	7,950				7,950	
Accounts receivable			(f) 1,800		1,800	
Store supplies	3,720			(b)1,050	2,670	
Prepaid insurance	2,400			(a) 100	2,300	
Copy equipment	26,000				26,000	
Accumulated depreciation, copy equipment				(c) 375		375
Accounts payable		6,200				6,200
Salaries payable				(e) 210		210
Unearned copy services revenue		3,000	(d) 250			2,750
Terry Dow, capital		30,000				30,000
Terry Dow, withdrawals	400				400	
Copy services revenue		3,900		(d) 250 (f) 1,800		5,950
Depreciation expense, copy equipment			(c) 375		375	
Salaries expense	1,400		(e) 210		1,610	
Insurance expense			(a) 100		100	
Rent expense	1,000				1,000	
Store supplies expense			(b)1,050		1,050	
Utilities expense	230				230	
Totals	43,100	43,100	3,785	3,785	45,485	45,485

An **unadjusted trial balance** is prepared before adjustments have been recorded. As you might expect, an **adjusted trial balance** uses the account balances after the adjusting entries have been posted to the ledger. In Illustration 3–3, parallel columns show the unadjusted trial balance, the adjustments, and the adjusted trial balance for Clear Copy as of December 31, 19X1. Notice that several new accounts have been added because of the adjusting entries. (The order of the accounts also has been changed to match the order of the account numbers listed inside the book's front and back covers.) Also notice that the letters in the adjustments columns identify the debits and credits that were recorded with adjusting entries presented earlier in the chapter.

Chapter 2 explained that the trial balance summarizes the information in the ledger by showing the account balances. This summary is easier to work with than the entire ledger when preparing financial statements. The accountant uses the adjusted trial balance for this purpose because it includes the balances that should appear in the statements.

Illustrations 3–4 and 3–5 show how the account balances are transferred from the adjusted trial balance to the statements. For completeness, the trial balance includes the identification numbers for the accounts.

Because the amount of net income is used on the statement of changes in owner's equity, the first phase of the preparation process produces the company's income statement. The arrows in the lower section of Illustration 3–4 show how the balances of the revenue and expense accounts are transferred into the income statement. The revenue is listed on the statement first, and then the expenses. The total expenses are subtracted from the revenues to find the net income of $1,585.

THE ADJUSTED TRIAL BALANCE

LO 3

Prepare a schedule that includes the unadjusted trial balance, the adjustments, and the adjusted trial balance; use the adjusted trial balance to prepare financial statements; and prepare entries to record cash receipts and cash disbursements related to accrued assets and liabilities.

PREPARING FINANCIAL STATEMENTS FROM THE ADJUSTED TRIAL BALANCE

Illustration 3-4 Preparing the Income Statement and the Statement of Changes in Owner's Equity from the Adjusted Trial Balance

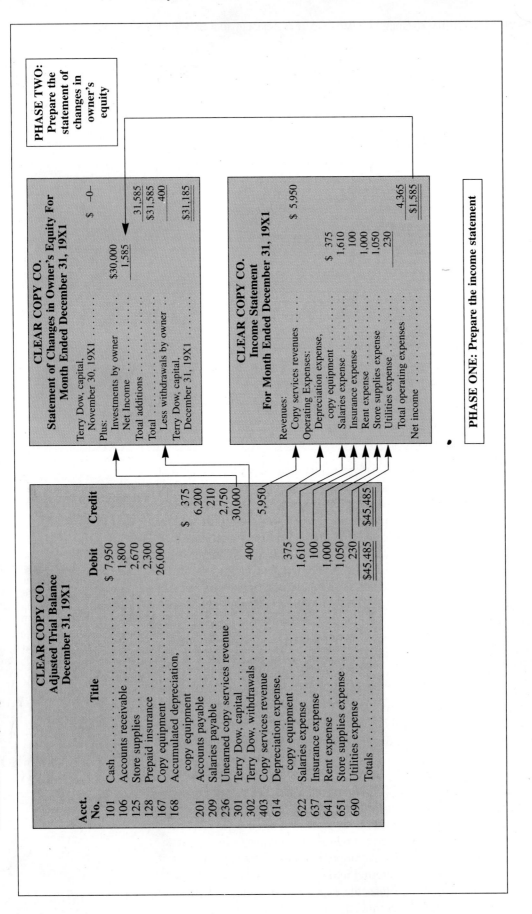

PHASE TWO: Prepare the statement of changes in owner's equity

CLEAR COPY CO.
Statement of Changes in Owner's Equity For
Month Ended December 31, 19X1

Terry Dow, capital, November 30, 19X1		$ –0–
Plus:		
Investments by owner	$30,000	
Net Income	1,585	
Total additions		31,585
Total		$31,585
Less withdrawals by owner		400
Terry Dow, capital, December 31, 19X1		$31,185

CLEAR COPY CO.
Income Statement
For Month Ended December 31, 19X1

Revenues:		
Copy services revenues		$ 5,950
Operating Expenses:		
Depreciation expense, copy equipment	$ 375	
Salaries expense	1,610	
Insurance expense	100	
Rent expense	1,000	
Store supplies expense	1,050	
Utilities expense	230	
Total operating expenses		4,365
Net income		$1,585

CLEAR COPY CO.
Adjusted Trial Balance
December 31, 19X1

Acct. No.	Title	Debit	Credit
101	Cash	$ 7,950	
106	Accounts receivable	1,800	
125	Store supplies	2,670	
128	Prepaid insurance	2,300	
167	Copy equipment	26,000	
168	Accumulated depreciation, copy equipment		$ 375
201	Accounts payable		6,200
209	Salaries payable		210
236	Unearned copy services revenue		2,750
301	Terry Dow, capital		30,000
302	Terry Dow, withdrawals	400	
403	Copy services revenue		5,950
614	Depreciation expense, copy equipment	375	
622	Salaries expense	1,610	
637	Insurance expense	100	
641	Rent expense	1,000	
651	Store supplies expense	1,050	
690	Utilities expense	230	
	Totals	$45,485	$45,485

PHASE ONE: Prepare the income statement

Illustration 3–5 Preparing the Balance Sheet from the Adjusted Trial Balance and the Statement of Changes in Owner's Equity

CLEAR COPY CO.
Adjusted Trial Balance
December 31, 19X1

Acct. No.	Title	Debit	Credit
101	Cash	$ 7,950	
106	Accounts receivable	1,800	
125	Store supplies	2,670	
128	Prepaid insurance	2,300	
167	Copy equipment	26,000	
168	Accumulated depreciation, copy equipment		$ 375
201	Accounts payable		6,200
209	Salaries payable		210
236	Unearned copy services revenue		2,750
301	Terry Dow, capital		30,000
302	Terry Dow, withdrawals	400	
403	Copy services revenue		5,950
614	Depreciation expense, copy equipment	375	
622	Salaries expense	1,610	
637	Insurance expense	100	
641	Rent expense	1,000	
651	Store supplies expense	1,050	
690	Utilities expense	230	
	Totals	$45,485	$45,485

PHASE THREE: Prepare the balance sheet

CLEAR COPY CO.
Balance Sheet
December 31, 19X1

Assets

Cash		$ 7,950
Accounts receivable		1,800
Store supplies		2,670
Prepaid insurance		2,300
Copy equipment	$26,000	
Less accumulated depreciation	(375)	25,625
Total assets		$40,345

Liabilities

Accounts payable	$ 6,200	
Salaries payable	210	
Unearned copy services revenue	2,750	
Total liabilities		$ 9,160

Owner's Equity

Terry Dow, capital, December 31, 19X1		31,185
Total liabilities and owner's equity		$40,345

Statement of Changes in Owner's Equity (from Illustration 3–4)

The second phase prepares the statement of changes in owner's equity. In developing this statement, the accountant combines the net income from the income statement with the balances of Terry Dow's capital and withdrawals accounts. The $30,000 capital account balance came from the initial investment in December. (In other situations, the accountant would have to analyze the capital account to identify the beginning balance and any new investments made during the period.) The bottom line of the statement shows the owner's equity on December 31.

The third phase of the preparation process is represented in Illustration 3–5. In this phase, the balances of the asset and liability accounts are transferred to the asset and liability sections of the balance sheet. Notice how the balance of the accumulated depreciation account is shown as a deduction from the cost of the copy equipment. Also, notice that the December 31 balance of Terry Dow's capital is taken from the statement of changes in owner's equity. The $30,000 balance of the capital account cannot be used on the balance sheet because it does not include the changes in equity created by the month's revenues, expenses, and withdrawals. (The next chapter explains how the capital account is updated through the closing process.) The completed balance sheet shows the total cost of the company's assets, its total liabilities, and the owner's equity.

REMOVING ACCRUED ASSETS AND LIABILITIES FROM THE ACCOUNTS

Revenues that are accrued at the end of an accounting period result in cash receipts from customers during the next period. In addition, expenses that were accrued at the end of an accounting period result in cash payments during the next period to settle the unpaid liabilities. This section explains how the accrued assets and accrued liabilities are removed from the accounts.

Accrued Expenses

Earlier, Clear Copy Co. recorded three days of accrued wages for its employee with this adjusting entry:

Dec.	31	Salaries Expense	210.00	
		Salaries Payable		210.00
		To record three days' accrued salary.		

When the next payday comes on Friday, January 9, the following entry removes the accrued liability and records additional salaries expense for January:

Jan.	9	Salaries Payable (3 days at $70)	210.00	
		Salaries Expense (7 days at $70)	490.00	
		Cash		700.00
		Paid two weeks' salary, including three days accrued		
		in December		

The first debit in the January 9 entry records the payment of the liability for the three days' salary accrued on December 31. The second debit records the salary for January's first seven working days (including the New Year's Day holiday) as an expense of the new accounting period. The credit records the total amount of cash paid to the employee.

Accrued Revenue

On December 31, the following adjusting entry was made to record 20 days' accrued revenue earned under Clear Copy's contract with the bank:

Dec.	31	Accounts Receivable	1,800.00	
		Copy Services Revenue		1,800.00
		To record 20 days' accrued revenue.		

When the first month's fee is received on January 11, the company makes the following entry to eliminate the receivable and recognize the revenue earned in January:

Jan.	11	Cash	2,700.00	
		Accounts Receivable		1,800.00
		Copy Services Revenue		900.00
		Received cash for accrued and earned copy services		
		revenue.		

The first credit in the entry records the collection of the receivable. The second credit records the earned revenue.

Progress Check

3-10 The following information has been taken from Jones Company's unadjusted and adjusted trial balances:

	Unadjusted		Adjusted	
	Debit	Credit	Debit	Credit
Prepaid insurance	$6,200		$5,900	
Salaries payable				$1,400

The adjusting entries must have included these items:
a. A $300 debit to Prepaid Insurance and a $1,400 credit to Salaries Payable.
b. A $300 credit to Prepaid Insurance and a $1,400 debit to Salaries Payable.
c. A $300 debit to Insurance Expense and a $1,400 debit to Salaries Expense.

3-11 What types of accounts are taken from the adjusted trial balance to prepare an income statement?

3-12 In preparing financial statements from an adjusted trial balance, which statement is prepared second?

3-13 On December 31, 19X1, Hall Company recorded $1,600 of accrued salaries. On January 5 (the next payday), salaries of $8,000 were paid. From this you know that: (a) The company uses cash basis accounting; (b) The January 5 entry includes a $6,400 credit to Cash; (c) The salaries expense assigned to 19X2 is $6,400.

Up to this point, we have presented only **unclassified balance sheets.** (For example, see Illustration 3–5.) However, the information on a balance sheet is more useful if assets and liabilities are classified into relevant groups. Readers of these **classified balance sheets** have more information to use in making their decisions. For example, they can use the data to assess the likelihood that funds will be available to meet the liabilities when they become due.

The balance sheet for National Electric Supply in Illustration 3–6 shows the most commonly used categories. Assets are classified as (1) current assets, (2) investments, (3) plant and equipment, and (4) intangible assets. Liabilities are either current or long-term. However, all companies do not use the same categories of assets and liabilities on their balance sheets. For example, **Whirlpool Corporation's** 1993 balance sheet has only three asset classes: current assets; other assets; and property, plant, and equipment.

CLASSIFYING BALANCE SHEET ITEMS

LO 4

Define each asset and liability category for the balance sheet, prepare a classified balance sheet, and calculate the current ratio.

Illustration 3–6   A Classified Balance Sheet

NATIONAL ELECTRICAL SUPPLY CO.
Balance Sheet
December 31, 19X1

Assets

Current assets:

Cash	$ 6,500	
Short-term investments	2,100	
Accounts receivable	4,400	
Notes receivable	1,500	
Merchandise inventory	27,500	
Prepaid expenses	2,400	
Total current assets		$ 44,400

Investments:

Chrysler Corporation common stock	$ 18,000	
Land held for future expansion	48,000	
Total investments		66,000

Plant and equipment:

Store equipment	$ 33,200		
Less accumulated depreciation	8,000	$ 25,200	
Buildings	$170,000		
Less accumulated depreciation	45,000	125,000	
Land		73,200	
Total plant and equipment			223,400

Intangible assets:

Trademark		10,000
Total assets		$343,800

Liabilities

Current liabilities:

Accounts payable	$ 15,300	
Wages payable	3,200	
Notes payable	3,000	
Current portion of long-term liabilities	7,500	
Total current liabilities		$ 29,000

Long-term liabilities:

Notes payable (net of current portion)	150,000	
Total liabilities		$179,000

Owner's Equity

B. Brown, capital		164,800
Total liabilities and owner's equity		$343,800

Current Assets

Current assets are cash and other assets that are reasonably expected to be sold, collected, or consumed within one year or within the normal **operating cycle of the business,** whichever is longer.[3] In addition to cash, current assets typically include short-term investments in marketable securities, accounts receivable, notes receivable, goods expected to be sold to customers (called *merchandise* or *inventory*), and prepaid expenses.

The Operating Cycle.   The length of a company's operating cycle depends on its activities. The diagrams in Illustration 3–7 represent the phases of operating cycles

---

[3]FASB, *Accounting Standards—Current Text* (Norwalk, CT, 1993), Sec. B05.105. First published as *Accounting Research Bulletin No. 43,* Chapter 3A, par. 4.

Illustration 3–7   The Phases of Operating Cycles for Companies that Sell Services and Merchandise

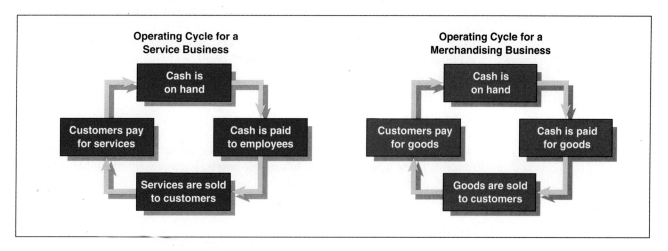

for service and merchandising companies. For a company that sells services, the operating cycle is the average time between paying the employees who perform the services and receiving the cash from customers. For a company that sells goods, the operating cycle is the average time between paying for the merchandise and receiving cash from customers.

Most operating cycles are shorter than one year. As a result, most companies use a one-year period in deciding which assets are current. However, a few companies have an operating cycle longer than one year. For example, a company may routinely allow customers to take several years to pay for their purchases. Some producers of beverages and other products allow their products to age for several years. In both cases, these companies use the longer operating cycle in deciding which assets are current.[4]

Other Details.   The balance sheet in Illustration 3–6 lists current assets first. This practice gives a prominent position to assets that are most easily converted into cash. Items within the current asset category are traditionally listed in the order of how quickly they will be converted to cash. Prepaid expenses are usually listed last because they will not be converted to cash.

A company's individual prepaid expenses are usually small compared to other assets on the balance sheet. As a result, they are often combined and shown as a single item. Thus, it is likely that the Prepaid expenses item in Illustration 3–6 includes such things as prepaid insurance, prepaid rent, office supplies, and store supplies.

Investments

The second balance sheet classification is long-term investments. In many cases, notes receivable and investments in stocks and bonds are not current assets because they will be held for more than one year (or one operating cycle). Investments also include land that is not being used in operations because it is held for future expansion. Notice that the short-term investments on the second line in Illustration 3–6 are current assets and are not presented in the Investments section. We explain the differences between short- and long-term investments in a later chapter.

Plant and Equipment

Earlier, we described plant and equipment as tangible long-lived assets that are used to produce or sell goods and services. Examples include equipment, vehicles, buildings, and land. Two key phrases in the definition are *long-lived* and *used to produce*

---

[4]In these unusual situations, the companies provide supplemental information about their current assets and liabilities to allow users to compare them with other companies.

or sell goods and services. Although it is tangible and has a long life, land held for future expansion is not a plant asset because it is not used to produce or sell goods and services.

The term *plant and equipment* is often used as a balance sheet caption. Other widely used titles for the same category are *Property, plant, and equipment,* or *Land, buildings, and equipment.* The order of the listing of the types of plant assets within the category varies among organizations.

Intangible Assets

Some assets that are used to produce or sell goods and services do not have a physical form. These assets are called **intangible assets.** Examples of intangible assets are goodwill, patents, trademarks, copyrights, and franchises. Their value comes from the privileges or rights granted to or held by the owner.

Current Liabilities

Obligations due to be paid or liquidated within one year (or the operating cycle) are classified as **current liabilities.** Current liabilities are usually satisfied by paying out current assets. Typical current liabilities are accounts payable, notes payable, wages payable, taxes payable, interest payable, and unearned revenues. Also, any portion of a long-term liability due to be paid within one year (or a longer operating cycle) is a current liability. Illustration 3–6 shows how the current portion of long-term liabilities is usually described on a balance sheet. Unearned revenues are classified as current liabilities because they will be settled by delivering goods or services within the year (or the operating cycle). Different companies present current liabilities in different orders. Generally, the first position goes to the liabilities that will be paid first.

Long-Term Liabilities

The second liability classification consists of **long-term liabilities.** These liabilities are not due to be paid within one year, or the operating cycle. Notes payable and bonds payable are usually long-term liabilities. If a company has both short- and long-term notes payable, it probably uses separate accounts for them in its ledger.

EQUITY ON THE BALANCE SHEET

The format of the balance sheet's equity section depends on whether the company is a single proprietorship, a partnership, or a corporation.

Single Proprietorships and Partnerships

If a business is a single proprietorship, the equity section consists of a single line showing the owner's equity as of the balance sheet date. For example, the balance sheet in Illustration 3–5 shows "Terry Dow, capital, December 31, 19X1" and the amount of $31,185. When total liabilities exceed total assets, the negative equity amount (often called a *deficit*) is subtracted from total liabilities.

If a business is organized as a partnership, separate equity accounts are used for each partner. Changes in each partner's equity are reported in a statement of changes in partners' equity that is similar to the statement of changes in owner's equity. The balance sheet shows the equity of each partner in a format like this:

Partners' Equity	
Shirley Tucker, capital	$17,300
Mark Jackson, capital	24,800
Total partners' equity	$42,100

Corporations

Corporations are established under state or federal laws. These laws may require the company's financial statements to distinguish between the equity created by investments from stockholders and the equity created by the corporation's net incomes less any reductions for **dividends.** A dividend is a distribution, generally a cash payment, made by a corporation to its stockholders. A cash dividend reduces the assets and the equity of a corporation in the same way that a withdrawal reduces the assets and equity of a proprietorship.

As described in Chapter 1, a corporation's total stockholders' equity is divided into *contributed capital* (also called *paid-in capital*) and *retained earnings.* Contributed capital is created by the stockholders' investments, and retained earnings are created by the corporation's profitable activities. The components of stockholders' equity are usually shown on a corporate balance sheet like this:

Stockholders' Equity	
Contributed capital: Common stock	$400,000
Retained earnings	124,400
Total stockholders' equity	$524,400

If a corporation issues only one kind of stock, it is called **common stock** or *capital stock*. (Other types of stock are described in Chapter 13.) The $400,000 amount assigned to common stock in the example is the amount invested in the corporation by its original stockholders when they bought the stock from the corporation. The retained earnings of $124,400 represents the stockholders' equity arising from prior years' net incomes in excess of any net losses and dividends paid to the stockholders.

ALTERNATIVE BALANCE SHEET FORMATS

Different companies choose different formats for their balance sheets. For example, the balance sheet in Illustration 1–8 (on p. 39) places the liabilities and stockholder's equity to the right of the assets. This format creates an **account form balance sheet.** If the items are arranged vertically, as shown in Illustration 3–6, the format creates a **report form balance sheet.** Both forms are widely used, and neither is considered more useful than the other.

USING CODE NUMBERS FOR ACCOUNTS

We described a possible three-digit account numbering system in Chapter 2. In these systems, the code number assigned to an account not only identifies the account but also provides information about the account's financial statement category.

In the following simple system, the first digit in an account's number identifies its primary balance sheet or income statement category. For example, account numbers beginning with a 1 are assigned to asset accounts and account numbers beginning with a 2 are assigned to liability accounts. Under this system, the following numbers could be assigned to the accounts of a company that buys and sells merchandise:

101–199	**Assets**
201–299	**Liabilities**
301–399	**Owner's Equity** (including withdrawals)
401–499	**Revenues**
501–599	**Cost of Goods Sold** (these accounts are described in Chapter 5)
601–699	**Operating Expenses**
701–799	**Gains**
801–899	**Losses**

In this system, the second digit of each account number identifies its subclassification within the primary category, as follows:

101–199   Assets
101–139   Current assets (second digit is 0, 1, 2, or 3)
141–149   Long-term investments (second digit is 4)
151–179   Plant assets (second digit is 5, 6, or 7)
181–189   Natural resources (second digit is 8)
191–199   Intangible assets (second digit is 9)
201–299   Liabilities
201–249   Current liabilities (second digit is 0, 1, 2, 3, or 4)
251–299   Long-term liabilities (second digit is 5, 6, 7, 8, or 9)

Finally, the third digit completes the unique code for each account. For example, specific current asset accounts might be assigned the following numbers:

101–199   Assets
101–139   Current assets
101   Cash
106   Accounts Receivable
110   Rent Receivable
128   Prepaid Insurance

This code is used for the accounts listed inside the front and back covers of the book.

A three-digit account numbering system may be adequate for many smaller businesses. However, a numbering system for a more complex business might use four, five, or even more digits.

USING THE INFORMATION— THE CURRENT RATIO

Most financial statement users find it helpful to evaluate a company's ability to pay its debts in the near future. This ability affects decisions by suppliers about allowing the company to buy on credit. It affects decisions by banks about lending money to the company and the terms of the loan, including the interest rate, due date, and any assets to be pledged as security against the loan. The ability to pay debts also affects a business owner's decisions about obtaining cash to pay existing debts when they come due.

The **current ratio** is widely used to describe the company's ability to pay its short-term obligations. It is calculated by dividing the current assets by the current liabilities:

$$\text{Current ratio} = \frac{\text{Current assets}}{\text{Current liabilities}}$$

Using the data for **Harley-Davidson, Inc.,** presented at the beginning of the chapter, the current ratios at the end of 1993 and 1992 are calculated as follows:

$$\text{December 31, 1993: Current ratio} = \frac{\$333,758}{\$190,762} = 1.75$$

$$\text{December 31, 1992: Current ratio} = \frac{\$265,465}{\$169,233} = 1.57$$

Note that the ratio improved from the end of 1992 to the end of 1993. Both values suggest that the company's short-term obligations could be satisfied with the short-term resources on hand. If the ratio were to be closer to one, the company might expect to face more difficulty in paying the liabilities. However, the company's sales may generate sufficient new cash to pay the liabilities. If the ratio were less than one, the company would be more likely to have difficulty because its current liabilities would be greater than its current assets.

Progress Check

3-14 Which of the following assets should be classified as current assets? Which should be classified as plant and equipment? *(a)* Land used in operating the business; *(b)* Office supplies; *(c)* Receivables from customers due in 10 months; *(d)* Insurance protection for the next nine months; *(e)* Trucks used to provide services to customers; *(f)* Trademarks used in advertising the company's services.

3-15 Identify two examples of assets classified as investments on the balance sheet.

3-16 Which category of liabilities is used in the calculation of the current ratio?

3-17 On the balance sheet of a corporation, the stockholders' equity is divided into two categories. What are they?

SUMMARY OF THE CHAPTER IN TERMS OF LEARNING OBJECTIVES

LO 1. Explain why financial statements are prepared at the end of regular accounting periods, why the accounts must be adjusted at the end of each period, and why the accrual basis of accounting produces more useful income statements and balance sheets than the cash basis. Companies prepare reports once each year. They also prepare interim financial statements because decision makers need information frequently and promptly. Adjusting entries are needed to capture information about unrecorded events that are not external transactions. The revenue recognition principle requires adjustments to ensure that revenue is reported when it is earned. The matching principle requires adjustments to ensure that expenses are reported in the same period as the revenue that was earned as a result of the expenses.

Accrual accounting is preferred to cash basis accounting because accrual accounting reports the economic effects of events when they occur, not when the cash flows happen. In addition to accrual basis financial statements, however, GAAP requires companies to report a statement of cash flows.

LO 2. Prepare adjusting entries for prepaid expenses, depreciation, unearned revenues, accrued expenses, and accrued revenues. Adjusting entries are used *(a)* to record expenses when prepaid expenses expire, *(b)* to record depreciation expense as the cost of using plant and equipment assets, *(c)* to record revenues when the company converts unearned revenues to earned revenues, *(d)* to accrue expenses and related liabilities, and *(e)* to accrue revenues and related assets.

LO 3. Prepare a schedule that includes the unadjusted trial balance, the adjustments, and the adjusted trial balance; use the adjusted trial balance to prepare financial statements; and prepare entries to record cash receipts and cash disbursements related to accrued assets and liabilities. The effects of adjustments can be shown in a six-column schedule that presents the unadjusted trial balance in the first two columns, the adjusting entries in the next two columns, and the adjusted trial balance in the final two columns. The adjusted trial balance shows all ledger accounts, including assets, liabilities, revenues, expenses, and owner's equity. As a result, it can be used to prepare the income statement, the statement of changes in owner's equity, and the balance sheet.

Payments of accrued expenses in the next accounting period are recorded with a debit to the accrued liability and may include another debit for any additional expense incurred since the beginning of the new period. When accrued revenues are collected, the entry credits the previously recorded asset (a receivable) and may include another credit for any additional revenue earned during the new period.

LO 4. Define each asset and liability category for the balance sheet, prepare a classified balance sheet, and calculate the current ratio. Classified balance sheets usually report four categories of assets: current assets, investments, plant and equipment, and intangible assets. The two categories of liabilities are current and long-term. Owner's equity for proprietorships and partners' equity for partnerships are reported by putting the capital account balances on the balance sheet. A corporation reports stockholders' equity as contributed capital and retained earnings. A company's current ratio describes its ability to pay its current liabilities out of its current assets. The value of the ratio equals the amount of the current assets divided by the current liabilities.

DEMONSTRATION PROBLEM

The following information relates to Best Plumbing Company on December 31, 19X2. The company uses the calendar year as its annual reporting period.

a. The company's weekly payroll is $2,800, paid every Friday for a five-day workweek. December 31, 19X2, falls on a Wednesday, but the employees will not be paid until Friday, January 2, 19X3.

b. Eighteen months earlier, on July 1, 19X1, the company purchased equipment that cost $10,000 and had no salvage value. Its useful life is predicted to be five years.

c. On October 1, 19X2, the company agreed to work on a new housing project. For installing plumbing in 24 new homes, the company was paid $144,000 in advance. When the $144,000 cash was received on October 1, 19X2, that amount was credited to the Unearned Plumbing Revenue account. Between October 1 and December 31, 19X2, work on 18 homes was completed.

d. On September 1, 19X2, the company purchased a one-year insurance policy for $1,200. The transaction was recorded with a $1,200 debit to Prepaid Insurance.

Required

1. Prepare the adjusting entries needed on December 31, 19X2, to record the previously unrecorded effects of the events.

2. Complete the following table describing your adjusting entries. Your answer should indicate the amount entered in the listed accounts by each entry; the amount of the asset or liability that will appear on the December 31, 19X2, balance sheet; and whether the item on the balance sheet will be a current asset, an item related to plant and equipment, a current liability, or a long-term liability:

Entry	Account	Amount in the Entry	Amount on the Balance Sheet	Balance Sheet Category
a	Wages Payable			
b	Accumulated Depreciation, Equipment			
c	Unearned Plumbing Revenue			
d	Prepaid Insurance			

3. Complete the following table describing your adjusting entries. Your answer should indicate how much the entry changed (if at all) the company's reported income, its reported total assets, and its reported total liabilities. If the change is a decrease, enter the amount in parentheses:

Entry	Reported Net Income	Reported Total Assets	Reported Total Liabilities
a			
b			
c			
d			

- Analyze the information for each situation to determine which accounts need to be updated with an adjustment.
- Calculate the size of each adjustment and prepare the necessary journal entries.
- Show the amount entered by each adjustment in the designated accounts, determine the adjusted balance, and then determine the balance sheet classification that the account falls within.
- Determine each entry's effect on reported net income, reported total assets, and reported total liabilities.

Planning the Solution

Adjusting journal entries.

Solution to Demonstration Problem

a.	Dec.	31	Wages Expense		1,680.00	
			Wages Payable			1,680.00
			To accrue wages for the last three days of the year ($2,800 × 3/5).			
b.	Dec.	31	Depreciation Expense, Equipment		2,000.00	
			Accumulated Depreciation, Equipment			2,000.00
			To record depreciation expense for the full year ($10,000/5 = $2,000).			
c.	Dec.	31	Unearned Plumbing Revenue		108,000.00	
			Plumbing Services Revenue			108,000.00
			To recognize plumbing revenues earned ($144,000 × 18/24).			
d.	Dec.	31	Insurance Expense		400.00	
			Prepaid Insurance			400.00
			To adjust for the expired portion of insurance ($1,200 × 4/12).			

Entry	Account	Amount in the Entry	Amount on the Balance Sheet	Balance Sheet Category
a	Wages Payable	$1,680 cr	$1,680	Current liability
b	Accumulated Depreciation, Equipment	$2,000 cr	$3,000	Plant and equipment
c	Unearned Plumbing Revenue	$108,000 dr	$36,000	Current liability
d	Prepaid Insurance	$400 cr	$800	Current asset

Entry	Reported Net Income	Reported Total Assets	Reported Total Liabilities
a	$(1,680)	no effect	$1,680
b	$(2,000)	$(2,000)	no effect
c	$108,000	no effect	$(108,000)
d	$(400)	$(400)	no effect

Recording Prepaid and Unearned Items in Income Statement Accounts

PREPAID EXPENSES

LO 6

Explain why some companies record prepaid and unearned items in income statement accounts and prepare adjusting entries when this procedure is used.

The discussion in Chapter 3 emphasized the fact that prepaid expenses are assets at the time they are purchased. Therefore, at the time of purchase, we recorded prepaid expenses with debits to asset accounts. Then, at the end of the accounting period, adjusting entries transferred the cost that had expired to expense accounts. We also recognized that some prepaid expenses are purchased and will fully expire before the end of the accounting period. In these cases, you can avoid having to make adjusting entries if you charge the prepaid items to expense accounts at the time of purchase.

Some companies follow a practice of recording all prepaid expenses with debits to expense accounts. Then, at the end of the accounting period, if any amounts remain unused or unexpired, adjusting entries are made to transfer the cost of the unused portions from the expense accounts to prepaid expense (asset) accounts. This practice is perfectly acceptable. The reported financial statements are exactly the same under either procedure.

To illustrate the differences between the two procedures, recall that on December 26, Clear Copy paid for 24 months of insurance coverage that began on December 1. We recorded that payment with a debit to an asset account, but could have recorded a debit to an expense account. The alternatives are as follows:

			Payment Recorded as Asset		Payment Recorded as Expense	
Dec.	26	Prepaid Insurance	2,400.00			
		Cash		2,400.00		
	26	Insurance Expense			2,400.00	
		Cash				2,400.00

At the end of the accounting period (December 31), insurance protection for one month has expired. That means $2,400/24 = $100 of the asset expired and became an expense of December. The required adjusting entry depends on how the original payment was recorded. The alternative adjusting entries are:

			Payment Recorded as Asset		Payment Recorded as Expense	
Adjusting entries:						
Dec.	31	Insurance Expense	100.00			
		Prepaid Insurance		100.00		
	31	Prepaid Insurance			2,300.00	
		Insurance Expense				2,300.00

When these entries are posted to the accounts, you can see that the two alternative procedures give the same results. Regardless of which procedure is followed, the December 31 adjusted account balances show prepaid insurance of $2,300 and insurance expense of $100.

Payment Recorded as Asset				**Payment Recorded as Expense**		
Prepaid Insurance				**Prepaid Insurance**		
Dec. 26	2,400	Dec. 31	100	Dec. 31	2,300	
	−100					
Bal.	2,300					

Insurance Expense				**Insurance Expense**		
Dec. 31	100			Dec. 26	2,400	Dec. 31	2,300
					−2,300		
				Bal.	100		

To continue the example for another month, assume that on January 1, Clear Copy paid $750 to purchase a second insurance policy. This policy provides protection for three months beginning January 1. Therefore, the total cost of unexpired insurance on January 1 was $2,300 + $750 = $3,050. On January 31, $250 of the second policy's cost (one month's worth) had expired. Since $100 of the first insurance policy and $250 of the second insurance policy expired during January, the adjusting entry on January 31 must be designed to report an insurance expense of $350 and a prepaid insurance asset of $3,050 − $350 = $2,700. Depending on how the original payments were recorded, the alternative adjusting entries are:

			Payment Recorded as Asset		**Payment Recorded as Expense**	
		Adjusting entries:				
Jan.	31	Insurance Expense	350.00			
		Prepaid Insurance		350.00		
	31	Prepaid Insurance			400.00	
		Insurance Expense				400.00

Note that if the insurance payments are debited to an expense account, the required adjusting entry increases the Prepaid Insurance account balance $400, from $2,300 to $2,700. The credit in the entry reduces the Insurance Expense account debit balance from $750 to $350.

UNEARNED REVENUES

The procedures for recording unearned revenues are similar to those used to record prepaid expenses. Receipts of unearned revenues may be recorded with credits to liability accounts (as described in Chapter 3) or they may be recorded with credits to revenue accounts. The adjusting entries at the end of the period are different, depending on which procedure is followed. Nevertheless, either procedure is acceptable. The amounts reported in the financial statements are exactly the same, regardless of which procedure is used.

To illustrate the alternative procedures of recording unearned revenues, recall that on December 26, Clear Copy received $3,000 in payment for copying services to be provided over the two-month period beginning December 15. In Chapter 3, that receipt was recorded with a credit to a liability account. The alternative would be to record it with a credit to a revenue account. Both alternatives follow:

Dec.				Receipt Recorded as a Liability	Receipt Recorded as a Revenue
Dec.	26	Cash		3,000.00	
		Unearned Copy Services Revenue			3,000.00	
	26	Cash			3,000.00
		Copy Services Revenue				3,000.00

By the end of the accounting period (December 31), Clear Copy had earned $750 of this revenue. That means $750 of the liability had been satisfied. Depending on how the original receipt was recorded, the required adjusting entry is as follows:

Dec.				Receipt Recorded as Liability	Receipt Recorded as Revenue
		Adjusting entries:			
Dec.	31	Unearned Copy Services Revenue . .		750.00	
		Copy Services Revenue			750.00	
	31	Copy Services Revenue			2,250.00
		Unearned Copy Services Revenue				2,250.00

After these entries are posted, you can see that the two alternative procedures give the same results. Regardless of which procedure is followed, the December 31 adjusted account balances show unearned copy services revenue of $2,250 and copy services revenue of $750.

Receipt Recorded as a Liability					**Receipt Recorded as a Revenue**			
Unearned Copy Services Revenue					**Unearned Copy Services Revenue**			
Dec. 31	750	Dec. 26	3,000				Dec. 31	2,250
			−750					
		Bal.	2,250					

Copy Services Revenue					**Copy Services Revenue**			
		Dec. 31	750		Dec. 31	2,250	Dec. 26	3,000
								−2,250
							Bal.	750

SUMMARY OF APPENDIX A IN TERMS OF LEARNING OBJECTIVE

LO 6. Explain why some companies record prepaid and unearned items in income statement accounts and prepare adjusting entries when this procedure is used. Because many prepaid expenses expire during the same period they are purchased, some companies choose to charge all prepaid expenses to expense accounts at the time they are purchased. When this is done, end-of-period adjusting entries are required to transfer any unexpired amounts from the expense accounts to appropriate asset accounts. Also, unearned revenues may be credited to revenue accounts at the time cash is received. If so, end-of-period adjusting entries are required to transfer any unearned amounts from the revenue accounts to appropriate unearned revenue accounts.

GLOSSARY

Account form balance sheet a balance sheet that places the liabilities and owner's equity to the right of the assets. p. 125

Accounting period the length of time covered by periodic financial statements and other reports. p. 106

Accrual basis accounting the approach to preparing financial statements based on recognizing revenues when they are earned and matching expenses to those revenues; the basis for generally accepted accounting principles. p. 109

Accrued expenses incurred but unpaid expenses that are recorded during the adjusting process; recorded with a debit to an expense and a credit to a liability. p. 114

Accrued revenues earned but uncollected revenues that are recorded during the adjusting process; recorded with a credit to a revenue and a debit to an expense. p. 115

Adjusted trial balance a trial balance prepared after adjustments have been recorded. p. 117

Adjusting entry a journal entry at the end of an accounting period that recognizes revenues earned or expenses incurred in that period while updating the related liability and asset accounts. p. 110

Cash basis accounting the approach to preparing financial statements based on recognizing revenues when the cash is received and reporting expenses when the cash is paid; not generally accepted. p. 109

Classified balance sheet a balance sheet that presents the assets and liabilities in relevant groups. p. 121

Common stock the most basic category of a corporation's stock; if the corporation issues only one class of stock, all of it is common. p. 125

Contra account an account the balance of which is subtracted from the balance of a related account so that more complete information than simply the net amount is provided. p. 113

Current assets cash or other assets that are reasonably expected to be sold, collected, or consumed within one year or within the normal operating cycle of the business, whichever is longer. p. 122

Current liabilities obligations due to be paid or liquidated within one year or the operating cycle, whichever is longer. p. 124

Current ratio a description of a company's ability to pay its short-term obligations, calculated by dividing current assets by current liabilities. p. 126

Depreciation the expense created by allocating the cost of plant and equipment to the periods in which they are used; represents the expense of using the assets. p. 112

Dividends a distribution, generally a cash payment, made by a corporation to its stockholders; similar to a withdrawal for a proprietorship. p. 125

Fiscal year the 12 consecutive months (or 52 weeks) selected as an organization's annual accounting period. p. 106

Intangible assets assets without a physical form that are used to produce or sell goods and services; their value comes from the privileges or rights that are granted to or held by the owner. p. 124

Interim financial reports financial reports covering less than one year; usually based on one- or three-month periods. p. 106

Long-term liabilities obligations that are not due to be paid within one year or the operating cycle, whichever is longer. p. 124

Matching principle the broad principle that requires expenses to be reported in the same period as the revenues that were earned as a result of the expenses. p. 108

Natural business year a 12-month period that ends when a company's sales activities are at their lowest point. p. 107

Operating cycle of a business the average time between paying cash for employee salaries or merchandise and receiving cash from customers. p. 122

Plant and equipment tangible long-lived assets used to produce goods or services. p. 112

Report form balance sheet a balance sheet that places the assets above the liabilities and owner's equity. p. 125

Time period principle a broad principle that requires identifying the activities of a business with specific time periods such as months, quarters, or years. p. 106.

Unadjusted trial balance a trial balance prepared before adjustments have been recorded. p. 117

Unclassified balance sheet a balance sheet that does not separate the assets and liabilities into categories. p. 121

The letter[A] *identifies the questions, quick studies, exercises, and problems that are based on Appendix A at the end of the chapter.*

QUESTIONS

1. What type of business is most likely to select a fiscal year that corresponds to the natural business year instead of the calendar year?

2. What kind of assets require adjusting entries to record depreciation?

3. What contra account is used when recording and reporting the effects of depreciation? Why is it used?

4. How is an unearned revenue classified on the balance sheet?

5. What is an accrued revenue? Give an example.

6. What is the difference between the cash and accrual bases of accounting?

7. What classes of assets and liabilities are shown on a typical classified balance sheet?

8. What is a company's operating cycle?

9. What are the characteristics of plant and equipment?

10. Review the consolidated balance sheets of Federal Express Corporation in Appendix G. Assume that all accrued expenses existing at the end of each year are paid within a few months. What was the total amount of accrued expenses in the company's adjusting entries at the end of the 1993 fiscal year?

11. Review the consolidated balance sheet of Ben & Jerry's Homemade, Inc., presented in Appendix G. As a simplification, assume that the company did not sell any property, plant, and equipment during 1992. How much depreciation was recorded in the adjusting entries at the end of 1992?

BEN&JERRY'S
VERMONT'S FINEST • ICE CREAM & FROZEN YOGURT™

A12. If a company initially records prepaid expenses with debits to expense accounts, what type of account is debited in the adjusting entries for prepaid expenses?

A13. Suppose that one company initially records unearned revenues with credits to a liability account while another records them with credits to revenue accounts. Will their financial statements differ as a result of this variation in their procedures? Why or why not?

QUICK STUDY (Five-Minute Exercises)

**QS 3–1
(LO 1)**

In its first year of operations, Blaine Company earned $26,000 in revenues and received $22,000 cash from customers. The company incurred expenses of $15,000, but had not paid for $1,500 of them at year-end. In addition, Blaine prepaid $2,500 for expenses that would be incurred the next year. Calculate the first year's net income under a cash basis and calculate the first year's net income under an accrual basis.

**QS 3–2
(LO 2)**

In recording its transactions during the year, Founder Company records prepayments of expenses in asset accounts and receipts of unearned revenues in liability accounts. At the end of its annual accounting period, the company must make three adjusting entries. They are (a) to accrue salaries expense, (b) to adjust the Unearned Services Revenue account to recognize earned revenue, and (c) to record the earning of services revenue for which cash will be received the following period. For each of these adjusting entries, use the numbers assigned to the following accounts to indicate the correct account to be debited and the correct account to be credited.

1. Prepaid Salaries Expense   5. Salaries Expense
2. Cash   6. Services Revenue Earned
3. Salaries Payable   7. Unearned Services Revenue
4. Accounts Receivable

**QS 3–3
(LO 2)**

In making adjusting entries at the end of its accounting period, Fulmer Company failed to record $700 of insurance premiums that had expired. This cost had been initially debited to the Prepaid Insurance account. The company also failed to record accrued salaries payable of $400. As a result of these oversights, the financial statements for the reporting period will: (a) Understate net income by $400; (b) Understate assets by $700; (c) Overstate liabilities by $400; (d) Understate expenses by $1,100.

**QS 3–4
(LO 3)**

The following information has been taken from Jones Company's unadjusted and adjusted trial balances:

	Unadjusted		Adjusted	
	Debit	Credit	Debit	Credit
Prepaid insurance	$6,200		$5,900	
Salaries payable				$1,400

The adjusting entries must have included these items:

a.   A $300 credit to Prepaid Insurance and a $1,400 debit to Salaries Payable.

b.   A $300 debit to Insurance Expense and a $1,400 debit to Salaries Payable.

c.   A $300 debit to Insurance Expense and a $1,400 debit to Salaries Expense.

Calculate Nickel Company's current ratio given the following information about its assets and liabilities:

QS 3–5
(LO 4)

Accounts receivable	$17,000
Accounts payable	11,000
Buildings	35,000
Cash	4,000
Long-term notes payable	20,000
Office supplies	800
Prepaid insurance	3,500
Unearned services revenue	3,000

Blalock Company initially records prepaid and unearned items in income statement accounts. In preparing adjusting entries at the end of the company's first accounting period:

ᴬQS 3–6
(LO 6)

a.   Unpaid salaries will be recorded with a debit to Prepaid Salaries and a credit to Salaries Expense.

b.   The cost of unused office supplies will be recorded with a debit to Supplies Expense and a credit to Office Supplies.

c.   Unearned fees will be recorded with a debit to Consulting Fees Earned and a credit to Unearned Consulting Fees.

d.   Earned but unbilled consulting fees will be recorded with a debit to Unearned Consulting Fees and a credit to Consulting Fees Earned.

e.   None of the above is correct.

EXERCISES

Prepare adjusting journal entries for the financial statements for the year ended December 31, 19X1, for each of these independent situations:

Exercise 3–1
Adjusting entries for expenses
(LO 2)

a.   The Supplies account had a $150 debit balance on January 1, 19X1; $1,340 of supplies were purchased during the year; and the December 31, 19X1, count showed that $177 of supplies are on hand.

b.   The Prepaid Insurance account had a $2,800 debit balance at December 31, 19X1, before adjusting for the costs of any expired coverage. An analysis of the company's insurance policies showed that $2,300 of coverage had expired.

c.   The Prepaid Insurance account had a $3,500 debit balance at December 31, 19X1, before adjusting for the costs of any expired coverage. An analysis of the company's insurance policies showed that $520 of unexpired insurance remained in effect.

d.   Depreciation on the company's equipment for 19X1 was estimated to be $8,000.

e.   Six months' property taxes are estimated to be $5,400. They have accrued since June 30, 19X1, but are unrecorded and unpaid at December 31, 19X1.

The Haywood Company has five part-time employees, and each earns $120 per day. They are normally paid on Fridays for work completed on Monday through Friday of the same week. They were all paid in full on Friday, December 28, 19X1. The next week, all five of the employees worked only four days because New Year's Day was an unpaid holiday. Show the adjusting entry that would be recorded on Monday, December 31, 19X1, and the journal entry that would be made to record paying the employees' wages on Friday, January 4, 19X2.

Exercise 3–2
Adjusting entries for accrued expenses
(LO 2, 3)

Exercise 3–3
Identifying adjusting entries
(LO 2)

For each of these adjusting entries, enter the letter of the explanation that most closely describes the transaction in the blank space beside the entry:

a. To record the year's consumption of a prepaid expense.

b. To record accrued interest expense.

c. To record accrued income.

d. To record the year's depreciation expense.

e. To record the earning of previously unearned income.

f. To record accrued salaries expense.

```
___ 1. Depreciation Expense ..............................  99,000.00
           Accumulated Depreciation .....................                99,000.00
___ 2. Insurance Expense ...............................   6,000.00
           Prepaid Insurance ...........................                 6,000.00
___ 3. Interest Receivable .............................  22,000.00
           Interest Earned .............................                22,000.00
___ 4. Salaries Expense ................................  37,500.00
           Salaries Payable ............................                37,500.00
___ 5. Interest Expense ................................  63,000.00
           Interest Payable ............................                63,000.00
___ 6. Unearned Professional Fees ......................  86,000.00
           Professional Fees Earned ....................                86,000.00
```

Exercise 3–4
Missing data in supplies
expense calculations
(LO 2)

Determine the missing amounts in each of these four independent situations:

	a.	b.	c.	d.
Supplies on hand—January 1	$100	$ 800	$ 680	?
Supplies purchased during the year	700	2,700	?	$12,000
Supplies on hand—December 31	250	?	920	1,600
Supplies expense for the year	?	650	4,800	13,150

Exercise 3–5
Adjustments and payments of
accrued items
(LO 2, 3)

The following three situations require adjusting journal entries to prepare financial statements as of June 30. For each situation, present the adjusting entry and the entry that would be made to record the payment of the accrued liability during July.

a. The total weekly salaries expense for all employees is $6,000. This amount is paid at the end of the day on Friday of each week with five working days. June 30 falls on Tuesday of this year, which means that the employees had worked two days since the last payday. The next payday is July 3.

b. The company has a $390,000 note payable that requires 0.8% interest to be paid each month on the 20th of the month. The interest was last paid on June 20 and the next payment is due on July 20.

c. On June 1, the company retained an attorney at a flat monthly fee of $1,000. This amount is payable on the 12th of the following month.

Exercise 3–6
Amounts of cash and accrual
basis expenses
(LO 1, 2)

On March 1, 19X1, a company paid a $32,400 premium on a three-year insurance policy for protection beginning on that date. Fill in the blanks in the following table:

	Balance Sheet Asset under the:			Insurance Expense under the:	
	Accrual Basis	**Cash Basis**		**Accrual Basis**	**Cash Basis**
12/31/X1	$_____	$_____	19X1	$_____	$_____
12/31/X2	_____	_____	19X2	_____	_____
12/31/X3	_____	_____	19X3	_____	_____
12/31/X4	_____	_____	19X4	_____	_____
			Total	$_____	$_____

The owner of a duplex apartment building prepares annual financial statements based on a March 31 fiscal year.

a. The tenants of one of the apartments paid five months' rent in advance on November 1, 19X1. The monthly rental is $1,000 per month. Because more than one month's rent was paid in advance, the journal entry credited the Unearned Rent account when the payment was received. No other entry had been recorded prior to March 31, 19X2. Give the adjusting journal entry that should be recorded on March 31, 19X2.

b. On January 1, 19X2, the tenants of the other apartment moved in and paid the first month's rent. The $900 payment was recorded with a credit to the Rent Earned account. However, the tenants have not paid the rent for February or March. They have agreed to pay it as soon as possible. Give the adjusting journal entry that should be recorded on March 31, 19X2.

c. On April 3, 19X2, the tenants described in part b paid $2,700 rent for February, March, and April. Give the journal entry to record the cash collection.

Exercise 3–7
Unearned and accrued revenues
(LO 2, 3)

Use the following adjusted trial balance of the Hamburg Trucking Company to prepare (a) an income statement for the year ended December 31, 19X1; (b) a statement of changes in owner's equity for the year ended December 31, 19X1; and (c) an unclassified balance sheet as of December 31, 19X1. The owner did not make any new investments during 19X1.

Exercise 3–8
Preparing financial statements
(LO 3)

	Debit	Credit
Cash	$ 5,500	
Accounts receivable	18,000	
Office supplies	2,000	
Trucks	180,000	
Accumulated depreciation, trucks		$ 45,000
Land	75,000	
Accounts payable		11,000
Interest payable		3,000
Long-term notes payable		52,000
B. Hamburg, capital		161,000
B. Hamburg, withdrawals	19,000	
Trucking fees earned		128,000
Depreciation expense, trucks	22,500	
Salaries expense	60,000	
Office supplies expense	7,000	
Repairs expense, trucks	11,000	
Total	$400,000	$400,000

Use the information provided in Exercise 3–8 to prepare a classified balance sheet for the Hamburg Trucking Company as of December 31, 19X1. Determine the value of the current ratio as of the balance sheet date.

Exercise 3–9
Preparing a classified balance sheet and calculating the current ratio
(LO 4)

Following are two income statements for the Carlton Financial Consulting Co. for the year ended December 31. The left column was prepared before any adjusting entries were recorded and the right column includes the effects of adjusting entries. Analyze the statements and prepare the adjusting entries that must have been recorded. Thirty percent of the additional consulting fees were earned but not billed and the other 70% were earned by performing services that the customers had paid for in advance.

Exercise 3–10
Identifying the effects of adjusting entries
(LO 2, 3)

CARLTON FINANCIAL CONSULTING CO.
Income Statements
For Year Ended December 31

	Before Adjustments	After Adjustments
Revenues:		
Consulting fees earned	$ 48,000	$ 60,000
Commissions earned	85,000	85,000
Total revenues	$133,000	$145,000
Operating expenses:		
Depreciation expense, computers		$ 3,000
Depreciation expense, office furniture		3,500
Salaries expense	$ 25,000	29,900
Insurance expense		2,600
Rent expense	9,000	9,000
Office supplies expense		960
Advertising expense	6,000	6,000
Utilities expense	2,500	2,640
Total operating expenses	$ 42,500	$ 57,600
Net income	$ 90,500	$ 87,400

Exercise 3–11
Calculating the current ratio
(LO 4)

Calculate the current ratio in each of the following cases:

	Current Assets	Current Liabilities
Case 1	$84,000	$31,000
Case 2	96,000	75,000
Case 3	45,000	48,000
Case 4	84,500	82,600
Case 5	65,000	97,000

^AExercise 3–12
Adjustments for prepaid items recorded in expense and revenue accounts
(LO 6)

The Elder Painting Co. was organized on December 1 by Terry Elder. In setting up the book-keeping procedures, Elder decided to debit expense accounts when the company prepays its expenses and to credit revenue accounts when customers pay for services in advance. Prepare journal entries for items *a* through *d* and adjusting entries as of December 31 for items *e* through *g:*

a. Shop supplies were purchased on December 1 for $1,000.

b. The company prepaid insurance premiums of $480 on December 2.

c. On December 15, the company received an advance payment of $4,000 from one customer for two painting projects.

d. On December 28, the company received $1,200 from a second customer for painting services to be performed in January.

e. By counting them on December 31, Elder determined that $640 of shop supplies were on hand.

f. An analysis of the insurance policies in effect on December 31 showed that $80 of insurance coverage had expired.

g. As of December 31, only one project had been completed. The fee for this particular project was $2,100.

^AExercise 3–13
Alternative procedures for revenues received in advance
(LO 6)

The Falcon Company experienced the following events and transactions during March:

Mar. 1 Received $1,000 in advance of performing work for T. Carson.

5 Received $4,200 in advance of performing work for B. Gamble.

10 Completed the job for T. Carson.

16 Received $3,750 in advance of performing work for S. Curtin.

25 Completed the job for B. Gamble.

31 The job for S. Curtin is still unfinished.

a. Give journal entries (including any adjusting entry as of the end of the month) to record these events using the procedure of initially crediting the Unearned Fees account when a payment is received from a customer in advance of performing services.

b. Give journal entries (including any adjusting entry as of the end of the month) to record these events using the procedure of initially crediting the Fees Earned account when a payment is received from a customer in advance of performing services.

c. Under each method, determine the amount of earned fees that should be reported on the income statement for March and the amount of unearned fees that should appear on the balance sheet as of March 31.

PROBLEMS

The Montgomery Company's annual accounting period ends on December 31, 19X2. The following information concerns the adjusting entries to be recorded as of that date:

Problem 3–1
Adjusting journal entries
(LO 2, 3)

a. The Office Supplies account started the year with a $1,000 balance. During 19X2, the company purchased supplies at a cost of $4,200, which was added to the Office Supplies account. The inventory of supplies on hand at December 31 had a cost of $880.

b. An analysis of the company's insurance policies provided these facts:

Policy	Date of Purchase	Years of Coverage	Total Cost
1	April 1, 19X1	2	$5,280
2	April 1, 19X2	3	4,356
3	August 1, 19X2	1	900

The total premium for each policy was paid in full at the purchase date, and the Prepaid Insurance account was debited for the full cost.

c. The company has five employees who earn a total of $700 in salaries for every working day. They are paid each Monday for their work in the five-day workweek ending on the preceding Friday. December 31, 19X2, falls on Tuesday, and all five employees worked the first two days of the week. Because New Year's Day is a paid holiday, they will be paid salaries for five full days on Monday, January 6, 19X3.

d. The company purchased a building on August 1, 19X2. The building cost $570,000 and is expected to have a $30,000 salvage value at the end of its predicted 30-year life.

e. Because the company is not large enough to occupy the entire building, it arranged to rent some space to a tenant at $800 per month, starting on November 1, 19X2. The rent was paid on time on November 1, and the amount received was credited to the Rent Earned account. However, the tenant has not paid the December rent. The company has worked out an agreement with the tenant, who has promised to pay both December's and January's rent in full on January 15. The tenant has agreed not to fall behind again.

f. On November 1, the company also rented space to another tenant for $725 per month. The tenant paid five months' rent in advance on that date. The payment was recorded with a credit to the Unearned Rent account.

Required

1. Use the information to prepare adjusting entries as of December 31, 19X2.

2. Prepare journal entries to record the subsequent cash transactions described in parts c and e.

CHECK FIGURE:
Insurance expense, $4,104

Problem 3–2
Adjusting entries and financial statements
(LO 3, 4)

Carl Carter owns and operates Carter Carpentry School. The school provides training to individuals who pay tuition directly to the business, and also offers extension training to groups in off-site locations. The school's unadjusted trial balance as of December 31, 19X1, follows. Facts that require eight adjusting entries on December 31, 19X1, are presented after the table:

CARTER CARPENTRY SCHOOL
Unadjusted Trial Balance

Cash	$ 13,000	
Accounts receivable		
Teaching supplies	5,000	
Prepaid insurance	7,500	
Prepaid rent	1,000	
Professional library	15,000	
Accumulated depreciation, professional library		$ 4,500
Equipment	35,000	
Accumulated depreciation, equipment		8,000
Accounts payable		18,000
Salaries payable		
Unearned extension fees		5,500
Carl Carter, capital		31,800
Carl Carter, withdrawals	20,000	
Tuition fees earned		51,000
Extension fees earned		19,000
Depreciation expense, equipment		
Depreciation expense, professional library		
Salaries expense	24,000	
Insurance expense		
Rent expense	11,000	
Teaching supplies expense		
Advertising expense	3,500	
Utilities expense	2,800	
Totals	$137,800	$137,800

Additional facts:

a. An analysis of the company's policies shows that $1,500 of insurance coverage has expired.

b. An inventory shows that teaching supplies costing $1,300 are on hand at the end of the year.

c. The estimated annual depreciation on the equipment is $6,000.

d. The estimated annual depreciation on the professional library is $3,000.

e. The school offers off-campus services for specific employers. On November 1, the company agreed to do a special six-month course for a client. The contract calls for a monthly fee of $1,100, and the client paid the first five months' fees in advance. When the cash was received, the Unearned Extension Fees account was credited.

f. On October 15, the school agreed to teach a four-month class for an individual for $1,500 tuition per month payable at the end of the class. The services have been provided as agreed, and no payment has been received.

g. The school's only employee is paid weekly. As of the end of the year, two days' wages have accrued at the rate of $100 per day.

h. The balance in the Prepaid Rent account represents the rent for December.

Required

1. Enter the unadjusted trial balance in the first two columns of a six-column table like the one shown in Illustration 3–3.

2. Enter the adjusting entries in the Adjustments columns of the table. Identify the debits and credits of each entry with the letters in the list of additional facts. Complete the adjusted trial balance.

3. Prepare the company's income statement and statement of changes in owner's equity for 19X1, and prepare the classified balance sheet as of December 31, 19X1. The owner did not make additional investments in the business during the year.

CHECK FIGURE:
Ending capital balance, $31,050

4. Calculate the current ratio and the debt ratio as of December 31, 19X1. Also, calculate the modified return on equity for the company, under the assumption that Carter's time in the business is worth $15,000 per year.

In the following six-column table for the Decker Company, the first two columns contain the unadjusted trial balance for the company as of March 31, 19X1. The last two columns contain the adjusted trial balance as of the same date.

Problem 3–3
Comparing the unadjusted and adjusted trial balances and preparing financial statements
(LO 3, 4)

	Unadjusted Trial Balance		Adjustments		Adjusted Trial Balance	
Cash	$ 13,500				$ 13,500	
Accounts receivable	6,000				11,230	
Office supplies	9,000				1,500	
Prepaid insurance	3,660				2,440	
Office equipment	36,000				36,000	
Accumulated depreciation, office equipment		$ 6,000				$ 9,000
Accounts payable		4,650				5,100
Interest payable						400
Salaries payable						3,300
Unearned consulting fees .		8,000				7,150
Long-term notes payable .		22,000				22,000
Webster Decker, capital ..		14,210				14,210
Webster Decker, withdrawals	15,000				15,000	
Consulting fees earned ..		78,000				84,080
Depreciation expense, office equipment					3,000	
Salaries expense	35,500				38,800	
Interest expense	700				1,100	
Insurance expense					1,220	
Rent expense	6,600				6,600	
Office supplies expense ..					7,500	
Advertising expense	6,900				7,350	
Totals	$132,860	$132,860			$145,240	$145,240

Required

Preparation component:

1. Prepare the company's income statement and the statement of changes in owner's equity for the year ended March 31, 19X1. The owner did not make any new investments during the year.

2. Prepare the company's classified balance sheet as of March 31, 19X1.

3. Calculate the company's current ratio and debt ratio as of March 31, 19X1.

CHECK FIGURE:
Current ratio, 1.8

Analysis component:

4. Analyze the differences between the unadjusted and adjusted trial balances to determine the adjustments that must have been made. Show the results of your analysis by inserting the adjusting journal entries that must have been recorded by the company in the two middle columns. Label each entry with a letter, and provide a short description of the purpose for recording it. (Use the Working Papers that accompany the text or recreate the table.)

Problem 3–4
Accrual basis income
(LO 1, 2, 3)

The records for Jan Kauffman's home nursing business were kept on the cash basis instead of the accrual basis. However, the company is now applying for a loan and the bank wants to know what its net income for 19X2 was under generally accepted accounting principles. Here is the income statement for 19X2 under the cash basis:

KAUFFMAN'S HOME NURSING
Income Statement (Cash Basis)
For Year Ended December 31, 19X2

Revenues	$175,000
Expenses	110,000
Net income	$ 65,000

This additional information was gathered to help the accountant convert the income statement to the accrual basis:

	As of 12/31/X1	As of 12/31/X2
Accrued revenues	$ 4,000	$5,500
Unearned revenues	22,000	7,000
Accrued expenses	4,900	3,000
Prepaid expenses	9,000	6,900

All prepaid expenses from the beginning of the year were consumed or expired, all unearned revenues from the beginning of the year were earned, and all accrued expenses and revenues from the beginning of the year were paid or collected.

Required

CHECK FIGURE:
Net income, $81,300

Prepare an accrual basis income statement for this business for 19X2. Provide schedules that explain how you converted from cash revenues and expenses to accrual revenues and expenses.

Problem 3–5
Identifying adjusting and subsequent entries
(LO 2)

For these adjusting and transaction entries, enter the letter of the explanation that most closely describes the adjustment or transaction in the blank space beside each entry. (You can use some letters more than once.)

a. To record collection of an accrued revenue.

b. To record the year's depreciation expense.

c. To record collection of an unearned revenue.

d. To record the earning of previously unearned income.

e. To record payment of an accrued expense.

f. To record an accrued expense.

g. To record accrued income.

h. To record payment of a prepaid expense.

i. To record the year's consumption of a prepaid expense.

——	1. Rent Expense	1,000.00	
	Prepaid Rent		1,000.00
——	2. Cash	6,500.00	
	Unearned Professional Fees		6,500.00
——	3. Depreciation Expense	3,000.00	
	Accumulated Depreciation		3,000.00
——	4. Interest Expense	4,000.00	
	Interest Payable		4,000.00
——	5. Prepaid Rent	3,500.00	
	Cash		3,500.00
——	6. Salaries Expense	5,000.00	
	Salaries Payable		5,000.00
——	7. Unearned Professional Fees	2,000.00	
	Professional Fees Earned		2,000.00

—	8. Cash	8,000.00	
	Accounts Receivable		8,000.00
—	9. Insurance Expense	6,000.00	
	Prepaid Insurance		6,000.00
—	10. Salaries Payable	1,500.00	
	Cash		1,500.00
—	11. Cash	9,000.00	
	Interest Receivable		9,000.00
—	12. Interest Receivable	7,000.00	
	Interest Earned		7,000.00

In the blank space beside each numbered balance sheet item, enter the letter of its balance sheet classification. If the item should not appear on the balance sheet, enter a *z* in the blank.

Problem 3–6
Balance sheet classifications
(LO 4)

a.	Current assets	*e.*	Current liabilities
b.	Investments	*f.*	Long-term liabilities
c.	Plant and equipment	*g.*	Owner's equity
d.	Intangible assets	*h.*	Stockholders' equity

___ 1. S. Sherman, capital
___ 2. Accounts payable
___ 3. Depreciation expense, trucks
___ 4. S. Sherman, withdrawals
___ 5. Investment in Ben & Jerry's
     Homemade, Inc. (long-term holding)
___ 6. Notes payable—due in three years
___ 7. Unearned fees revenue
___ 8. Prepaid insurance
___ 9. Common stock (issued)
___ 10. Interest receivable

___ 11. Accumulated depreciation, trucks
___ 12. Building
___ 13. Cash
___ 14. Retained earnings
___ 15. Office equipment
___ 16. Automobiles
___ 17. Repairs expense
___ 18. Prepaid property taxes
___ 19. Current portion of long-term note
     payable
___ 20. Land (in use)

This adjusted trial balance is for the Krumbell Wrecking Co. as of December 31, 19X1:

Problem 3–7
Preparing financial statements
from the adjusted trial balance
and computing ratios
(LO 3, 4)

	Debit	Credit
Cash	$ 11,000	
Accounts receivable	22,000	
Interest receivable	5,000	
Notes receivable (due in 90 days)	80,000	
Office supplies	4,000	
Trucks	90,000	
Accumulated depreciation, trucks		$ 36,000
Equipment	70,000	
Accumulated depreciation, equipment		5,000
Land	35,000	
Accounts payable		44,000
Interest payable		6,000
Salaries payable		5,500
Unearned wrecking fees		11,000
Long-term notes payable		65,000
W. Krumbell, capital		123,900
W. Krumbell, withdrawals	19,000	
Wrecking fees earned		210,000
Interest earned		8,000
Depreciation expense, trucks	9,000	
Depreciation expense, equipment	5,000	
Salaries expense	90,000	
Wages expense	16,000	
Interest expense	12,000	
Office supplies expense	13,000	
Advertising expense	25,000	
Repairs expense, trucks	8,400	
Total	$514,400	$514,400

Required

1. Use the information in the trial balance to prepare (*a*) the income statement for the year ended December 31, 19X1 (under the assumption that the owner made no new investments during the year); (*b*) the statement of changes in owner's equity for the year ended December 31, 19X1; and (*c*) the classified balance sheet as of December 31, 19X1.

2. Calculate the following ratios for the company:

    a.   Current ratio as of December 31, 19X1.

    b.   Debt ratio as of December 31, 19X1.

    c.   Modified return on equity for the year ended December 31, 19X1, under the assumption that the proprietor's efforts are valued at $30,000.

ᴬProblem 3–8
Recording prepaid expenses
and unearned revenues
(LO 2, 6)

The following events occurred for a company during the last two months of its fiscal year ended December 31:

Nov. 1   Paid $1,000 for future newspaper advertising.

     1   Paid $1,440 for insurance through October 31 of the following year.

   30   Received $2,200 for future services to be provided to a customer.

Dec. 1   Paid $1,800 for the services of a consultant, to be received over the next three months.

   15   Received $5,100 for future services to be provided to a customer.

   31   Of the advertising paid for on November 1, $600 worth had not yet been published by the newspaper.

   31   Part of the insurance paid for on November 1 had expired.

   31   Services worth $800 had not yet been provided to the customer who paid on November 30.

   31   One-third of the consulting services paid for on December 1 had been received.

   31   The company had performed $2,000 of the services that the customer had paid for on December 15.

Required

Preparation component:

1. Prepare entries for the above events under the approach that records prepaid expenses as assets and records unearned revenues as liabilities. Also, prepare adjusting entries at the end of the year.

2. Prepare journal entries under the approach that records prepaid expenses as expenses and records unearned revenues as revenues. Also, prepare adjusting entries at the end of the year.

Analysis component:

3. Explain why the alternative sets of entries in requirements 1 and 2 do not result in different financial statement amounts.

SERIAL PROBLEM

Emerald Computer Services

(This comprehensive problem was introduced in Chapter 2 and continues in Chapters 4 and 5. If the Chapter 2 segment has not been completed, the assignment can begin at this point. However, you will need to use the facts presented on pages 100-101 in Chapter 2. Because of its length, this problem is most easily solved if you use the Working Papers that accompany this text.)

After the success of its first two months, Tracy Green has decided to continue operating Emerald Computer Services. (The transactions that occurred in these months are described in Chapter 2.) Before proceeding into December, Green adds these new accounts to the chart of accounts for the ledger:

Account	No.
Accumulated Depreciation, Office Equipment	164
Accumulated Depreciation, Computer Equipment	168
Wages Payable	210
Unearned Computer Fees	233
Depreciation Expense, Office Equipment	612
Depreciation Expense, Computer Equipment	613
Insurance Expense	637
Rent Expense	640
Computer Supplies Expense	652

Required

1. Prepare journal entries to record each of the following transactions for Emerald Computer Services. Post the entries to the accounts in the ledger.

2. Prepare adjusting entries to record the events described on December 31. Post the entries to the accounts in the ledger.

3. Prepare an adjusted trial balance as of December 31, 19X1.

4. Prepare an income statement for the three months ended December 31, 19X1.

5. Prepare a statement of changes in owner's equity for the three months ended December 31, 19X1.

6. Prepare a balance sheet as of December 31, 19X1.

Transactions and other data:

Dec. 3   Paid $700 to the Town Center Mall for the company's share of mall advertising costs.

4   Paid $400 to repair the company's computer.

6   Received $2,500 from Alpha Printing Co. for the receivable from the prior month.

10   Paid Fran Sims for six days' work at the rate of $125 per day.

12   Notified by Alpha Printing Co. that Emerald's bid of $4,000 on a proposed project was accepted. The company paid an advance of $1,000.

13   Purchased $770 of computer supplies on credit from AAA Supply Co.

15   Sent a reminder to Fox Run Estates to pay the fee for services originally recorded on November 7.

19   Completed project for Delta Fixtures, Inc., and received $3,750 cash.

21   Paid $2,000 to Tracy Green as a cash withdrawal.

22–26   Took the week off for the holidays.

28   Received $1,900 from Fox Run Estates on their receivable.

29   Reimbursed Tracy Green's business automobile mileage of 400 miles at $0.25 per mile.

31   The following information was collected to be used in adjusting entries prior to preparing financial statements for the company's first three months:

a.   The December 31 inventory of computer supplies was $480.

b.   Three months have passed since the annual insurance premium was paid.

c.   As of the end of the year, Fran Sims has not been paid for four days of work at the rate of $125 per day.

d.   The computer is expected to have a four-year life with no salvage value.

e.   The office equipment is expected to have a three-year life with no salvage value.

f.   Prepaid rent for three of the four months has expired.

CRITICAL THINKING: ESSAYS, PROBLEMS, AND CASES

Analytical Essays

AE 3–1
(LO 1, 2)

Review the information presented in paragraphs *c, d,* and *e* of Problem 3–1. Describe how each of the following errors from 19X2 would affect the company's income statements for 19X2 and 19X3 and its balance sheets as of December 31, 19X2, and 19X3 (treat each case as independent from the others). None of the errors were repeated in 19X3, but they remained undiscovered until well into 19X4.

1. The company mistakenly recorded the $1,400 of accrued salary expense described in part *c* as if the amount was only $1,000. However, the employees were paid the correct amount of $1,400 on January 6, 19X3. At that time, the Salaries Payable account was debited for $1,000 and the remainder of the $3,500 payment to the employees was debited to the Salaries Expense account for 19X3.

2. The company failed to record the $7,500 depreciation expense on the building described in part *d.*

3. The company failed to record the $800 of accrued rent income described in part *e.* Instead, the revenue was recorded on January 15 as income earned in 19X3.

^AE 3–2
(LO 1, 2, 6)

On November 1, 19X1, Carson Company and Winslow Company each paid $6,000 for six months' rent on their offices. Carson recorded its payment with a debit to the Prepaid Rent account. On the other hand, Winslow debited the Rent Expense account for $6,000. Both companies use calendar years as their accounting periods. Describe the differences between the adjusting entries the two companies should make on December 31, 19X1. Be sure to explain how the two companies' different bookkeeping procedures affect the financial statements.

Financial Reporting Problems

FRP 3–1
(LO 1, 2)

The 19X1 and 19X2 balance sheets for Phillips Law Practice reported the following assets and liabilities:

	19X1	19X2
Accounts receivable ...	$45,000	$62,000
Prepaid insurance	4,800	3,600
Interest payable	5,750	9,250
Unearned legal fees	17,000	25,000

The company's records show that the following amounts of cash were spent and received during 19X2:

Cash spent to pay insurance premiums ..	$ 12,500
Cash spent to pay interest	14,000
Cash received on accounts receivable ...	120,000
Cash received in advance for legal fees ..	108,000

Calculate the amounts to be reported on Phillips Law Practice's 19X2 income statement for (*a*) insurance expense, (*b*) interest expense, and (*c*) total legal fees earned.

FRP 3–2
(LO 2, 3, 4, 6)

Early in January, Chris Williams created a new business called We-Fix-Anything. Unfortunately, Williams has not maintained any double-entry accounting records, although all cash receipts and disbursements have been carefully recorded. In addition, all unpaid invoices for the company's expenses and purchases are kept in a file until they are paid. The cash records have been summarized in this schedule:

Cash received:

Investment by owner	$43,000	
Customer repairs	66,000	
Total		$109,000
Cash paid:		
Shop equipment	$21,200	
Repair supplies	25,000	
Rent	8,400	
Insurance premiums	900	
Newspaper advertising	2,000	
Utility bills	1,600	
Employee's wages	8,000	
Chris Williams	20,000	
Total cash payments		87,100
Cash balance as of December 31		$ 21,900

Williams wants to know the net income for the first year and the company's financial position at the end of the year. Provide this information by preparing an accrual basis income statement, a statement of changes in owner's equity, and a classified balance sheet. Also compute the current ratio, the debt ratio, and the modified return on equity, assuming that Williams's efforts are worth $22,500 per year.

The following information will help you: The shop equipment was bought in January and is predicted to have a useful life of 10 years, with a $1,200 salvage value. There is a $4,000 unpaid invoice in the file; it is for supplies that have been purchased and received. An inventory shows that $8,200 of supplies are on hand at the end of the year. The shop space is rented for $600 per month under a five-year lease. The lease contract required Williams to pay the first and the final two months' rents in advance. The insurance premiums acquired two policies on January 2. The first is a one-year policy that cost $500, and the second is a two-year policy that cost $400. There are $190 of earned but unpaid wages and customers owe the shop $3,750 for services they have received.

Refer to the financial statements and related information for Apple Computer, Inc., in Appendix F. Find the answers to the following questions by analyzing the information in the report.

Financial Statement Analysis Case

(LO 4)

1. Does the company present a classified balance sheet? What title is given to the financial statement?

2. Identify the classifications of assets presented on the balance sheet.

3. What is the total amount of accumulated depreciation (and amortization) as of September 24, 1993? (*Amortization* is the term used for the depreciation of intangible assets.)

4. What is the company's current ratio at the end of its 1993 and 1992 fiscal years?

5. What is the company's debt ratio at the end of its 1993 and 1992 fiscal years? (Include deferred income taxes in the liabilities.)

Ethical Issues Essay   Review the As a Matter of Ethics case on page 116. Describe the ethical dilemma faced by Bill Palmer and describe the alternative courses of action that he might take. Explain how your answer would differ given the following assumptions: *(a)* Palmer knows that the company's financial statements are not going to be audited; *(b)* Palmer knows that the president's bonus depends on the amount of income reported in the first year; and *(c)* Palmer's job depends on complying with the president's wishes.

ANSWERS TO PROGRESS CHECKS

3–1   *a*

3–2   Interim financial statements are prepared to provide decision makers information frequently and promptly.

3–3   The revenue recognition principle and the matching principle.

3–4   No, the cash basis is not consistent with the matching principle because it does not always report expenses in the same period as the revenues that were earned as a result of the expenses.

3–5   No expense is reported in 19X2. Under the cash basis, the entire $4,800 is reported as expense in 19X1 when the premium was paid.

3–6   *c*

3–7   The balance of a contra account is subtracted from the balance of a related account so that more complete information than simply the net amount is provided.

3–8   An accrued expense is an incurred expense that is not recorded prior to adjusting entries because it has not

been paid. An example is unpaid salaries earned by employees prior to the year-end.

3–9   An unearned revenue arises when cash is received from a customer before the service is provided to the customer. Magazine subscription receipts are an example.

3–10   *c*

3–11   Revenue accounts and expense accounts.

3–12   The statement of changes in owner's equity is prepared second.

3–13   *c*

3–14   Current assets: *b, c, d.*
       Plant and equipment: *a, e.*

3–15   Stock investments that will be held longer than one year or the current operating cycle. Land held for plant expansion.

3–16   Current liabilities.

3–17   Contributed capital and retained earnings.

CHAPTER 4

The Work Sheet and the Closing Process

*O*ne day a Ben & Jerry's shareholder came into the company office and said: "Your annual report is great, but the financial statements are impossible to read for people who aren't trained in accounting."

Fran, the chief financial officer, responded: "I guess that's true. It's hard to make financial statements look friendly to nonfinancial people, because they are written in the language of business. That's the definition of accounting—the language of business. If we wrote the front half of the annual report in Martian, most creatures other than Martians wouldn't find that too friendly, either."

"Well can't you do something about it? Can't you just draw some pictures and write some clever things in them so we can understand them better?"

"Not really. The rules called 'generally accepted accounting principles,' are really specific, to make sure a company presents very clear, standardized information about its finances to its investors. Financial statements have footnotes and a 'management's discussion and analysis' that explain a lot of things about a company's finances. The footnotes and analysis may look imposing, but go ahead and look them over. Relax, have a bowl of Ben & Jerry's and unlock the secrets."

"Well, the language of business is a real secret to me. Help me out. I know the stuff in the front is important. That's one of the reasons why I bought stock. Now I want to learn more about the money side."[1]

Ben & Jerry's Homemade, Inc.
(In thousands)

| | Year Ended | | | | |
	12/26/92	12/28/91	12/29/90	12/30/89	12/31/88
Net sales	$131,969	$96,997	$77,024	$58,464	$47,561
Net income . .	6,675	3,739	2,609	2,053	1,618

[1]Quoted from the "Financial (not so very) Funnies" section of *Ben & Jerry's 1992 Annual Report,* ©1993, Ben & Jerry's Homemade, Inc., Waterbury, VT.

LEARNING OBJECTIVES

After studying Chapter 4, you should be able to:

1. **Explain why work sheets are useful, prepare a work sheet for a service business, and prepare financial statements from the information in a work sheet.**
2. **Explain why the temporary accounts are closed at the end of each accounting period and prepare closing entries and a post-closing trial balance for a service business.**
3. **Describe each step in the accounting cycle.**
4. **Calculate the profit margin ratio and describe what it reveals about a company's performance.**
5. **Define or explain the words and phrases listed in the chapter glossary.**

After studying Appendix B at the end of Chapter 4, you should be able to:

6. **Explain when and why reversing entries are used and prepare reversing entries.**

This chapter continues your study of the accounting process by describing procedures that the accountant performs at the end of each reporting period. You learn about an optional work sheet that accountants use to draft adjusting entries and the financial statements. Studying the work sheet allows you to get an overall perspective on the steps in the accounting cycle. The chapter also describes the closing process that prepares the revenue, expense, and withdrawals accounts for the next reporting period and updates the owner's capital account. In addition, the chapter describes the profit margin ratio that decision makers use to assess a company's performance.

USING WORK SHEETS AT THE END OF ACCOUNTING PERIODS

LO 1

Explain why work sheets are useful, prepare a work sheet for a service business, and prepare financial statements from the information in a work sheet.

When organizing the information presented in formal reports to internal and external decision makers, accountants prepare numerous analyses and informal documents. These informal documents are important tools for accountants. Traditionally, they are called **working papers.** One widely used working paper is the **work sheet.** Normally, the work sheet is not distributed to decision makers. It is prepared and used by accountants.

Why Study the Work Sheet?

As we stated previously, preparing a work sheet is an optional procedure. When a business has only a few accounts and adjustments, preparing a work sheet is not necessary. Also, computerized accounting systems provide financial statements without first generating a work sheet. Nevertheless, there are several reasons why an understanding of work sheets is helpful:

1. In a manual accounting system involving many accounts and adjustments, the work sheet helps the accountant avoid errors.
2. Studying the work sheet is an effective way for you to see the entire accounting process from beginning to end. In a sense, it gives a bird's-eye view of the process between the occurrence of economic events and the presentation of their effects in financial statements. This knowledge helps managers and other decision makers understand the information in the statements.
3. After a company has tentatively prepared its financial statements, the auditors of the statements often use a work sheet as a basis for planning and organizing the audit. Also, they may use a work sheet to reflect any additional adjustments that appear necessary as a result of the audit.

4. Accountants often use work sheets to prepare interim (monthly or quarterly) financial statements.

5. A modified form of the work sheet is sometimes used to show the effects of proposed transactions.

Where Does the Work Sheet Fit into the Accounting Process?

In practice, the work sheet is an optional step in the accounting process that can simplify the accountant's efforts in preparing financial statements. When a work sheet is used, it is prepared before making the adjusting entries at the end of the reporting period. The work sheet gathers information about the accounts, the needed adjustments, and the financial statements. When it is finished, the work sheet contains information that is recorded in the journal and then presented in the statements.

Illustration 4–1 shows a blank work sheet. Notice that it has five sets of double columns for the

PREPARING THE WORK SHEET

1. Unadjusted trial balance.
2. Adjustments.
3. Adjusted trial balance.
4. Income statement.
5. Statement of changes in owner's equity and the balance sheet.

Note that a separate set of double columns is not provided for the statement of changes in owner's equity. Because that statement includes only a few items, they are simply listed with the balance sheet items. A work sheet can be completed manually or with a computer. In fact, the format is well-suited for using a spreadsheet program.

Step 1—Enter the Unadjusted Trial Balance

Turn the first transparency over to create Illustration 4–2. This illustration shows how the accountant starts preparing the work sheet by listing the number and title of every account expected to appear on the company's financial statements. Then, the unadjusted debit or credit balances of the accounts are found in the ledger and recorded in the first two columns. Because these columns serve as the unadjusted trial balance, the totals of the columns should be equal.

Illustration 4–2 uses the information for Clear Copy Co. from Chapter 2 to show step 1. The account balances include the effects of December's external transactions. They do not reflect any of the adjustments described in Chapter 3.

In some cases, the accountant determines later that additional accounts need to be inserted on the work sheet. If the work sheet is completed manually, the additional accounts are inserted below the initial list. If a computer spreadsheet program is used, the new lines are easily inserted between existing lines.

Because a later phase in the example requires two lines for the Copy Services Revenue account, Illustration 4–2 includes an extra blank line below that account. If this need is not anticipated when the work sheet is being prepared manually, the accountant can squeeze two entries on one line.

Step 2—Enter the Adjustments and Prepare the Adjusted Trial Balance

Turn the next overlay page to create Illustration 4–3. The work sheet now appears as it would after step 2 is completed. Step 2 begins by entering adjustments for economic events that were not external transactions. These include adjustments for prepaid expenses, depreciation, unearned revenues, accrued expenses, and accrued revenues. The illustration shows the six adjustments for Clear Copy Co. that were explained in Chapter 3:

a. Expiration of $100 of prepaid insurance.
b. Consumption of $1,050 of store supplies.
c. Depreciation of copy equipment by $375.
d. Earning of $250 of previously unearned revenue.
e. Accrual of $210 of salaries owed to the employee.
f. Accrual of $1,800 of revenue owed by a customer.

To be sure that equal debits and credits are entered, the components of each adjustment are identified on the work sheet with a letter. Some accountants explain the adjustments with a list at the bottom of the work sheet or on a separate page.[2] To test for accuracy, they add the totals of the two columns to confirm that they are equal.

After the adjustments are entered on the work sheet, the adjusted trial balance is prepared by combining the adjustments with the unadjusted balances. Debits and credits are combined just as they would be in determining an account's balance. For example, the Prepaid Insurance account in Illustration 4–3 has a $2,400 debit balance in the unadjusted trial balance. This is combined with the $100 credit entry (a) in the Adjustments columns to give the account a $2,300 debit balance in the adjusted trial balance. Salaries Expense has a $1,400 balance in the unadjusted trial balance and is combined with the $210 debit entry (e) in the Adjustments columns. When the debit balance is combined with the debit from the adjustment, the account has a $1,610 debit balance in the adjusted trial balance. The totals of the Adjusted Trial Balance columns should confirm that debits equal credits.

Step 3—Extend the Adjusted Trial Balance Amounts to the Financial Statement Columns

Turn the third transparency over to create Illustration 4–4 and to see the effects of step 3. In this step, the accountant assigns each adjusted account balance to its financial statement. This is done by extending each amount to the appropriate column across the page. The revenue and expense balances are extended to the Income Statement columns. The asset, liability, and owner's capital and withdrawals account balances are extended to the Statement of Changes in Owner's Equity and Balance Sheet columns. Accounts with debit balances in the adjusted trial balance are extended to the Debit columns and accounts with credit balances are extended to the Credit columns.

Next, the columns are totaled. Notice that the paired column totals are not equal. This occurs because the sum of the expenses debit balances does not equal the sum of the revenue credit balances. This also creates an equal and opposite imbalance in the Statement of Changes in Owner's Equity and Balance Sheet columns. Step 4 deals with this imbalance.

Step 4—Enter the Net Income (or Loss) and Balance the Financial Statement Columns

To see the completed work sheet, turn the final transparent overlay to create Illustration 4–5. Step 4 begins by entering Net income and Totals on the next two lines in the account title column. Next, the accountant computes the net income by finding

---

[2]Auditors' work sheets cross-reference each adjustment to a detailed analysis and other supporting evidence.

the excess of the Income Statement Credit column total over the Debit column total. This amount is inserted on the net income line in the Debit column, and a new total is computed for each column. (If the initial total of the debits is greater than the initial total credits, the expenses exceed the revenues and the company has incurred a net loss. If so, the difference is entered in the Credit column instead of the Debit column.) The total debits and total credits in the Income Statement columns are now equal.

The accountant next enters the net income in the last Credit column of the work sheet. (If there is a net loss, it is entered in the last Debit column.) Notice that this entry causes the total debits in the last two columns to equal the total credits.

Even if all five pairs of columns balance, the work sheet may not be free of errors. For example, if the accountant incorrectly extends an asset account's balance to the Income Statement Debit column, the columns balance but net income is understated. Or, if an expense is extended to the Statement of Changes in Owner's Equity and Balance Sheet Debit column, the columns balance but the net income is overstated. Although these errors may not be immediately obvious, they are discovered when the accountant begins to actually prepare the financial statements. For example, it would be apparent that an asset does not belong on the income statement or that an expense does not belong on the balance sheet.

At this point, the work sheet is complete. If the accountant discovers new information or an error, the change can easily be included in the work sheet, especially if it is being prepared with a computer spreadsheet.

PREPARING ADJUSTING ENTRIES FROM THE WORK SHEET

Entering the adjustments in the Adjustments columns of a work sheet does not get these adjustments into the ledger accounts. Therefore, after completing the work sheet, adjusting entries like the ones described in Chapter 3 must be entered in the General Journal and posted to the accounts in the ledger. The work sheet makes this easy because its Adjustments columns provide the information for these entries. If adjusting entries are prepared from the information in Illustration 4–3, you will see that they are the same adjusting entries we discussed in the last chapter.

PREPARING FINANCIAL STATEMENTS FROM THE WORK SHEET

A work sheet is not a substitute for the financial statements. The work sheet is nothing more than a supporting tool that the accountant uses at the end of an accounting period to help organize the data. However, as soon as it is completed, the accountant uses the work sheet to prepare the financial statements.

The sequence is the same as we have seen before. The income statement is completed first. The net income is then combined with the owner's investments, withdrawals, and beginning capital balance on the statement of changes in owner's equity. In doing this, the accountant analyzes the owner's capital account to separate the beginning balance from any new investments made during the reporting period. Finally, the balance sheet is completed by using the ending balance of owner's equity from the statement of changes in owner's equity.

WHY USE A WORK SHEET?

At this point, it should be clear that we ended up with exactly the same financial statements and adjusting entries that we developed in Chapter 3 without using a work sheet. So, why prepare a work sheet?

First, the example in this chapter is greatly simplified. Real companies have many more adjusting entries and accounts than Clear Copy. A work sheet makes it easier to organize all the additional information. As we mentioned earlier in the chapter, auditors often use work sheets to plan and organize their work. In fact, they may request that a company provide a work sheet showing the adjustments made prior to the audit.

Illustration 4–1 Preparing the Work Sheet at the End of the Accounting Period

CLEAR COPY CO.
Work Sheet
For Month Ended December 31, 19X1

← The heading should identify the entity, the document, and the time period.

No.	Title	Unadjusted Trial Balance Dr.	Unadjusted Trial Balance Cr.	Adjustments Dr.	Adjustments Cr.	Adjusted Trial Balance Dr.	Adjusted Trial Balance Cr.	Income Statement Dr.	Income Statement Cr.	Statement of Changes in Owner's Equity and Balance Sheet Dr.	Statement of Changes in Owner's Equity and Balance Sheet Cr.

The work sheet can be prepared manually or with a computer spreadsheet program.

The worksheet collects and summarizes the information used to prepare financial statements, adjusting entries, and closing entries.

CLEAR COPY CO.
Income Statement
For Month Ended December 31, 19X1

Revenues:		
Copy services revenue		$5,950
Operating expenses:		
Depreciation expense, copy equipment	$ 375	
Salaries expense	1,610	
Insurance expense	100	
Rent expense	1,000	
Store supplies expense	1,050	
Utilities expense	230	
Total operating expenses		4,365
Net income		$1,585

CLEAR COPY CO.
Statement of Changes in Owner's Equity
For Month Ended December 31, 19X1

Terry Dow, Capital, November 30, 19X1		$ 0
Plus:		
Investments by owner	$30,000	
Net income	1,585	31,585
Total		$31,585
Less withdrawals by owner		400
Terry Dow, capital, December 31, 19X1		$31,185

CLEAR COPY CO.
Balance Sheet
December 31, 19X1

Assets

Cash		$ 7,950
Accounts receivable		1,800
Store supplies		2,670
Prepaid insurance		2,300
Copy equipment	$26,000	
Accumulated depreciation, copy equipment	(375)	25,625
Total assets		$40,345

Liabilities

Accounts payable		$ 6,200
Salaries payable		210
Unearned copy services revenue		2,750
Total liabilities		$ 9,160

Owner's Equity

Terry Dow, capital		31,185
Total liabilities and owner's equity		$40,345

Second, the work sheet can be used to prepare *interim* financial statements without recording the adjusting entries in the journal and ledger. Thus, a company can prepare statements each month or quarter and avoid taking the time to formally journalize and post the adjustments except once at the end of each year. All large companies with publically traded ownership prepare interim financial reports, usually on a quarterly basis. Some of them, such as **PepsiCo, Inc.,** also include summaries of the past year's quarterly data in their annual reports.

Also, companies may use a work sheet format to show the effects of proposed transactions. In doing this, they enter their adjusted financial statements amounts in the first two columns, arranging them to appear in the form of financial statements. Then, the proposed transactions are inserted in the second two columns. The extended amounts in the last columns show the effects of the proposed transactions on the financial statements. These final columns are called **pro forma statements,** because they show the statements as if the proposed transactions had already occurred.

ALTERNATE FORMATS OF THE WORK SHEET

Because the work sheet is an informal working paper, its format is not dictated by generally accepted accounting principles. For example, some accountants omit the Adjusted Trial Balance columns. Others use different work sheet columns to draft the *closing entries* described later in the chapter. Some work sheets have separate columns for the statement of changes in owner's equity and the balance sheet. The decision about which format is preferred rests with the accountant who creates the work sheet.

Progress Check
(Answers to Progress Checks are provided at the end of the chapter.)

4-1   On a work sheet, the $99,400 salaries expense balance was incorrectly extended from the Adjusted Trial Balance column to the Statement of Changes in Owner's Equity and Balance Sheet Debit column. As a result of this error: *(a)* The Adjusted Trial Balance columns will not balance; *(b)* Revenues on the work sheet will be understated; *(c)* Net income on the work sheet will be overstated.

4-2   Where does the accountant obtain the amounts entered in the Unadjusted Trial Balance columns of the work sheet?

4-3   What is the advantage of using a work sheet to prepare adjusting entries?

4-4   From a 10-column work sheet, the accountant prepares the financial statements in what order?

CLOSING ENTRIES

LO 2
Explain why the temporary accounts are closed at the end of each accounting period and prepare closing entries and a post-closing trial balance for a service business.

After the financial statements are completed and the adjusting entries are recorded, the next step in the accounting cycle is to journalize and post **closing entries.** Closing entries are designed to transfer the end-of-period balances in the revenue, expense, and withdrawals accounts to the owner's capital account. These entries are necessary because:

1. Revenues increase owner's equity, while expenses and withdrawals decrease owner's equity.

2. During an accounting period, these increases and decreases are temporarily accumulated in the revenue, expense, and withdrawals accounts rather than in the owner's capital account.

3. By transferring the effects of revenues, expenses, and withdrawals from the revenue, expense, and withdrawals accounts to the owner's capital account,

closing entries install the correct end-of-period balance in the owner's capital account.

4. Closing entries also cause the revenue, expense, and withdrawals accounts to begin each new accounting period with zero balances.

Remember that an income statement reports the revenues earned and expenses incurred during one accounting period and is prepared from information recorded in the revenue and expense accounts. Also, the statement of changes in owner's equity reports the changes in the owner's capital account during one period and uses the information accumulated in the withdrawals account. Because the revenue, expense, and withdrawals accounts accumulate information for only one period and then must be ready to do the same thing the next period, they must start each period with zero balances.

To close the revenue and expense accounts, the accountant transfers their balances first to a summary account called **Income Summary.** Then, the Income Summary balance, which is the net income or loss, is transferred to the owner's capital account. Finally, the accountant transfers the owner's withdrawals account balance to the owner's capital account. After the closing entries are posted, the revenue, expense, Income Summary, and withdrawals accounts have zero balances. Thus, these accounts are said to be closed or cleared.

Illustration 4–7 diagrams the four entries that close the revenue, expense, Income Summary, and withdrawals accounts of Clear Copy Co. on December 31, 19X1. The pre-closing balances of the accounts in the illustration are taken from the adjusted trial balance in Illustration 4–5.

Entry 1. The first closing entry transfers the credit balances in the revenue accounts to the Income Summary account. In general journal form, the entry is:

Dec.	31	Copy Services Revenue	5,950.00	
		Income Summary		5,950.00
		To close the revenue account and create the Income Summary account.		

Note that this entry closes the revenue account by giving it a zero balance. If the company had several different revenue accounts, this entry would be a compound entry that included a debit to each of them. This clearing of the accounts allows them to be used to record new revenues in the upcoming year.

The Income Summary account is created especially for the closing process and is used only during that process. The $5,950 credit balance in Income Summary equals the total revenues for the year.

Entry 2. The second closing entry transfers the debit balances in the expense accounts to the Income Summary account. This step concentrates all the expense account debit balances in the Income Summary account. It also closes each expense account by giving it a zero balance. That allows it to be used to record new expenses in the upcoming year. The second closing entry for Clear Copy is:

Dec.	31	Income Summary	4,365.00	
		Depreciation Expense, Copy Equipment		375.00
		Salaries Expense		1,610.00
		Insurance Expense		100.00
		Rent Expense		1,000.00
		Store Supplies Expense		1,050.00
		Utilities Expense		230.00
		To close the expense accounts.		

Illustration 4-7
Closing Entries for Clear
Copy Co.

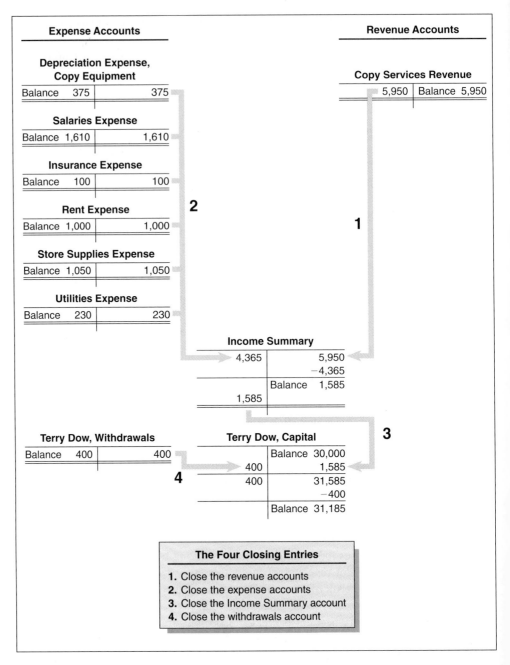

Illustration 4-7 shows that posting this entry gives each expense account a zero balance and prepares it to accept entries for expenses in 19X2. The entry also makes the balance of the Income Summary account equal to December's net income of $1,585. In effect, all the debit and credit balances of the expense and revenue accounts have now been concentrated in the Income Summary account.

Entry 3. The third closing entry transfers the balance of the Income Summary account to the owner's capital account. This entry closes the Income Summary account and adds the company's net income to the owner's capital account:

Dec.	31	Income Summary	1,585.00	
		Terry Dow, Capital		1,585.00
		To close the Income Summary account and add the net income to the capital account.		

After this entry is posted, the Income Summary account has a zero balance. It will continue to have a zero balance until the closing process occurs at the end of the next year. The owner's capital account has been increased by the amount of the net income, but still does not include the effects of the withdrawal that occurred in December.

Entry 4. The final closing entry transfers the debit balance of the withdrawals account to the capital account. This entry for Clear Copy is:

Dec.	31	Terry Dow, Capital	400.00	
		Terry Dow, Withdrawals		400.00
		To close the withdrawals account and reduce the balance		
		of the capital account.		

This entry gives the withdrawals account a zero balance, which allows it to accumulate the next year's payments to the owner. It also reduces the capital account balance to the $31,185 amount reported on the balance sheet.

SOURCES OF CLOSING ENTRY INFORMATION

The accountant can identify the accounts to be closed and the amounts to be used in the closing entries by referring to the individual revenue and expense accounts in the ledger. However, the work sheet provides this information in a more convenient format. To locate the information on the work sheet, look again at the income statement columns in Illustration 4–5. All accounts with balances in these columns are closed and the amounts in the work sheet are used in the closing entries. The balance of the owner's withdrawals account appears in the last debit column in the work sheet.

THE POST-CLOSING TRIAL BALANCE

The six-column table in Illustration 4–8 summarizes the effects of the closing process. The first two columns contain the adjusted trial balance from the work sheet, with two additional lines for the Income Summary account. The next two columns present the closing entries, numbered (1) through (4). The last two columns contain the **post-closing trial balance,** which lists the balances of the accounts that were not closed.[3] These accounts represent the company's assets, liabilities, and owner's equity as of the end of 19X1. These items and amounts are the same as those presented in the balance sheet in Illustration 4–6.

Instead of preparing the six-column table in Illustration 4–8, the post-closing trial balance is often prepared as a separate two-column table, as in Illustration 4–9. Regardless of the format, the post-closing trial balance is the last step in the annual accounting process.

Permanent (Real) Accounts and Temporary (Nominal) Accounts

Asset, liability, and owner's capital accounts are not closed as long as the company continues to own the assets, owe the liabilities, and have owner's equity. Because these accounts are not closed, they are called **permanent accounts** or **real accounts.** These accounts are permanent because they describe real conditions that are perceived to exist.

---

[3] Some accountants use work sheets that include these four columns instead of the financial statement columns. The financial statements are not changed by choosing one or the other.

Illustration 4–8   The Adjusted Trial Balance, Closing Entries, and Post-Closing Trial Balance for Clear Copy Co.

	Adjusted Trial Balance		Closing Entries		Post-Closing Trial Balance	
Cash	7,950				7,950	
Accounts receivable	1,800				1,800	
Store supplies	2,670				2,670	
Prepaid insurance	2,300				2,300	
Copy equipment	26,000				26,000	
Accumulated depreciation, copy equipment		375				375
Accounts payable		6,200				6,200
Salaries payable		210				210
Unearned copy services revenue		2,750				2,750
Terry Dow, capital		30,000	(4) 400	(3) 1,585		31,185
Terry Dow, withdrawals	400			(4) 400		
Copy services revenue		5,950	(1) 5,950			
Depreciation expense, copy equipment	375			(2) 375		
Salaries expense	1,610			(2) 1,610		
Insurance expense	100			(2) 100		
Rent expense	1,000			(2) 1,000		
Store supplies expense	1,050			(2) 1,050		
Utilities expense	230			(2) 230		
Income summary			(2) 4,365	(1) 5,950		
			(3) 1,585			
Totals	45,485	45,485	12,300	12,300	40,720	40,720

Illustration 4–9
Separate Post-Closing Trial Balance for Clear Copy Co.

Cash	$ 7,950	
Accounts receivable	1,800	
Store supplies	2,670	
Prepaid insurance	2,300	
Copy equipment	26,000	
Accumulated depreciation, copy equipment		$ 375
Accounts payable		6,200
Salaries payable		210
Unearned copy services revenue		2,750
Terry Dow, capital		31,185
Totals	$40,720	$40,720

In contrast, the terms **temporary accounts** and **nominal accounts** describe the revenue, expense, Income Summary, and withdrawals accounts. These terms are used because the accounts are opened at the beginning of the year, used to record events, and then closed at the end of the year. These accounts are temporary because they describe nominal events or changes that have occurred rather than real conditions that continue to exist.

Illustration 4–10   The Ledger for Clear Copy Co. as of December 31, 19X1 (after adjustments and closing entries have been posted)

Asset Accounts:

Cash   Acct. No. 101

Date		Expl.	Debit	Credit	Balance
19X1					
Dec.	1		30,000		30,000
	2			2,500	27,500
	3			20,000	7,500
	10		2,200		9,700
	12			1,000	8,700
	12			700	8,000
	22		1,700		9,700
	24			900	8,800
	24			400	8,400
	26		3,000		11,400
	26			2,400	9,000
	26			120	8,880
	26			230	8,650
	26			700	7,950

Store Supplies   Acct. No. 125

Date		Expl.	Debit	Credit	Balance
19X1					
Dec.	2		2,500		2,500
	6		1,100		3,600
	26		120		3,720
	31			1,050	2,670

Prepaid Insurance   Acct. No. 128

Date		Expl.	Debit	Credit	Balance
19X1					
Dec.	26		2,400		2,400
	31			100	2,300

Copy Equipment   Acct. No. 167

Date		Expl.	Debit	Credit	Balance
19X1					
Dec.	3		20,000		20,000
	6		6,000		26,000

Accounts Receivable   Acct. No. 106

Date		Expl.	Debit	Credit	Balance
19X1					
Dec.	12		1,700		1,700
	22			1,700	0
	31		1,800		1,800

Accumulated Depreciation, Copy Equipment   Acct. No. 168

Date		Expl.	Debit	Credit	Balance
19X1					
Dec.	31			375	375

Liability and Equity Accounts:

Accounts Payable   Acct. No. 201

Date		Expl.	Debit	Credit	Balance
19X1					
Dec.	6			7,100	7,100
	24		900		6,200

Terry Dow, Capital   Acct. No. 301

Date		Expl.	Debit	Credit	Balance
19X1					
Dec.	1			30,000	30,000
	31			1,585	31,585
	31		400		31,585

Salaries Payable   Acct. No. 209

Date		Expl.	Debit	Credit	Balance
19X1					
Dec.	31			210	210

Terry Dow, Withdrawals   Acct. No. 302

Date		Expl.	Debit	Credit	Balance
19X1					
Dec.	24		400		400
	31			400	0

Unearned Copy Services Revenue   Acct. No. 236

Date		Expl.	Debit	Credit	Balance
19X1					
Dec.	26			3,000	3,000
	31		250		2,750

Illustration 4–10   *(concluded)*

Revenue and Expense Accounts (including Income Summary):

Copy Services Revenue   **Acct. No.** 403

Date		Expl.	Debit	Credit	Balance
19X1					
Dec.	10			2,200	2,200
	12			1,700	3,900
	31			250	4,150
	31			1,800	5,950
	31		5,950		0

Depreciation Expense, Copy Equipment   **Acct. No.** 614

Date		Expl.	Debit	Credit	Balance
19X1					
Dec.	31		375		375
	31			375	0

Salaries Expense   **Acct. No.** 622

Date		Expl.	Debit	Credit	Balance
19X1					
Dec.	12		700		700
	26		700		1,400
	31		210		1,610
	31			1,610	0

Insurance Expense   **Acct. No.** 637

Date		Expl.	Debit	Credit	Balance
19X1					
Dec.	31		100		100
	31			100	0

Rent Expense   **Acct. No.** 641

Date		Expl.	Debit	Credit	Balance
19X1					
Dec.	12		1,000		1,000
	31			1,000	0

Store Supplies Expense   **Acct. No.** 651

Date		Expl.	Debit	Credit	Balance
19X1					
Dec.	31		1,050		1,050
	31			1,050	0

Utilities Expense   **Acct. No.** 690

Date		Expl.	Debit	Credit	Balance
19X1					
Dec.	26		230		230
	31			230	0

Income Summary   **Acct. No.** 901

Date		Expl.	Debit	Credit	Balance
19X1					
Dec.	31			5,950	5,950
	31		4,365		1,585
	31		1,585		0

THE LEDGER FOR CLEAR COPY CO.

To complete the Clear Copy example, look at Illustration 4–10, the company's entire ledger as of December 31, 19X1. Review the accounts and observe that the temporary accounts (the withdrawals account and all accounts with numbers greater than 400) have been closed.

CLOSING ENTRIES FOR CORPORATIONS

Up to this point, our examples of closing entries have related to the activities and accounts of single proprietorships. However, closing entries for corporations are very similar. The first two closing entries are exactly the same. In other words, a corporation's revenue and expense accounts are closed to the Income Summary account. The last two entries are different.

Recall from Chapter 3 that a corporation's balance sheet presents the stockholders' equity as contributed capital and retained earnings. As a result, the third closing entry for a corporation closes the Income Summary account to the Retained Earnings account. For example, **Dr Pepper/Seven-Up Companies, Inc.,** reported a net income of $77,925,000 in 1993, which means that was the credit balance in the Income Summary account after the revenue and expense accounts

were closed. The company's third closing entry would have updated the Retained Earnings account as follows:

Dec.	31	Income Summary	77,925,000.00	
		Retained Earnings		77,925,000.00
		To close the Income Summary account and		
		update Retained Earnings.		

The fourth closing entry is also different because corporations use a Dividends Declared account instead of a withdrawals account. The accounting practices for dividends paid to stockholders are described in Chapter 13.

Progress Check

4–5   When closing entries are prepared:
   a. **The accounts for expenses, revenues, and the owner's withdrawals are closed to the Income Summary account.**
   b. **The final balance of the Income Summary account equals net income or net loss for the period.**
   c. **All temporary accounts have zero balances when the process is completed.**

4–6   Why are revenue and expense accounts called temporary? Are there any other temporary accounts?

4–7   What accounts are listed on the post-closing trial balance?

4–8   What account is used by a corporation to close the Income Summary account?

Chapters 2, 3, and 4 have described the accounting procedures that are completed during each reporting period. They begin with recording external transactions in the journal and end with preparing the post-closing trial balance. Because these steps are repeated each period, they are often called the **accounting cycle.** In Illustration 4–11 a flow chart shows the steps in order. Steps 1 and 2 take place every day as the company engages in business transactions. The other steps are completed at the end of the accounting period. Review this illustration and the following list of the steps to be sure that you understand how each one helps accountants provide useful information in the financial statements:

A REVIEW OF THE ACCOUNTING CYCLE

LO 3
Describe each step in the accounting cycle.

Step	Description
1. **Journalizing**	Analyzing transactions and recording debits and credits in a journal.
2. **Posting**	Copying the debits and credits from the journal entries to the accounts in the ledger.
3. **Preparing an unadjusted trial balance**	Summarizing the ledger accounts and partially testing clerical accuracy. (If a work sheet is used, this is done on the work sheet.)
4. **Completing the work sheet (optional)**	Identifying the effects of adjustments on the financial statements before entering them in the ledger and posting them to the accounts; also drafting the adjusted trial balance, extending the adjusted amounts to the appropriate financial statement columns, and determining the size of the net income or net loss.
5. **Adjusting the accounts**	Identifying necessary adjustments to bring the account balances up to date; journalizing and posting entries to record the adjustments in the accounts. (If the work sheet is prepared, the information in the adjustments columns is used for the entries.)

6.	**Preparing the financial statements**	Using the information on the adjusted trial balance (or the work sheet) to prepare an income statement, a statement of changes in owner's equity, a balance sheet, and a statement of cash flows. (Techniques for preparing the cash flow statement are described in Chapter 16.)
7.	**Closing the temporary accounts**	Preparing journal entries to close the revenue, expense, and withdrawals accounts and to update the owner's capital (or retained earnings) account. These entries are posted to the ledger.
8.	**Preparing a post-closing trial balance**	Testing the clerical accuracy of the adjusting and closing procedures.

Illustration 4–11 also identifies an optional ninth step of making reversing entries at the beginning of the following period. These entries are described in Appendix B, which begins on page 168.

A Practical Point

Normally, accountants are not able to make all of the adjusting and closing entries on the last day of the fiscal year. Information about the economic events that require adjustments often is not available until after several days or even a few weeks. As a result, the adjusting and closing entries are recorded later but dated as of the last day of the year. This means the financial statements reflect what is known on the date that they are prepared instead of what was known on the financial statement date.

For example, a company might receive a utility bill on January 14 for costs incurred from December 1 through December 31. Upon receiving the bill, the company's accountant records the expense and the payable as of December 31. The income statement for December reflects the full expense and the December 31 balance sheet includes the payable, even though the exact amounts were not actually known on December 31.

Progress Check

4-9   The steps in the accounting cycle: *(a)* **Are concluded by preparing a post-closing trial balance;**   *(b)* **Are concluded by preparing a balance sheet;**   *(c)* **Begin with preparing the unadjusted trial balance.**

4-10   At what point in the accounting cycle is the work sheet prepared?

USING THE INFORMATION— THE PROFIT MARGIN

LO 4

Calculate the profit margin ratio and describe what it reveals about a company's performance.

By now, it should be clear that accountants go to great lengths to ensure that a company's financial statements reflect up-to-date information about its assets, liabilities, revenues, and expenses. A primary goal of this effort is to provide information that helps internal and external decision makers evaluate the results achieved in the reporting period. This includes evaluating management's success in generating profits. The information may suggest ways to achieve better results and also helps users predict future results.

In using accounting information to evaluate the results of operations, one widely used ratio relates the company's net income to its sales. The ratio is called the **profit margin** or the **return on sales,** and is calculated with this formula:

$$\text{Profit margin} = \frac{\text{Net income}}{\text{Revenues}}$$

In effect, this ratio measures the average portion of each dollar of revenue that ends up as profit.

Illustration 4–11   The Accounting Cycle

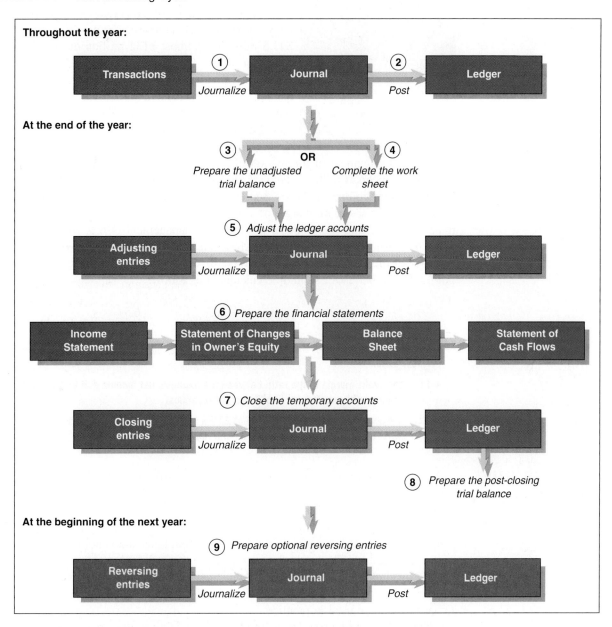

Recall from the beginning of the chapter the conversation between the chief financial officer of **Ben & Jerry's Homemade, Inc.,** and a Ben & Jerry's stockholder. The stockholder expressed a desire to learn more about the money side of the company. The company's profit margin is one measure the stockholder might use to evaluate the company's performance. The profit margins during several past years are as follows:

(In thousands)	Year Ended				
	12/26/92	**12/28/91**	**12/29/90**	**12/30/89**	**12/31/88**
Net income	$ 6,675	$ 3,739	$ 2,609	$ 2,053	$ 1,618
Net sales	131,969	96,997	77,024	58,464	47,561
Profit margin	5.1%	3.9%	3.4%	3.5%	3.4%

Note the positive trend in the company's profit margin. This appears even more favorable because the company's sales volume increased from a little more than $47.5 million to almost $132 million during the same period of time.

Although the trend in Ben & Jerry's profit margin is good, you cannot say that the absolute values are good without making comparisons to other companies. In fact, Ben & Jerry's is a relatively small competitor in the super-premium ice cream industry. As a result of selling in this segment of the market, the company's profit margins are higher than those of producers with more standard products. However, the competition from larger super-premium companies keeps Ben & Jerry's from enjoying a higher margin.

In evaluating the profit margin of a sole proprietorship, you should modify the formula by subtracting the value of the owner's management efforts from the net income. For example, assume that the efforts of Terry Dow, the owner of Clear Copy Co., are worth $1,200 per month. Based on this assumption, the company's profit margin for December 19X1 should be calculated as follows:

$$\text{Profit margin} = \frac{\$1,585 - \$1,200}{\$5950} = 6.5\%$$

Progress Check

4-11   The profit margin is the ratio between a company's net income and total: (a) expenses; (b) assets; (c) liabilities; (d) revenues.

4-12   If a company had a profit margin of 22.5% and net income of $1,012,500, what was the total amount of its revenues for the reporting period?

SUMMARY OF THE CHAPTER IN TERMS OF LEARNING OBJECTIVES

LO 1. Explain why work sheets are useful, prepare a work sheet for a service business, and prepare financial statements from the information in a work sheet. Accountants often use work sheets at the end of an accounting period in the process of preparing adjusting entries, the adjusted trial balance, and the financial statements. The work sheet is only a tool for accountants and is not distributed to investors or creditors. The work sheet described in this chapter has five pairs of columns for the unadjusted trial balance, the adjustments, the adjusted trial balance, the income statement, and the statement of changes in owner's equity and the balance sheet. Other formats are used in practice.

The income statement is prepared from the Income Statement columns of the work sheet by taking the revenues from the Credit column and the expenses from the Debit column. The net income is the difference between the debits and credits. The statement of changes in owner's equity combines the pre-closing balance of the capital account (including the beginning balance plus any new investments), the net income from the Income Statement columns, and the owner's withdrawals. The balance sheet combines all assets, contra assets, and liabilities from the last two columns of the work sheet with the ending balance of owner's equity presented in the statement of changes in owner's equity.

LO 2. Explain why the temporary accounts are closed at the end of each accounting period and prepare closing entries and a post-closing trial balance for a service business. The temporary accounts are closed at the end of each accounting period for two reasons. First, this process updates the owner's equity account to include the effects of all economic events recorded for the year. Second, it prepares the revenue, expense, and withdrawals accounts for the next reporting period by giving them zero balances. The revenue and expense account balances are initially transferred to the Income Summary account, which is then closed to the owner's capital account. Finally, the withdrawals account is closed to the capital account.

LO 3. Describe each step in the accounting cycle. The accounting cycle consists of eight steps: (1) journalizing external transactions and (2) posting the entries during the year, and, at the end of the year: (3) preparing either an unadjusted trial balance or (4) a work sheet, (5) preparing and posting adjusting entries, (6) preparing the financial statements, (7) preparing and posting closing entries, and (8) preparing the post-closing trial balance.

LO 4. Calculate the profit margin ratio and describe what it reveals about a company's performance. The profit margin ratio describes a company's income earning activities by showing the period's net income as a percentage of total revenue. It is found by dividing the reporting period's net income by the revenue for the same period. The ratio can be usefully interpreted only in light of additional facts about the company and its industry.

This six-column table shows the December 31, 19X1, adjusted trial balance of Westside Appliance Repair Company:

DEMONSTRATION PROBLEM

	Adjusted Trial Balance		Closing Entries		Post-Closing Trial Balance	
Cash	83,300					
Notes receivable	60,000					
Prepaid insurance	19,000					
Prepaid rent	5,000					
Equipment	165,000					
Accumulated depreciation, equipment .		52,000				
Accounts payable		37,000				
Long-term notes payable		58,000				
B. Westside, capital		173,500				
B. Westside, withdrawals	25,000					
Repair services revenue		294,000				
Interest earned		6,500				
Depreciation expense, equipment	26,000					
Wages expense	179,000					
Rent expense	47,000					
Insurance expense	7,000					
Interest expense	4,700					
Income summary						
Totals	621,000	621,000				

The beginning balance of the capital account was $140,500, and the owner invested $33,000 cash in the company on June 15, 19X1.

Required

1. Prepare closing entries for Westside Appliance Repair Co.
2. Complete the six-column schedule.
3. Post the closing entries to this capital account:

B. Westside, Capital   **Account No. 301**

Date	Explanation	Debit	Credit	Balance
19X1				
Jan. 1	Beginning balance			140,500.00
June 15	New investment		33,000.00	173,500.00

Planning the Solution

- Prepare entries to close the revenue accounts to Income Summary, to close the expense accounts to Income Summary, to close Income Summary to the capital account, and to close the withdrawals account to the capital account.

- Enter the four closing entries in the second pair of columns in the six-column schedule, and then extend the balances of the asset and liability accounts to the third pair of columns.

- Enter the post-closing balance of the capital account in the last column. Examine the totals of the columns to verify that they are equal.

- Post the third and fourth closing entries to the capital account.

Solution to Demonstration Problem

1.

Dec.	31	Repair Services Revenue	294,000.00	
		Interest Earned	6,500.00	
		Income Summary		300,500.00
		To close the revenue accounts and create the		
		Income Summary account.		
	31	Income Summary	263,700.00	
		Depreciation Expense, Equipment.		26,000.00
		Wages Expense		179,000.00
		Rent Expense		47,000.00
		Insurance Expense.		7,000.00
		Interest Expense		4,700.00
		To close the expense accounts.		
	31	Income Summary	36,800.00	
		B. Westside, Capital.		36,800.00
		To close the Income Summary account and add		
		the net income to the capital account.		
	31	B. Westside, Capital	25,000.00	
		B. Westside, Withdrawals		25,000.00
		To close the withdrawals account and reduce the		
		balance of the capital account.		

2.

	Adjusted Trial Balance		Closing Entries		Post-Closing Trial Balance	
Cash	83,300				83,300	
Notes receivable	60,000				60,000	
Prepaid insurance	19,000				19,000	
Prepaid rent	5,000				5,000	
Equipment	165,000				165,000	
Accumulated depreciation, equipment .		52,000				52,000
Accounts payable		37,000				37,000
Long-term notes payable		58,000				58,000
B. Westside, capital		173,500	(4) 25,000	(3) 36,800		185,300
B. Westside, withdrawals	25,000			(4) 25,000		
Repair services revenue		294,000	(1) 294,000			
Interest earned		6,500	(1) 6,500			
Depreciation expense, equipment	26,000			(2) 26,000		
Wages expense	179,000			(2) 179,000		
Rent expense	47,000			(2) 47,000		
Insurance expense	7,000			(2) 7,000		
Interest expense	4,700			(2) 4,700		
Income summary			(2) 263,700	(1) 300,500		
			(3) 36,800			
Totals	621,000	621,000	626,000	626,000	332,300	332,300

3.

B. Westside, Capital   **Account No.** 301

Date		Explanation	Debit	Credit	Balance
19X1					
Jan.	1	Beginning balance			140,500.00
June	15	New investment		33,000.00	173,500.00
Dec.	31	Net income		36,800.00	210,300.00
	31	Withdrawals	25,000.00		185,300.00

Reversing Entries

Reversing entries are optional entries that relate to accrued assets and liabilities created by adjusting entries at the end of a reporting period. Reversing entries are used for the practical purpose of simplifying a company's bookkeeping process.

Illustration B–1 shows how reversing entries work. The top of the diagram shows the adjusting entry that Clear Copy Co. recorded on December 31, 19X1, for the employee's earned but unpaid salary. The entry recorded three days' salary to increase December's total salary expense to $1,610. The entry also recognized a liability of $210. The expense is reported on December's income statement and the expense account is closed. As a result, the ledger on January 1, 19X2, reflects a $210 liability and a zero balance in the Salaries Expense account. At this point, the choice is made between using or not using reversing entries.

BOOKKEEPING WITHOUT REVERSING ENTRIES

The path down the left side of Illustration B–1 was described in Chapter 3. When the next payday occurs on January 9, the bookkeeper records the payment with a compound entry that debits both the expense and liability accounts. Posting the entry creates a $490 balance in the expense account and reduces the liability account balance to zero because the debt has been settled.

The disadvantage of this approach is the complex entry on January 9. Paying the accrued liability causes the entry to differ from the routine entries made on all other paydays. To construct the proper entry on January 9, the bookkeeper must be informed of the effect of the adjusting entry. Reversing entries overcome this disadvantage.

BOOKKEEPING WITH REVERSING ENTRIES

The right side of Illustration B–1 shows how a reversing entry on January 1 overcomes the disadvantage of the complex January 9 entry. The reversing entry is the exact opposite of the adjusting entry recorded on December 31. In other words, the Salaries Payable liability is debited for $210, with the result that the account has a zero balance after the entry is posted. Technically, the Salaries Payable account now understates the liability, but no problem exists because financial statements will not be prepared before the liability is settled on January 9.

The credit to the Salaries Expense account is unusual because it gives the account an *abnormal credit balance*. This account's balance is also temporary and does not cause a problem because financial statements will not be prepared before January 9.

As a result of the reversing entry, the January 9 entry to record the payment is simple. Notice that it debits the Salaries Expense account for the full $700 paid. This entry is the same as all other entries made to record 10 days' salary for the employee.

Look next at the accounts on the lower right side of Illustration B–1. After the payment entry is posted, the Salaries Expense account has the $490 balance that it should have to reflect seven days' salary of $70 per day. The zero balance in the Salaries Payable account is now correct. Then, the lower section of the illustration shows that the expense and liability accounts have exactly the same balances whether reversing occurs or not.

As a general rule, adjusting entries that create new asset or new liability accounts are the best candidates for reversing.

Illustration B–1 Reversing Entries for Accrued Expenses

Accrue salaries expense on December 31, 19X1

Salaries Expense ———————— 210
  Salaries Payable ———————— 210

Salaries Expense

Date	Expl.	Debit	Credit	Balance
19X1				
Dec. 12	(7)	700		700
26	(16)	700		1,400
31	(e)	210		1,610

Salaries Payable

Date	Expl.	Debit	Credit	Balance
19X1				
Dec. 31	(e)		210	210

No reversing entry recorded on January 1, 19X2

NO ENTRY

Salaries Expense

Date	Expl.	Debit	Credit	Balance
19X2				

Salaries Payable

Date	Expl.	Debit	Credit	Balance
19X1				
Dec. 31	(e)		210	210
19X2				

Reversing entry recorded on January 1, 19X2

Salaries Payable ———————— 210
  Salaries Expense ———————— 210

Salaries Expense

Date	Expl.	Debit	Credit	Balance
19X2				
Jan. 1			210	(210)

Salaries Payable

Date	Expl.	Debit	Credit	Balance
19X1				
Dec. 31	(e)		210	210
19X2				
Jan. 1		210		0

Pay the accrued and current salaries on January 9, the first payday in 19X2

Salaries Expense ———————— 490
Salaries Payable ———————— 210
  Cash ———————— 700

Salaries Expense

Date	Expl.	Debit	Credit	Balance
19X2				
Jan. 9		490		490

Salaries Payable

Date	Expl.	Debit	Credit	Balance
19X1				
Dec. 31	(e)		210	210
19X2				
Jan. 9		210		0

Salaries Expense ———————— 700
  Cash ———————— 700

Salaries Expense

Date	Expl.	Debit	Credit	Balance
19X2				
Jan. 1			210	(210)
9		700		490

Salaries Payable

Date	Expl.	Debit	Credit	Balance
19X1				
Dec. 31	(e)		210	210
19X2				
Jan. 1		210		0

Under both approaches, the expense and liability accounts have the same balances after the subsequent payment on January 9:

Salaries Expense ———————— $ 490
Salaries Payable ———————— $ 0

SUMMARY OF APPENDIX B IN TERMS OF LEARNING OBJECTIVE

LO 6. Explain when and why reversing entries are used and prepare reversing entries. Optional reversing entries can be applied to accrued assets and liabilities, including accrued interest earned, accrued interest expense, accrued taxes, and accrued salaries or wages. The goal of reversing entries is to simplify subsequent journal entries. The financial statements are not affected by the choice. Reversing entries are used simply as a matter of convenience in bookkeeping.

GLOSSARY

Accounting cycle eight recurring steps performed each accounting period, starting with recording transactions in the journal and continuing through the post-closing trial balance. p. 161

Closing entries journal entries recorded at the end of each accounting period to prepare the revenue, expense, and withdrawals accounts for the upcoming year and update the owner's capital account for the events of the year just finished. p. 154

Income Summary the special account used only in the closing process to temporarily hold the amounts of revenues and expenses before the net difference is added to (or subtracted from) the owner's capital account or the Retained Earnings account for a corporation. p. 155

Nominal accounts another name for *temporary accounts*. p. 158

Permanent accounts accounts that are used to describe assets, liabilities, and owner's equity; they are not closed as long as the company continues to own the assets, owe the liabilities, or have owner's equity; the balances of these accounts appear on the balance sheet. p. 157

Post-closing trial balance a trial balance prepared after the closing entries have been posted; the final step in the accounting cycle. p. 157

Profit margin the ratio of a company's net income to its revenues; measures the average proportion of each dollar of revenue that ends up as profit. p. 162

Pro forma statements statements that show the effects of the proposed transactions as if the transactions had already occurred. p. 154

Real accounts another name for *permanent accounts*. p. 157

Return on sales another name for *profit margin*. p. 162

Reversing entries optional entries recorded at the beginning of a new year that prepare the accounts for simplified journal entries subsequent to accrual adjusting entries. p. 168

Temporary accounts accounts that are used to describe revenues, expenses, and owner's withdrawals; they are closed at the end of the reporting period. p. 158

Work sheet a 10-column spreadsheet used to draft a company's unadjusted trial balance, adjusting entries, adjusted trial balance, and financial statements; an optional step in the accounting process. p. 150

Working papers analyses and other informal reports prepared by accountants when organizing the useful information presented in formal reports to internal and external decision makers. p. 150

The letter B identifies the questions, quick studies, exercises, and problems based on Appendix B at the end of the chapter.

QUESTIONS FOR CLASS DISCUSSION

1. What tasks are performed with the work sheet?
2. Why are the debit and credit entries in the Adjustments columns of the work sheet identified with letters?
3. What internal document is produced by combining the amounts in the Unadjusted Trial Balance columns with the amounts in the Adjustments columns of the work sheet?
4. What two purposes are accomplished by recording closing entries?
5. What are the four closing entries?
6. What accounts are affected by closing entries? What accounts are not affected?
7. Describe the similarities and differences between adjusting and closing entries.
8. What is the purpose of the Income Summary account?
9. Explain whether an error has occurred if a post-closing trial balance includes a Depreciation expense, building account.
10. Refer to the balance sheet for Federal Express Corporation in Appendix G at the end of the book. Assume that during 1992 Federal Express correctly recorded payments for all of the accrued expenses (liabilities) that were outstanding at the end of 1991. What amount of

accrued expenses was recorded in the process of preparing adjustments at the end of 1992?

11. Refer to the financial statements of Ben & Jerry's Homemade, Inc., in Appendix G at the end of the book. What journal entry was recorded as of December 26, 1992, to close the company's Income Summary account?

B12. How are the financial statements of a company affected by the accountant's choice to use or not use reversing entries?

B13. How do reversing entries simplify a company's bookkeeping efforts?

B14. If a company accrued unpaid salaries expense of $500 at the end of a fiscal year, what reversing entry could be made? When would it be made?

QUICK STUDY (Five-Minute Exercises)

In preparing a work sheet, indicate the financial statement debit column to which a normal balance of each of the following accounts should be extended. Use IS for the Income Statement Debit column and BS for the Statement of Changes in Owner's Equity or Balance Sheet Debit column.

QS 4–1
(LO 1)

1. Accounts receivable
2. Owner, withdrawals
3. Prepaid insurance
4. Insurance expense
5. Equipment
6. Depreciation expense, equipment

The following information is from the work sheet for Pursley Company as of December 31, 19X1. Using this information, determine the amount that should be reported for A. Pursley, capital on the December 31, 19X1, balance sheet.

QS 4–2
(LO 1)

	Income Statement		Statement of Changes in Owner's Equity and Balance Sheet	
	Dr.	Cr.	Dr.	Cr.
A. Pursley, capital				50,000
A. Pursley, withdrawals			32,000	
Totals	125,000	184,000		

Using the information presented in QS 4–2, prepare the entries to close the Income Summary and the withdrawals accounts.

QS 4–3
(LO 2)

List the following steps of the accounting cycle in the proper order:

QS 4–4
(LO 3)

a. Preparing the post-closing trial balance.
b. Journalizing and posting adjusting entries.
c. Preparing the unadjusted trial balance.
d. Journalizing and posting closing entries.
e. Journalizing transactions.
f. Posting the transaction entries.
g. Preparing the financial statements.
h. Completing the work sheet.

Gruene Corporation had net income of $75,850 and revenue of $410,000 for the year ended December 31, 19Xl. Calculate Gruene's profit margin.

QS 4–5
(LO 4)

On December 31, 19Xl, Ace Management Co. prepared an adjusting entry for $9,800 of earned but unrecorded rent revenue. On January 20, 19X2, Ace received rent payments in the amount of $15,500. Assuming Ace uses reversing entries, prepare the 19X2 entries pertaining to the rent transactions.

BQS 4–6
(LO 6)

EXERCISES

Exercise 4–1
Extending adjusted account
balances on a work sheet
(LO 1)

These accounts are from the Adjusted Trial Balance columns in a company's 10-column work sheet. In the blank space beside each account, write the letter of the appropriate financial statement column to which a normal account balance should be extended.

A. Debit column for the income statement

B. Credit column for the income statement

C. Debit column for the statement of changes in owner's equity and balance sheet

D. Credit column for the statement of changes in owner's equity and balance sheet

___ 1. R. Jefferson, Withdrawals	___ 9. Cash
___ 2. Interest Earned	___ 10. Office Supplies
___ 3. Accumulated Depreciation, Machinery	___ 11. R. Jefferson, Capital
___ 4. Service Fees Revenue	___ 12. Wages Payable
___ 5. Accounts Receivable	___ 13. Machinery
___ 6. Rent Expense	___ 14. Insurance Expense
___ 7. Depreciation Expense, Machinery	___ 15. Interest Expense
___ 8. Accounts Payable	___ 16. Interest Receivable

Exercise 4–2
Preparing adjusting entries from
work sheet information
(LO 1)

Use the following information from the Adjustments columns of a 10-column work sheet to prepare adjusting journal entries:

		Adjustments	
No.	**Title**	**Debit**	**Credit**
109	Interest receivable	(d) 380	
124	Office supplies		(b) 1,350
128	Prepaid insurance		(a) 1,000
164	Accumulated depreciation, office equipment ..		(c) 3,500
209	Salaries payable		(e) 660
409	Interest earned		(d) 380
612	Depreciation expense, office equipment	(c) 3,500	
620	Office salaries expense	(e) 660	
636	Insurance expense, office equipment	(a) 432	
637	Insurance expense, store equipment	(a) 568	
650	Office supplies expense	(b) 1,350	
	Totals	6,890	6,890

Exercise 4–3
Preparing a work sheet
(LO 1)

The following unadjusted trial balance contains the accounts and balances of the Fine Painting Co. as of December 31, 19X1, the end of its fiscal year:

No.	Title	Debit	Credit
101	Cash	$18,000	
126	Supplies	12,000	
128	Prepaid insurance	2,000	
167	Equipment	23,000	
168	Accumulated depreciation, equipment ..		$ 6,500
209	Salaries payable		
301	B. Fine, capital		31,900
302	B. Fine, withdrawals	6,000	
404	Services revenue		36,000
612	Depreciation expense, equipment		
622	Salaries expense	11,000	
637	Insurance expense		
640	Rent expense	2,400	
652	Supplies expense		
	Totals	$74,400	$74,400

Required

Use the following information about the company's adjustments to complete a 10-column work sheet for the company:

a. The cost of expired insurance coverage was $300.

b. The cost of unused supplies on hand at the end of the year was $1,600.

c. Depreciation of the equipment for the year was $3,250.

d. Earned but unpaid salaries at the end of the year were $250.

Use the information in Exercise 4–3 to prepare adjusting and closing journal entries for Fine Painting Co. (It is helpful but not mandatory to solve Exercise 4–3 first.)

Exercise 4–4
Adjusting and closing entries
(LO 2)

These partially completed Income Statement columns from a 10-column work sheet are for the Winston Sail'em Boat Rental Company. Use the information to determine the amount that should be entered on the Net income line of the work sheet. In addition, draft closing entries for the company. The owner's name is C. Winston, and the pre-closing balance of the withdrawals account is $18,000.

Exercise 4–5
Completing the income statement columns and preparing closing entries
(LO 1, 2)

	Debit	Credit
Rent earned		99,000
Salaries expense	35,300	
Insurance expense	4,400	
Dock rental expense	12,000	
Boat supplies expense	6,220	
Depreciation expense, boats	21,500	
Totals		
Net income		
Totals		

The Adjusted Trial Balance columns of a 10-column work sheet for the Plummer Plumbing Co. follow. Complete the work sheet by extending the account balances into the appropriate financial statement columns and by entering the amount of net income for the reporting period.

Exercise 4–6
Extending accounts in the work sheet
(LO 1)

No.	Title	Adjusted Trial Balance	
101	Cash	$ 8,200	
106	Accounts receivable	24,000	
153	Trucks	41,000	
154	Accumulated depreciation, trucks		$ 16,500
193	Franchise	30,000	
201	Accounts payable		14,000
209	Salaries payable		3,200
233	Unearned fees		2,600
301	F. Plummer, capital		64,500
302	F. Plummer, withdrawals	14,400	
401	Plumbing fees earned		79,000
611	Depreciation expense, trucks	11,000	
622	Salaries expense	31,500	
640	Rent expense	12,000	
677	Miscellaneous expenses	7,700	
	Totals	$179,800	$179,800
	Net income		
	Totals		

The adjusted trial balance for Plummer Plumbing Co. follows. Prepare a table with two columns under each of the following headings: Adjusted Trial Balance, Closing Entries, and Post-Closing Trial Balance. Complete the table by providing four closing entries and the post-closing trial balance.

Exercise 4–7
Preparing closing entries and the post-closing trial balance
(LO 2)

No.	Title	Adjusted Trial Balance	
101	Cash	$ 8,200	
106	Accounts receivable	24,000	
153	Trucks	41,000	
154	Accumulated depreciation, trucks		$ 16,500
193	Franchise	30,000	
201	Accounts payable		14,000
209	Salaries payable		3,200
233	Unearned fees		2,600
301	F. Plummer, capital		64,500
302	F. Plummer, withdrawals	14,400	
401	Plumbing fees earned		79,000
611	Depreciation expense, trucks	11,000	
622	Salaries expense	31,500	
640	Rent expense	12,000	
677	Miscellaneous expenses	7,700	
901	Income summary		
	Totals	$179,800	$179,800

Exercise 4–8
Closing entries for a corporation
(LO 2)

The following balances of the retained earnings and temporary accounts are for High Ridge, Inc., from its adjusted trial balance:

	Debit	Credit
Retained earnings		$43,200
Services revenue		62,000
Interest earned		5,800
Salaries expense	$23,500	
Insurance expense	4,050	
Rental expense	6,400	
Supplies expense	3,100	
Depreciation expense, trucks	10,600	

Required

a. Prepare the closing entries for this corporation.

b. Determine the amount of retained earnings to be reported on the company's balance sheet.

Exercise 4–9
Preparing and posting closing entries
(LO 2, 3)

Open the following T-accounts with the provided balances. Prepare closing journal entries and post them to the accounts.

B. Holley, Capital				Rent Expense	
	Dec. 31	44,000	Dec. 31	9,600	

B. Holley, Withdrawals				Salaries Expense	
Dec. 31	21,000		Dec. 31	24,000	

Income Summary			Insurance Expense	
		Dec. 31	3,500	

Services Revenue				Depreciation Expense	
	Dec. 31	77,000	Dec. 31	15,000	

Use the following information to calculate the profit margin for each case:

	Net Income	Revenue
a.	$ 1,745	$ 10,540
b.	48,372	131,651
c.	55,102	84,262
d.	27,513	450,266
e.	39,632	144,638

Exercise 4–10
Calculating the profit margin
(LO 4)

The following information was used to prepare adjusting entries for the Monterey Company as of August 31, the end of the company's fiscal year:

a. The company has earned $3,000 of unrecorded service fees.

b. The expired portion of prepaid insurance is $2,400.

c. The earned portion of the Unearned Fees account balance is $1,700.

d. Depreciation expense for the office equipment is $3,300.

e. Employees have earned but have not been paid salaries of $2,250.

Required

Prepare the reversing entries that would simplify the bookkeeping effort for recording subsequent events related to these adjustments.

^B**Exercise 4–11**
Reversing entries
(LO 6)

The following two conditions existed for Lomax Company on September 30, 19X1, the end of its fiscal year:

a. Lomax rents a building from its owner for $2,400 per month. By a prearrangement, the company delayed paying September's rent until October 5. On this date, the company paid the rent for both September and October.

b. Lomax rents space in a building it owns to a tenant for $655 per month. By prearrangement, the tenant delayed paying the September rent until October 8. On this date, the tenant paid the rent for both September and October.

^B**Exercise 4–12**
Reversing entries
(LO 6)

Required

1. Prepare the adjusting entries that Lomax should record for these situations as of September 30.

2. Assuming that Lomax does not use reversing entries, prepare journal entries to record Lomax's payment of rent on October 5 and the collection of rent on October 8 from Lomax's tenant.

3. Assuming that Lomax does use reversing entries, prepare those entries and the journal entries to record Lomax's payment of rent on October 5 and the collection of rent on October 8 from Lomax's tenant.

PROBLEMS

Problem 4–1
The work sheet, adjusting and closing entries, financial statements, and profit margin
(LO 1, 2, 4)

Dunagin's Repairs opened for business on January 1, 19X1. By the end of the year, the company's unadjusted trial balance appeared as follows:

DUNAGIN'S REPAIRS
Unadjusted Trial Balance
December 31, 19X1

No.	Title	Debit	Credit
101	Cash	$ 3,000	
124	Office supplies	3,800	
128	Prepaid insurance	2,650	
167	Equipment	48,000	
168	Accumulated depreciation, equipment		
201	Accounts payable		$ 12,000
210	Wages payable		
301	R. Dunagin, capital		30,000
302	R. Dunagin, withdrawals	15,000	
401	Repair fees earned		77,750
612	Depreciation expense, equipment		
623	Wages expense	36,000	
637	Insurance expense		
640	Rent expense	9,600	
650	Office supplies expense		
690	Utilities expense	1,700	
	Totals	$119,750	$119,750

Required

Preparation component:

1. Enter the unadjusted trial balance on a 10-column work sheet and complete the work sheet using this information:
   a. An inventory of the office supplies at the end of the year showed that $700 of supplies were on hand.
   b. The cost of expired insurance coverage was $660.
   c. The year's depreciation on the equipment was $4,000.
   d. The earned but unpaid wages at the end of the year were $500.

CHECK FIGURE:
Ending capital balance, $37,190

2. Present the adjusting entries and closing entries as they would appear in the journal.

3. Use the information in the work sheet to prepare an income statement, a statement of changes in owner's equity, and a classified balance sheet.

4. Determine the company's profit margin.

Analysis component:

5. Assume that the facts presented in requirement 1 differ as follows:
   a. None of the $2,650 prepaid insurance had expired.
   b. There were no earned but unpaid wages at the end of the year.
   Describe the changes in the financial statements that would result from these assumptions.

Problem 4–2
Work sheet, journal entries, financial statements, and profit margin
(LO 1, 2, 4)

This unadjusted trial balance is for Blue Mesa Construction as of the end of its fiscal year. The beginning balance of the owner's capital account was $12,660 and the owner invested another $15,000 cash in the company during the year.

BLUE MESA CONSTRUCTION
Unadjusted Trial Balance
September 30, 19X2

No.	Title	Debit	Credit
101	Cash	$ 18,000	
126	Supplies	9,400	
128	Prepaid insurance	6,200	
167	Equipment	81,000	
168	Accumulated depreciation, equipment		$ 20,250
201	Accounts payable		4,800
203	Interest payable		
208	Rent payable		
210	Wages payable		
213	Estimated property taxes payable		
251	Long-term notes payable		25,000
301	T. Morrison, capital		27,660
302	T. Morrison, withdrawals	36,000	
401	Construction fees earned		140,000
612	Depreciation expense, equipment		
623	Wages expense	41,000	
633	Interest expense	1,500	
637	Insurance expense		
640	Rent expense	13,200	
652	Supplies expense		
683	Property taxes expense	5,000	
684	Repairs expense	2,510	
690	Utilities expense	3,900	
	Totals	$217,710	$217,710

Required

Preparation component:

1. Prepare a 10-column work sheet for 19X2, starting with the unadjusted trial balance and including these additional facts:

   a. The inventory of supplies at the end of the year had a cost of $2,500.

   b. The cost of expired insurance for the year is $4,000.

   c. Annual depreciation on the equipment is $9,000.

   d. The September utilities expense was not included in the trial balance because the bill arrived after it was prepared. Its $400 amount needs to be recorded.

   e. The company's employees have earned $1,500 of accrued wages.

   f. The lease for the office requires the company to pay total rent for the year equal to 10% of the company's annual revenues. The rent is paid to the building owner with monthly payments of $1,100. If the annual rent exceeds the total monthly payments, the company must pay the excess before October 31. If the total is less than the amount previously paid, the building owner will refund the difference by October 31.

   g. Additional property taxes of $800 have been assessed on the equipment but have not been paid or recorded in the accounts.

   h. The long-term note payable bears interest at 1% per month, which the company is required to pay by the 10th of the following month. The balance of the Interest Expense account equals the amount paid during the year. The interest for September has not yet been paid or recorded. In addition, the company is required to make a $5,000 payment on the note on November 30, 19X2.

   CHECK FIGURE:
   Total assets, $74,450

2. Use the work sheet to prepare the adjusting and closing entries.

3. Prepare an income statement, a statement of changes in owner's equity, and a classified balance sheet. Calculate the company's profit margin for the year.

Analysis component:

4. Analyze the following independent errors and describe how each would affect the 10-column work sheet. Explain whether the error is likely to be discovered in completing the work sheet and, if not, the effect of the error on the financial statements.

    a. The adjustment for supplies consumption credited Supplies for $2,500 and debited the same amount to Supplies Expense.

    b. When completing the adjusted trial balance in the work sheet, the $18,000 cash balance was incorrectly entered in the Credit column.

Problem 4–3
Closing entries, financial
statements, ratios
(LO 1, 2, 4)

The adjusted trial balance for the Kessler Company as of December 31, 19X1, follows:

KESSLER COMPANY
Adjusted Trial Balance
December 31, 19X1

No.	Title	Debit	Credit
101	Cash	$ 14,000	
104	Short-term investments	16,000	
126	Supplies	6,100	
128	Prepaid insurance	3,000	
167	Equipment	40,000	
168	Accumulated depreciation, equipment ..		$ 15,000
173	Building	115,000	
174	Accumulated depreciation, building ...		35,000
183	Land	45,000	
201	Accounts payable		15,500
203	Interest payable		1,500
208	Rent payable		2,500
210	Wages payable		500
213	Estimated property taxes payable		800
233	Unearned professional fees		6,500
251	Long-term notes payable		66,000
301	H. Kessler, capital		86,700
302	H. Kessler, withdrawals	30,000	
401	Professional fees earned		112,000
406	Rent earned		12,000
407	Dividends earned		2,900
409	Interest earned		1,000
606	Depreciation expense, building	10,000	
612	Depreciation expense, equipment	5,000	
623	Wages expense	28,000	
633	Interest expense	4,100	
637	Insurance expense	9,000	
640	Rent expense	2,400	
652	Supplies expense	6,400	
682	Postage expense	3,200	
683	Property taxes expense	8,000	
684	Repairs expense	7,900	
688	Telephone expense	1,200	
690	Utilities expense	3,600	
	Totals	$357,900	$357,900

An analysis of other information reveals that the company is required to make a $3,900 payment on the long-term note payable during 19X2. Also, the owner invested $20,000 cash early in the year.

Required

1. Present the income statement, statement of changes in owner's equity, and balance sheet.

2. Present the four closing entries made at the end of the year.

3. Use the information in the financial statements to calculate these ratios:

   a. Return on equity (assuming the owner is not actively involved in managing the company).

   b. Modified return on equity assuming the owner's efforts are valued at $25,000 for the year.

   c. Debt ratio.

   d. Current ratio.

   e. Profit margin assuming the owner is not actively involved in managing the company.

   f. Profit margin assuming the owner's efforts are valued at $25,000 for the year.

On June 1, Jo Farr created a new travel agency called International Tours. These events occurred during the company's first month:

Problem 4–4
Performing the steps in the accounting cycle
(LO 1, 2, 3)

June 1 Farr created the new company by investing $20,000 cash and computer equipment worth $30,000.

2 The company rented furnished office space by paying $1,600 rent for the first month.

3 The company purchased $1,200 of office supplies for cash.

10 The company paid $3,600 for the premium on a one-year insurance policy.

14 The owner's assistant was paid $800 for two weeks' salary.

24 The company collected $6,800 of commissions from airlines on tickets obtained for customers.

28 The assistant was paid another $800 for two weeks' salary.

29 The company paid the month's $750 telephone bill.

30 The company paid $350 cash to repair the company's computer.

30 The owner withdrew $1,425 cash from the business.

The company's chart of accounts included these accounts:

101	Cash	405	Commissions Earned
106	Accounts Receivable	612	Depreciation Expense, Computer
124	Office Supplies		Equipment
128	Prepaid Insurance	622	Salaries Expense
167	Computer Equipment	637	Insurance Expense
168	Accumulated Depreciation,	640	Rent Expense
	Computer Equipment	650	Office Supplies Expense
209	Salaries Payable	684	Repairs Expense
301	J. Farr, Capital	688	Telephone Expense
302	J. Farr, Withdrawals	901	Income Summary

Required

1. Use the balance column format to create each of the listed accounts.

2. Prepare journal entries to record the transactions for June and post them to the accounts.

3. Prepare a 10-column work sheet that starts with the unadjusted trial balance as of June 30. Use the following information to draft the adjustments for the month:

   a. Two-thirds of one month's insurance coverage was consumed.

   b. There were $800 of office supplies on hand at the end of the month.

   c. Depreciation on the computer equipment was estimated to be $825.

   d. The assistant had earned $160 of unpaid and unrecorded salary.

   e. The company had earned $1,750 of commissions that had not yet been billed.

   Complete the remaining columns of the worksheet.

4. Prepare journal entries to record the adjustments drafted on the work sheet and post them to the accounts.

5. Prepare an income statement, a statement of changes in owner's equity, and a balance sheet.

6. Prepare journal entries to close the temporary accounts and post them to the accounts.

7. Prepare a separate post-closing trial balance.

ᴮProblem 4–5
Adjusting, reversing, and subsequent entries
(LO 6)

The unadjusted trial balance for Milton's Pool Parlor as of December 31, 19X1, follows:

MILTON'S POOL PARLOR
December 31, 19X1

	Unadjusted Trial Balance	
Cash	$ 11,000	
Accounts receivable		
Supplies	4,500	
Equipment	150,000	
Accumulated depreciation, equipment ..		$ 15,000
Interest payable		
Salaries payable		
Unearned membership fees		24,000
Notes payable		50,000
U. Milton, capital		58,250
U. Milton, withdrawals	30,000	
Membership fees earned		90,000
Depreciation expense, equipment		
Salaries expense	38,000	
Interest expense	3,750	
Supplies expense		
Totals	$237,250	$237,250

Required

1. Prepare a six-column table with two columns under each of the following headings: Unadjusted Trial Balance, Adjustments, and Adjusted Trial Balance. Complete the table by entering adjustments that reflect the following information:

    a. As of December 31, employees have earned $800 of unpaid and unrecorded wages. The next payday is January 4, and the total wages to be paid will be $1,200.

    b. The cost of supplies on hand at December 31 is $1,800.

    c. The note payable requires an interest payment to be made every three months. The amount of unrecorded accrued interest at December 31 is $1,250, and the next payment is due on January 15. This payment will be $1,500.

    d. An analysis of the unearned membership fees shows that $16,000 remains unearned at December 31.

    e. In addition to the membership fees included in the revenue account balance, the company has earned another $12,000 in fees that will be collected on January 21. The company is also expected to collect $7,000 on the same day for new fees earned during January.

    f. Depreciation expense for the year is $15,000.

2. Prepare journal entries for the adjustments drafted in the six-column table.

3. Prepare journal entries to reverse the effects of the adjusting entries that involve accruals.

4. Prepare journal entries to record the cash payments and collections that are described for January.

SERIAL PROBLEM

Emerald Computer Services

(The first two segments of this comprehensive problem were in Chapters 2 and 3, and the final segment is presented in Chapter 5. If the Chapter 2 and 3 segments have not been completed, the assignment can begin at this point. However, you should use the facts on pages 100–101 in Chapter 2 and pages 144–145 in Chapter 3. Because of its length, this problem is most easily solved if you use the Working Papers that accompany this text.)

The transactions of Emerald Computer Services for October through December 19X1 have been recorded in the problem segments in Chapters 2 and 3, as well as the year-end adjusting entries. Prior to closing the revenue and expense accounts for 19X1, the accounting system is modified to include the Income Summary account, which is given the number 901.

Required

1. Record and post the appropriate closing entries.
2. Prepare a post-closing trial balance.

CHECK FIGURE:

Total credits in post-closing trial balance, $49,440

CRITICAL THINKING: ESSAYS, PROBLEMS, AND CASES

On December 31, 19X1, the Castle Rock Company recorded a $10,000 liability to its employees for wages earned in 19X1 that will be paid on January 5, the first payday in 19X2. In addition, they will receive another $5,000 for wages earned in 19X2. The accountant did not prepare a reversing entry as of January 1, 19X2, but did not inform the bookkeeper about the liability accrued for the wages. As a result, the bookkeeper recorded a $15,000 debit to Wages Expense on January 5, and a $15,000 credit to Cash.

Describe the effects of this error on the financial statements for 19X1. Describe any erroneous account balances that will exist during 19X2. Suggest a reasonable point in time at which the error would be discovered.

The following balance sheet was prepared at the end of the company's fiscal year:

Analytical Essay
(LO 6)

Financial Reporting Problems

FRP 4–1
(LO 1)

TENDER TUNES
Balance Sheet
December 31, 19X1

Assets

Current assets:		
Cash	$ 6,500	
Office supplies	1,500	
Prepaid insurance	600	
Total current assets	$ 8,600	
Plant and equipment:		
Automobiles	$42,000	
Accumulated depreciation, automobiles	(17,000)	$25,000
Office equipment	$40,000	
Accumulated depreciation, office equipment	(13,500)	26,500
Total plant and equipment		$51,500
Total assets		$60,100

Liabilities

Current liabilities:

Accounts payable	$ 4,200
Interest payable	400
Salaries payable	1,100
Unearned fees	1,800
Total current liabilities	$ 7,500

Noncurrent liabilities:

Long-term notes payable	40,000
Total liabilities	$47,500

Owner's Equity

Charlie Griffin, capital	12,600
Total liabilities and owner's equity	$60,100

The company's accountant also prepared and posted the following adjusting and closing entries:

Dec.	31	Insurance Expense	800.00	
		Prepaid Insurance		800.00
		To record consumed insurance coverage.		
	31	Office Supplies Expense	4,100.00	
		Office Supplies		4,100.00
		To record consumed office supplies.		
	31	Depreciation Expense, Automobiles	8,500.00	
		Accumulated Depreciation,		
		Automobiles		8,500.00
		To record depreciation on automobiles.		
	31	Depreciation Expense, Office Equipment	3,500.00	
		Accumulated Depreciation,		
		Office Equipment		3,500.00
		To record depreciation on equipment.		
	31	Unearned Fees	730.00	
		Fees Earned		730.00
		To record earning of fees paid in advance.		
	31	Salaries Expense	1,100.00	
		Salaries Payable		1,100.00
		To record accrued salaries.		
	31	Interest Expense	400.00	
		Interest Payable		400.00
		To record accrued interest expense.		
	31	Fees Earned	61,000.00	
		Income Summary		61,000.00
		To close the revenue account and open the		
		Income Summary account.		
	31	Income Summary	45,960.00	
		Depreciation Expense, Automobiles ...		8,500.00
		Depreciation Expense, Office Equipment		3,500.00
		Salaries Expense		15,000.00
		Interest Expense		3,200.00
		Insurance Expense		800.00
		Rent Expense		7,200.00

	Office Supplies Expense	4,100.00
	Gas, Oil, and Repairs Expense	2,350.00
	Telephone Expense	1,310.00
	To close the expense accounts.	

31	Income Summary	15,040.00	
	Charlie Griffin, Capital		15,040.00
	To close Income Summary.		

31	Charlie Griffin, Capital	16,000.00	
	Charlie Griffin, Withdrawals		16,000.00
	To close withdrawals account.		

Use the information in the balance sheet and the journal entries to complete a 10-column work sheet. (The five steps should be completed in reverse order.)

Use the following information to complete a 10-column work sheet for California Car Wash. **FRP 4–2** Instead of the usual column headings, use the following headings on the work sheet: **(LO 1, 2, 3)**

Unadjusted Trial Balance: Debit and Credit

Adjustments: Debit and Credit

Adjusted Trial Balance: Debit and Credit

Closing Entries: Debit and Credit

Post-Closing Trial Balance: Debit and Credit

Unadjusted Trial Balance

No.	Title	Debit	Credit
101	Cash	$ 3,200	
106	Accounts receivable	500	
126	Soap supplies	6,000	
128	Prepaid insurance	2,100	
167	Equipment	15,000	
168	Accumulated depreciation, equipment ..		$ 4,000
201	Accounts payable		1,350
210	Salaries payable		
301	K. McGowan, capital		25,900
302	K. McGowan, withdrawals	13,500	
401	Fees earned		44,450
612	Depreciation expense, equipment		
623	Wages expense	18,000	
637	Insurance expense		
640	Rent expense	6,000	
652	Soap supplies expense		
690	Utilities expense	11,400	
901	Income summary		
	Totals	$75,700	$75,700

Use this information for the adjustments:

a. Three customers owe the company $550 for services provided but not billed.

b. A count of the supplies shows that $3,700 has been consumed.

c. The insurance coverage expired at the rate of $35 per month for 12 months.

d. The annual depreciation expense for the equipment is $2,000.

e. December's utility costs of $135 were not included in the unadjusted trial balance.

f. The employees had earned $623 of accrued wages as of December 31.

As the end of the calendar year is approaching, Controller Jerry James is getting the Woodward Company's accounting department ready to prepare the annual financial statements. One concern is the expense of the services provided by an external consultant under a three-month contract that runs from November 30, 19X1, through February 28, 19X2. The total fee for the contract is based on the hours of the consultant's time, with the result that the total fee is not known.

Business Communications Case
(LO 3)

The controller is concerned that the company's financial statements could not be prepared until March because the amount of consulting expense will not be known until then. To avoid this problem, the controller has asked you to prepare a letter to Pat Patterson, the consultant, that would ask for a progress report by the end of the first week of January. This report would specifically identify the hours and charges that will be billed for the consultant's time in December.

Draft the letter that will be sent to Patterson requesting this information. It will be signed by the controller on December 15, 19X1.

Financial Statement Analysis Case
(LO 2)

Review the consolidated balance sheet for Apple Computer, Inc., in Appendix F at the end of this book. Assume that a ledger account exists for each item in the balance sheet and prepare a post-closing trial balance for the company as of September 24, 1993. Also assume that the company uses an account with a credit balance called Allowance for Doubtful Accounts that is contra to the Accounts Receivable account. For simplicity, the amounts in the trial balance can be stated in thousands of dollars as they are presented in the balance sheet. (Note: The account for the accumulated translation adjustment is an owners' equity account.)

COMPREHENSIVE PROBLEM

Piper's Plumbing and Heating
(Review of Chapters 1–4)

Following is the unadjusted trial balance of Piper's Plumbing and Heating as of November 30, 19X1. The account balances include the effects of transactions during the first 11 months of the year.

PIPER'S PLUMBING AND HEATING
Unadjusted Trial Balance
November 30, 19X1

No.	Title	Debit	Credit
101	Cash	$ 17,000	
124	Office supplies	9,400	
126	Repair supplies	86,500	
128	Prepaid insurance	2,400	
153	Trucks	82,000	
154	Accumulated depreciation, trucks		$ 40,000
173	Building	185,000	
174	Accumulated depreciation, building		32,000
201	Accounts payable		13,500
210	Wages payable		
233	Unearned heating fees		3,700
301	Bill Piper, capital		174,600
302	Bill Piper, withdrawals	30,000	
401	Plumbing fees earned		180,000
402	Heating fees earned		95,000
606	Depreciation expense, building		
611	Depreciation expense, trucks		
623	Wages expense	65,000	
637	Insurance expense		
650	Office supplies expense		
652	Repair supplies expense		
669	Gas, oil, and repairs expense	13,500	
672	General and administrative expenses	48,000	
	Totals	$538,800	$538,800

The following transactions occurred during December 19X1:

Dec. 2 Received $1,000 for completed heating work.

　　5 Paid $11,325 on accounts payable.

　　6 Paid $4,100 insurance premium in advance.

　　7 Received $3,300 cash for plumbing work completed.

　　10 Purchased $1,500 of repair supplies on credit.

　　14 Paid $3,000 for wages earned December 1 to 14.

17 Purchased $325 of office supplies on credit.

21 Received $2,200 cash for plumbing work completed and $14,000 cash for heating work.

24 Paid $1,430 for truck repairs related to an accident.

28 Paid $3,300 for wages earned December 15 to 28.

30 Received $600 cash for plumbing work completed and $4,500 cash for heating work.

Required

1. Use the balance column format to create the accounts listed in the November 30 trial balance. Enter the unadjusted November 30 balances in the accounts.

2. Prepare and post journal entries to record the transactions for December; omit entering the account numbers in the posting reference column.

3. Prepare a 10-column work sheet as of December 31. Start by entering the unadjusted balances from the accounts as of that date. Continue by entering adjustments for the following items, and then complete the rest of the work sheet.

  a. At the end of the year, the office supplies inventory was $730.

  b. At the end of the year, the repair supplies inventory was $7,600.

  c. At the end of the year, the unexpired portion of the prepaid insurance was $3,800.

  d. Annual depreciation on the trucks was $20,000.

  e. Annual depreciation on the building was $5,000.

  f. At the end of the year, the employees had earned $990 in accrued wages.

  g. At the end of the year, the balance of unearned heating fees was $600.

4. Prepare adjusting journal entries and post them to the accounts.

5. Prepare an income statement and a statement of changes in owner's equity for 19X1 and a balance sheet as of December 31, 19X1. The owner did not make any new investments during the year.

6. Prepare closing journal entries and post them to the accounts.

7. Prepare a post-closing trial balance.

8. Calculate the following ratios for 19X1:

  a. Return on equity.

  b. Modified return on equity, assuming that the proprietor's management efforts are valued at $32,000 for the year.

  c. The profit margin.

ANSWERS TO PROGRESS CHECKS

4–1 c

4–2 The amounts in the Unadjusted Trial Balance columns are taken from the account balances in the ledger.

4–3 The work sheet offers the advantage of providing an overview of the information in the accounts and helps accountants organize the data.

4–4 Income statement, statement of changes in owner's equity, balance sheet.

4–5 c

4–6 Revenue and expense accounts are called temporary because they are opened and closed every reporting period. The Income Summary and owner's withdrawals accounts are also temporary accounts.

4–7 Permanent accounts are listed on the post-closing trial balance. These accounts include the asset, liability, and owner's capital accounts.

4–8 A corporation closes the Income Summary account to the Retained Earnings account.

4–9 a

4–10 A work sheet is prepared at the end of the reporting period after all transactions have been journalized and posted, but before adjustments have been recorded.

4–11 d

4–12 Profit margin = Net income/Total revenue. Therefore, Total revenue = Net income/Profit margin. Total revenue = $1,012,500/22.5% = $4,500,000.

Accounting for Merchandising Activities

J.C. Penney Company is a major retailer that has department stores in all 50 states and Puerto Rico. The primary products sold by the company include family apparel, shoes, jewelry, accessories, and home furnishings.

J.C. Penney uses a fiscal year of 52 weeks that ends in late January. Accordingly, the company describes its annual accounting period that ended on January 29, 1994, as the 1993 year. During the five-year period ending on January 29, 1994, the products the company owned for the purpose of reselling them to customers increased from $2,613 million to $3,545 million. During the same period, the receivables held by the company (primarily from customers) decreased from $4,872 million to $4,679 million. Thus, at the end of the 1993 year, the company's assets included $8,224 million ($3,545 million + $4,679 million) of products it held for sale and receivables. This amounted to nearly 56% of its total assets.

Many financial statement readers are interested in evaluating the effects of these large holdings of products and receivables on the company's ability to meet its current debt obligations. How might this issue be evaluated?

J.C. Penney Company
(In millions)

	End of Year	
	1993	1992
Current assets:		
Cash and short-term investments	$ 173	$ 426
Receivables, net	4,679	3,750
Merchandise inventories	3,545	3,258
Prepaid expenses	168	157
Total current assets	$8,565	$7,591
Total current liabilities	$3,883	$3,009

LEARNING OBJECTIVES

After studying Chapter 5, you should be able to:

1. **Describe merchandising activities, analyze their effects on financial statements, and record sales of merchandise.**
2. **Describe how the ending inventory and the cost of goods sold are determined with perpetual and periodic inventory accounting systems.**
3. **Describe various formats for income statements and prepare closing entries for a merchandising business.**
4. **Complete a work sheet for a merchandising company and explain the difference between the closing entry and adjusting entry approaches to updating the Merchandise Inventory account.**
5. **Calculate the acid-test ratio and describe what it reveals about a company's liquidity.**
6. **Define or explain the words and phrases in the chapter glossary.**

The first four chapters in this book used only service companies as examples of businesses that prepare financial statements. This chapter introduces some of the business and accounting practices used by companies that engage in merchandising activities. These companies buy goods and then resell them to customers. This chapter shows how the financial statements describe the special transactions and assets related to these activities. In particular, you will learn about the additional financial statement elements created by merchandising activities. To help you understand where the information comes from, we describe how accountants close the accounts of merchandising companies and design income statements.

THE NATURE OF MERCHANDISING ACTIVITIES

LO 1
Describe merchandising activities, analyze their effects on financial statements, and record sales of merchandise.

The first four chapters have described the financial statements and accounting records of Clear Copy Co. Because it provides services to its customers, Clear Copy is a service company. Other examples of service companies include Greyhound Lines Inc.; **Merrill Lynch & Co., Inc.;** America West Airlines, Inc.; Avis, Inc.; and Marriott International Inc. In return for services provided to its customers, a service company receives commissions, fares, or fees as revenue. Its net income for a reporting period is the difference between its revenues and the operating expenses incurred in providing the services.

In contrast, a merchandising company earns net income by buying and selling **merchandise,** which consists of goods that the company acquires for the purpose of reselling them to customers.[1] To achieve a net income, the revenue from selling the merchandise needs to exceed not only the cost of the merchandise sold to customers but also the company's other operating expenses for the reporting period.

The accounting term for the revenues from selling merchandise is *sales* and the term used to describe the expense of buying and preparing the merchandise is *cost of goods sold.*[2] The company's other expenses are often called *operating expenses.* This

---

[1]A merchandising company can be either a wholesaler or a retailer. Wholesalers buy goods from manufacturers and sell them to retailers or other wholesalers. Retailers buy goods from wholesalers and sell them to individual customers.

[2]Many service companies also use the word *sales* to describe their revenues.

Illustration 5-1   Classified Balance Sheet for a Merchandising Company

---

MEG'S MART
Balance Sheet
December 31, 19X2

Assets

Current assets:

Cash	$ 8,200	
Accounts receivable	11,200	
Merchandise inventory	21,000	
Prepaid expenses	1,100	
Total current assets		$41,500

Plant and equipment:

Office equipment	$ 4,200		
Less accumulated depreciation	1,400	$ 2,800	
Store equipment	$30,000		
Less accumulated depreciation	6,000	24,000	
Total plant and equipment			26,800
Total assets			$68,300

Liabilities

Current liabilities:

Accounts payable	$16,000	
Salaries payable	800	
Total liabilities		$16,800

Owner's Equity

Meg Harlowe, capital		51,500
Total liabilities and		
owner's equity		$68,300

---

condensed income statement for Meg's Mart shows you how these three elements of net income are related to each other:

MEG'S MART
Condensed Income Statement
For Year Ended December 31, 19X2

Net sales	$314,700
Cost of goods sold	(230,400)
Gross profit from sales	$ 84,300
Total operating expenses	(62,800)
Net income	$ 21,500

This income statement tells us that Meg's Mart sold goods to its customers for $314,700. The company acquired those goods at a total cost of $230,400. As a result, it earned $84,300 of **gross profit,** which is the difference between the net sales and the cost of goods sold. In addition, the company incurred $62,800 of operating expenses and achieved $21,500 of net income for the year.

A merchandising company's balance sheet includes an additional element that is not on the balance sheet of a service company. In Illustration 5–1, we present the classified balance sheet for Meg's Mart. Notice that the current asset section includes an item called **merchandise inventory.** Even though they also have inventories of supplies, most companies simply refer to merchandise on hand as *inventory.* This asset consists of goods the company owns on the balance sheet date and holds for the purpose of selling to its customers. The $21,000 amount listed for the inventory is the costs incurred to buy the goods, ship them to the store, and otherwise make them ready for sale.

The next sections of the chapter provide more information about these unique elements of the financial statements for merchandising companies.

TOTAL REVENUE FROM SALES

This schedule shows how Meg's Mart calculates its *net sales* for 19X2:

MEG'S MART
Calculation of Net Sales
For Year Ended December 31, 19X2

Sales		$321,000
Less: Sales returns and allowances	$2,000	
Sales discounts	4,300	6,300
Net sales		$314,700

The components of this calculation are described in the following paragraphs.

Sales

The sales item in this calculation is the total cash and credit sales made by the company during the year. Each cash sale was rung up on one of the company's cash registers. At the end of each day, the total cash sales for the day were recorded with a journal entry like this one for November 3:

Nov.	3	Cash	1,205.00	
		Sales		1,205.00
		Sold merchandise for cash.		

This entry records the fact that the cash received from customers represents sales revenue earned by the company.

In addition, a journal entry would be prepared each day to record the credit sales made on that day. For example, this entry records $450 of credit sales on November 3:

Nov.	3	Accounts Receivable	450.00	
		Sales		450.00
		Sold merchandise on credit.		

This entry records the increase in the company's assets in the form of the accounts receivable and records the revenue from the credit sales.[3]

Sales Returns and Allowances

To meet their customers' needs, most companies allow customers to return any unsuitable merchandise for a full refund. If a customer keeps the unsatisfactory goods and is given a partial refund of the selling price, the company is said to have provided

---

[3]Chapter 8 describes how stores account for sales to customers who use third-party credit cards, such as those issued by banks.

a sales *allowance.* Either way, returns and allowances involve dissatisfied customers and the possibility of lost future sales. To monitor the extent of these problems, managers need information about actual returns and allowances. Thus, many accounting systems record returns and allowances in a separate *contra-revenue* account like the one used in this entry to record a $200 cash refund:

Nov.	3	Sales Returns and Allowances	200.00	
		Cash		200.00
		Customer returned defective merchandise.		

The company could record the refund with a debit to the Sales account. Although this would provide the same measure of net sales, it would not provide information that the manager can use to monitor the refunds and allowances. By using the Sales Returns and Allowances contra account, the information is readily available. To simplify the reports provided to external decision makers, published income statements usually omit this detail and present only the amount of net sales.

Sales Discounts

When goods are sold on credit, the expected amounts and dates of future payments need to be clearly stated to avoid misunderstandings. The **credit terms** for a sale describe the amounts and timing of payments that the buyer agrees to make in the future. The specific terms usually reflect the ordinary practices of most companies in the industry. For example, companies in one industry might expect to be paid 10 days after the end of the month in which a sale occurred. These credit terms would be stated on sales invoices or tickets as "n/10 EOM," with the abbreviation **EOM** standing for "end of the month." In another industry, invoices may normally be due and payable 30 calendar days after the invoice date. These terms are abbreviated as "n/30," and the 30-day period is called the **credit period.**

When the credit period is long, the seller often grants a **cash discount** if the customer pays promptly. These early payments are desirable because the seller receives the cash more quickly and can use it to carry on its activities. In addition, prompt payments reduce future efforts and costs of billing customers. These advantages are usually worth the cost of offering the discounts.

If cash discounts for early payment are granted, they are described in the credit terms on the invoice. For example, the terms of 2/10, n/60 mean that a 60-day credit period passes before full payment is due. However, to encourage early payment, the seller allows the buyer to deduct 2% of the invoice amount from the payment if it is made within 10 days of the invoice date. The **discount period** is the period in which the reduced payment can be made.

At the time of a credit sale, the seller does not know that the customer will pay within the discount period and take advantage of a cash discount. As a result, the discount is usually not recorded until the customer pays within the discount period. For example, suppose that Meg's Mart completed a credit sale on November 12 at a gross selling price of $100, subject to terms of 2/10, n/60. This entry records the sale:

Nov.	12	Accounts Receivable	100.00	
		Sales		100.00
		Sold merchandise under terms of 2/10, n/60.		

Even though the customer may pay less than the gross price, the entry records the receivable and the revenue as if the full amount will be collected.

In fact, the customer has two alternatives. One option is to wait 60 days until January 11 and pay the full $100. If this is done, Meg's Mart records the collection as follows:

Jan.	11	Cash	100.00	
		Accounts Receivable		100.00
		Collected account receivable.		

The customer's other option is to pay $98 within a 10-day period that runs through November 22. If the customer pays on November 22, Meg's Mart records the collection with this entry:

Nov.	22	Cash	98.00	
		Sales Discounts	2.00	
		Accounts Receivable		100.00
		Received payment for the November 12 sale less		
		the discount.		

Cash discounts granted to customers are called **sales discounts.** Because management needs to monitor the amount of cash discounts to assess their effectiveness and their cost, they are recorded in a contra-revenue account called Sales Discounts. The balance of this account is deducted from the balance of the Sales account when calculating the company's net sales. Although information about the amount of discounts is useful internally, it is seldom reported on income statements distributed to external decision makers.

Progress Check

(Answers to Progress Checks are provided at the end of the chapter.)

5-1   Which of the following items is not unique to the financial statements of merchandising companies? *(a)* Cost of goods sold; *(b)* Accounts receivable; *(c)* Merchandise inventory.

5-2   What is a merchandising company's gross profit?

5-3   Why are sales returns and allowances and sales discounts recorded in contra-revenue accounts instead of in the Sales account? Is this information likely to be reported outside the company?

5-4   How long are the credit and discount periods under credit terms of 2/10, n/60?

MEASURING INVENTORY AND COST OF GOODS SOLD

A merchandising company's balance sheet includes a current asset called *inventory* and its income statement includes the item called *cost of goods sold*. Both of these items are affected by the company's merchandise transactions. The amount of the asset on the balance sheet equals the cost of the inventory on hand at the end of the fiscal year. The amount of the cost of goods sold is the cost of the merchandise that was sold to customers during the year.

Two different inventory accounting systems may be used to collect information about the cost of the inventory on hand and the cost of goods sold. They are described in the following paragraphs.

Periodic and Perpetual Inventory Systems

LO 2

Describe how the ending inventory and the cost of goods sold are determined with perpetual and periodic inventory accounting systems.

The two basic types of inventory accounting systems are called *perpetual* and *periodic*. As suggested by their name, **perpetual inventory systems** maintain a continuous record of the amount of inventory on hand. This perpetual record is maintained by adding the cost of each newly purchased item to the inventory account and subtracting the cost of each sold item from the account. When an item is sold, its cost is recorded in the Cost of Goods Sold account. Whenever posting is up to date during the period, users of perpetual systems can determine the cost of merchandise on hand by looking at the balance of the inventory account. They can also determine the cost of goods sold thus far during the period by referring to the Cost of Goods Sold account.

Before computers were used widely, perpetual systems were generally applied only by businesses that made a limited number of sales each day, such as automobile dealers or major appliance stores. Because there were relatively few transactions, the perpetual accounting system could be operated efficiently. However, the availability of improved technology has greatly increased the number of companies that use perpetual systems.

Under **periodic inventory systems,** a company does not continuously update its records of the quantity and cost of goods that are on hand or sold. Instead, the company simply records the cost of new merchandise in a temporary *Purchases* account. When merchandise is sold, only the revenue is recorded. Then, when financial statements are prepared, the company takes a *physical inventory* by counting the quantities of merchandise on hand. The total cost is determined by relating the quantities to records that show each item's original cost. This total cost is then used to determine the cost of goods sold.

Traditionally, periodic systems were used by companies such as drug and department stores that sold large quantities of low-valued items. Without computers and scanners, it was not feasible for accounting systems to track such small items as toothpaste, pain killers, clothing, and housewares through the inventory and into the customers' hands.

Although perpetual systems are now more affordable, they are still not used by all merchandising companies. As a result, it will be helpful for you to understand how periodic systems work. In addition, studying periodic systems will help you visualize the flow of goods through inventory without having to learn the more complicated sequence of journal entries used in perpetual systems. (More information on perpetual systems is provided in Chapter 9.)

As mentioned earlier, a store that uses a periodic inventory system does not record the cost of merchandise items when they are sold. Rather, the accountant waits until the end of the reporting period and determines the cost of all the goods sold during the period. To make this calculation, the accountant must have information about:

CALCULATING THE COST OF GOODS SOLD WITH A PERIODIC INVENTORY SYSTEM

1. The cost of merchandise on hand at the beginning of the period.
2. The cost of merchandise purchased during the period.
3. The cost of unsold goods on hand at the end of the period.

Look at Illustration 5–2 to see how this information can be used to measure the cost of goods sold for Meg's Mart.

In Illustration 5–2, note that Meg's Mart had $251,400 of goods available for sale during the period. They were available because the company had $19,000 of goods on hand when the period started and purchased an additional $232,400 of goods during the year.

Illustration 5–2
The Flow of Goods and
Costs through Inventory

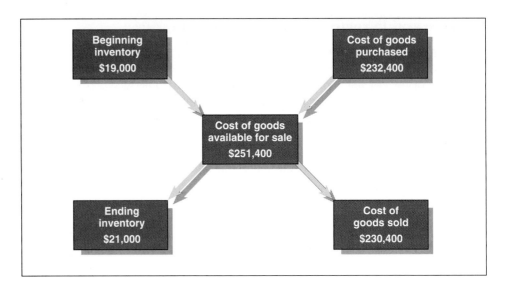

The available goods either were sold during the period or on hand at the end of the period. Because the count showed that $21,000 were on hand at the end of the year, we can conclude that $230,400 must have been sold. This schedule presents the calculation:

MEG'S MART	
Calculation of Cost of Goods Sold	
For Year Ended December 31, 19X2	
Beginning inventory	$ 19,000
Cost of goods purchased	232,400
Cost of goods available for sale	$251,400
Less ending inventory	(21,000)
Cost of goods sold	$230,400

Note that if any three of the items in this calculation are known, they can be used to calculate the fourth. For example, **Woolworth Corporation's** 1993 annual report disclosed the following information:

Beginning merchandise inventories	$2,269 million
Ending merchandise inventories	1,579 million
Cost of sales	$6,717 million

The cost of Woolworth's purchases during 1993 can be calculated as follows:

Ending merchandise inventories	$1,579 million
Cost of sales	6,717 million
Cost of goods that must have been available for sale	$8,296 million
Less beginning merchandise inventories	2,269 million
Cost of goods purchased	$6,027 million

The following paragraphs explain how the accounting system accumulates the information that the accountant needs to make these calculations.

Measuring and Recording Merchandise Inventory

Because a new reporting period starts as soon as the old period ends, the ending inventory of one period is always the beginning inventory of the next. When a periodic inventory system is used, the dollar amount of the ending inventory is determined by (1) counting the unsold items in the store and the stockroom, (2) multiplying the counted quantity of each type of good by its cost, and (3) adding all the costs of the different types of goods. The cost of goods sold is found by subtracting the cost of the ending inventory from the cost of the goods available for sale.

Through the closing process described later in the chapter, the periodic system records the cost of the ending inventory in the *Merchandise Inventory* account. The balance in this account is not changed during the next accounting period. In fact, entries are made to the Merchandise Inventory account only at the end of the period. Thus, neither the purchases of new merchandise nor the cost of goods sold is entered in the Merchandise Inventory account. As a result, as soon as any goods are purchased or sold in the current period, the account no longer shows the cost of the merchandise on hand. Because the account's balance describes the beginning inventory of the period, it cannot be used on a new balance sheet without being updated by the closing entries described later in this chapter.

Recording the Cost of Purchased Merchandise

To determine the cost of purchased merchandise, the gross purchase price must be adjusted for the effects of (1) any cash discounts provided by the suppliers, (2) any returns and allowances for unsatisfactory items received from the suppliers, and (3) any freight costs paid by the buyer to get the goods into the buyer's inventory. For example, the cost of the goods purchased by Meg's Mart for 19X2 is calculated as follows:

MEG'S MART
Calculation of Cost of Goods Purchased
For Year Ended December 31, 19X2

Purchases		$235,800
Less: Purchases returns and allowances	$1,500	
Purchases discounts	4,200	5,700
Net purchases		$230,100
Add transportation-in		2,300
Cost of goods purchased		$232,400

The following paragraphs explain how these amounts are accumulated in the accounts.

The Purchases Account. Under a periodic inventory system, the cost of merchandise bought for resale is debited to a temporary account called *Purchases*. For example, Meg's Mart records a $1,200 credit purchase of merchandise on November 2 with this entry:

Nov.	2	Purchases	1,200.00	
		Accounts Payable		1,200.00
		Purchased merchandise on credit, invoice dated		
		November 2, terms 2/10, n/30.		

The Purchases account accumulates the cost of all merchandise bought during a period. The account is a holding place for information used at the end of the period to calculate the cost of goods sold.

Trade Discounts. When a manufacturer or wholesaler prepares a catalog of the items it offers for sale, each item is given a **list price,** which is also called a *catalog price*. The list price generally is not the intended selling price of the item. Instead, the intended selling price equals the list price reduced by a given percentage called a **trade discount.**

The amount of the trade discount usually depends on whether the buyer is a wholesaler, a retailer, or the final consumer. For example, a wholesaler that buys large quantities is granted a larger discount than a retailer that buys smaller quantities. Regardless of its amount, a trade discount is a reduction in a list price that is applied to determine the actual sales price of the goods to a customer.

Trade discounts are commonly used by manufacturers and wholesalers to change selling prices without republishing their catalogs. When the seller wants to change the selling prices, it can notify its customers merely by sending them a new set of trade discounts to apply to the catalog prices.

Because list prices are not intended to reflect the negotiated sales value of the merchandise, neither the buyer nor the seller enters the list prices and the trade discounts in their accounts. Instead, they record the actual sales price (the list price less the trade discount). For example, if a manufacturer deducts a 40% trade discount on an item listed in its catalog at $2,000, the selling price is $1,200, which is [$2,000 − (40% × $2,000)]. The seller records the credit sale as follows:

Nov.	2	Accounts Receivable	1,200.00	
		Sales		1,200.00
		Sold merchandise on credit.		

The buyer also records the purchase at $1,200. For example, see the previous entry to record the purchase by Meg's Mart.

Purchases Discounts. When stores buy merchandise on credit, they may be offered cash discounts for paying within the discount period. The buyer refers to these cash discounts as **purchases discounts.** When the buyer pays within the discount period, the accounting system records a credit to a contra-purchases account called *Purchases Discounts*. The following entry uses this account to record the payment for the merchandise purchased on November 2:

Nov.	12	Accounts Payable	1,200.00	
		Purchases Discounts (2% × $1,200)		24.00
		Cash		1,176.00
		Paid for the purchase of November 2 less the discount.		

By recording the amount of discounts taken in a separate contra account, the accountant can help managers keep track of the company's performance in taking advantage of discounts. For example, if all purchases are made on credit and all suppliers offer a 2% discount, the balance of the Purchases Discounts contra account should equal 2% of the balance of the Purchases account. If the accountant did not use the contra account, the $24 credit entry would be recorded as a reduction of the Purchases account balance. As a result, it would be more difficult to determine whether discounts were taken.

The accountant uses the balance of the Purchases Discounts account to compute the net cost of the purchases for the period. However, published financial statements usually do not include this calculation because it is useful only for managers.

A Cash Management Technique. To ensure that discounts are not missed, most companies set up a system to pay all invoices within the discount period. Furthermore, careful cash management ensures that no invoice is paid until the last day of the discount period. A helpful technique for reaching both of these goals is to file each invoice in such a way that it automatically comes up for payment on the last day of its discount period. For example, a simple manual system uses 31 folders, one for each day in the month. After an invoice is recorded in the journal, it is placed in the file folder for the last day of its discount period. Thus, if the last day of an invoice's discount period is November 12, it is filed in folder number 12. Then, the invoice and any other invoices in the same folder are removed and paid on November 12. Computerized systems can accomplish the same result by using a code that identifies the last date in the discount period. When that date is reached, the computer automatically provides a reminder that the account should be paid.

Read the As a Matter of Ethics case and consider what you would do if you were faced with the situation it describes.

Purchases Returns and Allowances. Sometimes, merchandise received from a supplier is not acceptable and must be returned. In other cases, the purchaser may keep imperfect but marketable merchandise because the supplier grants an allowance, which is a reduction in the purchase price.

Even though the seller does not charge the buyer for the returned goods or gives an allowance for imperfect goods, the buyer incurs costs in receiving, inspecting, identifying, and possibly returning defective merchandise. The occurrence of these costs can be signaled to the manager by recording the cost of the returned merchandise or the seller's allowance in a separate contra-purchases account called *Purchases Returns and Allowances.* For example, this journal entry is recorded on November 14 when Meg's Mart returns defective merchandise for a $265 refund of the original purchase price:

Nov.	14	Accounts Payable	265.00	
		Purchases Returns and Allowances		265.00
		Returned defective merchandise.		

As we described for Purchases Discounts, the accountant uses the balance of the Purchases Returns and Allowances account to compute the net cost of goods purchased during the period. However, published financial statements generally do not include this detailed information.

Illustration 5-3   Identifying Ownership Responsibilities and Risks

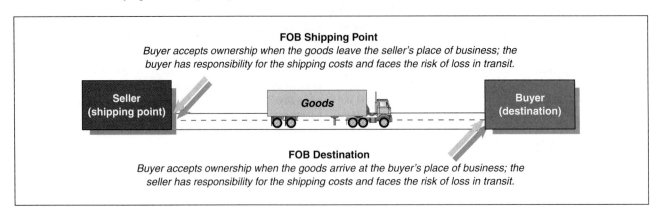

FOB Shipping Point
*Buyer accepts ownership when the goods leave the seller's place of business; the
buyer has responsibility for the shipping costs and faces the risk of loss in transit.*

**Seller
(shipping point)**

Goods

**Buyer
(destination)**

FOB Destination
*Buyer accepts ownership when the goods arrive at the buyer's place of business; the
seller has responsibility for the shipping costs and faces the risk of loss in transit.*

Discounts and Returned Merchandise. If part of a shipment of goods is returned within the discount period, the buyer can take the discount only on the remaining balance of the invoice. For example, suppose that Meg's Mart is offered a 2% cash discount on $5,000 of merchandise. Two days later, the company returns $800 of the goods before the invoice is paid. When the liability is paid within the discount period, Meg's Mart can take the 2% discount only on the $4,200 balance. Thus, the discount is $84 (2% × $4,200) and the cash payment must be $4,116 ($4,200 − $84).

Transportation Costs. Depending on the terms negotiated with its suppliers, a company may be responsible for paying the shipping costs for transporting the acquired goods to its own place of business. Because these costs are necessary to make the goods ready for sale, the cost principle requires them to be added to the cost of the purchased goods.

The freight charges could be recorded with a debit to the Purchases account. However, more complete information about these costs is provided to management if they are debited to a special supplemental account called *Transportation-In*. The accountant adds this account's balance to the net purchase price of the acquired goods to find the total cost of goods purchased. (See the schedule on page 00.)

The use of this account is demonstrated by the following entry, which records a $75 freight charge for incoming merchandise:

PRINCIPLE APPLICATION
Cost Principle p. 29
CompUSA Inc.'s 1993 annual report disclosed that the company had 57 stores in 32 major metropolitan markets across the United States. When the company purchases merchandise from a vendor and then distributes it among these stores, the cost of shipping the merchandise to the stores should be included in the costs of the store inventories according to the cost principle.

Nov.	24	Transportation-In	75.00	
		Cash		75.00
		Paid freight charges on purchased merchandise.		

Because detailed information about freight charges is relevant only for managers, it is seldom found in external financial statements.

Freight paid to bring purchased goods into the inventory is accounted for separately from freight paid on goods sent to customers. The shipping cost of incoming goods is included in the cost of goods sold, while the shipping cost for outgoing goods is a selling expense.

Identifying Ownership Responsibilities and Risks. When a merchandise transaction is planned, the buyer and seller need to establish which party will be responsible for paying any freight costs and which will bear the risk of loss during transit.

The basic issue to be negotiated is the point at which ownership is transferred from the buyer to the seller. The place of the transfer is called the **FOB** point, which is the abbreviation for the phrase, *free on board*. The meaning of different FOB points is explained by the diagram in Illustration 5–3.

Under an *FOB shipping point* agreement (also called *FOB factory*), the buyer accepts ownership at the seller's place of business. As a result, the buyer is responsible for paying the shipping costs and bears the risk of damage or loss while the goods are in shipment. In addition, the goods are part of the buyer's inventory while they are in transit because the buyer already owns them.

Alternatively, an *FOB destination* agreement causes ownership of the goods to pass at the buyer's place of business. If so, the seller is responsible for paying the shipping charges and bears the risk of damage or loss in transit. Furthermore, the seller should not record the sales revenue until the goods arrive at the destination because the transaction is not complete before that point in time.

Compaq Computer Corporation originally shipped all of its products under FOB factory agreements. However, customers' shipping companies proved to be undependable in picking up shipments at scheduled times and caused backups at the plant, missed deliveries, and disappointed end users. The company changed its agreements to FOB destination and cleared up these problems.

Debit and Credit Memoranda

Buyers and sellers often find they need to adjust the amount that is owed between them. For example, purchased merchandise may not meet specifications, unordered goods may be received, different quantities may be received than were ordered and billed, and billing errors may occur.

In some cases, the original balance can be adjusted by the buyer without a negotiation. For example, a seller may make an error on an invoice. If the buying company discovers the error, it can make its own adjustment and notify the seller by sending a **debit memorandum** or a **credit memorandum.** A debit memorandum is a business document that informs the recipient that the sender has *debited* the account receivable or payable. It provides the notification with words like these: "We debit your account," followed by the amount and an explanation. On the other hand, a credit memorandum informs the recipient that the sender has credited the receivable or payable. See Illustration 5–4 for two situations that involve these documents.

The debit memorandum in Illustration 5–4 is based on a case in which a buyer initially records an invoice as an account payable and later discovers an error by the seller that overstated the total bill by $100. The buyer corrects the balance of its liability and formally notifies the seller of the mistake with a debit memorandum reading: "We have debited your account for $100 because of an error." Additional information is provided about the invoice, its date, and the nature of the error. The buyer sends a *debit* memorandum because the correction debits the account payable to reduce its balance. The buyer's debit to the payable is offset by a credit to the Purchases account.

When the seller receives its copy of the debit memorandum, it records a *credit* to the buyer's account receivable to reduce its balance. An equal debit is recorded in the Sales account. Neither company uses a contra account because the adjustment was created by an error.

In other situations, an adjustment can be made only after negotiations between the buyer and the seller. For example, suppose that a buyer claims that some merchandise does not meet specifications. The amount of the allowance to be given by the seller can be determined only after discussion. Assume that a buyer accepts delivery of merchandise and records the transaction with a $750 debit to the Purchases account and an equal credit to Accounts Payable. Later, the buyer discovers that some

Illustration 5–4   The Use of Debit and Credit Memoranda

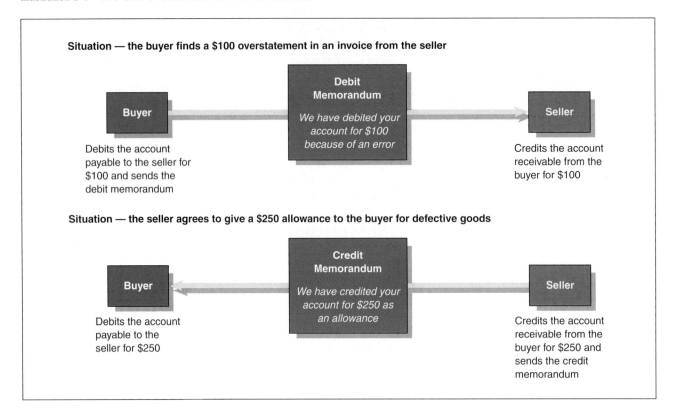

of the merchandise is flawed. After a phone call, the seller agrees to grant a $250 allowance against the original purchase price.

The seller records the allowance with a debit to the Sales Returns and Allowances contra account and a credit to Accounts Receivable. Then, the seller formally notifies the buyer of the allowance with a credit memorandum. A *credit* memorandum is used because the adjustment credited the receivable to reduce its balance. When the buyer receives the credit memorandum, it debits Accounts Payable and credits Purchases Returns and Allowances.

Inventory Shrinkage

Merchandising companies lose merchandise in a variety of ways, including shoplifting and deterioration while an item is on the shelf or in the warehouse. These losses are called **shrinkage.**

Even though perpetual inventory systems track all goods as they move into and out of the company, they are not able to directly measure shrinkage. However, these systems allow the accountant to calculate shrinkage by comparing a physical count with recorded quantities.

Because periodic inventory systems do not identify quantities on hand, they cannot provide direct measures of shrinkage. In fact, all that they can determine is the cost of the goods on hand and the goods that passed out of the inventory. The amount that passed out includes the cost of goods sold, stolen, or destroyed. For example, suppose that shoplifters took merchandise that cost $500. Because the goods were not on hand for a physical count, the ending inventory's cost is $500 smaller than it would have been. As a result, the $500 is included in the cost of the goods sold.

Chapter 9 describes perpetual systems and how they provide more complete information about shrinkage. Chapter 9 also describes how an accountant can estimate shrinkage when a periodic system is used.

Illustration 5–5   Classified Income Statement for Internal Use

MEG'S MART
Income Statement
For Year Ended December 31, 19X2

Sales			$321,000
Less: Sales returns and allowances		$2,000	
Sales discounts		4,300	6,300
Net sales			$314,700
Cost of goods sold:			
Merchandise inventory, December 31, 19X1 . . .		$19,000	
Purchases	$235,800		
Less: Purchases returns and allowances	$1,500		
Purchases discounts	4,200	5,700	
Net purchases		$230,100	
Add transportation-in		2,300	
Cost of goods purchased		232,400	
Goods available for sale		$251,400	
Merchandise inventory, December 31, 19X2 . .		21,000	
Cost of goods sold			230,400
Gross profit from sales			$ 84,300
Operating expenses:			
Selling expenses:			
Depreciation expense, store equipment	$ 3,000		
Sales salaries expense	18,500		
Rent expense, selling space	8,100		
Store supplies expense	1,200		
Advertising expense	2,700		
Total selling expenses		$33,500	
General and administrative expenses:			
Depreciation expense, office equipment	$ 700		
Office salaries expense	25,300		
Insurance expense	600		
Rent expense, office space	900		
Office supplies expense	1,800		
Total general and administrative expenses . .		29,300	
Total operating expenses			62,800
Net income			$ 21,500

Progress Check

5–5 Which of the following items is subtracted from the list price of merchandise to determine the actual sales price? *(a)* Freight-in; *(b)* Trade discount; *(c)* Purchases discount; *(d)* Purchases return and/or allowance.

5–6 How is the cost of goods sold determined with a periodic inventory accounting system?

5–7 What is the meaning of the abbreviation *FOB*? What is the meaning of the term *FOB destination?*

ALTERNATIVE INCOME STATEMENT FORMATS

Generally accepted accounting principles do not require companies to use exactly the same financial statement formats. In fact, practice shows that many different formats are used. This section of the chapter describes several possible formats that Meg's Mart could use for its income statement.

In Illustration 5–5, we present a **classified income statement** that would probably be distributed only to the company's managers because of the details that it includes. The sales and cost of goods sold sections are the same as the calculations presented

Illustration 5–6
Multiple-Step Income
Statement

MEG'S MART
Income Statement
For Year Ended December 31, 19X2

Net sales			$314,700
Cost of goods sold			230,400
Gross profit from sales			$ 84,300
Operating expenses:			
Selling expenses:			
Depreciation expense, store equipment	$ 3,000		
Sales salaries expense	18,500		
Rent expense, selling space	8,100		
Store supplies expense	1,200		
Advertising expense	2,700		
Total selling expenses		$33,500	
General and administrative expenses:			
Depreciation expense, office equipment	$ 700		
Office salaries expense	25,300		
Insurance expense	600		
Rent expense, office space	900		
Office supplies expense	1,800		
Total general and administrative expenses		29,300	
Total operating expenses			62,800
Net income			$ 21,500

LO 3

Describe various formats for income statements and prepare closing entries for a merchandising business.

earlier in the chapter. The difference between the net sales and cost of goods sold is the gross profit for the year.

Also notice that the operating expenses section classifies the expenses into two categories. **Selling expenses** include the expenses of promoting sales through displaying and advertising the merchandise, making sales, and

delivering goods to customers. **General and administrative expenses** support the overall operations of a business and include the expenses of activities such as accounting, human resource management, and financial management.

The income statement for **Apple Computer, Inc.,** in Appendix F presents only a single line item called Selling, general and administrative expenses. However, the annual report provides management's discussion and analysis of these expenses, changes in their amounts, and what they mean for the company.

Some expenses may be divided between categories because they contribute to both activities. For example, Illustration 5–5 reflects the fact that Meg's Mart divided the total rent expense of $9,000 for its store building between the two categories. Ninety percent ($8,100) was selling expense and the remaining 10% ($900) was general and administrative expense.[4] The cost allocation should reflect an economic relationship between the prorated amounts and the activities. For example, the allocation in this case could be based on relative rental values.

In Illustration 5–6, we use the **multiple-step income statement** format that is sometimes used in external reports. The only difference between this format and the one

---

[4]These expenses can be recorded in a single account or in two separate accounts. If they are recorded in one account, the accountant allocates its balance between the two expenses when preparing the statements.

Illustration 5-7
Single-Step Income
Statement

MEG'S MART
Income Statement
For Year Ended December 31, 19X2

Net sales		$314,700
Cost of goods sold	$230,400	
Selling expenses	33,500	
General and administrative expenses	29,300	
Total operating expenses		293,200
Net income		$ 21,500

in Illustration 5–5 is that it leaves out the detailed calculations of net sales and cost of goods sold. The format is called multiple-step because it shows several intermediate totals between sales and net income.

In contrast, we present a **single-step income statement** for Meg's Mart in Illustration 5–7. This simpler format includes cost of goods sold as an operating expense and presents only one intermediate total for total operating expenses. Many companies use this format in their published financial statements.

In practice, many companies use formats that combine some of the features of both the single- and multiple-step statements. For example, a combination format is used in the **Ben & Jerry's** income statement in Appendix G at the end of the book. As long as the income statement elements are presented logically, management can choose the format that it wants to use.[5]

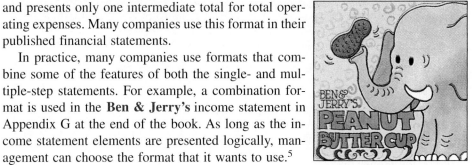

To help you understand how information flows through the accounting system into the financial statements, we now discuss the process for closing the temporary accounts of merchandising companies. The process is demonstrated with data from the adjusted trial balance for Meg's Mart in Illustration 5–8. In addition, the accountant knows from a physical count that the cost of the ending inventory is $21,000.

The trial balance includes these unique accounts for merchandising activities: Merchandise Inventory, Sales, Sales Returns and Allowances, Sales Discounts, Purchases, Purchases Returns and Allowances, Purchases Discounts, and Transportation-In. Their presence in the ledger causes the four closing entries to be slightly different from the ones described in Chapter 4.

CLOSING ENTRIES FOR MERCHANDISING COMPANIES

Entry 1—Record the Ending Inventory and Close the Temporary Accounts that Have Credit Balances

The first entry adds the $21,000 cost of the ending inventory to the balance of the Merchandise Inventory account. It also closes the temporary accounts that have credit

---

[5]Later chapters describe other possible elements, such as extraordinary gains and losses, that must be presented in specified locations on the income statement.

Illustration 5–8
Adjusted Trial Balance

MEG'S MART
Adjusted Trial Balance
December 31, 19X2

Cash	$ 8,200	
Accounts receivable	11,200	
Merchandise inventory	19,000	
Office supplies	550	
Store supplies	250	
Prepaid insurance	300	
Office equipment	4,200	
Accumulated depreciation, office equipment		$ 1,400
Store equipment	30,000	
Accumulated depreciation, store equipment		6,000
Accounts payable		16,000
Salaries payable		800
Meg Harlowe, capital		34,000
Meg Harlowe, withdrawals	4,000	
Sales		321,000
Sales returns and allowances	2,000	
Sales discounts	4,300	
Purchases	235,800	
Purchases returns and allowances		1,500
Purchases discounts		4,200
Transportation-in	2,300	
Depreciation expense, store equipment	3,000	
Depreciation expense, office equipment	700	
Office salaries expense	25,300	
Sales salaries expense	18,500	
Insurance expense	600	
Rent expense, office space	900	
Rent expense, selling space	8,100	
Office supplies expense	1,800	
Store supplies expense	1,200	
Advertising expense	2,700	
Totals	$384,900	$384,900

balances, including the Sales account and the two contra-purchases accounts. The first closing entry for Meg's Mart is:

Dec.	31	Merchandise Inventory	21,000.00	
		Sales	321,000.00	
		Purchases Returns and Allowances	1,500.00	
		Purchases Discounts	4,200.00	
		Income Summary		347,700.00
		To close temporary accounts with credit balances and record the ending inventory.		

Posting this entry gives zero balances to the three temporary accounts that had credit balances in the adjusted trial balance. It also momentarily increases the balance of the Merchandise Inventory account to $40,000. However, the next entry reduces the balance of this account.

Entry 2—Remove the Beginning Inventory and Close the Temporary Accounts that Have Debit Balances

The second entry subtracts the cost of the beginning inventory from the Merchandise Inventory account. It also closes the temporary accounts that have debit balances, including the expense accounts, the two contra-sales accounts, the Purchases account, and the Transportation-In account. The second closing entry for Meg's Mart is:

Dec.	31	Income Summary	326,200.00	
		Merchandise Inventory		19,000.00
		Sales Returns and Allowances		2,000.00
		Sales Discounts		4,300.00
		Purchases		235,800.00
		Transportation-In		2,300.00
		Depreciation Expense, Store Equipment		3,000.00
		Depreciation Expense, Office Equipment		700.00
		Office Salaries Expense		25,300.00
		Sales Salaries Expense		18,500.00
		Insurance Expense		600.00
		Rent Expense, Office Space		900.00
		Rent Expense, Selling Space		8,100.00
		Office Supplies Expense		1,800.00
		Store Supplies Expense		1,200.00
		Advertising Expense		2,700.00
		To close temporary accounts with debit balances and to remove the beginning inventory balance.		

Posting this entry reduces the balance of the Merchandise Inventory account to $21,000, which is the amount determined by the physical count on December 31, 19X2. It also gives zero balances to the 14 temporary accounts that had debit balances.

After posting the first two closing entries, the Merchandise Inventory account appears as follows:

Merchandise Inventory   **Acct. No.** 119

Date		Explanation	Debit	Credit	Balance
19X1					
Dec.	31	Ending balance for 19X1			19,000.00
19X2					
Dec.	31	First closing entry	21,000.00		40,000.00
	31	Second closing entry		19,000.00	21,000.00

As mentioned earlier in the chapter, the $21,000 balance will remain unchanged throughout 19X3 until the accounts are closed at the end of that year.

Entry 3—Close the Income Summary Account to the Owner's Capital Account

The third closing entry for a merchandising company is the same as the third closing entry for a service company. It closes the Income Summary account and updates the balance of the owner's capital account. The third closing entry for Meg's Mart is:

Dec.	31	Income Summary	21,500.00	
		Meg Harlowe, Capital		21,500.00
		To close the Income Summary account.		

The $21,500 amount in the entry is the net income reported on the income statement.

Entry 4—Close the Owner's Withdrawals Account to the Owner's Capital Account

The fourth closing entry for a merchandising company is the same as the fourth closing entry for a service company. It closes the owner's withdrawals account and reduces the balance of the owner's capital account to the amount shown on the balance sheet. The fourth closing entry for Meg's Mart is:

Dec.	31	Meg Harlowe, Capital	4,000.00	
		Meg Harlowe, Withdrawals		4,000.00
		To close the withdrawals account.		

When this entry is posted, all the temporary accounts are cleared and ready to record events in 19X3. In addition, the owner's capital account has been fully updated to reflect the events of 19X2.

Progress Check

5–8 Which of the following accounts is not unique to a merchandising company? *(a)* Merchandise Inventory; *(b)* Purchases Returns and Allowances; *(c)* Advertising Expense; *(d)* Transportation-In; *(e)* Purchases.

5–9 Which income statement format shows the detailed calculations of net sales and cost of goods sold? Which format does not present any intermediate totals (other than total expenses)?

5–10 Which of the four closing entries includes a credit to Merchandise Inventory?

A WORK SHEET FOR A MERCHANDISING COMPANY

LO 4

Complete a work sheet for a merchandising company and explain the difference between the closing entry and adjusting entry approaches to updating the Merchandise Inventory account.

Illustration 5–9 presents a version of the work sheet that the accountant for Meg's Mart could prepare in the process of developing its 19X2 financial statements. It differs in two ways from the 10-column work sheet described in Chapter 4.

The first difference is the deletion of the adjusted trial balance columns. Many accountants delete these columns simply to reduce the size of the worksheet. This has nothing to do with the fact that Meg's Mart is a retail business. The omission of the columns causes the accountant to first compute the adjusted balances and then extend them directly into the financial statement columns.

The second difference appears on the line for the Merchandise Inventory account. The unadjusted trial balance includes the beginning inventory balance of $19,000. This amount is extended into the Debit column for the income statement. Then, the ending balance is entered in the Credit column for the income statement and the Debit column for the balance sheet. This step allows the cost of goods sold to be included in net income while the correct ending balance is included for the balance sheet.

The adjustments in the work sheet reflect the following economic events:

(a) Expiration of $600 of prepaid insurance.

(b) Consumption of $1,200 of store supplies.

(c) Consumption of $1,800 of office supplies.

(d) Depreciation of the store equipment for $3,000.

(e) Depreciation of the office equipment for $700.

(f) Accrual of $300 of unpaid office salaries and $500 of unpaid store salaries.

Once the adjusted amounts are extended into the financial statement columns, the accountant uses the information to develop the company's financial statements.

Illustration 5-9   Work Sheet for Meg's Mart for the Year Ended December 31, 19X2

No.	Account	Unadjusted Trial Balance Dr.	Cr.	Adjustments Dr.	Cr.	Income Statement Dr.	Cr.	Statement of Changes in Owner's Equity and Balance Sheet Dr.	Cr.
101	Cash	8,200						8,200	
106	Accounts receivable	11,200						11,200	
119	**Merchandise inventory**	**19,000**				19,000	21,000	21,000	
124	Office supplies	2,350			(c) 1,800			550	
125	Store supplies	1,450			(b) 1,200			250	
128	Prepaid insurance	900			(a) 600			300	
163	Office equipment	4,200						4,200	
164	Accum. depr., office equipment		700		(e) 700				1,400
165	Store equipment	30,000						30,000	
166	Accum. depr., store equipment		3,000		(d) 3,000				6,000
201	Accounts payable		16,000						16,000
209	Salaries payable				(f) 800				800
301	Meg Harlowe, capital		34,000						34,000
302	Meg Harlowe, withdrawals	4,000						4,000	
413	Sales		321,000				321,000		
414	Sales returns and allowances	2,000				2,000			
415	Sales discounts	4,300				4,300			
505	Purchases	235,800				235,800			
506	Purchases returns and allowances		1,500				1,500		
507	Purchases discounts		4,200				4,200		
508	Transportation-in	2,300				2,300			
612	Depr. expense, store equipment			(d) 3,000		3,000			
613	Depr. expense, office equipment			(e) 700		700			
620	Office salaries expense	25,000		(f) 300		25,300			
621	Sales salaries expense	18,000		(f) 500		18,500			
637	Insurance expense			(a) 600		600			
641	Rent expense, office space	900				900			
642	Rent expense, selling space	8,100				8,100			
650	Office supplies expense			(c) 1,800		1,800			
651	Store supplies expense			(b) 1,200		1,200			
655	Advertising expense	2,700				2,700			
	Totals	380,400	380,400	8,100	8,100	326,200	347,700	79,700	58,200
	Net income					21,500			21,500
	Totals					347,700	347,700	79,700	79,700

THE ADJUSTING ENTRY APPROACH TO RECORDING THE CHANGE IN THE MERCHANDISE INVENTORY ACCOUNT

In the previous sections, the change in the Merchandise Inventory account was recorded in the process of making closing entries. This closing entry approach is widely used in practice. However, it is not the only bookkeeping method that can be applied at the end of the year. Another approach is to record the change in the Merchandise Inventory account with adjusting entries. When this approach is followed, the first two closing entries do not include changes in the Merchandise Inventory account. This adjusting entry approach is preferred by some accountants. It is also used by many computerized accounting systems that do not allow the Merchandise Inventory account (a permanent account) to be changed in the closing process.

The Adjusting Entries

Under the adjusting entry approach, Meg's Mart removes the beginning balance from the Merchandise Inventory account by recording this adjusting entry at the end of 19X2:

Dec.	31	Income Summary	19,000.00	
		Merchandise Inventory		19,000.00
		To remove the beginning balance from the		
		Merchandise Inventory account.		

The second adjusting entry produces the correct ending balance in the Merchandise Inventory account:

Dec.	31	Merchandise Inventory	21,000.00	
		Income Summary		21,000.00
		To insert the correct ending balance into the		
		Merchandise Inventory account.		

After this entry is posted, the Merchandise Inventory account has a $21,000 debit balance. In addition, the Income Summary account has a $2,000 credit balance.

The Closing Entries

If the two adjusting entries for inventory are used, the closing entries differ only by not including the Merchandise Inventory account. Thus, Meg's Mart records the following two closing entries for 19X2 under the adjusting entry approach:

Dec.	31	Sales	321,000.00	
		Purchases Returns and Allowances	1,500.00	
		Purchases Discounts ....'......................	4,200.00	
		Income Summary		326,700.00
		To close temporary accounts with credit balances.		

Dec.	31	Income Summary	307,200.00	
		Sales Returns and Allowances		2,000.00
		Sales Discounts		4,300.00
		Purchases		235,800.00
		Transportation-In		2,300.00
		Depreciation Expense, Store Equipment		3,000.00
		Depreciation Expense, Office Equipment		700.00
		Office Salaries Expense		25,300.00
		Sales Salaries Expense		18,500.00
		Insurance Expense		600.00
		Rent Expense, Office Space		900.00
		Rent Expense, Selling Space		8,100.00
		Office Supplies Expense		1,800.00
		Store Supplies Expense		1,200.00
		Advertising Expense		2,700.00
		To close temporary accounts with debit balances.		

The third and fourth entries are the same as before, although now the amount debited to the Income Summary account is based on four previous entries instead of two:

Dec.	31	Income Summary	21,500.00	
		Meg Harlowe, Capital		21,500.00
		To close the Income Summary account.		
Dec.	31	Meg Harlowe, Capital	4,000.00	
		Meg Harlowe, Withdrawals		4,000.00
		To close the withdrawals account.		

The Adjusting Entry Approach and the Work Sheet. If the accountant uses the adjusting entry approach to update the inventory account, the two adjustments are included in the adjustments columns in the work sheet, and a line for the Income Summary account is inserted at the bottom of the work sheet. This procedure is not demonstrated here.

Progress Check

5-11 In which of the following columns is the ending inventory entered on the work sheet when the closing entry approach is used to record the change in inventory? *(a)* Unadjusted Trial Balance Debit Column; *(b)* Adjustments Debit column; *(c)* Income Statement Debit column; *(d)* Income Statement Credit column; *(e)* Balance Sheet Credit column.

5-12 Will the reported amounts of ending inventory and net income differ if the adjusting entry approach to recording the change in inventory is used instead of the closing entry approach?

You have learned in this chapter that a company's current assets may include a merchandise inventory. Thus, you can understand that a major part of a company's current assets may not be available immediately for paying its existing liabilities. The inventory must be sold and the resulting accounts receivable must be collected before cash is available. As a result, the current ratio (which we described in Chapter 3) may not be an adequate indicator of a company's ability to pay its current liabilities.

Another measure that financial statement users often use to evaluate a company's ability to settle its current debts with its existing assets is the **acid-test ratio.** The acid-test ratio is similar to the current ratio, but differs because it excludes the less liquid current assets. The acid-test ratio is calculated just like the current ratio except that its numerator omits inventory and prepaid expenses. The remaining current assets (cash, short-term investments, and receivables) are called the company's *quick assets*. The formula for the ratio is

$$\text{Acid-test ratio} = \frac{\text{Quick assets}}{\text{Current liabilities}}$$

Recall the discussion of **J.C. Penney Company** at the beginning of the chapter. The acid-test ratios for J.C. Penney are computed as follows:

Acid-Test Ratios	End of Year	
	1993	1992
($173 + $4,679)/$3,883	1.2	
($426 + $3,750)/$3,009		1.4

USING THE INFORMATION— THE ACID-TEST RATIO

LO 5

Calculate the acid-test ratio and describe what it reveals about a company's liquidity.

In contrast, the current ratios (current assets/current liabilities) for J.C. Penney have these values:

	End of Year	
Current Ratios	**1993**	**1992**
$8,565/$3,883	2.2	
$7,591/$3,009		2.5

A traditional rule of thumb is that an acid-test ratio value of at least 1.0 suggests the company is not likely to face a liquidity crisis in the near future. However, a value less than 1.0 may not be threatening if the company can generate enough cash from sales or the accounts payable are not due until later in the year. On the other hand, a value more than 1.0 may hide a liquidity crisis if the payables are due at once but the receivables will not be collected until late in the year. These possibilities reinforce the point that a single ratio is seldom enough to indicate strength or weakness. However, it can identify areas that the analyst should look into more deeply.

Progress Check

5-13   Which assets are defined as quick assets for the purpose of calculating the acid-test ratio? *(a)* Cash, short-term investments, and prepaid expenses; *(b)* Merchandise inventory and prepaid expenses; *(c)* Merchandise inventory and short-term investments; *(d)* Cash, short-term investments, and receivables.

5-14   Which ratio is a more strict test of a company's ability to meet its obligations in the very near future, the acid-test ratio or the current ratio?

SUMMARY OF THE CHAPTER IN TERMS OF LEARNING OBJECTIVES

LO 1. Describe merchandising activities, analyze their effects on financial statements, and record sales of merchandise. Merchandising companies purchase and sell products. Their financial statements include the cost of the merchandise inventory in the current assets on the balance sheet and sales and cost of goods sold on the income statement. The difference between sales and cost of goods sold is called gross profit.

The seller of merchandise records the sale at the list price less any trade discount. Any returns or allowances are recorded in a contra account to provide information to the manager. When cash discounts from the sales price are offered and the customers pay within the discount period, the seller records the discounts in a contra-sales account.

LO 2. Describe how the ending inventory and the cost of goods sold are determined with perpetual and periodic inventory accounting systems. A perpetual inventory system continuously tracks the cost of goods on hand and the cost of goods sold. A periodic system merely accumulates the cost of goods purchased during the year and does not provide continuous information about the cost of the inventory or the sold goods. At year-end, the cost of the inventory is determined and used to calculate the cost of goods sold. The cost of goods available for sale equals the beginning inventory plus the cost of goods purchased. The cost of goods sold equals the cost of goods available for sale minus the cost of the ending inventory. The cost of goods purchased is affected by purchases discounts, purchases returns and allowances, and transportation-in. These amounts are recorded in contra and supplemental accounts to provide information to management. The contra and supplemental accounts are seldom reported in external statements.

LO 3. Describe various formats for income statements and prepare closing entries for a merchandising business. Companies have flexibility in choosing formats for their income statements. Internal statements show more details, including the calculations of net sales and the cost of goods sold. Classified income statements describe expenses incurred in different activities. Multiple-step statements include several intermediate totals and single-step statements do not.

In the closing entry approach, the Merchandise Inventory account is updated in the process of making closing entries. The ending inventory amount is added to the account as part of the entry that closes the income statement accounts with credit balances. The beginning inventory amount is removed from the account as part of the entry that closes the income statement accounts with debit balances.

LO 4. Complete a work sheet for a merchandising company and explain the difference between the closing entry and adjusting entry approaches to updating the Merchandise Inventory account. The work sheet for a merchandising company uses special entries to update the inventory. The beginning inventory balance is extended into the Income Statement Debit column and the cost of the ending inventory is entered in the Income Statement Credit column and Balance Sheet Debit column. Many accountants omit the adjusted trial balance columns to reduce the size of the work sheet. The adjusting entry approach to recording the ending inventory in the accounts uses two adjusting entries that remove the beginning cost from and add the ending cost to the Merchandise Inventory account. This approach is often used in computer systems.

LO 5. Calculate the acid-test ratio and describe what it reveals about a company's liquidity. The acid-test ratio is used to assess a company's ability to pay its current liabilities with its existing quick assets (cash, short-term investments, and receivables). The costs of the merchandise inventory and prepaid expenses are not included in the numerator. A ratio value equal to or greater than one is usually considered to be adequate.

Use the following adjusted trial balance and additional information to complete the requirements:

DEMONSTRATION PROBLEM

YE OLDE JUNQUE AND STUFF
Adjusted Trial Balance
December 31, 19X2

Cash	$ 19,000	
Merchandise inventory	52,000	
Store supplies	1,000	
Equipment	40,000	
Accumulated depreciation, equipment		$ 16,500
Accounts payable		8,000
Salaries payable		1,000
Ann Teak, capital		69,000
Ann Teak, withdrawals	8,000	
Sales		320,000
Sales discounts	20,000	
Purchases	147,000	
Purchases discounts		12,000
Transportation-in	11,000	
Depreciation expense	5,500	
Salaries expense	60,000	
Insurance expense	12,000	
Rent expense	24,000	
Store supplies expense	6,000	
Advertising expense	21,000	
Totals	$426,500	$426,500

A physical count shows that the cost of the year's ending inventory is $50,000.

Required

1. Prepare schedules that calculate the company's net sales and cost of goods sold for the year.
2. Present a single-step income statement for 19X2.
3. Prepare closing entries.

Planning the Solution

- The calculation of net sales deducts discounts from sales. The calculation of cost of goods sold adds the cost of goods purchased for the year to the beginning inventory and then subtracts the cost of the ending inventory.

- To prepare the single-step income statement, find the net sales and then list the operating expenses. Use the cost of goods sold number calculated in the first requirement.

- The first closing entry debits the inventory account for the cost of the ending inventory and debits all temporary accounts with credit balances. The second closing entry credits the inventory account with the cost of the beginning inventory and credits all temporary accounts with debit balances. The third entry closes the Income Summary account to the owner's capital account, and the fourth closing entry closes the owner's withdrawals account to the owner's capital account.

Solution to Demonstration Problem

1.

Sales		$320,000
Less sales discounts		(20,000)
Net sales		$300,000
Beginning inventory		$ 52,000
Purchases	$147,000	
Less purchases discounts	(12,000)	
Plus transportation-in	11,000	
Cost of goods purchased		146,000
Cost of goods available for sale		$198,000
Less ending inventory		(50,000)
Cost of goods sold		$148,000

2.

YE OLDE JUNQUE AND STUFF
Income Statement
For Year Ended December 31, 19X2

Net sales.		$300,000
Operating expenses:		
Cost of goods sold.	$148,000	
Depreciation expense	5,500	
Salaries expense	60,000	
Insurance expense	12,000	
Rent expense	24,000	
Store supplies expense	6,000	
Advertising expense.	21,000	
Total expenses.		276,500
Net income.		$ 23,500

3.

Dec.	31	Merchandise Inventory	50,000.00	
		Sales	320,000.00	
		Purchases Discounts	12,000.00	
		Income Summary		382,000.00
		To close temporary accounts with credit balances and record the ending inventory.		
Dec.	31	Income Summary	358,500.00	
		Merchandise Inventory		52,000.00
		Sales Discounts		20,000.00
		Purchases		147,000.00
		Transportation-In		11,000.00
		Depreciation Expense		5,500.00
		Salaries Expense		60,000.00
		Insurance Expense		12,000.00
		Rent Expense		24,000.00
		Store Supplies Expense		6,000.00
		Advertising Expense		21,000.00
		To close temporary accounts with debit balances and to remove the beginning inventory balance.		
Dec.	31	Income Summary	23,500.00	
		Ann Teak, Capital		23,500.00
		To close the Income Summary account.		
Dec.	31	Ann Teak, Capital	8,000.00	
		Ann Teak, Withdrawals		8,000.00
		To close the withdrawals account.		

GLOSSARY

Acid-test ratio a ratio used to assess the company's ability to settle its current debts with its existing assets; it is the ratio between a company's quick assets (cash, short-term investments, and receivables) and its current liabilities. p. 209

Cash discount a reduction in a debt that is granted by a seller to a purchaser in exchange for the purchaser's making payment within a specified period of time called the discount period. p. 191

Classified income statement an income statement format that classifies items in significant groups and shows detailed calculations of sales and cost of goods sold. p. 201

Credit memorandum a notification that the sender has entered a credit in the recipient's account maintained by the sender. p. 199

Credit period the time period that can pass before a customer's payment is due. p. 191

Credit terms the description of the amounts and timing of payments that a buyer agrees to make in the future. p. 191

Debit memorandum a notification that the sender has entered a debit in the recipient's account maintained by the sender. p. 199

Discount period the time period in which a cash discount is available. p. 191

EOM the abbreviation for *end-of-month*; used to describe credit terms for some transactions. p. 191

FOB the abbreviation for *free on board;* the designated point at which ownership of goods passes to the buyer; FOB shipping point (or factory) means that the buyer pays the shipping costs and FOB destination means that the seller pays the shipping costs. p. 198

General and administrative expenses expenses that support the overall operations of a business and include the expenses of such activities as providing accounting services, human resource management, and financial management. p. 202

Gross profit the difference between net sales and the cost of goods sold. p. 189

List price the nominal price of an item before any trade discount is deducted. p. 196

Merchandise goods acquired for the purpose of reselling them to customers. p. 188

Merchandise inventory goods a company owns on any given date and holds for the purpose of selling them to its customers. p. 189

Multiple-step income statement an income statement format that shows several intermediate totals between sales and net income. p. 202

Periodic inventory system a method of accounting that records the cost of inventory purchased but does not track the quantity on hand or sold to customers; the records are updated periodically to reflect the results of physical counts of the items on hand. p. 193

Perpetual inventory system a method of accounting that maintains continuous records of the amount of inventory on hand and sold. p. 193

Purchases discount a cash discount taken against an amount owed to a supplier of goods. p. 196

Sales discount a cash discount taken by customers against an amount owed to the seller. p. 192

Selling expenses the expenses of promoting sales by displaying and advertising the merchandise, making sales, and delivering goods to customers. p. 202

Shrinkage inventory losses that occur as a result of shoplifting or deterioration. p. 200

Single-step income statement an income statement format that does not present intermediate totals other than total expenses. p. 203

Trade discount a reduction below a list or catalog price that is negotiated in setting the selling price of goods. p. 196

QUESTIONS

1. What item on the balance sheet is unique to merchandising companies? What items on the income statement are unique to merchandising companies?

2. Explain how a business can earn a gross profit on its sales and still have a net loss.

3. Why would a company offer a cash discount?

4. What is the difference between a sales discount and a purchases discount?

5. In counting the ending inventory, an employee omitted the contents of one shelf that contained merchandise with a cost of $2,300. How would this omission affect the company's balance sheet and income statement?

6. Distinguish between cash discounts and trade discounts. Is the amount of a trade discount on purchased merchandise recorded in the Purchases Discounts account?

7. Why would a company's manager be concerned about the quantity of its purchases returns if its suppliers allow unlimited returns?

8. What do the sender and the recipient of a debit memorandum record in their accounts?

9. What is the difference between single-step and multiple-step income statement formats?

10. Does the beginning or ending inventory appear on the unadjusted trial balance of a company that uses a periodic inventory system?

11. Refer to the income statement for Ben & Jerry's Homemade, Inc., in Appendix G at the end of the book. What term is used instead of cost of goods sold? Does the company present the calculation of the cost of goods sold?

12. Use the income statement for Apple Computer, Inc., in Appendix F to calculate the gross profit for each of the three years to the nearest million dollars.

QUICK STUDY (Five-Minute Exercises)

QS 5–1
(LO 1)

Calculate net sales and gross profit in each of the following situations:

	a	b	c	d
Sales	$125,000	$505,000	$33,700	$256,700
Sales discounts	3,200	13,500	300	4,000
Sales returns and allowances	19,000	3,000	6,000	600
Cost of goods sold	67,600	352,700	22,300	123,900

QS 5–2
(LO 2)

A company purchased merchandise that cost $165,000 during the year that just ended. Determine the company's cost of goods sold in each of the following four situations:

a. There were no beginning or ending inventories.

b. There was a beginning inventory of $35,000 and no ending inventory.

c.   There was a $30,000 beginning inventory and a $42,000 ending inventory.

d.   There was no beginning inventory but there was a $21,000 ending inventory.

Given the following accounts with normal year-end balances, prepare the entry to close the income statement accounts that have debit balances (entry 2):

QS 5–3 (LO 3)

Merchandise inventory	$ 34,800
Jan Dean, capital	115,300
Jan Dean, withdrawals	4,000
Sales	157,200
Sales returns and allowances	3,500
Sales discounts	1,700
Purchases	102,000
Purchases returns and allowances	8,100
Purchases discounts	2,000
Transportation-in	5,400
Depreciation expense	7,300
Salaries expense	29,500
Miscellaneous expenses	1,900

Refer to the information in QS 5–3. Prepare the entry to close the income statement accounts that have debit balances (entry 2) assuming the business uses the adjusting entry approach to record the change in merchandise inventory.

QS 5–4 (LO 4)

Use the following information to calculate the acid-test ratio:

QS 5–5 (LO 5)

Cash	$1,000
Accounts receivable	2,500
Inventory	6,000
Prepaid expenses	500
Accounts payable	3,750
Other current liabilities	1,250

EXERCISES

Insert the letter for each term in the blank space beside the definition that it most closely matches:

Exercise 5–1 Merchandising terms (LO 1, 2)

A. Cash discount
B. Credit period
C. Discount period
D. FOB destination

E. FOB shipping point
F. Gross profit
G. Inventory

H. Purchases discount
I. Sales discount
J. Trade discount

___ 1.   An agreement that ownership of goods is transferred at the buyer's place of business.

___ 2.   The time period in which a cash discount is available.

___ 3.   The difference between net sales and the cost of goods sold.

___ 4.   A reduction in a receivable or payable that is granted if it is paid within the discount period.

___ 5.   A cash discount taken against an amount owed to a supplier of goods.

___ 6.   An agreement that ownership of goods is transferred at the seller's place of business.

___ 7.   A reduction below a list or catalog price that is negotiated in setting the selling price of goods.

___ 8. A cash discount taken by customers against an amount owed to the seller.

___ 9. The time period that can pass before a customer's payment is due.

___ 10. The goods that a company owns and expects to sell to its customers.

Exercise 5–2
Calculating cost of goods sold
(LO 2)

Determine each of the missing numbers in the following situations:

	a	b	c
Purchases	$45,000	$80,000	$61,000
Purchases discounts	2,000	?	1,300
Purchases returns and allowances	1,500	3,000	2,200
Transportation-in	?	7,000	8,000
Beginning inventory	3,500	?	18,000
Cost of goods purchased	44,700	79,000	?
Ending inventory	2,200	15,000	?
Cost of goods sold	?	83,200	68,260

Exercise 5–3
Recording journal entries for
merchandise transactions
(LO 2)

Prepare journal entries to record the following transactions for a retail store:

March 2 Purchased merchandise from Alfa Company under the following terms: $1,800 invoice price, 2/15, n/60, FOB factory.

3 Paid $125 for shipping charges on the purchase of March 2.

4 Returned to Alfa Company unacceptable merchandise that had an invoice price of $300.

17 Sent a check to Alfa Company for the March 2 purchase, net of the discount and the returned merchandise.

18 Purchased merchandise from Bravo Company under the following terms: $2,500 invoice price, 2/10, n/30, FOB destination.

21 After brief negotiations, received a credit memorandum from Bravo Company granting a $700 allowance on the purchase of March 18.

28 Sent a check to Bravo Company paying for the March 18 purchase, net of the discount and the allowance.

Exercise 5–4
Analyzing and recording
merchandise transactions and
returns
(LO 1, 2)

On May 12, Wilcox Company accepted delivery of $20,000 of merchandise and received an invoice dated May 11, with terms of 3/10, n/30, FOB Garner Company's factory. When the goods were delivered, Wilcox Company paid $185 to Express Shipping Service for the delivery charges on the merchandise. The next day, Wilcox Company returned $800 of defective goods to the seller, which received them one day later. On May 21, Wilcox Company mailed a check to Garner Company for the amount owed on that date. It was received the following day.

Required

a. Present the journal entries that Wilcox Company should record for these transactions.

b. Present the journal entries that Garner Company should record for these transactions.

Exercise 5–5
Analyzing and recording
merchandise transactions and
discounts
(LO 1, 2)

Sandra's Store purchased merchandise from a manufacturer with an invoice price of $11,000 and credit terms of 3/10, n/60, and paid within the discount period.

Required

a. Prepare the journal entries that the purchaser should record for the purchase and payment.

b. Prepare the journal entries that the seller should record for the sale and collection.

c. Assume that the buyer borrowed enough cash to pay the balance on the last day of the discount period at an annual interest rate of 8% and paid it back on the last day of the credit period. Calculate how much the buyer saved by following this strategy. (Use a 365-day year.)

The following information appeared in a company's income statement:

Exercise 5–6
Calculating expenses and cost
of goods sold
(LO 1, 2)

Sales	$300,000
Sales returns	15,000
Sales discounts	4,500
Beginning inventory	25,000
Purchases	180,000
Purchases returns and allowances	6,000
Purchases discounts	3,600
Transportation-in	11,000
Gross profit from sales	105,000
Net income	55,000

Required

Calculate the *(a)* total operating expenses, *(b)* cost of goods sold, and *(c)* ending inventory.

Fill in the blanks in the following income statements. Identify any losses by putting the amount in parentheses.

Exercise 5–7
Calculating expenses and
income
(LO 1, 2)

	a	b	c	d	e
Sales	$40,000	$85,000	$24,000	$?	$59,000
Cost of goods sold:					
Beginning inventory	$ 4,000	$ 6,200	$ 5,000	$ 3,500	$ 6,400
Purchases	24,000	?	?	16,000	14,000
Ending inventory	?	(5,400)	(6,000)	(3,300)	?
Cost of goods sold	$22,700	$31,800	$?	$?	$14,000
Gross profit	$?	$?	$ 2,500	$22,800	$?
Expenses	6,000	21,300	8,100	1,300	15,000
Net income (loss)	$?	$31,900	$ (5,600)	$21,500	$?

The following accounts and balances are taken from the year-end adjusted trial balance of the Vintage Shop, a single proprietorship. Use the information in these columns to complete the requirements.

Exercise 5–8
Multiple-step income
statement and other
calculations
(LO 3)

	Debit	Credit
Merchandise inventory	$ 28,000	
Sales		$425,000
Sales returns and allowances	16,500	
Sales discounts	4,000	
Purchases	240,000	
Purchases returns and allowances		18,000
Purchases discounts		2,000
Transportation-in	6,000	
Selling expenses	35,000	
General and administrative expenses	95,000	

The count of the ending inventory shows that its cost is $37,000.

Required

a. Calculate the company's net sales for the year.

b. Calculate the company's cost of goods purchased for the year.

c. Calculate the company's cost of goods sold for the year.

d. Prepare a multiple-step income statement for the year that lists net sales, cost of goods sold, gross profit, the operating expenses, and net income.

Use the information provided in Exercise 5–8 to prepare a classified income statement that shows the calculations of net sales and cost of goods sold.

Exercise 5–9
Classified income statement
(LO 3)

Closing entries
(LO 3)

The Vintage Shop described in Exercise 5–8 is owned and operated by Otto Vintage. The ending balance of Vintage's withdrawals account is $25,000. Prepare four closing entries for this company. Post the entries to a balance column account for Merchandise Inventory that includes the beginning balance.

Adjusting entry approach
(LO 4)

The Vintage Shop described in Exercise 5–8 is owned and operated by Otto Vintage. The ending balance of Vintage's withdrawals account is $25,000. Assume that the company uses the adjusting entry approach to update its inventory account. Prepare adjusting and closing journal entries for this company, and post them to a balance column account for Merchandise Inventory that includes the beginning balance.

Preparing reports from closing entries
(LO 3)

The following closing entries for Fox Fixtures Co. were made on March 31, the end of its annual accounting period:

1	Merchandise Inventory	11,000.00	
	Sales	445,000.00	
	Purchases Returns and Allowances	22,000.00	
	Purchases Discounts	11,400.00	
	Income Summary		489,400.00
	To close temporary accounts with credit balances and record the ending inventory.		

2.	Income Summary	453,300.00	
	Merchandise Inventory		15,000.00
	Sales Returns and Allowances		25,000.00
	Sales Discounts		16,000.00
	Purchases		286,000.00
	Transportation-In		8,800.00
	Selling Expenses		69,000.00
	General and Administrative Expenses . . .		33,500.00
	To close temporary accounts with debit balances and to remove the beginning inventory balance.		

Required

Use the information in the closing entries to prepare:

a.   A calculation of net sales.

b.   A calculation of cost of goods purchased.

c.   A calculation of cost of goods sold.

d.   A multiple-step income statement for the year that lists net sales, cost of goods sold, gross profit, the operating expenses, and net income.

Preparing a work sheet for a merchandising proprietorship
(LO 4)

The following unadjusted trial balance was taken from the ledger of Johnson's Newsstand at the end of its fiscal year. (To reduce your effort, the account balances are relatively small.)

JOHNSON'S NEWSSTAND
Unadjusted Trial Balance
December 31

No.	Title	Debit	Credit
101	Cash	$ 3,700	
106	Accounts receivable	1,800	
119	Merchandise inventory	1,200	
125	Store supplies	600	
201	Accounts payable		$ 140
209	Salaries payable		
301	Tod Johnson, capital		5,785
302	Tod Johnson, withdrawals	375	
413	Sales		6,000
414	Sales returns and allowances	145	
505	Purchases	3,200	
506	Purchases discounts		125
507	Transportation-in	80	
622	Salaries expense	700	
640	Rent expense	250	
651	Store supplies expense		
	Totals	$12,050	$12,050

Required

Use the preceding information and the following additional facts to complete an eight-column work sheet for the company (do not include columns for the adjusted trial balance).

a. The ending inventory of store supplies was $450.

b. Accrued salaries at the end of the year were $60.

c. The ending merchandise inventory was $1,360.

Calculate the current and acid-test ratios in each the following cases:

	Case X	Case Y	Case Z
Cash	$ 800	$ 910	$1,100
Short-term investments			500
Receivables		990	800
Inventory	2,000	1,000	4,000
Prepaid expenses	1,200	600	900
Total current assets	$4,000	$3,500	$7,300
Current liabilities	$2,200	$1,100	$3,650

Exercise 5–14
Acid-test ratio
(LO 5)

PROBLEMS

Prepare general journal entries to record the following transactions of the Belton Company and determine the cost of goods purchased and net sales for the month. (Use a separate account for each receivable and payable; for example, record the purchase on July 1 in Accounts Payable—Jones Co.)

Problem 5–1
Journal entries for merchandising activities
(LO 1, 2)

July 1   Purchased merchandise from the Jones Company for $3,000 under credit terms of 1/15, n/30, FOB factory.

2   Sold merchandise to Terra Co. for $800 under credit terms of 2/10, n/60, FOB shipping point.

3   Paid $100 for freight charges on the purchase of July 1.

8   Sold $1,600 of merchandise for cash.

9   Purchased merchandise from the Keene Co. for $2,300 under credit terms of 2/15, n/30, FOB destination.

July 12   Received a $200 credit memorandum acknowledging the return of merchandise purchased on July 9.

13   Received the balance due from the Terra Co. for the credit sale dated July 2, net of the discount.

16   Paid the balance due to the Jones Company within the discount period.

19   Sold merchandise to Urban Co. for $1,250 under credit terms of 2/10, n/60, FOB shipping point.

21   Issued a $150 credit memorandum to Urban Co. for an allowance on goods sold on July 19.

22   Received a debit memorandum from Urban Co. for an error that overstated the total invoice by $50.

24   Paid the Keene Co. the balance due after deducting the discount.

30   Received the balance due from the Urban Co. for the credit sale dated July 19, net of the discount.

31   Sold merchandise to Terra Co. for $5,000 under credit terms of 2/10, n/60, FOB shipping point.

CHECK FIGURE:
Total cost of goods purchased, $5,128

Problem 5–2
Income statement calculations and formats
(LO 1, 2, 3)

The following amounts appeared on the Gershwin Company's adjusted trial balance as of October 31, the end of its fiscal year:

	Debit	Credit
Merchandise inventory	$ 25,000	
Other assets	140,000	
Liabilities		$ 37,000
G. Gershwin, capital		117,650
G. Gershwin, withdrawals	17,000	
Sales		210,000
Sales returns and allowances	15,000	
Sales discounts	2,250	
Purchases	90,000	
Purchases returns and allowances		4,300
Purchases discounts		1,800
Transportation-in	3,100	
Sales salaries expense	28,000	
Rent expense, selling space	10,000	
Store supplies expense	3,000	
Advertising expense	18,000	
Office salaries expense	16,000	
Rent expense, office space	2,500	
Office supplies expense	900	
Totals	$370,750	$370,750

A physical count shows that the cost of the ending inventory is $27,000.

Required

1.   Calculate the company's net sales for the year.

2.   Calculate the company's cost of goods purchased for the year.

3.   Calculate the company's cost of goods sold for the year.

4.   Present a multiple-step income statement that lists the company's net sales, cost of goods sold, and gross profit, as well the components and amounts of selling expenses and general and administrative expenses.

CHECK FIGURE:
Part 5, total expenses, $163,400

5.   Present a condensed single-step income statement that lists these expenses: cost of goods sold, selling expenses, and general and administrative expenses.

Use the data for the Gershwin Company in Problem 5–2 to meet the following requirements:

Problem 5–3
Closing entries and interpreting information about discounts and returns
(LO 1, 3)

Required

Preparation component:

1. Prepare closing entries for the company as of October 31.

Analysis component:

2. All of the company's purchases were made on credit and the suppliers uniformly offer a 3% discount. Does it appear that the company's cash management system is accomplishing the goal of taking all available discounts?

3. In prior years, the company has experienced a 4% return rate on its sales, which means that approximately 4% of its gross sales were for items that were eventually returned outright or that caused the company to grant allowances to customers. How does this year's record compare to prior years' results?

CHECK FIGURE:
Second closing entry: debit to Income Summary, $213,750

Refer to the Gershwin Company data in Problem 5-2 and notice that the adjusted trial balance reflects the closing entry approach to accounting for merchandise inventory. Now assume that the company has decided to switch to the adjusting entry approach.

Problem 5–4
Adjusting entries, closing entries, and interpreting information about discounts and returns
(LO 1, 3, 4)

Required

Preparation component:

1. Prepare adjusting entries to update the Merchandise Inventory account at October 31 and then prepare closing entries for the company as of October 31.

Analysis component:

2. All of the company's purchases were made on credit and the suppliers uniformly offer a 2.1% discount. Does it appear that the company's cash management system is accomplishing the goal of taking all available discounts?

3. In prior years, the company has experienced a 9% return rate on its sales, which means that approximately 9% of its gross sales were for items that were eventually returned outright or that caused the company to grant allowances to customers. How does this year's record compare to prior years' results?

CHECK FIGURE:
Second closing entry: debit to Income Summary, $188,750

Problem 5–5
Work sheet, income
statements, and acid-test ratio
(LO 3, 4, 5)

The following unadjusted trial balance was prepared at the end of the fiscal year for Ruth's Place:

RUTH'S PLACE
Unadjusted Trial Balance
December 31

101	Cash	$ 4,000	
119	Merchandise inventory	9,900	
125	Store supplies	5,000	
128	Prepaid insurance	2,000	
165	Store equipment	45,000	
166	Accumulated depreciation, store equipment		$ 6,000
201	Accounts payable		8,000
301	Ruth Helm, capital		35,200
302	Ruth Helm, withdrawals	3,500	
413	Sales		90,000
415	Sales discounts	1,000	
505	Purchases	38,000	
506	Purchases returns and allowances		800
508	Transportation-in	1,800	
612	Depreciation expense, store equipment		
622	Salaries expense	16,000	
637	Insurance expense		
640	Rent expense	5,000	
651	Store supplies expense		
655	Advertising expense	8,800	
	Totals	$140,000	$140,000

Required

1. Use the unadjusted trial balance and the following information to prepare an eight-column work sheet for the company:

   a. The ending inventory of store supplies is $650.

   b. Expired insurance for the year is $1,200.

   c. Depreciation expense for the year is $9,000.

   d. The ending merchandise inventory is $11,500.

2. Prepare a detailed multiple-step income statement that would be used by the store's owner.

3. Prepare a single-step income statement that would be provided to decision makers outside the company.

CHECK FIGURE:
Part 3, total expenses, $81,750

4. Compute the company's current and acid-test ratios as of December 31.

SERIAL PROBLEM

Emerald Computer Services

(The first three segments of this comprehensive problem were presented in Chapters 2, 3, and 4. If those segments have not been completed, the assignment can begin at this point. However, the student will need to use the facts presented on pages 100–101 in Chapter 2, page 145 in Chapter 3, and page 181 in Chapter 4. Because of its length, this problem is most easily solved if students use the Working Papers that accompany this text.)

Earlier segments of this problem have described how Tracy Green created Emerald Computer Services on October 1, 19X1. The company has been successful, and its list of customers has started to grow. To accommodate the growth, the accounting system is ready to be modified to set up separate accounts for each customer. The following list of customers includes the account number used for each account and any balance as of the end of 19X1. Green decided to add a fourth digit with a decimal point to the 106 account number that had been used for the single Accounts Receivable account. This modification allows the existing chart of accounts to continue being used. The list also shows the balances that two customers owed as of December 31, 19X1:

Account	No.	Dec. 31 Balance
Alpha Printing Co.	106.1	
Bravo Productions	106.2	
Charles Company	106.3	$ 900
Delta Fixtures, Inc.	106.4	
Echo Canyon Ranch	106.5	
Fox Run Estates	106.6	$1,000
Golf Course Designs, Inc.	106.7	
Hotel Pollo del Mar	106.8	
Indiana Manuf. Co.	106.9	

In response to frequent requests from customers, Green has decided to begin selling computer software. The company will extend credit terms of 1/10, n/30 to customers who purchase merchandise. No cash discount will be available on consulting fees. The following additional accounts were added to the General Ledger to allow the system to account for the company's new merchandising activities:

Account	No.
Merchandise Inventory	119
Sales	413
Sales Returns and Allowances	414
Sales Discounts	415
Purchases	505
Purchases Returns and Allowances	506
Purchases Discounts	507
Transportation-In	508

Because the accounting system does not use reversing entries, all revenue and expense accounts have zero balances as of January 1, 19X2.

Required

1. Prepare journal entries to record each of the following transactions for Emerald Computer Services.

2. Post the journal entries to the accounts in the company's General Ledger. (Use asset, liability, and capital accounts that start with the balance as of December 31, 19X1.)

3. Prepare a six-column table similar to Illustration 3–3 that presents the unadjusted trial balance, the March 31 adjustments, and the adjusted trial balance.

   Do not prepare closing entries and do not journalize the adjusting entries or post them to the ledger.

4. Prepare an interim income statement for the three months ended March 31, 19X2. Use a detailed multiple-step format that shows calculations of net sales, total revenues, cost of goods sold, total expenses, and net income.

5. Prepare an interim statement of changes in owner's equity for the three months ended March 31, 19X2.

6. Prepare an interim balance sheet as of March 31, 19X2.

Transactions:

Jan. 4 Paid Fran Sims for five days, including one day in addition to the four unpaid days from the prior year.

6 Tracy Green invested an additional $12,000 cash in the business.

7 Purchased $2,800 of merchandise from SoftHead Co. on terms of 1/10, n/30, FOB shipping point.

8 Received $1,000 from Fox Run Estates as final payment on its account.

10 Completed 5-day project for Alpha Printing Co. and billed them $3,000, which is the total price of $4,000 less the advance payment of $1,000.

Jan. 13 Sold merchandise with a retail value of $2,100 to Delta Fixtures, Inc., with terms of 1/10, n/30, FOB shipping point.

14 Paid $350 for freight charges on the merchandise purchased on January 7.

16 Received $1,500 cash from Golf Course Designs, Inc., for computer services.

17 Paid SoftHead Co. for the purchase on January 7, net of the discount.

21 Delta Fixtures, Inc., returned $200 of defective merchandise from its purchase on January 13.

22 Received the balance due from Delta Fixtures, Inc., net of the discount and the credit for the returned merchandise.

23 Returned defective merchandise to SoftHead Co. and accepted credit against future purchases. Its cost, net of the discount, was $198.

26 Sold $2,900 of merchandise on credit to Hotel Pollo del Mar.

28 Purchased $4,000 of merchandise from SoftHead Co. on terms of 1/10, n/30, FOB destination.

29 Received a $198 credit memo from SoftHead Co. concerning the merchandise returned on January 23.

31 Paid Fran Sims for 10 days' work.

Feb. 1 Paid $2,250 to the Town Hall Mall for another three months' rent.

3 Paid SoftHead Co. for the balance due, net of the cash discount, less the $198 amount in the credit memo.

4 Paid $400 to the local newspaper for advertising.

11 Received the balance due from Alpha Printing Co. for fees billed on January 10.

16 Paid $2,000 to Tracy Green as a withdrawal.

23 Sold $1,600 of merchandise on credit to Golf Course Designs, Inc.

26 Paid Fran Sims for 8 days' work.

27 Reimbursed Tracy Green's business automobile mileage for 600 miles at $0.25 per mile.

Mar. 8 Purchased $1,200 of computer supplies from AAA Supply Co. on credit.

9 Received the balance due from Golf Course Designs, Inc., for merchandise sold on February 23.

15 Repaired the company's computer at the cost of $430.

16 Received $2,130 cash from Indiana Manuf. Co. for computing services.

19 Paid the full amount due to AAA Supply Co. including amounts created on December 13 and March 8.

24 Billed Bravo Productions for $2,950 of computing services.

25 Sold $900 of merchandise on credit to Echo Canyon Ranch.

30 Sold $1,110 of merchandise on credit to Charles Company.

31 Reimbursed Tracy Green's business automobile mileage for 400 miles at $0.25 per mile.

Information for the March 31 adjustments and financial statements:

a. The March 31 inventory of computing supplies is $670.

b. Three more months have passed since the company purchased the annual insurance policy at the cost of $1,440.

c. Fran Sims has not been paid for 7 days of work.

d. Three months have passed since any prepaid rent cost has been transferred to expense.

e. Depreciation on the computer for January through March is $750.

f. Depreciation on the office equipment for January through March is $500.

g. The March 31 inventory of merchandise is $2,182.

CRITICAL THINKING: ESSAYS, PROBLEMS, AND CASES

Analytical Essays

AE 5–1
(LO 1)

Briefly explain why a company's manager would want the accounting system to record a customer's return of unsatisfactory goods in the Sales Returns and Allowances account instead of the Sales account. In addition, explain whether the information would be useful for external decision makers.

AE 5–2
(LO 2)

A retail company's accountant recently compiled the cost of the ending merchandise inventory to use in preparing the financial statements. In developing the measure, the accountant did not know that $10,000 of incoming goods had been shipped by a supplier on December 31 under an FOB factory agreement. These goods had been recorded as a purchase, but they were not included in the physical count because they were not on hand. Explain how this overlooked fact would affect the company's financial statements and these ratios: return on equity, debt ratio, current ratio, profit margin, and acid-test ratio.

Financial Reporting Problem

(LO 1, 2, 3)

Wanda Wonder, the owner of the WonderFull Store, has operated the company for several years, but has never used an accrual accounting system. To have more useful information, Wonder has engaged you to help prepare an income statement for 19X2. Based on data that you have gathered from the cash-basis accounting system and other documents, you have been able to prepare the following balance sheets as of the beginning and end of 19X2:

	December 31	
	19X1	**19X2**
Cash	$ 5,400	$ 42,250
Accounts receivable	18,500	22,600
Merchandise inventory	39,700	34,000
Equipment (net of depreciation)	87,000	56,000
Total assets	$150,600	$154,850
Accounts payable	$ 28,300	$ 36,250
Wages payable	2,200	1,700
Wanda Wonder, capital	120,100	116,900
Total liabilities and owner's equity ..	$150,600	$154,850

The store's cash records also provided the following facts for 19X2:

Amount collected on accounts receivable ..	$339,900
Payments for:	
Accounts payable	198,050
Employees' wages	52,000
All other operating expenses	29,000
Withdrawals by the owner	24,000

You have determined that all merchandise purchases and sales were made on credit, and that no equipment was either purchased or sold during the year.

Use the preceding information to calculate the amounts of the company's sales, cost of goods purchased, cost of goods sold, depreciation expense, and wages expense for 19X2. Then, prepare a multiple-step income statement that shows the company's gross profit.

Financial Statement Analysis Cases

FSAC 5–1
(LO 5)

Calculate the current and acid-test ratios for each of these three cases, and comment on your findings.

	Case A	Case B	Case C
Current assets:			
Cash	$ 500	$3,100	$ 600
Short-term investments	1,500	2,600	400
Accounts receivable	3,000	2,800	1,100
Interest receivable	200	900	0
Merchandise inventory	4,000	1,000	7,000
Office supplies	300	500	1,000
Prepaid insurance	1,100	600	900
Prepaid rent	900	0	500
Current liabilities:			
Accounts payable	$1,300	$2,400	$4,000
Interest payable	300	700	100
Salaries payable	600	800	200
Notes payable	2,800	1,100	700

FSAC 5–2
(LO 1, 5)

Use the financial statements for Apple Computer, Inc., in Appendix F at the end of the book to find the answers to these questions:

a. Although Apple manufactures most of the goods that it sells, assume that the amounts reported for inventories and cost of sales were all purchased ready for resale and then calculate the total cost of goods purchased during the fiscal year ended September 24, 1993.

b. Calculate the current and acid-test ratios as of the end of the 1993 and 1992 fiscal years. (Assume that the Other current assets are not quick assets.) Comment on what you find.

Ethical Issues Essay

Describe the problem faced by Renee Fleck in the As a Matter of Ethics case on page 197 and evaluate her alternative courses of action.

ANSWERS TO PROGRESS CHECKS

5–1   *b*

5–2   Gross profit is the difference between net sales and cost of goods sold.

5–3   Keeping sales returns and allowances and sales discounts separate from sales makes useful information readily available to managers for internal monitoring and decision making. This information is not likely to be reported outside the company because it would not be useful for external decision makers.

5–4   Under credit terms of 2/10, n/60, the credit period is 60 days and the discount period is 10 days.

5–5   *b*

5–6   With a periodic inventory system, the cost of goods sold is determined at the end of an accounting period by adding the cost of goods purchased to the beginning inventory and subtracting the ending inventory.

5–7   FOB means free on board. The term *FOB destination* means that the seller does not transfer ownership of

the goods to the buyer until they arrive at the buyer's place of business. Thus, the seller is responsible for paying the shipping charges and bears the risk of damage during shipment.

5–8   *c*

5–9   The classified income statement; the single-step income statement.

5–10 The second closing entry, which closes the income statement accounts with debit balances, includes a credit to Merchandise Inventory to remove the beginning inventory amount.

5–11 *d*

5–12 Both approaches will report the same ending inventory and net income.

5–13 *d*

5–14 The acid-test ratio.

CHAPTER 6

Accounting Systems

Karly and Jeff Frankel own and operate a small business that sells nutritional supplements. During 1993, sales revenue amounted to $37,600. They use a simple accounting system and record the sales of their products in a single Sales account. The Frankels also own some Minnesota Mining and Manufacturing Company (3M) stock and have observed that 3M's accounting system must be much more complex than theirs. For example, 3M's 1993 income statement reported revenues of $14,020 million. In various notes to the statements, 3M provided substantially more details about these revenues. The Frankels wonder how this information can be captured by 3M's accounting system and whether their own management decisions might be better served by a more complex accounting system.

Minnesota Mining and Manufacturing Company—1993
(In millions)

Net sales:	
Industrial and consumer	$ 5,350
Information, imaging and electronic	4,520
Life sciences	4,132
Eliminations and other	18
Total company	$14,020

Net sales:	
United States	$7,126
Europe	3,646
Asia Pacific	2,154
Other areas	1,094
Total company	$14,020

LEARNING OBJECTIVES

After studying Chapter 6, you should be able to:

1. **Describe the five basic components of an accounting system.**
2. **Describe the types of computers used in large and small accounting systems, the role of software in those systems, and the different approaches to inputting and processing data, including the use of networking.**
3. **Explain special journals and controlling accounts, use them to record transactions, and explain how to test the posting of entries to the Accounts Receivable and Accounts Payable subsidiary ledgers.**
4. **Explain the use of special and general journals in accounting for sales taxes and sales returns and allowances, and explain how sales invoices can serve as a Sales Journal.**
5. **Explain the nature and use of business segment information.**
6. **Define or explain the words and phrases listed in the chapter glossary.**

Even in a small business such as the one operated by the Frankels, a large amount of information must be processed through the accounting system. Thus, the accounting system should be designed to process the information efficiently. As you study this chapter, you will learn some general concepts to follow in designing an efficient accounting system. The chapter begins by explaining the basic components of an accounting system, whether it is a manual or computer-based system. After considering some of the special characteristics of computer-based systems, the chapter then explains some of the labor-saving procedures employed in manual systems. These include efficient ways of processing routine transactions such as credit sales, cash receipts, credit purchases, and cash disbursements.

THE COMPONENTS OF AN ACCOUNTING SYSTEM

LO 1

Describe the five basic components of an accounting system.

Accounting systems consist of people, forms, procedures, and equipment. These systems must be designed to capture data about the transactions of the entity and to generate from that data a variety of financial, managerial, and tax accounting reports. Because all accounting systems must accomplish these same broad objectives, both manual and computerized accounting systems include the same basic components. However, computer-based systems provide more accuracy, speed, efficiency, and convenience.

The five common components of manual and computerized accounting systems are:

- Source documents.
- Input devices.
- Data processor.
- Data storage.
- Output devices.

Illustration 6–1 shows the relationships between these five components.

Source Documents

Chapter 2 described some of the business papers that companies use in the process of completing transactions. These business papers are called *source documents* because they provide a basis for making accounting entries. In other words, they provide the data that are entered in and processed by the accounting system. You are no doubt familiar with some kinds of source documents such as bank statements and checks received from other parties. Other examples of source documents include invoices from suppliers, billings to customers, and employee earnings records.

Illustration 6–1   The Components of an Accounting System

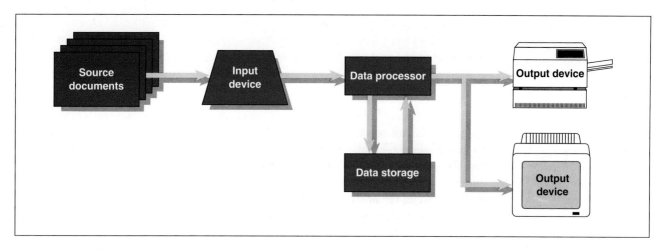

In manual accounting systems, source documents consist of paper documents. Paper documents are also very important for computerized systems, but some source documents take other forms. For example, some companies send invoices directly from their own computers to their customers' computers. The source documents in this case are computer files.

Accurate source documents are important for the proper functioning of an accounting system. If the information going into the system is faulty and incomplete, the information coming out of the system will also be faulty and incomplete. (In computer jargon, the results of defective input are described as garbage in, garbage out.)

Input Devices

The second component of an accounting system is one or more **input devices.** As shown in Illustration 6–1, an input device transfers the information from source documents to the data processing component of the accounting system. In a computer-based system, this often involves converting the data on the source documents from a written form into electronic signals. In addition to transferring data from source documents to the data processor, input devices are used to tell the data processing component how to process the data.

In prior chapters, you used an input device when you solved exercises and problems by recording the effects of transactions with journal entries. If you recorded transactions using the *GLAS* or *SPATS* supplements that accompany this text, you used the keyboard of a computer as the input device. When you recorded transactions using pencil and paper, you were using these items as the input device for a manual accounting system.

The most common input device for a computer-based accounting system is a keyboard. System operators use keyboards to transfer data from the source documents into the computer. Another input device is a *bar code reader* like those used in grocery and other retail stores. With a bar code reader, the clerk merely moves purchased items over the reader, which picks up their code numbers and sends the data to the computer. Other input devices include *scanners* that read words and numbers directly from source documents.

In both manual and computer systems, companies promote clerical accuracy by using routine procedures to input data. Also, controls should be in place to ensure that only authorized individuals can input data to the accounting system. Such controls help protect the integrity of the system and also allow incorrect input to be traced back to its source.

Data Processor

The third component of an accounting system is the **data processor** which interprets, manipulates, and summarizes recorded information so it can be used in analyses and reports. In manual systems, the primary data processor is the accountant's brain. However, the manual processing of data is not entirely a mental process. That is, the accountant uses the journal, the ledger, the working papers, and such procedures as posting to convert the journal entry data into more useful information. Of course, few if any accounting systems are completely manual. For example, calculators are essential equipment for manual systems.

As a result of technical developments over the last two decades, many manual accounting systems have been replaced by computer-based systems. The data processor in a computer-based system includes both *hardware* and *software*. Hardware is the machinery that performs the steps called for by the software.

The software consists of computer programs that specify the operations to be performed on the data. Software actually controls the whole system, including input, file management, processing, and output. The expanded use of computer-based systems has provided dramatic growth opportunities for companies that provide various kinds of software. For example, **Microsoft Corporation,** the world's largest producer of software with revenues in excess of $3.7 billion in 1993, began operations in 1975.

Data Storage

Data storage is an essential component of both manual and computer-based systems. As data is inputted and processed, it must be saved so it can be used as output or processed further. This stockpile of data (a database) should be readily accessible so periodic financial reports can be compiled quickly. In addition, data storage should support the preparation of special purpose reports that managers may request. The accounting database also serves as the primary source of information auditors use when they audit the financial statements. Companies also maintain files of source documents for use by auditors and to clear up errors or disputes.

In manual systems, data storage consists of files of paper documents. However, with a computer-based system, most of the data is stored on floppy diskettes, hard disks, or magnetic tapes. As a result of recent improvements, these devices can store very large amounts of data. For example, floppy diskettes can hold up to two megabytes of information (one megabyte is roughly equivalent to 500 double-spaced typed pages). Small digital-audio-tape (DAT) cassettes can hold hundreds of megabytes of information. Some hard disks can hold thousands of megabytes (1,000 megabytes is a gigabyte). Because of the recent improvements in data storage, accounting systems now can store much more detailed and extensive databases than was possible in the past. As a result, managers have much more information available to help them plan and control business activities.

In a computer-based system, data storage can be on-line (usually on a hard disk), which means that the data can be accessed whenever it is needed by the software. In contrast, when data is stored off-line, the data cannot be accessed until the computer operator inserts a disk or a magnetic tape into a drive.

Generally, we do not use the concepts of on-line and off-line storage in reference to manual accounting systems. However, one might argue that in a manual system, only the data stored in the accountant's brain is on-line; everything else is off-line.

Output Devices

The fifth component of an accounting system is the **output devices.** These allow information to be taken out of the system and placed in the hands of its users. Examples of output include bills to customers, checks payable to suppliers and employees, financial statements, and a variety of other internal reports.

For computer-based systems, the most common output devices are video screens and printers. Other output devices include telephones or direct phone line connections to the computer systems of suppliers or customers. When requests for output are entered, the data processor searches the database for the needed data, organizes it in the form of a report, and sends the information to an output device.

Depending on the output device, the information may be displayed on a screen, printed on paper, or expressed as a voice over the telephone. For example, a bank customer may call to find out the balance in his or her checking account. If a touchtone telephone serves as an input/output device, a recording may ask the customer to enter appropriate identifying information including the number of the account. With this input, the computer searches the database for the information and sends it back over the telephone. If the telephone is not used as an input/output device, the bank employee who answers the phone inputs the information request using a keyboard. The employee then reads the output on a video screen and relays it over the phone to the customer.

Another kind of output involves paying employees without writing paychecks. Instead, the company's computer system may send the payroll data directly to the computer system of the company's bank. Thus, the output of the company's system is an electronic fund transfer (EFT) from the company's bank account to the employees' bank accounts. The output device in this instance is the connection or interface between the computer systems of the company and the bank. Large companies are increasingly using EFTs. In other situations, the company's computer outputs the payroll data on a magnetic tape or disk. The tape or disk is then used by the bank to transfer the funds to the employees' bank accounts.

In addition to the preceding forms of output, many situations require printed output that computer systems produce on laser, impact, or ink-jet printers.

For companies using manual accounting systems, the production of output involves physically searching the records to find the needed data and then organizing it in a written report.

Progress Check

(Answers to Progress Checks are provided at the end of the chapter.)

6-1　Which one of the following components of an accounting system is not likely to include paper documents? *(a)* Source documents; *(b)* Data processor; *(c)* Data storage; *(d)* Output devices.

6-2　What does the data processor component of an accounting system accomplish?

6-3　What uses are made of the data that are stockpiled in the data storage component of an accounting system?

SMALL AND LARGE COMPUTER-BASED SYSTEMS

LO 2

Describe the types of computers used in large and small accounting systems, the role of software in those systems, and the different approaches to inputting and processing data, including the use of networking.

CUSTOM-DESIGNED AND OFF-THE-SHELF PROGRAMS

The world has seen radical changes in the use of computers since the first Apple computer was sold in 1980. Many of you are already proficient users of personal computers (PCs) such as those produced by **International Business Machines Corporation (IBM)** or by Apple Computer, Inc. These computers (often called *microcomputers*) are physically small, easy to operate, and increasingly inexpensive.

Although the use of microcomputers in business has greatly expanded in recent years, many companies also use larger computers called *mainframes*. These machines are able to process huge quantities of accounting data quickly. In addition, they help businesses perform other important tasks such as analyzing the results of market research, compiling stockholder information, and doing engineering design work for products and production lines. These computers include the AS series of machines produced by IBM and the VAX family manufactured by **Digital Equipment Corporation (DEC).**

Regardless of its size and speed, every computer does nothing more than execute instructions that are organized as programs. A program consists of a series of very specific instructions for obtaining data from input or storage, processing it, returning it to storage for later use, and sending it to an output device to produce a report.

Illustration 6–2 presents a flowchart of the steps that a computer program might use to process a stack of customer orders for merchandise. When this program is executed in a normal situation, the system creates a shipping order that identifies the products to be sent to customers. If a shipment causes the quantity on hand to fall below the minimum level, the system generates a purchase order to be approved by a manager. If the quantity on hand is less than the customer ordered, the system produces a partial shipping order as well as a report to the customer that the remainder is on back order. Then, if replacements have not been ordered already, the system produces a purchase order. If no units of the desired product are on hand, the system notifies the customer of the back order and issues a purchase order, unless one already exists. The system follows this process for each item ordered by each customer until the stack of orders is exhausted.

Despite the apparent complexity of the instructions in Illustration 6–2, this routine is actually incomplete. For example, it does not update the accounting records for sales and accounts receivable, nor does it deal with cash and trade discounts that might be offered to customers.

In the early days of computer systems, each program had to be custom designed using a programming language such as COBOL or FORTRAN. Since then, programmers have developed more flexible and easier-to-use languages. However, programming is a skill that only a limited number of people need to master. Instead, the expanded used of microcomputers has resulted in an increasing variety of off-the-shelf programs that are ready to be used.

Some off-the-shelf programs are general, multipurpose applications that accomplish a variety of different tasks. These programs include familiar word processor programs (such as Microsoft Word® and WordPerfect®), spreadsheet programs (such as Microsoft Excel® and Lotus® 1-2-3®), and database management programs (such as dBase®).

Other off-the-shelf programs are designed to meet very specific needs of users. These programs include a large number of accounting programs such as DacEasy® Accounting, Peachtree® Complete Accounting, and Great Plains® Accounting Series. Off-the-shelf programs are designed to be so user-friendly they guide users through the input steps and then ask which reports are desired.

Illustration 6–2 Flowchart for an Order-Processing Program

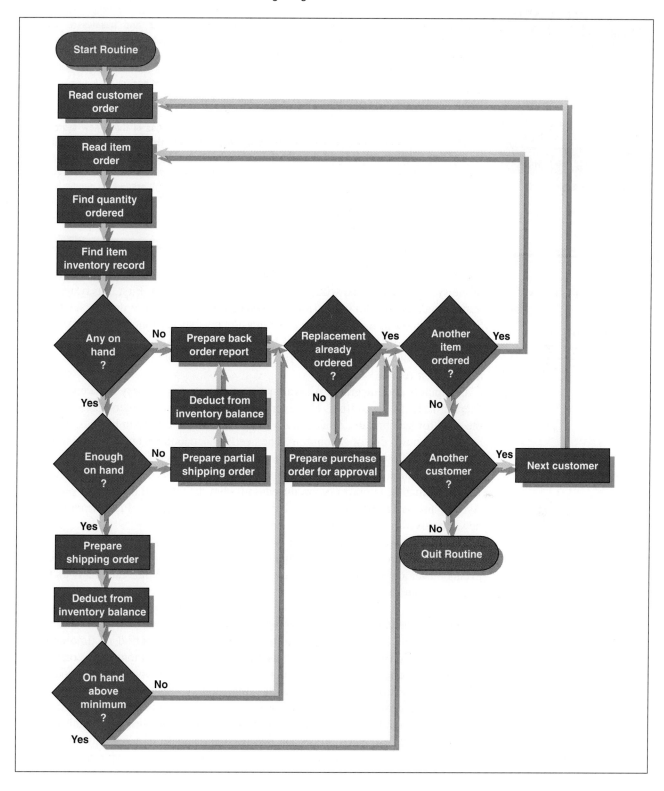

Many of the off-the-shelf accounting programs save time and minimize errors because they operate as *integrated* systems. In an integrated system, actions taken in one part of the system also produce results in related parts.

For example, when a credit sale is recorded in an integrated system, several parts

Brenda Smith, CPA

As a Matter of Opinion

Ms. Smith received her B.A. in accounting from the University of Colorado at Colorado Springs. She is a partner in Baird, Kurtz and Dobson, a public accounting firm in Colorado Springs. She has served as the chairperson of the Colorado Springs Chamber of Commerce, and on the governing boards of the American Group of CPAs and the Christian Management Association.

Successful business managers need information, and they need computers to get it for them. Yet, many people are still held back by a fear of computers. We need to learn to be as comfortable with computers as we are with our calculators.

The systems available to today's small businesses are great savers of time and effort. For example, many banks and businesses have linked their computers. This system instantly records deposits to a store's checking account and updates its sales and inventory records at the same time. A lot of paperwork is eliminated, and managers and employees can devote their skills to the business instead of bookkeeping.

Despite the abilities of these new systems, we have to know the appropriate accounting principles to avoid getting "garbage-in-garbage-out" results. While we don't need to understand how to program computers, we do need a basic understanding of their processes. And, we need to understand accounting so that we can make them work for us.

of the system are updated with one or two simple commands. First, the system stores transaction data (as in a journal) so that you can review the entire entry at a later time. Second, it updates the Cash and Accounts Receivable accounts. Third, it updates a detailed record of the amount owed by the customer. Fourth, it might update a detailed record of the products held for sale to show the number of units sold and the number that remain on hand.

Computers and integrated software programs have dramatically reduced the bookkeeping tasks in accounting. However, do not think that computers have eliminated the need for accountants. Nor should you conclude that success in business no longer requires a knowledge of accounting. The need for accountants and accounting knowledge is created by the need for information, not by the need for pencil and paper. Accountants continue to be in demand because their expertise is necessary to determine what information ought to be produced and what data should be used to produce it. Accountants are also needed to analyze and explain the output. Furthermore, writing new, improved programs requires a knowledge of accounting.

In short, the value of accounting knowledge does not disappear just because mechanical steps are done with a computer. You still need to understand the effects of events on the company and how they are reflected in financial statements and management reports.

BATCH AND ON-LINE SYSTEMS

Accounting systems also differ in how the input is entered and processed. With **batch processing,** the source documents are accumulated for a period of time and then processed all at the same time, such as once a day, week, or month. By comparison, with **on-line processing,** data are entered and processed as soon as source documents are available. As a result, the database is immediately updated.

The disadvantage of batch processing is that the database is not kept up to date during the times that source documents are being accumulated. In many situations, however, companies use batch processing because the database requires only periodic updating. For example, records used in sending bills to customers may require updating only once each month.

On-line processing has the advantage of keeping the database always up to date. However, it is more expensive because the software is more complicated and because it usually requires a much larger investment in hardware. On-line processing applications include airline reservations, credit card records, and rapid response mail-order processing.

As a Matter of Ethics

A CPA has a client whose business has grown significantly over the last couple of years and has reached the point where its accounting system has become inadequate for handling both the volume of transactions and management's needs for financial information. The client asks the CPA which software system would work best for the company.

The CPA has been offered a 10% commission by a software company for each purchase of its system by one of the CPA's clients. The price of one of these systems falls within the range specified by the client. Do you think that the CPA's evaluation of the alternative systems could be affected by this commission arrangement? Should it be? Should the CPA feel compelled to tell the client about the commission arrangement before making a recommendation?

COMPUTER NETWORKS

In many circumstances, firms create advantages by linking or networking computers with each other. **Computer networks** allow different users to share access to the same data and the same programs. A relatively small computer network is called a *local area network (LAN)*. This type of network links the machines within an office by special *hard-wired* hookups. For example, many universities have networks in their computer labs. Larger computer networks that are spread over long distances communicate over telephone lines by using *modems*.

In some cases, the need for information requires very large networks. Examples include the system used by Federal Express Corporation for tracking its packages and billing its customers and the system used by **Wal-Mart Stores, Inc.,** for monitoring inventory levels in each of its stores. These networks involve many computers (desktops and mainframes) and satellite communications to gather information and to provide ready access to the database from all locations.

We now turn to a discussion of some of the labor-saving procedures used to process transactions in manual systems. However, remember that accounting systems have similar purposes whether they are computer-based or manual in operation. Thus, your understanding of computer-based systems will be improved when you understand manual procedures.

Progress Check

6-4 In a computer-based accounting system:
   a. The accounting software is more efficient if it operates as an integrated system.
   b. The need for accountants is nearly eliminated.
   c. Data about transactions must be entered with on-line processing.
   d. The accountant must have the ability to program the computer.

6-5 What advantages do computer systems offer over manual systems?

6-6 Which of the following allows different computer users to access the same data and programs? (a) On-line processing; (b) Electronic Fund Transfers; (c) Bar code readers; (d) Local area networks.

SPECIAL JOURNALS

LO 3

Explain special journals and controlling accounts, use them to record transactions, and explain how to test the posting of entries to the Accounts Receivable and Accounts Payable subsidiary ledgers.

The General Journal is a flexible journal in which you can record any transaction. However, each debit and credit entered in a General Journal must be individually posted. As a result, a firm that uses a General Journal to record all the transactions of its business requires much time and labor to post the individual debits and credits.

One way to reduce the writing and the posting labor is to divide the transactions of a business into groups of similar transactions and to provide a separate **special journal** for recording the transactions in each group. For example, most of the transactions of a merchandising business fall into four groups: sales on credit, purchases on credit, cash receipts, and cash disbursements. When a special journal is provided for each group, the journals are:

1. A Sales Journal for recording credit sales.
2. A Purchases Journal for recording credit purchases.
3. A Cash Receipts Journal for recording cash receipts.
4. A Cash Disbursements Journal for recording cash payments.
5. A General Journal for the miscellaneous transactions not recorded in the special journals and also for adjusting, closing, and correcting entries.

The following illustrations show how special journals save time in journalizing and posting transactions. They do this by providing special columns for accumulating the debits and credits of similar transactions. These journals allow you to post the amounts entered in the special columns as column totals rather than as individual amounts. For example, you can save posting labor if you record credit sales for a month in a Sales Journal like the one at the top of Illustration 6–3. As the illustration shows, you do not post the credit sales to the general ledger accounts until the end of the month. Then, you calculate the total sales for the month and post the total as one debit to Accounts Receivable and as one credit to Sales. Only seven sales are recorded in the illustrated journal. However, if you assume the 7 sales represent 700 sales, you can better appreciate the posting labor saved by making only one debit to Accounts Receivable and one credit to Sales.

The special journal in Illustration 6–3 is also called a **columnar journal** because it has columns for recording the date, the customer's name, the invoice number, and the amount of each credit sale. Only credit sales are recorded in it, and they are recorded daily with the information about each sale placed on a separate line. Normally, the information is taken from a copy of the sales ticket or invoice prepared at the time of the sale. However, before discussing the journal further, you need to understand the role played by subsidiary ledgers.

KEEPING A SEPARATE ACCOUNT FOR EACH CREDIT CUSTOMER

In previous chapters, when we recorded credit sales, we debited a single account called Accounts Receivable. However, when a business has more than one credit customer, the accounts must show how much each customer has purchased, how much each customer has paid, and how much remains to be collected from each customer. To provide this information, businesses with credit customers must maintain a separate Account Receivable for each customer.

One possible way of keeping a separate account for each customer would be to keep all of these accounts in the same ledger that contains the financial statement accounts. However, this usually is not done. Instead, the ledger that contains the financial statement accounts, now called the **General Ledger,** continues to hold a single Accounts Receivable account. Then, a supplementary record is established in which a separate account is maintained for each customer. This supplementary record is called the **Accounts Receivable Ledger.** This subsidiary ledger may exist on tape or disk storage in a computerized system. In a manual system, the Accounts Receivable Ledger may take the form of a book or tray that contains the customer accounts. In either case, the customer accounts in the subsidiary ledger are kept separate from the Accounts Receivable account in the General Ledger.

Understand that when debits (or credits) to Accounts Receivable are posted twice (once to Accounts Receivable and once to the customer's account), this does not

Illustration 6–3   Posting from the Sales Journal

Sales Journal				Page 3
Date	Account Debited	Invoice Number	PR	Amount
Feb. 2	James Henry	307	√	450.00
7	Albert Smith	308	√	500.00
13	Sam Moore	309	√	350.00
15	Paul Roth	310	√	200.00
22	James Henry	311	√	225.00
25	Frank Booth	312	√	175.00
28	Albert Smith	313	√	250.00
28	Total—Accounts Receivable, Dr.; Sales, Cr.			2,150.00
				(106/413)

Individual amounts are posted daily to the subsidiary ledger.

Total is posted at the end of the month to the general ledger accounts.

Accounts Receivable Ledger

Frank Booth

Date	PR	Debit	Credit	Balance
Feb. 25	S3	175.00	5	175.00

James Henry

Date	PR	Debit	Credit	Balance
Feb. 2	S3	450.00		450.00
22	S3	225.00		675.00

Sam Moore

Date	PR	Debit	Credit	Balance
Feb. 13	S3	350.00		350.00

Paul Roth

Date	PR	Debit	Credit	Balance
Feb. 15	S3	200.00		200.00

Albert Smith

Date	PR	Debit	Credit	Balance
Feb. 7	S3	500.00		500.00
28	S3	250.00		750.00

General Ledger

Accounts Receivable   No. 106

Date	PR	Debit	Credit	Balance
Feb. 28	S3	2,150.00		2,150.00

Sales   No. 413

Date	PR	Debit	Credit	Balance
Feb. 28	S3		2,150.00	2,150.00

Note that the customer accounts are in a subsidiary ledger and the financial statement accounts are in the General Ledger.
Explanation columns are omitted from the accounts due to a lack of space.

Illustration 6–4   The Accounts Receivable Controlling Account and Subsidiary Ledger

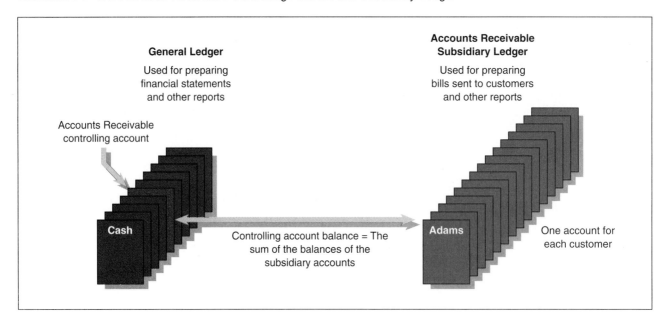

violate the requirement that debits equal credits. The equality of debits and credits is maintained in the General Ledger. The Accounts Receivable Ledger is simply a supplementary record that provides detailed information concerning each customer.

Illustration 6–4 shows the relationship between the Accounts Receivable controlling account and the accounts in the subsidiary ledger. Note that after all items are posted, the balance in the Accounts Receivable account should equal the sum of the balances in the customers' accounts. As a result, the Accounts Receivable account controls the Accounts Receivable Ledger and is called a **controlling account.** Since the Accounts Receivable Ledger is a supplementary record controlled by an account in the General Ledger, it is called a **subsidiary ledger.** After posting is completed, if the Accounts Receivable balance does not equal the sum of the customer account balances, you know an error has been made.

MAINTAINING A SEPARATE RECORD FOR EACH ACCOUNT PAYABLE

The Accounts Receivable account and the Accounts Receivable Ledger are not the only examples of controlling accounts and subsidiary ledgers. Most companies buy on credit from several suppliers. As a result, a company must keep a separate account for each creditor. To accomplish this, the firm maintains an Accounts Payable controlling account in the General Ledger and a separate account for each creditor in a subsidiary **Accounts Payable Ledger.** The controlling account, subsidiary ledger, and columnar journal techniques demonstrated thus far with accounts receivable also apply to the creditor accounts. The only difference is that a Purchases Journal and a Cash Disbursements Journal are used to record most of the transactions that affect these accounts. You will learn about these journals later in the chapter.

Another situation in which a subsidiary ledger often is used involves equipment. For example, a company with many items of office equipment might keep only one Office Equipment account in its General Ledger. This account would control a subsidiary ledger in which each item of equipment is recorded in a separate account.

Recall from the beginning of the chapter the detailed sales information **Minnesota Mining and Manufacturing Company** presented in its 1993 annual report. The presentation included the revenue of each major business segment and also the revenue earned in different regions of the world. However, 3M's accounting system undoubtedly keeps far more detailed sales records than reflected in the annual report. In fact, the company sells thousands of different products and no doubt is able to analyze the sales performance of each one of them.

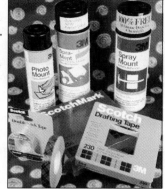

To some extent, this kind of detail is captured by having many different general ledger sales accounts. However, it also may be captured by using supplementary records that function like subsidiary ledgers. In fact, the concept of a subsidiary ledger may be applied in many different ways to ensure that the accounting system captures sufficient details to support possible analyses managers may want to make.

POSTING THE SALES JOURNAL

When customer accounts are maintained in a subsidiary ledger, a Sales Journal is posted as shown in Illustration 6–3. The individual sales recorded in the Sales Journal are posted each day to the proper customer accounts in the Accounts Receivable Ledger. These daily postings keep the customer accounts up-to-date. This is important in granting credit because the person responsible for granting credit should know the amount the credit-seeking customer currently owes. The source of this information is the customer's account; if the account is not up-to-date, an incorrect decision may be made.

Note the check marks in the Sales Journal's Posting Reference column. They indicate that the sales recorded in the journal were individually posted to the customer accounts in the Accounts Receivable Ledger. Check marks rather than account numbers are used because customer accounts may not be numbered. When the accounts are not numbered, they are arranged alphabetically in the Accounts Receivable Ledger so they can be located easily.

In addition to the daily postings to customer accounts, the Sales Journal's Amount column is totaled at the end of the month. Then, the total is debited to Accounts Receivable and credited to Sales. The credit records the month's revenue from charge sales. The debit records the resulting increase in accounts receivable.

IDENTIFYING POSTED AMOUNTS

When posting several journals to ledger accounts, you should indicate in the Posting Reference column before each posted amount the journal and the page number of the journal from which the amount was posted. Indicate the journal by using its initial. Thus, items posted from the Cash Disbursements Journal carry the initial *D* before their journal page numbers in the Posting Reference columns. Likewise, items from the Cash Receipts Journal carry the letter *R*. Those from the Sales Journal carry the initial *S*. Items from the Purchases Journal carry the initial *P*, and from the General Journal, the letter *G*.

6-7   **When special journals are used:**
       a. **A General Journal is not used.**
       b. **All cash payments by check are recorded in the Cash Disbursements Journal.**
       c. **All purchase transactions are recorded in the Purchases Journal.**
       d. **All sales transactions are recorded in the Sales Journal.**

6-8   **Why does a columnar journal save posting labor?**

6-9   **How can debits and credits remain equal when credit sales to customers are posted twice (once to Accounts Receivable and once to the customer's account)?**

6-10   **How can you identify the journal from which a particular amount in a ledger account was posted?**

CASH RECEIPTS JOURNAL

LO 3

Explain special journals and controlling accounts, use them to record transactions, and explain how to test the posting of entries to the Accounts Receivable and Accounts Payable subsidiary ledgers.

A Cash Receipts Journal that is designed to save labor through posting column totals must be a multicolumn journal. A multicolumn journal is necessary because different accounts are credited when cash is received from different sources. For example, the cash receipts of a store normally fall into three groups: (1) cash from credit customers in payment of their accounts, (2) cash from cash sales, and (3) cash from other sources. Note in Illustration 6–5 that a special column is provided for the credits that result when cash is received from each of these sources.

Cash from Credit Customers

When a Cash Receipts Journal similar to Illustration 6–5 is used to record cash received in payment of a customer's account, the customer's name is entered in the journal's Account Credited column. The amount credited to the customer's account is entered in the Accounts Receivable Credit column, and the debits to Sales Discounts and Cash are entered in the journal's last two columns.

Look at the Accounts Receivable Credit column. First, observe that this column contains only credits to customer accounts. Second, the individual credits are posted daily to the customer accounts in the subsidiary Accounts Receivable Ledger. Third, the column total is posted at the end of the month as a credit to the Accounts Receivable controlling account. This is the normal recording and posting procedure when using special journals and controlling accounts with subsidiary ledgers. Transactions are normally entered in a special journal column. Then, the individual amounts are posted to the subsidiary ledger accounts and the column totals are posted to the general ledger accounts.

Cash Sales

After cash sales are entered on one or more cash registers and totaled at the end of each day, the daily total is recorded with a debit to Cash and a credit to Sales. When using a Cash Receipts Journal like Illustration 6–5, the debits to Cash are entered in the Cash Debit column, and the credits in a special column headed Sales Credit. By using a separate Sales Credit column, the bookkeeper can post the total cash sales for a month as a single amount, the column total. (Although cash sales are normally journalized daily based on the cash register reading, cash sales are journalized only once each week in Illustration 6–5 to shorten the illustration.)

At the time they record daily cash sales in the Cash Receipts Journal, some bookkeepers, as in Illustration 6–5, place a check mark in the Posting Reference (PR) column to indicate that no amount is individually posted from that line of the journal. Other bookkeepers use a double check (√√) to distinguish amounts that are not posted to customer accounts from amounts that are posted.

Illustration 6-5 Posting from the Cash Receipts Journal

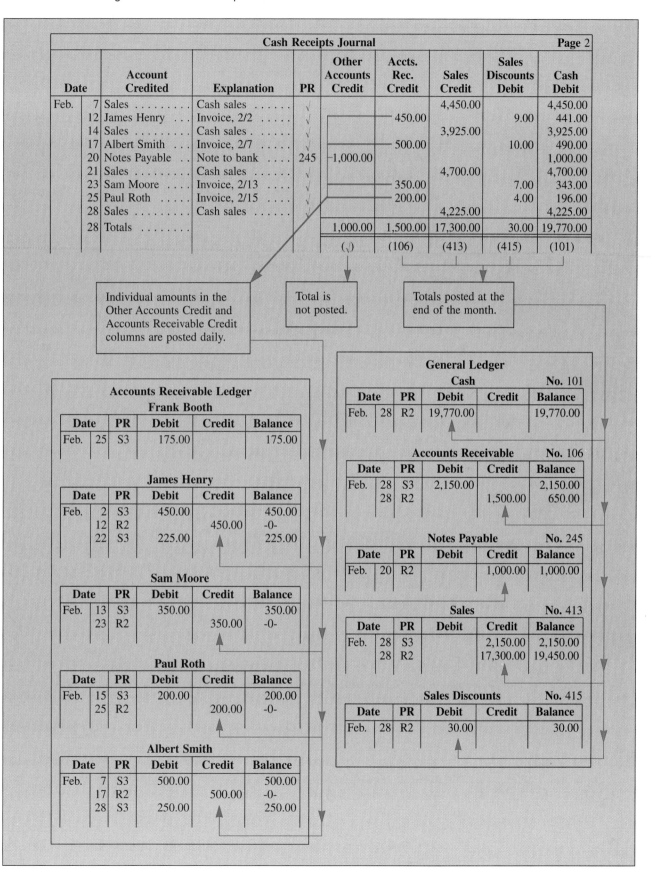

Miscellaneous Receipts of Cash

Most cash receipts are from collections of accounts receivable and from cash sales. However, other sources of cash include borrowing money from a bank or selling un-needed assets. The Other Accounts Credit column is for receipts that do not occur often enough to warrant a separate column. In most companies, the items entered in this column are few and are posted to a variety of general ledger accounts. As a result, postings are less apt to be omitted if these items are posted daily.

The Cash Receipts Journal's Posting Reference column is used only for daily postings from the Other Accounts and Accounts Receivable columns. The account numbers in the Posting Reference column indicate items that were posted to general ledger accounts. The check marks indicate either that an item (like a day's cash sales) was not posted or that an item was posted to the subsidiary Accounts Receivable Ledger.

Month-End Postings

At the end of the month, the amounts in the Accounts Receivable, Sales, Sales Discounts, and Cash columns of the Cash Receipts Journal are posted as column totals. However, the transactions recorded in any journal must result in equal debits and credits to general ledger accounts. Therefore, to be sure that the total debits and credits in a columnar journal are equal, the bookkeeper must *crossfoot* the column totals before posting them. To *foot* a column of numbers is to add it. To crossfoot, add the debit column totals and add the credit column totals; then compare the two sums for equality. For Illustration 6–5, the two sums appear as follows:

Debit Columns		Credit Columns	
Sales discounts debit	$ 30	Other accounts credit	$ 1,000
Cash debit	19,770	Accounts receivable credit	1,500
		Sales credit	17,300
Total	$19,800	Total	$19,800

After crossfooting the journal to confirm that debits equal credits, the bookkeeper posts the totals of the last four columns as indicated in each column heading. Because the individual items in the Other Accounts column are posted daily, the column total is not posted. Note in Illustration 6–5 the check mark below the Other Accounts column. The check mark indicates that the column total was not posted. The account numbers of the accounts to which the remaining column totals were posted are in parentheses below each column.

Posting items daily from the Other Accounts column with a delayed posting of the offsetting items in the Cash column (total) causes the General Ledger to be out of balance during the month. However, this does not matter because posting the Cash column total causes the offsetting amounts to reach the General Ledger before the trial balance is prepared.

POSTING RULE

Now that we have explained the procedures for posting from two different journals to a subsidiary ledger and its controlling account, the rule that governs all such postings should be clear. The rule for posting to a subsidiary ledger and its controlling account is: *The controlling account must be debited periodically for an amount or amounts equal to the sum of the debits to the subsidiary ledger, and it must be credited periodically for an amount or amounts equal to the sum of the credits to the subsidiary ledger.*

A Purchases Journal with one money column can be used to record purchases of merchandise on credit. However, a Purchases Journal usually is more useful if it is a multicolumn journal in which all credit purchases on account are recorded. Such a journal may have columns similar to those in Illustration 6–6. In the illustrated journal, the invoice date and terms together indicate the date on which payment for each purchase is due. The Accounts Payable Credit column is used to record the amounts credited to each creditor's account. These amounts are posted daily to the individual creditor accounts in a subsidiary Accounts Payable Ledger.

In Illustration 6–6, note that each line of the Account column shows the subsidiary ledger account that should be posted for the amount in the Accounts Payable Credit column. The Account column also shows the general ledger account to be debited when a purchase involves an amount recorded in the Other Accounts Debit column.

In this illustration, note the separate column provided for purchases of office supplies on credit. A separate column such as this is useful whenever several transactions involve debits to a particular account. The Other Accounts Debit column in Illustration 6–6 allows the Purchases Journal to be used for all purchase transactions involving credits to Accounts Payable. The individual amounts in the Other Accounts Debit column typically are posted daily to the indicated general ledger accounts.

At the end of the month, all of the column totals except the Other Accounts Debit column are posted to the appropriate general ledger accounts. After this is done, the balance in the Accounts Payable controlling account should equal the sum of the account balances in the subsidiary Accounts Payable Ledger.

The Cash Disbursements Journal, like the Cash Receipts Journal, has columns so that you can post repetitive debits and credits in column totals. The repetitive cash payments involve debits to the Accounts Payable controlling account and credits to both Purchases Discounts and Cash. Most companies usually purchase merchandise on credit. Therefore, a Purchases column is not needed. Instead, the occasional cash purchase is recorded as shown on line 2 of Illustration 6–7.

Observe that the illustrated journal has a column headed Check Number (Ck. No.). To gain control over cash disbursements, all payments except for very small amounts should be made by check.[1] The checks should be prenumbered by the printer and should be entered in the journal in numerical order with each check's number in the column headed Ck. No. This makes it possible to scan the numbers in the column for omitted checks. When a Cash Disbursements Journal has a column for check numbers, it is often called a **Check Register.**

The individual amounts in the Other Accounts Debit column of a Cash Disbursements Journal are normally posted to the appropriate general ledger accounts on a daily basis. The individual amounts in the Accounts Payable Debit column are also posted daily to the named creditors' accounts in the subsidiary Accounts Payable Ledger. At the end of the month, the bookkeeper crossfoots the column totals and posts the Accounts Payable Debit column total to the Accounts Payable controlling account. Then, the Purchases Discounts Credit column total is posted to the Purchases Discounts account and the Cash Credit column total is posted to the Cash account. The Other Accounts column total is not posted.

Periodically, after all posting is completed, the account balances in the General Ledger and the subsidiary ledgers should be tested for accuracy. To do this, the bookkeeper first prepares a trial balance of the General Ledger to confirm that debits equal credits. If the trial balance balances, the accounts in the General Ledger, including the

PURCHASES JOURNAL

THE CASH DISBURSEMENTS JOURNAL OR CHECK REGISTER

TESTING THE ACCURACY OF THE LEDGERS

---

[1]In Chapter 7, we discuss a system that is used to control small payments made with currency and coins.

Illustration 6-6 Posting from the Purchases Journal

Purchases Journal								Page 1
Date	Account	Date of Invoice	Terms	PR	Purchases Debit	Office Supplies Debit	Other Accounts Debit	Accounts Payable Credit
Feb. 3	Horn Supply Co.	2/2	n/30	√	275.00	75.00		350.00
5	Acme Mfg. Co.	2/5	2/10,n/30	√	200.00			200.00
13	Wycoff & Co.	2/10	2/10,n/30	√	150.00			150.00
20	Smith & Co.	2/18	2/10,n/30	√	300.00			300.00
25	Acme Mfg. Co.	2/24	2/10,n/30	√	100.00			100.00
28	Store Supplies/HAG Co.	2/28	n/30	125/√	125.00	25.00	75.00	225.00
28	Totals				1,150.00	100.00	75.00	1,325.00
					(505)	(124)	(√)	(201)

These totals are posted at the end of the month.

Individual amounts in the Other Accounts Debit and Accounts Payable Credit columns are posted daily.

General Ledger

Office Supplies   No. 124

Date	PR	Debit	Credit	Balance
Feb. 28	P1	100.00		100.00

Store Supplies   No. 125

Date	PR	Debit	Credit	Balance
Feb. 28	P1	75.00		75.00

Accounts Payable   No. 201

Date	PR	Debit	Credit	Balance
Feb. 28	P1		1,325.00	1,325.00

Purchases   No. 505

Date	PR	Debit	Credit	Balance
Feb. 28	P1	1,150.00		1,150.00

Accounts Payable Ledger

Acme Mfg. Company

Date	PR	Debit	Credit	Balance
Feb. 5	P1		200.00	200.00
25	P1		100.00	300.00

HAG Company

Date	PR	Debit	Credit	Balance
Feb. 28	P1		225.00	225.00

Horn Supply Company

Date	PR	Debit	Credit	Balance
Feb. 3	P1		350.00	350.00

Smith & Company

Date	PR	Debit	Credit	Balance
Feb. 20	P1		300.00	300.00

Wycoff & Company

Date	PR	Debit	Credit	Balance
Feb. 13	P1		150.00	150.00

Illustration 6-7 Posting from the Cash Disbursements Journal

Cash Disbursements Journal — Page 2

Date	Ch. No.	Payee	Account Debited	PR	Other Accounts Debit	Accounts Payable Debit	Purchases Discounts Credit	Cash Credit
Feb. 3	105	L. & N. Railroad	Transportation-In	508	15.00			15.00
12	106	East Sales Co.	Purchases	505	25.00			25.00
15	107	Acme Mfg. Co.	Acme Mfg. Co	√		200.00	4.00	196.00
15	108	Jerry Hale	Salaries Expense . . .	622	250.00			250.00
20	109	Wycoff & Co.	Wycoff & Co.	√		150.00	3.00	147.00
28	110	Smith & Co.	Smith & Co.	√		300.00	6.00	294.00
28		Totals			290.00	650.00	13.00	927.00
					(√)	(201)	(507)	(101)

Individual amounts in the Other Accounts Debit column and Accounts Payable Debit column are posted daily.

Totals posted at the end of the month.

Accounts Payable Ledger

Acme Mfg. Company

Date	PR	Debit	Credit	Balance
Feb. 5	P1		200.00	200.00
15	D2	200.00		-0-
25	P1		100.00	100.00

HAG Company

Date	PR	Debit	Credit	Balance
Feb. 28	P1		225.00	225.00

Horn Supply Company

Date	PR	Debit	Credit	Balance
Feb. 3	P1		350.00	350.00

Smith & Company

Date	PR	Debit	Credit	Balance
Feb. 20	P1		300.00	300.00
28	D2	300.00		-0-

Wycoff & Company

Date	PR	Debit	Credit	Balance
Feb. 13	P1		150.00	150.00
20	D2	150.00		-0-

General Ledger

Cash — No. 101

Date	PR	Debit	Credit	Balance
Feb. 28	R2	19,770.00		19,770.00
28	D2		927.00	18,843.00

Accounts Payable — No. 201

Date	PR	Debit	Credit	Balance
Feb. 28	P1		1,325.00	1,325.00
28	D2	650.00		675.00

Purchases — No. 505

Date	PR	Debit	Credit	Balance
Feb. 12	D2	25.00		25.00
28	P1	1,150.00		1,175.00

Purchases Discounts — No. 507

Date	PR	Debit	Credit	Balance
Feb. 28	D2		13.00	13.00

Transportation-In — No. 508

Date	PR	Debit	Credit	Balance
Feb. 3	D2	15.00		15.00

Salaries Expense — No. 622

Date	PR	Debit	Credit	Balance
Feb. 15	D2	250.00		250.00

Illustration 6–8
Schedule of Accounts
Payable, December 31, 19—

Acme Mfg. Company	$100
HAG Company	225
Horn Supply Company	350
Total accounts payable	$675

controlling accounts, are assumed to be correct. Second, the subsidiary ledgers are tested by preparing schedules of accounts receivable and accounts payable.

A **schedule of accounts payable** is prepared by listing the accounts in the Accounts Payable Ledger with their balances and calculating the sum of the balances. If the total is equal to the balance of the Accounts Payable controlling account, the accounts in the Accounts Payable Ledger are presumably correct. Illustration 6–8 shows a schedule of accounts payable drawn from the Accounts Payable Ledger of Illustration 6–7.

A **schedule of accounts receivable** is prepared in the same way as a schedule of accounts payable. Also, if its total equals the balance of the Accounts Receivable controlling account, you can assume the accounts in the Accounts Receivable Ledger are correct.

Progress Check

6-11   When special journals and controlling accounts with subsidiary ledgers are used, which of the following is not true?
   a. Transactions are first entered in the appropriate special journal.
   b. All column totals, except Other Accounts, are posted to the general ledger accounts at month-end.
   c. Individual transactions in the Other Accounts columns are posted to the appropriate general ledger accounts at month-end.

6-12   What is the rule for posting to a subsidiary ledger and its controlling account?

6-13   To test the accuracy of amounts posted to Accounts Receivable and Accounts Payable controlling accounts and their subsidiary ledgers:
   a. Prepare a trial balance of the General Ledger accounts.
   b. Foot and crossfoot the column totals in the journals.
   c. Prepare schedules of accounts receivable and accounts payable.
   d. Both a and c.

SALES TAXES

LO 4

Explain how sales taxes are recorded in special journals, how sales invoices can serve as a Sales Journal, and how sales returns and allowances are recorded.

Many cities and states require retailers to collect sales taxes from their customers and to periodically remit these taxes to the city or state treasurer. When using a columnar Sales Journal, you can have a record of the taxes collected by adding special columns in the journal as shown in Illustration 6–9.

As we described earlier in the chapter, the column totals of a Sales Journal are typically posted at the end of each month. This, of course, includes crediting the Sales Taxes Payable account for the total of the Sales Taxes Payable column. The individual amounts in the Accounts Receivable column are posted daily to the customer accounts in the Accounts Receivable Ledger. The individual amounts in the Sales Taxes Payable and Sales columns are not posted.

A business that collects sales taxes on its cash sales may use a special Sales Taxes Payable column in its Cash Receipts Journal.

SALES INVOICES AS A SALES JOURNAL

To save labor, some retailers avoid using Sales Journals for credit sales. Instead, they post each sales invoice total directly to the customer's account in the subsidiary Accounts Receivable Ledger. Then, they place copies of the invoices in numerical order in a binder. At the end of the month, they total all the invoices of that month and make a

Illustration 6-9   A Sales Journal with a Column for Sales Taxes Payable

		Sales Journal				
Date	**Account Debited**	**Invoice Number**	**PR**	**Accounts Receivable Debit**	**Sales Taxes Payable Credit**	**Sales Credit**
Dec. 1	D. R. Horn	7-1698		103.00	3.00	100.00

Illustration 6-10

		Sales Returns and Allowances Journal				
Date	**Account Credited**	**Explanation**	**Credit Memo No.**	**PR**	**Amount**	
Oct. 7	Robert Moore	Defective merchandise	203	√	10.00	
14	James Warren	Defective merchandise	204	√	12.00	
18	T. M. Jones	Not ordered	205	√	6.00	
23	Sam Smith	Defective merchandise	206	√	18.00	
31	Sales Returns and Allowances, Dr.; Accts. Receivable, Cr.				46.00	
					(414/106)	

general journal entry to debit Accounts Receivable and credit Sales for the total. In effect, the bound invoice copies act as a Sales Journal. Such a procedure is known as direct posting of sales invoices.

A business that has only a few sales returns may record them in a General Journal with an entry like the following:

SALES RETURNS

Oct.	17	Sales Returns and Allowances	414	17.50	
		Accounts Receivable—George Ball	106/√		17.50
		Customer returned merchandise.			

The debit of the entry is posted to the Sales Returns and Allowances account. The credit is posted to both the Accounts Receivable controlling account and to the customer's account. Note the account number and the check mark, 106/√, in the PR column on the credit line. This indicates that both the Accounts Receivable controlling account in the General Ledger and the George Ball account in the Accounts Receivable Ledger were credited for $17.50. Both were credited because the balance of the controlling account in the General Ledger will not equal the sum of the customer account balances in the subsidiary ledger unless both are credited.

A company with a large number of sales returns can save posting labor by recording them in a special Sales Returns and Allowances Journal similar to Illustration 6–10. Note that this is in keeping with the idea that a company can design and use a special journal for any group of similar transactions if there are enough transactions to warrant the journal. When using a Sales Returns and Allowances Journal to record returns, the amounts in the journal are posted daily to the customers' accounts. Then, at the end of the month, the journal total is posted as a debit to Sales Returns and Allowances and as a credit to Accounts Receivable.

GENERAL JOURNAL ENTRIES

When special journals are used, a General Journal is always necessary for adjusting, closing, and correcting entries and for a few transactions that cannot be recorded in the special journals. Some of these transactions are purchases returns, purchases of plant assets financed by notes payable, and if a Sales Returns and Allowances Journal is not provided, sales returns.

Progress Check

6-14   If sales taxes must be recorded and special journals are used: *(a)* **The sales taxes must be recorded in the General Journal;**   *(b)* **A separate column for sales taxes should be included in the Cash Receipts Journal and the Sales Journal;**   *(c)* **A special Sales Taxes Journal should be used.**

6-15   **What is direct posting of sales invoices?**

6-16   **If a company uses special journals for sales, purchases, cash receipts, and cash disbursements, why does it need a General Journal?**

USING THE INFORMATION— BUSINESS SEGMENTS

LO 5

Explain the the nature and use of business segment information.

The accounting system a company uses is more complicated when a company is large and operates in more than one line of business. When information is provided about each **business segment** of the company, outside users of the financial statements can gain a better understanding of the overall business. A business segment is a portion of the company that can be separately identified by the products or services that it provides or a geographic market that it serves.

Companies that have securities traded in public markets must publish segment information if they have material operations in more than one industry.[2] The required information for each segment includes:

1. Revenues or net sales.
2. Operating profits (before interest and taxes).
3. Capital expenditures.
4. Depreciation and amortization expense.
5. Identifiable assets.

In addition, they may be required to report (1) a geographical distribution of sales and (2) sales to each major customer that accounts for 10% or more of total sales.

Look again at the net sales information for **3M** presented on page 227. This is a typical example of business segment information. Note that the company identified three primary segments: industrial and consumer; information, imaging, and electronic; life sciences. In addition, the company reported its geographic distribution of sales.

The usefulness of segment information comes from the fact that different industries and geographical areas often face different levels of risk, profitability, and opportunities for growth. The information helps financial statement readers gain insight about the performance of the segments and the dependence of the entire company on the profits derived from each of the segments.

---

[2]FASB, *Accounting Standards Current Text* (Norwalk, CT, 1994), sec. S20.101. First published as *FASB Statement No. 15.*

Progress Check

6-17 The requirements for segment information include presenting each segment's: *(a)*
Revenues; *(b)* Operating expenses; *(c)* Income taxes; *(d)* Capital expenditures;
(e) Both *a* and *d.*

LO 1. Describe the five basic components of an accounting system. The components of accounting systems include source documents, input devices, the data processor, data storage, and output devices. Both manual and computerized systems must have all five components.

LO 2. Describe the types of computers used in large and small accounting systems, the role of software in those systems, and the different approaches to inputting and processing data, including the use of networking. Depending on the complexity of a company's accounting system, the computers used may be large mainframe computers or smaller microcomputers. If a mainframe computer is used, the software that provides the computer instructions is likely to be custom made for the company. However, an increasing variety of off-the-shelf programs are available, especially for microcomputers. There are many different ways to set up computer systems, including batch and on-line processing, and computer networks.

LO 3. Explain special journals and controlling accounts, use them to record transactions, and explain how to test the posting of entries to the Accounts Receivable and Accounts Payable subsidiary ledgers. Columnar journals are designed so that repetitive debits or credits are entered in separate columns. A typical set of special journals includes a Sales Journal, a Purchases Journal, a Cash Receipts Journal, and a Cash Disbursements Journal (or Check Register). Any transactions that cannot be entered in the special journals are entered in the General Journal.

When many accounts of the same type are required, such as an account receivable for each credit customer, they usually are kept in a separate subsidiary ledger. Then, a single controlling account is maintained in the General Ledger. After all transactions are posted to the accounts in the subsidiary ledger and to the controlling account, the controlling account balance should equal the sum of the account balances in the subsidiary ledger.

LO 4. Explain the use of special and general journals in accounting for sales taxes and sales returns and allowances, and explain how sales invoices can serve as a Sales Journal. To record sales taxes, the Sales Journal and the Cash Receipts Journal should include a separate Sales Taxes Payable column. When sales invoices substitute for a Sales Journal, the customer accounts in the Accounts Receivable Ledger are posted directly from the sales invoices. Copies of the invoices for each month are then bound and totaled as a basis for recording the sales in the General Ledger. Sales returns and allowances may be recorded in the General Journal, or a special journal for sales returns and allowances may be used.

LO 5. Explain the nature and use of business segment information. Public companies with material operations in more than one industry must provide separate information for each segment. The information includes revenues, operating profits, capital expenditures, depreciation, and identifiable assets. It also includes a geographical distribution of sales and sales to major customers.

SUMMARY OF THE CHAPTER IN TERMS OF LEARNING OBJECTIVES

GLOSSARY

Accounting system   the people, forms, procedures, and equipment that are used to capture data about the transactions of an entity and to generate from that data a variety of financial, managerial, and tax accounting reports. p. 228

Accounts Payable Ledger   a subsidiary ledger that contains a separate account for each party that grants credit on account to the entity. p. 238

Accounts Receivable Ledger   a subsidiary ledger that contains an account for each credit customer. p. 236

Batch processing   an approach to inputting data that accumulates source documents for a period such as a day, week, or month and inputs all of them at the same time. p. 234

Business segment   a portion of a company that can be separately identified by the products or services that it provides or a geographic market that it serves. p. 248

Check Register   a book of original entry for recording cash payments by check. p. 243

Columnar journal   a book of original entry having columns, each of which is designated as the place for entering specific data about each transaction of a group·of similar transactions. p. 236

Computer network   a system in which computers are linked with each other so that different users on different computers can share access to the same data and the same programs. p. 235

Controlling account   a general ledger account the balance of which (after posting) equals the sum of the balances of the accounts in a related subsidiary ledger. p. 238

Data processor   the component of an accounting system that interprets, manipulates, and summarizes the recorded information so that it can be used in analyses and reports. p. 230

Data storage   the component of an accounting system that keeps the inputted data in a readily accessible manner so that financial reports can be drawn from it efficiently. p. 230

General Ledger   the ledger that contains the financial statement accounts of a business. p. 236

Input device   a means of transferring information from source documents to the data processing component of an accounting system. p. 229

On-line processing   an approach to inputting data whereby the data on each source document is inputted as soon as the document is available. p. 234

Output devices   the means by which information is taken out of the accounting system and made available for use. p. 231

Schedule of accounts payable   a list of the balances of all the accounts in the accounts payable ledger that is summed to show the total amount of accounts payable outstanding. p. 246

Schedule of accounts receivable   a list of the balances of all the accounts in the Accounts Receivable Ledger that is summed to show the total amount of accounts receivable outstanding. p. 246

Special journal   a book of original entry that is designed and used for recording only a specified type of transaction. p. 235

Subsidiary ledger   a group of accounts that show the details underlying the balance of a controlling account in the General Ledger. p. 238

QUESTIONS

1. What are the five basic components of an accounting system?

2. What are source documents? Give some examples.

3. What is the purpose of an input device? Give some examples of input devices for computer systems.

4. What is the difference between data that is stored off-line and data that is stored on-line?

5. What purpose is served by the output devices of an accounting system?

6. What is the difference between batch and on-line processing?

7. When special journals are used, separate special journals normally are used to record each of four different types of transactions. What are these four types of transactions?

8. Why should sales to and receipts of cash from credit customers be recorded and posted daily?

9. Both credits to customer accounts and credits to miscellaneous accounts are individually posted from a Cash Receipts Journal similar to the one in Illustration 6–5. Why not put both kinds of credits in the same column and thus save journal space?

10. What procedures allow copies of a company's sales invoices to be used as a Sales Journal?

11. When a general journal entry is used to record a returned credit sale, the credit of the entry must be posted twice. Does this cause the trial balance to be out of balance? Why or why not?

12. Look in Appendix F at Apple Computer's financial statements. What amount of operating income in 1993 came from operations in Europe? What geographic area generated the largest operating income?

QUICK STUDY (Five-Minute Exercises)

Identify the role in an accounting system played by each of the lettered items by assigning a number from the list on the left:

1. Source documents
2. Input devices
3. Data processor
4. Data storage
5. Output devices

_____ a. Bar code reader
_____ b. Filing cabinet
_____ c. Bank statement
_____ d. Calculator
_____ e. Computer keyboard
_____ f. Floppy diskette
_____ g. Computer monitor
_____ h. Invoice from a supplier
_____ i. Computer hardware and software
_____ j. Computer printer

Fill in the blanks:

a. Personal computers, often called _____, are physically small, easy to operate, and increasingly inexpensive.

b. Off-the-shelf programs designed so that actions taken in one part of the system also produce results in related parts are known as _____ systems.

c. With _____ processing, source documents are accumulated for a period of time and then processed all at the same time, such as once a day, week, or month.

d. A computer _____ allows different computer users to share access to the same data and programs.

Sampson Iron Works uses a Sales Journal, a Purchases Journal, a Cash Receipts Journal, a Cash Disbursements Journal, and a General Journal. Sampson recently completed the following transactions. List the transaction letters and next to each letter give the name of the journal in which the transaction should be recorded.

a. Paid a creditor.
b. Sold merchandise for cash.
c. Purchased merchandise on credit.
d. Sold merchandise on credit.
e. Borrowed money from the bank.
f. Purchased shop supplies on credit.
g. Paid an employee's salary.

The Nostalgic Book Shop uses a Sales Journal, a Purchases Journal, a Cash Receipts Journal, a Cash Disbursements Journal, and a General Journal. The following transactions occurred during the month of November. Journalize the November transactions that should be recorded in the General Journal.

Nov. 2 Purchased merchandise on credit for $1,900 from the Randolph Co., terms 2/10, n/30.

12 The owner, I. M. Nowalski, contributed an automobile worth $13,500 to the business.

16 Sold merchandise on credit to W. Ryder for $1,100, terms n/30.

19 W. Ryder returned $90 of merchandise originally purchased on November 16.

28 Returned $170 of defective merchandise to the Randolph Co. from the November 2 purchase.

QS 6–5
(LO 5)

A company with publicly traded securities operates in more than one industry. Which of the following items of information about each business segment must the company report?

a.	Revenues	e.	Capital expenditures
b.	Net sales	f.	Amortization and depreciation
c.	Operating profits	g.	Cash flows
d.	Operating expenses	h.	Identifiable assets

EXERCISES

Exercise 6–1
The Sales Journal
(LO 3)

Fletcher's Frozen Foods uses a Sales Journal, a Purchases Journal, a Cash Receipts Journal, a Cash Disbursements Journal, and a General Journal. The following transactions occurred during the month of February:

Feb. 2 Sold merchandise to M. Stohl for $356 cash, Invoice No. 5703.

5 Purchased merchandise on credit from Campbell Company, $2,035.

7 Sold merchandise to E. Jason for $950, terms 2/10, n/30, Invoice No. 5704.

8 Borrowed $5,000 by giving a note to the bank.

12 Sold merchandise to L. Patrick for $223, terms n/30, Invoice No. 5705.

16 Received $931 from E. Jason to pay for the purchase of February 7.

19 Sold used store equipment to Green Acres for $500.

25 Sold merchandise to P. Sumo for $428, terms n/30, Invoice No. 5706.

Required

On a sheet of notebook paper, draw a Sales Journal like the one that appears in Illustration 6–3. Journalize the February transactions that should be recorded in the Sales Journal.

Exercise 6–2
The Cash Receipts Journal
(LO 3)

Landmark Map Company uses a Sales Journal, a Purchases Journal, a Cash Receipts Journal, a Cash Disbursements Journal, and a General Journal. The following transactions occurred during the month of September:

Sept. 3 Purchased merchandise on credit for $2,900 from Pace Supply Co.

7 Sold merchandise on credit to N. Jamal for $800, subject to a $16 sales discount if paid by the end of the month.

9 Borrowed $1,750 by giving a note to the bank.

13 Received a capital contribution of $3,500 from R. Galindo, the owner of the company.

18 Sold merchandise to T. Byrd for $199 cash.

22 Paid Pace Supply $2,900 for the merchandise purchased on September 3.

27 Received $784 from N. Jamal in payment of the September 7 purchase.

30 Paid salaries of $1,500.

Required

On a sheet of notebook paper, draw a multicolumn Cash Receipts Journal like the one that appears in Illustration 6–5. Journalize the September transactions that should be recorded in the Cash Receipts Journal.

Exercise 6–3
The Purchases Journal
(LO 3)

Gem Industries uses a Sales Journal, a Purchases Journal, a Cash Receipts Journal, a Cash Disbursements Journal, and a General Journal. The following transactions occurred during the month of July:

July 1 Purchased merchandise on credit for $7,190 from Angel, Inc., terms n/30.

8 Sold merchandise on credit to H. Baruk for $1,300, subject to a $26 sales discount if paid by the end of the month.

10 J. Powers, the owner of the business, contributed $2,500 cash to the business.

14 Purchased store supplies from Steck & Vaughn on credit for $145, terms n/30.

17 Purchased office supplies on credit from King Mart for $310, terms n/30.

24 Sold merchandise to V. Valdi for $467 cash.

28 Purchased store supplies from Hadlock's for $79 cash.

29 Paid Angel, Inc., $7,190 for the merchandise purchased on July 1.

Required

On a sheet of notebook paper, draw a multicolumn Purchases Journal like the one that appears in Illustration 6–6. Journalize the July transactions that should be recorded in the Purchases Journal.

Neon Art Supply uses a Sales Journal, a Purchases Journal, a Cash Receipts Journal, a Cash Disbursements Journal, and a General Journal. The following transactions occurred during the month of March:

Exercise 6–4
The Cash Disbursements Journal
(LO 3)

Mar. 3 Purchased merchandise for $1,850 on credit from Paige, Inc., terms 2/10, n/30.

9 Issued Check No. 210 to Mott & Son to buy store supplies for $369.

12 Sold merchandise on credit to C. Klempt for $625, terms n/30.

17 Issued Check No. 211 for $1,000 to repay a note payable to City Bank.

20 Purchased merchandise for $4,700 on credit from LeBeck's, terms 2/10, n/30.

29 Issued Check No. 212 to LeBeck's to pay the amount due for the purchase of March 20, less the discount.

31 Paid salary of $1,500 to B. Eldon by issuing Check No. 213.

31 Issued Check No. 214 to Paige, Inc., to pay the amount due for the purchase of March 3.

Required

On a sheet of notebook paper, draw a multicolumn Cash Disbursements Journal like the one that appears in Illustration 6–7. Journalize the March transactions that should be recorded in the Cash Disbursements Journal.

Simonetti Pharmacy uses the following journals: Sales Journal, Purchases Journal, Cash Receipts Journal, Cash Disbursements Journal, and General Journal. On June 5, Simonetti purchased merchandise priced at $15,000, subject to credit terms of 2/10, n/30. On June 14, the pharmacy paid the net amount due. However, in journalizing the payment, the bookkeeper debited Accounts Payable for $15,000 and failed to record the cash discount. Cash was credited for the actual amount paid. In what journals would the June 5 and the June 14 transactions have been recorded? What procedure is likely to discover the error in journalizing the June 14 transaction?

Exercise 6–5
Special journal transactions
(LO 3)

At the end of May, the Sales Journal of Cowtown Leather Goods appeared as follows:

Exercise 6–6
Posting to subsidiary ledger accounts
(LO 3)

Sales Journal

Date		Account Debited	Invoice Number	PR	Amount
May	6	Bud Smith	190		1,780.00
	10	Don Holly	191		2,040.00
	17	Sandy Ford	192		960.00
	25	Don Holly	193		335.00
	31	Total			5,115.00

Cowtown also had recorded the return of merchandise with the following entry:

May	20	Sales Returns and Allowances	165.00	
		Accounts Receivable—Sandy Ford		165.00
		Customer returned merchandise.		

Required

1. On a sheet of notebook paper, open a subsidiary Accounts Receivable Ledger that has a T-account for each customer listed in the Sales Journal. Post to the customer accounts the entries in the Sales Journal, and any portion of the general journal entry that affects a customer's account.

2. Open a General Ledger that has T-accounts for Accounts Receivable, Sales, and Sales Returns and Allowances. Post the Sales Journal and any portion of the general journal entry that affects these accounts.

3. Prepare a list or schedule of the accounts in the subsidiary Accounts Receivable Ledger and add their balances to show that the total equals the balance in the Accounts Receivable controlling account.

Exercise 6–7
Accounts Receivable Ledger
(LO 3, 4)

Skillern Company posts its sales invoices directly and then binds the invoices to make them into a Sales Journal. Skillern had the following sales during January:

Jan.	2	Jay Newton	$ 3,600
	8	Adrian Carr	6,100
	10	Kathy Olivas	13,400
	14	Lisa Mack	20,500
	20	Kathy Olivas	11,200
	29	Jay Newton	7,300
		Total	$62,100

Required

1. On a sheet of notebook paper, open a subsidiary Accounts Receivable Ledger having a T-account for each customer. Post the invoices to the subsidiary ledger.

2. Give the general journal entry to record the end-of-month total of the Sales Journal.

3. Open an Accounts Receivable controlling account and a Sales account and post the general journal entry.

4. Prepare a list or schedule of the accounts in the subsidiary Accounts Receivable Ledger and add their balances to show that the total equals the balance in the Accounts Receivable controlling account.

Exercise 6–8
Posting from special journals and subsidiary ledgers to T-accounts
(LO 3)

Following are the condensed journals of Tip-Top Trophy Shop. The journal column headings are incomplete in that they do not indicate whether the columns are debit or credit columns.

Sales Journal

Account	Amount
Jack Heinz	2,700
Trudy Stone	7,400
Wayne Day	3,000
Total	13,100

Purchases Journal

Account	Amount
Frasier Corp.	3,400
Sultan, Inc.	6,500
McGraw Company	1,700
Total	11,600

General Journal

...	..	Sales Returns and Allowances	400.00	
		Accounts Receivable—Jack Heinz		400.00
	..	Accounts Payable—Frasier Corp.	850.00	
		Purchases Returns and Allowances		850.00

Cash Receipts Journal

Account	Other Accounts	Accounts Receivable	Sales	Sales Discounts	Cash
Jack Heinz		2,300		46	2,254
Sales			1,950		1,950
Notes Payable	3,500				3,500
Sales			525		525
Trudy Stone		7,400		148	7,252
Store Equipment	200				200
Totals	3,700	9,700	2,475	194	15,681

Cash Disbursements Journal

Account	Other Accounts	Accounts Payable	Purchases Discounts	Cash
Prepaid Insurance	960			960
Sultan, Inc.		6,500	195	6,305
Frasier Corp.		2,550	51	2,499
Store Equipment	1,570			1,570
Totals	2,530	9,050	246	11,334

Required

1. Prepare T-accounts on notebook paper for the following general ledger and subsidiary ledger accounts. Separate the accounts of each ledger group as follows:

General Ledger Accounts
Cash
Accounts Receivable
Prepaid Insurance
Store Equipment
Accounts Payable
Notes Payable
Sales
Sales Returns and Allowances
Sales Discounts
Purchases
Purchases Returns and Allowances
Purchases Discounts

Accounts Receivable Ledger Accounts
Wayne Day
Jack Heinz
Trudy Stone

Accounts Payable Ledger Accounts
Frasier Corp.
McGraw Company
Sultan, Inc.

2. Without referring to any of the illustrations in the chapter that show complete column headings for the journals, post the journals to the proper T-accounts.

A company that records credit purchases in a Purchases Journal and records purchases returns in its General Journal made the following errors. List each error by letter, and opposite each letter tell when the error should be discovered:

Exercise 6–9
Errors related to the Purchases Journal
(LO 3, 4)

a. Made an addition error in determining the balance of a creditor's account.

b. Made an addition error in totaling the Office Supplies column of the Purchases Journal.

c. Posted a purchases return to the Accounts Payable account and to the creditor's account but did not post to the Purchases Returns and Allowances account.

d.   Posted a purchases return to the Purchases Returns and Allowances account and to the Accounts Payable account but did not post to the creditor's account.

e.   Correctly recorded a $4,000 purchase in the Purchases Journal but posted it to the creditor's account as a $400 purchase.

PROBLEMS

Problem 6–1

Special journals, subsidiary ledgers, schedule of accounts receivable

(LO 3)

Niagara Company completed these transactions during April of the current year:

Apr. 2   Purchased merchandise on credit from Flott Company, invoice dated April 2, terms 2/10, n/60, $13,300.

      3   Sold merchandise on credit to Linda Hobart, Invoice No. 760, $2,000. (The terms of all credit sales are 2/10, n/30.)

      3   Purchased office supplies on credit from Whitewater Inc., $1,380. Invoice dated April 2, terms n/10 EOM.

      4   Issued Check No. 587 to *U.S. Times* for advertising expense, $815.

      5   Sold merchandise on credit to Paul Abrams, Invoice No. 761, $6,000.

      6   Received an $85 credit memorandum from Whitewater Inc. for office supplies received on April 3 and returned for credit.

      9   Purchased store equipment on credit from Cooper's Supply, invoice dated April 9, terms n/10 EOM, $11,125.

     11   Sold merchandise on credit to Kelly Schaefer, Invoice No. 762, $9,500.

     12   Issued Check No. 588 to Flott Company in payment of its April 2 invoice, less the discount.

     13   Received payment from Linda Hobart for the April 3 sale, less the discount.

     13   Sold merchandise on credit to Linda Hobart, Invoice No. 763, $4,100.

     14   Received payment from Paul Abrams for the April 5 sale, less the discount.

     16   Issued Check No. 589, payable to Payroll, in payment of the sales salaries for the first half of the month, $9,750. Cashed the check and paid the employees.

     16   Cash sales for the first half of the month were $50,840. (Cash sales are usually recorded daily from the cash register readings. However, they are recorded only twice in this problem to reduce the repetitive transactions.)

     17   Purchased merchandise on credit from Sprague Company, invoice dated April 16, terms 2/10, n/30, $12,750.

     18   Borrowed $40,000 from First State Bank by giving a long-term note payable.

     20   Received payment from Kelly Schaefer for the April 11 sale, less the discount.

     20   Purchased store supplies on credit from Cooper's Supply, invoice dated April 19, terms n/10 EOM, $730.

     23   Received a $400 credit memorandum from Sprague Company for defective merchandise received on April 17 and returned.

     23   Received payment from Linda Hobart for the April 13 sale, less the discount.

     25   Purchased merchandise on credit from Flott Company, invoice dated April 24, terms 2/10, n/60, $10,375.

     26   Issued Check No. 590 to Sprague Company in payment of its April 16 invoice, less the return and the discount.

     27   Sold merchandise on credit to Paul Abrams, Invoice No. 764, $3,070.

     27   Sold merchandise on credit to Kelly Schaefer, Invoice No. 765, $5,700.

     30   Issued Check No. 591, payable to Payroll, in payment of the sales salaries for the last half of the month, $9,750.

     30   Cash sales for the last half of the month were $70,975.

Required

Preparation component:

1. Open the following general ledger accounts: Cash, Accounts Receivable, Long-Term Notes Payable, Sales, and Sales Discounts. Also open subsidiary accounts receivable ledger accounts for Paul Abrams, Linda Hobart, and Kelly Schaefer.

2. Prepare a Sales Journal and a Cash Receipts Journal like the ones illustrated in this chapter.

3. Review the transactions of Niagara Company and enter those transactions that should be journalized in the Sales Journal and those that should be journalized in the Cash Receipts Journal. Ignore any transactions that should be journalized in a Purchases Journal, a Cash Disbursements Journal, or a General Journal.

4. Post the items that should be posted as individual amounts from the journals. (Normally, such items are posted daily; but since they are few in number in this problem you are asked to post them only once.)

5. Foot and crossfoot the journals and make the month-end postings.

6. Prepare a trial balance of the General Ledger and test the accuracy of the subsidiary ledger by preparing a schedule of accounts receivable.

CHECK FIGURE:
Trial balance totals, $192,185

Analysis component:

7. Assume that the sum of the account balances on the schedule of accounts receivable does not equal the balance of the controlling account in the General Ledger. Describe the steps you would go through to discover the error(s).

On March 31, Niagara Company had a cash balance of $167,000 and a Long-Term Notes Payable balance of $167,000. The April transactions of Niagara Company included those listed in Problem 6–1.

Problem 6–2
Special journals, subsidiary ledgers, schedule of accounts payable
(LO 3, 4)

Required

1. Open the following general ledger accounts: Cash, Office Supplies, Store Supplies, Store Equipment, Accounts Payable, Long-Term Notes Payable, Purchases, Purchases Returns and Allowances, Purchases Discounts, Sales Salaries Expense, and Advertising Expense. Enter the March 31 balances of Cash and Long-Term Notes Payable ($167,000 each).

2. Open subsidiary accounts payable ledger accounts for Cooper's Supply, Flott Company, Sprague Company, and Whitewater Inc.

3. Prepare a General Journal and a Cash Disbursements Journal like the ones illustrated in this chapter. Prepare a Purchases Journal with a debit column for purchases, a debit column for other accounts, and a credit column for accounts payable.

4. Review the April transactions of Niagara Company and enter those transactions that should be journalized in the General Journal, the Purchases Journal, or the Cash Disbursements Journal. Ignore any transactions that should be journalized in a Sales Journal or Cash Receipts Journal.

5. Post the items that should be posted as individual amounts from the journals. (Normally, such items are posted daily; but since they are few in number in this problem you are asked to post them only once.)

6. Foot and crossfoot the journals and make the month-end postings.

7. Prepare a trial balance and a schedule of accounts payable.

CHECK FIGURE:
Trial balance totals, $191,438

(If the Working Papers that accompany this text are not being used, omit this problem.)

Problem 6–3
Special journals, subsidiary ledgers, trial balance
(LO 3, 4)

It is December 16 and you have just taken over the accounting work of Outdoor Outfitters, whose annual accounting periods end each December 31. The company's previous accountant journalized its transactions through December 15 and posted all items that required posting as individual amounts, as an examination of the journals and ledgers in the Working Papers will show.

The company completed these transactions beginning on December 16:

Dec. 16   Sold merchandise on credit to Ambrose Fielder, Invoice No. 916, $7,700. (Terms of all credit sales are 2/10, n/30.)

17   Received a $1,040 credit memorandum from Weathers Company for merchandise received on December 15 and returned for credit.

17   Purchased office supplies on credit from Gray Supply Company, $615. Invoice dated December 16, terms n/10 EOM.

18   Received a $40 credit memorandum from Gray Supply Company for office supplies received on December 17 and returned for credit.

20   Issued a credit memorandum to Amy Oakley for defective merchandise sold on December 15 and returned for credit, $500.

21   Purchased store equipment on credit from Gray Supply Company, invoice dated December 21, terms n/10 EOM, $6,700.

22   Received payment from Ambrose Fielder for the December 12 sale less the discount.

23   Issued Check No. 623 to Sunshine Company in payment of its December 15 invoice less the discount.

24   Sold merchandise on credit to Wilson Wilde, Invoice No. 917, $1,200.

24   Issued Check No. 624 to Weathers Company in payment of its December 15 invoice less the return and the discount.

25   Received payment from Amy Oakley for the December 15 sale less the return and the discount.

26   Received merchandise and an invoice dated December 25, terms 2/10, n/60, from Sunshine Company, $8,100.

29   Sold a neighboring merchant five boxes of file folders (office supplies) for cash at cost, $50.

30   Marlin Levy, the owner of Outdoor Outfitters, used Check No. 625 to withdraw $2,500 cash from the business for personal use.

31   Issued Check No. 626 to Jamie Forster, the company's only sales employee, in payment of her salary for the last half of December, $1,620.

31   Issued Check No. 627 to Countywide Electric Company in payment of the December electric bill, $510.

31   Cash sales for the last half of the month were $29,600. (Cash sales are usually recorded daily but are recorded only twice in this problem to reduce the repetitive transactions.)

Required

1.   Record the transactions in the journals provided.

2.   Post to the customer and creditor accounts and also post any amounts that should be posted as individual amounts to the general ledger accounts. (Normally, these amounts are posted daily, but they are posted only once by you in this problem because they are few in number.)

3.   Foot and crossfoot the journals and make the month-end postings.

CHECK FIGURE:
Trial balance totals, $221,160

4.   Prepare a December 31 trial balance and test the accuracy of the subsidiary ledgers by preparing schedules of accounts receivable and payable.

Problem 6–4
Special journals, subsidiary ledgers, trial balance
(LO 3)

The Flutie Company completed these transactions during March of the current year:

Mar. 2   Sold merchandise on credit to Leroy Hazzard, Invoice No. 854, $15,800. (Terms of all credit sales are 2/10, n/30.)

3   Purchased office supplies on credit from Arnot Company, $1,120. Invoice dated March 3, terms n/10 EOM.

Mar. 3   Sold merchandise on credit to Sam Segura, Invoice No. 855, $9,200.

     5   Received merchandise and an invoice dated March 3, terms 2/10, n/30, from Defore Industries, $42,600.

     6   Borrowed $36,000 by giving Commerce Bank a long-term promissory note payable.

     9   Purchased office equipment on credit from Jett Supply, invoice dated March 9, terms n/10 EOM, $20,850.

   10   Sold merchandise on credit to Marjorie Cobb, Invoice No. 856, $4,600.

   12   Received payment from Leroy Hazzard for the March 2 sale less the discount.

   13   Sent Defore Industries Check No. 416 in payment of its March 3 invoice less the discount.

   13   Received payment from Sam Segura for the March 3 sale less the discount.

   14   Received merchandise and an invoice dated March 13, terms 2/10, n/30, from the Welch Company, $31,625.

   15   Issued Check No. 417, payable to Payroll, in payment of sales salaries for the first half of the month, $15,900. Cashed the check and paid the employees.

   15   Cash sales for the first half of the month were $134,680. (Normally, cash sales are recorded daily; however, they are recorded only twice in this problem to reduce the repetitive entries.)

   15   *Post to the customer and creditor accounts and also post any amounts that should be posted as individual amounts to the general ledger accounts. (Normally, such items are posted daily; but you are asked to post them on only two occasions in this problem because they are few in number.)*

   16   Purchased store supplies on credit from Arnot Company, $1,670. Invoice dated March 16, terms n/10 EOM.

   17   Received a credit memorandum from the Welch Company for unsatisfactory merchandise received on March 14 and returned for credit, $2,425.

   19   Received a credit memorandum from Jett Supply for office equipment received on March 9 and returned for credit, $630.

   20   Received payment from Marjorie Cobb for the sale of March 10 less the discount.

   23   Issued Check No. 418 to the Welch Company in payment of its invoice of March 13 less the return and the discount.

   27   Sold merchandise on credit to Marjorie Cobb, Invoice No. 857, $13,910.

   28   Sold merchandise on credit to Sam Segura, Invoice No. 858, $5,315.

   31   Issued Check No. 419, payable to Payroll, in payment of sales salaries for the last half of the month, $15,900. Cashed the check and paid the employees.

   31   Cash sales for the last half of the month were $144,590.

   31   *Post to the customer and creditor accounts and post any amounts that should be posted as individual amounts to the general ledger accounts.*

   31   *Foot and crossfoot the journals and make the month-end postings.*

Required

1. Open the following general ledger accounts: Cash, Accounts Receivable, Office Supplies, Store Supplies, Office Equipment, Accounts Payable, Long-Term Notes Payable, Sales, Sales Discounts, Purchases, Purchases Returns and Allowances, Purchases Discounts, and Sales Salaries Expense.

2. Open the following accounts receivable ledger accounts: Marjorie Cobb, Leroy Hazzard, and Sam Segura.

3. Open the following accounts payable ledger accounts: Arnot Company, Defore Industries, Jett Supply, and the Welch Company.

4.   Enter the transactions in a Sales Journal, a Purchases Journal, a Cash Receipts Journal, a Cash Disbursements Journal, and a General Journal similar to the ones illustrated in this chapter. Post when instructed to do so.

CHECK FIGURE:
Trial balance totals, $390,966

5.   Prepare a trial balance and test the accuracy of the subsidiary ledgers by preparing schedules of accounts receivable and payable.

CRITICAL THINKING: ESSAYS, PROBLEMS, AND CASES

Analytical Essays

AE 6–1
(LO 3)

Small Company uses a Cash Disbursements Journal similar to the one shown in Illustration 6–7. In the process of crossfooting the journal at the end of the current month, the company's bookkeeper found that the sum of the debits did not equal the sum of the credits. Describe the procedures you would follow to discover the reason why the journal does not crossfoot correctly.

AE 6–2
(LO 2)

Lorber's is a merchandising company that uses the special journals described in this chapter. At the end of the accounting period, the bookkeeper for the company prepared a trial balance and a schedule of accounts receivable. The trial balance is in balance but the sum of the account balances on the schedule of accounts receivable does not equal the balance in the controlling account. Describe the procedures you would follow to discover the reason for the imbalance between the controlling account and the total shown on the schedule of accounts receivable.

Ethical Issues Essay

Review the As a Matter of Ethics case presented on page 235. Discuss the problem faced by the CPA and the factors the CPA should consider in deciding on a course of action.

COMPREHENSIVE PROBLEM

Regis Company
(LO 3, 4)

(If the Working Papers that accompany this text are not available, omit this comprehensive problem.)

Assume it is Monday, August 1, the first business day of the month, and you have just been hired as the accountant for Regis Company, which operates with monthly accounting periods. All of the company's accounting work has been completed through the end of July and its ledgers show July 31 balances. During your first month on the job, you record the following transactions:

Aug. 1   Issued Check No. 1236 to Republic Management Co. in payment of the August rent, $2,650. (Use two lines to record the transaction. Charge 80% of the rent to Rent Expense, Selling Space and the balance to Rent Expense, Office Space.)

2   Sold merchandise on credit to L&M Company, Invoice No. 5725, $4,300. (The terms of all credit sales are 2/10, n/30.)

2   Issued a $125 credit memorandum to Prime, Inc., for defective merchandise sold on July 28 and returned for credit. The total selling price (gross) was $3,375.

3   Received a $570 credit memorandum from Signature Products for merchandise received on July 29 and returned for credit.

4   Purchased on credit from Discount Supplies: merchandise, $26,480; store supplies, $410; and office supplies, $59. Invoice dated August 4, terms n/10 EOM.

5   Received payment from Prime, Inc., for the remaining balance from the sale of July 28 less the August 2 return and the discount.

8   Issued Check No. 1237 to Signature Products to pay for the $5,070 of merchandise received on July 29 less the August 3 return and a 2% discount.

Aug. 9 Sold store supplies to the merchant next door at cost for cash, $250.

10 Purchased office equipment on credit from Discount Supplies, invoice dated August 10, terms n/10 EOM, $2,910.

11 Received payment from L&M Company for the August 2 sale less the discount.

11 Received merchandise and an invoice dated August 10, terms 2/10, n/30, from Mayfair Corp., $6,300.

12 Received a $610 credit memorandum from Discount Supplies for defective office equipment received on August 10 and returned for credit.

15 Issued Check No. 1238, payable to Payroll, in payment of sales salaries, $3,800, and office salaries, $2,250. Cashed the check and paid the employees.

15 Cash sales for the first half of the month, $42,300. (Such sales are normally recorded daily. They are recorded only twice in this problem to reduce the repetitive entries.)

15 *Post to the customer and creditor accounts. Also, post individual items that are not included in column totals at the end of the month to the general ledger accounts. (Such items are normally posted daily, but you are asked to post them only twice each month because they are few in number.)*

16 Sold merchandise on credit to L&M Company, Invoice No. 5726, $2,850.

17 Received merchandise and an invoice dated August 14, terms 2/10, n/60, from Tranh Industries, $9,750.

19 Issued Check No. 1239 to Mayfair Corp. in payment of its August 10 invoice less the discount.

22 Sold merchandise on credit to Anchor Services, Invoice No. 5727, $4,900.

23 Issued Check No. 1240 to Tranh Industries in payment of its August 14 invoice less the discount.

24 Purchased on credit from Discount Supplies: merchandise, $5,800; store supplies, $450; and office supplies, $200. Invoice dated August 24, terms n/10 EOM.

25 Received merchandise and an invoice dated August 23, terms 2/10, n/30, from Signature Products, $2,200.

26 Sold merchandise on credit to Franzetti Corp., Invoice No. 5728, $10,150.

26 Issued Check No. 1241 to HP&L in payment of the July electric bill, $918.

29 The owner of Regis Company, Walt Regis, used Check No. 1242 to withdraw $5,000 from the business for personal use.

30 Received payment from Anchor Services for the August 22 sale less the discount.

30 Issued Check No. 1243, payable to Payroll, in payment of sales salaries, $3,800, and office salaries, $2,250. Cashed the check and paid the employees.

31 Cash sales for the last half of the month were $47,180.

31 *Post to the customer and creditor accounts. Also, post individual items that are not included in column totals at the end of the month to the general ledger accounts.*

31 Foot and crossfoot the journals and make the month-end postings.

Required

1. Enter the transactions in the appropriate journals and post when instructed to do so.

2. Prepare a trial balance in the Trial Balance columns of the provided work sheet form and complete the work sheet using the following information:

   a. Expired insurance, $395.

   b. Ending store supplies inventory, $1,880.

   c. Ending office supplies inventory, $360.

   d. Estimated depreciation of store equipment, $405.

     e.   Estimated depreciation of office equipment, $235.

     f.   Ending merchandise inventory, $126,000.

3. Prepare a multiple-step classified August income statement, an August statement of changes in owner's equity, and an August 31 classified balance sheet.

4. Prepare and post adjusting and closing entries.

5. Prepare a post-closing trial balance. Also prepare a list of the Accounts Receivable Ledger accounts and a list of the Accounts Payable Ledger accounts. Total the balances of each to confirm that the totals equal the balances in the controlling accounts.

ANSWERS TO PROGRESS CHECKS

6–1 *b*

6–2 The data processor component interprets, manipulates, and summarizes the recorded information so that it can be used in analyses and reports.

6–3 The data that is saved in data storage is used to prepare periodic financial reports, to prepare special-purpose reports for managers, and to provide a source of information for independent auditors.

6–4 *a*

6–5 Compared to manual systems, computer systems offer more accuracy, speed, efficiency, and convenience.

6–6 *d*

6–7 *b*

6–8 Columnar journals allow you to accumulate repetitive debits and credits and post them as column totals rather than as individual amounts.

6–9 The equality of debits and credits is still maintained within the General Ledger. The subsidiary ledger containing the customer's individual account is used only for supplementary information.

6–10 The initial and page number of the journal from which the amount was posted is entered in the Posting Reference column of the ledger account next to the amount.

6–11 *c*

6–12 The controlling account must be debited periodically for an amount or amounts equal to the sum of the debits to the subsidiary ledger, and it must be credited periodically for an amount or amounts equal to the sum of the credits to the subsidiary ledger.

6–13 *d*

6–14 *b*

6–15 This refers to the procedure of using copies of sales invoices as a Sales Journal. Each invoice total is posted directly to the customer's account, and all the invoices are totaled at month-end for posting to the General Ledger accounts.

6–16 The General Journal would still be needed for adjusting, closing, and correcting entries, and for miscellaneous transactions such as sales returns, purchases returns, and plant asset purchases.

6–17 *e*

CHAPTER 7

Accounting for Cash and the Principles of Internal Control

Robert, left, and Susanna Scaretta, owners of Revere Armored Inc., arriving at Federal court on Long Island for their arraignment. (*The New York Times*, May 14, 1993.)

*W*hite-collar crimes continue to increase in the United States causing substantial financial loss, in some cases, to cause bankruptcy. Many could have been prevented if the victims had used appropriate procedures to protect their assets.

In the infamous Revere Armored Inc. case, federal prosecutors concluded that the fraud involved up to $45 million in bank funds. The banks placed their cash in the custodianship of Revere and overlooked the red flags that should have prompted an audit.[1] In a second case involving a $60,000 embezzlement from a church, an analysis of the facts attributed the fraud to the governing board's lack of basic accounting knowledge. In a third case, police arrested a bookkeeper who allegedly embezzled at least $600,000 from seven small businesses in southern California.

Other news reports indicate that a wide range of business entities are victims of substantial embezzlement. In addition, accounting literature indicates that small businesses and not-for-profits often have weak internal control structures that leave them vulnerable to embezzlement.

It is management's responsibility to ensure the safeguarding of business assets, including cash. To do so, management and employees of organizations should understand and be able to apply the basic principles of internal control.

---

[1]*New York Times*, July 11, 1994, p. A9.

LEARNING OBJECTIVES

After studying Chapter 7, you should be able to:

1. **Explain the concept of liquidity and the difference between cash and cash equivalents.**
2. **Explain why internal control procedures are needed in a large organization and state the broad principles of internal control.**
3. **Describe internal control procedures used to protect cash received from cash sales, cash received through the mail, and cash disbursements.**
4. **Explain the operation of a petty cash fund and be able to prepare journal entries to record petty cash fund transactions.**
5. **Explain why the bank balance and the book balance of cash should be reconciled and be able to prepare a reconciliation.**
6. **Explain how recording invoices at net amounts helps gain control over cash discounts taken, and calculate days' sales uncollected.**
7. **Define or explain the words and phrases listed in the chapter glossary.**

Cash is an asset that every business owns and uses. Most organizations own at least some assets known as cash equivalents, which are very similar to cash. In studying this chapter, you will learn the general principles of internal control and the specific principles that guide businesses in managing and accounting for cash. If these internal control principles had been followed by the victims described on the previous page, many of the entities might have been saved from financial loss.

The chapter shows you how to establish and use a petty cash fund and how to reconcile a checking account. Also, you will learn a method of accounting for purchases that helps management determine whether cash discounts on purchases are being lost and, if so, how much has been lost.

CASH, CASH EQUIVALENTS, AND THE CONCEPT OF LIQUIDITY

LO 1

Explain the concept of liquidity and the difference between cash and cash equivalents.

In previous chapters, you learned that a company can own many different kinds of assets such as accounts receivable, merchandise inventory, equipment, buildings, and land. These assets all have value, but most of them are not easily used as a means of payment when buying other assets, acquiring services, or paying off liabilities. Usually, cash must be used as the method of payment. Another way to state this is to say that cash is more *liquid* than these other assets.

In more general terms, the **liquidity** of an asset refers to how easily the asset can be converted into other types of assets or be used to buy services or satisfy obligations. All assets can be evaluated in terms of their relative liquidity. Assets such as cash are said to be **liquid assets** because they can be converted easily into other types of assets or used to buy services or pay liabilities.

As you know, a company needs more than valuable assets to stay in business. That is, the company must own some liquid assets so that bills are paid on time and purchases can be made for cash when necessary.

For financial accounting, the asset *cash* includes not only currency and coins but also amounts on deposit in bank accounts, including checking accounts (sometimes called demand deposits) and some savings accounts (also called time deposits). In addition, cash includes items that are acceptable for deposit in those accounts, especially customers' checks made payable to the company.

To increase their return, many companies invest their idle cash balances in assets called **cash equivalents.** These assets are short-term, highly liquid investments that satisfy two criteria:

1. The investment must be readily convertible to a known amount of cash.
2. The investment must be sufficiently close to its maturity date so that its market value is relatively insensitive to interest rate changes.

In general, only investments purchased within three months of their maturity dates satisfy these criteria.[2] Examples of cash equivalents include short-term investments in U.S. treasury bills, commercial paper (short-term corporate notes payable), and money market funds.

Because cash equivalents are so similar to cash, most companies combine them with cash as a single item on the balance sheet. For example, **Chrysler Corporation's** balance sheet on December 31, 1993, reported the following:

Cash and cash equivalents . . . . $4,040 (million)

As another example, **Mattel Inc.'s** December 31, 1993, balance sheet does not mention cash equivalents. It simply reports cash with a balance of $506,113,000 on its December 31, 1993, balance sheet. However, Mattel discloses the following in a footnote:

> Cash includes cash equivalents. Highly liquid investments with maturities of three months or less when purchased are considered to be cash equivalents. Because of the short maturities of these instruments, the carrying amount is a reasonable estimate of fair value.

As you would expect, cash is an important asset for every business. Because cash is so important, companies need to be careful about keeping track of it. They also need to carefully control access to cash by employees and others who might want to take it for their own use. A good accounting system supports both goals. It can keep track of how much cash is on hand, and it helps control who has access to the cash. Because of the special importance of cash, this chapter describes the practices companies follow to account for and protect cash.

The importance of accounting for cash and cash equivalents is highlighted by the fact that a complete set of financial statements includes a statement of cash flows. That statement identifies the types of activities that caused changes in cash and cash equivalents. You learn more about that statement in Chapter 16.

Progress Check

(Answers to Progress Checks are provided at the end of the chapter.)

7-1   Why does a company need to own liquid assets?

7-2   Why does a company own cash equivalent assets in addition to cash?

7-3   Which of the following assets should be classified as a cash equivalent? *(a)* Land purchased as an investment; *(b)* Accounts receivable; *(c)* Common stock purchased as a short-term investment; *(d)* A 90-day Treasury bill issued by the U.S. government.

---

[2]FASB, *Accounting Standards—Current Text* (Norwalk, CT, 1994), sec. C25.106. First published in *Statement of Financial Accounting Standards No. 95,* par. 8.

INTERNAL CONTROL

LO 2

Explain why internal control procedures are needed in a large organization and state the broad principles of internal control.

In a small business, the manager often controls the entire operation through personal supervision and direct participation in all its activities. For example, he or she commonly buys all the assets and services used in the business. The manager also hires and supervises all employees, negotiates all contracts, and signs all checks. As a result, the manager knows from personal contact and observation whether the business actually received the assets and services for which the checks were written. However, as a business grows, it becomes increasingly difficult to maintain this close personal contact. At some point, the manager must delegate responsibilities and rely on formal procedures rather than personal contact in controlling the operations of the business.

The procedures a company uses to control its operations make up its **internal control system.** A properly designed internal control system encourages adherence to prescribed managerial policies. In doing so, it promotes efficient operations and protects the assets from waste, fraud, and theft. The system also helps ensure that accurate and reliable accounting data are produced.

Specific internal control procedures vary from company to company and depend on such factors as the nature of the business and its size. However, the same broad principles of internal control apply to all companies. These broad principles are:

1. Clearly establish responsibilities.
2. Maintain adequate records.
3. Insure assets and bond employees.
4. Separate record-keeping and custody over assets.
5. Divide responsibility for related transactions.
6. Use mechanical devices whenever feasible.
7. Perform regular and independent reviews.

We discuss these seven principles in the following paragraphs. Throughout, we describe how various internal control procedures prevent fraud and theft. Remember, however, that these procedures are needed to ensure that the accounting records are complete and accurate.

Clearly Establish Responsibilities

To have good internal control, responsibility for each task must be clearly established and assigned to one person. When responsibility is not clearly spelled out, it is difficult to determine who is at fault when something goes wrong. For example, if two sales clerks share access to the same cash register and there is a shortage, it may not be possible to tell which clerk is at fault. Neither can prove that he or she did not cause the shortage. To prevent this problem, one clerk should be given responsibility for making all change. Alternately, the business can use a register with separate cash drawers for each operator.

Maintain Adequate Records

A good record-keeping system helps protect assets and ensures that employees follow prescribed procedures. Reliable records are also a source of information that management uses to monitor the operations of the business. For example, if detailed records of manufacturing equipment and tools are maintained, items are unlikely to be lost or otherwise disappear without any discrepancy being noticed. As another example, expenses and other expenditures are less likely to be debited to the wrong accounts if a comprehensive chart of accounts is established and followed carefully. If the chart is not in place or is not used correctly, management may never discover that some expenses are excessive.

Numerous preprinted forms and internal business papers should be designed and properly used to maintain good internal control. For example, if sales slips are properly designed, sales personnel can record the needed information efficiently without errors or delays to customers. And, if all sales slips are prenumbered and controlled, each salesperson can be held responsible for the sales slips issued to him or her. As a result, a salesperson is not able to pocket cash by making a sale and destroying the sales slip. Computerized point-of-sale systems can achieve the same control results.

Insure Assets and Bond Key Employees

Assets should be covered by adequate casualty insurance, and employees who handle cash and negotiable assets should be bonded. An employee is said to be *bonded* when the company purchases an insurance policy, or a bond, against losses from theft by that employee. Bonding clearly reduces the loss suffered by a theft. It also tends to discourage theft because bonded employees know that an impersonal bonding company must be dealt with when a theft is discovered.

Separate Record-Keeping and Custody over Assets

A fundamental principle of internal control is that the person who has access to or is otherwise responsible for an asset should not maintain the accounting record for that asset. When this principle is followed, the custodian of an asset, knowing that a record of the asset is being kept by another person, is not as likely to misplace, steal, or waste the asset. And, the record-keeper, who does not have access to the asset, has no reason to falsify the record. As a result, two people would have to agree to commit a fraud (called *collusion*) if the asset were stolen and the theft concealed in the records. Because collusion is necessary to commit the fraud, it is less likely to happen.

Divide Responsibility for Related Transactions

Responsibility for a transaction or a series of related transactions should be divided between individuals or departments so that the work of one acts as a check on the other. However, this principle does not call for duplication of work. Each employee or department should perform an unduplicated portion.

For example, responsibility for placing orders, receiving the merchandise, and paying the vendors should not be given to one individual or department. Doing so creates a situation in which mistakes and perhaps fraud are more likely to occur. Having a different person check incoming goods for quality and quantity may encourage more care and attention to detail than having it done by the person who placed the order. And, designating a third person to approve the payment of the invoice offers additional protection against error and fraud. Finally, giving a fourth person the authority to actually write checks adds another measure of protection.

Use Mechanical Devices Whenever Feasible

Cash registers, check protectors, time clocks, and mechanical counters are examples of control devices that should be used whenever feasible. A cash register with a locked-in tape makes a record of each cash sale. A check protector perforates the amount of a check into its face, and makes it difficult to change the amount. A time clock registers the exact time an employee arrives on the job and the exact time the employee departs. Using mechanical change and currency counters is faster and more accurate than counting by hand and reduces the possibility of loss.

Perform Regular and Independent Reviews

Even a well-designed internal control system has a tendency to deteriorate as time passes. Changes in personnel and computer equipment present opportunities for short-cuts and other omissions. The stress of time pressures tends to bring about the same results. Thus, regular reviews of internal control systems are needed to be sure that the standard procedures are being followed. Where possible, these reviews should be performed by internal auditors who are not directly involved in operations. From their independent perspective, internal auditors can evaluate the overall efficiency of operations as well as the effectiveness of the internal control system.

Many companies also have audits by independent auditors who are CPAs. After testing the company's financial records, the CPAs give an opinion as to whether the company's financial statements are presented fairly in accordance with generally accepted accounting principles. However, before CPAs decide on how much testing they must do, they evaluate the effectiveness of the internal control system. When making their evaluation, they can find areas for improvement and offer suggestions.

In the **Revere Armored Inc.** case cited in the opening scenario, if the banks that placed their cash in Revere's custodianship had periodically sent auditors to conduct a joint audit, the fraud could have been avoided. Instead, the audits for each bank were not coordinated and Revere avoided discovery by moving funds from one bank vault to another.

COMPUTERS AND INTERNAL CONTROL

LO 2

Explain why internal control procedures are needed in a large organization and state the broad principles of internal control.

The broad principles of internal control should be followed for both manual and computerized accounting systems. However, computers have several important effects on internal control. Perhaps the most obvious is that computers provide rapid access to large quantities of information. As a result, management's ability to monitor and control business operations can be greatly improved.

Computers Reduce Processing Errors

Computers reduce the number of errors in processing information. Once the data are entered correctly, the possibility of mechanical and mathematical errors is largely eliminated. On the other hand, data entry errors may occur because the process of entering data may be more complex in a computerized system. Also, the lack of human involvement in later processing may cause data entry errors to go undiscovered.

Computers Allow More Extensive Testing of Records

The regular review and audit of computerized records can include more extensive testing because information can be accessed so rapidly. To reduce costs when manual methods are used, managers may select only small samples of data to test. But, when computers are used, large samples or even complete data files can be reviewed and analyzed.

Computerized Systems May Limit Hard Evidence of Processing Steps

Because many data processing steps are performed by the computer, fewer items of documentary evidence may be available for review. However, computer systems can create additional evidence by recording more information, such as who made entries and even when they were made. And, the computer can be programmed to require the use of passwords before making entries so that access to the system is limited. Therefore, internal control may depend more on reviews of the design and operation of the computerized processing system and less on reviews of the documents left behind by the system.

Separation of Duties Must Be Maintained

Because computerized systems are so efficient, companies often need fewer employees. This savings carries the risk that the separation of critical responsibilities may not be maintained. In addition, companies that use computers need employees with special skills to program and operate them. The duties of such employees must be controlled to minimize undetected errors and the risk of fraud. For example, better control is maintained if the person who designs and programs the system does not serve as the operator. Also, control over programs and files related to cash receipts and disbursements should be separated. To prevent fraud, check-writing activities should not be controlled by the computer operator. However, achieving a suitable separation of duties can be especially difficult in small companies that have only a few employees.

Recall from the first page of the chapter the case in which $600,000 was embezzled from seven small businesses in Southern California. The bookkeeper in that case was responsible for making deposits and handling computerized general ledger records. Although other employees prepared and verified deposit slips, they were replaced by slips prepared by the bookkeeper who took deposits to the bank. Manipulation of computerized records hid shortfalls that he pocketed.

Progress Check

7-4 **The broad principles of internal control require that:**
   a. Responsibility for a series of related transactions (such as placing orders for, receiving, and paying for merchandise) should be given to one person so that responsibility is clearly assigned.
   b. Responsibility for specific tasks should be shared by more than one employee so that one serves as a check on the other.
   c. Employees who handle cash and negotiable assets should be bonded.

7-5 **What are some of the effects of computers on internal control?**

Now that we have covered the principles of good internal control in general, it is helpful to see how they are applied to cash, the most liquid of all assets. A good system of internal control for cash should provide adequate procedures for protecting both cash receipts and cash disbursements. In the procedures, three basic guidelines should always be observed:

1. Duties should be separated so that people responsible for actually handling cash are not responsible for keeping the cash records.
2. All cash receipts should be deposited in the bank, intact, each day.
3. All cash payments should be made by check.

The reason for the first principle is that a division of duties helps avoid errors. It also requires two or more people to collude if cash is to be embezzled (stolen) and the theft concealed in the accounting records. One reason for the second guideline is that the daily deposit of all receipts produces a timely independent test of the accuracy of the count of the cash received and the deposit. It also helps prevent loss or theft and keeps an employee from personally using the money for a few days before depositing it.

Finally, if all payments are made by check, the bank records provide an independent description of cash disbursements. This arrangement also tends to prevent thefts of cash. (One exception to this principle allows small disbursements of currency and coins to be made from a petty cash fund. Petty cash funds are discussed later in this

INTERNAL CONTROL FOR CASH

LO 3

Describe internal control procedures used to protect cash received from cash sales, cash received through the mail, and cash disbursements.

chapter.) Note especially that the daily intact depositing of receipts and making disbursements by check allows you to use the bank records as a separate and external record of essentially all cash transactions. Later in the chapter, you learn how to use bank records to confirm the accuracy of your own records.

The exact procedures used to achieve control over cash vary from company to company. They depend on such factors as company size, number of employees, the volume of cash transactions, and the sources of cash. Therefore, the procedures described in the following paragraphs illustrate many but not all situations.

Cash from Cash Sales

Cash sales should be recorded on a cash register at the time of each sale. To help ensure that correct amounts are entered, each register should be placed so that customers can read the amounts displayed. Also, clerks should be required to ring up each sale before wrapping the merchandise and should give the customer a receipt. Finally, each cash register should be designed to provide a permanent, locked-in record of each transaction. In some systems, the register is directly connected to a computer. The computer is programmed to accept cash register transactions and enter them in the accounting records. In other cases, the register simply prints a record of each transaction on a paper tape locked inside the register.

We stated earlier that custody over cash should be separated from record-keeping for cash. For cash sales, this separation begins with the cash register. The salesclerk who has access to the cash in the register should not have access to its locked-in record. At the end of each day, the salesclerk should count the cash in the register, record the result, and turn over the cash and this record of the count to an employee in the cashier's office. The employee in the cashier's office, like the salesclerk, has access to the cash and should not have access to the computerized accounting records (or the register tape). A third employee, preferably from the accounting department, examines the computerized record of register transactions (or the register tape) and compares its total with the cash receipts reported by the cashier's office. The computer record (or register tape) becomes the basis for the journal entry to record cash sales. Note that the accounting department employee has access to the records for cash but does not have access to the actual cash. The salesclerk and the employee from the cashier's office have access to the cash but not to the accounting records. Thus, their accuracy is automatically checked, and none of them can make a mistake or divert any cash without the difference being revealed.

Cash Received through the Mail

Control of cash that comes in through the mail begins with the person who opens the mail. Preferably, two people should be present when the mail is opened. One should make a list (in triplicate) of the money received. The list should record each sender's name, the amount, and the purpose for which the money was sent. One copy is sent to the cashier with the money. A second copy goes to the accounting department. A third copy is kept by the clerk who opened the mail. The cashier deposits the money in the bank, and the bookkeeper records the amounts received in the accounting records. Then, when the bank balance is reconciled by a fourth person (this process is discussed later in the chapter), errors or fraud by the clerk, the cashier, or the bookkeeper are detected. They will be detected because the bank's record of the amount of cash deposited and the records of three people must agree. Note how this arrangement makes errors and fraud nearly impossible, unless the employees enter into collusion. If the clerk does not report all receipts accurately, the customers will question their account balances. If the cashier does not deposit all receipts intact, the bank balance does not agree with the bookkeeper's cash balance. The bookkeeper and the fourth person who reconciles the bank balance do not have access to cash and, therefore, have no opportunity to divert any to themselves. Thus, undetected errors and fraud are made highly unlikely.

Cash Disbursements

The previous discussions clearly show the importance of gaining control over cash from sales and cash received through the mail. Most large embezzlements, however, are actually accomplished through payments of fictitious invoices. Therefore, controlling cash disbursements is perhaps even more critical than controlling cash receipts.

As described earlier, the key to controlling cash disbursements is to require all expenditures to be made by check, except very small payments from petty cash. And, if authority to sign checks is assigned to some person other than the business owner, that person should not have access to the accounting records. This separation of duties helps prevent an employee from concealing fraudulent disbursements in the accounting records.

In a small business, the manager usually signs checks and normally knows from personal contact that the items being paid for were actually received. However, this arrangement is impossible in a larger business. Instead, internal control procedures must be substituted for personal contact. The procedures are designed to assure the check signer that the obligations to be paid were properly incurred and should be paid. Often these controls are achieved through a voucher system.

A **voucher system** is a set of procedures designed to control the incurrence of obligations and disbursements of cash. This kind of system:

1. Establishes procedures for incurring obligations that result in cash disbursements, such as permitting only authorized individuals to make purchase commitments.
2. Provides established procedures for verifying, approving, and recording these obligations.
3. Permits checks to be issued only in payment of properly verified, approved, and recorded obligations.
4. Requires that every obligation be recorded at the time it is incurred and that every purchase be treated as an independent transaction, complete in itself.

A good voucher system produces these results for every transaction, even if several purchases are made from the same company during a month or other billing period.

When a voucher system is used, control over cash disbursements begins as soon as the company incurs an obligation that will result in cash being paid out. A key factor in making the system work is that only specified departments and individuals are authorized to incur such obligations. Managers should also limit the kind of obligations that each department or individual can incur. For example, in a large retail store, only a specially created purchasing department should be authorized to incur obligations through merchandise purchases. In addition, the procedures for purchasing, receiving, and paying for merchandise should be divided among several departments. These departments include the one that originally requested the purchase, the purchasing department, the receiving department, and the accounting department. To coordinate and control the responsibilities of these

THE VOUCHER SYSTEM AND CONTROL

LO 3
Describe internal control procedures used to protect cash received from cash sales, cash received through the mail, and cash disbursements.

Illustration 7-1　The Accumulation of Documents in the Voucher

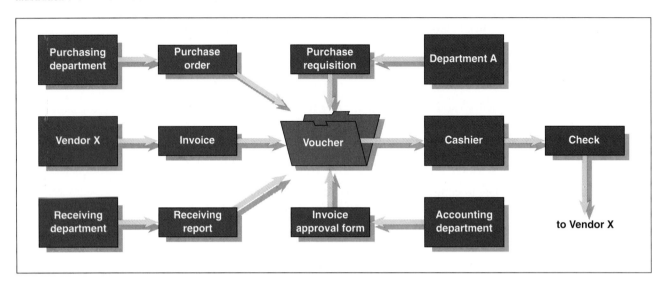

departments, several different business papers are used. Illustration 7–1 shows how these papers are accumulated in a **voucher.** A voucher is an internal business paper that is used to accumulate other papers and information needed to control the disbursement of cash and to ensure that the transaction is properly recorded. The following explanation of each paper going into the voucher will show you how companies use this system to gain control over cash disbursements for merchandise purchases.

Purchase Requisition

In a large retail store, department managers generally are not allowed to place orders directly with suppliers. If each manager could deal directly with suppliers, the amount of merchandise purchased and the resulting liabilities would not be well controlled. Therefore, to gain control over purchases and the resulting liabilities, department managers usually are required to place all orders through the purchasing department. When merchandise is needed, the department managers inform the purchasing department of their needs by preparing and signing a **purchase requisition.** On the requisition, the manager lists the merchandise needed by the department and requests that it be purchased. Two copies of the purchase requisition are sent to the Purchasing Department. The manager of the requisitioning department (identified in Illustration 7–1 as Department A) keeps a third copy as a backup. The purchasing department sends one copy to the accounting department. When it is received, the accounting department creates a new voucher.

Purchase Order

A **purchase order** is a business paper used by the purchasing department to place an order with the seller or **vendor,** which usually is a manufacturer or wholesaler. The purchase order authorizes the vendor to ship the ordered merchandise at the stated price and terms.

When a purchase requisition is received by the purchasing department, it prepares at least four copies of a purchase order. The copies are distributed as follows:

Copy 1 is sent to the vendor as a request to purchase and as authority to ship the merchandise.

Copy 2, with a copy of the purchase requisition attached, is sent to the accounting department, where it is used in approving the payment of the invoice for the purchase; this copy is shown in Illustration 7–1.

Copy 3 is sent to the department originally issuing the requisition to inform its manager that the action has been taken.

Copy 4 is retained on file by the purchasing department.

Invoice

An **invoice** is an itemized statement of goods prepared by the vendor that lists the customer's name, the items sold, the sales prices, and the terms of sale. In effect, the invoice is the bill sent to the buyer by the seller. (From the vendor's point of view, it is a *sales invoice*.) The vendor sends the invoice to the buyer or **vendee,** who treats it as a *purchase invoice*. On receiving a purchase order, the vendor ships the ordered merchandise to the buyer and mails a copy of the invoice that covers the shipment. The goods are delivered to the buyer's receiving department and the invoice is sent directly to the buyer's accounting department, where it is placed in the voucher. Illustration 7–1 also presents this document flow.

Receiving Report

Most large companies maintain a special department that receives all merchandise or other purchased assets. When each shipment arrives, this receiving department counts the goods and checks them for damage and agreement with the purchase order. Then, it prepares four or more copies of a **receiving report.** This report is a form used within the business to notify the appropriate persons that ordered goods were received and to describe the quantities and condition of the goods. As shown in Illustration 7–1, one copy is sent to the accounting department and placed in the voucher. Copies are also sent to the original requisitioning department and the purchasing department to notify them that the goods have arrived. The receiving department retains a copy in its files.

Invoice Approval Form

After the receiving report arrives, the accounting department should have copies of these papers on file in the voucher:

1. The *purchase requisition* listing the items to be ordered.
2. The *purchase order* listing the merchandise that was actually ordered.
3. The *invoice* showing the quantity, description, price, and total cost of the goods shipped by the seller.
4. The *receiving report* listing the quantity and condition of the items actually received by the buyer.

With the information on these papers, the accounting department is in a position to make an entry recording the purchase and to approve its eventual payment before the end of the discount period. In approving the invoice for payment, the accounting department checks and compares the information on all the papers. To facilitate the checking procedure and to ensure that no step is omitted, the department commonly

Illustration 7-2
An Invoice Approval Form

	By	Date
Purchase order number	___	___
Requisition check	___	___
Purchase order check	___	___
Receiving report check	___	___
Invoice check:		
Price approval	___	___
Calculations	___	___
Terms	___	___
Approved for payment	___	___

uses an **invoice approval form.** (See Illustration 7–2.) This form is a document on which the accounting department notes that it has performed each step in the process of checking an invoice and approving it for recording and payment. An invoice approval form may be a separate business paper that is filed in the voucher or it may be preprinted on the voucher. It also may be stamped on the invoice. For clarity, the flowchart in Illustration 7–1 shows the form as a separate document.

As each step in the checking procedure is finished, the clerk initials the invoice approval form and records the current date. Initials in each space on the form indicate that the following administrative actions have been taken:

1. **Requisition check** . . . . The items on the invoice were actually requisitioned, as shown on the copy of the purchase requisition.

2. **Purchase order check** . . . . The items on the invoice were actually ordered, as shown on the copy of the purchase order.

3. **Receiving report check** . . . The items on the invoice were actually received, as shown on the copy of the receiving report.

4. **Invoice check:**
   Price approval . . . . The invoice prices are stated as agreed with the vendor.

   Calculations . . . . The invoice has no mathematical errors.

   Terms . . . . The terms are stated as agreed with the vendor.

The Voucher

After an invoice is checked and approved, the voucher is complete. At this point, the voucher is a record that summarizes the transaction. The voucher shows that the transaction has been certified as correct and authorizes its recording as an obligation of the buyer. The voucher also contains approval for paying the obligation on the appropriate date. Of course, the actual physical form used for vouchers varies substantially from company to company. In general, they are designed so that the invoice and other documents from which they are prepared are placed inside the voucher, which is often a folder. The information printed on the inside of a typical voucher is shown in Illustration 7–3, and the information on the outside is shown in Illustration 7–4.

The preparation of a voucher requires a clerk to enter the specified information in the proper blanks. The information is taken from the invoice and all the supporting documents filed inside the voucher. Once the steps are completed, the voucher is sent to the appropriate authorized individual (sometimes called the *auditor*), who completes one final review of the information, approves the accounts and amounts to be debited (called the *accounting distribution*), and approves the voucher for recording.

After a voucher is approved and recorded, it is filed until its due date, when it is sent to the cashier's office for payment. Here, the person responsible for issuing checks

Illustration 7–3
Inside of a Voucher

VALLEY SUPPLY COMPANY   Voucher No. _93–767_
Eugene, Oregon

Date _____Oct. 1, 19X1_____

Pay to _____A. B. Seay Wholesale Company_____

City _____Salem_____   State_____Oregon_____

For the following: (attach all invoices and supporting papers)

Date of Invoice	Terms	Invoice Number and Other Details	Amount
Sept. 30, 19X1	2/10, n/60	Invoice No. C-11756 Less discount Net amount payable	800.00 16.00 784.00

Payment approved

N. O. Neal
Auditor

Illustration 7–4
Outside of a Voucher

Voucher No. _93–767_

ACCOUNTING DISTRIBUTION

Account Debited	Amount
Purchases	800.00
Transportation-In	
Store Supplies	
Office Supplies	
Sales Salaries	
Other	
Total Vouch. Pay. Cr.	800.00

Due date _____October 10, 19X1_____

Pay to _A. B. Seay Wholesale Company_
City_____Salem_____
State_____Oregon_____

Summary of charges:
Total charges _____800.00_____
Discount _____16.00_____
Net payment _____784.00_____

Record of payment:
Paid _____
Check No. _____

relies on the approved voucher and its signed supporting documents as proof that the obligation was properly incurred and should be paid. As described earlier, the purchase requisition and purchase order attached to the voucher confirm that the purchase was authorized. The receiving report shows that the items were received, and the invoice approval form verifies that the invoice was checked for errors. As a result, there is little chance for error. There is even less chance for fraud without collusion, unless all the documents and signatures are forged.

Under a voucher system, obligations should be approved for payment and recorded as liabilities as soon as possible after they are incurred. As shown in the example, this practice should be followed for all purchases. It also should be followed for all expenses. For example, when a company receives a monthly telephone bill, the charges (especially long-distance calls) should be examined for accuracy. A voucher should be prepared, and the telephone bill should be filed inside the voucher. The voucher

THE VOUCHER SYSTEM AND EXPENSES

then is recorded with a journal entry. If the amount is due at once, a check should be issued. Otherwise, the voucher should be filed for payment on the due date.

The requirement that vouchers be prepared for expenses as they are incurred helps ensure that every expense payment is approved only when adequate information is available. However, invoices or bills for such things as equipment repairs are sometimes not received until weeks after the work is done. If no records of the repairs exist, it may be difficult to determine whether the invoice or bill correctly states the amount owed. Also, if no records exist, it may be possible for a dishonest employee to arrange with an outsider for more than one payment of an obligation, or for payment of excessive amounts, or for payment for goods and services not received. A properly functioning voucher system helps prevent all of these undesirable results.

Progress Check

7-6   **Regarding internal control procedures for cash receipts:**
    a. **All cash disbursements, other than from petty cash, should be made by check.**
    b. **An accounting employee should count the cash received from sales and promptly deposit the receipts.**
    c. **Mail containing cash receipts should be opened by an accounting employee who is responsible for recording and depositing the receipts.**

7-7   **Do all companies need a voucher system? At what approximate point in a company's growth would you recommend installing a voucher system?**

THE PETTY CASH FUND

LO 4

Explain the operation of a petty cash fund and be able to prepare journal entries to record petty cash fund transactions.

A basic principle for controlling cash disbursements requires that all disbursements be made by check. However, an exception to this rule is made for *petty cash disbursements.* Every business must make many small payments for items such as postage, express charges, repairs, and small items of supplies. If firms made such payments by check, they would end up writing many checks for small amounts. This arrangement would be both time consuming and expensive. Therefore, to avoid writing checks for small amounts, a business should establish a petty cash fund and use the money in this fund to make payments like those listed earlier.

Establishing a petty cash fund requires estimating the total amount of small payments likely to be made during a short period, such as a month. Then, a check is drawn by the company cashier's office for an amount slightly in excess of this estimate. This check is recorded with a debit to the Petty Cash account (an asset) and a credit to Cash. The check is cashed, and the currency is turned over to a member of the office staff designated as the *petty cashier.* This person is responsible for the safekeeping of the cash, for making payments from this fund, and for keeping accurate records.

The petty cashier should keep the petty cash in a locked box in a safe place. As each disbursement is made, the person receiving payment signs a *petty cash receipt* (see Illustration 7–5). The receipt is then placed in the petty cashbox with the remaining money. Under this system, the sum of all the receipts plus the remaining cash should always equal the amount of the fund. For example, a $100 petty cash fund could have *(a)* $100 in cash, *(b)* $80 in cash and $20 in receipts, or *(c)* $10 in cash and $90 in receipts. Notice that each disbursement reduces the cash and increases the sum of the receipts in the petty cashbox. When the cash is nearly gone, the fund should be reimbursed.

To reimburse the fund, the petty cashier presents the receipts to the company cashier. The company cashier stamps all receipts *paid* so that they cannot be reused, retains them, and gives the petty cashier a check for their sum. When this check is cashed and the proceeds returned to the cashbox, the money in the box is restored to its original amount, and the fund is ready to begin a new cycle of operations.

Illustration 7-5
A Petty Cash Receipt

No. _- 1 -_ $ _10.00_

RECEIVED OF PETTY CASH

Date _Nov. 2_ 19 _X1_

For_Washing windows_

Charge to_____ _Miscellaneous Expenses_

Approved by
CAB

Received by
Bob Tone

TOPS-Form 3008

At the time a check is written to reimburse the petty cash fund, the petty cashier should sort the paid receipts according to the type of expense or other accounts to be debited in recording payments from the fund. Each group is then totaled, and the totals are used in making the entry to record the reimbursement.

**ILLUSTRATION OF
A PETTY CASH
FUND**

To avoid writing numerous checks for small amounts, a company established a petty cash fund on November 1, designating one of its office clerks, Carl Burns, as petty cashier. A $75 check was drawn, cashed, and the proceeds turned over to Burns. The following entry recorded the check:

Nov.	1	Petty Cash	75.00	
		Cash		75.00
		Established a petty cash fund.		

Notice that this entry transfers $75 from the regular Cash account to the Petty Cash account. After the petty cash fund is established, the Petty Cash account is not debited or credited again unless the size of the total fund is changed. For example, the fund should be increased if it is being exhausted and reimbursed too frequently. Another entry like the preceding one would be made to record an increase in the size of the fund. That is, there would be a debit to Petty Cash and credit to Cash for the amount of the increase. If the fund is too large, some of the money in the fund should be redeposited in the checking account. Such a reduction in the fund is recorded with a debit to Cash and a credit to Petty Cash.

During November, Carl Burns, the petty cashier, made several payments from the petty cash fund. Each time, he asked the person who received payment to sign a receipt. On November 27, after making a $26.50 payment for repairs to an office computer, Burns noticed that only $3.70 cash remained in the fund. Therefore, he summarized and totaled the petty cash receipts as shown in Illustration 7–6. Then, he gave the summary and the petty cash receipts to the company cashier in exchange for a $71.30 check to reimburse the fund. Burns cashed the check, put the $71.30 proceeds in the petty cashbox, and was ready to make additional payments from the fund. The reimbursing check is recorded with the following journal entry:

Illustration 7-6
Summary of Petty Cash
Payments

Miscellaneous expenses:		
Nov. 2, washing windows	$10.00	
Nov. 17, washing windows	10.00	
Nov. 27, computer repairs	26.50	$46.50
Transportation-in:		
Nov. 5, delivery of merchandise purchased . . .	$ 6.75	
Nov. 20, delivery of merchandise purchased . .	8.30	15.05
Delivery expense:		
Nov. 18, customer's package delivered		5.00
Office supplies:		
Nov. 15, purchased office supplies		4.75
Total		$71.30

Nov.	27	Miscellaneous Expenses	46.50	
		Transportation-In	15.05	
		Delivery Expense	5.00	
		Office Supplies	4.75	
		Cash		71.30
		Reimbursed petty cash.		

Information for this entry came from the petty cashier's summary of payments. Note that the debits in the entry record the petty cash payments. Even if the petty cash fund is not low on funds at the end of an accounting period, it may be reimbursed at that time to record the expenses in the proper period. Otherwise, the financial statements show an overstated petty cash asset and understated expenses or assets that were paid for out of petty cash. (Of course, the amounts involved are seldom if ever significant to users of the financial statements.)

CASH OVER AND SHORT

Sometimes, a petty cashier fails to get a receipt for a payment. Then, when the fund is reimbursed, he or she may forget the purpose of the expenditure. This mistake causes the fund to be short. If, for whatever reason, the petty cash fund is short at reimbursement time, the shortage is recorded as an expense in the reimbursing entry with a debit to the **Cash Over and Short account.** This account is an income statement account that records the income effects of cash overages and cash shortages arising from omitted petty cash receipts and from errors in making change.

Errors in making change are discovered when there are differences between the cash in a cash register and the record of the amount of cash sales. Even though a cashier is careful, some customers may be given too much or too little change. As a result, at the end of a day, the actual cash from a cash register may not equal the cash sales rung up. For example, assume that a cash register shows cash sales of $550 but the actual count of cash in the register is $555. The entry to record the cash sales and the overage would be:

Nov.	23	Cash	555.00	
		Cash Over and Short		5.00
		Sales		550.00
		Day's cash sales and overage.		

On the other hand, if there were a shortage of cash in the register on the next day, the entry to record cash sales and the shortage would look like the following:

Nov.	24	Cash	621.00	
		Cash Over and Short	4.00	
		Sales		625.00
		Day's cash sales and shortage.		

Because customers are more likely to dispute being shortchanged, the Cash Over and Short account usually has a debit balance by the end of the accounting period. Because it is a debit, this balance represents an expense. This expense may be shown on the income statement as a separate item in the general and administrative expense section. Or, because the amount is usually small, you can combine it with other small expenses and report them as a single item called *miscellaneous expenses*. If Cash Over and Short has a credit balance at the end of the period, it usually is included as part of *miscellaneous revenues* on the income statement.

Progress Check

7-8   Why are some cash payments made from a petty cash fund?

7-9   Why should a petty cash fund be reimbursed at the end of an accounting period?

7-10   What are two results of reimbursing the petty cash fund?

RECONCILING THE BANK BALANCE

LO 5

Explain why the bank balance and the book balance of cash should be reconciled and be able to prepare a reconciliation.

At least once every month, banks send depositors bank statements that show the activity in their accounts during the month. Different banks use a variety of formats for their bank statements. However, all of them include the following items of information in one place or another:

1. The balance of the depositor's account at the beginning of the month.
2. Deposits and any other amounts added to the account during the month.
3. Checks and any other amounts deducted from the account during the month.
4. The account balance at the end of the month.

Of course, all this information is presented as it appears in the bank's records. Examine Illustration 7–7, an example of a typical bank statement, to find the four items just listed.

Note that section A of Illustration 7–7 summarizes the changes in the account. Section B lists specific debits and credits to the account (other than canceled checks). Section C lists all paid checks in numerical order, and section D shows the daily account balances.

Illustration 7-7   A Typical Bank Statement

First National Bank P.O. BOX 1727 AUSTIN, TEXAS 78767 512/473-4343

VALLEY COMPANY
1300 FALCON LEDGE
AUSTIN, TEXAS 78746

ACCOUNT NUMBER	DATE OF THIS STATEMENT	DATE OF LAST STATEMENT	PAGE NO.
494 504 2	10/31/X5	9/30/X5	1

A

BALANCE OF PREVIOUS STATEMENT ON 9/30/X5	1,609.58
5 DEPOSITS AND OTHER CREDITS TOTALING	1,155.00
10 CHECKS AND OTHER DEBITS TOTALING	723.00
SERVICE CHARGE AMOUNT	.00
INTEREST AMOUNT AT 5.2500%	8.42
CURRENT BALANCE AS OF THIS STATEMENT	2,050.00
AVERAGE BALANCE AS OF THIS STATEMENT	1,924.95
TOTAL INTEREST PAID TO DATE	124.00

B

CHECKING ACCOUNT TRANSACTIONS

DATE	AMOUNT	TRANSACTION DESCRIPTION ....
10/02	240.00 +	DEPOSIT
10/09	180.00 +	DEPOSIT
10/12	23.00 −	CHARGE FOR PRINTING NEW CHECKS
10/15	100.00 +	DEPOSIT
10/16	150.00 +	DEPOSIT
10/23	485.00 +	NOTE COLLECTION LESS FEE
10/25	30.00 −	NSF CHECK AND NSF CHARGE
10/31	8.42 +	INTEREST PAID

C

DATE	CHECK NO	AMOUNT	DATE	CHECK NO	AMOUNT
10/03	119	55.00	10/16	123	25.00
10/19	120	200.00	10/23	125*	10.00
10/10	121	120.00	10/26	127*	50.00
10/14	122	75.00	10/29	128	135.00

*INDICATES A SKIP IN CHECK NUMBER SEQUENCE

D

DAILY BALANCE SUMMARY

DATE	BALANCE	DATE	BALANCE	DATE	BALANCE
10/01	1,609.58	10/12	1,831.58	10/23	2,256.58
10/02	1,849.58	10/14	1,756.58	10/25	2,226.58
10/03	1,794.58	10/15	1,856.58	10/26	2,176.58
10/09	1,974.58	10/16	1,981.58	10/29	2,041.58
10/10	1,854.58	10/19	1,781.58	10/31	2,050.00

FOR QUESTIONS ON DIRECT DEPOSITS, PLEASE CALL 473-4522, BETWEEN 9:00–4:00 MONDAY-FRIDAY
OR WRITE P.O. BOX 1727, AUSTIN, TEXAS 78767.

Enclosed with the monthly statement are the depositor's **canceled checks** and any debit or credit memoranda that have affected the account. Canceled checks are checks that the bank has paid and deducted from the customer's account during the month. Additional deductions that may appear on the bank statement for an individual include withdrawals through automatic teller machines (ATM withdrawals) and periodic payments arranged in advance by the depositor.[3] Other deductions from the depositor's account may include service charges and fees assessed by the bank, customers' checks deposited that prove to be uncollectible, and corrections of previous errors. Except for the service charges, the bank notifies the depositor of the de-

---

[3]Because of the need to make all disbursements by check, most business checking accounts do not allow ATM withdrawals.

duction in each case with a debit memorandum at the time that the bank reduces the balance. For completeness, a copy of each debit memorandum is usually sent with the monthly statement.[4]

In addition to deposits made by the depositor, the bank may add amounts to the depositor's account. Examples of additions would be amounts the bank has collected on behalf of the depositor and corrections of previous errors. Credit memoranda notify the depositor of all additions when they are first recorded. For completeness, a copy of each credit memorandum may be sent with the monthly statement.

Another item commonly added to the bank balance on the statement is interest earned by the depositor. Many checking accounts pay the depositor interest based on the average cash balance maintained in the account. The bank calculates the amount of interest earned and credits it to the depositor's account each month. In Illustration 7–7, note that the bank credited $8.42 of interest to the account of Valley Company. (The methods used to calculate interest are discussed in the next chapter.)

When the business deposits all receipts intact and when all payments (other than petty cash payments) are drawn from the checking account, the bank statement is a device for proving the accuracy of the depositor's cash records. The test of the accuracy begins by preparing a **bank reconciliation;** this analysis explains the difference between the balance of a checking account in the depositor's records and the balance on the bank statement.

Need for Reconciling the Bank Balance

For virtually all checking accounts, the balance on the bank statement does not agree with the balance in the depositor's accounting records. Therefore, to prove the accuracy of both the depositor's records and those of the bank, you must *reconcile* the two balances. In other words, you must explain or account for the differences between them.

Numerous factors cause the bank statement balance to differ from the depositor's book balance. Some are:

1. **Outstanding checks.** These checks were written (or drawn) by the depositor, deducted on the depositor's records, and sent to the payees. However, they did not reach the bank for payment and deduction before the statement date.

2. **Unrecorded deposits.** Companies often make deposits at the end of each business day, after the bank is closed. These deposits made in the bank's night depository are not recorded by the bank until the next business day. Therefore, a deposit placed in the night depository on the last day of the month cannot appear on the bank statement for that month. In addition, deposits mailed to the bank toward the end of the month may be in transit and unrecorded when the statement is prepared.

3. **Charges for uncollectible items and for service.** Occasionally, a company deposits a customer's check that bounces, or turns out to be uncollectible. Usually, the balance in the customer's account is not large enough to cover the check. In these cases, the check is called a nonsufficient funds (NSF) check. In other situations, the customer's account has been closed. In processing deposited checks, the bank credits the depositor's account for the full amount. Later, when the bank learns that the check is uncollectible, it debits (reduces) the depositor's account for the amount of the check. Also, the bank may charge the depositor a fee for processing the uncollectible check. At the same time, the bank notifies the depositor of each deduction by mailing a debit memorandum. Although each deduction should be recorded by the depositor on the day the debit memorandum is received, sometimes an entry is not made until the bank reconciliation is prepared.

---

[4]A depositor's account is a liability on the bank's records. Thus, a deposit increases the account balance, and the bank records it with a *credit* to the account. Debit memos from the bank produce *credits* on the depositor's books, and credit memos lead to *debits*.

Other charges to a depositor's account that a bank might report on the bank statement include the printing of new checks. Also, the bank may assess a monthly service charge for maintaining the account. Notification of these charges is *not* provided until the statement is mailed.

4. **Credits for collections and for interest.** Banks sometimes act as collection agents for their depositors by collecting promissory notes and other items. When the bank collects an item, it deducts a fee and adds the net proceeds to the depositor's account. At the same time, it sends a credit memorandum to notify the depositor of the transaction. As soon as the memorandum is received, it should be recorded by the depositor. However, these items may remain unrecorded until the time of the bank reconciliation.

    Many bank accounts earn interest on the average cash balance in the account during the month. If an account earns interest, the bank statement includes a credit for the amount earned during the past month. Notification of earned interest is provided only by the bank statement.

5. **Errors.** Regardless of care and systems of internal control for automatic error detection, both banks and depositors make errors. Errors by the bank may not be discovered until the depositor completes the bank reconciliation. Also, the depositor's errors often are not discovered until the balance is reconciled.

Steps in Reconciling the Bank Balance

To obtain the benefits of separated duties, an employee who does not handle cash receipts, process checks, or maintain cash records should prepare the bank reconciliation. In preparing to reconcile the balance, this employee must gather information from the bank statement and from other sources in the records. The person who performs the reconciliation must do the following:

*   Compare the deposits listed on the bank statement with the deposits shown in the accounting records. Identify any discrepancies and determine which is correct. Make a list of any errors or unrecorded deposits.

*   Examine all other credits on the bank statement and determine whether each was recorded in the books. These items include collections by the bank, correction of previous bank statement errors, and interest earned by the depositor. List any unrecorded items.

*   Compare the canceled checks listed on the bank statement with the actual checks returned with the statement. For each check, make sure that the correct amount was deducted by the bank and that the returned check was properly charged to the company's account. List any discrepancies or errors.

*   Compare the canceled checks listed on the bank statement with the checks recorded in the books. (To make this process easier, the bank statement normally lists canceled checks in numerical order.) Prepare a list of any outstanding checks.

    Although an individual may occasionally write a check and fail to record it in the books, companies with reasonable internal controls rarely if ever write a check without recording it. Nevertheless, prepare a list of any canceled checks unrecorded in the books.

*   Determine whether any outstanding checks listed on the previous month's bank reconciliation are not included in the canceled checks listed on the bank statement. Prepare a list of any of these checks that remain outstanding at the end of the current month. Send this list to the cashier's office for follow-up with the payees to see if the checks were actually received.

Illustration 7–8
A Typical Bank Reconciliation

VALLEY COMPANY
Bank Reconciliation
October 31, 19X5

①Bank statement balance	$2,050.00	⑤Book balance		$1,404.58
②Add:		⑥Add:		
Deposit of 10/31	145.00	Proceeds of note less		
		collection fee		$ 485.00
		Interest earned		8.42
		Total		$ 493.42
Total	$2,195.00	Total		$1,898.00
③Deduct:		⑦Deduct:		
Outstanding checks:		NSF check plus service		
No. 124	$ 150.00	charge		$ 30.00
No. 126	200.00	Check printing charge		23.00
Total	$ 350.00	Total		$ 53.00
④Reconciled balance	$1,845.00	⑧Reconciled balance		$1,845.00

⑨The two balances both equal $1,845.00

- Examine all other debits to the account shown on the bank statement and determine whether each was recorded in the books. These include bank charges for newly printed checks, NSF checks, and monthly service charges. List those not yet recorded.

When this information has been gathered, the employee can complete the reconciliation like the one in Illustration 7–8 by using these steps:

1. Start with the bank balance of the cash account.
2. Identify and list any unrecorded deposits and any bank errors that understated the bank balance. Add them to the bank balance.
3. Identify and list any outstanding checks and any bank errors that overstated the bank balance. Subtract them from the bank balance.
4. Compute the adjusted balance. This amount is also called the correct or reconciled balance.
5. Start with the book balance of the cash account.
6. Identify and list any unrecorded credit memoranda from the bank (perhaps for the proceeds of a collected note), interest earned, and any errors that understated the balance. Add them to the book balance.
7. Identify and list any unrecorded debit memoranda from the bank (perhaps for a NSF check from a customer), service charges, and any errors that overstated the book balance. Subtract them from the book balance.
8. Compute the reconciled balance. This is also the correct balance.
9. Verify that the two adjusted balances from steps 4 and 8 are equal. If so, they are reconciled. If not, check for mathematical accuracy and for any missing data.

When the reconciliation is complete, the employee should send a copy to the accounting department so that any needed journal entries can be recorded. For example, entries are needed to record any unrecorded debit and credit memoranda and any of the company's mistakes. Another copy should go to the cashier's office, especially if the bank has made an error that needs to be corrected.

ILLUSTRATION OF A BANK RECONCILIATION

We can illustrate a bank reconciliation by preparing one for Valley Company as of October 31. In preparing to reconcile the bank account, the Valley Company employee gathered the following facts:

- The bank balance shown on the bank statement was $2,050.
- The cash balance according to the accounting records was $1,404.58.
- A $145 deposit was placed in the bank's night depository on October 31 and was unrecorded by the bank when the bank statement was mailed.
- Enclosed with the bank statement was a copy of a credit memorandum showing that the bank had collected a note receivable for the company on October 23. The note's proceeds of $500 (less a $15 collection fee) were credited to the company's account. This credit memorandum had not been recorded by the company.
- The bank statement also showed a credit of $8.42 for interest earned on the average cash balance in the account. Because there had been no prior notification of this item, it had not been recorded on the company's books.
- A comparison of canceled checks with the company's books showed that two checks were outstanding—No. 124 for $150 and No. 126 for $200.
- Other debits on the bank statement that had not been previously recorded on the books included (a) a $23 charge for checks printed by the bank; and (b) an NSF (nonsufficient funds) check for $20 plus the related processing fee of $10. The NSF check had been received from a customer, Frank Green, on October 16 and had been included in that day's deposit.

Illustration 7–8 shows the bank reconciliation that reflects these items. The numbers in the circles beside the various parts of the reconciliation correspond to the numbers of the steps listed earlier.

Preparing a bank reconciliation helps locate any errors made by either the bank or the depositor. It also identifies unrecorded items that should be recorded on the company's books. For example, in Valley Company's reconciliation, the adjusted balance of $1,845.00 is the correct balance as of October 31, 19X5. However, at that date, Valley Company's accounting records show a $1,404.58 balance. Therefore, journal entries must be made to increase the book balance to the correct balance. This process requires four entries. The first is:

Nov.	2	Cash	485.00	
		Collection Expense	15.00	
		Notes Receivable		500.00
		To record the collection fee and proceeds of a note collected by the bank.		

This entry records the net proceeds of Valley Company's note receivable that had been collected by the bank, the expense of having the bank perform that service, and the reduction in the Notes Receivable account.

The second entry records the interest credited to Valley Company's account by the bank:

Nov.	2	Cash	8.42	
		Interest Earned		8.42
		To record interest earned on the average cash balance maintained in the checking account.		

Interest earned is a revenue, and the entry recognizes both the revenue and the related increase in Cash.

The third entry records the NSF check that was returned as uncollectible. The $20 check was received from Green in payment of his account and deposited. The bank charged $10 for handling the NSF check and deducted $30 from Valley Company's account. Therefore, the company must reverse the entry made when the check was received and also record the $10 processing fee:

Nov.	2	Accounts Receivable—Frank Green	30.00	
		Cash		30.00
		To charge Frank Green's account for his NSF check and for the bank's fee.		

This entry reflects the fact that Valley Company followed customary business practice and added the NSF $10 fee to Green's account. Thus, it will try to collect the entire $30 from Green.

The fourth entry debits Miscellaneous Expenses for the check printing charge. The entry is:

Nov.	2	Miscellaneous Expenses	23.00	
		Cash		23.00
		Check printing charge.		

After these entries are recorded, the balance of cash is increased to the correct amount of $1,845.00 ($1,404.58 + $485.00 + $8.42 − $30.00 − $23.00).

Progress Check

7-11 What is a bank statement?

7-12 What is the meaning of the phrase *to reconcile a bank balance?*

7-13 Why should you reconcile the bank statement balance of cash and the depositor's book balance of cash?

7-14 List items that commonly affect the bank side of a reconciliation and indicate if the items are added or subtracted.

7-15 List items that commonly affect the book side of a reconciliation and indicate if the items are added or subtracted.

OTHER INTERNAL CONTROL PROCEDURES

LO 6

Explain how recording invoices at net amounts helps gain control over cash discounts taken, and calculate days' sales uncollected.

Internal control principles apply to every phase of a company's operations including merchandise purchases, sales, cash receipts, cash disbursements, and owning and operating plant assets. Many of these procedures are discussed in later chapters. At this point, we consider a way that a company can gain more control over *purchases discounts.*

Recall that entries such as the following have recorded the receipt and payment of an invoice for a purchase of merchandise:

Oct.	2	Purchases	1,000.00	
		Accounts Payable		1,000.00
		Purchased merchandise, terms 2/10, n/60.		
	12	Accounts Payable	1,000.00	
		Purchases Discounts		20.00
		Cash		980.00
		Paid the invoice of October 2.		

These entries reflect the **gross method of recording purchases.** That is, the invoice was recorded at its gross amount of $1,000 before considering the cash discount. Many companies record invoices in this way. However, the **net method of recording purchases** records invoices at their *net* amounts (after cash discounts). This method is widely thought to provide more useful information to management.

To illustrate the net method, assume that a company purchases merchandise with a $1,000 invoice price, and terms of 2/10, n/60. On receiving the goods, the purchasing company deducted the offered $20 discount from the gross amount and recorded the purchase at the $980 net amount:

Oct.	2	Purchases	980.00	
		Accounts Payable		980.00
		Purchased merchandise on credit.		

If the invoice for this purchase is paid within the discount period, the entry to record the payment debits Accounts Payable and credits Cash for $980. However, if payment is not made within the discount period and the discount is *lost,* an entry such as the following must be made either before or when the invoice is paid:

Dec.	1	Discounts Lost	20.00	
		Accounts Payable		20.00
		To record the discount lost.		

A check for the full $1,000 invoice amount is then written, recorded, and mailed to the creditor.[5]

Advantage of the Net Method

When invoices are recorded at *gross* amounts, the amount of discounts taken is deducted from the balance of the Purchases account on the income statement to arrive at the cost of merchandise purchased. However, the amount of any lost discounts does not appear in any account or on the income statement. Therefore, lost discounts may not come to the attention of management.

On the other hand, when purchases are recorded at *net* amounts, the amount of discounts taken does not appear on the income statement. Instead, an expense for **discounts lost** is brought to management's attention through its appearance on the income statement as an operating expense.

Recording invoices at their net amounts supplies management with useful information about the amount of discounts missed through oversight, carelessness, or some other reason. Thus, this practice gives management better control over the people responsible for paying bills on time so that cash discounts can be taken. When the accounts record the fact that discounts are missed, someone has to explain why. As a result, it is likely that fewer discounts are lost through carelessness.

USING THE INFORMATION—DAYS' SALES UNCOLLECTED

Many companies attract customers by selling to them on credit. As a result, cash flows from customers are postponed until the accounts receivable are collected. To evaluate the liquidity of a company's assets, investors want to know how quickly the company converts its accounts receivable into cash. One way financial statement users

---

[5]Alternatively, the lost discount can be recorded with the late payment in a single entry.

evaluate the liquidity of the receivables is to look at the **days' sales uncollected.** This is calculated by taking the ratio between the present balance of receivables and the credit sales over the preceding year, and then multiplying by the number of days in the year. Since the amount of credit sales usually is not reported, net sales is typically used in the calculation. Thus, the formula for the calculation is:

$$\text{Days' sales uncollected} = \frac{\text{Accounts receivable}}{\text{Net sales}} \times 365$$

For example, Meg's Mart (see p. 189) had accounts receivable of $11,200 at the end of 19X2 and net sales of $314,700 (see page 201) for the year. By dividing $11,200 by $314,700, we find that the receivables balance represents 3.56% of the year's sales. Because there are 365 days in a year, the $11,200 balance is 3.56% of 365 days of sales, or 13 days of sales.

The number of days' sales uncollected is used as an estimate of how much time is likely to pass before cash receipts from credit sales equal the amount of the existing accounts receivable. In evaluating this number, financial statement users should compare it to days' sales uncollected calculations for other companies in the same industry. In addition, they may make comparisons between the current and prior periods. To illustrate such a comparison, selected data from the annual reports of two toy manufacturing companies are used to compute days' sales uncollected:

(In thousands)	1993		
	TYCO	**MATTEL**	
Accounts receivable	$219,036	$580,313	
Net sales	$730,179 $\times$ 365	$2,704,448 $\times$ 365	
Days' sales uncollected	110 days	78 days	

If TYCO Toys, Inc.'s management made the preceding comparison, the resulting figures might motivate them to investigate how this compares to last year and how they could improve this ratio. Continuation of a financially sound business requires continuous monitoring of the liquidity of the firm's assets.

Progress Check

7-16 When invoices are recorded at net amounts:
   a. The amount of purchases discounts taken is not recorded in a separate account.
   b. Purchases discounts taken are recorded in a Purchases Discounts account.
   c. The cash expenditures for purchases will always be less than if the invoices are recorded at gross amounts.

7-17 Why is the days' sales uncollected calculation usually based on net sales instead of credit sales?

SUMMARY OF THE CHAPTER IN TERMS OF LEARNING OBJECTIVES

LO 1. Explain the concept of liquidity and the difference between cash and cash equivalents. The liquidity of an asset refers to how easily the asset can be converted into other types of assets or used to buy services or satisfy obligations. Cash is the most liquid asset. To increase their return, companies may invest their idle cash balances in cash equivalents. These investments are readily convertible to a known amount of cash and are purchased so close to their maturity date that their market values are relatively insensitive to interest rate changes.

LO 2. Explain why internal control procedures are needed in a large organization and state the broad principles of internal control. Internal control systems are designed to encourage adherence to prescribed managerial policies. In doing so, they promote efficient operations and protect assets against theft or misuse. They also help ensure that accurate and reliable accounting data are produced. Principles of good internal control include establishing clear responsibilities, maintaining adequate records, insuring assets and bonding employees, separating record-keeping and custody of assets, dividing responsibilities for related transactions, using mechanical devices whenever feasible, and performing regular independent reviews of internal control practices.

LO 3. Describe internal control procedures used to protect cash received from cash sales, cash received through the mail, and cash disbursements. To maintain control over cash, custody must be separated from record-keeping for cash. All cash receipts should be deposited intact in the bank on a daily basis, and all payments (except for minor petty cash payments) should be made by check. A voucher system helps maintain control over cash disbursements by ensuring that payments are made only after full documentation and approval.

LO 4. Explain the operation of a petty cash fund and be able to prepare journal entries to record petty cash fund transactions. The petty cashier, who should be a responsible employee, makes small payments from the petty cash fund and obtains signed receipts for the payments. The Petty Cash account is debited when the fund is established or increased in size. Petty cash disbursements are recorded with a credit to cash whenever the fund is replenished.

LO 5. Explain why the bank balance and the book balance of cash should be reconciled and be able to prepare a reconciliation. A bank reconciliation is produced to prove the accuracy of the depositor's and the bank's records. In completing the reconciliation, the bank statement balance is adjusted for such items as outstanding checks and unrecorded deposits made on or before the bank statement date but not reflected on the statement. The depositor's cash account balance is adjusted to the correct balance. The difference arises from such items as service charges, collections the bank has made for the depositor, and interest earned on the average checking account balance.

LO 6. Explain how recording invoices at net amounts helps gain control over cash discounts taken, and calculate days' sales uncollected. When the net method of recording invoices is used, missed cash discounts are reported as an expense in the income statement. In contrast, when the gross method is used, discounts taken are reported as reductions in the cost of the purchased goods. Therefore, the net method directs management's attention to instances where the company failed to take advantage of discounts. In evaluating the liquidity of a company, financial statement users may calculate days' sales uncollected.

DEMONSTRATION PROBLEM

Set up a table with the following headings for a bank reconciliation as of September 30:

Bank Balance		Book Balance			Not Shown on the Reconciliation
Add	Deduct	Add	Deduct	Must Adjust	

For each item that follows, place an *x* in the appropriate columns to indicate whether the item should be added to or deducted from the book or bank balance, or whether it should not appear on the reconciliation. If the book balance is to be adjusted, place a *Dr.* or *Cr.* in the Must Adjust column to indicate whether the Cash balance should be debited or credited.

1. Interest earned on the account.
2. Deposit made on September 30 after the bank was closed.

3. Checks outstanding on August 31 that cleared the bank in September.
4. NSF check from customer returned on September 15 but not recorded by the company.
5. Checks written and mailed to payees on September 30.
6. Deposit made on September 5 that was processed on September 8.
7. Bank service charge.
8. Checks written and mailed to payees on October 5.
9. Checks written by another depositor but charged against the company's account.
10. Principal and interest collected by the bank but not recorded by the company.
11. Special charge for collection of note in No. 10 on company's behalf.
12. Check written against the account and cleared by the bank; erroneously omitted by the bookkeeper.

Planning the Solution

- Examine each item to determine whether it affects the book balance or the bank balance.
- If it acts to increase the balance, place an *x* in the Add column. If it acts to decrease the balance, place an *x* in the Deduct column.
- If the item increases or decreases the book balance, enter a *Dr.* or *Cr.* in the adjustment column.
- If the item does not affect either balance, place an × in the Not Shown on the Reconciliation column.

Solution to Demonstration Problem

	Bank Balance		Book Balance			Not Shown on the Reconciliation
	Add	Deduct	Add	Deduct	Must Adjust	
1. Interest earned on the account.			×		Dr.	
2. Deposit made on September 30 after the bank was closed.	×					
3. Checks outstanding on August 31 that cleared the bank in September.						×
4. NSF check from customer returned on September 15 but not recorded by the company.				×	Cr.	
5. Checks written and mailed to payees on September 30.		×				
6. Deposit made on September 5 that was processed on September 8.						×
7. Bank service charge.				×	Cr.	
8. Checks written and mailed to payees on October 5.						×
9. Check written by another depositor but charged against the company's account.	×					
10. Principal and interest collected by the bank but not recorded by the company.			×		Dr.	
11. Special charge for collection of note in No. 10 on company's behalf.				×	Cr.	
12. Check written against the account and cleared by the bank; erroneously omitted by the bookkeeper.				×	Cr.	

GLOSSARY

Bank reconciliation an analysis that explains the difference between the balance of a checking account shown in the depositor's records and the balance shown on the bank statement. p. 281

Canceled checks checks that the bank has paid and deducted from the customer's account during the month. p. 280

Cash equivalents temporary liquid investments that can be easily and quickly converted to cash. p. 264

Cash Over and Short account an income statement account used to record cash overages and cash shortages arising from omitted petty cash receipts and from errors in making change. p. 278

Days' sales uncollected the number of days of average credit sales volume accumulated in the accounts receivable balance, calculated as the product of 365 times the ratio of the accounts receivable balance divided by credit (or net) sales. p. 287

Discounts lost an expense resulting from failing to take advantage of cash discounts on purchases. p. 286

Gross method of recording purchases a method of recording purchases at the full invoice price without deducting any cash discounts. p. 286

Internal control system procedures adopted by a business to encourage adherence to prescribed managerial policies; in doing so, the system also promotes operational efficiencies and protects the business assets from waste, fraud, and theft, and helps ensure that accurate and reliable accounting data are produced. p. 266

Invoice an itemized statement prepared by the vendor that lists the customer's name, the items sold, the sales prices, and the terms of sale. p. 273

Invoice approval form a document on which the accounting department notes that it has performed each step in the process of checking an invoice and approving it for recording and payment. p. 274

Liquid asset an asset, such as cash, that is easily converted into other types of assets or used to buy services or pay liabilities. p. 264

Liquidity a characteristic of an asset that refers to how easily the asset can be converted into another type of asset or used to buy services or satisfy obligations. p. 264

Net method of recording purchases a method of recording purchases at the full invoice price less any cash discounts. p. 286

Outstanding checks checks that were written (or drawn) by the depositor, deducted on the depositor's records, and sent to the payees; however, they had not reached the bank for payment and deduction before the statement date. p. 281

Purchase order a business paper used by the purchasing department to place an order with the vendor; authorizes the vendor to ship the ordered merchandise at the stated price and terms. p. 272

Purchase requisition a business paper used to request that the Purchasing Department buy the needed merchandise or other items. p. 272

Receiving report a form used within the business to notify the appropriate persons that ordered goods were received and to describe the quantities and condition of the goods. p. 273

Vendee the buyer or purchaser of goods or services. p. 273

Vendor the seller of goods or services, usually a manufacturer or wholesaler. p. 272

Voucher an internal business paper used to accumulate other papers and information needed to control the disbursement of cash and to ensure that the transaction is properly recorded. p. 272

Voucher system a set of procedures designed to control the incurrence of obligations and disbursements of cash. p. 271

QUESTIONS

1. Which of the following assets is most liquid? Which is least liquid? Merchandise inventory, building, accounts receivable, cash.

2. List the seven broad principles of internal control.

3. Why should the person who keeps the record of an asset not be the person responsible for custody of the asset?

4. Internal control procedures are important in every business, but at what stage in the development of a business do they become critical?

5. Why should responsibility for a sequence of related transactions be divided among different departments or individuals?

6. Why should all receipts be deposited intact on the day of receipt?

7. When merchandise is purchased for a large store, why are department managers not permitted to deal directly with suppliers?

8. What is a petty cash receipt? Who signs a petty cash receipt?

9. Apple Computer's consolidated statements of cash flows (see Appendix F) describes the changes in cash and cash equivalents that occurred during the year ended September 25, 1992. What amount was provided (or used) by investing activities and what amount was provided (or used) by financing activities?

10. Refer to the Federal Express financial statements in Appendix G. What was the difference in the number of days' sales uncollected on May 31, 1993, and 1992? (In making the calculations, use the amounts that are reported as "receivables, less allowance for doubtful accounts.")

QUICK STUDY (Five-Minute Exercises)

What is the difference between the terms *liquidity* and *cash equivalent*?

QS 7–1
(LO 1)

a. What is the main objective of internal control and how is it accomplished?

b. Why should record-keeping for assets be separated from custody over the assets?

QS 7–2
(LO 2)

In a good system of internal control for cash that provides adequate procedures for protecting both cash receipts and cash disbursements, three basic guidelines should always be observed. What are these guidelines?

QS 7–3
(LO 3)

a. The Petty Cash Fund of the No-Fear Ski Club was established at $50. At the end of the month, the fund contained $4.35 and had the following receipts: film rental $12.50, refreshments for meetings $20.15 (both expenditures to be classified as Entertainment Expenses), postage $4.00, and printing $9.00. Prepare the journal entries to record (a) the establishment of the fund; (b) the reimbursement at the end of the month.

b. Explain when the Petty Cash account would be credited in a journal entry.

QS 7–4
(LO 4)

a. Identify whether each of the following items affects the bank or book side of the reconciliation and indicate if the amount represents an addition or a subtraction.

QS 7–5
(LO 5)

  (1) Bank service charges.

  (2) Outstanding checks.

  (3) Debit memos.

  (4) Unrecorded deposits.

  (5) Interest on average monthly balance.

  (6) NSF checks.

  (7) Credit memos.

b. Which of the previous items require a journal entry?

Which accounting method uses a Discounts Lost account and what is the advantage of this method?

QS 7–6
(LO 6)

Refer to Ben & Jerry's Homemade financial statements in Appendix G. What was the difference in the number of days' sales uncollected in 1991 and 1992? (In making calculations, use amounts that are reported as "receivables less allowance for doubtful accounts.") According to this ratio analysis, is Ben & Jerry's collection of receivables improving? Explain your answer.

QS 7–7
(LO 6)

BEN&JERRY'S
VERMONT'S FINEST • ICE CREAM & FROZEN YOGURT.

EXERCISES

Exercise 7–1
Analyzing internal control
(LO 2)

Seinfeld Company is a young business that has grown rapidly. The company's bookkeeper, who was hired two years ago, left town suddenly after the company's manager discovered that a great deal of money had disappeared over the past 18 months. An audit disclosed that the bookkeeper had written and signed several checks made payable to the bookkeeper's sister, and then recorded the checks as salaries expense. The sister, who cashed the checks but had never worked for the company, left town with the bookkeeper. As a result, the company incurred an uninsured loss of $123,000.

Evaluate Seinfeld Company's internal control system and indicate which principles of internal control appear to have been ignored in this situation.

Exercise 7–2
Recommending internal control procedures
(LO 2, 3)

What internal control procedures would you recommend in each of the following situations?

a. An antique store has one employee who is given cash and sent to garage sales each weekend. The employee pays cash for merchandise to be resold at the antique store.

b. Fun in the Sun has one employee who sells sun visors and beach chairs at the beach. Each day, the employee is given enough visors and chairs to last through the day and enough cash to make change. The money is kept in a box at the stand.

Exercise 7–3
Internal control over cash receipts
(LO 2, 3)

Some of Carver Company's cash receipts from customers are sent to the company in the mail. Carver's bookkeeper opens the letters and deposits the cash received each day. What internal control problem is inherent in this arrangement? What changes would you recommend?

Exercise 7–4
Petty cash fund
(LO 4)

A company established a $400 petty cash fund on March 1. One week later, on March 8, the fund contained $74.50 in cash and receipts for these expenditures: postage, $73.00; transportation-in, $38.00; miscellaneous expenses, $122.00; and store supplies, $92.50.

Prepare the journal entries to *(a)* establish the fund and *(b)* reimburse it on March 8. *(c)* Now assume that the fund was not only reimbursed on March 8 but also increased to $600 because it was exhausted so quickly. Give the entry to reimburse the fund and increase it to $600.

Exercise 7–5
Petty cash fund
(LO 4)

A company established a $300 petty cash fund on May 9. On May 31, the fund had $123.20 in cash and receipts for these expenditures: transportation-in, $24.20; miscellaneous expenses, $66.10; and store supplies, $84.90. The petty cashier could not account for the $1.60 shortage in the fund. Prepare *(a)* the May 9 entry to establish the fund and *(b)* the May 31 entry to reimburse the fund and reduce it to $225.

Exercise 7–6
Bank reconciliation
(LO 5)

Cisco Company deposits all receipts intact on the day received and makes all payments by check. On April 30, 19X1, after all posting was completed, its Cash account showed a $9,540 debit balance. However, Cisco's April 30 bank statement showed only $7,881 on deposit in the bank on that day. Prepare a bank reconciliation for Cisco, using the following information:

a. Outstanding checks, $1,440.

b. Included with the April canceled checks returned by the bank was a $15 debit memorandum for bank services.

c. Check No. 658, returned with the canceled checks, was correctly drawn for $327 in payment of the utility bill and was paid by the bank on April 22. However, it had been recorded with a debit to Utilities Expense and a credit to Cash as though it were for $372.

d. The April 30 cash receipts, $3,129, were placed in the bank's night depository after banking hours on that date and were unrecorded by the bank at the time the April bank statement was prepared.

Give the journal entries that Cisco Company should make as a result of having prepared the bank reconciliation in the previous exercise.

Exercise 7–7
Adjusting entries resulting from bank reconciliation
(LO 5)

Complete the following bank reconciliation by filling in the missing amounts:

Exercise 7–8
Completion of bank reconciliation
(LO 5)

SAZAR COMPANY
Bank Reconciliation
September 30, 19X1

Bank statement balance	$19,260	Book balance of cash	$?
Add:		Add:	
Deposit of September 30	$ 8,575	Collection of note	$15,000
Bank error	?	Interest earned	450
Total	$?	Total	$?
Total	$27,915	Total	$23,640
Deduct:		Deduct:	
Outstanding checks	?	NSF check	$ 550
		Recording error	?
		Service charge	20
		Total	$?
Reconciled balance	$23,010	Reconciled balance	$?

Tiny's Toys had the following transactions during the month of September. Prepare entries to record the transactions assuming Tiny's Toys records invoices *(a)* at gross amounts and *(b)* at net amounts.

Exercise 7–9
Recording invoices at gross or net amounts
(LO 6)

Sept. 3   Received merchandise purchased at a $3,150 invoice price, invoice dated August 31, terms 2/10, n/30.

      8   Received a $650 credit memorandum (invoice price) for merchandise received on September 3 and returned for credit.

     15   Received merchandise purchased at a $7,000 invoice price, invoice dated September 13, terms 2/10, n/30.

     22   Paid for the merchandise received on September 15, less the discount.

     29   Paid for the merchandise received on September 3. Payment was delayed because the invoice was mistakenly filed for payment today. This error caused the discount to be lost. The filing error occurred after the credit memorandum received on September 8 was attached to the invoice dated August 31.

Electric Services Company reported net sales for 19X1 and 19X2 of $345,000 and $520,000. The end-of-year balances of accounts receivable were December 31, 19X1, $30,000; and December 31, 19X2, $76,000. Calculate the days' sales uncollected at the end of each year and describe any changes in the apparent liquidity of the company's receivables.

Exercise 7–10
Liquidity of accounts receivable
(LO 6)

PROBLEMS

Serrapede's Trading Company completed the following petty cash transactions during July of the current year:

Problem 7–1
Establishing, reimbursing, and increasing petty cash fund
(LO 4)

July   1   Drew a $250 check, cashed it, and gave the proceeds and the petty cash box to Tom Albertson, the petty cashier.

      3   Purchased stationery, $37.00.

     11   Paid $12.50 postage to express mail a contract to a customer.

14   Paid $11.25 COD charges on merchandise purchased for resale.

17   Paid $29.00 for stamps.

19   Purchased paper for the copy machine, $16.25.

22   Reimbursed Sarah Oliver, the manager of the business, $24.00 for business car mileage.

24   Paid $37.50 COD charges on merchandise purchased for resale.

26   Paid City Delivery $12.00 to deliver merchandise sold to a customer.

31   Albertson sorted the petty cash receipts by accounts affected and exchanged them for a check to reimburse the fund for expenditures. However, there was only $65.35 in cash in the fund, and he could not account for the shortage. In addition, the size of the petty cash fund was increased to $300.

Required

Preparation component:

1. Prepare a journal entry to record establishing the petty cash fund.

2. Prepare a summary of petty cash payments that has these categories: Office supplies, Postage expense, Transportation-in, Mileage expense, and Delivery expense. Sort the payments into the appropriate categories and total the expenses in each category.

CHECK FIGURE:
July 31, Cash, $234.65 Cr.

3. Prepare the journal entry to record the reimbursement and the increase of the fund.

Analysis component:

4. Assume that the July 31 transaction reimbursed but did not increase the size of the fund. Also assume that when the payments from petty cash were recorded, the company's bookkeeper made an entry in the following general form:

July	31	xxxxxxxxxxxx (Expense)	xxx	
		xxxxxxxxxxxx (Expense)	xxx	
		xxxxxxxxxxxx (Asset)	xxx	
		Petty Cash		xxx

Explain why this entry is not correct. Also explain the effects of the error on the General Ledger and on the balance sheet.

Problem 7–2
Petty cash fund; reimbursement and analysis of errors
(LO 4)

The Thayer Company has only a General Journal in its accounting system and uses it to record all transactions. However, the company recently set up a petty cash fund to facilitate payments of small items. The following petty cash transactions were noted by the petty cashier as occurring during October (the last month of the company's fiscal year):

Oct. 2 Received a company check for $275 to establish the petty cash fund.

16 Received a company check to replenish the fund for the following expenditures made since October 2 and to increase the fund to $375.

   a. Payment of $63.50 to *Travis Times* for an advertisement in the newspaper.

   b. Purchased postage stamps for $58.

   c. Purchased office supplies for $70.75.

   d. Payment of $75 for janitorial service.

   e. Discovered that $12.35 remained in the petty cash box.

31 The petty cashier noted that $182.20 remained in the fund. Having decided that the October 16 increase in the fund was too large, received a company check to replenish the fund for the following expenditures made since October 16 but causing the fund to be reduced to $325.

 f. Reimbursement to office manager for business mileage, $36.

 g. Purchased office supplies for $57.80.

 h. Paid $52 to Austin Trucking Co. to deliver merchandise sold to a customer.

 i. Payment of $47 COD delivery charges on merchandise purchased for resale.

Required

1. Prepare journal entries to record the establishment of the fund on October 2 and its replenishments on October 16 and on October 31.

2. Explain how the company's financial statements would be affected if the petty cash fund is not replenished and no entry is made on October 31. (Hint: The amount of office supplies that appears on a balance sheet is determined by a physical count of the supplies on hand.)

CHECK FIGURE:
Cash credits, $362.65, $142.80

The following information was available to reconcile Kramer Company's book cash balance with its bank statement balance as of March 31, 19X1:

a. The March 31 cash balance according to the accounting records was $24,789, and the bank statement balance for that date was $34,686.

b. Check No. 573 for $834 and Check No. 582 for $300, both written and entered in the accounting records in March, were not among the canceled checks returned. Two checks, No. 531 for $1,761 and No. 542 for $285, were outstanding on February 28 when the bank and book statement balances were last reconciled. Check No. 531 was returned with the March canceled checks but Check No. 542 was not.

c. When the March checks were compared with entries in the accounting records, it was found that Check No. 567 had been correctly drawn for $1,925 to pay for office supplies but was erroneously entered in the accounting records as though it were drawn for $1,952.

d. Two debit memoranda were included with the returned checks and were unrecorded at the time of the reconciliation. One of the debit memoranda was for $570 and dealt with an NSF check for $555 that had been received from a customer, Barbara White, in payment of her account. It also assessed a $15 fee for processing. The second debit memorandum covered check printing and was for $67. These transactions were not recorded by Kramer before receiving the statement.

e. A credit memorandum indicated that the bank had collected a $15,000 note receivable for the company, deducted a $15 collection fee, and credited the balance to the company's account. This transaction was not recorded by Kramer before receiving the statement.

f. The March 31 cash receipts, $5,897, had been placed in the bank's night depository after banking hours on that date and did not appear on the bank statement.

Problem 7–3
Preparation of bank reconciliation and recording adjustments
(LO 5)

Required

Preparation component:

1. Prepare a bank reconciliation for the company as of March 31.

2. Prepare the general journal entries necessary to bring the company's book balance of cash into conformity with the reconciled balance.

CHECK FIGURE:
Reconciled balance, $39,164

Analysis component:

3. Explain the nature of the messages conveyed by a bank to one of its depositors when the bank sends a debit memo and a credit memo to the depositor.

Problem 7–4
Preparation of bank
reconciliation and recording
adjustments
(LO 5)

Mountainview Co. reconciled its bank and book statement balances of cash on October 31 and showed two checks outstanding at that time, No. 1388 for $1,597 and No. 1393 for $745. The following information was available for the November 30, 19X1, reconciliation:

From the November 30 bank statement:

Balance of previous statement on 10/31/X1	27,418.00
6 Deposits and other credits totaling	17,176.00
9 Checks and other debits totaling	16,342.00
Current balance as of 11/30/X1	28,252.00

═══════Checking Account Transactions═══════

Date	Amount	Transaction Description
11/5	1,698.00 +	Deposit
11/12	3,426.00 +	Deposit
11/17	905.00 −	NSF check
11/21	6,297.00 +	Deposit
11/25	3,618.00 +	Deposit
11/30	17.00 +	Interest
11/30	2,120.00 +	Credit memorandum

Date	Check No.	Amount	Date	Check No.	Amount
11/3	1388	1,597.00	11/22	1404	3,185.00
11/7	1401*	4,363.00	11/20	1405	1,442.00
11/4	1402	1,126.00	11/28	1407*	329.00
11/22	1403	614.00	11/29	1409*	2,781.00

*Indicates a skip in check sequence

From Mountainview Co.'s accounting records:

		Cash			Account No. 101

Date		Explanation	PR	Debit	Credit	Balance
Oct.	31	Balance				25,076.00
Nov.	30	Total receipts	R12	17,474.00		42,550.00
	30	Total disbursements	D23		15,537.00	27,013.00

Cash Receipts Deposited

Date		Cash Debit
Nov.	5	1,698.00
	12	3,426.00
	21	6,297.00
	25	3,618.00
	30	2,435.00
		17,474.00

Cash Disbursements

Check No.		Cash Credit
1401		4,363.00
1402		1,126.00
1403		614.00
1404		3,135.00
1405		1,442.00
1406		1,322.00
1407		329.00
1408		425.00
1409		2,781.00
		15,537.00

Check No. 1404 was correctly drawn for $3,185 to pay for computer equipment; however, the bookkeeper misread the amount and entered it in the accounting records with a debit to Computer Equipment and a credit to Cash as though it were for $3,135.

The NSF check was originally received from a customer, Jerry Skyles, in payment of his account. Its return was not recorded when the bank first notified the company. The credit memorandum resulted from the collection of a $2,150 note for Mountainview by the bank. The bank had deducted a $30 collection fee. The collection has not been recorded.

Required

Preparation component:

1. Prepare a November 30 bank reconciliation for the company.

2. Prepare the general journal entries needed to adjust the book balance of cash to the reconciled balance.

Analysis component:

3. The preceding bank statement discloses three places where the canceled checks returned with the bank statement are not numbered sequentially. In other words, some of the prenumbered checks in the sequence are missing. Several possible situations would explain why the canceled checks returned with a bank statement might not be numbered sequentially. Describe three situations, each of which is a possible explanation of why the canceled checks returned with a bank statement are not numbered sequentially.

CRITICAL THINKING: ESSAYS, PROBLEMS, AND CASES

The Commerce Company has enjoyed rapid growth since it was created several years ago. Last year, for example, its sales exceeded $4 million. However, its purchasing procedures have not kept pace with its growth. A plant supervisor or department head who needs raw materials, plant assets, or supplies telephones a request to the purchasing department manager. The purchasing department manager then prepares a purchase order in duplicate, sends one copy to the company selling the goods, and keeps the other copy in the files. When the seller's invoice is received, it is sent directly to the purchasing department. When the goods arrive, receiving department personnel count and inspect the items and prepare only one copy of a receiving report, which is then sent to the purchasing department. The purchasing department manager attaches the receiving report and the file copy of the purchase order to the invoice. If all is in order, the invoice is stamped *approved for payment* and signed by the purchasing department manager. The invoice and its supporting documents then are sent to the accounting department to be recorded and filed until due. On its due date, the invoice and its supporting documents are sent to the office of the company treasurer, and a check is prepared and mailed. The number of the check is entered on the invoice and the invoice is sent to the accounting department for an entry to record its payment.

Do the procedures of Commerce make it fairly easy for someone in the company to initiate the payment of fictitious invoices by the company? If so, who is most likely to commit the fraud and what would that person have to do to receive payment of a fictitious invoice? What changes should be made in the company's purchasing procedures, and why should each change be made?

Analytical Essay
(LO 2, 3)

On March 26, Summerfield Office Supply received Miles Brokaw's check number 629, dated March 24, in the amount of $1,420. The check was to pay for merchandise Brokaw had purchased on February 25. The merchandise was shipped from Summerfield's office at 1715 Westgate Boulevard, Austin, Texas, 78704 to Brokaw's home at 823 Congress, Austin, Texas, 78701. On March 27, Summerfield's cashier deposited the check in the company's bank account. The bank returned the check to Summerfield with the March 31 bank statement. Also included was a debit memorandum indicating that Brokaw's check was returned for nonsufficient funds and the bank was charging Summerfield a $25 NSF processing fee. Immediately after reconciling the bank statement on April 2, Marla Decker, Summerfield's accountant, asks you to write a letter for her signature using the company's letterhead stationery. Your letter to Brokaw should explain the amount owed and request prompt payment.

**Business
Communications
Case**
(LO 5)

For this problem, turn to the financial statements of Apple Computer, Inc., in Appendix F. Use the information presented in the financial statements to answer these questions:

1. For both 1993 and 1992, determine the total amount of cash and cash equivalents that Apple held at the end of the fiscal year. Determine the percentage that this amount

**Financial Statement
Analysis Case**
(LO 1, 6)

represents of total current assets, total current liabilities, total shareholders' equity, and total assets.

2. For both 1993 and 1992, determine the total amount of cash, cash equivalents, and short-term investments that Apple held at the end of the year. Determine the percentage that this amount represents of total current assets, total current liabilities, total shareholders' equity, and total assets.

3. For 1993, use the information in the statement of cash flows to determine the percentage change between the beginning of the year and end of the year holding of cash and cash equivalents.

4. What was the number of days' sales uncollected at the end of the 1993 fiscal year and at the end of the 1992 fiscal year? (In making the calculations, use the amounts that are reported as "accounts receivable, net of allowance for doubtful accounts.")

Ethical Issues Essay   Review the As a Matter of Ethics case on page 279. Discuss the nature of the problem faced by Nancy Tucker and evaluate the alternative courses of action she should consider.

CONCEPT TESTER

Test your understanding of the concepts introduced in this chapter by completing the following crossword puzzle.

Across Clues

1. Two words; a business paper that tells a vendor to ship ordered merchandise at the stated terms.
3. The seller of goods or services.
5. A statement showing the items sold, price, and terms given by a vendor to a customer.
7. The buyer or purchaser of goods or services
8. Two words; an expense resulting from failing to take a cash discount on purchases.

Down Clues

2. Two words; investments convertible to a known amount of cash, generally within three months.
4. Business paper used to accumulate information needed to control disbursements of cash.
6. Asset characteristic; refers to how quickly the asset can be used to pay for other assets.

ANSWERS TO PROGRESS CHECKS

7–1 A company needs to own liquid assets to be able to acquire other assets, buy services, and pay its obligations.

7–2 A company owns cash equivalents because they earn more income than cash does.

7–3 *d*

7–4 *c*

7–5 Computers reduce processing errors, allow more extensive testing of records, tend to limit the amount of hard evidence of processing steps that is available, and highlight the importance of maintaining a separation of duties.

7–6 *a*

7–7 Not necessarily. A voucher system should be used when the manager can no longer control the purchasing procedures through personal supervision and direct participation in the activities of the business.

7–8 If all cash payments were made by check, numerous checks for small amounts would be written. Because this practice would be expensive and often would take too long, a petty cash fund is established to avoid writing checks for small amounts.

7–9 If the petty cash fund is not reimbursed at the end of an accounting period, the transactions for which petty cash expenditures were made are unrecorded in the accounts and the asset petty cash is overstated. However, these amounts are seldom large enough to affect the financial statements.

7–10 When the petty cash fund is reimbursed, the petty cash transactions are recorded in the accounts. The reimbursement also allows the fund to continue being used for its intended purpose.

7–11 A bank statement is a report prepared by the bank that describes the activity in a depositor's account.

7–12 To reconcile a bank balance means to explain the difference between the cash balance in the depositor's accounting records and the balance on the bank statement.

7–13 The purpose of the bank reconciliation is to determine if any errors have been made by the bank or by the depositor and to determine if the bank has completed any transactions affecting the depositor's account that the depositor has not recorded.

7–14 Outstanding checks—subtracted
Unrecorded deposits—added

7–15 Bank services charges—subtracted
Debit memos—subtracted
NSF checks—subtracted
Interest earned—added
Credit memos—added

7–16 *a*

7–17 The calculation is based on net sales because the amount of credit sales normally is not known by statement readers.

CHAPTER 8

Short-Term Investments and Receivables

*P*epsiCo, Inc., an internationally known manufacturer of soft drinks, reported having one-third of the industry's sales in 1993, for a total volume of $28.2 billion. In the information from the company's balance sheet that follows, note that PepsiCo's short-term investments and accounts and notes receivable represent 68% of the firm's total current assets. Sound financial management of these assets is vital to ensure future liquidity and growth potential. Accounting for these highly liquid assets provides important information to help managers assess the risk and success of their decisions regarding these assets. Economic conditions causing many businesses and consumers to take longer to pay their bills and an increasing amount of defaults due to bankruptcies have made receivables management a top priority today.

PEPSICO, INC.
(In millions)
December 25, 1993

	Current Assets	
Short-term investments	. . . .	$1,629.3
Accounts receivable,		
less $128.3 allowance	. . . .	1,883.4
Total current assets	. . . .	$5,164.1

LEARNING OBJECTIVES

After studying Chapter 8, you should be able to:

1. **Prepare journal entries to account for short-term investments and explain how fair (market) value gains and losses on such investments are reported.**

2. **Prepare entries to account for credit card sales.**

3. **Prepare entries to account for transactions with credit customers, including accounting for bad debts under the allowance method and the direct write-off method.**

4. **Calculate the interest on promissory notes and prepare entries to record the receipt of promissory notes and their payment or dishonor.**

5. **Explain how receivables can be converted into cash before they are due and calculate accounts receivable turnover.**

6. **Define or explain the words and phrases listed in the chapter glossary.**

The focus of the prior chapter was on accounting for cash, the most liquid of all assets. This chapter continues the discussion of liquid assets by focusing on short-term investments, accounts receivable, and short-term notes receivable. You will learn about current business trends relating to receivables and about new accounting regulations for short-term investments. You will then be better able to understand and use the financial statement information related to these current assets.

Because companies use cash to acquire assets and to pay expenses and obligations, good managers plan to maintain a cash balance large enough to meet expected payments plus some surplus for unexpected needs. Also, idle cash balances may exist during some months of each year because of seasonal fluctuations in sales volume. Rather than leave these idle cash balances in checking accounts that pay little or no interest, most companies invest them in securities that earn higher returns.

SHORT-TERM INVESTMENTS

LO 1

Prepare journal entries to account for short-term investments and explain how fair (market) value gains and losses on such investments are reported.

Recall from Chapter 7 that cash equivalents are investments that can be easily converted into a known amount of cash; generally, they mature no more than three months after purchase. Some investments of idle cash balances do not meet these criteria of cash equivalents but, nevertheless, are classified as current assets. Although these **short-term investments** or **temporary investments** do not qualify as cash equivalents, they serve a similar purpose. Like cash equivalents, short-term investments can be converted into cash easily and are an available source of cash to satisfy the needs of current operations. Management usually expects to convert them into cash within one year or the current operating cycle of the business, whichever is longer.[1]

Short-term investments may be made in the form of government or corporate debt

obligations (called *debt securities*) or in the form of stock (called *equity securities*). Some short-term investments in debt securities mature within one year or the current operating cycle of the business and will be held until they mature. Other securities that do not mature in the short term can be classified as current assets only if they are marketable. In other words, the reporting company must be able to sell them without excessive delays.

In the notes to their financial statements, companies usually give their definition of cash equivalents and short-term investments. **Texas Instruments Incorporated,** for example, includes this note:

---

[1]FASB, *Accounting Standards—Current Text* (Norwalk, CT, 1994), sec. B05.105. First published as *Accounting Research Bulletin No. 43,* chap. 3A, par. 4.

Short-term investments consist primarily of commercial paper, notes, and short-term U.S. government securities with original maturities beyond three months, stated at cost, which approximates market value. Similar items with original maturities of three months or less are considered cash equivalents.

When short-term investments are purchased, you should record them at cost. For example, assume that on January 10 Alpha Company purchased Ford Motor Company's short-term notes payable for $40,000. Alpha's entry to record the transaction is:

Jan.	10	Short-Term Investments	40,000.00	
		Cash		40,000.00
		Bought $40,000 of Ford Motor Company notes due		
		May 10.		

Assume that these notes mature on May 10 and that the cash proceeds are $40,000 plus $1,200 interest. When the receipt is recorded, this entry credits the interest to a revenue account:

May	10	Cash	41,200.00	
		Short-Term Investments		40,000.00
		Interest Earned		1,200.00
		Received cash proceeds from matured notes.		

To determine the cost of an investment, you must include any commissions paid. For example, assume that on June 2, 19X1, Bailey Company purchased 1,000 shares of Xerox Corporation common stock as a short-term investment. The purchase price was 70⅛ ($70.125 per share) plus a $625 broker's commission. The entry to record the transaction is:[2]

June	2	Short-Term Investments	70,750.00	
		Cash		70,750.00
		Bought 1,000 shares of Xerox stock at 70⅛ plus $625		
		broker's commission.		

Notice that the commission is not recorded in a separate account.

When cash dividends are received on stock held as a short-term investment, they are credited to a revenue account, as follows:

Dec.	12	Cash	1,000.00	
		Dividends Earned		1,000.00
		Received dividend of $1 per share on 1,000 shares of		
		Xerox stock.		

---

[2]Stock prices are quoted on stock exchanges on the basis of dollars and ⅛ dollars per share. For example, a stock quoted at 23⅛ sold for $23.125 per share and one quoted at 36½ sold for $36.50 per share.

Reporting Short-Term Investments in the Financial Statements

In past years, companies reported their short-term investments at the lower of cost or market value. The losses on reducing cost to market value were subtracted in the calculation of net income on the income statement. Recently, however, these reporting requirements have changed.

In May 1993, the FASB issued a new standard that requires companies to report most short-term investments at their fair (market) values.[3] The exact requirements of the new standard vary, depending on whether the investments are classified as (1) investments in securities held to maturity, (2) investments in trading securities, or (3) investments in securities available for sale.

Short-Term Investments in Securities Held to Maturity

If a company has the positive intent and ability to hold investments in debt securities until they mature, the investments are classified as **investments in securities held to maturity.**[4] For example, in the summary of significant accounting policies in the notes to their 1993 financial statements, **International Dairy Queen, Inc.,** stated:

Management determines the appropriate classification of debt securities at the time of purchase and reevaluates such designation as of each balance sheet date. Debt securities are classified as held-to-maturity because the Company has the positive intent and ability to hold such securities to maturity.

As we mentioned earlier, these investments cannot qualify as current assets unless their maturity dates fall within one year or the current operating cycle of the business. Short-term investments in debt securities (that will be) held until maturity are reported at cost.

Short-Term Investments in Trading Securities

Some short-term investments in securities are actively managed. In other words, frequent purchases and sales generally are made with the objective of generating profits on short-term differences in price. Most often, such investments are made by financial institutions such as banks or insurance companies. The FASB notes that these **investments in trading securities** are bought principally for the purpose of selling them in the near term.

According to SFAS 115, companies must report investments in trading securities at their fair (market) values. The related gains and losses of fair (market) value are reported on the income statement as part of net income or loss.

Short-Term Investments in Securities Available for Sale

Investments in securities available for sale include all securities investments that do not qualify as investments in trading securities or as investments in securities held to maturity. Securities available for sale are purchased to earn interest, dividends, and perhaps increases in market value. They are not actively managed like trading secu-

---

[3]FASB, "Accounting for Certain Investments in Debt and Equity Securities," *Statement of Financial Accounting Standards No. 115* (Norwalk, CT, 1994). The requirements of SFAS 115 also apply to long-term investments in debt and marketable equity securities. You learn more about this in Chapter 11.

[4]Ibid., par. 7.

rities. Many industrial and commercial companies have short-term investments in securities available for sale.

As in the case of trading securities, SFAS 115 requires companies to adjust the reported amount of securities available for sale to reflect all changes in fair value. Unlike trading securities, however, the fair value gains and losses on securities available for sale are not reported on the income statement. Instead, they are reported in the equity section of the balance sheet.

For example, assume that the J. Bailey Company did not have any short-term investments prior to its purchase of the Xerox stock on June 2, 19X1. Later during 19X1, Bailey purchased two other short-term investments. Assume that all three are classified as securities available for sale. On December 31, 19X1, the cost and fair values of these securities are:

Short-Term Investments in Securities Available for Sale on December 31, 19X1	Costs	Fair (Market) Values
Sears, Roebuck & Co. common stock	$ 42,600	$ 43,500
Chrysler Corporation notes payable	30,500	30,200
Xerox Corporation common stock	70,750	78,250
Total	$143,850	$151,950

The difference between the $143,850 cost and the $151,950 fair (market) value amounts to a $8,100 gain in fair value. Because the amount of the gain has not yet been confirmed by the sale of the security, accountants describe this gain as an **unrealized holding gain.** The following entry records the gain:

Dec.	31	Short-Term Investments, Fair Value Adjustment	8,100.00	
		Unrealized Holding Gain (Loss)		8,100.00
		To reflect fair values of short-term investments in securities available for sale.		

After posting this entry, the cost and fair value adjustment of the short-term investments appear in the accounts as follows:

Short-term investments	$143,850
Short-term investments, fair value adjustment . .	8,100
Total	$151,950

Note that the cost of the investments is maintained in one account and the adjustment to fair values is recorded in a separate account. Keeping the Short-Term Investments account at cost facilitates calculating realized gains or losses that must be recorded when securities are sold.

Depending on whether the fair value adjustment account has a debit or credit balance, it is added or subtracted from the cost to determine the fair value amount reported on the balance sheet. Bailey's December 31, 19X1, balance sheet includes the following:

Assets

Current assets:

Cash and cash equivalents	$ xx,xxx
Short-term investments	151,950
Accounts receivable	xxx,xxx

Owner's Equity

J. Bailey, capital	$xxx,xxx
Unrealized holding gain on securities held for sale . .	8,100
Total owner's equity	$xxx,xxx

Notice that the unrealized holding gain is reported as a separate item in the equity section. It is not reported on the income statement and is not closed. If the fair value of the securities available for sale had been less than cost, the **unrealized holding loss** would have appeared in owner's equity as a deduction.

When a short-term investment in securities available for sale is sold, the cash proceeds from the sale are compared with the cost of the investment to determine the *realized* gain or loss. This realized gain or loss is reported on the income statement and closed as part of the net income or loss.

For example, assume that on May 14, 19X2, Bailey sold its investment in Xerox common stock for $81,000. The entry to record the sale is:

May	14	Cash	81,000.00	
		Short-Term Investments		70,750.00
		Gain on Sale of Short-Term Investments		10,250.00
		To record sale of Xerox common stock.		

Note that the realized gain is calculated by comparing the proceeds with cost, not with the previously reported fair value of the stock. Then, at the next balance sheet date, the unrealized gain or loss account is adjusted so the securities available for sale are reported at their new fair values.

For example, assume that Bailey did not buy or sell any other securities during 19X2. As a result, the securities available for sale on December 31, 19X2, include the Sears common stock and the Chrysler notes payable. The costs and December 31, 19X2, fair values of these securities are as follows:

Short-Term Investments in Securities Available for Sale on December 31, 19X2	Costs	Fair (Market) Values
Sears common stock	$42,600	$41,200
Chrysler notes payable	30,500	29,900
Total	$73,100	$71,100

Recall the December 31, 19X1, entry that recorded the $8,100 excess of fair values over costs. That entry gave the Short-Term Investments, Fair Value Adjustment account a debit balance of $8,100, and gave the Unrealized Holding Gain (Loss) account a credit balance of $8,100. On December 31, 19X2, these account balances must be revised to show that the $73,100 costs exceed the $71,100 fair values by $2,000. The required adjustments are calculated as follows:

	Short-Term Investments, Fair Value Adjustment	Unrealized Holding Gain (Loss)
Existing balances	$ 8,100 Debit	$ 8,100 Credit
Required balances, December 31, 19X2	2,000 Credit	2,000 Debit
Necessary adjustment	$10,100 Credit	$10,100 Debit

The following adjusting entry updates the account balances:

Dec.	31	Unrealized Holding Gain (Loss)	10,100.00	
		Short-Term Investments, Fair Value Adjustment		10,100.00
		To reflect fair values of short-term investments in securities held for sale.		

Progress Check

(Answers to Progress Checks are provided at the end of the chapter.)

8-1 How are securities held to maturity reported on the balance sheet—at cost or fair (market) values? How are investments in trading securities reported?

8-2 On what statement are unrealized holding gains and losses on investments in securities available for sale reported?

8-3 Where are unrealized holding gains and losses on investments in trading securities reported?

CREDIT SALES AND RECEIVABLES

In addition to cash, cash equivalents, and short-term investments, the liquid assets of a business include receivables that result from credit sales to customers. In the following sections, we discuss the procedures to account for sales when customers use credit cards issued by banks or credit card companies. Then, we focus on accounting for credit sales when a business grants credit directly to its customers. This situation requires the company (1) to maintain a separate account receivable for each customer and (2) to account for bad debts that result from credit sales. In addition, we discuss how to account for notes receivable, many of which arise from extending credit to customers.

CREDIT CARD SALES

LO 2

Prepare entries to account for credit card sales.

Many customers use credit cards such as Visa, MasterCard, or American Express to charge purchases from various businesses. This practice gives the customers the ability to make purchases without carrying cash or writing checks. It also allows them to defer their payments to the credit card company. Further, once credit is established with the credit card company, the customer does not have to open an account with each store. Finally, customers who use credit cards can make single monthly payments instead of several to different creditors.

There are good reasons why businesses allow customers to use credit cards instead of maintaining their own accounts receivable. First, the business does not have to evaluate the credit standing of each customer or make decisions about who should get

credit and how much. Second, the business avoids the risk of extending credit to customers who cannot or do not pay. Instead, this risk is faced by the credit card company. Third, the business typically receives cash from the credit card company sooner than it would if it granted credit directly to its customers. Fourth, a variety of credit options for customers offers a potential increase in sales volume. **Sears, Roebuck & Co.,** one the nation's largest credit providers among retailers, historically offered credit only to customers using SearsCharge cards. Their 1993 annual report notes the following in the management discussion:

> As a strategic measure to increase merchandise sales and to provide customers a choice of payment vehicles, the Company began accepting additional third party payment products (American Express, MasterCard and Visa) in the third quarter of 1993. Since the introduction of third party payment products, SearsCharge sales as a percentage of sales have been above prior year levels.

In dealing with some credit cards, usually those issued by banks, the business deposits a copy of each credit card sales receipt in its bank account just like it deposits a customer's check. Thus, the business receives a credit to its checking account without delay. Other credit cards require the business to send a copy of each receipt to the credit card company. Until payment is received, the business has an account receivable from the credit card company. In return for the services provided by the credit card company, a business pays a fee ranging from 2 to 5% of credit card sales. This charge is deducted from the credit to the checking account or the cash payment to the business.

The procedures used in accounting for credit card sales depend on whether cash is received immediately on deposit or is delayed until paid by the credit card company. If cash is received immediately, the entry to record $100 of credit card sales with a 4% fee is:

Jan.	25	Cash	96.00	
		Credit Card Expense	4.00	
		Sales		100.00
		To record credit card sales less a 4% credit card		
		expense.		

If the business must send the receipts to the credit card company and wait for payment, this entry on the date of the sales records them:

Jan.	25	Accounts Receivable—Credit Card Company	100.00	
		Sales		100.00
		To record credit card sales.		

When cash is received from the credit card company, the entry to record the receipt and the deduction of the fee is:

Feb.	10	Cash	96.00	
		Credit Card Expense	4.00	
		Accounts Receivable—Credit Card Co		100.00
		To record cash receipt less 4% credit card expense.		

In the last two entries, notice that the credit card expense was not recorded until cash was received from the credit card company. This practice is merely a matter of convenience. By following this procedure, the business avoids having to calculate and record the credit card expense each time sales are recorded. Instead, the expense related to many sales can be calculated once and recorded when cash is received. However, the *matching principle* requires reporting credit card expense in the same period as the sale. Therefore, if the sale and the cash receipt occur in different periods, you must accrue and report the credit card expense in the period of the sale by using an adjusting entry at the end of the year. For example, this year-end adjustment accrues $24 of credit card expense on a $600 receivable that the Credit Card Company has not yet paid.

PRINCIPLE APPLICATION
Matching Principle, p. 108
In 1993, J.C. Penney Company had retail sales of $18,983 million. In addition to bad debt expenses, the credit costs the company matched with these revenues included operating expenses and third-party credit costs of $260 million.

Dec.	31	Credit Card Expense	24.00	
		Accounts Receivable—Credit Card Company		24.00
		To accrue credit card expense that is unrecorded at the end of the year.		

Then, the following entry records the cash collection in January:

Jan.	5	Cash	576.00	
		Accounts Receivable—Credit Card Company		576.00
		To record collection of the amount due from Credit Card Company.		

Some firms report credit card expense in the income statement as a type of discount that is deducted from sales to get net sales. Other companies classify it as a selling expense or even as an administrative expense. Arguments can be made for all three alternatives but there is little practical difference in the result.

Progress Check

8-4 **In recording credit card sales, when do you debit Accounts Receivable and when do you debit Cash?**

8-5 **When are credit card expenses recorded in situations where sales receipts must be accumulated before they can be sent to the credit card company? When are these expenses incurred?**

8-6 **If payment for a credit card sale has not been received by the end of the accounting period, how do you account for the credit card expense associated with that sale?**

Illustration 8-1   The Accounts Receivable Account and the Accounts Receivable Ledger

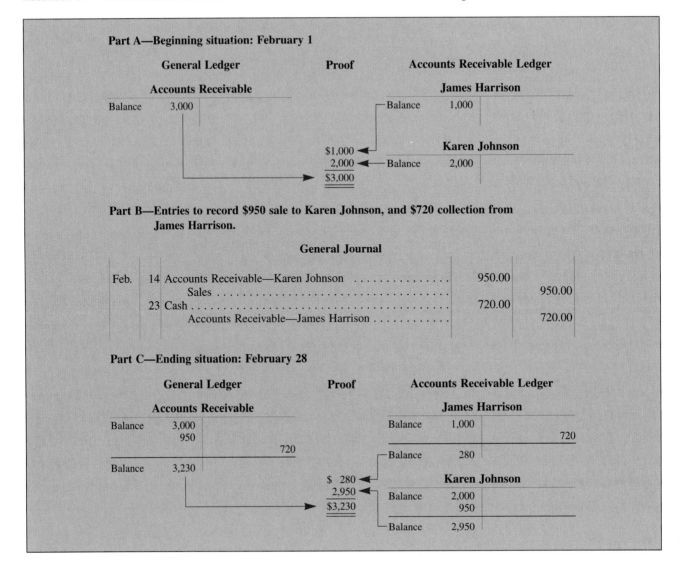

MAINTAINING A SEPARATE ACCOUNT FOR EACH CREDIT CUSTOMER

LO 3

Prepare entries to account for transactions with credit customers, including accounting for bad debts under the allowance method and the direct write-off method.

In previous chapters, we recorded credit sales by debiting a single Accounts Receivable account. However, a business with more than one credit customer must design its accounting system to show how much each customer has purchased, how much each customer has paid, and how much remains to be collected from each customer. This information provides the basis for sending bills to the customers. To have this information on hand, businesses that extend credit directly to their customers must maintain a separate account receivable for each of them.

One possible way of keeping a separate account for each customer would be to include all of these accounts in the same ledger that contains the financial statement accounts. However, this approach usually is not used because there are too many customers. Instead, the **General Ledger,** which is the ledger that contains the financial statement accounts, has only a single Accounts Receivable account. In addition, a supplementary record is established in which a separate account is maintained for each customer. This supplementary record is the **Accounts Receivable Ledger.**

Illustration 8–1 shows the relationship between the Accounts Receivable account in the General Ledger and the individual customer accounts in the Accounts Receivable Ledger. In Part A of Illustration 8–1, notice that the $3,000 sum of the two balances in the Accounts Receivable Ledger is equal to the balance of the Accounts Receivable account in the General Ledger as of February 1. To maintain this relationship, each time that credit sales are posted with a debit to the Accounts Receivable account in the General Ledger, they are also posted with debits to the appropriate customer accounts in the Accounts Receivable Ledger. Also, cash receipts from credit customers must be posted with credits to both the Accounts Receivable account in the General Ledger and to the appropriate customer accounts.

Part B shows the general journal entry to record a credit sale on February 14 to customer Karen Johnson. It also shows the entry to record the collection of $720 from James Harrison.

Part C presents the general ledger account and the Accounts Receivable Ledger as of February 28. Notice how the General Ledger account shows the effects of the sales and the collection, and that it has a $3,230 balance. The same events are reflected in the accounts for the two customers: Harrison now has a balance of only $280, and Johnson owes $2,950. The $3,230 sum of their accounts equals the debit balance of the General Ledger account.

Note that posting debits or credits to Accounts Receivable twice does not violate the requirement that debits equal credits. The equality of debits and credits is maintained *in the General Ledger*. The Accounts Receivable Ledger is simply a supplementary record that provides detailed information concerning each customer.

Because the balance in the Accounts Receivable account is always equal to the sum of the balances in the customers' accounts, the Accounts Receivable account is said to control the Accounts Receivable Ledger and is an example of a **controlling account.** And, the Accounts Receivable Ledger is an example of a supplementary record that is controlled by an account in the General Ledger; this kind of supplementary record is called a **subsidiary ledger.**

The Accounts Receivable account and the Accounts Receivable Ledger are not the only examples of controlling accounts and subsidiary ledgers. Most companies buy on credit from several suppliers and must use a controlling account and subsidiary ledger for accounts payable. Another example might be an Office Equipment account that would control a subsidiary ledger in which the cost of each item of equipment is recorded in a separate account.

BAD DEBTS

When a company grants credit to its customers, there usually are a few who do not pay what they promised. The accounts of such customers are called **bad debts.** These bad debt amounts that cannot be collected are an expense of selling on credit.

You might ask why merchants sell on credit if it is likely that some of the accounts prove to be uncollectible. The answer is that they believe granting credit will increase revenues and profits. They are willing to incur bad debt losses if the net effect is to increase sales and profits. Therefore, bad debt losses are an expense of selling on credit that is incurred to increase sales.

The reporting of bad debts expense on the income statement is governed by the *matching principle*. This principle requires that the expenses from bad debts be reported in the same accounting period as the revenues they helped produce.

PRINCIPLE APPLICATION
Matching Principle, p. 108
In a note to their 1994 financial statements, Pier 1 Imports explained that bad debt expense for the period is netted against revenues generated by credit sales (finance charges) and charged as a selling, general, and administrative expense.

MATCHING BAD DEBT EXPENSES WITH SALES

Managers realize that some portion of credit sales result in bad debts. However, the fact that a specific credit sale will not be collected does not become apparent until later. If a customer fails to pay within the credit period, most businesses send out several repeat billings and make other efforts to collect. Usually, they do not accept the fact that the customer is not going to pay until every reasonable means of collection has been exhausted. In many cases, this point may not be reached until one or more accounting periods after the period in which the sale was made. Thus, matching this expense with the revenue it produced requires the company to estimate its unknown amount at the end of the year. The **allowance method of accounting for bad debts** accomplishes this matching of bad debts expense with revenues.

ALLOWANCE METHOD OF ACCOUNTING FOR BAD DEBTS

At the end of each accounting period, the allowance method of accounting for bad debts requires estimating the total bad debts expected to result from the period's sales. An allowance is then provided for the loss. This method has two advantages: (1) the expense is charged to the period in which the revenue is recognized; and (2) the accounts receivable are reported on the balance sheet at the estimated amount of cash to be collected.

Recording the Estimated Bad Debts Expense

Under the allowance method of accounting for bad debts, you calculate the estimated bad debts expense at the end of each accounting period. Then, you record it with an adjusting entry. For example, assume that Fritz Company had credit sales of $300,000 during the first year of its operations. At the end of the year, $20,000 remains uncollected. Based on the experience of similar businesses, Fritz Company estimates that $1,500 of accounts receivable will be uncollectible. This estimated expense is recorded with the following adjusting entry:

Dec.	31	Bad Debts Expense	1,500.00	
		Allowance for Doubtful Accounts		1,500.00
		To record the estimated bad debts.		

The debit in this entry causes the expense to appear on the income statement of the year in which the sales were made. As a result, the estimated $1,500 expense of selling on credit is matched with the $300,000 of revenue it helped produce.

Note that the credit of the entry is to a contra account called **Allowance for Doubtful Accounts.** A contra account must be used because at the time of the adjusting entry, you do not know which customers will not pay. Therefore, because specific bad accounts are not identifiable at the time of the adjusting entry, they cannot be removed from the subsidiary Accounts Receivable Ledger. Because the customer accounts are left in the subsidiary ledger, the controlling account for Accounts Receivable cannot be reduced. Instead, the Allowance for Doubtful Accounts account *must* be credited.

Bad Debts in the Accounts and in the Financial Statements

The process of evaluating customers and approving them for credit usually is not assigned to the selling department of a business. Otherwise, given the primary objective of increasing sales, the selling department might not use good judgment in approving customers for credit. Because the sales department is not responsible for granting credit, it should not be held responsible for bad debts expense. Therefore, bad debts expense often appears on the income statement as an administrative expense rather than a selling expense.

Recall from the previous example that Fritz Company has $20,000 of outstanding accounts receivable at the end of its first year of operations. Thus, after the bad debts adjusting entry is posted, the company's Accounts Receivable and Allowance for Doubtful Accounts accounts show these balances:

Accounts Receivable		Allowance for Doubtful Accounts	
Dec. 31 20,000			Dec. 31 1,500

The Allowance for Doubtful Accounts credit balance of $1,500 has the effect of reducing accounts receivable (net of the allowance) to their estimated **realizable value.** The term *realizable value* means the expected proceeds from converting the assets into cash. Although $20,000 is legally owed to Fritz Company by all of its customers, only $18,500 is likely to be realized in cash collections from customers.

When the balance sheet is prepared, the allowance for doubtful accounts is subtracted from the accounts receivable to show the amount expected to be realized from the accounts. For example, this information could be reported as follows:

Current assets:		
Cash and cash equivalents		$11,300
Short-term investments, at fair		
market value (cost is $16,200)		14,500
Accounts receivable	$20,000	
Less allowance for doubtful accounts	(1,500)	18,500
Merchandise inventory		52,700
Prepaid expenses		1,100
Total current assets		$98,100

In this example, compare the presentations of short-term investments and accounts receivable, and note that contra accounts are subtracted in both cases. Even though the contra account to the Short-Term Investments account is not shown on the statement, you can easily determine that its balance is $1,700 by comparing the $16,200 cost with the $14,500 net amount. Sometimes, the contra account to Accounts Receivable is presented in a similar fashion, as follows:

Accounts receivable (net of $1,500 estimated	
uncollectible accounts)	$18,500

Writing off a Bad Debt

When specific accounts are identified as uncollectible, they are written off against the Allowance for Doubtful Accounts. For example, after spending a year trying to collect from Jack Vale, the Fritz Company finally decided that his $100 account was uncollectible and made the following entry to write it off:

Jan.	23	Allowance for Doubtful Accounts	100.00	
		Accounts Receivable—Jack Vale		100.00
		To write off an uncollectible account.		

Posting the credit of the entry to the Accounts Receivable account removes the amount of the bad debt from the controlling account. Posting it to the Jack Vale account removes the amount of the bad debt from the subsidiary ledger. By removing it from the subsidiary ledger, Fritz Company avoids the cost of sending additional bills to Vale. After the entry is posted, the general ledger accounts appear as follows:

Accounts Receivable				**Allowance for Doubtful Accounts**			
Dec. 31	20,000					Dec. 31	1,500
		Jan. 23	100	Jan. 23	100		

Notice two aspects of the entry and the accounts. First, although bad debts are an expense of selling on credit, the allowance account is debited in the write-off. The expense account is not debited. The expense account is not debited because the estimated expense was previously recorded at the end of the period in which the sale occurred. At that time, the expense was estimated and recorded with an adjusting entry.

Second, although the write-off removed the amount of the account receivable from the ledgers, it did not affect the estimated realizable value of Fritz Company's net accounts receivable, as the following tabulation shows:

	Before	After
Accounts receivable	$20,000	$19,900
Less allowance for doubtful accounts	1,500	1,400
Estimated realizable accounts receivable	$18,500	$18,500

Thus, neither total assets nor net income are affected by the decision to write off a specific account. However, both total assets and net income are affected by the recognition of the year's bad debts expense in the adjusting entry. Again, a primary purpose of writing off a specific account is to avoid the cost of additional collection efforts.

Bad Debt Recoveries

When a customer fails to pay and the account is written off, his or her credit standing is jeopardized. Therefore, the customer may choose to voluntarily pay all or part of the amount owed after the account is written off as uncollectible. This payment helps restore the credit standing. Thus, when this event happens, it should be recorded in the customer's subsidiary account where the information will be retained for use in future credit evaluations.

When a company collects an account that was previously written off, it makes two journal entries. The first reverses the original write-off and reinstates the customer's account. The second entry records the collection of the reinstated account. For example, assume that on August 15 Jack Vale pays in full the account that Fritz Company had previously written off. The entries to record the bad debt recovery are:

Aug.	15	Accounts Receivable—Jack Vale	100.00	
		Allowance for Doubtful Accounts		100.00
		To reinstate the account of Jack Vale written off on		
		January 23.		
	15	Cash	100.00	
		Accounts Receivable—Jack Vale		100.00
		Received full payment of account.		

In this case, Jack Vale paid the entire amount previously written off. In other situations, the customer may pay only a portion of the amount owed. The question then arises of whether the entire balance of the account should be returned to accounts receivable or just the amount paid. The answer is a matter of judgment. If you believe the customer will later pay in full, the entire amount owed should be returned. However, only the amount paid should be returned if you believe that no more will be collected.

8-7 In meeting the requirements of the matching principle, why must bad debts expenses be estimated?

8-8 What term describes the balance sheet valuation of accounts receivable less the allowance for doubtful accounts?

8-9 Why is estimated bad debts expense credited to a contra account rather than to the Accounts Receivable controlling account?

As you already learned, the allowance method of accounting for bad debts requires an adjusting entry at the end of each accounting period to record management's estimate of the bad debts expense for the period. That entry takes the following form:

ESTIMATING THE AMOUNT OF BAD DEBTS EXPENSE

Dec.	31	Bad Debts Expense	????	
		Allowance for Doubtful Accounts		????
		To record the estimated bad debts.		

How does a business determine the amount to record in this entry? There are two alternative approaches. One focuses on the income statement relationship between bad debts expense and sales. The other focuses on the balance sheet relationship between accounts receivable and allowance for doubtful accounts. Both alternatives require a careful analysis of past experience.

Estimating Bad Debts by Focusing on the Income Statement

The income statement approach to estimating bad debts is based on the idea that some particular percentage of a company's credit sales for the period will become uncollectible.[5] Hence, in the income statement, the amount of bad debts expense should equal that amount.

For example, suppose that Baker Company had credit sales of $400,000 in 19X2. Based on past experience and the experience of similar companies, Baker Company estimates that 0.6% of credit sales will be uncollectible. Using this prediction, Baker Company can expect $2,400 of bad debts expense to result from the year's sales ($400,000 × 0.006 = $2,400). The adjusting entry to record this estimated expense is:

Dec.	31	Bad Debts Expense	2,400.00	
		Allowance for Doubtful Accounts		2,400.00
		To record the estimated bad debts.		

This entry does not mean the December 31, 19X2, balance in Allowance for Doubtful Accounts will be $2,400. A $2,400 balance would occur only if the account had a zero balance immediately prior to posting the adjusting entry. For several reasons, however, the unadjusted balance of Allowance for Doubtful Accounts is not likely to be zero.

---

[5]Note that the factor to be considered is *credit* sales. Naturally, cash sales do not produce bad debts, and they generally should not be used in the calculation. However, if cash sales are relatively small compared to credit sales, there is no practical difference in the result.

First, unless Baker Company was created during the current year, the Allowance for Doubtful Accounts would have had a credit balance at the beginning of the year. The beginning-of-year credit balance would have resulted from entries made in past years to record estimated bad debts expense and to write off uncollectible accounts. The cumulative effect of these entries would show up as a credit balance at the beginning of the current year.

Second, because bad debts expense must be estimated each year, the total amount of expense recorded in past years is not likely to equal the amounts that were written off as uncollectible. Although annual expense estimates are based on past experience, some residual difference between recorded expenses and amounts written off should be expected to show up in the unadjusted Allowance for Doubtful Accounts balance.

Third, some of the amounts written off as uncollectible during the current year probably relate to credit sales made during the current year. These debits affect the unadjusted Allowance for Doubtful Accounts balance. In fact, they may cause the account to have a debit balance prior to posting the adjusting entry for bad debts expense.

For these reasons, you should not expect the Allowance for Doubtful Accounts to have an unadjusted balance of zero at the end of the year. As we stated earlier, this means that the adjusted balance reported on the balance sheet normally does not equal the amount of expense reported on the income statement.

Remember that expressing bad debts expense as a percentage of sales is an estimate based on past experience. As new experience is gained over time, the percentage used may appear to have been too large or too small. When this happens, a different rate should be used in future periods.

Estimating Bad Debts by Focusing on the Balance Sheet

The balance sheet approach to estimating bad debts is based on the idea that some portion of the end-of-period accounts receivable balance will not be collected. From this point of view, the goal of the bad debts adjusting entry is to make the Allowance for Doubtful Accounts balance equal to the portion of outstanding accounts receivable estimated to be uncollectible. To obtain this required balance in the Allowance for Doubtful Accounts account, simply compare its balance before the adjustment with the required balance. The difference between the two is debited to Bad Debts Expense and credited to Allowance for Doubtful Accounts. Estimating the required balance of the Allowance account can be done in two ways: (1) by using the simplified approach and (2) by aging the accounts receivable.

The Simplified Balance Sheet Approach.

Using the simplified balance sheet approach, a company estimates that a certain percentage of its outstanding receivables will prove to be uncollectible. This estimated percentage is based on past experience and the experience of similar companies. It also may be affected by current conditions such as recent prosperity or economic difficulties faced by the firm's customers. Then, the total dollar amount of all outstanding receivables is multiplied by the estimated percentage to determine the estimated dollar amount of uncollectible accounts. This amount must appear in the balance sheet as the balance of the Allowance for Doubtful Accounts. To put this balance in the account, you must prepare an adjusting entry that debits Bad Debts Expense and credits Allowance for Doubtful Accounts. The amount of the adjustment is the amount necessary to provide the required balance in Allowance for Doubtful Accounts.

For example, assume that Baker Company (of the previous illustration) has $50,000 of outstanding accounts receivable on December 31, 19X2. Past experience suggests that 5% of the outstanding receivables are uncollectible. Thus, after the adjusting entry is posted, the Allowance for Doubtful Accounts should have a $2,500 credit balance (5% of $50,000). Assume that before the adjustment the account appears as follows:

Allowance for Doubtful Accounts

		Dec. 31, 19X1, balance	2,000
Feb. 6	800		
July 10	600		
Nov. 20	400		
		Unadjusted balance	200

The $2,000 beginning balance appeared on the December 31, 19X1, balance sheet. During 19X2, accounts of specific customers were written off on February 6, July 10, and November 20. As a result, the account has a $200 credit balance prior to the December 31, 19X2, adjustment. The adjusting entry to give the Allowance the required $2,500 balance is:

Dec.	31	Bad Debts Expense	2,300.00	
		Allowance for Doubtful Accounts		2,300.00
		To record the estimated bad debts.		

After this entry is posted, the Allowance has a $2,500 credit balance, as shown here:

Allowance for Doubtful Accounts

		Dec. 31, 19X1, balance	2,000
Feb. 6	800		
July 10	600		
Nov. 20	400		
		Unadjusted balance	200
		Dec. 31	2,300
		Dec. 31, 19X2, balance	2,500

Aging Accounts Receivable. Both the income statement approach and the simplified balance sheet approach use knowledge gained from past experience to estimate the amount of bad debts expense. Another balance sheet approach produces a more refined estimate based on past experience and on information about current conditions.

This method involves **aging of accounts receivable.** Under this method, each account receivable is examined in the process of estimating the amount that is uncollectible. Specifically, the receivables are classified by how long they have been outstanding. Then, estimates of uncollectible amounts are made under the assumption that the longer an amount is outstanding, the more likely it will be uncollectible.

To age the accounts receivable outstanding at the end of the period, you must examine each account and classify the outstanding amounts by how much time has passed since they were created. The selection of the classes to be used depends on the judgment of each company's management. However, the classes are often based on 30-day (or one month) periods. After the outstanding amounts have been classified (or aged), past experience is used to estimate a percentage of each class that will become uncollectible. These percentages are applied to the amounts in the classes to determine the required balance of the Allowance for Doubtful Accounts. The calculation is completed by setting up a schedule like the one in Illustration 8–2 for Baker Company.

In Illustration 8–2, notice that each customer's account is listed with its total balance. Then, each balance is allocated to five categories based on the age of the unpaid charges that make up the balance. (In computerized systems, this allocation is done automatically.)

Illustration 8-2 Estimating Bad Debts by Aging the Accounts

BAKER COMPANY
Schedule of Accounts Receivable by Age
December 31, 19X2

Customer's Name	Total	Not Due	1 to 30 Days Past Due	31 to 60 Days Past Due	61 to 90 Days Past Due	Over 90 Days Past Due
Charles Abbot	$ 450.00	$ 450.00				
Frank Allen	710.00			$ 710.00		
George Arden	500.00	300.00	$ 200.00			
Paul Baum	740.00				$ 100.00	$ 640.00
ZZ Services	1,000.00	810.00	190.00			
Totals	$49,900.00	$37,000.00	$6,500.00	$3,500.00	$1,900.00	$1,000.00
Rate		× 2%	× 5%	× 10%	× 25%	× 40%
Estimated uncollectible accounts	$ 2,290.00	$ 740.00	$ 325.00	$ 350.00	$ 475.00	$ 400.00

When all accounts have been aged, the amounts in each category are totaled and multiplied by the estimated percentage of uncollectible accounts for each category. The reasonableness of the percentages used must be reviewed regularly and frequently reflect reactions to the state of the economy. The following excerpt from the management discussion in the 1993 annual report of **Sears, Roebuck & Co.** illustrates this point:

The provision for uncollectible accounts fell 8.2% in 1993, primarily reflecting a decline in bankruptcy experience. Domestic retail customer receivables delinquent three months or more as a percentage of gross customer receivables were 3.55% at Dec. 31, 1993, compared with 2.99% at Dec. 31, 1992.

For example, in Illustration 8–2, Baker Company is owed $3,500 that is 31 to 60 days past due. Baker's management estimates that 10% of the amounts in this age category will not be collected. Thus, the dollar amount of uncollectible accounts in this category is $350 ($3,500 × 10%). The total in the first column tells us that the adjusted balance in Baker Company's Allowance for Doubtful Accounts should be $2,290 ($740 + $325 + $350 + $475 + $400). Because the Allowance has an unadjusted credit balance of $200, the aging of accounts receivable approach requires the following change in its balance:

Unadjusted balance	$ 200 credit
Required balance	2,290 credit
Required adjustment	$2,090 credit

As a result, Baker should record the following adjusting entry:

Dec.	31	Bad Debts Expense	2,090.00	
		Allowance for Doubtful Accounts		2,090.00
		To record the estimated bad debts.		

For instructional purposes, suppose that Baker's Allowance had an unadjusted *debit* balance of $500. In this case, the calculation of the adjustment amount and the entry would be:

Unadjusted balance	$ 500 debit
Required balance	2,290 credit
Required adjustment	$2,790 credit

Dec.	31	Bad Debts Expense	2,790.00	
		Allowance for Doubtful Accounts		2,790.00
		To record the estimated bad debts.		

Recall from page 315 that when the income statement approach was used, Baker's bad debts expense for 19X2 was estimated to be $2,400. When the simplified balance sheet approach was used (see page 316), the estimate was $2,300. And when aging of accounts receivable was used the first time, the estimate was $2,090. Do not be surprised that the amounts are different; after all, each approach is only an estimate of what will prove to be true. However, the aging of accounts receivable is based on a more detailed examination of specific outstanding accounts and is usually the most reliable.[6]

The allowance method of accounting for bad debts satisfies the requirements of the *matching principle*. Therefore, it is the method that should be used in most cases. However, another method may be suitable under certain limited circumstances. Under this **direct write-off method of accounting for bad debts,** no attempt is made to estimate uncollectible accounts or bad debts expense at the end of each period. In fact, no adjusting entry is made. Instead, bad debts expense is recorded when specific accounts are written off as uncollectible. For example, note the following entry to write off a $52 uncollectible account:

DIRECT WRITE-OFF METHOD OF ACCOUNTING FOR BAD DEBTS

Nov.	23	Bad Debts Expense	52.00	
		Accounts Receivable—Dale Hall		52.00
		To write off the uncollectible account under the direct write-off method.		

The debit of the entry charges the uncollectible amount directly to the current year's Bad Debts Expense account. The credit removes the balance of the account from the subsidiary ledger and from the controlling account.

If an account previously written off directly to Bad Debts Expense is later collected in full, the following entries record the recovery:

Mar.	11	Accounts Receivable—Dale Hall	52.00	
		Bad Debts Expense		52.00
		To reinstate the account of Dale Hall previously written off.		
	11	Cash	52.00	
		Accounts Receivable—Dale Hall		52.00
		In full payment of account.		

---

[6]In many cases, the aging analysis is supplemented with information about specific customers that allows management to decide whether those accounts should be classified as uncollectible. This information often is supplied by the sales and credit department managers.

Sometimes an amount previously written off directly to Bad Debts Expense is recovered in the year following the write-off. If there is no balance in the Bad Debts Expense account from previous write-offs and no other write-offs are expected, the credit portion of the entry recording the recovery can be made to a Bad Debt Recoveries revenue account.

The direct write-off method usually mismatches revenues and expenses. The mismatch occurs because bad debts expense is not recorded until an account becomes uncollectible, which often does not occur during the same period as the credit sale. Despite this weakness, the direct write-off method may be used when a company's bad debts expenses are very small in relation to other financial statement items such as total sales and net income. In such cases, the direct write-off method is justified by the *materiality principle*, which we explain next.

THE MATERIALITY PRINCIPLE

The basic idea of the **materiality principle** is that the requirements of accounting principles may be ignored if the effect on the financial statements is unimportant to their users. In other words, failure to follow the requirements of an accounting principle is acceptable when the failure does not produce an error or misstatement large enough to influence a financial statement reader's judgment of a given situation.

INSTALLMENT ACCOUNTS AND NOTES RECEIVABLE

Many companies allow their credit customers to make periodic payments over several months. When this is done, the selling company's assets may be in the form of **installment accounts receivable** or notes receivable. As is true for other accounts receivable, the evidence behind installment accounts receivable includes sales slips or invoices that describe the sales transactions. A note receivable, on the other hand, is a written document that promises payment and is signed by the customer. In either case, when payments are made over several months or if the credit period is long, the customer is usually charged interest. Although the credit period of installment accounts and notes receivable may be more than one year, they should be classified as current assets if the company regularly offers customers such terms.

Generally, creditors prefer notes receivable over accounts receivable when the credit period is long and the receivable relates to a single sale for a fairly large amount. Notes also can replace accounts receivable when customers ask for additional time to pay their past-due accounts. In these situations, creditors prefer notes to accounts receivable for legal reasons. If a lawsuit is needed to collect from a customer, a note represents a clear written acknowledgment by the debtor of the debt, its amount, and its terms.

Progress Check

D & C Boutiques International estimated that, based on an aging of accounts receivable, $6,142 would be uncollectible. The year end 12/31/X1 balance of the allowance account is a credit of $440.

8-10   **Prepare the year-end adjusting entry.**

8-11   **Using the following information, prepare the appropriate journal entries:**
On January 10, 19X2, the $300 account of customer Felix Arthur was determined uncollectible. On April 12, 19X2, Felix Arthur paid the account that was determined uncollectible on January 10, 19X2.

PROMISSORY NOTES

A **promissory note** is an unconditional written promise to pay a definite sum of money on demand or at a fixed or determinable future date. In the promissory note shown in Illustration 8–3, Hugo Brown promises to pay Frank Tomlinson or to his order (that is, according to Tomlinson's instructions) a definite sum of money ($1,000), called

Illustration 8–3
A Promissory Note

```
  _____$1,000.00_____        ____Eugene, Oregon____        ____March 9, 19X1____

  ____Thirty days____  after date  _____I_____  promise to pay to

  the order of _____Frank Tomlinson_____

  One thousand and no / 100 ------------------------------------------------  dollars

  for value received with interest at  _____12%_____

  payable at  ___First National Bank of Eugene, Oregon___

                                            _____Hugo Brown_____
```

the **principal of the note** at a fixed future date (April 8, 19X1). As the one who signed the note and promised to pay it at maturity, Hugo Brown is the **maker of the note.** As the person to whom the note is payable, Frank Tomlinson is the **payee of the note.** To Hugo Brown, the illustrated note is a liability called a *note payable.* To Frank Tomlinson, the same note is an asset called a *note receivable.*

The Hugo Brown note bears **interest** at 12%. Interest is the charge assessed for the use of money. To a borrower, interest is an expense. To a lender, it is a revenue. The rate of interest that a note bears is stated on the note.

Calculating Interest

Unless otherwise stated, the rate of interest on a note is the rate charged for the use of the principal for one year. The formula for calculating interest is:

$$\text{Principal of the note} \times \text{Annual rate of interest} \times \text{Time of the note expressed in years} = \text{Interest}$$

For example, interest on a $1,000, 12%, six-month note is calculated as:

$$\$1{,}000 \times 12\% \times \frac{6}{12} = \$60$$

The **maturity date of a note** is the day on which the note (principal and interest) must be repaid. Many notes mature in less than a full year, and the period covered by them often is expressed in days. When the time of a note is expressed in days, the maturity date is the specified number of days after the note's date. As a simple example, a one-day note dated June 15 matures and is due on June 16. Also, a 90-day note dated July 10 matures on October 8. This October 8 due date is calculated as follows:

Number of days in July	31
Minus the date of the note	10
Gives the number of days the note runs in July	21
Add the number of days in August	31
Add the number of days in September	30
Total through September 30	82
Days in October needed to equal the 90-day time of the note, also the maturity date of the note (October 8)	8
Total time the note runs in days	90

In other situations, the period of a note is expressed in months. In these cases, the note matures and is payable in the month of its maturity on the same day of the month as its original date. For example, a three-month note dated July 10 is payable on October 10.

LO 4

Calculate the interest on promissory notes and prepare entries to record the receipt of promissory notes and their payment or dishonor.

To simplify interest calculations for notes that have periods expressed in days, a common practice has been to treat a year as having just 360 days. Although this practice is not applied as frequently as it used to be, we use it in this book to make it easier for you to work the exercises and problems assigned by your instructor. We also assume a 360-day year in the following discussion. Suppose, for example, that there is a 90-day, 12%, $1,000 note. The amount of interest is calculated as follows:

$$\text{Interest} = \text{Principal} \times \text{Rate} \times \frac{\text{Exact days}}{360}$$

or

$$\text{Interest} = \$1,000 \times 12\% \times \frac{90}{360} = \$30$$

Recording the Receipt of a Note

To simplify record-keeping, notes receivable are usually recorded in a single Notes Receivable account. Only one account is needed because the individual original notes are on hand. Therefore, the maker, rate of interest, due date, and other information may be learned by examining each note.[7]

When a company receives a note at the time of a sale, an entry such as this one is recorded:

Dec.	5	Notes Receivable	650.00	
		Sales		650.00
		Sold merchandise, terms six-month, 9% note.		

A business also may accept a note from an overdue customer as a way of granting a time extension on the past-due account receivable. When this happens, the business may collect part of the past-due balance in cash. This partial payment forces a concession from the customer, reduces the customer's debt (and the seller's risk), and produces a note for a smaller amount. For example, Symplex Company agrees to accept $232 in cash and a $600, 60-day, 15% note from Joseph Cook to settle his $832 past-due account. Symplex makes the following entry to record the receipt of the cash and note:

Oct.	5	Cash	232.00	
		Notes Receivable	600.00	
		Accounts Receivable—Joseph Cook		832.00
		Received cash and a note in settlement of an account.		

When Cook pays the note on the due date, Symplex records the receipt as follows:

Dec.	4	Cash	615.00	
		Notes Receivable		600.00
		Interest Earned		15.00
		Collected the Joseph Cook note including interest of		
		$600 × 15% × 60/360.		

---

[7]If the company holds a large number of notes, it may be more efficient to set up a controlling account and a subsidiary ledger.

Dishonored Notes Receivable

Sometimes, the maker of a note is not able to pay the note at maturity. When a note's maker is unable or refuses to pay at maturity, the note is said to be dishonored. This act of **dishonoring a note** does not relieve the maker of the obligation to pay. Furthermore, the payee should use every legitimate means to collect. However, collection may require lengthy legal proceedings.

The usual practice is to have the balance of the Notes Receivable account show only the amount of notes that have not matured. Therefore, when a note is dishonored, you should remove the amount of the note from the Notes Receivable account and charge it back to an account receivable from its maker. To illustrate, Symplex Company holds an $800, 12%, 60-day note of George Hart. At maturity, Hart dishonors the note. To remove the dishonored note from the Notes Receivable account, the company makes the following entry:

Oct.	14	Accounts Receivable—George Hart	816.00	
		Interest Earned		16.00
		Notes Receivable		800.00
		To charge the account of George Hart for his dishonored note including interest of $800 × 12% × 60/360.		

Charging a dishonored note back to the account of its maker serves two purposes. First, it removes the amount of the note from the Notes Receivable account, leaving in the account only notes that have not matured. It also records the dishonored note in the maker's account. The second purpose is important. If the maker of the dishonored note again applies for credit in the future, his or her account will show all past dealings, including the dishonored note. Restoring the account also reminds the business to continue collection efforts.

Note that Hart owes both the principal and the interest. Therefore, the entry records the full amount owed in Hart's account and credits the interest to Interest Earned. This procedure assures that the interest will be included in future efforts to collect from Hart.

End-of-Period Adjustments

When notes receivable are outstanding at the end of an accounting period, the accrued interest should be calculated and recorded. This procedure recognizes the interest revenue when it is earned and recognizes the additional asset owned by the note's holder. For example, on December 16, Perry Company accepted a $3,000, 60-day, 12% note from a customer in granting an extension on a past-due account. When the company's accounting period ends on December 31, $15 of interest will have accrued on this note ($3,000 × 12% × 15/360). The following adjusting entry records this revenue:

Dec.	31	Interest Receivable	15.00	
		Interest Earned		15.00
		To record accrued interest.		

The adjusting entry causes the interest earned to appear on the income statement of the period in which it was earned. It also causes the interest receivable to appear on the balance sheet as a current asset.

Collecting Interest Previously Accrued

When the note is collected, Perry Company's entry to record the cash receipt is:

Feb.	14	Cash	3,060.00	
		Interest Earned		45.00
		Interest Receivable		15.00
		Notes Receivable		3,000.00
		Received payment of a note and its interest.		

Observe that the entry's credit to Interest Receivable records collection of the interest accrued at the end of the previous period. Only the $45 of interest earned between January 1 and February 14 is recorded as revenue.

Progress Check

8-12 White Corporation purchased $7,000 of merchandise from Stamford Company on December 16, 19X1. Stamford accepted White's $7,000, 90-day, 12% note as payment. Assuming Stamford's annual accounting period ends on December 31 and it does not make reversing entries, prepare entries for Stamford Company on December 16, 19X1, and December 31, 19X1.

8-13 Based on the facts in 8-12, prepare the March 16, 19X2, entry assuming White dishonors the note.

CONVERTING RECEIVABLES INTO CASH BEFORE THEY ARE DUE

LO 5

Explain how receivables can be converted into cash before they are due and calculate accounts receivable turnover.

Many companies grant credit to customers and then hold the receivables until they are paid by the customers. However, some companies convert receivables into cash without waiting until they are due. This is done either by selling the receivables or by using them as security for a loan. In certain industries such as textiles and furniture, this has been a common practice for years. More recently, the practice has spread to other industries, in particular the apparel industry. More small businesses are using sale of receivables as a source of cash, especially those selling to other businesses and government agencies that often delay payment.

Selling Accounts Receivable

A business may sell its accounts receivable to a finance company or bank. The buyer, which is called a *factor,* charges the seller a *factoring fee* and then collects the receivables as they come due. By incurring the factoring fee cost, the seller receives the cash earlier and passes the risk of bad debts to the factor. The seller also avoids the cost of billing and accounting for the receivables.

For example, assume that a business sells $20,000 of its accounts receivable and is charged a 2% factoring fee. The seller records the sale with the following entry:

Aug.	15	Cash	19,600.00	
		Factoring Fee Expense	400.00	
		Accounts Receivable		20,000.00
		Sold accounts receivable for cash, less a 2% factoring fee.		

Factoring has become big business today. **CIT Group/Commercial Services,** the factoring firm with the largest volume in recent years, posted a 7.6% increase in volume to $3.738 billion in the first half of 1993. It is interesting to note that 90% of the factoring industry's business comes from textile and apparel businesses.

Pledging Accounts Receivable as Security for a Loan

When a business borrows money and pledges its accounts receivable as security for the loan, the business records the loan with an entry such as the following:

Aug.	20	Cash	35,000.00	
		Notes Payable		35,000.00
		Borrowed money on a note secured by the pledge of accounts receivable.		

Under the pledging arrangement, the risk of bad debts is not transferred to the lender. The borrower retains ownership of the receivables. However, if the borrower defaults on the loan, the creditor has the right to be paid from the cash receipts as the accounts receivable are collected.

Because pledged receivables are committed as security for a loan from a particular creditor, the borrower's financial statements should disclose the fact that accounts receivable have been pledged. For example, the following footnote to the financial statements provides the necessary information: "Accounts receivable in the amount of $40,000 are pledged as security for a $35,000 note payable to Western National Bank."

Discounting Notes Receivable

Notes receivable also can be converted into cash before they mature, usually by discounting the notes receivable at a bank. For example, if a company discounts a $50,000 note receivable at a cost of $700, it records the discounting with the following entry:

Aug.	25	Cash	49,300.00	
		Interest Expense	700.00	
		Notes Receivable		50,000.00
		Discounted a note receivable.		

Notes receivable may be discounted with recourse or without recourse. If a note is discounted with recourse and the original maker of the note fails to pay the bank when the note matures, the original payee of the note must pay. Thus, a company that discounts a note with recourse has a contingent liability until the bank is paid. A **contingent liability** is an obligation to make a future payment if, and only if, an uncertain future event actually occurs. The company should disclose the contingent liability in its financial statements with a footnote such as: "The company is contingently liable for a $50,000 note receivable discounted with recourse."

In the preceding entry, notice the debit to Interest Expense. This indicates that the discounting transaction is understood to be a loan. In some cases, discounting a note with recourse is considered to be a sale.[8] When the transaction is a sale, the debit should be to Loss on Sale of Notes instead of to Interest Expense.

When a note is discounted *without recourse,* the bank assumes the risk of a bad

debt loss and the original payee does not have a contingent liability. A note discounted without recourse is clearly understood to be sold.

Accounting Trends and Techniques, an annual survey of accounting practices followed in 600 stockholders' reports, shows that 127 of the surveyed companies disclosed either the sale of receivables or the pledging of receivables as collateral. The following footnote from Pitney Bowes, Inc.'s annual report illustrates disclosure of substantial receivables sold with recourse:

> The company has sold net finance receivables with varying amounts of recourse in privately-placed transactions with third-party investors. The uncollected principal balance of receivables sold and residual guarantee contracts totaled $342.3 million and $551.0 million at December 31, 1993 and 1992, respectively. These contracts are supported by the underlying equipment value and creditworthiness of customers. Adequate provisions have been made for sold receivables which may be uncollectible.

FULL-DISCLOSURE PRINCIPLE

The disclosure of contingent liabilities in footnotes is consistent with the **full-disclosure principle.** This principle requires financial statements (including the footnotes) to present all relevant information about the operations and financial position of the entity. A company should report any facts important enough to affect a statement reader's evaluation of the company's operations, financial position, or cash flows. This principle does not require companies to report excessive detail. It simply means that significant information should not be withheld and that enough information should be provided to make the reports understandable. Examples of items that are reported to satisfy the full-disclosure principle include the following:

Contingent Liabilities. In addition to discounted notes, a company should disclose any items for which the company is contingently liable. Examples are possible additional tax assessments, debts of other parties that the company has guaranteed, and unresolved lawsuits against the company. Information about these facts helps users pre-

dict events that might affect the company. In October of 1994, *The Wall Street Journal* reported "Pennzoil said it agreed to pay the IRS $454 million in back taxes and interest to resolve a claim stemming from its 1988 settlement with Texaco." Those that had a financial interest in Pennzoil were aware of this potential tax liability because following GAAP requirements Pennzoil Company made the following disclosure in the footnotes to their 1993 annual report:

> In January 1994, Pennzoil received a letter and examination report from the District Director of the IRS that proposes a tax deficiency based on an audit of Pennzoil's 1988 federal income tax return. The examination report proposes two principal adjustments with which Pennzoil disagrees. . . . The proposed tax deficiency relating to this proposed adjustment is $550.9 million, net of available offsets. Pennzoil estimates that the additional after-tax interest on this proposed deficiency would be approximately $234.3 million as of December 31, 1993.

---

[8]The criteria for deciding whether discounting with recourse is a loan or a sale are explained in more advanced accounting courses.

Another example is the 1991 annual report of **The Quaker Oats Company** which disclosed in a footnote a $42.6 million judgment for infringement on trademark rights of another company in their advertisement for Gatorade. The footnote indicated appeal was in process and "the amount of any liability which might finally exist cannot reasonably be estimated and no provision for loss has been made in the accompanying financial statements."

Long-Term Commitments under Contracts. A company should disclose that it has signed a long-term lease requiring material annual payments, even though the obligation does not appear in the accounts. Also, a company should reveal that it has pledged certain of its assets as security for loans. These facts show statement readers that the company has restricted its flexibility.

Accounting Methods Used. When more than one accounting method can be applied, a company must describe the one it uses, especially when the choice can materially affect reported net income.[9] For example, a company must describe the methods it uses to account for inventory and depreciation. (These methods are explained in future chapters.) This information helps users understand how the company determines its net income.

In Chapter 7, you learned how to calculate *days' sales uncollected,* which provides information about the short-term liquidity of a company. In evaluating short-term liquidity, you also may want to calculate **accounts receivable turnover.** The formula for this ratio is:

$$\text{Accounts receivable turnover} = \frac{\text{Net sales}}{\text{Average accounts receivable}}$$

USING THE INFORMATION— ACCOUNTS RECEIVABLE TURNOVER

Recall that days' sales uncollected relates to the accounts receivable balance at the end of the year. In contrast, notice that the denominator in the turnover formula is the average accounts receivable balance during the year. The average is often calculated as:

$$\frac{(\text{The beginning balance} + \text{The ending balance})}{2}$$

This method of estimating the average balance provides a useful result if the seasonal changes in the accounts receivable balances during the year are not too large.

Accounts receivable turnover indicates how often the company converted its average accounts receivable balance into cash during the year. Thus, a turnover of 12 suggests that the average accounts receivable balance was converted into cash 12 times during the year.

Accounts receivable turnover also provides useful information for evaluating how efficient management has been in granting credit to produce revenues. A ratio that is high in comparison with competing companies suggests that management should consider using more liberal credit terms to increase sales. A low ratio suggests that management should consider less liberal credit terms and more aggressive collection efforts to avoid an excessive investment in accounts receivable. The following data were

---

[9]FASB, *Accounting Standards—Current Text* (Norwalk, CT, 1994), sec. A10.105. First published as *APB Opinion No. 22,* pars. 12, 13.

extracted from 1993 annual reports of competing companies to illustrate the calculations and comparisons:

Dr Pepper/Seven-Up Companies (In thousands)

$$\text{Accounts receivable turnover} = \frac{\$707,378}{(\$70,255 + \$57,267)/2} = 11.09 \text{ times}$$

PepsiCo, Inc. (In millions)

$$\text{Accounts receivable turnover} = \frac{\$25,020.7}{(\$1,883.4 + \$1,588.5)/2} = 14.41 \text{ times}$$

Progress Check

8-14   **A garment manufacturer is short of cash but has substantial accounts receivable. What alternatives are available for gaining cash from the accounts receivable prior to receiving payments from the credit customers? Show the entry that would be made for each alternative.**

8-15   **Calculate the 1992 accounts receivable turnover for Ben & Jerry's Homemade, Inc., using the annual report in Appendix G.**

SUMMARY OF THE CHAPTER IN TERMS OF LEARNING OBJECTIVES

LO 1. Prepare journal entries to account for short-term investments and explain how fair (market) value gains and losses on such investments are reported. Short-term investments are recorded at cost; dividends and interest on the investments are recorded in appropriate income statement accounts. On the balance sheet, investments in securities held to maturity are reported at cost; investments in trading securities and securities available for sale are reported at their fair values. Unrealized gains and losses on trading securities are included in income, but unrealized gains and losses on securities available for sale are reported as a separate stockholders' equity item.

LO 2. Prepare entries to account for credit card sales. When credit card receipts are deposited in a bank account, the credit card expense is recorded at the time of the deposit. When credit card receipts must be submitted to the credit card company for payment, Accounts Receivable is debited for the sales amount. Then, credit card expense is recorded when cash is received from the credit card company. However, any unrecorded credit card expense should be accrued at the end of each accounting period.

LO 3. Prepare entries to account for transactions with credit customers, including accounting for bad debts under the allowance method and the direct write-off method. Under the allowance method, bad debts expense is recorded with an adjustment at the end of each accounting period that debits the expense and credits the Allowance for Doubtful Accounts. The amount of the adjustment is determined by focusing on either (*a*) the income statement relationship between bad debts expense and credit sales or (*b*) the balance sheet relationship between accounts receivable and the Allowance for Doubtful Accounts. The latter approach may involve using a simple percentage relationship or aging the accounts. Uncollectible accounts are written off with a debit to the Allowance for Doubtful Accounts. The direct write-off method charges Bad Debts Expense when accounts are written off as uncollectible. This method is suitable only when the amount of bad debts expense is immaterial.

LO 4. Calculate the interest on promissory notes and prepare entries to record the receipt of promissory notes and their payment or dishonor. Interest rates are typically stated in annual terms. When a note's time to maturity is more or less than one year, the amount of interest on the note must be determined by expressing the time as a fraction of one year and multiplying the note's principal by that fraction and the annual interest rate. Dishonored notes are credited to Notes Receivable and debited to Accounts Receivable and to the account of the maker.

LO 5. Explain how receivables can be converted into cash before they are due and calculate accounts receivable turnover. To obtain cash from receivables before they are due, a company may sell accounts receivable to a factor, who charges a factoring fee. Also, a company may borrow money by signing a note payable that is secured by pledging the accounts receivable. Notes receivable may be discounted at a bank, with or without recourse. The full-disclosure principle requires companies to disclose the amount of accounts receivable that have been pledged and the contingent liability for notes discounted with recourse.

DEMONSTRATION PROBLEM

Garden Company had the following transactions during 19X2:

May 8 Purchased 300 shares of Federal Express common stock as a short-term investment in a security available for sale. The cost of $40 per share plus $975 in broker's commissions was paid in cash.

July 14 Wrote off a $750 account receivable arising from a sale several months ago. (Garden Company uses the allowance method.)

Aug. 15 Accepted a $2,000 down payment and a $10,000 note receivable from a customer in exchange for an inventory item that normally sells for $12,000. The note was dated August 15, bears 12% interest, and matures in six months.

Sept. 2 Sold 100 shares of Federal Express stock at $47 per share, and continued to hold the other 200 shares. The broker's commission on the sale was $225.

Sept. 15 Received $9,850 in return for discounting without recourse the $10,000 note (dated August 15) at the local bank.

Dec. 2 Purchased 400 shares of McDonald's Corp. stock for $60 per share plus $1,600 in commissions. The stock is to be held as a short-term investment in a security available for sale.

Required

1. Prepare journal entries to record these transactions on the books of Garden Company.
2. Prepare adjusting journal entries as of December 31, 19X2, for the following items (assume 19X2 is the first year of operations):
   a. The market prices of the equity securities held by Garden Company are $48 per share for the Federal Express stock, and $55 per share for the McDonald's stock.
   b. Bad debts expense is estimated by an aging of accounts receivable. The unadjusted balance of the Allowance for Doubtful Accounts account is a $1,000 debit, while the required balance is estimated to be a $20,400 credit.

Planning the Solution

- Examine each item to determine which accounts are affected, and produce the needed journal entries.
- With respect to the year-end adjustments, adjust stock investments to fair value and record the bad debts expense.

May	8	Short-Term Investments		12,975.00	
		Cash			12,975.00
		Purchased 300 shares of Federal Express. Cost is (300 × $40) + $975.			
July	14	Allowance for Doubtful Accounts		750.00	
		Accounts Receivable			750.00
		Wrote off an uncollectible account.			
Aug.	15	Cash		2,000.00	
		Notes Receivable		10,000.00	
		Sales			12,000.00
		Sold merchandise to customer for $2,000 cash and $10,000 note receivable.			
Sept.	2	Cash		4,475.00	
		Gain on Sale of Investment			150.00
		Short-Term Investments			4,325.00
		Sold 100 shares of Federal Express for $47 per share less a $225 commission. The original cost is $12,975 × 100/300.			
	15	Cash		9,850.00	
		Loss on Sale of Notes		150.00	
		Notes Receivable			10,000.00
		Discounted note receivable dated August 15.			
Dec.	2	Short-Term Investments		25,600.00	
		Cash			25,600.00
		Purchased 400 shares of McDonald's for $60 per share plus $1,600 in commissions.			
	31	Unrealized Holding Gain (Loss)		2,650.00	
		Short-Term Investments, Fair Value Adjustment			2,650.00
		To reflect fair values of short-term investments in securities available for sale.			

Short-Term Investments in Securities Available for Sale	Shares	Cost per Share	Total Cost	Market Value per Share	Total Market Value	Difference
Federal Express	200	$43.25	$ 8,650	$48.00	$ 9,600	
McDonald's	400	64.00	25,600	55.00	22,000	
Total			$34,250		$31,600	$2,650

	31	Bad Debts Expense		21,400.00	
		Allowance for Doubtful Accounts			21,400.00
		To adjust the allowance account from $1,000 debit balance to $20,400 credit balance.			

GLOSSARY

Accounts Receivable Ledger a supplementary record (also called a subsidiary ledger) having an account for each customer. p. 310

Accounts receivable turnover a measure of how long it takes a company to collect its accounts, calculated by dividing credit sales (or net sales) by the average accounts receivable balance. p. 327

Aging of accounts receivable a process of classifying accounts receivable by how long they have been outstanding for the purpose of estimating the amount of uncollectible accounts. p. 317

Allowance for Doubtful Accounts a contra asset account with a balance equal to the estimated amount of accounts receivable that will be uncollectible. p. 312

Allowance method of accounting for bad debts an accounting procedure that (1) estimates and reports bad debt expense from credit sales during the period of the sales, and (2) reports accounts receivable at the amount of cash proceeds that is expected from their collection (their estimated realizable value). p. 312

Bad debts accounts receivable from customers that are not collected; the amount is an expense of selling on credit. p. 311

Contingent liability an obligation to make a future payment if, and only if, an uncertain future event actually occurs. p. 325

Controlling account a general ledger account with a balance that is always equal to the sum of the balances in a related subsidiary ledger. p. 311

Direct write-off method of accounting for bad debts a method that makes no attempt to estimate uncollectible accounts or bad debts expense at the end of each period; instead, when an account is found to be uncollectible, it is written off directly to Bad Debts Expense; this method is generally considered to be inferior to the allowance method. p. 319

Dishonoring a note failure by a promissory note's maker to pay the amount due at maturity. p. 323

Full-disclosure principle the accounting principle that requires financial statements (including the footnotes) to contain all relevant information about the operations and financial position of the entity; it also requires that the information be presented in an understandable manner. p. 326

General Ledger the ledger that contains all the financial statement accounts of an organization. p. 310

Installment accounts receivable accounts receivable that allow the customer to make periodic payments over several months and that typically earn interest for the seller. p. 320

Interest the charge assessed for the use of money. p. 321

Investments in securities available for sale investments in debt and equity securities that do not qualify as investments in trading securities or as investments in securities held to maturity. p. 304

Investments in securities held to maturity investments in debt securities that the owner positively intends to hold and has the ability to hold until maturity. p. 304

Investments in trading securities investments in debt and equity securities that the owner actively manages, so that frequent purchases and sales generally are made with the objective of generating profits on short-term differences in price. p. 304

Maker of a note one who signs a note and promises to pay it at maturity. p. 321

Materiality principle the idea that the requirements of an accounting principle may be ignored if the effect on the financial statements is unimportant to their users. p. 320

Maturity date of a note the date on which a note and any interest are due and payable. p. 321

Payee of a note the one to whom a promissory note is made payable. p. 321

Principal of a note the amount that the signer of a promissory note agrees to pay back when it matures, not including the interest. p. 321

Promissory note an unconditional written promise to pay a definite sum of money on demand or at a fixed or determinable future date. p. 320

Realizable value the expected proceeds from converting assets into cash. p. 313

Short-term investments investments that can be converted into cash quickly (but less quickly than cash equivalents), and that management intends to sell as a source of cash to satisfy the needs of current operations; short-term investments include such things as government or corporate debt obligations and marketable equity securities. p. 302

Subsidiary ledger a collection of accounts (other than general ledger accounts) that contains the details underlying the balance of a controlling account in the General Ledger. p. 311

Temporary investments another name for *short-term investments*. p. 302

Unrealized holding gain an increase in the fair (market) value of a security that has not yet been confirmed by the sale of the security. p. 305

Unrealized holding loss a decrease in the fair (market) value of a security that has not yet been confirmed by the sale of the security. p. 306

QUESTIONS

1. Under what conditions should investments be classified as current assets?

2. If a short-term investment in securities held for sale cost $6,780 and was sold for $7,500, how should the difference between the two amounts be recorded?

3. On a balance sheet, what valuation must be reported for short-term investments in trading securities?

4. If a company purchases short-term investments in securities available for sale for the first time, and their fair (market) values fall below cost, what account is credited for the amount of the unrealized loss?

5. For which category of short-term investments are unrealized holding gains included in earnings and reported on the income statement?

6. How do businesses benefit from allowing their customers to use credit cards?

7. Explain why writing off a bad debt against the allowance account does not reduce the estimated realizable value of a company's accounts receivable.

8. Why does the Bad Debts Expense account usually not have the same adjusted balance as the Allowance for Doubtful Accounts?

9. Why does the direct write-off method of accounting for bad debts commonly fail to match revenues and expenses?

10. What is the essence of the accounting principle of materiality?

11. Why might a business prefer a note receivable to an account receivable?

12. Review the consolidated balance sheets of Federal Express Corporation presented in Appendix G. Assuming the company records all of its receivables in one controlling account, what was the balance of that account on May 31, 1993?

13. Review the consolidated balance sheets of Federal Express Corporation presented in Appendix G. Assuming that during the year ended May 31, 1993, $5 million of Federal Express Corporation's receivables were written off as uncollectible and no amounts written off were subsequently collected during the year, what amount of bad debts expense did the company record during that year?

QUICK STUDY (Five-Minute Exercises)

QS 8–1
(LO 1)

On January 20, Smythe and O'Shea Co. made a short-term investment in 100 shares of Computer Links common stock. The intent is to actively manage these stocks. The purchase price was $62^1/_5$ and the broker's fee was $200. March 20, they received $2 per share in dividends. Prepare the January 20 and March 20 journal entries.

QS 8–2
(LO 1)

During this year, Balzarini Associates acquired short-term investments securities at a cost of $46,000. These securities were classified as available for sale. At December 31 year-end, these securities had a market (fair) value of $44,000.

a. Prepare the necessary year-end adjustment.

b. Explain how each account used in requirement *a* would affect or be reported in the financial statements.

QS 8–3
(LO 2)

Journalize the following transactions:

a. Sold $2,000 in merchandise on Visa credit cards. The sales receipts were deposited in our business account. Visa charges us a 5% fee.

b. Sold $5,000 on miscellaneous credit cards. Cash will be received within two weeks and a 4% fee will be charged.

QS 8–4
(LO 3)

Arnold Equipment Co. uses the allowance method to account for uncollectibles. On March 1, they wrote off a $4,000 account of a customer, Trukin Co. On May 1, they received a $1,000 payment from Trukin Co.

a. Make the appropriate entry or entries for March 1.

b. Make the appropriate entry or entries for May 1.

The year-end trial balance of Harpson Co. shows Accounts Receivable of $164,000, Allowance for Doubtful Accounts of $200 (credit), Sales of $600,000. Uncollectibles are estimated to be 1.5% of outstanding Accounts Receivable.

QS 8–5
(LO 3)

a. Prepare the December 31 year-end adjustment.

b. What amount would have been used in the year-end adjustment if the allowance account had a year-end debit balance of $100?

c. Assume the same facts, except Harpson Co. estimated uncollectibles as 1% of sales. What amount would be used in the adjustment?

On May 2, 19X1, Building American Corp. received a $9,000, 90-day, 12% note from customer Sean Conrad as payment on account. Prepare the May 2 and maturity date entries assuming the note is honored by Conrad.

QS 8–6
(LO 4)

The December 31 trial balance shows a $5,000 balance in Notes Receivable. This balance is from one note dated December 1, with a period of 120 days and 9% interest. Prepare the December 31 and maturity date entries assuming the note is honored.

QS 8–7
(LO 4)

The following facts were extracted from Orion Corp.'s comparative balance sheets:

QS 8–8
(LO 5)

	19X2	19X1
Accounts receivable	514,000	426,000
Sales (net)	1,600,000	1,200,000

Compute the accounts receivable turnover for 19X2.

EXERCISES

Prepare general journal entries to record the following transactions involving Best Plumbing's short-term investments, all of which occurred during 19X1:

Exercise 8–1
Transactions involving short-term investments
(LO 1)

a. On April 15, paid $90,000 to purchase $90,000 of Westside Company's short-term (60-day) notes payable, which are dated April 15 and pay interest at an 8% rate.

b. On May 10, bought 600 shares of American Steel common stock at $10^{1}/_{2}$ plus a $126 brokerage fee.

c. On June 15, received a check from Westside Company in payment of the principal and 60 days' interest on the notes purchased in transaction a.

d. On June 25, paid $75,000 to purchase Stockard Corporation's 7% notes payable, $75,000 principal value, due June 25, 19X2.

e. On August 16, received a $1.25 per share cash dividend on the American Steel common stock purchased in transaction b.

f. On September 3, sold 300 shares of American Steel common stock for $15 per share, less a $90 brokerage fee.

g. On December 26, received a check from Stockard Corporation for six months' interest on the notes purchased in transaction d.

Exercise 8–2
Recording fair values of short-term investments
(LO 1)

On December 31, 19X1, Compustat Company held the following short-term investments in securities available for sale:

	Cost	Fair Value
J.C. Penney Company common stock	$37,200	$41,100
Exxon Corporation bonds payable	50,400	48,500
Transamerica Corporation notes payable ..	69,600	63,900
Times Mirror Company common stock ...	85,500	84,100

Compustat had no short-term investments prior to 19X1. Prepare the December 31 adjusting entry to record the change in fair value of the investments.

Exercise 8–3
Adjusting the short-term investment accounts to reflect changes in fair value
(LO 1)

Rexlon Company's annual accounting period ends on December 31. The total cost and fair (market) value of the company's short-term investments in securities available for sale were as follows:

	Total Cost	Total Fair Value
Short-term investments in securities available for sale:		
On December 31, 19X1	$56,250	$52,500
On December 31, 19X2	63,750	68,125

Prepare the December 31, 19X2, adjusting entry to update the fair values of the short-term investments.

Exercise 8–4
Credit card transactions
(LO 2)

Nickels Company allows customers to use two credit cards in charging purchases. With the Southwest Bank card, Nickels receives an immediate credit on depositing sales receipts in its checking account. Southwest Bank assesses a 3% service charge for credit card sales. The second credit card that Nickels accepts is Americard. Nickels sends their accumulated receipts to Americard on a weekly basis and is paid by Americard approximately 15 days later. Americard charges 2.5% of sales for using its card. Prepare entries in journal form to record the following credit card transactions of Nickels Company:

May 4 Sold merchandise for $2,500, accepting the customers' Southwest Bank cards. At the end of the day, the Southwest Bank card receipts were deposited in the company's account at the bank.

   5 Sold merchandise for $550, accepting the customer's Americard.

  12 Mailed $9,520 of credit card receipts to Americard, requesting payment.

  28 Received Americard's check for the May 12 billing, less the normal service charge.

Exercise 8–5
Subsidiary ledger accounts
(LO 3)

Littlefield Corporation recorded the following transactions during April 19X1:

Apr.	2	Accounts Receivable—Barbara Fowler	2,500.00	
		Sales		2,500.00
	10	Accounts Receivable—Robert Guerrero	260.00	
		Sales		260.00
	18	Accounts Receivable—Chris Layton	1,800.00	
		Sales		1,800.00
	23	Sales Returns and Allowances	562.00	
		Accounts Receivable—Chris Layton		562.00
	30	Accounts Receivable—Barbara Fowler	1,125.00	
		Sales		1,125.00

Required

1. Open a General Ledger having T-accounts for Accounts Receivable, Sales, and Sales Returns and Allowances. Also, open a subsidiary Accounts Receivable Ledger having a T-account for each customer. Post the preceding entries to the general ledger accounts and the customer accounts.

2. List the balances of the accounts in the subsidiary ledger, total the balances, and compare the total with the balance of the Accounts Receivable controlling account.

On December 31, at the end of its annual accounting period, a company estimated its bad debts as one-fourth of 1% of its $1,240,000 of credit sales made during the year, and made an addition to its Allowance for Doubtful Accounts equal to that amount. On the following February 3, management decided the $1,390 account of Colin Smith was uncollectible and wrote it off as a bad debt. Two months later, on April 2, Smith unexpectedly paid the amount previously written off. Give the journal entries required to record these events.

Exercise 8–6
Allowance for doubtful accounts
(LO 3)

At the end of each year, a company uses the simplified balance sheet approach to estimate bad debts. On December 31, 19X1, it has outstanding accounts receivable of $176,600 and estimates that 3.5% will be uncollectible. (a) Give the entry to record bad debts expense for 19X1 under the assumption that the Allowance for Doubtful Accounts had a $1,470 credit balance before the adjustment. (b) Give the entry under the assumption that the Allowance for Doubtful Accounts has a $1,235 debit balance before the adjustment.

Exercise 8–7
Bad debts expense
(LO 3)

Prepare journal entries to record these transactions:

Exercise 8–8
Dishonor of a note
(LO 4)

Aug. 12   Accepted a $4,500, three-month, 10% note dated today from Clive Nelson in granting a time extension on his past-due account.

Nov. 12   Nelson dishonored his note when presented for payment.

Dec. 31   After exhausting all legal means of collecting, wrote off the account of Nelson against the Allowance for Doubtful Accounts.

On March 31, Jester Company had accounts receivable in the amount of $82,500. Prepare journal entries to record the following transactions for April. Also, prepare any footnotes to the April 30 financial statements that should be reported as a result of these transactions.

Exercise 8–9
Selling and pledging accounts receivable
(LO 5)

Apr. 5   Sold merchandise to customers on credit, $23,600.

8   Sold $6,800 of accounts receivable to Union Bank. Union Bank charges a 1.5% fee.

17   Received payments from customers, $5,200.

24   Borrowed $15,000 from Union Bank, pledging $22,000 of accounts receivable as security for the loan.

The following information is from the financial statements of Fine Furniture Company:

Exercise 8–10
Accounts receivable turnover
(LO 5)

	19X3	19X2	19X1
Net sales	$1,080,000	$860,000	$750,000
Accounts receivable (December 31)	81,900	80,100	76,800

Calculate Fine Furniture's accounts receivable turnover for 19X2 and 19X3. Compare the two results and give a possible explanation for any significant change.

PROBLEMS

Problem 8–1
Accounting for short-term investments
(LO 1)

Ridgeway Company had no short-term investments prior to 19X1, but had the following transactions involving short-term investments in securities available for sale during 19X1:

Jan. 3 Purchased 1,200 shares of General Mills, Inc., common stock at 62¼ plus a $1,494 brokerage fee.

26 Paid $250,000 to buy six-month U.S. Treasury bills, $250,000 principal amount, 6%, dated January 26.

Mar. 11 Purchased 3,000 shares of Texaco Inc. common stock at 59½ plus a $3,570 brokerage fee.

May 4 Purchased 700 shares of Unisys Corp. common stock at 11½ plus a $161 brokerage fee.

July 28 Received a check for the principal and accrued interest on the U.S. Treasury bills that matured on July 26.

29 Received a $1.60 per share cash dividend on the General Mills common shares.

Aug. 4 Sold 600 shares of General Mills common stock at 76 less a $912 brokerage fee.

19 Received a $3.10 per share cash dividend on the Texaco common shares.

Oct. 28 Received a $1.75 per share cash dividend on the remaining General Mills common shares owned.

Nov. 19 Received a $2.95 per share cash dividend on the Texaco common shares.

On December 31, 19X1, the market prices of the securities held by Ridgeway were General Mills, 79¼; Texaco, 61⅞; and Unisys, 14¾.

Required

Preparation component:

1. Prepare journal entries to record the preceding transactions.
2. Prepare a schedule to compare the cost and fair (market) values of Ridgeway's short-term investments in securities available for sale.

CHECK FIGURE:
Unrealized Holding Gain
(Loss), $15,122 Cr.

3. Prepare an adjusting entry, if necessary, to record the fair value adjustment of the short-term investments.

Analytical component:

4. Explain the balance sheet presentation of the fair value adjustment.
5. How did the short-term investments of Ridgeway Company affect the reported profitability for the year and the final equity figure?

Problem 8–2
Credit sales and credit card sales
(LO 2)

Werner Company allows a few customers to make purchases on credit. Other customers may use either of two credit cards. West Bank deducts a 2% service charge for sales on its credit card but credits the checking accounts of its commercial customers immediately when credit card receipts are deposited. Werner deposits the West Bank credit card receipts at the close of each business day.

When customers use SilverCard, Werner accumulates the receipts for several days before submitting them to SilverCard for payment. SilverCard deducts a 3% service charge and usually pays within one week of being billed. (Terms of all credit sales are 2/15, n/30; all sales are recorded at the gross price.) Werner completed the following transactions.

June 3 Sold merchandise on credit to Sandra Kish for $985.

9 Sold merchandise for $3,980 to customers who used their West Bank credit cards. Sold merchandise for $4,300 to customers who used their SilverCards.

11 Sold merchandise for $2,460 to customers who used their SilverCards.

June 13 Wrote off the account of John Farlow against Allowance for Doubtful Accounts. The $278 balance in Farlow's account stemmed from a credit sale in October of last year.

14 The SilverCard receipts accumulated since June 9 were submitted to the credit card company for payment.

18 Received Kish's check paying for the purchase of June 3.

23 Received the amount due from SilverCard.

Required

Prepare journal entries to record the preceding transactions and events.

On December 31, 19X1, Hallmart Company's records showed the following results for the year:

Problem 8–3
Estimating bad debts expense
(LO 3)

Cash sales	$ 601,250
Credit sales	1,178,000

In addition, the unadjusted trial balance included the following items:

Accounts receivable	$356,700 debit
Allowance for doubtful accounts	5,250 debit

Required

1. Prepare the adjusting entry needed on the books of Hallmart to recognize bad debts under each of the following independent assumptions:

   a. Bad debts are estimated to be 1% of total sales.

   b. Bad debts are estimated to be 2% of credit sales.

   c. An analysis suggests that 5% of outstanding accounts receivable on December 31, 19X1, will become uncollectible.

2. Show how Accounts Receivable and the Allowance for Doubtful Accounts would appear on the December 31, 19X1, balance sheet given the facts in requirement 1(b).

3. Show how Accounts Receivable and the Allowance for Doubtful Accounts would appear on the December 31, 19X1, balance sheet given the facts in requirement 1(c).

CHECK FIGURE:
Bad Debts Expense, (1.a.)
$17,792.50 Dr.

Artex Company had credit sales of $1.3 million in 19X1. On December 31, 19X1, the company's Allowance for Doubtful Accounts had a credit balance of $6,700. The accountant for Artex has prepared a schedule of the December 31, 19X1, accounts receivable by age, and on the basis of past experience has estimated the percentage of the receivables in each age category that will become uncollectible. This information is summarized as follows:

Problem 8–4
Aging accounts receivable
(LO 3)

December 31, 19X1 Accounts Receivable	Age of Accounts Receivable	Expected Percentage Uncollectible
$365,000	Not due (under 30 days)	1.00%
177,000	1 to 30 days past due	2.50
38,000	31 to 60 days past due	7.75
20,000	61 to 90 days past due	45.00
6,000	over 90 days past due	70.00

Required

Preparation component:

1. Calculate the amount that should appear in the December 31, 19X1, balance sheet as the Allowance for Doubtful Accounts.

2. Prepare the journal entry to record bad debts expense for 19X1.

CHECK FIGURE:
Bad Debts Expense, $17,520 Dr.

Analysis component:

3. On June 30, 19X2, Artex concluded that a customer's $1,875 receivable (created in 19X1) was uncollectible and that the account should be written off. What effect will this action have on Artex's 19X2 net income? Explain your answer.

Problem 8–5
Recording accounts receivable transactions and bad debt adjustments
(LO 3)

Gilcrest Company began operations on January 1, 19X1. During the next two years, the company completed a number of transactions involving credit sales, accounts receivable collections, and bad debts. These transactions are summarized as follows:

19X1

a. Sold merchandise on credit for $817,500, terms n/30.

b. Wrote off uncollectible accounts receivable in the amount of $12,500.

c. Received cash of $476,500 in payment of outstanding accounts receivable.

d. In adjusting the accounts on December 31, concluded that 1.5% of the outstanding accounts receivable would become uncollectible.

19X2

e. Sold merchandise on credit for $1,017,000, terms n/30.

f. Wrote off uncollectible accounts receivable in the amount of $19,200.

CHECK FIGURE:
19X2 Bad Debts Expense, $22,339.50 Dr.

g. Received cash of $788,500 in payment of outstanding accounts receivable.

h. In adjusting the accounts on December 31, concluded that 1.5% of the outstanding accounts receivable would become uncollectible.

Required

Prepare journal entries to record the 19X1 and 19X2 summarized transactions of Gilcrest and the adjusting entries to record bad debts expense at the end of each year.

Problem 8–6
Analysis and journalizing of notes receivable transactions
(LO 4, 5)

Following are transactions of Brackenridge Company:

19X1

Dec. 1 Accepted a $6,000, 90-day, 10% note dated this day in granting Tish McCoy a time extension on her past-due account.

      31 Made an adjusting entry to record the accrued interest on the McCoy note.

      31 Closed the Interest Earned account.

19X2

Mar. 1 Received McCoy's payment for the principal and interest on the note dated December 1.

      5 Accepted a $3,200, 9%, 60-day note dated this day in granting a time extension on the past-due account of Gary Roster.

      17 Accepted a $1,000, 90-day, 10% note dated this day in granting T. Z. Hanks a time extension on his past-due account.

      31 Discounted, with recourse, the Roster note at First Bank at a cost of $20. The transaction was considered to be a loan.

May   5 Received notice from First Bank that Roster defaulted on the note. Paid the bank the principal plus interest due on the note. (Hint: Create an account receivable for the maturity value of the note.)

June 16 Hanks dishonored his note when presented for payment.

July 5 Received payment from Roster of the maturity value of his dishonored note plus interest for 60 days beyond maturity at 9%.

      16 Accepted a $3,400, 90-day, 12% note dated this day in granting a time extension on the past-due account of Stanley Frasier.

Aug. 6 Accepted a $1,300, 60-day, 10% note dated this day in granting Susan Faltinski a time extension on her past-due account.

Aug. 31   Discounted, without recourse, the Faltinski note at First Bank at a cost of $10.

Oct. 14   Received payment of principal plus interest from Frasier for the note of July 16.

Dec. 1   Wrote off the T. Z. Hanks account against Allowance for Doubtful Accounts.

Required

Preparation component:

Prepare journal entries to record these transactions.

Analysis component:

What reporting is necessary when a business discounts notes receivable with recourse and these notes have not reached maturity by the end of the fiscal period? Explain the reason for this requirement and what accounting principle is being satisfied.

Reitz Company has relatively large idle cash balances and invests them in common stocks that it holds available for sale. Following is a series of events and other facts relevant to the short-term investment activity of the company:

Problem 8–7
Entries and fair value adjustments for short-term investments
(LO 1)

19X1

Mar. 2   Purchased 1,600 shares of Borden, Inc., at $18.75 plus $900 commission.

Apr. 6   Purchased 700 shares of Chrysler Corporation at $56.00 plus $1,176 commission.

Aug. 15   Purchased 1,800 shares of Pennzoil Company at $55.50 plus $2,997 commission.

Dec. 31   These per share market values were known for the stocks in the portfolio: Borden, $20.15; Chrysler, $49.00; Pennzoil, $57.25.

19X2

Jan. 10   Sold 1,600 shares of Borden at $21.75 less $1,044 commission.

May 3   Sold 1,800 shares of Pennzoil at $49.50 less $2,673 commission.

Oct. 22   Purchased 2,000 shares of H. J. Heinz Company at $36.25 plus $2,175 commission.

Nov. 5   Purchased 800 shares of Reebok Intl. Ltd. at $28.00 plus $672 commission.

Dec. 31   These per share market values were known for the stocks in the portfolio: Chrysler, $36.75; Heinz, $32.50; Reebok, $30.00.

19X3

Feb. 19   Purchased 3,800 shares of Continental Airlines at $23.00 plus $2,622 commission.

Apr. 11   Sold 2,000 shares of Heinz at $31.25 less a $1,875 commission.

Aug. 9   Sold 700 shares of Chrysler at $40.00 less an $840 commission.

Sept. 6   Purchased 2,000 shares of Goodyear Tire & Rubber at $47.50 plus a $2,850 commission.

Dec. 12   Sold 800 shares of Reebok at $45.50 less a $1,092 commission.

31   These per share market values were known for the stocks in the portfolio: Continental Airlines, $25.75; Goodyear, $56.50.

Required

1. Prepare journal entries to record the events and any year-end adjustments needed to record the fair values of the short-term investments.

2. Prepare a schedule that shows the total cost, total fair value adjustment, and total fair value of the investments at the end of each year.

3. For each year, prepare a schedule that shows the realized gains and losses included in earnings and the total unrealized gain or loss at the end of each year.

CHECK FIGURE:
12/31/X3, Short-Term Investments, Fair Value Adjustment, $46,376 Dr.

CRITICAL THINKING: ESSAYS, PROBLEMS, AND CASES

Analytical Essays

AE 8–2
(LO 1)

Cloron Company did not own any short-term investments prior to 19X2. After purchasing some short-term investments in 19X2, the company's accountant made the following December 31, 19X2, adjusting entry:

Dec.	31	Short-Term Investments, Fair Value Adjustment	5,670.00	
		Holding Gain (Loss)		5,670.00
		To record fair value of short-term investments in		
		securities available for sale.		

When Cloron's accountant reviewed the year-end adjustments with an office manager of the company, the accountant commented that the previous adjustment might have been different if the company had owned short-term investments on December 31, 19X1. The office manager thought the accountant must be confused. The manager said that the December 31, 19X2, adjustment was supposed to record a gain that occurred during 19X2, and therefore should not be affected by any events that occurred during 19X1.

Required

Explain why the accountant's comment is correct.

AE 8–2
(LO 3)

Review the facts about Hallmart Company in Problem 8–3.

Required

Recall that Allowance for Doubtful Accounts is a contra asset account. Nevertheless, Hallmart's unadjusted trial balance shows that this account has a $5,250 debit balance. Explain how this contra asset account could have a debit balance.

In Problem 8–3, requirement 1(c) indicates that 5% of the outstanding accounts receivable ($356,700 × 5% = $17,835) will become uncollectible. Given this conclusion, explain why the adjusting entry should not include a $17,835 credit to Accounts Receivable.

Business Communications Case

(LO 3)

As the accountant for JWest Company, you recently attended a sales managers' meeting devoted to a discussion of the company's credit policies. At the meeting, you reported that bad debts expense for the past year was estimated to be $35,000 and accounts receivable at the end of the year amounted to $645,000 less a $21,000 allowance for doubtful accounts. Chris Albertson, one of the sales managers, expressed confusion over the fact that bad debts expense and the allowance for doubtful accounts were different amounts. To save time at the meeting, you agreed to discuss the matter with Albertson after the meeting.

Because the meeting lasted longer than expected, Albertson had to leave early to catch a plane back to his sales district. As a result, you need to write a memorandum to him explaining why a difference in bad debts expense and the allowance for doubtful accounts is not unusual. (Assume that the company estimates bad debts expense to be 2% of sales.)

Financial Reporting Problem

(LO 3)

Builders Depot has been in business for six years and has used the direct write-off method of accounting for bad debts. The following information is available from the accounting records for the first five years:

	19X5	19X4	19X3	19X2	19X1
Sales	$2,243,000	$1,170,000	$2,600,000	$3,400,000	$950,000
Net income	336,200	175,000	390,200	509,500	142,200
Bad debts written off					
during year	13,940	18,410	47,960	11,720	2,100
Bad debts by year of sale* . .	21,300	11,990	29,790	32,910	10,640

*Results from classifying bad debt losses so that the losses appear in the same years as the sales that produced them. For example, the $21,300 for 19X5 includes $12,500 of bad debts that became uncollectible during 19X6.

You are the manager of Builders Depot and want to change the method of accounting for bad debts from the direct write-off method to the allowance method. Kelly Skyles, the president of the company, feels this is not necessary. Prepare a five-year schedule for Skyles showing:

a. Net income if bad debts expense is defined to be bad debts by year of sale.

b. The dollar amount of difference between net income using the direct write-off method and the answer to requirement a.

c. The answer to requirement b as a percentage of the answer to requirement a.

d. Bad debts by year of sale as a percentage of sales.

e. Bad debts written off during the year as a percentage of sales.

Use the schedule to support your argument for using the allowance method to account for bad debts.

Refer to the financial statements and related disclosures from Apple Computer, Inc.'s 1993 annual report in Appendix F. Based on your examination of this information, answer the following:

Financial Statement Analysis Case

(LO 1, 5)

1. Apple's most liquid assets include cash and cash equivalents, short-term investments, and accounts receivable. What total amount of those assets did Apple have on September 24, 1993?

2. Express Apple's total liquid assets as of September 24, 1993, (as previously defined) as a percentage of current liabilities. Do the same for 1992. Comment on Apple's ability to satisfy current liabilities at the end of fiscal year 1993, as compared to the end of fiscal year 1992.

3. What criteria did Apple use to classify items as cash equivalents? Short-term investments?

4. Calculate Apple's accounts receivable turnover for 1993. (In making the calculations, use accounts receivable net of allowance for doubtful accounts.)

ANSWERS TO PROGRESS CHECKS

8–1 Securities held to maturity are reported at cost; investments in trading securities are reported at fair (market) value.

8–2 The equity section of the balance sheet.

8–3 The income statement.

8–4 If cash is received as soon as copies of credit card sales receipts are deposited in the bank, the business debits Cash at the time of the sale. If the business does not receive payment until after it submits the receipts to the credit card company, it debits Accounts Receivable at the time of the sale.

8–5 The credit card expenses are recorded when the cash is received from the credit card company; however, they are incurred at the time of the related sales.

8–6 An adjusting entry must be made to satisfy the matching principle. The credit card expense must be reported in the same period as the sale.

8–7 Bad debts expense must be matched with the sales that gave rise to the accounts receivable. This requires that companies estimate bad debts before they learn which accounts are uncollectible.

8–8 Realizable value.

8–9 The estimated amount of bad debts expense cannot be credited to the Accounts Receivable account because the specific customer accounts that will prove uncollectible cannot be identified and removed from the subsidiary Accounts Receivable Ledger. If the controlling account were credited directly, its balance would not equal the sum of the subsidiary account balances.

8–10

19X1			
Dec. 31	Bad Debts Expense	5,702	
	Allow. for Doubtful Acc.		5,702

8–11

19X2			
Jan. 10	Allowance for Doubtful Accounts	300	
	Acc. Rec.—Felix Arthur		300
Apr. 12	Acc. Rec.—Felix Arthur	300	
	Allow. for Doubtful Acc.		300
12	Cash	300	
	Acc. Rec.—Felix Arthur		300

8–12

19X1

| Dec. 16 | Notes Receivable | 7,000 | |
| | Sales | | 7,000 |

Dec. 31	Interest Receivable	35	
	Interest Earned		35
	$7,000 \times 12\% \times 15/360$		

8–13

19X2

Mar. 16	Acc. Rec.—White Corp.	7,210	
	Interest Earned		175
	Interest Receivable		35
	Notes Receivable		7,000

8–14 Alternatives are (1) selling their accounts receivable to a factor, and (2) pledging the accounts receivable as security for a loan. The entries to record these transactions would take the following form:

(1) Cash

  Factoring Fee Expense

    Accounts Receivable

(2) Cash

    Notes Payable

8–15 Receivable turnover =

$$\frac{140,327,757}{(11,679,222 + 8,849,326)/2} = 13.67 \text{ times}$$

CHAPTER 9

Inventories and Cost of Goods Sold

*C*an the choice of an accounting method affect the amount of income or loss that a company reports? Often the choice of one acceptable accounting approach over another can have a dramatic impact on net income. To illustrate, in 1994 Mobil Corporation changed the method it used to account for inventory and disclosed that the change caused a $680 million charge against revenues. The following information was extracted from the news release prepared by Mobil. Note that Mobil's change in accounting method (principle) for inventory required that the company restate its results from a net income of $733 million to $53 million for the first six months of 1994.

FAIRFAX, VA, July 29—Mobil Corporation announced today that it is making a change in its method of applying the lower-of-cost-or-market test for crude oil and product inventories. Accordingly, it will reduce previously reported first quarter 1994, and therefore year-to-date, net income by a $680 million after-tax, noncash charge. This inventory accounting change was adopted by Mobil at its board meeting today. . . . The previously reported 1994 first quarter and estimated six months net income will be restated as follows (in millions of dollars):

	Three Months Ended March 31, 1994	Six Months Ended June 30, 1994 Estimated
Net income as previously reported	$ 535	$ 733
Cumulative effect of change in accounting principle	(680)	(680)
Restated net income (loss)	$ (145)	$ 53

LEARNING OBJECTIVES

After studying Chapter 9, you should be able to:

1. Describe *(a)* how the matching principle relates to accounting for merchandise, *(b)* the types of items that should be included in merchandise inventory, and *(c)* the elements that make up the cost of merchandise.

2. Calculate the cost of an inventory based on *(a)* specific invoice prices, *(b)* weighted-average cost, *(c)* FIFO, and *(d)* LIFO, and explain the financial statement effects of choosing one method over the others.

3. Explain the effect of an inventory error on the income statements of the current and succeeding years.

4. Describe perpetual inventory systems and prepare entries to record merchandise transactions and maintain subsidiary inventory records under a perpetual inventory system.

5. Calculate the lower-of-cost-or-market amount of an inventory.

6. Use the retail method and the gross profit method to estimate an inventory and calculate merchandise turnover and days' stock on hand.

7. Define or explain the words and phrases listed in the chapter glossary.

The operations of merchandising businesses involve the purchase and resale of tangible goods. In Chapter 5, when we first introduced the topic of accounting for merchandisers, we left several important matters for later consideration. In this chapter, we return to the topic and examine the methods businesses use at the end of each period to assign dollar amounts to merchandise inventory and to cost of goods sold. The principles and procedures that we explain in this chapter are used in department stores, grocery stores, automobile dealerships, and any other businesses that purchase goods for resale. Since these procedures affect the reported amounts of income, assets, and equity, understanding the fundamental concepts of inventory accounting will enhance your ability to use and interpret financial statements.

The assets that a business buys and holds for resale are called *merchandise inventory*. As a rule, the items held as merchandise inventory are sold within one year or one operating cycle. Therefore, merchandise inventory is a current asset, usually the largest current asset on the balance sheet of a merchandiser.

MATCHING MERCHANDISE COSTS WITH REVENUES

LO 1

Describe *(a)* how the matching principle relates to accounting for merchandise; *(b)* the types of items that should be included in merchandise inventory; and *(c)* the elements that make up the cost of merchandise.

Accounting for inventories affects both the balance sheet and the income statement. However, "the major objective [in accounting for the goods in the inventory] is the matching of appropriate costs against revenues in order that there may be a proper determination of the realized income."[1] The matching process is already a familiar topic. For inventories, it consists of deciding how much of the cost of the goods that were available for sale during a period should be deducted from the period's revenue and how much should be carried forward as inventory to be matched against a future period's revenue.

In a periodic inventory system, when the cost of goods available for sale is allocated between cost of goods sold and ending inventory, the key problem is assigning a cost to the ending inventory. Remember, however, that by assigning a cost to the ending inventory, you are also determining cost of goods sold. This is true because the ending inventory is subtracted from the cost of goods available for sale to determine cost of goods sold.

---

[1]FASB, *Accounting Standards—Current Text* (Norwalk, CT, 1994), sec. I78.104. First published as *Accounting Research Bulletin No. 43*, chap. 4, par. 4

The merchandise inventory of a business includes all goods owned by the business and held for sale, regardless of where the goods may be located at the time inventory is counted. In applying this rule, most items present no problem. All that is required is to see that all items are counted, that nothing is omitted, and that nothing is counted more than once. However, goods in transit, goods sold but not delivered, goods on consignment, and obsolete and damaged goods require special attention.

Should merchandise be included in the inventory of a business if the goods are in transit from a supplier to a business on the date the business takes an inventory? The answer to this question depends on whether the rights and risks of ownership have passed from the supplier to the purchaser. If ownership has passed to the purchaser, they should be included in the purchaser's inventory. If the buyer is responsible for paying the freight charges, ownership usually passes as soon as the goods are loaded on the means of transportation. (As mentioned in Chapter 5, the terms would be FOB the seller's factory or warehouse.) On the other hand, if the seller is to pay the freight charges, ownership passes when the goods arrive at their destination (FOB destination).

Goods on consignment are goods shipped by their owner (known as the **consignor**) to another person or firm (called the **consignee**) who is to sell the goods for the owner. Consigned goods belong to the consignor and should appear on the consignor's inventory. For example, **Score Board Inc.** pays sports celebrities such as Shaquille O'Neal and Joe DiMaggio to sign memorabilia. The autographed baseballs, jerseys, photos, and so on, are then offered to the shopping networks on consignment as well as sold through catalogs and dealers.

Damaged goods and deteriorated or obsolete goods should not be counted in the inventory if they are not salable. If such goods can be sold at a reduced price, they should be included in the inventory at a conservative estimate of their **net realizable value** (sales price less the cost of making the sale). Thus, the accounting period in which the goods deteriorated, were damaged, or became obsolete suffers the resultant loss.

As applied to merchandise, cost means the sum of the expenditures and charges directly or indirectly incurred in bringing an article to its existing condition and location.[2] Therefore, the cost of an inventory item includes the invoice price, less any discount, plus any additional or incidental costs necessary to put the item into place and condition for sale. The additional costs may include import duties, transportation-in, storage, insurance, and any other related costs such as those incurred during an aging process (for example, the aging of wine).

All of these costs should be included in the cost of merchandise. When calculating the cost of a merchandise inventory, however, some concerns do not include the incidental costs of acquiring merchandise. They price the inventory on the basis of invoice prices only. As a result, the incidental costs are allocated to cost of goods sold during the period in which they are incurred.

In theory, a share of each incidental cost should be assigned to every unit purchased. This causes a portion of each to be carried forward in the inventory to be matched against the revenue of the period in which the inventory is sold. However, the effort of computing costs on such a precise basis may outweigh the benefit from the extra accuracy. Therefore, many businesses take advantage of the *materiality principle* and charge such costs to cost of goods sold.

ITEMS TO INCLUDE IN MERCHANDISE INVENTORY

ELEMENTS OF MERCHANDISE COST

PRINCIPLE APPLICATION
Materiality Principle, p. 320
In 1993, Colgate-Palmolive Company reported net sales of $7,141.3 million, cost of sales of $3,728.9 million, and net income of $189.9 million. End-of-year inventories were $678.0 million and total assets were $5,761.2 million. Consider whether a $1 million or $10 million error in allocating a cost between inventory and cost of goods sold could be ignored under the materiality principle. (In general, determining whether an amount is material is a matter of professional judgment.)

---

[2]Ibid., sec. I78.402. First published as *Accounting Research Bulletin No. 43*, ch. 4, par. 5.

Illustration 9-1   Inventory Tickets Used to Tag Inventory Items as They Are Counted

INVENTORY TICKET NO. _786_	Quantity counted _____
Item _____	Sales price $ _____
Counted by _____	Cost price $ _____
Checked by _____	Purchase date _____

TAKING AN ENDING INVENTORY

As you learned in Chapter 5, when a *periodic inventory system* is used, the dollar amount of the ending inventory is determined as follows: count the units of each product on hand, multiply the count for each product by its cost per unit, and add the costs for all products. In making the count, items are less likely to be counted twice or omitted from the count if you use prenumbered **inventory tickets** like the one in Illustration 9–1.

Before beginning the inventory count, a sufficient number of the tickets, at least one for each product on hand, is issued to the employees who make the count. Next, the employees count the quantity of each product. From the count and the price tag attached to the merchandise, the required inventory tickets are filled in and attached to the counted items. By the time the count is completed, inventory tickets should have been attached to all counted items. After checking for uncounted items, the employees remove the tickets and send them to the accounting department. To ensure that no ticket is lost or left attached to merchandise, the accounting department verifies that all the prenumbered tickets issued have been returned.

In the accounting department, the unit and cost data on the tickets are aggregated by multiplying the number of units of each product by its unit cost. This gives the dollar amount of each product in the inventory and the total for all the products is the dollar total of the inventory.

Progress Check

(Answers to Progress Checks are provided at the end of the chapter.)

9-1   Which accounting principle most directly governs the allocation of cost of goods available for sale between the ending inventory and cost of goods sold?

9-2   If Campbell sells goods to Thompson, FOB Campbell's factory, and the goods are still in transit from Campbell to Thompson, which company should include the goods in its inventory?

9-3   Kramer Gallery purchased an original painting for $11,400. Additional costs incurred in obtaining and offering the artwork for sale included $130 for transportation-in, $150 for import duties, $100 for insurance during shipment, $180 for advertising costs, $400 for framing, and $800 for sales salaries. In calculating the cost of inventory, what total cost should be assigned to the painting?   (a) $11,400;   (b) $11,530; (c) $11,780;   (d) $12,180.

ASSIGNING COSTS TO INVENTORY ITEMS

One of the major issues in accounting for merchandise involves determining the unit cost amounts that will be assigned to items in the inventory. When all units are purchased at the same unit cost, this process is easy. However, when identical items are purchased at different costs, a problem arises as to which costs apply to the ending inventory and which apply to the goods sold. There are four commonly used methods of assigning costs to goods in the ending inventory and to goods sold. They are (1) specific invoice prices; (2) weighted-average cost; (3) first-in, first-out; and (4) last-in, first-out. All four methods are generally accepted.

To illustrate the four methods, assume that a company has 12 units of Product X on hand at the end of its annual accounting period. Also, assume that the inventory at the beginning of the year and the purchases during the year were as follows:

LO 2

Calculate the cost of an inventory based on (a) specific invoice prices, (b) weighted-average cost, (c) FIFO, and (d) LIFO, and explain the financial statement effects of choosing one method over the others.

Jan.	1	Beginning inventory	10 units @ $100 =	$1,000
Mar.	13	Purchased	15 units @ $108 =	1,620
Aug.	17	Purchased	20 units @ $120 =	2,400
Nov.	10	Purchased	10 units @ $125 =	1,250
Total		....	55 units	$6,270

Specific Invoice Prices

When each item in an inventory can be clearly related to a specific purchase and its invoice, **specific invoice inventory pricing** may be used to assign costs. For example, assume that 6 of the 12 unsold units of Product X were from the November purchase and 6 were from the August purchase. With this information, specific invoice prices can be used to assign costs to the ending inventory and to goods sold as follows:

Total cost of 55 units available for sale		$6,270
Less ending inventory priced by means of specific invoices:		
6 units from the November purchase at $125 each	$750	
6 units from the August purchase at $120 each	720	
12 units in the ending inventory		1,470
Cost of goods sold		$4,800

Weighted Average

When using **weighted-average inventory pricing,** multiply the per unit costs of the beginning inventory and of each purchase by the number of units in the beginning inventory and each purchase. Then, divide the total of these amounts by the total number of units available for sale to find the weighted-average cost per unit as follows:

10 units @ $100 = $1,000
15 units @ $108 = 1,620
20 units @ $120 = 2,400
10 units @ $125 = 1,250
55                $6,270
$6,270/55 = $114 weighted-average cost per unit

After determining the weighted-average cost per unit, use this average to assign costs to the inventory and to the units sold as follows:

Total cost of 55 units available for sale	$6,270
Less ending inventory priced on a weighted average	
cost basis: 12 units at $114 each	1,368
Cost of goods sold	$4,902

First-In, First-Out

First-in, first-out inventory pricing (FIFO) assumes the items in the beginning inventory are sold first. Additional sales are assumed to come in the order in which they were purchased. Thus, the costs of the last items received are assigned to the ending inventory, and the remaining costs are assigned to goods sold. For example, when first-in, first-out is used, the costs of Product X are assigned to the inventory and goods sold as follows:

Total cost of 55 units available for sale		$6,270
Less ending inventory priced on a basis of FIFO:		
10 units from the November purchase at $125 each	$1,250	
2 units from the August purchase at $120 each	240	
12 units in the ending inventory		1,490
Cost of goods sold		$4,780

Understand that FIFO is acceptable whether or not the physical flow of goods actually follows a first-in, first-out pattern. The physical flow of products depends on the nature of the product and the way the products are stored. If a product is perishable (for example, fresh tomatoes), the business attempts to sell them in a first-in, first-out pattern. Other products, for example, bolts or screws kept in a large bin, may tend to be sold on a last-in, first-out basis. In either case, the FIFO method of allocating cost may be used.

Last-In, First-Out

Under the **last-in, first-out inventory pricing (LIFO)** method, the costs of the last goods received are charged to cost of goods sold and matched with revenue from sales. Again, this method is acceptable even though the physical flow of goods may not be on a last-in, first-out basis.

One argument for the use of LIFO is based on the fact that a going concern must replace the inventory items it sells. When goods are sold, replacements are purchased. Thus, a sale causes the replacement of goods. From this point of view, a correct matching of costs with revenues would be to match replacement costs with the sales that made replacements necessary. Although the costs of the most recent purchases are not quite the same as replacement costs, they usually are close approximations of replacement costs. Because LIFO assigns the most recent purchase costs to the income statement, LIFO (compared to FIFO or weighted average) comes closest to matching replacement costs with revenues.

Under LIFO, costs are assigned to the 12 remaining units of Product X and to the goods sold as follows:

Total cost of 55 units available for sale		$6,270
Less ending inventory priced on a basis of LIFO:		
10 units in the beginning inventory at $100 each	$1,000	
2 units from the March purchase at $108 each	216	
12 units in the ending inventory		1,216
Cost of goods sold		$5,054

Notice that when LIFO is used to match costs and revenues, the ending inventory cost is the cost of the oldest 12 units.

	Specific Invoice Prices	Weighted Average	FIFO	LIFO
Sales	$6,000	$6,000	$6,000	$6,000
Cost of goods sold:				
Merchandise inventory, January 1	$1,000	$1,000	$1,000	$1,000
Purchases	5,270	5,270	5,270	5,270
Cost of goods available for sale	$6,270	$6,270	$6,270	$6,270
Merchandise inventory, December 31	1,470	1,368	1,490	1,216
Cost of goods sold	$4,800	$4,902	$4,780	$5,054
Gross profit	$1,200	$1,098	$1,220	$ 946
Operating expenses	500	500	500	500
Income before taxes	$ 700	$ 598	$ 720	$ 446
Income taxes expense (30%)	210	179	216	134
Net income	$ 490	$ 419	$ 504	$ 312

Illustration 9–2
The Income Statement Effects of Alternative Inventory Pricing Methods

Comparison of Methods

In a stable market where prices remain unchanged, the choice of an inventory pricing method is not important. When prices are unchanged over a period of time, all methods give the same cost figures. However, in a changing market where prices are rising or falling, each method may give a different result. These differences are shown in Illustration 9–2, where we assume that Product X sales were $6,000 and operating expenses were $500.

In Illustration 9–2, note the differences that resulted from the choice of an inventory pricing method. Because purchase prices were rising throughout the period, FIFO resulted in the lowest cost of goods sold, the highest gross profit, and the highest net income. On the other hand, LIFO resulted in the highest cost of goods sold, the lowest gross profit, and the lowest net income. As you would expect, the results of using the weighted-average method fall between FIFO and LIFO. The results of using specific invoice prices depend entirely on which units were actually sold.

Some companies' financial statements indicate what the difference would be if another method were used. For example, footnote 4 in **Ford Motor Company's** 1993 annual report states:

Inventories are stated at the lower of cost or market. The cost of most U.S. inventories is determined by the last-in, first-out ("LIFO") method. The cost of the remaining inventories is determined substantially by the first-in, first-out ("FIFO") method.

If FIFO was the only method of inventory accounting used by the company, inventories would have been $1,342 million and $1,365 million higher than reported at December 31, 1993, and 1992, respectively.

If you refer to the financial statements for **Ben & Jerry's Homemade** in the Appendix G, you will be able to determine a great deal about their inventories. The ending inventory is $13,452,863 and consists of ice cream and ingredients with a cost of

$12,001,189; paper goods with a cost of $595,227; and food, beverage, and gift items valued at $856,447. The firm used the FIFO method to determine costs and stated inventories at the lower of cost or market (to be discussed later in the chapter). Although the FIFO method best describes the physical flow of goods for a business like Ben & Jerry's, it was not required that they use this method.

Each of the four pricing methods is generally accepted, and arguments can be made for using each. In one sense, one might argue that specific invoice prices exactly match costs and revenues. It is clearly the most appropriate method when each unit of product has unique features that affect the cost of that particular unit. However, this method may not be practical except for relatively high-priced items when just a few units are kept in stock and sold. Weighted-average costs tend to smooth out price fluctuations. FIFO provides an inventory valuation on the balance sheet that most closely approximates current replacement cost. LIFO causes the last costs incurred to be assigned to cost of goods sold. Therefore, it results in a better matching of current costs with revenues on the income statement.

Because the choice of an inventory pricing method often has material effects on the financial statements, the choice of a method should be disclosed in the footnotes to the statements. This information is important to an understanding of the statements and is required by the *full-disclosure principle*.[3]

PRINCIPLE APPLICATION
Full-Disclosure Principle,
p. 326
The Home Depot states in Note 1 to its 1993 financial statements that: "Inventories are stated at the lower of cost (first-in, first-out) or market, as determined by the retail inventory method."

Tax Effect of LIFO

The income statements in Illustration 9–2 are assumed to be those of a corporation. Therefore, the income statements include income taxes expense (at an assumed rate of 30%). Note a tax advantage was gained by using LIFO because purchase prices were rising. This advantage arises because LIFO assigns the largest dollar amounts to cost of goods sold when purchase prices are increasing. As a result, the smallest income is reported when LIFO is used. This in turn results in the smallest income tax expense.

The Consistency Principle

Because the choice of an inventory pricing method can have a material effect on the financial statements, some companies might be inclined to make a new choice each year. Their objective would be to select whichever method would result in the most favorable financial statements. If this were allowed, however, readers of financial statements would find it extremely difficult to compare the company's financial statements from one year to the next. If income increased, the reader would have difficulty deciding whether the increase resulted from more successful operations or from the change in the accounting method. The **consistency principle** is used to avoid this problem.

The *consistency principle* requires that a company use the same accounting methods period after period, so that the financial statements of succeeding periods will be comparable.[4] The *consistency principle* is not limited just to inventory pricing methods. Whenever a company must choose between alternative accounting methods, consistency requires that the company continue to use the selected method period after period. As a result, a reader of a company's financial statements may assume that in keeping its records and in preparing its statements, the company used the same

---

[3]Ibid., sec. A10.105, 106. First published as *APB Opinion No. 22,* pars. 12, 13.

[4]FASB, *Statement of Financial Accounting Concepts No. 2,* "Qualitative Characteristics of Accounting Information" (Norwalk, CT, 1980), par. 120.

procedures employed in previous years. Only on the basis of this assumption can meaningful comparisons be made of the data in a company's statements year after year.

The consistency principle does not require a company to use one inventory valuation method exclusively, however; it can use different methods to value different categories of inventory. For example, Texaco, Inc., includes the following note in its financial statements:

> Virtually all inventories of crude oil, petroleum products, and petrochemicals are stated at cost, determined on the last-in, first-out (LIFO) method. Other merchandise inventories are stated at cost, determined on the first-in, first-out (FIFO) method. Inventories are valued at the lower of cost or market. Materials and supplies are stated at average cost.

In achieving comparability, the *consistency principle* docs not mcan that a company can never change from one accounting method to another. Rather, if a company justifies a different acceptable method or procedure as an improvement in financial reporting, a change may be made. However, when such a change is made, the *full-disclosure principle* requires that the nature of the change, justification for the change, and the effect of the change on net income be disclosed in footnotes to the statements.[5]

Progress Check

9-4   A company with the following beginning inventory and purchases ended the period with 30 units on hand:

	Units	Unit Cost
Beginning Inventory	100	$10
Purchases #1	40	12
Purchases #2	20	14

   a. Determine ending inventory using FIFO.
   b. Determine cost of goods sold using LIFO.

9-5   In a period of rising prices, which method (LIFO or FIFO) reports the higher net income?

9-6   In a period of rising prices, what effect will LIFO as compared to FIFO have on the balance sheet?

Companies that use the *periodic inventory system* must be especially careful in taking the end-of-period inventory. If an error is made, it will cause misstatements in cost of goods sold, gross profit, net income, current assets, and owner's equity. Also, the ending inventory of one period is the beginning inventory of the next. Therefore, the error will carry forward and cause misstatements in the succeeding period's cost of goods sold, gross profit, and net income. Furthermore, since the amount involved in an inventory often is large, the misstatements can materially reduce the usefulness of the financial statements.

To illustrate the effects of an inventory error, assume that in each of the years 19X1, 19X2, and 19X3, a company had $100,000 in sales. If the company maintained a $20,000 inventory throughout the period and made $60,000 in purchases in each of the years,

INVENTORY ERRORS— PERIODIC SYSTEM

LO 3

Explain the effect of an inventory error on the income statements of the current and succeeding years.

---

[5]FASB, *Accounting Standards—Current Text* (Norwalk, CT, 1994), sec. A06.113. First published as *APB Opinion No. 20,* par. 17.

Illustration 9-3 Effects of Inventory Errors—Periodic Inventory System

	19X1		19X2		19X3	
Sales		$100,000		$100,000		$100,000
Cost of goods sold:						
Beginning inventory	$20,000		$16,000*		$20,000	
Purchases	60,000		60,000		60,000	
Goods for sale	$80,000		$76,000		$80,000	
Ending inventory	16,000*		20,000		20,000	
Cost of goods sold		64,000		56,000		60,000
Gross profit		$ 36,000		$ 44,000		$ 40,000

*Should have been $20,000.

its cost of goods sold each year was $60,000 and its annual gross profit was $40,000. However, assume the company incorrectly calculated its December 31, 19X1, inventory at $16,000 rather than $20,000. Note the effects of the error in Illustration 9–3.

Observe in Illustration 9–3 that the $4,000 understatement of the December 31, 19X1, inventory caused a $4,000 overstatement in 19X1 cost of goods sold and a $4,000 understatement in gross profit and net income. Also, because the ending inventory of 19X1 became the beginning inventory of 19X2, the error caused an understatement in the 19X2 cost of goods sold and a $4,000 overstatement in gross profit and net income. However, by 19X3 the error had no effect.

In Illustration 9–3, the December 31, 19X1, inventory is understated. Had it been overstated, it would have caused opposite results—the 19X1 net income would have been overstated and the 19X2 income understated.

Because inventory errors correct themselves by causing offsetting errors in the next period, you might be inclined to think that they are not serious. Do not make this mistake. Management, creditors, and owners base many important decisions on fluctuations in reported net income. Therefore, inventory errors must be avoided.

Progress Check

9-7 **Falk Company maintains its inventory records on a periodic basis. In making the physical count of inventory at 19X1 year-end, an error was made that overstated the 19X1 ending inventory by $10,000. Will this error cause cost of goods sold to be over- or understated in 19X1? In 19X2? By how much?**

PERPETUAL INVENTORY SYSTEMS

LO 4

Describe perpetual inventory systems and prepare entries to record merchandise transactions and maintain subsidiary inventory records under a perpetual inventory system.

The previous discussion of inventories focused on the periodic inventory system. Under the periodic system, the Merchandise Inventory account is updated only once each accounting period, at the end of the period. Then, the Merchandise Inventory account reflects the current balance of inventory only until the first purchase or sale in the following period. Thereafter, the Merchandise Inventory account no longer reflects the current balance.

By contrast, a *perpetual inventory system* updates the Merchandise Inventory account after each purchase and after each sale. As long as all entries have been posted, the account shows the current amount of inventory on hand. The system takes its name from the fact that the Merchandise Inventory account is perpetually up to date. When a perpetual system is used, management is able to monitor the inventory on hand on a regular basis. This aids in planning future purchases.

Before the widespread use of computers in accounting, only companies that sold a limited number of products of relatively high value used perpetual inventory systems. The cost and effort of maintaining perpetual inventory records were simply too

Illustration 9-4 A Comparison of Entries under Periodic and Perpetual Inventory Systems

X Company purchases merchandise for $15 per unit and sells it for $25. The company begins the current period with five units of product on hand, which cost a total of $75.

Periodic			**Perpetual**		
1. *Purchased on credit 10 units of merchandise for $15 per unit:*					
Purchases	150		Merchandise Inventory	150	
Accounts Payable		150	Accounts Payable		150
2. *Returned 3 units of merchandise originally purchased in (1):*					
Accounts Payable	45		Accounts Payable	45	
Purchases Returns and			Merchandise Inventory		45
Allowances		45			
3. *Sold eight units for $200 cash:*					
Cash	200		Cash	200	
Sales		200	Sales		200
			Cost of Goods Sold	120	
			Merchandise Inventory		120
4. *Closing entries:*					
Merchandise Inventory (Ending)	60		Income Summary	120	
Sales	200		Cost of Goods Sold		120
Purchases Returns and Allowances		45			
Income Summary		305	Sales	200	
			Income Summary		200
Income Summary 225					
Merchandise Inventory (Beginning)		75			
Purchases		150			

	Units	Cost
Beginning inventory	5	$ 75
Purchases	10	150
Purchases returns	(3)	(45)
Goods available	12	$180
Goods sold	(8)	(120)
Ending inventory	4	$ 60

great for other types of companies. However, since computers have made the record-keeping chore much easier, an increasing number of firms are switching from periodic to perpetual systems.

By using parallel columns in Illustration 9–4, we show the typical journal entries made under periodic and perpetual inventory systems. Observe the entries for the purchase of transaction 1. The perpetual system does not use a Purchases account. Instead, the cost of the items purchased is debited directly to Merchandise Inventory. Also, in transaction 2, the perpetual system credits the cost of purchase returns directly to the Merchandise Inventory account instead of using a Purchases Returns and Allowances account.

    Transaction 3 involves the sale of merchandise. Note that the perpetual system requires two entries to record the sale, one to record the revenue and another to record

COMPARING JOURNAL ENTRIES UNDER PERIODIC AND PERPETUAL INVENTORY SYSTEMS

cost of goods sold. Thus, the perpetual system uses a Cost of Goods Sold account. In the periodic system the elements of cost of goods sold are not transferred to such an account. Instead, they are transferred to Income Summary in the process of recording the closing entries.

The closing entries under the two systems are shown as item 4 in Illustration 9–4. Under the periodic system, all of the cost elements related to inventories are transferred to Income Summary. By comparison, under the perpetual system, those cost elements were already recorded in a Cost of Goods Sold account. Thus, the closing entries simply transfer the balance in the Cost of Goods Sold account to Income Summary. Of course, Sales must be closed under both inventory systems. In Illustration 9–4, both inventory systems result in the same amounts of sales, cost of goods sold, and end-of-period merchandise inventory.

SUBSIDIARY INVENTORY RECORDS— PERPETUAL SYSTEM

When a company sells more than one product and uses the perpetual inventory system, the Merchandise Inventory account serves as a controlling account to a subsidiary Merchandise Inventory Ledger. This ledger contains a separate record for each product in stock. This ledger may be computerized or kept on a manual basis. In either case, the record for each product shows the number of units and cost of each purchase, the number of units and cost of each sale, and the resulting balance of product on hand.

Illustration 9–5 shows an example of a subsidiary merchandise inventory record. This particular record is for Product Z, which is stored in Bin 8 of the stockroom. In this case, the record also shows the company's policy of maintaining no more than 25 or no less than 5 units of Product Z on hand.

In Illustration 9–5, note that the beginning inventory consisted of 10 units that cost $10 each. The first transaction occurred on January 5 and was a sale of five units at $17 per unit. Next, 20 units were purchased on January 8 at a cost of $10.50 per unit. Then, three units were sold on January 10 for $17 per unit. The entries to record the January 10 sale are:

Jan.	10	Cash (or Accounts Receivable)	51.00	
		Sales		51.00
		3 × $17.00 = $51		
	10	Cost of Goods Sold	30.00	
		Merchandise Inventory		30.00
		3 × $10.00 = $30		

In the second entry, notice that the cost per unit assigned to these three units was $10. This indicates that a first-in, first-out basis is being assumed for this product. In addition to FIFO, perpetual inventory systems can be designed to accommodate an average cost flow assumption. Perpetual inventory systems rarely use LIFO in the subsidiary records. If a company wants its financial statements to reflect LIFO, special adjustments are made at the end of each accounting period to convert the balances from FIFO or weighted average to LIFO. The details of using weighted average and LIFO with perpetual systems are explained in a more advanced accounting course.

All companies should take a physical inventory at least annually, even if a perpetual inventory system is used. By taking a physical inventory, management confirms the accuracy of the perpetual inventory records. When the physical inventory shows that the perpetual records are incorrect, a special adjusting entry should be prepared to update the accounts.

Illustration 9–5   A Subsidiary Inventory Record Using FIFO

Item	Product Z				Location in stock room		Bin 8			
Maximum	25				Minimum		5			

Date	Received			Sold			Balance		
	Units	Cost	Total	Units	Cost	Total	Units	Cost	Balance
1/1							10	10.00	100.00
1/5				5	10.00	50.00	5	10.00	50.00
1/8	20	10.50	210.00				5	10.00	
							20	10.50	260.00
1/10				3	10.00	30.00	2	10.00	
							20	10.50	230.00

Progress Check

9–8   What account is used in a perpetual inventory system but not in a periodic system?

9–9   In a perpetual inventory system, which of the following statements are true?
 a. The Merchandise Inventory account balance shows the amount of merchandise on hand.
 b. Subsidiary inventory records are maintained for each type of product.
 c. A sale of merchandise requires two entries, one to record the revenue and one to record the cost of goods sold.
 d. A separate Cost of Goods Sold account is used.
 e. All of the above are correct.

LOWER OF COST OR MARKET

LO 5
Calculate the lower-of-cost-or-market amount of an inventory.

As we have discussed, the cost of the ending inventory is determined by using one of the four pricing methods (FIFO, LIFO, weighted average, or specific invoice prices). However, the cost of the inventory is not necessarily the amount reported on the balance sheet. Generally accepted accounting principles require that the inventory be reported at market value whenever market is lower than cost. Thus, merchandise inventory is shown on the balance sheet at the **lower of cost or market (LCM).**

Market Normally Means Replacement Cost

In applying lower of cost or market to merchandise inventories, what do accountants mean by the term *market?* In this situation, market does not mean the expected sales price. Instead, market normally means *replacement cost.*[6] That is the price a company would pay if it bought new items to replace those in its inventory.

The theory underlying LCM is that when the sales price of merchandise falls, the replacement cost also is likely to fall. The decline from the previously incurred cost to replacement cost represents a loss of value that should be recognized when the loss occurs. This is accomplished at the end of the period by writing the ending merchandise down from cost to replacement cost.

---

[6]Exceptions to the normal definition of market as replacement cost are explained in more advanced accounting courses.

Product	Units on Hand	Per Unit Cost	Per Unit Replacement Cost	Total Cost	Total Replacement Cost	Lower of Cost or Replacement Cost
X	20	$8	$7	$160	$140	$140
Y	10	5	6	50	60	50
Z	5	9	7	45	35	35
Total cost originally incurred				$255		
LCM (applied to whole inventory)					$235	
LCM (applied to each product)						$225

Note that when LCM is applied to the whole inventory, the total is $235, which is $20 lower than the $255 cost. And when the method is applied separately to each product, the sum is only $225. In general, a company may apply LCM three different ways:

1. LCM may be applied separately to each product.
2. LCM may be applied to major categories of products.
3. If the products are not too different, LCM may be applied to the inventory as a whole.

Recall that the opening of the chapter discussed **Mobil Corporation's** decision to change the method it uses to determine the LCM of its inventories. The company's news release did not explain exactly how the LCM method was changed, but it did indicate the effect of the change on net income. Following the full disclosure principle, Mobil will repeat this information in its financial statements.

THE CONSERVATISM PRINCIPLE

Generally accepted accounting principles require writing inventory down to market when market is less than cost. On the other hand, inventory generally cannot be written up to market when market exceeds cost. If writing inventory down to market is justified, why not also write inventory up to market? What is the reason for this apparent inconsistency?

The reason is that the gain from a market value increase is not realized until a sales transaction provides verifiable evidence of the amount of the gain. But why, then, are inventories written down when market is below cost?

Accountants often justify the lower-of-cost-or-market rule by citing the **conservatism principle.** This principle attempts to guide the accountant in uncertain situations where amounts must be estimated. In general terms, it implies that when "two estimates of amounts to be received or paid in the future are about equally likely, . . . the less optimistic" should be used.[7] Because the value of inventory is uncertain, writing the inventory down when its market value falls is clearly the less optimistic estimate of the inventory's value to the company.

Progress Check

9-10   A company's ending inventory includes the following items:

Product	Units on Hand	Unit Cost	Market Value per Unit
A	20	$ 6	$ 5
B	40	9	8
C	10	12	15

The inventory's lower of cost or market, applied separately to each product, is:
(a) $520;   (b) $540;   (c) $570;   (d) $600.

---

[7]FASB, *Statement of Financial Accounting Concepts No. 2* (Norwalk, CT, 1980) par. 95.

Illustration 9–6
Calculating the Ending
Inventory Cost by the Retail
Method

		At Cost	At Retail
(Step 1)	Goods available for sale:		
	Beginning inventory	$20,500	$ 34,500
	Net purchases	39,500	65,500
	Goods available for sale	$60,000	$100,000
(Step 2)	Cost ratio: ($60,000/$100,000) × 100 = 60%		
(Step 3)	Deduct net sales at retail		70,000
	Ending inventory at retail		$ 30,000
(Step 4)	Ending inventory at cost ($30,000 × 60%)	$18,000	

Most companies prepare financial statements on a quarterly or monthly basis. These monthly or quarterly statements are called **interim statements,** because they are prepared between the regular year-end statements. The cost of goods sold information that is necessary to prepare interim statements is readily available if a perpetual inventory system is used. However, a periodic system requires a physical inventory to determine cost of goods sold. To avoid the time-consuming and expensive process of taking a physical inventory each month or quarter, some companies use the **retail inventory method** to estimate cost of goods sold and ending inventory. Then, they take a physical inventory at the end of each year. Other companies also use the retail inventory method to prepare the year-end statements. However, all companies should take a physical inventory at least once each year to correct any errors or shortages.

Estimating an Ending Inventory by the Retail Method

When the retail method is used to estimate an inventory, the company's records must show the amount of inventory it had at the beginning of the period both at *cost* and at *retail*. You already understand the cost of an inventory. The retail amount of an inventory simply means the dollar amount of the inventory at the marked selling prices of the inventory items.

In addition to the beginning inventory, the accounting records must show the net amount of goods purchased during the period both at cost and at retail. This is the balance of the Purchases account less returns and discounts. Also, the records must show the amount of net sales at retail. With this information, you estimate the ending inventory as follows:

Step 1: Compute the amount of goods available for sale during the period both at cost and at retail.

Step 2: Divide the goods available at cost by the goods available at retail to obtain a **retail method cost ratio.**

Step 3: Deduct sales (at retail) from goods available for sale (at retail) to determine the ending inventory at retail.

Step 4: Multiply the ending inventory at retail by the cost ratio to reduce the inventory to a cost basis.

Look at Illustration 9–6 to see these calculations.

This is the essence of Illustration 9–6: (1) The company had $100,000 of goods (at marked selling prices) for sale during the period. (2) The cost of these goods was 60% of their $100,000 marked retail sales value. (3) The company's records (its Sales account) showed that $70,000 of these goods were sold, leaving $30,000 (retail value) of unsold merchandise in the ending inventory. (4) Since cost in this store is 60% of retail, the estimated cost of this ending inventory is $18,000.

THE RETAIL METHOD OF ESTIMATING INVENTORIES

LO 6

Use the retail method and the gross profit method to estimate an inventory and calculate merchandise turnover and days' stock on hand.

An ending inventory calculated as in Illustration 9–6 is an estimate arrived at by deducting sales (goods sold) from goods available for sale. As we said before, this method may be used for interim statements or even for year-end statements. Nevertheless, a store must take a physical count of the inventory at least once each year to correct any errors or shortages.

Using the Retail Method to Reduce a Physical Inventory to Cost

In retail stores, items for sale normally have price tags attached that show selling prices. So, when a store takes a physical inventory, it commonly takes the inventory at the marked selling prices of the items on hand. It then reduces the dollar total of this inventory to a cost basis by applying its cost ratio. It does this because the selling prices are readily available and the application of the cost ratio eliminates the need to look up the invoice price of each item on hand.

For example, assume that the company in Illustration 9–6 estimates its inventory by the retail method and takes a physical inventory at the marked selling prices of the goods. Also assume that the total retail amount of this physical inventory is $29,600. The company can calculate the cost for this inventory simply by applying its cost ratio to the inventory total as follows:

$$\$29,600 \times 60\% = \$17,760$$

The $17,760 cost figure for this company's ending physical inventory is a satisfactory figure for year-end statement purposes. It is also acceptable to the Internal Revenue Service for tax purposes.

Inventory Shortage

An inventory determined as in Illustration 9–6 is an estimate of the amount of goods on hand. Since it is determined by deducting sales from goods for sale, it does not reveal any shortages due to breakage, loss, or theft. However, you can estimate the amount of such shortages by comparing the inventory as calculated in Illustration 9–6 with the amount that results from taking a physical inventory.

For example, in Illustration 9–6, we estimated that the ending inventory at retail was $30,000. Then, we assumed that this same company took a physical inventory and counted only $29,600 of merchandise on hand (at retail). Therefore, the company must have had an inventory shortage at retail of $30,000 − $29,600 = $400. Stated in terms of cost, the shortage is $400 × 60% = $240.

GROSS PROFIT METHOD OF ESTIMATING INVENTORIES

Sometimes, a business that does not use a perpetual inventory system or the retail method may need to estimate the cost of its inventory. For example, if the inventory is destroyed by fire or is stolen, the business must estimate the inventory so that it can file a claim with its insurance company. In cases such as this, the cost of the inventory can be estimated by the **gross profit method.** With this method, the historical relationship between cost of goods sold and sales is applied to sales of the current period as a way of estimating cost of goods sold during the current period. Then, cost of goods sold is subtracted from the cost of goods available for sale to get the estimated cost of the ending inventory.

To use the gross profit method, several items of accounting information must be available. This includes information about the normal gross profit margin or rate, the cost of the beginning inventory, the cost of net purchases, transportation-in, and the amount of sales and sales returns.

For example, assume that the inventory of a company was totally destroyed by a fire on March 27, 19X1. The company's average gross profit rate during the past five

Illustration 9-7
The Gross Profit Method of
Estimating Inventory

Goods available for sale:		
Inventory, January 1, 19X1		$12,000
Net purchases	$20,000	
Add transportation-in	500	20,500
Goods available for sale		$32,500
Less estimated cost of goods sold:		
Sales	$31,500	
Less sales returns	(1,500)	
Net sales	$30,000	
Estimated cost of goods sold (70% × $30,000)		(21,000)
Estimated March 27 inventory and inventory loss		$11,500

years has been 30% of net sales. On the date of the fire, the company's accounts showed the following balances:

Sales	$31,500
Sales returns	1,500
Inventory, January 1, 19X1	12,000
Net purchases	20,000
Transportation-in	500

With this information, the gross profit method may be used to estimate the company's inventory loss. To apply the gross profit method, the first step is to recognize that whatever portion of each dollar of net sales was gross profit, the remaining portion was cost of goods sold. Thus, if the company's gross profit rate averages 30%, then 30% of each net sales dollar was gross profit, and 70% was cost of goods sold. In Illustration 9-7, we show how the 70% is used to estimate the inventory that was lost.

To understand Illustration 9-7, recall that an ending inventory is normally subtracted from goods available for sale to determine the cost of goods sold. Then, observe in Illustration 9-7 that the opposite subtraction is made. Estimated cost of goods sold is subtracted from goods available for sale to determine the estimated ending inventory.

As we mentioned, the gross profit method is often used to estimate the amount of an insurance claim. Accountants also use this method to see if an inventory amount determined by management's physical count of the items on hand is reasonable.

In prior chapters, we explained some ratios that you can use to evaluate a company's short-term liquidity. These ratios include the current ratio, the acid-test ratio, days' sales uncollected, and accounts receivable turnover. A company's ability to pay its short-term obligations also depends on how rapidly it sells its merchandise inventory. To evaluate this, you may calculate **merchandise turnover.** The formula for this ratio is:

USING THE INFORMATION— MERCHANDISE TURNOVER AND DAYS' STOCK ON HAND

$$\text{Merchandise turnover} = \frac{\text{Cost of goods sold}}{\text{Average merchandise inventory}}$$

In this ratio, the average merchandise inventory is usually calculated by adding the beginning and ending inventory amounts and dividing the total by two. However, if the company's sales vary by season of the year, you may want to take an average of the inventory amounts at the end of each quarter.

Analysts use merchandise turnover in evaluating short-term liquidity. In addition, they may use it to assess whether management is doing a good job of controlling the amount of inventory kept on hand. A ratio that is high compared to the ratios of competing companies may indicate that the amount of merchandise held in inventory is too low. As a result, sales may be lost because customers are unable to find what they want. A ratio that is low compared to other companies may indicate an inefficient use of assets. In other words, the company may be holding more merchandise than is needed to support its sales volume.

Earlier, we explained how the choice of an inventory costing method affects the reported amounts of inventory and cost of goods sold. The choice also affects merchandise turnover. Therefore, comparing the merchandise turnover ratios of different companies may be misleading unless they use the same costing method.

Another inventory statistic used to evaluate the liquidity of the merchandise inventory is **days' stock on hand.** This is similar to the days' sales uncollected measure described in Chapter 7. The formula for days' stock on hand is:

$$\text{Days' stock on hand} = \frac{\text{Ending inventory}}{\text{Cost of goods sold}} \times 365$$

Notice the difference in the focus of merchandise turnover and days' stock on hand. Merchandise turnover is an average that occurred during an accounting period. By comparison, the focus of days' stock on hand is on the end-of-period inventory. Days' stock on hand is an estimate of how many days it will take to convert the inventory on hand at the end of the period into accounts receivable or cash.

In **The GAP, Inc.'s** 1993 annual report, management reported that they had initiated an aggressive new strategy of selling a more creative mix of merchandise and improving inventory management. This enabled The GAP to realize a 22.6% increase in net earnings for 1993 based on sales that only increased by 11.3%. The following data from The GAP's financial statements show that GAP's days' stock on hand decreased from 68.2 days in 1992 to 56.9 days in 1993 and inventory turnover increased from 5.8 to 6.1 times.

	1993	1992	1991
Cost of goods sold and occupancy expenses ..	$2,121,789	$1,955,553	
Ending merchandise inventory	331,155	365,692	$313,899

Days' stock on hand:

$$1993: \frac{\$331,155}{\$2,121,789} \times 365 = 56.9 \text{ days}$$

$$1992: \frac{\$365,692}{\$1,955,553} \times 365 = 68.2 \text{ days}$$

Progress Check

9-11 **The following data relate to Taylor Company's inventory during the year:**

	Cost	Retail
Beginning inventory	$324,000	$530,000
Purchases	204,000	348,000
Purchases returns	9,000	13,000
Sales		320,000

Using the retail method, the estimated cost of the ending inventory is:
(a) $545,000; (b) $324,200; (c) $333,200; (d) $314,000; (e) $327,000.

9-12 **Refer to the financial statements of Ben & Jerry's Homemade, Inc., in Appendix G. Calculate the merchandise turnover for 1992.**

LO 1. Describe (a) how the matching principle relates to accounting for merchandise, (b) the types of items that should be included in merchandise inventory, and (c) the elements that make up the cost of merchandise. The allocation of the cost of goods available for sale between cost of goods sold and ending inventory is an accounting application of the *matching principle*. Merchandise inventory should include all goods that are owned by the business and held for resale. This includes items the business has placed on consignment with other parties but excludes items that the business has taken on consignment from other parties. The cost of merchandise includes not only the invoice price less any discounts but also any additional or incidental costs incurred to put the merchandise into place and condition for sale.

LO 2. Calculate the cost of an inventory based on (a) specific invoice prices, (b) weighted-average cost, (c) FIFO, and (d) LIFO, and explain the financial statement effects of choosing one method over the others. When specific invoice prices are used to price an inventory, each item in the inventory is identified and the cost of the item is determined by referring to the item's purchase invoice. With weighted-average cost, the total cost of the beginning inventory and of purchases is divided by the total number of units available to determine the weighted-average cost per unit. Multiplying this cost by the number of units in the ending inventory yields the cost of the inventory. FIFO prices the ending inventory based on the assumption that the first units purchased are the first units sold. LIFO is based on the assumption that the last units purchased are the first units sold. All of these methods are acceptable.

LO 3. Explain the effect of an inventory error on the income statements of the current and succeeding years. When the periodic inventory system is used, an error in counting the ending inventory affects assets (inventory), net income (cost of goods sold), and owner's equity. Since the ending inventory is the beginning inventory of the next period, an error at the end of one period affects the cost of goods sold and the net income of the next period. These next period effects offset the financial statement effects in the previous period.

LO 4. Describe perpetual inventory systems and prepare entries to record merchandise transactions and maintain subsidiary inventory records under a perpetual inventory system. Under a perpetual inventory system, purchases and purchases returns are recorded in the Merchandise Inventory account. At the time sales are recorded, the cost of goods sold is credited to Merchandise Inventory. As a result, the Merchandise Inventory is kept up to date throughout the accounting period.

LO 5. Calculate the lower-of-cost-or-market amount of an inventory. When lower of cost or market is applied to merchandise inventory, market usually means replacement cost. Lower of cost or market may be applied separately to each product, to major categories of products, or to the merchandise inventory as a whole.

LO 6. Use the retail method and the gross profit method to estimate an inventory and calculate merchandise turnover and days' stock on hand. When the retail method is used, sales are subtracted from the retail amount of goods available for sale to determine the ending inventory at retail. This is multiplied by the cost ratio to reduce the inventory amount to cost. To calculate the cost ratio, divide the cost of goods available by the retail value of goods available.

With the gross profit method, multiply sales by (1 − the gross profit rate) to estimate cost of goods sold. Then, subtract the answer from the cost of goods available for sale to estimate the cost of the ending inventory.

Analysts use merchandise turnover and days' stock on hand in evaluating a company's short-term liquidity. They also use merchandise turnover to evaluate whether the amount of merchandise kept in inventory is too high or too low.

DEMONSTRATION PROBLEM

Tale Company uses a periodic inventory system and had the following beginning inventory and purchases during 19X1:

	Date		Units	Unit Cost
	1/1	Inventory	400	$14
	3/10	Purchase	200	15
	5/9	Purchase	300	16
	9/22	Purchase	250	20
	11/28	Purchase	100	21

(header: **Item X**)

At December 31, 19X1, there were 550 units of X on hand.

Required

1. Using the preceding information, apply FIFO inventory pricing and calculate the cost of goods available for sale in 19X1, the ending inventory, and the cost of goods sold.

2. In preparing the financial statements for 19X1, the bookkeeper was instructed to use FIFO but failed to do so and computed the cost of goods sold according to LIFO. Determine the size of the misstatement of 19X1's income from this error. Also determine the effect of the error on the 19X2 income. Assume no income taxes.

Planning the Solution

*   Multiply the units of each purchase and the beginning inventory by the appropriate unit costs to determine the total costs. Then, calculate the cost of goods available for sale.

*   For FIFO, calculate the ending inventory by multiplying the units on hand by the unit costs of the latest purchases. Then, subtract the ending inventory from the cost of goods available for sale.

*   For LIFO, calculate the ending inventory by multiplying the units on hand by the unit costs of the beginning inventory and the earliest purchases. Then, subtract the total ending inventory from the cost of goods available for sale.

*   Compare the ending 19X1 inventory amounts under FIFO and LIFO to determine the misstatement of 19X1 income that resulted from using LIFO. The 19X2 and 19X1 errors are equal in amount but have opposite effects.

Solution to Demonstration Problem

1. FIFO basis:

1/1 inventory (400 @ $14)		$ 5,600
Purchases:		
3/10 purchase (200 @ $15)	$3,000	
5/9 purchase (300 @ $16)	4,800	
9/22 purchase (250 @ $20)	5,000	
11/28 purchase (100 @ $21)	2,100	14,900
Cost of goods available for sale		$20,500
Ending inventory at FIFO cost:		
11/28 purchase (100 @ $21)	$2,100	
9/22 purchase (250 @ $20)	5,000	
5/9 purchase (200 @ $16)	3,200	
FIFO cost of ending inventory . . .		10,300
Cost of goods sold		$10,200

2. LIFO basis:

Cost of goods available for sale		$20,500
Ending inventory at LIFO cost:		
1/1 inventory (400 @ $14)	$5,600	
3/10 purchase (150 @ $15)	2,250	
LIFO cost of ending inventory . . .		7,850
Cost of goods sold		$12,650

If LIFO is mistakenly used when FIFO should have been used, cost of goods sold in 19X1 would be overstated by $2,450, which is the difference between the FIFO and LIFO amounts of ending inventory. Income would be understated in 19X1 by $2,450. In 19X2, income would be overstated by $2,450 because of the understatement of the beginning inventory.

GLOSSARY

Conservatism principle the accounting principle that guides accountants to select the less optimistic estimate when two estimates of amounts to be received or paid are about equally likely. p. 356

Consignee one who receives and holds goods owned by another party for the purpose of selling the goods for the owner. p. 345

Consignor an owner of goods who ships them to another party who will then sell the goods for the owner. p. 345

Consistency principle the accounting requirement that a company use the same accounting methods period after period so that the financial statements of succeeding periods will be comparable. p. 350

Days' stock on hand an estimate of how many days it will take to convert the inventory on hand at the end of the period into accounts receivable or cash; calculated by dividing the ending inventory by cost of goods sold and multiplying the result by 365. p. 360

First-in, first-out inventory pricing (FIFO) the pricing of an inventory under the assumption that the first items received were the first items sold. p. 348

Gross profit inventory method a procedure for estimating an ending inventory in which the past gross profit rate is used to estimate cost of goods sold, which is then subtracted from the cost of goods available for sale to determine the estimated ending inventory. p. 358

Interim statements monthly or quarterly financial statements prepared in between the regular year-end statements. p. 357

Inventory ticket a form attached to the counted items in the process of taking a physical inventory. p. 346

Last-in, first-out inventory pricing (LIFO) the pricing of an inventory under the assumption that the last items received were the first items sold. p. 348

Lower of cost or market (LCM) the required method of reporting merchandise inventory in the balance sheet, in which market is normally defined as replacement cost on the date of the balance sheet. p. 355

Merchandise turnover the number of times a company's average inventory was sold during an accounting period, calculated by dividing cost of goods sold by the average merchandise inventory balance. p. 359

Net realizable value the expected sales price of an item less any additional costs to sell. p. 345

Retail inventory method a method for estimating an ending inventory based on the ratio of the amount of goods for sale at cost to the amount of goods for sale at marked selling prices. p. 357

Retail method cost ratio the ratio of goods available for sale at cost to goods available for sale at retail prices. p. 357

Specific invoice inventory pricing the pricing of an inventory where the purchase invoice of each item in the ending inventory is identified and used to determine the cost assigned to the inventory. p. 347

Weighted-average inventory pricing an inventory pricing system in which the unit prices of the beginning inventory and of each purchase are weighted by the number of units in the beginning inventory and each purchase. The total of these amounts is then divided by the total number of units available for sale to find the unit cost of the ending inventory and of the units that were sold. p. 347

QUESTIONS

1. Where is merchandise inventory disclosed in the financial statements?

2. Why are incidental costs often ignored in pricing an inventory? Under what accounting principle is this permitted?

3. Give the meanings of the following when applied to inventory: (a) FIFO; (b) LIFO; (c) cost; and (d) perpetual inventory.

4. If prices are falling, will the LIFO or the FIFO method of inventory valuation result in the lower cost of goods sold?

5. May a company change its inventory pricing method each accounting period?

6. Does the accounting principle of consistency preclude any changes from one accounting method to another?

7. What effect does the full-disclosure principle have if a company changes from one acceptable accounting method to another?

8. What is meant when it is said that under a periodic inventory system, inventory errors correct themselves?

9. If inventory errors under a periodic inventory system correct themselves, why be concerned when such errors are made?

10. What guidance for accountants is provided by the principle of conservatism?

11. What accounts are used in a periodic inventory system but not in a perpetual inventory system?

12. What is the usual meaning of the word *market* as it is used in determining the lower of cost or market for merchandise inventory?

13. In deciding whether to reduce an item of merchandise to the lower of cost or market, what is the importance of the item's net realizable value?

14. Refer to Ben & Jerry's Homemade, Inc.'s financial statements in Appendix G. On December 26, 1992, what percentage of Ben & Jerry's current assets was represented by inventory?

VERMONT'S FINEST • ICE CREAM & FROZEN YOGURT™

QUICK STUDY (Five Minute Exercises)

QS 9–1
(LO 1)

a. Explain how the matching principle applies to the accounting for inventory.

b. Fun Stuff Inc., a distributor of novelty items, operates out of owner Margaret Falcaro's home. At the end of the accounting period, Falcaro tells us she has 2,000 units of product in her basement, 50 of which were damaged by water leaks and cannot be sold. She also has another 400 units in her van ready to deliver to fill a customer order, terms FOB destination, and has another 100 units out on consignment to a friend who owns a stationery store. How many units should be included in the end-of-the-period inventory?

QS 9–2
(LO 1)

The Victorian Attic, an antique dealer, purchased the contents of an estate for a bulk bid price of $45,000. The terms of the purchase were FOB shipping point and the cost of transporting the goods to Victorian Attic was $2,000. Victorian Attic insured the shipment at the cost of $200. Prior to placing the goods in the store, they cleaned and refurbished some merchandise at a cost of $600 for labor and parts. Determine the cost of the inventory acquired in the purchase of the estate contents.

QS 9–3
(LO 2)

A company had the following beginning inventory and purchases during a period. What is the cost of the 110 units that remain in the ending inventory, assuming (a) FIFO, (b) LIFO, and (c) weighted average?

	Units	Unit Cost
Beginning inventory on January 1	200	$6.00
Purchase on March 20	50	$6.50
Purchase on July 2	80	$7.00

QS 9–4
(LO 2)

Identify the inventory costing method most closely related to each of the following statements assuming a period of rising costs:

a. Results in a balance sheet inventory closest to replacement costs.

b. Matches recent costs against revenue.

c. Provides a tax advantage.

d. Is best because each unit of product has unique features that affect cost.

e. Understates current value of inventory on a balance sheet.

QS 9–5
(LO 3)

Gardner Company maintains its inventory records on a periodic basis. In taking a physical inventory at the end of 19X1, certain units were counted twice. Explain how this error affects the following: (a) cost of goods sold, (b) gross profit, (c) 19X1 net income, (d) 19X2 net income, (e) the combined two-year income, (f) income in years after 19X2.

QS 9–6
(LO 4)

a. Journalize the following transactions under the periodic inventory system and under the perpetual inventory system:

Nov. 2   Purchased and received 100 cases of soda for $11 per case, FOB destination.

5   Sold 20 cases of soda on account for $15 per case.

17   Returned 30 cases of soda to supplier.

b.   Under which of the two alternative inventory systems would the inventory account have a November 17 balance that represented the cost of the 50 cases of soda that remain on hand?

Media-Tec has the following products in its ending inventory:

QS 9–7
(LO 5)

Product	Quantity	Cost	Market
A	4	$300	$240
B	15	400	420
C	8	200	180

Calculate lower of cost or market (a) for the inventory as a whole, and (b) applied separately to each product.

The inventory of Abba Cadabba was destroyed by a fire on April 15. The following data were found in the accounting records:

QS 9–8
(LO 6)

Jan. 1 inventory	$20,000
Jan. 1–Apr. 15 purchases (net)	38,000
Sales	86,000
Estimated gross profit rate	54%

Determine the cost of the inventory destroyed in the fire.

Using the financial statements in Appendix G, calculate the days' stock on hand for Ben & Jerry's on December 26, 1992.

QS 9–9
(LO 7)

EXERCISES

Serges Company began a year and purchased merchandise as follows:

Exercise 9–1
Alternative cost flow assumptions, periodic inventory system
(LO 2)

Jan. 1	Beginning inventory	80 units @ $60.00 =	$ 4,800
Feb. 16	Purchased	400 units @ $56.00 =	22,400
Sept. 2	Purchased	160 units @ $50.00 =	8,000
Nov. 26	Purchased	320 units @ $46.00 =	14,720
Dec. 4	Purchased	240 units @ $40.00 =	9,600
	Total	1,200 units	$59,520

Required

The company uses a periodic inventory system, and the ending inventory consists of 300 units, 100 from each of the last three purchases. Determine the share of the $59,520 cost of the units for sale that should be assigned to the ending inventory and to goods sold under each of the following: (a) costs are assigned on the basis of specific invoice prices, (b) costs are assigned on a weighted-average cost basis, (c) costs are assigned on the basis of FIFO, and (d) costs are assigned on the basis of LIFO. Assuming the company has enough income to require that it pay income taxes, which method provides a current tax advantage?

Finest Company began a year and purchased merchandise as follows:

Exercise 9–2
Alternative cost flow assumptions, periodic inventory system
(LO 2)

Jan. 1	Beginning inventory	80 units @ $40.00 =	$ 3,200
Feb. 16	Purchased	400 units @ $46.00 =	18,400
Sept. 2	Purchased	160 units @ $50.00 =	8,000
Nov. 26	Purchased	320 units @ $56.00 =	17,920
Dec. 4	Purchased	240 units @ $60.00 =	14,400
	Total	1,200 units	$61,920

Required

The company uses a periodic inventory system, and the ending inventory consists of 300 units, 100 from each of the last three purchases. Determine the share of the $61,920 cost of the units for sale that should be assigned to the ending inventory and to goods sold under each of the following: (a) costs are assigned on the basis of specific invoice prices, (b) costs are assigned on a weighted-average cost basis, (c) costs are assigned on the basis of FIFO, and (d) costs are assigned on the basis of LIFO. Assuming the company has enough income to require that it pay income taxes, which method provides a current tax advantage?

Exercise 9–3
Analysis of inventory errors
(LO 3)

Coe Company had $435,000 of sales during each of three consecutive years, and it purchased merchandise costing $300,000 during each of the years. It also maintained a $105,000 inventory from the beginning to the end of the three-year period. However, in accounting under a periodic inventory system, it made an error at the end of year 1 that caused its ending year 1 inventory to appear on its statements at $90,000 rather than the correct $105,000.

Required

1. State the actual amount of the company's gross profit in each of the years.
2. Prepare a comparative income statement like Illustration 9–3 to show the effect of this error on the company's cost of goods sold and gross profit in year 1, year 2, and year 3.

Exercise 9–4
Perpetual inventory system— FIFO cost flow
(LO 4)

In its beginning inventory on January 1, 19X1, Stable Company had 120 units of merchandise that cost $8 per unit. Prepare general journal entries for Stable to record the following transactions during 19X1, assuming a perpetual inventory system and a first-in, first-out cost flow.

Apr. 3   Purchased on credit 300 units of merchandise at $10.00 per unit.

      9   Returned 60 defective units from the April 3 purchase to the supplier.

July 16   Purchased for cash 180 units of merchandise at $8.50 per unit.

Aug. 5   Sold 200 units of merchandise for cash at a price of $12.50 per unit.

Dec. 31   Prepare entries to close the revenue and expense accounts to the Income Summary.

Exercise 9–5
Lower of cost or market
(LO 5)

Crystal Corporation's ending inventory includes the following items:

Product	Units on Hand	Unit Cost	Replacement Cost per Unit
W	40	$30	$34
X	50	48	40
Y	60	26	24
Z	44	20	20

Replacement cost is determined to be the best measure of market. Calculate lower of cost or market for the inventory (a) as a whole, and (b) applied separately to each product.

Exercise 9–6
Estimating ending inventory— retail method
(LO 6)

During an accounting period, Felder Company sold $220,000 of merchandise at marked retail prices. At the period end, the following information was available from its records:

	At Cost	At Retail
Beginning inventory	$ 62,180	$102,000
Net purchases	115,820	176,125

Use the retail method to estimate Felder's ending inventory at cost.

Exercise 9–7
Reducing physical inventory to cost—retail method
(LO 6)

Assume that in addition to estimating its ending inventory by the retail method, Felder Company of Exercise 9–6 also took a physical inventory at the marked selling prices of the inventory items. Assume further that the total of this physical inventory at marked selling prices was $50,500. Then, (a) determine the amount of this inventory at cost and (b) determine the store's inventory shrinkage from breakage, theft, or other causes at retail and at cost.

On January 1, a store had a $216,000 inventory at cost. During the first quarter of the year, it purchased $735,000 of merchandise, returned $10,500, and paid freight charges on purchased merchandise totaling $22,300. During the past several years, the store's gross profit on sales has averaged 25%. Under the assumption the company had $890,000 of sales during the first quarter of the year, use the gross profit method to estimate its inventory at the end of the first quarter.

Exercise 9–8
Estimating ending inventory—
gross profit method
(LO 6)

From the following information for Jester Company, calculate merchandise turnover for 19X3 and 19X2 and days' stock on hand at December 31, 19X3, and 19X2.

Exercise 9–9
Merchandise turnover and
days' stock on hand
(LO 6)

	19X3	19X2	19X1
Cost of goods sold	$367,900	$243,800	$223,600
Inventory (December 31)	77,120	69,400	73,200

Comment on Jester's efficiency in using its assets to support increasing sales from 19X2 to 19X3.

PROBLEMS

Hart Company began a year with 3,000 units of Product A in its inventory that cost $25 each, and it made successive purchases of the product as follows:

Problem 9–1
Alternative cost flows—
periodic system
(LO 2)

Jan. 29	4,500 units @ $30 each
Apr. 4	5,000 units @ $35 each
Sept. 8	4,800 units @ $40 each
Dec. 9	4,500 units @ $45 each

The company uses a periodic inventory system. On December 31, a physical count disclosed that 6,000 units of Product A remained in inventory.

Required

1. Prepare a calculation showing the number and total cost of the units available for sale during the year.

2. Prepare calculations showing the amounts that should be assigned to the ending inventory and to cost of goods sold assuming (a) a FIFO basis, (b) a LIFO basis, and (c) a weighted-average cost basis. Round your calculation of the weighted-average cost per unit to three decimal places.

CHECK FIGURE:
Cost of units sold, $517,000;
$614,000; $564,958

MDI Company sold 7,800 units of its product at $55 per unit during 19X1. Incurring operating expenses of $8 per unit in selling the units, it began the year and made successive purchases of the product as follows:

Problem 9–2
Income statement comparisons
and cost flow assumptions
(LO 2)

January 1 beginning inventory	800 units costing $30.00 per unit
Purchases:	
March 3	1,000 units costing $31.00 per unit
June 9	2,000 units costing $32.00 per unit
October 17	4,500 units costing $33.00 per unit
December 6	600 units costing $34.00 per unit

Required

Preparation component:

1. Prepare a comparative income statement for the company, showing in adjacent columns the net incomes earned from the sale of the product assuming the company uses a periodic inventory system and prices its ending inventory on the basis of: (a) FIFO, (b) LIFO, and (c) weighted-average cost. Assume an income tax rate of 30%. Round your calculation of the weighted-average cost per unit to three decimal places.

CHECK FIGURE:
Net income, $80,920; $78,400;
$79,998

Analysis component:

2. In comparing the results of the three alternatives, how would they change if MDI had been experiencing declining prices in the acquisition of additional inventory?

3. What specific advantages and disadvantages are offered by using LIFO and by using FIFO assuming the cost trends given at the beginning of this problem?

Problem 9–3

Analysis of inventory errors

(LO 3)

Ying Company keeps its inventory records on a periodic basis. The following amounts were reported in the company's financial statements:

	Financial Statements for Year Ended December 31		
	19X1	**19X2**	**19X3**
(a) Cost of goods sold	$130,000	$154,000	$140,000
(b) Net income	40,000	50,000	42,000
(c) Total current assets	210,000	230,000	200,000
(d) Owner's equity	234,000	260,000	224,000

In making the physical counts of inventory, the following errors were made:

Inventory on December 31, 19X1	Understated	$12,000
Inventory on December 31, 19X2	Overstated	6,000

Required

Preparation component:

1. For each of the preceding financial statement items—*(a)*, *(b)*, *(c)*, and *(d)*—prepare a schedule similar to the following and show the adjustments that would have been necessary to correct the reported amounts.

	19X1	**19X2**	**19X3**
Cost of goods sold:			
Reported	___	___	___
Adjustments: 12/31/X1 error	___	___	___
12/31/X2 error	___	___	___
Corrected	___	___	___

Analysis component:

2. What is the error in the aggregate net income for the three-year period that resulted from the inventory errors? Explain why this result occurs. Also explain why the understatement of inventory by $12,000 in year 1 resulted in an understatement of equity by the same figure that year.

Problem 9–4

Lower of cost or market

(LO 5)

The following information pertains to the physical inventory of Home Appliance Center taken at December 31:

		Per Unit	
Product	**Units on Hand**	**Cost**	**Replacement Cost**
Kitchen:			
Refrigerators	165	$380	$405
Stoves	120	203	181
Dishwashers	158	140	165
Microwaves	200	50	40
Entertainment:			
Stereos	140	250	312
Televisions	360	304	320
Cleaning/Maintenance:			
Washers	245	190	146
Dryers	280	188	162
Vacuum Cleaners	104	67	79

Required

Calculate the lower of cost or market *(a)* for the inventory as a whole, *(b)* for the inventory by major category, and *(c)* for the inventory, applied separately to each product.

CHECK FIGURE:
Lower of cost or market,
$369,778; $352,966; $347,078

The records of The Unlimited provided the following information for the year ended December 31:

Problem 9–5
Retail inventory method
(LO 6)

	At Cost	At Retail
January 1 beginning inventory	$ 160,450	$ 264,900
Purchases	1,113,140	1,828,200
Purchases returns	17,600	34,100
Sales		1,570,200
Sales returns		15,600

Required

1. Prepare an estimate of the company's year-end inventory by the retail method.

2. Under the assumption the company took a year-end physical inventory at marked selling prices that totaled $478,800, prepare a schedule showing the store's loss from theft or other cause at cost and at retail.

CHECK FIGURE:
Inventory shortage at cost,
$15,616

Cafferty Company wants to prepare interim financial statements for the first quarter of 19X1. The company uses a periodic inventory system but would like to avoid making a physical count of inventory. During the last five years, the company's gross profit rate has averaged 35%. The following information for the year's first quarter is available from its records:

Problem 9–6
Gross profit method
(LO 6)

January 1 beginning inventory	$ 600,520
Purchases	1,890,400
Purchases returns	26,100
Transportation-in	13,800
Sales	2,382,300
Sales returns	18,900

Required

Use the gross profit method to prepare an estimate of the company's March 31 inventory.

CHECK FIGURE:
Estimated March 31 inventory,
$942,410

CRITICAL THINKING: ESSAYS, PROBLEMS, AND CASES

Starlite Furniture uses a periodic inventory system to account for its merchandise. Describe what effect, if any, the following independent errors would have on Starlite's financial statements for 19X2 and 19X3:

Analytical Essay

(LO 3)

a. Goods held on consignment by Starlite were included in its December 31, 19X2, inventory.

b. Merchandise stored in one of Starlite's warehouses was double counted in the inventory taken on December 31, 19X1.

c. Starlite purchased and received merchandise in December 19X2, but did not record the purchase until 19X3. (Assume payment for the merchandise was not due until January 19X3.)

Financial Reporting Problems

The Dow Chemical Company manufactures and supplies more than 2,000 products and services, including chemicals and performance products, plastics, hydrocarbons and energy, and consumer specialities. In the company's 1992 annual report, the footnotes to the financial statements included the following note.

FRP 9–1
(LO 2)

Inventories

A reduction of certain inventories resulted in the liquidation of some quantities of LIFO inventory, which decreased pretax income by $6 [million] in
1992 and which increased pretax income by $11 [million] in 1991 and $44
[million] in 1990.

The amount of reserve required to reduce inventories from the first-in, first-
out basis to the last-in, first-out basis on December 31, 1992 and 1991, was
$162 [million] and $216 [million], respectively. The inventories that were
valued on a LIFO basis represented 42 percent and 40 percent of the total
inventories on December 31, 1992 and 1991, respectively.
Courtesy of Dow Chemical Company

Discuss the financial statement effects of experiencing a reduction in inventory when LIFO is
used and explain how this applies to Dow Chemical.

FRP 9–2
(LO 2)

The Times Mirror Company is a media and information company that does business in three
principal areas: print media, professional information and book publishing, and electronic
media. Times Mirror uses the FIFO method for books and certain finished products and
LIFO for newsprint, paper, and certain other inventories. The 1993 annual report of Times
Mirror included the following footnote in its financial statements:

Note G—Inventories

Inventories consist of the following (in thousands):

	1993	1992	1991
Newsprint, paper, and other raw materials	$ 39,066	$ 50,633	$ 59,557
Books and other finished products	94,675	91,205	71,788
Work-in-process	27,510	25,330	20,596
	$161,251	$167,168	$151,941

Inventories determined on the last-in, first-out method were $26,994,000,
$40,177,000, and $51,133,000 at December 31, 1993, 1992, and 1991,
respectively, and would have been higher by $8,232,000 in 1993, $4,631,000
in 1992 and $7,427,000 in 1991 had the first-in, first-out method (which
approximates current cost) been used exclusively.

Courtesy of Times Mirror Company

Times Mirror reported a net income of $317,159,000 in 1993. Retained earnings on Decem-
ber 31, 1993, was $1,687,574. If Times Mirror had used FIFO for all of its inventories, what
would the total inventories reported on December 31, 1993, and December 31, 1992, have
been? Assuming the average income tax rate applicable to the company was 30% in all past
years, what would have been reported as the 1993 net income if FIFO had been used for all
inventories? What would have been the balance of retained earnings on December 31, 1993?
Comment on Times Mirror's policy of using FIFO for some inventories and LIFO for other
inventories in light of the consistency principle.

**Financial Statement
Analysis Case**

(LO 1, 2)

Refer to the financial statements and related disclosures from Apple Computer, Inc.'s 1993
annual report in Appendix F. Based on your examination of this information, answer the
following:

1. What was the total amount of inventories held as current assets by Apple at September
    24, 1993? At September 25, 1992?

2. Inventories represented what percentage of total assets at September 24, 1993? At Sep-
    tember 25, 1992?

3. Comment on the relative size of inventories Apple holds compared to other types
    of assets.

4. What method did Apple use to determine the inventory amounts reported on its balance sheet?
5. Calculate merchandise turnover for fiscal year 1993 and days' stock on hand at September 24, 1993, and September 25, 1992. (Use cost of sales for cost of goods sold.)

CONCEPT TESTER

Test your understanding of the concepts introduced in this chapter by completing the following crossword puzzle:

Across Clues

1. One who holds goods for sale that are owned by another party.
2. Principle that calls for less optimistic estimate when two estimates are equally likely.
5. Inventory pricing method that assumes units sold first come from units purchased first.
6. Two words; inventory estimation method based on ratio of cost of goods available to selling price.
7. Two words; financial statements prepared on a monthly or quarterly basis.

Down Clues

1. Owner of goods who transfers them to another party who will attempt to sell them for the owner.
2. Principle that calls for using the same accounting methods period after period.
3. Inventory pricing method that assumes units sold come from latest purchases.
4. Required method of reporting inventory at replacement cost when that is less than cost.

ANSWERS TO PROGRESS CHECKS

9–1 The matching principle.
9–2 Thompson.
9–3 *d*
9–4 a. $(20 \times \$14) + (10 \times \$12) = \$400$
   b. $(20 \times \$14) + (40 \times \$12) + (70 \times \$10) = \$1,460$
9–5 FIFO. LIFO results in a higher cost of goods sold and therefore a lower gross profit, which carries through to a lower net income.

9–6 LIFO will result in a smaller inventory figure on the balance sheet, as compared to FIFO which will result in an inventory figure that is close to current replacement costs.
9–7 The cost of goods sold will be understated by $10,000 in 19X1 and overstated by $10,000 in 19X2.
9–8 An account used only in a perpetual inventory system is Cost of Goods Sold.

9–9 *e*

9–10 *b*

9–11 *e*

9–12 Merchandise turnover

$$= \frac{\text{Cost of goods sold}}{\text{Average inventory}}$$

$$= \frac{\$94,389,391}{(\$17,089,857 + \$8,999,666)/2}$$

$$= 7.24 \text{ times}$$

Plant and Equipment

Coca-Cola Bottling Co. Consolidated intensified the fruit drink wars in 1994 when it announced that it had invested $150 million to expand production of its Fruitopia beverage by purchasing additional plants in Waco, Texas, and Northampton, Massachusetts, and by upgrading bottling lines in existing production facilities. The excerpt below from the company's 1993 annual report shows the plant asset holdings prior to this acquisition. The magnitude of the plant asset investment is apparent when compared to the 1993 holdings. As an analyst from Solomon Brothers said: "This shows that Coca-Cola is serious about Fruitopia. The $150 million investment is half of Coca-Cola's domestic capital expenditure budget." (*New York Times*, November 11, 1994, p. D4.)

COCA-COLA BOTTLING CO. CONSOLIDATED
CONSOLIDATED BALANCE SHEETS
(In thousands)

ASSETS	January 2, 1994
Property, plant and equipment, at cost	$297,561
Less—Accumulated depreciation and amortization	134,546
Property, plant and equipment, net	$163,015

LEARNING OBJECTIVES

After studying Chapter 10, you should be able to:

1. Describe the differences between plant assets and other kinds of assets, and calculate the cost and record the purchase of plant assets.

2. Explain depreciation accounting (including the reasons for depreciation), calculate depreciation by the straight-line and units-of-production methods, and calculate depreciation after revising the estimated useful life of an asset.

3. Describe the use of accelerated depreciation for financial accounting and tax accounting purposes and calculate accelerated depreciation under *(a)* the declining-balance method, and *(b)* the Modified Accelerated Cost Recovery System.

4. Describe the difference between revenue and capital expenditures and account properly for costs such as repairs and betterments incurred after the original purchase of plant assets.

5. Prepare entries to account for the disposal or exchange of plant assets and explain the use of total asset turnover in evaluating a company's efficiency in using its assets.

6. Define or explain the words and phrases listed in the chapter glossary.

The focus of this chapter is long-term, tangible assets used in the operation of a business. These plant assets represent a major category of investment by businesses. Recent financial press predictions call for an approximate 8% increase in spending related to plant assets. For example, in the Sony Corporation annual report for the year ended March 31, 1994, management made the following statement: "For the past two fiscal years, Sony has reduced its capital investments, but in the fiscal year ending March 31, 1995, it intends to boost its level of investment, primarily in manufacturing facilities for audio equipment in Asia and computer displays in the United States."

As another example, Wendy's International Inc.'s 1993 annual report indicated that the company had acquired 33 domestic restaurants in 1993 for cash of $8.7 million and assumption of certain liabilities. Further expansion was projected for 1994 through construction of 125 new company-owned restaurants and 225 new franchised restaurants.

Learning fundamental concepts of accounting for plant and equipment will enable you to recognize the direct financial statement impact of business activities like those described for Coca-Cola, Sony, and Wendy's. In studying this chapter, you will learn what distinguishes plant and equipment from other types of assets, how to determine their cost, and how companies allocate their costs to the periods that benefit from their use.

PLANT ASSETS COMPARED TO OTHER TYPES OF ASSETS

Tangible assets that are used in the production or sale of other assets or services and that have a useful life longer than one accounting period are called *plant assets*. In the past, such assets were often described as *fixed assets*. However, more descriptive terms such as *plant and equipment* or perhaps *property, plant, and equipment* are now used.

The main difference between plant assets and merchandise is that plant assets are held for use while merchandise is held for sale. For example, a business that buys a computer for the purpose of reselling it should report the computer on the balance sheet as merchandise inventory. If the same retailer owns another computer that is used to account for business operations and to prepare reports, it is classified as plant and equipment.

The characteristic that distinguishes plant assets from current assets is the length of their useful lives. For example, supplies are usually consumed within a short time after they are placed in use. Thus, their cost is assigned to the single period in which they are used. By comparison, plant assets have longer useful lives that extend over more than one accounting period. As the usefulness of plant assets expires over these periods, their cost must be allocated among them. This allocation should be accomplished in a systematic and rational manner.[1]

Plant a plant assets are also different than the items that are reported on the balance sheet as long-term investments. Although both are held for more than one accounting period, long-term investments are not used in the primary operations of the business. For example, land that is held for future expansion is classified as a long-term investment. On the other hand, land on which the company's factory is located is a plant asset. In addition, standby equipment held for use in case of a breakdown or during peak periods of production is a plant asset. However, equipment that is removed from service and held for sale is no longer considered a plant asset.

When a plant asset is purchased, it should be recorded at cost. This cost includes all normal and reasonable expenditures necessary to get the asset in place and ready to use. For example, the cost of a factory machine includes its invoice price, less any cash discount for early payment, plus freight, unpacking, and assembling costs. The cost of an asset also includes the costs of installing a machine before placing it in service. Examples are the costs to build a concrete base or foundation for a machine, to provide electrical connections, and to adjust the machine before using it in operations.

An expenditure cannot be charged to and reported as part of the cost of a plant asset unless the expenditure is reasonable and necessary. For example, if a machine is damaged by being dropped during unpacking, the repairs should not be added to its cost. Instead, they should be charged to an expense account. Also, a fine paid for moving a heavy machine on city streets without proper permits is not part of the cost of the machine. However, if proper permits are obtained, their cost is included in the cost of the asset. Sometimes, costs in addition to the purchase price are incurred to modify or customize a new plant asset. These items should be charged to the asset's cost.

When a plant asset is constructed by a business for its own use, cost includes material and labor costs plus a reasonable amount of indirect overhead costs such as the costs of heat, lights, power, and depreciation on the machinery used to construct the asset. Cost also includes design fees, building permits, and insurance during construction. However, insurance costs for coverage after the asset has been placed in service are an operating expense.

When land is purchased for a building site, its cost includes the total amount paid for the land, including any real estate commissions. Its cost also includes fees for insuring the title, legal fees, and any accrued property taxes paid by the purchaser. Payments for surveying, clearing, grading, draining, and landscaping are also included in the cost of land. Other costs of land include assessments by the local government, whether incurred at the time of purchase or later, for such things as installing streets,

LO 1

Describe the differences between plant assets and other kinds of assets, and calculate the cost and record the purchase of plant assets.

COST OF A PLANT ASSET

---

[1]See FASB, *Statement of Financial Accounting Concepts No. 6,* "Elements of Financial Statements of Business Enterprises" (Norwalk, CT, 1985), par. 149.

sewers, and sidewalks. These assessments are included because they add a more or less permanent value to the land.

Land purchased as a building site may have an old building that must be removed. In such cases, the total purchase price should be charged to the Land account. Also, the cost of removing the old building, less any amounts recovered through the sale of salvaged materials, should be charged to the Land account.

Because land has an unlimited life and is not consumed when it is used, it is not subject to depreciation. However, **land improvements,** such as parking lot surfaces, fences, and lighting systems, have limited useful lives. Although these costs increase the usefulness of the land, they must be charged to separate Land Improvement accounts so that they can be depreciated. Of course, a separate Building account must be charged for the costs of a building that will be used as a plant asset.

Land, land improvements, and buildings often are purchased in a single transaction for a lump-sum price. When this occurs, you must allocate the cost of the purchase among the different types of assets, based on their relative market values. These market values may be estimated by appraisal or by using the tax-assessed valuations of the assets.

For example, assume that a company pays $90,000 cash to acquire land appraised at $30,000, land improvements appraised at $10,000, and a building appraised at $60,000. The $90,000 cost is allocated on the basis of appraised values as follows:

	Appraised Value	Percentage of Total	Apportioned Cost
Land	$ 30,000	30%	$27,000
Land improvements	10,000	10	9,000
Building	60,000	60	54,000
Totals	$100,000	100%	$90,000

Progress Check

(Answers to Progress Checks are provided at the end of the chapter.)

10-1   Identify the asset classification for: *(a)* office supplies; *(b)* office equipment; *(c)* merchandise; *(d)* land held for future expansion; *(e)* trucks used in operations.

10-2   Identify the account charged for each of the following expenditures: *(a)* the purchase price of a vacant lot; *(b)* the cost of paving that vacant lot.

10-3   What amount should be recorded as the cost of a new production machine, given the following items related to the machine: gross purchase price, $700,000; sales tax, $49,000; purchase discount taken, $21,000; freight to move machine to plant, $3,500; assembly costs, $3,000; cost of foundation for machine, $2,500; cost of spare parts to be used in maintaining the machine, $4,200?

NATURE OF DEPRECIATION

LO 2

Explain depreciation accounting (including the reasons for depreciation), calculate depreciation by the straight-line and units-of-production methods, and calculate depreciation after revising the estimated useful life of an asset.

Because plant assets are purchased for use, you can think of a plant asset as a quantity of usefulness that contributes to the operations of the business throughout the service life of the asset. And, because the life of any plant asset (other than land) is limited, this quantity of usefulness expires as the asset is used. This expiration of a plant asset's quantity of usefulness is generally described as *depreciation*. In accounting, this term describes the process of allocating and charging the cost of the usefulness to the accounting periods that benefit from the asset's use.

For example, when a company buys an automobile for use as a plant asset, it acquires a quantity of usefulness in the sense that it obtains a quantity of transportation. The total cost of the transportation is the cost of the car less the expected proceeds to be received when the car is sold or traded in at the end of its service life. This net cost must be allocated to the accounting periods that benefit from the car's use. In other words, the asset's cost must be depreciated. Note that the depreciation process does not measure the decline in the car's market value each period. Nor does it measure the physical deterioration of the car each period. Under generally accepted accounting principles, depreciation is a process of allocating a plant asset's cost to income statements of the years in which it is used.

Because depreciation represents the cost of using a plant asset, you should not begin recording depreciation charges until the asset is actually put to use providing services or producing products.

The **service life** of a plant asset is the length of time it will be used in the operations of the business. This service life (or useful life) may not be as long as the asset's potential life. For example, although computers have a potential life of six to eight years, a company may plan to trade in its old computers for new ones every three years. In this case, the computers have a three-year service life. Therefore, this company should charge the cost of the computers (less their expected trade-in value) to depreciation expense over this three-year period.

SERVICE (USEFUL) LIFE OF A PLANT ASSET

Several factors often make the service life of a plant asset hard to predict. Wear and tear from use determine the service life of many assets. However, two additional factors, **inadequacy** and **obsolescence,** often need to be considered.

When a business grows more rapidly than anticipated, the capacity of the assets may become too small for the productive demands of the business. As this happens, the assets become inadequate. Obsolescence, like inadequacy, is hard to anticipate because the timing of new inventions and improvements normally cannot be predicted. Yet, new inventions and improvements may cause a company to discard an obsolete asset long before it wears out.

Many times, a company is able to predict the service life of a new asset based on the company's past experience with similar assets. In other cases, when it has no experience with a particular type of asset, a company must depend on the experience of others or on engineering studies and judgment.

In its 1993 annual report, **Microsoft Corporation** disclosed the following information regarding its depreciation procedures:

Property, plant, and equipment is stated at cost and depreciated using the straight-line method over the following estimated useful lives:

Buildings	30 years
Leasehold improvements	Lease term
Computer equipment and other	3–5 years

SALVAGE VALUE

The total amount of depreciation that should be taken over an asset's service life is the asset's cost minus its estimated **salvage value.** The salvage value of a plant asset is the amount that you expect to receive from selling the asset at the end of its life. If you expect an asset to be traded in on a new asset, the salvage value is the expected trade-in value.

Sometimes, a company must incur additional costs to dispose of plant assets. For example, a company may plan to clean and paint an old machine before offering it for sale. In this case, the estimated salvage value is the expected proceeds from the sale of the asset less the cleaning and painting costs.

ALLOCATING DEPRECIATION

Many depreciation methods for allocating a plant asset's total cost among the several accounting periods in its service life have been suggested and used in the past. However, at present, most companies use the *straight-line method* of depreciation in their financial accounting records for presentation in their financial statements. Some types of assets are depreciated according to the *units-of-production method.* We explain these two methods next and then consider some *accelerated depreciation* methods.

Straight-Line Method

Straight-line depreciation charges each year in the asset's life with the same amount of expense. To determine the annual expense, the total cost to be depreciated over the asset's life is calculated by first subtracting the asset's estimated salvage value from its cost. This total amount to be depreciated is then divided by the estimated number of accounting periods in the asset's service life.

For example, if an asset costs $7,000, has an estimated service life of five years, and has an estimated $2,000 salvage value, its depreciation per year by the straight-line method is $1,000. This amount is calculated as follows:

$$\frac{\text{Cost} - \text{Salvage}}{\text{Service life in years}} = \frac{\$7,000 - \$2,000}{5 \text{ years}} = \$1,000 \text{ per year}$$

If this asset is purchased on December 31, 19X1, and used throughout its predicted service life of five years, the straight-line method will allocate an equal amount of depreciation to each of those years (19X2 through 19X6). The left graph in Illustration 10–1 shows that this $1,000 per year amount will be reported each year as an expense. The right graph shows the amount that will be reported on each of the six balance sheets that will be produced while the company actually owns the asset. This **book value** of the asset is its original cost less accumulated depreciation. The book

value goes down by $1,000 each year. Both graphs show why this method is called *straight-line.*

Although most companies use straight-line depreciation, other methods are common in certain industries. For example, **Boise Cascade Corporation** uses the units-of-production method in nearly all of its facilities that manufacture paper and wood products.

Units-of-Production Method

The purpose of recording depreciation is to provide relevant information about the cost of consuming an asset's usefulness. In general, this means that each accounting period an asset is used should be charged with a fair share of its cost. The straight-line method charges an equal share to each period. If plant assets are used about the same amount in each accounting period, this method produces a reasonable result. However, the use of some plant assets varies greatly from one accounting period to another. For example, a contractor may use a particular piece of construction equipment for a month and then not use it again for a few months.

Because the use of such equipment varies from period to period, **units-of-production depreciation** may provide a better matching of expenses with revenues than straight-line depreciation. Under the units-of-production method, the cost of an asset minus its estimated salvage value is divided by the total number of units that management predicts it will produce during its service life. Units of production may be expressed as units of product or in any other unit of measure such as hours of use

Illustration 10-1 The Financial Statement of Straight-Line Depreciation

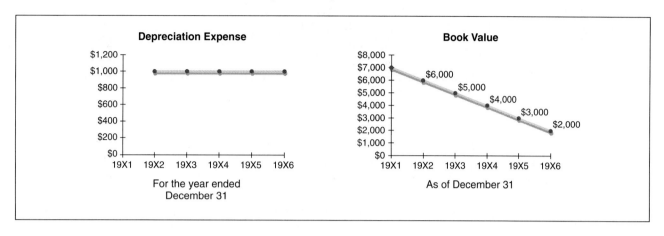

Illustration 10-1 The Financial Statement of Straight-Line Depreciation

or miles driven. In effect, this method computes the amount of depreciation per unit of service provided by the asset. Then, the amount of depreciation taken in an accounting period is determined by multiplying the units produced in that period by the depreciation per unit.

For example, a truck that cost $24,000 has a predicted salvage value of $4,000 and an estimated service life of 125,000 miles. The depreciation per mile, or the depreciation per unit of service, is $0.16, which is calculated as follows:

$$\text{Depreciation per unit of production} = \frac{\text{Cost} - \text{Salvage value}}{\text{Predicted units of production}}$$

$$= \frac{\$24,000 - \$4,000}{125,000 \text{ miles}}$$

$$= \$0.16 \text{ per mile}$$

If the truck is driven 20,000 miles during its first year, depreciation for the first year is $3,200 (20,000 miles at $0.16 per mile). If the truck is driven 15,000 miles in the second year, depreciation for the second year is 15,000 miles times $0.16 per mile, or $2,400.

Of course, plant assets may be purchased or disposed of at any time during the year. When an asset is purchased (or disposed of) at some time other than the beginning or end of an accounting period, depreciation must be recorded for part of a year. Otherwise, the year of purchase or the year of disposal is not charged with its share of the asset's depreciation.

DEPRECIATION FOR PARTIAL YEARS

For example, assume that a machine was purchased and placed in service on October 8, 19X1, and that the annual accounting period ends on December 31. The machine cost $4,600; it has an estimated service life of five years and an estimated salvage value of $600. Because the machine was purchased and used nearly three months during 19X1, the annual income statement should reflect depreciation expense on the machine for that part of the year. The amount of depreciation to be reported is often based on the assumption that the machine was purchased on the first of the month nearest the actual date of purchase. Therefore, since the purchase occurred on October 8, three months' depreciation is recorded on December 31. If the purchase had been on October 16 or later during October, depreciation would be calculated as if the purchase had been on November 1. Using straight-line depreciation, the three months' depreciation of $200 is calculated as follows:

$$\frac{\$4,600 - \$600}{5} \times \frac{3}{12} = \$200$$

A similar calculation is necessary when the disposal of an asset occurs during a year. For example, suppose that the preceding asset is sold on June 24, 19X6. On the date of the disposal, depreciation should be recognized. The partial year's depreciation, calculated to the nearest whole month, is:

$$\frac{\$4,600 - \$600}{5} \times \frac{6}{12} = x400$$

DEPRECIATION ON THE BALANCE SHEET

In presenting information about the plant assets of a business, both the cost and accumulated depreciation of plant assets should be reported. For example, **Apple Computer, Inc.'s** balance sheet at the close of its 1993 fiscal year included the following:

(Dollars in thousands)	1993	1992
Property, plant, and equipment:		
Land and buildings	$ 404,688	$ 255,808
Machinery and equipment	578,272	516,335
Office furniture and equipment	167,905	155,317
Leasehold improvements	261,792	208,180
	$1,412,657	$1,135,640
Accumulated depreciation and amortization . .	(753,111)	(673,419)
Net property, plant, and equipment	$ 659,546	$ 462,221

PRINCIPLE APPLICATION
Full Disclosure Principle,
p. 326
In the footnotes to its 1993 financial statements, Sara Lee Corporation states: "Property is stated at cost, and depreciation is computed using principally the straight-line method at annual rates of 2% to 20% for buildings and improvements, and 5% to 50% for machinery and equipment."

Notice that Apple reported only the total amount of accumulated depreciation and amortization for all plant and equipment. This is the usual practice in published financial statements. In fact, many companies show plant and equipment on one line with the net amount of cost less accumulated depreciation. When this is done, however, the amount of accumulated depreciation is disclosed in a footnote. To satisfy the *full-disclosure principle,* companies also describe the depreciation method or methods used.[2] Usually, they do this in a footnote.

Reporting both the cost and the accumulated depreciation of plant assets may help balance sheet readers compare the status of different companies. For example, a company that holds assets having an original cost of $50,000 and accumulated depreciation of $40,000 may be in quite a different situation than another company with new assets that cost $10,000. Although the net undepreciated cost is the same in both cases, the first company may have more productive capacity available but probably is facing the need to replace its older assets. These differences are not conveyed if the balance sheets report only the $10,000 book values.

From the discussion so far, you should recognize that depreciation is a process of cost allocation rather than valuation. Plant assets are reported on balance sheets at their remaining undepreciated costs (book value), not at market values.

---

[2]FASB, *Accounting Standards—Current Text* (Norwalk, CT, 1994), sec. D40.101. First published as *APB Opinion No. 12,* par. 5.

Some people argue that financial statements should report the market value of plant assets. However, this practice has not gained general acceptance. Instead, most accountants believe that financial statements should be based on the *going-concern principle* described in Chapter 1. This principle states that, unless there is adequate evidence to the contrary, the accountant should assume the company will continue in business. This leads to a related assumption that plant assets will be held and used long enough to recover their original cost through the sale of products and services. Therefore, since the plant assets will not be sold, their market values are not reported in the financial statements. Instead, the assets are carried on the balance sheet at cost less accumulated depreciation. This is the remaining portion of the original cost that is expected to be recovered in future periods.

Inexperienced financial statement readers may make the mistake of thinking that the accumulated depreciation shown on a balance sheet represents funds accumulated to buy new assets when the presently owned assets must be replaced. However, you know that accumulated depreciation is a contra account with a credit balance that cannot be used to buy anything. If a business has funds available to buy assets, the funds are shown on the balance sheet as liquid assets such as *Cash,* not as accumulated depreciation.

REVISING DEPRECIATION RATES

Because the calculation of depreciation must be based on an asset's *predicted* useful life, depreciation expense is an estimate. Therefore, during the life of an asset, new information may indicate that the original prediction of useful life was inaccurate. If your estimate of an asset's useful life changes, what should be done? The answer is to use the new estimate of the remaining useful life to calculate depreciation in the future. In other words, revise the estimate of annual depreciation expense in the future by spreading the remaining cost to be depreciated over the revised remaining useful life. This approach should be followed whether the depreciation method is straight-line, units-of-production, or some other method.

For example, assume that a machine was purchased seven years ago at a cost of $10,500. At that time, the machine was predicted to have a 10-year life with a $500 salvage value. Therefore, it was depreciated by the straight-line method at the rate of $1,000 per year [($10,500 − $500)/10 = $1,000]. At the beginning of the asset's eighth year, its book value is $3,500, calculated as follows:

Cost	$10,500
Less seven years' accumulated depreciation	7,000
Book value	$ 3,500

At the beginning of its eighth year, the predicted number of years remaining in the useful life is changed from three to five years. The estimated salvage value is also changed to $300. Depreciation for each of the machine's five remaining years should be calculated as follows:

$$\frac{\text{Book value} - \text{Revised salvage value}}{\text{Revised remaining useful life}} = \frac{\$3,500 - \$300}{5 \text{ years}} = \$640 \text{ per year}$$

Thus, $640 of depreciation should be recorded for the machine at the end of the eighth and each remaining year in its useful life.

Because this asset was depreciated at the rate of $1,000 per year for the first seven years, you might contend that depreciation expense was overstated during the first seven years. While that view may have merit, accountants have concluded that past

As a Matter of Ethics

Fascar Company has struggled financially for more than two years. The economic situation surrounding the company has been depressed and there are no signs of improvement for at least two more years. As a result, net income has been almost zero, and the future seems bleak.

The operations of Fascar require major investments in equipment. As a result, depreciation is a large factor in the calculation of income. Because competition in Fascar's industry normally has required frequent replacements of equipment, the equipment has been depreciated over only three years. However, Fascar's president has recently in-structed Sue Ann Meyer, the company's accountant, to revise the estimated useful lives of existing equipment to six years and to use a six-year life on new equipment.

Meyer suspects that the president's instruction is motivated by a desire to improve the reported income of the company. In trying to determine whether to follow the president's instructions, Meyer is torn between her loyalty to her employer and her responsibility to the public, the stockholders, and others who use the company's financial statements. She also wonders what the independent CPA who audits the financial statements will think about the change.

years' financial statements generally should not be restated to reflect facts that were not known when the statements were originally prepared.

A revision of the predicted useful life of a plant asset is an example of a **change in an accounting estimate.** Such changes result "from new information or subsequent developments and accordingly from better insight or improved judgment." Generally accepted accounting principles require that changes in accounting estimates, such as a change in estimated useful life or salvage value, be reflected only in future financial statements, not by modifying past statements.[3]

Progress Check

10-4 For accounting purposes, what is the meaning of the term *depreciation?*

10-5 Clandestine Gift Shop purchased a new machine for $96,000 on January 1, 19X1. Its predicted useful life is five years or 100,000 units of product, and salvage value is $8,000. During 19X1, 10,000 units of product were produced. Find the book value of the machine on December 31, 19X1, assuming *(a)* straight-line depreciation and *(b)* units-of-production depreciation.

10-6 In early January of 19X1, Betty's Brownies acquired mixing equipment at a cost of $3,800. The company estimated that this equipment would be used for three years and then have a salvage of $200. Early in 19X3, they changed the estimate to a four-year life with no residual value. Assuming straight-line depreciation, how much will be reported as depreciation on this equipment for the year ended 19X3?

ACCELERATED DEPRECIATION

LO 3

Describe the use of accelerated depreciation for financial accounting and tax accounting purposes and calculate accelerated depreciation under *(a)* the declining-balance method, and *(b)* the Modified Accelerated Cost Recovery System.

An annual survey of 600 industrial companies indicates that straight-line is the most widely used method of depreciation. However, note in the following table that **accelerated depreciation** methods were used 13% of the time in 1993:

	Depreciation Methods Used	
	1993	1992
Straight-line	80%	78%
An accelerated method	13	14
Units-of-production	6	7
Other	1	1
Total	100%	100%

Source: *Accounting Trends & Techniques,* Copyright © 1994 (1993) by American Institute of Certified Public Accountants, Inc., Table 3–13, p. 361.

---

[3]FASB, *Accounting Standards—Current Text* (Norwalk, CT, 1994), sec. A35.104 and sec. A06.130. First published as *APB Opinion No. 20,* par. 13 and par. 31.

Accelerated depreciation methods produce larger depreciation charges during the early years of an asset's life and smaller charges in the later years. Although more than one accelerated method is used in financial reporting, the most commonly used is the declining-balance method.

Declining-Balance Method

Under **declining-balance depreciation,** a depreciation rate of up to twice the straight-line rate is applied each year to the book value of the asset at the beginning of the year. Because the book value *declines* each year, the amount of depreciation gets smaller each year.

When the depreciation rate used is twice the straight-line rate, the method is called the *double-declining-balance method.* To use the double-declining-balance method: (1) calculate the straight-line depreciation rate for the asset; (2) double it; and (3) calculate depreciation expense for the year by applying this rate to the asset's book value at the beginning of that year. Note that the salvage value is not used in the calculation.

For example, assume that the double-declining-balance method is used to calculate depreciation on a new $10,000 asset; it has an estimated life of five years and an estimated salvage value of $1,000. The steps to follow are:

1. Divide 100% by five years to determine the straight-line annual depreciation rate of 20% per year.
2. Double this 20% rate to get a declining-balance rate of 40% per year.
3. Calculate the annual depreciation charges as shown in the following table:

Year	Beginning Book Value	Annual Depreciation (40% of Book Value)	Accumulated Depreciation at Year-End	Ending Book Value ($10,000 Cost Less Accumulated Depreciation)
First	$10,000	$4,000	$4,000	$6,000
Second	6,000	2,400	6,400	3,600
Third	3,600	1,440	7,840	2,160
Fourth	2,160	864	8,704	1,296
Fifth	1,296	296*	9,000	1,000
Total		$9,000		

*Fifth year depreciation is $1,296 − $1,000 = $296.

In the fifth year of the table, notice that the annual depreciation of $296 for the fifth year does not equal 40% × $1,296, or $518.40. Instead, the $296 was calculated by subtracting the $1,000 salvage value from the $1,296 book value at the beginning of the fifth year. This was done because, according to generally accepted accounting principles, an asset should not be depreciated below its salvage value. If the declining-balance procedure had been applied in the fifth year, the $518.40 of annual depreciation would have reduced the ending book value to $777.60, which is less than the $1,000 estimated salvage value.

Earlier in the chapter we discussed the calculation of a partial year's depreciation when the straight-line method is used. Recall that when an asset is purchased (or disposed of) at some time other than the end of an accounting period, depreciation must be recorded for part of a year. Declining-balance depreciation does not complicate this calculation. For example, if depreciation must be calculated for three months, the annual amount of depreciation is simply multiplied by $^3/_{12}$. So, if an asset that cost $10,000 is purchased three months before the end of the year and the annual declining-balance depreciation rate is 20%, depreciation for the last three months is $10,000 × 20% × $^3/_{12}$ = $500.

	Asset Classes		
Year	**Three-Year**	**Five-Year**	**Seven-Year**
1	33.33%	20.00%	14.29%
2	44.45	32.00	24.49
3	14.81	19.20	17.49
4	7.41	11.52	12.49
5		11.52	8.93
6		5.76	8.92
7			8.93
8			4.46
Total	100.00%	100.00%	100.00%

Accelerated Depreciation for Tax Purposes

Some people fail to understand why the records a company keeps for financial accounting purposes may be different from the records it keeps for tax accounting purposes. Some may even suspect fraud when they hear there are differences between the two sets of records. In fact, differences between the two are normal and to be expected. Accelerated depreciation provides an example of this.

Many companies prefer to use accelerated depreciation for the purpose of calculating their taxable income. Accelerated methods reduce taxable income in the early years of an asset's life and increase taxable income in the later years. The effect of this is to defer income tax payments. Taxes are decreased in the early years and increased in the later years.

Beginning in 1981, a United States federal income tax law installed new rules for depreciating assets. Those rules were revised beginning in 1987 and are now called the **Modified Accelerated Cost Recovery System (MACRS).** MACRS allows straight-line depreciation and for most kinds of property also provides an accelerated method. MACRS separates depreciable assets purchased after December 31, 1986, into eight different types or classes. These include 3-year, 5-year, 7-year, 10-year, 15-year, 20-year, 27$\frac{1}{2}$-year, 31$\frac{1}{2}$-year, and 39-year classes. For example, computer equipment and general-purpose, heavy trucks are in the five-year class while office furniture is in the seven-year class.

When calculating depreciation for tax purposes, salvage values are ignored. Also, depreciation methods for personal property are based on the assumption that the asset is purchased half-way through the year and sold or retired half-way through the year. This *half-year convention* is required regardless of when the asset was actually purchased or sold.[4]

To simplify accelerated calculations under MACRS, the Internal Revenue Service provides a table for each class of assets. The tables show the percentage of original cost to be deducted as depreciation on each year's tax return. For example, Illustration 10–2 shows the accelerated depreciation rates for the three-year, five-year, and seven-year classes. In the table, note that it takes four years to fully depreciate the assets in the three-year class. Also, it takes six years to depreciate the assets in the five-year class, and eight years to depreciate the assets in the seven-year class. This happens because the half-year convention provides one-half of one year's depreciation during the first year and one-half of one year's depreciation during the last year.

Remember that the half-year convention also applies to straight-line depreciation under MACRS. Thus, under straight-line, it also takes four years to fully depreciate an asset in the three-year class.

[4]Under certain conditions, a half-quarter convention must be used. Depreciation methods for real property are based on a half-month convention.

As an example of how MACRS is applied, assume an asset in the five-year class (for example, a general-purpose, heavy truck) is purchased in 19X1 at a cost of $10,000. In the following table, the second column shows the MACRS accelerated rates for assets in the five-year class, which includes the truck. The remaining columns in the table show the effects of applying accelerated depreciation under MACRS to the $10,000 truck:

Year	MACRS Accelerated Depreciation Rate	Beginning Tax Basis	(Depreciation Rate × $10,000)	Ending Tax Basis
19X1	20.00%	$10,000	$2,000	$8,000
19X2	32.00	8,000	3,200	4,800
19X3	19.20	4,800	1,920	2,880
19X4	11.52	2,880	1,152	1,728
19X5	11.52	1,728	1,152	576
19X6	5.76	576	576	0
Total	100.00%			

While MACRS is now required for tax purposes, MACRS is not consistent with *generally accepted accounting principles.* It is not consistent because it allocates depreciation over an arbitrary period that usually is much shorter than the estimated service life of the asset. For example, general-purpose, heavy trucks in the 5-year class normally have useful lives of up to 10 years. Even when straight-line depreciation is used under MACRS, acceleration occurs because the length of life assumed for tax purposes is shorter than the expected service life of the asset. As a result, companies typically have to keep one set of depreciation records for tax purposes and another set for financial accounting purposes.

Progress Check

10-7   On January 1, 19X1, Temperware Industries paid $77,000 to purchase office furniture having an estimated salvage value of $14,000. The furniture has an estimated service life of 10 years, but it is in the 7-year class for tax purposes. What is the 19X1 depreciation on the furniture using (1) the double-declining-balance method for financial accounting purposes and (2) the straight-line method under MACRS with the half-year convention?

By this time, you have learned that some expenditures are recorded as expenses right away while others are recorded as assets with expenses coming later. After a plant asset is acquired and put into service, additional expenditures may be incurred to operate, maintain, repair, and improve it. In recording these additional expenditures, the accountant must decide whether they should be debited to expense accounts or asset accounts. The issue is whether more useful information is provided by reporting these expenditures as current expenses or by adding them to the plant asset's cost and depreciating them over its remaining useful life.

Expenditures that are recorded as expenses and deducted from revenues on the current period's income statement are called **revenue expenditures.** They are reported on the income statement because they do not provide material benefits in future periods. Examples of revenue expenditures that relate to plant assets are supplies, fuel, lubricants, and electrical power.

In contrast to revenue expenditures, **capital expenditures** produce economic benefits that do not fully expire before the end of the current period. Because they are

REVENUE AND CAPITAL EXPENDITURES

LO 4

Describe the difference between revenue and capital expenditures and account properly for costs such as repairs and betterments incurred after the original purchase of plant assets.

debited to asset accounts and reported on the balance sheet, they are also called **balance sheet expenditures.** Capital expenditures increase or improve the kind or amount of service that an asset provides.

Because the information in the financial statements is affected for several years by the choice you make in recording costs as revenue or capital expenditures, managers must be careful in deciding how to classify them. In making these decisions, it is helpful to identify the costs as ordinary repairs, extraordinary repairs, betterments, or purchases of assets with low costs.

Ordinary Repairs

Ordinary repairs are made to keep an asset in normal, good operating condition. These expenditures are necessary if an asset is to provide its expected level of service over its estimated useful life. However, ordinary repairs do not extend the useful life beyond the original estimate and do not increase the productivity of the asset beyond the levels originally estimated. For example, machines must be cleaned, lubricated, and adjusted, and small parts must be replaced when they wear out. These

ordinary repairs typically are made every year, and accountants treat them as *revenue expenditures.* Thus, their costs should be reported on the current income statement as expenses.

Consistent with the guidelines given here, America West Airlines, Inc., expenses routine maintenance and repairs as incurred. In addition, the cost of scheduled airframe and engine overhauls is capitalized because such expenditures are expected to benefit future periods.

Extraordinary Repairs

In contrast to ordinary repairs that keep a plant asset in its normal, good operating condition, **extraordinary repairs** extend the asset's service life beyond the original estimate. Because they benefit future periods, the costs of extraordinary repairs are *capital expenditures.* They may be debited to the asset account. However, by tradition, they are debited to the repaired asset's accumulated depreciation account to show that they restore the effects of past years' depreciation. For example, a machine was purchased for $8,000 and depreciated under the assumption it would last eight years and have no salvage value. At the beginning of the machine's seventh year, when the machine's book value is $2,000, it is given a major overhaul at a cost of $2,100. The overhaul extends the machine's estimated useful life three years. Thus, the company now predicts that the machine will be used for five more years. The $2,100 cost of the extraordinary repair should be recorded as follows:

Jan.	12	Accumulated Depreciation, Machinery	2,100.00	
		Cash		2,100.00
		To record extraordinary repairs.		

This entry increases the book value of the asset from $2,000 to $4,100. For the remaining five years of the asset's life, depreciation should be based on this new book value. The effects of the extraordinary repairs are as follows:

	Before	Extraordinary Repair	After
Original cost	$ 8,000		$ 8,000
Accumulated depreciation	(6,000)	$2,100	(3,900)
Book value	$ 2,000		$ 4,100
Annual depreciation expense for remaining years ($4,100/5 years)			$820

Notice that because the $2,100 cost of the extraordinary repairs is included in the $4,100 book value, it is depreciated over the asset's remaining life of five years.

Betterments

A **betterment** (or an improvement) occurs when a plant asset is modified to make it more efficient or productive. A betterment often involves adding a component to an asset or replacing one of its old components with an improved or superior component. While a betterment makes an asset more productive, it may not increase the asset's useful life. For example, replacing the manual controls on a machine with automatic controls reduces future labor costs. But, the machine still wears out just as fast as it would have with the manual controls.

A betterment benefits future periods and should be debited to the asset account as a capital expenditure. Then, the new book value (less salvage) should be depreciated over the remaining service life of the asset. For example, suppose that a company paid $80,000 for a machine with an eight-year service life and no salvage value. On January 2, after three years and $30,000 of depreciation, it adds an automatic control system to the machine at a cost of $18,000. As a result, the company's labor cost to operate the machine in future periods will be reduced. The cost of the betterment is added to the Machinery account with this entry:

Jan.	2	Machinery	18,000.00	
		Cash		18,000.00
		To record the installation of the automatic control system.		

At this point, the remaining cost to be depreciated is $80,000 + $18,000 − $30,000 = $68,000. Because five years remain in the useful life, the annual depreciation expense hereafter will be $13,600 per year ($68,000/5 years).

Plant Assets with Low Costs

Even with the help of computers, keeping individual plant asset records can be expensive. Therefore, many companies do not keep detailed records for assets that cost less than some minimum amount such as $50 or $100. Instead, they treat the acqui-

sition as a revenue expenditure and charge the cost directly to an expense account at the time of purchase. As long as the amounts are small, this practice is acceptable under the *materiality principle*. That is, treating these capital expenditures as revenue expenditures is unlikely to mislead a user of the financial statements.

In its 1993 annual report, Coca-Cola Bottling Co. Consolidated discloses the following aspects of its accounting policies related to plant assets:

Property, plant and equipment are recorded at cost and depreciated using the straight-line method over the estimated useful lives of the assets. Additions and major replacements or betterments are added to the assets at cost. Maintenance and repair costs and minor replacements are charged to expense when incurred. When assets are replaced or otherwise disposed of, the cost and accumulated depreciation are removed from the accounts, and the gain or loss, if any, is reflected in income.

Progress Check

10-8 **At the beginning of the fifth year of a machine's estimated six-year useful life, the machine was completely overhauled and its estimated useful life was extended to nine years in total. The machine originally cost $108,000, and the overhaul cost was $12,000. Prepare the journal entry to record the cost of the overhaul.**

10-9 **What is the difference between revenue expenditures and capital expenditures and how should they be recorded?**

10-10 **What is a betterment? How should a betterment to a machine be recorded?**

PLANT ASSET DISPOSALS

LO 5

Prepare entries to account for the disposal or exchange of plant assets and explain the use of total asset turnover in evaluating a company's efficiency in using its assets.

A variety of events might lead to the disposal of plant assets. Some assets wear out or become obsolete. Other assets may be sold because of changing business plans. Sometimes, an asset is discarded or sold because it is damaged by a fire or other accident. Regardless of what leads to a disposal, the journal entry or entries related to the disposal should:

1. Record depreciation expense up to the date of the disposal and bring the accumulated depreciation account up to date.
2. Remove the asset and accumulated depreciation account balances that relate to the disposal.
3. Record any cash received or paid as a result of the disposal.
4. Record any gain or loss that results from comparing the book value of the asset with the cash received or paid as a result of the disposal.

For example, assume a machine that cost $9,000 was totally destroyed in a fire on June 25. Accumulated depreciation at the end of the previous year was $3,000 and unrecorded depreciation for the first six months of the current year is $500. The following entry brings the accumulated depreciation account up to date:

June	25	Depreciation Expense	500.00	
		Accumulated Depreciation, Machinery		500.00
		To record depreciation up to the date of the fire.		

Assume the owner of the machine carried insurance against fire losses and received a $4,400 cash settlement for the loss. The following entry records the loss of the machine and the cash settlement:

June	25	Cash	4,400.00	
		Loss on Fire[5]	1,100.00	
		Accumulated Depreciation, Machinery	3,500.00	
		Machinery		9,000.00
		To record the destruction of machinery, the receipt of insurance settlement, and the net loss resulting from the fire.		

Notice that the two entries accomplish all four of the necessary changes that occurred as a result of the asset disposal. Of course, an asset disposal might involve a gain instead of a loss. Also, a disposal might involve a cash payment instead of a receipt. Regardless of the specific facts, entries similar to these must be made so the income statement shows any gain or loss resulting from the disposal and the balance sheet reflects the necessary changes in the asset and accumulated depreciation accounts.

In recent years, many corporations have restructured and downsized their operations. These activities frequently involve disposing of plant assets. For example, as part of its restructuring, **Woolworth Corporation** sold approximately 120 of its Woolco discount stores to Wal-Mart Stores. At the same time, Woolworth planned to continue expanding in the area of specialty operations such as Foot Locker, Northern Reflections, and Accessory Lady. The disposition of the Woolco stores resulted in a $168 million loss that was charged against revenues and contributed to a $495 million reported net loss. It is also interesting to note that the disposition of the Woolco stores generated net cash of approximately $200 million.

Many plant assets are sold for cash when they are retired from use. Others, such as machinery, automobiles, and office equipment, are commonly exchanged for new assets. In a typical exchange of assets, a trade-in allowance is received on the old asset, and any balance is paid in cash.

EXCHANGING PLANT ASSETS

Accounting for the exchange of nonmonetary assets depends on whether the old and the new assets are similar in the functions they perform. For example, trading an old truck for a new truck is an exchange of similar assets. An example of exchanging dissimilar assets would be trading a parcel of land for a truck.

Exchanges of Dissimilar Assets

If a company exchanges a plant asset for another asset that is *dissimilar* in use or purpose, any gain or loss on the exchange must be recorded. The gain or loss can be determined by comparing the book value of the assets given up with the fair market value of the assets received. For example, assume that a company exchanges an old machine plus $16,500 cash for some merchandise inventory. The old machine originally cost $18,000 and had accumulated depreciation of $15,000 at the time of the

---

[5]Note that the recorded loss of $1,100 probably does not equal the economic loss from the fire. The economic loss depends on the difference between the cost of replacing the asset and any insurance settlement. A difference between this economic loss and the reported loss arises from the fact that the accounting records do not attempt to reflect the replacement value of plant assets.

exchange. Also assume that the fair market value of the merchandise received in the exchange was $21,000. This entry would record the exchange:

Jan.	5	Merchandise Inventory (or Purchases)	21,000.00	
		Accumulated Depreciation, Machinery	15,000.00	
		Machinery		18,000.00
		Cash		16,500.00
		Gain on Exchange of Machinery		1,500.00
		Exchanged old machine and cash for merchandise		
		inventory.		

Note that the book value of the assets given up totaled $19,500, which included $16,500 cash plus $3,000 ($18,000 − $15,000) for the machine. Because the merchandise had a fair market value of $21,000, the entry recorded a gain of $1,500 ($21,000 − $19,500).

Another way to calculate the gain or loss is to compare the machine's book value with the trade-in allowance granted for the machine. Since the fair market value of the merchandise was $21,000 and the cash paid was $16,500, the trade-in allowance granted for the machine was $4,500. The difference between the machine's $3,000 book value and the $4,500 trade-in allowance equals the $1,500 gain on the exchange.

Exchanges of Similar Assets

In general, accounting for exchanges of similar assets depends on whether the book value of the asset given up is less or more than the trade-in allowance received for the asset.[6] When the trade-in allowance is less than the book value, the difference is recognized as a loss. However, when the trade-in allowance is more than the book value, no gain is recognized.

Recognition of a Loss. To illustrate the recognition of a loss on an exchange of similar assets, assume the machine that cost $18,000 and has accumulated depreciation of $15,000 is traded in on a similar but new machine. The new machine has a $21,000 cash price, and a $1,000 trade-in allowance is received. The $20,000 balance of the cost is paid in cash. Under these assumptions, the book value of the old machine and the loss on the exchange are calculated as follows:

Cost of old machine	$18,000
Less accumulated depreciation	15,000
Book value	$ 3,000
Less trade-in allowance	1,000
Loss on exchange	$ 2,000

---

[6]These general rules apply to exchanges of similar assets when the exchange includes a cash payment or when no cash is received or paid. The accounting is more complex when the exchange involves a cash receipt. Such cases are explained in more advanced accounting texts. See FASB, *Accounting Standards— Current Text* (Norwalk, CT, 1994), sec. N35.109. First published as *APB Opinion No. 29,* par. 22.

The entry to record this exchange transaction is:

Jan.	5	Machinery	21,000.00	
		Loss on Exchange of Machinery	2,000.00	
		Accumulated Depreciation, Machinery	15,000.00	
		Machinery		18,000.00
		Cash		20,000.00
		Exchanged old machine and cash for a similar machine.		

The $21,000 debit to Machinery puts the new machine in the accounts at its cash price. The debit to Loss on Exchange of Machinery records the loss. The old machine is removed from the accounts with the $15,000 debit to Accumulated Depreciation, Machinery and the $18,000 credit to Machinery.

Nonrecognition of a Gain. When similar assets are exchanged and the trade-in allowance of the asset given up is more than its book value, the difference between the trade-in allowance and the book value may be perceived as a gain. However, generally accepted accounting principles do not allow the recognition of this gain. Instead, the new asset is recorded at the sum of the old asset's book value plus any cash paid.

For example, assume that the exchange for the $21,000 machine in the previous section involved a trade-in allowance of $4,500 instead of $1,000. As a result, the balance to be paid in cash is only $16,500. Since the $4,500 trade-in allowance exceeds the $3,000 book value of the old asset, the difference is a gain. However, you cannot recognize the gain in the accounts. Rather, it is absorbed into the cost of the new machine, which is calculated as follows:

Cost of old machine	$18,000
Less accumulated depreciation	15,000
Book value of old machine	$ 3,000
Cash given in the exchange	16,500
Cost recorded for the new machine	$19,500

The following entry records the exchange:

Jan.	5	Machinery	19,500.00	
		Accumulated Depreciation, Machinery	15,000.00	
		Machinery		18,000.00
		Cash		16,500.00
		Exchanged old machine and cash for a similar but new machine.		

Observe that the $19,500 recorded for the new machine equals its cash price less the unrecognized $1,500 gain on the exchange ($21,000 − $1,500 = $19,500). In other words, the $1,500 gain was absorbed into the amount at which the new machine was recorded. The $19,500 is the *cost basis* of the new machine and is the amount used to calculate its depreciation and/or any gain or loss on its sale.

In summary, when similar plant assets are exchanged and there is a cash payment, losses are recognized but gains are not recognized. This rule is based on the opinion that "revenue [or a gain] should not be recognized merely because one productive asset is substituted for a similar productive asset but rather should be considered to flow from the production and sale of the goods or services to which the substituted productive asset is committed."[7] As a result, the effect of a gain is delayed. In future income statements, the gain appears in the form of smaller depreciation charges or perhaps as a gain on the sale of the asset. In the previous example, depreciation calculated on the recorded $19,500 cost basis of the new machine is smaller than it would be if it was based on the machine's $21,000 cash price.

USING THE INFORMATION— TOTAL ASSET TURNOVER

We have not yet discussed all of the different assets a business might own. Nevertheless, you can see from this and previous chapters that a company's assets are usually very important factors in determining the company's ability to earn profits. Managers spend a great deal of time and energy deciding which assets a company should acquire, how much should be acquired, and how the assets can be used most efficiently. Outside investors and other financial statement readers are also interested in evaluating whether a company uses its assets efficiently.

One way to describe the efficiency of a company's use of its assets is to calculate **total asset turnover.** The formula for this calculation is:

$$\text{Total asset turnover} = \frac{\text{Net sales}}{\text{Average total assets}}$$

In this calculation, average total assets is often approximated by averaging the total assets at the beginning of the year with total assets at the end of the year.

For example, suppose that a company with total assets of $9,650,000 at the beginning of the year and $10,850,000 at the end of the year generated sales of $44,000,000 during the year. The company's total asset turnover for the year is calculated as follows:

$$\text{Total asset turnover} = \frac{\$44,000,000}{(\$9,650,000 + \$10,850,000)/2} = 4.3$$

Thus, in describing the efficiency of the company in using its assets to generate sales, we can say that it turned its assets over 4.3 times during the year. Or, we might say that each $1.00 of assets produced $4.30 of sales during the year.

As is true for other financial ratios, a company's total asset turnover is meaningful only when compared to the results in other years and of similar companies. Interpreting the total asset turnover also requires that users understand the company's operations. Some operations are capital intensive, meaning that a relatively large amount must be invested in assets to generate sales. This suggests a relatively low total asset turnover. On the other hand, if operations are labor intensive, sales are generated more by the efforts of people than the use of assets. Thus, we would expect a higher total asset turnover.

Fortune magazine conducts an annual Corporate Reputations Survey, in which more than 10,000 senior executives, outside directors, and financial analysts are asked to rate the 10 largest companies in their own industries on eight attributes of reputation. One of eight attributes is "use of corporate assets." In this category for 1993 the top scorer was **Rubbermaid Incorporated**. Rubbermaid's total asset turnover in 1993 was:

$$\text{Total asset turnover} = \frac{\$1,960,207,000}{(1,513,124,000 + 1,326,569,000)/2} = 1.38$$

---

[7]APB, "Accounting for Nonmonetary Transactions," *APB Opinion No. 29* (New York: AICPA, May 1973), par. 16.

Progress Check

10–11 Melanie Co. acquired equipment on January 10, 19X1, at a cost of $42,000. Straight-line depreciation was used assuming a five year life and $7,000 salvage value. On June 27, 19X2, the company decided to change their manufacturing methods and sold this equipment for $32,000. Prepare the appropriate entry or entries for June 27, 19X2.

10–12 Standard Company traded an old truck for a new one. The original cost of the old truck was $30,000, and its accumulated depreciation at the time of the trade was $23,400. The new truck had a cash price of $45,000. Prepare entries to record the trade assuming Standard received (a) a $3,000 trade-in allowance or (b) a $7,000 trade-in allowance.

10–13 Using the annual report for Federal Express Corporation in Appendix G, calculate the total asset turnover for the year ended September 24, 1993.

SUMMARY OF THE CHAPTER IN TERMS OF LEARNING OBJECTIVES

LO 1. **Describe the differences between plant assets and other kinds of assets, and calculate the cost and record the purchase of plant assets.** Plant assets are tangible items that have a useful life longer than one accounting period. Plant assets are not held for sale but are used in the production or sale of other assets or services. The cost of plant assets includes all normal and reasonable expenditures necessary to get the assets in place and ready to use. The cost of a lump-sum purchase should be allocated among the individual assets based on their relative market values.

LO 2. **Explain depreciation accounting (including the reasons for depreciation), calculate depreciation by the straight-line and units-of-production methods, and calculate depreciation after revising the estimated useful life of an asset.** The cost of plant assets that have limited service lives must be allocated to the accounting periods that benefit from their use. The straight-line method of depreciation divides the cost minus salvage value by the number of periods in the service life of the asset to determine the depreciation expense of each period. The units-of-production method divides the cost minus salvage value by the estimated number of units the asset will produce to determine the depreciation per unit. If the estimated useful life of a plant asset is changed, the remaining cost to be depreciated is spread over the remaining (revised) useful life of the asset.

LO 3. **Describe the use of accelerated depreciation for financial accounting and tax accounting purposes and calculate accelerated depreciation under (a) the declining-balance method, and (b) the Modified Accelerated Cost Recovery System.** Accelerated depreciation methods such as the declining-balance method are acceptable for financial accounting purposes if they are based on realistic estimates of useful life. However, they are not widely used at the present time. The Modified Accelerated Cost Recovery System (MACRS), which is used for tax purposes, is not based on realistic estimates of useful life. Thus, MACRS is not acceptable for financial accounting purposes.

LO 4. **Describe the difference between revenue and capital expenditures and account properly for costs such as repairs and betterments incurred after the original purchase of plant assets.** The benefit of revenue expenditures expires during the current period. Thus, revenue expenditures are debited to expense accounts and matched with current revenues. Capital expenditures are debited to asset accounts because they benefit future periods. Ordinary repairs are revenue expenditures. Examples of capital expenditures include extraordinary repairs and betterments. Amounts paid for assets with low costs are technically capital expenditures but can be treated as revenue expenditures if they are not material.

LO 5. **Prepare entries to account for the disposal or exchange of plant assets and explain the use of total asset turnover in evaluating a company's efficiency in using its assets.** When a plant asset is discarded or sold, the cost and accumulated depreciation are removed from the accounts. Any cash proceeds are recorded and compared to the asset's book value to determine gain or loss. When nonmonetary assets are exchanged and they are dissimilar, the new asset is recorded at its fair value, and either a gain or a loss on disposal is recognized. When similar assets are exchanged, losses are recognized but gains are not. Instead, the new asset account is debited for the book value of the old asset plus any cash paid. Total asset turnover measures the efficiency of a company's use of its assets to generate sales.

DEMONSTRATION PROBLEM

On July 14, 19X1, Tulsa Company paid $600,000 to acquire a fully equipped factory. The purchase included the following:

Asset	Appraised Value	Estimated Salvage Value	Estimated Service Life	Depreciation Method
Land	$160,000			Not depreciated
Land improvements ..	80,000	$ —0—	10 years	Straight line
Building	320,000	100,000	10 years	Double declining balance
Machinery	240,000	20,000	10,000 units	Units of production*
Total	$800,000			

*The machinery was used to produce 700 units in 19X1 and 1,800 units in 19X2.

Required

1. Allocate the total $600,000 cost among the separate assets.
2. Calculate the 19X1 (six months) and 19X2 depreciation expense for each type of asset and calculate the total each year for all assets.

Planning the Solution

* Complete a three-column worksheet showing these amounts for each asset: appraised value, percent of total value, and allocated cost.
* Using the allocated costs, compute the amount of depreciation for 19X1 (only one-half year) and 19X2 for each asset. Then, summarize those calculations in a table showing the total depreciation for each year.

Solution to Demonstration Problem

1. Allocation of total cost among the assets:

Asset	Appraised Value	Percent of Total Value	Allocated Cost
Land	$160,000	20%	$120,000
Land improvements	80,000	10	60,000
Building	320,000	40	240,000
Machinery	240,000	30	180,000
Total	$800,000	100%	$600,000

2. Depreciation for each asset:

Land Improvements:

Cost	$60,000
Salvage value	—0—
Net cost	$60,000
Service life	10 years
Annual expense ($60,000/10)	$6,000
19X1 depreciation ($6,000 × 6/12)	$3,000
19X2 depreciation	$6,000

Building:
   Straight-line rate = 100%/10 = 10%
   Double-declining-balance rate = 10% × 2 = 20%

19X1 depreciation ($240,000 × 20% × 6/12)	$24,000
19X2 depreciation [($240,000 − $24,000) × 20%] . .	$43,200

Machinery:

Cost	$180,000
Salvage value	20,000
Net cost	160,000
Total expected units	10,000
Expected cost per unit ($160,000/10,000)	$ 16

Year	Units × Unit Cost	Depreciation
19X1	700 × $16	$11,200
19X2	1,800 × $16	28,800

Total depreciation expense:

	19X2	19X1
Land improvements	$ 6,000	$ 3,000
Building	43,200	24,000
Machinery	28,800	11,200
Total	$78,000	$38,200

GLOSSARY

Accelerated depreciation depreciation methods that produce larger depreciation charges during the early years of an asset's life and smaller charges in the later years. p. 382

Balance sheet expenditure another name for *capital expenditure.* p. 386

Betterment a modification to an asset to make it more efficient, usually by replacing one of its components with an improved or superior component. p. 387

Book value the amount assigned to an item in the accounting records and in the financial statements; for a plant asset, book value is its original cost less accumulated depreciation. p. 378

Capital expenditure an expenditure that produces economic benefits that do not fully expire before the end of the current period; because it creates or adds to existing assets, it should appear on the balance sheet as the cost of an asset. Also called a *balance sheet expenditure.* p. 385

Change in an accounting estimate a change in a calculated amount used in the financial statements that results from new information or subsequent developments and from better insight or improved judgment. p. 382

Declining-balance depreciation a depreciation method in which a plant asset's depreciation charge for the period is determined by applying a constant depreciation rate (up to twice the straight-line rate) each year to the asset's beginning book value. p. 383

Extraordinary repairs major repairs that extend the service life of a plant asset beyond original expectations; treated as a capital expenditure. p. 386

Inadequacy a condition in which the capacity of plant assets becomes too small for the productive demands of the business. p. 377

Land improvements assets that increase the usefulness of land but that have a limited useful life and are subject to depreciation. p. 376

Modified Accelerated Cost Recovery System (MACRS) the system of depreciation required by federal income tax law for assets placed in service after 1986. p. 384

Obsolescence a condition in which, because of new inventions and improvements, a plant asset can no longer be used to produce goods or services with a competitive advantage. p. 377

Ordinary repairs repairs made to keep a plant asset in normal, good operating condition; treated as a revenue expenditure. p. 386

Revenue expenditure an expenditure that should appear on the current income statement as an expense and be deducted from the period's revenues because it does not provide a material benefit in future periods. p. 385

Salvage value the amount that management predicts will be recovered at the end of a plant asset's service life through a sale or as a trade-in allowance on the purchase of a new asset. p. 377

Service life the length of time in which a plant asset will be used in the operations of the business. p. 377

Straight-line depreciation a method that allocates an equal portion of the total depreciation for a plant asset (cost minus salvage) to each accounting period in its service life. p. 378

Total asset turnover a measure of how efficiently a company uses its assets to generate sales; calculated by dividing net sales by average total assets. p. 392

Units-of-production depreciation a method that allocates an equal portion of the total depreciation for a plant asset

(cost minus salvage) to each unit of product or service that it produces, or on a similar basis, such as hours of use or miles driven. p. 378

QUESTIONS

1. What characteristics of a plant asset make it different from other assets?

2. What is the balance sheet classification of land held for future expansion? Why is the land not classified as a plant asset?

3. In general, what is included in the cost of a plant asset?

4. What is the difference between land and land improvements?

5. Does the balance of the account, Accumulated Depreciation, Machinery, represent funds accumulated to replace the machinery when it wears out? What does the balance of Accumulated Depreciation represent?

6. Why is the Modified Accelerated Cost Recovery System not generally accepted for financial accounting purposes?

7. What is the difference between ordinary repairs and extraordinary repairs and how should they be recorded?

8. What accounting principle justifies charging the $75 cost of a plant asset immediately to an expense account?

9. What are some of the events that might lead to the disposal of a plant asset?

10. Should a gain on an exchange of plant assets be recorded?

11. How is total asset turnover calculated? Why would a financial statement user be interested in calculating total asset turnover?

12. Refer to the consolidated balance sheets for Federal Express Corporation in Appendix G. What phrase does Federal Express use to describe its plant assets? What is the book value of plant assets as of May 31, 1993, and May 31, 1992?

13. Using the consolidated balance sheet and consolidated statement of income for Ben & Jerry's Homemade, Inc., in Appendix G, calculate total asset turnover for the year ended December 26, 1992.

QUICK STUDY (Five-Minute Exercises)

QS 10–1
(LO 1)

Explain the difference between *(a)* plant assets and long-term investments; *(b)* plant assets and inventory; and *(c)* plant assets and current assets.

QS 10–2
(LO 1)

Mattituck Lanes installed automatic score-keeping equipment. The electrical work required to prepare for the installation was $12,000. The invoice price of the equipment was $120,000. Additional costs were $2,000 for delivery and $8,400, sales tax. During the installation, a component of the equipment was damaged because it was carelessly left on a lane and hit by the automatic lane cleaning machine during a daily maintenance run. The cost of repairing the component was $1,500. What is the cost of the automatic scorekeeping equipment?

QS 10–3
(LO 2)

January 5, 19X1, Blind Man's Sun acquired sound equipment for concert performances at a cost of $111,800. The rock band estimated that they would use this equipment for four years, during which time they anticipated performing about 12 concerts. They estimated at that point they could sell the equipment for $3,800. During 19X1, the band performed four concerts. Calculate the 19X1 depreciation using *(a)* straight-line method and *(b)* the units-of-production method.

QS 10–4
(LO 2)

Refer to the facts in QS 10–3. Assume that Blind Man's Sun chose straight-line depreciation but recognized during the second year that due to concert bookings beyond expectations, this equipment would only last a total of three years. The salvage value would remain unchanged. Calculate the revised depreciation for the second year and the third year.

A fleet of refrigerated delivery trucks acquired on January 4, 19X1, at a cost of $620,000 had an estimated useful life of eight years and an estimated salvage value of $100,000. Calculate the 19X1 depreciation under *(a)* the double-declining-balance method for financial accounting purposes and *(b)* the accelerated method under MACRS with the half-year convention for tax purposes. (MACRS classifies this asset in a five-year category.)

QS 10–5
(LO 3)

a. Classify the following expenditures as revenue or capital expenditures:

    (1) Monthly replacement cost of filters on an air conditioning system, $120.

    (2) Cost of replacing a compressor for a meatpacking firm's refrigeration system that extends the estimated life of the system four years, $40,000.

    (3) The cost of $175,000 for an addition of a new wing on an office building.

    (4) The cost of annual tune-ups for delivery trucks.

b. Prepare the journal entry to record (2) and (3).

QS 10–6
(LO 4)

Dean's Carpet Stores owned an automobile with a $20,000 cost and $18,000 accumulated depreciation. In a transaction with a neighboring computer retailer, Dean exchanged this auto for a computer with a fair market value of $6,000. Dean was required to pay an additional $5,000 cash. Prepare the entry to record this transaction for Dean.

QS 10–7
(LO 5)

Frolic, Inc., owns an industrial machine that cost $19,200 and has been depreciated $10,200. Frolic exchanged the machine for a newer model that has a fair value of $24,000. Record the exchange assuming a trade-in allowance of *(a)* $8,000 and *(b)* $12,000.

QS 10–8
(LO 5)

Goodyear Tire & Rubber Company reported the following facts in its 1993 annual report: net sales of $11,643.4 million for 1993 and $11,784.9 million for 1992; total end-of-year assets of $8,436.1 million for 1993 and $8,563.7 million for 1992. Calculate the total asset turnover for 1993.

QS 10–9
(LO 5)

EXERCISES

Hot Sox purchased a machine for $23,000, terms 2/10, n/60, FOB shipping point. The seller prepaid the freight charges, $520, adding the amount to the invoice and bringing its total to $23,520. The machine required a special steel mounting and power connections costing $1,590, and another $750 was paid to assemble the machine and get it into operation. In moving the machine onto its steel mounting, it was dropped and damaged. The repairs cost $380. Later, $60 of raw materials were consumed in adjusting the machine so that it would produce a satisfactory product. The adjustments were normal for this type of machine and were not the result of the damage. However, the items produced while the adjustments were being made were not sellable. Prepare a calculation to show the cost of this machine for accounting purposes. (Assume Hot Sox pays for the purchase within the discount period.)

Exercise 10–1
Cost of a plant asset
(LO 1)

Piper Plumbing Company paid $184,125 for real estate plus $9,800 in closing costs. The real estate included land appraised at $83,160; land improvements appraised at $27,720; and a building appraised at $87,120. Prepare a calculation showing the allocation of the total cost among the three purchased assets and present the journal entry to record the purchase.

Exercise 10–2
Lump-sum purchase of plant assets
(LO 1)

After planning to build a new manufacturing plant, Jammers Casual Wear purchased a large lot on which a small building was located. The negotiated purchase price for this real estate was $150,000 for the lot plus $80,000 for the building. The company paid $23,000 to have the old building torn down and $34,000 for landscaping the lot. Finally, it paid $960,000 in construction costs, which included the cost of a new building plus $57,000 for lighting and paving a parking lot next to the building. Present a single journal entry to record the costs incurred by Jammers, all of which were paid in cash.

Exercise 10–3
Recording costs of real estate
(LO 1)

Exercise 10–4
Alternative depreciation methods
(LO 2, 3)

Moon Paper Company installed a computerized machine in its factory at a cost of $84,600. The machine's useful life was estimated at 10 years, or 363,000 units of product, with a $12,000 trade-in value. During its second year, the machine produced 35,000 units of product. Determine the machine's second-year depreciation under the *(a)* straight-line, *(b)* units-of-production, and *(c)* double-declining-balance methods.

Exercise 10–5
Alternative depreciation methods; partial year's depreciation
(LO 2, 3)

On April 1, 19X1, Lake Excavating Services purchased a trencher for $500,000. The machine was expected to last five years and have a salvage value of $50,000. Calculate depreciation expense for 19X2, using *(a)* the straight-line method and *(b)* the double-declining-balance method.

Exercise 10–6
Revising depreciation rates
(LO 2)

Gemini Fitness Club used straight-line depreciation for a machine that cost $43,500, under the assumption it would have a four-year life and a $4,500 trade-in value. After two years, Gemini determined that the machine still had three more years of remaining useful life, after which it would have an estimated $3,600 trade-in value. *(a)* Calculate the machine's book value at the end of its second year. *(b)* Calculate the amount of depreciation to be charged during each of the remaining years in the machine's revised useful life.

Exercise 10–7
Income statement effects of alternative depreciation methods
(LO 2, 3)

Starnes Enterprises recently paid $156,800 for equipment that will last five years and have a salvage value of $35,000. By using the machine in its operations for five years, the company expects to earn $57,000 annually, after deducting all expenses except depreciation. Present a schedule showing income before depreciation, depreciation expense, and net income for each year and the total amounts for the five-year period, assuming *(a)* straight-line depreciation and *(b)* double-declining-balance depreciation.

Exercise 10–8
MACRS depreciation
(LO 2, 3)

In January 19X1, Labenski Labs purchased computer equipment for $98,000. The equipment will be used in research and development activities for four years and then sold at an estimated salvage value of $20,000. The equipment is in the five-year class for tax purposes, and the half-year convention is required. Prepare schedules showing the depreciation under MACRS for each year's tax return, assuming *(a)* straight-line depreciation and *(b)* accelerated depreciation. (To calculate accelerated depreciation, use the MACRS rates shown in Illustration 10–2.)

Exercise 10–9
Ordinary repairs, extraordinary repairs, and betterments
(LO 4)

Eden Extract Company paid $175,000 for equipment that was expected to last four years and have a salvage value of $20,000. Prepare journal entries to record the following costs related to the equipment:

a. During the second year of the equipment's life, $14,000 cash was paid for a new component that was expected to increase the equipment's productivity by 10% each year.

b. During the third year, $3,500 cash was paid for repairs necessary to keep the equipment in good working order.

c. During the fourth year, $9,300 was paid for repairs that were expected to increase the service life of the equipment from four to six years.

Exercise 10–10
Extraordinary repairs
(LO 4)

Hot Dog Heaven owns a building that appeared on its balance sheet at the end of last year at its original $374,000 cost less $280,500 accumulated depreciation. The building has been depreciated on a straight-line basis under the assumption that it would have a 20-year life and no salvage value. During the first week in January of the current year, major structural repairs were completed on the building at a cost of $44,800. The repairs did not increase the building's capacity, but they did extend its expected life for 7 years beyond the 20 years originally estimated.

a. Determine the building's age as of the end of last year.

b. Give the entry to record the repairs, which were paid with cash.

c. Determine the book value of the building after the repairs were recorded.

d. Give the entry to record the current year's depreciation.

Plum Hill Industries purchased and installed a machine on January 1, 19X1, at a total cost of $185,500. Straight-line depreciation was taken each year for four years, based on the assumption of a seven-year life and no salvage value. The machine was disposed of on July 1, 19X5, during its fifth year of service. Present the entries to record the partial year's depreciation on July 1, 19X5, and to record the disposal under each of the following unrelated assumptions: *(a)* The machine was sold for $70,000 cash; and *(b)* Plum Hill received an insurance settlement of $60,000 resulting from the total destruction of the machine in a fire.

Exercise 10–11
Partial year's depreciation; disposal of plant asset
(LO 2, 5)

The Rourke Group traded in an old tractor for a new tractor, receiving a $56,000 trade-in allowance and paying the remaining $164,000 in cash. The old tractor cost $190,000, and straight-line depreciation of $105,000 had been recorded under the assumption that it would last eight years and have a $22,000 salvage value. Answer the following questions:

Exercise 10–12
Exchanging plant assets
(LO 5)

a.   What was the book value of the old tractor?

b.   What is the loss on the exchange?

c.   What amount should be debited to the new Tractor account?

On January 2, 19X1, Kelly Camera Shop disposed of a machine that cost $84,000 and had been depreciated $45,250. Present the journal entries to record the disposal under each of the following unrelated assumptions:

Exercise 10–13
Recording plant asset disposal or exchange
(LO 5)

a.   The machine was sold for $32,500 cash.

b.   The machine was traded in on a new machine of like purpose having a $117,000 cash price. A $40,000 trade-in allowance was received, and the balance was paid in cash.

c.   A $30,000 trade-in allowance was received for the machine on a new machine of like purpose having a $117,000 cash price. The balance was paid in cash.

d.   The machine was traded for vacant land adjacent to the shop to be used as a parking lot. The land had a fair value of $75,000, and Kelly paid $25,000 cash in addition to giving the seller the machine.

Lamb's Antiques reported net sales of $2,431,000 for 19X2 and $3,771,000 for 19X3. End of year balances for total assets were: 19X1, $793,000; 19X2, $850,000; and 19X3, $941,000. Calculate Lamb's total asset turnover for 19X2 and 19X3, and comment on the store's efficiency in the use of its assets.

Exercise 10–14
Evaluating efficient use of assets
(LO 5)

PROBLEMS

In 19X1, ProSports paid $1,400,000 for a tract of land and two buildings on it. The plan was to demolish Building One and build a new store in its place. Building Two was to be used as a company office and was appraised at a value of $291,500, with a useful life of 20 years and an $80,000 salvage value. A lighted parking lot near Building One had improvements (Land Improvements One) valued at $185,500 that were expected to last another 14 years and have no salvage value. Without considering the buildings or improvements, the tract of land was estimated to have a value of $848,000. ProSports incurred the following additional costs:

Problem 10–1
Real estate costs; partial year's depreciation
(LO 1, 2)

Cost to demolish Building One	$ 211,300
Cost of additional landscaping	83,600
Cost to construct new building (Building Three), having a useful life of 25 years and a $195,050 salvage value . .	1,009,500
Cost of new land improvements near Building Two (Land Improvements Two) which have a 20-year useful life and no salvage value	79,000

Required

1. Prepare a schedule having the following column headings: Land, Building Two, Building Three, Land Improvements One, and Land Improvements Two. Allocate the costs incurred by ProSports to the appropriate columns and total each column.

2. Prepare a single journal entry dated March 31 to record all the incurred costs, assuming they were paid in cash on that date.

CHECK FIGURE:
Depreciation Expense, Land Improvements, $2,962.50

3. Using the straight-line method, prepare December 31 adjusting entries to record depreciation for the nine months of 19X1 during which the assets were in use.

Problem 10–2

Plant asset costs; partial year's depreciation; alternative methods, including MACRS
(LO 1, 2, 3)

Valley Wide Industries recently negotiated a lump-sum purchase of several assets from a vending machine service company that was going out of business. The purchase was completed on March 1, 19X1, at a total cash price of $1,575,000, and included a building, land, certain land improvements, and 12 vehicles. The estimated market value of each asset was: building, $816,000; land, $578,000; land improvements, $85,000; and vehicles, $221,000.

Required

Preparation component:

1. Prepare a schedule to allocate the lump-sum purchase price to the separate assets that were purchased. Also present the journal entry to record the purchase.

2. Calculate the 19X1 depreciation expense on the building using the straight-line method, assuming a 15-year life and a $51,300 salvage value.

CHECK FIGURE:
19X1, depreciation expense on land improvements, $16,406.25

3. Calculate the 19X1 depreciation expense on the land improvements assuming an eight-year life and double-declining-balance depreciation.

4. The vehicles are in the five-year class for tax purposes, but are expected to last seven years and have a salvage value of $29,400. Prepare a schedule showing each year's depreciation for the vehicles under MACRS, assuming (a) straight-line and (b) accelerated depreciation. (To calculate accelerated depreciation, use the MACRS rates in Illustration 10–2.)

Analysis component:

5. Defend or refute this statement: Accelerated depreciation results in lower taxes over the life of the asset.

Problem 10–3

Alternative depreciation methods; partial year's depreciation; disposal of plant asset
(LO 2, 3, 5)

CHECK FIGURE:
Year 4, units-of-production depreciation expense, $22,320

Part 1. A machine that cost $105,000, with a four-year life and an estimated $10,000 salvage value, was installed in Patterson Company's factory on January 1. The factory manager estimated that the machine would produce 237,500 units of product during its life. It actually produced the following units: year 1, 60,700; year 2, 61,200; year 3, 59,800; and year 4, 59,100. Note the total number of units produced by the end of year 4 exceeded the original estimate. Nevertheless, the machine should not be depreciated below the estimated salvage value.

Required

1. Prepare a calculation showing the amount that should be charged to depreciation over the machine's four-year life.

2. Prepare a form with the following column headings:

Year	Straight Line	Units of Production	Double-Declining Balance

Then show the depreciation for each year and the total depreciation for the machine under each depreciation method.

Part 2. Patterson purchased a used machine for $83,500 on January 2. It was repaired the next day at a cost of $1,710 and installed on a new platform that cost $540. The company predicted that the machine would be used for six years and would then have a $7,300 salvage value. Depreciation was to be charged on a straight-line basis. A full year's depreciation was charged on December 31, the end of the first year of the machine's use. On September 30 of its sixth year in service, it was retired.

Required

1. Prepare journal entries to record the purchase of the machine, the cost of repairing it, and the installation. Assume that cash was paid.

2. Prepare entries to record depreciation on the machine on December 31 of its first year and on September 30 in the year of its disposal.

3. Prepare entries to record the retirement of the machine under each of the following unrelated assumptions: (*a*) it was sold for $6,750; (*b*) it was sold for $18,000; and (*c*) it was destroyed in a fire and the insurance company paid $12,000 in full settlement of the loss claim.

Finlay General Contractors completed these transactions involving the purchase and operation of heavy equipment:

19X1

June 30   Paid $127,720 cash for a new front-end loader, plus $7,600 in state sales tax and $1,250 for transportation charges. The loader was estimated to have a four-year life and a $17,370 salvage value.

Oct. 4   Paid $1,830 to enclose the cab and install air conditioning in the loader. This increased the estimated salvage value of the loader by $555.

Dec. 31   Recorded straight-line depreciation on the loader.

19X2

Feb. 16   Paid $460 to repair the loader after the operator backed it into a tree.

July 1   Paid $2,250 to overhaul the loader's engine. As a result, the estimated useful life of the loader was increased by two years.

Dec. 31   Recorded straight-line depreciation on the loader.

Required

Prepare journal entries to record the transactions.

Syracuse Systems completed the following transactions involving delivery trucks:

19X1

Mar. 29   Paid cash for a new delivery truck, $38,830 plus $2,330 state sales tax. The truck was estimated to have a five-year life and a $6,000 trade-in value.

Dec. 31   Recorded straight-line depreciation on the truck.

19X2

Dec. 31   Recorded straight-line depreciation on the truck. However, due to new information obtained earlier in the year, the original estimated service life of the truck was changed from five years to four years, and the original estimated trade-in value was increased to $7,000.

19X3

July 5   Traded in the old truck and paid $27,130 in cash for a new truck. The new truck was estimated to have a six-year life and a $6,250 trade-in value. The invoice for the exchange showed these items:

Price of the new truck	$45,100
Trade-in allowance granted on the old truck . .	(19,500)
Balance of purchase price	$25,600
State sales tax	1,530
Total paid in cash	$27,130

Dec. 31   Recorded straight-line depreciation on the new truck.

Problem 10–4
Partial year's depreciation; revising depreciation rates; revenue and capital expenditures
(LO 2, 3, 4)

CHECK FIGURE:
Dec. 31, 19X2, Accum. Depr., Heavy Equipment, $24,337

Problem 10–5
Partial year's depreciation; revising depreciation rates; exchanging plant assets
(LO 2, 3, 5)

Required

Prepare journal entries to record the transactions.

Problem 10–6
Partial year's depreciation;
alternative methods; disposal of
plant assets
(LO 2, 3, 5)

Menck Interiors completed the following transactions involving machinery:

Machine No. 15–50 was purchased for cash on May 1, 19X1, at an installed cost of $52,900. Its useful life was estimated to be six years with a $4,300 trade-in value. Straight-line depreciation was recorded for the machine at the end of 19X1, 19X2, and 19X3. On April 29, 19X4, it was traded for Machine No. 17–95, a similar asset with an installed cash price of $61,900. A trade-in allowance of $30,110 was received for Machine No. 15–50, and the balance was paid in cash.

Machine No. 17–95's life was predicted to be four years with an $8,200 trade-in value. Double-declining-balance depreciation was recorded on each December 31 of its life. On November 2, 19X5, it was traded for Machine No. BT–311, which was a dissimilar asset with an installed cash price of $179,000. A trade-in allowance of $27,000 was received for Machine No. 17–95, and the balance was paid in cash.

It was estimated that Machine No. BT–311 would produce 200,000 units of product during its five-year useful life, after which it would have a $35,000 trade-in value. Units-of-production depreciation was recorded for the machine for 19X5, a period in which it produced 31,000 units of product. Between January 1, 19X6, and August 21, 19X8, the machine produced 108,000 more units. On the latter date, it was sold for $81,200.

Required

Prepare journal entries to record: *(a)* the purchase of each machine, *(b)* the depreciation expense recorded on the first December 31 of each machine's life, and *(c)* the disposal of each machine. (Only one entry is needed to record the exchange of one machine for another.)

CRITICAL THINKING: ESSAYS, PROBLEMS, AND CASES

Analytical Essays

AE 10–1
(LO 4)

It is January 9, 19X2, and you have just been hired as an accountant for Brinks Supply Company. The previous accountant brought the accounting records up to date through December 31, 19X1, the end of the fiscal year, including the year-end adjusting entries. In reviewing the entries made last year, you discover the following three items:

a. An expenditure to have a factory machine reconditioned by the manufacturer so it would last three years longer than originally estimated was recorded as a debit to Repairs Expense, Machinery.

b. The lubrication of factory machinery was recorded as a debit to Machinery.

c. The installation of a security system for the building was recorded as a debit to Building Improvements. The new system allowed the company to reduce the number of security guards.

Required

For each of the three items, explain why you think a correction is or is not necessary. Also, describe any correcting entry that should be made.

AE 10–2
(LO 3)

Prepare brief answers for each of the following:

a. What are the conflicting objectives of financial accounting and tax accounting when accounting for depreciation?

b. Refer to the annual report for Federal Express Corporation in Appendix G. Explain how they have resolved this conflict in terms of their accounting for depreciation.

c. Defend or refute this statement:

Although it is commonplace for publicly held corporations like Federal Express to use different depreciation methods for tax accounting and financial accounting purposes, it is not necessary for a privately held business to do so.

While examining the accounting records of Fortunato Company on December 15, 19X5, you discover two 19X5 entries that appear questionable. The first entry recorded the cash proceeds from an insurance settlement as follows:

Apr.	30	Cash	29,000.00	
		Loss on Fire	8,800.00	
		Accumulated Depreciation, Machinery	25,200.00	
		Machinery		63,000.00
		Received payment of fire loss claim.		

Your investigation shows that this entry was made to record the receipt of an insurance company's $29,000 check to settle a claim resulting from the destruction of a machine in a small fire on April 2, 19X5. The machine originally cost $58,800 and was put into operation on January 3, 19X2. It was depreciated on a straight-line basis for three years, under the assumptions that it would have a seven-year life and no salvage value. During the first week of January 19X5, the machine was overhauled at a cost of $4,200. The overhaul did not increase the machine's capacity or its salvage value. However, it was expected that the overhaul would lengthen the machine's service life two years beyond the seven originally expected.

The second entry that appears questionable was made to record the receipt of a check from selling a portion of a tract of land. The land was adjacent to the company's plant and had been purchased the year before. It cost $105,000, and another $18,000 was paid for clearing and grading it. Both amounts had been debited to the Land account. The land was to be used for storing finished products but, sometime after the grading was completed, it became obvious the company did not need the entire tract. Fortunato received an offer from a purchaser to buy the north section for $94,550 or the south section for $60,450. The company decided to sell the north section and recorded the receipt of the purchaser's check with the following entry:

Nov.	16	Cash	94,550.00	
		Land		94,550.00
		Sold unneeded land.		

Required

Write a memo to the company's Corrections File describing any errors made in recording these transactions. Since the Corrections File is used in making the year-end adjusting journal entries, show the entry or entries needed to correct each error described in your memo.

Manufax Company temporarily recorded the costs of a new plant in a single account called Land and Buildings. Now, management has asked you to examine this account and prepare any necessary entries to correct the account balances. In doing so, you find the list of debits and credits to the account that follows.

An account called Depreciation Expense, Land and Buildings was debited in recording the $9,358 of depreciation. Your investigation suggests that 40 years is a reasonable life expectancy for a building of the type involved and that an assumption of zero salvage value is reasonable.

To summarize your analysis, set up a schedule with columns headed Date, Description, Total Amount, Land, Buildings, and Other Accounts. Next, enter the items found in the Land and Buildings account on the schedule, distributing the amounts to the proper columns. Show credits on the schedule by enclosing the amounts in parentheses. Also, draft any required correcting entry or entries, under the assumption that the accounts have not been closed.

Debits

Jan.	4	Cost of land and building acquired for new plant site	$ 564,000
	9	Attorney's fee for title search	1,500
	18	Cost of demolishing old building on plant site	37,500
	30	Nine months' liability and fire insurance during construction	6,075
Sept.	28	Payment to building contractor on completion	819,000
Oct.	1	Architect's fee for new building	25,200
	10	City assessment for street improvements	42,000
	21	Cost of landscaping new plant site	10,500
			$1,505,775

Credits

Jan.	21	Proceeds from sale of salvaged materials from building	$ 7,900
Oct.	5	Refund of one month's liability and fire insurance premium	675
Dec.	31	Depreciation at 2-1/2% per year	9,358
			$ 17,933
		Debit balance	$1,487,842

Financial Statement Analysis Case

(LO 1, 2)

Refer to the annual report for Apple Computer, Inc., in Appendix F. Give particular attention to the balance sheet, statement of income, and notes to financial statements before answering the following questions:

1. What percentage of the original cost of Apple's property, plant, and equipment remains to be depreciated as of September 24, 1993, and September 25, 1992? (Assume the assets have no salvage value.)

2. What method of depreciation does Apple use in depreciating its plant assets?

3. What was the net change in total property, plant, and equipment (before depreciation) during the year ended September 24, 1993? What was the amount of cash generated by (or used for) investment in property, plant, and equipment during the year ended September 24, 1993? What is one possible explanation for the difference between these two amounts?

4. Calculate Apple's total asset turnover for the year ended September 24, 1993.

Ethical Issues Essay

Review the As a Matter of Ethics case on page 382 and write a short essay discussing the situation faced by Sue Ann Meyer. Include a discussion of the alternative courses of action available to Meyer and indicate how you think she should deal with the situation.

CONCEPT TESTER

Test your understanding of the concepts introduced in this chapter by completing the following crossword puzzle:

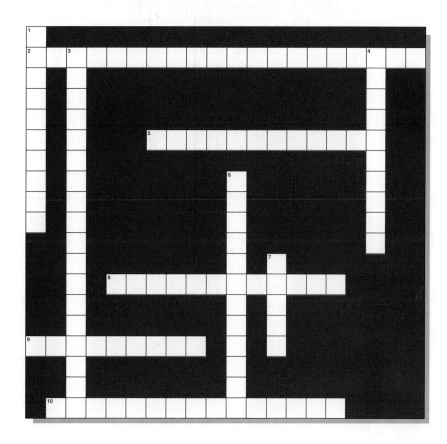

Across Clues

2. Two words; major repairs that extend the service life of a plant asset.
5. Two words; depreciation method that allocates an equal amount to each period.
8. Two words; the expected amount to be recovered at the end of an asset's life.
9. Two words; the original cost of an asset less the accumulated depreciation.
10. Two words; repairs made to keep an asset in normal, good operating condition.

Down Clues

1. A cost incurred to make an asset more efficient.
3. Three words; a measure of how efficiently a company uses its assets.
4. A condition in which the capacity of an asset becomes too small for the demands of the business.
6. A condition in which an asset has lost its usefulness because of new inventions and improvements.
7. Acronym for the depreciation method required under the tax law.

ANSWERS TO PROGRESS CHECKS

by completing the following crossword puzzle:

10–1 *(a)* office supplies—current assets
    (b) office equipment—plant assets
    (c) merchandise—current assets
    (d) land held for future expansion—long-term investments
    (e) trucks used in operations—plant assets

10–2 *(a)* Land
    (b) Land Improvements

10–3 $700,000 + $49,000 − $21,000 + $3,500 + $3,000 + $2,500 = $737,000

10–4 Depreciation is a process of allocating and charging the cost of plant assets to the accounting periods that benefit from the asset's use.

10–5 *(a)* Book value using straight-line depreciation:
       $96,000 − [($96,000 − $8,000)/5] = $78,400
    (b) Book value using units of production:
       $96,000 − [($96,000 − $8,000) × (10,000/100,000)] = $87,200

10–6 ($3,800 − $200)/3 = $1,200
    $1,200 × 2 = $2,400
    ($3,800 − $2,400)/2 = $700

10–7 Double-declining-balance depreciation: $77,000 × (10% × 2) = $15,400
    Straight-line MACRS: ($77,000/7) × 1/2 = $5,500

10–8 Accumulated Depreciation Machinery 12,000.00
      Cash 12,000.00

10–9 A revenue expenditure benefits only the current period and should be charged to the expense of the current period. A capital expenditure has benefit that extends beyond the end of the current period and should be charged to an asset.

10–10 A betterment involves modifying an existing plant asset to make it more efficient,

10–11 Depreciation Expense   3,500
      Accumulated Depreciation   3,500
    Cash   32,000
    Accumulated Depreciation   10,500
      Gain on Sale of Equipment   500
      Equipment   42,000

10–12
(a) Truck   45,000
    Loss on Trade-in   3,600
    Accumulated Depreciation   23,400
      Truck   30,000
      Cash   42,000
(b) Truck   44,600
    Accumulated Depreciation   23,400
      Truck   30,000
      Cash   38,000

10–13 Total asset turnover:
$$\frac{\$7,808,043}{(\$5,793,064 + \$5,463,186)/2} = 1.4 \text{ times}$$

CHAPTER 11

Natural Resources, Intangible Assets, and Long-Term Investments

THE FAR SIDE By GARY LARSON

"Well, shoot. I just can't figure it out. I'm movin' over 500 doughnuts a day, but I'm still just barely squeakin' by."

*T*he question posed in the *New York Times's* business section (October 17, 1994) was "What, exactly, lies beyond 'The Far Side'?" when cartoonist Gary Larson announced that he planned to stop drawing the widely popular cartoon in January of 1995. Analysts anticipated that the $500 million merchandising empire related to "Far Side" would be shaken by his move.

Manufacturers had invested huge sums for the rights to manufacture "Far Side" products such as books, calendars, greeting cards, mugs, and T-shirts. Without the newspaper exposure of this cartoon, demand for these products would drop. The manufacturers of "Far Side" products would probably experience a dramatic reduction in related revenues in the years to come. Other financial disclosures by these firms also might be affected.

LEARNING OBJECTIVES

After studying Chapter 11, you should be able to:

1. **Identify assets that should be classified as natural resources or as intangible assets and prepare entries to account for them, including entries to record depletion and amortization.**

2. **State the criteria for classifying assets as long-term investments and describe the categories of securities that are classified as long-term investments.**

3. **Describe the methods used to report long-term securities investments in the financial statements.**

4. **Describe the primary accounting problems of having investments in international operations and prepare entries to account for sales to foreign customers.**

5. **Explain the use of return on total assets in evaluating a company's efficiency in using its assets.**

6. **Define or explain the words and phrases listed in the chapter glossary.**

In Chapters 7 through 10, you learned about current assets and plant assets. This chapter concludes the focus on assets with a discussion of natural resources, intangible assets, and long-term investments. Natural resources and intangible assets may be particularly important in evaluating the future prospects of some companies. For example, the rights to manufacture "Far Side" products are intangible assets of the companies that purchased these rights from the cartoon's creator or the copyright owner. Gary Larson's decision to lay down his pen no doubt would have an impact on the amounts reported for these assets.

Many companies make long-term investments in assets such as real estate and debt and equity securities issued by other companies. Also, an increasing number of companies invest in foreign countries or have international operations. The financial statement effects of these investments are often very important. As a result, your study of these topics in this chapter will enrich your ability to understand and interpret financial reports.

NATURAL RESOURCES

LO 1

Identify assets that should be classified as natural resources or as intangible assets and prepare entries to account for them, including entries to record depletion and amortization.

Natural resources include such things as standing timber, mineral deposits, and oil reserves. Because they are physically consumed when they are used, they are known as *wasting assets*. In their natural state, they represent inventories of raw materials that will be converted into a product by cutting, mining, or pumping. However, until the conversion takes place, they are noncurrent assets and appear on a balance sheet un-

der captions such as "Timberlands," "Mineral deposits," or "Oil reserves." Sometimes, this caption appears under the property, plant, and equipment category of assets and sometimes it is a separate category. **Aluminum Company of America** combines its natural resources with other fixed assets in one balance sheet item called *Properties, plant, and equipment.* However, a note to the financial statements provides more detailed information by separating the total into the following categories: land and land rights, including mines; structures; machinery and equipment; and construction work in progress.

Natural resources are initially recorded at cost. Like the cost of plant assets, the cost of natural resources is allocated to the periods in which they are consumed. The cost created by consuming the usefulness of natural resources is called **depletion.** On the balance sheet, natural resources are shown at cost less *accumulated depletion.* The amount by which such assets are depleted each year by cutting, mining, or pumping is usually calculated on a units-of-production basis. For example, **Exxon Corporation** uses the units-of-production method to amortize the costs of discovering and operating its oil wells.

To illustrate the units-of-production method, assume that a mineral deposit has an estimated 500,000 tons of available ore and is purchased for $500,000. The units-of-production depletion charge per ton of ore mined is $1. Thus, if 85,000 tons are mined and sold during the first year, the depletion charge for the year of $85,000 is recorded as follows:

Dec.	31	Depletion Expense, Mineral Deposit	85,000.00	
		Accumulated Depletion, Mineral Deposit		85,000.00
		To record depletion of the mineral deposit.		

On the balance sheet prepared at the end of the first year, the mineral deposit should appear at its $500,000 cost less accumulated depletion of $85,000. Because the 85,000 tons of ore were sold during the year, the entire $85,000 depletion charge is reported on the income statement. However, if a portion of the ore had remained unsold at year-end, the depletion cost related to the unsold ore should be carried forward on the balance sheet as part of the cost of the unsold ore inventory, which is a current asset.

The conversion of natural resources through mining, cutting, or pumping often requires the use of machinery and buildings. Because the usefulness of these assets is related to the depletion of the natural resource, their costs should be depreciated over the life of the natural resource in proportion to the annual depletion charges. In other words, depreciation should be calculated using the units-of-production method. For example, if a machine is installed in a mine and one-eighth of the mine's ore is mined and sold during a year, one-eighth of the machine's cost (less salvage value) should be charged to depreciation expense.

INTANGIBLE ASSETS

Some assets represent certain legal rights and economic relationships beneficial to the owner. Because they have no physical existence, they are called **intangible assets.** Patents, copyrights, leaseholds, leasehold improvements, goodwill, and trademarks are intangible assets. We discuss each of these intangible items in more detail in the following sections. Although notes and accounts receivable are also intangible in nature, they are not used to produce products or provide services. Therefore, they are not listed on the balance sheet as intangible assets; instead, they are classified as current assets or investments.

When an intangible asset is purchased, it is recorded at cost. Thereafter, its cost must be systematically written off to expense over its estimated useful life through the process of **amortization.** Generally accepted accounting principles require that the amortization period for an intangible asset be 40 years or less.[1] Companies often disclose the amortization periods they apply to their intangibles. For example, **Corning Incorporated's** annual report

[1]FASB, *Accounting Standards—Current Text* (Norwalk, CT, 1994), sec. I60.110. First published as *APB Opinion No. 17*, par. 29.

discloses that it amortizes goodwill over a maximum of 40 years and other intangible assets over a maximum of 15 years.

In many cases, the estimated life of an intangible asset is highly subjective and influenced by a myriad of factors. The selected useful life can have a dramatic impact on reported profits. A few years ago, **Blockbuster Entertainment Corporation** was criticized for changing its amortization period for videotape rights from 9 to 36 months. The change added $3 million, or nearly 20% to Blockbuster's reported income.[2]

Amortization of intangible assets is similar to depreciation of plant assets and depletion of natural resources in that all three are processes of cost allocation. However, only the straight-line method can be used for amortizing intangibles unless the reporting company can demonstrate that another method is more appropriate. Also, while the effects of depreciation and depletion on the assets are recorded in a contra account (Accumulated Depreciation or Accumulated Depletion), amortization is usually credited directly to the intangible asset account. As a result, the full original cost of intangible assets generally is not reported on the balance sheet. Instead, only the remaining amount of unamortized cost is reported.

Normally, intangible assets are shown in a separate section of the balance sheet that follows immediately after plant and equipment. However, not all companies follow this tradition. The following paragraphs describe several specific intangible assets.

Patents

The federal government grants **patents** to encourage the invention of new machines, mechanical devices, and production processes. A patent gives its owner the exclusive right to manufacture and sell a patented machine or device, or to use a process, for 17 years. When patent rights are purchased, the cost of acquiring the rights is debited to an account called Patents. Also, if the owner engages in lawsuits to defend a patent, the cost of the lawsuits should be debited to the Patents account. However, the costs of research and development leading to a new patent are not debited to an asset account.[3]

Although a patent gives its owner exclusive rights to the patented device or process for 17 years, the cost of the patent should be amortized over its predicted useful life, which might be less than the full 17 years. For example, if a patent that cost $25,000 has an estimated useful life of 10 years, the following adjusting entry is made at the end of each of those years to write off one-tenth of its cost:

Dec.	31	Amortization Expense, Patents	2,500.00	
		Patents		2,500.00
		To write off patent costs over the expected 10-year life.		

The entry's debit causes $2,500 of patent costs to appear on the income statement as one of the costs of the product manufactured and sold under the protection of the patent. Note that we have followed the convention of crediting the Patents account

---

[2]*Forbes,* June 12, 1989, p. 150.

[3]FASB, *Accounting Standards—Current Text* (Norwalk, CT, 1994), sec. R50.108. First published as *Statement of Financial Accounting Standards No. 2,* par. 12.

patent. Note that we have followed the convention of crediting the Patents account rather than a contra account.

Copyrights

A **copyright** is granted by the federal government or by international agreement. In most cases, a copyright gives its owner the exclusive right to publish and sell a musical, literary, or artistic work during the life of the composer, author, or artist and for 50 years thereafter. Most copyrights have value for a much shorter time, and their costs should be amortized over the shorter period. Often, the only identifiable cost of a copyright is the fee paid to the Copyright Office. If this fee is not material, it may be charged directly to an expense account. Otherwise, the copyright costs should be capitalized (recorded as a capital expenditure), and the periodic amortization of a copyright should be debited to an account called *Amortization Expense, Copyrights.*

Leaseholds

Property is rented under a contract called a **lease.** The person or company that owns the property and grants the lease is called the **lessor.** The person or company that secures the right to possess and use the property is called the **lessee.** The rights granted to the lessee by the lessor under the lease are called a **leasehold.** A leasehold is an intangible asset for the lessee.

Some leases require no advance payment from the lessee but do require monthly rent payments. In such cases, a Leasehold account is not needed and the monthly payments are debited to a Rent Expense account. Sometimes, a long-term lease requires the lessee to pay the final year's rent in advance when the lease is signed. If so, the lessee records the advance payment with a debit to its Leasehold asset account. Because the usefulness of the advance payment is not consumed until the final year is reached, the Leasehold account balance remains intact until that year. At that time, the balance is transferred to Rent Expense.[4]

Often, a long-term lease gains value because the current rental rates for similar property increase while the required payments under the lease remain constant. In such cases, the increase in value of the lease is not reported on the lessee's balance sheet since no extra cost was incurred to acquire it. However, if the property is subleased and the new tenant makes a cash payment to the original lessee for the rights under the old lease, the new tenant should debit the payment to a Leasehold account. Then, the balance of the Leasehold account should be amortized to Rent Expense over the remaining life of the lease.

To appreciate how the changing value of a lease can affect business decisions, consider La Côte Basque, one of the world's most esteemed and historic restaurants located in New York City. Late in 1994, La Côte Basque sold the two years remaining on its lease to **The Walt Disney Company.** La Côte Basque knew that it would not be able to renew the lease when it expired, because Disney had negotiated a long-term lease of the property with the building owner, **The Coca-Cola Company.** La Côte Basque, had been operating in this location for 36 years, but could not compete with the rental fees being offered by Disney. The inevitability of nonrenewal prompted the restaurant to sell the remainder of its lease for a sizable amount and attempt to relocate sooner rather than later.

---

[4]Some long-term leases give the lessee essentially the same rights as a purchaser, and result in tangible assets and liabilities reported by the lessee. Chapter 12 describes these leases.

Leasehold Improvements

Long-term leases often require the lessee to pay for any alterations or improvements to the leased property, such as new partitions and store fronts. Normally, the costs of these **leasehold improvements** are debited to an account called Leasehold Improvements. Also, since the improvements become part of the property and revert to the lessor at the end of the lease, the lessee must amortize the cost of the improvements over the life of the lease or the life of the improvements, whichever is shorter. The amortization entry commonly debits Rent Expense and credits Leasehold Improvements.

Goodwill

The term **goodwill** has a special meaning in accounting. In theory, a business has an intangible asset called goodwill when its rate of expected future earnings is greater than the rate of earnings normally realized in its industry. Above-average earnings and the existence of theoretical goodwill may be demonstrated with the following information about Companies A and B, both of which are in the same industry:

	Company A	Company B
Net assets (other than goodwill)	$100,000	$100,000
Normal rate of return in this industry	10%	10%
Normal return on net assets	$ 10,000	$ 10,000
Expected net income	10,000	15,000
Expected earnings above average	$ –0–	$ 5,000

Company B is expected to have an above-average earnings rate compared to its industry and, therefore, is said to have goodwill. This goodwill may be the result of excellent customer relations, the location of the business, the quality and uniqueness of its products, monopolistic market advantages, a superior management and workforce, or a combination of these and other factors.[5] Consequently, a potential investor would be willing to pay more for Company B than for Company A. Thus, goodwill is theoretically an asset that has value.

Normally, goodwill is purchased only when an entire business operation is acquired. In determining the purchase price of a business, the buyer and seller may estimate the amount of goodwill in several different ways. If the business is expected to have $5,000 each year in above-average earnings, its goodwill may be valued at, say, four times its above-average earnings, or $20,000. Or, if the $5,000 is expected to continue indefinitely, they may think of it as a return on an investment at a given

rate of return, say, 10%. In this case, the estimated amount of goodwill is $5,000/10% = $50,000. However, in the final analysis, the value of goodwill is confirmed only by the price the seller is willing to accept and the buyer is willing to pay.

To keep financial statement information from being too subjective, accountants have agreed that goodwill should not be recorded unless it is purchased. The amount of goodwill is measured by subtracting the fair market value of the purchased

---

[5]Of course, the value of the location may be reflected in a higher cost for the land owned and used by the company.

As A Matter of Fact

Intangible Assets Disclosed	Number of Companies			
	1993	1992	1991	1990
Goodwill recognized in a business combination	385	383	383	379
Patents, patent rights	69	62	59	62
Trademarks, brand names, copyrights	51	50	48	46
Noncompete covenants	26	21	18	20
Licenses, franchises, memberships	19	17	17	16
Other—described	48	45	42	37

Excerpted with permission from *Accounting Trends & Techniques,* Annual Survey of Accounting Practices Followed in 600 Stockholders' Reports, Forty-Seventh Edition, Copyright © 1993 by American Institute of Certified Public Accountants, Inc., Table 2–18, p. 177.

business's net assets (excluding goodwill) from the purchase price. In many business acquisitions, goodwill represents a major component of total cost. For example, **Procter & Gamble Company's** purchase of Revlon, Inc.'s worldwide Max Factor and Betrix lines of cosmetics for $1,025 million (net of cash acquired) included goodwill and other intangibles of $927 million.

Like other intangible assets, goodwill must be amortized on a straight-line basis over its estimated useful life. However, estimating the useful life of goodwill is very difficult and highly arbitrary in most situations. As a result, you can expect to find companies reporting amortization expense for goodwill based on an estimated useful life of 5 years upward, but not more than 40 years.

Trademarks and Trade Names

Companies often adopt unique symbols or select unique names that they use in marketing their products. Sometimes, the ownership and exclusive right to use such a **trademark** or **trade name** can be established simply by demonstrating that one company has used the trademark or trade name before other businesses. However, ownership generally can be established more definitely by registering the trademark or trade name at the U.S. Patent Office. The cost of developing, maintaining, or enhancing the value of a trademark or trade name, perhaps through advertising, should be charged to expense in the period or periods incurred. However, if a trademark or trade name is purchased, the purchase cost should be debited to an asset account and amortized over time.

Amortization of Intangibles

Some intangibles, such as patents, copyrights, and leaseholds, have limited useful lives that are determined by law, contract, or the nature of the asset. Other intangibles, such as goodwill, trademarks, and trade names, have indeterminable lives. In general, the cost of intangible assets should be amortized over the periods expected to be benefited by their use, which in no case is longer than their legal existence. However, as we stated earlier, generally accepted accounting principles require that the amortization period of intangible assets never be longer than 40 years. This limitation applies even if the life of the asset (for example, goodwill) may continue indefinitely into the future.

11–1　Give an example of an intangible asset and a natural resource.

11–2　Prospect Mining Company paid $650,000 for an ore deposit. The deposit had an estimated 325,000 tons of ore that would be fully mined during the next 10 years. During the current year, 91,000 tons were mined, processed, and sold. What is the amount of depletion for the year?

11–3　On January 6, 19X1, Fun-4-U Toy Company paid $120,000 for a patent with a 17-year legal life to produce a toy that is expected to be marketable for about 3 years. Prepare the entries necessary to record the acquisition and the December 31, 19X1, adjustment.

CLASSIFYING INVESTMENTS

LO 2

State the criteria for classifying securities investments as long-term investments and describe the categories of securities that are reported as long-term investments.

In Chapter 8, you learned how to account for short-term investments in debt and equity securities. (We encourage you to review pages 302–307 before you study this section.) Recall that short-term investments are current assets; they are expected to be converted into cash within one year or the current operating cycle of the business, whichever is longer. In general, short-term investments are held as "an investment of cash available for current operations."[6] They either mature within one year or the current operating cycle or are easily sold and therefore qualify as being *marketable.*

Securities investments that do not qualify as current assets are called **long-term investments.** Long-term investments include investments in bonds and stocks that are not marketable or that, although marketable, are not intended to serve as a ready source of cash. Long-term investments also include funds earmarked for a special purpose, such as bond sinking funds, and land or other assets owned but not used in the regular operations of the business. In general, these assets are reported on the balance sheet in a separate *Long-term investments* section.

Recall from Chapter 8 that accounting for short-term investments depends on whether the investments are in (1) trading securities, (2) debt securities held to maturity, or (3) debt and equity securities available for sale. Investments in trading securities always are short-term investments; they are reported as current assets. The other two types of investments may be long-term or short-term.

In Illustration 11–1, the boxes on the left side show the different long-term investments in securities. Note that they include (1) debt securities held to maturity, (2) debt and equity securities available for sale, (3) equity securities which give the investor a significant influence over the investee, and (4) equity securities which give the investor control over the investee. We discuss each of these types of investments in the following sections.

11–4　What types of assets are classified as long-term investments?

11–5　Under what conditions should a stock investment be classified on the balance sheet as a long-term investment?

LONG-TERM INVESTMENTS IN SECURITIES

Much of what you learned about short-term investments in Chapter 8 also applies to long-term investments. For example, at the time of purchase, investments are recorded at cost, which includes any commissions or brokerage fees paid to make the purchase. After the purchase, the accounting treatment depends on the type of investment.

[6]FASB, *Accounting Standards—Current Text,* (Norwalk, CT, 1994) sec. B05.105. Previously published in *Accounting Research Bulletin No. 43,* ch. 3, sec. A, par. 4.

Illustration 11-1 Accounting for Long-Term Investments in Securities

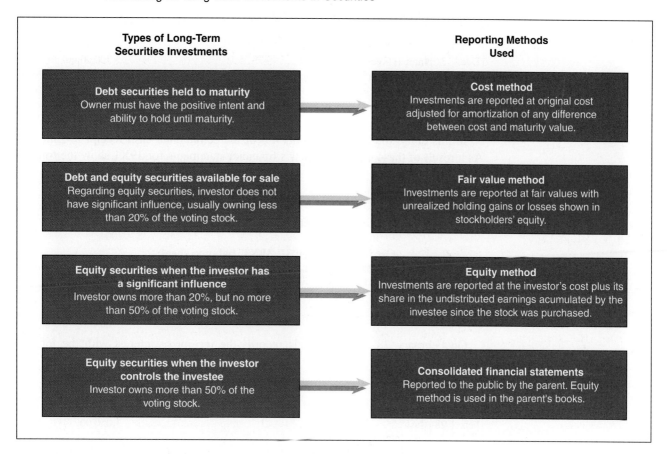

Investments in Debt Securities Held to Maturity

Debt securities held to maturity may be short-term or long-term investments. In either case, the owner must have the positive intent and the ability to hold the securities until they mature.[7] At the time of purchase, these investments are recorded at cost. Then, interest revenue is recorded as it accrues.

The cost of an investment in debt securities may be more or less than the maturity value of the securities. When the investment is long-term, any difference between cost and maturity value must be amortized over the remaining life of the security. Chapter 12 explains the process of amortizing this difference. In this chapter, however, we assume that the costs of debt investments equal their maturity values.

For example, on August 31, 19X1, Francis, Inc., paid $29,500 plus a brokerage fee of $500 to buy $30,000 par value of Candice Corp.'s 7% bonds payable. The bonds pay interest semiannually on August 31 and February 28. The amount of each payment is $30,000 × 7% × 6/12 = $1,050. Francis has the positive intent to hold the bonds until they mature on August 31, 19X3. The following entry records the purchase:

19X1					
Aug.	31	Investment in Candice Corp. Bonds	30,000.00	
		Cash		30,000.00
		Purchased bonds to be held to maturity.		

LO 3

Describe the methods used to report long-term securities investments in the financial statements.

---

[7]FASB, "Accounting for Certain Investments in Debt and Equity Securities," *Statement of Accounting Standards No. 115* (Norwalk, CT, 1994), par. 6.

On December 31, 19X1, at the end of its accounting period, Francis accrues interest receivable with the following entry:

Dec.	31	Interest Receivable	700.00	
		Interest Earned		700.00
		$1,050 × 4/6 = $700.		

In this entry, the $700 represents 4/6 of the semiannual cash receipt for interest. As a result of these entries, Francis's financial statements for 19X1 show the following items:

On the income statement for 19X1:
  Interest earned .... $ 700
On the December 31, 19X1, balance sheet:
  Assets:
    Long-term investments:
      Investment in Candice Corp. bonds $30,000

On February 28, 19X2, Francis records the receipt of interest with the following entry:

19X2 Feb.	28	Cash	1,050.00	
		Interest Receivable		700.00
		Interest Earned		350.00
		Received 6 months' interest on Candice Corp. bonds.		

When the bonds mature, this entry records the proceeds from the matured bonds:

19X3 Aug.	31	Cash	30,000.00	
		Investment in Candice Corp. Bonds		30,000.00
		Received cash from matured bonds.		

Investments in Securities Available for Sale

On the left side of Illustration 11–1, notice that only the top two boxes include debt securities. In other words, debt securities that do not qualify as securities held to maturity are classified as securities available for sale. In the second box on the left side of Illustration 11–1, you can see that securities available for sale also include certain equity securities. To be included in this group of long-term investments, the investor in equity securities must not have a significant influence over the investee. Normally, this means that the investor owns less than 20% of the investee corporation's voting stock.[8]

---

[8]The 20% limit is not an absolute rule. Other factors may overrule. FASB, *Accounting Standards—Current Text* (Norwalk, CT, 1994), sec. I82.107–108. First published in *FASB Interpretation No. 35,* pars. 3–4.

Debt Securities Available for Sale. Accounting for debt securities available for sale is similar to debt securities held to maturity. At the time of purchase, the debt securities are recorded at cost. Then, interest is recorded as it accrues.

For example, assume that in the previous discussion, the bonds purchased by Francis, Inc., were not classified as debt securities held to maturity. Instead, assume they were securities available for sale. In other words, assume that Francis did not necessarily intend to hold the bonds to maturity. The previous entries to record the purchase of the bonds on August 31, the accrual of interest on December 31, 19X1, and the receipt of interest on February 28, 19X2, would be exactly the same. If Francis were to sell the bonds before they mature, any gain or loss realized on the sale would be reported in the income statement.

The only difference between debt securities held to maturity and debt securities available for sale involves the amount reported on the balance sheet. Debt securities held to maturity are reported at cost (adjusted for the amortized amount of any difference between cost and maturity value). Debt securities available for sale are reported at their fair value. We explain this more completely after discussing equity securities available for sale.

Equity Securities Available for Sale. Chapter 8 (pages 304–307) explained the procedures of accounting for short-term investments in equity securities available for sale. These same procedures are used for long-term investments. At the time of purchase, the investments are recorded at cost. As dividends are received, they are credited to Dividends Earned and reported in the income statement. When the shares are sold, the proceeds from the sale are compared with the cost of the investment and any gain or loss realized on the sale is reported in the income statement.

Continuing with Francis, Inc., assume that on October 10, 19X1, Francis purchased 1,000 shares of Intex Corp.'s common stock at their par value of $86,000. The following entry records the purchase:

Oct.	10	Investment in Intex Corp. Common Stock	86,000.00	
		Cash		86,000.00
		Purchased 1,000 shares.		

On November 2, Francis received a $1,720 quarterly dividend on the Intex shares. The following entry records the receipt:

Nov.	2	Cash	1,720.00	
		Dividends Earned		1,720.00
		Received dividend of $1.72 per share.		

On December 20, Francis sold 500 of the Intex shares for $45,000, and records the sale with the following entry:

Dec.	20	Cash	45,000.00	
		Investment in Intex Corp. Common Stock		43,000.00
		Gain on Sale of Long-Term Investment		2,000.00
		$86,000/2 = $43,000		

Reporting the Fair Values of Securities Available for Sale. On the balance sheet, long-term investments in securities available for sale are reported at their fair values. This includes both debt and equity securities. Unrealized holding gains (losses) are reported as a separate item in the equity section.

For example, assume that Francis had no prior investments in securities available for sale, other than the bonds purchased on August 31 and the stock purchased on October 10. The following table shows the book values and fair values of these investments on December 31, 19X1:

	Book Value	Fair (Market) Value
Candice Corp. bonds payable	$30,000	$29,050
Intex Corp. common stock, 500 shares	43,000	45,500
Total	$73,000	$74,550

The entry to record the fair value of the investments is:

Dec.	31	Long-Term Investments, Fair Value Adjustment	1,550.00	
		Unrealized Holding Gain (Loss)		1,550.00
		To record change in fair value of securities available for sale.		

In preparing Francis's December 31, 19X1, balance sheet, the cost of the investments normally would be combined with the balance in the Long-Term Investments, Fair Value Adjustment account and reported as a single amount. Thus, Francis's balance sheet would include the following items:

Assets:	
Long-term investments:	
Securities available for sale (at fair value) . .	$74,550
Stockholders' equity:	
Common stock	xxx
Retained earnings	xxx
Unrealized holding gain	1,550

Investment in Equity Securities; Investor Has a Significant Influence or Has Control

Sometimes, an investor buys a large block of a corporation's voting stock and is able to exercise a significant influence over the investee corporation. An investor who owns 20% or more of a corporation's voting stock is normally presumed to have a significant influence over the investee. There may be cases, however, where the accountant concludes that the 20% test of significant influence should be overruled by other, more persuasive, evidence.

An investor who owns more than 50% of a corporation's voting stock can dominate all of the other stockholders in electing the corporation's board of directors. Thus, the investor usually has control over the investee corporation's management.[9]

As we stated earlier, the method of accounting for a stock investment depends on the relationship between the investor and the investee. In studying Illustration 11–1, note that if the investor has a significant influence, the *equity method* of accounting and reporting is used. Finally, if the investor controls the investee, the investor uses the equity method in its records, but reports *consolidated financial statements* to the public. We discuss the equity method and consolidated statements in the following sections.

The Equity Method of Accounting for Common Stock Investments

If a common stock investor has significant influence over the investee, the **equity method** of accounting for the investment must be used. When the stock is acquired, the investor records the purchase at cost. For example, on January 1, 19X1, Gordon Company purchased 3,000 shares (30%) of JWM, Inc., common stock for a total cost of $70,650. This entry records the purchase on Gordon's books:

Jan.	1	Investment in JWM Common Stock	70,650.00	
		Cash		70,650.00
		Purchased 3,000 shares.		

Under the equity method, the earnings of the investee corporation not only increase the investee's net assets but also increase the investor's equity claims against the investee's assets. Therefore, when the investee closes its books and reports the amount of its earnings, the investor takes up its share of those earnings in its investment account. For example, assume that JWM reported net income of $20,000 for 19X1. Gordon's entry to record its 30% share of these earnings is:

Dec.	31	Investment in JWM Common Stock	6,000.00	
		Earnings from Investment in JWM, Inc.		6,000.00
		To record 30% equity in investee's earnings of $20,000.		

The debit records the increase in Gordon Company's equity in JWM. The credit causes 30% of JWM's net income to appear on Gordon Company's income statement as earnings from the investment. As with any other revenue, Gordon closes the earnings to Income Summary.

If the investee corporation incurs a net loss instead of a net income, the investor records its share of the loss and reduces (credits) its investment account. Then, the investor closes the loss to Income Summary.

Under the equity method, the receipt of cash dividends is not recorded as revenue because the investor has already recorded its share of the earnings reported by the investee. Instead, dividends received from the investee simply convert the form of the investor's asset from a stock investment to cash. Thus, the equity method records dividends as a reduction in the balance of the investment account.

---

[9]Ibid., sec. C51.102. First published in *Statement of Financial Accounting Standards No. 94,* par. 13.

For example, assume that JWM declared and paid $10,000 in cash dividends on its common stock. Gordon's entry to record its 30% share of these dividends, which it received on January 9, 19X2, is:

Jan.	9	Cash	3,000.00	
		Investment in JWM Common Stock		3,000.00
		To record receipt of 30% of the $10,000 dividend paid by JWM, Inc.		

Thus, when the equity method is used, the carrying value of a common stock investment equals the cost of the investment plus the investor's equity in the *undistributed* earnings of the investee. For example, after the preceding transactions are recorded on the books of Gordon Company, the investment account appears as follows:

Investment in JWM Common Stock

Date		Explanation	Debit	Credit	Balance
19X1					
Jan.	1	Investment	70,650		70,650
Dec.	31	Share of earnings	6,000		76,650
19X2					
Jan.	9	Share of dividend		3,000	73,650

If Gordon prepared a balance sheet on January 9, the investment in JWM would be reported as $73,650. This is the original cost of the investment, plus Gordon's equity in JWM's earnings since the date of purchase, less Gordon's equity in JWM's dividends since the date of purchase.

When an equity method stock investment is sold, the gain or loss on the sale is determined by comparing the proceeds from the sale with the carrying value (book value) of the investment on the date of sale. For example, suppose that Gordon Company sold its JWM stock for $80,000 on January 10, 19X2. The entry to record the sale is:

Jan.	10	Cash	80,000.00	
		Investment in JWM Common Stock		73,650.00
		Gain on Sale of Investments		6,350.00
		Sold 3,000 shares of stock for $80,000.		

Investments that Require Consolidated Financial Statements

Corporations often own stock in and may even control other corporations. For example, if Par Company owns more than 50% of the voting stock of Sub Company, Par Company can elect Sub Company's board of directors and thus control its activities and resources. The controlling corporation, Par Company, is known as the **parent company** and Sub Company is called a **subsidiary.**

Many large companies are parents with subsidiaries. For example, **PepsiCo, Inc.** is the parent of several subsidiaries, including Taco Bell, Pizza Hut, Kentucky Fried Chicken, and Frito-Lay.

When a corporation owns all the outstanding stock of a subsidiary, it can take over the subsidiary's assets, cancel the subsidiary's stock, and merge the subsidiary into the parent company. However, there often are financial, legal, and tax advantages if a large business is operated as a parent corporation that controls one or more subsidiary corporations. In fact, many large companies are parent corporations that own one or more subsidiaries.

When a business operates as a parent company with subsidiaries, separate accounting records are maintained by each corporation. From a legal viewpoint, the parent and each subsidiary are still separate entities with all the rights, duties, and responsibilities of individual corporations. However, investors in the parent company indirectly are investors in the subsidiaries. To evaluate their investments, parent company investors must consider the financial status and operations of the subsidiaries as well as the parent. This information is provided in **consolidated financial statements.**

Consolidated statements show the financial position, the results of operations, and the cash flows of all corporations under the parent's control, including the subsidiaries. These statements are prepared as if the business is organized as a single company. Although the parent uses the equity method in its accounts, the investment account is not reported on the parent's financial statements. Instead, the individual assets and liabilities of the affiliated companies are combined on a single balance sheet. Also, their revenues and expenses are combined on a single income statement and their cash flows are combined on a single statement of cash flows. More detailed explanations of consolidated statements are included in advanced accounting courses.

Progress Check

11-6 **What are the similarities and differences in accounting for long-term investments in debt securities that are held to maturity and those that are available for sale?**

11-7 **What are the three categories of long-term equity investments? Describe the criteria for each category and the method used to account for each.**

In today's complex world, many companies conduct business activities in more than one country. In fact, the operations of some large corporations involve so many different countries that they are called **multinational businesses.** The problems of managing and accounting for companies that have international operations can be very complex. Because of this complexity, the following pages present only a brief discussion. A more detailed study of these issues is reserved for advanced business courses.

Two primary problems in accounting for international operations occur because businesses with transactions in more than one country have to deal with more than one currency. These two problems are (1) accounting for sales or purchases denominated in a foreign currency and (2) preparing consolidated financial statements with foreign subsidiaries. To simplify the discussion of these problems, we assume that the companies have a base of operations in the United States and prepare their financial statements in the U.S. dollar. Hence, the **reporting currency** of such firms is the U.S. dollar.

INVESTMENTS IN INTERNATIONAL OPERATIONS

LO 4

Describe the primary accounting problems of having investments in international operations and prepare entries to account for sales to foreign customers.

Exchange Rates between Currencies

Active markets for the purchase and sale of foreign currencies exist all over the world. In these markets, U.S. dollars can be exchanged for Canadian dollars, British pounds, French francs, Japanese yen, or other currencies. The price of one currency stated in terms of another currency is called a **foreign exchange rate.** For example, assume that the current exchange rate for British pounds and U.S. dollars was $1.7515 on

January 31, 19X1. This rate means that one pound could have been acquired for $1.7515. On the same day, assume that the exchange rate between German marks and U.S. dollars was $0.5321. This number means that one mark could be purchased for $0.5321. Foreign exchange rates fluctuate daily (or even hourly) in accordance with the changing supply and demand for each currency and expectations about future events.

Sales or Purchases Denominated in a Foreign Currency

When a U.S. company makes a credit sale to a foreign customer, a special problem can arise in accounting for the sale and the account receivable. If the sales terms require the foreign customer's payment to be in U.S. dollars, no special accounting problem arises. But, if the terms of the sale state that payment is to be made in a foreign currency, the U.S. company must go through special steps to account for the sale and the account receivable.

For example, suppose that a U.S. company, the Boston Company, makes a credit sale to London Outfitters, a British company. The sale occurs on December 12, 19X1, and the price is £10,000, which is due on February 10, 19X2. Naturally, Boston Company keeps its accounting records in U.S. dollars. Therefore, to record the sale, Boston Company must translate the sales price from pounds to dollars. This is done using the current exchange rate on the date of the sale. Assuming that the current exchange rate on December 12 is $1.80, Boston records the sale as follows:

Dec.	12	Accounts Receivable—London Outfitters	18,000.00	
		Sales (10,000 × $1.80)		18,000.00
		To record a sale of £10,000, when the exchange rate		
		equals $1.80.		

Now, assume that Boston Company prepares annual financial statements on December 31, 19X1. On that date, the current exchange rate has increased to $1.84. Therefore, the current dollar value of Boston Company's receivable is $18,400 (10,000 × $1.84). This amount is now $400 greater than the amount originally recorded on December 12. According to generally accepted accounting principles, the receivable must be reported in the balance sheet at its current dollar value. Hence, Boston Company must make the following entry to record the increase in the dollar value of the receivable:

Dec.	31	Accounts Receivable—London Outfitters	400.00	
		Foreign Exchange Gain or Loss		400.00
		To record the effects of the increased value of the		
		British pound on our receivable.		

The Foreign Exchange Gain or Loss is closed to the Income Summary account and reported on the income statement.[10]

Assume that Boston Company receives London Outfitters' payment of £10,000 on February 10, and immediately exchanges the pounds for U.S. dollars. On this date, the exchange rate for pounds has declined to $1.78. Therefore, Boston Company re-

---

[10] Ibid., sec. F60.122. First published as FASB, *Statement of Financial Accounting Standards No. 52*, par. 15.

ceives only $17,800 (10,000 × $1.78). The firm records the receipt and the loss associated with the decline in the exchange rate as follows:

Feb.	10	Cash	17,800.00	
		Foreign Exchange Gain or Loss	600.00	
		Accounts Receivable—London Outfitters		18,400.00
		Received foreign currency payment of account and converted it into dollars.		

Accounting for credit purchases from a foreign supplier is similar to the previous example of a credit sale to a foreign customer. If the U.S. company is required to make a payment in a foreign currency, the account payable must be translated into dollars before it can be recorded by the U.S. company. Then, if the exchange rate changes, an exchange gain or loss must be recognized by the U.S. company at any intervening balance sheet date and at the payment date.

Consolidated Statements with Foreign Subsidiaries

A second problem of accounting for international operations involves the preparation of consolidated financial statements when the parent company has one or more foreign subsidiaries. For example, suppose that a U.S. company owns a controlling interest in a French subsidiary. The reporting currency of the U.S. parent is the dollar. However, the French subsidiary maintains its financial records in francs. Before preparing consolidated statements, the parent must translate financial statements of the French company into U.S. dollars. After the translation is completed, the preparation of consolidated statements is not any different than for any other subsidiary.[11]

The procedures for translating a foreign subsidiary's account balances depend on the nature of the subsidiary's operations. In simple terms, the general process requires the parent company to select appropriate foreign exchange rates and then to apply those rates to the account balances of the foreign subsidiary.

Progress Check

11-8 **If a U.S. company makes a credit sale of merchandise to a French customer and the sales terms require payment in francs:**

  a. **The U.S. company will incur an exchange loss if the foreign exchange rate between francs and dollars increases from $0.189 at the date of sale to $0.199 at the date the account is settled.**

  b. **The French company may eventually have to record an exchange gain or loss.**

  c. **The U.S. company may be required to record an exchange gain or loss on the date of the sale.**

  d. **None of the above is correct.**

After studying this and the previous chapters, you have learned about all of the important classes of assets that businesses own. Recall from Chapter 10 that in evaluating the efficiency of a company in using its assets, a ratio that is often calculated and reviewed is total asset turnover. Another ratio that provides information about a

USING THE INFORMATION— RETURN ON TOTAL ASSETS

LO 5

Explain the use of return on total assets in evaluating a company's efficiency in using its assets.

---

[11]The problem grows much more complicated when the accounts of the French subsidiary are maintained in acccordance with the French version of GAAP. The French statements must be converted to U.S. GAAP before the consolidation can be completed.

company's efficiency in using its assets is **return on total assets.** You can calculate the return on total assets with this formula:

$$\text{Return on total assets} = \frac{\text{Net income}}{\text{Average total assets}}$$

For example, **Reebok International,** a worldwide distributor of sports and fitness products, earned a net income of $222.4 million during 1993. At the beginning of 1993, Reebok had total assets of $1,345.3 million, and at the end of the year total assets were $1,391.7 million. If the average total assets owned during the year is approximated by averaging the beginning and ending asset balances, Reebok's return on total assets for 1993 was:

$$\text{Return on total assets} = \frac{\$222.4}{(\$1,345.3 + \$1,391.7)/2} = 16.3\%$$

As we have seen for other ratios, a company's return on total assets should be compared with past performance and with the ratios of similar companies. In addition, you must be careful not to place too much importance on the evaluation of any single ratio. For past performance comparisons, Reebok's return on total assets and total asset turnover over a four-year period were as follows:

Year	Return on Total Assets	Total Asset Turnover
1993	16.3%	2.1
1992	8.3	2.2
1991	16.7	1.9
1990	13.9	1.7
1989	15.8	1.6

Notice that the change in return on total assets suggests that the company's efficiency in using its assets declined. However, the total asset turnover improved each year. A possible explanation for this might be that Reebok decided to increase expenses at a faster rate than sales in an effort to gain an increasing share of the market for its products. Such a strategy would explain a reduced return on total assets and an increased total asset turnover.

Comparing Reebok to a similar company, **Nike, Inc.** reported a 13.1% return on assets for the year ended May 31, 1994. A more general basis for comparison is provided by Dun & Bradstreet's *Industry Norms and Key Ratios.* The 1993–94 edition indicates that the average return on assets for manufacturers of athletic footwear was 15%. It is interesting to note that Reebok was above the norm whereas Nike was below it.

Progress Check

11-9   A company had net income of $140,000 for 19X1 and $100,000 for 19X2. At December 31, 19X1 and 19X2, total assets reported were $800,000 and $900,000, respectively. What was the return on total assets for 19X2?

LO 1. **Identify assets that should be classified as natural resources or as intangible assets and prepare entries to account for them, including entries to record depletion and amortization.** The cost of a natural resource is recorded in an asset account. Then, depletion of the natural resource is recorded by allocating the cost to expense according to a units-of-production basis. The depletion is credited to an accumulated depletion account. Intangible assets are recorded at the cost incurred to purchase the assets. The allocation of intangible asset cost to expense is done on a straight-line basis and is called amortization. Normally, amortization is recorded with credits made directly to the asset account instead of a contra account.

LO 2. **State the criteria for classifying assets as long-term investments and describe the categories of securities that are classified as long-term investments.** Securities investments are classified as current assets if they are held as a source of cash to be used in current operations and if they mature within one year or the current operating cycle of the business or are marketable. All other investments in securities are long-term investments, which also include assets held for a special purpose and not used in operations.

Long-term investments in securities are classified in four groups: (*a*) debt securities held to maturity, (*b*) debt and equity securities available for sale, (*c*) equity securities when the investor has a significant influence over the investee, and (*d*) equity securities when the investor controls the investee.

LO 3. **Describe the methods used to report long-term securities investments in the financial statements.** Debt held to maturity is reported at its original cost adjusted for amortization of any difference between cost and maturity value. Debt and equity securities available for sale are reported at their fair values with unrealized gains or losses shown in the stockholders' equity section of the balance sheet. Gains and losses realized on the sale of the investments are reported in the income statement.

The equity method is used if the investor has a significant influence over the investee. This situation usually exists when the investor owns 20% or more of the investee's voting stock. If an investor owns more than 50% of another corporation's voting stock and controls the investee, the investor's financial reports are prepared on a consolidated basis.

Under the equity method, the investor records its share of the investee's earnings with a debit to the investment account and a credit to a revenue account. Dividends received satisfy the investor's equity claims, and reduce the investment account balance.

LO 4. **Describe the primary accounting problems of having investments in international operations and prepare entries to account for sales to foreign customers.** If a U.S. company makes a credit sale to a foreign customer and the sales terms call for payment with a foreign currency, the company must translate the foreign currency into dollars to record the receivable. If the exchange rate changes before payment is received, foreign exchange gains or losses are recognized in the year in which they occur. The same treatment is used if a U.S. company makes a credit purchase from a foreign supplier and is required to make payment in a foreign currency. Also, if a U.S. company has a foreign subsidiary that maintains its accounts in a foreign currency, the account balances must be translated into dollars before they can be consolidated with the parent's accounts.

LO 5. **Explain the use of return on total assets in evaluating a company's efficiency in using its assets.** Return on total assets is used along with other ratios such as total asset turnover to evaluate the efficiency of a company in using its assets. Return on total assets is usually calculated as the annual net income divided by the average amount of total assets.

SUMMARY OF THE CHAPTER IN TERMS OF LEARNING OBJECTIVES

DEMONSTRATION PROBLEM

The following transactions relate to Brown Company's long-term investment activities during 19X1 and 19X2. Brown did not own any long-term investments prior to 19X1. Show the appropriate journal entries and the portions of each year's balance sheet and income statement that describe these transactions.

19X1

Sept. 9 Purchased 1,000 shares of Packard, Inc., common stock for $80,000 cash. These shares represent 30% of Packard's outstanding shares.

Oct. 2 Purchased 2,000 shares of AT&T common stock for $60,000 cash. These shares represent less than a 1% ownership in AT&T.

17 Purchased as a long-term investment 1,000 shares of Apple Computer common stock for $40,000 cash. These shares are less than 1% of Apple's outstanding shares.

Nov. 1 Received $5,000 cash dividend from Packard.

30 Received $3,000 cash dividend from AT&T.

Dec. 15 Received $1,400 cash dividend from Apple.

31 Packard's 19X1 net income was $70,000.

31 Market values for the investments in marketable equity securities are Packard, $84,000; AT&T, $48,000; and Apple Computer, $45,000.

Dec. 31 After closing the accounts, selected account balances on Brown Company's books are:

Common stock.	$500,000
Retained earnings. . . .	350,000

19X2

Jan. 1 Packard, Inc., was taken over by other investors, and Brown sold its shares for $108,000 cash.

May 30 Received $3,100 cash dividend from AT&T.

June 15 Received $1,600 cash dividend from Apple.

Aug. 17 Sold the AT&T stock for $52,000 cash.

19 Purchased 2,000 shares of Coca-Cola common stock for $50,000 as a long-term investment. The stock represents less than a 5% ownership in Coca-Cola.

Dec. 15 Received $1,800 cash dividend from Apple.

31 Market values of the investments in marketable equity securities are Apple, $39,000 and Coca-Cola, $48,000.

31 After closing the accounts, selected account balances on Brown Company's books are:

Common stock.	$500,000
Retained earnings. . . .	410,000

Planning the Solution

* Account for the investment in Packard under the equity method.
* Account for the investments in AT&T, Apple, and Coca-Cola as long-term investments in securities available for sale.
* Prepare the information for the two balance sheets by including the appropriate assets and stockholders' equity accounts.

Solution to Demonstration Problem

Journal entries during 19X1:

Sept.	9	Investment in Packard Common Stock	80,000.00	
		Cash		80,000.00
		Acquired 1,000 shares representing a 30% equity in Packard, Inc.		

Oct.	2	Investment in AT&T Common Stock	60,000.00	
		Cash		60,000.00
		Acquired 2,000 shares as a long-term investment in securities available for sale.		
	17	Investment in Apple Common Stock	40,000.00	
		Cash		40,000.00
		Acquired 1,000 shares as a long-term investment in securities available for sale.		
Nov.	1	Cash	5,000.00	
		Investment in Packard Common Stock		5,000.00
		Received dividend from Packard, Inc.		
	30	Cash	3,000.00	
		Dividends Earned		3,000.00
		Received dividend from AT&T.		
Dec.	15	Cash	1,400.00	
		Dividends Earned		1,400.00
		Received dividend from Apple.		
	31	Investment in Packard Common Stock	21,000.00	
		Earnings from Investment in Packard		21,000.00
		To record our 30% share of Packard's annual earnings of $70,000.		
	31	Unrealized Holding Gain (Loss)	7,000.00	
		Long-Term Investments, Fair Value Adjustment		7,000.00
		To record change in fair value of securities available for sale.		

	Cost	Fair (Market) Value
AT&T	$ 60,000	$48,000
Apple	40,000	45,000
Total	$100,000	$93,000

Required credit balance of Long-Term Investments, Fair Value Adjustment account ($100,000 − $93,000)	$ 7,000
Existing balance	–0–
Necessary credit	$ 7,000

December 31, 19X1, balance sheet items:

Assets

Long-term investments:		
Securities available for sale (at fair value)	$93,000	
Investment in Packard, Inc.	96,000	
Total		$189,000

Stockholders' Equity

Common stock	$500,000
Retained earnings	350,000
Unrealized holding gain (loss)	(7,000)

Income statement items for the year ended December 31, 19X1:

Dividends earned	$ 4,400
Earnings from equity method investment ..	21,000

Journal entries during 19X2:

Jan.	1	Cash	108,000.00	
		Investment in Packard Common Stock		96,000.00
		Gain on Sale of Investments		12,000.00
		Sold 1,000 shares for cash.		
May	30	Cash	3,100.00	
		Dividends Earned		3,100.00
		Received dividend from AT&T.		
June	15	Cash	1,600.00	
		Dividends Earned		1,600.00
		Received dividend from Apple.		
Aug.	17	Cash	52,000.00	
		Loss on Sale of Investments	8,000.00	
		Investment in AT&T Common Stock		60,000.00
		Sold 2,000 shares for cash.		
	19	Investment in Coca-Cola Common Stock	50,000.00	
		Cash		50,000.00
		Acquired 2,000 shares as a long-term investment in securities available for sale.		
Dec.	15	Cash	1,800.00	
		Dividends Earned		1,800.00
		Received dividend from Apple.		
	31	Long-Term Investments, Fair Value Adjustment	4,000.00	
		Unrealized Holding Gain (Loss)		4,000.00
		To record change in fair value of securities available for sale.		

	Cost	Fair (Market) Value
Apple	$40,000	$39,000
Coca-Cola	50,000	48,000
Total	$90,000	$87,000

Required credit balance of Long-Term Investments, Fair Value Adjustment account ($90,000 − $87,000)	$3,000
Existing credit balance	7,000
Necessary debit	$4,000

December 31, 19X2, balance sheet items:

Assets

Long-term investments:	
Securities available for sale (at fair value)	$87,000

Stockholders' Equity

Common stock	$500,000
Retained earnings	410,000
Unrealized holding gain (loss)	(3,000)

Income statement items for the year ended December 31, 19X2:

Dividends earned	$ 6,500
Gain on sale of investments	12,000
Loss on sale of investments	(8,000)

GLOSSARY

Amortization the process of systematically writing off the cost of an intangible asset to expense over its estimated useful life. p. 409

Consolidated financial statements financial statements that show the results of all operations under the parent's control, including those of any subsidiaries; assets and liabilities of all affiliated companies are combined on a single balance sheet, revenues and expenses are combined on a single income statement, and cash flows are combined on a single statement of cash flows as though the business were in fact a single company. p. 421

Copyright an exclusive right granted by the federal government or by international agreement to publish and sell a musical, literary, or artistic work for a period of years. p. 411

Depletion the cost created by consuming the usefulness of natural resources. p. 408

Equity method an accounting method used when the investor has influence over the investee; the investment account is initially debited for cost and then is increased to reflect the investor's share of the investee's earnings and decreased to reflect the investor's receipt of dividends paid by the investee. p. 419

Foreign exchange rate the price of one currency stated in terms of another currency. p. 421

Goodwill an intangible asset of a business that represents future earnings greater than the average in its industry; recognized in the financial statements only when a business is acquired at a price in excess of the fair market value of its net assets (excluding goodwill). p. 412

Intangible asset an asset representing certain legal rights and economic relationships; it has no physical existence but is beneficial to the owner. p. 409

Lease a contract under which the owner of property (the lessor) grants to a lessee the right to use the property. p. 411

Leasehold the rights granted to a lessee by the lessor under the terms of a lease contract. p. 411

Leasehold improvements improvements to leased property made and paid for by the lessee. p. 412

Lessee the individual or company that acquires the right to use property under the terms of a lease. p. 411

Lessor the individual or company that owns property to be used by a lessee under the terms of a lease. p. 411

Long-term investments investments in stocks and bonds that are not marketable or, if marketable, are not intended to be a ready source of cash in case of need; also funds earmarked for a special purpose, such as bond sinking funds, and land or other assets not used in regular operations. p. 414

Multinational business a company that operates in a large number of different countries. p. 421

Parent company a corporation that owns a controlling interest in another corporation (more than 50% of the voting stock is required). p. 420

Patent exclusive right granted by the federal government to manufacture and sell a patented machine or device, or to use a process, for 17 years. p. 410

Reporting currency the currency in which a company presents its financial statements. p. 421

Return on total assets a measure of a company's operating efficiency, calculated by expressing net income as a percentage of average total assets. p. 424

Subsidiary a corporation that is controlled by another corporation (the parent) because the parent owns more than 50% of the subsidiary's voting stock. p. 420

Trademark a unique symbol used by a company in marketing its products or services. p. 413

Trade name a unique name used by a company in marketing its products or services. p. 413

QUESTIONS

1. What is the name for the process of allocating the cost of natural resources to expense as the natural resources are used?

2. What are the characteristics of an intangible asset?

3. Is the declining-balance method an acceptable means of calculating depletion of natural resources?

4. What general procedures are followed in accounting for intangible assets?

5. When does a business have goodwill? Under what conditions can goodwill appear in a company's balance sheet?

6. X Company bought an established business and paid for goodwill. If X Company plans to incur substantial advertising and promotional costs each year to maintain the value of the goodwill, must the company also amortize the goodwill?

7. In accounting for common stock investments, when should the equity method be used?

8. Under what circumstances would a company prepare consolidated financial statements?

9. Under what circumstances are long-term investments in debt securities reported at their original cost adjusted for amortization of any difference between cost and maturity value?

10. What are two basic problems of accounting for international operations?

11. If a U.S. company makes a credit sale to a foreign customer and the customer is required to make payment in U.S. dollars, can the U.S. company have an exchange gain or loss as a result of the sale?

12. A U.S. company makes a credit sale to a foreign customer, and the customer is required to make payment in a foreign currency. The foreign exchange rate was $1.40 on the date of the sale and is $1.30 on the date the customer pays the receivable. Will the U.S. company record an exchange gain or an exchange loss?

13. Refer to Federal Express Corporation's consolidated balance sheets in Appendix G. What percentage of total assets is represented by goodwill at May 31, 1993?

14. Refer to Ben & Jerry's Homemade, Inc., financial statements in Appendix G. Calculate the return on total assets for 1992.

QUICK STUDY (Five-Minute Exercises)

**QS 11–1
(LO 1)**

Three Z Mining Co. acquired an ore mine at a cost of $615,000. It was necessary to incur a $60,000 cost to access the mine. The mine is estimated to hold 200,000 tons of ore and the estimated value of the land after the ore is removed is $80,000.

   a.   Prepare the entry to record the acquisition.

   b.   Prepare the year-end adjusting entry assuming that 46,000 tons of ore were removed from the mine this year.

**QS 11–2
(LO 1)**

Which of the following assets should be reported on the balance sheet as an intangible asset? Which should be reported as a natural resource? (*a*) copper mine, (*b*) copyright, (*c*) building, (*d*) goodwill, (*e*) timberland.

**QS 11–3
(LO 1)**

In early January of the current year, Big Mountain Ski Shop incurred a $160,000 cost to modernize the shop. The improvements included new floors, lighting, and fitting platforms for rental equipment. These improvements would last for 10 years of use. Big Mountain leases its retail space and has eight years remaining on the lease. Prepare the entry to record the modernization, and the adjusting entry at the end of the current year.

**QS 11–4
(LO 2)**

On April 1, 19X1, Demi Dean purchased 8% bonds of Multi Media Inc. at a cost of $50,000, which equals their par value. The bonds carry an 8% rate of interest to be paid semiannually on September 30 and March 31. Prepare the entries to record the September 30 receipt of interest and the December 31 accrual.

**QS 11–5
(LO 2)**

On January 2, 19X1, Nassau Co. paid $500,000 to acquire 10,000 (10%) of Suffolk Corp.'s outstanding common shares as a long-term investment. On March 25, 19X3, Nassau sold half of the shares for $260,000. What method should be used to account for this stock investment? Prepare entries to record the acquisition of the stock and the stock sale.

**QS 11–6
(LO 3)**

Assume the same facts as in QS 11–5 except assume that the stock acquired represented 30% of the outstanding stock. Suffolk Co. paid a $100,000 dividend on October 12, 19X1, and reported a net income of $400,000 for the 19X1 year. Prepare the entry to record the receipt of the dividend and the year-end adjustment of the investment account.

**QS 11–7
(LO 4)**

On November 21, 19X1, a U.S. company, NCN, made a sale with credit terms requiring payment in 30 days to a German company, Ehlers Inc. The price of the sale was 50,000 marks. Assuming the exchange rate between German marks and U.S. dollars was $0.6214 on the date of sale and $0.5942 on December 21, prepare the entries to record the sale and cash receipt on December 21.

**QS 11–8
(LO 5)**

How is the return on total assets calculated? What does this ratio evaluate?

EXERCISES

On March 30, 19X1, Clementine Investments paid $7,275,000 for an ore deposit containing 4,850,000 tons. The company also installed machinery in the mine that cost $339,500, had an estimated 10-year life with no salvage value, and was capable of removing all the ore in 8 years. The machine will be abandoned when the ore is completely mined. Clementine began operations on July 1, 19X1, and mined and sold 582,000 tons of ore during the remaining six months of the year. Give the December 31, 19X1, entries to record the depletion of the ore deposit and the depreciation of the mining machinery.

Exercise 11–1
Depletion of natural resources
(LO 1)

Majestic Productions purchased the copyright to a painting for $369,000 on January 1, 19X1. The copyright legally protects its owner for 24 more years. However, the company plans to market and sell prints of the original for only 15 more years. Prepare journal entries to record the purchase of the copyright and the annual amortization of the copyright on December 31, 19X1.

Exercise 11–2
Amortization of intangible assets
(LO 1)

Rocky Lane has devoted years to developing a profitable business that earns an attractive return. Lane is now considering the possibility of selling the business and is attempting to estimate the value of the goodwill in the business. The fair value of the net assets of the business (excluding goodwill) is $625,000, and in a typical year net income is about $90,000. Most businesses of this type are expected to earn a return of about 12% on net assets. Estimate the value of the goodwill assuming (a) the value is equal to eight times the excess earnings above average, and (b) the value can be found by capitalizing the excess earnings above average at a rate of 10%.

Exercise 11–3
Estimating goodwill
(LO 1)

During 19X1, Stockton Company's investments in securities included five items. These securities, with their December 31, 19X1, market values, are as follows:

Exercise 11–4
Classifying stock investments, recording fair values
(LO 2, 3)

a. Antel Corporation bonds payable: $167,400 cost; $182,000 market value. Stockton positively intends and is able to hold these bonds until they mature in 19X4.

b. Foxfire, Inc., common stock: 30,800 shares; $132,980 cost; $143,500 market value. Stockton owns 22% of Foxfire's voting stock and has a significant influence on Foxfire.

c. Techcon Corp. common stock: 10,300 shares; $67,900 cost; $73,240 market value. The goal of this investment is to earn dividends over the next few years.

d. Bali common stock: 4,500 shares; $46,120 cost; $45,770 market value. The goal of this investment is an expected increase in market value of the stock over the next three to five years. Bali has 30,000 common shares outstanding.

e. Joskey common stock: 18,400 shares; $57,100 cost; $59,900 market value. This stock is marketable and is held as an investment of cash available for operations.

State whether each of these investments should be classified as a current asset or as a long-term investment. Also, for each of the long-term items, indicate in which of the four types of long-term investments the item should be classified. Then, prepare a journal entry dated December 31, 19X1, to record the fair value of the long-term investments in securities available for sale. Assume that Stockton had no long-term investments prior to 19X1.

Pratt Company began operations in 19X1 and regularly makes long-term investments in securities available for sale. The total cost and fair value of these investments at the end of several years were:

Exercise 11–5
Investments in securities available for sale
(LO 3)

	Cost	Market Value
On December 31, 19X1	$170,000	$164,800
On December 31, 19X2	194,000	206,000
On December 31, 19X3	264,000	312,000
On December 31, 19X4	398,000	354,000

Required

Prepare journal entries to record the fair value of Pratt's investments at the end of each year.

Exercise 11–6
Stock investment transactions;
equity method
(LO 3)

Prepare general journal entries to record the following events on the books of MCM Company:

19X1

Jan. 14   Purchased 18,000 shares of Putnam, Inc., common stock for $156,900 plus broker's fee of $1,000. Putnam has 90,000 shares of common stock outstanding and has acknowledged the fact that its policies will be significantly influenced by MCM.

Oct. 1   Putnam declared and paid a cash dividend of $2.60 per share.

Dec. 31   Putnam announced that net income for the year amounted to $650,000.

19X2

Apr. 1   Putnam declared and paid a cash dividend of $2.70 per share.

Dec. 31   Putnam announced that net income for the year amounted to $733,100.

     31   MCM sold 6,000 shares of Putnam for $119,370.

Exercise 11–7
Receivables denominated in a
foreign currency
(LO 4)

On June 2, 19X1, Comco Company made a credit sale to a French company. The terms of the sale required the French company to pay 980,000 francs on January 3, 19X2. Comco prepares quarterly financial statements on March 31, June 30, September 30, and December 31. The foreign exchange rates for francs during the time the receivable was outstanding were:

June 2, 19X1	$0.16720
June 30, 19X1	0.17100
September 30, 19X1	0.17225
December 31, 19X1	0.16885
January 3, 19X2	0.17310

Calculate the foreign exchange gain or loss that Comco should report on each of its quarterly income statements during the last three quarters of 19X1 and the first quarter of 19X2. Also calculate the amount that should be reported on Comco's balance sheets at the end of the last three quarters of 19X1.

Exercise 11–8
Foreign currency transactions
(LO 4)

Donham Company of Montvale, New Jersey, sells its products to customers in the United States and in England. On December 3, 19X1, Donham sold merchandise on credit to Swensons, Ltd., of London, England, at a price of 6,500 pounds. The exchange rate on that day was 1 pound equals $1.4685. On December 31, 19X1, when Donham prepared its financial statements, the exchange rate was 1 pound for $1.4230. Swensons, Ltd., paid its bill in full on January 3, 19X2, at which time the exchange rate was 1 pound for $1.4460. Donham immediately exchanged the 6,500 pounds for U.S. dollars. Prepare journal entries on December 3, December 31, and January 3, to account for the sale and account receivable on the books of Donham.

Exercise 11–9
Return on total assets
(LO 5)

The following information is available from the financial statements of NRE Company:

	19X1	19X2	19X3
Total assets, December 31	$320,000	$580,000	$1,200,000
Net income	46,000	75,000	106,000

Calculate NRE's return on total assets for 19X2 and 19X3. Comment on the company's efficiency in using its assets in 19X2 and 19X3.

PROBLEMS

Part 1. Five years ago, Zeno Insurance Company leased space in a building for 15 years. The lease contract calls for annual rental payments of $28,000 to be made on each July 1 throughout the life of the lease and also provides that the lessee must pay for all additions and improvements to the leased property. Because recent nearby construction has made the location more valuable, Zeno decided to sublease the space to Bogart & Company for the remaining 10 years of the lease. On June 25, Bogart paid $75,000 to Zeno for the right to sublease the property and agreed to assume the obligation to pay the $28,000 annual rental charges to the building owner, beginning the next July 1. After taking possession of the leased space, Bogart paid for improving the office portion of the leased space at a cost of $90,950. The improvement was paid for on July 8 and is estimated to have a life equal to the 17 years remaining in the life of the building.

Problem 11–1
Intangible assets and natural resources
(LO 1)

Required

Prepare entries for Bogart & Company to record (*a*) its payment to Zeno for the right to sublease the building space, (*b*) its payment of the next annual rental charge to the building owner, and (*c*) payment for the improvements. Also, prepare the adjusting entries required at the end of the first year of the sublease to amortize (*d*) a proper share of the $75,000 cost of the sublease and (*e*) a proper share of the office improvement.

Part 2. On February 20 of the current year, Amazon Industries paid $8,700,000 for land estimated to contain 11.6 million tons of recoverable ore of a valuable mineral. It installed machinery costing $348,000, which had a 12-year life and no salvage value, and was capable of exhausting the ore deposit in 9 years. The machinery was paid for on May 24, six days before mining operations began. The company removed 744,000 tons of ore during the first seven months' operations.

Required

Preparation component:

Prepare entries to record (*a*) the purchase of the land, (*b*) the installation of the machinery, (*c*) the first seven months' depletion under the assumption that the land will be valueless after the ore is mined, and (*d*) the first seven months' depreciation on the machinery, which will be abandoned after the ore is fully mined.

CHECK FIGURE:
Depletion of Mineral Deposit,
$558,000

Analysis component:

Describe the similarities and differences in amortization, depletion, and depreciation.

Flowers Unlimited has the following balance sheet on December 31, 19X1:

Problem 11–2
Goodwill
(LO 1)

Cash	$ 57,800
Merchandise inventory	43,650
Buildings	320,000
Accumulated depreciation	(112,000)
Land	101,750
Total assets	$411,200
Accounts payable	$ 9,400
Long-term note payable	124,925
D. E. Flowers, capital	276,875
Total liabilities and owner's equity . .	$411,200

In this industry, earnings average 32% of owner's equity. Flowers Unlimited, however, is expected to earn $100,000 annually. The owner believes that the balance sheet amounts are reasonable estimates of fair market values for all assets except goodwill, which does not appear on the financial statement. In discussing a plan to sell the company, D. E. Flowers has suggested to the potential buyer that goodwill can be measured by capitalizing the amount of above-average earnings at a rate of 12%. On the other hand, the potential buyer thinks that goodwill should be valued at six times the amount of excess earnings above the average for the industry.

Required

1. Calculate the amount of goodwill claimed by Flowers.

2. Calculate the amount of goodwill according to the potential buyer.

3. Suppose that the buyer finally agrees to pay the full price requested by Flowers. If the amount of expected earnings (before amortization of goodwill) is obtained and the goodwill is amortized over the longest permissible time period, what amount of net income will be reported for the first year after the company is purchased?

4. If the buyer pays the full price requested by Flowers, what rate of return on the purchaser's investment will be earned as net income the first year?

Problem 11–3
Accounting for stock investments
(LO 3)

Austex Company was organized on January 2, 19X1. The following transactions and events subsequently occurred:

19X1

Jan.   7   Austex purchased 50,000 shares (20%) of Staat, Inc.'s outstanding common stock for $565,500.

Apr. 30   Staat declared and paid a cash dividend of $1.10 per share.

Dec. 31   Staat announced that its net income for 19X1 was $480,000. Market value of the stock was $11.80 per share.

19X2

Nov. 30   Staat declared and paid a cash dividend of $0.70 per share.

Dec. 31   Staat announced that its net income for 19X2 was $630,000. Market value of the stock was $12.18 per share.

19X3

Jan. 5   Austex sold all of its investment in Staat for $682,000 cash.

Part 1. Assume that Austex has a significant influence over Staat because it owns 20% of the stock.

Required

1. Give the entries on the books of Austex to record the preceding events.

2. Calculate the carrying value per share of Austex's investment as reflected in the investment account on January 4, 19X3.

3. Calculate the change in Austex's equity from January 7, 19X1, through January 5, 19X3, that resulted from its investment in Staat.

Part 2. Assume that even though Austex owns 20% of Staat's outstanding stock, a thorough investigation of the surrounding circumstances indicates that it does not have a significant influence over the investee.

Required

1. Give the entries on the books of Austex to record the preceding events. Also prepare an entry dated January 5, 19X3, to remove any balances related to the fair value adjustment.

2. Calculate the cost per share of Austex's investment as reflected in the investment account on January 4, 19X3.

3. Calculate the change in Austex's equity from January 7, 19X1, through January 5, 19X3, that resulted from its investment in Staat.

Leling Company's long-term investments portfolio at December 31, 19X1, consisted of the following:

Problem 11–4
Accounting for long-term investments
(LO 2, 3)

Securities Available for Sale	Cost	Fair (Market) Value
10,000 shares of Company X common stock	$163,500	$145,000
1,500 shares of Company Y common stock	65,000	62,000
120,000 shares of Company Z common stock	40,000	35,600

Leling made the following long-term investments transactions during 19X2:

Jan. 17 Sold 750 shares of Company Y common stock for $36,000 less a brokerage fee of $180.

Mar. 3 Purchased 5,000 shares of Company A common stock for $300,000 plus a brokerage fee of $1,500. The shares represent a 30% ownership in Company A.

May 12 Purchased 3,000 shares of Company B common stock for $96,000 plus a brokerage fee of $400. The shares represent a 10% ownership in Company B.

Sept. 2 Purchased 250,000 shares of Company C common stock for $480,000 plus a brokerage fee of $2,400. The shares represent a 51% ownership in Company C.

Dec. 11 Purchased 10,000 shares of Company D common stock for $89,000 plus a brokerage fee of $445. The shares represent a 5% ownership in Company D.

Dec. 20 Sold 10,000 shares of Company X common stock for $160,000 less a brokerage fee of $800.

The fair (market) values of Leling's investments at December 31, 19X2, follow: A, $18,000; B, $92,000; C, $506,500; D, $90,800; Y, $38,200; Z, $31,000.

Required

1. Determine what amount should be reported on Leling's December 31, 19X2, balance sheet for its investments in equity securities available for sale.

2. Prepare a December 31, 19X2, adjusting entry, if necessary, to record the fair value adjustment of the long-term investments in securities available for sale.

3. What amount of gain or loss on those transactions relating to securities available for sale should be reported on Leling's December 31, 19X2, income statement?

CHECK FIGURE:
Unrealized Holding Gain (Loss), $19,555 Cr.

Lupold Company is a U.S. company that has customers in several foreign countries. The company had the following transactions in 19X1 and 19X2:

Problem 11–5
Foreign currency transactions
(LO 4)

19X1

May 22 Sold merchandise for 15,000 marks to Weishaar Imports of Germany, payment in full to be received in 90 days. On this day, the foreign exchange rate for marks was $0.5654.

Sept. 9 Sold merchandise to Campos Company of Mexico for $24,780 cash. The exchange rate for pesos was $0.322154.

Aug. 25 Received Weishaar Imports' payment for its purchase of May 22, and exchanged the marks for dollars. The current foreign exchange rate for marks was $0.5995.

Nov. 29 Sold merchandise on credit to ONI Company located in Japan. The price of 1.1 million yen was to be paid 60 days from the date of sale. The exchange rate for yen was $0.009195 on November 29.

Dec. 23 Sold merchandise for 158,000 francs to Martinique Company of France, payment in full to be received in 30 days. The exchange rate for francs was $0.16722.

Dec. 31 Prepared adjusting entries to recognize exchange gains or losses on the annual financial statements. Rates for exchanging foreign currencies on this day included the following:

Marks (Germany)	$0.5690
Pesos (Mexico)	0.331256
Yen (Japan)	0.010110
Francs (France)	0.16530

19X2

Jan. 24   Received full payment from Martinique for the sale of December 23 and immediately exchanged the francs for dollars. The exchange rate for francs was $0.16342.

30   Received ONI's full payment for the sale of November 29 and immediately exchanged the yen for dollars. The exchange rate for yen was $0.010290.

Required

Preparation component:

CHECK FIGURE:
19X1 total foreign exchange gain, $1,214.64

1.   Prepare general journal entries to account for these transactions of Lupold.

2.   Calculate the foreign exchange gain or loss to be reported on Lupold's 19X1 income statement.

Analysis component:

3.   What actions might Lupold consider to reduce its risk of foreign exchange gains or losses?

CRITICAL THINKING: ESSAYS, PROBLEMS, AND CASES

Analytical Essay

(LO 3)

On January 3, Tragor Company purchased 20,000 shares of Entech Company common stock for $10 per share, or $200,000. Tragor's purchase represents a 30% ownership in Entech. Tragor did not own any investments prior to the Entech stock purchase. Entech did not declare any dividends on its common stock during the year, and on December 31 reported a net loss of $80,000. The market value of the Entech stock on December 31 was $11.00 per share. The accountant for Tragor made the following adjusting entry to update the account balances for the investment in Entech:

Dec.	31	Long-Term Investments, Fair Value Adjustment	20,000.00	
		Unrealized Holding Gain (Loss)		20,000.00
		(20,000 × $11) − $200,000 = $20,000		

Describe the method that Tragor's accountant used to account for the investment in Entech. Explain why this method is incorrect. Without providing specific amounts, determine what impact the accountant's error had on the financial statements.

Business Communications Case

(LO 2, 3)

You are the accountant for PCI Company. The owner of PCI, Lester Murphy, has finished reviewing the financial statements you prepared for 19X3 and questions the $40,000 loss reported on PCI's sale of its investment in the stock of Runyan Company.

PCI acquired 100,000 shares of Runyan's outstanding common stock on December 31, 19X1, at a cost of $500,000. This stock purchase represented a 30% interest in Runyan. The 19X2 income statement showed that the investments made by PCI proved to be very profitable and that the earnings from all investments were $340,000. On January 5, 19X3, PCI sold the Runyan stock for $580,000. Runyan did not pay any dividends during 19X2 and reported $400,000 net income for the year.

Murphy believes that because the purchase price of the Runyan stock was $500,000 and it was sold for $580,000, the 19X3 income statement should report an $80,000 gain on the sale.

Draft a memo to Murphy explaining why the $40,000 loss on the sale of the Runyan stock is correctly reported.

UNI Company is considering buying either Riteway Company or Best Company, similar businesses that acquired their equipment and began operating four years ago. In evaluating the two companies, UNI has determined that they have not used the same accounting procedures so their financial statements are not comparable. Over the past four years, Riteway has reported an average annual net income of $197,840 and Best has reported $254,190. The current balance sheets of the two companies show the following:

	Riteway	Best
Cash	$ 131,500	$ 144,400
Accounts receivable	972,400	1,077,000
Allowance for doubtful accounts	(57,000)	–0–
Merchandise inventory	1,268,200	1,666,000
Store equipment	496,800	420,800
Accumulated depreciation, store equipment	(293,310)	(168,320)
Total assets	$2,518,590	$3,139,880
Total liabilities	$1,176,800	$1,408,600

Riteway has used the allowance method of accounting for bad debts and Best has used the direct write-off method. An examination of each company's accounts revealed that only $30,000 of Riteway's accounts are probably uncollectible and that Best's estimated uncollectible accounts total $54,000.

Because Best uses FIFO, its ending inventory amounts approximate replacement cost. However, Riteway uses LIFO. As a result, Riteway's current inventory is reported $176,000 below replacement cost.

In taking depreciation for the past four years, both companies have assumed 10-year lives and no salvage value for their equipment. However, Riteway has used double-declining-balance depreciation, while Best has used straight-line. UNI believes that straight-line depreciation results in reporting equipment on the balance sheet at its approximate fair market value.

UNI is willing to pay fair market value for the net assets (including goodwill) of either business. UNI estimates goodwill to be four times the average annual earnings in excess of 14% of the fair market value of the net tangible assets (assets, other than goodwill, minus liabilities).

Required

Prepare the following schedules: (*a*) the net tangible assets of each company at fair market values assessed by UNI, (*b*) the revised net incomes of the companies based on adjusted amounts of bad debts expense, FIFO inventories, and straight-line depreciation, (*c*) the calculation of each company's goodwill, and (*d*) the maximum purchase price UNI would pay for each business, if it assumed the liabilities of the purchased business. (Note: Round all calculations to the nearest dollar.)

Examine Apple Computer, Inc.'s financial statements and supplemental information in Appendix F and answer the following questions:

1. Are Apple's financial statements consolidated? How can you tell?

2. Does Apple have more than one subsidiary? How can you tell?

3. Does Apple have any foreign operations? How can you tell?

4. Is there a foreign exchange gain or loss on the income statement? Provide an explanation for what you find or do not find.

5. What intangible assets does Apple own? Assuming it will not take advantage of any renewal options, what is the maximum time period that Apple can use to amortize these intangibles?

6. Calculate Apple's return on total assets for 1993.

CONCEPT TESTER

Test your understanding of the concepts introduced in this chapter by completing the following crossword puzzle.

Across Clues

1. A unique symbol used by a company in marketing its products or services.
4. The individual or company that acquires the right to use property under a lease.
6. Exclusive right granted by government to manufacture and sell a device or use a process.
9. 2 words; A valuable legal right or economic relationship that has no physical existence.
10. 3 words; the price of one currency stated in terms of another currency.
12. 2 words; a unique name used by a company in marketing its products or services.
13. An exclusive right granted by the government to sell a musical, literary, or artistic work.

Down Clues

2. The cost created by consuming the usefulness of natural resources.
3. 2 words; the currency in which a company presents its financial statements.
5. A corporation that is controlled by another corporation (the parent.)
7. The individual or company that owns property to be used by a lessee under a lease.
8. An intangible asset that represents future earnings greater than average.
11. A contract under which the owner of property grants a lessee the right to use the property.

ANSWERS TO PROGRESS CHECKS

11–1 Some possible answers:
Intangible Assets:
Patents
Copyrights
Leaseholds
Leasehold Improvements
Goodwill
Trademarks
Exclusive Licenses
Natural Resources:
Timberlands
Mineral Deposits
Oil Reserves

11–2 $650,000 \times (91,000/325,000) = \$182,000$

11–3
Jan.	6	Patents	120,000	
		Cash		120,000
Dec.	31	Amortization Expense	40,000	
		Patents		40,000

11–4 Long-term investments include funds earmarked for a special purpose, bonds and stocks that do not meet the test of a current asset, and other assets that are not used in the regular operations of the business.

11–5 A stock investment is classified as a long-term investment if it is not marketable or, if marketable, it is not held as an available source of cash to meet the needs of current operations.

11–6 Debt securities held to maturity and debt securities available for sale are recorded at cost and interest on both is accrued as earned. However, only securities held to maturity require amortizing the difference between cost and maturity value. In addition, only securities available for sale require end-of-period adjustments to fair market value.

11–7 Long-term equity investments are placed in the following three categories and accounted for using the method indicated:
a. Noninfluential holding (less than 20% of outstanding stock) — Fair Value Method.
b. Significantly influential holding (20% to 50% of outstanding stock) — Equity Method.
c. Controlling holding (more than 50%) — Consolidated Statements.

11–8 d

11–9 ($800,000 + $900,000)/2 = $850,000
$100,000/$850,000 = 11.8%

Current and Long-Term Liabilities

Safeway, Inc. is one of the world's largest food retailers. At the end of its 1993 year, Safeway operated approximately 1,080 stores in the United States and Canada. The company's 1993 annual report appears to indicate that Safeway has been successfully emerging from a very difficult period of losses. At the end of its 1989 year, total stockholders' equity was a negative $388.9 million (a deficit). In other words, total liabilities exceeded total assets by $388.9 million. This situation improved each year until, at the end of 1993, total stockholders' equity was a positive $382.9 million.

C. A. Smith is considering investing in Safeway. In evaluating Safeway's financial condition, Smith is confused about the nature of the company's liabilities. The balance sheet reports four different categories of liabilities, and the differences between these categories are not clear to Smith.

Safeway Inc. and Subsidiaries
(In millions)

	Year-end 1993	Year-end 1992
Current liabilities:		
Current maturities of notes and debentures	$ 188.6	$ 92.0
Current obligations under capital leases	19.3	20.4
Accounts payable	880.5	811.0
Accrued salaries and wages	216.3	192.5
Other accrued liabilities	406.7	385.9
Total current liabilities	$1,711.4	$1,501.8
Long-term debt:		
Notes and debentures	$2,287.7	$2,736.6
Obligations under capital leases	193.6	199.6
Total long-term debt	$2,481.3	$2,936.2
Deferred income taxes	145.5	176.0
Accrued claims and other liabilities	353.6	368.7
Total liabilities	$4,691.8	$4,982.7

LEARNING OBJECTIVES

After studying Chapter 12, you should be able to:

1. **Define liabilities, explain the difference between current and long-term liabilities, and describe the uncertainties related to some liabilities.**
2. **Describe how accountants record and report estimated liabilities such as warranties and income taxes and how they report contingent liabilities.**
3. **Describe payroll expenses and liabilities and prepare journal entries to account for them.**
4. **Describe how accountants record and report short-term notes payable.**
5. **Explain and calculate the present value of an amount to be paid at a future date and the present value of a series of equal amounts to be paid at future dates.**
6. **Describe how accountants use present value concepts in accounting for long-term notes, and how liabilities may result from leasing assets.**
7. **Calculate the number of times a company earns its fixed interest charges and describe what it reveals about a company's situation.**
8. **Define or explain the words and phrases listed in the chapter glossary.**

Previous chapters have described liabilities for accounts payable, notes payable, wages payable, and unearned revenues. In this chapter, you will learn about liabilities arising from warranties, income taxes, borrowing, asset purchases, leases, and payrolls. We also describe contingent liabilities and the important concept of present value. As you study this chapter, you will learn how accountants define, classify, and measure liabilities for the purpose of reporting useful information about them.

DEFINING AND CLASSIFYING LIABILITIES

LO 1

Define liabilities, explain the difference between current and long-term liabilities, and describe the uncertainties related to some liabilities.

In general, a liability means that because of a past event, a business has a present obligation to make a future payment. More precisely, liabilities are probable future payments of assets or services that an entity is presently obligated to make as a result of past transactions or events.[1] As shown in the diagram, this definition involves three dimensions in time:

- The company is obligated in the present

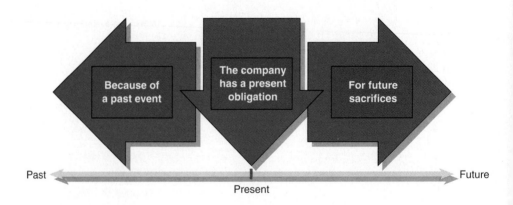

Past ← | → Future
Present

---

[1]Financial Accounting Standards Board, *Statement of Financial Accounting Concepts No. 6*, "Elements of Financial Statements" (Norwalk, CT, 1985), par. 35.

- To pay out assets or deliver services in the future
- Because of an event in the past

This definition also tells us that liabilities do not include all expected future payments. For example, suppose that a company expects to pay wages to its employees in the coming months. These future payments are not liabilities because the company is not presently obligated to pay them. The company is not presently obligated because the employees have not yet earned the future wages. In other words, no past transaction has resulted in a present obligation. The liabilities will be created in the future only when the employees actually perform the work.

Current and Long-Term Liabilities

Information about liabilities is more useful when the balance sheet identifies the liabilities as current and long-term. *Current liabilities* are expected to be paid by using existing current assets or creating other current liabilities.[2] Current liabilities are due within one year or the company's operating cycle, whichever is longer. Typical current liabilities include accounts payable, short-term notes payable, wages payable, warranty liabilities, lease liabilities, payroll and other taxes payable, and unearned revenues.

The specific current liabilities reported by a company depend on the nature of its operations. For example, the 1993 balance sheet for **Southern Company** (an electric utility) reports more than $100 million in its current liabilities for customer deposits. As another example, **US West, Inc.'s** 1993 balance sheet included a $455.7 million liability for the current portion of restructuring charges.

Obligations that are not expected to be paid within one year (or a longer operating cycle) should be classified as *long-term liabilities.* Typical long-term liabilities include long-term notes payable, warranty liabilities, lease liabilities, and bonds payable. On the balance sheet, these may be presented in a single long-term liabilities section. However, many companies show them as two or more items such as *long-term debt* and *other liabilities.* For example, the liabilities of Safeway Inc., on page 441 include long-term debt, deferred income taxes, and accrued claims and other liabilities. All of these are reported below current liabilities and are understood to be non-current (long-term) liabilities.

Some kinds of liabilities may be either current or long term. A specific debt is assigned to a category on the basis of how soon it will be paid. In fact, a single liability is divided between the two categories if the company expects to make payments in both the near and more distant future. For example, recall the liabilities of **Safeway Inc.** Notice that the first two current liabilities represent the current portions of the two items listed as long-term debt.

A few liabilities do not have a fixed due date because they are payable on the creditor's demand. They are reported as current liabilities because they may have to be paid within the year or a longer operating cycle.

[2]FASB, *Accounting Standards—Current Text* (Norwalk, CT, 1994), sec. B05.402. First published as *Accounting Research Bulletin No. 43,* Ch. 3A, par. 7.

UNCERTAIN ASPECTS OF SOME LIABILITIES

Three important questions concerning liabilities are: Who must be paid? When is payment due? How much is to be paid? In many situations, the answers to these three questions are determined at the time the liability is incurred. For example, assume that Coleman Company has an account payable for precisely $100, payable on August 15, 19X1, to R. L. Tucker. There is no uncertainty about any of the questions. The company knows who to pay, when to pay, and how much to pay. Other types of liabilities may be uncertain with respect to one or more of the three questions.

When the Identity of the Creditor Is Uncertain. Some liabilities have uncertainty about who will be paid. For example, a corporation's board of directors creates a liability with a known amount when it declares a dividend payable to the stockholders. Because the dividend will be paid to the investors who actually own stock on a specified future date, the recipients are not known with certainty until that date. Despite this uncertainty, the corporation has a liability that is reported on the balance sheet.

When the Due Date Is Uncertain. In other situations, a company may have an obligation of a known amount to a known creditor, but not know exactly when the debt must be settled. For example, a copy services company may accept fees in advance from a customer who expects to need copies later. Thus, the copy service company has a liability that will be settled by providing services at an unknown future date. Even though this uncertainty exists, the company's balance sheet is complete only if it includes this liability to its customer. (These obligations are reported as current liabilities because may have to be settled in the short term.)

When the Amount Is Uncertain. In addition, a company may know that an obligation exists but may not know exactly how much will be required to settle it. For example, a company uses electrical power every day but is billed only after the meter has been read. The cost has been incurred and the liability has been created, even though the bill has not been received. As a result, a liability to the power company is reported with an estimated amount if the balance sheet is prepared before the bill arrives.

Progress Check
(Answers to Progress Checks are provided at the end of the chapter.)

12-1 What is a liability?

12-2 Is every expected future payment a liability?

12-3 If a liability is payable in 15 months, should it be classified as current or long-term?

ESTIMATED LIABILITIES

LO 2

Describe how accountants record and report estimated liabilities such as warranties and income taxes, and how they report contingent liabilities.

Obligations of uncertain amounts that can be reasonably estimated are called **estimated liabilities.** A common example of an estimated liability involves warranties offered by a seller. Other estimated liabilities are created for contracts to provide future services, income taxes, property taxes, and employee benefits such as pensions and health care.

Warranty Liabilities

An estimated liability is created when a company sells products covered by a warranty. In effect, a **warranty** obligates the seller or manufacturer to pay for replacing or repairing the product when it breaks or otherwise fails to perform within a specified period. For example, a used car might be sold with a warranty that covers parts and labor.

To comply with the *full disclosure* and the *matching principles,* the seller must report the expense of providing a warranty during the same period as the revenue from the sales of the product. The seller must also report the obligation under the warranty as a liability, even though it is uncertain about the existence, amount, payee, and date of its future sacrifices. The seller's warranty obligation does not require payments unless the products break and are returned for repairs. Nonetheless, future payments are probable, and the amount of the liability can be estimated using the company's past experience with warranties.

For example, suppose that a dealer sells a used car for $8,000 on December 1, 19X1, with a one-year or 12,000-mile warranty that covers repair parts and labor charges. Experience shows that the warranty expense averages about 4% of a car's selling price. In this case, the expense is expected to be $320 ($8,000 × 4%). The dealer records the expense and liability with this entry:

19X1				
Dec.	1	Warranty Expense	320.00	
		Estimated Warranty Liability		320.00
		To record the warranty expense and liability at 4% of the selling price.		

This entry causes the expense to be reported on the 19X1 income statement. It also causes the warranty liability to appear on the balance sheet for December 31, 19X1.

Now, suppose that the customer returns the car for warranty repairs on January 9, 19X2. The dealer performs the work by replacing parts that cost $90 and using labor at a cost of $110. This entry records the partial settlement of the estimated warranty liability:

19X2				
Jan.	9	Estimated Warranty Liability	200.00	
		Auto Parts Inventory		90.00
		Cash		110.00
		To record the cost of warranty repairs.		

Notice that this entry does not record any additional expense in 19X2. Instead, the entry reduces the balance of the estimated warranty liability. The warranty expense was already recorded in 19X1, the year the car was sold under the warranty.

What happens if the total warranty costs actually turn out to be more or less than the predicted $320? In fact, some difference is highly likely for any particular car. Over the long term, management should monitor the actual warranty costs to see whether the 4% rate provides useful information. If actual experience reveals a large difference, the rate should be modified for future sales.

Income Tax Liabilities for Corporations

A proprietorship's financial statements do not include income taxes because they do not pay income taxes; instead, they are assessed directly against the owner. However, corporations are subject to income taxes and must estimate the amount of their income tax liability when they prepare interim financial statements. We explain this process in the following paragraphs. Then, in the next section, we discuss deferred income tax liabilities that arise from temporary differences between GAAP and income tax rules.

Income tax expense for a corporation creates a liability that exists until payments are made to the government. Because the taxes are created by the process of earning income, a liability is incurred as soon as the income is earned. However, the taxes must be paid quarterly under federal regulations.

PRINCIPLE APPLICATION
Full Disclosure Principle,
p. 326
At the end of its 1993 year, General Motors Corporation reported that the $38,474.8 million of other liabilities and deferred credits reported on its balance sheet included $12,552.1 million for warranties, dealer and customer allowances, claims, discounts, etc.

For example, suppose that a corporation, Foster, Inc., prepares monthly financial statements. Based on the income earned in January, the company estimates that it owes income taxes of $12,100. The following adjusting entry records the estimate:

Jan.	31	Income Taxes Expense	12,100.00	
		Income Taxes Payable		12,100.00
		Accrued income tax expense and liability based on the		
		estimated income for the month of January.		

The liability is adjusted each month until the first quarterly payment is made. Assuming the taxes for the first three months total $50,000, the following entry records the payment:

Apr.	10	Income Taxes Payable	50,000.00	
		Cash		50,000.00
		Paid the quarterly income taxes based on the estimated		
		income for the first quarter of the year.		

The process of accruing and then paying the taxes continues throughout the year. However, by the time the annual financial statements are prepared at the end of the year, the company's accountant knows the amount of income that has been earned and the actual amount of income taxes that must be paid. This information allows the accountant to update the expense and liability accounts.

For example, suppose that Foster, Inc.'s accounts include a $22,000 credit balance in the Income Taxes Liability account at December 31, 19X1. Information about the company's income for the year shows that the actual liability should be $33,500. This entry records the additional expense and liability:

Dec.	31	Income Taxes Expense	11,500.00	
		Income Taxes Payable		11,500.00
		To record additional tax expense and liability.		

The liability will be settled when the company makes its final quarterly payment early in 19X2.

Deferred Income Tax Liabilities

Another special type of income tax liability may be incurred when the amount of income before taxes reported on a corporation's income statement is not the same as the amount of income reported on its income tax return. These differences arise because income tax laws define income differently from GAAP.[3]

Some of the differences between the tax law and GAAP are temporary. These *temporary differences* arise when the tax return and the income statement report a revenue or expense in different years. As an example, for tax purposes, companies are often able to deduct higher amounts of depreciation in the early years of an asset's life and smaller amounts in the later years. On their income statements, they often re-

---

[3]The differences between the tax laws and GAAP arise because Congress uses the tax law to generate receipts, stimulate the economy, and otherwise influence behavior. GAAP, on the other hand, are intended to provide financial information that is useful for decision making.

port an equal amount of depreciation expense in each year. Thus, in the early years, depreciation for tax purposes is more than depreciation expense on the income statement. Then, in the later years, depreciation for tax purposes is less than depreciation expense on the income statement.

When there are temporary differences between taxable income on the tax return and income before taxes on the income statement, GAAP requires corporations to calculate income tax expense based on the income reported on the income statement. In the previous example involving depreciation, the result is that the income tax expense reported in the early years is more than the amount of income tax payable. This difference is called **deferred income tax liability.**

For example, assume that after making and recording its quarterly income tax payments, a company determines at the end of the year that an additional $25,000 of income tax expense should be recorded. It also determines that only $21,000 is currently due and $4,000 is deferred to future years. The following entry records the end-of-year adjustment:

Dec.	31	Income Taxes Expense	25,000.00	
		Income Taxes Payable		21,000.00
		Deferred Income Tax Liability		4,000.00
		To record tax expense and deferred tax liability.		

In this entry, the credit to Income Taxes Payable represents the amount that is currently due to be paid. The credit to Deferred Income Tax Liability represents the tax payments that are deferred until future years when the temporary difference reverses.

Many companies report deferred income tax liabilities. For example, **Ford Motor Company's** December 31, 1993, balance sheet shows that Ford had a deferred income tax liability of $2,287 million.

In some circumstances, temporary differences may cause a company to pay income taxes before they are reported on the income statement as an expense. If so, the company usually reports a *deferred income tax asset* on its balance sheet that is similar to a prepaid expense. For example, **The Clorox Company's** June 30, 1993, balance sheet reported deferred income taxes of $19,360,000 as a current asset.

Progress Check

12-4 Estimated liabilities would include an obligation to pay:
 a. An uncertain but reasonably estimated amount to a specific person on a specific date.
 b. A known amount to a specific person on an uncertain due date.
 c. A known amount to an uncertain person on a known due date.
 d. All of the above.

12-5 An automobile was sold for $15,000 on June 1, 19X1, with a one-year warranty that covers parts and labor. Based on past experience, warranty expense is estimated at 1.5% of the selling price. On March 1, 19X2, the customer returned the car for warranty repairs that used replacement parts at a cost of $75 and labor at a cost of $60. The amount that should be recorded as warranty expense at the time of the March 1 repairs is: *(a)* $0, *(b)* $60, *(c)* $75, *(d)* $135, *(e)* $225.

12-6 Why would a corporation accrue an income tax liability for interim reports?

CONTINGENT LIABILITIES

LO 2

Describe how accountants record and report estimated liabilities such as warranties and income taxes and how they report contingent liabilities.

Sometimes, past transactions have the effect of requiring a future payment only if some uncertain future event takes place. If the likelihood that the uncertain future event will occur is remote, the company is not required to report a liability in the statements or the footnotes. However, if the uncertain future event is probable and the amount of the payment can be reasonably estimated, the company is required to report the payment as a liability.[4]

Contingent liabilities involve situations that fall between these two extremes. One situation is when the uncertain future event is probable but the amount of the payment cannot be reasonably estimated. The other is when the uncertain future event is not probable but has a reasonable possibility of occurring. These contingent liabilities are not recorded in the books as liabilities. However, the *full-disclosure principle* requires disclosure of contingent liabilities in the financial statements or in the footnotes.

Distinguishing Between Liabilities and Contingent Liabilities

Contingent liabilities become definite obligations only if some previously uncertain event actually takes place. For example, a typical contingent liability is a discounted note receivable that becomes a definite obligation only if the original signer of the note fails to pay it at maturity. We discussed this example in Chapter 8.

Does a product warranty create a liability or a contingent liability? A product warranty requires service or payment only if the product fails and the customer returns it for service. These conditions make it appear to be like a contingent liability. However, the contingent obligation should be recorded in the books as a liability if the occurrence of the future contingency is probable and if the amount of the liability can be reasonably estimated. Therefore, product warranties are usually recorded as liabilities because: (1) the failure of some percentage of the sold products is probable, and (2) past experience allows the seller to develop a reasonable estimate of the amount to be paid.

Other Examples of Contingent Liabilities

Potential Legal Claims. In today's legal environment, many companies find themselves being sued for damages for a variety of reasons. The accounting question is this: Should the defendant recognize a liability on the balance sheet or disclose a contingent liability in the footnotes while a lawsuit is outstanding and not yet settled? The answer is that the potential claim should be recorded as a liability only if a payment for damages is probable and the amount can be reasonably estimated. If the potential claim cannot be reasonably estimated or is less than probable but is reasonably possible, it should be described as a contingent liability.

For example, a footnote in a recent annual report for **The Quaker Oats Company** disclosed that a $43 million judgment had been entered against the company. The case involved the company's practices in advertising Gatorade. Despite the judgment, the company did not record a loss in the financial statements because the company's attorneys said that they believed that an appeal of the decision would eliminate the claim.

Debt Guarantees. Sometimes a company will guarantee the payment of a debt owed by a supplier, customer, or other company. Usually, the guarantor describes the guarantee in the financial statement footnotes as

---

[4]FASB, *Accounting Standards—Current Text* (Norwalk, CT, 1994), sec. C59.105. First published as *FASB Statement No. 5*, par. 8.

As a Matter of Opinion

Diana Scott is a graduate of Wittenberg University. She worked for Price Waterhouse in its national office in New York before joining the FASB staff as a project manager in 1985. After leaving that position in 1991, she joined the management consulting firm of Towers Perrin in Chicago, where she is an accounting and financial consultant in the Technical Services Group.

Over the past several years, accountants have begun to pay much more attention to the potential future payments that businesses may be obligated to make as a result of current operations. A good example involves the promises of employers to pay health care benefits for their retired employees. Prior to the FASB's standard on this topic (*SFAS 106*), companies generally did not report this obligation except by reporting an expense for actual payments they had already made. The standard requires them to provide information about their obligations and to recognize the expenses for probable future payments.

Are there other obligations that we presently ignore but someday may have to recognize as liabilities? I would not be surprised. One that comes to mind is potential claims from injuries to product users. Some juries have given large awards many years after a product was sold. Another possible liability is the cost of cleaning up toxic wastes discarded before anyone was aware of the danger.

Nobody can say whether these particular examples will eventually result in new liabilities or disclosures. But, I have no doubt that accounting will continue to evolve in response to an increasing emphasis on the obligations of doing business responsibly.

Diana J. Scott, CPA

a contingent liability. However, if it is probable that the original debtor will default, the guarantor needs to record and report the guarantee as a liability.

Other Uncertainties

All companies and other organizations face major uncertainties from future economic events, including natural disasters and the development of new competing products. If these events do occur, they may destroy the company's assets or drive it out of business. However, these uncertainties are not liabilities because they are future events that are not a result of past transactions. Financial statements are not useful if they include speculation about possible effects of events that have not yet occurred.

Be sure to read the comment by Diana Scott in As a Matter of Opinion. She discusses additional liabilities that companies may need to describe in the future if accounting principles are changed.

Progress Check

12-7 A future payment should be reported as a liability on a company's balance sheet if the payment is contingent on a future event that:
   a. Is not probable but is reasonably possible and the amount of the payment cannot be reasonably estimated.
   b. Is probable and the amount of the payment can be reasonably estimated.
   c. Is not probable but the amount of the payment is known.

12-8 Under what circumstances should a future payment be reported in the financial statements as a contingent liability?

Most liabilities arise in situations with little uncertainty. The procedures used to account for these debts are described in the following sections of the chapter. The topics include:

- Payroll liabilities.
- Short-term notes payable.
- Long-term notes payable.
- Lease liabilities.

ACCOUNTING FOR KNOWN LIABILITIES

In addition, we introduce you to present value calculations that accountants use when accounting for long-term liabilities and interest expense.

PAYROLL LIABILITIES

LO 3

Describe payroll expenses and liabilities and prepare journal entries to account for them.

An employer typically incurs several expenses and liabilities as a result of having employees. The expenses and liabilities arise from the salaries or wages earned by employees, from employee benefits, and from payroll taxes levied on the employer. These items are discussed in the next sections. In addition, you can learn more about payroll reports, records, and procedures by studying Appendix C at the end of the book.

FICA Taxes on Employees

The federal Social Security system provides qualified workers who retire at age 62 with monthly cash payments for the rest of their lives. The retirees also receive *Medicare benefits* beginning at age 65. In addition, the system provides monthly payments to deceased workers' families who qualify for the assistance. These benefits are paid with **FICA taxes** collected under the Federal Insurance Contributions Act. The taxes for retirees and survivors are often called *Social Security taxes* to distinguish them from *Medicare taxes.*

Among other things, the law requires employers to withhold FICA taxes from each employee's salary or wages paid on each payday. The two components of these taxes for Social Security and Medicare are calculated separately. In 1995, the amount withheld from each employee's pay for Social Security was 6.2% of the first $61,200 earned by the employee in the calendar year. The Medicare tax was 1.45% of all wages earned by the employee.

The employer is required to promptly pay the withheld taxes to the Internal Revenue Service. Substantial penalties can be levied against those who fail to turn the withheld taxes over to the IRS on time. Until all these taxes are paid, they are included in the employer's current liabilities.

Employees' Federal Income Tax Withholdings

With very few exceptions, employers must withhold an amount of federal income tax from each employee's paycheck. The amount withheld is determined from tables published by the IRS. The amount depends on the employee's annual earnings rate and the number of *withholding allowances* claimed by the employee. Employees can claim allowances for themselves and their dependents. They can also claim additional allowances if they anticipate major reductions in their taxable income for medical expenses or other deductible items. The income taxes withheld from employees must be paid promptly to the IRS. Until they are paid, withholdings are reported as a current liability on the employer's balance sheet.

Other Withholdings from Wages

In addition to Social Security, Medicare, and income taxes, employers may withhold other amounts from employees' earnings according to their instructions. These withholdings may include amounts for charitable contributions, medical insurance premiums, investment purchases, and union dues. Until they are paid, these withholdings are current liabilities of employers.

Recording Payroll Expenses and Other Withholdings

Employers must accrue the payroll expenses and liabilities at the end of each pay period. As an example, this entry shows a typical entry to accrue the payroll:

Jan.	31	Salaries Expense	2,000.00	
		FICA Taxes Payable		153.00
		Employees' Federal Income Taxes Payable		213.00
		Employees' Medical Insurance Payable		85.00
		Employees' Union Dues Payable		25.00
		Accrued Payroll Payable		1,524.00
		To record the payroll for the pay period ended		
		January 31.		

The debit to Salaries Expense records the fact that the company's employees earned gross salaries of $2,000. The first four credits record liabilities that the employer owes on behalf of its employees for their FICA taxes, income taxes, medical insurance, and union dues. The credit to the Accrued Payroll Payable account records the $1,524 net pay that the employees will receive from the $2,000 that they earned.

When employees are actually paid, another entry (or a series of entries) is required to record the checks actually written and distributed. To record the payments, Accrued Payroll Payable is debited and Cash is credited.

In addition to the taxes assessed on the employees, other taxes must be paid by employers. They include FICA and unemployment taxes.

EMPLOYER'S PAYROLL TAXES

Employer's FICA Tax

Employers must pay FICA taxes equal in amount to the FICA taxes withheld from their employees. An employer's tax is credited to the same FICA Taxes Payable account used to record the FICA taxes withheld from the employees. The debit is recorded in a Payroll Taxes Expense account.

Federal and State Unemployment Taxes

The federal government participates with the states in a joint federal-state unemployment insurance program. Under this joint program, each state administers its own program. These programs provide unemployment benefits to covered workers. The federal government approves the state programs and pays a portion of their administrative expenses.

The Federal Unemployment Tax (FUTA). Employers are subject to a federal unemployment tax on wages paid to their employees. In 1995, the Federal Unemployment Tax Act (called FUTA) required employers to pay a tax of as much as 6.2% of the first $7,000 in salary or wages paid to each employee. However, the federal tax can be reduced by a credit of up to 5.4% for taxes paid to a state program. As a result, the net federal unemployment tax is normally only 0.8%.

State Unemployment Insurance Taxes (SUTA). All states support their unemployment insurance programs by placing a payroll tax on employers. In most states, the basic rate is 5.4% of the first $7,000 paid each employee. However, the employer's experience in creating or avoiding unemployment is described in a **merit rating** assigned by the state. A good rating is based on high stability and allows the employer to pay less than the basic 5.4% rate. A history of high turnover or seasonal hiring and layoffs may cause the employer to pay more.

A favorable merit rating may offer important cash savings. For example, an employer with 100 employees who each earn $7,000 or more per year would save $34,300 annually if it received a merit rating that reduced the rate from 5.4% to 0.5%. At the 5.4% rate, it would pay $37,800, but only $3,500 at the 0.5% rate.

Recording the Employer's Payroll Taxes

The employer's payroll taxes are an additional expense above the salaries earned by the employees. As a result, these taxes are usually recorded in a journal entry separate from the one recording the basic payroll expense and withholding liabilities.

For example, assume that the previously recorded $2,000 salaries expense was earned by employees who have earned less than $7,000 so far in the year. Also, assume that the federal unemployment tax rate was 0.8% and that the state unemployment tax rate was 5.4%.

The FICA portion of the employer's tax expense is $153, which equals 7.65% (6.2% + 1.45%) of the $2,000 gross pay. The state unemployment (SUTA) taxes are $108, which is 5.4% of the $2,000 gross pay. The federal unemployment (FUTA) taxes are $16, which is 0.8% of $2,000. This entry records the employer's payroll tax expense and the related liabilities:

Jan.	31	Payroll Taxes Expense	277.00	
		FICA Taxes Payable		153.00
		State Unemployment Taxes Payable		108.00
		Federal Unemployment Taxes Payable		16.00
		To record payroll taxes.		

EMPLOYEE BENEFITS

In addition to salaries and wages earned by employees and payroll taxes paid by employers, many companies provide a variety of **employee benefits.** For example, an employer may pay all or part of the premiums for medical, dental, life, and disability insurance. Many employers also contribute to pension plans or offer special stock purchase plans for their employees.

By the time that payroll taxes and employee benefits costs are added to the employees' basic earnings, employers often find that their total payroll cost exceeds the employees' gross earnings by 25% or more. The following paragraphs describe two specific employee benefits.

Employer Contributions to Insurance and Pension Plans

The entries that record employee benefit costs are similar to the entries for payroll taxes. Returning to the previous example, suppose that the employer agreed to pay an amount for medical insurance equal to the $85 withheld from the employees' paychecks and to contribute an additional 10% of the employees' $2,000 gross salary to a retirement program. This entry would record these benefits:

Jan.	7	Employee Benefits Expense	285.00	
		Employees' Medical Insurance Payable		85.00
		Employees' Retirement Program Payable		200.00
		To record employee benefits.		

Vacation Pay

Another widely offered benefit is paid vacations. For example, many employees earn 2 weeks' vacation by working 50 weeks. This benefit increases the employer's payroll expenses above their apparent amount because the employees are paid for 50 weeks of work over the 52 weeks in the year. Although the total annual salary is the same, the cost per week worked is greater than the amount paid per week. For example, suppose than an employee is paid $20,800 for 52 weeks of employment, but works only 50 weeks. The weekly salary expense to the employer is $416 ($20,800/50 weeks) instead of the $400 paid weekly to the employee ($20,800/52 weeks). The $16 difference between these two amounts is recorded as salary expense and a liability for vacation pay. When the employee actually takes a vacation, the employer reduces the vacation pay liability and does not record additional expense.

Progress Check

12-9   **Midtown Repairs pays its one employee $3,000 per month. The company's net FUTA rate is 0.8% on the first $7,000 earned by the employee, the SUTA rate is 4.0% on the first $7,000, the Social Security tax rate is 6.2% of the first $61,200, and the Medicare tax rate is 1.45% of all amounts earned by the employee. The entry to record the company's payroll taxes for March would include a total expense of:** (a) **$277.50;** (b) **$293.50;** (c) **$373.50;** (d) **$1,120.50;** (e) **$4,093.20.**

12-10   **Indicate whether the employer or the employee pays each of these taxes:** (a) **FICA taxes;** (b) **FUTA taxes;** (c) **SUTA taxes; and** (d) **withheld income taxes.**

A short-term note payable may be created when a company purchases merchandise on credit and then extends the credit period by signing a note that replaces the account. Short-term notes payable also arise when money is borrowed from a bank.

Note Given to Extend a Credit Period

In some cases, a company may create a note payable to replace an account payable. For example, a creditor may ask that an interest-bearing note be substituted for an account that does not bear interest. In other situations, the borrower's weak financial condition may encourage the creditor to obtain a note and close the account to ensure that additional credit sales are not made to this customer.

For example, assume that on August 23, Broke Company asks to extend its past-due $600 account payable to Smart Company. After some negotiations, Smart agrees to accept $100 cash and a 60-day, 12%, $500 note payable to replace the account payable. The accountant for Broke records the substitution with this entry:

Aug.	23	Accounts Payable—Smart Company	600.00	
		Cash		100.00
		Notes Payable		500.00
		Paid $100 cash and gave a 60-day, 12% note to extend the due date on the account.		

Notice that signing the note does not pay off the debt. Instead, the debt's form is merely changed from an account to a note payable. Smart Company may prefer to have the note because it earns interest and because it provides reliable documentation of the debt's existence, term, and amount.

When the note becomes due, Broke will pay the note and interest by giving Smart a check for $510 and then record the payment with this entry:

Oct.	22	Notes Payable	500.00	
		Interest Expense	10.00	
		Cash		510.00
		Paid note with interest ($500 × 12% × 60/360).		

SHORT-TERM NOTES PAYABLE

LO 4
Describe how accountants record and report short-term notes payable.

(Note that the interest expense is calculated by multiplying the principal of the note by the original rate for the fraction of the year the note was outstanding.)

Borrowing from a Bank

When making a loan, a bank typically requires the borrower to sign a promissory note. When the note matures, the borrower pays back a larger amount. The difference between the two amounts is *interest.* In many situations, the note states that the signer of the note promises to pay the *principal* (the amount borrowed) plus the interest. If so, the *face value* of the note equals the principal.

In other situations, the bank may have the borrower sign a note with a face value that includes both the principal and the interest. In these cases, the signer of the note borrows less than the note's face value. The difference between the borrowed amount and the note's face value is interest. Because the borrowed amount is less than the face value, the difference is sometimes called the **discount on note payable.** To illustrate these two kinds of loans, assume that Robin Goode borrows $2,000 from a bank on behalf of the Goode Company. The loan is made on September 30 and will be repaid in 60 days. It has a 12% annual interest rate.

Face Value Equals the Amount Borrowed. Suppose that the bank requires Goode to sign a loan with a face value equal to the borrowed $2,000. If so, the note will include the following phrase: "I promise to pay $2,000 plus interest at 12% sixty days after September 30." The Goode Company records the increase in cash and the new liability with this entry:

Sept.	30	Cash	2,000.00	
		Notes Payable		2,000.00
		Borrowed cash with a 60-day, 12% note.		

When the note and interest are paid 60 days later, Goode records the event with this entry:

Nov.	29	Notes Payable	2,000.00	
		Interest Expense	40.00	
		Cash		2,040.00
		Paid note with interest ($2,000 × 12% × 60/360).		

Face Value Equals the Amount Borrowed and the Interest. If Goode's bank wishes, it may draw up a note that includes the 12% interest in its face value. If so, the note contains the following promise: "I promise to pay $2,040 sixty days after September 30." Notice that the note does not refer to the rate that was used to compute the $40 of interest included in the $2,040 face value. In all other respects, the note is exactly the same. However, the lack of a stated rate of interest sometimes causes an agreement like this one to be called a **noninterest-bearing note.** In fact, this widely used term is not precise because the note does bear interest, which is included in the face value.

When the face value of the note includes principal and interest, Goode could record the debt with an entry exactly like the previous September 30 entry. However, the more typical practice is to credit Notes Payable for the face value of the note and record the discount in a contra account. The following entry takes this approach:

Sept.	30	Cash	2,000.00	
		Discount on Notes Payable	40.00	
		Notes Payable		2,040.00
		Borrowed cash with a 60-day, 12% note (Discount		
		= $2,000 × 12% × 60/360).		

The Discount on Notes Payable account is contra to the Notes Payable account. If a balance sheet is prepared on September 30, the $40 discount is subtracted from the $2,040 balance in the Notes Payable account to reflect the $2,000 net amount borrowed.

When the note matures 60 days later on November 29, the entry to record Goode's $2,040 payment to the bank is:

Nov.	29	Notes Payable	2,040.00	
		Interest Expense	40.00	
		Cash		2.040.00
		Discount on Notes Payable		40.00
		Paid note with interest.		

ADJUSTMENTS AT
THE END OF THE
REPORTING
PERIOD

If the end of an accounting period falls between the signing of a note payable and its maturity date, the *matching principle* requires the accountant to record the accrued but unpaid interest on the note. For example, suppose that Robin Goode borrowed $2,000 on December 16, 19X1, instead of September 30. The 60-day note matures on February 14, 19X2. Because the company's fiscal year ends on December 31, the accountant records interest expense for the 15 days in December. The entries depend on the form of the note.

Face Value Equals the Amount Borrowed. If the note's face value equals the amount borrowed, the accrued interest is charged to expense and credited to an Interest Payable account. To illustrate, assume that the $2,000 note signed by Goode on December 16 bears 12% interest. Because 15 out of the 60 days covered by the note have elapsed by December 31, one-fourth (15 days/60 days) of the $40 total interest is an expense of 19X1. Goode records this expense with the following adjusting entry at the end of 19X1:

19X1				
Dec.	31	Interest Expense	10.00	
		Interest Payable		10.00
		To record accrued interest on note payable ($2,000 ×		
		12% × 15/360).		

When the note matures on February 14, Goode records this entry:

19X2				
Feb.	14	Interest Expense ($2,000 × 12% × 45/360)	30.00	
		Interest Payable	210.00	
		Notes Payable	2,000.00	
		Cash		2,040.00
		Paid note with interest.		

The entry recognizes the 45 days of interest expense for 19X2 and removes the balances of the two liability accounts.

Face Value Equals the Amount Borrowed and the Interest.   Now assume that the face value of the note includes the interest. For example, assume that Goode signed a $2,040 noninterest-bearing note on December 15. In recording the note, Goode credited the $2,040 face value of the note to Notes Payable and debited the $40 discount to a contra account. This adjusting entry is needed to record the accrual of 15 days of interest at the end of 19X1:

Dec.	31	Interest Expense	10.00	
		Discount on Notes Payable		10.00
		To record accrued interest on note payable ($2,000 ×		
		12% × 15/360).		

Observe that the accrued interest is not credited to Interest Payable. Instead, the entry reduces the balance of the contra account from $40 to $30. As a result, it increases the net liability to $2,010 ($2,040 − $30).

When the note matures, the following entry accrues the interest expense for the last 45 days of the note and records its payment:

19X2				
Feb.	14	Interest Expense	30.00	
		Notes Payable	2,040.00	
		Discount on Notes Payable		30.00
		Cash		2,040.00
		Paid note with interest ($2,000 × 12% × 45/360).		

Progress Check

12-11   **Why would a creditor want a past-due account to be replaced by a note?**

12-12   **A company borrows money for six months by signing a $1,050 note payable. In recording the transaction, the company's bookkeeper correctly debited $50 to Discount on Notes Payable. How much was borrowed? What annual rate of interest was charged?**

LONG-TERM LIABILITIES

In addition to current liabilities, companies often have liabilities that are repaid after one year (or a longer operating cycle). These *long-term liabilities* can arise when money is borrowed from a bank or when a note is issued to buy an asset. A long-term liability also may be created when a company enters into a multiyear lease agreement that is similar to buying the asset. Each of these liability arrangements is described in this chapter. In addition, large companies often borrow money by issuing *bonds* to a number of creditors. These securities are usually long-term liabilities that exist as long as 30 years or more. Accounting for bonds is described in Chapter 15.

Because of the extended lives of long-term liabilities, accounting for them is often more complicated than accounting for short-term liabilities. In particular, the accountant may need to apply present value techniques to measure a long-term liability when it is created and to assign interest expense to each of the years in the liability's life.

Information based on the concept of **present value** enters into many financing and investing decisions. It also enters into accounting for liabilities resulting from those decisions. Therefore, an understanding of present value is important for all business students.

Because this chapter focuses on liabilities, we explain present value concepts by referring to future cash outflows, payables, and interest expense. However, the same concepts also apply to future cash inflows, receivables, and interest income. The most fundamental present value concept is based on the idea that an amount of cash to be paid (or received) in the future has less value now than the same amount of cash to be paid (or received) today.

For example, $1 to be paid one year from now has a present value that is less than $1. To see why this is true, assume that $0.9259 is borrowed for one year at 8% interest. The amount of interest that will be incurred is $0.9259 × 8% = $0.0741. When the $0.0741 interest is added to the $0.9259, the sum equals the $1 payment that is necessary to repay the debt with interest, as shown here:

Amount borrowed	$0.9259
Interest for one year at 8%	0.0741
Total debt after one year	$1.0000

In this example, the $0.9259 borrowed amount is the present value of the $1 future payment. To state the concept more generally, a borrowed amount is the present value of a future payment if the borrowed amount generates interest at a given rate and the future payment will repay the debt with interest.[5]

To carry this example of present value further, assume that the $1 payment is to be made after two years and the 8% interest is to be compounded annually. Compounding means that interest during the second period is based on the sum of the amount borrowed plus the interest accrued during the first period. In other words, the second period's interest is 8% multiplied by the sum of the original amount borrowed plus the interest earned during the first period.

In this example, where $1 is to be paid back after two years, the amount that can be borrowed (the present value) is $0.8573. The following calculation shows why $0.8573 is the present value:

Amount borrowed during first year	$0.8573
Interest during first year ($0.8573 × 8%) . . .	0.0686
Amount borrowed during second year	$0.9259
Interest during second year ($0.9259 × 8%) .	0.0741
Total debt after one year	$1.0000

Notice that the first year's interest is added to the principal amount borrowed so that the second year's interest is based on $0.9259.[6]

---

[5]Exactly the same analysis applies to an investment. If $0.9259 is invested at 8%, it will generate $0.0741 interest revenue in one year, thereby amounting to a $1 receipt of principal and interest.

[6]Benjamin Franklin is said to have described compounding with this expression: "The money money makes makes more money."

PRESENT VALUE CONCEPTS

LO 5

Explain and calculate the present value of an amount to be paid at a future date and the present value of a series of equal amounts to be paid at future dates.

Chapter 12

Table 12-1
Present Value of $1

			Rate		
Periods	**2%**	**4%**	**6%**	**8%**	**10%**
1	0.9804	0.9615	0.9434	0.9259	0.9091
2	0.9612	0.9246	0.8900	0.8573	0.8264
3	0.9423	0.8890	0.8396	0.7938	0.7513
4	0.9238	0.8548	0.7921	0.7350	0.6830
5	0.9057	0.8219	0.7473	0.6806	0.6209
6	0.8880	0.7903	0.7050	0.6302	0.5645
7	0.8706	0.7599	0.6651	0.5835	0.5132
8	0.8535	0.7307	0.6274	0.5403	0.4665
9	0.8368	0.7026	0.5919	0.5002	0.4241
10	0.8203	0.6756	0.5584	0.4632	0.3855

Present Value Tables

The present value of $1 to be paid after a number of periods in the future can be calculated by using this formula: $1/(1 + i)^n$. The symbol i in the equation is the interest rate per period and n is the number of periods until the future payment must be made. For example, the present value of $1 to be paid after two periods at 8% is $1/(1.08)^2$, which equals $0.8573.

Although you can use this formula to find present values, other techniques are available. For example, many electronic calculators are preprogrammed to find present values. You can also use a **present value table** that shows present values computed with the formula at various interest rates for different time periods. In fact, many students find it helpful to learn how to make the calculations with the tables, and then move on to use a calculator when they become comfortable with present value concepts.

Table 12–1 shows present values of a future payment of $1 for up to 10 periods at five different interest rates. The present values in the table have been rounded to four decimal places.[7] (This table is taken from a larger and more complete table in Appendix E at the end of the book.)

To use this table, notice that the first value in the 8% column in Table 12–1 is 0.9259. We used this value in the previous section as the present value of $1 at 8%. Go down one row in the same 8% column to find the present value of $1 discounted at 8% for two years. You should find the value of 0.8573 that we used in the second example. This value means that $0.8573 is the present value of the obligation to pay $1 after two periods, discounted at 8% per period.

Using a Present Value Table

To demonstrate how an accountant can measure a liability by using a present value table like Table 12–1, assume that a company plans to borrow cash and then repay it as follows:

To be paid back after one year	$ 2,000
To be paid back after two years	3,000
To be paid back after three years	5,000
Total to be paid back	$10,000

---

[7]Four decimal places are sufficient for the applications described in this book. Other situations may require more precision.

Illustration 12-1
Finding the Present Value of
a Series of Unequal
Payments

Years from Now	Expected Payments	Present Value of $1 at 10%	Present Value of Expected Payments
1	$2,000	0.9091	$1,818
2	3,000	0.8264	2,479
3	5,000	0.7513	3,757
Total present value of the payments ..			$8,054

Illustration 12-2
Finding the Present Value of
a Series of Equal Payments
(an Annuity) by Discounting
Each Payment

Years from Now	Expected Payments	Present Value of $1 at 6%	Present Value of Expected Payments
1	$5,000	0.9434	$ 4,717
2	5,000	0.8900	4,450
3	5,000	0.8396	4,198
4	5,000	0.7921	3,961
Total		3.4651	$17,326

If the company will have to pay 10% interest on this loan, how much will it be able to borrow? The answer is that it can borrow the present value of the three future payments, discounted at 10%. This is calculated in Illustration 12–1 with values from Table 12–1. The illustration shows that the company can borrow $8,054 at 10% in exchange for its promise to make the three payments at the scheduled dates.

Present Values of Annuities

The $8,054 present value of the loan in Illustration 12–1 is the sum of the present values of the three different payments. If the expected cash flows for a liability are not equal, their combined present value must be found by calculating each of their individual present values. In other cases, a loan may create an **annuity,** this is a series of equal payments occurring at equal time intervals. The present value of an annuity can be found with fewer calculations.

For example, suppose that a company can repay a 6% loan by making a $5,000 payment at the end of each year for the next four years. The amount to be borrowed under this loan equals the present value of the four payments discounted at 6%. The present value is calculated in Illustration 12–2 by multiplying each payment by the appropriate value from Table 12–1. The illustration shows that the company can borrow $17,326 under these terms.

Because the series of $5,000 payments is an annuity, the accountant can determine the present value with either of two shortcuts. As shown in the third column of Illustration 12–2, the total of the present values of $1 at 6% for 1 through 4 periods equals 3.4651. One short cut multiplies this total of 3.4651 by the $5,000 annual payment to get the combined present value of $17,326. This shortcut requires only one multiplication instead of four.

The second shortcut uses an *annuity table* such as Table 12–2.[8] (Table 12–2 is taken

---

[8]The formula for finding the table values is: $\dfrac{1 - \dfrac{1}{(1 + i)^n}}{i}$

However, the present values in Table 12–2 can be found by adding the values of the individual payments in Table 12–1. (Because the tables show only four decimal places, there are some ±0.0001 rounding differences between them.)

Table 12-2
Present Value of An Annuity
of $1

Payments	Rate				
	2%	**4%**	**6%**	**8%**	**10%**
1	0.9804	0.9615	0.9434	0.9259	0.9091
2	1.9416	1.8861	1.8334	1.7833	1.7355
3	2.8839	2.7751	2.6730	2.5771	2.4869
4	3.8077	3.6299	3.4651	3.3121	3.1699
5	4.7135	4.4518	4.2124	3.9927	3.7908
6	5.6014	5.2421	4.9173	4.6229	4.3553
7	6.4720	6.0021	5.5824	5.2064	4.8684
8	7.3255	6.7327	6.2098	5.7466	5.3349
9	8.1622	7.4353	6.8017	6.2469	5.7590
10	8.9826	8.1109	7.3601	6.7101	6.1446

from a more complete table in Appendix E at the end of the book.) Instead of having to take the sum of the individual present values from Table 12–1, you can go directly to the annuity table to find the present (table) value that relates to a specific number of payments and a specific interest rate. Then, you multiply this table value by the amount of the payment to find the present value of all the payments in the annuity.

To continue the example, the second shortcut proceeds as follows: Enter Table 12–2 on the row for four payments and go across until you reach the column for 6%, where we find the value of 3.4651. This amount equals the present value of an annuity with four payments of $1, discounted at 6%. Then, multiply 3.4651 times $5,000 to get the $17,326 present value of the annuity.

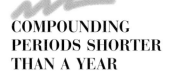

COMPOUNDING PERIODS SHORTER THAN A YEAR

In the previous examples, the interest rates were applied to periods of one year. However, in many situations, interest is compounded over shorter periods. For example, the interest rate on bonds is usually described as an annual rate but the interest is actually paid every six months. As a result, the present value of the interest payments to be received from these bonds must be based on interest periods that are six months long.

To illustrate a calculation based on six-month interest periods, suppose that a borrower wants to know the present value of a series of ten $4,000 semiannual payments to be made over five years. These payments are to be discounted with an *annual* interest rate of 8%. Although the interest rate is described as an annual rate of 8%, it is actually a rate of 4% per six-month interest period. To find the present value of the series of $4,000 payments, enter Table 12–2 on row 10 and go across to the 4% column. The table value is 8.1109, and the present value of the annuity is $32,444 (8.1109 × $4,000).

Study Appendix E at the end of the book to learn more about present value concepts. The appendix includes more complete present value tables and provides future value tables. It also includes exercises that will help you understand discounting.

Progress Check

12-13 A company enters into an agreement to make four annual payments of $1,000 each, starting one year from now. The annual interest rate is 8%. The present value of these four payments is: *(a)* $2,923; *(b)* $2,940; *(c)* $3,312; *(d)* $4,000; *(e)* $6,733.

12-14 Suppose that a company has an option to pay either $10,000 after one year or $5,000 after six months and another $5,000 after one year. Which choice always has the smaller present value?

Illustration 12-3   Allocation of Interest on a Note with All Interest Paid at Maturity

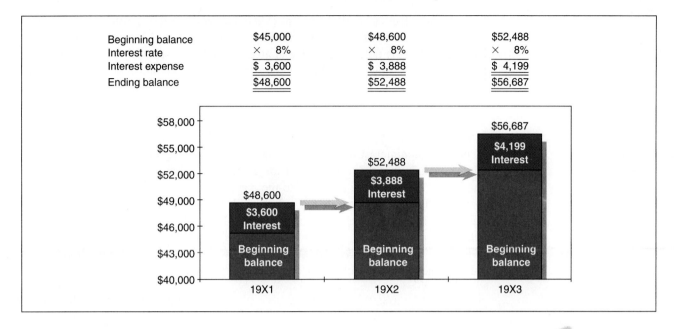

Beginning balance	$45,000	$48,600	$52,488
Interest rate	× 8%	× 8%	× 8%
Interest expense	$ 3,600	$ 3,888	$ 4,199
Ending balance	$48,600	$52,488	$56,687

Earlier in the chapter, we stated that accountants use present value concepts to measure liabilities and to assign or allocate interest expense to each reporting period in a liability's life. In doing this, the liability is initially measured as the present value of the future payments. Over the life of the note, the amount of interest allocated to each period equals the product of multiplying the original interest rate by the balance of the liability at the beginning of the period. The balance at any point in time equals the original balance plus any allocated interest less any payments.[9]

Interest-Bearing Notes That Require a Single Payment

Suppose that a company buys equipment on January 2 with a fair market value of $45,000 by issuing an 8%, three-year note. If the 8% interest is at the prevailing market rate, the face value of the note should be $45,000. The buyer records the purchase with this entry:

Jan.	2	Store Equipment	45,000.00	
		Notes Payable		45,000.00
		Issued a $45,000, three-year, 8% note payable for		
		store equipment.		

Over the life of the note, the issuer reports annual interest expense equal to the original interest rate times each year's beginning balance for the liability. Illustration 12–3 shows the interest allocation. Note that the interest is allocated by multiplying each year's beginning balance by the original 8% interest rate. Then, the interest is added to the beginning balance to find the ending balance, which then becomes the next year's beginning balance. Because the balance grows through compounding, the amount of interest allocated to each year increases over the life of the note. The final ending balance of $56,687 equals the original $45,000 borrowed plus the total interest of $11,687.

APPLYING PRESENT VALUE CONCEPTS TO LONG-TERM NOTES

LO 6

Describe how accountants use present value concepts in accounting for long-term notes and how liabilities may result from leasing assets.

---

[9]The liability's balance at any date also equals the present value of all remaining future payments, discounted at the original interest rate.

Noninterest-Bearing Notes

Earlier in the chapter, we described so-called noninterest-bearing notes, which include the interest in their initial face values. When a noninterest-bearing note is used to purchase an asset, the note's face value is greater than the asset's fair value. As a result, the asset and the note should be recorded at the asset's fair value or at the note's fair value, whichever is more clearly determinable.[10] The note's fair value can be estimated by finding the present value of its payments discounted at the market interest rate when it was issued.

For example, suppose that Harborg Company buys machinery on January 2, 19X1, by issuing a noninterest-bearing, five-year, $10,000 note payable. The company's managers conclude that their estimate of the asset's fair value is less reliable than is the current 10% interest rate available to the company.

When the note is issued, its fair value equals the present value of the $10,000 payment due after five years discounted at 10%. Table 12–1 shows us that the present value of 1 discounted at 10% for five years is 0.6209. Thus, the present (fair) value of the note is calculated as $10,000 × 0.6209 = $6,209. This is also the implied fair value of the asset. The following entry records the purchase:

19X1					
Jan.	2	Machinery	6,209.00	
		Discount on Notes Payable	3,791.00	
		Long-Term Notes Payable		10,000.00
		Exchanged a five-year noninterest-bearing note		
		for a machine.		

By recording the maturity value in one account and the discount in a contra account, the entry follows the typical approach of recording a noninterest-bearing note. In the entry, the $3,791 debit to Discount on Notes Payable equals the total amount of interest that must be allocated to the five years in the note's life.

In Illustration 12–4, we calculate each year's interest and show the effect of the allocation on the discount and the net liability. The net liability balance grows over the five years until it reaches the maturity amount of $10,000. Note also that the discount balance decreases to $0 after five years. Because the discount is gradually reduced to zero, this process is often referred to as *amortizing the discount.*

Notice that the process of calculating each year's interest is the same as it was in the previous discussion of interest-bearing notes that require a single payment. The net liability balance at the beginning of each year is multiplied by the 10% interest rate to determine the interest for the year.

The first year's interest and reduction of the discount are recorded when the accountant makes this year-end adjusting entry:

19X1					
Dec.	31	Interest Expense	621.00	
		Discount on Notes Payable		621.00
		To record interest expense accrued on a		
		noninterest-bearing note.		

---

[10]FASB, *Accounting Standards—Current Text* (Norwalk, CT, 1994), sec. I69.105. First published as *APB Opinion No. 21, par.* 12.

Illustration 12-4   Allocating Interest Expense over the Life of a Noninterest-Bearing Note

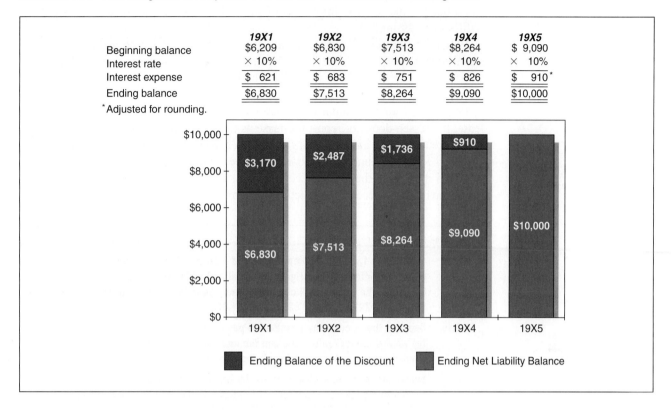

	19X1	19X2	19X3	19X4	19X5
Beginning balance	$6,209	$6,830	$7,513	$8,264	$ 9,090
Interest rate	× 10%	× 10%	× 10%	× 10%	× 10%
Interest expense	$ 621	$ 683	$ 751	$ 826	$ 910*
Ending balance	$6,830	$7,513	$8,264	$9,090	$10,000

*Adjusted for rounding.

Similar entries are recorded at the end of each year until the balance of the discount account equals $0, and the net liability balance equals $10,000.

When the note matures on January 2, 19X6, the issuer records the payment with this entry:

19X6 Jan.	2	Long-Term Notes Payable	10,000.00	
		Cash		10,000.00
		Paid noninterest-bearing note.		

As an alternative to purchasing property, companies can lease it by agreeing to make a series of rental payments to the property owner, who is called the *lessor*. Because a lease gives the property's user (called the *lessee*) exclusive control over the property's usefulness, the lessee can use it to earn revenues. In addition, a lease creates a liability if it has essentially the same effect as purchasing the asset on credit.

LIABILITIES FROM LEASING

According to the generally accepted accounting principles described in *Statement of Financial Accounting Standards No. 13,* the lessee's financial statements must report a leased asset and a lease liability if the lease qualifies as a **capital lease.** The essence of a capital lease is that the lease agreement gives the lessee the risks and benefits normally associated with ownership. In general, a capital lease covers a number of years and creates a long-term liability that is paid off with a series of equal payments. For example, **Federal Express Corporation** reported that its

capital leases for equipment and facilities covered assets with a cost of $513 million and a book value of $183 million as of May 31, 1994. The leases also involved liabilities of $199 million.

When a capital lease is created, the lessee recognizes a leased asset and depreciates it over its useful life. The lessee also recognizes a lease liability and allocates interest expense to the years in the lease. The interest allocation process is the same as we have seen for notes payable.

Leases that are not capital leases are called **operating leases.** With an operating lease, the lessee does not report the lease as an asset. The lessee's income statement reports rent expense and does not report either interest or depreciation expense.

Intermediate accounting textbooks describe more details about the characteristics of leases that cause them to be accounted for as capital or operating. They also describe the financial accounting practices used by the lessor and lessee for capital leases.

Progress Check

12-15 On January 1, 19X1, Fairview Co. signed a $6,000 three-year note payable bearing 6% annual interest. The original principal and all interest is to be paid on December 31, 19X3. The interest will compound every year. How much interest should be allocated to 19X2? *(a)* $0; *(b)* $360; *(c)* $381.60; *(d)* $404.50.

12-16 Suppose that a company promises to pay a lender $4,000 at the end of four years. If the annual interest rate is 8% and the interest is included in the $4,000, what is the amount that the company originally borrowed?

12-17 Which one of the following requires the lessee to record a liability? *(a)* Operating lease; *(b)* Lessor; *(c)* Contingent liability; *(d)* Capital lease.

USING THE INFORMATION — TIMES FIXED INTEREST CHARGES EARNED

LO 7

Calculate the number of times a company earns its fixed interest charges and describe what it reveals about a company's situation.

A company incurs interest expense when it issues notes or bonds and when it enters into capital leases. Many of these liabilities are long-term obligations that are likely to remain outstanding for a substantial period of time even if the company experiences a decline in sales. As a result, interest expense is often viewed as a fixed cost. That is, the amount of interest is not likely to fluctuate much as a result of changes in sales volume.

Although fixed costs can be advantageous when a company is growing, they create the risk that the company might not be able to pay them if sales decline. The following example shows a company's results for the current year and two possible outcomes for the next year:

| | | Next Year | |
	Current Year	If Sales Increase	If Sales Decrease
Sales	$600,000	$900,000	$300,000
Expenses (75% of sales)	450,000	675,000	225,000
Income before interest	$150,000	$225,000	$ 75,000
Interest expense (fixed)	60,000	60,000	60,000
Net income	$ 90,000	$165,000	$ 15,000

As we show in the table, expenses other than interest are projected to stay at 75% of sales. In contrast, the interest is expected to remain at $60,000 per year. Note in the second column that the company's income would nearly double if its sales increased by 50%. However, the company's profits would fall drastically if the sales decreased by 50%. These numbers show that a company's risk is affected by the amount of fixed interest charges that it incurs each year.

The risk created by these fixed expenses can be described numerically with the **times fixed interest charges earned** ratio. You can use the following formula to find the ratio:

$$\text{Times fixed interest charges earned} = \frac{\text{Income before interest}}{\text{Interest expense}}$$

For this company's current year, the income before interest is $150,000. Therefore, the ratio is $150,000/$60,000, which equals 2.5 times. This result suggests that the company faces a relatively low degree of risk. Its sales would have to go down by a large amount before the company would not be able to cover its interest expenses. This condition should provide comfort to the company's creditors and its owners.

Care must be taken in calculating the times fixed interest charges earned ratio for a corporation. Because interest is deducted in determining taxable income, the numerator for a corporation can be expressed as follows:

Income before interest = Net income + Interest expense + Income taxes expense

The times fixed interest charges earned ratio is best interpreted in light of information about the variability of the company's net income before interest. If this amount is stable from year to year, or is growing, the company can afford to take on some of the risk created by borrowing. However, if the company's income before interest varies greatly from year to year, fixed interest charges can increase the risk that the owner will not earn a return or that the company will be unable to pay the interest.

Progress Check

12-18 **The times fixed interest charges earned ratio:**
   a. **Equals interest expense divided by net income.**
   b. **Takes on a larger value as the amount of fixed interest charges gets larger.**
   c. **Is best interpreted in light of information about the variability of the company's net income before interest.**

12-19 **Two companies each have net income after interest of $100,000. First Company has fixed interest charges of $200,000 and Second Company has fixed interest charges of $40,000. Which one is in a more risky situation in terms of being affected by a drop in sales?**

SUMMARY OF THE CHAPTER IN TERMS OF LEARNING OBJECTIVES

LO 1. Define liabilities, explain the difference between current and long-term liabilities, and describe the uncertainties related to some liabilities. Liabilities are probable future payments of assets or services that an entity is presently obligated to make as a result of past events. Current liabilities are due within one year or one operating cycle, whichever is longer. All other liabilities are long-term liabilities. Potential uncertainties about a liability include the identity of the creditor, the due date, and the amount to be paid.

LO 2. Describe how accountants record and report estimated liabilities such as warranties and income taxes, and how they report contingent liabilities. If an uncertain future payment depends on a probable future event and the amount can be reasonably estimated, the payment should be reported as a liability. The future payment must be described as a contingent liability if (*a*) the future event is reasonably possible but not probable, or (*b*) the event is probable but the amount of the payment cannot be reasonably estimated.

Liabilities for warranties and income taxes are recorded with estimated amounts to be paid. This practice recognizes the expenses in the time period that they are incurred. Deferred income tax liabilities are recognized if temporary differences between GAAP and tax rules result in recording more income tax expense than the amount to be currently paid.

LO 3. Describe payroll expenses and liabilities and prepare journal entries to account for them. An employer's payroll expenses include gross earnings of the employees, additional employee benefits, and payroll taxes levied against the employer. Payroll liabilities include the net pay of employees, amounts withheld from the employees' wages, employee benefits, and the employer's payroll taxes. Payroll taxes are assessed for Social Security, Medicare, and unemployment programs.

LO 4. Describe how accountants record and report short-term notes payable. Short-term notes payable may be interest-bearing, in which case the face value of the note equals the amount borrowed and the note specifies a rate of interest to be paid until maturity. Noninterest-bearing notes include interest in their face value; thus, the face value equals the amount to be paid when the note matures.

LO 5. Explain and calculate the present value of an amount to be paid at a future date and the present value of a series of equal amounts to be paid at future dates. The primary present value concept is that today's value of an amount of cash to be paid or received in the future is less than today's value of the same amount of cash to be paid or received today. Another present value concept is that interest is compounded, which means that the interest is added to the balance and used to determine interest for succeeding periods. An annuity is a series of equal payments occurring at equal time intervals.

LO 6. Describe how accountants use present value concepts in accounting for long-term notes, and how liabilities may result from leasing assets. Accountants may use present value concepts to determine the fair value of assets purchased in return for issuing debt. They also use present value concepts to allocate interest expense among the periods in a note's life by multiplying the note's beginning-of-period balance by the original interest rate. Noninterest-bearing notes are normally recorded with a discount account that is contra to the liability account. The balance of the discount account is amortized in the process of recognizing interest expense over the note's life.

Leases are an alternative to purchases as a means of gaining the use of assets. Capital leases give the lessee essentially the same risks and potential rewards as ownership. As a result, the leases and related lease obligations are recorded as assets and liabilities. Other leases, which are called operating leases, involve recording rent expense as the asset is used.

LO 7. Calculate the number of times a company earns its fixed interest charges and describe what it reveals about a company's situation. Times fixed interest charges earned is calculated by dividing a company's net income before interest by the amount of fixed interest charges incurred. This ratio describes the cushion that exists to protect the company's ability to pay interest and earn a profit for its owners against declines in its sales.

DEMONSTRATION PROBLEM

The following series of transactions and other events took place at the Kern Company during its calendar reporting year. Describe their effects on the financial statements by presenting the journal entries described in each situation.

a. Throughout September 19X1, Kern sold $140,000 of merchandise that was covered by a 180-day warranty. Prior experience shows that the costs of fulfilling the warranty will equal 5% of the sales revenue. Calculate September's warranty expense and the increase in the warranty liability and show how it would be recorded with a September 30 adjusting entry. Also show the journal entry that would be made on October 8 to record an expenditure of $300 cash to provide warranty service on an item sold in September.

b. On October 12, Kern arranged with a supplier to replace an overdue $10,000 account payable by paying $2,500 cash and signing a note for the remainder. The note matured in 90 days and had a 12% interest rate. Show the entries that would be recorded on October 12, December 31, and January 10, 19X2 (when the note matures).

c. Kern acquired a machine on December 1 by giving a $60,000 noninterest-bearing note due in one year. The market rate of interest for this type of debt was 10%. Show the entries that would be made when the note is created; as of December 31, 19X1, and at maturity on December 1, 19X2.

- For *(a)*, compute the warranty expense for September and record it with an estimated liability. Record the October expenditure as a decrease in the liability.
- For *(b)*, eliminate the liability for the account payable and create the liability for the note payable. Calculate the interest expense for the 80 days that the note is outstanding in 19X1 and record it as an additional liability. Record the payment of the note, being sure to include the interest for the 10 days in 19X2.
- For *(c)*, measure the cost of the machinery by finding the present value of the $60,000 cash expected to be paid when the note matures. Record the note at its face value, and use a contra-liability account to record the discount. Accrue 30 days' interest at December 31 by reducing the discount account. At maturity, the journal entry should record additional interest expense for 19X2, eliminate the note payable account balance, and eliminate the discount account balance.

a. Warranty expense = 5% × $140,000 = $7,000

Sept.	30	Warranty Expense	7,000.00	
		Estimated Warranty Liability		7,000.00
		To record warranty expense and liability at 5% of sales for the month.		

Oct.	8	Estimated Warranty Liability	300.00	
		Cash		300.00
		To record the cost of the warranty service.		

b. Interest expense for 19X1 = 12% × $7,500 × 80/360 = $200
Interest expense for 19X2 = 12% × $7,500 × 10/360 = $25

Oct.	12	Accounts Payable	10,000.00	
		Notes Payable		7,500.00
		Cash		2,500.00
		Paid $2,500 cash and gave a 90-day, 12% note to extend the due date on the account.		
Dec.	31	Interest Expense	200.00	
		Interest Payable		200.00
		To accrue interest on note payable.		
Jan.	10	Interest Expense	25.00	
		Interest Payable	200.00	
		Notes Payable	7,500.00	
		Cash		7,725.00
		Paid note with interest, including accrued interest payable.		

c. Cost of the asset = Present value of the note
Present value of the note = $60,000 × Table 12–1 value for
n = 1 and i = 10%
Present value of the note = $60,000 × 0.9091 = $54,546
Discount on the note   = $60,000 − $54,546 = $5,454

Dec.	1	Machinery	54,546.00	
		Discount on Notes Payable	5,454.00	
		Notes Payable		60,000.00
		Exchanged a one-year, noninterest-bearing note for a machine.		

Interest expense for 19X1 = 10% × $54,546 × 30/360 = $455
Interest expense for 19X2 = $5,454 − $455 = $4,999

Dec.	31	Interest Expense	455.00	
		Discount on Notes Payable		455.00
		To accrue interest on noninterest-bearing note payable.		
19X2				
Dec.	1	Interest Expense	4,999.00	
		Notes Payable	60,000.00	
		Cash		60,000.00
		Discount on Notes Payable		4,999.00
		Paid noninterest-bearing note payable.		

GLOSSARY

Annuity a series of equal payments occurring at equal time intervals. p. 459

Capital lease a lease that gives the lessee the risks and benefits normally associated with ownership. p. 463

Deferred income tax liability payments of income taxes that are deferred until future years because of temporary differences between GAAP and tax rules. p. 447

Discount on note payable the difference between the face value of a noninterest-bearing note payable and the amount borrowed; represents interest that will be paid on the note over its life. p. 454

Employee benefits additional compensation paid to or on behalf of employees, such as premiums for medical, dental, life, and disability insurance, contributions to pension plans, and vacations. p. 452

Estimated liability an obligation that is reported as a liability even though the amount to be paid is uncertain. p. 444

FICA taxes taxes assessed on both employers and employees under the Federal Insurance Contributions Act; these taxes fund Social Security and Medicare programs. p. 450

Merit rating a rating assigned to an employer by a state according to the employer's past record for creating or not creating unemployment; a higher rating produces a lower unemployment tax rate. p. 451

Noninterest-bearing note a note that does not have a stated rate of interest; the interest is included in the face value of the note. p. 454

Operating lease a lease that is not a capital lease. p. 464

Present value the amount that can be invested (borrowed) at a given interest rate to generate a total future investment (debt) that will equal the amount of a specified future receipt (payment). p. 457

Present value table a table that shows the present values of an amount to be received when discounted at various interest rates for various periods of time, or the present values of a series of equal payments to be received for a varying number of periods when discounted at various interest rates. p. 458

Times fixed interest charges earned the ratio of a company's income before interest divided by the amount of interest charges; used to evaluate the risk of being committed to make interest payments when income varies. p. 465

Warranty an agreement that obligates the seller or manufacturer to repair or replace a product that fails to perform properly within a specified period. p. 444

QUESTIONS

1. What is the difference between a current and a long-term liability?

2. What is an estimated liability?

3. What are the three important questions concerning the certainty of liabilities?

4. Suppose that a company has a facility located in an area where disastrous weather conditions often occur. Should it report a probable loss from a future disaster as a liability on its balance sheet? Why?

5. Why are warranty liabilities usually recognized on the balance sheet as liabilities even when they are uncertain?

6. What is an employer's unemployment merit rating? Why are these ratings assigned to employers?

7. What factors affect the present value of a future $2,000 payment?

8. How would a lease create an asset and a liability for the lessee?

9. Examine the 1993 balance sheet for Federal Express Corporation in Appendix G. How much of the com-

pany's long-term debt is due to be paid during the 1994 fiscal year?

10. Examine the balance sheet for Ben & Jerry's in Appendix G. Has the company entered into any capital leases for its equipment? How do you know?

QUICK STUDY (Five Minute Exercises)

Which of the following items would normally be classified as a current liability for a company that has a 14-month operating cycle?

**QS 12–1
(LO 1)**

a. A note payable due in 18 months.

b. Salaries payable.

c. Bonds payable that mature in two years.

d. A note payable due in 10 months.

e. The portion of a long-term note that is due to be paid in 14 months.

On December 20, Compu sold a computer for $3,500 with a one-year warranty that covers parts and labor. Warranty expense was estimated at 2% of sales. On March 2, the computer was turned in for repairs covered under the warranty requiring $50 in parts and $30 of labor. Prepare the March 2 journal entry to record the warranty repairs.

**QS 12–2
(LO 2)**

Tracon Co. has six employees, each of whom earns $3,000 per month. FICA taxes are 7.65% of gross pay, and FUTA taxes are 0.8% and SUTA taxes are 3.5% of the first $7,000 paid to each employee. Prepare the March 31 journal entry to record payroll taxes expense.

**QS 12–3
(LO 3)**

On December 11, 19X1, the Snyder Company borrowed $42,000 and signed a 60-day, 9% note payable with a face value of $42,000. (a) Calculate the accrued interest payable on December 31, and (b) present the journal entry to record the paying of the note at maturity.

**QS 12–4
(LO 4)**

Determine the amount that can be borrowed under each of the following circumstances:

**QS 12–5
(LO 5)**

a. A promise to pay $50,000 in six years at an interest rate of 10%.

b. An agreement made on January 2, 19X1, to make four payments of $4,200 on January 2 of 19X2 through 19X5. The annual interest rate was 8%.

On January 1, 19X1, a company borrowed $40,000 in exchange for an interest-bearing note. The note plus compounded interest at an annual rate of 12% is due on December 31, 19X3. Determine the amount that the company will pay on the due date.

**QS 12–6
(LO 6)**

Calculate the times fixed interest charges earned for a company that has income before interest of $462,000 and interest expense of $98,000.

**QS 12–7
(LO 7)**

EXERCISES

The following list of items might appear as liabilities on the balance sheet of a company that has a two-month operating cycle. Identify the proper classification of each item. In the space beside each item write C if it is a current liability, an L if it is a long-term liability, or an N if it is not a liability.

**Exercise 12–1
Classifying liabilities
(LO 1)**

___ a. Wages payable.

___ b. Notes payable in 60 days.

___ c. Mortgage payable (payments due after next 12 months).

___ d. Notes receivable in 90 days.

___ e. Bonds payable (mature in 10 years).

___ f. Mortgage payable (payments due in next 12 months).

___ g. Notes payable in 6–12 months.

___ h. Income taxes payable.

___ i. Accounts receivable.

___ j. Notes payable in 13–24 months.

Exercise 12–2
Warranty expense and liability
(LO 2)

Sassower Co. sold a computer to a customer on December 4, 19X1, for $8,000 cash. Based on prior experience, the company expects to eventually incur warranty costs equal to 5% of this selling price. On January 18, 19X2, the customer returned the computer for repairs that were completed on the same day. The cost of the repairs consisted of $198 for the materials taken from the parts inventory and $40 of labor that was fully paid with cash.

a. How much warranty expense should the company report for December for this computer?

b. How large is the warranty liability for this computer as of December 31, 19X1?

c. How much warranty expense should the company report for January for this computer?

d. How large is the warranty liability for this computer as of January 31, 19X2?

e. Show the journal entries that would be made to record (1) the sale; (2) the adjustment as of December 31, 19X1, to record the warranty expense; and (3) the repairs that occurred in January.

Exercise 12–3
Accounting for income taxes
(LO 2)

McKeag Corp. prepares interim financial statements each month. As part of the process, estimated income taxes are accrued each month as 30% of the company's income for that month. The estimated income taxes are paid in the first month of each quarter for the amount accrued in the prior quarter. These facts are known about the last quarter of 19X1:

a. The company determined that the following amounts of net income occurred for these months:

October 19X1	$ 8,500
November 19X1	6,000
December 19X1	10,000

b. After the tax return was completed in early January, the accountant determined that the Income Taxes Payable account balance should be $7,480 on December 31.

Required

1. Determine the amount of the adjustment needed to produce the proper ending balance in the Income Taxes Payable account.

2. Present the journal entries to record the adjustment to the Income Taxes Payable account upon completion of the return and to record the January 15 payment of the fourth-quarter taxes.

Exercise 12–4
Payroll taxes
(LO 3)

The Juneau Co. has a single employee on its payroll. The employee and the company are subject to the following taxes:

Tax	Rate	Applied to
FICA—Social Security	6.20%	First $61,200
FICA—Medicare	1.45	Gross pay
FUTA	0.80	First $7,000
SUTA	3.20	First $7,000

Compute the amounts of the four taxes on the employee's gross earnings for July under each of these three separate situations:

	Gross Salary Through June	Gross Salary for July
a.	$ 5,000	$ 900
b.	20,000	3,500
c.	60,600	10,000

Use the data in requirement *a* of Exercise 12–4 to prepare journal entries to record the gross salary and withholdings for the employee and the company's payroll taxes. The employee's withheld income taxes are $125.

Exercise 12–5
Payroll tax journal entries
(LO 3)

The Knightwood Co. borrowed $50,000 on September 1, 19X1, for 90 days at 8% interest by signing a note.

a. On what date will this note mature?

b. How much interest expense is created by this note? (Assume a 360-day year.)

c. Suppose that the face value of the note equals the principal of the loan. Show the general journal entries to record issuing the note and paying it at maturity.

d. Suppose that the face value of the note includes the principal of the loan and the interest to be paid at maturity. Show the general journal entries to record issuing the note and paying it at maturity.

Exercise 12–6
Interest-bearing and noninterest-bearing notes payable
(LO 4)

The Shelby Co. borrowed $30,000 on December 1, 19X1, for 90 days at 10% interest by signing a note.

a. On what date will this note mature?

b. How much interest expense is created by this note in 19X1? (Assume a 360-day year.)

c. How much interest expense is created by this note in 19X2? (Assume a 360-day year.)

d. Suppose that the face value of the note equals the principal of the loan. Show the general journal entries to record issuing the note, to accrue interest at the end of 19X1, and to record paying the note at maturity.

e. Suppose that the face value of the note includes the principal of the loan and the interest to be paid at maturity. Show the general journal entries to record issuing the note, to accrue interest at the end of 19X1, and to record paying the note at maturity.

Exercise 12–7
Interest-bearing and noninterest-bearing short-term notes payable with year-end adjustments
(LO 4)

On January 1, 19X1, a company has agreed to pay $15,000 after three years. If the annual interest rate is 6%, determine how much cash the company can borrow with this promise. Present a three-column table that shows the beginning balance, interest, and ending balance for 19X1, 19X2, and 19X3.

Exercise 12–8
Present value of a future payment and accumulating interest
(LO 5)

Find the amount of money that can be borrowed with each of the following promises:

	Future Payment	Number of Years	Interest Rate
a.	$80,000	1	6%
b.	80,000	5	6
c.	80,000	5	8
d.	60,000	7	10
e.	10,000	1	2
f.	25,000	9	4

Exercise 12–9
Present value of liabilities
(LO 5)

A company recently borrowed money and agreed to pay it back with a series of three annual payments of $10,000 each. The firm also borrowed cash and agreed to pay it back with a

Exercise 12–10
Present value of annuities
(LO 5)

series of seven annual payments of $4,000 each. The annual interest rate for the loans was 10%.

a. Use Table 12–1 to find the present value of these two annuities.

b. Use Table 12–2 to find the present value of these two annuities.

Exercise 12–11
Semiannual compounding
(LO 5)

A company borrowed cash on January 2, 19X1, by promising to make four payments of $3,000 each at June 30, 19X1; December 31, 19X1; June 30, 19X2; and December 31, 19X2.

a. How much cash was the company able to borrow if the interest rate was 12%, compounded semiannually?

b. How much cash was the company able to borrow if the interest rate was 16%, compounded semiannually?

c. How much cash was the company able to borrow if the interest rate was 20%, compounded semiannually?

Exercise 12–12
Recording an asset purchase in exchange for a note
(LO 6)

The Carson Company purchased some machinery on March 10 that had a cost of $56,000. Show the journal entry that would record this purchase under these four separate situations:

a. The company paid cash for the full purchase price.

b. The company gave an interest-bearing note for the full purchase price.

c. The company gave a noninterest-bearing one-year note for $61,600.

Exercise 12–13
Calculations concerning a noninterest-bearing note
(LO 6)

On January 2, 19X1, the Brewster Co. acquired land by issuing a noninterest-bearing note for $20,000. The fair market value of the land was not reliably known, but the company knew that the market interest rate for the note was 6%. The note matures in three years on January 1, 19X4.

a. What is the present value of the note at the time of the purchase?

b. What is the initial balance of the discount on the note payable?

c. Prepare a table that shows the amount of interest that will be allocated to each of the three years in the note's life and the ending balance of the net liability for each year.

d. Prepare a table that determines the ending balance of the discount on the note for each of the three years.

Exercise 12–14
Journal entries for a noninterest-bearing note
(LO 6)

Use the data in Exercise 12–13 to prepare journal entries for these dates:

a. January 2, 19X1 (land purchase).

b. December 31, 19X1 (accrual entry).

c. December 31, 19X2 (accrual entry).

d. December 31, 19X3 (accrual entry).

e. January 1, 19X4 (the payment of the note).

Exercise 12–15
Times fixed interest charges earned
(LO 7)

Use the following information for a proprietorship to compute times fixed interest charges earned:

	Net Income or (Loss)	Interest Expense
a.	$ 85,000	$ 16,000
b.	85,000	40,000
c.	85,000	90,000
d.	240,000	120,000
e.	(25,000)	60,000
f.	96,000	6,000

PROBLEMS

On November 10, 19X1, Bright Beam Co. began to buy and resell high-powered flashlights for $40 each. The flashlights are covered under a warranty that requires the company to replace any nonworking flashlight within 90 days. When a flashlight is returned, the company simply throws it away and mails a new one from inventory to the customer. The company's cost for a new flashlight is only $7. The manufacturer has advised the company to expect warranty costs to equal 8% of the total sales. These events occurred in 19X1 and 19X2:

Problem 12–1
Estimated product warranty liabilities
(LO 2)

19X1

Nov. 15   Sold flashlights for $8,000 cash.

     30   Recognized warranty expense for November with an adjusting entry.

Dec. 8   Replaced 15 flashlights that were returned under the warranty.

     15   Sold flashlights for $22,000 cash.

     29   Replaced 40 flashlights that were returned under the warranty.

     31   Recognized warranty expense for December with an adjusting entry.

19X2

Jan. 14   Sold flashlights for $11,000 cash.

     20   Replaced 63 flashlights that were returned under the warranty.

     31   Recognized warranty expense for January with an adjusting entry.

Required

1. How much warranty expense should be reported for November and December of 19X1?
2. How much warranty expense should be reported for January 19X2?
3. What is the balance of the estimated warranty liability as of December 31, 19X1?
4. What is the balance of the estimated warranty liability as of January 31, 19X2?
5 Prepare journal entries to record the transactions and adjustments.

CHECK FIGURE:
12/31/X1 estimated liability balance, $2,015

The Northside Co. entered into the following transactions involving short-term liabilities during 19X1 and 19X2:

Problem 12–2
Transactions with short-term notes payable
(LO 4)

19X1

Mar. 14   Purchased merchandise on credit from Pete Winston Co. for $12,500. The terms were 1/10, n/30.

Apr. 14   Replaced the account payable to Pete Winston Co. with a 60-day note bearing 10% annual interest. Northside paid $3,500 cash, with the result that the balance of the note was $9,000.

May 21   Borrowed $20,000 from Central Bank by signing an interest-bearing note for $20,000. The annual interest rate was 12%, and the note has a 90-day term.

?   Paid the note to Pete Winston Co. at maturity.

?   Paid the note to Central Bank at maturity.

Dec. 15   Borrowed $35,000 from Eastern Bank by signing a noninterest-bearing note for $36,050 that matures in 120 days. (This amount is based on a 9% interest rate.)

     31   Recorded an accrual adjusting entry for the interest on the note to Eastern Bank.

19X2

?   Paid the note to Eastern Bank at maturity.

Required

1. Determine the maturity dates of the three notes just described.
2. Determine the interest due at maturity for the three notes. (Assume a 360-day year.)
3. Determine the interest to be recorded in the adjusting entry at the end of 19X1.
4. Determine the interest to be recorded in 19X2.
5. Present journal entries for all the preceding events and adjustments.

Problem 12–3
Payroll costs, withholdings, and taxes
(LO 3)

The Boston Company pays its employees every week. The employees' gross earnings are subject to these taxes:

	Rate	Applied to
FICA—Social Security	6.20%	First $61,200
FICA—Medicare	1.45	Gross pay
FUTA	0.80	First $7,000
SUTA	3.20	First $7,000

The company is preparing its payroll calculations for the week ended October 20. The payroll records show the following information for the company's four employees:

Name	Gross Pay Through 10/13	This Week Gross Pay	This Week Withholding Tax
Fran	$21,000	$1,500	$165
Lynn	85,000	2,500	325
Shane	60,600	2,000	285
Terry	5,500	1,000	122

In addition to the gross pay, the company and each employee pay one-half of the weekly health insurance premium of $66. The company also contributes 10% of each employee's gross earnings to a pension fund.

Required

Use this information to determine:

1. Each employee's FICA withholdings for Social Security.
2. Each employee's FICA withholdings for Medicare.
3. The employer's FICA taxes for Social Security.
4. The employer's FICA taxes for Medicare.
5. The employer's FUTA taxes.
6. The employer's SUTA taxes.

7. Each employee's take-home pay.
8. The employer's total payroll-related expense for each employee.

Problem 12–4
Present values of possible liabilities
(LO 5, 6)

Sherlock Enterprises is negotiating the purchase of a new building. The seller has offered Sherlock the following three payment plans:

Plan A: $100,000 cash would be paid at once.
Plan B: $114,000 cash would be paid after two years.
Plan C: $58,000 cash would be paid at the end of each of the next two years.

The company's owner knows that the market interest rate is 8%.

Required

1. Use the market interest rate to determine present value of each of the three possible payment plans.

2. Show the journal entry that would be made to record the acquisition under each of the three plans. (Assume that the note's face value would include all interest to be paid.)

3. Identify the plan that creates the lowest cost for the company.

4. Assume that Plan B is adopted and the present value of the cash flows is used as the building's cost. Determine the amount of interest expense that will be reported in each of the two years in the note's life.

On January 2, 19X1, Watts Company acquired an item of equipment by issuing a $55,000 non-interest-bearing five-year note payable on December 31, 19X5. A reliable cash price for the equipment was not readily available. The market annual rate of interest for similar notes was 4% on the day of the exchange.

Problem 12–5
Exchanging a noninterest-bearing note for a plant asset
(LO 6)

Required

(Round all amounts in your answers to the nearest whole dollar.)

1. Determine the initial net liability created by issuing this note.

2. Present a table showing the calculation of the amount of interest expense allocated to each year the note is outstanding and the carrying amount of the net liability at the end of each of those years.

3. Present a table that shows the balance of the discount at the end of each year the note is outstanding.

4. Prepare general journal entries to record the purchase of the equipment, the accrual of interest expense at the end of 19X1 and 19X2, and the accrual of interest expense and the payment of the note on December 31, 19X5.

5. Show how the note should be presented on the balance sheet as of December 31, 19X3.

CHECK FIGURE:
Net liability as of December 31, 19X3, $50,850

These condensed income statements are for two companies:

Problem 12–6
Understanding times fixed interest charges earned
(LO 7)

Adams Co.		Beene Co.	
Sales	$100,000	Sales	$100,000
Variable expenses (65%) ...	65,000	Variable expenses (85%) ...	85,000
Net income before interest ..	$ 35,000	Net income before interest ..	$ 15,000
Interest (fixed)	25,000	Interest (fixed)	5,000
Net income	$ 10,000	Net income	$ 10,000

Required

Preparation component:

1. What times fixed interest charges earned for Adams Co.?

2. What times fixed interest charges earned for Beene Co.?

3. What happens to each company's net income if sales increase by 20%?

4. What happens to each company's net income if sales increase by 40%?

5. What happens to each company's net income if sales increase by 80%?

6. What happens to each company's net income if sales decrease by 10%?

7. What happens to each company's net income if sales decrease by 20%?

8. What happens to each company's net income if sales decrease by 50%?

CHECK FIGURE:
Part 3: Net income for Adams Co., $17,000

Analysis component:

9. Comment on what you observe and relate it to the ratio values that you found in questions 1 and 2.

CRITICAL THINKING: ESSAYS, PROBLEMS, AND CASES

Analytical Essays

AE 12-1
(LO 6)

This problem requires you to demonstrate your understanding of noninterest-bearing notes, interest allocation, and present values by explaining how it would be possible to use incomplete information to discover other facts about a loan. Suppose that a company borrowed some cash on January 1, 19X1, with a four-year noninterest-bearing note payable. A year later, on December 31, 19X1, you know only these two items of information:

a. The net liability (net of the remaining discount) as of December 31, 19X1.

b. The interest expense reported for the year ended December 31, 19X1.

Write brief explanations of the calculations you would make to identify the following additional facts about the loan:

1. The amount borrowed on January 1, 19X1.
2. The market interest rate on January 1, 19X1.
3. The amount of interest that will be reported for 19X2.

AE 12-2
(LO 6)

After a long analysis, the manager of the Greenfield Company has decided to acquire a truck through a long-term noncancellable lease instead of buying it outright. Under the terms of the lease, Greenfield must make regular monthly payments throughout the four year term of the lease and provide for all the operating costs, including gas, insurance, and repairs. At the end of the lease, the lessor will simply give Greenfield the legal title to the truck. Describe why Greenfield should account for the lease as if it is essentially a purchase.

Management Decision Case

(LO 3)

All 60 regular employees of the Excellent Shirt Company earn at least $7,000 per year. The company operates in a state with a maximum SUTA tax rate of 5.4% on the first $7,000 gross wages of each employee. The company's excellent record has earned a merit rating that reduces its SUTA rate to 3.5%.

The company has recently received an order for a line of leather vests from a chain of clothing stores. The order should be very profitable and probably will be repeated each year for at least three or four years. The company can produce the vests with its present production facility, but it will have to add 10 more workers for six weeks at 40 hours per week to make the vests and pack them for shipment.

The company is considering two different approaches to getting the workers. That is, it can either go through a local temporary employment service (called Temployees) or actually hire them as employees and then lay them off after six weeks. Excellent Shirt would pay Temployees $12 per hour for each worker, and Temployees would pay their wages and all payroll taxes and benefits. Alternatively, Excellent Shirt would pay its new employees a wage rate of $8.50 per hour, plus these additional payroll taxes: FICA tax, 7.65%; FUTA tax, 0.8%; and SUTA tax, 5.0%. The SUTA rate would jump to 5.0% because the company would receive a less favorable merit rating from the state because of the unemployment claims it would create by laying off the workers every year. This higher rate would apply to all of the company's employees. In addition, Excellent Shirt would provide health care insurance to these employees at the rate of $24 per employee per week.

Compare the total costs under the two alternatives to determine whether Excellent Shirt should use the services of Temployees or hire the additional workers that it needs. Provide a complete analysis and explanation.

Business Communications Case

(LO 2)

Sam Ishikawa is the new manager of accounting and finance for a medium-sized manufacturing company. Now that the end of the year is approaching, his problem is determining whether and how to describe some of the company's contingencies in the financial statements. The general manager, Sue Peebles, raised objections to two specific contingencies in his preliminary proposal.

First, Peebles objected to the proposal to report nothing about a patent infringement suit that the company has filed against a competitor. The manager's written comment on his proposal was, "We KNOW that we have them cold on this one! There is no way that we're not going to win a very large settlement!"

Second, she objected to his proposal to recognize an expense and a liability for warranty service on units of a new product that was just introduced in the company's fourth quarter. Her scribbled comment on this point was "There is no way that we can estimate this warranty cost. Besides, we don't owe anybody anything until the products break down and are returned for service. Let's just report an expense if and when we do the repairs."

Develop a short written response for Ishikawa to the objections raised by the general manager in a one-page memorandum dated December 15.

Answer the following questions by using the information in the financial statements and footnotes for Apple Computer, Inc., that appear in Appendix F at the end of the book:

Financial Statement Analysis Case

(LO 1, 2, 6, 7)

1. Examine the company's balance sheet to find the amount of long-term debt that it had on September 24, 1993. Also, what is the amount of the company's current notes payable?

2. Examine the supplemental cash flow disclosures on the statement of cash flows to find the amount of interest paid during fiscal years 1993 and 1992. Assume that the interest paid represents interest expense. Calculate times fixed interest charges earned for both years and comment on any significant change in the ratio.

3. Does the footnote on "Commitments and Contingencies" provide information that allows the reader to determine whether the company has entered into any operating or capital leases?

4. What evidence would you look for as an indication that the company has any temporary differences between the income reported on the income statement and the income reported on its tax return? Can you find any evidence of these differences for Apple?

CONCEPT TESTER

Test your understanding of the concepts introduced in this chapter by completing the following crossword puzzle.

Across Clues

3. 2 words; an employer's rating that reflects the employers past record for creating unemployment

6. 2 words; an obligation reported as a liability even though the amount to be paid is uncertain.

7. A series of equal payments occurring at equal time intervals.

8. 2 words; compensation to or on behalf of employees in addition to their wages or salaries.

9. 2 words; a lease that gives the lessee the risks and benefits normally related to ownership.

Down Clues

1. 2 words; taxes assessed under the Federal Insurance Contributions Act.

2. 2 words; an amount that, if invested now, will generate a specified future receipt.

4. 2 words; a lease that is not a capital lease.

5. An obligation of a seller or manufacturer to repair or replace products that fail.

COMPREHENSIVE PROBLEM

Schwartz Exterminator Company (Review of Chapters 1–12)

The Schwartz Exterminator Company provides pest control services and sells extermination products manufactured by other companies. The following six-column table contains the company's unadjusted trial balance as of December 31, 19X4.

SCHWARTZ EXTERMINATOR COMPANY
Six-column Table
December 31, 19X4

	Unadjusted Trial Balance		Adjustments		Adjusted Trial Balance	
Cash	$ 15,000					
Accounts receivable	24,000					
Allowance for doubtful accounts			$ 3,064			
Merchandise inventory	18,000					
Trucks	22,000					
Accum. depreciation, trucks ..			0			
Equipment	75,000					
Accum. depreciation, equipment			21,500			
Accounts payable			6,000			
Estimated warranty liability ..			1,200			
Unearned extermination services revenue			0			
Long-term notes payable			60,000			
Discount on notes payable ...	15,898					
Arnold Schwartz, capital			58,800			
Arnold Schwartz, withdrawals	21,000					
Extermination services revenue			70,000			
Interest earned			436			
Sales			135,000			
Purchases	81,000					
Depreciation expense, trucks ..	0					
Depreciation expense, equip. ...	0					
Wages expense	45,000					
Interest expense	0					
Rent expense	16,000					
Bad debts expense	0					
Miscellaneous expenses	6,202					
Repairs expense	11,000					
Utilities expense	5,900					
Warranty expense	0					
Totals	$356,000	$356,000				

The following information applies to the company and its situation at the end of the year:

a. The bank reconciliation as of December 31, 19X4, includes these facts:

Balance per bank	$13,200
Balance per books	15,000
Outstanding checks	2,600
Deposit in transit	3,500
Interest earned	44
Service charges (miscellaneous expense) ..	17

Included with the bank statement was a canceled check that the company had failed to record. (This information allows you to determine the amount of the check, which was a payment of an account payable.)

b. An examination of customers' accounts shows that accounts totaling $2,500 should be written off as uncollectible. In addition, the owner has determined that the ending balance of the Allowance for Doubtful Accounts account should be $4,300.

c. A truck was purchased and placed in service on July 1, 19X4. Its cost is being depreci-
    ated with the straight-line method using these facts and predictions:

    Original cost $22,000
    Expected salvage value   6,000
    Useful life (years)   4

d. Two items of equipment (a sprayer and an injector) were purchased and put into service
    early in January 19X2. Their costs are being depreciated with the straight-line method
    using these facts and predictions:

	Sprayer	Injector
Original cost	$45,000	$30,000
Expected salvage value	3,000	2,500
Useful life (years)	8	5

e. On October 1, 19X4, the company was paid $2,640 in advance to provide monthly ser-
    vice on an apartment complex for one year. The company began providing the services
    in October. When the cash was received, the full amount was credited to the Extermina-
    tion Services Revenue account.

f. The company offers a warranty for all of the products it sells. The expected cost of pro-
    viding warranty service is 2% of sales. No warranty expense has been recorded for
    19X4. All costs of servicing products under the warranties in 19X4 were properly deb-
    ited to the liability account.

g. The $60,000 long-term note is a five-year, noninterest-bearing note that was given to
    Second National Bank on December 31, 19X2. The market interest rate on the date of
    the loan was 8%.

h. The ending inventory of merchandise was counted and determined to have a cost of
    $16,300.

Required

1. Use the provided information to determine the amounts of the following items:

    a. The correct ending balance of Cash and the amount of the omitted check.

    b. The adjustment needed to obtain the correct ending balance of the Allowance for
        Doubtful Accounts.

    c. The annual depreciation expense for the truck that was acquired during the year
        (calculated to the nearest month).

    d. The annual depreciation expense for the two items of equipment that were used
        during the year.

    e. The correct ending balances of the Extermination Services Revenue and Unearned
        Extermination Services Revenue accounts.

    f. The correct ending balances of the accounts for Warranty Expense and the Esti-
        mated Warranty Liability.

    g. The correct ending balances of the accounts for Interest Expense and the Discount
        on Notes Payable.

    h. The cost of goods sold for the year.

2. Use the results of requirement 1 to complete the six-column table by first entering the
    appropriate adjustments for items a through g and then completing the adjusted trial
    balance columns. (Hint: item b requires two entries.)

3. Present general journal entries to record the adjustments entered on the six-column
    table.

4. Present a single-step income statement, a statement of changes in owner's equity, and a
    classified balance sheet.

ANSWERS TO PROGRESS CHECKS

12–1 Liabilities are probable future payments of assets or services that an entity is presently obligated to make as a result of past transactions or events.

12–2 No; an expected future payment is not a liability unless an obligation was created by a past event or transaction.

12–3 In most cases, a liability due in 15 months should be classified as long-term. However, it should be classified as a current liability if the company's operating cycle is at least 15 months long.

12–4 *a*

12–5 *a*

12–6 A corporation would accrue an income tax liability for its interim financial statements because income tax expense is incurred when income is earned, not just at the end of the year.

12–7 *b*

12–8 A future payment should be reported as a contingent liability if *(a)* the uncertain future event is probable but the amount of the payment cannot be reasonably estimated, and *(b)* the uncertain future event is not probable but has a reasonable possibility of occurring.

12–9 *a*
$1,000(.008 + .04) + $3,000(.062 + .0145) = $277.50

12–10 *(a)* FICA taxes are paid by both the employee and the employer.
(b) FUTA taxes are paid by the employer.

(c) SUTA taxes are paid by the employer.
(d) Withheld income taxes are paid by the employee.

12–11 A creditor might want to have a note payable instead of an account payable in order to *(a)* start charging interest and/or *(b)* have positive evidence of the debt and its terms.

12–12 The amount borrowed was $1,000 ($1,050 − $50). The rate of interest was 5% ($50/$1,000) for six months, which is an annual rate of 10%.

12–13 *c*
3.3121 × $1,000 = $3,312

12–14 The option of paying $10,000 after a year always has a lower present value. In effect, it postpones paying the first $5,000 by six months. As a result, the present value of the delayed payment is always less.

12–15 *c*
[$6,000 + ($6,000 × .06)] × .06 = $381.60

12–16 $4,000 × 0.7350 = $2,940

12–17 *d*

12–18 *c*

12–19 The risk can be described by the ratio that shows the number of times the fixed interest charges are covered by the net income *before* interest. The ratio for the first company is only 1.5 [($100,000 + $200,000)/$200,000], while the ratio for the second company is 3.5 [($100,000 + $40,000)/$40,000]. This analysis shows that First Company is more susceptible to the risk of incurring a loss if its sales decline.

Corporations and Partnerships

*B*ecause his father worked for Mobil Corporation for 30 years until retirement, Barry Foster has been interested in the company since childhood. He has always been impressed by the fact that Mobil has paid dividends every year since 1902. It has operations in more than 100 countries involving oil and gas, petrochemicals, plastics, mining, and land development. In 1993, these operations generated total revenues in excess of $63 billion.

Late in 1994, Foster began to examine the company's dividend record more closely. In doing so, he noted that during the 10-year period from 1983 to 1993, dividends to common stock increased from $2.00 per share to $3.25 per share. Dividends in 1994 were running at a rate that would accumulate to $3.40 per share. In attempting to evaluate the company, Foster also gathered information about several other companies. However, he was unsure about how to compare them.

Company	Common Dividend per Share		November 1994 Stock Price
	1994*	1993	
Mobil Corporation	$3.40	$3.25	$82¼
Minnesota Mining & Manufacturing Co.	1.76	1.66	53¼
Texaco Inc.	3.20	3.20	60⅞
AT&T Corp.	1.32	1.32	54
GAP, Inc.	0.48	0.38	37⅞
Microsoft Corp.	0	0	64½

*Estimated 1994 amounts.

LEARNING OBJECTIVES

After studying Chapter 13, you should be able to:

1. **Explain the unique characteristics of the corporate form of business.**
2. **Record the issuance of par value stock and no-par stock with or without a stated value, and explain the concept of minimum legal capital.**
3. **Record transactions that involve dividends and stock subscriptions and explain the effects of stock subscriptions on the balance sheet.**
4. **State the differences between common and preferred stock, and allocate dividends between the common and preferred stock of a corporation.**
5. **Describe convertible preferred stock and explain the meaning of the par value, call price, market value, and book value of corporate stock.**
6. **Explain the concepts of mutual agency and unlimited liability for a partnership, record the investments and withdrawals of partners, and allocate the net incomes or losses of a partnership among the partners.**
7. **Calculate dividend yield and describe its meaning.**
8. **Define or explain the words and phrases listed in the chapter glossary.**

Of the three common types of business organizations (proprietorships, partnerships, and corporations), corporations are fewest in number. However, they transact more business than the other two combined. Large businesses like Mobil Corporation are almost all corporations. In the United States, the dollar sales volume of corporations is approximately nine times the combined sales of unincorporated businesses. Thus, from an overall economic point of view, corporations are clearly the most important form of business organization. As you study this chapter, you will learn how corporations are organized and operated, and about some of the procedures used to account for corporations. You will also learn about partnerships.

CORPORATIONS

CHARACTERISTICS OF CORPORATIONS

LO 1

Explain the unique characteristics of the corporate form of business.

Corporations have become the dominant type of business because of the advantages created by their unique characteristics. We describe these characteristics in the following sections.

Corporations Are Separate Legal Entities

A corporation is a separate legal entity. As a separate entity, a corporation conducts its affairs with the same rights, duties, and responsibilities as a person. However, because it is not a real person, a corporation can act only through its agents, who are its officers and managers.

Stockholders Are Not Liable for the Corporation's Debts

Because a corporation is a separate legal entity, it is responsible for its own acts and its own debts. Its shareholders are not liable for either. From the viewpoint of an investor, this lack of stockholders' liability is, perhaps, the most important advantage of the corporate form of business.

Ownership Rights of Corporations Are Easily Transferred

The ownership of a corporation is represented by shares of stock that, in general, are easily bought or sold. Also, the transfer of shares from one stockholder to another usually has no effect on the corporation or its operations.[1] Many companies have thousands or even millions of their shares bought and sold every day through major stock exchanges located throughout the world. For example, *The Wall Street Journal* reported that on November 15, 1994, 5,552,600 shares of **American Express Company** stock were traded on the New York Stock Exchange.

Corporations Have Continuity of Life

A corporation's life may continue indefinitely because it is not tied to the physical lives of its owners. In some cases, a corporation's life may be initially limited by the laws of the state of its incorporation. However, the corporation's charter can be renewed and its life extended when the stated time expires. Thus, a corporation may have a perpetual life as long as it continues to be successful.

Stockholders Are Not Agents of the Corporation

As we previously stated, a corporation acts through its agents, who are the officers or managers of the corporation. Stockholders who are not officers or managers of the corporation do not have the power to bind the corporation to contracts. Instead, stockholders participate in the affairs of the corporation only by voting in the stockholders' meetings.

Ease of Capital Accumulation

Buying stock in a corporation often is more attractive to investors than investing in other forms of business. Stock investments are attractive because: (1) stockholders are not liable for the corporation's actions and debts, (2) stock usually can be transferred easily, (3) the life of the corporation is not limited, and (4) stockholders are not agents of the corporation. These advantages make it possible for some corporations to accumulate large amounts of capital from the combined investments of many stockholders. In a sense, a corporation's capacity for raising capital is limited only by its ability to convince investors that it can use their funds profitably.

Governmental Regulation of Corporations

Corporations are created by fulfilling the requirements of a state's incorporation laws. These laws subject a corporation to state regulation and control. Single proprietorships and partnerships may escape some of these regulations. In addition, they may avoid having to file some governmental reports required of corporations.

Taxation of Corporations

Corporations are subject to the same property and payroll taxes as single proprietorships and partnerships. In addition, corporations are subject to taxes that are not levied

---

[1]However, a transfer of ownership can create significant effects if it brings about a change in who controls the company's activities.

on either of the other two. The most burdensome of these are federal and state income taxes that together may take 40% or more of a corporation's pretax income. However, the tax burden does not end there. The income of a corporation is taxed twice, first as income of the corporation and again as personal income to the stockholders when cash is distributed to them as dividends. This differs from single proprietorships and partnerships, which are not subject to income taxes as business units. Their income is taxed only as the personal income of their owners.[2]

The tax situation of a corporation is generally viewed as a disadvantage. However, in some cases, it can work to the advantage of stockholders because corporation and individual tax rates are progressive. That is, higher levels of income are taxed at higher rates and lower levels of income are taxed at lower rates. Therefore, taxes may be saved or at least delayed if a large amount of income is divided among two or more tax-paying entities. Thus, an individual who has a large personal income and pays taxes at a high rate may benefit if some of the income is earned by a corporation that person owns, as long as the corporation avoids paying dividends. By not paying dividends, the corporation's income is taxed only once at the lower corporate rate, at least temporarily until dividends are paid.

ORGANIZING A CORPORATION

A corporation is created by securing a charter from a state government. The requirements that must be met to be chartered vary among the states. Usually, a charter application must be signed by three or more subscribers to the prospective corporation's stock (such persons are called the *incorporators* or *promoters*). Then, the application must be filed with the appropriate state official. When it is properly completed and all fees are paid, the charter is issued and the corporation is formed. The subscribers then purchase the corporation's stock, meet as stockholders, and elect a board of directors. The directors are responsible for guiding the company's business affairs.

ORGANIZATION COSTS

The costs of organizing a corporation, such as legal fees, promoters' fees, and amounts paid to secure a charter, are called **organization costs.** On the corporation's books, these costs are debited to an asset account called Organization Costs. In a sense, this intangible asset benefits the corporation throughout its life. Thus, you could argue that the cost should be amortized over the life of the corporation, which may be unlimited. However, generally accepted accounting principles require any intangible asset to be amortized over a period that is no longer than 40 years.[3]

Income tax rules permit a corporation to write off organization costs as a tax deduction over a minimum of five years. Thus, to make record-keeping simple, many corporations use a five-year amortization period for financial statement purposes. Although the five-year period is arbitrary, it is widely used in practice. Because organization costs usually are not material in amount, the *materiality principle* also supports the arbitrarily short amortization period.

MANAGEMENT OF A CORPORATION

Although the organizational structures of all corporations are not always the same, the ultimate control of a corporation rests with its stockholders. However, this control is exercised only indirectly through the election of the board of directors. Indi-

---

[2]Some corporations that have a limited number of shareholders can elect to be treated like a partnership for tax purposes. These companies are called *Sub-Chapter S Corporations.*

[3]FASB, *Accounting Standards—Current Text* (Norwalk, CT, 1994), sec. I60.110. First published in *APB Opinion No. 17,* par. 29.

vidual stockholders' rights to participate in management begin and end with a vote in the stockholders' meetings, where each of them has one vote for each share of stock owned.

Normally, a corporation holds a stockholders' meeting once each year to elect directors and transact other business as required by the corporation's bylaws. A group of stockholders that owns or controls the votes of 50% plus one share of a corporation's stock can easily elect the board and thereby control the corporation. However, in many companies, very few stockholders attend the annual meeting or even care about getting involved in the voting process. As a result, a much smaller percentage may be able to dominate the election of board members.

Stockholders who do not attend stockholders' meetings must be given an opportunity to delegate their voting rights to an agent. A stockholder does this by signing a document called a **proxy** that gives a designated agent the right to vote the stock. Prior to a stockholders' meeting, a corporation's board of directors typically mails to each stockholder an announcement of the meeting and a proxy that names the existing board chairperson as the voting agent of the stockholder. The announcement asks the stockholder to sign and return the proxy.

A corporation's board of directors is responsible for and has final authority for managing the corporation's activities. However, it can act only as a collective body. An individual director has no power to transact corporate business. Although the board has final authority, it usually limits its actions to establishing broad policy. Day-to-day direction of corporate business is delegated to executive officers appointed by the board.

Traditionally, the chief executive officer (CEO) of the corporation is the president. Under the president, several vice presidents may be assigned specific areas of management responsibility, such as finance, production, and marketing. In addition, the corporation secretary keeps the minutes of the meetings of the stockholders and directors and ensures that all legal responsibilities are fulfilled. In a small corporation, the secretary is also responsible for keeping a record of the stockholders and the changing amounts of their stock interest.

Many corporations have a different structure in which the chairperson of the board of directors is also the chief executive officer. With this arrangement, the president is usually designated the chief operating officer (COO), and the rest of the structure is essentially the same.

STOCK CERTIFICATES AND THE TRANSFER OF STOCK

When investors buy a corporation's stock, they may receive a stock certificate as proof that they purchased the shares.[4] In many corporations, only one certificate is issued for each block of stock purchased. This certificate may be for any number of shares. Other corporations may use preprinted certificates, each of which represents 100 shares, plus blank certificates that may be made out for any number of shares.

When selling shares of a corporation, a stockholder completes and signs a transfer endorsement on the back of the certificate and sends it to the corporation's secretary or the transfer agent. The secretary or agent cancels and files the old certificate, and issues a new certificate to the new stockholder. If the old certificate represents more shares than were sold, the corporation issues two new certificates. One certificate goes to the new stockholder for the sold shares and the other to the original stockholder for the remaining unsold shares.

---

[4] The issuance of certificates is less common than it used to be. Instead, many stockholders maintain accounts with the corporation or their stockbrokers and never receive certificates.

Registrar and Transfer Agent

If a corporation's stock is traded on a major stock exchange, the corporation must have a *registrar* and a *transfer agent.* The registrar keeps the stockholder records and prepares official lists of stockholders for stockholders' meetings and for dividend payments. Registrars and transfer agents usually are large banks or trust companies that have the computer facilities and staff to carry out this kind of work.

When a corporation has a transfer agent and a stockholder wants to transfer ownership of some shares to another party, the owner completes the transfer endorsement on the back of the stock certificate and sends the certificate to the transfer agent, usually with the assistance of a stockbroker. The transfer agent cancels the old certificate and issues one or more new certificates and sends them to the registrar. The registrar enters the transfer in the stockholder records and sends the new certificate or certificates to the proper owners.

Progress Check

(Answers to Progress Checks are provided at the end of the chapter.)

13–1   Which of the following is not a characteristic of the corporate form of business?
(a) Ease of capital accumulation;   *(b)* Stockholders are liable for corporate debts;
(c) Ownership rights are easily transferred.

13–2   Why is the income of a corporation said to be taxed twice?

13–3   What is a proxy?

AUTHORIZATION AND ISSUANCE OF STOCK

LO 2

Record the issuance of par value stock and no-par stock with or without a stated value, and explain the concept of minimum legal capital.

When a corporation is organized, its charter authorizes it to issue a specified number of shares of stock. If all of the authorized shares have the same rights and characteristics, the stock is called **common stock.** However, a corporation may be authorized to issue more than one class of stock, including different classes of common stock and preferred stock. (We discuss preferred stock later in this chapter.) For example, **American Greetings Corporation** has two types of common stock outstanding. Class A stock has one vote per share and Class B stock has ten votes per share.

Because a corporation cannot issue more than the number of shares authorized in its charter, its founders usually obtain authorization to issue more shares than they plan to sell when the company is first organized. By doing so, the corporation avoids

having to get the state's approval to sell more shares when additional capital is needed to finance an expansion of the business. A corporation's balance sheet must disclose the numbers of shares authorized and issued. These facts are reported in the stockholders' equity section of the statement. For example, **Federal Express Corporation's** balance sheet in Appendix G shows this information:

	1993	1992
Common stock, $.10 par value; 100,000,000 shares authorized, 54,743,000 and 54,100,000 shares issued	$5,474,300	$5,410,000

Sale of Stock for Cash

When stock is sold for cash and immediately issued, an entry like the following is made to record the sale and issuance:

June	5	Cash	300,000.00	
		Common Stock, $10 Par Value		300,000.00
		Sold at par and issued 30,000 shares of $10 par value		
		common stock.		

Exchanging Stock for Noncash Assets

A corporation may accept assets other than cash in exchange for its stock. In the process, the corporation also may assume some liabilities, such as a mortgage on some of the property. These transactions are recorded with an entry like this:

June	10	Machinery	10,000.00	
		Buildings	65,000.00	
		Land	15,000.00	
		Long-Term Notes Payable		50,000.00
		Common Stock, $10 Par Value		40,000.00
		Exchanged 4,000 shares of $10 par value common stock		
		for machinery, buildings, and land.		

This entry records the acquired assets and the new liability at their fair market values as of the date of the transaction. It also records the difference between the combined fair values of the assets and the liability as an increase in stockholders' equity. If reliable fair values for the assets and liabilities cannot be determined, the fair market value of the stock may be used to estimate their values.

A corporation also may give shares of its stock to its promoters in exchange for their services in organizing the company. In this case, the corporation receives the intangible asset of being organized in exchange for its stock. The company's bookkeeper records this transaction as follows:

June	5	Organization Costs	5,000.00	
		Common Stock, $10 Par Value		5,000.00
		Gave the promoters 500 shares of $10 par value common		
		stock in exchange for their services in organizing the		
		corporation.		

PAR VALUE AND MINIMUM LEGAL CAPITAL

Many stocks have a **par value,** which is an arbitrary value assigned to the stock when it is authorized. A corporation may choose to issue stock with a par value of any amount. For example, **Sara Lee Corporation's** common stock has a par value of $1.33⅓. Widely used par values are $100, $25, $10, $5, $1, and $0.01. When a corporation issues par value stock, the par value is printed on each certificate and used in accounting for the stock.

In many states, the par value of a corporation's stock also establishes the **minimum legal capital** for the corporation. Laws that establish minimum legal capital normally require stockholders to invest assets equal in value to at least that amount.

Otherwise, the stockholders are liable to the corporation's creditors for the deficiency. Usually, the minimum legal capital is defined as the par value of the issued stock. In other words, persons who buy stock from a corporation must give the corporation assets equal in value to at least the par value of the stock or be subject to making up the difference later. For example, if a corporation issues 1,000 shares of $100 par value stock, the minimum legal capital of the corporation is $100,000. Minimum legal capital requirements also make it illegal to pay any dividends if they will reduce the stockholders' equity below the minimum amount.

The requirements for minimum legal capital are intended to protect the creditors of a corporation. Because a corporation's creditors cannot demand payment from the personal assets of the stockholders, the assets of the corporation are all that is available to satisfy the creditors' claims. To protect a corporation's creditors under these conditions, the minimum legal capital requirement limits a corporation's ability to distribute its assets to its stockholders. The idea is that assets equal to the amount of minimum legal capital cannot be paid to the stockholders unless all creditor claims are paid first.

Because par value determines the amount of minimum legal capital in many states, it is traditionally used in accounting for the part of stockholders' equity derived from the issuance of stock. However, par value does not establish a stock's market value or the price at which a corporation must issue the stock. If purchasers are willing to pay more, a corporation may sell and issue its stock at a price above par.

STOCK PREMIUMS AND DISCOUNTS

Premiums on Stock

When a corporation sells its stock at a price above the par value, the stock is said to be issued at a premium. For example, if a corporation sells and issues its $10 par value common stock at $12 per share, the stock is sold at a $2 per share premium. A **premium on stock** is an amount in excess of par paid by the purchasers of newly issued stock. It is not a revenue and does not appear on the income statement. Rather, a premium is reported on the balance sheet as part of the stockholders' investment.

In accounting for stock sold at a price greater than its par value, the premium is recorded separately from the par value and is called *contributed capital in excess of par value*. For example, assume that a corporation sells and issues 10,000 shares of its $10 par value common stock for cash at $12 per share. The sale is recorded as follows:

Dec.	1	Cash	120,000.00	
		Common Stock, $10 Par Value		100,000.00
		Contributed Capital in Excess of Par Value, Common Stock		20,000.00
		Sold and issued 10,000 shares of $10 par value common stock at $12 per share.		

When a balance sheet is prepared, any contributed capital in excess of par value is added to the par value of the stock in the equity section, as shown in the following example:

Stockholders' Equity

Common stock, $10 par value, 25,000 shares authorized, 20,000 shares issued and outstanding	$200,000
Contributed capital in excess of par value, common stock . .	30,000
Total contributed capital	$230,000
Retained earnings	82,400
Total stockholders' equity	$312,400

Discounts on Stock

If stock is issued at a price below par value, the difference between par and the issue price is called a **discount on stock.** Most states prohibit the issuance of stock at a discount because the stockholders would be investing less than minimum legal capital. In states that allow stock to be issued at a discount, its purchasers usually become contingently liable to the corporation's creditors for the amount of the discount. Therefore, stock is seldom issued at a discount. However, if stock is issued at less than par, the discount is not an expense and does not appear on the income statement. Rather, the amount of the discount is debited to a discount account that is contra to the common stock account. The balance of the discount account is subtracted from the par value of the stock on the balance sheet.

At one time, all stocks were required to have a par value. Today, nearly all states permit the issuance of stocks that do not have a par value. The primary advantage of **no-par stock** is that it may be issued at any price without having a discount liability attached. Also, printing a par value of, say, $100 on a stock certificate may cause an inexperienced person to think that the share must be worth $100. Therefore, eliminating par value may encourage a closer analysis of the factors that give a stock value. These factors include such things as expected future earnings and dividends, and prospects for the economy as a whole.

NO-PAR STOCK

In some states, the entire proceeds from the sale of no-par stock becomes minimum legal capital. In this case, the entire proceeds are credited to a no-par stock account. For example, if a corporation issues 1,000 shares of no-par stock at $42 per share, the transaction is recorded like this:

Oct.	20	Cash	42,000.00	
		Common Stock, No-Par		42,000.00
		Sold and issued 1,000 shares of no-par common stock at $42 per share.		

In other states, the board of directors of a corporation places a **stated value** on its no-par stock. The stated value becomes the minimum legal capital and is credited to the no-par stock account. If the stock is issued at an amount in excess of stated value, the excess is credited to Contributed Capital in Excess of Stated Value, No-Par Common Stock. For example, suppose that a corporation issues 1,000 shares of no-par common stock with a stated value of $25 per share for cash of $42 per share. The transaction is recorded as follows:

Oct.	20	Cash	42,000.00	
		Common Stock, No-Par		25,000.00
		Contributed Capital in Excess of		
		Stated Value, No-Par Common Stock		17,000.00
		Sold 1,000 shares of no-par stock having a $25 per share stated value at $42 per share.		

Progress Check

13–4 **A company issued 7,000 shares of its $10 par value common stock in exchange for equipment valued at $105,000. The entry to record the transaction would include a credit to:**
a. **Contributed Capital in Excess of Par Value, Common Stock for $35,000;**
b. **Retained Earnings for $35,000;**
c. **Common Stock, $10 Par Value for $105,000.**

13-5 What is a stock premium?

13-6 Who is intended to be protected by minimum legal capital?

SALE OF STOCK THROUGH SUBSCRIPTIONS

LO 3

Record transactions that involve dividends and stock subscriptions and explain the effects of stock subscriptions on the balance sheet.

Usually, stock is sold for cash and immediately issued. However, corporations sometimes sell stock through **stock subscriptions.** For example, when a new corporation is formed, the organizers may realize that the new business has limited immediate needs for cash but will need additional capital in the future. To get the corporation started on a sound footing, the organizers may sell the stock to investors who agree to contribute some cash now and to make additional contributions in the future. When stock is sold through subscriptions, the investor agrees to buy a certain number of the shares at a specified price. The agreement also states when payments are to be made.

To illustrate the sale of stock through subscriptions, assume that Northgate Corporation accepted subscriptions on May 6 to 5,000 shares of its $10 par value common stock at $12 per share. The subscription contracts called for a 10% down payment with the balance to be paid in two equal installments due after three and six months. Northgate records the subscriptions with the following entry:

May	6	Subscriptions Receivable, Common Stock	60,000.00	
		Common Stock Subscribed		50,000.00
		Contributed Capital in Excess of Par Value, Common Stock		10,000.00
		Accepted subscriptions to 5,000 shares of $10 par value common stock at $12 per share.		

At the time that subscriptions are accepted, the firm debits the Subscriptions Receivable account for the sum of the stock's par value and premium. This is the total amount the subscribers agreed to pay. Notice that the *Common Stock Subscribed* account (an equity) is credited for par value and that the premium is credited to Contributed Capital in Excess of Par Value, Common Stock.

The receivables are converted into cash when the subscribers pay for their stock. And, when all the payments are received, the subscribed stock is issued. Northgate records the receipt of the down payment and the two installment payments with these entries:

May	6	Cash	6,000.00	
		Subscriptions Receivable, Common Stock		6,000.00
		Collected 10% down payments on the common stock subscriptions.		
Aug.	6	Cash	27,000.00	
		Subscriptions Receivable, Common Stock		27,000.00
		Collected the first installment payments on the common stock subscriptions.		
Nov.	6	Cash	27,000.00	
		Subscriptions Receivable, Common Stock		27,000.00
		Collected the second installment payments on the common stock subscriptions.		

In this case, the down payments accompanied the subscriptions. Therefore, the accountant could have combined the May 6 entries to record the subscriptions and the down payments as follows:

May	6	Cash	6,000.00	
		Subscriptions Receivable, Common Stock	54,000.00	
		Common Stock Subscribed		50,000.00
		Contributed Capital in Excess of Par		
		Value, Common Stock		10,000.00
		Accepted subscriptions to 5,000 shares of $10 par value common stock at $12 per share and received down payments of 10% of the subscription price.		

When stock is sold through subscriptions, the stock usually is not issued until the subscriptions are paid in full. Also, if dividends are declared before subscribed stock has been issued, the dividends go only to the holders of outstanding shares, not to the subscribers. However, as soon as the subscriptions are paid, the stock is issued. The entry to record the issuance of the Northgate common stock is as follows:

Nov.	6	Common Stock Subscribed	50,000.00	
		Common Stock, $10 Par Value		50,000.00
		Issued 5,000 shares of common stock sold through subscriptions.		

Subscriptions are usually collected in full, but not always. Sometimes, a subscriber fails to pay the agreed amount. When this default happens, the subscription contract is canceled. If the subscriber has made a partial payment on the contract, the amount may be refunded. Or, the company may issue a smaller amount of stock with a fair value equal to the partial payment. Or, the state law may allow the subscriber's partial payment to be kept by the corporation to compensate it for any damages.

Subscriptions Receivable and Subscribed Stock on the Balance Sheet

If the collection of stock subscriptions is questionable, they should be subtracted from contributed capital on the balance sheet. Otherwise, if the corporation is confident of collection, they may be reported on the balance sheet as current or long-term assets, depending on when collection is expected. If a corporation prepares a balance sheet after accepting subscriptions to its stock but before the stock is issued, both the issued stock and the subscribed stock should be reported on the balance sheet as follows:

Common stock, $10 par value, 25,000 shares authorized, 20,000 shares issued and outstanding	$200,000	
Common stock subscribed, 5,000 shares	50,000	
Total common stock issued and subscribed . .	$250,000	
Contributed capital in excess of par value, common stock		40,000
Total contributed capital		$290,000

Many corporations pay cash dividends to their stockholders in regular amounts at regular dates. These cash flows provide a return to the investors and usually affect the stock's market value. Three dates are involved in the process of declaring dividends.

The day the directors vote to pay a dividend is called the **date of declaration.** Stockholders receive a dividend only if the directors formally vote to declare one. By

CORPORATE DIVIDENDS

declaring a dividend, the directors create a legal liability of the corporation to its stock-holders.

In its declaration, the directors specify a future date on which the persons listed in the corporation's records are identified as those who will receive the dividend. In most cases, this **date of record** follows the date of declaration by at least two weeks. Persons who buy stock in time to be recorded as stockholders on the date of record will receive the dividend.

The declaration by the board of directors also specifies a **date of payment,** which follows the date of record by enough time to allow the corporation to prepare checks payable to the stockholders. If a balance sheet is prepared between the date of declaration and the date of payment, the liability for the dividend is reported as a current liability.

Accounting for Dividends

Because the act of declaring a dividend creates a liability for the corporation, the accountant needs to record the new obligation. This entry would be recorded if the directors of a company with 5,000 outstanding shares declare a $1 per share dividend on January 9, payable on February 1:

Jan.	9	Cash Dividends Declared	5,000.00	
		Common Dividend Payable		5,000.00
		Declared a $1 per share cash dividend on the common stock.		

Cash Dividends Declared is a temporary account that accumulates information about the total dividends declared during the reporting period. It serves the same purpose as the Withdrawals account for a proprietorship. Note that it is not an expense account. The credited account describes the corporation's liability to its stockholders.

No entry is needed at the date of record. And on the payment date, the following entry records the settlement of the liability and the reduction of the cash balance:

Feb.	1	Common Dividend Payable	5,000.00	
		Cash		5,000.00
		Paid the $1 per share cash dividend to the common stockholders.		

At the end of the annual reporting period, the balance of the Cash Dividends Declared account is closed to Retained Earnings. For example, if the company declared four quarterly dividends of $5,000, the account has a $20,000 balance at the end of the year, and the accountant makes this closing entry:

Dec.	31	Retained Earnings	20,000.00	
		Cash Dividends Declared		20,000.00
		To close the Cash Dividends Declared account.		

If one of the declared dividends remains unpaid on December 31, this closing entry is still recorded because the act of declaration reduces retained earnings. The liability account continues to have a balance until the dividends are paid, and its amount is presented on the December 31 balance sheet.

Deficits and Dividends

A corporation with a debit balance of retained earnings is said to have a **deficit.** A deficit arises when a company incurs cumulative losses and pays dividends greater than the cumulative profits earned in other years. A deficit is deducted on a corporation's balance sheet, as in this example:

Stockholders' Equity

Common stock, $10 par value, 5,000 shares authorized and outstanding	$50,000
Deduct retained earnings deficit	(6,000)
Total stockholders' equity	$44,000

In most states, a corporation with a deficit is not allowed to pay a cash dividend to its stockholders. This legal restriction is designed to protect the creditors of the corporation by preventing the distribution of assets to stockholders at a time when the company is in financial difficulty.

Progress Check

13-7   Siskel Co. accepted subscriptions for 9,000 shares of $10 par value common stock at $48 per share. A 10% down payment was made on the date of the contract, the balance to be paid in full in six months. The entries to record receipt of the final balance and the issuance of the stock would include a credit to: *(a)* Subscriptions Receivable, Common Stock for $432,000;   *(b)* Common Stock Subscribed for $432,000;   *(c)* Common Stock, $10 Par Value for $90,000.

13-8   How is the Common Stock Subscribed account classified on the balance sheet?

13-9   In accounting for cash dividends that have been declared but not paid, the Cash Dividends Declared account is: *(a)* Reported on the balance sheet as a liability;   *(b)* Closed to Income Summary;   *(c)* Closed to Retained Earnings.

13-10   What three dates are normally involved in the declaration and payment of a cash dividend?

When investors buy a corporation's common stock, they acquire all the *specific* rights granted by the corporation's charter to its common stockholders. They also acquire the *general* rights granted stockholders by the laws of the state in which the company is incorporated. State laws vary, but common stockholders usually have the following general rights:

1. The right to vote at stockholders' meetings.
2. The right to sell or otherwise dispose of their stock.
3. The right of first opportunity to purchase any additional shares of common stock issued by the corporation. This right is called the common stockholders' **preemptive right**. It gives stockholders the opportunity to protect their proportionate interest in the corporation. For example, a stockholder who owns 25% of a corporation's common stock has the first opportunity to buy 25% of any new common stock issued. This arrangement enables the stockholder to maintain a 25% interest.

RIGHTS OF COMMON STOCKHOLDERS

LO 4

State the differences between common and preferred stock, and allocate dividends between the common and preferred stock of a corporation.

4. The right to share equally with other common stockholders in any dividends, with the result that each common share receives the same amount.

5. The right to share equally in any assets that remain after creditors are paid when the corporation is liquidated, with the result that each common share receives the same amount.

In addition, stockholders have the right to receive timely reports that describe the corporation's financial position and the results of its activities.

PREFERRED STOCK

As mentioned earlier in this chapter, a corporation may be authorized to issue more than one kind or class of stock. If two classes of common stock are issued, the primary difference between them often is only a matter of voting rights. However, some companies issue two classes of stock with one class being a **preferred stock** and the other class being a common stock.

Preferred stock often has a par value, but like common stock, may be sold at a price that differs from par. Separate contributed capital accounts are used to record the issuance of preferred stock. For example, if 50 shares of preferred stock with a $100 par value are issued for $6,000 cash, the entry is:

June	1	Cash	6,000.00	
		Preferred Stock		5,000.00
		Contributed Capital in Excess of Par Value, Preferred Stock		1,000.00
		Issued preferred stock for cash.		

The term *preferred* is used because the preferred shares have a higher priority (or senior status) relative to common shares in one or more ways. These typically include a preference for receiving dividends and a preference in the distribution of assets if the corporation is liquidated.

In addition to the preferences it receives, preferred stock carries all the rights of common stock, unless they are nullified in the corporation's charter. For example, most preferred stock does not have the right to vote.

Preferred Dividends

A preference for dividends gives preferred stockholders the right to receive their dividends before the common stockholders receive a dividend. In other words, a dividend cannot be paid to common stockholders unless preferred stockholders also receive one. The amount of dividends that the preferred stockholders must receive is usually expressed as a dollar amount per share or as a percentage applied to the par value. For example, the December 31, 1993, balance sheet of **Pitney Bowes, Inc.**, showed that the company had 4%, $50 par value, preferred stock outstanding. These shares required the company to pay quarterly dividends of $0.50 per share (an annual rate of $2 or 4% of par) before the common shareholders could receive a dividend.

A preference for dividends does not, however, grant an absolute right to dividends. If the board of directors does not declare a dividend, neither the preferred nor the common stockholders receive one.

Cumulative and Noncumulative Preferred Stock

Most preferred stock is **cumulative** but some is **noncumulative**. For noncumulative, the right to receive dividends is forfeited in any year that the dividends are not declared. When preferred stock is cumulative and the board of directors fails to declare a dividend to the preferred stockholders, the unpaid dividend is called a **dividend in arrears.** The accumulation of dividends in arrears on cumulative preferred stock does not guarantee that they will be paid. However, the cumulative preferred stockholders must be paid both the current dividend and all dividends in arrears before any dividend can be paid to the common stockholders.

To show the difference between cumulative and noncumulative preferred stock, assume that a corporation's outstanding stock includes 1,000 shares of $100 par, 9% preferred stock and 4,000 shares of $50 par, common stock. During 19X1, the first year of the corporation's operations, the board of directors declared cash dividends of $5,000. During 19X2, it declared $42,000. The allocations of the total dividends are as follows:

	Preferred	Common
Assuming noncumulative preferred:		
19X1	$ 5,000	$ 0
19X2:		
First: current preferred dividend	$ 9,000	
Remainder to common		$33,000
Assuming cumulative preferred:		
19X1	$ 5,000	$ 0
19X2:		
First: dividends in arrears	$ 4,000	
Next: current preferred dividend	9,000	
Remainder to common		$29,000
Totals	$13,000	$29,000

Notice that the allocation of the 19X2 dividends depends on whether the preferred stock is noncumulative or cumulative. With noncumulative preferred stock, the preferred stockholders never receive the $4,000 that was skipped in 19X1. However, when the preferred stock is cumulative, the $4,000 in arrears is paid in 19X2 before the common stockholders receive a dividend.

Disclosure of Dividends in Arrears in the Financial Statements

Dividends are not like interest expense, which is incurred as time passes and therefore must be accrued. A liability for a dividend does not come into existence until the dividend is declared by the board of directors. Thus, if a preferred dividend date passes and the corporation's board fails to declare the dividend on its cumulative preferred stock, the dividend in arrears is not a liability. However, when preparing the financial statements, the *full-disclosure principle* requires the corporation to report the amount of preferred dividends in arrears as of the balance sheet date. Normally, this information is given in a footnote.

Participating Preferred Stock—A Defense Against Hostile Takeovers

The dividends on most preferred stocks are limited to a maximum amount each year. The maximum is defined as a stated percentage of the stock's par value or as a specific dollar amount per share. Once the preferred stockholders receive this amount, the common stockholders receive any and all additional dividends. Preferred stocks that have this limitation are called *nonparticipating*. However, the owners of **participating preferred stock** have the right to share with the common stockholders in any additional dividends paid in excess of the stated percentage dividend on the preferred.

Although many corporations are authorized to issue participating preferred stock, the shares are rarely issued. That is, companies obtain authorization to issue the shares even though management does not expect to ever sell them. They do this to defend against a *takeover* of the corporation by an unfriendly investor (or a group of investors) who would buy enough voting common stock to gain control over operations. Using terminology from spy novels, the financial world refers to this kind of a plan as a *poison pill* that the company will swallow if it is threatened with capture by an enemy.

A typical poison pill works as follows: The common stockholders on a given date are granted the right to purchase a large amount of participating preferred stock at a very low price. This right cannot be transferred. Thus, if the stock is sold, the buyer does not gain the right. In addition, this right cannot be exercised unless the directors identify a buyer of a large block of common shares as an unfriendly buyer.

If an unfriendly investor were identified and the preferred stock were issued, future dividends would be divided between the preferred shares and the common shares. This would transfer some of the value of the common shares to the preferred shares. As a result, the stock owned by the unfriendly buyer would lose much of its value and be worth much less than the buyer's cost. The ultimate effect is to eliminate the potential benefit of attempting a hostile takeover.

WHY PREFERRED STOCK IS ISSUED

A corporation might issue nonparticipating preferred stock for several reasons. One reason is to raise capital without sacrificing control of the corporation. For example, suppose that the organizers of a business have $100,000 cash to invest but wish to organize a corporation that needs $200,000 of capital to get off to a good start. If they sold $200,000 of common stock, they would have only 50% control and would have to negotiate extensively with the other stockholders in making policy. However, if they issue $100,000 of common stock to themselves and can sell outsiders $100,000 of 8%, cumulative preferred stock that has no voting rights, they can retain control of the corporation.

A second reason for issuing preferred stock is to boost the return earned by the common stockholders. Using the previous example to illustrate, suppose that the corporation's organizers expect the new company to earn an annual after-tax income of $24,000. If they sell and issue $200,000 of common stock, this income produces a 12% return on the $200,000 of common stockholders' equity. However, if they issue $100,000 of 8% preferred stock to the outsiders and $100,000 of common stock to themselves, their own return increases to 16% per year, as shown here:

Net after-tax income	$24,000
Less preferred dividends at 8%	(8,000)
Balance to common stockholders (equal to 16% on their $100,000 investment)	$16,000

In this case, the common stockholders earn 16% because the assets contributed by the preferred stockholders are invested to earn $12,000 while the preferred dividend payments amount to only $8,000.

The use of preferred stock to increase the return to common stockholders is an example of **financial leverage.** Whenever the dividend rate on preferred stock is less than the rate that the corporation earns on its assets, the effect of issuing preferred stock is to increase (or *lever*) the rate earned by common stockholders. Financial leverage also occurs when debt is issued and paid an interest rate less than the rate earned from using the assets the creditors loaned to the corporation.

There are other reasons for issuing preferred stock. For example, a corporation's preferred stock may appeal to some investors who believe that its common stock is too risky or that the dividend rate on the common stock will be too low. Also, if a corporation's management wants to issue common stock but believes the current market price for the common stock is too low, the corporation may issue preferred stock that is convertible into common stock. If and when the price of the common stock increases, the preferred stockholders can convert their shares into common shares.

Progress Check

13-11 In what ways may preferred stock have a priority status to common stock?

13-12 Increasing the return to common stockholders by including preferred stock in the capital structure is an example of: (a) Financial leverage; (b) Cumulative earnings; (c) Dividends in arrears.

13-13 MBI Corp. has 9,000 shares of $50 par value, 10% cumulative and nonparticipating preferred stock and 27,000 shares of $10 par value common stock issued and outstanding. No dividends have been declared for the past two years, but during the current year, MBI declares a $288,000 dividend. The amount to be paid to common shareholders is: (a) $243,000; (b) $153,000; (c) $135,000.

As we just mentioned, an issue of preferred stock can be made more attractive to some investors by giving them the right to exchange the preferred shares for a fixed number of common shares. **Convertible preferred stock** offers investors a higher potential return than does nonconvertible preferred stock. If the company prospers and its common stock increases in value, the convertible preferred stockholders can share in the prosperity by converting their preferred stock into the more valuable common stock. Conversion is at the option of the investors and therefore does not occur unless it is to their advantage. (The investors can enjoy the results of the increased value of the common stock without converting the preferred stock because the preferred stock's market value reflects the change in the common stock's value.)

In addition to a par value, stocks may have a *call price,* a *market value,* and a *book value.*

Call Price of Callable Preferred Stock

Some issues of preferred stock are callable. This means that the issuing corporation has the right to retire the **callable preferred stock** by paying a specified amount to the preferred stockholders. The amount that must be paid to call and retire a preferred share is its **call price** or *redemption value.* This amount is set at the time the stock is issued. Normally, the call price includes the par value of the stock plus a premium that provides the stockholders with some additional return on their investment. When the issuing corporation calls and retires a preferred stock, it must pay not only the call price but also any dividends in arrears.

CONVERTIBLE PREFERRED STOCK

LO 5

Explain convertible preferred stock and describe the meaning of the par value, call price, market value, and book value of corporate stock.

STOCK VALUES

Illustration 13-1
Stockholders' Equity with
Preferred and Common
Stock

Stockholders' Equity		
Preferred stock, $100 par value, 7% cumulative,		
2,000 shares authorized, 1,000 shares		
issued and outstanding	$100,000	
Contributed capital in excess of par		
value, preferred stock	5,000	
Total capital contributed by preferred stockholders		$105,000
Common stock, $25 par value, 12,000 shares authorized,		
10,000 shares issued and outstanding	$250,000	
Contributed capital in excess of par		
value, common stock	10,000	
Total capital contributed by common stockholders		260,000
Total contributed capital		$365,000
Retained earnings		82,000
Total stockholders' equity		$447,000

Market Value

The market value of a share of stock is the price at which it can be bought or sold. Market values are influenced by a wide variety of factors including expected future earnings, dividends, and events in the economy at large. Market values of frequently traded stocks are reported daily in newspapers such as *The Wall Street Journal*. The market values of stocks that are not actively traded can be more difficult to determine. Analysts use a variety of techniques to estimate the value of such stocks, and most of these techniques use accounting information as an important input to the valuation process.

Book Value

The **book value of a share of stock** equals the share's portion of the stockholders' equity as it is recorded in the company's accounts. If a corporation has only common stock, the book value per share equals the total stockholders' equity divided by the number of outstanding shares. For example, if a company has 10,000 outstanding shares and total stockholders' equity of $285,000, the stock's book value is $28.50 per share ($285,000/10,000 shares).

Computing the book value of stock is more complex when both common and preferred shares are outstanding. To calculate the book values of each class of stock, you begin by allocating the total stockholders' equity between the two classes. The preferred stockholders' portion equals the preferred stock's call price (or par value if the preferred is not callable) plus any cumulative dividends in arrears. Then allocate the remaining stockholders' equity to the common shares. To determine the book value per share of preferred, divide the portion of stockholders' equity assigned to preferred by the number of preferred shares outstanding. Similarly, the book value per share of common is the stockholders' equity assigned to common divided by the number of outstanding common shares. For example, assume a corporation has the stockholders' equity as shown in Illustration 13–1.

If the preferred stock is callable at $108 per share and two years of cumulative preferred dividends are in arrears, the book values of the corporation's shares are calculated as follows:

Total stockholders' equity		$ 447,000
Less equity applicable to preferred shares:		
Call price (1,000 × $108)	$108,000	
Cumulative dividends in arrears ($100,000 × 7% × 2) . . .	14,000	(122,000)
Equity applicable to common shares		$ 325,000
Book value of preferred shares ($122,000/1,000)		$ 122.00
Book value of common shares ($325,000/10,000)		$ 32.50

In their annual reports to shareholders, corporations sometimes report the increase in the book value of the corporation's shares that has occurred during a year. Also, book value may have significance in contracts. For example, a stockholder may enter into a contract to sell shares at their book value at some future date. However, remember that book value normally does not approximate market value. For example, the book value per share of Anheuser-Busch Companies, Inc.'s common stock on December 31, 1993, was $15.94; this is significantly lower than its $49.125 market value on the same date.

Similarly, book value should not be confused with the liquidation value of a stock. If a corporation is liquidated, its assets probably will sell at prices that are quite different from the amounts at which they are carried on the books.

Progress Check

13-14 Potter Co.'s outstanding stock includes 1,000 shares of $90 par value cumulative preferred stock and 12,000 shares of $20 par value common stock. The call price of the preferred stock is $90 and dividends of $18,000 are in arrears. Total stockholders' equity is $630,000. What is the book value per share of the common shares?

13-15 The price at which a share of stock can be bought or sold is the: *(a)* Call price; *(b)* Redemption value; *(c)* Market value.

PARTNERSHIPS

A **partnership** can be defined as *an unincorporated association of two or more persons to carry on a business for profit as co-owners.* Many businesses, such as small retail and service businesses, are organized as partnerships. Also, many professional practitioners—including physicians, lawyers, and certified public accountants—have traditionally organized their practices as partnerships.

LO 6

Explain the concepts of mutual agency and unlimited liability for a partnership, record investments and withdrawals of partners, and allocate the net incomes or losses of a partnership among the partners.

A partnership is a voluntary association between the partners. All that is required to form a partnership is that two or more legally competent people (that is, people who are of age and of sound mental capacity) must agree to be partners. Their agreement becomes a **partnership contract.** Although it should be in writing, the contract is binding even if it is only expressed orally.[5]

The life of a partnership is always limited. Death, bankruptcy, or anything that takes away the ability of one of the partners to enter into or fulfill a contract

CHARACTERISTICS OF PARTNERSHIPS

---

[5] In some cases, courts have ruled that partnerships have been created by the actions of the partners, even when there was no expressed agreement to form a partnership.

automatically ends a partnership. In addition, a partnership may be terminated at will by any one of the partners. Before agreeing to join a partnership, you should understand clearly two important characteristics of a partnership: mutual agency and unlimited liability.

Mutual Agency

Generally, the relationship between the partners in a partnership involves **mutual agency.** Under normal circumstances, every partner is a fully authorized agent of the partnership. As its agent, a partner can commit or bind the partnership to any contract that is within the apparent scope of the partnership's business. For example, a partner in a merchandising business can sign contracts that bind the partnership to buy merchandise, lease a store building, borrow money, or hire employees. These activities are all within the scope of the business of a merchandising firm. On the other hand, a partner in a law firm, acting alone, cannot bind his or her partners to a contract to buy merchandise for resale or rent a retail store building. These actions are not within the normal scope of a law firm's business.

Partners may agree to limit the power of any one or more of the partners to negotiate certain contracts for the partnership. Such an agreement is binding on the partners and on outsiders who know that it exists. However, it is not binding on outsiders who do not know that it exists. Outsiders who are not aware of the agreement have the right to assume that each partner has normal agency powers for the partnership.

Because mutual agency exposes all partners to the risk of unwise actions by any one partner, people should carefully evaluate potential partners before agreeing to join a partnership. The importance of this advice is underscored by the fact that most partnerships are also characterized by unlimited liability.

Unlimited Liability of Partners

When a partnership cannot pay its debts, the creditors normally can satisfy their claims from the *personal* assets of the partners. Also, if some partners do not have enough assets to meet their share of the partnership's debts, the creditors can turn to the assets of the remaining partners who are able to pay. Because partners may be called on to pay all the debts of the partnership, each partner is said to have **unlimited liability** for the partnership's debts. Mutual agency and unlimited liability are the main reasons why most partnerships have only a few members.

Limited Partnerships and Limited Liability Partnerships

Partnerships in which all of the partners have unlimited liability are called **general partnerships.** Sometimes, however, individuals who want to invest in a partnership are not willing to accept the risk of unlimited liability. Their needs may be met by using a **limited partnership.** A limited partnership has two classes of partners, general and limited. At least one partner has to be a **general partner** who must assume unlimited liability for the debts of the partnership. The remaining **limited partners** have no personal liability beyond the amounts that they invest in the business. Usually, a limited partnership is managed by the general partner or partners. The limited partners have no active role except for major decisions specified in the partnership agreement.

A similar form of partnership that an increasing number of states are allowing professionals such as lawyers to use is the **limited liability partnership.** This type of partnership is designed to protect innocent partners from malpractice or negligence claims that result from the acts of another partner. When a partner provides service that results in a malpractice claim, that partner has personal liability for the claim. The remaining partners who were not responsible for the actions that resulted in the claim are not personally liable for the claim. However, all partners have personal liability for other partnership debts.

Accounting for a partnership does not differ from accounting for a proprietorship except for transactions that directly affect the partners' equity. Because ownership rights in a partnership are divided among the partners, partnership accounting:

- Uses a capital account for each partner.
- Uses a withdrawals account for each partner.
- Allocates net incomes or losses to the partners according to the provisions of the partnership agreement.

When partners invest in a partnership, their capital accounts are credited for the invested amounts. Partners' withdrawals of assets are debited to their withdrawals accounts. In closing the accounts at the end of the year, the partners' capital accounts are credited or debited for their shares of the net income or loss. Finally, the withdrawals account of each partner is closed to that partner's capital account. These closing procedures are like those used for a single proprietorship. The only difference is that separate capital and withdrawals accounts are maintained for each partner.

PARTNERSHIP ACCOUNTING

Because they are its owners, partners are not employees of the partnership. If partners devote their time and services to the affairs of their partnership, they are understood to do so for profit, not for salary. Therefore, when the partners calculate the net income of a partnership, salaries to the partners are not deducted as expenses on the income statement. However, when the net income or loss of the partnership is allocated among the partners, the partners may agree to base part of the allocation on salary allowances that reflect the relative values of service provided by the partners.

Partners are also understood to have invested in a partnership for profit, not for interest. Nevertheless, partners may agree that the division of partnership earnings should include a return based on their invested capital. For example, if one partner contributes five times as much capital as another, it is only fair that this fact be considered when earnings are allocated among the partners. Thus, a partnership agreement may provide for interest allowances based on the partners' capital balances. Like salary allowances, interest allowances are not expenses to be reported on the income statement.

NATURE OF PARTNERSHIP EARNINGS

In the absence of a contrary agreement, the law states that the income or loss of a partnership should be shared equally by the partners. However, partners may agree to any method of sharing. If they agree on how they will share income but say nothing about losses, then losses are shared in the same way as income.

Several methods of sharing partnership earnings can be used. Three frequently used methods divide earnings: (1) on a stated fractional basis, (2) in the ratio of capital investments, or (3) using salary and interest allowances and any remainder in a fixed ratio.

DIVISION OF EARNINGS

Earnings Allocated on a Stated Fractional Basis

An easy way to divide partnership earnings is to give each partner a fraction of the total. All that is necessary is for the partners to agree on the fractional share that each will receive. For example, assume that the partnership agreement of B. A. Jones and

	Share to Stanley	Share to Breck	Income to be Allocated
Total net income			$70,000
Allocated as salary allowances:			
Stanley	$36,000		
Breck		$24,000	
Total allocated as salary allowances			60,000
Balance of income after salary allowances			$10,000
Allocated as interest:			
Stanley (10% on $30,000)	3,000		
Breck (10% on $10,000)		1,000	
Total allocated as interest			4,000
Balance of income after salary and interest allowances			$ 6,000
Balance allocated equally:			
Stanley	3,000		
Breck		3,000	
Total allocated equally			6,000
Balance of income			$ 0
Shares of the partners	$42,000	$28,000	
Percentages of total net income	60%	40%	

S. A. Meyers states that Jones will receive two-thirds and Meyers will receive one-third of the partnership earnings. If the partnership's net income is $30,000, the earnings are allocated to the partners and the Income Summary account is closed with the following entry:

Dec.	31	Income Summary	30,000.00	
		B. A. Jones, Capital		20,000.00
		S. A. Meyers, Capital		10,000.00
		To close the Income Summary account and allocate the earnings.		

When earnings are shared on a fractional basis, the fractions may reflect the relative capital investments of the partners. For example, suppose that B. Donner and H. Flack formed a partnership and agreed to share earnings in the ratio of their investments. Because Donner invested $50,000 and Flack invested $30,000, Donner will receive five-eighths of the earnings ($50,000/$80,000) while Flack will receive three-eighths of the earnings ($30,000/$80,000).

Salaries and Interest as Aids in Sharing

As we have mentioned, the service contributions and capital contributions of the partners often are not equal. If the service contributions are not equal, salary allowances can compensate for the differences. Or, when capital contributions are not equal, interest allowances can compensate for the unequal investments. When both investment and service contributions are unequal, the allocation of net incomes and losses may include both interest and salary allowances.

For example, in Kathy Stanley and David Breck's new partnership, Stanley is to provide services that they agree are worth an annual salary of $36,000. Breck is less

Illustration 13-3
Sharing Income When
Interest and Salary
Allowances Exceed Income

	Share to Stanley	Share to Breck	Income to be Allocated
Total net income			$ 50,000
Allocated as salary allowances:			
Stanley	$36,000		
Breck		$24,000	
Total allocated as salary allowances			60,000
Balance of income after salary allowances			$ (10,000)
Allocated as interest:			
Stanley (10% on $30,000)	3,000		
Breck (10% on $10,000)		1,000	
Total allocated as interest			4,000
Balance of income after salary and interest allowances			$ (14,000)
Balance allocated equally:			
Stanley	(7,000)		
Breck		(7,000)	
Total allocated equally			(14,000)
Balance of income			$ 0
Shares of the partners	$32,000	$18,000	
Percentages of total net income	64%	36%	

experienced in the business, so his service contribution is worth only $24,000. Also, Stanley will invest $30,000 in the business and Breck will invest $10,000. To compensate Stanley and Breck fairly in light of the differences in their service and capital contributions, they agree to share incomes or losses as follows:

1. Annual salary allowances of $36,000 to Stanley and $24,000 to Breck.
2. Interest allowances equal to 10% of each partner's beginning-of-year capital balance.
3. The remaining balance of income or loss is to be shared equally.

Note that the provisions for salaries and interest in this partnership agreement are called *allowances*. These allowances are not reported on the income statement as salaries and interest expense. They are only a means of splitting up the net income or net loss of the partnership.

Under the Stanley and Breck partnership agreement, a first year's net income of $70,000 is shared as shown in Illustration 13–2. Notice that Stanley gets $42,000, or 60% of the income, while Breck gets $28,000, or 40%.

In Illustration 13–2, notice that the $70,000 net income exceeds the salary and interest allowances of the partners. However, the method of sharing agreed to by Stanley and Breck must be followed even if the net income is smaller than the salary and interest allowances. For example, if the first year's net income was $50,000, it would be allocated to the partners as shown in Illustration 13–3. Notice that this circumstance provides Stanley with 64% of the total income, while Breck gets only 36%.

A net loss would be shared by Stanley and Breck in the same manner as the $50,000 net income. The only difference is that the income-and-loss-sharing procedure would begin with a negative amount of income because of the net loss. After the salary and interest allowances, the remaining balance to be allocated equally would then be a larger negative amount.

13–16   A partnership is automatically terminated in the event: *(a)* **The partnership agree-ment is not in writing;**   *(b)* **A partner dies;**   *(c)* **A partner exercises mutual agency.**

13–17   **Mixon and Reed form a partnership by contributing $70,000 and $35,000 respec-tively. They agree to an interest allowance equal to 10% of each partner's capital balance at the beginning of the year with the remaining income to be shared equally. Allocate the first-year net income of $40,000 to the partners.**

13–18   **What does the term *unlimited liability* mean when it is applied to a partnership?**

USING THE INFORMATION— DIVIDEND YIELD

LO 7

Calculate dividend yield and de-scribe its meaning.

Investors buy shares of a company's stock in anticipation of receiving a return from cash dividends and from increases in the stock's value. Stocks that pay large divi-dends on a regular basis are sometimes called *income stocks.* They are attractive to investors who want dependable cash flows from their investments. In contrast, other stocks pay few or no dividends, but are still attractive to investors because they ex-pect the market value of the stocks to increase rapidly. The stocks of companies that do not distribute cash but use it to finance rapid expansion are often called *growth stocks.*

One way to evaluate whether a company stock should be viewed as an income stock or growth stock is to examine the **dividend yield.** The following formula shows that this ratio is a rate of return based on the annual cash dividends and the stock's market value:

$$\text{Dividend yield} = \frac{\text{Annual cash dividends per share}}{\text{Market value per share}}$$

Dividend yield may be calculated on a historical basis using the prior year's actual dividends or on an expected basis. For example, recall from the first page of this chap-ter the discussion of Mobil Corporation and the dividend and stock price information for several companies. The dividend yields for those companies were as follows:

Company	Common Dividend per share		November 1994 Stock Price	Dividend Yield	
	1994*	1993		1994*	1993
Mobil Corporation	$3.40	$3.25	$82¼	4.1%	4.0%
Minnesota Mining & Mfg. Co.	1.76	1.66	53¼	3.3	3.1
Texaco Inc.	3.20	3.20	60⅝	5.3	5.3
AT&T Corp.	1.32	1.32	54	2.4	2.4
GAP, Inc.	0.48	0.38	37⅞	1.3	1.0
Microsoft Corp.	0	0	64½	—	—

*Estimated 1994 amounts.

An investor can compare these dividend yields to evaluate the relative importance of dividends to the prices of the stocks. Current dividends obviously have no impact on Microsoft Corp.'s stock price and very little impact on the GAP, Inc.'s stock price. The values of these two stocks must stem from expected increases in their stock prices (and the eventual dividends that may be paid.)

On the other hand, Mobil Corporation and Texaco Inc. pay substantial dividends of 4.0 to 5.3%. These are less than one would expect from investments in corporate debt securities, but still high enough to conclude that dividends are a very important factor in establishing their stock prices.

Although income stocks tend to have relatively stable market values, their values can vary substantially in anticipation of changes in the company's ability to pay future dividends or changes in rates of returns on other available investments. Thus, investors should examine much more information in addition to the dividend yield before deciding to buy, sell, or keep a stock.

Progress Check

13-19   **Which of the following produces an expected dividend yield of 10% for common stock?**

  a. **Dividends of $100,000 are expected to be paid next year and expected net income is $1,000,000.**

  b. **Dividends of $50,000 were paid during the prior year and net income was $500,000.**

  c. **Dividends of $2 per share are expected to be paid next year and the current market value of the stock is $20 per share.**

SUMMARY OF THE CHAPTER IN TERMS OF LEARNING OBJECTIVES

LO 1.   Explain the unique characteristics of the corporate form of business. Corporations are separate legal entities. As such, their stockholders are not liable for the corporate debts. Stocks issued by corporations are easily transferred between stockholders, and the life of corporations does not end with the incapacity or death of a stockholder. A corporation acts through its agents, who are its officers and managers, not its stockholders. Corporations tend to be closely regulated by government and are subject to income taxes.

LO 2.   Record the issuance of par value stock and no-par stock with or without a stated value, and explain the concept of minimum legal capital. When stock is issued, the par or stated value is credited to the stock account and any excess is credited to a separate contributed capital account. If the stock has no par or stated value, the entire proceeds are credited to the stock account. Stockholders must contribute assets equal to the minimum legal capital of a corporation or be potentially liable for the deficiency. And, as long as any liabilities remain unpaid, the minimum legal capital cannot be paid to stockholders.

LO 3.   Record transactions that involve dividends and stock subscriptions and explain the effects of stock subscriptions on the balance sheet. If a corporation sells stock through subscriptions, the unpaid portion is recorded as a receivable, and the subscribers' equity is recorded in contributed capital accounts. The balance of the Common Stock Subscribed account is transferred to the Common Stock account when the shares are issued, which normally occurs after all payments are received. Three dates are involved when cash dividends are distributed to stockholders. The board of directors binds the company to pay the dividend on the date of declaration. The recipients of the dividend are identified on the date of record. The cash is paid to the stockholders on the date of payment.

LO 4.   State the differences between common and preferred stock, and allocate dividends between the common and preferred stock of a corporation. Preferred stock has a priority (or senior status) relative to common stock in one or more ways. Usually, common stockholders cannot be paid dividends unless a specified amount of dividends also is paid to preferred shareholders. Preferred stock also may have a priority status if the corporation is liquidated. The dividend preference for most preferred stocks is cumulative. Many companies are authorized to issue participating preferred stocks as a poison pill against hostile takeovers.

LO 5.   Describe convertible preferred stock and explain the meaning of the par value, call price, market value, and book value of corporate stock. Convertible preferred stock can be exchanged by its holders for common stock. If preferred stock is callable, the amount that must be paid to retire the stock is its call price plus any dividends in arrears. Market value is the price that a stock commands when it is bought or sold. The book value of preferred stock is any dividends in arrears plus its par value or, if it is callable, its call price. The remaining stockholders' equity is divided by the number of outstanding common shares to determine the book value per share of the common stock.

LO 6. Explain the concepts of mutual agency and unlimited liability for a partnership, record the investments and withdrawals of partners, and allocate the net incomes or losses of a partnership among the partners. Mutual agency means that every partner can bind a partnership to contracts that are within the normal scope of the business. In a general partnership, each partner has unlimited liability for the debts of the partnership. A partnership agreement should specify the method for allocating the partnership's net income or loss among the partners. This allocation may be done on a fractional basis, or it may use salary and interest allowances to compensate partners for differences in their service and capital contributions.

LO 7. Calculate dividend yield and describe its meaning. The dividend yield is the ratio between a stock's annual dividends per share and its market value per share. It describes the rate of return provided to the stockholders from the company's dividends. The yield can be compared with the rates of return offered by other kinds of investments to determine whether the stock should be viewed as an income or growth stock.

DEMONSTRATION PROBLEM

Barton Corporation was created on January 1, 19X1. The following transactions relating to stockholders' equity occurred during the first two years of the company's operations. Prepare the journal entries to record these transactions. Also prepare the balance sheet presentation of the organization costs, liabilities, and stockholders' equity as of December 31, 19X1, and December 31, 19X2. Include appropriate footnotes.

19X1

Jan. 1 Authorized the issuance of 2 million shares of $5 par value common stock and 100,000 shares of $100 par value preferred stock. The preferred stock pays a 10% annual dividend and is cumulative.

1 Issued 200,000 shares of common stock for cash at $12 per share.

1 Issued 100,000 shares of common stock in exchange for a building valued at $820,000 and merchandise inventory valued at $380,000.

1 Accepted subscriptions for 150,000 shares of common stock at $12 per share. The subscribers made no down payments, and the full purchase price was due on April 1, 19X1.

1 Paid a cash reimbursement to the company's founders for $100,000 of organization costs; these costs are to be amortized over 10 years.

1 Issued 12,000 shares of preferred stock for cash at $110 per share.

Apr. 1 Collected the full subscription price for the January 1 common stock and issued the stock.

Dec. 31 The Income Summary account for 19X1 had a $125,000 credit balance before being closed to Retained Earnings; no dividends were declared on either the common or preferred stocks.

19X2

June 4 Issued 100,000 shares of common stock for cash at $15 per share.

Dec. 10 Declared dividends payable on January 10, 19X3, as follows:

To preferred stockholders for 19X1	$120,000
To preferred stockholders for 19X2	120,000
To common stockholders for 19X2	300,000

31 The Income Summary account for 19X2 had a $1 million credit balance before being closed to Retained Earnings.

Planning the Solution

- Record journal entries for the events in 19X1 and 19X2.
- Close the accounts related to retained earnings at the end of each year.
- Determine the balances for the 19X1 and 19X2 balance sheets, including the following amounts to use in the balance sheet and the accompanying note:
  - *a.* The number of shares issued.
  - *b.* The amount of dividends in arrears.
  - *c.* The unamortized balance of organization costs.
- Prepare the specified portions of the 19X1 and 19X2 balance sheets.

Solution to
Demonstration
Problem

19X1				
Jan.	1	Cash	2,400,000.00	
		Common Stock		1,000,000.00
		Contributed Capital in Excess of		
		Par Value, Common Stock		1,400,000.00
		Issued 200,000 shares of common stock.		
	1	Building	820,000.00	
		Merchandise Inventory	380,000.00	
		Common Stock		500,000.00
		Contributed Capital in Excess of		
		Par Value, Common Stock		700,000.00
		Issued 100,000 shares of common stock.		
Jan.	1	Subscriptions Receivable	1,800,000.00	
		Common Stock Subscribed		750,000.00
		Contributed Capital in Excess of		
		Par Value, Common Stock		1,050,000.00
		Accepted subscriptions for 150,000 shares of		
		common stock.		
	1	Organization Costs	100,000.00	
		Cash...............................		100,000.00
		Reimbursed the founders for organization		
		costs.		
	1	Cash	1,320,000.00	
		Preferred Stock		1,200,000.00
		Contributed Capital in Excess of		
		Par Value, Preferred Stock		120,000.00
		Issued 12,000 shares of preferred stock.		
Apr.	1	Cash	1,800,000.00	
		Subscriptions Receivable		1,800,000.00
		Collected balance due on subscribed common		
		stock.		
	1	Common Stock Subscribed	750,000.00	
		Common Stock		750,000.00
		Issued 150,000 shares of subscribed common		
		stock.		
Dec.	31	Income Summary	125,000.00	
		Retained Earnings		125,000.00
		To close the Income Summary account and		
		update Retained Earnings.		

19X2					
June	4	Cash	1,500,000.00		
		Common Stock			500,000.00
		Contributed Capital in Excess of			
		Par Value, Common Stock			1,000,000.00
		Issued 100,000 shares of common stock.			
Dec.	10	Cash Dividends Declared	540,000.00		
		Common Dividend Payable			300,000.00
		Preferred Dividend Payable			240,000.00
		Declared current dividends and dividends in			
		arrears to common and preferred stockholders,			
		payable on January 10, 19X3.			
	31	Income Summary	1,000,000.00		
		Retained Earnings			1,000,000.00
		To close the Income Summary account and			
		update Retained Earnings.			
	31	Retained Earnings	540,000.00		
		Cash Dividends Declared			540,000.00
		To close the Cash Dividends Declared			
		account.			

Balance sheet presentations:

	As of December 31,	
	19X1	**19X2**
Assets		
Organization costs	$ 90,000	$ 80,000
Liabilities		
Common dividend payable		$ 300,000
Preferred dividend payable		240,000
Total liabilities		$ 540,000
Stockholders' Equity		
Contributed capital:		
Preferred stock, $100 par value,		
10% cumulative dividends, 100,000		
shares authorized, 12,000 shares issued		
and outstanding	$1,200,000	$1,200,000
Contributed capital in excess of		
par value, preferred stock	120,000	120,000
Total capital contributed by		
preferred stockholders	$1,320,000	$1,320,000
Common stock, $5 par value, 2,000,000		
shares authorized, 450,000 shares		
issued and outstanding in 19X1, and		
550,000 shares in 19X2	$2,250,000	$2,750,000
Contributed capital in excess of par value,		
common stock	3,150,000	4,150,000
Total capital contributed by		
common stockholders	$5,400,000	$6,900,000
Total contributed capital	$6,720,000	$8,220,000
Retained Earnings (see Note 1)	125,000	585,000
Total stockholders' equity	$6,845,000	$8,805,000

Note 1: As of December 31, 19X1, there were $120,000 of dividends in arrears on the preferred stock.

GLOSSARY

Book value of a share of stock one share's portion of the stockholders' equity recorded in the accounts. p. 500

Callable preferred stock preferred stock that the issuing corporation, at its option, may retire by paying a specified amount (the call price) to the preferred stockholders plus any dividends in arrears. p. 499

Call price of preferred stock the amount that must be paid to call and retire a preferred share. p. 499

Common stock stock of a corporation that has only one class of stock, or if there is more than one class, the class that has no preferences over the corporation's other classes of stock. p. 488

Convertible preferred stock a preferred stock that can be exchanged for shares of the issuing corporation's common stock at the option of the preferred stockholder. p. 499

Cumulative preferred stock preferred stock on which undeclared dividends accumulate until they are paid; common stockholders cannot receive a dividend until all cumulative dividends have been paid. p. 497

Date of declaration the date on which a corporation's board of directors votes to pay a dividend; the dividend becomes a liability on this date. p. 493

Date of payment the date on which a corporation actually disburses a cash dividend directly to the stockholders. p. 494

Date of record the date on which the corporation's records are examined to identify the stockholders who will receive a dividend. p. 494

Deficit a debit balance in the Retained Earnings account; this situation arises when a company's cumulative losses and dividends are greater than the cumulative profits earned in other years. p. 495

Discount on stock the difference between the par value of stock and its issue price when it is issued at a price below par value. p. 491

Dividend in arrears an unpaid dividend on cumulative preferred stock; it must be paid before any regular dividends on the preferred stock and before any dividends on the common stock. p. 497

Dividend yield a company's annual cash dividends per share divided by the market value per share. p. 506

Financial leverage the achievement of an increased return on common stock by paying dividends on preferred stock or interest at a rate that is less than the rate of return earned with the assets invested in the corporation by the preferred stockholders or creditors. p. 499

General partner a partner who assumes unlimited liability for the debts of the partnership; the general partner in a limited partnership is usually responsible for its management. p. 502

General partnership a partnership in which all partners have unlimited liability for partnership debts. p. 502

Limited liability partnership a partnership in which each partner is not personally liable for malpractice claims unless the partner was responsible for providing the service that resulted in the claim. p. 502

Limited partners partners who have no personal liability for debts of the partnership beyond the amounts they have invested in the partnership. p. 502

Limited partnership a partnership that has two classes of partners, limited partners and one or more general partners. p. 502

Minimum legal capital an amount of assets defined by state law that stockholders must invest and leave invested in a corporation; this provision is intended to protect the creditors of the corporation. p. 489

Mutual agency the legal relationship among the partners whereby each partner is an agent of the partnership and is able to bind the partnership to contracts within the apparent scope of the partnership's business. p. 502

Noncumulative preferred stock a preferred stock on which the right to receive dividends is forfeited for any year that the dividends are not declared. p. 497

No-par stock a class of stock that does not have a par value; no-par stock can be issued at any price without creating a discount liability. p. 491

Organization costs the costs of bringing a corporation into existence, including legal fees, promoters' fees, and amounts paid to the state to secure the charter. p. 486

Par value an arbitrary value assigned to a share of stock when the stock is authorized. p. 489

Participating preferred stock preferred stock that gives its owners the right to share in dividends in excess of the stated percentage or amount. p. 498

Partnership an unincorporated association of two or more persons to carry on a business for profit as co-owners. p. 501

Partnership contract the agreement between partners that sets forth the terms under which the affairs of the partnership will be conducted. p. 501

Preemptive right the right of common stockholders to protect their proportionate interest in a corporation by having the first opportunity to buy additional shares of common stock issued by the corporation. p. 495

Preferred stock stock that gives its owners a priority status over common stockholders in one or more ways, such as the payment of dividends or the distribution of assets upon liquidation. p. 496

Premium on stock the difference between the par value of stock and its issue price when it is issued at a price above par value. p. 490

Proxy a legal document that gives an agent of a stockholder the power to exercise the voting rights of that stockholder's shares. p. 487

Stated value of no-par stock   an arbitrary amount assigned to no-par stock by the corporation's board of directors; this amount is credited to the no-par stock account when the stock is issued. p. 491

Stock subscription   a contractual commitment by an investor to purchase unissued shares of stock and become a stockholder. p. 492

Unlimited liability of partners   the legal relationship among general partners that makes each of them responsible for paying all the debts of the partnership if the other partners are unable to pay their shares. p. 502

QUESTIONS

1. Who is responsible for directing the affairs of a corporation?

2. What are organization costs? List several examples of these costs.

3. How are organization costs classified on the balance sheet?

4. What are the duties and responsibilities of a corporation's registrar and transfer agent?

5. List the general rights of common stockholders.

6. What is the preemptive right of common stockholders?

7. What is the main advantage of no-par stock?

8. What is the difference between the par value and the call price of a share of stock?

9. Why would an investor find convertible preferred stock attractive?

10. Kurt and Ellen are partners in operating a store. Without consulting Kurt, Ellen contracts to purchase merchandise for the store. Kurt contends that he did not authorize the order and refuses to take delivery. Is the partnership obligated to pay? Why or why not?

11. Would your answer to Question 10 differ if Kurt and Ellen were partners in a public accounting firm?

12. Examine the balance sheet for Ben & Jerry's Homemade, Inc., in Appendix G at the end of the book and determine the classes of stock that the company has issued.

13. Examine the statement of changes in stockholders' equity (called the *consolidated statement of changes in common stockholders' investment*) for Federal Express Corporation in Appendix G at the end of the book and determine how many shares of common stock the company issued during the year ended May 31, 1993. Examine the company's balance sheet and determine the par value per share.

QUICK STUDY (Five-Minute Exercises)

QS 13–1
(LO 1)

Of the following statements, which are true for the corporate form of business?

a. Capital often is more easily accumulated than with other forms of organization.

b. It has a limited life.

c. Owners have unlimited liability for corporate debts.

d. Distributed income is taxed twice in normal circumstances.

e. It is a separate legal entity.

f. Ownership rights cannot be easily transferred.

g. Owners are not agents of the corporation.

QS 13–2
(LO 2)

On June 1, YMI Corporation issued 25,000 shares of $5 par value common stock for $168,000 cash. Present the entry to record this transaction.

QS 13–3
(LO 3)

On August 15, Retro Company accepted subscriptions to 12,000 shares of $1 par value common stock at $10 per share. A 20% down payment was made on this date with the remainder to be paid in six months. Prepare an entry to record this transaction.

Nosar Company's stockholders' equity includes 50,000 shares of $5 par value, 8%, cumulative, nonparticipating preferred stock and 200,000 shares of $1 par value common stock. Nosar did not declare any dividends during the prior year and now declares and pays a $72,000 cash dividend. Determine the amount distributed to each class of stockholders.

QS 13–4
(LO 4)

Prepare journal entries to record the following transactions for Gruene Corporation:

June 15 Declared a $24,000 cash dividend payable to common stockholders.

July 31 Paid the dividend declared on June 15.

Dec. 31 Closed the Cash Dividends Declared account.

QS 13–5
(LO 4)

The stockholders' equity section of Roscoe Company's balance sheet follows:

QS 13–6
(LO 5)

Stockholders' Equity

Preferred stock, 5% cumulative, $10 par value, 20,000 shares authorized, issued and outstanding	$ 200,000
Common stock, $5 par value, 200,000 shares authorized, 150,000 shares issued and outstanding	750,000
Retained earnings	890,000
Total stockholders' equity	$1,840,000

The call price of the preferred stock is $45 and one year's dividends are in arrears. Determine the book value per share of the common stock.

Fred Earnest and Jackie Magness are partners in a business they started two years ago. The partnership agreement states that Earnest should receive a salary allowance of $15,000 and that Magness should receive $20,000. Any remaining income or loss is to be shared equally. Determine each partner's share of the current year's net income of $52,000.

QS 13–7
(LO 6)

SOS Company expects to pay out a $4.50 per share cash dividend next year on its common stock. The current market price per share is $52.20. Calculate the expected dividend yield on the SOS stock.

QS 13–8
(LO 7)

EXERCISES

Present the general journal entries that an accountant would prepare to record the following issuances of stock in three different situations:

Exercise 13–1
Recording stock issuances
(LO 2)

a. Two thousand shares of $10 par value common stock are issued for $35,000 cash.

b. One thousand shares of no-par common stock are issued to the corporation's promoters in exchange for their efforts in creating it. Their efforts are estimated to be worth $15,000, and the stock has no stated value.

c. One thousand shares of no-par common stock are issued to the corporation's promoters in exchange for their efforts in creating it. Their efforts are estimated to be worth $15,000, and the stock has a $1 per share stated value.

Printers, Inc., issued 4,000 shares of its common stock for $96,000 cash on March 16. Present the journal entries that the company's accountant would use to record this event under each of the following situations:

Exercise 13–2
Accounting for par and no-par stock issuances
(LO 2)

a. The stock has no par or stated value.

b. The stock has a stated value of $8 per share.

c. The stock has a $20 par value.

Exercise 13–3
Interpreting journal entries for stock issuances and subscriptions
(LO 2, 3)

Each of these entries was recently recorded by a different corporation. Provide an explanation for the event or transaction described by each entry.

a.	Cash	40,000.00	
	Common Stock, No-Par	40,000.00	

b.	Merchandise Inventory	45,000.00	
	Machinery	65,000.00	
	Notes Payable		72,000.00
	Common Stock, $25 Par Value		20,000.00
	Contributed Capital in Excess of		
	Par Value, Common Stock		18,000.00

c.	Organization Costs	45,000.00	
	Common Stock, No-Par		33,000.00
	Contributed Capital in Excess of		
	Stated Value, No-Par Common Stock		12,000.00

d.	Cash	25,000.00	
	Subscriptions Receivable, Common Stock	75,000.00	
	Common Stock Subscribed		60,000.00
	Contributed Capital in Excess of		
	Par Value, Common Stock		40,000.00

Exercise 13–4
Stock subscriptions
(LO 3)

On February 15, Quality Care Corp. accepted subscriptions at $19 per share for 8,000 shares of its $10 par value common stock. The subscriptions called for 40% of the subscription price to be paid as a down payment with the balance due on April 15. Show the journal entries that the company's accountant would make to record these three events:

a. Accepting the subscriptions and the down payments.

b. Receiving the balance of the subscriptions on the due date.

c. Issuing the stock on the same date.

Exercise 13–5
Dividends on common and noncumulative preferred stock
(LO 4)

The outstanding stock of D. B. Copper Corp. includes 20,000 shares of noncumulative preferred stock with a $10 par value and a 7.5% dividend rate, as well as 50,000 shares of common stock with a $1 par value. During its first four years of operation, the corporation declared and paid the following total amounts of dividends:

19X1	$ 5,000
19X2	12,000
19X3	50,000
19X4	98,000

Determine the amount of dividends paid in each year to each class of stockholders. Also determine the total dividends paid to each class in the four years combined.

Exercise 13–6
Dividends on common and cumulative preferred stock
(LO 4)

Use the data in Exercise 13–5 to determine the amount of dividends paid in each year to each class of stockholders, assuming that the preferred stock is cumulative. Also determine the total dividends paid to each class in the four years combined.

Exercise 13–7
Using preferred stock to create leverage
(LO 4)

An individual entrepreneur is planning to start a new business and needs $625,000 of start-up capital. This person has $500,000 in personal assets that can be invested and thus needs to raise another $125,000 in cash. The founder will buy 10,000 shares of common stock for $500,000 and has two alternative plans for raising the additional cash. One plan is to sell 2,500 shares of common stock to one or more other investors for $125,000 cash. The second is to sell 1,250 shares of cumulative preferred stock to one or more investors for $125,000 cash (this stock has a $100 par value, an annual 8% dividend rate, and would be issued at par).

1. If the business is expected to earn $90,000 of after-tax net income in the first year, what rate of return on beginning equity will the founder earn under each alternative? Which of the two plans will provide the higher return to the founder?

2. If the business is expected to earn $21,000 of after-tax net income in the first year, what rate of return on beginning equity will the founder earn under each alternative? Which of the two plans will provide the higher return to the founder?

Match each of the numbered descriptions with the characteristic of preferred stock that it best describes. Indicate your answer by writing the letter for the correct characteristic in the blank space next to each description.

Exercise 13–8
Identifying characteristics of preferred stock
(LO 5)

A. Callable
B. Convertible
C. Cumulative

D. Noncumulative
E. Nonparticipating
F. Participating

__1. The holders of the stock can exchange it for shares of common stock.
__2. The issuing corporation can retire the stock by paying a prearranged price.
__3. The holders of the stock are entitled to receive dividends in excess of the stated rate under some conditions.

__4. The holders of the stock are not entitled to receive dividends in excess of the stated rate.
__5. The holders of the stock lose any dividends that are not declared.
__6. The holders of the stock are entitled to receive current and all past dividends before common stockholders receive any dividends.

On the following list of eight general characteristics of business organizations, write a brief description of how each characteristic applies to corporations and partnerships.

Exercise 13–9
Characteristics of corporations and partnerships
(LO 1, 6)

		Corporations	**Partnerships**
1.	Life		
2.	Owners' liability		
3.	Legal status		
4.	Tax status of income		
5.	Owners' authority		
6.	Ease of formation		
7.	Transferability of ownership		
8.	Ability to raise large amounts of capital		

Andy Anderson and Bobbie Buelow created a new business on April 11 when they each invested $60,000 cash in the company. On December 15, they decided that they would each receive $15,000 of the company's cash as a distribution. The checks were prepared and given to Anderson and Buelow on December 20. On December 31, the company's accountant determined that the company's net income was $44,000.

Exercise 13–10
Comparative entries for partnership and corporation
(LO 1, 6)

1. Assume that this company is a partnership and present the journal entries that the accountant would make to record these events: *(a)* investments by the owners, *(b)* the

cash distribution to the owners, and *(c)* the closing of the Income Summary and the owners' withdrawals accounts.

2. Assume that this company is a corporation and present the journal entries that the accountant would make to record these events: *(a)* investments by the owners, *(b)* the cash distribution to the owners, and *(c)* the closing of the Income Summary and dividends accounts. When the company was created, each owner acquired 2,000 shares of $25 par value common stock.

Exercise 13–11
Book value per share of stock
(LO 5)

The balance sheet for High Beams, Inc., includes the following information:

Stockholders' Equity

Preferred stock, 6% cumulative, $50 par value, $60 call price, 5,000 shares issued and outstanding	$ 250,000
Common stock, $20 par value, 40,000 shares issued and outstanding	800,000
Retained earnings	535,000
Total stockholders' equity	$1,585,000

Determine the book value per share of the preferred and common stock under these two situations:

a. No preferred dividends are in arrears.

b. Three years of preferred dividends are in arrears.

Exercise 13–12
Income allocation for a partnership
(LO 6)

Sells and Haskins began a partnership by investing $120,000 and $80,000, respectively. During its first year, the partnership earned $40,000. Show how the partnership's income would be allocated to the partners under each of the following situations:

a. The partners did not establish a method of sharing income.

b. The partners agreed to share incomes and losses in proportion to their initial investments.

c. The partners agreed to share incomes and losses with an $18,000 per year salary allowance to Sells, a $10,000 per year salary allowance to Haskins, 8% interest on their initial investments, and the balance equally.

Exercise 13–13
Calculating dividend yield
(LO 7)

Calculate the dividend yield for each of these situations:

		Annual Dividend per Share	Stock's Market Price per Share
a.	......	$6.00	$ 64.00
b.	......	3.00	30.50
c.	......	5.50	65.00
d.	......	0.60	43.00
e.	......	1.00	25.00
f.	......	7.50	108.00

PROBLEMS

Problem 13–1
Stock subscriptions
(LO 2, 3, 4)

On March 1, Mercer Corporation received authorization to issue up to 20,000 shares of $10 par value preferred stock that pays a 9% cumulative dividend. The company also is authorized to issue up to 100,000 shares of common stock that has no par value; however, the board of directors established a $2 stated value for this stock. The company then completed these transactions over the next three months:

Mar. 6 Accepted subscriptions to 15,000 shares of common stock at $5 per share. The subscribers each made down payments of 30% of the subscription price. The balance is due on May 6.

20 Issued 1,000 shares of common stock to the corporation's promoters for their services in organizing the corporation. The board valued the services at $5,000.

30 Accepted subscriptions to 4,000 shares of preferred stock at $12 per share. The subscribers each made down payments of 40% of the subscription price. The balance is due on May 30.

May 6 Collected the balance due on the March 6 common stock subscriptions and issued the shares.

12 Accepted subscriptions to 2,500 shares of preferred stock at $14 per share. The subscribers each made down payments of 40% of the subscription price. The balance is due on July 12.

30 Collected the balance due on the March 30 preferred stock subscriptions and issued the shares.

At the end of May, the balance of retained earnings is $16,000.

Required

Use the information about the transactions to prepare the stockholders' equity section of the company's balance sheet as of May 31. (Note: You will find it useful to prepare journal entries for the transactions to help you process the data.)

CHECK FIGURE:
Total equity, $179,000

Alabama Energy, Inc., was chartered at the beginning of the year and engaged in a number of transactions. The following journal entries affected its stockholders' equity during its first year of operations:

Problem 13–2
Stockholders' equity transactions
(LO 2, 3, 5, 7)

a.	Cash	300,000.00	
	Common Stock, $25 Par Value		250,000.00
	Contributed Capital in Excess of		
	Par Value, Common Stock		50,000.00
b.	Organization Costs	150,000.00	
	Common Stock, $25 Par Value		125,000.00
	Contributed Capital in Excess of		
	Par Value, Common Stock		25,000.00
c.	Cash	43,000.00	
	Accounts Receivable	15,000.00	
	Office Equipment	21,500.00	
	Building	60,000.00	
	Accounts Payable		22,000.00
	Notes Payable		37,500.00
	Common Stock, $25 Par Value		50,000.00
	Contributed Capital in Excess of		
	Par Value, Common Stock		30,000.00
d.	Cash	120,000.00	
	Common Stock, $25 Par Value		75,000.00
	Contributed Capital in Excess of		
	Par Value, Common Stock		45,000.00
e.	Cash Dividends Declared	15,000.00	
	Common Dividend Payable		15,000.00
f.	Common Dividend Payable	15,000.00	
	Cash		15,000.00

g.   Income Summary 60,000.00
         Retained Earnings 60,000.00

h.   Retained Earnings 15,000.00
         Cash Dividends Declared 15,000.00

Required

1.   Provide explanations for the journal entries.

2.   Prepare answers for the following questions:

   a.   What is the net income for the year?

   b.   How many shares of common stock are outstanding?

   c.   What is the minimum legal capital?

   d.   What is the total contributed capital?

   e.   What is the total retained earnings?

   f.   What is the total stockholders' equity?

   g.   What is the book value per share of the common stock at the end of the year?

   h.   The dividend yield on this stock is 2%. Expected dividends for the upcoming year are $1 per share. What is the stock's current market value?

   i.   The market interest rate on bonds ranges from 8 to 10%. Does the value of this company's stock appear to be based on income or growth?

CHECK FIGURE:
Total equity, $695,000

Problem 13–3
Allocating dividends between preferred and common stock
(LO 4)

Moving Along, Inc., has 5,000 outstanding shares of $100 par value, 5% preferred stock and 40,000 shares of $1 par value common stock. During the last seven-year period, the company paid out the following total amounts in dividends to its preferred and common stockholders:

19X1	$ 5,000
19X2	11,000
19X3	22,500
19X4	65,000
19X5	18,000
19X6	35,000
19X7	45,000

CHECK FIGURE:
Requirement *b:* total to common, $26,500

No dividends were in arrears for years prior to 19X1.

Required

1.   Determine the amounts of dividends paid to the two classes of stock in each year and for all seven years combined under these two assumptions:

   a.   The preferred stock is noncumulative.

   b.   The preferred stock is cumulative.

2.   Comment on the difference between the answers in requirement 1.

Problem 13–4
Calculating book values
(LO 5)

Duplex Communications, Inc.'s common stock is currently selling on a stock exchange today at $85 per share, and a recent balance sheet shows the following information:

Stockholders' Equity

Preferred stock, 5%, $? par value, 1,000 shares authorized, issued and outstanding	$ 50,000
Common stock, $? par value, 4,000 shares authorized, issued, and outstanding	80,000
Retained earnings	150,000
Total stockholders' equity	$280,000

Required

Preparation component:

1. What is the market value of the corporation's common stock?

2. What are the par values of the preferred stock and the common stock?

3. If no dividends are in arrears, what are the book values of the preferred stock and the common stock?

4. If two years' preferred dividends are in arrears, what are the book values of the preferred stock and the common stock?

5. If two years' preferred dividends are in arrears and the preferred stock is callable at $55 per share, what are the book values of the preferred stock and the common stock?

CHECK FIGURE:
Requirement 4: book value of common, $56.25

Analysis component:

6. What are some factors that may contibute to the difference between the book value of common stock and its market value?

Tinker, Evers, and Chance created a partnership and invested $42,000, $83,000, and $75,000, respectively, at the beginning of the year. During its first year, the partnership achieved a net income of $78,000. Tinker, Evers, and Chance each withdrew $15,000 cash from the partnership on December 31.

Problem 13–5
Allocating partnership income
(LO 6)

Required

Preparation component:

1. Prepare schedules that show how the partners would allocate the partnership's net income among themselves under each of the following agreements:

   a. The partners divide the income equally.

   b. The partners share the income in proportion to their initial investments.

   c. The partners agreed to provide annual salary allowances of $30,000 to Tinker, $13,000 to Evers, and $13,000 to Chance and 8% interest allowances on the partners' initial investments. Any remaining income (or deficit) is to be shared equally.

CHECK FIGURE:
Agreement c: income to Evers, $21,640

2. Prepare a schedule that shows the equity balances of each of the three partners as of the end of the year under agreement *c*.

Analysis component:

3. For each of the partnership agreements in requirement 1, describe a probable situation which would result in the partners agreeing that the agreement was a fair allocation of future earnings.

CRITICAL THINKING: ESSAYS, PROBLEMS, AND CASES

Jan Carston and Carey Glenwood want to create a new software development business. Each of them can contribute fairly large amounts of capital. However, they know that the business will need additional equity capital from other investors after its first year. With respect to their individual activities, they are both planning to devote full-time effort to getting the first products out the door within the year. They plan to hire three employees initially and expect to distribute a substantial amount of cash every year for their personal expenses Carston has proposed organizing the business as a general partnership, but Glenwood thinks that a corporation offers more advantages. They have asked you to prepare a brief analysis that supports choosing the corporate form. What main points would you include in your analysis?

Analytical Essay
(LO 1, 6)

Financial Reporting Problem

(LO 2, 6)

For a number of years, Berry Benson and Connie Karle have operated a retailing company called We've Got It. They organized the company as a partnership and have shared income and losses in a 2:3 ratio. (Benson gets 40% while Karle gets 60%.) Because the business is growing beyond their ability to keep up with it, they have agreed to accept a third person, Mickey Rogers, into the business. Part of the new arrangement involves creating a new corporation, called We've Got It, Inc. The corporate charter authorizes 50,000 shares of $10 par value common stock. The deal requires three steps. First, the partners must settle up the old business by revaluing the assets to their fair market values and dividing the previously unrecognized gains and losses. Second, the partnership must transfer its assets and liabilities to the corporation, which will issue shares to the partners in exchange for their equity in the partnership. The shares will be considered to be worth $10 each when the exchange is made. Third, Rogers will pay $10 cash for all authorized shares not issued to the former partners. You have been engaged to help the three phases of the deal go smoothly.

The following spreadsheet has been developed to help you accomplish the first phase of modifying the partnership's accounts to reflect the fair market values for the assets and to modify the partners' equity balances:

WE'VE GOT IT
Account Modification Spreadsheet
July 31

Accounts	Unmodified Trial Balance	Modifications (a)	(b)	(c)	(d)	(e)	Modified Trial Balance
Debits:							
Cash	21,000						
Accounts receivable	31,000						
Merchandise inventory	150,000	(25,000)					
Store equipment	128,000						
Buildings	280,000						
Land	87,000						
Total	697,000						
Credits:							
Allowance for doubtful accounts	(3,000)						
Accum. depreciation, equip.	(48,000)						
Accum. depreciation, bldgs.	(82,000)						
Accounts Payable	(32,000)						
Notes payable	(172,000)						
Benson, capital	(160,000)	10,000					
Karle, capital	(200,000)	15,000					
Total	(697,000)						

Numbers in parentheses are credits.

The partners have agreed that the following modifications need to be included in the first phase (they will divide any gains and losses from the changes in recorded value according to their regular income and loss ratio):

a.   The merchandise inventory is to be written down to its fair value of $125,000.

b.   An account receivable from a customer for $1,000 is known to be uncollectible and will be written off against the allowance for doubtful accounts.

c.   After writing off that account, the allowance for doubtful accounts will be adjusted to 5% of the gross accounts receivable.

d.   The net recorded value of the store equipment will be decreased to $65,000 by increasing the balance of the accumulated depreciation account.

e. The gross recorded value of the building is to be increased to its replacement cost of $360,000. At the same time, the balance of the accumulated depreciation account is to be adjusted to equal 25% of the replacement cost to represent the fact the building's fair market value is 75% of its replacement cost.

Your first task is to complete the spreadsheet by entering the effects of each of the five modifications as debits and credits to the affected accounts. The first items have been entered in the spreadsheet as an example. You should provide supporting calculations as needed. Second, determine how many shares each partner is entitled to receive in exchange for the partner's equity. Third, determine how many shares Rogers will purchase for cash. Fourth, present the journal entries that the corporation will use to record the issuance of the shares to all three stockholders. Finally, present a balance sheet for the corporation immediately after the transactions are completed (the notes payable are due within 90 days).

Financial Statement Analysis Cases

FSAC 13-1
(LO 4)

Having received a large lump sum of severance pay, Lou Franklin is thinking about investing the money in one of two securities, either Endor Corporation common stock or the preferred stock issued by Kenobe Company. The companies manufacture similar products and compete in the same market, and both have been operating about the same length of time—four years for Endor and three years for Kenobe. The two companies also have similar amounts of stockholders' equity, as shown here:

Endor Corporation

Common stock, $1 par value, 800,000 shares authorized, 500,000 shares issued and outstanding . .	$ 500,000
Retained earnings	820,000
Total stockholders' equity	$1,320,000

Kenobe Company

Preferred stock, $50 par value, 6% cumulative, 6,000 shares authorized, issued, and outstanding . . .	$ 300,000*
Common stock, $20 par value, 50,000 shares authorized, issued, and outstanding	1,000,000
Retained earnings	60,000
Total stockholders' equity	$1,360,000

*The current and two prior years' dividends are in arrears on the preferred stock.

Endor did not pay a dividend on its common stock during its first year's operations; however, it has paid a cash dividend of $0.09 per share in each of the past three years. The stock is currently selling for $3.00 per share. In contrast, the preferred stock of Kenobe Company is selling for $45 per share. Franklin has expressed a leaning for the preferred stock as an investment because it appears to be a bargain at $5 below par value and $14 below book value. Besides, Franklin has told you, "The dividends are guaranteed because it is a preferred stock." Franklin also believes that the common stock of Endor is overpriced at 14% above book value and 200% above par value, while it is paying only a $0.09 per share dividend. In conclusion, your friend asks how anyone could prefer a common stock yielding only 3% to a preferred stock that is supposed to pay 6%.

1. Is the preferred stock of Kenobe Company actually selling at $14 below its book value, and is the common stock of Endor Corporation actually selling at 14% above book value and 200% above par?

2. Analyze the stockholders' equity sections and express your opinion of the two stocks as investments by describing some of the factors Franklin should consider in choosing between them.

FSAC 13-2
(L.O. 3, 4, 5, 7)

Use the information provided in the financial statements of Apple Computer, Inc., and the footnotes in Appendix F to answer the following questions:

1. Does it appear that Apple has been authorized to issue any preferred stock? If so, has any been issued as of September 24, 1993?

2. How many shares of common stock have been authorized? How many have been issued as of September 24, 1993?

3. What is the par value of the common stock? What is its book value at September 24, 1993?

4. Are any shares of common stock subscribed? Are there any shares that cannot be issued to the public because they have been promised to others?

5. What was the highest market value of the stock during 1993? What was the lowest?

6. Did Apple declare any dividends on its capital stock during 1993? If so, how large were the dividends (in total, and per share)? If the price of the stock was $48 per share at the end of fiscal year 1993, and dividends were expected to continue at the same rate, what was the dividend yield of the stock? Does it appear that Apple is a growth or income stock?

ANSWERS TO PROGRESS CHECKS

13–1 *b*

13–2 A corporation must pay taxes on its income and its stockholders must pay personal income taxes on dividends received from the corporation.

13–3 A proxy is a legal document used to transfer a stockholder's right to vote to another person.

13–4 *a*

13–5 A stock premium is an amount in excess of par paid by purchasers of newly issued stock.

13–6 Creditors of the corporation are intended to be protected by minimum legal capital.

13–7 *c*

13–8 Common Stock Subscribed is classfied as contributed capital in the stockholders' equity section of the balance sheet.

13–9 *c*

13–10 The three dates are the date of declaration, the date of record, and the date of payment.

13–11 Typically, preferred stock has a preference in receiving dividends and in the distribution of assets in the case of a company's liquidation.

13–12 *a*
13–13 *b*

Total dividend	$288,000
To preferred shareholders	135,000*
Remainder to common shareholders	$153,000

*9,000 × $50 × .10 × 3 = $135,000

13–14

Total stockholders' equity		$630,000
Less equity applicable to preferred shares:		
Call price (1,000 × $90)	$90,000	
Dividends in arrears	18,000	108,000
Equity applicable to common shares		$522,000
Book value of common shares ($522,000/12,000)		$ 43.50

13–15 *c*

13–16 *b*

13–17

	Mixon	Reed	Income to be Allocated
Total net income			$40,000
Allocated as interest	$ 7,000	$ 3,500	10,500
Remaining balance			$29,500
Balance allocated equally	14,750	14,750	29,500
Remaining balance			$ –0–
Shares of partners	$21,750	$18,250	

13–18 Unlimited liability means that the creditors of a partnership have the right to require each partner to be personally responsible for all partnership debts.

13–19 *c*

CHAPTER 14

Additional Corporate Transactions; Reporting Income and Retained Earnings; Earnings per Share

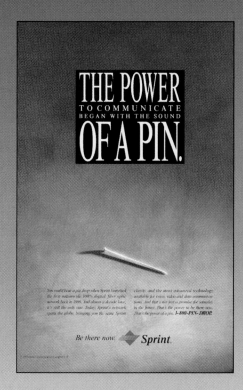

*S*print Corporation is a diversified telecommunications company that provides global voice, data, and video conferencing services and related products. The company's 1993 annual report stated that net operating revenues had tripled since 1984, increasing from $3.7 to $11.4 billion. During the three-year period from 1991 to 1993, income from continuing operations increased from $472.7 to $480.6 million. Nevertheless, during the same three years, the earnings applicable to common stock declined from $516.1 to $52.1 million.

Considering the sharp differences in these trends, a common stockholder might wonder how to assess the company's future prospects. How might Sprint describe the results in its financial statements? What additional information would you expect to find in the income statement beyond the items in the following table?

Sprint Corporation
(In millions)

	1993	1992	1991
Net operating revenues	$11,367.8	$10,420.3	$9,933.3
Income from continuing operations	480.6	496.1	472.7
Net income	54.9	502.8	520.2
Preferred stock dividends	(2.8)	(3.5)	(4.1)
Earnings applicable to common stock	52.1	499.3	516.1

LEARNING OBJECTIVES

After studying Chapter 14 you should be able to:

1. **Describe stock dividends and stock splits and explain their effects on a corporation's assets and stockholders' equity.**

2. **Record purchases and sales of treasury stock and retirements of stock and describe their effects on stockholders' equity. Also, describe restrictions and appropriations of retained earnings and explain how they are described in financial reports.**

3. **Explain how to report the income effects of discontinued segments, extraordinary items, changes in accounting principles and estimates, and prior period adjustments.**

4. **Calculate earnings per share for companies with simple capital structures and explain the difference between primary and fully diluted earnings per share.**

5. **Calculate the price-earnings ratio and describe its meaning.**

6. **Define or explain the words and phrases listed in the chapter glossary.**

Corporations often enter into special financing transactions that involve changes in stockholders' equity. The first section of this chapter explains several of these transactions, including stock dividends, stock splits, and transactions involving the company's own stock. The second section of the chapter expands your understanding of financial statements by explaining how information about income and retained earnings is classified and reported. The third section explains how corporations report earnings per share. Understanding these topics will help you interpret and use financial statements. In fact, the discussion in this chapter helps clarify some of the reporting issues implied by the previous discussion of Sprint Corporation.

CORPORATE DIVIDENDS AND OTHER STOCK TRANSACTIONS

In Chapter 1, we briefly described a corporation's retained earnings as the stockholders' equity that is created by the company's profitable activities. It is equal to the total cumulative amount of the reported net income less any net losses and dividends declared since the company started operating. In effect, retained earnings are the stockholders' residual interest in the corporation that was not created by their investments. Information about retained earnings is helpful to investors and other users of financial statements for predicting future cash flows for dividends and other events.

RETAINED EARNINGS AND DIVIDENDS

LO 1

Describe stock dividends and stock splits and explain their effects on a corporation's assets and stockholders' equity.

Most state laws allow a corporation to pay cash dividends if retained earnings exist. However, in addition to retained earnings, a corporation must have enough cash to pay the dividend. And, even if there is sufficient cash and retained earnings, the directors may decide against declaring a dividend because the cash is needed in the business. Although cash may be paid out in dividends, companies also keep some cash in reserve to meet emergencies, to take advantage of unexpected opportunities, or to avoid having to borrow for future expansion.

Chapter 13 described how cash dividends are recorded in the accounts. The declaration of a dividend reduces the retained earnings and creates a current liability to the stockholders. On the date of record, the recipients of the dividend are identified, but no entry is recorded in the accounts. On the date of payment, cash is sent to the qualifying stockholders and the liability is removed from the books.

Generally, the Dividends Declared account is closed to the Retained Earnings account. However, in limited circumstances, some state laws allow cash dividends to be paid as a return of capital contributed by the stockholders. If so, the Dividends Declared account is closed with a debit entry to one of the contributed capital accounts instead of Retained Earnings. Because these dividends return part of the original investment to the stockholders, they are often called **liquidating dividends.** They usually occur when the company is completing a major downsizing, perhaps in preparation for a merger or even dissolution. In most cases, the equity that originated from the par or stated value of the outstanding stock cannot be used as a basis for liquidating dividends until all creditors have been paid. This situation normally occurs only when the corporation is actually going out of business.

DIVIDENDS BASED ON CONTRIBUTED CAPITAL

Sometimes, a corporation's directors may declare a **stock dividend.** This means the company distributes additional shares of its own stock to its stockholders without receiving any payment in return. Stock dividends and cash dividends are very different. A cash dividend reduces the corporation's assets and stockholders' equity, and a stock dividend does neither. A stock dividend simply transfers some equity from retained earnings into contributed capital.

STOCK DIVIDENDS

Why Stock Dividends Are Distributed

If stock dividends do not affect assets or total stockholders' equity, why are they declared and distributed? Directors can use stock dividends to keep the market value of the stock affordable. For example, if a profitable corporation grows but does not pay cash dividends, the price of its common stock increases in anticipation of continued growth and future dividends. Eventually, the price of a share may become so high that it discourages some investors from buying the stock. Thus, the corporation may declare stock dividends to increase the number of outstanding shares and thereby keep the per share price of its stock low enough to be attractive to smaller investors.

Another reason for declaring a stock dividend is to provide tangible evidence of management's confidence that the company is doing well. The stock dividend may substitute for a cash dividend, thereby saving cash that can be used to expand the business.

The Effect of Stock Dividends on Stockholders' Equity Accounts

Although a stock dividend does not affect the corporation's assets or total stockholders' equity, it does affect the components of stockholders' equity. This effect is recorded by transferring part of the retained earnings to the contributed capital accounts. Because this treatment increases the company's contributed capital, it is often described as *capitalizing* retained earnings.

If a corporation declares a **small stock dividend,** accounting principles require it to capitalize retained earnings equal to the market value of the shares to be distributed. This practice is based on the concept that a small stock dividend is likely to be perceived as similar to a cash dividend because it has a small impact on the price of the stock. A dividend is considered small if it is less than or equal to 25% of the previously outstanding shares.

A **large stock dividend,** one that distributes more than 25% of the outstanding shares before the dividend, is likely to have a noticeable effect on the stock's market price per share. It is not likely to be perceived as a substitute for a cash dividend. Therefore, a large stock dividend is recorded by capitalizing an amount of retained earnings only to the minimum required by the state law governing the corporation. In most cases, the law requires capitalizing retained earnings equal to the par or stated value of the shares.

For example, assume that Northwest Corporation's stockholders' equity consists of the following amounts just before the declaration of a stock dividend:

NORTHWEST CORPORATION
Stockholders' Equity
December 31, 19X1

Common stock, $10 par value, 15,000 shares authorized, 10,000 shares issued and outstanding	$100,000
Contributed capital in excess of par value, common stock ..	8,000
Total contributed capital	$108,000
Retained earnings	35,000
Total stockholders' equity	$143,000

Recording a Small Stock Dividend

To illustrate how a small stock dividend is recorded, let's assume that the directors of Northwest Corporation declare a 10% stock dividend on December 31. The 1,000 dividend shares (10% of the 10,000 outstanding shares) are to be distributed on January 20 to the January 15 stockholders of record.

If the market value of Northwest Corporation's stock on December 31 is $15 per share, the dividend declaration is recorded with this entry:

Dec.	31	Stock Dividends Declared	15,000.00	
		Common Stock Dividend Distributable		10,000.00
		Contributed Capital in Excess of		
		Par Value, Common Stock		5,000.00
		To record the declaration of a 1,000-share common		
		stock dividend.		

The debit is recorded in the temporary account called Stock Dividends Declared. This account serves the same purpose as the Cash Dividends Declared account described in the preceding chapter. A complete chart of accounts includes separate accounts for cash and stock dividends because the financial statements must report stock and cash dividends as separate events. If stock dividends are not frequently declared, a company can get by without a separate account for Stock Dividends Declared. Instead, it can record the debit directly to Retained Earnings. This approach is acceptable as long as the information is reported correctly in the financial statements.

In the previous entry, the first credit puts the par value of the dividend shares in a contributed capital account called Common Stock Dividend Distributable. This account balance exists only until the shares are actually issued. The second credit records the premium on the dividend shares at this time, even though the shares have not yet been issued. This account is the same one that is used for all other issuances at an amount more than par value.

Illustration 14-1
The Effect of Northwest Corporation's 10% Stock Dividend

Before the 10% stock dividend
Stockholders' equity:

Common stock (10,000 shares)	$100,000
Contributed capital in excess of par value, common stock ..	8,000
Retained earnings	35,000
Total stockholders' equity	$143,000

Book value per share = $143,000/10,000 shares = $14.30
Book value of Johnson's 200 shares = $14.30 × 200 = $2,860

After the 10% stock dividend
Stockholders' equity:

Common stock (11,000 shares)	$110,000
Contributed capital in excess of par value, common stock ..	13,000
Retained earnings	20,000
Total stockholders' equity	$143,000

Book value per share = $143,000/11,000 shares = $13.00
Book value of Johnson's 220 shares = $13 × 220 = $2,860

As part of the year-end closing process, the accountant for the Northwest Corporation closes the Stock Dividends Declared account to Retained Earnings with this entry:

Dec.	31	Retained Earnings	15,000.00	
		Stock Dividends Declared		15,000.00
		To close the Stock Dividends Declared account.		

On January 20, the company distributes the new shares to the stockholders and records the event with this entry:

Jan.	20	Common Stock Dividend Distributable	10,000.00	
		Common Stock		10,000.00
		To record the distribution of a 1,000-share common stock dividend.		

The combined effect of these three entries is the transfer (or capitalization) of $15,000 of retained earnings to contributed capital. The amount of capitalized retained earnings equals the market value of the 1,000 issued shares ($15 × 1,000 shares).

This example demonstrates that a stock dividend has no effect on the corporation's assets or total stockholders' equity. Nor does the dividend affect the percentage of the company owned by individual stockholders. For example, assume that Pat Johnson owned 200 shares of Northwest Corporation's stock prior to the 10% stock dividend. When the corporation sent each stockholder one new share for each 10 shares held, Johnson received 20 new shares (10% × 200 shares).

Looking at Illustration 14–1, you can see what the 10% stock dividend does to Northwest Corporation's total contributed capital and retained earnings. Note that nothing happens to the total book value of Johnson's shares. Before the stock dividend, Johnson owned 2% of the corporation's stock, which is 200 of the 10,000 outstanding shares. The book value of this holding was $2,860 (2% × $143,000, or 200

× $14.30 per share). After the dividend, Johnson holds 220 shares, but the holding still equals 2% of the 11,000 shares now outstanding. The book value is still $2,860 (2% × $143,000, or 220 × $13.00 per share). In other words, the only change in Johnson's 2% investment is that now it is represented by 220 shares instead of 200 shares. Also, the only effect on the stockholders' equity is a transfer of $15,000 from retained earnings to contributed capital. There is no change in the corporation's total assets, in its total equity, or in the percentage of equity owned by Johnson. Of course, Johnson's main concern is whether the 220 shares are now worth more than the 200 shares used to be.

Stock Dividends on the Balance Sheet

Because a stock dividend does not reduce the corporation's assets, it is never a liability on a balance sheet prepared between the declaration and distribution dates. Instead, the amount of any declared but undistributed stock dividend appears on the balance sheet as a component of the contributed capital in the stockholders' equity section. For example, the stockholders' equity of Northwest Corporation looks like this just after the 10% stock dividend is declared on December 31:

NORTHWEST CORPORATION
Stockholders' Equity
December 31, 19X1

Common stock, $10 par value, 15,000 shares authorized, 10,000 shares issued and outstanding	$100,000
Common stock dividend distributable, 1,000 shares	10,000
Total common stock issued and to be issued	$110,000
Contributed capital in excess of par value, common stock . .	13,000
Total contributed capital	$123,000
Retained earnings	20,000
Total stockholders' equity	$143,000

This updated section of the balance sheet is changed in three ways. First, the amount of equity attributed to the common stock increased from $100,000 to $110,000 because 1,000 additional shares are ready to be issued. Second, the contributed capital in excess of par increased by $5,000, which equals the excess of the $15 per share market value over the $10 per share par value for the 1,000 shares. Finally, the balance of retained earnings decreased by $15,000 from the predividend amount of $35,000 to $20,000.

Recording a Large Stock Dividend

When a stock dividend exceeds 25% of the outstanding shares, the corporation capitalizes retained earnings equal to the minimum amount required by the law. Usually, that is the par or stated value of the newly issued shares. For example, suppose Northwest Corporation's board declared a 30% stock dividend on December 31 instead of 10%. Because the dividend is greater than the arbitrary limit of 25%, it is considered to be large. As a result, only the par value of the new 3,000 shares is capitalized. Thus, the company would record the declaration with this entry:

Dec.	31	Stock Dividends Declared	30,000.00	
		Common Stock Dividend Distributable		30,000.00
		To record the declaration of a 3,000-share stock dividend at par value.		

This entry causes the company's retained earnings to be decreased by the $30,000 par value of the dividend shares. It also causes the company's contributed capital to increase by the same amount.

STOCK SPLITS

Recall that one goal for stock dividends is to reduce the stock's market price. Stock dividends divide the company into a larger number of smaller pieces. The total value of the company is unchanged, but the price of each new share is smaller. The same result can be accomplished through a **stock split.** When a stock split occurs, the corporation calls in its outstanding shares and issues two or more new shares in exchange for each of the old ones.[1]

Suppose that a company has 100,000 outstanding shares of $20 par value common stock that have a current market value of $88 per share. The market value can be cut in half by a two-for-one split. The split replaces the 100,000 $20 par value shares with 200,000 $10 par value shares that have a market value in the neighborhood of $44 per share.

Splits can be accomplished at any ratio, including two-for-one, three-for-one, or even higher. In fact, it is possible for the ratio to be less than one to one, causing stockholders to end up with fewer shares. These **reverse stock splits** are intended to increase the stock's market price per share.

A stock split does not affect the total stockholders' equity reported on the balance sheet. It also does not affect a stockholder's percentage interest in the corporation. The contributed capital and retained earnings accounts are unchanged by a split, and no journal entry is made. The only effect on the accounts is a change in the account title used for the common stock. The earlier example described a two-for-one split for a $20 par value stock. After the split, the account name would be changed to Common Stock, $10 Par Value. Although nothing else changes in the accounts, the disclosures about the stock on the balance sheet are changed to reflect the additional outstanding shares and the revised par value per share.

Many companies accomplish the effect of a stock split by declaring large stock dividends. This practice avoids a great deal of the administrative cost that would be incurred by splitting the stock. **Harley-Davidson, Inc.,** accomplished the effect of a 2-for-1 stock split in 1992 by distributing one new share for each old share.

Progress Check

(Answers to Progress Checks are provided at the end of the chapter.)

14-1 Which of the following statements is correct?

a. A large stock dividend is recorded by capitalizing retained earnings equal to the market value of the distributable shares.

b. Stock dividends and stock splits have the same effect on the total assets and retained earnings of the issuing corporation.

c. A stock dividend does not transfer corporate assets to the stockholders but does require that retained earnings be capitalized.

14-2 What distinguishes a large stock dividend from a small stock dividend?

14-3 When accounting for a small stock dividend, what amount of retained earnings should be capitalized?

---

[1]To reduce the administrative cost, most splits are accomplished by simply issuing new certificates to the stockholders for the additional shares they are entitled to receive. The stockholders do not have to turn in the old certificates.

As a Matter of Ethics

Falcon Corporation's board of directors and officers have been planning the agenda for the corporation's 19X1 annual stockholders' meeting. The first item considered by the directors and officers was whether to report a large government contract that Falcon has just signed. Although this contract will significantly increase income and cash flows in 19X1 and beyond, management saw no need to reveal the news at the stockholders' meeting. "After all," one officer said, "the meeting is intended to be the forum for describing the past year's activities, not the plans for the next year."

After agreeing not to mention the contract, the group moved on to the next topic for the stockholders' meeting. This topic was a motion for the stockholders to approve a compensation plan award-ing managers options to acquire large quantities of shares over the next several years. According to the plan, the managers will have a three-year option to buy shares at a fixed price that equals the market value of the stock as measured 30 days after the upcoming stockholders' meeting. In other words, the managers will be able to buy stock in 19X2, 19X3, or 19X4 by paying the 19X1 market value. Obviously, if the stock increases in value over the next several years, the managers will realize large profits without having to invest any cash. The financial vice president asked the group whether they should reconsider the decision about the government contract in light of its possible relevance to the vote on the stock option plan.

TREASURY STOCK

LO 2

Record purchases and sales of treasury stock and retirements of stock and describe their effects on stockholders' equity. Also, describe restrictions and appropriations of retained earnings and explain how they are described in financial reports.

For a variety of reasons, corporations often acquire shares of their own stock. They may use the shares to acquire control of other corporations. Sometimes, they repurchase shares to avoid a hostile takeover by an investor seeking control of the company. Many buy shares and reissue them to employees as compensation. For example, **Hewlett-Packard Company** reports that it has a stock repurchase program to meet future employee stock plan requirements. In 1993, the company purchased 4,345,000 shares under this program.

Less frequently, a corporation may buy a large number of shares to maintain a suitable market for the stock. This practice was widespread in 1987 after many stocks lost a great deal of market value very quickly. By buying the shares, corporations helped their stockholders get a better price and brought more stability to the market.

Regardless of the reason for their acquisition, a corporation's reacquired shares are called **treasury stock.** In many respects, treasury stock is similar to unissued stock. Neither unissued nor treasury stock is an asset of the corporation. Neither receive cash or stock dividends, and no one can exercise the vote attached to the shares. However, treasury stock does have one potentially significant difference from unissued stock. Specifically, if treasury stock was originally issued at its par value or higher, the company can resell the stock at less than par without having the buyers incur a discount liability.

In addition, treasury stock purchases require management to exercise ethical sensitivity. Corporate funds are being paid to specific stockholders instead of all stockholders. As a result, managers must be careful to be sure that the purchase is in the best interest of all the stockholders. These concerns cause most companies to be very open with their stockholders about their treasury stock and other activities related to stock. Read As a Matter of Ethics and consider whether Falcon Corporation's management is showing proper consideration for its stockholders.

PURCHASING TREASURY STOCK

The act of purchasing treasury stock reduces the corporation's assets and stockholders' equity by equal amounts.[2] This effect is illustrated by the two balance sheets of the Curry Corporation in Illustrations 14–2 and 14–3. The first balance sheet shows the account balances on April 30, 19X1, before a treasury stock purchase. The sec-

---

[2]This text discusses the *cost method* of accounting for treasury stock; it is the most widely used. The *par value* method is discussed in more advanced accounting courses.

CURRY CORPORATION
Balance Sheet
April 30, 19X1

Assets		Stockholders' Equity		
Cash	$ 30,000	Contributed capital:		
Other assets	95,000	Common stock, $10 par value, authorized and issued		
		10,000 shares	$100,000	
		Retained earnings	25,000	
Total assets	$125,000	Total stockholders' equity	$125,000	

CURRY CORPORATION
Balance Sheet
April 30, 19X1

Assets		Stockholders' Equity		
Cash	$ 18,500	Contributed capital:		
Other assets	95,000	Common stock, $10 par value, authorized and issued 10,000 shares, of which 1,000 are in the treasury	$100,000	
		Retained earnings, of which $11,500 is restricted by the purchase of treasury stock	25,000	
		Total	$125,000	
		Less cost of treasury stock	(11,500)	
Total assets	$113,500	Total stockholders' equity	$113,500	

ond balance sheet shows the account balances after the company purchased 1,000 of its own shares for $11,500 cash.

This entry records the purchase of the 1,000 shares:

May	1	Treasury Stock, Common	11,500.00	
		Cash		11,500.00
		Purchased 1,000 shares of treasury stock at $11.50 per share.		

The entry reduces the stockholders' equity by debiting the Treasury Stock account, which is *contra* to equity. To see the effects of the transaction, look at the balance sheet in Illustration 14-3.

Notice that the purchase reduces the company's cash, total assets, and total equity by $11,500. The equity reduction is reflected on the balance sheet by deducting the cost of the treasury stock in the equity section. The purchase does not reduce the balance of either the Common Stock account or the Retained Earnings account. However, two disclosures in this section describe the effects of the transaction. First, the statement tells the reader that 1,000 of the issued shares are in the treasury of the corporation. Thus, only 9,000 shares are outstanding. Second, the purchase has placed a restriction on the company's retained earnings. This restriction is described in the next section.

Restricting Retained Earnings by the Purchase of Treasury Stock

Cash dividends and purchases of treasury stock have a similar effect on a corporation's assets and stockholders' equity. That is, they both transfer corporate cash to stockholders and reduce assets and equity. Therefore, most states restrict the amount of cash dividends and treasury stock purchases to the amount of retained earnings.

Unlike a cash dividend, a treasury stock purchase does not directly reduce the balance of the Retained Earnings account. However, the corporation should disclose any statutory restrictions on retained earnings. Thus, the balance sheet in Illustration 14–3 identifies the amount of the **restricted retained earnings** created by the treasury stock purchase. In many cases, the restriction is described in a footnote to the financial statements. In addition to this restriction, other limits on dividends may be established by statute and by contract.

Appropriated Retained Earnings

In contrast to statutory or contractual retained earnings restrictions, a corporation's directors may voluntarily limit dividends because of a special need for cash, such as to purchase new facilities. When the directors do this, management usually explains in a letter attached to the financial statements why dividends have not been declared. However, they may notify the stockholders and other financial statement users of this change in policy by setting up an amount of **appropriated retained earnings.** These appropriations are strictly voluntary and nonbinding. They serve only to notify the statement readers of the directors' decision to not pay out cash.

REISSUING TREASURY STOCK

Treasury stock may be reissued by selling it at cost, above cost, or below cost. If it is reissued by being sold at its cost, the entry is the opposite of the entry that was made to record the purchase.

If treasury stock is sold for more than cost, the amount received in excess of cost is credited to a special account called Contributed Capital, Treasury Stock Transactions. For example, if Curry Corporation receives $12 cash per share for 500 treasury shares originally purchased at $11.50 per share, the accountant records the transaction with the following entry:

June	3	Cash	6,000.00	
		Treasury Stock, Common		5,750.00
		Contributed Capital, Treasury Stock		
		Transactions		250.00
		Received $12 per share for 500 treasury shares that cost		
		$11.50 per share.		

Notice that the company does not report a gain from this transaction.

When treasury stock is sold at less than its cost, the entry to record the sale depends on whether there is a credit balance in the Contributed Capital, Treasury Stock Transactions account. If there is no balance, the excess of cost over the sales price is debited to Retained Earnings. However, if the contributed capital account has a credit balance, the excess of the cost over the sales price is debited for an amount up to the balance in that account. When the credit balance in the contributed capital account is eliminated, any remaining difference between the cost and the selling price is debited to Retained Earnings.

For example, if Curry Corporation sells its remaining 500 shares of treasury stock at $10 per share, the company's equity is reduced by $750 (500 shares ×$1.50 per share excess of cost over selling price). The reissuance is recorded with this entry:

July	10	Cash..	5,000.00	
		Contributed Capital, Treasury Stock Transactions........	250.00	
		Retained Earnings	500.00	
		Treasury Stock, Common		5,750.00
		Received $10 per share for 500 treasury shares that cost $11.50 per share.		

This entry eliminates the $250 credit balance in the contributed capital account created on June 3 and then reduces the Retained Earnings balance by the remaining $500 of the excess of the cost over the selling price. Thus, the purchase and reissuance of the treasury shares caused the Curry Corporation to incur a $500 decrease in retained earnings and total stockholders' equity. Notice that the company does not report a loss from this transaction.

RETIRING STOCK

Instead of acquiring treasury stock with the intent of reissuing it in the future, a corporation may simply purchase its own stock and retire it. It cancels the shares, which become the same as unissued stock. For example, the **Wm. Wrigley Jr. Company** reported in the notes to its 1993 financial statements that "on August 19, 1992, the Board of Directors adopted a resolution retiring the entire balance of shares of Common Stock held in the corporate treasury at that time and all subsequent acquisitions to the extent not required for issuance [under the company's management Incentive Plan.]" Like purchases of treasury stock, purchases and retirements of stock are permissible under state laws only if they do not jeopardize the best interests of creditors and other stockholders.

When stock is purchased for retirement, the accountant must remove all the contributed capital amounts related to the retired shares. If the purchase price for the shares exceeds the net amount removed from contributed capital, the excess is debited to Retained Earnings. On the other hand, if the purchase price is less than the net amount removed from contributed capital, the difference is credited to a special contributed capital account.

For example, assume that the Carolina Corporation originally issued its $10 par value common stock at $12 per share. As a result, the $2 per share premium was credited to the Contributed Capital in Excess of Par Value, Common Stock account. When the corporation purchased and retired 1,000 shares of this stock at $12 per share on April 12, it recorded the effects of this event with this entry:

Apr.	12	Common Stock	10,000.00	
		Contributed Capital in Excess of Par Value, Common Stock	2,000.00	
		Cash		12,000.00
		Purchased and retired 1,000 shares of common stock at $12 per share.		

This entry restores the accounts to the balances that they would have had if the stock had never been issued.

On the other hand, if the corporation paid only $11 per share instead of $12, the retirement causes equity to increase by $1 per share, the difference between cost and the original issuance price. This increase in equity is recorded as follows:

Apr.	12	Common Stock	10,000.00	
		Contributed Capital in Excess of Par Value, Common Stock	2,000.00	
		Cash		11,000.00
		Contributed Capital from the Retirement of		
		Common Stock		1,000.00
		Purchased and retired 1,000 shares of common stock at $11 per share.		

Even though this transaction increased equity, the amount is not a gain. The concept underlying this treatment is that transactions in a corporation's own stock cannot affect income or increase retained earnings.

The same idea governs the accounting for a retirement accomplished with a purchase price that is greater than the stock's original issuance price. For example, suppose that the Carolina Corporation retired 1,000 shares of its stock at $15 per share, which is $3 per share greater than the $12 original issue price. This entry would be used to account for the event:

Apr.	12	Common Stock	10,000.00	
		Contributed Capital in Excess of Par Value, Common Stock	2,000.00	
		Retained Earnings	3,000.00	
		Cash		15,000.00
		Purchased and retired 1,000 shares of common stock at $15 per share.		

Even though this transaction decreased equity, the $3 per share is not a loss. In this case, the $3,000 is debited to Retained Earnings. If there had been a credit balance in a contributed capital account related to retirements, it would have been debited up to the amount of its balance.

All three retirement examples reduced the company's assets and equity by the amount paid for the stock. However, no income effects are recognized. The only effects on equity are recorded in the contributed capital and retained earnings accounts.

Progress Check

14-4 **A corporation's purchase of treasury stock:** *(a)* **Has no effect on total assets;** *(b)* **Reduces total assets and total stockholders' equity by equal amounts;** *(c)* **Is recorded with a debit to Retained Earnings.**

14-5 **Southern Co. purchased shares of Northern Corp. Should these shares be classified as treasury stock by either company?**

14-6 **How does treasury stock affect the number of authorized, issued, and outstanding shares of stock?**

14-7 **When a corporation purchases treasury stock:** *(a)* **Retained earnings is restricted by the amount paid for the stock;** *(b)* **It is recorded with a credit to Appropriated Retained Earnings;** *(c)* **It is always retired.**

REPORTING INCOME AND RETAINED EARNINGS INFORMATION

When a company's only revenue and expense transactions are created by routine, continuing operations, a single-step income statement is adequate for describing the results of its activities. This format shows the revenues followed by a list of operating expenses and the net income. In today's complex business world, however, activities often include many income-related events that are not part of a company's continuing and otherwise normal activities.

The accountant's goal is to provide useful information in a format that helps the statement users understand the past-period events and predict future-period results. To see how this goal is accomplished, look at the income statement in Illustration 14–4. Notice that the income statement is separated into five different sections.

CONTINUING OPERATIONS

Section 1 of the income statement shows the revenues, expenses, and income generated by the company's continuing operations. This portion looks like the single-step income statement that we first discussed in Chapter 5. Income statement users rely on the information in this section to develop predictions of what will happen in the future. As such, this section usually contains the most important information in the income statement. Previous chapters have explained the nature of the items and measures included in income from continuing operations.

DISCONTINUED SEGMENTS

Most large companies have several different lines of business and deal with different groups of customers. For example, **International Business Machines** not only produces and sells computer hardware and software but also delivers system design and repair services. Information about these **segments of the business** is of particular interest to users of the company's financial statements. According to GAAP, a segment is a component of a company's operations that serves a particular line of business or class of customers. A segment has assets, activities, and financial results of operations that can be distinguished from other parts of the business. Large companies with operations in different segments are required to provide supplemental footnote information about each of their major segments.

Reporting Income Statement Information about Discontinued Segments

When a company incurs a gain or loss from selling or closing down a segment, the gain or loss must be reported in a separate section of the income statement.[3] Section 2 of the income statement in Illustration 14–4 includes this information. Note that the income from operating the discontinued segment prior to its disposal also is reported in section 2. When the income statement presents the results of several years side by side, it is necessary to go back and restate the prior years' results to separate out the revenues and expenses of the discontinued segment.

Separate information about a discontinued segment can be useful on its own. However, the primary purpose of reporting the gains or losses from discontinued operations separately is to more clearly present the results of continuing operations. The effect is to provide useful information for predicting the income that will be earned by the segments that continue to operate in the future.

LO 3

Explain how to report the income effects of discontinued segments, extraordinary items, changes in accounting principles and estimates, and prior period adjustments.

---

[3]FASB, *Accounting Standards—Current Text* (Norwalk, CT, 1994), sec. I13.105. Originally published as *APB Opinion No. 30,* par. 8.

Illustration 14–4   Income Statement for a Corporation

CONNELLY CORPORATION
Income Statement
For Year Ended December 31, 19X4

	Net sales		$8,440,000
	Gain on sale of equipment		38,000
	Total		$8,478,000
	Expenses:		
	Cost of goods sold	$5,950,000	
	Depreciation expense	35,000	
1	Other selling, general, and administrative expenses	515,000	
	Interest expense	20,000	
	Income taxes expense	595,500	
	Total expenses		(7,115,500)
	Unusual loss on relocating a plant		(45,000)
	Infreqent gain on sale of surplus land		72,000
	Income from continuing operations		$1,389,500
Discontinued segment:			
	Income from operating Division A		
	(net of $180,000 income taxes)	$ 420,000	
2	Loss on disposal of Division A		
	(net of $66,000 tax benefit)	(154,000)	266,000
	Income before extraordinary items and cumulative		
	effect of a change in accounting principle		$1,655,500
Extraordinary items:			
	Gain on sale of unused land condemned by the		
	state for a highway interchange		
3	(net of $61,200 income taxes)	$ 142,800	
	Loss from earthquake damage		
	(net of $270,000 income tax benefit)	(630,000)	(487,200)
Cumulative effect of a change in accounting			
principle:			
	Effect on prior years' income (through December 31, 19X3)		
4	of changing to a different depreciation method		
	(net of $24,000 income taxes)		56,000
	Net inome		$1,224,300
Earnings per common share (200,000 outstanding shares):			
	Income from continuing operations		$ 6.95
	Discontinued operations		1.33
	Income before extraordinary items and cumulative		
5	effect of a change in accounting principle		$ 8.28
	Extraordinary items		(2.44)
	Cumulative effect of a change in accounting principle		0.28
	Net income		$ 6.12

Distinguishing the Results of Operating a Discontinued Segment from the Gain or Loss on Disposal

Section 2 of Illustration 14–4 reports both the income from operating the discontinued Division A during the year and the loss that occurred from disposing of the division's assets. The income tax effects of operating and disposing of the segment are also disclosed in section 2. As a result, the tax effects related to the discontinued segment are separated from the presentation of continuing operations in section 1. If the tax effects of the discontinued segment were not separated from the continuing operations, the result would not be as useful.

This discussion presents only a highly summarized description of the requirements for reporting the results of discontinued segments. The details are covered in more advanced accounting courses.

EXTRAORDINARY ITEMS

Section 3 of the income statement in Illustration 14–4 reports **extraordinary gains and losses** that occurred during the year. Extraordinary gains and losses are both unusual and infrequent. An **unusual gain or loss** is abnormal or otherwise unrelated to the ordinary activities and environment of the business. An **infrequent gain or loss** is not expected to occur again in the company's operating environment.[4] Reporting extraordinary items in a separate category makes it easier for users to predict what will happen in the future, apart from these extraordinary events.

In light of these definitions of *unusual* and *infrequent,* very few items qualify as extraordinary gains or losses by meeting both criteria. For example, none of the following events are considered extraordinary:

1. Write-downs or write-offs of assets, unless the change in value is caused by a major unusual and infrequent calamity, a condemning or expropriating of property by a domestic or foreign government, or a prohibition against using the assets under a newly enacted law.

2. Gains or losses from exchanging foreign currencies or translating account balances expressed in one currency into another currency.

3. Gains and losses from disposing of a business segment.

4. Effects of a labor action, including one against the company, its competitors, or its major suppliers.

5. Adjustment of accruals on long-term contracts.[5]

Gains or losses that are neither unusual nor infrequent are reported as part of the results of continuing operations. Gains or losses that are either unusual or infrequent but not both are not extraordinary. These items are listed on the income statement in the continuing operations section below the regular revenues, expenses, gains, and losses. For example, **Duracell International Inc.'s** 1993 income statement reported a $65 million charge for restructuring. The charge related to organizational integration and streamlining, including the closure of a Brazilian manufacturing facility and upgrading global manufacturing capabilities.

Section 1 of Illustration 14–4 includes a "Gain on sale of equipment" that is neither unusual nor infrequent with the revenues. However, an unusual loss and an infrequent gain are reported at the end of the section. The proper classification of these items is not always clear without carefully examining the circumstances.

In addition, GAAP require a few items to be reported as extraordinary gains or losses, even if they do not otherwise meet the normal criteria. For example, *FASB Statement No. 4* requires a gain or loss from retiring debt to be reported as extraordinary. Thus, in 1992, **Maybelline, Inc.** reported an extraordinary loss of $13,568,000 from the retirement of debt.

---

[4]Ibid., sec. I17.107. Originally published as *APB Opinion No. 30,* par. 20.

[5]Ibid., sec. I17.110. Originally published as *APB Opinion No. 30,* par. 23.

Illustration 14–5   Calculating the Cumulative Effect of a Change in Accounting Principle

Year	Double-Declining-Depreciation Amount	Straight-Line Depreciation Amount	Pre-Tax Difference	Tax Rate	After-Tax Cumulative Effect
Prior to change:					
19X1	$ 80,000	$ 35,000	$45,000		
19X2	60,000	35,000	25,000		
19X3	45,000	35,000	10,000		
Subtotal	$185,000	$105,000	$80,000	30%	$56,000†
Year of change:					
19X4	$ 33,750	35,000*			
Years after change:					
19X5		35,000			
19X6		35,000			
19X7		35,000			
19X8		35,000			
Total		$210,000			

*Reported on the 19X4 income statement as depreciation expense.
†Reported on the 19X4 income statement as the cumulative adjustment for differences in the three years
prior to the change in 19X4, net of $24,000 additional taxes to be paid (30% × $80,000).

CHANGES IN ACCOUNTING PRINCIPLES

In general, the *consistency principle* requires a company to continue applying a specific accounting method or principle once it is chosen. (In this context, the term *accounting principles* describes accounting methods, such as FIFO and straight-line depreciation.) However, a company may change from one acceptable accounting principle to another as long as it justifies the change as an improvement in the information provided in its financial statements. In addition, companies often change accounting principles when they adopt new standards issued by the FASB.

When a company changes accounting principles, it usually affects the amount of reported income in more than one way. For example, let's consider Connelly Corporation's income statement in Illustration 14–4. The company purchased its only depreciable asset early in 19X1 for $320,000. The asset has a $40,000 salvage value and has been depreciated with the double-declining balance method for three of the eight years in its predicted useful life. (This company is subject to a 30% income tax rate.) During 19X4, the company decided that its income statement would be more useful if the annual depreciation were calculated with the straight-line method instead of double-declining balance.

In Illustration 14–5, we compare the results of applying the two depreciation methods to the first three years in the asset's service life and show how the company would determine what to report on its 19X4 income statement. The table shows that the accelerated method caused $185,000 of depreciation to be allocated to 19X1 through 19X3. If the straight-line method had been used from the beginning, only $105,000 of depreciation would have been allocated to those years. To give the accounts the balances that they would have had under the straight-line method, the company needs to decrease accumulated depreciation for this asset by the $80,000 gross difference. Offsetting this debit is a credit of $24,000 (30% × $80,000) to a deferred income tax liability for additional taxes to be paid in the future. The remaining $56,000 is the resulting credit to equity created by this change. Because the change increases equity, the company adds it to the income for the year in which the change is made effective.

Reporting Requirements for Changes in Accounting Principles

The income statement in Illustration 14–4 on page 538 shows the acceptable method of reporting the effects of a change in accounting principles by the Connelly Corporation. Section 1 of the income statement includes $35,000 of depreciation expense for the current year. This amount is shown in the straight-line method column for 19X4 in Illustration 14–5. Thus, the income for the year of the change is based on the new accounting principle. The annual depreciation of $35,000 also will be used in 19X5 through 19X8. In Illustration 14–5, we calculate the $56,000 catch-up adjustment reported in section 4 of the income statement in Illustration 14–4. This item is the cumulative effect of the change in accounting principle.

In many cases, the cumulative effect may be millions or even billions of dollars. Many large companies reported cumulative effects when they changed their accounting for employees' benefits other than pensions and income taxes. These changes were made because the FASB implemented *Statement No. 106*. For example, Deere & Company reported a $1,095 million reduction in net income when it first applied *Statement No. 106* in 1993.

In addition to the information in the financial statements, two points about the change should be explained: First, a footnote should describe the change and why it is an improvement over the old principle. Second, the footnote should describe what 19X4's income would have been under the old method if the change had not occurred. For this example, the footnote would reveal that leaving the method unchanged would have caused the depreciation for 19X4 to be $33,750 under double-declining instead of $35,000 under straight-line. This footnoted amount appears in Illustration 14–5 as the declining balance depreciation for 19X4.

EARNINGS PER SHARE SECTION OF THE INCOME STATEMENT

Section 5 of Illustration 14–4 provides detailed information about earnings per share results for the year. This information is included on the face of the income statement in accordance with GAAP. This section is more complete than the minimum reporting requirements to show the possible categories companies can and often do report. A later section of the chapter explains the basic procedures to compute earnings per share.

PRIOR PERIOD ADJUSTMENTS FOR CORRECTING MATERIAL ERRORS

Companies do not report the effect of a **prior period adjustment** on their current income statements. Instead, prior period adjustments appear in the statement of retained earnings (or the statement of changes in stockholders' equity), net of any income tax effects. Prior period adjustments modify the beginning balance of retained earnings for events occurring prior to the earliest year described in the financial statements. Under GAAP, prior period adjustments only record the effects of correcting material errors in earlier years. These errors include arithmetic mistakes, using unacceptable accounting principles, or failing to consider relevant facts.[6] An error would occur if an accountant mistakenly omits depreciation, applies an unacceptable depreciation method, or overlooks important facts in predicting an asset's useful life. For example, assume that the accountant for the Connelly Corporation failed to detect an error

---

[6]Ibid, sec. A35.104. Originally published as *APB Opinion No. 20,* par. 13.

in a 19X2 journal entry for the purchase of land incorrectly debited to an expense account. This statement of retained earnings includes a prior period adjustment to correct this error discovered in 19X4:

CONNELLY CORPORATION
Statement of Retained Earnings
For Year Ended December 31, 19X4

Retained earnings, December 31, 19X3, as previously stated . .	$4,745,000
Prior period adjustment:	
Cost of land incorrectly charged to expense	
(net of $63,000 income taxes)	147,000
Retained earnings, December 31, 19X3, as adjusted	$4,892,000
Plus net income	1,162,500
Less cash dividends declared	(240,000)
Retained earnings, December 31, 19X4	$5,814,500

CHANGES IN ACCOUNTING ESTIMATES

Many of the items disclosed in financial statements are based on estimates and predictions. Future events are certain to reveal that some of these estimates and predictions were inaccurate, even though they were based on the best data available at the time. Because these inaccuracies are not the result of mistakes, they are not considered to be accounting errors. Thus, any corrections of these estimates are not reported as prior period adjustments. Instead, they are **changes in accounting estimates.** For example, depreciation is based on predicted useful lives and salvage values. As new information becomes available, it may be used to change the predictions and modify the amounts reported as depreciation expense. Unlike changes in accounting principles, changes in accounting estimates are not accounted for with cumulative catch-up adjustments. Instead, the revised estimates are applied in determining revenues and expenses for the current and future periods. In Chapter 10, we explained one common change in an accounting estimate when we discussed revising depreciation rates.

STATEMENT OF CHANGES IN STOCKHOLDERS' EQUITY

Most corporations actually do not present a separate statement of retained earnings. Instead, they provide a **statement of changes in stockholders' equity** that lists the beginning and ending balances of each equity account and describes all the changes that occurred during the year. For example, **Albertson's Inc.,** which operates a large chain of retail food-drug stores, presents this information in a format that provides a column for each component of equity, and uses the rows to describe the events of the year. (See Illustration 14–6.) Notice that the company acquired treasury stock in fiscal year 1994 and then either sold or retired all the shares. The statement also indicates a stock split, but the credit to the Common Stock account reveals it was actually a 100% stock dividend. (For reasons not explained in the report, the dividend was recorded with a partial transfer of contributed capital in excess of par to the common stock account.)

Progress Check

14-8   Which of the following is an extraordinary item?   *(a)* A settlement paid to a customer injured while using the company's product;   *(b)* A loss from damages to a plant caused by a meteorite;   *(c)* A loss from selling old equipment.

Illustration 14-6

ALBERTSON'S INC.
Consolidated Stockholders' Equity
(In thousands, except per share data)

	Common Stock $1.00 Par Value	Capital in Excess of Par	Retained Earnings	Treasury Stock	Total
Balance at January 30, 1992	$132,131	$ 718	$1,066,603		$1,199,452
Exercise of stock options	199	4,191			4,390
Cash dividends, $0.32 per share			(84,631)		(84,631)
Net earnings			269,217		269,217
Balance at January 28, 1993	132,330	4,909	1,251,189		1,388,428
Exercise of stock options	245	4,238			4,483
Purchase treasury shares				$(517,526)	(517,526)
Issue treasury shares		19,615		244,912	264,527
Retire treasury shares	(5,788)	(25,010)	(241,816)	272,614	
Two-for-one stock split	126,620	(1,635)	(124,985)		
Other			953		953
Cash dividends, $0.36 per share			(91,167)		(91,167)
Net earnings			339,681		339,681
Balance at February 3, 1994	$253,407	$ 2,117	$1,133,855		$1,389,379

Courtesy of Albertson's Inc.

14-9   Identify the four possible major sections of the income statement that might appear below income from continuing operations.

14-10 A company that used FIFO for the past 15 years has decided to switch to LIFO. The effect of this event on past years' net income should be: *(a)* Reported as a prior period adjustment to retained earnings; *(b)* Ignored as it is a change in an accounting estimate; *(c)* Reported on the current year's income statement.

EARNINGS PER SHARE

Among the most widely quoted items of accounting information is **earnings per share.** This number represents the amount of income earned by each share of a corporation's common stock. For example, this excerpt from *The Wall Street Journal* reported the earnings per share **J. C. Penney Co.** achieved and expected to achieve:

LO 4

Calculate earnings per share for companies with simple capital structures and explain the difference between primary and fully diluted earnings per share.

> J. C. Penney Co. expects to post another record year for earnings and revenue, William R. Howell, chairman and chief executive, said at the company's annual meeting. Mr. Howell said he is comfortable with analysts' estimates of earnings between $4.15 and $4.22 a share for the fiscal year ending Jan. 29, 1995, a gain of 10% to 12% from fiscal 1994 earnings of $944 million, or $3.77 a share.[7]

---

[7]"J. C. Penney Expects to have Record Year for Sales and Profit," *The Wall Street Journal,* May 23, 1994, p. C16.

As this excerpt suggests, investors and their advisers use earnings per share to evaluate a corporation's past performance, project its future performance, and compare its prospects with other investment opportunities.

Because of the importance and widespread use of earnings per share numbers, accountants have developed detailed guidelines for calculating it. One important factor that shapes the presentation of earnings per share is the company's capital structure, which can be either simple or complex.

COMPANIES WITH SIMPLE CAPITAL STRUCTURES

Earnings per share calculations can be simple or complicated, depending on a company's situation. The calculations are not difficult for a company with a **simple capital structure** because it has only common stock and perhaps nonconvertible preferred stock outstanding. That is, a simple capital structure cannot include any options or rights to purchase common stock or any convertible preferred stock or bonds.

Calculating Earnings per Share When the Number of Common Shares Does Not Change

The earnings per share calculation is simple if: (1) a company has only common stock and nonconvertible preferred stock outstanding, and (2) the number of outstanding common shares does not change during the period. In this situation, the calculation involves determining the amount of the net income that is available to the common stockholders and dividing it by the number of common shares. The amount of income available to the common stockholders is the year's net income less any dividends declared or accumulated on the preferred stock. (If the preferred stock is cumulative, the current year's dividend must be subtracted even if it was not declared.) The following formula applies:

$$\text{Earnings per share} = \frac{\text{Net income} - \text{Preferred dividends}}{\text{Outstanding common shares}}$$

For example, assume that Blackwell Company earned $40,000 net income in 19X1 and declared dividends of $7,500 on its noncumulative preferred stock. The company had 5,000 common shares outstanding throughout the entire year. Thus:

$$\text{Earnings per share} = \frac{\$40,000 - \$7,500}{5,000 \text{ shares}} = \$6.50$$

The calculation is more complex if the number of outstanding shares changes during the year. The number of shares outstanding may change for a variety of reasons such as sales of additional shares, purchases of treasury stock, and stock dividends or splits.

Finding the Denominator When a Company Sells or Purchases Common Shares

If a company sells additional shares or purchases treasury shares during the year, the denominator of the formula is the weighted-average number of outstanding shares. The idea behind this change is to produce an average amount of earnings accruing to the average number of shares outstanding during the year the income was earned.

For example, suppose that Blackwell Company earned $40,000 in 19X2 and declared preferred dividends of $7,500. As a result, the earnings available to the common stock is again $32,500. Also assume that Blackwell sold 4,000 additional common shares on July 1, 19X2, and purchased 3,000 treasury shares on November 1, 19X2. As a result, 5,000 shares were outstanding for six months, 9,000 shares were outstanding for four months, and 6,000 shares were outstanding for two months. We calculate the weighted-average number of shares outstanding as follows:

Time Period	Outstanding Shares	Fraction of Year	Weighted Average
January–June	5,000	6/12	2,500
July–October	9,000	4/12	3,000
November–December	6,000	2/12	1,000
Weighted-average outstanding shares ..			6,500

Using the weighted-average number of common shares outstanding for Blackwell, the earnings per share calculation is:

$$\text{Earnings per share} = \frac{\$40,000 - \$7,500}{6,500 \text{ shares}} = \$5.00$$

Blackwell reports this number at the bottom of its 19X2 income statement.

Adjusting the Denominator for Stock Splits and Stock Dividends

The number of outstanding shares also can be affected by a stock split or stock dividend during the year. These events do not bring in any additional assets; thus, they do not affect the company's ability to produce earnings for the common stockholders. In effect, the earnings for the year are simply spread out over a larger number of shares. As a result, in calculating the weighted-average number of shares outstanding, stock splits and stock dividends are not treated like stock sales and purchases.

When a stock split or stock dividend occurs, the number of shares that were outstanding earlier in the year are retroactively restated to reflect the effects of the stock split or dividend as if it occurred at the beginning of the year. For example, reconsider the Blackwell Company example and assume that the stock transactions in 19X2 included a two-for-one stock split on December 1. This split caused the percentage ownership of each share to be cut in half while doubling the number of outstanding shares. The situation is described by this table:

Time Period	Original Shares	Effect of Split	Post-Split Shares
January–June	5,000	2	10,000
July–October	9,000	2	18,000
November	6,000	2	12,000

Then, the numbers in the third column can be inserted into the weighted-average calculation for the new shares:

Time Period	Post-Split Shares	Fraction of Year	Weighted Average
January–June	10,000	6/12	5,000
July–October	18,000	4/12	6,000
November–December	12,000	2/12	2,000
Weighted-average outstanding shares			13,000

The Blackwell Company's earnings per share for 19X2 under this set of assumptions are:

$$\text{Earnings per share} = \frac{\$40,000 - \$7,500}{13,000 \text{ shares}} = \$2.50$$

The same sort of modification is used when stock dividends occur. For example, if the two-for-one stock split had been a 10% stock dividend, the numbers of old outstanding shares would have been multiplied by 1.1 instead of two.

COMPANIES WITH COMPLEX CAPITAL STRUCTURES

Companies with **complex capital structures** have outstanding options or rights to purchase common stock and/or securities such as bonds or preferred stock that are convertible into common stock. Earnings per share calculations for companies with complex capital structures are more complicated. Often, such companies must present two types of earnings per share calculations. One is called **primary earnings per share,** and the other is called **fully diluted earnings per share.**

Suppose that a corporation has convertible preferred stock outstanding throughout the current year. However, consider what the effects would have been if the preferred shares had been converted at the beginning of the year. The result of this assumed conversion would have been to increase the number of common shares outstanding and to reduce preferred dividends. The net result may have been to reduce earnings per share, or to increase earnings per share. When the assumed conversion of a security reduces earnings per share, the security is said to be **dilutive;** those that increase earnings per share are **antidilutive.**

Primary Earnings per Share

Based on detailed rules, convertible securities are evaluated at the time they are issued.[8] If eventual conversion appears highly probable, the convertible security is called a **common stock equivalent.** Primary earnings per share is calculated as if dilutive common stock equivalents had already been converted at the beginning of the period.

Fully Diluted Earnings per Share

Common stock equivalents have terms that make their eventual conversion very probable. Other convertible securities are less apt to be converted. Nevertheless, if we assume those securities were converted at the beginning of the period, the effect may be to reduce earnings per share; in other words, the assumed conversion may have a dilutive effect. Fully diluted earnings per share is calculated as if all dilutive securities had already been converted.

PRESENTING EARNINGS PER SHARE ON THE INCOME STATEMENT

Because information about earnings per share is important, corporations must report it on the face of their income statements. Furthermore, they usually report the amount of earnings per share for net income and each of the four subcategories of income (continuing operations, discontinued segments, extraordinary items, and the effect of accounting principle changes). Illustration 14–4 on page 538 shows Connelly Corporation's earnings per share in section 5.

Even though GAAP is flexible in where some earnings per share information should be reported, many companies present all the details in one place for the convenience of the financial statement users. Illustration 14–7 provides real earnings per share presentations by **Sprint Corporation** and the **Colgate-Palmolive Company.**

---

[8]FASB, *Accounting Standards—Current Text* (Norwalk, CT, 1990), sec. E09.122–127. First published as *APB Opinion No. 15,* par. 31, 33, 35–37. Also see FASB, *Statement of Financial Accounting Standards No. 85* (March 1985), par. 2.

Illustration 14–7 Reporting Earnings per Share on the Income Statement

SPRINT CORPORATION:
Showing multiple components:

	1993	1992	1991
Earnings per common share			
Continuing operations	$1.39	$1.46	$1.41
Discontinued operations	(0.04)		0.15
Extraordinary item	(0.08)	(0.05)	(0.01)
Cumulative effect of changes in accounting principles	(1.12)	0.07	
Total	$0.15	$1.48	$1.55

COLGATE-PALMOLIVE COMPANY
Showing primary and fully diluted results:

	1993	1992	1991
Earnings per common share, primary			
Income before changes in accounting	$ 3.38	$2.92	$0.77
Cumulative effect on prior years of accounting changes	(2.30)		
Net income	$ 1.08	$2.92	$0.77
Earnings per common share, fully diluted			
Income before changes in accounting	$ 3.15	$2.74	$0.75
Cumulative effect on prior years of accounting changes	(2.10)		
Net income	$ 1.05	$2.74	$0.75

Courtesy of Sprint Corporation and Colgate-Palmolive Company.

Sprint shows the per-share effects of the various components of its income for three fiscal years. Colgate-Palmolive shows the primary and fully diluted results for the same three years.

Progress Check

14–11   During 19X1, FDI Co. had net income of $250,000 and paid preferred dividends of $70,000. On January 1, the company had 25,000 outstanding common shares and purchased 5,000 treasury shares on July 1. Earnings per share for 19X1 is: *(a)* $8.00; *(b)* $9.00; *(c)* $10.00.

14–12   How are stock splits and stock dividends treated in calculating the weighted-average number of outstanding common shares?

14–13   What two sets of earnings per share results are reported for a company with a complex capital structure?

USING THE INFORMATION— THE PRICE-EARNINGS RATIO

LO 5

Calculate the price-earnings ratio and describe its meaning.

You learned in Chapter 13 that a stock's market value is largely affected by the stream of future dividends expected to be paid out to stockholders. Market value is also affected by expected future changes in value. By comparing the company's earnings per share and its market price per share, investors and other decision makers can obtain information about the stock market's apparent expectations for growth in future earnings, dividends, and market values.

Although it would be possible to make this comparison as a rate of return by dividing the earnings per share by the market price per share, the ratio has traditionally been turned upside-down and calculated as the **price-earnings ratio.** Thus, this ratio is found by dividing the stock's market price by the earnings per share, as shown in this formula:

$$\text{Price-earnings ratio} = \frac{\textbf{Market value per share}}{\textbf{Earnings per share}}$$

The ratio may be calculated using the earnings per share reported in the past period. However, analysts often calculate the ratio based on the expected earnings per share for the next period. Suppose, for example, that the stock's current market price is $100 per share and that its next year's earnings are expected to be $8 per share. Its price-earnings ratio (often abbreviated as the PE ratio) is found as $100/$8, which is 12.5.

As a general rule, stocks with higher PE ratios (generally greater than 12 to 15) are considered more likely to be overpriced while stocks with lower PE ratios (generally less than 5 to 8) are considered more likely to be underpriced. Thus, some investors prefer to sell or avoid buying stocks with high PE ratios while they prefer to buy or hold stocks that have low PE ratios. Investment decisions are not quite that simple, however, because a stock with a high PE ratio may prove to be a good investment if its earnings increase rapidly. On the other hand, a stock with a low PE ratio may prove to be a low performer. Although the price-earnings ratio is clearly important for investment decisions, it is only one piece of information that investors should consider.

Progress Check

14-14   Calculate the price-earnings ratio for a company with earnings per share of $4.25 and stock with a market value of $34.00.

14-15   Two companies in the same industry face similar levels of risk, have nearly the same level of earnings, and are expected to continue their historical record of paying $1.50 annual dividends per share. Yet, one of the companies has a PE ratio of 6 while the other has a PE ratio of 10. Which company does the market apparently expect to have a higher future growth rate in earnings?

SUMMARY OF CHAPTER IN TERMS OF LEARNING OBJECTIVES

LO 1. Describe stock dividends and stock splits and explain their effects on a corporation's assets and stockholders' equity. In contrast to cash dividends, stock dividends do not transfer corporate assets to stockholders. Stock dividends and stock splits do not affect assets, total stockholders' equity, or the equity attributed to each stockholder. Small stock dividends ($\leq 25\%$) are recorded by capitalizing retained earnings equal to the market value of the distributed shares. Large stock dividends ($>25\%$) are recorded by capitalizing retained earnings equal to the par or stated value of the issued shares. Stock splits are not recorded through journal entries but should lead to changing the account title for the common stock if it includes the par or stated value.

LO 2. Record purchases and sales of treasury stock and retirements of stock and describe their effects on stockholders' equity. Also, describe restrictions and appropriations of retained earnings and explain how they are described in financial reports. When outstanding treasury shares are repurchased by the corporation that issued them, the cost of the shares is debited to Treasury Stock. Its balance is subtracted from total stockholders' equity in the balance sheet. When treasury stock is later reissued, the amount of any proceeds in excess of cost is credited to Contributed Capital, Treasury Stock Transactions. If the proceeds are less than cost, the difference is debited to Contributed Capital, Treasury Stock Transactions to the extent a credit balance exists in that account. Any remaining amount is debited to Retained Earnings.

Most states limit dividends and treasury stock purchases to the amount of retained earnings. Companies also enter into contracts that may limit the amount of dividends, even though the companies have both the cash and the retained earnings to pay them.

Corporations may voluntarily appropriate retained earnings to inform stockholders why dividends are not larger. Often, however, this information is expressed in a letter to the stockholders.

LO 3. Explain how to report the income effects of discontinued segments, extraordinary items, changes in accounting principles and estimates, and prior period adjustments. If a company has decided to discontinue a segment, the income effects of operating and disposing of the segment are separately reported on the income statement below income from continuing operations. Extraordinary gains or losses also are separated from continuing operations and reported lower in the income statement. A similar treatment is required for the cumulative effects of changes in accounting principles. Prior period adjustments for error corrections are not reported on the income statement, but appear on the retained earnings statement or the statement of changes in stockholders' equity. Changes in accounting estimates arise when new information shows the old estimates to be inaccurate. If an accounting estimate is changed, the firm uses the new estimate to calculate income in the current and future periods.

LO 4. Calculate earnings per share for companies with simple capital structures and explain the difference between primary and fully diluted earnings per share. The outstanding securities of companies with simple capital structures do not include any securities that are convertible into common stock. These companies calculate earnings per share by dividing net income (less any preferred dividends) by the weighted-average number of outstanding common shares. Companies with complex capital structures have issued securities that are convertible into common stock. These companies often have to report both primary earnings per share and fully diluted earnings per share.

LO 5. Calculate the price-earnings ratio and describe its meaning. The price-earnings ratio of a common stock is closely watched by investors and other decision makers. The ratio is calculated by dividing the current market value per share by earnings per share. A high ratio may suggest that a stock is overvalued while a low ratio may suggest that a stock is undervalued. However, selecting stocks to buy or sell requires a great deal more information.

DEMONSTRATION PROBLEM

The Precision Company began 19X1 with the following balances in its stockholders' equity accounts:

Common stock, $10 par, 500,000 shares authorized, 200,000 shares issued and outstanding	$2,000,000
Contributed capital in excess of par	1,000,000
Retained earnings	5,000,000
Total	$8,000,000

All of the outstanding stock was issued for $15 when the company was created.

Part 1

Prepare journal entries to account for the following transactions during 19X1:

Mar. 31 Declared a 20% stock dividend. The market value of the stock was $18 per share.

Apr. 15 Distributed the stock dividend declared on March 31.

June 30 Purchased 30,000 shares of treasury stock at $20 per share.

Aug. 31 Sold 20,000 treasury shares at $26 per share.

Nov. 30 Purchased and retired 50,000 shares at $24 per share.

Part 2

Use the following information to prepare an income statement for 19X1, including earnings per share results for each category of income.

Cumulative effect of a change in depreciation method (net of tax benefit)	$ (136,500)
Expenses related to continuing operations	(2,072,500)
Extraordinary gain on debt retirement (net of tax)	182,000
Gain on disposal of discontinued segment's assets (net of tax)	29,000
Gain on sale of stock investment	400,000
Loss from operating discontinued segment (net of tax benefit)	(120,000)
Income taxes on income from continuing operations	(225,000)
Prior period adjustment for error (net of tax benefit)	(75,000)
Sales	4,140,000
Infrequent loss	(650,000)

Planning the Solution

- Decide whether the stock dividend is a small or large dividend. Then, analyze each event to determine the accounts affected and the appropriate amounts to be recorded.
- Based on the shares of outstanding stock at the beginning of the year and the transactions during the year, calculate the weighted-average number of outstanding shares for the year.
- Assign each of the listed items to an appropriate income statement category.
- Prepare an income statement similar to Illustration 14–4, including appropriate earnings per share results.

Solution to Demonstration Problem

Part 1

			Debit	Credit
Mar. 31	Stock Dividends Declared	720,000.00	
		Common Stock Dividend Distributable		400,000.00
		Contributed Capital in Excess of Par Value, Common Stock		320,000.00
		Declared a small stock dividend of 20% or 40,000 shares; market value is $18 per share.		
Apr. 15	Common Stock Dividend Distributable	400,000.00	
		Common Stock		400,000.00
		Distributed 40,000 shares of common stock.		
June 30	Treasury Stock, Common	600,000.00	
		Cash		600,000.00
		Purchased 30,000 shares of common stock at $20 per share.		
Aug. 31	Cash	520,000.00	
		Treasury Stock, Common		400,000.00
		Contributed Capital, Treasury Stock Transactions		120,000.00
		Sold 20,000 shares of treasury stock at $26 per share.		

Nov.	30	Common Stock	500,000.00	
		Contributed Capital in Excess of Par Value,		
		Common Stock	250,000.00	
		Retained Earnings	450,000.00	
		Cash		1,200,000.00
		Purchased and retired 50,000 shares at $24 per share.		

Part 2

Calculating the weighted average of outstanding shares:

Time Period	Original Shares	Effect of Dividend	Post-Dividend Shares
January–April 15	200,000	1.2	240,000

Time Period	Post-Dividend Shares	Fraction of Year	Weighted Average
January–June	240,000	6/12	120,000
July–August	210,000	2/12	35,000
September–November	230,000	3/12	57,500
December	180,000	1/12	15,000
Weighted-average outstanding shares			227,500

PRECISION COMPANY
Income Statement
For Year Ended December 31, 19X1

Sales	$4,140,000
Expenses	(2,072,500)
Income taxes	(225,000)
Gain on sale of stock investment	400,000
Infrequent loss	(650,000)
Income from continuing operations	$1,592,500

Discontinued operations:

Loss from operating discontinued segment (net of tax benefit)	$(120,000)	
Gain on disposal of discontinued segment's assets (net of tax)	29,000	
Loss from discontinued division		(91,000)
Income before extraordinary items and cumulative effect of a change in accounting principle		$1,501,500

Extraordinary items:

Extraordinary gain on debt retirement (net of tax)	182,000

Cumulative effect of a change in accounting principle:

Cumulative effect of a change in depreciation method (net of tax benefit)	(136,500)
Net income	$1,547,000

Earnings per share (227,500 average shares outstanding):

Income from continuing operations	$ 7.00
Loss from discontinued segment	(0.40)
Income before extraordinary gain and cumulative effect of change in accounting principle	$ 6.60
Extraordinary gain	0.80
Cumulative effect of change in accounting principle	(0.60)
Net income	$ 6.80

GLOSSARY

Antidilutive securities securities the assumed conversion or exercise of which has the effect of decreasing earnings per share. p. 546

Appropriated retained earnings retained earnings that are voluntarily restricted as a way of informing stockholders that dividends will not be paid. p. 534

Changes in accounting estimates modifications to previous estimates or predictions about future events and outcomes, such as salvage values and the useful lives of operating assets. p. 542

Common stock equivalent a convertible or exercisable security the eventual conversion of which is highly probable. p. 546

Complex capital structure a capital structure that includes outstanding rights or options to purchase common stock or securities that are convertible into common stock. p. 546

Dilutive securities securities the assumed conversion or exercise of which has the effect of decreasing earnings per share. p. 546

Earnings per share the amount of income earned by each share of a company's common stock. p. 543

Extraordinary gain or loss a gain or loss that is reported separate from continuing operations because it is both unusual and infrequent. p. 539

Fully diluted earnings per share earnings per share calculated as if all dilutive securities had already been converted. p. 546

Infrequent gain or loss a gain or loss that is not expected to occur again, given the operating environment of the business. p. 539

Large stock dividend a stock dividend that is more than 25% of the corporation's previously outstanding shares. p. 528

Liquidating dividends distributions of corporate assets as a dividend that returns part of the original investment to the stockholders; these distributions are charged to contributed capital accounts. p. 527

Price-earnings ratio the ratio between a company's current market value and its earnings per share; used to gain under-standing of the market's expectations for the stock. p. 547

Primary earnings per share earnings per share calculated as if dilutive common stock equivalents had already been converted or exercised. p. 546

Prior period adjustment a correction of an error in a previous year that is reported in the statement of retained earnings. p. 541

Restricted retained earnings retained earnings that are not available for dividends because of legal or contractual limitations. p. 534

Reverse stock split an act by a corporation to call in its stock and replace each share with less than one new share. p. 531

Segment of a business a component of a company's operations that serves a particular line of business or class of customers and that has assets, activities, and financial results of operations that can be distinguished from other parts of the business. p. 537

Simple capital structure a capital structure that consists of no more than common stock and nonconvertible preferred stock; it cannot include any options or rights to purchase common stock or any convertible preferred stocks or bonds. p. 544

Small stock dividend a stock dividend that is 25% or less of the corporation's previously outstanding shares. p. 527

Statement of changes in stockholders' equity a financial statement that lists the beginning and ending balances of each equity account and describes all the changes that occurred during the year. p. 542

Stock dividend a corporation's distribution of its own stock to its stockholders without receiving any payment in return. p. 527

Stock split an act by a corporation to call in its stock and replace each share with more than one new share. p. 531

Treasury stock stock that was reacquired and is still held by the issuing corporation. p. 532

Unusual gain or loss a gain or loss that is abnormal or otherwise unrelated to the ordinary activities and environment of the business. p. 539

QUESTIONS

1. Why is the term *liquidating dividend* used to describe cash dividends that are debited against contributed capital accounts?

2. What effects does declaring a stock dividend have on the corporation's assets, liabilities, and total stockholders' equity? What effects does the distribution of the stock have?

3. What is the difference between a stock dividend and a stock split?

4. Courts have determined that a stock dividend is not taxable income to stockholders. What concept justifies this decision?

5. How does the purchase of treasury stock affect the purchaser's assets and total stockholders' equity?

6. Why do state laws place limits on purchases of treasury stock?

7. Where on the income statement would a company report an abnormal gain that is not expected to occur more often than once every two years?

8. After taking five years' straight-line depreciation expense for an asset that was expected to have an eight-year useful life, a company decided that the asset would last another six years. Is this decision a change in accounting principle? How would the financial statements describe this change?

9. How are earnings per share results calculated for a corporation with a simple capital structure?

10. Refer to the statement of changes in common stockholders' investment for Federal Express Corporation in Appendix G at the end of the book. Can you determine the purpose for the company's annual purchases of treasury stock?

11. Refer to the balance sheet for Ben & Jerry's Homemade, Inc., in Appendix G at the end of the book. How many treasury shares of Class A and Class B stock did the company have at the end of its 1992 fiscal year?

QUICK STUDY (Five-Minute Exercises)

The stockholders' equity section of Baylor Co.'s balance sheet as of June 1 follows:

QS 14–1
(LO 1)

Common stock, $5 par value, 250,000 shares authorized, 100,000 shares issued and outstanding.	$ 500,000
Contributed capital in excess of par value, common stock	235,000
Total contributed capital	$ 735,000
Retained earnings.	422,000
Total stockholders' equity	$1,157,000

On June 1, Baylor declares and distributes a 10% stock dividend. The market value of the stock on this date is $25. Prepare the stockholders' equity section for Baylor immediately following the stock dividend.

On September 2, Garrett Corp. purchased 2,000 shares of its own stock for $18,000. On December 5, Garrett reissued 500 shares of the treasury stock for $4,725. Prepare the December 5 journal entry Garrett should make to record the sale of the treasury stock.

QS 14–2
(LO 2)

Answer the questions about each of the following items related to a company's activities for the year:

QS 14–3
(LO 3)

a. After using an expected useful life of seven years and no salvage value to depreciate its office equipment over the preceding three years, the company decided early this year that the equipment will last only two more years. How should the effects of this decision be reported in the current financial statements?

b. In reviewing the notes payable files, it was discovered that last year the company reported the entire amount of a payment on an installment note payable as interest expense. The mistake had a material effect on the amount of income in the prior year. How should the correction be reported in the current year financial statements?

On January 1, Star Company had 50,000 shares of common stock issued and outstanding. On April 1, it purchased 4,000 treasury shares and on June 5, declared a 20% stock dividend. Calculate Star's weighted-average outstanding shares for the year.

QS 14–4
(LO 4)

Calculate a company's price-earnings ratio if its common stock has a market value of $63 per share and if its earnings per share is $7.20.

QS 14–5
(LO 5)

EXERCISES

Exercise 14–1
Stock dividends and per share values
(LO 1)

The stockholders' equity of Porter Construction, Inc., on March 8 consisted of the following:

Common stock, $25 par value, 100,000 shares authorized, 40,000 shares issued and outstanding	$1,000,000
Contributed capital in excess of par value, common stock	350,000
Total contributed capital	$1,350,000
Retained earnings	450,000
Total stockholders' equity	$1,800,000

On March 8, the stock's market value was $40. On that date, the directors declared a 20% stock dividend distributable on March 31 to the March 20 stockholders of record. The stock's market value was $38 on April 10.

Required

1. Prepare entries to record the dividend declaration and distribution.

2. One stockholder owned 500 shares on March 8. Calculate the per share and total book values of the investor's shares immediately before and after the dividend on March 8.

3. Calculate the market values of the investor's shares as of March 8 and April 10.

Exercise 14–2
Stock dividends and splits
(LO 1)

On March 31, 19X1, Pacific Management Corporation's common stock was selling for $62 per share and the following information appeared in the stockholders' equity section of its balance sheet as of that date:

Common stock, $20 par value, 60,000 shares authorized, 25,000 shares issued and outstanding	$ 500,000
Contributed capital in excess of par value, common stock	200,000
Total contributed capital	$ 700,000
Retained earnings	660,000
Total stockholders' equity	$1,360,000

Required

1. Assume that the company declares and immediately distributes a 100% stock dividend. The event is recorded by capitalizing the required minimum amount of retained earnings. Answer these questions about the stockholders' equity as it exists after issuing the new shares:

   a. What is the retained earnings balance?

   b. What is the total amount of stockholders' equity?

   c. How many shares are outstanding?

2. Assume that the company implements a two-for-one stock split instead of the stock dividend. Answer these questions about the stockholders' equity as it exists after issuing the new shares:

   a. What is the retained earnings balance?

   b. What is the total amount of stockholders' equity?

   c. How many shares are outstanding?

3. Briefly explain the difference, if any, that an investor would experience if new shares are distributed under a large dividend or a stock split.

Exercise 14–3
Reporting a treasury stock purchase
(LO 2)

On August 15, the stockholders' equity section of the balance sheet for Indelible, Inc., included this information:

Stockholders' Equity

Contributed capital:
Common stock, $10 par value, 12,000 shares authorized,
issued, and outstanding.............................. $120,000
Contributed capital in excess of par value, common stock 36,000
Total contributed capital.................................. $156,000
Retained earnings 144,000
Total stockholders' equity $300,000

On the next day, the corporation purchased 1,500 shares of treasury stock at $30 per share. Present the stockholders' equity section as it would appear immediately after the purchase.

Use the information in Exercise 14–3 to develop the accountant's journal entries to record these events for Indelible, Inc.:

1. The purchase of the treasury shares on August 16.
2. The sale of 400 treasury shares on September 1 for cash at $36 per share.
3. The sale of all the remaining treasury shares on September 29 for cash at $25 per share.

Exercise 14–4
Journal entries for treasury stock transactions
(LO 2)

This information appeared in the stockholders' equity section of Winter Sports, Inc.'s balance sheet as of December 31, 19X1:

Common stock, $5 par value, 40,000 shares
authorized, 15,000 shares issued and outstanding .... $ 75,000
Contributed capital in excess of par value, common stock. . . 165,000
Total contributed capital.......................... $240,000
Retained earnings 190,000
Total stockholders' equity $430,000

Exercise 14–5
Journal entries for stock retirements
(LO 2)

On January 1, 19X2, the company purchased and retired 800 shares of common stock.

1. Determine the average amount of contributed capital per share of outstanding stock.
2. Prepare the journal entries to record the retirement under the following separate situations:
   a. The stock was purchased for $13 per share.
   b. The stock was purchased for $16 per share.
   c. The stock was purchased for $30 per share.

During 19X1, Simon's Club, Inc., sold its assets in a chain of wholesale outlets. This sale took the company out of the wholesaling business completely. The company still operates its retail outlets. Following is a lettered list of sections of an income statement:

Exercise 14–6
Income statement categories
(LO 3)

A. Income from continuing operations
B. Income from operating a discontinued segment
C. Gain or loss from disposing of a discontinued segment
D. Extraordinary gain or loss
E. Cumulative effect of a change in accounting principle

Indicate where each of the nine income-related items for the company would appear on the 19X1 income statement by writing the letter of the appropriate section in the blank beside each item.

		Debit	Credit
____ 1.	Depreciation expense	$175,000	
____ 2.	Gain on sale of segment (net of tax)		$ 450,000
____ 3.	Loss from operating segment (net of tax)	370,000	
____ 4.	Salaries expense	360,000	
____ 5.	Sales		1,800,000
____ 6.	Gain on state's condemnation of company property (net of tax)		220,000
____ 7.	Cost of goods sold	920,000	
____ 8.	Effect of change from declining-balance to straight-line depreciation (net of tax)		90,000
____ 9.	Income taxes expense	138,000	

Exercise 14–7
Income statement
presentation
(LO 3)

Use the data for the company described in Exercise 14–6 to present the income statement for 19X1.

Exercise 14–8
Accounting for a change in
accounting principle
(LO 3)

The Long Company put an asset in service on January 1, 19X1. Its cost was $900,000, its predicted service life was six years, and its expected salvage value was $90,000. The company decided to use double-declining-balance depreciation and recorded these amounts of depreciation expense in the first two years of the asset's life:

19X1 .... $300,000
19X2 200,000

The scheduled depreciation expense for 19X3 was $133,000. After consulting with the company's auditors, management decided to change to straight-line depreciation in 19X3, without changing either the predicted service life or salvage value. Under this system, the annual depreciation expense for all years in the asset's life would be $135,000. The company faces a 35% income tax rate.

1. Prepare a table like Illustration 14–5 that deals with this situation.
2. How much depreciation expense will be reported on the company's income statement for this asset in 19X3 and in each of the remaining years of the asset's life?
3. What amount will be reported on the company's 19X3 income statement as the after-tax cumulative effect of the change?

Exercise 14–9
Weighted-average
outstanding shares and
earnings per share
(LO 4)

A company reported $450,000 of net income for 19X1. It also declared $65,000 of dividends on preferred stock for the same year. At the beginning of 19X1, the company had 90,000 outstanding shares of common stock. These two events changed the number of outstanding shares during the year:

Apr. 30 Sold 60,000 common shares for cash.

Oct. 31 Purchased 36,000 shares of common stock for the treasury.

a. What is the amount of net income available to the common stockholders?
b. What is the weighted-average number of shares of common stock for the year?
c. What is the earnings per share for the year?

Exercise 14–10
Weighted-average shares
outstanding and earnings
per share
(LO 4)

A company reported $240,000 of net income for 19X1. It also declared $32,500 of dividends on preferred stock for the same year. At the beginning of 19X1, the company had 25,000 outstanding shares of common stock. These three events changed the number of outstanding shares during the year:

June 1 Sold 15,000 common shares for cash.

Aug. 31 Purchased 6,500 shares of common stock for the treasury.

Oct. 1 Completed a three-for-one stock split.

a.   What is the amount of net income available to the common stockholders?

b.   What is the weighted-average number of shares of common stock for the year?

c.   What is the earnings per share for the year?

Use the following information to calculate the price-earnings ratio for each case:

Exercise 14–11
Computing the price-earnings ratio
(LO 5)

	Earnings per Share	Market Value per Share
a.	$ 4.50	$ 43.00
b.	18.00	120.00
c.	3.25	45.00
d.	0.75	18.00
e.	5.00	83.00

Match each of the numbered definitions with the term it best defines. Indicate your answer by writing the letter for the correct term in the blank space next to each description.

Exercise 14–12
Identifying corporate capital structure terms
(LO 6)

A.   Common stock equivalent

B.   Extraordinary gain or loss

C.   Large stock dividend

D.   Reverse stock split

E.   Small stock dividend

F.   Stock split

G.   Treasury stock

___ 1.   Gain or loss that is reported separate from continuing operations because it is both unusual and infrequent.

___ 2.   Stock that was reacquired and is still held by the issuing corporation.

___ 3.   Stock dividend that is more than 25% of the corporation's previously outstanding shares.

___ 4.   Action by a corporation to call in its stock and replace it with less than one new share.

___ 5.   Convertible or exercisable security that is reasonably expected to be converted or exercised.

___ 6.   Action by a corporation to call in its stock and replace it with more than one new share.

___ 7.   Stock dividend that is 25% or less of the corporation's previously outstanding shares.

PROBLEMS

The balance sheet for Elizabeth Manufacturing, Inc., reported the following components of stockholders' equity on December 31, 19X1:

Problem 14–1
Treasury stock transactions and stock dividends
(LO 1, 2)

Common stock, $10 par value, 100,000 shares authorized, 40,000 shares issued and outstanding.	$400,000
Contributed capital in excess of par value, common stock	60,000
Retained earnings	270,000
Total stockholders' equity	$730,000

The company completed these transactions during 19X2:

Jan. 6   Purchased 4,000 shares of treasury stock at $20.00 cash per share.

Mar. 10   The directors declared a $1.50 per share cash dividend payable on April 10 to the April 2 stockholders of record.

Apr. 10   Paid the dividend declared on March 10.

Aug. 1   Sold 1,500 of the treasury shares at $24.00 per share.

Sept. 6   Sold 2,500 of the treasury shares at $17.00 per share.

Dec. 10   The directors declared a $1.60 per share cash dividend payable on January 10, 19X3, to the December 15 stockholders of record. They also declared a 20% stock dividend distributable on January 10, 19X3, to the December 15 stockholders of record. The market value of the stock was $25.00 per share.

      31   Closed the $388,000 credit balance in the Income Summary account to Retained Earnings.

      31   Closed the Cash Dividends Declared and Stock Dividends Declared accounts.

Required

CHECK FIGURE:
Retained earnings,
Dec. 31, 19X2,
$338,500

1. Prepare general journal entries to record the transactions and closings for 19X2.
2. Prepare a statement of retained earnings for 19X2.
3. Prepare the stockholders' equity section of the company's balance sheet as of December 31, 19X2.

Problem 14–2
Describing equity changes with journal entries and account balances
(LO 1)

At September 30, the end of the third quarter for Astronomical Adventures, Inc., these balances existed in its stockholders' equity accounts:

Common stock, $12 par value.	$360,000
Contributed capital in excess of par value	90,000
Retained earnings.	320,000

Over the next three months, the following journal entries were recorded in the company's equity accounts:

Oct.	5	Cash Dividends Declared	60,000.00	
		Common Dividend Payable		60,000.00
	20	Common Dividend Payable	60,000.00	
		Cash		60,000.00
	31	Stock Dividends Declared	75,000.00	
		Common Stock Dividend Distributable		36,000.00
		Contributed Capital in Excess of		
		Par Value, Common Stock		39,000.00
Nov.	15	Common Stock Dividend Distributable	36,000.00	
		Common Stock, $12 Par Value		36,000.00
Dec.	1	Memo—change the title of the common stock		
		account to reflect the new par value of $4 per share.		
	31	Income Summary	210,000.00	
		Retained Earnings		210,000.00
	31	Retained Earnings	135,000.00	
		Cash Dividends Declared		60,000.00
		Stock Dividends Declared		75,000.00

Required

CHECK FIGURE:
Total equity, Dec. 31,
$920,000

1. Provide explanations for each of the journal entries.
2. Complete the following table showing the balances of the company's equity accounts (including the dividends declared accounts) at each of the indicated dates:

Date	Oct. 5	Oct. 20	Oct. 31	Nov. 15	Dec. 1	Dec. 31
Common stock	$	$	$	$	$	$
Stock dividend distributable						
Contributed capital in excess of par						
Retained earnings						
Less:						
Cash dividends declared ..						
Stock dividends declared ..						
Combined balances of equity accounts	$	$	$	$	$	$

The equity sections from the 19X1 and 19X2 balance sheets of New Haven Corporation appeared as follows:

Problem 14–3
Changes in retained earnings
(LO 1, 2)

Stockholders' Equity
(As of December 31, 19X1)

Common stock, $4 par value, 100,000 shares authorized, 40,000 shares issued and outstanding	$160,000
Contributed capital in excess of par value, common stock ..	120,000
Total contributed capital	$280,000
Retained earnings	320,000
Total stockholders' equity	$600,000

Stockholders' Equity
(As of December 31, 19X2)

Common stock, $4 par value, 100,000 shares authorized, 47,400 shares issued, 3,000 in the treasury	$189,600
Contributed capital in excess of par value, common stock ..	179,200
Total contributed capital	$368,800
Retained earnings ($30,000 restricted)	400,000
Total	$768,800
Less cost of treasury stock	(30,000)
Total stockholders' equity	$738,800

The following events occurred during 19X2:

Jan. 10 A $0.50 per share cash dividend was declared, and the date of record was five days later.

Mar. 17 The treasury stock was purchased.

Apr. 10 A $0.50 per share cash dividend was declared, and the date of record was five days later.

July 10 A $0.50 per share cash dividend was declared, and the date of record was five days later.

Aug. 15 A 20% stock dividend was declared when the market value was $12.00 per share.

Sept. 8 The dividend shares were issued.

Oct. 10 A $0.50 per share cash dividend was declared, and the date of record was five days later.

Required

1. How many shares were outstanding on each of the cash dividend dates?
2. How large were each of the four cash dividends?
3. How large was the capitalization of retained earnings for the stock dividend?
4. What was the price per share paid for the treasury stock?
5. How much income did the company achieve during 19X2?

CHECK FIGURE:
Net income, $248,000

Problem 14–4
Presenting items in an
income statement
(LO 3)

The following table shows the balances from various accounts in the adjusted trial balance for McHenry Corp. as of December 31, 19X1:

		Debit	Credit
a.	Interest earned		$ 8,000
b.	Depreciation expense, equipment	$ 24,000	
c.	Loss on sale of office equipment	16,500	
d.	Accounts payable		28,000
e.	Other operating expenses	65,000	
f.	Accumulated depreciation, equipment		49,000
g.	Gain from settling a lawsuit		28,000
h.	Cumulative effect of change in accounting principle (pre-tax) ..	42,000	
i.	Accumulated depreciation, buildings		109,000
j.	Loss from operating a discontinued segment (pre-tax)	13,000	
k.	Gain on early settlement of debt (pre-tax)		19,000
l.	Sales		647,000
m.	Depreciation expense, buildings	36,000	
n.	Correction of overstatement of prior year's sales (pre-tax)	10,000	
o.	Gain on sale of discontinued segment's assets (pre-tax)		22,000
p.	Loss from settling a lawsuit	16,000	
q.	Income taxes expense	?	
r.	Cost of goods sold	325,000	

Required

Answer each of these questions by providing detailed schedules:

1. Assuming that the company's income tax rate is 30%, what are the tax effects and after-tax measures of the items labeled as pre-tax?
2. What is the amount of the company's income from continuing operations before income taxes? What is the amount of the company's income taxes expense? What is the amount of the company's income from continuing operations?
3. What is the amount of after-tax income associated with the discontinued segment?
4. What is the amount of income before extraordinary items and the cumulative effect of the change in principle?
5. What is the amount of net income for the year?

CHECK FIGURE:
Net income, $130,550

Problem 14–5
Changes in accounting
principles
(LO 3)

On January 1, 19X1, Fields, Inc., purchased some equipment. Its cost was $400,000 and it was expected to have a salvage value of $20,000 at the end of its five-year useful life. Depreciation was allocated to 19X1, 19X2, and 19X3 with the declining-balance method at twice the straight-line rate. Early in 19X4, the company concluded that changing to the straight-line method would produce more useful financial statements because it would be consistent with the practices of other firms in the industry.

Required

Preparation component:

1. Do generally accepted accounting principles allow Fields, Inc., to change depreciation methods in 19X4?
2. Prepare a schedule that shows the amount of depreciation expense allocated to 19X1 through 19X3 under the declining-balance method.
3. Prepare a schedule that shows the amount of depreciation expense that would have been allocated to 19X1 through 19X3 under the straight-line method.
4. Combine the information from your answers to Requirements 2 and 3 in a table like Illustration 14–5 that computes the before- and after-tax cumulative effects of the change.

CHECK FIGURE:
After-tax cumulative effect, $59,920

The company's income tax rate is 30%. (For simplicity, round your answers to the nearest dollar.)

5. How should the cumulative effect be reported by the company? Does the cumulative effect increase or decrease net income?

6. How much depreciation expense will be reported on the income statement for 19X4?

Analysis component

7. Assume that in error, Fields, Inc., treats the change in depreciation methods as a change in an accounting estimate. Using your answers from requirements 2, 3, and 4, describe the effect this error would have on the 19X4 financial statements.

The income statements for Safeco, Inc., presented the following information when they were first published in 19X2, 19X3, and 19X4:

Problem 14–6
Earnings per share calculations and presentation
(LO 4)

	19X2	19X3	19X4
Sales	$740,000	$850,000	$825,000
Expenses	465,000	520,000	491,000
Income from continuing operations	$275,000	$330,000	$334,000
Loss on discontinued segment	(105,000)		
Income before extraordinary items	$170,000	$330,000	$334,000
Extraordinary gain (loss)		66,000	(140,000)
Net income	$170,000	$396,000	$194,000

The company also experienced some changes in the number of outstanding shares through the following events:

Outstanding shares on December 31, 19X1	10,000
19X2:	
Treasury stock purchase on April 1	− 1,000
Issuance of new shares on June 30	+ 3,000
10% stock dividend on October 1	+ 1,200
Outstanding shares on December 31, 19X2	13,200
19X3:	
Issuance of new shares on July 1	+ 4,000
Treasury stock purchase on November 1	− 1,200
Outstanding shares on December 31, 19X3	16,000
19X4:	
Issuance of new shares on August 1	+ 5,000
Treasury stock purchase on September 1	− 1,000
Three-for-one split on October 1	+ 40,000
Outstanding shares on December 31, 19X4	60,000

Required

Preparation component:

1. Calculate the weighted average of the outstanding common shares as of the end of 19X2.

2. Calculate the 19X2 earnings per share amounts to report on the 19X2 income statement for income from continuing operations, loss on discontinued segment, and net income.

3. Calculate the weighted average of the outstanding common shares as of the end of 19X3.

4. Calculate the 19X3 earnings per share amounts to report on the 19X3 income statement for income from continuing operations, the extraordinary gain, and net income.

5. Calculate the weighted average of the outstanding common shares as of the end of 19X4.

CHECK FIGURE:
19X4 earnings per share
for net income, $3.64

6. Calculate the 19X4 earnings per share amounts to report on the 19X4 income statement for income from continuing operations, the extraordinary gain, and net income.

Analysis component:

7. Write a brief explanation of how you would use the earnings per share statistics from requirement 6 to estimate earnings per share for 19X5.

CRITICAL THINKING: ESSAYS, PROBLEMS, AND CASES

Analytical Essays

AE 14-1
(LO 1)

As of December 31, the balance sheet for Helmer Corporation provided this information about the stockholders' equity:

Common stock, $10 par value, 50,000 shares authorized, 30,000 shares issued and outstanding . .	$300,000
Contributed capital in excess of par value, common stock	150,000
Retained earnings	500,000
Total stockholders' equity	$950,000

The company's board of directors wants to decrease the market value of the company's outstanding stock from its current level of $50 per share by increasing the number of outstanding shares from 30,000 to 60,000. They are considering a choice between a two-for-one stock split and a 100% stock dividend.

Required

Write a short essay describing the difference between the two alternatives in terms of:

1. Their effects on the stock.
2. How they would be recorded in the accounts.
3. Their effects on the balance sheet.

AE 14-2
(LO 4)

The bookkeeper for Catamaran Corporation, who has almost finished preparing the 19X1 financial statements, has come to you for some advice. This draft of the balance sheet accurately describes the company's stockholders' equity situation:

Preferred stock, $80 par value, 5%, cumulative, 10,000 shares authorized, 6,000 shares issued and outstanding . .	$480,000
Common stock, $1 par value, 50,000 shares authorized, 36,000 shares issued and outstanding	36,000
Contributed capital in excess of par value, common stock	260,000
Retained earnings	125,000
Total stockholders' equity	$901,000

The net income for 19X1 has been correctly measured as $250,000, and the accounts show that no cash dividends were declared on the preferred or common stock. In fact, the only stock transaction that occurred during the year was the sale of 3,000 shares of common stock on May 1, 19X1. The bookkeeper has tentatively calculated earnings per share as follows:

$$\frac{\text{Net income}}{\text{Outstanding common plus preferred as of Dec. 31}} = \frac{\$250,000}{36,000 + 6,000} = \$5.95$$

Required

1. Describe any errors that you find in the calculation of earnings per share and specify the corrections that should be made.

2. Explain how the calculation would be different if the preferred stock is not cumulative and if the additional common shares had been issued through a stock dividend instead of a sale.

Financial Reporting Problems

On January 1, 19X1, QualTech, Inc., had the following balances in its stockholders' equity accounts:

FRP 14-1 (LO 1, 2)

Common stock	$ 750,000
Contributed capital in excess of par value, common stock ..	150,000
Retained earnings	650,000
Total	$1,550,000

The company was authorized to issue 100,000 shares, but had issued only 25,000 shares as of January 1, 19X1. The par value per share was $30. The common stock had the following book values as of December 31:

19X1	$70.00
19X2	30.00
19X3	36.00

At the end of each year, the company paid the following dividends per share:

19X1	$3.50
19X2	1.00
19X3	2.00

On March 1, 19X1, the company declared a 20% stock dividend. The market value of the shares was $40 per share. On August 10, 19X2, the stockholders approved a three-for-one split by increasing the number of authorized shares and reducing the par value per share. On April 5, 19X3, the company purchased 10,000 shares of treasury stock at the price of $50 per share.

Required

Use the preceding facts to find the following information (present your work in appropriate schedules):

1. Determine the par value per share of common stock as of the end of 19X1, 19X2, and 19X3.

2. Determine the number of authorized, issued, and outstanding shares as of the end of 19X1, 19X2, and 19X3.

3. Determine the total par value of the issued shares as of the end of 19X1, 19X2, and 19X3.

4. Determine the balance of contributed capital in excess of par as of the end of 19X1, 19X2, and 19X3.

5. Use the book value per share to determine the total stockholders' equity at the end of 19X1, 19X2, and 19X3.

6. Determine the total amount of retained earnings as of the end of 19X1, 19X2, and 19X3.

7. Use the answer to requirement 6 and information about the dividends to determine the amount of net income reported in 19X1, 19X2, and 19X3.

Finally, use the information to complete this table:

	1/1/X1	12/31/X1	12/31/X2	12/31/X3
Common stock:				
Par value per share	____	____	____	____
Authorized shares	____	____	____	____
Issued shares	____	____	____	____
Treasury shares	____	____	____	____
Outstanding shares	====	====	====	====
Account balances:				
Common stock	____	____	____	____
Contributed capital in excess of par	____	____	____	____
Retained earnings	____	____	____	____
Total	____	____	____	____
Less treasury stock	____	____	____	____
Total stockholders' equity	====	====	====	====

FRP 14-2
(LO 3)

Over the last three years, Commonwealth Enterprises, Inc., has experienced the following income results (all numbers are rounded to the nearest thousand dollars):

	19X1	19X2	19X3
Revenues	$11,000	$11,900	$14,600
Expenses	(7,000)	(7,900)	(7,700)
Gains	3,200	2,400	0
Losses	(1,200)	(1,900)	(3,900)
Net income	$ 6,000	$ 4,500	$ 3,000

Part 1

Use the information to develop a general prediction of the company's net income for 19X4.

Part 2

A closer analysis of the information shows that the company discontinued a segment of its operations in 19X3. The company's accountant has determined that the discontinued segment produced the following amounts of income:

	19X1	19X2	19X3
Revenues	$7,000	$2,600	$1,600
Expenses	(5,000)	(5,000)	(4,000)
Gains		400	
Losses	(1,200)	(1,500)	(900)
Loss on disposal of segment assets			(1,200)

Use the information to calculate the company's income without the discontinued segment and then develop a general prediction of the company's net income for 19X4.

Part 3

A more in-depth analysis of the company's activity reveals that the company experienced these extraordinary items during the three years when it retired some of its debts before their scheduled maturity dates:

	19X1	19X2	19X3
Extraordinary gain	$2,200	$2,000	
Extraordinary loss			$(1,700)

Use the information to calculate the company's income from continuing operations and to develop a general prediction of the company's net income for 19X4.

The financial statements and footnotes from Apple's 1993 annual report are presented in Appendix F at the end of the book. Use that information to answer the following questions:

1. Does Apple have a simple or complex capital structure?

2. What was Apple's earnings per share in fiscal year 1993? How does this figure compare with the results for 1992?

3. What was the dollar amount of cash dividends declared during 1993?

4. What was the dollar amount of cash dividends paid during 1993? How does this number compare with the dividends declared?

5. What is the par value of the common stock?

6. How many shares of common stock were outstanding at the end of the 1993 fiscal year?

7. Does Apple own shares of treasury stock?

8. Did Apple have any extraordinary gains or losses during 1993?

9. Did Apple have any gains or losses on the disposal of a business segment during 1993?

Financial Statement Analysis Case
(LO 1, 2, 3, 4)

Review the As a Matter of Ethics case on page 532 and discuss the ethical implications of the directors' tentative decision to avoid announcing Falcon Corporation's new government contract. What actions would you take if you were the financial vice president?

Ethical Issues Essay

CONCEPT TESTER

(LO 6)

Test your understanding of the concepts introduced in this chapter by completing the following crossword puzzle:

Across Clues

2. Three words; the calling in of stock to replace each share with less than one new share.
5. Three words; a distribution of shares to stockholders without receiving anything in return.
7. Three words; stock that was reacquired and is still held by the issuing corporation.
8. Three words; a gain that is both infrequent and unusual.

Down Clues

1. Three words; replacing each share of a corporation's stock with more than one new share.
3. Three words; the amounmt of income earned by each share of a corporation's stock.
6. Two words; a gain that is not expected to occur again, given the environment of the business.

ANSWERS TO PROGRESS CHECKS

14–1 *c*

14–2 A small stock dividend is 25% or less of the previous oustanding shares. A large stock dividend is greater than 25%.

14–3 Retained earnings equal to the market value of the distributable shares should be capitalized.

14–4 *b*

14–5 No. The shares are an investment for Southern Co. and issued outstanding shares for Northern Corp.

14–6 Treasury stock does not affect the number of both authorized and issued shares. It reduces the amount of outstanding shares.

14–7 *a*

14–8 *b*

14–9 The four major sections are discontinued segments, extraordinary items, cumulative effects of changes in accounting principles, and earnings per share.

14–10 *c*

14–11 *a* Weighted-average shares: $(25,000 \times 6/12) + (20,000 \times 6/12) = 22,500$

Earnings per share: $(\$250,000 - \$70,000)/22,500 = \$8.00$

14–12 The number of shares previously outstanding are retroactively restated to reflect the stock split or stock dividend as if it occurred at the beginning of the year.

14–13 The two sets are primary earnings per share and fully diluted earnings per share.

14–14 $\$34.00/\$4.25 = \$8.00$

14–15 The company with the highest PE ratio.

CHAPTER 15

Installment Notes Payable and Bonds

L. A. Gear Inc. designs, develops, and markets a broad range of athletic and lifestyle footwear for adults and children. Its innovative products include lighted shoes sold under the names of *L. A. LIGHTS*™ and *Light Gear*™. The company's 1993 annual report disclosed the sale of approximately 4.5 million pairs of children's lighted shoes during 1993. Based on industry estimates for 1993, the company had the fourth largest share of the United States market for branded athletic footwear.

Nevertheless, during the three-year period of 1991 through 1993, L. A. Gear experienced substantial net losses that resulted from reduced sales. Fiscal year net losses decreased from $66,200,000 in 1991 to $32,513,000 in 1993. To counter this trend, the company initiated a long-term restructuring plan late in 1991. That effort, which continued throughout the 1993 year, included a program of international expansion. Primarily to finance that effort, the company issued $50 million of bonds payable during December of 1992. These bonds were described on the company's November 30, 1993, balance sheet as 7¾% convertible subordinated debentures due 2002.

L. A. Gear Inc. (In thousands)	1993	1992	1991
Net sales	$398,358	$430,194	$619,175
Net income (loss)	(32,513)	(71,901)	(66,200)
Total assets	254,613	250,144	327,751
Convertible subordinated debentures	50,000	—	—
Shareholders' equity	46,797	87,451	131,715

LEARNING
OBJECTIVES

After studying Chapter 15, you should be able to:

1. **Calculate the payments on an installment note payable and describe their effects on the financial statements.**

2. **Describe the various characteristics of different types of bonds and prepare entries to record bond issuances and retirements.**

3. **Estimate the price of bonds issued at a discount and describe their effects on the issuer's financial statements.**

4. **Estimate the price of bonds issued at a premium and describe their effects on the issuer's financial statements.**

5. **Calculate and describe how to use the ratio of pledged assets to secured liabilities.**

6. **Define or explain the words and phrases listed in the chapter glossary.**

In Chapter 12, you learned that some notes payable require a single payment on the date the note matures. In those cases, the single payment includes the borrowed amount plus interest. You also learned about other notes requiring a series of payments that include interest plus a part of the principal. We begin this chapter with a more complete discussion of these installment notes. Then, we turn to bonds, which are securities issued by corporations and government bodies. The discussion explains the nature of bonds such as the convertible subordinated debentures issued by **L. A. Gear, Inc.**

INSTALLMENT
NOTES PAYABLE

LO 1

Calculate the payments on an installment note payable and describe their effects on the financial statements.

When an **installment note** is used to borrow money, the borrower records the note with an entry similar to the one used for a single-payment note. That is, the increase in cash is recorded with a debit and the increase in the liability is recorded with a credit to Notes Payable. For example, suppose that a company borrows $60,000 by signing an 8% installment note that requires six annual payments. The borrower records the note as follows:

19X1				
Dec.	31	Cash	60,000.00	
		Notes Payable		60,000.00
		Borrowed $60,000 by signing an 8% installment note.		

Installment notes payable like this one require the borrower to pay back the debt with a series of periodic payments. Usually, each payment includes all interest expense that has accrued up to the date of the payment plus some portion of the original amount borrowed (the *principal*). Installment notes generally specify one of two alternative payment patterns. Some notes require payments that include interest and equal amounts of principal while other notes simply call for equal payments.

Installment Notes with Payments of Accrued Interest and Equal Amounts of Principal

Installment note agreements requiring payments of accrued interest plus equal amounts of principal create cash flows that decrease in size over the life of the note. This pattern occurs because each payment reduces the liability's principal balance, with the result that the following period's interest expense is reduced. The next payment is smaller because the amount of interest is reduced. For example, suppose the $60,000,

Illustration 15–1   Installment Note with Payments of Accrued Interest and Equal Amounts of Principal

| | (a) | Payments | | | (e) |
| | | (b) Debit Interest Expense 8% × (a) | (c) Debit Notes Payable $60,000/6 | (d) Credit Cash (b) + (c) | |
Period Ending	Beginning Balance Prior (e)		+	=	Ending Balance (a) − (c)
12/31/X2 ...... $60,000		$ 4,800	$10,000	$14,800	$50,000
12/31/X3 50,000		4,000	10,000	14,000	40,000
12/31/X4 40,000		3,200	10,000	13,200	30,000
12/31/X5 30,000		2,400	10,000	12,400	20,000
12/31/X6 20,000		1,600	10,000	11,600	10,000
12/31/X7 10,000		800	10,000	10,800	0
Total		$16,800 +	$60,000 =	$76,800	

Payments on the note payable:

Payments decrease

Interest decreases with each payment

Each payment includes $10,000 of principal

Interest   Principal

8% note that we just recorded requires the borrower to make six payments at the end of each year equal to the accrued interest plus $10,000 of principal.

We describe the payments, interest, and changes in the balance of this note in Illustration 15–1. Column *a* of the illustration contains the beginning balance of the note. Columns *b*, *c*, and *d* describe each cash payment and how it is divided between interest and principal. Column *b* calculates the interest expense that accrues during each year at 8% of the beginning balance. Column *c* shows the portion of the payment applied to principal. It shows that each payment reduces the liability with a $10,000 debit to the Notes Payable account. Column *d* calculates each annual payment, which consists of the interest in column b plus $10,000. (Notice that the credit to the Cash account equals the sum of the debits to the expense and the liability account.) Finally, column *e* shows the ending balance of the liability, which equals the beginning balance in column *a* minus the principal portion of the payment in column *c*. Over the life of the note, the table shows that the total interest expense is $16,800 and the total reduction in principal is $60,000. Thus, the total cash payments are $76,800.

The graph in the lower section of Illustration 15–1 shows these three points: (1) the total payment gets smaller as the loan balance is reduced, (2) the amount of interest included in each payment gets steadily smaller, and (3) the amount of principal in each payment remains constant at $10,000.

Illustration 15–2
Installment Note with Equal
Payments

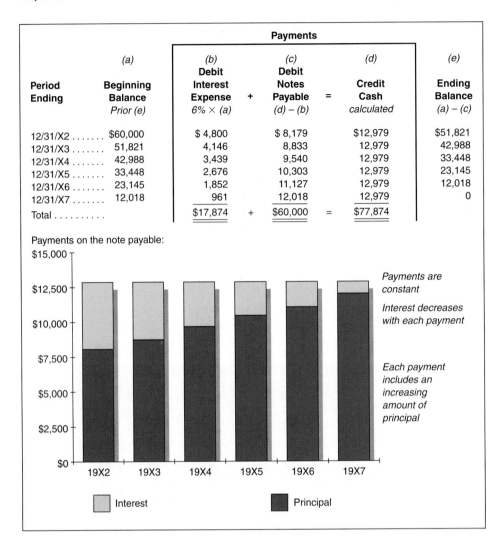

	(a)	Payments			(e)
		(b)	(c)	(d)	
		Debit	Debit		
Period	**Beginning**	**Interest**	**Notes**	**Credit**	**Ending**
Ending	**Balance**	**Expense** +	**Payable** =	**Cash**	**Balance**
	Prior (e)	*6% × (a)*	*(d) – (b)*	*calculated*	*(a) – (c)*
12/31/X2	$60,000	$ 4,800	$ 8,179	$12,979	$51,821
12/31/X3	51,821	4,146	8,833	12,979	42,988
12/31/X4	42,988	3,439	9,540	12,979	33,448
12/31/X5	33,448	2,676	10,303	12,979	23,145
12/31/X6	23,145	1,852	11,127	12,979	12,018
12/31/X7	12,018	961	12,018	12,979	0
Total		$17,874 +	$60,000 =	$77,874	

Payments on the note payable:

Payments are constant

Interest decreases with each payment

Each payment includes an increasing amount of principal

The borrower records the effects of the first two payments with these entries:

19X2				
Dec.	31	Interest Expense	4,800.00	
		Notes Payable	10,000.00	
		Cash		14,800.00
		To record first installment payment.		

19X3				
Dec.	31	Interest Expense	4,000.00	
		Notes Payable	10,000.00	
		Cash		14,000.00
		To record second installment payment.		

After all six payments are recorded, the balance of the Notes Payable account for the note is eliminated.

Installment Notes with Equal Payments

In contrast to the previous pattern, many installment notes require the borrower to make a series of equal payments. These payments consist of changing amounts of interest and principal. To demonstrate this type of note, assume that a $60,000 note requires the borrower to make a series of six equal payments of $12,979 at the end of each year. Illustration 15–2 shows the effects of making the payments on this note. (The payments are $12,979 because $60,000 is the present value of an annuity of six annual payments of $12,979, discounted at 8%. We show you how to make this calculation later in this section.)

Allocating Each Payment between Interest and Principal. Each payment of $12,979 includes both interest and principal. Look at Illustration 15–2 to see how an accountant allocates the total amount of each payment between interest and principal.

The table is essentially the same as the table in Illustration 15–1. Again, column *a* shows the liability's beginning balance for each year. Column *b* presents the interest that accrues each year at 8% of the beginning balance. Column *c* calculates the change in the principal of the liability caused by each payment. The debit to the liability account in this column is the difference between the total payment in column *d* and the interest expense in column *b*. Finally, column *e* presents the ending balance after each payment is made.

Even though all six payments are equal, the amount of interest decreases each year because the balance of the liability gets smaller. Then, because the amount of interest gets smaller, the amount of the payment applied to the principal gets larger. This effect is presented graphically in Illustration 15–2. Because the tables in Illustrations 15–1 and 15–2 show how the principal balance is reduced (or amortized) by the periodic payments, they are often referred to as *installment note amortization schedules*.[1]

The bookkeeper records the effects of the first two payments with these journal entries:

19X2					
Dec.	31	Interest Expense		4,800.00	
		Notes Payable		8,179.00	
		Cash			12,979.00
		To record first installment payment.			

19X3					
Dec.	31	Interest Expense		4,146.00	
		Notes Payable		8,833.00	
		Cash			12,979.00
		To record second installment payment.			

The amounts in these entries come from the table in Illustration 15–2. The borrower would record similar entries for each of the remaining payments. Over the six years, the Notes Payable account balance will be eliminated.

---

[1] Many business calculators are programmed to make these amortization calculations for annuities.

To be sure that you understand the differences between the two payment patterns, compare the numbers and graphs in Illustrations 15–1 and 15–2. Notice that the series of equal payments leads to a greater amount of interest expense over the life of the note. This result occurs because the first three payments in Illustration 15–2 are smaller and thus do not reduce the principal as quickly as the first three payments in Illustration 15–1.

Calculating the Equal Periodic Payments on an Installment Note. In the previous example, we simply gave you the size of the equal annual payments on the installment note. Now, we show you how to calculate the size of the payment.

When a note requires a series of equal payments, you can calculate the size of each payment with a present value table for an annuity such as Table 15–2 on page 594.[2] To make the calculation with the table, start with this equation:

$$\text{Payment} \times \text{Annuity table value} = \text{Present value of the annuity}$$

Then, modify the equation to get this version:

$$\text{Payment} = \frac{\text{Present value of the annuity}}{\text{Annuity table value}}$$

Because the balance of an installment note equals the present value of the series of payments, the equation can again be modified to become this formula:

$$\text{Payment} = \frac{\text{Note balance}}{\text{Annuity table value}}$$

For this example, the initial note balance is $60,000. The annuity table value in the formula is based on the note's interest rate and the number of payments. The interest rate is 8% and there are six payments. Therefore, enter Table 15–2 on the sixth row and go across to the 8% column, where you will find the value of 4.6229. These numbers now can be substituted into the formula to find the payment:

$$\text{Payment} = \frac{\$60,000}{4.6229} = \$12,979$$

This formula can be used for all installment notes that require equal periodic payments.[3]

Progress Check
(Answers to Progress Checks are provided at the end of the chapter.)

15–1   Which of the following is true for an installment note that requires a series of equal payments?
    a. The payments consist of an increasing amount of interest and a decreasing amount of principal.
    b. The payments consist of changing amounts of principal, but the interest portion of the payment remains constant.
    c. The payments consist of a decreasing amount of interest and an increasing amount of principal.

15–2   How is the interest portion of an installment note payment calculated?

15–3   When a borrower records an interest payment on an installment note, how are the balance sheet and income statement affected?

---

[2]Appendix E provides present value tables that include additional interest rates and additional periods (or payments). You should use them to solve the exercises and problems at the end of the chapter.

[3]Business calculators can also be used to find the size of the payments.

	Plan A Don't Expand	Plan B Increase Equity	Plan C Issue Bonds
Income before interest ..	$ 100,000	$ 225,000	$ 225,000
Interest			(50,000)
Net income	$ 100,000	$ 225,000	$ 175,000
Equity	$1,000,000	$1,500,000	$1,000,000
Return on equity	10.0%	15.0%	17.5%

Illustration 15–3
Financing with Bonds or Stock

BORROWING BY ISSUING BONDS

LO 2

Describe the various characteristics of different types of bonds and prepare entries to record bond issuances and retirements.

Business corporations often borrow money by issuing **bonds.**[4] Bonds involve written promises to pay interest at a stated annual rate and to make a final payment of an amount identified on the bonds as the **par value of the bonds.** Most bonds require the borrower to pay the interest semiannually. The par value of the bonds (also known as the *face amount*) is paid at a specified future date called the *maturity date of the bonds*. The amount of interest that must be paid each year is determined by multiplying the par value of the bonds by the stated rate of interest established when the bonds were issued.

Differences between Notes Payable and Bonds

When a business borrows money by signing a note payable, the money is generally obtained from a single lender, such as a bank. In contrast, a group of bonds (often called a *bond issue*) typically consists of a large number of bonds, usually in denominations of $1,000, that are sold to many different lenders. After bonds are originally issued, they often are bought and sold by these investors. Thus, any particular bond may actually be owned by a number of people before it matures.

Differences between Stocks and Bonds

Stocks and bonds are different types of securities. A share of stock represents an ownership right in the corporation. For example, a person who owns 1,000 of a corporation's 10,000 outstanding shares controls one-tenth of the total stockholders' equity. On the other hand, if a person owns a $1,000, 11%, 20-year bond, the bondholder has a receivable from the issuer. The bond owner has the right to receive 11% interest ($110) each year that the bond is outstanding and $1,000 when the bond matures 20 years after its issue date. The issuing company is obligated to make these payments and thus has a liability to the bondholder.

Companies that issue bonds are usually trying to increase their rate of return on equity. For example, assume a company that has $1 million of equity is considering spending $500,000 to expand its capacity. Management predicts that the $500,000 will allow the company to earn an additional $125,000 of income before paying any interest. The managers are considering three possible plans. Under Plan A, the expansion will not occur. Under Plan B, the expansion will occur, and the needed funds will be obtained from the owners. Under Plan C, the company will sell $500,000 of bonds that pay 10% annual interest ($50,000). Illustration 15–3 shows how the plans would affect the company's net income, equity, and return on equity.

ADVANTAGES OF ISSUING BONDS

---

[4]Bonds are also issued by nonprofit corporations, as well as the federal government and other governmental units, such as cities, states, and school districts. Although the examples in this chapter deal with business situations, all issuers use the same practices to account for their bonds.

Analysis of the alternatives in the illustration shows that the owners will enjoy a greater rate of return and be better off if the expansion is made and if the funds are obtained by issuing the bonds. Even though the projected total income under Plan C would be smaller than Plan B's income, the rate of return on the equity would be larger because there would be less equity. This result occurs whenever the expected rate of return from the new assets is greater than the rate of interest on the bonds. In addition, issuing bonds allows the current owner or owners of a business to remain in control of the company.

CHARACTERISTICS OF BONDS

Over the years, financial experts have created many different kinds of bonds with various characteristics. We describe some of the more common features of bonds in the following paragraphs.

Serial Bonds

Some companies issue several groups of bonds that mature at different dates. As a result, the bonds are repaid gradually over a number of years. Because these bonds mature in series, they are called **serial bonds.** For example, $1 million of serial bonds might mature at the rate of $100,000 each year from 6 to 15 years after the bonds were issued. There would be 10 groups (or series) of bonds of $100,000 each. One series would mature after six years, another after seven years, and another each successive year until the final series is repaid.

Sinking Fund Bonds

As an alternative to serial bonds, **sinking fund bonds** all mature on the same date. To reduce some of the risk for owners, these bonds require the issuer to create a *sinking fund,* which is a separate pool of assets used only to retire the bonds at maturity. In effect, the issuer must start to set aside the cash to pay off the bonds long before they mature.

Convertible Bonds

Some companies issue **convertible bonds** that can be exchanged by the bondholders for a fixed number of shares of the issuing company's common stock. These bonds offer issuers the advantage that they might be settled without paying back the cash initially borrowed. Convertible bonds also offer the bondholders the potential to participate in future increases in the market value of the stock. However, if the stock does not appreciate, the bondholders continue to receive periodic interest and will receive the par value when the bond matures. In most cases, the bondholders can decide whether and when to convert the bonds to stock. However, the issuer can force conversion by exercising an option to buy the bonds back at a price less than the market value of the stock.

Registered Bonds and Bearer Bonds

A company that issues **registered bonds** keeps a record of the names and addresses of the bonds' owners. Then, over the life of the bonds, the company makes interest payments by sending checks to these registered owners. When one investor sells a bond to another investor, the issuer must be notified of the change. Registered bonds offer the issuer the practical advantage of not having to actually issue bond certificates to the investors. This arrangement also protects investors against loss or theft of the bonds.

Unregistered bonds are called **bearer bonds,** because they are payable to whoever holds them (the *bearer*). Since there may be no record of sales or exchanges, the holder of a bearer bond is presumed to be its rightful owner. As a result, lost or stolen bonds are difficult to replace.

Many bearer bonds are also **coupon bonds.** This term reflects the fact that interest coupons are attached to each bond. Each coupon matures on a specific interest payment date. The owner detaches each coupon when it matures and presents it to a bank or broker for collection. At maturity, the owner follows the same process and presents the bond certificates to a bank or broker. Because there is no readily available record of who actually receives the interest, the income tax law discourages companies from issuing new coupon bonds.

Secured Bonds and Debentures

When bonds are secured, specific assets of the issuing company are pledged (or *mortgaged*) as collateral. This arrangement gives the bondholders additional protection against default by the issuer. If the issuing company fails to pay the interest or maturity value, the secured bondholders can demand that the collateral be sold and the proceeds used to repay the debt.

In contrast to secured bonds, unsecured bonds are potentially more risky because they are supported by only the issuer's general credit standing. Unsecured bonds are also called **debentures.** Because of the greater risk of default, a company generally must be financially strong to successfully issue debentures at a favorable rate of interest.

Sometimes, companies issue debentures that rank below certain other unsecured liabilities of the company. Debentures such as this are called subordinated debentures. Recall from the discussion at the beginning of the chapter that **L. A. Gear Inc.** issued *subordinated debentures.* In a liquidation, the subordinated debentures would not be repaid until the claims of the more senior, unsecured liabilities were first satisfied.

Bond Market Values

Bonds are securities and can be easily traded between investors. Because they are bought and sold in the market, they have a market value. As a matter of convenience, bond market values are expressed as a percentage of their face value. For example, a company's bonds might be trading at $103\frac{1}{2}$, which means that they can be bought or sold for 103.5% of their par value. If other bonds are trading at 95, they can be bought or sold at 95% of their par value.

When a company issues bonds, it normally sells them to an investment firm called an *underwriter*. In turn, the underwriter resells the bonds to the public. In some situations, the issuer may sell the bonds directly to investors as the cash is needed.

The legal document that identifies the rights and obligations of the bondholders and the issuer is called the **bond indenture.** In effect, the bond indenture is the legal contract between the issuer and the bondholders. Although the practice is less common today, each bondholder may receive an actual bond certificate as evidence of the company's debt. However, most companies reduce their costs by not issuing certificates to registered bondholders.

If the underwriter sells the bonds to a large number of investors, the bondholders' interests are represented and protected by a *trustee*. The trustee monitors the issuer's actions to ensure that it complies with the obligations in the bond indenture. Most trustees are large banks or trust companies.

THE PROCESS OF ISSUING BONDS

Accounting for the Issuance of Bonds

Before bonds are issued, the terms of the indenture are drawn up and accepted by the trustee. If the bonds are to be offered to the general public by the underwriter, they must be registered with the Securities and Exchange Commission (SEC), which means that the issuer must provide extensive financial information in special reports.

For example, suppose that the Barnes Company receives authorization from the SEC to issue $800,000 of 9%, 20-year bonds dated January 1, 1995, that are due on December 31, 2014. They will pay interest semiannually on each June 30 and December 31. After the bond indenture is accepted by the trustee on behalf of the bondholders, all or a portion of the bonds may be sold to the underwriter. If all the bonds are sold at their par value, Barnes Company makes this entry to record the sale:

1995 Jan.	1	Cash	800,000.00	
		Bonds Payable		800,000.00
		Sold bonds at par.		

This entry reflects the fact that the company's cash and long-term liabilities are increased.

Six months later, the first semiannual interest payment is made, and Barnes records the payment with this entry:

1995 June	30	Interest Expense	36,000.00	
		Cash		36,000.00
		Paid semiannual interest on bonds.		
		(9% × $800,000 × 1/2).		

When the bonds mature 20 years later, Barnes Company will record its payment of the maturity value with the following entry:

2014 Dec.	31	Bonds Payable	800,000.00	
		Cash		800,000.00
		Paid bonds at maturity.		

SELLING BONDS BETWEEN INTEREST DATES

Like the previous example, many bonds are sold on their original issue date. However, circumstances may cause a company to actually sell some of the bonds later. If so, it is likely that the selling date will fall between interest payment dates. When this happens, the purchasers normally pay the issuer the purchase price plus any interest accrued since the issue date or the preceding interest payment date. This accrued interest is then refunded to the purchasers on the next interest date. For example, assume that the Fields Company sold $100,000 of its 9% bonds at par on March 1, 19X1, which was two months after the original issue date. The interest on the bonds is payable semiannually on each June 30 and December 31. Because two months have passed, the issuer collects two months' interest from the buyer at the time of the sale. This amount is $1,500 ($100,000 × 9% × 2/12). This situation is represented by the following diagram:

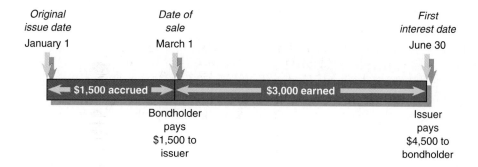

The issuer's entry to record the sale is:

Mar.	1	Cash	101,500.00	
		Interest Payable		1,500.00
		Bonds Payable		100,000.00
		Sold $100,000 of bonds with two months' accrued interest.		

Note that the liabilities for the interest and the bonds are recorded in separate accounts.

When the June 30 semiannual interest date arrives, the issuer pays a full six months' interest of $4,500 ($100,000 × 9% × 1/2) to the bondholder. This payment includes the four months' interest of $3,000 earned by the bondholder from March 1 to June 30 plus the refund of the two months' accrued interest collected by the issuer when the bonds were sold. The issuer's entry to record this first payment is:

June	30	Interest Payable	1,500.00	
		Interest Expense	3,000.00	
		Cash		4,500.00
		Paid semiannual interest on the bonds.		

The practice of collecting and then refunding the accrued interest with the next interest payment may seem like a roundabout way to do business. However, it greatly simplifies the bond issuer's administrative efforts. To understand this point, suppose that a company sells bonds on 15 or 20 different dates between the original issue date and the first interest payment date. If the issuer did not collect the accrued interest from the buyers, it would have to pay different amounts of cash to each of them in accordance with how much time had passed since they purchased their bonds. To make the correct payments, the issuer would have to keep detailed records of the purchasers and the dates on which they bought their bonds. Issuers avoid this extra record-keeping by having each buyer pay in the accrued interest at the time of purchase. Then, the company pays a full six months' interest to all purchasers, regardless of when they bought the bonds.

BOND INTEREST RATES

The interest rate to be paid by the issuer of bonds is specified in the indenture and on the bond certificates. Because it is stated in the indenture, this rate is called the **contract rate** of the bonds. (This rate is also known as the *coupon rate*, the *stated rate*, or the *nominal rate*.) The amount of interest to be paid each year is determined by multiplying the par value of the bonds by the contract rate. The contract rate is usually stated on an annual basis, even if the interest is to be paid semiannually. For example, suppose that a company issues a $1,000, 8% bond that pays interest semiannually. As a result, the annual interest of $80 (8% × $1,000) will be paid in two semiannual payments of $40 each.

Although the contract rate sets the amount of interest that the issuer pays in *cash,* the contract rate is not necessarily the rate of interest *expense* actually incurred by the issuer. In fact, the interest expense depends on the market value of the issuer's bonds, which depends on the purchasers' opinions about the risk of lending to the issuer. This perceived risk (as well as the supply of and demand for bonds) is reflected in the **market rate** for bond interest. The market rate is the consensus rate that borrowers are willing to pay and that lenders are willing to earn at the level of risk inherent in the bonds. This rate changes often (even daily) in response to changes in the supply of and demand for bonds. The market rate tends to go up when the demand for bonds decreases or the supply increases. The rate tends to go down when the supply of bonds decreases or the demand increases.

Because many factors affect the bond market, various companies face different interest rates for their bonds. The market rate for a specific set of bonds depends on the level of risk investors assign to them. As the level of risk increases, the rate increases. Market rates also are affected by the length of the bonds' life. Long-term bonds generally have higher rates because they are more risky.

Many bond issuers offer a contract rate of interest equal to the rate they expect the market to demand as of the bonds' issuance date. If the contract and market rates are equal, the bonds sell at their par value. However, if the contract and market rates are not equal, the bonds are not sold at their par value. Instead, they are sold at a *premium* above their par value or at a *discount* below their par value. Observe the relationship between the interest rates and the issue price of the bonds' values in this table:

When the contract rate is		The bond sells
Above the market rate	⇒	At a premium
At the market rate	⇒	At par value
Below the market rate	⇒	At a discount

Over the last two decades, some companies have issued *zero-coupon bonds* that do not provide any periodic interest payments. Because this contract rate of 0% is always below the market rate, these bonds are always issued at prices less than their face values.

Progress Check

15-4   Unsecured bonds that are backed only by the issuer's general credit standing are called: (a) Serial bonds; (b) Debentures; (c) Registered bonds; (d) Convertible bonds; (e) Bearer bonds.

15-5   How do you calculate the amount of interest a bond issuer will pay each year?

15-6   On May 1, a company sold $500,000 of 9% bonds that pay semiannual interest on each January 1 and July 1. The bonds were sold at par value plus accrued interest since January 1. The bond issuer's entry to record the first semiannual interest payment on July 1 should include: (a) A debit to Interest Payable for $15,000; (b) A debit to Interest Expense for $22,500; (c) A credit to Interest Payable for $7,500.

15-7   When the contract rate is above the market rate, do the bonds sell at a premium or a discount? Do the purchasers pay more or less than the par value of the bonds?

As we described in the previous section, a **discount on bonds payable** arises when a company issues bonds with a contract rate less than the market rate. The expected issue price of the bonds can be found by calculating the *present value* of the expected cash flows, discounted at the market rate of interest.

To illustrate, assume that a company offers to issue bonds with a $100,000 par value, an 8% annual contract rate, and a five-year life. Also assume that the market rate of interest for this company's bonds is 10%.[5] In exchange for the purchase price received from the buyers, these bonds obligate the issuer to pay out two different future cash flows:

1. $100,000 at the end of the bonds' five-year life.
2. $4,000 (4% × $100,000) at the end of each six-month interest period throughout the five-year life of the bonds.

To estimate the bonds' issue price, use the market rate of interest to calculate the present value of the future cash flows. Using an annuity table of present values, you must work with *semiannual* compounding periods. Thus, the annual market rate of 10% is changed to the semiannual rate of 5%. Likewise, the five-year life of the bonds is changed to 10 semiannual periods.

The actual calculation requires two steps: First, you find the present value of the $100,000 maturity payment. Second, find the present value of the annuity of 10 payments of $4,000 each.

The present values can be found by using Table 15–1 (on page 594) for the single maturity payment and Table 15–2 for the annuity. To complete the first step, enter Table 15–1 on row 10 and go across to the 5% column. The table value is 0.6139. Second, enter Table 15–2 on row 10 and go across to the 5% column, where the table value is 7.7217. This schedule shows the results when you multiply the cash flow amounts by the table values and add them together:

Cash Flow	Table	Table Value	Amount	Present Value
Par value	15–1	0.6139	$100,000	$61,390
Interest (annuity) . .	15–2	7.7217	4,000	30,887
Total				$92,277

If 5% is the appropriate semiannual interest rate for the bonds in the current market, the maximum price that informed buyers would offer for the bonds is $92,277. This amount is also the minimum price that the issuer would accept.

If the issuer accepts $92,277 cash for its bonds on the original issue date of December 31, 19X1, it records the event with this entry:

19X1					
Dec.	31	Cash	92,277.00	
		Discount on Bonds Payable	7,723.00	
		Bonds Payable		100,000.00
		Sold bonds at a discount on the original issue date.		

[5]The spread between the contract rate and the market rate of interest on a new bond issue is seldom more than a fraction of a percent. However, we use a difference of 2% here to emphasize the effects.

BONDS SOLD AT A DISCOUNT

LO 3

Estimate the price of bonds issued at a discount and describe their effects on the issuer's financial statements.

This entry causes the bonds to appear in the long-term liability section of the issuer's balance sheet as follows:

Long-term liabilities:		
Bonds payable, 8%, due December 31, 19X6 ..	$100,000	
Less discount	7,723	$92,277

This presentation shows that the discount is deducted from the par value of the bonds to produce the **carrying amount** of the bonds payable. As we saw in the last chapter for notes payable, the carrying amount is the net amount at which the bonds are reflected on the balance sheet.

Allocating Interest and Amortizing the Discount

In the previous example, the issuer received $92,277 for its bonds and will pay the bondholders $100,000 after five years have passed. Because the $7,723 discount is eventually paid to the bondholders at maturity, it is part of the cost of using the $92,277 for five years. This table shows that the total interest cost of $47,723 is the difference between the amount repaid and the amount borrowed:

Amount repaid:	
Ten payments of $4,000	$ 40,000
Maturity amount	100,000
Total repaid	$140,000
Less amount borrowed	(92,277)
Total interest expense	$ 47,723

The total expense also equals the sum of the 10 cash payments and the discount:

Ten payments of $4,000	$40,000
Plus discount	7,723
Total interest expense	$47,723

In describing these bonds and the interest expense, the issuer's accountant must accomplish two things: First, the total interest expense of $47,723 must be allocated among the 10 six-month periods in the bonds' life. Second, the carrying value of the bonds must be updated for each balance sheet. Two alternative methods accomplish these objectives. They are the straight-line and the interest methods of allocating interest. Because the process involves reducing the original discount on the bonds over the life of the bonds, it is also called *amortizing the bond discount.*

Straight-Line Method.   The **straight-line method** of allocating the interest is the simpler of the two methods. This method allocates an equal portion of the total interest expense to each of the six-month interest periods.

   In applying the straight-line method to the present example, the accountant divides the five years' total expense of $47,723 by 10 (the number of semiannual periods in the bonds' life). The result is $4,772 per period.[6] The same number can be found by

----

[6] For simplicity, all calculations have been rounded to the nearest whole dollar. Use the same practice when solving the exercises and problems at the end of the chapter.

dividing the $7,723 original discount by 10. That result is $772, which is the amount of discount to be amortized in each interest period. When the $772 of amortized discount is added to the $4,000 cash payment, the total interest expense for each six-month period is $4,772.

When the semiannual cash payment is made, the issuer uses the following entry to record the interest expense and update the balance of the bond liability:

19X2					
June	30	Interest Expense	4,772.00	
		Discount on Bonds payable		772.00
		Cash		4,000.00
		To record six months' interest and discount amortization		

Note that the $772 credit to the Discount on Bonds Payable account actually *increases* the bonds' carrying value. The increase comes about by *decreasing* the balance of the contra account that is subtracted from the Bonds Payable account.

As an example of this, **Chiquita Brands International's** 1993 Annual Report disclosed debentures with a par value of $110,820,000 and a contract rate of $10\frac{1}{2}\%$. A footnote explained that the bonds had an "imputed interest rate of 12.1%" and "unamortized discount of $10,391,000 and $10,887,000" at the end of 1993 and 1992, respectively. The carrying value was $100,429,000 and $99,933,000 at the end of 1993 and 1992, respectively. Thus, the unamortized discount decreased by $496,000 and the carrying value of the bonds increased by exactly the same amount.

Illustration 15–4 presents a table similar to the amortization tables that you have studied for notes payable. It shows how the interest expense is allocated among the 10 six-month periods in the bonds' life. It also shows how amortizing the bond discount causes the balance of the net liability to increase until it reaches $100,000 at the end of the bonds' life. Notice the following points as you analyze Illustration 15–4:

1. The $92,277 beginning balance in column *a* equals the cash received from selling the bonds. It also equals the $100,000 face amount of the bonds less the initial $7,723 discount from selling the bonds for less than par.

2. The semiannual interest expense of $4,772 in column *b* for each row equals the amount obtained by dividing the total expense of $47,723 by 10.

3. The credit to the Discount on Bonds Payable account in column *c* equals one-tenth of the total discount of $7,723.

4. The $4,000 interest payment in column *d* is the result of multiplying the $100,000 par value of the bonds by the 4% semiannual contract rate of interest.

5. The ending balance in column *e* equals the beginning balance in column *a* plus the $772 discount amortization in column *c*. This ending balance then becomes the beginning balance on the next row in the table.

6. The balance in column *e* continues to grow each period by the $772 of discount amortization until it finally equals the par value of the bonds when they mature.

The three payment columns show that the company incurs a $4,772 interest expense

Illustration 15-4   Allocating Interest Expense and Amortizing the Bond Discount with the Straight-Line Method

Period Ending	(a) Beginning Balance	(b) Debit Interest Expense		(c) Credit Discount on Bonds	+	(d) Credit Cash	(e) Ending Balance
	Prior (e)	$47,723/10	=	$7,723/10	+	4% × $100,000	(a) + (c)
6/30/X2	$92,277	$ 4,772		$ 772		$ 4,000	$ 93,049
12/31/X2	93,049	4,772		772		4,000	93,821
6/30/X3	93,821	4,772		772		4,000	94,593
12/31/X3	94,593	4,772		772		4,000	95,365
6/30/X4	95,365	4,772		772		4,000	96,137
12/31/X4	96,137	4,772		772		4,000	96,909
6/30/X5	96,909	4,772		772		4,000	97,681
12/31/X5	97,681	4,772		772		4,000	98,453
6/30/X6	98,453	4,772		772		4,000	99,225
12/31/X6	99,225	4,775*		775		4,000	100,000
Total		$47,723	=	$7,723	+	$40,000	

*Adjusted for rounding.

each period, but pays only $4,000. The $772 unpaid portion of the expense is appropriately added to the balance of the liability. It is added to the liability by being taken from the contra account balance. This table shows you how the balance of the discount is partially amortized every six months until it is eliminated:

Period Ending	Beginning Discount Balance	Amount Amortized	Ending Discount Balance
6/30/X2	$7,723	$ (772)	$6,951
12/31/X2	6,951	(772)	6,179
6/30/X3	6,179	(772)	5,407
12/31/X3	5,407	(772)	4,635
6/30/X4	4,635	(772)	3,863
12/31/X4	3,863	(772)	3,091
6/30/X5	3,091	(772)	2,319
12/31/X5	2,319	(772)	1,547
6/30/X6	1,547	(772)	775
12/31/X6	775	(775)	0
Total		$(7,723)	

Interest Method.   Straight-line allocations of interest used to be widely applied in practice. However, generally accepted accounting principles now allow the straight-line method to be used only if the results do not differ materially from those obtained by using the **interest method** to allocate the interest over the life of the bonds.[7]

The interest method is exactly the same process for allocating interest that you first learned in Chapter 12 for notes payable. Interest expense for a period is found by multiplying the balance of the liability at the beginning of that period by the original market interest rate.

---

[7] FASB, *Accounting Standards—Current Text* (Norwalk, CT, 1994), sec. I69.108. First published in *APB Opinion No. 21*, par. 15.

Illustration 15-5 Allocating Interest Expense and Amortizing the Bond Discount with the Interest Method

Period Ending	(a) Beginning Balance	(b) Debit Interest Expense	=	(c) Credit Discount on Bonds	+	(d) Credit Cash	(e) Ending Balance
	Prior (e)	5% × (a)		(b) − (d)		4% × $100,000	(a) + (c)
6/30/X2	$92,277	$ 4,614		$ 614		$ 4,000	$ 92,891
12/31/X2	92,891	4,645		645		4,000	93,536
6/30/X3	93,536	4,677		677		4,000	94,213
12/31/X3	94,213	4,711		711		4,000	94,924
6/30/X4	94,924	4,746		746		4,000	95,670
12/31/X4	95,670	4,784		784		4,000	96,454
6/30/X5	96,454	4,823		823		4,000	97,277
12/31/X5	97,277	4,864		864		4,000	98,141
6/30/X6	98,141	4,907		907		4,000	99,048
12/31/X6	99,048	4,952		952		4,000	100,000
Total		$47,723	=	$7,723	+	$40,000	

In Illustration 15–5, we present an amortization table for our example. The key difference between Illustrations 15–4 and 15–5 lies in the calculation of the interest expense in column *b*. Instead of assigning an equal amount of interest to each interest period, the interest method assigns an increasing amount of interest over the bonds' life because the balance of the liability increases over the five years. The interest expense in column *b* equals the original 5% market interest rate times the balance of the liability at the beginning of each period. Notice that both methods allocate the same $47,723 of total expense among the five years, but with different patterns.

The amount of discount amortized in any period is the difference between the interest expense in column *b* and the cash payment in column *d*. In effect, the accrued but unpaid portion of the interest expense in column *c* is added to the net liability in column *a* to get the ending balance in column *e*.

In the following table, you can see how the balance of the discount is amortized by the interest method until it reaches zero:

Period Ending	Beginning Discount Balance	Amount Amortized	Ending Discount Balance
6/30/X2	$7,723	$ (614)	$7,109
12/31/X2	7,109	(645)	6,464
6/30/X3	6,464	(677)	5,787
12/31/X3	5,787	(711)	5,076
6/30/X4	5,076	(746)	4,330
12/31/X4	4,330	(784)	3,546
6/30/X5	3,546	(823)	2,723
12/31/X5	2,723	(864)	1,859
6/30/X6	1,859	(907)	952
12/31/X6	952	(952)	0
Total		$(7,723)	

Except for the differences in the amounts, journal entries that record the expense and update the liability balance are the same under the interest method and the straight-line method. For example, the entry to record the interest payment at the end of the first interest period is:

19X2					
June	30	Interest Expense	4,614.00	
		Discount on Bonds Payable		614.00
		Cash		4,000.00
		To record six months' interest and discount amortization.		

The accountant uses the numbers in Illustration 15-5 to make similar entries throughout the five-year life of the bonds.

Comparing the Straight-Line and Interest Methods. With this background in place, we can now look more closely at the differences between the straight-line and interest methods of allocating interest among the periods in the bonds' life. In Illustration 15–6, the two graphs illustrate the differences for bonds issued at a discount.

The horizontal line in the first graph in Illustration 15–6 represents the amounts of interest expense reported each period under straight-line. The upward sloping line represents the increasing amounts of interest reported under the interest method. The amounts increase because the constant 5% rate is applied to the growing balance of the liability.

The horizontal line in the second graph represents the constant rate of 5% that the interest method uses to determine the interest expense for every six-month period. The downward sloping line represents the changing interest rates produced by the straight-line method when the bond is issued at a discount. The interest rates decrease each period because the amount of interest expense remains constant while the balance of the liability increases.

The interest method is preferred over the straight-line method because it provides a more reasonable description of the growth of the liability and the amount of interest expense incurred each period. As we mentioned, the straight-line method can be used only if the results do not differ materially from those obtained by using the interest method.

Progress Check

A company recently issued a group of five-year, 6% bonds with a $100,000 par value. The interest is to be paid semiannually, and the market interest rate was 8% on the issue date. Use this information to answer the following questions:

15-8   What is the bonds' selling price? *(a)* $100,000; *(b)* $92,393; *(c)* $91,893; *(d)* $100,321; *(e)* $92,016.

15-9   What is the journal entry to record the sale?

15-10   What is the amount of interest expense recorded at the time of the first semiannual cash payment *(a)* using the straight-line method of allocating interest and *(b)* using the interest method of allocating interest?

BONDS SOLD AT A PREMIUM

LO 4

Estimate the price of bonds issued at a premium and describe their effects on the issuer's financial statements.

When bonds carry a contract interest rate that is greater than the market rate, the bonds sell at a price greater than the par value and the difference between the par and market values is called the **premium.** In effect, buyers bid up the price of the bonds until it reaches the level that creates the current market rate of interest. As we explained for the discount situation, this premium market price can be estimated by finding the present value of the expected cash flows from the bonds at the market interest rate.

Illustration 15–6 Comparing the Straight-Line and Interest Methods of Allocating Interest on a Bond Sold at a Discount

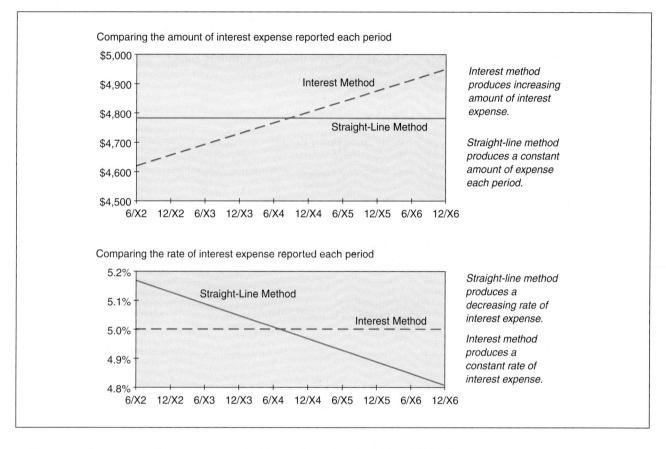

For example, assume that a company decides to issue bonds with a $100,000 par value, a 12% annual contract rate, and a five-year life. On the issue date, the market interest rate for the bonds is only 10%. Thus, potential buyers of these bonds bid up their market price until the effective rate equals the market rate. To estimate this price, we use the 5% semiannual market rate to find the present value of the expected cash flows. The cash flows consist of:

1. $100,000 at the end of the bonds' five-year life.
2. $6,000 (6% × $100,000) at the end of each six-month interest period throughout the five-year life of the bonds.

The present values can be found by using Table 15–1 (page 594) for the single maturity payment and Table 15–2 for the annuity. To complete the first step, enter Table 15–1 on row 10 and go across to the 5% column. The table value is 0.6139. Second, enter Table 15–2 on row 10 and go across to the 5% column, where the table value is 7.7217. Finally, use these table values to reduce the future cash flows to their present value. This schedule shows the results when you multiply the cash flow amounts by the table values and add them together:

Cash Flow	Table	Table Value	Amount	Present Value
Par value	15–1	0.6139	$100,000	$ 61,390
Interest (annuity)	15–2	7.7217	6,000	46,330
Total				$107,720

If 5% is the appropriate semiannual interest rate for the bonds in the current market, the maximum price that informed buyers would offer for the bonds is $107,720. This amount is also the minimum price that the issuer would accept.

If the issuer does accept $107,720 cash for its bonds on the original issue date of December 31, 19X1, it records the event with this entry:

19X1				
Dec.	31	Cash	107,720.00	
		Premium on Bonds Payable		7,720.00
		Bonds Payable		100,000.00
		Sold bonds at a premum on the original issue date.		

This entry causes the bonds to appear in the long-term liability section of the issuer's balance sheet as follows:

Long-term liabilities:
    Bonds payable, 8%, due December 31, 19X6 .... $100,000
    Plus premium 7,720 $107,720

This presentation shows that the premium is added to the par value of the bonds to produce their carrying amount.

Allocating Interest Expense and Amortizing the Premium

Over the life of these premium bonds, the issuer pays back $160,000, which consists of the 10 periodic interest payments of $6,000 plus the $100,000 par value. Because it borrowed $107,720, the total interest expense will be $52,280. This table shows the calculation:

Amount repaid:
    Ten payments of $6,000 .... $ 60,000
    Maturity amount   100,000
    Total repaid $160,000
  Less amount borrowed ...... (107,720)
  Total interest expense .... $ 52,280

The following calculation confirms that the total expense also equals the difference between the 10 cash payments and the premium:

Ten payments of $6,000 .... $ 60,000
Less premium .... (7,720)
Total interest expense .... $ 52,280

Illustration 15-7   Allocating Interest Expense and Amortizing the Bond Premium with the Interest Method

Period Ending	(a) Beginning Balance	(b) Debit Interest Expense	+	(c) Debit Premium on Bonds	=	(d) Credit Cash	(e) Ending Balance
	Prior (e)	*5% × (a)*		*(d) – (b)*		*6% × $100,000*	*(a) – (c)*
6/30/X2	$107,720	$ 5,386		$ 614		$ 6,000	$107,106
12/31/X2	107,106	5,355		645		6,000	106,461
6/30/X3	106,461	5,323		677		6,000	105,784
12/31/X3	105,784	5,289		711		6,000	105,073
6/30/X4	105,073	5,254		746		6,000	104,327
12/31/X4	104,327	5,216		784		6,000	103,543
6/30/X5	103,543	5,177		823		6,000	102,720
12/31/X5	102,720	5,136		864		6,000	101,856
6/30/X6	101,856	5,093		907		6,000	100,949
12/31/X6	100,949	5,051 *		949		6,000	100,000
Total		$52,280	+	$7,720	=	$60,000	

*Adjusted for rounding.

The premium is subtracted because it will not be paid to the bondholders when the bonds mature.

This total interest expense can be allocated over the 10 semiannual periods with either the straight-line or the interest method. Because the interest method is preferred, it is the only one illustrated for these bonds. Illustration 15–7 shows an amortization schedule for the bonds using this method.

Again, column *a* of the illustration shows the beginning balance, and column *b* shows the amount of expense at 5% of the beginning balance. But, the amount of cash paid out in column *d* is larger than the expense because the payment is based on the higher 6% contract rate. As a result, the excess payment over the expense reduces the principal. These amounts are shown in column *c*. Finally, column *e* shows the new ending balance after the amortized premium in column *c* is deducted from the beginning balance in column *a*.

The following table shows how the premium is reduced by the amortization process over the life of the bonds:

Period Ending	Beginning Premium Balance	Amount Amortized	Ending Premium Balance
6/30/X2	$7,720	$ (614)	$7,106
12/31/X2	7,106	(645)	6,461
6/30/X3	6,461	(677)	5,784
12/31/X3	5,784	(711)	5,073
6/30/X4	5,073	(746)	4,327
12/31/X4	4,327	(784)	3,543
6/30/X5	3,543	(823)	2,720
12/31/X5	2,720	(864)	1,856
6/30/X6	1,856	(907)	949
12/31/X6	949	(949)	0
Total		$(7,720)	

The effect of premium amortization on interest expense and on the liability can be seen in this journal entry on June 30, 19X2, when the issuer makes the first semiannual interest payment:

19X2				
June	30	Interest Expense	5,386.00	
		Premium on Bonds Payable	614.00	
		Cash		6,000.00
		To record six months' interest and premium amortization.		

Similar entries are recorded at each payment date until the bonds mature at the end of 19X6. However, the interest method causes the company to report decreasing amounts of interest expense and increasing amounts of premium amortization.

ACCOUNTING FOR ACCRUED INTEREST EXPENSE

If a bond's interest period does not coincide with the issuing company's accounting period, an adjusting entry is necessary to recognize the interest expense that has accrued since the most recent interest payment. For example, assume that the bonds described in Illustration 15–7 were issued on September 1, 19X1, instead of December 31, 19X1. As a result, four months' interest (and premium amortization) accrue before the end of the 19X1 calendar year. Because the reporting period ends on that date, an adjusting entry is needed to capture this information about the bonds.

Interest for the four months ended December 31, 19X1, equals $3,591, which is 4/6 of the first six months' interest of $5,386. The premium amortization is $409, which is 4/6 of the first six months' amortization of $614. The sum of the interest expense and the amortization is $4,000 ($3,591 + $409), which also equals 4/6 of the $6,000 cash payment that is due on March 1, 19X2. The accountant records these effects with this adjusting entry:

19X1				
Dec.	31	Interest Expense	3,591.00	
		Premium on Bonds Payable	409.00	
		Interest Payable		4,000.00
		To record four months' accrued interest and premium amortization.		

Similar entries are made on each December 31 throughout the five-year life of the bonds.

When the $6,000 cash payment occurs on the next interest date, the journal entry recognizes the interest expense and amortization for January and February of 19X2 and eliminates the interest payable liability created by the adjusting entry. For this example, the accountant makes the following entry to record the payment on March 1, 19X2:

19X2				
Mar.	1	Interest Payable	4,000.00	
		Interest Expense ($5,386 × 2/6)	1,795.00	
		Premium on Bonds Payable ($614 × 2/6)	205.00	
		Cash		6,000.00
		To record two months' interest and amortization and eliminate the accrued interest liability.		

The interest payments made each September are recorded normally because the entire six-month interest period is included within a single fiscal year.

Progress Check

On December 31, 19X1, Cello Corporation issued 16%, 10-year bonds with a par value of $100,000. Interest is paid on June 30 and December 31. The bonds were sold to yield a 14% annual market rate of interest. Use this information to solve the following:

15-11   What is the selling price of the bonds?

15-12   Using the interest method of allocating interest expense, Cello would record the second interest payment (on December 31, 19X2) with a debit to Premium on Bonds Payable in the amount of: *(a)* $7,470; *(b)* $7,741; *(c)* $259; *(d)* $530; *(e)* $277.

15-13   How would the bonds appear in the long-term liability section of Cello's balance sheet as of December 31, 19X2?

For various reasons, companies may want to retire some or all of their bonds prior to maturity. For example, if market interest rates decline significantly, a company may wish to replace old high-interest debt obligations with new lower-interest debt. Many companies reserve the right to retire bonds early by issuing **callable bonds.** This means the bond indenture gives the issuing company an option to *call* the bonds before they mature by paying the par value plus a *call premium*

to the bondholders. When interest rates were high in the 1980s, **AT&T Corporation** and many other companies issued callable bonds. When market rates dropped dramatically in the early 1990s, many of these bonds were called and retired.

Even if a specific bond issue is not callable, the issuer may be able to retire its bonds by repurchasing them on the open market at the current market price. Whether bonds are called or repurchased, the issuer is unlikely to pay a price that equals the bonds' carrying value. In a repurchase, this is because a bond's market value changes as the market interest rate changes.

If there is a difference between the bonds' carrying value and the amount paid in a bond retirement transaction, the issuer must record a gain or loss equal to the difference.[8] For example, in **Mattel Inc.'s** 1993 Annual Report, a footnote to the financial statements explained that in July 1991, the company "redeemed its 14 3/4% debentures with a remaining principal amount of $99.1 million at 105.9% of par. The write-off of unamortized discount associated with the debt together with the early redemption premium resulted in an extraordinary charge of $4.5 million, net of an income tax benefit of $2.6 million."

As another example, assume that a company issued callable bonds with a par value of $100,000. The call option required the issuer to pay a call premium of $3,000 to the bondholders in addition to the par value. Also

RETIRING BONDS PAYABLE

LO 2

Describe the various characteristics of different types of bonds and prepare entries to record bond issuances and retirements.

---

[8]Any material gain or loss from retiring bonds or other debt must be reported on the debtor's income statement as an extraordinary gain or loss. FASB, *Accounting Standards—Current Text* (Norwalk, CT, 1994), sec. D14.104. First published in FASB, *Statement of Financial Accounting Standards No. 4,* par. 8.

assume that immediately after a June 30 interest payment, the bonds had a carrying value of $104,500. Then, on July 1, the issuer called all of the bonds and paid $103,000 to the bondholders. The issuer must recognize a $1,500 gain as a result of the difference between the bonds' carrying value of $104,500 and the retirement price of $103,000. This entry records the bond retirement:

July	1	Bonds Payable	100,000.00	
		Premium on Bonds Payable	4,500.00	
		Gain on Retirement of Bonds		1,500.00
		Cash		103,000.00
		To record the retirement of bonds.		

Although a company generally must call all of its bonds when it exercises a call option, it may retire as many or as few bonds as it desires through open market transactions. If it retires less than the entire set of bonds, it recognizes a gain or loss for the difference between the carrying value of those bonds and the amount paid to acquire them.

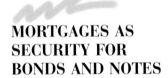

MORTGAGES AS SECURITY FOR BONDS AND NOTES

Earlier in this chapter, we said that some bonds are secured by collateral agreements, while others, called *debentures,* are not secured. These risk-reducing arrangements also are widely used for notes payable, including car and home loans. Unsecured bonds and notes are more risky because the issuer's obligation to pay interest and principal has the same priority as all other unsecured liabilities in the event of bankruptcy. If the company's financial troubles leave it unable to pay its debts in full, the unsecured creditors (including the holders of debentures) lose a proportion or all of their balances.

Thus, a company's ability to borrow money with or without collateral agreements depends on its credit rating. In many cases, debt financing is simply unavailable if the borrower cannot provide security to the creditors with a collateral agreement. Even if unsecured loans are available, the creditors are likely to charge a higher rate of interest to compensate for the additional risk. To borrow the funds at a more economical rate, many notes payable and bonds are secured by collateral agreements called *mortgages.*

A **mortgage** is a legal agreement that helps protect a lender if a borrower fails to make the required payments on a note payable or on bonds payable. A mortgage gives the lender the right to be paid out of the cash proceeds from the sale of the borrower's specific assets identified in the mortgage.

A separate legal document, called the *mortgage contract,* describes the terms of a mortgage. The mortgage contract is given to the lender who accepts a note payable or to the trustee for the bondholders. Mortgage contracts usually require a borrower to pay all property taxes on the mortgaged assets, to maintain them properly, and to carry adequate insurance against fire and other types of losses. These requirements are designed to keep the property from losing value and thus avoid diminishing the lender's security. Importantly, mortgage contracts grant the lender the right to *foreclose* on the property if the borrower fails to pay in accordance with the terms of the debt agreement. If a foreclosure occurs, a court either orders the property to be sold or simply grants legal title of the mortgaged property to the lender. If the property is sold, the proceeds are first applied to court costs and then to the claims of the mortgage holder. If there are any additional proceeds, the borrower is entitled to receive them. However, this cash is subject to any claims from the company's unsecured creditors.

Given the relevance of information about a company's security agreements with its lenders, the footnotes to the financial statements may describe the amounts of assets pledged as security against liabilities. The next section describes a ratio that can be used to assess a borrower's situation with respect to its security agreements.

Progress Check

15-14 Six years ago, a company issued $500,000 of 6%, 8-year bonds at a price of 95. The current carrying value is $493,750. The company retired 50% of the bonds by buying them on the open market at a price of 102$\frac{1}{2}$. What is the amount of gain or loss on retirement of the bonds?

15-15 A mortgage is:
   a. A promissory note that requires the borrower to make a series of payments consisting of interest and principal.
   b. A legal agreement that protects a lender by giving the lender the right to be paid out of the cash proceeds from the sale of specific assets owned by the borrower.
   c. A company's long-term liability that requires periodic payments of interest and a final payment of its par value when it matures.

As you have learned in this chapter, creditors can reduce their risk with agreements that can force borrowers to sell specific assets to settle overdue debts. Investors who consider buying a company's secured debt obligations need to determine whether the pledged assets of the debtor provide adequate security. One method of evaluating this is to calculate the ratio of **pledged assets to secured liabilities.** This is calculated by dividing the book value of the company's assets pledged as collateral by the book value of the liabilities secured by these collateral agreements:

USING THE INFORMATION — PLEDGED ASSETS TO SECURED LIABILITIES

LO 5

Calculate and describe how to use the ratio of pledged assets to secured liabilities.

$$\text{Pledged assets to secured liabilities} = \frac{\textbf{Book value of pledged assets}}{\textbf{Book value of secured liabilities}}$$

For example, suppose that a company has assets with a book value of $2,300,000 that are pledged to secure liabilities with a balance of $1,000,000. The ratio is $2,300,000/$1,000,000 = 2.3 to 1. Although there are no hard and fast guidelines for interpreting the values of this ratio, 2.3 to 1 may be sufficiently high to provide the existing secured creditors with some comfort that the debts are safely covered by the assets.

The pledging of assets for the benefit of secured creditors also affects unsecured creditors. As an increasing portion of the assets are pledged, the unsecured creditors are less likely to receive a full repayment. In evaluating their position, unsecured creditors may gain some information from the ratio of pledged assets to secured creditors. For two reasons, an unusually large ratio may suggest that the unsecured creditors are at risk. First, secured creditors may have demanded an unusually large ratio because the value of the assets in liquidation is low. Second, the secured creditors may perceive that the ability of the company to meet its obligations from operating cash flows is weak.

In using this ratio, a creditor must be aware that the reported book value of the company's assets is unlikely to reflect their fair value. Thus, creditors would have better information if they could determine the assets' current market value and then use it in the ratio instead of book value. Major creditors may be able to get this information directly by asking the borrower to provide recent appraisals or other evidence of the assets' fair value. Other creditors may not have this option. In addition, using the ratio requires knowledge about the amounts of secured liabilities and pledged assets. This information may or may not be clearly identified in the financial statements.

Progress Check

15-16   At the end of 19X3, A to Z Company has $350,000 of unsecured liabilities and $575,000 of secured liabilities. The book value of pledged assets is $1,265,000. Calculate the ratio of pledged assets to secured liabilities.

15-17   Would the secured creditors or the unsecured creditors be more concerned if A to Z's ratio of pledged assets to secured liabilities was 1.7 to 1 the previous year?

PRESENT VALUE TABLES

Table 15-1
Present Value of $1

Periods	3%	4%	5%	6%	7%	8%	10%	12%
				Rate				
1	0.9709	0.9615	0.9524	0.9434	0.9346	0.9259	0.9091	0.8929
2	0.9426	0.9246	0.9070	0.8900	0.8734	0.8573	0.8264	0.7972
3	0.9151	0.8890	0.8638	0.8396	0.8163	0.7938	0.7513	0.7118
4	0.8885	0.8548	0.8227	0.7921	0.7629	0.7350	0.6830	0.6355
5	0.8626	0.8219	0.7835	0.7473	0.7130	0.6806	0.6209	0.5674
6	0.8375	0.7903	0.7462	0.7050	0.6663	0.6302	0.5645	0.5066
7	0.8131	0.7599	0.7107	0.6651	0.6227	0.5835	0.5132	0.4523
8	0.7894	0.7307	0.6768	0.6274	0.5820	0.5403	0.4665	0.4039
9	0.7664	0.7026	0.6446	0.5919	0.5439	0.5002	0.4241	0.3606
10	0.7441	0.6756	0.6139	0.5584	0.5083	0.4632	0.3855	0.3220
20	0.5537	0.4564	0.3769	0.3118	0.2584	0.2145	0.1486	0.1037
30	0.4120	0.3083	0.2314	0.1741	0.1314	0.0994	0.0573	0.0334

Table 15-2   Present Value of an Annuity of $1

Payments	3%	4%	5%	6%	7%	8%	10%	12%
				Rate				
1	0.9709	0.9615	0.9524	0.9434	0.9346	0.9259	0.9091	0.8929
2	1.9135	1.8861	1.8594	1.8334	1.8080	1.7833	1.7355	1.6901
3	2.8286	2.7751	2.7232	2.6730	2.6243	2.5771	2.4869	2.4018
4	3.7171	3.6299	3.5460	3.4651	3.3872	3.3121	3.1699	3.0373
5	4.5797	4.4518	4.3295	4.2124	4.1002	3.9927	3.7908	3.6048
6	5.4172	5.2421	5.0757	4.9173	4.7665	4.6229	4.3553	4.1114
7	6.2303	6.0021	5.7864	5.5824	5.3893	5.2064	4.8684	4.5638
8	7.0197	6.7327	6.4632	6.2098	5.9713	5.7466	5.3349	4.9676
9	7.7861	7.4353	7.1078	6.8017	6.5152	6.2469	5.7590	5.3282
10	8.5302	8.1109	7.7217	7.3601	7.0236	6.7101	6.1446	5.6502
20	14.8775	13.5903	12.4622	11.4699	10.5940	9.8181	8.5136	7.4694
30	19.6004	17.2920	15.3725	13.7648	12.4090	11.2578	9.4269	8.0552

SUMMARY OF THE CHAPTER IN TERMS OF LEARNING OBJECTIVES

LO 1. Calculate the payments on an installment note payable and describe their effects on the financial statements. Typical installment notes require one of two alternative payment patterns: *(a)* payments that include interest plus equal amounts of principal or *(b)* equal payments. In either case, interest is allocated to each period in a note's life by multiplying the carrying value by the original interest rate. If a note is repaid with equal payments, the payment's size is found by dividing the borrowed amount by the annuity table value for the interest rate and the number of payments.

LO 2. Describe the various characteristics of different types of bonds and prepare entries to record bond issuances and retirements. Bonds usually are issued to many investors. Serial bonds mature at different points in time. Companies that issue sinking fund bonds must accumulate a fund of assets to use to pay out the par value of the bonds at the maturity date. Convertible bonds can be exchanged by the bondholders for shares of the issuing company's stock. When bonds are registered, each bondholder's name and address is recorded by the issuing company. In contrast, bearer bonds are payable to whoever holds the bonds.

Some bonds are secured by mortgages on the issuer's assets while other bonds, called debentures, are unsecured. When bonds are sold between interest dates, the accrued interest is collected from the purchasers, who are then refunded that amount on the next interest payment date. Bonds can be retired early by the issuer by exercising a call option or by purchases on the open market. The issuer must recognize a gain or loss for the difference between the amount paid out and the bonds' carrying value.

LO 3. Estimate the price of bonds issued at a discount and describe their effects on the issuer's financial statements. The cash paid to bondholders on semiannual interest payment dates is calculated as one-half of the result of multiplying the par value of the bonds by their contract interest rate. The market value of a bond can be estimated by using the market interest rate to find the present values of the interest payments and the par value. Bonds are issued at a discount when the contract rate is less than the market rate. Then, the issuer records the issuance with a credit to the Bonds Payable account for the par value and a debit to Discount on Bonds Payable. The amount of interest assigned to each interest period can be allocated with the straight-line method if the result is not materially different from the results of applying the interest method. The interest method assigns interest to a period by multiplying the beginning carrying value by the original market interest rate.

LO 4. Estimate the price of bonds issued at a premium and describe their effects on the issuer's financial statements. Bonds are issued at a premium when the contract rate is higher than the market interest rate. The issuer records the premium in a supplemental account. The balance of this account is reduced over the life of the bonds through the interest allocation process.

LO 5. Calculate and describe how to use the ratio of pledged assets to secured liabilities. Secured and unsecured creditors are both concerned about the relationship between the amounts of assets owned by the debtor and the amounts of secured liabilities. The secured creditors are safer when the ratio of pledged assets to secured liabilities is larger, while the risks of unsecured creditors may be increased in this circumstance.

DEMONSTRATION PROBLEM

The Staley Tile Company patented and successfully test-marketed a new product. However, to expand its ability to produce and market the product, the company needed to raise $800,000 of additional financing. On January 1, 19X1, the company borrowed the money under these arrangements:

a. Staley signed a $400,000, 10% installment note that will be repaid with five equal annual installments. The payments will be made on December 31 of 19X1 through 19X5.

b. Staley issued five-year bonds with a par value of $400,000. The bonds have a 12% annual contract rate and pay interest on June 30 and December 31. The annual market interest rate for the bonds was 10% on January 1, 19X1.

Required

1. For the installment note, (a) calculate the size of each payment, (b) prepare an amortization table, and (c) present the entry for the first payment.

2. For the bonds, *(a)* estimate the issue price of the bonds; *(b)* present the January 1, 19X1, entry to record issuing the bonds; *(c)* prepare an amortization table using the interest method; *(d)* present the June 30, 19X1, entry to record the first payment of interest; and *(e)* present an entry to record retiring the bonds at the call price of $416,000 on January 1, 19X3.

Planning the Solution

• For the installment note, divide the borrowed amount by the annuity table factor (from Table 15–2 on page 594) for 10% and five payments. Prepare a table similar to Illustration 15–2 and use the numbers in the first line for the entry.

• For the bonds, estimate the issue price by using the market rate to find the present values of the bonds' cash flows. Then, use this result to record issuing the bonds. Next, develop an amortization table like Illustration 15–7, and use it to get the numbers that you need for the journal entry. Finally, use the table to find the carrying value as of the date of the retirement of the bonds that you need for the journal entry.

Solution to Demonstration Problem

Part 1:

Payment = Note balance/Table value = $400,000/3.7908 = $105,519
Table value is for 5 payments and an interest rate of 10%.

Table:

			Payments			
		(a)	*(b)*	*(c)*	*(d)*	*(e)*
			Debit	**Debit**		
	Period Ending	**Beginning Balance**	**Interest Expense** +	**Notes Payable** =	**Credit Cash**	**Ending Balance**
19X1		$400,000	$ 40,000	$ 65,519	$105,519	$334,481
19X2		334,481	33,448	72,071	105,519	262,410
19X3		262,410	26,241	79,278	105,519	183,132
19X4		183,132	18,313	87,206	105,519	95,926
19X5		95,926	9,593	95,926	105,519	0
Total			$127,595	$400,000	$527,595	

Journal entry:

19X1				
Dec.	31	Interest Expense	40,000.00	
		Notes Payable	65,519.00	
		Cash		105,519.00
		To record first installment payment.		

Part 2:

Estimated issue price of the bonds:

Cash Flow	Table	**Table Value**	Amount	**Present Value**
Par value	15–1	0.6139	$400,000	$245,560
Interest (annuity)	15–2	7.7217	24,000	185,321
Total				$430,881

Table value is for 10 payments and an interest rate of 5%.

Journal entry:

19X1					
Jan.	1	Cash	430,881.00		
		Premium on Bonds Payable		30,881.00	
		Bonds Payable		400,000.00	
		Sold bonds at a premium.			

Table:

	(a)	(b)	(c)	(d)	(e)
		Payments			
		Debit	Debit		
Period	**Beginning**	**Interest**	**Premium**	**Credit**	**Ending**
Ending	**Balance**	**Expense** +	**on Bonds** =	**Cash**	**Balance**
	Prior (e)	*5% × (a)*	*(d) – (b)*	*6% × $400,000*	*(a) – (c)*
6/30/X1	$430,881	$ 21,544	$ 2,456	$ 24,000	$428,425
12/31/X1	428,425	21,421	2,579	24,000	425,846
6/30/X2	425,846	21,292	2,708	24,000	423,138
12/31/X2	423,138	21,157	2,843	24,000	420,295
6/30/X3	420,295	21,015	2,985	24,000	417,310
12/31/X3	417,310	20,866	3,134	24,000	414,176
6/30/X4	414,176	20,709	3,291	24,000	410,885
12/31/X4	410,885	20,544	3,456 .	24,000	407,429
6/30/X5	407,429	20,371	3,629	24,000	403,800
12/31/X5	403,800	20,200*	3,800	24,000	400,000
Total		$209,119	$30,881	$240,000	

*Adjusted for rounding.

Journal entries:

19X1					
June	30	Interest Expense	21,544.00		
		Premium on Bonds Payable	2,456.00		
		Cash		24,000.00	
		Paid semiannual interest on the bonds.			
19X3					
Jan.	1	Bonds Payable	400,000.00		
		Premium on Bonds Payable	20,295.00		
		Cash		416,000.00	
		Gain on Retirement of Bonds		4,295.00	
		To record the retirement of bonds (carrying value			
		determined as of December 31, 19X2).			

GLOSSARY

Bearer bonds bonds that are made payable to whoever holds them (called the bearer); these bonds are not registered. p. 576

Bond a company's long-term liability that requires periodic payments of interest and final payment of its par value when it matures; usually issued in denominations of $1,000. p. 575

Bond indenture the contract between the bond issuer and the bondholders; it identifies the rights and obligations of the parties. p. 577

Callable bonds bonds that give the issuer an option of retiring them before they mature. p. 591

Carrying amount the net amount at which bonds are reflected on the balance sheet; equals the par value of the bonds less any unamortized discount or plus any unamortized premium. p. 582

Contract rate the interest rate specified in the bond indenture; it is multiplied by the par value of the bonds to determine the amount of interest to be paid each year. p. 579

Convertible bonds bonds that can be exchanged by the bondholders for a fixed number of shares of the issuing company's common stock. p. 576

Coupon bonds bonds that have interest coupons attached to their certificates; the bondholders detach the coupons when they mature and present them to a bank for collection. p. 577

Debentures unsecured bonds that are supported by only the general credit standing of the issuer. p. 577

Discount on bonds payable the difference between the par value of a bond and its lower issue price or paying amount; arises when the contract rate is lower than the market rate. p. 581

Installment notes promissory notes that require the borrower to make a series of payments consisting of interest and principal. p. 570

Interest method (interest allocation) a method that allocates interest expense to a reporting period by multiplying the beginning paying value by the original market interest rate. p. 584

Market rate the consensus interest rate that borrowers are willing to pay and that lenders are willing to earn at the level of risk inherent in the bonds. p. 580

Mortgage a legal agreement that protects a lender by giving the lender the right to be paid out of the cash proceeds from the sale of the borrower's specific assets identified in the mortgage. p. 592

Par value of a bond the amount that the bond issuer agrees to pay at maturity and the amount on which interest payments are based; also called the *face amount.* p. 575

Pledged assets to secured liabilities the ratio of the book value of a company's pledged assets to the book value of its secured liabilities. p. 593

Premium on bonds payable the difference between the par value of a bond and its higher issue price or paying amount; arises when the contract rate is higher than the market rate. p. 586

Registered bonds bonds owned by investors whose names and addresses are recorded by the issuing company; the interest payments are made with checks to the bondholders. p. 576

Serial bonds bonds that mature at different dates with the result that the entire debt is repaid gradually over a number of years. p. 576

Sinking fund bonds bonds that require the issuing company to make deposits to a separate pool of assets; the bondholders are repaid at maturity from the assets in this pool. p. 576

Straight-line method (interest allocation) a method that allocates an equal amount of interest to each accounting period in the life of bonds. p. 582

QUESTIONS

1. Describe two alternative payment patterns for installment notes.
2. What is the difference between notes payable and bonds payable?
3. What is the primary difference between a share of stock and a bond?
4. What is the main advantage of issuing bonds instead of obtaining funds from the company's owners?
5. What is a bond indenture? What provisions are usually included in an indenture?
6. What are the duties of a trustee for bondholders?
7. Why does a company that issues bonds between interest dates collect accrued interest from the bonds' purchasers?
8. What are the *contract* and *market interest rates* for bonds?
9. What factors affect the market interest rates for bonds?
10. If you know the par value of bonds, the contract rate and the market interest rate, how can you estimate the market value of the bonds?
11. Does the straight-line or interest method produce an allocation of interest that creates a constant rate of interest over a bond's life? Explain your answer.
12. What is the cash price of a $2,000 bond that is sold at 98 1/4? What is the cash price of a $6,000 bond that is sold at 101 1/2?
13. Explain why unsecured creditors should be alarmed when the pledged assets to secured liabilities ratio for a borrower has grown substantially.
14. Refer to the financial statements for Ben & Jerry's Homemade, Inc., presented in Appendix G. Is there any indication in the balance sheet that the company has issued bonds?

QUICK STUDY (Five-Minute Exercises)

QS 15–1
(LO 1)

The owner of Ripley's Restaurant borrowed $80,000 from a bank and signed an installment note that calls for eight annual payments of equal size, with the first payment due one year after the note was signed. Use Table 15–2 on page 594 to calculate the size of the annual payment for each of the following annual interest rates: *a.* 5%, *b.* 7%, *c.* 10%.

Match the following terms and phrases by entering the letter of the phrase that best describes each term in the blank next to the term.

QS 15–2
(LO 2)

_____ serial bonds   _____ bearer bonds
_____ sinking fund bonds   _____ secured bonds
_____ convertible bonds   _____ debentures
_____ registered bonds   _____ bond indenture

a. Issuer records the bondholders' names and addresses.

b. Unsecured; backed only by the issuer's general credit standing.

c. Varying maturity dates.

d. Identifies the rights and responsibilities of the issuer and bondholders.

e. Can be exchanged for shares of the issuer's common stock.

f. Unregistered; interest is paid to whoever possesses them.

g. Issuer maintains a separate pool of assets from which bondholders are paid at maturity.

h. Specific assets of the issuer are mortgaged as collateral.

The Carraway Co. issued 10%, 10-year bonds with a par value of $200,000. On the issue date, the annual market rate of interest for the bonds was 12%, and they sold for $177,059. The straight-line method is used to allocate the interest.

QS 15–3
(LO 3)

a. What is the total amount of interest expense that will be recognized over the life of the bonds?

b. What is the amount of interest expense recorded on the first interest payment date?

The Downhome Co. issued 12%, 10-year bonds with a par value of $60,000 and semiannual interest payments. On the issue date, the annual market rate of interest for the bonds was 10%, and they were sold for $67,478. The interest method is used to allocate the interest.

QS 15–4
(LO 4)

a. What is the total amount of interest expense that will be recognized over the life of the bonds?

b. What is the amount of interest expense recorded on the first interest payment date?

Use the following information to compute the ratio of pledged assets to secured liabilities for both companies:

QS 15–5
(LO 5)

	Red Co.	Blue Co.
Pledged assets	$155,000	$ 87,000
Total assets	180,000	300,000
Secured liabilities	90,000	66,000
Unsecured liabilities	140,000	160,000

EXERCISES

When solving the following exercises, round all dollar amounts to the nearest whole dollar. Also assume that none of the companies use reversing entries.

On December 31, 19X1, Akron Co. borrowed $16,000 by signing a four-year, 5% installment note. The note requires annual payments of accrued interest and equal amounts of principal on December 31 of each year from 19X2 through 19X5.

Exercise 15–1
Installment note with payments of accrued interest and equal amounts of principal
(LO 1)

a. How much principal will be included in each of the four payments?

b. Prepare an amortization table for this installment note like the one presented in Illustration 15–1 on page 571.

Use the data in Exercise 15–1 to prepare journal entries that Akron Co. would make to record the loan on December 31, 19X1, and the four payments starting on December 31, 19X2, through the final payment on December 31, 19X5.

Exercise 15–2
Entries for payments of accrued interest and equal amounts of principal
(LO 1)

Exercise 15–3
Installment note with equal payments
(LO 1)

On December 31, 19X1, Gates Co. borrowed $10,000 by signing a four-year, 5% installment note. The note requires four equal payments of accrued interest and principal on December 31 of each year from 19X2 through 19X5.

a. Calculate the size of each of the four equal payments.

b. Prepare an amortization table for this installment note like the one presented in Illustration 15–2 on page 572.

Exercise 15–4
Journal entries for a note with equal payments
(LO 1)

Use the data in Exercise 15–3 to prepare journal entries that Gates Co. would make to record the loan on December 31, 19X1, and the four payments starting on December 31, 19X2, through the final payment on December 31, 19X5.

Exercise 15–5
Journal entries for bond issuance and interest payments
(LO 2)

On January 1, 19X1, the Tennyson Co. issued $300,000 of 20-year bonds that pay 8% interest semiannually on June 30 and December 31. The bonds were sold to investors at their par value.

a. How much interest will the issuer pay to the holders of these bonds every six months?

b. Show the journal entries that the issuer would make to record (1) the issuance of the bonds on January 1, 19X1, (2) the first interest payment on June 30, 19X1, and (3) the second interest payment on December 31, 19X1.

Exercise 15–6
Journal entries for bond issuance with accrued interest
(LO 2)

On March 1, 19X1, the Tennyson Co. issued $300,000 of 20-year bonds dated January 1, 19X1. The bonds pay 8% interest semiannually on June 30 and December 31. The bonds were sold to investors at their par value plus the two months' interest that had accrued since the original issue date.

a. How much accrued interest was paid to the issuer by the purchasers of these bonds on March 1, 19X1?

b. Show the journal entries that the issuer would make to record (1) the issuance of the bonds on March 1, 19X1; (2) the first interest payment on June 30, 19X1; and (3) the second interest payment on December 31, 19X1.

Exercise 15–7
Calculating the present value of a bond and recording the issuance
(LO 3)

The Sesame Co. issued bonds with a par value of $150,000 on their initial issue date. The bonds mature in 15 years and pay 8% annual interest in two semiannual payments. On the issue date, the annual market rate of interest for the bonds turned out to be 10%.

a. What is the size of the semiannual interest payment for these bonds?

b. How many semiannual interest payments will be made on these bonds over their life?

c. Use the information about the interest rates to decide whether the bonds were issued at par, a discount, or a premium.

d. Estimate the market value of the bonds as of the date they were issued.

e. Present the journal entry that would be made to record the bonds' issuance.

Exercise 15–8
Straight-line allocation of interest for bonds sold at a discount
(LO 3)

The Columbia Company issued bonds with a par value of $50,000 on January 1, 19X2. The annual contract rate on the bonds is 8%, and the interest is paid semiannually. The bonds mature after three years. The annual market interest rate at the date of issuance was 12%, and the bonds were sold for $45,085.

a. What is the amount of the original discount on these bonds?

b. How much total interest expense will be recognized over the life of these bonds?

c. Present an amortization table like Illustration 15–4 on page 584 for these bonds; use the straight-line method of allocating the interest and amortizing the discount.

Exercise 15–9
Interest method allocation of interest for bonds sold at a discount
(LO 3)

The Cheyenne Company issued bonds with a par value of $30,000 on January 1, 19X2. The annual contract rate on the bonds is 8%, and the interest is paid semiannually. The bonds mature after three years. The annual market interest rate at the date of issuance was 10%, and the bonds were sold for $28,477.

a.   What is the amount of the original discount on these bonds?

b.   How much total interest expense will be recognized over the life of these bonds?

c.   Present an amortization table like Illustration 15–5 on page 585 for these bonds; use the interest method of allocating the interest and amortizing the discount.

The Allan Co. issued bonds with a par value of $25,000 on their initial issue date. The bonds mature in 15 years and pay 8% annual interest in two semiannual payments. On the issue date, the annual market rate of interest for the bonds turned out to be 6%.

Exercise 15–10
Calculating the present value of a bond and recording the issuance
(LO 3)

a.   What is the size of the semiannual interest payment for these bonds?

b.   How many semiannual interest payments will be made on these bonds over their life?

c.   Use the information about the interest rates to decide whether the bonds were issued at par, a discount, or a premium.

d.   Estimate the market value of the bonds as of the date they were issued.

e.   Present the journal entry that would be made to record the bonds' issuance.

The Cypress Company issued bonds with a par value of $40,000 on January 1, 19X2. The annual contract rate on the bonds was 12%, and the interest is paid semiannually. The bonds mature after three years. The annual market interest rate at the date of issuance was 10%, and the bonds were sold for $42,030.

Exercise 15–11
Interest method allocation of interest for bonds sold at a premium
(LO 3)

a.   What is the amount of the original premium on these bonds?

b.   How much total interest expense will be recognized over the life of these bonds?

c.   Present an amortization table like Illustration 15–7 on page 589 for these bonds; use the interest method of allocating the interest and amortizing the premium.

On January 1, 19X1, the Amsterdam Co. issued $700,000 of its 10%, 15-year bonds at a price of 95$1/2$. Three years later, on January 1, 19X4, the company retired 30% of these bonds by buying them on the open market at 105$3/4$. All interest had been properly accounted for and paid through December 31, 19X3, the day before the purchase. The company used the straight-line method to allocate the interest and amortize the original discount.

Exercise 15–12
Retiring bonds payable
(LO 2)

a.   How much money did the company receive when it first issued the entire group of bonds?

b.   How large was the original discount on the entire group of bonds?

c.   How much amortization did the company record on the entire group of bonds between January 1, 19X1, and December 31, 19X3?

d.   What was the carrying value of the entire group of bonds as of the close of business on December 31, 19X3? What was the carrying value of the retired bonds on this date?

e.   How much money did the company pay on January 1, 19X4, to purchase the bonds that it retired?

f.   What is the amount of the gain or loss from retiring the bonds?

g.   Provide the general journal entry that the company would make to record the retirement of the bonds.

The Schaffner Co. issued bonds with a par value of $100,000 and a five-year life on May 1, 19X1. The contract interest rate is 7%. The bonds pay interest on October 31 and April 30. They were issued at a price of $95,948.

Exercise 15–13
Straight-line amortization table and accrued interest
(LO 3, 4, 5)

a.   Prepare an amortization table for these bonds that covers their entire life. Use the straight-line method of allocating interest.

b.   Show the journal entries that the issuer would make to record the first two interest payments and to accrue interest as of December 31, 19X1.

PROBLEMS

When solving the following problems, round all dollar amounts to the nearest whole dollar. Also assume that none of the companies use reversing entries.

Problem 15–1
Installment notes
(LO 1)

On November 30, 19X1, the Stanley Company borrowed $50,000 from a bank by signing a four-year installment note bearing interest at 12%. The terms of the note require equal payments each year on November 30.

Required

1. Calculate the size of each installment payment. (Use Table 15–2 on page 594.)
2. Complete an installment note amortization schedule for this note similar to Illustration 15–2 on page 594.
3. Present the journal entries that the borrower would make to record accrued interest as of December 31, 19X1 (the end of the annual reporting period) and the first payment on the note.
4. Now assume that the note does not require equal payments but does require four payments that include accrued interest and an equal amount of principal in each payment. Complete an installment note amortization schedule for this note similar to Illustration 15–1 on page 591. Present the journal entries that the borrower would make to record accrued interest as of December 31, 19X1 (the end of the annual reporting period) and the first payment on the note.

CHECK FIGURE:
Requirement 2: Interest for period ending 11/30/X4, $3,339

Problem 15–2
Calculating bond prices and recording issuances with journal entries
(LO 2, 3, 4)

Helmer Co. issued a group of bonds on January 1, 19X1, that pay interest semiannually on June 30 and December 31. The par value of the bonds is $40,000, the annual contract rate is 8%, and the bonds mature in 10 years.

Required

For each of these three situations, *(a)* determine the issue price of the bonds and *(b)* show the journal entry that would record the issuance.

CHECK FIGURE:
Requirement 1: Premium, $5,952

1. The market interest rate at the date of issuance was 6%.
2. The market interest rate at the date of issuance was 8%.
3. The market interest rate at the date of issuance was 10%.

Problem 15–3
Straight-line method of allocating interest and amortizing a bond discount
(LO 3)

Abbot Company issued $125,000 of bonds that pay 6% annual interest with two semiannual payments. The date of issuance was January 1, 19X1, and the interest is paid on June 30 and December 31. The bonds mature after 10 years and were issued at the price of $108,014.

Required

1. Prepare a general journal entry to record the issuance of the bonds.
2. Determine the total interest expense that will be recognized over the life of these bonds.
3. Prepare the first four lines of an amortization table like Illustration 15–4 based on the straight-line method of allocating the interest.
4. Prepare the first four lines of a separate table that shows the beginning balance of the discount, the amount of straight-line amortization of the discount, and the ending balance.

CHECK FIGURE:
Total interest expense, $91,986

5. Present the journal entries that the bond issuer would make to record the first two interest payments.

Problem 15–4
Interest method of allocating bond interest and amortizing a discount
(LO 2, 3)

The Martin Company issued $50,000 of bonds that pay 4% annual interest with two semiannual payments. The date of issuance was January 1, 19X1, and the interest is paid on June 30 and December 31. The bonds mature after three years and were issued at the price of $47,292. The market interest rate was 6%.

Required

Preparation component:

1. Prepare a general journal entry to record the issuance of the bonds.
2. Determine the total interest expense that will be recognized over the life of these bonds.
3. Prepare the first four lines of an amortization table like Illustration 15–5 based on the interest method.
4. Prepare the first four lines of a separate table that shows the beginning balance of the discount, the amount of interest method amortization of the discount, and the ending balance.
5. Present the journal entries that the bond issuer would make to record the first two interest payments.

Analysis component:

6. Instead of the facts described in the problem, assume that the market interest rate on January 1, 19X1, was 3% instead of 6%. Without presenting any specific numbers, describe how this change would affect the amounts presented on the company's financial statements.

The Jones Company issued $100,000 of bonds that pay 9% annual interest with two semiannual payments. The date of issuance was January 1, 19X1, and the interest is paid on June 30 and December 31. The bonds mature after three years and were issued at the price of $102,619. The market interest rate was 8%.

Problem 15–5
Interest method of amortizing bond premium and retiring bonds
(LO 2, 4)

Required

1. Prepare a general journal entry to record the issuance of the bonds.
2. Determine the total interest expense that will be recognized over the life of these bonds.
3. Prepare the first four lines of an amortization table like Illustration 15–7 based on the interest method.
4. Prepare the first four lines of a separate table that shows the beginning balance of the premium, the amount of interest method amortization of the premium, and the ending balance.
5. Present the journal entries that the bond issuer would make to record the first two interest payments.
6. Present the journal entry that would be made to record the retirement of these bonds on December 31, 19X2, at the price of 98.

The Briggs Company issued bonds with a par value of $80,000 and a five-year life on January 1, 19X1. The bonds pay interest on June 30 and December 31. The contract interest rate is 8.5%. The bonds were issued at a price of $81,625. The market interest rate was 8% on the original issue date.

Problem 15–6
Bond premium amortization and finding the present value of remaining cash flows
(LO 3, 4)

Required

1. Prepare an amortization table for these bonds that covers their entire life. Use the interest method.
2. Show the journal entries that the issuer would make to record the first two interest payments.
3. Use the original market interest rate to calculate the present value of the remaining cash flows for these bonds as of December 31, 19X3. Compare your answer with the amount shown on the amortization table as the balance for that date, and explain your findings.

On January 1, 19X2, Alpha Company issued $45,000 of 10%, five-year bonds secured by a mortgage that specifies assets totaling $75,000 as collateral. On the same date, Beta Company isssued 10%, five-year bonds with a par value of $20,000. Beta is securing its bonds with a

Problem 15–7
Computing and analyzing ratio of pledged assets to secured liabilities
(LO 5)

mortgage that includes $50,000 of pledged assets. Following is December 31, 19X1, balance sheet information for both companies:

	Alpha Co.	Beta Co.
Total assets	$300,000*	$150,000†
Liabilities:		
Secured	$ 70,000	$ 25,000
Unsecured	50,000	55,000
Owners' equity	180,000	70,000
Total liabilities and owners' equity	$300,000	$150,000
Footnote	*33% pledged	†42% pledged

Required

Preparation component:

1. Calculate the ratio of pledged assets to secured liabilities for each company after January 1, 19X2.

Analysis component:

2. Which company's bonds appear to offer the best security? What other information might be helpful in evaluating the risk of the bonds?

CRITICAL THINKING: ESSAYS, PROBLEMS, AND CASES

When solving the following, round all dollar amounts to the nearest whole dollar.

Analytical Essay

(LO 5)

An unsecured major creditor of the Hawkins Company has been monitoring the company's financing activities. Two years before, the ratio of its pledged assets to secured liabilities had been 1.4. One year ago, the ratio had climbed to 2.0, and the most recent financial report shows that the ratio value is now 3.1. Briefly describe what this trend may indicate about the company's activities, specifically from the point of view of this creditor.

Management Decision Case

(LO 2, 3, 4)

Star Manufacturing Company is planning major additions to its operating capacity and needs approximately $400,000 to finance the expansion. The company has been considering three alternative proposals for issuing bonds that pay annual interest over the eight years in their lives. The alternatives are:

Plan A: Issue $400,000 of 8% bonds.
Plan B: Issue $450,000 of 6% bonds.
Plan C: Issue $360,000 of 10% bonds.

The market rate of interest for all of these bonds is expected to be 8%.

Required

1. For each plan, calculate:
   a. The expected cash proceeds from issuing the bonds.
   b. The expected annual cash outflow for interest.
   c. The expected interest expense for the first year. (Use the interest method to amortize bond premium or discount.)
   d. The amount that must be paid at maturity.
2. Which plans have the smallest and largest cash demands on the company prior to the final payment at maturity? Which plans require the smallest and largest payment at maturity?

The Angela Company issued $500,000 of zero-coupon bonds on January 1, 19X1. These bonds are scheduled to mature seven years later on December 31, 19X7. Under the terms of the bond agreement, the company will pay out $500,000 to the bondholders on the maturity date without making any periodic interest payments. The market rate of interest for these bonds was 10% when they were issued.

Financial Reporting Problem

(LO 3)

Required

1. Estimate the amount of cash that Angela received when it issued these bonds (assume annual compounding).
2. Present the journal entry that Angela's accountant would use to record the issuance of these bonds.
3. Calculate the total amount of interest expense that will be incurred over the life of the bonds.
4. Prepare an amortization table that shows the amount of interest expense that will be allocated to each year in the bonds' life with the interest method.
5. Present the journal entry that Angela's accountant would use to record the interest expense from these bonds for the year ended December 31, 19X1.

Use the financial statements and the footnotes in Appendix F to answer these questions about Apple Computer, Inc.

Financial Statement Analysis Case

(LO 1)

a. Has Apple issued any bonds or long-term notes payable?
b. What is the carrying value of Apple's short-term notes payable at the end of the 1993 fiscal year?
c. Are the notes payable secured or unsecured?
d. What was the average life of the notes?
e. What was the average interest rate on the notes outstanding at the end of the 1993 fiscal year?

ANSWERS TO PROGRESS CHECKS

15–1 c

15–2 The interest portion of an installment payment equals the beginning balance for the period multiplied by the original interest rate.

15–3 On the balance sheet, the balances of the liability and cash are decreased. On the income statement, interest expense is increased.

15–4 b

15–5 Multiply the par value of the bonds by the contract rate of interest.

15–6 a

15–7 The bonds sell at a premium, and the purchasers pay more than the par value of the bonds.

15–8 c. (Present values of $100,000 and a semiannual annuity of $3,000, both at 4% for 10 semiannual periods.)

15–9 Cash 91,893.00
       Discount on Bonds Payable 8,107.00
          Bonds Payable 100,000.00

15–10 a. $3,811 (Total interest equal to $38,107, or 10 payments of $3,000 plus the $8,107 discount, divided by 10 periods.)
       b. $3,676 (Beginning balance of $91,893 times 4% market interest rate.)

15–11 $110,592 (Present value of $100,000 plus the semiannual annuity of $8,000, both at 7% for 20 semiannual periods.)

15–12   *e.* (On 6/30/X2: $110,592 × 7% = $7,741 interest expense;
        $8,000 − $7,741 = $259 premium amortization; $110,592 − $259 = $110,333
        ending balance. On 12/31/X2: $110,333 × 7% = $7,723 interest expense;
        $8,000 − $7,723 = $277 premium amortization.)

15–13   Bonds payable, 16%, due December 31,
        19X0 .... $100,000
        Plus premium 10,056* $110,056

        *Beginning premium balance of $10,592 less $259 and $277 amortized on 6/30/X2
        and 12/31/X2.

15–14 $9,375 loss (Difference between repurchase price of $256,250 [50% of ($500,000 ×
        102.5%)] and carrying value of $246,875 [50% of $493,750].)

15–15   *b*

15–16   2.2 to 1 ($1,265,000/$575,000)

15–17   Unsecured creditors. They may be less likely to receive full repayment if the portion
        of assets pledged increases.

CHAPTER 16

Reporting and Using Cash Flows in Decision Making

*F*inancial news reports indicate that Hollywood studios and other corporations in the entertainment industries are battling to take over television studios. In 1994, *The Wall Street Journal* described a widespread rumor that The Walt Disney Company considered bidding to acquire NBC. Supposedly, the initial offer being considered was $5 billion. Why might Disney have been interested? Cash flow! The networks' libraries of TV episodes are considered to be major prizes in winning acquisitions. Episodes of "Home Improvement," a successful sitcom owned by Disney, are selling for $3.4 million an episode, and Paramount Pictures' production of "Seinfeld" is expected to sell for $2 to $3 million per episode! (*The Wall Street Journal*, Sept. 9, 1994, p. R4)

As the following excerpt from Disney's 1993 annual report shows, the company's cash position had declined substantially since 1991. Continued drains on cash were expected as a result of ongoing renovations and expansion of theme parks and stores, plans to build cruise ships, new parks, and the demands of EuroDisney. Under these circumstances, management must pay particular attention to cash inflows and outflows.

THE WALT DISNEY COMPANY—CONSOLIDATED STATEMENT OF CASH FLOW
(In millions)

Year ended September 30	1993	1992	1991
Increase (Decrease) in Cash and Cash Equivalents	$(401.8)	$(121.3)	$ 66.3
Cash and Cash Equivalents, Beginning of Year	764.8	886.1	819.8
Cash and Cash Equivalents, End of Year	$363.0	$764.8	$886.1

LEARNING OBJECTIVES

After studying Chapter 16, you should be able to:

1. **Explain why cash flow information is important to decision making and describe the information in a statement of cash flows and the methods used to disclose noncash investing and financing activities.**

2. **Calculate cash inflows and outflows by inspecting the noncash account balances and prepare a statement of cash flows using the direct method.**

3. **Calculate the net cash provided or used by operating activities according to the indirect·method and prepare the statement of cash flows.**

4. **Prepare a working paper for a statement of cash flows so that the net cash flow from operating activities is calculated by the indirect method.**

5. **Define or explain the words or phrases listed in the chapter glossary.**

Up to this point in your study of accounting, profitability may have seemed to be the sole focus of business managers. Profits certainly are important to business success. However, a business cannot achieve or maintain profitability without carefully managing its cash. Cash is the lifeblood of a business enterprise. In a sense, cash is the fuel that keeps a business moving forward.

Managers and external parties such as investors and creditors pay close attention to a company's cash position and the events and transactions causing that position to change. Information about these events and transactions is reported in a financial statement called the **statement of cash flows.** By studying this chapter, you will learn how to prepare and interpret a statement of cash flows. You will also begin to appreciate the importance of cash flow information as the basis for projecting future cash flows and making a variety of decisions.

WHY CASH FLOW INFORMATION IS IMPORTANT

LO 1

Explain why cash flow information is important to decision making and describe the information in a statement of cash flows and the methods used to disclose noncash investing and financing activities.

Information about cash flows can influence decision makers in many ways. For example, if a company's regular operations bring in more cash than they use, investors will value the company higher than if property and equipment must be sold to finance operations. Information about cash flows can help creditors decide whether a company will have enough cash to pay its existing debts as they mature. And, investors, creditors, managers, and other users of financial statements use cash flow information to evaluate a company's ability to meet unexpected obligations. Cash flow in-

formation is used by decision makers outside as well as inside the firm to evaluate a company's ability to take advantage of new business opportunities that may arise. Managers within a company use cash flow information to plan day-to-day operating activities and make long-term investment decisions.

An example of how careful analysis and management of cash flows can lead to improved financial stability is **R. H. Macy & Company's** dramatic turnaround. The company obtained temporary protection from the bankruptcy court in January 1992 and desperately needed to improve its cash flows. Management did so by engaging in aggressive cost-cutting measures. As a result of this effort, Macy's cash inflow rose to $210 million in its fiscal year ended July 1993 from a negative cash flow of $38.9 million in fiscal 1992. This improvement allowed Macy's to avoid bankruptcy and probably influenced its combination with Federated Department Stores.

The story of **W. T. Grant Co.** is a classic example of why cash flow information should be considered in predicting a firm's future stability and performance. From

1970 to 1973, Grant was reporting net income of more than $40 million per year. At the same time, it was experiencing an alarming decrease in cash provided by operations. Net cash *outflow* exceeded $90 million by 1973.[1] In spite of its earnings performance, Grant went bankrupt within a few years.

The **W. T. Grant** investors who relied solely on earnings per share figures in the early 1970s were unpleasantly surprised. In more recent years, investors generally have learned to evaluate cash flows as well as income statement and balance sheet information as they make their investment decisions.[2]

The importance of cash flow information to decision makers has directly influenced the thinking of accounting authorities. For example, the FASB's objectives of financial reporting clearly reflect the importance of cash flow information. The FASB stated that financial statements should include information about:

- How a business obtains and spends cash.
- Its borrowing and repayment activities.
- The sale and repurchase of its ownership securities.
- Dividend payments and other distributions to its owners.
- Other factors affecting a company's liquidity or solvency.[3]

To accomplish these objectives, a financial statement is needed to summarize, classify, and report the periodic cash inflows and outflows of a business. This information is provided in a statement of cash flows.

STATEMENT OF CASH FLOWS

In November 1987, the FASB issued *Statement of Financial Accounting Standards No. 95,* "Statement of Cash Flows." This standard requires businesses to include a statement of cash flows in all financial reports that contain both a balance sheet and an income statement. The purpose of this statement is to present information about a company's cash receipts and disbursements during the reporting period.

Illustration 16–1 is a diagram of the information reported in a statement of cash flows. The illustration shows three categories of cash flows: cash flows from operating activities, cash flows from investing activities, and cash flows from financing activities. Both inflows and outflows are included within each category. Because all cash inflows and outflows are reported, the statement reconciles the beginning-of-period and end-of-period balances of cash plus cash equivalents.

Direct Method of Presenting Cash Flows from Operating Activities

When preparing a statement of cash flows, you can calculate the net cash provided (or used) by operating activities two different ways. One is the **direct method of calculating net cash provided (or used) by operating activities.** The other is the indirect method. When using the direct method, you separately list each major class of operating cash receipts (for example, cash received from customers) and each major

---

[1] James Largay and Clyde Stickney, "Cash Flow, Ratio Analysis and the W. T. Grant Company Bankruptcy," *Financial Analysts Journal,* July–August 1980, pp. 51–56.

[2] Marc J. Epstein and Moses L. Pava, "How Useful Is the Statement of Cash Flows," *Management Accounting,* July 1992.

[3] FASB, *Statement of Financial Accounting Concepts No. 1,* "Objectives of Financial Reporting by Business Enterprises" (Norwalk, CT, 1978), par. 49.

As a Matter of Opinion

Ms. Garza earned a BBA degree with a major in accounting at the University of Houston. Upon graduation she joined the audit staff of Ernst & Young where she specialized in bank auditing. She continued her education at The University of Texas at Austin, completing an MBA degree in 1982. Thereafter, Ms. Garza entered banking as a professional and executive lender. Presently, she is senior vice president and metropolitan manager of the Austin area, NationsBank of Texas, N.A.

Ms. Garza has served in a variety of public service positions with organizations such as United Way, the American Heart Association, and Easter Seals.

After I left public accounting and entered the banking industry, there was not much emphasis placed on cash flow analysis. As a loan officer,

the review of financial statements centered primarily on profitability. However, during the years I have been in banking, there has been a shift in focus to the analysis of cash flows.

We now recognize that a lender must have a complete understanding of a borrower's cash flow in order to better assess both the borrowing needs and repayment sources. This requires historical and projected information about the major types of cash inflows and outflows.

The truth is that cash, and cash alone, is the source of repayment for all loans. Over the years, I have seen many companies, whose financial statements indicated good profitability, experience severe financial problems because the owners or managers lacked a good understanding of the companies' cash flow.

Mary E. Garza

class of cash payments (such as payments for merchandise). Then, you subtract the payments from the receipts to determine the net cash provided (or used) by operating activities.

Indirect Method of Presenting Cash Flows from Operating Activities

The **indirect method of calculating net cash provided (or used) by operating activities** is not as informative as the direct method. The indirect method is not as informative because it does not disclose the individual categories of cash inflows and outflows from operating activities. Instead, the indirect method discloses only the net cash provided (or used) by operating activities.

When using the indirect method, list net income first. Next, adjust it for items that are necessary to reconcile net income to the net cash provided (or used) by operating activities. For example, in the calculation of net income, we subtract depreciation expense. However, depreciation expense does not involve a current cash payment. Therefore, add depreciation expense back to net income in the process of reconciling net income to the net cash provided (or used) by operating activities.

The direct method is most informative and is the method that the FASB recommends. However, most companies use the indirect method in spite of the FASB's recommendation. By learning the direct method first, you will find the indirect method easier to understand. Also, managers use the direct method to predict future cash requirements and cash availability. Thus, we explain the direct method next.

The Format of the Statement of Cash Flows (Direct Method)

Illustration 16–2 shows the statement of cash flows for Grover Company. Notice that the major classes of cash inflows and cash outflows are listed separately in the operating activities section of the statement. This is the format of the direct method. The operating cash outflows are subtracted from the operating cash inflows to determine the net cash provided (or used) by operating activities.

Also observe in Illustration 16–2 the other two categories of cash flows reported on the statement of cash flows. In both categories—investing activities and financing activities—we subtract the cash outflows from the cash inflows to determine the net cash provided (or used).

Illustration 16–1   Categories of Information in the Statement of Cash Flows

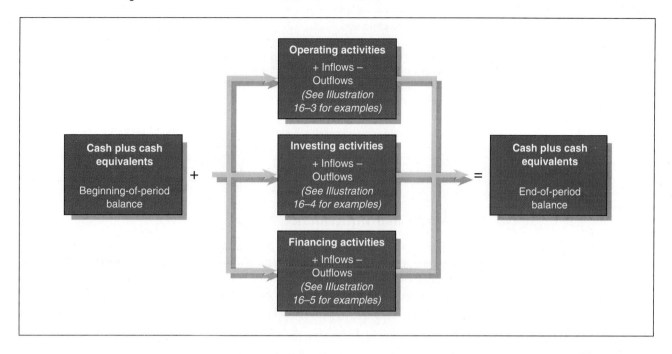

Illustration 16–2
Statement of Cash Flows
(Direct Method)

GROVER COMPANY
Statement of Cash Flows
For Year Ended December 31, 19X2

Cash flows from operating activities:
Cash received from customers	$570,000	
Cash paid for merchandise	(319,000)	
Cash paid for wages and other operating expenses ..	(218,000)	
Cash paid for interest	(8,000)	
Cash paid for taxes	(5,000)	
Net cash provided by operating activities		$20,000

Cash flows from investing activities:
Cash received from sale of plant assets	$12,000	
Cash paid for purchase of plant assets	(10,000)	
Net cash provided by investing activities		2,000

Cash flows from financing activities:
Cash received from issuing stock	$15,000	
Cash paid to retire bonds	(18,000)	
Cash paid for dividends	(14,000)	
Net cash used in financing activities		(17,000)
Net increase in cash		$ 5,000
Cash balance at beginning of 19X2		12,000
Cash balance at end of 19X2		$17,000

Compare the statement in Illustration 16–2 with the chart in Illustration 16–1. Notice that the beginning and ending balances are called *cash plus cash equivalents* in Illustration 16–1. However, in Illustration 16–2, the beginning and ending balances refer only to *cash.* The balances in Illustration 16–2 are called *cash* because Grover Company does not own any cash equivalents.

Illustration 16-3
Cash Flows from Operating
Activities

Cash Inflows	Cash Outflows
Cash sales to customers.	Payments to employees for salaries and wages.
Cash collections from credit customers.	Payments to suppliers of goods and services.
Receipts of cash dividends from stock investments in other entities.	Payments to government agencies for taxes, fines, and penalties.
Receipts of interest payments.	Interest payments, net of amounts capitalized.
Refunds from suppliers.	Cash refunds to customers.
Cash collected from a lawsuit.	Contributions to charities.

Cash and Cash Equivalents

In *Statement of Financial Accounting Standards No. 95,* the FASB concluded that a statement of cash flows should explain the difference between the beginning and ending balances of cash and cash equivalents. Prior to this new standard, cash equivalents were generally understood to be short-term, temporary investments of cash. As you learned in Chapter 7, however, a cash equivalent must satisfy these two criteria:

1. The investment must be readily convertible to a known amount of cash.
2. The investment must be sufficiently close to its maturity date so that its market value is relatively insensitive to interest rate changes.

In general, only investments purchased within three months of their maturity dates satisfy these criteria.[4]

The idea of classifying short-term, highly liquid investments as cash equivalents is based on the assumption that companies make these investments to earn a return on idle cash balances. Sometimes, however, items that meet the criteria of cash equivalents are not held as temporary investments of idle cash balances. For example, an investment company that specializes in the purchase and sale of securities may buy cash equivalents as part of its investing strategy. Companies that have such investments are allowed to exclude them from the cash equivalents category. However, the companies must develop a clear policy for determining which items to include and which to exclude. These policies must be disclosed in the footnotes to the financial statements and must be followed consistently from period to period.

CLASSIFYING CASH TRANSACTIONS

On a statement of cash flows, cash and cash equivalents are treated as a single item. In other words, the statement reports the changes in cash plus cash equivalents. Therefore, cash payments to purchase cash equivalents and cash receipts from selling cash equivalents do not appear on the statement. All other cash receipts and payments are classified and reported on the statement as operating, investing, or financing activities. Within each category, individual cash receipts and payments are summarized in a manner that clearly describes the general nature of the company's cash transactions. Then, the summarized cash receipts and payments within each category are netted against each other. A category provides a net cash inflow if the receipts in the category exceed the payments. And, if the payments in a category exceed the receipts, the category is a net cash outflow during the period.

---

[4]FASB, *Accounting Standards—Current Text* (Stamford, CT, 1994), sec. C25.106. First published in *Statement of Financial Accounting Standards No. 95,* par. 8.

Cash Inflows	Cash Outflows
Proceeds from selling productive assets (for example, land, buildings, equipment, natural resources, and intangible assets).	Payments to purchase property, plant, and equipment or other productive assets (excluding merchandise inventory).
Proceeds from selling investments in the equity securities of other companies.	Payments to acquire equity securities of other companies.
Proceeds from selling investments in the debt securities of other entities, except cash equivalents.	Payments to acquire debt securities of other entities, except cash equivalents.
Proceeds from collecting the principal amount of loans.	Payments in the form of loans made to other parties.
Proceeds from the sale (discounting) of loans made by the enterprise.	

Illustration 16–4
Cash Flows from Investing Activities

Operating Activities

Look at the cash flows classified as **operating activities** in Illustration 16–2. Notice that operating activities generally include transactions that relate to the calculation of net income. However, some income statement items are not related to operating activities. We discuss these items later.

As disclosed in a statement of cash flows, operating activities involve the production or purchase of merchandise and the sale of goods and services to customers. Operating activities also include expenditures that relate to administering the business. In fact, cash flows from operating activities include all cash flows from transactions that are not defined as investing or financing activities. Illustration 16–3 shows typical cash inflows and outflows from operating activities.

Investing Activities

Transactions that involve making and collecting loans or that involve purchasing and selling plant assets, other productive assets, or investments (other than cash equivalents) are called **investing activities.** Usually, investing activities involve the purchase or sale of assets classified on the balance sheet as plant and equipment, intangible assets, or long-term investments. However, the purchase and sale of short-term investments other than cash equivalents are also investing activities. Illustration 16–4 shows examples of cash flows from investing activities.

The fourth type of receipt listed in Illustration 16–4 involves proceeds from collecting the principal amount of loans. Regarding this item, carefully examine any cash receipts that relate to notes receivable. If the notes resulted from sales to customers, classify the cash receipts as operating activities. Use this classification even if the notes are long-term notes. But, if a company loans money to other parties, classify the cash receipts from collecting the principal of the loans as inflows from investing activities. Nevertheless, the FASB concluded that collections of interest are not investing activities. Instead, they are reported as operating activities.

Financing Activities

The **financing activities** of a business include transactions with its owners and transactions with creditors to borrow money or to repay the principal amounts of loans. Financing activities include borrowing and repaying both short-term loans and long-term debt. However, cash payments to settle credit purchases of merchandise, whether

Illustration 16–5
Cash Flows from Financing
Activities

Cash Inflows	**Cash Outflows**
Proceeds from issuing equity securities (e.g., common and preferred stock).	Payments of dividends and other distributions to owners.
Proceeds from issuing bonds and notes payable.	Payments to purchase treasury stock.
Proceeds from other short- or long-term borrowing transactions.	Repayments of cash loans.
	Payments of the principal amounts involved in long-term credit arrangements.

Illustration 16–6
Decco Company—Footnote
Describing Noncash
Investing and Financing
Activities

The company issued 1,000 shares of common stock for the purchase of land and buildings with fair values of $5,000 and $15,000, respectively.

The company entered into a capital lease obligation of $12,000 for new computer equipment.

The company exchanged old machinery with a fair value of $7,000 and a book value of $8,000 for new machinery valued at $12,000. The balance of $5,000 was paid in cash.

on account or by note, are operating activities. Payments of interest expense are also operating activities. Illustration 16–5 shows examples of cash flows from financing activities.

NONCASH INVESTING AND FINANCING ACTIVITIES

Some important investing and financing activities do not involve cash receipts or payments during the current period. For example, a company might purchase land and buildings and finance 100% of the purchase by giving a long-term note payable. Although this transaction clearly involves both investing and financing activities, we do not report it in the current period's statement of cash flows because it does not involve a cash inflow or outflow.

Other investing and financing activities may involve some cash receipt or payment as well as giving or receiving other types of consideration. For example, suppose that you purchase machinery for $12,000 by paying cash of $5,000 and trading in old machinery that has a market value of $7,000. In this case, the statement of cash flows reports only the $5,000 cash outflow for the purchase of machinery. As a result, this $12,000 investing transaction is only partially described in the statement of cash flows.

The noncash portions of investing and financing activities should *not* be reported in the statement of cash flows. However, they are important events that should be disclosed. To accomplish this disclosure, a company may describe its noncash investing and financing activities in a footnote or a separate schedule. Illustration 16–6 shows an example of how a company might disclose its noncash investing and financing activities.

In Illustration 16–6, notice that the last item describes an exchange of machinery including both the cash and noncash aspects of this transaction. The $5,000 cash payment is reported in Decco Company's statement of cash flows as an investing activity. Nevertheless, the description of noncash investing and financing activities includes both the cash and noncash aspects of the transaction.

Examples of transactions that must be disclosed as noncash investing and financing activities include the following:

- The retirement of debt securities by issuing equity securities.
- The conversion of preferred stock to common stock.

- The leasing of assets in a transaction that qualifies as a capital lease.
- The purchase of long-term assets by issuing a note payable to the seller.
- The exchange of a noncash asset for other noncash assets.
- The purchase of noncash assets by issuing equity or debt securities.

Progress Check
(Answers to Progress Checks are provided at the end of the chapter.)

16-1   Does a statement of cash flows disclose payments of cash to purchase cash equivalents? Does it disclose receipts of cash from the liquidation of cash equivalents?

16-2   What are the categories of cash flows reported separately on the statement of cash flows?

16-3   Concerning the direct and indirect methods of presenting cash flows from operating activities, which is most informative? Which is used most often in practice?

16-4   Identify the category for each of the following cash flow activities: *(a)* purchase of equipment for cash; *(b)* payment of wages; *(c)* sale of common stock; *(d)* receipt of cash dividends on stock investment; *(e)* collection from customers; *(f)* issuance of bonds for cash.

The information you need to prepare a statement of cash flows comes from a variety of sources. These include comparative balance sheets at the beginning and the end of the accounting period, an income statement for the period, and a careful analysis of each noncash balance sheet account in the general ledger. However, because cash inflows and cash outflows are to be reported, you might wonder why we do not focus our attention on the Cash account. For the moment, we should at least consider this approach.

Analyzing the Cash Account

All of a company's cash receipts and cash payments are recorded in the Cash account in the General Ledger. Therefore, the Cash account would seem to be the logical place to look for information about cash flows from operating, investing, and financing activities. To demonstrate, review this summarized Cash account of Grover Company:

Summarized Cash Account

Balance, 12/31/X1	12,000		
Receipts from customers	570,000	Payments for merchandise	319,000
Proceeds from sale of plant		Payments for wages and other	
assets	12,000	operating expenses	218,000
Proceeds from stock issuance	15,000	Interest payments	8,000
		Tax payments	5,000
		Payments for purchase of	
		plant assets	10,000
		Payments to retire bonds	18,000
		Dividend payments	14,000
Balance, 12/31/X2	17,000		

In this account, the individual cash transactions are already summarized in terms of major types of receipts and payments. For example, the account has only one debit entry for the total receipts from all customers. All that remains is to determine whether each type of cash inflow or outflow is an operating, investing, or financing activity and then place it in its proper category on the statement of cash flows. The completed statement of cash flows appears in Illustration 16–2 on page 611.

PREPARING A STATEMENT OF CASH FLOWS

LO 2
Calculate cash inflows and outflows by inspecting the noncash account balances and prepare a statement of cash flows using the direct method.

Illustration 16-7   Why an Analysis of the Noncash Accounts Explains the Change in Cash

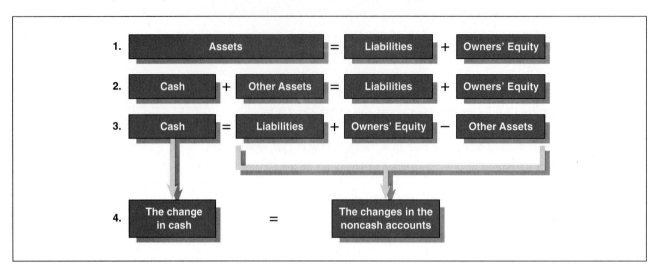

While an analysis of the Cash account may appear to be an easy way to prepare a statement of cash flows, it has two serious drawbacks. First, most companies have so many individual cash receipts and disbursements that it is not practical to review them all. Imagine what a problem this analysis would present for IBM, General Motors, Kodak, or Exxon, or even for a relatively small business. Second, the Cash account usually does not contain a description of each cash transaction. Therefore, even though the Cash account shows the amount of each debit and credit, you generally cannot determine the type of transaction by looking at the Cash account. Thus, the Cash account does not readily provide the information you need to prepare a statement of cash flows. To obtain the necessary information, you must analyze the changes in the noncash accounts.

Analyzing Noncash Accounts to Determine Cash Flows

When a company records cash inflows and outflows with debits and credits to the Cash account, it also records credits and debits in other accounts. Some of these accounts are balance sheet accounts. Others are revenue and expense accounts that are closed to Retained Earnings, a balance sheet account. As a result, all cash transactions eventually affect noncash balance sheet accounts. Therefore, we can determine the nature of the cash inflows and outflows by examining the changes in the noncash balance sheet accounts. Illustration 16–7 shows this important relationship between the Cash account and the noncash balance sheet accounts.

In Illustration 16–7, notice that the balance sheet equation labeled (1) is expanded in (2) so that cash is separated from the other assets. Then, the equation is rearranged in (3) so that cash is set equal to the sum of the liability and equity accounts less the noncash asset accounts. The illustration then points out in (4) that changes in one side of the equation (cash) must be equal to the changes in the other side (noncash accounts). Part (4) shows that you can fully explain the changes in cash by analyzing the changes in liabilities, owners' equity, and noncash assets.

This overall process has another advantage. The examination of each noncash account also identifies any noncash investing and financing activities that occurred during the period. As you learned earlier, these noncash items must be disclosed, but not on the statement of cash flows.

Illustration 16–8   Analysis of the Noncash Accounts Explains the Change in Cash

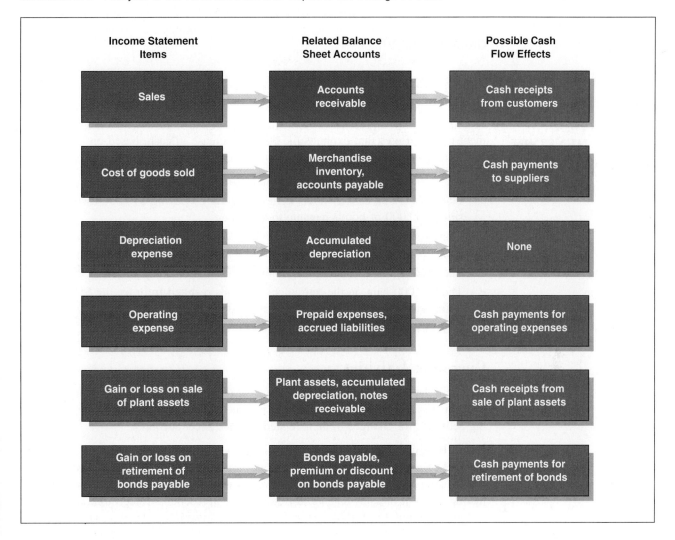

When beginning to analyze the changes in the noncash balance sheet accounts, recall that Retained Earnings is affected by revenues, expenses, and dividend declarations. Therefore, look at the income statement accounts to help explain the change in Retained Earnings. In fact, the income statement accounts provide important information that relates to the changes in several balance sheet accounts.

Illustration 16–8 summarizes some of these relationships between income statement accounts, balance sheet accounts, and possible cash flows. For example, to determine the cash receipts from customers during a period, adjust the amount of sales revenue for the increase or decrease in Accounts Receivable.[5] If the Accounts Receivable balance did not change, the cash collected from customers is equal to sales revenue. On the other hand, if the Accounts Receivable balance decreased, cash collections must have been equal to sales revenue *plus* the reduction in Accounts Receivable. And, if the Accounts Receivable balance increased, the cash collected from customers must have been equal to Sales *less* the increase in Accounts Receivable.

---

[5]This introductory explanation assumes that there is no bad debts expense. However, if bad debts occur and are written off directly to Accounts Receivable, the change in the Accounts Receivable balance will be due in part to the write-off. The remaining change results from credit sales and from cash receipts. This chapter does not discuss the allowance method of accounting for bad debts since it would make the analysis unnecessarily complex at this time.

By analyzing all noncash balance sheet accounts and related income statement accounts in this fashion, you can obtain the necessary information for a statement of cash flows. Next, we illustrate this process by examining the noncash accounts of Grover Company.

GROVER COMPANY—A COMPREHENSIVE EXAMPLE

Grover Company's December 31, 19X1, and 19X2 balance sheets and its 19X2 income statement are presented in Illustration 16–9. Our objective is to prepare a statement of cash flows that explains the $5,000 increase in cash, based on these financial statements and this additional information about the 19X2 transactions:

a. All accounts payable balances resulted from merchandise purchases.

b. Plant assets that cost $70,000 were purchased by paying $10,000 cash and issuing $60,000 of bonds payable to the seller.

c. Plant assets with an original cost of $30,000 and accumulated depreciation of $12,000 were sold for $12,000 cash. The result was a $6,000 loss.

d. The proceeds from issuing 3,000 shares of common stock were $15,000.

e. The $16,000 gain on the retirement of bonds resulted from paying $18,000 to retire bonds that had a book value of $34,000.

f. Cash dividends of $14,000 were declared and paid.

Operating Activities

We begin the analysis by calculating the cash flows from operating activities. In general, this process involves adjusting the income statement items that relate to operating activities for changes in their related balance sheet accounts.

Cash Received from Customers The calculation of cash receipts from customers begins with sales revenue. If all sales are for cash, the amount of cash received from customers is equal to sales. However, when sales are on account, you must adjust the amount of sales revenue for the change in Accounts Receivable.

In Illustration 16–9, look at the Accounts Receivable balances on December 31, 19X1, and 19X2. The beginning balance was $40,000, and the ending balance was $60,000. The income statement shows that sales revenue was $590,000. With this information, you can reconstruct the Accounts Receivable account and determine the amount of cash received from customers, as follows:

Accounts Receivable

Balance, 12/31/X1	40,000		
Sales, 19X2	590,000	Collections =	570,000
Balance, 12/31/X	260,000		

This account shows that the balance of Accounts Receivable increased from $40,000 to $60,000. It also shows that cash receipts from customers are $570,000, which is equal to sales of $590,000 plus the $40,000 beginning balance less the $60,000 ending balance. This calculation can be restated in more general terms like this:

Cash received from customers = Sales − Increase in accounts receivable

And, if the balance of Accounts Receivable decreases, the calculation is:

Cash received from customers = Sales + Decrease in accounts receivable

Now turn back to Illustration 16–2 on page 611. Note that the $570,000 of cash Grover Company received from customers appears on the statement of cash flows as a cash inflow from operating activities.

Illustration 16–9
Financial Statements

GROVER COMPANY
Balance Sheet
December 31, 19X2 and 19X1

			19X2			19X1
Assets						
Current assets:						
Cash			$ 17,000			$ 12,000
Accounts receivable			60,000			40,000
Merchandise inventory			84,000			70,000
Prepaid expenses			6,000			4,000
Total current assets			$167,000			$126,000
Long-term assets:						
Plant assets	$250,000			$210,000		
Less accumulated depreciation	60,000		190,000	48,000		162,000
Total assets			$357,000			$288,000
Liabilities						
Current liabilities:						
Accounts payable			$ 35,000			$ 40,000
Interest payable			3,000			4,000
Income taxes payable			22,000			12,000
Total current liabilities			$ 60,000			$ 56,000
Long-term liabilities:						
Bonds payable			90,000			64,000
Total liabilities			$150,000			$120,000
Stockholders' Equity						
Contributed capital:						
Common stock, $5 par value			$ 95,000			$ 80,000
Retained earnings			112,000			88,000
Total stockholders' equity			207,000			168,000
Total liabilities and						
stockholders' equity			$357,000			$288,000

GROVER COMPANY
Income Statement
For Year Ended December 31, 19X2

Sales		$590,000
Cost of goods sold	$300,000	
Wages and other operating expenses	216,000	
Interest expense	7,000	
Income taxes expense	15,000	
Depreciation expense	24,000	(562,000)
Loss on sale of plant assets		(6,000)
Gain on retirement of debt		16,000
Net income		$ 38,000

Cash Payments for Merchandise. The calculation of cash payments for merchandise begins with cost of goods sold and merchandise inventory. For a moment, suppose that all merchandise purchases are for cash and that the ending balance of Merchandise Inventory is unchanged from the beginning balance. In this case, the total cash paid for merchandise equals the cost of goods sold. However, this case is not typical. Usually, you expect some change in a company's Merchandise Inventory balance during a period. Also, purchases of merchandise usually are made on account, causing some change in the Accounts Payable balance.

When the balances of Merchandise Inventory and Accounts Payable change, you must adjust cost of goods sold for the changes in these accounts to determine the cash payments for merchandise. This adjustment has two steps. First, combine the change in the balance of Merchandise Inventory with cost of goods sold to determine the cost of purchases during the period.[6] Second, combine the change in the balance of Accounts Payable with the cost of purchases to determine the total cash payments to suppliers of merchandise.

Consider again the Grover Company example. Begin by combining the reported amount of cost of goods sold ($300,000) with the Merchandise Inventory beginning balance ($70,000) and with the ending balance ($84,000) to determine the amount that was purchased during the period. To accomplish this, reconstruct the Merchandise Inventory account as follows:

Merchandise Inventory

Balance, 12/31/X1	70,000		
Purchases =	**314,000**	Cost of goods sold	300,000
Balance, 12/31/X2	84,000		

This account shows that we add the $14,000 increase in merchandise inventory to cost of goods sold of $300,000 to get purchases of $314,000.

To determine the cash paid for merchandise, you adjust purchases for the change in accounts payable. This can be done by reconstructing the Accounts Payable account as follows:

Accounts Payable

		Balance, 12/31/X1	40,000
Payments =	**319,000**	Purchases	314,000
		Balance, 12/31/X2	35,000

In this account, purchases of $314,000 plus a beginning balance of $40,000 less the ending balance of $35,000 equals cash payments of $319,000. In other words, purchases of $314,000 plus the $5,000 decrease in accounts payable equals cash payments of $319,000.

To summarize the adjustments to cost of goods sold that are necessary to calculate cash payments for merchandise:

$$\textbf{Purchases} = \textbf{Cost of goods sold} \begin{bmatrix} + & \textbf{Increase in merchandise inventory} \\ & or \\ - & \textbf{Decrease in merchandise inventory} \end{bmatrix}$$

And,

$$\textbf{Cash payments for merchandise} = \textbf{Purchases} \begin{bmatrix} + & \textbf{Decrease in accounts payable} \\ & or \\ - & \textbf{Increase in accounts payable} \end{bmatrix}$$

Now, look at Illustration 16–2 on page 611. Notice that Grover Company's payments of $319,000 for merchandise are reported on the statement of cash flows as a cash outflow for operating activities.

Cash Payments for Wages and Other Operating Expenses. Grover Company's income statement shows wages and other operating expenses of $216,000 (see Illustration 16–9 on page 619). To determine the amount of cash paid during the period for wages and other operating expenses, we need to combine this amount with the changes in any related balance sheet accounts. In Grover Company's beginning and ending balance sheets in Illustration 16–9, you must look for prepaid expenses and any accrued liabilities that relate to wages and other operating expenses. In this example, the balance sheets show that Grover Company has prepaid expenses but does

---

[6]The amount of purchases is also in the Purchases account in the General Ledger.

not have any accrued liabilities. Thus, the adjustment to the expense item is limited to the change in prepaid expenses. The amount of the adjustment can be determined by assuming that all cash payments of wages and other operating expenses were originally debited to Prepaid Expenses. With this assumption, we can reconstruct the Prepaid Expenses account as follows:

Prepaid Expenses			
Balance, 12/31/X1	4,000		
Payments =	218,000	Wages and other operating expenses	216,000
Balance, 12/31/X2	6,000		

This account shows that prepaid expenses increased by $2,000 during the period. Therefore, the cash payments for wages and other operating expenses were $2,000 greater than the reported expense. Thus, the amount paid for wages and other operating expenses is $216,000 plus $2,000, or $218,000.

In reconstructing the Prepaid Expenses account, we assumed that all cash payments for wages and operating expenses were debited to Prepaid Expenses. However, this assumption does not have to be true for the analysis to work. If cash payments were debited directly to the expense account, the total amount of cash payments would be the same. In other words, the cash paid for operating expenses still equals the $216,000 expense plus the $2,000 increase in prepaid expenses.

On the other hand, if Grover Company's balance sheets had shown accrued liabilities, we would have to adjust the expense for the change in those accrued liabilities. In general terms, the calculation is as follows:

$$
\begin{array}{ccc}
\text{Cash paid for} & \text{Wages and} & \begin{bmatrix} + \text{ Increase in prepaid} \\ \text{expenses} \\ or \\ - \text{ Decrease in prepaid} \\ \text{expenses} \end{bmatrix} \begin{bmatrix} + \text{ Decrease in accrued} \\ \text{liabilities} \\ or \\ - \text{ Increase in accrued} \\ \text{liabilities} \end{bmatrix} \\
\text{wages and other} & = & \text{other} \\
\text{operating} & & \text{operating} \\
\text{expenses} & & \text{expenses}
\end{array}
$$

Payments for Interest and Taxes. Grover Company's remaining operating cash flows involve cash payments for interest and for taxes. The analysis of these items is similar because both require adjustments for changes in related liability accounts. Grover Company's income statement shows interest expense of $7,000 and income taxes expense of $15,000. To calculate the related cash payments, adjust interest expense for the change in interest payable and adjust income taxes expense for the change in income taxes payable. These calculations are accomplished by reconstructing the liability accounts as follows:

Interest Payable			
		Balance, 12/31/X1	4,000
Interest paid =	8,000	Interest expense	7,000
		Balance, 12/31/X2	3,000

Income Taxes Payable			
		Balance, 12/31/X1	12,000
Income taxes paid =	5,000	Income taxes expense	15,000
		Balance, 12/31/X2	22,000

These reconstructed accounts show that interest payments were $8,000 and income tax payments were $5,000. The general form of each calculation is:

$$
\text{Cash payment} = \text{Expense} \begin{bmatrix} + \text{ Decrease in related payable} \\ or \\ - \text{ Increase in related payable} \end{bmatrix}
$$

Both of these cash payments appear as operating items on Grover Company's statement of cash flows in Illustration 16–2 on page 611.

Investing Activities

Investing activities usually involve transactions that affect long-term assets. Recall from the information provided about Grover Company's transactions that the company purchased and also sold plant assets. Both of these transactions are investing activities.

Purchase of Plant Assets. Grover Company purchased plant assets that cost $70,000 by issuing $60,000 of bonds payable to the seller and paying the $10,000 balance in cash. The $10,000 payment is reported as a cash outflow on the statement of cash flows (see Illustration 16–2). Also, because $60,000 of the purchase was financed by issuing bonds payable, this transaction involves noncash investing and financing activities. It might be described in a footnote as follows:

Noncash investing and financing activities:	
Purchased plant assets	$70,000
Issued bonds payable to finance purchase . .	60,000
Balance paid in cash	$10,000

Sale of Plant Assets. Grover Company sold plant assets that cost $30,000 when they had accumulated depreciation of $12,000. The result of the sale was a loss of $6,000 and a cash receipt of $12,000. This cash receipt is reported in the statement of cash flows as a cash inflow from investing activities (see Illustration 16–2).

Recall from Grover Company's income statement that depreciation expense was $24,000. Depreciation does not use or provide cash. Note, however, the effects of depreciation expense, the plant asset purchase, and the plant asset sale on the Plant Assets and Accumulated Depreciation accounts. These accounts are reconstructed as follows:

Plant Assets					Accumulated Depreciation, Plant Assets		
Balance, 12/31/X1	210,000					Balance, 12/31/X1	48,000
Purchase	70,000	Sale	30,000	Sale	12,000	Depreciation expense	24,000
Balance, 12/31/X2	250,000					Balance, 12/31/X2	60,000

The beginning and ending balances of these accounts were taken from Grover Company's balance sheets (Illustration 16–9). Reconstructing the accounts shows that the beginning and ending balances of both accounts are completely reconciled by the purchase, the sale, and the depreciation expense. Therefore, we did not omit any of the investing activities that relate to plant assets.

Financing Activities

Financing activities usually relate to a company's long-term debt and stockholders' equity accounts. In the information about Grover Company, four transactions involved financing activities. We already discussed one of these, the $60,000 issuance of bonds payable to purchase plant assets, as a noncash investing and financing activity. The remaining three transactions were the retirement of bonds, the issuance of common stock, and the payment of cash dividends.

Payment to Retire Bonds Payable. Grover Company's December 31, 19X1, balance sheet showed total bonds payable of $64,000. Included within this beginning balance for 19X2 were bonds with a carrying value of $34,000 that were retired for an $18,000 cash payment during the year. The income statement reports the $16,000 difference as a gain. The statement of cash flows shows the $18,000 payment as a cash outflow for financing activities (see Illustration 16–2 on page 611).

Notice that the beginning and ending balances of Bonds Payable are reconciled by the $60,000 issuance of new bonds and the retirement of $34,000 of old bonds. The following reconstructed Bonds Payable account shows the results of these activities:

Bonds Payable

		Balance, 12/31/X1	64,000
Retired bonds	34,000	Issued bonds	60,000
		Balance, 12/31/X2	90,000

Receipt from Common Stock Issuance. During 19X2, Grover Company issued 3,000 shares of common stock at par for $5 per share. This $15,000 cash receipt is reported on the statement of cash flows as a financing activity. Look at the December 31, 19X1, and 19X2 balance sheets in Illustration 16–9. Notice that the Common Stock account balance increased from $80,000 at the end of 19X1 to $95,000 at the end of 19X2. Thus, the $15,000 stock issue explains the change in the Common Stock account.

Payment of Cash Dividends. According to the facts provided about Grover Company's transactions, it paid cash dividends of $14,000 during 19X2. This payment is reported as a cash outflow for financing activities. Also, note that the effects of this $14,000 payment and the reported net income of $38,000 fully reconcile the beginning and ending balances of Retained Earnings. This is shown in the reconstructed Retained Earnings account that follows:

Retained Earnings

		Balance, 12/31/X1	88,000
Cash dividend	14,000	Net income	38,000
		Balance, 12/31/X2	112,000

We have described all of Grover Company's cash inflows and outflows and one noncash investing and financing transaction. In the process of making these analyses, we reconciled the changes in all of the noncash balance sheet accounts. The change in the Cash account is reconciled by the statement of cash flows, as seen in Illustration 16–2 on page 611.

Progress Check

16–5 Net sales during a period were $590,000, beginning accounts receivable were $120,000, and ending accounts receivable were $90,000. What amount was collected from customers during the period?

16–6 Merchandise Inventory account balance decreased during a period from a beginning balance of $32,000 to an ending balance of $28,000. Cost of goods sold for the period was $168,000. If the Accounts Payable balance increased $2,400 during the period, what was the amount of cash paid for merchandise?

16–7 Hargrave Inc. reports wages and other operating expenses incurred totaled $112,000. At the end of last year prepaid expenses totaled $1,200 and this year the balance was $4,200. The current balance sheet does show wages payable of $5,600 whereas last year's did not show any accrued liabilities. How much was paid for wages and other operating expenses this year?

16–8 Equipment that cost $80,000 and had accumulated depreciation of $30,000 was sold at a loss of $10,000. What was the cash receipt from the sale? In what category of the statement of cash flows should it be reported?

Illustration 16–10
Statement of Cash Flows
(Indirect Method)

GROVER COMPANY
Statement of Cash Flows
For Year Ended December 31, 19X2

Cash flows from operating activities:		
Net income	$ 38,000	
Adjustments to reconcile net income to net		
cash provided by operating activities:		
(1) Increase in accounts receivable	(20,000)	
Increase in merchandise inventory . . .	(14,000)	
Increase in prepaid expenses	(2,000)	
Decrease in accounts payable	(5,000)	
Decrease in interest payable	(1,000)	
Increase in income taxes payable	10,000	
(2) Depreciation expense	24,000	
(3) Loss on sale of plant assets	6,000	
Gain on retirement of bonds	(16,000)	
Net cash provided by operating activities		$ 20,000
Cash flows from investing activities:		
Cash received from sale of plant assets . . .	$ 12,000	
Cash paid for purchase of plant assets	(10,000)	
Net cash provided by investing activities . .		2,000
Cash flows from financing activities:		
Cash received from issuing stock	$ 15,000	
Cash paid to retire bonds	(18,000)	
Cash paid for dividends	(14,000)	
Net cash used in financing activities		(17,000)
Net increase in cash		$ 5,000
Cash balance at beginning of 19X2		12,000
Cash balance at end of 19X2		$ 17,000

RECONCILING NET INCOME TO NET CASH PROVIDED (OR USED) BY OPERATING ACTIVITIES

As you learned earlier, the FASB recommends that the operating activities section of the statement of cash flows be prepared according to the direct method. Under this method, the statement reports each major class of cash inflows and outflows from operating activities. *However, when the direct method is used, the FASB also requires that companies disclose a reconciliation of net income to the net cash provided (or used) by operating activities.* This reconciliation is precisely what is accomplished by the *indirect* method of calculating the net cash provided (or used) by operating activities. We explain the indirect method next.

THE INDIRECT METHOD OF CALCULATING NET CASH PROVIDED (OR USED) BY OPERATING ACTIVITIES

LO 3

Calculate the net cash provided or used by operating activities according to the indirect method and prepare the statement of cash flows.

When using the indirect method, list net income first. Then, adjust net income to reconcile its amount to the net amount of cash provided (or used) by operating activities. To see the results of the indirect method, look at Illustration 16–10. This illustration shows Grover Company's statement of cash flows with the reconciliation of net income to the net cash provided by operating activities.

In Illustration 16–10, notice that the net cash provided by operating activities is $20,000. This is the same amount that was reported on the statement of cash flows (direct method) in Illustration 16–2 on page 611. However, these illustrations show entirely different ways of calculating the $20,000 net cash inflow. Under the direct method in Illustration 16–2, we subtracted major classes of operating cash outflows from major classes of cash inflows. By comparison, we include none of the individual cash inflows or cash outflows under the indirect method used in Illustration 16–10. Instead, we modify net income to exclude those amounts included in the determination of net income but not involved in operating cash inflows or outflows during the period. Net income also is modified to include operating cash inflows and outflows not recorded as revenues and expenses.

Illustration 16–10 shows three types of adjustments to net income. The adjustments grouped under section (1) are for changes in noncash current assets and current liabilities that relate to operating activities. Adjustment (2) is for an income statement item that relates to operating activities but that did not involve a cash inflow or outflow during the period. The adjustments grouped under (3) eliminate gains and losses that resulted from investing and financing activities. These gains and losses do not relate to operating activities.

ADJUSTMENTS FOR CHANGES IN CURRENT ASSETS AND CURRENT LIABILITIES

To help you understand why adjustments for changes in noncash current assets and current liabilities are part of the reconciliation process, we use the transactions of a very simple company as an example. Assume that Simple Company's income statement shows only two items, as follows:

Sales	$20,000
Operating expenses	(12,000)
Net income	$ 8,000

For a moment, assume that all of Simple Company's sales and operating expenses are for cash. The company has no current assets other than cash and has no current liabilities. Given these assumptions, the net cash provided by operating activities during the period is $8,000, which is the cash received from customers less the cash paid for operating expenses.

Adjustments for Changes in Noncash Current Assets

Now assume that Simple Company's sales are on account. Also assume that its Accounts Receivable balance was $2,000 at the beginning of the year and $2,500 at the end of the year. Under these assumptions, cash receipts from customers equal sales of $20,000 minus the $500 increase in Accounts Receivable, or $19,500. Therefore, using the *direct* method, the net cash provided by operating activities is $7,500 ($19,500 − $12,000).

When the *indirect* method is used to calculate the net cash flow, net income of $8,000 is adjusted for the $500 increase in Accounts Receivable to get $7,500 as the net amount of cash provided by operating activities. Both calculations are as follows:

Direct Method:	
Receipts from customers ($20,000 − $500)	$19,500
Payments for operating expenses	(12,000)
Cash provided (or used) by operating activities . .	$ 7,500
Indirect Method:	
Net income	$8,000
Less the increase in accounts receivable	(500)
Cash provided (or used) by operating activities . .	$7,500

Notice that the direct method calculation subtracts the increase in Accounts Receivable from Sales, while the indirect method calculation subtracts the increase in Accounts Receivable from net income.

As another example, assume instead that the Accounts Receivable balance decreased from $2,000 to $1,200. Under this assumption, cash receipts from customers equal sales of $20,000 plus the $800 decrease in Accounts Receivable, or $20,800. By the direct method, the net cash provided by operating activities is $8,800 ($20,800 − $12,000). And, when the indirect method is used, the $800 decrease in Accounts Receivable is *added* to the $8,000 net income to get $8,800 net cash provided by operating activities.

When the indirect method is used, adjustments like those for Accounts Receivable are required for all noncash current assets related to operating activities. When a non-cash current asset increases, part of the assets derived from operating activities goes into the increase. This leaves a smaller amount as the net cash inflow. Therefore, when you calculate the net cash inflow using the indirect method, subtract the noncash current asset increase from net income. But, when a noncash current asset decreases, additional cash is produced, and you should add this amount to net income. These modifications of income for changes in current assets related to operating activities are as follows:

Net income
Add: Decreases in current assets
Subtract: Increases in current assets
Net cash provided (or used) by operating activities

Adjustments for Changes in Current Liabilities

To illustrate the adjustments for changes in current liabilities, return to the original assumptions about Simple Company. Sales of $20,000 are for cash, and operating expenses are $12,000. However, assume now that Simple Company has Interest Payable as its only current liability. Also assume that the beginning-of-year balance in Interest Payable was $500 and the end-of-year balance was $900. This increase means that the operating expenses of $12,000 were $400 larger than the amount paid in cash during the period. Therefore, the cash payments for operating expenses were only $11,600, or ($12,000 − $400). Under these assumptions, the direct method calculation of net cash provided by operating activities is $8,400, or $20,000 receipts from customers less $11,600 payments for expenses. The indirect method calculation of $8,400 is net income of $8,000 plus the $400 increase in Interest Payable.

Alternatively, if the Interest Payable balance decreased, for example by $300, the cash outflow for operating expenses would have been the $12,000 expense plus the $300 liability decrease, or $12,300. Then, the direct calculation of net cash flow is $20,000 − $12,300 = $7,700. The indirect calculation is $8,000 − $300 = $7,700. In other words, when using the indirect method, subtract a *decrease* in Interest Payable from net income.

Using the indirect method requires adjustments like those for Interest Payable for all current liabilities related to operating activities. When a current liability decreases, part of the cash derived from operating activities pays for the decrease. Therefore, subtract the decrease from net income to determine the remaining net cash inflow. And, when a current liability increases, it finances some operating expenses. In other words, cash was not used to pay for the expense and the liability increase must be *added* to net income when you calculate cash provided by operating activities. These adjustments for changes in current liabilities related to operating activities are:

Net income
Add: Increases in current liabilities
Subtract: Decreases in current liabilities
Net cash provided (or used) by operating activities

One way to remember how to make these modifications to net income is to observe that a *debit* change in a noncash current asset or a current liability is *subtracted* from net income. And, a *credit* change in a noncash current asset or a current liability is *added* to net income.

Adjustments for Operating Items that Do Not Provide or Use Cash

Some operating items that appear on an income statement do not provide or use cash during the current period. One example is depreciation. Other examples are amortization of intangible assets, depletion of natural resources, and bad debts expense.

Record these expenses with debits to expense accounts and credits to noncash accounts. They reduce net income but do not require cash outflows during the period. Therefore, when adjustments to net income are made under the indirect method, add these noncash expenses back to net income.

In addition to noncash expenses such as depreciation, net income may include some revenues that do not provide cash inflows during the current period. An example is equity method earnings from a stock investment in another entity (see Chapter 11). If net income includes revenues that do not provide cash inflows, subtract the revenues from net income in the process of reconciling net income to the net cash provided by operating activities.

The indirect method adjustments for expenses and revenues that do not provide or use cash during the current period are as follows:

Net income
Add: Expenses that do not use cash
Subtract: Revenues that do not provide cash
Net cash provided (or used) by operating activities

Adjustments for Nonoperating Items

Some income statement items are not related to the operating activities of the company. These gains and losses result from investing and financing activities. Examples are gains or losses on the sale of plant assets and gains or losses on the retirement of bonds payable.

Remember that the indirect method reconciles net income to the net cash provided (or used) by operating activities. Therefore, net income must be modified to exclude gains and losses created by investing and financing activities. In making the modifications under the indirect method, subtract gains from financing and investing activities from net income and add losses back to net income:

Net income
Add: Losses from investing or financing activities
Subtract: Gains from investing or financing activities
Net cash provided (or used) by operating activities

16–9 Determine the net cash provided (or used) by operating activities based on the following data:

Net income	$74,900
Decrease in accounts receivable	4,600
Increase in inventory	11,700
Decrease in accounts payable	1,000
Loss on sale of equipment	3,400
Payment of dividends	21,500

16–10 Why are expenses such as depreciation and amortization of goodwill added to net income when cash flow from operating activities is calculated by the indirect method?

16–11 A company reports a net income of $15,000 that includes a $3,000 gain on the sale of plant assets. Why is this gain subtracted from net income in calculating cash flow from operating activities according to the indirect method?

APPLYING THE INDIRECT METHOD TO GROVER COMPANY

LO 4

Prepare a working paper for a statement of cash flows so that the net cash flow from operating activities is calculated by the indirect method.

Determining the net cash flows provided (or used) by operating activities according to the indirect method requires balance sheets at the beginning and end of the period, the current period's income statement, and other information about selected transactions. Illustration 16–9 on page 619 shows the income statement and balance sheet information for Grover Company. Based on this information, Illustration 16–10 presents the indirect method of reconciling net income to net cash provided by operating activities.

Preparing the Indirect Method Working Paper

When a company has a large number of accounts and many operating, investing, and financing transactions, the analysis of noncash accounts can be difficult and confusing. In these situations, a working paper can help organize the information you need to prepare a statement of cash flows. A working paper also makes it easier to check the accuracy of your work.

In addition to Grover Company's comparative balance sheets and income statement presented in Illustration 16–9, the information needed to prepare the working paper follows. The letters identifying each item of information also cross-reference related debits and credits in the working paper.

a. Net income was $38,000.

b. Accounts receivable increased by $20,000.

c. Merchandise inventory increased by $14,000.

d. Prepaid expenses increased by $2,000.

e. Accounts payable decreased by $5,000.

f. Interest payable decreased by $1,000.

g. Income taxes payable increased by $10,000.

h. Depreciation expense was $24,000.

i. Loss on sale of plant assets was $6,000; assets that cost $30,000 with accumulated depreciation of $12,000 were sold for $12,000 cash.

j. Gain on retirement of bonds was $16,000; bonds with a book value of $34,000 were retired with a cash payment of $18,000.

k. Plant assets that cost $70,000 were purchased; the payment consisted of $10,000 cash and issuing $60,000 of bonds payable.

Illustration 16–11

GROVER COMPANY
Working Paper for Statement of Cash Flows (Indirect Method)
For Year Ended December 31, 19X2

	December 31, 19X1	Analysis of Changes		December 31, 19X2
		Debit	Credit	
Balance sheet—debits:				
Cash	12,000			17,000
Accounts receivable	40,000	(b) 20,000		60,000
Merchandise inventory	70,000	(c) 14,000		84,000
Prepaid expenses	4,000	(d) 2,000		6,000
Plant assets	210,000	(k1) 70,000	(i) 30,000	250,000
	336,000			417,000
Balance sheet—credits:				
Accumulated depreciation	48,000	(i) 12,000	(h) 24,000	60,000
Accounts payable	40,000	(e) 5,000		35,000
Interest payable	4,000	(f) 1,000		3,000
Income taxes payable	12,000		(g) 10,000	22,000
Bonds payable	64,000	(j) 34,000	(k2) 60,000	90,000
Common stock, $5 par value	80,000		(l) 15,000	95,000
Retained earnings	88,000	(m) 14,000	(a) 38,000	112,000
	336,000			417,000
Statement of cash flows:				
Operating activities:				
Net income		(a) 38,000		
Increase in accounts receivable ...			(b) 20,000	
Increase in merchandise inventory .			(c) 14,000	
Increase in prepaid expenses			(d) 2,000	
Decrease in accounts payable			(e) 5,000	
Decrease in interest payable			(f) 1,000	
Increase in income taxes payable ..		(g) 10,000		
Depreciation expense		(h) 24,000		
Loss on sale of plant assets		(i) 6,000		
Gain on retirement of bonds			(j) 16,000	
Investing activities:				
Receipts from sale of plant assets .		(i) 12,000		
Payment for purchase of plant assets .			(k1) 10,000	
Financing activities:				
Payments to retire bonds			(j) 18,000	
Receipts from issuing stock		(l) 15,000		
Payments of dividends			(m) 14,000	
Noncash investing and financing activities:				
Purchase of plant assets financed by bonds		(k2) 60,000	(k1) 60,000	
		337,000	337,000	

l. Sold 3,000 shares of common stock for $15,000.

m. Paid cash dividends of $14,000.

Illustration 16–11 shows the indirect method working paper for Grover Company. Notice that the beginning and ending balance sheets are recorded on the working paper the same as when using the direct method. Following the balance sheets, we enter information in the Analysis of Changes columns about cash flows from operating, investing, and financing activities and about noncash investing and financing activities. Note that the working paper does not reconstruct the income statement. Instead, net income is entered as the first item used in computing the amount of cash flows from operating activities.

Entering the Analysis of Changes on the Working Paper

After the balance sheets are entered, we recommend using the following sequence of procedures to complete the working paper:

1. Enter net income as an operating cash inflow (a debit) and as a credit to Retained Earnings.
2. In the Statement of Cash Flows section, adjustments to net income are entered as debits if they increase cash inflows and as credits if they decrease cash inflows. Following this rule, adjust net income for the change in each noncash current asset and current liability related to operating activities. For each adjustment to net income, the offsetting debit or credit should reconcile the beginning and ending balances of a current asset or current liability.
3. Enter the adjustments to net income for income statement items, such as depreciation, that did not provide or use cash during the period. For each adjustment, the offsetting debit or credit should help reconcile a noncash balance sheet account.
4. Adjust net income to eliminate any gains or losses from investing and financing activities. Because the cash associated with a gain must be excluded from operating activities, the gain is entered as a credit in the operating activities section. On the other hand, losses are entered with debits. For each of these adjustments, the related debits and/or credits help reconcile balance sheet accounts and also involve entries to show the cash flow from investing or financing activities.
5. After reviewing any unreconciled balance sheet accounts and related information, enter the reconciling entries for all remaining investing and financing activities. These include items such as purchases of plant assets, issuances of long-term debt, sales of capital stock, and dividend payments. Some of these may require entries in the noncash investing and financing activities section of the working paper.
6. Confirm the accuracy of your work by totaling the Analysis of Changes columns and by determining that the change in each balance sheet account has been explained.

For Grover Company, these steps were performed in Illustration 16–11:

Step	Entries
1	(a)
2	(b) through (g)
3	(h)
4	(i) through (j)
5	(k) through (m)

Because adjustments *i, j,* and *k* are more complex, we show them in the following debit and credit format. This format is similar to the one used for general journal entries, except that the changes in the Cash account are identified as sources or uses of cash.

i.	Loss from Sale of Plant Assets	6,000.00	
	Accumulated Depreciation	12,000.00	
	Receipt from Sale of Plant Assets	12,000.00	
	Plant Assets		30,000.00
	To describe the sale of plant assets.		
j.	Bonds Payable	34,000.00	
	Payments to Retire Bonds		18,000.00
	Gain on Retirement of Bonds		16,000.00
	To describe the retirement of bonds.		
k1.	Plant Assets	70,000.00	
	Payment to Purchase Plant Assets		10,000.00
	Purchase of Plant Assets Financed by Bonds		60,000.00
	To describe the purchase of plant assets, the cash payment, and the use of noncash financing.		
k2.	Purchase of Plant Assets Financed by Bonds	60,000.00	
	Bonds Payable		60,000.00
	To show the issuance of bonds payable to finance the purchase of plant assets.		

Progress Check

16-12 **In preparing a working paper for a statement of cash flows with the cash flows from operating activities reported according to the indirect method, which of the following is true?**

(a) **A decrease in accounts receivable is analyzed with a debit in the statement of cash flows section and a credit in the balance sheet section.**

(b) **A cash dividend paid is analyzed with a debit to retained earnings and a credit in the investing activities section.**

(c) **The analysis of a cash payment to retire bonds payable at a loss would require one debit and two credits.**

(d) **Depreciation expense would not require analysis on the working paper because there is no cash inflow or outflow.**

Numerous ratios are used to analyze income statement and balance sheet data. By comparison, ratios related to the statement of cash flows are not widely used.[7] Only one ratio of that nature, cash flow per share, has received much attention. Some financial analysts use that ratio, usually calculated as net income adjusted for noncash items such as depreciation and amortization. Currently, however, the FASB does not allow reporting cash flow per share, apparently because it might be misinterpreted as a measure of earnings performance.

Mary Garza (As a Matter of Opinion, page 610) typifies the attitude of most managers when she emphasizes the importance of understanding and predicting cash flows. Many business decisions are based on cash flow evaluations. For example, creditors evaluate a company's ability to generate cash before deciding whether to loan money to the company. Investors often make similar evaluations before they buy a company's stock. In making these evaluations, cash flows from investing and financing activities are considered. However, special attention is given to the company's ability to generate cash flows from its operations. The cash flows statement facilitates this by separating the investing and financing activity cash flows from the operating cash flows.

USING THE INFORMATION—CASH FLOWS

LO 1

Explain why cash flow information is important to decision making and describe the information in a statement of cash flows and the methods used to disclose noncash investing and financing activities.

---

[7]To consider some suggested cash flow ratios, see Don E. Giacomino and David E. Mielke, "Cash Flows: Another Approach to Ratio Analysis," *Journal of Accountancy,* March 1993.

To see the importance of identifying cash flows as operating, investing, and financing activities, consider the following three companies. Assume they operate in the same industry and have been in business for several years.

	First Company	Second Company	Third Company
Cash provided (used) by operating activities	$90,000	$40,000	$(24,000)
Cash provided (used) by investing activities:			
Proceeds from sale of operating assets			26,000
Purchase of operating assets	(48,000)	(25,000)	
Cash provided (used) by financing activities:			
Proceeds from issuance of debt			13,000
Repayment of debt	(27,000)		
Net increase (decrease) in cash	$15,000	$15,000	$ 15,000

Each of the three companies generated a $15,000 net increase in cash. Their means of accomplishing this, however, were very different. First Company's operating activities provided $90,000, which allowed the company to purchase additional operating assets for $48,000 and repay $27,000 of debt. By comparison, Second Company's operating activities provided only $40,000, enabling it to purchase only $25,000 of operating assets. By comparison, Third Company's net cash increase was obtained only by selling operating assets and incurring additional debt; operating activities resulted in a net cash outflow of $24,000.

The implication of this comparison is that First Company is more capable of generating cash to meet its future obligations than is Second Company; and Third Company is least capable. This evaluation is, of course, tentative and may be contradicted by other information.

Managers analyze cash flows in making a variety of short-term decisions. In deciding whether borrowing will be necessary, managers use the procedures you learned in this chapter to predict cash flows for the next period or periods. These short-term planning situations also may lead to decisions about investing idle cash balances. Another example is deciding whether a customer's offer to buy a product at a reduced price should be accepted or rejected.

Long-term decisions involving new investments usually require detailed cash flow predictions. Companies must estimate cash inflows and outflows over the life of the investment, often extending many years into the future. Other decisions that require cash flow information include deciding whether a product should be manufactured by the company or purchased from an outside supplier, and deciding whether a product or a department should be eliminated or retained.

Progress Check

16-13   Refer to the consolidated statements of cash flows for Ben & Jerry's Homemade, Inc., in Appendix G. What type and amount of investing activities took place during the year ended December 26, 1992? What was the largest source of cash to finance these activities?

SUMMARY OF CHAPTER IN TERMS OF LEARNING OBJECTIVES

LO 1. Explain why cash flow information is important to decision making and describe the information in a statement of cash flows and the methods used to disclose noncash investing and financing activities. Many decisions involve evaluating cash flows. Examples are investor and creditor decisions to invest in or loan money to a company. The evaluations include paying attention to the activities that provide or use cash. Managers evaluate cash flows in deciding whether borrowing is necessary, whether cash balances should be invested, and in a variety of other short-term and long-term decisions.

The statement of cash flows reports cash receipts and disbursements as operating, investing, or financing activities. Operating activities include transactions related to producing or purchasing merchandise, selling goods and services to customers, and performing administrative functions. Investing activities include purchases and sales of noncurrent assets and short-term investments that are not cash equivalents. Financing activities include transactions with owners and transactions to borrow or repay the principal amounts of long-term and short-term debt.

For external reporting, a company must supplement its statement of cash flows with a description of its noncash investing and financing activities. Two examples of these activities are the retirement of debt obligations by issuing equity securities and the exchange of a note payable for plant assets.

LO 2. Calculate cash inflows and outflows by inspecting the noncash account balances and prepare a statement of cash flows using the direct method. To identify the cash receipts and cash payments, analyze the changes in the noncash balance sheet accounts created by income statement transactions and other events. For example, the amount of cash collected from customers is calculated by modifying sales revenues for the change in accounts receivable. Also, cash paid for interest is calculated by adjusting interest expense for the change in interest payable.

In using the direct method to report the net cash provided (or used) by operating activities, major classes of operating cash inflows and outflows are separately disclosed. Then, operating cash outflows are subtracted from operating cash inflows to derive the net inflow or outflow from operating activities. This method is encouraged by the FASB but is not required. Company managers generally use the direct method to predict future cash inflows and outflows.

LO 3. Calculate the net cash provided or used by operating activities according to the indirect method and prepare the statement of cash flows. In using the indirect method to calculate the net cash provided (or used) by operating activities, first list the net income and then modify it for these three types of events: *(a)* changes in noncash current assets and current liabilities related to operating activities, *(b)* revenues and expenses that did not provide or use cash, and *(c)* gains and losses from investing and financing activities. If using the direct method, report the reconciliation between net income and net cash provided (or used) by operating activities on a separate schedule.

LO 4. Prepare a working paper for a statement of cash flows so that the net cash flow from operating activities is calculated by the indirect method. To prepare an indirect method working paper, first enter the beginning and ending balances of the balance sheet accounts in columns 1 and 4. Then, establish the three sections of the statement of cash flows. Net income is entered as the first item in the operating activities section. Then, adjust the net income for events *(a)* through *(c)* identified in the preceding paragraph. This process reconciles the changes in the noncash current assets and current liabilities related to operations. Reconcile any remaining balance sheet account changes and report their cash effects in the appropriate sections. Enter noncash investing and financing activities at the bottom of the working paper.

DEMONSTRATION PROBLEM

The following summarized journal entries show the total debits and credits to the Pyramid Corporation's Cash account during 19X2. Use the information to prepare a statement of cash flows for 19X2. The cash provided (or used) by operating activities should be presented according to the direct method. In the statement, identify the entry that records each item of cash flow. Assume that the beginning balance of cash was $133,200.

a.	Cash	1,440,000.00	
	Common Stock, $10 par value		360,000.00
	Contributed Capital in Excess of		
	Par Value, Common Stock		1,080,000.00
	Issued common stock for cash.		
b.	Cash	2,400,000.00	
	Notes Payable		2,400,000.00
	Borrowed cash with a note payable.		
c.	Purchases	480,000.00	
	Cash		480,000.00
	Purchased merchandise for cash.		
d.	Accounts Payable	1,200,000.00	
	Cash		1,200,000.00
	Paid for credit purchases of merchandise.		
e.	Wages Expense	600,000.00	
	Cash		600,000.00
	Paid wages to employees.		
f.	Rent Expense	420,000.00	
	Cash		420,000.00
	Paid rent for buildings.		
g.	Cash	3,000,000.00	
	Sales		3,000,000.00
	Made cash sales to customers.		
h.	Cash	1,800,000.00	
	Accounts Receivable		1,800,000.00
	Collected accounts from credit customers.		
i.	Machinery	2,136,000.00	
	Cash		2,136,000.00
	Purchased machinery for cash.		
j.	Investments	2,160,000.00	
	Cash		2,160,000.00
	Purchased investments for cash.		
k.	Interest Expense	216,000.00	
	Notes Payable	384,000.00	
	Cash		600,000.00
	Paid notes and accrued interest.		
l.	Cash	206,400.00	
	Dividends Earned		206,400.00
	Collected dividends from investments.		
m.	Cash	210,000.00	
	Loss on Sale of Investments	30,000.00	
	Investments		240,000.00
	Sold investments for cash.		
n.	Cash	720,000.00	
	Accumulated Depreciation, Machinery	420,000.00	
	Machinery		960,000.00
	Gain on Sale of Machinery		180,000.00
	Sold machinery for cash.		
o.	Common Dividend Payable	510,000.00	
	Cash		510,000.00
	Paid cash dividends to stockholders.		

p.	Income Taxes Payable	480,000.00	
	Cash		480,000.00
	Paid income taxes owed for the year.		
q.	Treasury Stock, Common	228,000.00	
	Cash		228,000.00
	Acquired treasury stock for cash.		

- Prepare a blank statement of cash flows with sections for operating, investing, and financing activities.

- Examine each journal entry to determine whether it describes an operating, investing, or financing activity and whether it describes an inflow or outflow of cash.

- Enter the cash effects of the entry in the appropriate section of the statement, being sure to combine similar events, including c and d, as well as g and h. For entry k, identify the portions of the cash flow that should be assigned to operating and financing activities.

- Total each section of the statement, determine the total change in cash, and add the beginning balance to get the ending balance.

Planning the Solution

PYRAMID CORPORATION
Statement of Cash Flows
For Year Ended December 31, 19X2

Solution to Demonstration Problem

Cash flows from operating activities:

g,h.	Cash received from customers	$ 4,800,000	
l.	Cash received as dividends	206,400	
c,d.	Cash paid for merchandise	(1,680,000)	
e.	Cash paid for wages	(600,000)	
f.	Cash paid for rent	(420,000)	
k.	Cash paid for interest	(216,000)	
p.	Cash paid for taxes	(480,000)	
	Net cash provided by operating activities		$ 1,610,400

Cash flows from investing activities:

i.	Cash paid for purchases of machinery	$(2,136,000)	
j.	Cash paid for purchases of investments	(2,160,000)	
m.	Cash received from sale of investments	210,000	
n.	Cash received from sale of machinery	720,000	
	Net cash used in investing activities		(3,366,000)

Cash flows from financing activities:

a.	Cash received from issuing stock	$ 1,440,000	
b.	Cash received from borrowing	2,400,000	
k.	Cash paid for repayment of note payable	(384,000)	
o.	Cash paid for dividends	(510,000)	
q.	Cash paid for purchases of treasury stock	(228,000)	
	Net cash provided by financing activities		2,718,000
Net increase in cash			$ 962,400
Beginning balance of cash			133,200
Ending balance of cash			$ 1,095,600

GLOSSARY

Direct method of calculating net cash provided (or used) by operating activities a calculation of the net cash provided or used by operating activities that lists the major classes of operating cash receipts, such as receipts from customers, and subtracts the major classes of operating cash disbursements, such as cash paid for merchandise. p. 609

Financing activities transactions with the owners of a business or transactions with its creditors to borrow money or to repay the principal amounts of loans. p. 613

Indirect method of calculating net cash provided (or used) by operating activities a calculation that begins with net income and then adjusts the net income amount by adding and subtracting items that are necessary to reconcile net income to the net cash provided or used by operating activities. p. 610

Investing activities transactions that involve making and collecting loans or that involve purchasing and selling plant assets, other productive assets, or investments other than cash equivalents. p. 613

Operating activities activities that involve the production or purchase of merchandise and the sale of goods and services to customers, including expenditures related to administering the business. p. 613

Statement of cash flows a financial statement that reports the cash inflows and outflows for an accounting period, and that classifies those cash flows as operating activities, investing activities, and financing activities. p. 608

QUESTIONS

1. What are some examples of items reported on a statement of cash flows as investing activities?

2. What are some examples of items reported on a statement of cash flows as financing activities?

3. When a statement of cash flows is prepared by the direct method, what are some examples of items reported as cash flows from operating activities?

4. If a corporation pays cash dividends, where on the corporation's statement of cash flows should the payment be reported?

5. A company purchases land for $100,000, paying $20,000 cash and borrowing the remainder on a long-term note payable. How should this transaction be reported on a statement of cash flows?

6. What is the direct method of reporting cash flows from operating activities?

7. What is the indirect method of reporting cash flows from operating activities?

8. Is depreciation a source of cash?

9. On June 3, a company borrowed $50,000 by giving its bank a 60-day, interest-bearing note. On the statement of cash flows, where should this item be reported?

10. If a company reports a net income for the year, is it possible for the company to show a net cash outflow from operating activities? Explain your answer.

11. Refer to Federal Express Corporation's consolidated statement of cash flows shown in Appendix G.
    (a) Which method was used to calculate net cash provided by operating activities? *(b)* Why was the increase in receivables subtracted rather than added in the calculation of net cash provided by operating activities during the year ended May 31, 1993?

QUICK STUDY (Five-Minute Exercises)

**QS 16–1
(LO 1)**

Describe the content of a statement of cash flows.

**QS 16–2
(LO 1)**

Classify the following cash flows as operating, investing, or financing activities:

1. Purchased merchandise for cash.
2. Paid interest on outstanding bonds.
3. Sold delivery equipment at a loss.
4. Paid property taxes on the company offices.
5. Collected proceeds from sale of long-term investments.

6. Issued common stock for cash.

7. Received payments from customers.

8. Paid wages.

9. Paid dividends.

10. Received interest on investment.

List three examples of transactions that are noncash financing and investing transactions.   **QS 16–3**
(LO 1)

Use the following information in QS 16–4 through QS 16–9.   **QS 16–4**
(LO 2)

KUNG ATTIRE, INC.
Comparative Balance Sheet

Assets	19X2	19X1
Cash	$ 47,900	$ 12,500
Accounts receivable (net)	21,000	26,000
Inventory	43,400	48,400
Prepaid expenses	3,200	2,600
Furniture	55,000	60,000
Accumulated depreciation, furniture	(9,000)	(5,000)
Total assets	$161,500	$144,500

Liabilities and Stockholders' Equity		
Accounts payable	$ 8,000	$ 11,000
Wages payable	5,000	3,000
Income taxes payable	1,200	1,800
Notes payable (long-term)	15,000	35,000
Common stock, $5 par value	115,000	90,000
Retained earnings	17,300	3,700
Total liabilities and stockholders' equity	$161,500	$144,500

KUNG ATTIRE, INC.
Income Statement
For Year Ended June 30, 19X2

Sales		$234,000
Cost of goods sold		156,000
Gross profit		$ 78,000
Operating expenses:		
Depreciation expense	$19,300	
Other expenses	28,500	
Total operating expenses		47,800
Net income from operations		$ 30,200
Income taxes		12,300
Net income		$ 17,900

How much cash was received from customers during Year 2?

Refer to the facts in QS 16–4. How much cash was paid for merchandise during 19X2?   **QS 16–5**
(LO 5)

Refer to the facts in QS 16–4. How much cash was paid for operating expenses during 19X2?   **QS 16–6**
(LO 2)

Refer to the facts in QS 16–4 and assume furniture that cost $27,000 was sold at its book value and all furniture acquisitions were for cash. What was the cash inflow related to the sale of furniture?   **QS 16–7**
(LO 2)

QS 16–8
(LO 2)

Refer to the facts in QS 16–4 and assume that all stock was issued for cash. How much cash was disbursed for dividends?

QS 16–9
(LO 3)

Refer to the facts in QS 16–4. Using the indirect method, calculate cash provided or used from operating activities.

QS 16–10
(LO 4)

When a working paper for a statement of cash flows is prepared, all changes in noncash balance sheet accounts are accounted for on the working paper. Explain why this occurs.

EXERCISES

Exercise 16–1
Classifying transactions
on statement of cash flows
(direct method)
(LO 1)

The following events occurred during the year. Assuming that the company uses the direct method of reporting cash provided by operating activities, indicate the proper accounting treatment for each event by placing an *x* in the appropriate column.

		Statement of Cash Flows		Footnote Describing Noncash Investing and Financing Activities	Not Reported on Statement or in Footnote
	Operating Activities	Investing Activities	Financing Activities		
a. Long-term bonds payable were retired by issuing common stock.	————	————	————	————	————
b. Surplus merchandise inventory was sold for cash.	————	————	————	————	————
c. Borrowed cash from the bank by signing a nine-month note payable.	————	————	————	————	————
d. Paid cash to purchase a patent.	————	————	————	————	————
e. A six-month note receivable was accepted in exchange for a building that had been used in operations.	————	————	————	————	————
f. Recorded depreciation expense on all plant assets.	————	————	————	————	————
g. A cash dividend that was declared in a previous period was paid in the current period.	————	————	————	————	————

Exercise 16–2
Organizing the statement of
cash flows and supporting
footnote
(LO 1)

Use the following information about the 19X2 cash flows of Forrest Company to prepare a statement of cash flows under the direct method and a footnote describing noncash investing and financing activities.

Cash and cash equivalents balance, December 31, 19X1 ..	$ 50,000
Cash and cash equivalents balance, December 31, 19X2 ..	140,000
Cash received as interest	5,000
Cash paid for salaries	145,000
Bonds payable retired by issuing common stock (there was no gain or loss on the retirement)	375,000
Cash paid to retire long-term notes payable	250,000
Cash received from sale of equipment	122,500
Cash borrowed on six-month note payable	50,000
Land purchased and financed by long-term note payable ..	212,500
Cash paid for store equipment	47,500
Cash dividends paid	30,000
Cash paid for other expenses	80,000
Cash received from customers	970,000
Cash paid for merchandise	505,000

In each of the following cases, use the information provided about the 19X1 operations of Benzar Company to calculate the indicated cash flow:

Exercise 16–3
Calculating cash flows
(LO 2)

Case A: Calculate cash received from customers:

Sales revenue	$255,000
Accounts receivable, January 1	12,600
Accounts receivable, December 31	17,400

Case B: Calculate cash paid for insurance:

Insurance expense	$ 34,200
Prepaid insurance, January 1	5,700
Prepaid insurance, December 31	8,550

Case C: Calculate cash paid for salaries:

Salaries expense	$102,000
Salaries payable, January 1	6,300
Salaries payable, December 31	7,500

In each of the following cases, use the information provided about the 19X1 operations of CNA Company to calculate the indicated cash flow:

Exercise 16–4
Calculating cash flows
(LO 2)

Case A: Calculate cash paid for rent:

Rent expense	$ 20,400
Rent payable, January 1	4,400
Rent payable, December 31	3,600

Case B: Calculate cash received from interest:

Interest revenue	$ 68,000
Interest receivable, January 1	6,000
Interest receivable, December 31	7,200

Case C: Calculate cash paid for merchandise:

Cost of goods sold	$352,000
Merchandise inventory, January 1	106,400
Accounts payable, January 1	45,200
Merchandise inventory, December 31	87,600
Accounts payable, December 31	56,000

Use the following income statement and information about changes in noncash current assets and current liabilities to present the cash flows from operating activities using the direct method:

Exercise 16–5
Cash flows from operating
activities (direct method)
(LO 2)

ALAMO DATA COMPANY
Income Statement
For Year Ended December 31, 19X1

Sales		$606,000
Cost of goods sold		297,000
Gross profit from sales		$309,000
Operating expenses:		
Salaries expense	$82,845	
Depreciation expense	14,400	
Rent expense	16,200	
Amortization expense, patents	1,800	
Utilities expense	6,375	121,620
Total		$187,380
Gain on sale of equipment		2,400
Net income		$189,780

Changes in current asset and current liability accounts during the year, all of which related to operating activities, were as follows:

Accounts receivable	$13,500 increase
Merchandise inventory	9,000 increase
Accounts payable	4,500 decrease
Salaries payable	1,500 decrease

Exercise 16–6
Cash flows from operating
activities (indirect method)
(LO 3)

Refer to the information about Alamo Data Company presented in Exercise 16–5. Use the indirect method and calculate the cash provided (or used) by operating activities.

Exercise 16–7
Cash flows from operating
activities (indirect method)
(LO 3)

Trador Company's 19X1 income statement showed the following: net income, $728,000; depreciation expense, $90,000; amortization expense, $16,400; and gain on sale of plant assets, $14,000. An examination of the company's current assets and current liabilities showed that the following changes occurred because of operating activities: accounts receivable decreased $36,200; merchandise inventory decreased $104,000; prepaid expenses increased $7,400; accounts payable decreased $18,400; other payables increased $2,800. Use the indirect method to calculate the cash flow from operating activities.

Exercise 16–8
Classifying transactions on
statement of cash flows (indirect
method)
(LO 3)

The following events occurred during the year. Assuming that the company uses the indirect method of reporting cash provided by operating activities, indicate the proper accounting treatment for each event listed below by placing an x in the appropriate column.

	Statement of Cash Flows			Footnote Describing Noncash Investing and Financing Activities	Not Reported on Statement or in Footnote
	Operating Activities	Investing Activities	Financing Activities		
a. Land for a new plant was purchased by issuing common stock.	_____	_____	_____	_____	_____
b. Recorded depreciation expense.	_____	_____	_____	_____	_____
c. Income taxes payable increased by 15% from prior year.	_____	_____	_____	_____	_____
d. Declared and paid a cash dividend.	_____	_____	_____	_____	_____
e. Paid cash to purchase merchandise inventory.	_____	_____	_____	_____	_____
f. Sold plant equipment at a loss.	_____	_____	_____	_____	_____
g. Accounts receivable decreased during the year.	_____	_____	_____	_____	_____

PROBLEMS

Problem 16–1
Statement of cash flows
(direct method)
(LO 1, 2)

Helix Corporation's 19X2 and 19X1 balance sheets carried the following items:

	December 31	
Debits	**19X2**	**19X1**
Cash	$116,000	$ 78,000
Accounts receivable	62,000	54,000
Merchandise inventory	406,000	356,000
Equipment	222,000	198,000
Totals	$806,000	$686,000

Credits		
Accumulated depreciation, equipment	$104,000	$ 68,000
Accounts payable	46,000	64,000
Income taxes payable	18,000	16,000
Common stock, $2 par value	388,000	372,000
Contributed capital in excess of par value, common stock	132,000	108,000
Retained earnings	118,000	58,000
Totals	$806,000	$686,000

An examination of the company's activities during 19X2, including the income statement, shows the following:

a.	Sales (all on credit)		$1,328,000
b.	Credits to Accounts Receivable during the period were receipts from customers.		
c.	Cost of goods sold	$796,000	
d.	Purchases of merchandise were on credit.		
e.	Debits to Accounts Payable during the period resulted from payments for merchandise.		
f.	Depreciation expense	36,000	
g.	Other operating expenses (paid with cash)	334,000	
h.	Income taxes expense	28,000	1,194,000
i.	The only decreases in Income Taxes Payable were payments of taxes.		
j.	Net income		$ 134,000
k.	Equipment was purchased for $24,000 cash.		
l.	Eight thousand shares of stock were issued for cash at $5 per share.		
m.	The company declared and paid $74,000 of cash dividends during the year.		

Required

Prepare a statement of cash flows that reports the cash inflows and outflows from operating activities according to the direct method. Show your supporting calculations.

CHECK FIGURE:
Net cash provided by operating activities, $96,000

Refer to Helix Corporation's balance sheets presented in Problem 16–1. The additional information about the company's activities during 19X2 is restated as follows:

a. Net income was $134,000.

b. Accounts receivable increased.

c. Merchandise inventory increased.

d. Accounts payable decreased.

e. Income taxes payable increased.

f. Depreciation expense was $36,000.

g. Equipment was purchased for $24,000 cash.

h. Eight thousand shares of stock were issued for cash at $5 per share.

i. The company declared and paid $74,000 of cash dividends during the year.

Problem 16–2
Statement of cash flows (indirect method)
(LO 3)

Required

Prepare a statement of cash flows that reports the cash inflows and outflows from operating activities according to the indirect method.

CHECK FIGURE:
Net cash provided by operating activities, $96,000

Refer to the facts about Helix Corporation presented in Problem 16–1 and Problem 16–2. Prepare a statement of cash flows working paper that follows the indirect method of calculating cash flows from operating activities. Identify the debits and credits in the Analysis of Changes columns with letters that correspond to the list in Problem 16–2.

Problem 16–3
Cash flows working paper (indirect method)
(LO 4)

Purcell Company's 19X2 and 19X1 balance sheets included the following items:

CHECK FIGURE:
Analysis of Changes column totals, $386,000

	December 31	
Debits	**19X2**	**19X1**
Cash	$ 107,750	$153,250
Accounts receivable	130,000	99,250
Merchandise inventory	547,500	505,000
Prepaid expenses	10,750	12,500
Equipment	319,000	220,000
Totals	$1,115,000	$990,000

Problem 16–4
Statement of cash flows (direct method)
(LO 1, 2)

	December 31	
Credits	**19X2**	**19X1**
Accumulated depreciation, equipment . .	$ 69,250	$ 88,000
Accounts payable	176,250	233,250
Short-term notes payable	20,000	12,500
Long-term notes payable	187,500	107,500
Common stock, $5 par value	337,500	312,500
Contributed capital in excess of		
par value, common stock	65,000	
Retained earnings	259,500	236,250
Totals	$1,115,000	$990,000

Additional information about the 19X2 activities of the company is as follows:

a. Sales revenue, all on credit $992,500
b. Credits to Accounts Receivable during the period
    were receipts from customers.
c. Cost of goods sold $500,000
d. All merchandise purchases were on credit.
e. Debits to Accounts Payable during the period
    resulted from payments to creditors.
f. Depreciation expense   37,500
g. Other expenses   273,000
h. The other expenses were paid in advance and were
    initially debited to Prepaid Expenses.
i. Income taxes expense (paid with cash)   24,250
j. Loss on sale of equipment   10,250   845,000
    The equipment cost $93,750, was depreciated by
    $56,250, and was sold for $27,250.
k. Net income $147,500

l. Equipment that cost $192,750 was purchased by paying cash of
    $50,000 and by signing a long-term note payable for the balance.
m. Borrowed $7,500 by signing a short-term note payable.
n. Paid $62,750 to reduce a long-term note payable.
o. Issued 5,000 shares of common stock for cash at $18 per share.
p. Declared and paid cash dividends of $124,250.

Required

Preparation component:

1. Prepare a statement of cash flows that reports the cash inflows and outflows from oper-
    ating activities according to the direct method. Show your supporting calculations. Also
    prepare a footnote describing noncash investing and financing activities.

CHECK FIGURE:
Net cash provided by operating
activities, $66,750

Analysis component:

2. Analyze and discuss the information contained in your answer to requirement 1, giving
    special attention to the wisdom of the dividend payment.

Problem 16–5
Statement of cash flows
(indirect method)
(LO 3)

Refer to Purcell Company's balance sheets presented in Problem 16–4. The additional information about the company's activities during 19X2 is restated as follows:

a. Net income was $147,500.
b. Accounts receivable increased.
c. Merchandise inventory increased.
d. Prepaid expenses decreased.
e. Accounts payable decreased.
f. Depreciation expense was $37,500.
g. Equipment that cost $93,750 with accumulated depreciation of $56,250 was sold for
    $27,250 cash, which caused a loss of $10,250.

h. Equipment that cost $192,750 was purchased by paying cash of $50,000 and (*i*) by signing a long-term note payable for the balance.

j. Borrowed $7,500 by signing a short-term note payable.

k. Paid $62,750 to reduce a long-term note payable.

l. Issued 5,000 shares of common stock for cash at $18 per share.

m. Declared and paid cash dividends of $124,250.

Required

Prepare a statement of cash flows that reports the cash inflows and outflows from operating activities according to the indirect method.

CHECK FIGURE:
Net cash provided by operating activities, $66,750

Refer to the facts about Purcell Company presented in Problem 16–4 and Problem 16–5. Prepare a statement of cash flows working paper that follows the indirect method of calculating cash flows from operating activities. Identify the debits and credits in the Analysis of Changes columns with letters that correspond to the list for the company presented in Problem 16–5.

Problem 16–6
Cash flows working paper (indirect method)
(LO 4)

CHECK FIGURE:
Analysis of Changes column totals, $1,030,750

CRITICAL THINKING: ESSAYS, PROBLEMS, AND CASES

Analytical Essays

Write a brief essay explaining why, in preparing a statement of cash flows according to the direct method, it is generally better to determine the changes in cash by analyzing the changes in the noncash accounts rather than by examining the Cash account directly. You should include in your essay an explanation of why the changes in cash for the period equal the changes in the noncash balance sheet accounts.

AE 16–1
(LO 2)

The following items might be found on a working paper for a statement of cash flows. Write a brief essay describing where each item appears on a working paper for a statement of cash flows according to the indirect method. Also describe the nature of any debits and/or credits that should be entered in the Analysis of Changes columns next to each item, and any balancing entries.

AE 16–2
(LO 4)

a. Accounts receivable.

b. Depreciation expense.

c. Payment for purchase of plant assets.

Financial Reporting Problem

(LO 4)

Griffin Company's 19X2 statement of cash flows appeared as follows:

Cash flows from operating activities:

Cash received from customers	$903,600	
Cash paid for merchandise	(473,550)	
Cash paid for other operating expenses	(244,500)	
Cash paid for income taxes	(26,100)	
Net cash provided by operating activities		$159,450

Cash flows from investing activities:

Cash received from sale of office equipment ..	$ 13,950	
Cash paid for store equipment	(21,000)	
Net cash used in investing activities		(7,050)

Cash flows from financing activities:

Cash paid to retire bonds payable	$(76,650)	
Cash paid for dividends	(37,500)	
Net cash used in financing activities		(114,150)
Net increase in cash		$ 38,250
Cash balance at beginning of year		47,850
Cash balance at end of year		$ 86,100

Griffin's beginning and ending balance sheets were as follows:

	December 31	
Debits	**19X2**	**19X1**
Cash	$ 86,100	$ 47,850
Accounts receivable	68,250	79,650
Merchandise inventory	312,000	292,950
Prepaid expenses	7,200	3,300
Equipment	271,650	293,400
Totals	$745,200	$717,150

	December 31	
Credits	**19X2**	**19X1**
Accumulated depreciation, equipment ..	$123,900	$ 95,100
Accounts payable	57,600	67,500
Income taxes payable	10,200	8,850
Dividends payable	–0–	9,000
Bonds payable	–0–	75,000
Common stock, $10 par value	337,500	337,500
Retained earnings	216,000	124,200
Totals	$745,200	$717,150

An examination of the company's statements and accounts showed:

a. All sales were made on credit.

b. All merchandise purchases were on credit.

c. Accounts Payable balances resulted from merchandise purchases.

d. Prepaid expenses relate to other operating expenses.

e. Equipment that cost $42,750 with accumulated depreciation of $22,200 was sold for cash.

f. Equipment was purchased for cash.

g. The change in the balance of Accumulated Depreciation resulted from depreciation expense and from the sale of equipment.

h. The change in the balance of Retained Earnings resulted from dividend declarations and net income.

Required

Present Griffin's income statement for 19X2. Show your supporting calculations.

Look in Appendix F at the end of the book to find Apple Computer, Inc.'s statement of cash flows. Based on your examination of that statement, answer the following questions:

Financial Statement Analysis Case

(LO 1)

1. Was Apple's statement of cash flows prepared according to the direct method or the indirect method?

2. During each of the fiscal years 1993, 1992, and 1991, was the cash provided by operating activities more or less than the cash paid for dividends?

3. What was the major reason for the difference between net income and cash flow from operating activities?

4. Describe the major cash inflows and outflows during 1993.

5. Describe the major differences in Apple's 1993 cash flows compared to its 1992 cash flows.

ANSWERS TO PROGRESS CHECKS

16–1 No. The statement of cash flows reports changes in the sum of cash plus cash equivalents. It does not report transfers between cash and cash equivalents.

16–2 The three categories of cash inflows and outflows are operating activities, investing activities, and financing activities.

16–3 The direct method is most informative. The indirect method is used most often.

16–4 *a.* Investing
   b. Operating
   c. Financing
   d. Operating
   e. Operating
   f. Financing

16–5 $590,000 + ($120,000 − $90,000) = $620,000

16–6 $168,000 − ($32,000 − $28,000) − $2,400 = $161,600

16–7 $112,000 + ($4,200 − $1,200) − $5,600 = $109,400

16–8 $80,000 − $30,000 − $10,000 = $40,000
   The $40,000 cash receipt should be reported as an investment activity.

16–9 $74,900 + $4,600 − $11,700 − $1,000 + $3,400 = $70,200

16–10 In the calculation of net income, expenses such as depreciation and amortization are subtracted because these expenses do not require current cash outflows. Therefore, adding these expenses back to net income eliminates noncash items from the net income number, converting it to a cash basis.

16–11 In the process of reconciling net income to net cash provided (or used) by operating activities, a gain on the sale of plant assets is subtracted from net income because a sale of plant assets is not an operating activity; it is an investing activity.

16–12 *a*

16–13 Investing activities during the year ended December 26, 1992, used net cash of $36,378,580. Cash outflows that contributed to this included additions to property, plant, and equipment for $10,447,007; increase in investments amounting to $25,200,000; and changes in other assets amounting to $836,657. An investing activity that produced a cash inflow was the sale of property, plant, and equipment for $105,084. The largest source of cash to finance these activities was $33,661,528 obtained through the issuance of common stock.

Analyzing Financial Statements

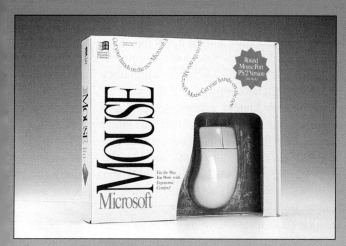

A group of high-tech wizards have a vision and a desire to create a computer software corporation. In their enthusiasm, they have told a few potential investors that their proposed company was likely to be so successful it would rival the current giants in the industry. Microsoft Corporation was named as an example of what the new venture was likely to become. The investors were quite familiar with the history of Microsoft and suggested that the wizards might be wise to be a little more moderate in their expectations. When the wizards disagreed, the investors pointed out that Microsoft was formed in 1975 and by 1993 had revenues of $3.75 billion. They added that it operated in 41 countries and had revenues outside the United States of more than $2 billion.

In concluding the conversation, the investors gave the wizards a copy of Microsoft's 1993 annual report and suggested that they study it carefully to see if it really represented a goal they could achieve.

MICROSOFT CORPORATION
Growth percentages increase

	Year Ended June 30				
	1993	1992	1991	1990	1989
Net revenues	36%	50%	56%	47%	36%
Net income	35	53	66	63	38
Earnings per share	31	47	58	55	37
Book value per share	43	56	44	57	47

LEARNING OBJECTIVES

After studying Chapter 17, you should be able to:

1. **Explain the relationship between financial reporting and general purpose financial statements.**

2. **Describe, prepare, and interpret comparative financial statements and common-size comparative statements.**

3. **Calculate and explain the interpretation of the ratios, turnovers, and rates of return used to evaluate (*a*) short-term liquidity, (*b*) long-term risk and capital structure, and (*c*) operating efficiency and profitability.**

4. **State the limitations associated with using financial statement ratios and the sources from which standards for comparison may be obtained.**

5. **Define or explain the words and phrases listed in the chapter glossary.**

Chapter 17 demonstrates how to use the information in financial statements to evaluate the activities and financial status of a business. By explaining how you can relate the numbers in financial statements to each other, this chapter expands your ability to interpret the ratios we described in previous chapters.

FINANCIAL REPORTING

LO 1

Explain the relationship between financial reporting and general purpose financial statements.

Many people receive and analyze financial information about business firms. These people include managers, employees, directors, customers, suppliers, current and potential owners, current and potential lenders, brokers, regulatory authorities, lawyers, economists, labor unions, financial advisors, and financial analysts. Some of these, such as managers and some regulatory agencies, are able to gain access to specialized financial reports that meet their specific interests. However, the others must rely on the **general purpose financial statements** that companies publish periodically. General purpose financial statements include the (1) income statement, (2) balance sheet, (3) statement of changes in stockholders' equity (or statement of retained earnings), (4) statement of cash flows, and (5) footnotes related to the statements.

    Financial reporting is intended to provide useful information to investors, creditors, and others for making investment, credit, and similar decisions. The infor-

mation should help the users assess the amounts, timing, and uncertainty of prospective cash inflows and outflows.

    Financial reporting includes communicating through a variety of means in addition to the financial statements. Some examples are reports filed with the Securities and Exchange Commission, news releases, and management letters or analyses included in annual reports. For an example, in Appendix F look at the section of Apple Computer, Inc.'s annual report called Management Discussion and Analysis of Financial Condition and Results of Operations.

Progress Check

(Answers to Progress Checks are provided at the end of the chapter.)

17-1   Who are the intended users of general purpose financial statements?

17-2   What statements are usually included in the general purpose financial statements published by corporations?

In analyzing financial information, individual items usually are not very revealing. However, important relationships exist between items and groups of items. As a result, financial statement analysis involves identifying and describing relationships between items and groups of items and changes in those items.

You can see changes in financial statement items more clearly when amounts for two or more successive accounting periods are placed side by side in columns on a single statement. Statements prepared in this manner are called **comparative statements.** Each financial statement can be presented in this comparative format.

In its simplest form, a comparative balance sheet consists of the amounts from two or more successive balance sheet dates arranged side by side. However, the usefulness of the statement can be improved by also showing each item's dollar amount of change and percentage change. When this is done, large dollar or percentage changes are more readily apparent. Illustration 17–1 shows this type of comparative balance sheet for Microsoft Corporation.

A comparative income statement is prepared in the same way. Amounts for two or more successive periods are placed side by side, with dollar and percentage changes in additional columns. Look at Illustration 17–2 to see **Microsoft Corporation's** comparative income statement.

COMPARATIVE STATEMENTS

LO 2

Describe, prepare, and interpret comparative financial statements and common-size comparative statements.

Calculating Percentage Increases and Decreases

To calculate the percentage increases and decreases on comparative statements, divide the dollar increase or decrease of an item by the amount shown for the item in the base year. If no amount is shown in the base year, or if the base year amount is negative (such as a net loss), a percentage increase or decrease cannot be calculated.

In this text, percentages and ratios typically are rounded to one or two decimal places. However, there is no uniform practice on this matter. In general, percentages should be carried out far enough to be meaningful. They should not be carried out so far that the important relationships become lost in the length of the numbers.

Analyzing and Interpreting Comparative Statements

In analyzing comparative data, study any items that show significant dollar or percentage changes. Then, try to identify the reasons for each change and, if possible, determine whether they are favorable or unfavorable. For example, in Illustration 17–1, the first item, "Cash and short-term investments," shows a $945 million increase (70.3%). To a large extent, this may be explained by the increase in two other items: the $429 million increase in "Common stock and paid-in capital" and the $620 million increase in "Retained earnings."

Note that **Microsoft Corporation's** liabilities increased by $116 million. In light of this, the $945 million increase in "Cash and short-term investments" might appear to be an excessive investment in highly liquid assets that usually earn a low return. However, the company's very strong and liquid financial position indicates an outstanding ability to respond to new opportunities such as the acquisition of other companies.

Now look at the comparative income statement for

Illustration 17-1

	June 30		Amount of Increase or (Decrease) during 1993	Percentage Increase or (Decrease) during 1993
	1993	1992		
Assets				
Current assets:				
Cash and short-term investments	$2,290	$1,345	$ 945	70.3
Accounts receivable, net of				
allowances of $76 and $57	338	270	68	25.2
Inventories	127	86	41	47.7
Other	95	69	26	37.7
Total current assets	$2,850	$1,770	$1,080	61.0
Property, plant, and equipment—net	867	767	100	13.0
Other assets	88	103	(15)	(14.6)
Total assets	$3,805	$2,640	$1,165	44.1
Liabilities and Stockholders' Equity				
Current liabilities:				
Accounts payable	$ 239	$ 196	$ 43	21.9
Accrued compensation	86	62	24	38.7
Income taxes payable	127	73	54	74.0
Other	111	116	(5)	(4.3)
Total current liabilities	$ 563	$ 447	$ 116	26.0
Commitments and contingencies	—	—		
Stockholders' equity:				
Common stock and paid-in capital—				
shares authorized 500; issued and				
outstanding 282 and 272	$1,086	$ 657	$ 429	65.3
Retained earnings	2,156	1,536	620	40.4
Total stockholders' equity	$3,242	$2,193	$1,049	47.8
Total liabilities and stockholders' equity . .	$3,805	$2,640	$1,165	44.1

MICROSOFT CORPORATION
Comparative Balance Sheet
June 30, 1993, and June 30, 1992
(in millions)

Microsoft in Illustration 17–2. Microsoft's rapid growth is reflected by its 36% increase in net revenues. In fact, we should point out that the growth in 1993 continued a very strong trend established in prior years. (Later, we present data showing that net revenues in 1993 were 467% of net revenues in 1989.) Perhaps the most fundamental reason for this is the company's commitment to research and development. Note that research and development expenses were $470 million in 1993, up $118 million from 1992.

All of the income statement items (except "Other") reflect the company's rapid growth. The increases ranged from 30.7 to 46.4%. Especially note the large $351 million or 41.1% increase in "Sales and marketing." This suggests the company's leadership and strong response to competition in the software industry. Although the dollar increase in "Interest income—net" was only $26 million, this amounted to a 46.4% increase. This is consistent with the large increase in Cash and short-term investments reported on the balance sheet.

Illustration 17–2

MICROSOFT CORPORATION **Comparative Income Statement** **For Years Ended June 30, 1993, and 1992** **(in millions)**				
	Years Ended June 30		**Amount of Increase or (Decrease) during 1993**	**Percentage Increase or (Decrease) during 1993**
	1993	**1992**		
Net revenues	$3,753	$2,759	$994	36.0
Cost of revenues	633	467	166	35.6
Gross profit	$3,120	$2,292	$828	36.1
Operating expenses:				
Research and development	$ 470	$ 352	$118	33.5
Sales and marketing	1,205	854	351	41.1
General and administrative	119	90	29	32.2
Total operating expenses	$1,794	$1,296	$498	38.4
Operating income	$1,326	$ 996	$330	33.1
Interest income—net	82	56	26	46.4
Other*	(7)	(11)	(4)	(36.4)
Income before income taxes	$1,401	$1,041	$360	34.6
Provision for income taxes	448	333	115	34.5
Net income	$ 953	$ 708	$245	34.6
Earnings per share	$ 3.15	$ 2.41	$0.74	30.7
Weighted-average shares outstanding	303	294		

*On this line, the (7) and (11) are shown in parentheses because they represent expenses that are subtracted in the calculation of income. The (4) is in parentheses because the Other item decreased from 11 to 7. In the third column, the expense decrease (4) must be added to the $330 and $26 increases in operating income and interest income to reconcile the $360 increase in Income before income taxes.

Trend Percentages

Trend percentages (also known as *index numbers*) can be used to describe changes that have occurred from one period to the next. They are also used to compare data that cover a number of years. To calculate trend percentages:

1. Select a base year and assign each item on the base year statement a weight of 100%.

2. Express each item from the statements for the other years as a percentage of its base year amount. To determine these percentages, divide the amounts in the nonbase years by the amount of the item in the base year.

For example, consider the following data for Microsoft Corporation:

	1993	1992	1991	1990	1989
Net revenues	$3,753	$2,759	$1,843	$1,183	$804
Cost of revenues	633	467	362	253	204
Gross profit	$3,120	$2,292	$1,481	$ 930	$600

Using 1989 as the base year, we calculate the trend percentages for each year by dividing the dollar amounts in each year by the 1989 dollar amounts. When the percentages are calculated, the trends for these items appear as follows:

Illustration 17-3   Trend Lines Showing Percentage Changes in Net Revenues, Cost of Revenues, and Gross Profit

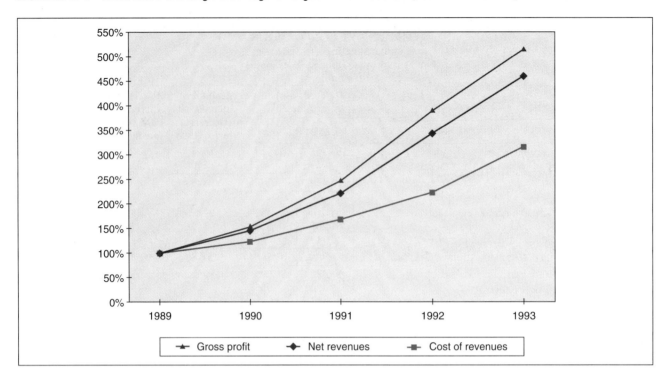

	1993	1992	1991	1990	1989
Net revenues	466.8%	343.2%	229.2%	147.1%	100%
Cost of revenues	310.3	228.9	177.5	124.0	100
Gross profit	520.0	382.0	246.8	155.0	100

Illustration 17–3 presents the same data in a graph. A graph can help you identify trends and detect changes in their strength or direction. For example, note that the gross profit line and the net revenues line were bending upward from 1989 to 1991 but were essentially straight from 1991 to 1993. In other words, the rates of increase were improving from 1989 to 1991 but were basically unchanged from 1991 to 1993.

A graph also may help you identify and understand the relationships between items. For example, the graph in Illustration 17–3 shows that through 1993, cost of revenues increased at a rate that was somewhat less than the increase in net revenues. Further, the differing trends in these two items had a clear effect on the percentage changes in gross profit. That is, gross profit increased each year at a faster rate than net revenues or cost of revenues.

The analysis of financial statement items also may include the relationships between items on different financial statements. For example, note the following comparison of Microsoft's total assets and net revenues:

			1993 Amount as a
	1993	1989	Percentage of 1989
Net revenues	$3,753	$804	466.8%
Total assets (fiscal year-end)	3,805	721	527.7

The rate of increase in total assets was even larger than the increase in net revenues. Was this change favorable? We cannot say for sure. It might suggest that the

Illustration 17–4

	June 30		Common-size Percentages	
	1993	1992	1993	1992
MICROSOFT CORPORATION Common-Size Comparative Balance Sheet June 30, 1993, and June 30, 1992 (in millions)				
Assets				
Current assets:				
Cash and short-term investments	$2,290	$1,345	60.2	50.9
Accounts receivable, net of allowances of $76 and $57	338	270	8.9	10.2
Inventories	127	86	3.3	3.3
Other	95	69	2.5	2.6
Total current assets	$2,850	$1,770	74.9	67.0
Property, plant, and equipment—net	867	767	22.8	29.1
Other assets	88	103	2.3	3.9
Total assets	$3,805	$2,640	100.0	100.0
Liabilities and Stockholders' Equity				
Current liabilities:				
Accounts payable	$ 239	$ 196	6.3	7.4
Accrued compensation	86	62	2.3	2.3
Income taxes payable	127	73	3.3	2.8
Other	111	116	2.9	4.4
Total current liabilities	$ 563	$ 447	14.8	16.9
Commitments and contingencies	—	—		
Stockholders' equity:				
Common stock and paid-in capital— shares authorized 500; issued and outstanding 282 and 272	$1,086	$ 657	28.5	24.9
Retained earnings	2,156	1,536	56.7	58.2
Total stockholders' equity	$3,242	$2,193	85.2	83.1
Total liabilities and stockholders' equity . .	$3,805	$2,640	100.0	100.0

company is no longer able to use its assets as efficiently as in earlier years. On the other hand, it might mean that the company is poised for even greater growth in future years. Financial statement analysis often leads the analyst to ask questions, without providing one clear answer.

Common-Size Comparative Statements

Although the comparative statements illustrated so far show how each item has changed over time, they do not emphasize the relative importance of each item. Changes in the relative importance of each financial statement item are shown more clearly by **common-size comparative statements.**

In common-size statements, each item is expressed as a percentage of a *base amount.* For a common-size balance sheet, the base amount is usually the amount of total assets. This total is assigned a value of 100%. (Of course, the total amount of liabilities plus owners' equity also equals 100%.) Then, each asset, liability, and owners' equity item is shown as a percentage of total assets (or total liabilities plus owners' equity). If you present a company's successive balance sheets in this way, changes in the mixture of the assets or liabilities and equity are more readily apparent.

Illustration 17-5

MICROSOFT CORPORATION
Common-Size Comparative Income Statement
For Years Ended June 30, 1993, and 1992
(in millions)

	Years Ended June 30		Common-size Percentages	
	1993	1992	1993	1992
Net revenues	$3,753	$2,759	100.0	100.0
Cost of revenues	633	467	16.9	16.9
Gross profit	$3,120	$2,292	83.1	83.1
Operating expenses:				
Research and development	$ 470	$ 352	12.5	12.8
Sales and marketing	1,205	854	32.1	31.0
General and administrative	119	90	3.2	3.3
Total operating expenses	$1,794	$1,296	47.8	47.0*
Operating income	$1,326	$ 996	35.3	36.1
Interest income—net	82	56	2.2	2.0
Other	(7)	(11)	(0.2)	(0.4)
Income before income taxes	$1,401	$1,041	37.3	37.7
Provision for income taxes	448	333	11.9	12.1
Net income	$ 953	$ 708	25.4	25.7*
Earnings per share	$ 3.15	$ 2.41		
Weighted-average shares outstanding	303	294		

*Does not foot due to rounding.

For example, look at the common-size comparative balance sheet for Microsoft in Illustration 17–4. Note that Cash and short-term investments amounted to 50.9% of

total assets at the end of the 1992 fiscal year. By comparison, they were 60.2% of total assets at the end of 1993.

In producing a common-size income statement, the amount of net sales is usually the base amount and is assigned a value of 100%. Then, each statement item appears as a percentage of net sales. If you think of the 100% sales amount as representing one sales dollar, the remaining items show how each sales dollar was distributed among costs, expenses, and profit. For example, the comparative income statement in Illustration 17–5 shows that for each dollar of **Microsoft's** net revenue during 1993, research and development expenses amounted to 12.5 cents. In 1992, research and development consumed 12.8 cents of each sales dollar. Common-size percentages help the analyst see any potentially important changes in a company's expenses. For Microsoft, the relative size of each expense changed very little from 1992 to 1993.

Many corporate annual reports include graphic presentations such as those in Illustration 17–6 from Microsoft's 1993 Annual Report. The pie chart on the left side of the illustration shows the revenues generated by each of the company's product groups. The pie chart on the right shows the revenues by sales channel. In that chart, OEM refers to original equipment manufacturers. In the annual report, the data for these charts did not appear in the financial statements. Instead, they were included as part of the discussion and analysis by management.

Illustration 17-6   Pie-Chart Presentations, Microsoft Corporation

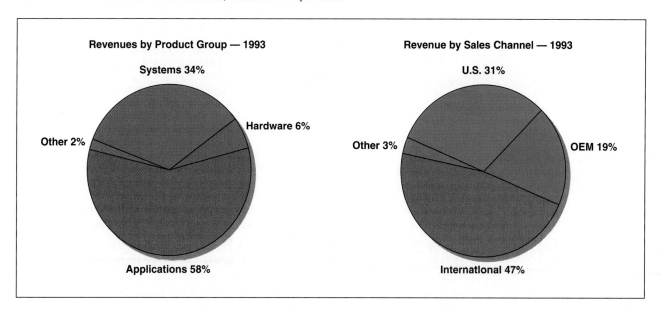

ANALYSIS OF SHORT-TERM LIQUIDITY

LO 3

Calculate and explain the interpretation of the ratios, turnovers, and rates of return used to evaluate *(a)* short-term liquidity, *(b)* long-term risk and capital structure, and *(c)* operating efficiency and profitability.

The amount of current assets less current liabilities is called the **working capital** or *net working capital* of a business. A business must maintain an adequate amount of working capital to meet current debts, carry sufficient inventories, and take advantage of cash discounts. Indeed, a business that runs out of working capital cannot meet its current obligations or continue operations.

Current Ratio

When evaluating the working capital of a business, you must look beyond the dollar amount of current assets less current liabilities. Also consider the relationship between the amounts of current assets and current liabilities. Recall from Chapter 3 that the *current ratio* describes a company's ability to pay its short-term obligations. The current ratio relates current assets to current liabilities, as follows:

$$\text{Current ratio} = \frac{\text{Current assets}}{\text{Current liabilities}}$$

For example, using the information in Illustration 17–1, Microsoft's working capital positions and current ratios at the end of its 1993 and 1992 years were:

	June 30, 1993	June 30, 1992
(In millions)		
Current assets	$2,850	$1,770
Current liabilities	563	447
Working capital	$2,287	$1,323
Current ratio:		
$2,850/$563	5.1 to 1	
$1,770/$447		4.0 to 1

A high current ratio generally indicates a strong position because a high ratio suggests the company is capable of meeting its current obligations. On the other hand, a company might have a current ratio that is too high. This condition means that the company has invested too much in current assets compared to its needs. Normally, current assets do not generate very much additional revenue. Therefore, if a company invests too much in current assets, the investment is not being used efficiently.

Years ago, bankers and other creditors often used a current ratio of 2 to 1 as a rule of thumb in evaluating the debt-paying ability of a credit-seeking company. A company with a 2 to 1 current ratio was generally thought to be a good credit risk in the short run. However, most lenders realize that the 2 to 1 rule of thumb is not a good test of debt-paying ability. Whether a company's current ratio is good or bad depends on at least three factors:

1. The nature of the company's business.
2. The composition of its current assets.
3. The turnover rate for some of its current assets.

Whether a company's current ratio is adequate depends on the nature of its business. A service company that has no inventories other than supplies and that grants little or no credit may be able to operate on a current ratio of less than 1 to 1 if its sales generate enough cash to pay its current liabilities on time. On the other hand, a company that sells high-fashion clothing or furniture may occasionally misjudge customer demand. If this happens, the company's inventory may not generate as much cash as expected. A company that faces risks like these may need a current ratio of much more than 2 to 1 to protect its liquidity.

Therefore, when you study the adequacy of working capital, consider the type of business under review. Before you decide that a company's current ratio is too low or too high, compare the company's current ratio with ratios of other successful companies in the same industry. Another important source of insight is to observe how the ratio has changed over time.

Keep in mind that the current ratio can be affected by a company's choice of an inventory flow assumption. For example, a company that uses LIFO tends to report a smaller amount of current assets than if it uses FIFO. Therefore, consider the underlying factors before deciding that a given current ratio is acceptable.

Also consider the composition of a company's current assets when you evaluate its working capital position. Cash and short-term investments are more liquid than accounts and notes receivable. And, short-term receivables normally are more liquid than merchandise inventory. Cash can be used to pay current debts at once. But, accounts receivable and merchandise inventory must be converted into cash before payments can be made. Therefore, an excessive amount of receivables and inventory could weaken the company's ability to pay its current liabilities.

One way to take the composition of current assets into account is to evaluate the acid-test ratio. We discuss this next; then, we examine the turnover rates for receivables and inventories.

Acid-Test Ratio

Recall from Chapter 5 that an easily calculated check on current asset composition is the *acid-test ratio*, also called the *quick ratio*. Quick assets are cash, short-term investments, accounts receivable, and notes receivable. These are the most liquid types of current assets. Calculate the ratio as follows:

$$\text{Acid-test ratio} = \frac{\text{Quick assets}}{\text{Current liabilities}}$$

Using the information in Illustration 17–1, we calculate Microsoft's acid-test ratios as follows:

	June 30, 1993	June 30, 1992
(In millions)		
Cash and short-term investments	$2,290	$1,345
Accounts receivable, net of		
allowances	338	270
Total quick assets	$2,628	$1,615
Current liabilities	$ 563	$ 447
Acid-test ratio:		
$2,628/$563	4.7 to 1	
$1,615/$447		3.6 to 1

A traditional rule of thumb for an acceptable acid-test ratio is 1 to 1. However, as is true for all financial ratios, you should be skeptical about rules of thumb. The working capital requirements of a company are also affected by how frequently the company converts its current assets into cash. Thus, a careful analysis of a company's short-term liquidity should include additional analyses of its receivables and inventories.

Accounts Receivable Turnover

One way to measure how frequently a company converts its receivables into cash is to calculate the accounts receivable turnover. As you learned in Chapter 8, this is calculated as follows:

$$\text{Accounts receivable turnover} = \frac{\text{Net sales}}{\text{Average accounts receivable}}$$

Although this ratio is widely known as accounts receivable turnover, all short-term receivables from customers normally are included in the denominator. Thus, if a company has short-term notes receivable, those balances should be included with the accounts receivable. In the numerator, the calculation would be more precise if credit sales were used. Usually, however, net sales is used because information about credit sales is not available.

Applying the formula to Microsoft's 1993 fiscal year results, the company's accounts receivable turnover was:

$$\frac{\$3,753}{(\$338 + \$270)/2} = 12.3 \text{ times}$$

If accounts receivable are collected quickly, the accounts receivable turnover is high. In general, this is favorable because it means that the company does not have to commit large amounts of capital to accounts receivable. However, an accounts receivable turnover may be too high. This might occur when credit terms are so restrictive they negatively affect sales volume.

Sometimes, the ending accounts receivable balance can substitute for the average balance in calculating accounts receivable turnover. This is acceptable if the effect is not significant. Also, some analysts prefer using gross accounts receivable before subtracting the allowance for doubtful accounts. However, balance sheets may report only the net amount of accounts receivable.

Days' Sales Uncollected

Accounts receivable turnover is only one way to measure how frequently a company collects its accounts. Another method is to calculate the days' sales uncollected, which we defined in Chapter 7 as:

$$\text{Days' sales uncollected} = \frac{\text{Accounts receivable}}{\text{Net sales}} \times 365$$

Although this formula takes the usual approach of placing accounts receivable in the numerator, short-term notes receivable from customers should be included. To illustrate, we refer to the information about Microsoft in Illustrations 17–1 and 17–2. The days' sales uncollected on June 30, 1993, was:

$$\frac{\$338}{\$3,753} \times 365 = 32.9 \text{ days}$$

Days' sales uncollected has more meaning if you know the credit terms. A rule of thumb is that days' sales uncollected: *(a)* should not exceed one and one-third times the days in the credit period, if discounts are not offered; *(b)* should not exceed one and one-third times the days in its discount period, if discounts are offered.

Turnover of Merchandise Inventory

Working capital requirements are also affected by how long a company holds merchandise inventory before selling it. This effect can be measured by calculating merchandise turnover, which we defined in Chapter 9 as:

$$\text{Merchandise turnover} = \frac{\text{Cost of goods sold}}{\text{Average merchandise inventory}}$$

Using the cost of revenues and inventories information in Illustrations 17–1 and 17–2, we calculate Microsoft's merchandise turnover during 1993 as follows (cost of goods sold is called cost of revenues on Microsoft's income statement):

$$\frac{\$633}{(\$127 + \$86)/2} = 5.9 \text{ times}$$

In this calculation, the average inventory was estimated by averaging the beginning and the ending inventories for 1993. In case the beginning and ending inventories do not represent the amount normally on hand, an average of the quarterly inventories may be used, if that is available.

From a working capital point of view, a company with a high turnover requires a smaller investment in inventory than one that produces the same sales with a low turnover. On the other hand, the merchandise turnover may be too high if a company keeps such a small inventory that sales volume is restricted.

Days' Stock on Hand

Recall from Chapter 9 that days' stock on hand is another means of evaluating the liquidity of a company's inventory. It relates to inventory in a similar fashion as day's sales uncollected relates to receivables. The calculation is:

$$\text{Days' stock on hand} = \frac{\text{Ending inventory}}{\text{Cost of goods sold}} \times 365$$

Applying the formula to Microsoft's 1993 information, we calculate days' stock on hand as:

$$\frac{\$127}{\$633} \times 365 = 73.2 \text{ days}$$

Assuming the particular products in inventory are those customers demand, the formula estimates that the inventory will be converted into receivables (or cash) in 73.2 days. If all of Microsoft's sales were credit sales, the conversion of inventory to receivables in 73.2 days plus the conversion of receivables to cash in 32.9 days would suggest that the inventory would be converted into cash in about 106 days (73.2 + 32.9 = 106.1).

Progress Check

17-6 The following is taken from the 12/31/X2 balance sheet of Paff Company: cash, $820,000; accounts receivable, $240,000; inventories, $470,000; plant and equipment, $910,000; accounts payable, $350,000; and income taxes payable, $180,000. Calculate the *(a)* current ratio and *(b)* acid-test ratio.

17-7 On 12/31/X1, Paff Company (see 17-6) had accounts receivable of $290,000 and inventories of $530,000. Also, during 19X2, net sales amounted to $2,500,000 and cost of goods sold was $750,000. Calculate the *(a)* accounts receivable turnover, *(b)* days' sales uncollected, *(c)* merchandise turnover, and *(d)* days' stock on hand.

An analysis of working capital evaluates the short-term liquidity of the company. However, analysts are also interested in a company's ability to meet its obligations and provide security to its creditors over the long run. Indicators of this ability include *debt* and *equity* ratios, the relationship between *pledged assets* and *secured liabilities*, and the company's capacity to earn *sufficient income to pay its fixed interest charges*.

ANALYSIS OF LONG-TERM RISK AND CAPITAL STRUCTURE

LO 3

Calculate and explain the interpretation of the ratios, turnovers, and rates of return used to evaluate *(a)* short-term liquidity, *(b)* long-term risk and capital structure, and *(c)* operating efficiency and profitability.

Debt and Equity Ratios

Financial analysts are always interested in the portion of a company's assets contributed by its owners and the portion contributed by creditors. This relationship is described by the debt ratio you learned about in Chapter 2. Recall that the debt ratio expresses total liabilities as a percentage of total assets. The **equity ratio** provides complementary information by expressing total stockholders' equity as a percentage of total assets.

We calculate the debt and equity ratios of Microsoft Corporation as follows:

	1993	1992
a. Total liabilities (all short-term)	$ 563	$ 447
b. Total stockholders' equity	3,242	2,193
c. Total liabilities and stockholders' equity	$3,805	$2,640
Percentages provided by creditors: (*a/c*)	14.8%	16.9%
Percentages provided by stockholders: (*b/c*)	85.2%	83.1%

Microsoft's financial statements reflect very little debt compared to most companies. It has no long-term liabilities and, at the end of the 1993 year, its current liabilities provide only 14.8% of the total assets. In general, a company is less risky if it has only a small amount of debt in its capital structure. The larger the portion provided by stockholders, the more losses can be absorbed by stockholders before the remaining assets become inadequate to satisfy the claims of creditors.

From the stockholders' point of view, however, including debt in the capital structure of a company may be desirable, so long as the risk is not too great. If a business can earn a return on borrowed capital that is higher than the cost of borrowing, the difference represents increased income to stockholders. Because debt can have the effect of increasing the return to stockholders, the inclusion of debt is sometimes described as financial leverage. Companies are said to be highly leveraged if a large portion of their assets is financed by debt.

Pledged Assets to Secured Liabilities

In Chapter 15, we explained how to use the ratio of pledged assets to secured liabilities to evaluate the risk of nonpayment faced by secured creditors. Recall that the ratio also may provide information of interest to unsecured creditors. The ratio is calculated as follows:

$$\text{Pledged assets to secured liabilities} = \frac{\text{Book value of pledged assets}}{\text{Secured liabilities}}$$

Regardless of how helpful this ratio might be in evaluating the risk faced by creditors, the information needed to calculate the ratio is seldom presented in published financial statements. Thus, it is used primarily by persons who have the ability to obtain the information directly from the company managers.

The usual rule-of-thumb minimum value for this ratio is 2 to 1. However, the ratio needs careful interpretation because it is based on the book value of the pledged assets. As you know, book values are not intended to reflect the amount that would be received for the assets in a liquidation sale. Also, the long-term earning ability of the company with pledged assets may be more important than the value of the pledged assets. Creditors prefer that a debtor be able to pay with cash generated by operating activities rather than with cash obtained by liquidating assets.

Times Fixed Interest Charges Earned

As you learned in Chapter 12, the times fixed interest charges earned ratio is often calculated to describe the security of the return offered to creditors. The amount of income before the deduction of interest charges and income taxes is the amount available to pay the interest charges. Calculate the ratio as follows:

$$\text{Times fixed interest charges earned} = \frac{\text{Income before interest and income taxes}}{\text{Interest expense}}$$

The larger this ratio, the greater the security for the lenders. A rule of thumb for this statistic is that creditors are reasonably safe if the company earns its fixed interest charges two or more times each year. Look in Illustration 17–2 and observe that Microsoft did not report interest expense as a separate item. Apparently interest expense is not material; probably it is offset against interest income which is reported as "Interest income—net." Also recall from Illustration 17–1 that Microsoft did not have any long-term debt. Furthermore, few if any of the company's current liabilities would be likely to generate interest expense. As a result, we are not able to calculate a times fixed interest charges earned ratio for Microsoft. Yet, we should again recognize that there appears to be little risk for Microsoft's creditors.

Financial analysts are especially interested in the ability of a company to use its assets efficiently to produce profits for its owners and thus provide cash flows to them. Several ratios are available to help you evaluate operating efficiency and profitability.

Profit Margin

The operating efficiency of a company can be expressed in two components. The first is the company's *profit margin.* As you learned in Chapter 4, this ratio describes a company's ability to earn a net income from sales. It is measured by expressing net income as a percentage of revenues. For example, we can use the information in Illustration 17–2 to calculate **Microsoft's** 1993 profit margin as follows:

$$\text{Profit margin} = \frac{\text{Net income}}{\text{Revenues}} = \frac{\$953}{\$3,753} = 25.4\%$$

To evaluate the profit margin of a company, consider the nature of the industry in which the company operates. For example, a publishing company might be expected to have a profit margin between 10 and 15%, while a retail supermarket might have a normal profit margin of 1 or 2%.

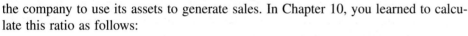

Total Asset Turnover

The second component of operating efficiency is *total asset turnover,* which describes the ability of the company to use its assets to generate sales. In Chapter 10, you learned to calculate this ratio as follows:

$$\text{Total asset turnover} = \frac{\text{Net sales}}{\text{Average total assets}}$$

In calculating Microsoft's total asset turnover for 1993, we follow the usual practice of averaging the total assets at the beginning and the end of the year. Taking the information from Illustrations 17-1 and 17-2, the calculation is:

$$\frac{\$3,753}{(\$3,805 + \$2,640)/2} = 1.165 \text{ times*}$$

*Carried to three decimal places to avoid later rounding error.

Both profit margin and total asset turnover describe the two basic components of operating efficiency. However, they also evaluate management performance because the management of a company is fundamentally responsible for its operating efficiency.

Return on Total Assets

Because operating efficiency has two basic components (profit margin and total asset turnover), analysts frequently calculate a summary measure of these components. This summary measure is the *return on total assets* that we discussed in Chapter 11. Recall that the calculation is:

$$\text{Return on total assets} = \frac{\text{Net income}}{\text{Average total assets}}$$

Applying this to Microsoft's 1993 year, we calculate return on total assets as:

$$\frac{\$953}{(\$3,805 + \$2,640)/2} = 29.6\%$$

Microsoft's 29.6% return on total assets appears very favorable compared to most businesses. However, you should make comparisons with competing companies and alternative investment opportunities before reaching a final conclusion. Also, you should evaluate the trend in the rates of return earned by the company in recent years.

Earlier, we said that the return on total assets summarizes the two components of operating efficiency—profit margin and total asset turnover. The following calculation shows the relationship between these three measures. Notice that both profit margin and total asset turnover contribute to overall operating efficiency, as measured by return on total assets.

Profit margin	$\times$	Total asset turnover	$=$	Return on total assets
$\dfrac{\text{Net income}}{\text{Net sales}}$	$\times$	$\dfrac{\text{Net sales}}{\text{Average total assets}}$	$=$	$\dfrac{\text{Net income}}{\text{Average total assets}}$
For Microsoft Corporation:				
25.4%	$\times$	1.165	$=$	29.6%

Return on Common Stockholders' Equity

Perhaps the most important reason for operating a business is to earn a net income for its owners. The *return on common stockholders' equity* measures the success of a business in reaching this goal. In Chapter 1, we simplified this calculation by basing it on the beginning balance of owners' equity. However, many companies have frequent transactions that involve issuing and perhaps repurchasing stock during each year. Thus, you should allow for these events by calculating the return based on the average stockholders' equity, as follows:

$$\text{Return on common stockholders' equity} = \frac{\text{Net income} - \text{Preferred dividends}}{\text{Average common stockholders' equity}}$$

Recall from Illustration 17–1 that Microsoft did not have any preferred stock outstanding. As a result, we determine Microsoft's 1993 return as follows:

$$\frac{\$953}{(\$3,242 + \$2,193)/2} = 35.1\%$$

When preferred stock is outstanding, the denominator in the calculation should be the book value of the common stock. In the numerator, the dividends on cumulative preferred stock must be subtracted whether they were declared or are in arrears. If the preferred is not cumulative, the dividends are subtracted only if declared.

Price Earnings Ratio

Recall from Chapter 14 that the price earnings ratio is calculated as follows:

$$\text{Price earnings ratio} = \frac{\text{Market price per share}}{\text{Earnings per share}}$$

Sometimes, the predicted earnings per share for the next period is used in the denominator of the calculation. Other times, the reported earnings per share for the most recent period is used. In either case, the ratio is an indicator of the future growth of and risk related to the company's earnings as perceived by investors who establish the market price of the stock.

During the last three months of Microsoft's 1993 year, the market price of its common stock ranged from a low of $65.50 to a high of $98. Using the $3.15 earnings per share that was reported after the year-end, the price earnings ratios for the low and the high were:

$$\text{Low: } \frac{\$65.50}{\$3.15} = 20.8 \qquad \text{High: } \frac{\$98.00}{\$3.15} = 31.1$$

In its 1993 annual report, Microsoft's management reported that it did not expect the 1994 revenue growth rates to be as high as those for 1993. Management also indicated that operating expenses as a percentage of revenues might increase. Nevertheless, the price earnings ratios are much higher than for most companies. No doubt, Microsoft's high ratios reflect the expectation of investors that the company would continue to grow at a much higher rate than most companies.

Dividend Yield

As you learned in Chapter 13, *dividend yield* is a statistic used to compare the dividend-paying performance of different investment alternatives. The formula is:

$$\text{Dividend yield} = \frac{\text{Annual dividends per share}}{\text{Market price per share}}$$

Some companies may not declare dividends because they need the cash in the business. For example, Microsoft's 1993 Annual Report stated that the company had not declared any dividends.

Progress Check

17-8   Which ratio describes the security of the return offered to creditors?   *(a)* Debt ratio; *(b)* Equity ratio;   *(c)* Times fixed interest charges earned;   *(d)* Pledged assets to secured liabilities.

17-9   Which ratio measures the success of a business in earning net income for its owners?   *(a)* Profit margin;   *(b)* Return on common stockholders' equity;   *(c)* Price earnings ratio;   *(d)* Dividend yield.

17-10   If BK Company has net sales of $8,500,000, net income of $945,000, and total asset turnover of 1.8 times, what is BK's return on total assets?

To evaluate short-term liquidity, use these ratios:

$$\text{Current ratio} = \frac{\text{Current assets}}{\text{Current liabilities}}$$

$$\text{Acid-test ratio} = \frac{\text{Cash} + \text{Short-term investments} + \text{Current receivables}}{\text{Current liabilities}}$$

$$\text{Accounts receivable turnover} = \frac{\text{Net sales}}{\text{Average accounts receivable}}$$

$$\text{Days' sales uncollected} = \frac{\text{Accounts receivable}}{\text{Net sales}} \times 365$$

$$\text{Merchandise turnover} = \frac{\text{Cost of goods sold}}{\text{Average merchandise inventory}}$$

$$\text{Days' stock on hand} = \frac{\text{Ending inventory}}{\text{Cost of goods sold}} \times 365$$

To evaluate long-term risk and capital structure, use these ratios:

$$\text{Debt ratio} = \frac{\text{Total liabilities}}{\text{Total assets}}$$

$$\text{Equity ratio} = \frac{\text{Total stockholders' equity}}{\text{Total assets}}$$

REVIEW OF FINANCIAL STATEMENT RATIOS AND STATISTICS FOR ANALYSIS

$$\text{Pledged assets to secured liabilities} = \frac{\text{Book value of pledged assets}}{\text{Secured liabilities}}$$

$$\text{Times fixed interest charges earned} = \frac{\text{Income before interest and taxes}}{\text{Interest expense}}$$

To evaluate operating efficiency and profitability, use these ratios:

$$\text{Profit margin} = \frac{\text{Net income}}{\text{Net sales}}$$

$$\text{Total asset turnover} = \frac{\text{Net sales}}{\text{Average total assets}}$$

$$\text{Return on total assets} = \frac{\text{Net income}}{\text{Average total assets}}$$

$$\text{Return on common stockholders' equity} = \frac{\text{Net income} - \text{Preferred dividends}}{\text{Average common stockholders' equity}}$$

$$\text{Price earnings ratio} = \frac{\text{Market price per common share}}{\text{Earnings per share}}$$

$$\text{Dividend yield} = \frac{\text{Annual dividends per share}}{\text{Market price per share}}$$

STANDARDS OF COMPARISON

LO 4

State the limitations associated with using financial statement ratios and the sources from which standards for comparison may be obtained.

After computing ratios and turnovers in the process of analyzing financial statements, you have to decide whether the calculated amounts suggest good, bad, or merely average performance by the company. To make these judgments, you must have some bases for comparison. The following are possibilities:

1. An experienced analyst may compare the ratios and turnovers of the company under review with *subjective* standards acquired from past experiences.

2. For purposes of comparison, an analyst may calculate the ratios and turnovers of a selected group of competing companies in the same *industry.*

3. *Published* ratios and turnovers (such as those provided by Dun & Bradstreet) may be used for comparison.

4. Some local and national trade associations gather data from their members and publish *standard* or *average* ratios for their trade or industry. When available, these data can give the analyst a useful basis for comparison.

5. *Rule-of-thumb* standards can be used as a basis for comparison.

Of these five standards, the ratios and turnovers of a selected group of competing companies normally are the best bases for comparison. Rule-of-thumb standards should be applied with great care and then only if they seem reasonable in light of past experience and the industry's norms.

Progress Check

17-11 **Which of the following would not be used as a basis for comparison when analyzing ratios and turnovers?**
   a. **Companies in different industries.**
   b. **Subjective standards from past experience.**
   c. **Rule-of-thumb standards.**
   d. **Averages within a trade or industry.**

17-12 **Which of the typical bases of comparison is usually best?**

LO 1. **Explain the relationship between financial reporting and general purpose financial statements.** Financial reporting is intended to provide information that is useful to investors, creditors, and others in making investment, credit, and similar decisions. The information is communicated in a variety of ways, including general purpose financial statements. These statements normally include an income statement, balance sheet, statement of changes in stockholders' equity or statement of retained earnings, statement of cash flows, and the related footnotes.

LO 2. **Describe, prepare, and interpret comparative financial statements and common-size comparative statements.** Comparative financial statements show amounts for two or more successive periods, sometimes with the changes in the items disclosed in absolute and percentage terms. In common-size statements, each item is expressed as a percentage of a base amount. The base amount for the balance sheet is usually total assets, and the base amount for the income statement is usually net sales.

LO 3. **Calculate and explain the interpretation of the ratios, turnovers, and rates of return used to evaluate (a) short-term liquidity, (b) long-term risk and capital structure, and (c) operating efficiency and profitability.** To evaluate the short-term liquidity of a company, calculate a current ratio, an acid-test ratio, the accounts receivable turnover, the days' sales uncollected, the merchandise turnover, and the days' stock on hand.

In evaluating the long-term risk and capital structure of a company, calculate debt and equity ratios, pledged assets to secured liabilities, and the number of times fixed interest charges were earned.

In evaluating operating efficiency and profitability, calculate profit margin, total asset turnover, return on total assets, and return on common stockholders' equity. Other statistics used to evaluate the profitability of alternative investments include the price earnings ratio and the dividend yield.

LO 4. **State the limitations associated with using financial statement ratios and the sources from which standards for comparison may be obtained.** In deciding whether financial statement ratio values are satisfactory, too high, or too low, you must have some bases for comparison. These bases may come from past experience and personal judgment, from ratios of similar companies, or from ratios published by trade associations or other public sources. Traditional rules of thumb should be applied with great care and only if they seem reasonable in light of past experience.

SUMMARY OF THE CHAPTER IN TERMS OF LEARNING OBJECTIVES

Use the financial statements of Precision Co. to satisfy the following requirements:

1. Prepare a comparative income statement showing the percentage increase or decrease for 19X2 over 19X1.
2. Prepare a common-size comparative balance sheet for 19X2 and 19X1.
3. Compute the following ratios as of December 31, 19X2, or for the year ended December 31, 19X2:

   a. Current ratio.
   b. Acid-test ratio.
   c. Accounts receivable turnover.
   d. Days' sales uncollected.
   e. Merchandise turnover.
   f. Debt ratio

   g. Pledged assets to secured liabilities.
   h. Times fixed interest charges earned.
   i. Profit margin.
   j. Total asset turnover.
   k. Return on total assets.
   l. Return on common stockholders' equity.

DEMONSTRATION PROBLEM

PRECISION COMPANY
Comparative Income Statement
For Years Ended December 31, 19X2 and 19X1

	19X2	19X1
Sales	$2,486,000	$2,075,000
Cost of goods sold	1,523,000	1,222,000
Gross profit from sales	$ 963,000	$ 853,000
Operating expenses:		
Advertising expense	$ 145,000	$ 100,000
Sales salaries expense	240,000	280,000
Office salaries expense	165,000	200,000
Insurance expense	100,000	45,000
Supplies expense	26,000	35,000
Depreciation expenses	85,000	75,000
Miscellaneous expense	17,000	15,000
Total operating expenses	$ 778,000	$ 750,000
Operating income	$ 185,000	$ 103,000
Less interest expense	44,000	46,000
Income before taxes	$ 141,000	$ 57,000
Income taxes	47,000	19,000
Net income	$ 94,000	$ 38,000
Earnings per share	$ 0.99	$ 0.40

PRECISION COMPANY
Comparative Balance Sheet
December 31, 19X2, and December 31, 19X1

	19X2	19X1
Assets		
Current assets:		
Cash	$ 79,000	$ 42,000
Short-term investments	65,000	96,000
Accounts receivable (net)	120,000	100,000
Merchandise inventory	250,000	265,000
Total current assets	$ 514,000	$ 503,000
Plant and equipment:		
Store equipment (net)	$ 400,000	$ 350,000
Office equipment (net)	45,000	50,000
Buildings (net)	625,000	675,000
Land	100,000	100,000
Total plant and equipment	$1,170,000	$1,175,000
Total assets	$1,684,000	$1,678,000
Liabilities		
Current liabilities:		
Accounts payable	$ 164,000	$ 190,000
Short-term notes payable	75,000	90,000
Taxes payable	26,000	12,000
Total current liabilities	$ 265,000	$ 292,000
Long-term liabilities:		
Notes payable (secured by		
mortgage on building and land)	400,000	420,000
Total liabilities	$ 665,000	$ 712,000
Stockholders' Equity		
Contributed capital:		
Common stock, $5 par value	$ 475,000	$ 475,000
Retained earnings	544,000	491,000
Total stockholders' equity	$1,019,000	$ 966,000
Total liabilities and		
stockholders' equity	$1,684,000	$1,678,000

- Set up a four-column income statement; enter the 19X2 and 19X1 amounts in the first two columns, and then enter the dollar change in the third column and the percentage change from 19X1 in the fourth column.
- Set up a four-column balance sheet; enter the 19X2 and 19X1 amounts in the first two columns, and then compute and enter the amount of each item as a percent of total assets.
- Compute the given ratios using the provided numbers; be sure to use the average of the beginning and ending amounts where appropriate.

Planning the Solution

1.

PRECISION COMPANY
Comparative Income Statement
For Years Ended December 31, 19X2 and 19X1

Solution to Demonstration Problem

	19X2	19X1	Increase (Decrease) in 19X2 Amount	Percentage
Sales	$2,486,000	$2,075,000	$411,000	19.8
Cost of goods sold	1,523,000	1,222,000	301,000	24.6
Gross profit from sales	$ 963,000	$ 853,000	$110,000	12.9
Operating expenses:				
Advertising expense	$ 145,000	$ 100,000	$ 45,000	45.0
Sales salaries expense	240,000	280,000	(40,000)	(14.3)
Office salaries expense	165,000	200,000	(35,000)	(17.5)
Insurance expense	100,000	45,000	55,000	122.2
Supplies expense	26,000	35,000	(9,000)	(25.7)
Depreciation expense	85,000	75,000	10,000	13.3
Miscellaneous expenses	17,000	15,000	2,000	13.3
Total operating expenses	$ 778,000	$ 750,000	$ 28,000	3.7
Operating income	$ 185,000	$ 103,000	$ 82,000	79.6
Less interest expense	44,000	46,000	(2,000)	(4.3)
Income before taxes	$ 141,000	$ 57,000	$ 84,000	147.4
Income taxes	47,000	19,000	28,000	147.4
Net income	$ 94,000	$ 38,000	$ 56,000	147.4
Earnings per share	$ 0.99	$ 0.40	$ 0.59	147.5

2.

PRECISION COMPANY
Common-Size Comparative Balance Sheet
December 31, 19X2, and December 31, 19X1

	December 31		Common-size Percentages	
	19X2	19X1	19X2*	19X1*
Assets				
Current assets:				
Cash	$ 79,000	$ 42,000	4.7	2.5
Short-term investments	65,000	96,000	3.9	5.7
Accounts receivable (net)	120,000	100,000	7.1	6.0
Merchandise inventory	250,000	265,000	14.8	15.8
Total current assets	$ 514,000	$ 503,000	30.5	30.0
Plant and equipment:				
Store equipment (net)	$ 400,000	$ 350,000	23.8	20.9
Office equipment (net)	45,000	50,000	2.7	3.0
Buildings (net)	625,000	675,000	37.1	40.2
Land	100,000	100,000	5.9	6.0
Total plant and equipment	$1,170,000	$1,175,000	69.5	70.0
Total assets	$1,684,000	$1,678,000	100.0	100.0

	December 31		Common-size Percentages	
	19X2	**19X1**	**19X2***	**19X1***
Liabilities				
Current liabilities:				
Accounts payable	$ 164,000	$ 190,000	9.7	11.3
Short-term notes payable	75,000	90,000	4.5	5.4
Taxes payable	26,000	12,000	1.5	0.7
Total current liabilities	$ 265,000	$ 292,000	15.7	17.4
Long-term liabilities:				
Notes payable (secured by				
mortgage on building and land)	400,000	420,000	23.8	25.0
Total liabilities	$ 665,000	$ 712,000	39.4	42.4
Stockholders' Equity				
Contributed capital:				
Common stock, $5 par value	$ 475,000	$ 475,000	28.2	28.3
Retailed earnings	544,000	491,000	32.3	29.3
Total stockholders' equity	$1,019,000	$ 966,000	60.5	57.6
Total liabilities and equity	$1,684,000	$1,678,000	100.0	100.0

*Columns may not foot due to rounding.

3. Ratios for 19X2:

a. Current ratio: $514,000/$265,000 = 1.9 to 1

b. Acid-test ratio: ($79,000 + $65,000 + $120,000)/$265,000 = 1.0 to 1

c. Average receivables: ($120,000 + $100,000)/2 = $110,000
Accounts receivable turnover: $2,486,000/$110,000 = 22.6 times

d. Days' sales uncollected: ($120,000/$2,486,000) × 365 = 17.6 days

e. Average inventory: ($250,000 + $265,000)/2 = $257,500
Merchandise turnover: $1,523,000/$257,500 = 5.9 times

f. Debt ratio: $665,000/$1,684,000 = 39.5%

g. Pledged assets to secured liabilities:
($625,000 + $100,000)/$400,000 = 1.8 to 1

h. Times fixed interest charges earned: $185,000/$44,000 = 4.2 times

i. Profit margin: $94,000/$2,486,000 = 3.8%

j. Average total assets: ($1,684,000 + $1,678,000)/2 = $1,681,000
Total asset turnover: $2,486,000/$1,681,000 = 1.48 times

k. Return on total assets: $94,000/$1,681,000 = 5.6% or 3.8% × 1.48 = 5.6%

l. Average total equity: ($1,019,000 + $966,000)/2 = $992,500
Return on common stockholders' equity: $94,000/$992,500 = 9.5%

GLOSSARY

Common-size comparative statements comparative financial statements in which each amount is expressed as a percentage of a base amount. In the balance sheet, the amount of total assets is usually selected as the base amount and is expressed as 100%. In the income statement, net sales is usually selected as the base amount. p. 653

Comparative statement a financial statement with data for two or more successive accounting periods placed in columns side by side, sometimes with changes shown in dollar amounts and percentages. p. 649

Equity ratio the portion of total assets provided by stockholders' equity, calculated as stockholders' equity divided by total assets. p. 659

Financial reporting the process of providing information that is useful to investors, creditors, and others in making investment, credit, and similar decisions. p. 648

General purpose financial statements statements published periodically for use by a wide variety of interested parties; include the income statement, balance sheet, statement of changes in stockholders' equity (or statement of retained earnings), statement of cash flows, and related footnotes. p. 648

Working capital current assets minus current liabilities. p. 655

QUESTIONS

1. Explain the difference between financial reporting and financial statements.

2. What is the difference between comparative financial statements and common-size comparative statements?

3. Which items are usually assigned a value of 100% on a common-size comparative balance sheet and a common-size comparative income statement?

4. Why is working capital given special attention in the process of analyzing balance sheets?

5. What are three factors that would influence your decision as to whether a company's current ratio is good or bad?

6. Suggest several reasons why a 2 to 1 current ratio may not be adequate for a particular company.

7. What does a relatively high accounts receivable turnover indicate about a company's short-term liquidity?

8. What is the significance of the number of days' sales uncollected?

9. Why does merchandise turnover provide information about a company's short-term liquidity?

10. Why is the capital structure of a company, as measured by debt and equity ratios, of importance to financial statement analysts?

11. Why must the ratio of pledged assets to secured liabilities be interpreted with caution?

12. Why would a company's return on total assets be different from its return on common stockholders' equity?

13. What ratios would you calculate for the purpose of evaluating management performance?

14. Using the financial statements for Federal Express Corporation in Appendix G, calculate Federal Express's return on total assets for the fiscal year ended May 31, 1993.

15. Refer to the financial statements for Ben & Jerry's Homemade, Inc., in Appendix G. Calculate Ben & Jerry's equity ratio as of December 26, 1992.

QUICK STUDY (Five-Minute Exercises)

Which of the following items are means of accomplishing the objective of financial reporting but are not included within general purpose financial statements? *(a)* Income statements; *(b)* Company news releases; *(c)* Balance sheets; *(d)* Certain reports filed with the Securities and Exchange Commission; *(e)* Statements of cash flows; *(f)* Management discussions and analyses of financial performance.

**QS 17–1
(LO 1)**

Given the following information for Moyers Corporation, determine *(a)* the common-size percentages for gross profit from sales, and *(b)* the trend percentages for net sales, using 19X1 as the base year.

**QS 17–2
(LO 2)**

	19X2	19X1
Net sales	$134,400	$114,800
Cost of goods sold	72,800	60,200

a. Which two terms describe the difference between current assets and current liabilities?

b. Which two short-term liquidity ratios measure how frequently a company collects its accounts?

c. Which two ratios are the basic components in measuring a company's operating efficiency? Which ratio is the summary of these two components?

**QS 17–3
(LO 3)**

What are five possible bases of comparison you can use when analyzing financial statement ratios? Which of these is generally considered to be the most useful? Which one is least likely to provide a good basis for comparison?

**QS 17–4
(LO 4)**

EXERCISES

Exercise 17–1
Calculating trend percentages
(LO 2)

Calculate trend percentages for the following items, using 19X0 as the base year. Then, state whether the situation shown by the trends appears to be favorable or unfavorable.

	19X4	19X3	19X2	19X1	19X0
Sales	$377,600	$362,400	$338,240	$314,080	$302,000
Cost of goods sold	172,720	164,560	155,040	142,800	136,000
Accounts receivable	25,400	24,400	23,200	21,600	20,000

Exercise 17–2
Reporting percentage changes
(LO 2)

Where possible, calculate percentages of increase and decrease for the following:

	19X2	19X1
Short-term investments	$145,200	$110,000
Accounts receivable	28,080	32,000
Notes payable	38,000	–0–

Exercise 17–3
Calculating common-size percentages
(LO 2)

Express the following income statement information in common-size percentages and assess whether the situation is favorable or unfavorable:

CLEARWATER CORPORATION
Comparative Income Statement
For Years Ended December 31, 19X2, and 19X1

	19X2	19X1
Sales	$960,000	$735,000
Cost of goods sold	576,000	382,200
Gross profit from sales	$384,000	$352,800
Operating expenses	216,000	148,470
Net income	$168,000	$204,330

Exercise 17–4
Evaluating short-term liquidity
(LO 3)

TGA Company's December 31 balance sheets included the following data:

	19X3	19X2	19X1
Cash	$ 61,600	$ 71,250	$ 73,600
Accounts receivable, net	177,000	125,000	98,400
Merchandise inventory	223,000	165,000	106,000
Prepaid expenses	19,400	18,750	8,000
Plant assets, net	555,000	510,000	459,000
Total assets	$1,036,000	$890,000	$745,000
Accounts payable	$ 257,800	$150,500	$ 98,500
Long-term notes payable secured by mortgages on plant assets	195,000	205,000	165,000
Common stock, $10 par value	325,000	325,000	325,000
Retained earnings	258,200	209,500	156,500
Total liabilities and stockholders' equity	$1,036,000	$890,000	$745,000

Required

Compare the short-term liquidity positions of the company at the end of 19X3, 19X2, and 19X1 by calculating: (*a*) the current ratio and (*b*) the acid-test ratio. Comment on any changes that occurred.

Refer to the information in Exercise 17–4 about TGA Company. The company's income statements for the years ended December 31, 19X3, and 19X2 included the following data:

Exercise 17–5
Evaluating short-term liquidity
(LO 3)

	19X3	19X2
Sales	$1,345,000	$1,060,000
Cost of goods sold	$ 820,450	$ 689,000
Other operating expenses	417,100	267,960
Interest expense	22,200	24,600
Income taxes	17,050	15,690
Total costs and expenses	$1,276,800	$ 997,250
Net income	$ 68,200	$ 62,750
Earnings per share	$ 2.10	$ 1.93

Required

For the years ended December 31, 19X3, and 19X2, assume all sales were on credit and calculate the following: (*a*) days' sales uncollected, (*b*) accounts receivable turnover, (*c*) merchandise turnover, and (*d*) days' stock on hand. Comment on any changes that occurred from 19X2 to 19X3.

Refer to the information in Exercises 17–4 and 17–5 about TGA Company. Compare the long-term risk and capital structure positions of the company at the end of 19X3 and 19X2 by calculating the following ratios: (*a*) debt and equity ratios, (*b*) pledged assets to secured liabilities, and (*c*) times fixed interest charges earned. Comment on any changes that occurred.

Exercise 17–6
Evaluating long-term risk and capital structure
(LO 3)

Refer to the financial statements of TGA Company presented in Exercises 17–4 and 17–5. Evaluate the operating efficiency and profitability of the company by calculating the following: (*a*) profit margin, (*b*) total asset turnover, and (*c*) return on total assets. Comment on any changes that occurred.

Exercise 17–7
Evaluating operating efficiency and profitability
(LO 3)

Refer to the financial statements of TGA Company presented in Exercises 17–4 and 17–5. This additional information about the company is known:

Exercise 17–8
Evaluating profitability
(LO 3)

Common stock market price, December 31, 19X3	$30.00
Common stock market price, December 31, 19X2	28.00
Annual cash dividends per share in 19X3	.60
Annual cash dividends per share in 19X2	.30

Required

To evaluate the profitability of the company, calculate the following for 19X3 and 19X2: (*a*) return on common stockholders' equity, (*b*) price earnings ratio on December 31, and (*c*) dividend yield.

Common-size and trend percentages for a company's sales, cost of goods sold, and expenses follow:

Exercise 17–9
Determining income effects from common-size and trend percentages
(LO 2)

	Common-Size Percentages			Trend Percentages		
	19X3	19X2	19X1	19X3	19X2	19X1
Sales	100.0%	100.0%	100.0%	106.5%	105.3%	100.0%
Cost of goods sold	64.5	63.0	60.2	104.1	102.3	100.0
Expenses	16.4	15.9	16.2	96.0	94.1	100.0

Required

Determine whether the company's net income increased, decreased, or remained unchanged during this three-year period.

PROBLEMS

Problem 17–1
Calculating ratios and percentages
(LO 2, 3)

The condensed statements of Stellar Company follow:

STELLAR COMPANY
Comparative Income Statement
For Years Ended December 31, 19X3, 19X2, and 19X1
($000)

	19X3	19X2	19X1
Sales	$148,000	$136,000	$118,000
Cost of goods sold	89,096	85,000	75,520
Gross profit from sales	$ 58,904	$ 51,000	$ 42,480
Selling expenses	$ 20,898	$ 18,768	$ 15,576
Administrative expenses	13,379	11,968	9,735
Total expenses	$ 34,277	$ 30,736	$ 25,311
Income before taxes	$ 24,627	$ 20,264	$ 17,169
State and federal income taxes	4,588	4,148	3,481
Net income	$ 20,039	$ 16,116	$ 13,688

STELLAR COMPANY
Comparative Balance Sheet
December 31, 19X3, 19X2, and 19X1
($000)

	19X3	19X2	19X1
Assets			
Current assets	$24,240	$18,962	$25,324
Long-term investments	–0–	250	1,860
Plant and equipment	45,000	48,000	28,500
Total assets	$69,240	$67,212	$55,684
Liabilities and Stockholders' Equity			
Current liabilities	$10,100	$ 9,980	$ 9,740
Common stock	36,000	36,000	27,000
Other contributed capital	4,500	4,500	3,000
Retained earnings	18,640	16,732	15,944
Total liabilities and stockholders' equity ..	$69,240	$67,212	$55,684

Required

Preparation component:

1. Calculate each year's current ratio.

CHECK FIGURE:
19X3, total assets, 124.34

2. Express the income statement data in common-size percentages.

3. Express the balance sheet data in trend percentages with 19X1 as the base year.

Analysis component:

4. Comment on any significant relationships revealed by the ratios and percentages.

Problem 17–2
Calculation and analysis of trend percentages
(LO 2)

The condensed comparative statements of Jasper Company follow:

JASPER COMPANY
Comparative Income Statement
For Years Ended December 31, 19X7–19X1
($000)

	19X7	19X6	19X5	19X4	19X3	19X2	19X1
Sales	$797	$698	$635	$582	$543	$505	$420
Cost of goods sold	573	466	401	351	326	305	250
Gross profit from sales	$224	$232	$234	$231	$217	$200	$170
Operating expenses	170	133	122	90	78	77	65
Net income	$ 54	$ 99	$112	$141	$139	$123	$105

JASPER COMPANY
Comparative Balance Sheet
December 31, 19X7–19X1
($000)

	19X7	19X6	19X5	19X4	19X3	19X2	19X1
Assets							
Cash	$ 34	$ 44	$ 46	$ 47	$ 49	$ 48	$ 50
Accounts receivable, net	240	252	228	175	154	146	102
Merchandise inventory	869	632	552	466	418	355	260
Other current assets	23	21	12	22	19	19	10
Long-term investments	0	0	0	68	68	68	68
Plant and equipment, net . . .	1,060	1,057	926	522	539	480	412
Total assets	$2,226	$2,006	$1,764	$1,300	$1,247	$1,116	$902
Liabilities and Equity							
Current liabilities	$ 560	$ 471	$ 309	$ 257	$ 223	$ 211	$136
Long-term liabilities	597	520	506	235	240	260	198
Common stock	500	500	500	420	420	320	320
Other contributed capital . . .	125	125	125	90	90	80	80
Retained earnings	444	390	324	298	274	245	168
Total liabilities and equity . .	$2,226	$2,006	$1,764	$1,300	$1,247	$1,116	$902

Required

Preparation component:

1. Calculate trend percentages for the items of the statements using 19X1 as the base year.

Analysis component:

2. Analyze and comment on the situation shown in the statements.

The 19X2 financial statements of Oltorf Corporation follow:

OLTORF CORPORATION
Income Statement
For Year Ended December 31, 19X2

Sales		$697,200
Cost of goods sold:		
Merchandise inventory, December 31, 19X1	$ 64,800	
Purchases	455,800	
Goods available for sale	$520,600	
Merchandise inventory, December 31, 19X2	62,300	
Cost of goods sold		458,300
Gross profit from sales		$238,900
Operating expenses		122,700
Operating income		$116,200
Interest expense		7,100
Income before taxes		$109,100
Income taxes		17,800
Net income		$ 91,300

CHECK FIGURE:
19X7 total assets, 246.8

Problem 17–3
Calculation of financial
statement ratios
(LO 3)

OLTORF CORPORATION
Balance Sheet
December 31, 19X2

Assets		Liabilities and Stockholders' Equity	
Cash	$ 18,000	Accounts payable	$ 32,600
Short-term investments	14,700	Accrued wages payable	4,200
Accounts receivable, net	55,800	Income taxes payable	4,800
Notes receivable (trade)	6,200	Long-term note payable,	
Merchandise inventory	62,300	secured by mortgage on	
Prepaid expenses	2,800	plant assets	125,000
Plant assets, net	306,300	Common stock, $1 par value .	180,000
		Retained earnings	119,500
		Total liabilities and	
Total assets	$466,100	stockholders' equity	$466,100

Assume that all sales were on credit. On the December 31, 19X1, balance sheet, the assets totaled $367,500, common stock was $180,000, and retained earnings were $86,700.

Required

Calculate the following: (*a*) current ratio, (*b*) acid-test ratio, (*c*) days' sales uncollected, (*d*) merchandise turnover, (*e*) days' stock on hand, (*f*) ratio of pledged assets to secured liabilities, (*g*) times fixed interest charges earned, (*h*) profit margin, (*i*) total asset turnover, (*j*) return on total assets, and (*k*) return on common stockholders' equity.

Problem 17–4
Comparative analysis of financial statement ratios
(LO 3)

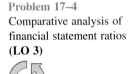

Two companies that compete in the same industry are being evaluated by a bank that can lend money to only one of them. Summary information from the financial statements of the two companies follows:

	Payless Company	Capital Company
Data from the current year-end balance sheets:		
Assets		
Cash	$ 37,400	$ 66,000
Accounts receivable	73,450	112,900
Notes receivable (trade)	16,200	13,100
Merchandise inventory	167,340	263,100
Prepaid expenses	8,000	11,900
Plant and equipment, net	568,900	606,400
Total assets	$ 871,290	$1,073,400
Liabilities and Stockholders' Equity:		
Current liabilities	$ 120,200	$ 184,600
Long-term notes payable	159,800	210,000
Common stock, $5 par value	350,000	410,000
Retained earnings	241,290	268,800
Total liabilities and stockholders' equity	$ 871,290	$1,073,400
Data from the current year's income statements:		
Sales	$1,325,000	$1,561,200
Cost of goods sold	970,500	1,065,000
Interest expense	14,400	23,000
Income tax expense	24,840	38,700
Net income	135,540	210,400
Beginning-of-year data:		
Accounts receivable, net	$ 57,800	$ 106,200
Notes receivable	–0–	–0–
Merchandise inventory	109,600	212,400
Total assets	776,400	745,100
Common stock, $5 par value	350,000	410,000
Retained earnings	189,300	181,200

Required

1. Calculate the current ratio, acid-test ratio, accounts (including notes) receivable turnover, merchandise turnover, days' stock on hand, and days' sales uncollected for the two companies. Then, identify the company that you consider to be the better short-term credit risk and explain why.

2. Calculate the profit margin, total asset turnover, return on total assets, and return on common stockholders' equity for the two companies. Assuming that each company paid cash dividends of $2.00 per share and each company's stock can be purchased at $25 per share, calculate their price earnings ratios and dividend yields. Also, identify which company's stock you would recommend as the better investment and explain why.

Metro Corporation began the month of March with $750,000 of current assets, a current ratio of 2.5 to 1, and an acid-test ratio of 1.1 to 1. During the month, it completed the following transactions:

Problem 17–5
Analysis of working capital
(LO 3)

Mar. 4 Bought $85,000 of merchandise on account. (The company uses a perpetual inventory system.)

10 Sold merchandise that cost $68,000 for $113,000.

12 Collected a $29,000 account receivable.

17 Paid a $31,000 account payable.

19 Wrote off a $13,000 bad debt against the Allowance for Doubtful Accounts account.

24 Declared a $1.25 per share cash dividend on the 40,000 shares of outstanding common stock.

28 Paid the dividend declared on March 24.

29 Borrowed $85,000 by giving the bank a 30-day, 10% note.

30 Borrowed $100,000 by signing a long-term secured note.

31 Used the $185,000 proceeds of the notes to buy additional machinery.

Required

Prepare a schedule showing Metro's current ratio, acid-test ratio, and working capital after each of the transactions. Round calculations to two decimal places.

CRITICAL THINKING: ESSAYS, PROBLEMS, AND CASES

Analytical Essays

Kerbey Company and Telcom Company are similar firms that operate within the same industry. The following information is available:

AE 17–1
(LO 3)

	Kerbey			Telcom		
	19X3	**19X2**	**19X1**	**19X3**	**19X2**	**19X1**
Current ratio	1.8	1.9	2.2	3.3	2.8	2.0
Acid-test ratio	1.1	1.2	1.3	2.9	2.6	1.7
Accounts receivable						
turnover	30.5	25.2	29.2	16.4	15.2	16.0
Merchandise turnover	24.2	21.9	17.1	14.5	13.0	12.6
Working capital	$65,000	$53,000	$47,000	$126,000	$98,000	$73,000

Required

Write a brief essay comparing Kerbey and Telcom based on the preceding information. Your discussion should include their relative ability to meet current obligations and to use current assets efficiently.

AE 17–2
(LO 3)

Snowden Company and Comet Company are similar firms that operate within the same industry. Comet began operations in 19X7 and Snowden in 19X1. In 19X9, both companies paid 7% interest to creditors. The following information is available:

	Snowden			Comet		
	19X9	**19X8**	**19X7**	**19X9**	**19X8**	**19X7**
Total asset turnover	3.3	3.0	3.2	1.9	1.7	1.4
Return on total assets ...	9.2	9.8	9.0	6.1	5.8	5.5
Profit margin	2.6	2.7	2.5	3.0	3.2	3.1
Sales	$800,000	$740,000	$772,000	$400,000	$320,000	$200,000

Required

Write a brief essay comparing Snowden and Comet based on the preceding information. Your discussion should include their relative ability to use assets efficiently to produce profits. Also comment on their relative success in employing financial leverage in 19X9.

Financial Statement Analysis Cases

FSAC 17–1
(LO 2, 3)

In your position as controller of Skinner Company, you are responsible for keeping the board of directors informed about the financial activities and status of the company. In preparing for the next board meeting, you have calculated the following ratios, turnovers, and percentages to enable you to answer questions:

	19X6	**19X5**	**19X4**
Sales trend	137.00	125.00	100.00
Selling expenses to net sales	9.8%	13.7%	15.3%
Sales to plant assets	3.5 to 1	3.3 to 1	3.0 to 1
Current ratio	2.6 to 1	2.4 to 1	2.1 to 1
Acid-test ratio	0.8 to 1	1.1 to 1	1.2 to 1
Merchandise turnover	7.5 times	8.7 times	9.9 times
Accounts receivable turnover	6.7 times	7.4 times	8.2 times
Total asset turnover	2.6 times	2.6 times	3.0 times
Return on total assets	8.8%	9.4%	10.1%
Return on stockholders' equity ...	9.75%	11.50%	12.25%
Profit margin	3.3%	3.5%	3.7%

Required

Using the preceding data, answer each of the following questions and explain your answers:

a. Is it becoming easier for the company to meet its current debts on time and to take advantage of cash discounts?

b. Is the company collecting its accounts receivable more rapidly?

c. Is the company's investment in accounts receivable decreasing?

d. Are dollars invested in inventory increasing?

e. Is the company's investment in plant assets increasing?

f. Is the stockholders' investment becoming more profitable?

g. Is the company using its assets efficiently?

h. Did the dollar amount of selling expenses decrease during the three-year period?

Refer to the 11-year financial history and the consolidated balance sheet contained in the financial statements of Apple Computer, Inc., in Appendix F, to answer the following questions:

a. Using 1991 as the base year, calculate trend percentages for 1991–1993 for the total net sales, total costs and expenses, operating income, and net income.

b. Calculate common-size percentages for 1993 and 1992 for the following categories of assets: total current assets; net property, plant, and equipment; and other assets.

c. Calculate the high and low price earnings ratio for 1993.

d. Calculate the dividend yield for 1993 using the high stock price for the year.

e. Calculate the debt and equity ratios for 1993.

ANSWERS TO PROGRESS CHECKS

17–1 General purpose financial statements are intended for the large variety of users who are interested in receiving financial information about a business but who do not have the ability to require the company to prepare specialized financial reports designed to meet their specific interests.

17–2 General purpose financial statements include the income statement, balance sheet, statement of changes in stockholders' equity (or statement of retained earnings), and statement of cash flows, plus footnotes related to the statements.

17–3 d

17–4 Percentages on a comparative income statement show the increase or decrease in each item from one period to the next. On a common-size comparative income statement, each item is shown as a percentage of net sales for a specific period.

17–5 c

17–6 (a) ($820,000 + $240,000 + $470,000)/($350,000 + $180,000) = 2.9 to 1
(b) ($820,000 + $240,000)/($350,000 + $180,000) = 2 to 1

17–7 (a) $2,500,000/[($290,000 + $240,000)/2] = 9.43 times
(b) ($240,000/$2,500,000) × 365 = 35 days
(c) $750,000/[($530,000 + $470,000)/2] = 1.5 times
(d) ($470,000/$750,000) × 365 = 228.7 days

17–8 c

17–9 b

17–10 Profit margin × Total asset turnover = Return on total assets ($945,000/$8,500,000) × 1.8 = 20%

17–11 a

17–12 The ratios and turnovers of a selected group of competing companies.

Payroll Reports, Records, and Procedures

After studying Appendix C, you should be able to:

1. Describe an employer's payroll reports and records, and the procedures used to calculate tax withholdings and issue checks to employees.
2. Define or explain the terms and phrases listed in the appendix glossary.

LEARNING OBJECTIVES

A typical feature of many small businesses that get into financial trouble is that they have failed to file required payroll reports. Understanding the importance of following appropriate payroll procedures and keeping adequate payroll records is essential to business success.

Payroll expenses involve liabilities to individual employees, to federal and state governments, and usually to other organizations such as insurance companies. In addition to paying these liabilities, employers are required to prepare and submit a variety of reports that explain how the payments were determined.

PAYROLL REPORTS

LO 1
Describe an employer's payroll reports and records, and the procedures used to calculate tax withholdings and issue checks to employees.

Reporting FICA Taxes and Income Tax Withholdings to the Federal Government

According to the Federal Insurance Contributions Act, each employer must file an Employer's Quarterly Federal Tax Return within one month after the end of each calendar quarter. (An example of this tax information return, known as Form 941, is shown in Illustration C–1.)

In Illustration C–1, notice that on line 2 of Form 941, an employer reports the total payments of wages subject to income tax withholding. The amount of income tax withheld is reported on lines 3 and 5. The combined amount of the employees' and employer's FICA (Social Security) taxes is reported on line 6a where it says, "Taxable social security wages" $34,370.50 \times 12.4\% =$ Tax, $4,261.94. The 12.4% is the sum of the (1995) 6.2% tax withheld from the employees' wages for the quarter plus the 6.2% tax levied on the employer. The combined amount of the employees' and employer's Medicare wages is reported on line 7. Total FICA taxes (Social Security plus Medicare) are reported on lines 8 and 10, and then are added to the total income taxes withheld. Finally, the total of the amounts deposited in a **federal depository bank** during the quarter is subtracted to determine if a balance remains to be paid. Federal depository banks are authorized to accept deposits of amounts payable to the federal government.

Deposit requirements depend on the amount of tax owed. If the sum of the FICA taxes plus the employees' income taxes is less than $500 for a quarter, the taxes may be paid when the Form 941 is filed. Companies with larger payrolls may have to pay monthly or semiweekly. If the taxes are $100,000 or more at the end of any day, they must be paid by the end of the next banking day.

Illustration C–1 Employer's Quarterly Report of Federal Taxes Withheld

Form **941**
(Rev. April 1994)
Department of the Treasury
Internal Revenue Service (O)

4141

Employer's Quarterly Federal Tax Return
▶ See separate instructions for information on completing this return.
Please type or print.

OMB No. 1545-0029

Enter state code for state in which deposits made ▶ (see page 2 of instructions).

Name (as distinguished from trade name)

Date quarter ended
Sept. 30, 1995

Trade name, if any
Graphic Planners, Inc.

Employer identification number
74-1633163

Address (number and street)
907 Falcon Trail

City, state, and ZIP code
Austin, TX 78746

T	
FF	
FD	
FP	
I	
T	

If address is different from prior return, check here ▶

IRS Use

1 1 1 1 1 1 1 1 1 1   2   3 3 3 3 3 3   4 4 4

5 5 5   6   7   8 8 8 8 8   9 9 9   10 10 10 10 10 10 10 10 10 10

If you do not have to file returns in the future, check here ▶ ☐ and enter date final wages paid ▶

If you are a seasonal employer, see **Seasonal employers** on page 2 and check here (see instructions) ▶ ☐

1	Number of employees (except household) employed in the pay period that includes March 12th ▶			
2	Total wages and tips subject to withholding, plus other compensation	**2**	34,370	50
3	Total income tax withheld from wages, tips, and sick pay	**3**	3,820	20
4	Adjustment of withheld income tax for preceding quarters of calendar year	**4**		
5	Adjusted total of income tax withheld (line 3 as adjusted by line 4—see instructions) . . .	**5**	3,820	20
6a	Taxable social security wages . . . . $ 34,370 50 × 12.4% (.124) =	**6a**	4,261	94
b	Taxable social security tips . . . . $ × 12.4% (.124) =	**6b**		
7	Taxable Medicare wages and tips . . . . . $ 34,370 50 × 2.9% (.029) =	**7**	996	74
8	Total social security and Medicare taxes (add lines 6a, 6b, and 7). Check here if wages are not subject to social security and/or Medicare tax . . . . ▶ ☐	**8**	5,258	68
9	Adjustment of social security and Medicare taxes (see instructions for required explanation) Sick Pay $ _____ ± Fractions of Cents $ _____ ± Other $ _____ =	**9**		
10	Adjusted total of social security and Medicare taxes (line 8 as adjusted by line 9—see instructions)	**10**	5,258	68
11	**Total taxes** (add lines 5 and 10)	**11**	9,078	88
12	Advance earned income credit (EIC) payments made to employees, if any	**12**		
13	Net taxes (subtract line 12 from line 11). **This should equal line 17, column (d) below** (or line D of Schedule B (Form 941))	**13**	9,078	88
14	Total deposits for quarter, including overpayment applied from a prior quarter	**14**	9,078	88
15	**Balance due** (subtract line 14 from line 13). Pay to Internal Revenue Service	**15**	-0-	

16 **Overpayment,** if line 14 is more than line 13, enter excess here ▶ $ _____
and check if to be: ☐ Applied to next return **OR** ☐ Refunded.

- **All filers:** If line 13 is less than $500, you need not complete line 17 or Schedule B.
- **Semiweekly depositors:** Complete Schedule B and check here . . . . ▶ ☐
- **Monthly depositors:** Complete line 17, columns (a) through (d) and check here . . . . ▶ ☒

17	**Monthly Summary of Federal Tax Liability.**		
(a) First month liability	**(b)** Second month liability	**(c)** Third month liability	**(d)** Total liability for quarter
3,026.29	3,026.29	3,026.30	9,078.88

Sign Here

Under penalties of perjury, I declare that I have examined this return, including accompanying schedules and statements, and to the best of my knowledge and belief, it is true, correct, and complete.

Signature ▶

Print Your Name and Title ▶ **President**

Date ▶ Oct. 25, 1995

For Paperwork Reduction Act Notice, see page 1 of separate instructions.   Cat. No. 17001Z   Form **941** (Rev. 4-94)

*U.S. Government Printing Office: 1995 — 387-095/00360

Illustration C–2 Reporting an Employee's Annual Wages and Taxes

a Control number		OMB No. 1545-0008	
b Employer's identification number 74-1633163		**1** Wages, tips, other compensation 24,560.60	**2** Federal income tax withheld 2,460.00
c Employer's name, address, and ZIP code Graphic Planners, Inc 907 Falcon Trail Austin, TX 78746		**3** Social security wages 24,560.60	**4** Social security tax withheld 1,522.76
		5 Medicare wages and tips 24,560.60	**6** Medicare tax withheld 356.13
		7 Social security tips	**8** Allocated tips
d Employee's social security number 302-02-0222		**9** Advance EIC payment	**10** Dependent care benefits
e Employee's name, address, and ZIP code Charles Robert Lusk 1310 East 5th Street Austin, TX 78711		**11** Nonqualified plans	**12** Benefits included in box 1
		13 See Instrs. for box 13	**14** Other

15 Statutory employee	Deceased	Pension plan	Legal rep.	942 emp.	Subtotal	Deferred compensation
☐	☐	☐	☐	☐	☐	☐

16 State	Employer's state I.D. No.	17 State wages, tips, etc.	18 State income tax	19 Locality name	20 Local wages, tips, etc.	21 Local income tax

Department of the Treasury—Internal Revenue Service

Form W-2 **Wage and Tax Statement** **1994**   This information is being furnished to the Internal Revenue Service.

Copy B To Be Filed With Employee's FEDERAL Tax Return

Reporting FUTA Taxes and SUTA Taxes

An employer's federal unemployment taxes are reported on an annual basis. The report is filed on an Annual Federal Unemployment Tax Return, Form 940. It must be mailed on or before January 31 following the end of each tax year. (Ten additional days are allowed for filing if all required tax deposits are made on a timely basis and the full amount of the tax is paid on or before January 31.) Payments of FUTA taxes are made quarterly to a federal depository bank if the total amount due exceeds $100. If $100 or less is due, the taxes are remitted annually with the Form 940.

Requirements for the payment and reporting of state unemployment taxes vary depending on the laws of the state. A requirement of quarterly payments and quarterly reports is typical.

Reporting Wages to Employees

Employers are required to provide each employee an annual report of the employee's wages subject to FICA and federal income taxes and the amounts of such taxes withheld. The report, a Wage and Tax Statement or Form W-2, must be given to the

Illustration C–3 A Payroll Register

				Daily Time					Total Hours	O.T. Hours	Reg- ular Pay Rate	Reg- ular Pay	O.T. Pre- mium Pay	Gross Pay
														Payroll Week Ended
													Earnings	
Employees	Clock Card No.	M	T	W	T	F	S	S						
Robert Austin	114	8	8	8	8	8			40		10.00	400.00		400.00
Judy Cross	102	8	8	8	8	8			40		15.00	600.00		600.00
John Cruz	108	0	8	8	8	8	8		40		14.00	560.00		560.00
Kay Keife	109	8	8	8	8	8	8		48	8	14.00	672.00	56.00	728.00
Lee Miller	112	8	8	8	8	0			32		14.00	448.00		448.00
Dale Sears	103	8	8	8	8	8	4		44	4	15.00	660.00	30.00	690.00
Totals												3,340.00	86.00	3,426.00

employee before January 31 following the year covered by the report. (Illustration C–2 shows an example of a Form W-2.)

Copies of the W-2 Forms must also be sent to the Social Security Administration, which posts to each employee's Social Security account the amount of the employee's wages subject to FICA tax and the FICA tax withheld. These posted amounts become the basis for determining the employee's retirement and survivors' benefits. The Social Security Administration also transmits to the Internal Revenue Service the amount of each employee's wages subject to federal income tax and the amount of such tax withheld.

PAYROLL RECORDS MAINTAINED BY EMPLOYERS

In addition to reports and payment of taxes, all employers must maintain certain payroll records. These generally include a **Payroll Register** for each pay period showing the pay period dates and the hours worked, gross pay, deductions, and net pay of each employee. An individual earnings record for each employee is also required.

The Payroll Register

Illustration C–3 shows a typical Payroll Register for a weekly pay period. Note that the columns under the heading Daily Time show the hours worked each day by each employee. If hours worked include overtime hours, these are entered in the column headed O.T. Hours.

The Regular Pay Rate column shows the hourly pay rate of each employee. Total hours worked multiplied by the regular pay rate equals regular pay. Overtime hours multiplied by the overtime premium rate equals overtime premium pay. Note that the overtime premium rate in this case is 50%. If employers are engaged in interstate commerce, federal law sets the minimum wage and overtime rate that must be paid to employees. In 1995, the minimum wage was $4.25 per hour. Also, the minimum overtime premium was 50% of the regular rate for hours worked in excess of 40 during any week. In other words, workers must earn at least 150% of their regular rate for hours in excess of 40 per week.

In Illustration C–3, notice the separate columns for each type of payroll deduction and for the expense accounts to which the payroll cost should be charged. As a result, the Payroll Register contains all of the data necessary to record the payroll in the General Journal.

March 23, 19___

	Deductions					Payment		Distribution	
FICA Taxes		Federal Income Taxes	Hosp. Ins.	Union Dues	Total Deductions	Net Pay	Check No.	Sales Salaries	Office Salaries
Medicare	Social Security								
5.80	24.80	37.00	40.00		107.60	292.40	893		400.00
8.70	37.20	93.00	56.00	10.00	204.90	395.10	894	600.00	
8.12	34.72	82.00	56.00	10.00	190.84	369.16	895	560.00	
10.56	45.14	127.00	56.00	10.00	248.70	479.30	896	728.00	
6.50	27.78	53.00	56.00	10.00	153.28	294.72	897	448.00	
10.00	42.78	118.00	56.00		226.78	463.22	898		690.00
49.68	212.42	510.00	320.00	40.00	1,132.10	2,293.90		2,336.00	1,090.00

Employee's Individual Earnings Record

An **Employee's Individual Earnings Record,** as shown in Illustration C–4, provides a full year's summary of an employee's working time, gross earnings, deductions, and net pay. In addition, it accumulates information that indicates when an employee's earnings have reached the tax-exempt points for FICA and state and federal unemployment taxes. It also supplies the data the employer needs to prepare the Wage and Tax Statement, Form W-2. The payroll information on an Employee's Individual Earnings Record is taken from the Payroll Register.

CALCULATING FEDERAL INCOME TAX WITHHOLDINGS

The amount of tax to be withheld from each employee's wages is determined by the amount of the wages earned and the number of the employee's personal **withholding allowances.** Each employee indicates the number of withholding allowances claimed on a withholding allowance certificate (Form W-4) and gives it to the employer. As the number of withholding allowances claimed increases, the amount of income tax to be withheld decreases.

Most employers use a **wage bracket withholding table** similar to the one shown in Illustration C–5 to determine the federal income taxes to be withheld from each employee's gross pay. The illustrated table is for single employees who are paid weekly. Different tables are provided for married employees and for biweekly, semimonthly, and monthly pay periods.

When using the tables to determine the federal income tax to be withheld from an employee's gross wages, locate the employee's wage bracket in the first two columns of the appropriate withholding table. Then, find the amount to be withheld by looking in the withholding allowance column appropriate for the employee.

PAYING THE EMPLOYEES

In a company that has few employees, employees are paid with checks drawn on the regular bank account. A business with many employees normally uses a special **payroll bank account** to pay its employees. When such an account is used, one check for the total payroll is drawn on the regular bank account and deposited in the special payroll bank account. The entry to record this transaction is:

Mar.	23	Accrued Payroll Payable	2,293.90	
		Cash		2,293.90
		Transfer of cash to payroll bank account.		

Illustration C-4 Employee's Individual Earnings Record

Employee's Name	Robert Austin			S.S. Acct. No. 307-03-2195					Employee No. 114			
Home Address	111 South Greenwood			Notify in Case of Emergency	Margaret Austin				Phone No. 964-9834			
Employed	June 7, 1980			Date of Termination					Reason			
Date of Birth	June 6, 1962		Date Becomes 65	June 6, 2027	Male (X) Female ( )	Married (X) Single ( )	Number of Exemptions 1		Pay Rate $10.00			
Occupation	Clerk					Place			Office			

| Date | | Time Lost | | Time Worked | | Reg. Pay | O.T. Prem. Pay | Gross Pay | FICA Taxes | | Fed. Income Taxes | Hosp. Ins. | Total Deduc-tions | Net Pay | Check No. | Cumu-lative Pay |
Per. Ends	Paid	Hrs.	Rea-son	Total	O.T. Hours				Medi-care	Soc. Secur-ity						
1/5	1/5			40		400.00		400.00	5.80	24.80	50.00	40.00	120.60	279.40	173	400.00
1/12	1/12			40		400.00		400.00	5.80	24.80	50.00	40.00	120.60	279.40	201	800.00
1/19	1/19			40		400.00		400.00	5.80	24.80	50.00	40.00	120.60	279.40	243	1,200.00
1/26	1/26	4	Sick	36		360.00		360.00	5.22	22.32	43.00	40.00	110.54	249.46	295	1,560.00
2/2	2/2			40		400.00		400.00	5.80	24.80	50.00	40.00	120.60	279.40	339	1,960.00
2/9	2/9			40		400.00		400.00	5.80	24.80	50.00	40.00	120.60	279.40	354	2,360.00
2/16	2/16			40		400.00		400.00	5.80	24.80	50.00	40.00	120.60	279.40	397	2,760.00
2/23	2/23			40		400.00		400.00	5.80	24.80	50.00	40.00	120.60	279.40	446	3,160.00
3/23	3/23			40		400.00		400.00	5.80	24.80	50.00	40.00	120.60	279.40	893	4,760.00

Then, individual payroll checks are drawn on the payroll bank account. Because only one check for the payroll total is drawn on the regular bank account each payday, use of a special payroll bank account simplifies internal control, especially the reconciliation of the regular bank account.

When companies use a payroll bank account, they often add a Check Number column to the Payroll Register. In this column, they enter the number of each employee's check. For example, look at Illustration C–3 and notice that check 893 was issued to Robert Austin. With this additional column, the Payroll Register serves as a permanent supplementary record of the wages earned by and paid to employees.

Progress Check

C–1 Which of the following steps must be completed when a company uses a special payroll bank account?
   a. Record the information shown on the Payroll Register with a general journal entry.
   b. Write a check to the payroll bank account for the total amount of the payroll and record it with a debit to Accrued Payroll Payable and a credit to Cash.
   c. Deposit a check for the total amount of the payroll in the payroll bank account.
   d. Write individual payroll checks to be drawn on the payroll bank account.
   e. All of the above.

C–2 What determines the amount that must be deducted from an employee's wages for federal income taxes?

C–3 What amount of income tax should be withheld from the salary of a single employee who has three withholding allowances and earned $675 in a week? (Use the wage bracket withholding table in Illustration C–5 to find the answer.)

Illustration C–5   A Wage Bracket Withholding Table

SINGLE Persons—WEEKLY Payroll Period
(For Wages Paid in 1995)

| If the wages are— | | And the number of withholding allowances claimed is— | | | | | | | | | | |
At least	But less than	0	1	2	3	4	5	6	7	8	9	10
		The amount of income tax to be withheld is—										
$600	$610	100	87	73	62	54	47	40	33	26	18	11
610	620	103	89	76	63	56	49	41	34	27	20	13
620	630	106	92	79	65	57	50	43	36	29	21	14
630	640	108	95	82	68	59	52	44	37	30	23	16
640	650	111	98	84	71	60	53	46	39	32	24	17
650	660	114	101	87	74	62	55	47	40	33	26	19
660	670	117	103	90	76	63	56	49	42	35	27	20
670	680	120	106	93	79	66	58	50	43	36	29	22
680	690	122	109	96	82	69	59	52	45	38	30	23
690	700	125	112	98	85	71	61	53	46	39	32	25
700	710	128	115	101	88	74	62	55	48	41	33	26
710	720	131	117	104	90	77	64	56	49	42	35	28
720	730	134	120	107	93	80	66	58	51	44	36	29
730	740	136	123	110	96	83	69	59	52	45	38	31
740	750	139	126	112	99	85	72	61	54	47	39	32
750	760	142	129	115	102	88	75	62	55	48	41	34
760	770	145	131	118	104	91	78	64	57	50	42	35
770	780	148	134	121	107	94	80	67	58	51	44	37
780	790	150	137	124	110	97	83	70	60	53	45	38
790	800	153	140	126	113	99	86	72	61	54	47	40
800	810	156	143	129	116	102	89	75	63	56	48	41
810	820	159	145	132	118	105	92	78	65	57	50	43
820	830	162	148	135	121	108	94	81	67	59	51	44
830	840	164	151	138	124	111	97	84	70	60	53	46
840	850	167	154	140	127	113	100	86	73	62	54	47
850	860	170	157	143	130	116	103	89	76	63	56	49
860	870	173	159	146	132	119	106	92	79	65	57	50
870	880	176	162	149	135	122	108	95	81	68	59	52
880	890	178	165	152	138	125	111	98	84	71	60	53
890	900	181	168	154	141	127	114	100	87	74	62	55

LO 1. Describe an employer's payroll reports and records, and the procedures used to calculate tax withholdings and issue checks to employees. Employers report FICA taxes and federal income tax withholdings quarterly on Form 941. FUTA taxes are reported annually on Form 940. Annual earnings and deduction information are reported to each employee and to the federal government on Form W-2. An employer's payroll records include a Payroll Register for each pay period and an Employee's Individual Earnings Record for each employee.

Federal income tax withholdings depend on the employee's earnings and the number of withholding allowances claimed by the employee. Various wage bracket withholding tables are available for pay periods of different lengths and for several classes of employees such as single or married.

Employers with a large number of employees often use a separate payroll bank account. When this is done, the payment of employees is recorded with a single credit to Cash. This entry records the transfer of cash from the regular checking account to the payroll checking account.

SUMMARY OF THE APPENDIX IN TERMS OF LEARNING OBJECTIVE

GLOSSARY

Employee's Individual Earnings Record a record of an employee's hours worked, gross pay, deductions, net pay, and certain personal information about the employee. p. AP–5

Federal depository bank a bank authorized to accept deposits of amounts payable to the federal government. p. AP–1

Payroll bank account a special bank account a company uses solely for the purpose of paying employees, by depositing in the account each pay period an amount equal to the total employees' net pay and drawing the employees' payroll checks on that account. p. AP–5

Payroll Register a record for a pay period that shows the pay period dates and the hours worked, gross pay, deductions, and net pay of each employee. p. AP–4

Wage bracket withholding table a table that shows the amounts of income tax to be withheld from employees' wages at various levels of earnings. p. AP–5

Withholding allowance a number that is used to reduce the amount of federal income tax withheld from an employee's pay. p. AP–5

EXERCISE

Exercise C–1
Calculating gross and net pay
(LO 1)

Nancy Bode, an unmarried employee of a company subject to the Fair Labor Standards Act, worked 48 hours during the week ended January 12. Her pay rate is $16 per hour, and her wages are subject to no deductions other than FICA and federal income taxes. She claims two withholding allowances. Calculate her regular pay, overtime premium pay, gross pay, FICA tax deduction at an assumed rate of 6.2% for the Social Security portion and 1.45% for the Medicare portion, income tax deduction (use the wage bracket withholding table of Illustration C–5), total deductions, and net pay.

PROBLEMS

Problem C–1
General journal entries for payroll transactions
(LO 1)

Vaughn Company has 10 employees, each of whom earns $2,600 per month and is paid on the last day of each month. All 10 have been employed continuously at this amount since January 1. Vaughn uses a payroll bank account and special payroll checks to pay its employees. On March 1, the following accounts and balances appeared in its ledger:

a. FICA Taxes Payable, $3,978. (The balance of this account represents the liability for both the employer's and employees' FICA taxes for the February payroll only.)
b. Employees' Federal Income Taxes Payable, $3,900 (liability for February only).
c. Federal Unemployment Taxes Payable, $416 (liability for January and February together).
d. State Unemployment Taxes Payable, $2,080 (liability for January and February together).

During March and April, the company had the following payroll transactions:

Mar. 15   Issued check payable to Union Bank, a federal depository bank authorized to accept employers' payments of FICA taxes and employee income tax withholdings. The $7,878 check was in payment of the February FICA and employee income taxes.

       31   Prepared general journal entries to record the March Payroll Record, which had the following column totals, and to transfer the funds from the regular bank account to the payroll bank account:

Office Salaries	Shop Wages	Gross Pay	FICA Taxes	Federal Income Taxes	Total Deductions	Net Pay
$10,400	$15,600	$26,000	$1,989	$3,900	$5,889	$20,111

       31   Issued checks payable to each employee in payment of the March payroll.

Mar. 31 Prepared a general journal entry to record the employer's payroll taxes resulting from the March payroll. The company has a merit rating that reduces its state unemployment tax rate to 4.0% of the first $7,000 paid each employee. The federal rate is 0.8%.

Apr. 15 Issued check payable to Union Bank in payment of the March FICA and employee income taxes.

15 Issued check to the State Tax Commission for the January, February, and March state unemployment taxes. Mailed the check along with the second quarter tax return to the State Tax Commission.

30 Issued check payable to Union Bank. The check was in payment of the employer's federal unemployment taxes for the second quarter of the year.

30 Mailed Form 941 to the IRS, reporting the FICA taxes and the employees' federal income tax withholdings for the second quarter.

Required

Prepare general journal entries to record the transactions.

ANSWERS TO PROGRESS CHECKS

C–1 *e*

C–2 An employee's gross earnings and the number of withholding allowances the employee claims determine the amount that must be deducted for federal income taxes.

C–3 $79

Accounting Principles, the FASB's Conceptual Framework, and Alternative Valuation Methods

LEARNING OBJECTIVES

After studying Appendix D, you should be able to:

1. Explain the difference between descriptive concepts and prescriptive concepts, and the difference between bottom-up and top-down approaches to the development of accounting concepts.
2. Describe the major components in the FASB's conceptual framework.
3. Explain why conventional financial statements fail to adequately account for price changes.
4. Use a price index to restate historical cost/nominal dollar costs into constant purchasing power amounts and to calculate purchasing power gains and losses.
5. Explain the current cost approach to valuation, including its effects on the income statement and balance sheet.
6. Explain the current selling price approach to valuation.
7. Define or explain the words and phrases listed in the appendix glossary.

Accounting principles or concepts are not laws of nature. They are broad ideas developed as a way of *describing* current accounting practices and *prescribing* new and improved practices. In studying Appendix D, you will learn about some new accounting concepts that the FASB developed in an effort to guide future changes and improvements in accounting. You also will learn about some major alternatives to the historical cost measurements reported in conventional financial statements. Studying these alternatives will help you understand the nature of the information that is contained in conventional statements. In addition, it will help you grasp the meaning of new reporting practices that may occur in future years.

ACCOUNTING PRINCIPLES AND THE FASB'S CONCEPTUAL FRAMEWORK

DESCRIPTIVE AND PRESCRIPTIVE ACCOUNTING CONCEPTS

To fully understand the importance of financial accounting concepts or principles, you must realize that they serve two purposes. First, they provide general descriptions of existing accounting practices. In doing this, concepts and principles serve as guidelines that help you learn about accounting. Thus, after learning how the concepts or principles are applied in a few situations, you develop the ability to apply them in different situations. This is easier and more effective than memorizing a very long list of specific practices.

Second, these concepts or principles help accountants analyze unfamiliar situations and develop procedures to account for those situations. This purpose is especially important for the Financial Accounting Standards Board (FASB), which is charged with developing uniform practices for financial reporting in the United States and with improving the quality of such reporting.

In prior chapters, we defined and illustrated several important accounting principles. These principles, which follow, describe in general terms the practices currently used by accountants.

(LO 1)

Explain the difference between descriptive concepts and prescriptive concepts, and the difference between bottom-up and top-down approaches to the development of accounting concepts.

Generally Accepted Principles

Business entity principle	Full-disclosure principle	Objectivity principle
Conservatism principle	Going-concern principle	Revenue recognition
Consistency principle	Matching principle	principle
Cost principle	Materiality principle	Time period principle

To help you learn accounting, we introduced these principles in Chapter 1 (p. 25) and have referred to them frequently in later chapters. Although these ideas are labeled *principles,* in this discussion we use the term *concepts* to include both these principles as well as other general rules developed by the FASB. The FASB also uses the word *concepts* in this general manner.

The preceding concepts are useful for teaching and learning about accounting practice and are helpful for dealing with some unfamiliar transactions. As business practices have evolved in recent years, however, these concepts have become less useful as guides for accountants to follow in dealing with new and different types of transactions. This problem has occurred because the concepts are intended to provide general descriptions of current accounting practices. In other words, they describe what accountants currently do; they do not necessarily describe what accountants should do. Also, since these concepts do not identify weaknesses in accounting practices, they do not lead to major changes or improvements in accounting practices.

Because the FASB is charged with improving financial reporting, its first members decided that a new set of concepts should be developed. They also decided that the new set of concepts should not merely *describe* what was being done under current practice. Instead, the new concepts should *prescribe* what ought to be done to make things better. The project to develop a new set of prescriptive concepts was initiated in 1973 and quickly became known as the FASB's *conceptual framework project.*

However, before we examine the concepts developed by the FASB, we need to look more closely at the differences between descriptive and prescriptive uses of accounting concepts.

THE PROCESSES OF DEVELOPING DESCRIPTIVE AND PRESCRIPTIVE ACCOUNTING CONCEPTS

Sets of concepts differ in how they are developed and used. In general, when concepts are intended to describe current practice, they are developed by looking at accepted specific practices and then making some general rules to encompass them. This bottom-up approach is diagrammed in Illustration D–1 that shows the arrows going from the practices to the concepts. The outcome of the process is a set of general rules that summarize practice and that can be used for education and for solving some new problems. For example, this approach leads to the concept that asset purchases are recorded at cost. However, these kinds of concepts often fail to show how new problems should be solved. To continue the example, the concept that assets are recorded at cost does not provide much direct guidance for situations in which assets have no cost because they are donated to a company by a local government. Further, because

Illustration D-1 A Bottom-Up
Process of Developing
Descriptive Accounting
Concepts

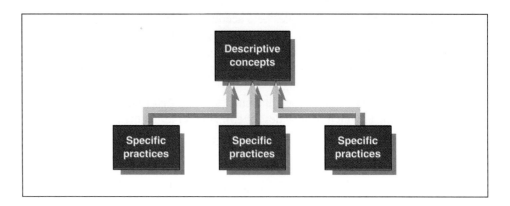

these concepts are based on the presumption that current practices are adequate, they do not lead to the development of new and improved accounting methods. To continue the example, the concept that assets are initially recorded at cost does not encourage asking the question of whether they should always be carried at that amount.

In contrast, if concepts are intended to *prescribe* improvements in accounting practices, they are likely to be designed by a top-down approach (Illustration D–2). Note that the top-down approach starts with broad accounting objectives. The process then generates broad concepts about the types of information that should be reported. Finally, these concepts should lead to specific practices that ought to be used. The advantage of this approach is that the concepts are good for solving new problems and evaluating old answers; its disadvantage is that the concepts may not be very descriptive of current practice. In fact, the suggested practices may not be in current use.

Since the FASB uses accounting concepts to prescribe accounting practices, the Board used a top-down approach to develop its conceptual framework. The Board's concepts are not necessarily more correct than the previously developed concepts. However, the new concepts are intended to provide better guidelines for developing new and improved accounting practices. The Board has stated that it will use them as a basis for its future actions and already has used them to justify important changes in financial reporting.

Progress Check

D–1 The FASB's conceptual framework is intended to:
   a. Provide a historical analysis of accounting practice.
   b. Describe current accounting practice.
   c. Provide concepts that are prescriptive of what should be done in accounting practice.

D–2 What is the starting point in a top-down approach to developing accounting concepts?

D–3 What is the starting point in a bottom-up approach to developing accounting concepts?

THE FASB'S CONCEPTUAL FRAMEWORK

(LO 2)

Describe the major components in the FASB's conceptual framework.

The FASB's approach to developing its conceptual framework is diagrammed in Illustration D–3. Between 1978 and 1985, the Board issued six *Statements of Financial Accounting Concepts (SFAC)*. These concepts statements are not the same as the FASB's *Statements of Financial Accounting Standards (SFAS)*. The *SFAS*s are authoritative statements of generally accepted accounting principles that must be followed. The *SFAC*s are guidelines the Board uses in developing new standards. Accountants are not required to follow the *SFAC*s in practice.

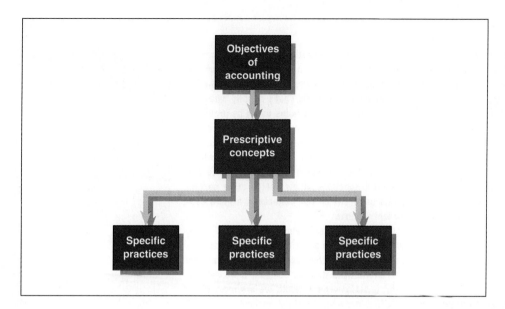

The Objectives of Financial Reporting

The FASB's first *Statement of Financial Accounting Concepts (SFAC 1)* identified the broad objectives of financial reporting (Illustration D–3). The first and most general objective stated in *SFAC 1* is to "provide information that is useful to present and potential investors and creditors and other users in making rational investment, credit, and similar decisions."[1] From this beginning point in *SFAC 1,* the Board expressed other more specific objectives. These objectives recognize (1) that financial reporting should help users predict future cash flows, and (2) that information about a company's resources and obligations is useful in making such predictions. All the concepts in the conceptual framework are intended to be consistent with these general objectives. Of course, present accounting practice already provides information about a company's resources and obligations. Thus, although the conceptual framework is intended to be prescriptive of new and improved practices, the concepts in the framework also are descriptive of many current practices.

The Qualities of Useful Information

Illustration D–3 shows that the next step in the conceptual framework project was to identify the qualities (or qualitative characteristics) that financial information should have if it is to be useful in decision making. The Board discussed the fact that information can be useful only if it is understandable to users. However, the users are assumed to have the training, experience, and motivation to analyze financial reports. With this decision, the Board indicated that financial reporting should not try to meet the needs of unsophisticated or other casual report users.

In *SFAC 2,* the FASB said that information is useful if it is (1) relevant, (2) reliable, and (3) comparable. Information is *relevant* if it can make a difference in a decision. Information has this quality when it helps users predict the future or evaluate the past, and when it is received in time to affect their decisions.

---

[1]FASB, *Statement of Financial Accounting Concepts No. 1,* "Objectives of Financial Reporting by Business Enterprises" (Norwalk, CT, 1978), par. 34.

As a Matter of Opinion

Mr. Beresford graduated from the University of Southern California in 1961 with a B.A. degree in accounting. After working 10 years in the Los Angeles office of Ernst & Ernst (now Ernst & Young), he was assigned to that firm's national office and made a partner. In 1987, he was appointed to the Financial Accounting Standards Board and named as its chairman. In 1991, he was reappointed for a second term, which will expire in 1997. Among his honors is the designation as the Beta Alpha Psi "Accountant of the Year" for 1986.

When the conceptual framework was being created, some thought that it would provide immediate answers for standard-setting issues. However, it could never do that all by itself. Rather, the framework is a tool that helps the FASB do its job.

Because getting to right answers depends on asking the right questions, I've come to realize that perhaps the most critical part of the standard-setting process is identifying and stating the issues properly. That's exactly what the conceptual framework helps us do by providing us with common objectives and terms. In effect, the conceptual framework brings discipline to those who participate in the standard-setting process. This discipline helps the Board to ask the right questions. It also helps other participants comment on our projects in a more consistent manner.

Although all Board members might not agree which answer to a question is best, the odds are much higher that the best answer will be among the alternatives that we consider if we ask the right questions. As a result, we are more likely to ultimately adopt the best answer.

Dennis R. Beresford, C.P.A.

Information is *reliable* if users can depend on it to be free from bias and error. Reliable information is verifiable and faithfully represents what is supposed to be described. In addition, users can depend on information only if it is neutral. This means that the rules used to produce information should not be designed to lead users to accept or reject any specific decision alternative.

Information is *comparable* if users can use it to identify differences and similarities between companies. Comparability is possible only if companies follow uniform practices. However, even if all companies uniformly follow the same practices, comparable reports do not result if the practices are not appropriate. For example, comparable information would not be provided if all companies were to ignore the useful lives of their assets and depreciate all assets over two years.

Comparability also requires consistency (see Chapter 9, page 350), which means that a company should not change its accounting practices unless the change is justified as a reporting improvement. Another important concept discussed in *SFAC 2* is materiality (see Chapter 8, page 320).

Elements of Financial Statements

Illustration D–3 shows that another important step in developing the conceptual framework was to determine the elements of financial statements. This involved defining the categories of information that should be contained in financial reports. The Board's discussion of financial statement elements includes definitions of important elements such as assets, liabilities, equity, revenues, expenses, gains, and losses. In earlier chapters, we referred to many of these definitions when we explained various accounting procedures. The Board's pronouncement on financial statement elements was first published in 1980 as *SFAC 3*. In 1985, *SFAC 3* was replaced by *SFAC 6*, which modified the discussion of financial statement elements to include several elements for not-for-profit accounting entities.[2]

---

[2]Among the six *Statements of Financial Accounting Concepts* issued by the FASB, one *(SFAC 4)* is directed toward accounting by not-for-profit organizations. Although *SFAC 4* is important, it is beyond the scope of this course.

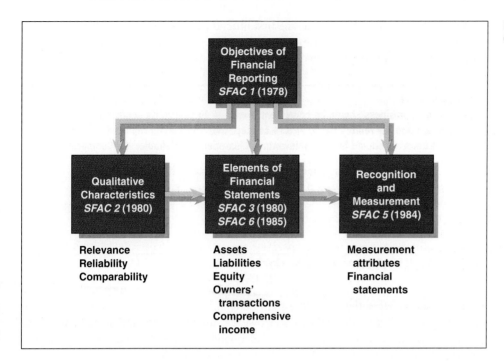

Recognition and Measurement

In *SFAC 5,* "Recognition and Measurement in Financial Statements of Business Enterprises," the FASB established concepts for deciding (1) when items should be presented (or recognized) in the financial statements, and (2) how to assign numbers to (or measure) those items. In general, the Board concluded that items should be recognized in the financial statements if they meet the following criteria:

- *Definitions.* The item meets the definition of an element of financial statements.
- *Measurability.* It has a relevant attribute measurable with sufficient reliability.
- *Relevance.* The information about it is capable of making a difference in user decisions.
- *Reliability.* The information is representationally faithful, verifiable, and neutral.

The question of how items should be measured raises the fundamental question of whether financial statements should be based on cost or on value. Since this question is quite controversial, the Board's discussion of this issue is more descriptive of current practice than it is prescriptive of new measurement methods.

In *SFAC 5,* the Board stated that a full set of financial statements should show:

1. Financial position at the end of the period.
2. Earnings for the period. (This concept is very similar to the concept of net income used in current practice.)
3. Comprehensive income for the period. (This new concept is broader than earnings and includes all changes in owner's equity other than those that resulted from transactions with the owners. Some changes in asset values are included in this concept but are excluded from earnings.)
4. Cash flows during the period.
5. Investments by and distributions to owners during the period.

We should note that *SFAC 5* was the first official pronouncement to call for the presentation of a statement of cash flows. The statement of cash flows is now required under *SFAS 95,* which was issued two years after *SFAC 5.*

Progress Check

D–4   That a business should be consistent from year to year in its accounting practices most directly relates to the FASB's concept that information reported in financial statements should be: *(a)* Relevant; *(b)* Material; *(c)* Reliable; *(d)* Comparable.

D–5   Which characteristics of accounting information make it reliable?

D–6   What is the meaning of the phrase *elements of financial statements?*

ALTERNATIVE ACCOUNTING VALUATION SYSTEMS

CONVENTIONAL FINANCIAL STATEMENTS FAIL TO ACCOUNT FOR PRICE CHANGES

(LO 3)

Explain why conventional financial statements fail to adequately account for price changes.

All accountants agree that conventional financial statements provide useful information for making economic decisions. However, many accountants also believe that conventional financial statements fail to adequately account for the impact of changing prices. Sometimes, this makes the statements misleading. That is, the statements may imply certain facts that are inconsistent with the real state of affairs. As a result, the information in the statements may lead decision makers to make decisions inconsistent with their objectives.

Failure to Account for Price Changes on the Balance Sheet

In what ways do conventional financial statements fail to account for changing prices? The general problem is that transactions are recorded in the historical number of dollars paid. Usually, these amounts are not adjusted even though subsequent price changes may dramatically change the value of the purchased items.[3] For example, Old Company purchased 10 acres of land for $25,000. Then, at the end of each accounting period, Old Company presented a balance sheet showing "Land . . . $25,000." Six years later, after price increases of 97%, New Company purchased 10 acres of land that was next to and nearly identical to Old Company's land. New Company paid $49,250 for the land. Comparing the conventional balance sheets of the two companies reveals the following balances:

	Old Company	New Company
Land	$25,000	$49,250

Without knowing the details that led to these balances, a statement reader is likely to conclude that either New Company has more land than Old Company or that New Company's land is more valuable. In reality, both companies own 10 acres that are of equal value. The entire difference between the prices paid by the two companies is explained by the 97% price increase between the two purchase dates. That is, $25,000 \times 1.97 = $49,250$.

---

[3]An exception to this general rule is the reporting of certain investments in debt and equity securities at their fair (market) values. This exception is explained in Chapters 8 and 11.

Failure to Account for Price Changes on the Income Statement

The failure of conventional financial statements to adequately account for changing prices also shows up in the income statement. For example, assume that in the previous example, the companies purchased machines instead of land. Also, assume that the machines of Old Company and New Company are identical except for age; both are being depreciated on a straight-line basis over a 10-year period with no salvage value. As a result, the annual income statements of the two companies show the following:

	Old Company	New Company
Depreciation expense, machinery	$2,500	$4,925

Although assets of equal value are being depreciated, the income statements show depreciation expense for New Company that is 97% higher than Old Company's. This is inconsistent with the fact that both companies own identical machines affected by the same depreciation factors. Furthermore, although Old Company appears more profitable, it must pay more income taxes due to the apparent extra profits. Also, if Old Company's selling prices are linked to its costs, it may not recover the full replacement cost of its machinery through the sale of its products.

There are three basic alternatives to the historical cost measurements presented in conventional financial statements without adjustment for changing prices. These alternatives are:

1. Historical costs adjusted for changes in the general price level.
2. Current replacement cost valuations.
3. Current selling price valuations.

We discuss each of these in the remaining sections of Appendix D.

VALUATION ALTERNATIVES TO CONVENTIONAL MEASUREMENTS OF COST

Progress Check

D-7   The following selected information is from the conventional balance sheets of A Company and B Company:

	A Company	B Company
Cash	$ 24,000	$ 40,000
Equipment, net	96,000	102,200
Land	130,000	157,800
Total assets	$250,000	$300,000

Based on this information, which of the following statements is true?
a. Company B's assets are worth $50,000 more than Company A's assets.
b. If Company A and Company B own identical tracts of land, Company B must have purchased its land at a later date than Company A.
c. The relative values of Company A's and Company B's assets cannot be determined from this conventional balance sheet information.

Illustration D–4 Expressing Costs in Constant Purchasing Power

Year Cost Was Incurred	Monetary Units Expended (a)	Price Index Factor for Adjustment to 19X2 Dollars (b)	Historical Cost Stated in 19X2 Dollars (a × b = c)	Price Index Factor for Adjustment to 19X7 Dollars (d)	Historical Cost Stated in 19X7 Dollars (c × d)
19X1	$1,000	100/92.5 = 1.08108	$1,081	168/100 = 1.68000	$1,816*
19X2	1,500		1,500	168/100 = 1.68000	2,520
Total cost	$2,500		$2,581		$4,336

*An alternative calculation is $1,000 × (168.0/92.5) = $1,816.

ADJUSTING HISTORICAL COSTS FOR GENERAL PRICE LEVEL CHANGES

(LO 4)

Use a price index to restate historical cost/nominal dollar costs into constant purchasing power amounts and to calculate purchasing power gains and losses.

One alternative to conventional financial statements is to restate dollar amounts of cost incurred in earlier years for changes in the general price level. In other words, a specific dollar amount of cost in a previous year can be restated as the number of dollars that would have been expended if the cost had been paid with dollars that have the current amount of purchasing power.

For example, assume the following general price index for December of 19X1 through 19X7:

Year	Price Index
19X1	92.5
19X2	100.0
19X3	109.5
19X4	123.7
19X5	135.0
19X6	150.0
19X7	168.0

Then, assume that a firm purchased assets for $1,000 in December 19X1 and for $1,500 in December 19X2. The 19X1 cost of $1,000 correctly states the number of monetary units (dollars) expended in 19X1. Also, the 19X2 cost of $1,500 correctly states the number of monetary units expended in 19X2. However, in a very important way, the 19X1 monetary units do not mean the same thing as the 19X2 monetary units. A dollar (one monetary unit) in 19X1 represents a different amount of purchasing power than a dollar in 19X2. Both of these dollars represent different amounts of purchasing power than a dollar in 19X7.

To communicate the total amount of purchasing power given up for the assets, the historical number of monetary units must be restated in dollars with the same amount of purchasing power. For example, the total amount of cost incurred during 19X1 and 19X2 may be stated in the purchasing power of 19X2 dollars, or stated in the purchasing power of 19X7 dollars. These calculations are presented in Illustration D–4.

Conventional financial statements disclose revenues, expenses, assets, liabilities, and owners' equity in the historical monetary units exchanged when the transactions occurred. As such, they are sometimes called **historical cost/nominal dollar financial statements.** This emphasizes the difference between conventional statements and historical cost/constant purchasing power statements. **Historical cost/constant purchasing power accounting** uses a general price index to restate the dollar amounts on conventional financial statements into amounts that represent current general purchasing power.

The same principles for determining depreciation expense, cost of goods sold, accruals of revenue, and so forth, apply to both historical cost/nominal dollar statements and historical cost/constant purchasing power statements. The same generally accepted accounting principles apply to both. The only difference between the two is that constant purchasing power statements reflect adjustments for general price level changes and nominal dollar statements do not.

The Impact of General Price Changes on Monetary Items

Some assets and liabilities are defined as monetary items. **Monetary assets** represent money or claims to receive a fixed amount of money. **Monetary liabilities** are obligations that are fixed in terms of the amount owed. The number of dollars to be received or paid does not change even though the purchasing power of the dollar may change. Examples of monetary items include cash, accounts receivable, accounts payable, and notes payable.

Because the amount of money that will be received or paid is fixed, a monetary item is not adjusted for general price level changes on a historical cost/constant purchasing power balance sheet. For example, assume that $800 in cash was owned at the end of 19X2. Regardless of how the price level has changed since the cash was acquired, the amount to be reported on the December 31, 19X2, historical cost/constant purchasing power balance sheet is $800.

Although monetary items are not adjusted on the balance sheet, they do involve special risks. When the general price level changes, monetary items create **purchasing power gains and losses.** Owning monetary assets during a period of inflation results in a loss of purchasing power. Owing monetary liabilities during a period of inflation results in a gain of purchasing power. During a period of deflation, the effects are just the opposite. Monetary assets result in purchasing power gains and monetary liabilities result in purchasing power losses.

For example, assume that a company has a cash balance of $800 on December 31, 19X2, which resulted from the following:

Cash balance, December 31, 19X1	$ 200
Cash receipts, assumed to have been received uniformly throughout the year	1,500
Cash disbursements, assumed to have been made uniformly throughout the year	(900)
Cash balance, December 31, 19X2	$ 800

Also assume that the general price index was 150.0 at the end of 19X1; that it averaged 160.0 throughout 19X3; and was 168.0 at the end of that year. As the price level increased throughout 19X2, the purchasing power of the cash declined. To calculate the loss during the year, the beginning cash balance and each receipt or disbursement must be adjusted for price changes to the end of the year. Then, the adjusted balance is compared with the actual balance to determine the loss. The calculation is as follows:

	Nominal Dollar Amounts	Price Index Factor for Restatement to December 31, 19X2	Restated to December 31, 19X2	Gain or (Loss)
Beginning balance	$ 200	168.0/150.0 = 1.12000	$ 224	
Receipts	1,500	168.0/160.0 = 1.05000	1,575	
Disbursements	(900)	168.0/160.0 = 1.05000	(945)	
Ending balance, adjusted			$ 854	
Ending balance, actual	$ 800		(800)	
Purchasing power loss				$(54)

Stated in terms of general purchasing power at year-end, the beginning cash balance plus receipts less disbursements was $854. Since the company has only $800 on hand, the $54 difference is a loss of general purchasing power.

In the preceding calculation, note that we adjusted the receipts and disbursements from the *average* price level during the year (160.0) to the ending price level (168.0). Because we assumed the receipts and disbursements occurred uniformly throughout the year, we used the average price level to approximate the price level at the time each receipt and disbursement took place. If receipts and disbursements do not occur uniformly, then we must separately adjust each receipt and each disbursement from the price level at the time of the receipt or disbursement to the price level at year-end.

The calculation of purchasing power gains and losses that result from owing monetary liabilities is the same as it is for monetary assets. Assume, for example, that a note payable for $300 was outstanding on December 31, 19X1, when the price index was 150.0. On April 5, 19X2, when the price index was 157.0, a $700 increase in the note resulted in a $1,000 balance that remained outstanding throughout the rest of 19X2. On December 31, 19X2, the price index was 168.0. On the historical cost/constant purchasing power balance sheet for December 31, 19X2, the note payable is reported at $1,000. The purchasing power gain or loss during 19X2 is calculated as follows:

	Nominal Dollar Amounts	Price Index Factor for Restatement to December 31, 19X2	Restated to December 31, 19X2	Gain or (Loss)
Beginning balance	$ 300	168.0/150.0 = 1.120	$ 336	
April 5 increase	700	168.0/157.0 = 1.070	749	
Ending balance, adjusted			$ 1,085	
Ending balance, actual	$1,000		(1,000)	
Purchasing power gain				$85

Stated in terms of general purchasing power at year-end, the amount borrowed was $1,085. Since the company can pay the note with $1,000, the $85 difference is a gain in general purchasing power earned by the firm.

To determine a company's total purchasing power gain or loss during a year, the accountant must analyze each monetary asset and each monetary liability. The final gain or loss is then described as the *purchasing power gain (or loss) on net monetary items owned or owed.*

The Impact of General Price Changes on Nonmonetary Items

Nonmonetary items include stockholders' equity and all assets and liabilities that are not fixed in terms of the number of monetary units to be received or paid. Land, equipment, intangible assets, and many product warranty liabilities are examples of non-

Illustration D–5 Reporting the Effects of Price Changes on Monetary and Nonmonetary Items

Financial Statement Item	When the General Price Level Rises (Inflation)		When the General Price Level Falls (Deflation)	
	Balance Sheet Adjustment Required	Income Statement Gain or Loss	Balance Sheet Adjustment Required	Income Statement Gain or Loss
Monetary assets	No	Loss	No	Gain
Nonmonetary assets	Yes	None	Yes	None
Monetary liabilities	No	Gain	No	Loss
Nonmonetary equities and liabilities	Yes	None	Yes	None

monetary items. The prices of **nonmonetary assets** tend to increase or decrease over time as the general price level increases or decreases. Similarly, the amounts needed to satisfy **nonmonetary liabilities** tend to change with changes in the general price level.

To reflect these changes on historical cost/constant purchasing power balance sheets, nonmonetary items are adjusted for price level changes that occur after the items were acquired. For example, assume that $500 was invested in land (a nonmonetary asset) at the end of 19X1, and the investment was still held at the end of 19X7. During this time, the general price index increased from 92.5 to 168.0. The historical cost/constant purchasing power balance sheets would disclose the following amounts:

Asset	December 31, 19X1, Historical Cost/Constant Purchasing Power Balance Sheet (a)	Price Index Factor for Adjustment to December 31, 19X7 (b)	December 31, 19X7, Historical Cost/Constant Purchasing Power Balance Sheet (a × b)
Land	$500	168.0/92.5 = 1.81622	$908

The $908 shown as the investment in land at the end of 19X7 reflects the same amount of general purchasing power as $500 at the end of 19X1. Thus, no change in general purchasing power is recognized from holding the land.

Illustration D–5 summarizes the impact of general price level changes on monetary and nonmonetary items. The illustration shows which items require adjustments to prepare a historical cost/constant purchasing power balance sheet. It also shows which items generate purchasing power gains and losses that are recognized on a constant purchasing power income statement.

Progress Check

D–8 Foster Company purchased 150 acres of land for $100,000 in 19X1 when the general price index was 125.0. In December 19X4, the general price index was 150.0. What amount should be reported for the land on the 19X4 historical cost/constant purchasing power balance sheet?

D–9 Refer to D–8. Should any purchasing power gain or loss pertaining to the land be reported on the 19X4 historical cost/constant purchasing power income statement?

CURRENT COST VALUATIONS

(LO 5)

Explain the current cost approach to valuation, including its effects on the income statement and balance sheet.

As we said before, all prices do not change at the same rate. In fact, when the general price level is rising, some specific prices may be falling. If this were not so, and if all prices changed at the same rate, then historical cost/constant purchasing power accounting would report current values on the financial statements.

For example, suppose that a company purchased land for $50,000 on January 1, 19X1, when the general price index was 135.0. Then, the price level increased until December 19X2, when the price index was 168.0. A December 31, 19X2, historical cost/constant purchasing power balance sheet for this company would report the land at $50,000 \times 168.0/135.0 = $62,222$. If all prices increased at the same rate during that period, the market value of the land would have increased from $50,000 to $62,222, and the company's historical cost/constant purchasing power balance sheet would coincidentally disclose the land at its current value.

Because all prices do not change at the same rate, however, the current value of the land may differ substantially from the historical cost/constant dollar amount of $62,222. For example, assume that the company had the land appraised and determined that its current value on December 31, 19X2, was $80,000. The difference between the original purchase price of $50,000 and the current value of $80,000 is explained as follows:

Unrealized holding gain	$80,000 − $62,222 = $17,778
Adjustment for general price level increase	$62,222 − $50,000 = 12,222
Total change	$80,000 − $50,000 = $30,000

In this case, the historical cost/constant purchasing power balance sheet would report land at $62,222, which is $17,778 ($80,000 − $62,222) less than its current value. This illustrates an important fact about historical cost/constant purchasing power accounting; it does not attempt to report current value. Rather, historical cost/constant purchasing power accounting restates original transaction prices into equivalent amounts of current, *general* purchasing power. The balance sheets display current values only if current, *specific* purchasing power is the basis of valuation.

Current Costs on the Income Statement

When the current cost approach to accounting is used, the reported amount of each expense, or **current cost,** is the number of dollars that would have been needed at the time the expense was incurred to acquire the consumed resources. For example, assume that the annual sales of a company included an item sold in May for $1,500. The item had been acquired on January 1 for $500. Also, suppose that in May, at the time of the sale, the cost to replace this item was $700. Then, the annual current cost income statement would show sales of $1,500 less cost of goods sold of $700. In other words, when an asset is acquired and then held for a time before it expires, the historical cost of the asset usually is different from its current cost at the time it expires. Current cost accounting measures the amount of expense as the cost to replace the asset at the time the asset expires or is sold.

The result of measuring expenses in current costs is that revenue is matched with the current (at the time of the sale) cost of the resources used to earn the revenue. Thus, operating profit is not greater than zero unless revenues are large enough to replace all of the resources consumed in the process of producing those revenues. Those who argue for current costs believe that operating profit measured in this fashion provides an improved basis for evaluating the effectiveness of operating activities.

Current Costs on the Balance Sheet

On the balance sheet, current cost accounting reports assets at the amounts that would have to be paid to purchase them as of the balance sheet date. Liabilities are reported at the amounts that would have to be paid to satisfy the liabilities as of the balance sheet date. Note that this valuation basis is similar to historical cost/constant purchasing power accounting in that a distinction exists between monetary and nonmonetary assets and liabilities. Monetary assets and liabilities are fixed in amount regardless of price changes. Therefore, monetary items are not adjusted for price changes. All of the nonmonetary items, however, must be evaluated at each balance sheet date to determine the best estimate of current cost.

For a moment, think about the large variety of assets reported on balance sheets. Given that there are so many different assets, you should not be surprised that accountants have difficulty obtaining reliable estimates of current costs. In some cases, they use price indexes that relate to specific categories of assets. Such specific price indexes may provide the most reliable source of current cost information. In other cases, when an asset is not new and has been partially depreciated, accountants may estimate its current cost by determining the cost to acquire a similar but new asset. Depreciation on the old asset is then based on the current cost of the new asset. Clearly, the accountant's professional judgment is an important factor in developing current cost data.

Progress Check

D-10   **On a balance sheet prepared under the current cost approach to accounting:**
   a. **Monetary items are not adjusted for price changes.**
   b. **Nonmonetary items are restated to reflect general price level changes.**
   c. **Monetary items are restated to reflect general price level changes.**

D-11   **Describe the meaning of *operating profit* under a current cost accounting system.**

In the previous discussion, you learned that conventional financial statements generally report historical costs in nominal dollars. That is, adjustments usually are not made for price changes. We also explained how accountants use a general price level index to adjust the nominal dollar amounts to measure the historical costs in terms of a constant purchasing power. Next, we discussed the alternative of reporting current (replacement) costs in the financial statements.

The final alternative to be considered is the reporting of assets (and liabilities) at current selling prices. On the balance sheet, this means assets would be reported at the amounts that would be received if the assets were sold. Similarly, liabilities would be reported at the amounts that would have to be paid to settle or eliminate the liabilities. The financial press describes this selling price approach to valuation as mark-to-market accounting.

The argument for reporting the current selling prices of assets is based on the idea that the alternative to owning an asset is to sell it. Thus, the sacrifice a business makes to hold an asset is the amount it would receive if the asset were sold. Further, the benefit derived from owing a liability is the amount the business avoids paying by not eliminating the liability. If these current selling prices are reported on the balance sheet, the stockholders' equity represents the net amount of cash that would be realized by liquidating the business. This net liquidation value is the amount that could be invested in other projects if the business were liquidated. Therefore, one can argue that net liquidation value is the most relevant basis for evaluating whether the income the company earns is enough to justify remaining in business.

CURRENT SELLING PRICE VALUATIONS

(LO 6)
Explain the current selling price approach to valuation.

Some proponents of the current selling price approach believe that it should be applied to assets but not to liabilities. Others argue that it applies equally well to both. Still others believe that it should be applied only to assets held for sale. They would not apply it to assets held for use in the business.

A related issue is whether to report the adjustments to selling price as gains and losses in the income statement. Some businesses, especially banks, argue that reporting such gains or losses causes excessive fluctuations in their reported net incomes. As an alternative to reporting the gains or losses on the income statement, they may be shown in stockholders' equity on the balance sheet as "unrealized gains and losses."

As Chapters 8 and 11 explain, a very recent pronouncement by the FASB *(SFAS 115)* requires companies to use the selling price approach to valuation for some assets. Investments in trading securities are reported at their fair (market) values, with the related changes in fair values reported on the income statement. Investments in securities available for sale are also reported at their fair values, but the related changes in fair values are not reported on the income statement. Instead, they are reported as part of stockholders' equity.

Progress Check

D–12   **If current selling price valuations were used to account for the assets and liabilities of a business:**
  a. **Gains and losses from changing market values would not be recorded.**
  b. **Losses from changing market values would be recorded but not gains.**
  c. **The accounting system might be described as mark-to-market accounting.**

D–13   **What is meant by the current selling price valuation of a liability?**

SUMMARY OF APPENDIX D IN TERMS OF LEARNING OBJECTIVES

LO 1. Explain the difference between descriptive concepts and prescriptive concepts, and the difference between bottom-up and top-down approaches to the development of accounting concepts. Some accounting concepts provide general descriptions of current accounting practices and are most useful in learning about accounting. Other accounting concepts prescribe the practices accountants should follow. These prescriptive concepts are most useful in developing accounting procedures for new types of transactions and making improvements in accounting practice. A bottom-up approach to developing concepts begins by examining the practices currently in use. Then, concepts are developed that provide general descriptions of those practices. In contrast, a top-down approach begins by stating the objectives of accounting. From these objectives, concepts are developed that prescribe the types of accounting practices accountants should follow.

LO 2. Describe the major components in the FASB's conceptual framework. The FASB's conceptual framework begins with *SFAC 1* by stating the broad objectives of financial reporting. Next, *SFAC 2* identifies the qualitative characteristics accounting information should possess. The elements contained in financial reports are defined in *SFAC 6* and the recognition and measurement criteria to be used are identified in *SFAC 5*.

LO 3. Explain why conventional financial statements fail to adequately account for price changes. Conventional financial statements report transactions in terms of the historical number of dollars received or paid. Therefore, the statements are not adjusted to reflect general price level changes or changes in the specific prices of the items reported.

LO 4. Use a price index to restate historical cost/nominal dollar costs into constant purchasing power amounts and to calculate purchasing power gains and losses. To restate a historical cost/nominal dollar cost in constant purchasing power terms, multiply the nominal dollar cost by a factor that represents the change in the general price level since the cost was incurred. On the balance sheet, monetary assets and liabilities should not be adjusted for changes in prices. However, purchasing power gains or losses result from holding monetary assets and owing monetary liabilities during a period of general price changes.

LO 5. Explain the current cost approach to valuation, including its effects on the income statement and balance sheet. Current costs on the balance sheet are the dollar amounts that would be spent to purchase the assets at the balance sheet date. On the income statement, current costs are the dollar amounts that would be necessary to acquire the consumed assets on the date they were consumed.

LO 6. Explain the current selling price approach to valuation. Reporting current selling prices of assets and liabilities is supported by those who believe the balance sheet should show the net cost of not selling the assets and settling the liabilities. Some argue for applying selling price valuations to all assets and liabilities, or to marketable investments and marketable liabilities only, or to assets only. The related gains and losses may be reported on the income statement, but some would show them as unrealized stockholders' equity items on the balance sheet. The FASB's newly issued *SFAS 114* requires companies to use the selling price approach in reporting certain securities investments.

GLOSSARY

Current cost in general, the cost that would be required to acquire (or replace) an asset or service at the present time. On the income statement, the number of dollars that would be required, at the time the expense is incurred, to acquire the resources consumed. On the balance sheet, the amounts that would have to be paid to replace the assets or satisfy the liabilities as of the balance sheet date. p. AP–22

Historical cost/constant purchasing power accounting an accounting system that adjusts historical cost/nominal dollar financial statements for changes in the general purchasing power of the dollar. p. AP–19

Historical cost/nominal dollar financial statements conventional financial statements that disclose revenues, expenses, assets, liabilities, and owners' equity in terms of the historical monetary units exchanged at the time the transactions occurred. p. AP–18

Monetary assets money or claims to receive a fixed amount of money; the number of dollars to be received does not change regardless of changes in the purchasing power of the dollar. p. AP–19

Monetary liabilities fixed amounts that are owed; the number of dollars to be paid does not change regardless of changes in the general price level. p. AP–19

Nonmonetary assets assets that are not claims to a fixed number of monetary units, the prices of which therefore tend to fluctuate with changes in the general price level. p. AP–21

Nonmonetary liabilities obligations that are not fixed in terms of the number of monetary units needed to satisfy them, and that therefore tend to fluctuate in amount with changes in the general price level. p. AP–21

Purchasing power gains or losses the gains or losses that result from holding monetary assets and/or owing monetary liabilities during a period in which the general price level changes. p. AP–19

QUESTIONS

1. Can a concept be used descriptively and prescriptively?

2. Explain the difference between the FASB's Statements of Financial Accounting Concepts and the Statements of Financial Accounting Standards.

3. Which three qualitative characteristics of accounting information did the FASB identify as being necessary if the information is to be useful?

4. What is implied by saying that financial information should have the qualitative characteristic of relevance?

5. What are the four criteria an item should satisfy to be recognized in the financial statements?

6. Some people argue that conventional financial statements fail to adequately account for inflation. What general problem with conventional financial statements generates this argument?

7. What is the fundamental difference in the adjustments made under current cost accounting and under historical cost/constant purchasing power accounting?

8. What are historical cost/nominal dollar financial statements?

9. What is the difference between monetary and nonmonetary assets?

EXERCISES

Exercise D–1
Adjusting costs for historical cost/constant purchasing power statements
(LO 5)

A company's plant and equipment consisted of land purchased in late 19X1 for $460,000, machinery purchased in late 19X3 for $154,000, and a building purchased in late 19X5 for $210,000. Values of the general price index for December of 19X1 through 19X8 are as follows:

19X1	....	100.0	19X5	128.0
19X2	....	106.5	19X6	139.0
19X3	....	111.0	19X7	144.0
19X4	....	121.3	19X8	153.0

Required

1. Assuming the preceding price index adequately represents end-of-year price levels, calculate the amount of each asset's cost that would be shown on a historical cost/constant purchasing power balance sheet for *(a)* December 31, 19X7, and *(b)* December 31, 19X8. Ignore any accumulated depreciation. Round calculations to three decimals.

2. Would the historical cost/constant purchasing power income statement for 19X8 disclose any purchasing power gain or loss as a consequence of holding these assets? If so, how much?

Exercise D–2
Classifying monetary and nonmonetary items
(LO 5, 6)

Determine whether the following are monetary or nonmonetary items:

1. Notes payable.
2. Merchandise inventory.
3. Copyrights.
4. Savings accounts.
5. Common stock.
6. Product warranties liability.
7. Wages payable.
8. Contributed capital in excess of par value, common stock.
9. Accounts receivable.
10. Goodwill.
11. Prepaid insurance.
12. Computer equipment.
13. Retained earnings.
14. Prepaid rent.

Exercise D–3
Calculating amounts for current cost statements
(LO 6)

A company purchased land in 19X1 at a cost of $730,000 and in 19X2 at a cost of $357,000. What is the current cost of these land purchases in *(a)* 19X3 and *(b)* 19X4, given the following specific price index for land costs?

19X1	....	104.0
19X2	....	100.0
19X3	....	109.2
19X4	....	117.0

Exercise D–4
Calculating general purchasing power gain or loss
(LO 5)

Calculate the general purchasing power gain or loss in 19X2 given the following information (round calculations to three decimals):

Time Period	Price Index
December 19X1	95.6
Average during 19X2	100.2
December 19X2	105.0

a. The cash balance on December 31, 19X1, was $74,000. During 19X2, cash sales occurred uniformly throughout the year and amounted to $452,000. Payments of expenses also occurred evenly throughout the year and amounted to $315,000. Accounts payable of $22,500 were paid in December.

b. Accounts payable amounted to $52,000 on December 31, 19X1. Additional accounts payable amounting to $97,000 were recorded evenly throughout 19X2. The only payment of accounts during the year was $22,500 in late December.

PROBLEMS

Garson Company purchased machinery for $330,000 on December 31, 19X1. It expected the equipment to last five years and to have no salvage value; straight-line depreciation was to be used. It sold the equipment on December 31, 19X5, for $82,000. End-of-year general price index numbers were as follows:

Problem D–1
Adjusting costs to historical cost/constant purchasing power amounts
(LO 5)

19X1	106.0
19X2	110.1
19X3	117.0
19X4	122.3
19X5	128.9

Required

(Round answers to the nearest whole dollar.)

1. What should be presented for the machinery and accumulated depreciation on a historical cost/constant purchasing power balance sheet dated December 31, 19X4? Hint: Depreciation is the total amount of cost that has been allocated to expense. Therefore, the price index number that is used to adjust the nominal dollar cost of the asset should also be used to adjust the nominal dollar amount of depreciation.

2. How much depreciation expense should be shown on the historical cost/constant purchasing power income statement for 19X4?

3. How much depreciation expense should be shown on the historical cost/constant purchasing power income statement for 19X5?

4. How much gain on the sale of the machinery should be reported on the historical cost/nominal dollar income statement for 19X5?

5. After adjusting the machinery's cost and accumulated depreciation to the end-of-19X5 price level, how much gain in (loss of) purchasing power was realized on the sale of the machinery?

Parker Company had three monetary items during 19X2: cash, accounts receivable, and accounts payable. The changes in these accounts during the year were as follows:

Problem D–2
Calculating purchasing power gain or loss
(LO 5)

Cash:

Beginning balance.	$ 90,500
Cash proceeds from sale of building (in May 19X2)	51,200
Cash receipts from customers (spread evenly throughout the year)	359,400
Payments of accounts payable (spread evenly throughout the year)	(274,700)
Dividends declared and paid in July 19X2	(44,000)
Payments of other cash expenses during August 19X2	(77,800)
Ending balance	$104,600

Accounts receivable:	
Beginning balance	$ 92,800
Sales to customers (spread evenly throughout the year)	375,600
Cash receipts from customers (spread evenly throughout the year)	(359,400)
Ending balance	$109,000
Accounts payable:	
Beginning balance	$115,000
Merchandise purchases (spread evenly throughout the year)	231,600
Special purchase December 31, 19X2	47,500
Payments of accounts payable (spread evenly throughout the year)	(274,700)
Ending balance	$119,400

General price index numbers at the end of 19X1 and during 19X2 are as follows:

December 19X1	196.4
January 19X2	202.1
May 19X2	211.0
July 19X2	214.1
August 19X2	215.6
December 19X2	217.0
Average for 19X2	214.8

Required

Calculate the general purchasing power gain or loss experienced by Parker Company in 19X2. Round all amounts to the nearest whole dollar.

Problem D–3
Historical cost/nominal dollars, historical cost/constant purchasing power, and current costs
(LO 4, 5, 6)

Longhorn Corporation purchased a tract of land for $574,000 in 19X1, when the general price index was 127.4. At the same time, a price index for land values in the area of Longhorn's tract was 133.1. In 19X2, when the general price index was 134.6 and the specific price index for land was 142.5, Longhorn bought another tract of land for $296,000. In late 19X7, the general price index is 157.2 and the price index for land values is 174.0.

Required

Preparation Component:

1. In preparing a balance sheet at the end of 19X7, show the amount that should be reported for land based on:

   a. Historical cost/nominal dollars.

   b. Historical cost/constant purchasing power.

   c. Current costs.

   (Round all amounts to the nearest whole dollar.)

Analysis Component:

2. In Longhorn's December 19X7 meeting of the board of directors, one director insists that Longhorn has earned a gain in purchasing power as a result of owning the land. A second director argues that there could not have been a purchasing power gain or loss since land is a nonmonetary asset. Which director do you think is correct? Explain your answer.

CRITICAL THINKING: ESSAYS, PROBLEMS, AND CASES

Write a brief essay that explains the difference between descriptive and prescriptive concepts and that explains why the FASB's conceptual framework is designed to be prescriptive. Also discuss the question of whether specific concepts can be both descriptive and prescriptive.

Analytical Essay

(LO 1, 2, 3)

ANSWERS TO PROGRESS CHECKS

D–1 c

D–2 A top-down approach to developing accounting concepts begins by identifying appropriate objectives of accounting reports.

D–3 A bottom-up approach to developing accounting starts by examining existing accounting practices and determining the general features that characterize those procedures.

D–4 d

D–5 To have the qualitative characteristic of being reliable, accounting information should be free from bias and error, should be verifiable, should faithfully represent what is supposed to be described, and should be neutral.

D–6 The elements of financial statements are the objects and events that financial statements should describe, for example, assets, liabilities, revenues, and expenses.

D–7 c

D–8 $100,000 \times (150/125) = $120,000

D–9 No. Land is a nonmonetary asset and therefore no purchasing power gain or loss is generated.

D–10 a

D–11 Operating profit is measured as revenues less the current (at the time of sale) cost of the resources that were used to earn those revenues.

D–12 c

D–13 The current selling price of a liability is the amount that would have to be paid to settle or eliminate the liability.

Present and Future Values: An Expansion

LEARNING OBJECTIVES

After studying Appendix E, you should be able to:

1. Explain what is meant by the present value of a single amount and the present value of an annuity, and be able to use tables to solve present value problems.
2. Explain what is meant by the future value of a single amount and the future value of an annuity, and be able to use tables to solve future value problems.

The concept of present value is introduced and applied to accounting problems in Chapters 12 and 15. This appendix supplements those presentations with additional discussion, more complete tables, and additional homework exercises. In studying this appendix, you also learn about the concept of future value.

PRESENT VALUE OF A SINGLE AMOUNT

LO 1

Explain what is meant by the present value of a single amount and the present value of an annuity, and be able to use tables to solve present value problems.

The present value of a single amount to be received or paid at some future date may be expressed as:

$$p = \frac{f}{(1 + i)^n}$$

where

p = Present value
f = Future value
i = Rate of interest per period
n = Number of periods

For example, assume that $2.20 is to be received one period from now. It would be useful to know how much must be invested now, for one period, at an interest rate of 10% to provide $2.20. We can calculate that amount with this formula:

$$p = \frac{f}{(1 + i)^n} = \frac{\$2.20}{(1 + .10)^1} = \$2.00$$

Alternatively, we can use the formula to find how much must be invested for two periods at 10% to provide $2.42:

$$p = \frac{f}{(1 + i)^n} = \frac{\$2.42}{(1 + .10)^2} = \$2.00$$

Note that the number of periods (n) does not have to be expressed in years. Any period of time such as a day, a month, a quarter, or a year may be used. However, whatever period is used, the interest rate (i) must be compounded for the same period. Thus, if a problem expresses n in months, and i equals 12% per year, then 1% of the amount invested at the beginning of each month is earned during that month and added to the investment. Thus, the interest is compounded monthly.

A present value table shows present values for a variety of interest rates (i) and a variety of numbers of periods (n). Each present value is based on the assumption that the future value (f) is 1. The following formula is used to construct a table of present values of a single future amount:

$$p = \frac{1}{(1 + i)^n}$$

Table E–1 on page AP–36 is a table of present values of a single future amount and often is called a *present value of 1* table.

Progress Check

E-1   **Lamar Company is considering an investment that will yield $70,000 after six years. If Lamar requires an 8% return, how much should it be willing to pay for the investment?**

The following formula for the present value of a single amount can be modified to become the formula for the future value of a single amount with a simple step:

$$p = \frac{f}{(1 + i)^n}$$

By multiplying both sides of the equation by $(1 + i)^n$, the result is:

$$f = p \times (1 + i)^n$$

For example, we can use this formula to determine that $2.00 invested for one period at an interest rate of 10% will increase to a future value of $2.20:

$$f = p \times (1 + i)^n$$
$$= \$2.00 \times (1 + .10)^1$$
$$= \$2.20$$

Alternatively, assume that $2.00 will remain invested for three periods at 10%. The $2.662 amount that will be received after three periods is calculated with the formula as follows:

$$f = p \times (1 + i)^n$$
$$= \$2.00 \times (1 + .10)^3$$
$$= \$2.662$$

A future value table shows future values for a variety of interest rates (i) and a variety of numbers of periods (n). Each future value is based on the assumption that the present value (p) is 1. Thus, the formula used to construct a table of future values of a single amount is:

$$f = (1 + i)^n$$

Table E–2 on page AP–37 is a table of future values of a single amount and often is called a *future value of 1* table.

In Table E–2, look at the row where $n = 0$ and observe that the future value is 1 for all interest rates because no interest is earned.

Observe that a table showing the present values of 1 and a table showing the future values of 1 contain exactly the same information because both tables are based on the same equation:

$$p = \frac{f}{(1 + i)^n}$$

This equation is nothing more than a reformulation of:

$$f = p \times (1 + i)^n$$

FUTURE VALUE OF A SINGLE AMOUNT

LO 2
Explain what is meant by the future value of a single amount and the future value of an annuity, and be able to use tables to solve future value problems.

Both tables reflect the same four variables, p, f, i, and n. Therefore, any problem that can be solved with one of the two tables can also be solved with the other table.

For example, suppose that a person invests $100 for five years and expects to earn 12% per year. How much should the person receive after five years? To solve the problem using Table E–2, find the future value of 1, five periods from now, compounded at 12%. In the table, $f = 1.7623$. Thus, the amount to be accumulated over five years is $176.23 ($100 × 1.7623).

Table E–1 shows that the present value of 1, discounted five periods at 12% is 0.5674. Recall that the relationship between present value and future value may be expressed as:

$$p = \frac{f}{(1 + i)^n}$$

This formula can be restated as:

$$p = f \times \frac{1}{(1 + i)^n}$$

In turn, it can be restated as:

$$f = \frac{p}{\dfrac{1}{(1 + i)^n}}$$

Because we know from Table E–1 that $1/(1 + i)^n$ equals 0.5674, the future value of $100 invested for five periods at 12% is:

$$f = \frac{\$100}{0.5674} = \$176.24$$

In summary, the future value can be found two ways. First, we can multiply the amount invested by the future value found in Table E–2. Second, we can divide the amount invested by the present value found in Table E–1. As you can see in this problem, immaterial differences can occur between these two methods through rounding.

Progress Check

E-2 On May 9, Cindy Huber was notified that she had won $150,000 in a sweepstakes. She decided to deposit the money in a savings account that yields an 8% annual rate of interest and plans on quitting her job when the account equals $299,850. How many years will it be before Cindy is able to quit working? (a) 2; (b) 8; (c) 9.

PRESENT VALUE OF AN ANNUITY

LO 1

Explain what is meant by the present value of a single amount and the present value of an annuity, and be able to use tables to solve present value problems.

An annuity is a series of equal payments occurring at equal intervals, such as three annual payments of $100 each. The present value of an annuity is defined as the present value of the payments one period prior to the first payment. Graphically, this annuity and its present value (p) may be represented as follows:

One way to calculate the present value of this annuity finds the present value of each payment with the formula and adds them together. For this example, assuming an interest rate of 15%, the calculation is:

$$p = \frac{\$100}{(1 + .15)^1} + \frac{\$100}{(1 + .15)^2} + \frac{\$100}{(1 + .15)^3} = \$228.32$$

Another way calculates the present value of the annuity by using Table E–1 to compute the present value of each payment then taking their sum:

First payment: $p = \$100 \times 0.8696 = \$\ 86.96$
Second payment: $p = \$100 \times 0.7561 = \ \ \ 75.61$
Third payment: $p = \$100 \times 0.6575 = \ \ \ \underline{65.75}$
Total: $p = \underline{\$228.32}$

We can also use Table E–1 to solve the problem by first adding the table values for the three payments and then multiplying this sum by the $100 amount of each payment:

From Table E–1: $i = 15\%, n = 1, p = \ \ 0.8696$
                   $i = 15\%, n = 2, p = \ \ 0.7561$
                   $i = 15\%, n = 3, p = \ \ \underline{0.6575}$
                                      2.2832
                   $2.2832 \times \$100 = \underline{\$228.32}$

An easier way to solve the problem uses a different table that shows the present values of annuities like Table E–3 on page AP–38, which often is called a *present value of an annuity of 1* table. Look in Table E–3 on the row where $n = 3$ and $i = 15\%$ and observe that the present value is 2.2832. Thus, the present value of an annuity of 1 for three periods, discounted at 15%, is 2.2832.

Although a formula is used to construct a table showing the present values of an annuity, you can construct one by adding the amounts in a present value of 1 table.[1] Examine Table E–1 and Table E–3 to confirm that the following numbers were drawn from those tables:

From Table E–1		From Table E–3	
$i = 8\%, n = 1$	0.9259		
$i = 8\%, n = 2$	0.8573		
$i = 8\%, n = 3$	0.7938		
$i = 8\%, n = 4$	0.7350		
Total	3.3120	$i = 8\%, n = 4$	3.3121

The minor difference in the results occurs only because the numbers in the tables have been rounded.

In addition to the preceding methods, you can use preprogrammed business calculators and spreadsheet computer programs to find the present value of annuities.

Progress Check

E–3   **Smith & Company is considering an investment that would pay $10,000 every six months for three years. The first payment would be received in six months. If Smith & Company requires an annual return of 8%, they should be willing to invest no more than: (a) $25,771; (b) $46,229; (c) $52,421.**

---

[1]The formula for the present value of an annuity of 1 is:

$$p = \frac{1 - \frac{1}{(1 + i)^n}}{i}$$

FUTURE VALUE OF AN ANNUITY

LO 2

Explain what is meant by the future value of a single amount and the future value of an annuity, and be able to use tables to solve problems that involve future values.

Just as an annuity has a present value, it also has a future value. The future value of an annuity is the accumulated value of the annuity payments and interest as of the date of the final payment. Consider the earlier annuity of three annual payments of $100. These are the points in time at which the present value (*p*) and the future value (*f*) occur:

$100 $100 $100

p   *f*

Note that the first payment is made two periods prior to the point at which the future value is determined. Therefore, for the first payment, $n = 2$. For the second payment, $n = 1$. Since the third payment occurs on the future value date, $n = 0$.

One way to calculate the future value of this annuity uses the formula to find the future value of each payment and adds them together. Assuming an interest rate of 15%, the calculation is:

$$f = \$100 \times (1 + .15)^2 + \$100 \times (1 + .15)^1 + \$100 \times (1 + .15)^0 = \$347.25$$

Another way calculates the future value of the annuity by using Table E–2 to find the sum of the future values of each payment:

First payment:	$f = \$100 \times 1.3225 =$	$132.25
Second payment:	$f = \$100 \times 1.1500 =$	115.00
Third payment:	$f = \$100 \times 1.0000 =$	100.00
Total:		$f = \$347.25

A third approach adds the future values of three payments of 1 and multiplies the sum by $100:

From Table E–2:	$i = 15\%, n = 2, f =$	1.3225
	$i = 15\%, n = 1, f =$	1.1500
	$i = 15\%, n = 0, f =$	1.0000
	Sum =	3.4725

Future value = 3.4725 × $100 = $347.25

A fourth and easier way to solve the problem uses a table that shows the future values of annuities, often called a *future value of an annuity of 1* table. Table E–4 on page AP–39 is such a table. Note in Table E–4 that when $n = 1$, the future values are equal to 1 ($f = 1$) for all rates of interest because the annuity consists of only one payment and the future value is determined on the date of the payment. Thus, the future value equals the payment.

Although a formula is used to construct a table showing the future values of an annuity of 1, you can construct one by adding together the amount in a future value of 1 table like Table E–2.[2] Examine Table E–2 and Table E–4 to confirm that the following numbers were drawn from those tables:

From Table E–2		**From Table E–4**	
$i = 8\%, n = 0$	1.0000		
$i = 8\%, n = 1$	1.0800		
$i = 8\%, n = 2$	1.1664		
$i = 8\%, n = 3$	1.2597		
Total	4.5061	$i = 8\%, n = 4$	4.5061

---

[2]The formula for the future value of an annuity of 1 is:

$$f = \frac{(1 + i)^n - 1}{i}$$

Minor differences may occur because the numbers in the tables have been rounded.

You can also use business calculators and spreadsheet computer programs to find the future values of annuities.

Observe that the future value in Table E–2 is 1.0000 when $n = 0$ but the future value in Table E–4 is 1.0000 when $n = 1$. Why does this apparent contradiction arise? When $n = 0$ in Table E–2, the future value is determined on the date that the single payment occurs. Thus, no interest is earned and the future value equals the payment. However, Table E–4 describes annuities with equal payments occurring each period. When $n = 1$, the annuity has only one payment, and its future value also equals 1 on the date of its final and only payment.

Progress Check

E–4   Syntel Company invests $45,000 per year for five years at 12%. Calculate the value of the investment at the end of five years.

SUMMARY OF THE APPENDIX IN TERMS OF LEARNING OBJECTIVES

LO 1. Explain what is meant by the present value of a single amount and the present value of an annuity, and be able to use tables to solve present value problems. The present value of a single amount to be received at a future date is the amount that could be invested now at the specified interest rate to yield that future value. The present value of an annuity is the amount that could be invested now at the specified interest rate to yield that series of equal periodic payments. Present value tables and business calculators simplify calculating present values.

LO 2. Explain what is meant by the future value of a single amount and the future value of an annuity, and be able to use tables to solve future value problems. The future value of a single amount invested at a specified rate of interest is the amount that would accumulate at a future date. The future value of an annuity to be invested at a specified rate of interest is the amount that would accumulate at the date of the final equal periodic payment. Future value tables and business calculators simplify calculating future values.

Table E-1   Present Value of 1 Due in *n* Periods

					Rate							
Periods	**1%**	**2%**	**3%**	**4%**	**5%**	**6%**	**7%**	**8%**	**9%**	**10%**	**12%**	**15%**
1	0.9901	0.9804	0.9709	0.9615	0.9524	0.9434	0.9346	0.9259	0.9174	0.9091	0.8929	0.8696
2	0.9803	0.9612	0.9426	0.9246	0.9070	0.8900	0.8734	0.8573	0.8417	0.8264	0.7972	0.7561
3	0.9706	0.9423	0.9151	0.8890	0.8638	0.8396	0.8163	0.7938	0.7722	0.7513	0.7118	0.6575
4	0.9610	0.9238	0.8885	0.8548	0.8227	0.7921	0.7629	0.7350	0.7084	0.6830	0.6355	0.5718
5	0.9515	0.9057	0.8626	0.8219	0.7835	0.7473	0.7130	0.6806	0.6499	0.6209	0.5674	0.4972
6	0.9420	0.8880	0.8375	0.7903	0.7462	0.7050	0.6663	0.6302	0.5963	0.5645	0.5066	0.4323
7	0.9327	0.8706	0.8131	0.7599	0.7107	0.6651	0.6227	0.5835	0.5470	0.5132	0.4523	0.3759
8	0.9235	0.8535	0.7894	0.7307	0.6768	0.6274	0.5820	0.5403	0.5019	0.4665	0.4039	0.3269
9	0.9143	0.8368	0.7664	0.7026	0.6446	0.5919	0.5439	0.5002	0.4604	0.4241	0.3606	0.2843
10	0.9053	0.8203	0.7441	0.6756	0.6139	0.5584	0.5083	0.4632	0.4224	0.3855	0.3220	0.2472
11	0.8963	0.8043	0.7224	0.6496	0.5847	0.5268	0.4751	0.4289	0.3875	0.3505	0.2875	0.2149
12	0.8874	0.7885	0.7014	0.6246	0.5568	0.4970	0.4440	0.3971	0.3555	0.3186	0.2567	0.1869
13	0.8787	0.7730	0.6810	0.6006	0.5303	0.4688	0.4150	0.3677	0.3262	0.2897	0.2292	0.1625
14	0.8700	0.7579	0.6611	0.5775	0.5051	0.4423	0.3878	0.3405	0.2992	0.2633	0.2046	0.1413
15	0.8613	0.7430	0.6419	0.5553	0.4810	0.4173	0.3624	0.3152	0.2745	0.2394	0.1827	0.1229
16	0.8528	0.7284	0.6232	0.5339	0.4581	0.3936	0.3387	0.2919	0.2519	0.2176	0.1631	0.1069
17	0.8444	0.7142	0.6050	0.5134	0.4363	0.3714	0.3166	0.2703	0.2311	0.1978	0.1456	0.0929
18	0.8360	0.7002	0.5874	0.4936	0.4155	0.3503	0.2959	0.2502	0.2120	0.1799	0.1300	0.0808
19	0.8277	0.6864	0.5703	0.4746	0.3957	0.3305	0.2765	0.2317	0.1945	0.1635	0.1161	0.0703
20	0.8195	0.6730	0.5537	0.4564	0.3769	0.3118	0.2584	0.2145	0.1784	0.1486	0.1037	0.0611
25	0.7798	0.6095	0.4776	0.3751	0.2953	0.2330	0.1842	0.1460	0.1160	0.0923	0.0588	0.0304
30	0.7419	0.5521	0.4120	0.3083	0.2314	0.1741	0.1314	0.0994	0.0754	0.0573	0.0334	0.0151
35	0.7059	0.5000	0.3554	0.2534	0.1813	0.1301	0.0937	0.0676	0.0490	0.0356	0.0189	0.0075
40	0.6717	0.4529	0.3066	0.2083	0.1420	0.0972	0.0668	0.0460	0.0318	0.0221	0.0107	0.0037

Table E-2 Future Value of 1 Due in *n* Periods

Periods	1%	2%	3%	4%	5%	6%	7%	8%	9%	10%	12%	15%
0	1.0000	1.0000	1.0000	1.0000	1.0000	1.0000	1.0000	1.0000	1.0000	1.0000	1.0000	1.0000
1	1.0100	1.0200	1.0300	1.0400	1.0500	1.0600	1.0700	1.0800	1.0900	1.1000	1.1200	1.1500
2	1.0201	1.0404	1.0609	1.0816	1.1025	1.1236	1.1449	1.1664	1.1881	1.2100	1.2544	1.3225
3	1.0303	1.0612	1.0927	1.1249	1.1576	1.1910	1.2250	1.2597	1.2950	1.3310	1.4049	1.5209
4	1.0406	1.0824	1.1255	1.1699	1.2155	1.2625	1.3108	1.3605	1.4116	1.4641	1.5735	1.7490
5	1.0510	1.1041	1.1593	1.2167	1.2763	1.3382	1.4026	1.4693	1.5386	1.6105	1.7623	2.0114
6	1.0615	1.1262	1.1941	1.2653	1.3401	1.4185	1.5007	1.5869	1.6771	1.7716	1.9738	2.3131
7	1.0721	1.1487	1.2299	1.3159	1.4071	1.5036	1.6058	1.7138	1.8280	1.9487	2.2107	2.6600
8	1.0829	1.1717	1.2668	1.3686	1.4775	1.5938	1.7182	1.8509	1.9926	2.1436	2.4760	3.0590
9	1.0937	1.1951	1.3048	1.4233	1.5513	1.6895	1.8385	1.9990	2.1719	2.3579	2.7731	3.5179
10	1.1046	1.2190	1.3439	1.4802	1.6289	1.7908	1.9672	2.1589	2.3674	2.5937	3.1058	4.0456
11	1.1157	1.2434	1.3842	1.5395	1.7103	1.8983	2.1049	2.3316	2.5804	2.8531	3.4785	4.6524
12	1.1268	1.2682	1.4258	1.6010	1.7959	2.0122	2.2522	2.5182	2.8127	3.1384	3.8960	5.3503
13	1.1381	1.2936	1.4685	1.6651	1.8856	2.1329	2.4098	2.7196	3.0658	3.4523	4.3635	6.1528
14	1.1495	1.3195	1.5126	1.7317	1.9799	2.2609	2.5785	2.9372	3.3417	3.7975	4.8871	7.0757
15	1.1610	1.3459	1.5580	1.8009	2.0789	2.3966	2.7590	3.1722	3.6425	4.1772	5.4736	8.1371
16	1.1726	1.3728	1.6047	1.8730	2.1829	2.5404	2.9522	3.4259	3.9703	4.5950	6.1304	9.3576
17	1.1843	1.4002	1.6528	1.9479	2.2920	2.6928	3.1588	3.7000	4.3276	5.0545	6.8660	10.7613
18	1.1961	1.4282	1.7024	2.0258	2.4066	2.8543	3.3799	3.9960	4.7171	5.5599	7.6900	12.3755
19	1.2081	1.4568	1.7535	2.1068	2.5270	3.0256	3.6165	4.3157	5.1417	6.1159	8.6128	14.2318
20	1.2202	1.4859	1.8061	2.1911	2.6533	3.2071	3.8697	4.6610	5.6044	6.7275	9.6463	16.3665
25	1.2824	1.6406	2.0938	2.6658	3.3864	4.2919	5.4274	6.8485	8.6231	10.8347	17.0001	32.9190
30	1.3478	1.8114	2.4273	3.2434	4.3219	5.7435	7.6123	10.0627	13.2677	17.4494	29.9599	66.2118
35	1.4166	1.9999	2.8139	3.9461	5.5160	7.6861	10.6766	14.7853	20.4140	28.1024	52.7996	133.176
40	1.4889	2.2080	3.2620	4.8010	7.0400	10.2857	14.9745	21.7245	31.4094	45.2593	93.0510	267.864

Rate

Table E-3　Present Value of an Annuity of 1 per Period

						Rate						
Periods	**1%**	**2%**	**3%**	**4%**	**5%**	**6%**	**7%**	**8%**	**9%**	**10%**	**12%**	**15%**
1	0.9901	0.9804	0.9709	0.9615	0.9524	0.9434	0.9346	0.9259	0.9174	0.9091	0.8929	0.8696
2	1.9704	1.9416	1.9135	1.8861	1.8594	1.8334	1.8080	1.7833	1.7591	1.7355	1.6901	1.6257
3	2.9410	2.8839	2.8286	2.7751	2.7232	2.6730	2.6243	2.5771	2.5313	2.4869	2.4018	2.2832
4	3.9020	3.8077	3.7171	3.6299	3.5460	3.4651	3.3872	3.3121	3.2397	3.1699	3.0373	2.8550
5	4.8534	4.7135	4.5797	4.4518	4.3295	4.2124	4.1002	3.9927	3.8897	3.7908	3.6048	3.3522
6	5.7955	5.6014	5.4172	5.2421	5.0757	4.9173	4.7665	4.6229	4.4859	4.3553	4.1114	3.7845
7	6.7282	6.4720	6.2303	6.0021	5.7864	5.5824	5.3893	5.2064	5.0330	4.8684	4.5638	4.1604
8	7.6517	7.3255	7.0197	6.7327	6.4632	6.2098	5.9713	5.7466	5.5348	5.3349	4.9676	4.4873
9	8.5660	8.1622	7.7861	7.4353	7.1078	6.8017	6.5152	6.2469	5.9952	5.7590	5.3282	4.7716
10	9.4713	8.9826	8.5302	8.1109	7.7217	7.3601	7.0236	6.7101	6.4177	6.1446	5.6502	5.0188
11	10.3676	9.7868	9.2526	8.7605	8.3064	7.8869	7.4987	7.1390	6.8052	6.4951	5.9377	5.2337
12	11.2551	10.5753	9.9540	9.3851	8.8633	8.3838	7.9427	7.5361	7.1607	6.8137	6.1944	5.4206
13	12.1337	11.3484	10.6350	9.9856	9.3936	8.8527	8.3577	7.9038	7.4869	7.1034	6.4235	5.5831
14	13.0037	12.1062	11.2961	10.5631	9.8986	9.2950	8.7455	8.2442	7.7862	7.3667	6.6282	5.7245
15	13.8651	12.8493	11.9379	11.1184	10.3797	9.7122	9.1079	8.5595	8.0607	7.6061	6.8109	5.8474
16	14.7179	13.5777	12.5611	11.6523	10.8378	10.1059	9.4466	8.8514	8.3126	7.8237	6.9740	5.9542
17	15.5623	14.2919	13.1661	12.1657	11.2741	10.4773	9.7632	9.1216	8.5436	8.0216	7.1196	6.0472
18	16.3983	14.9920	13.7535	12.6593	11.6896	10.8276	10.0591	9.3719	8.7556	8.2014	7.2497	6.1280
19	17.2260	15.6785	14.3238	13.1339	12.0853	11.1581	10.3356	9.6036	8.9501	8.3649	7.3658	6.1982
20	18.0456	16.3514	14.8775	13.5903	12.4622	11.4699	10.5940	9.8181	9.1285	8.5136	7.4694	6.2593
25	22.0232	19.5235	17.4131	15.6221	14.0939	12.7834	11.6536	10.6748	9.8226	9.0770	7.8431	6.4641
30	25.8077	22.3965	19.6004	17.2920	15.3725	13.7648	12.4090	11.2578	10.2737	9.4269	8.0552	6.5660
35	29.4086	24.9986	21.4872	18.6646	16.3742	14.4982	12.9477	11.6546	10.5668	9.6442	8.1755	6.6166
40	32.8347	27.3555	23.1148	19.7928	17.1591	15.0463	13.3317	11.9246	10.7574	9.7791	8.2438	6.6418

Table E-4   Future Value of an Annuity of 1 per Period

						Rate						
Periods	**1%**	**2%**	**3%**	**4%**	**5%**	**6%**	**7%**	**8%**	**9%**	**10%**	**12%**	**15%**
1	1.0000	1.0000	1.0000	1.0000	1.0000	1.0000	1.0000	1.0000	1.0000	1.0000	1.0000	1.0000
2	2.0100	2.0200	2.0300	2.0400	2.0500	2.0600	2.0700	2.0800	2.0900	2.1000	2.1200	2.1500
3	3.0301	3.0604	3.0909	3.1216	3.1525	3.1836	3.2149	3.2464	3.2781	3.3100	3.3744	3.4725
4	4.0604	4.1216	4.1836	4.2465	4.3101	4.3746	4.4399	4.5061	4.5731	4.6410	4.7793	4.9934
5	5.1010	5.2040	5.3901	5.4163	5.5256	5.6371	5.7507	5.8666	5.9847	6.1051	6.3528	6.7424
6	6.1520	6.3081	6.4684	6.6330	6.8019	6.9753	7.1533	7.3359	7.5233	7.7156	8.1152	8.7537
7	7.2135	7.4343	7.6625	7.8983	8.1420	8.3938	8.6540	8.9228	9.2004	9.4872	10.0890	11.0668
8	8.2857	8.5830	8.8923	9.2142	9.5491	9.8975	10.2598	10.6366	11.0285	11.4359	12.2997	13.7268
9	9.3685	9.7546	10.1591	10.5828	11.0266	11.4913	11.9780	12.4876	13.0210	13.5795	14.7757	16.7858
10	10.4622	10.9497	11.4639	12.0061	12.5779	13.1808	13.8164	14.4866	15.1929	15.9374	17.5487	20.3037
11	11.5668	12.1687	12.8078	13.4864	14.2068	14.9716	15.7836	16.6455	17.5603	18.5312	20.6546	24.3493
12	12.6825	13.4121	14.1920	15.0258	15.9171	16.8699	17.8885	18.9771	20.1407	21.3843	24.1331	29.0017
13	13.8093	14.6803	15.6178	16.6268	17.7130	18.8821	20.1406	21.4953	22.9534	24.5227	28.0291	34.3519
14	14.9474	15.9739	17.0863	18.2919	19.5986	21.0151	22.5505	24.2149	26.0192	27.9750	32.3926	40.5047
15	16.0969	17.2934	18.5989	20.0236	21.5786	23.2760	25.1290	27.1521	29.3609	31.7725	37.2797	47.5804
16	17.2579	18.6393	20.1569	21.8245	23.6575	25.6725	27.8881	30.3243	33.0034	35.9497	42.7533	55.7175
17	18.4304	20.0121	21.7616	23.6975	25.8404	28.2129	30.8402	33.7502	36.9737	40.5447	48.8837	65.0751
18	19.6147	21.4123	23.4144	25.6454	28.1324	30.9057	33.9990	37.4502	41.3013	45.5992	55.7497	75.8364
19	20.8109	22.8406	25.1169	27.6712	30.5390	33.7600	37.3790	41.4463	46.0185	51.1591	63.4397	88.2118
20	22.0190	24.2974	26.8704	29.7781	33.0660	36.7856	40.9955	45.7620	51.1601	57.2750	72.0524	102.444
25	28.2432	32.0303	36.4593	41.6459	47.7271	54.8645	63.2490	73.1059	84.7009	98.3471	133.334	212.793
30	34.7849	40.5681	47.5754	56.0849	66.4388	79.0582	94.4608	113.283	136.308	164.494	241.333	434.745
35	41.6603	49.9945	60.4621	73.6522	90.3203	111.435	138.237	172.317	215.711	271.024	431.663	881.170
40	48.8864	60.4020	75.4013	95.0255	120.800	154.762	199.635	259.057	337.882	442.593	767.091	1,779.09

EXERCISES

Jasper Company is considering an investment which, if paid for immediately, is expected to return $172,500 five years hence. If Jasper demands a 9% return, how much will it be willing to pay for this investment?

Exercise E–1
Present value of an amount
(LO 1)

LCV Company invested $529,000 in a project expected to earn a 12% annual rate of return. The earnings will be reinvested in the project each year until the entire investment is liquidated 10 years hence. What will the cash proceeds be when the project is liquidated?

Exercise E–2
Future value of an amount
(LO 2)

Cornblue Distributing is considering a contract that will return $200,400 annually at the end of each year for six years. If Cornblue demands an annual return of 7% and pays for the investment immediately, how much should it be willing to pay?

Exercise E–3
Present value of an annuity
(LO 1)

Sarah Oliver is planning to begin an individual retirement program in which she will invest $1,200 annually at the end of each year. Oliver plans to retire after making 30 annual investments in a program that earns a return of 10%. What will be the value of the program on the date of the last investment?

Exercise E–4
Future value of an annuity
(LO 2)

Kevin Smith has been offered the possibility of investing $0.3152 for 15 years, after which he will be paid $1. What annual rate of interest will Smith earn? (Use Table E–1 to find the answer.)

Exercise E–5
Interest rate on an investment
(LO 1)

Laura Veralli has been offered the possibility of investing $0.5268. The investment will earn 6% per year and will return Veralli $1 at the end of the investment. How many years must Veralli wait to receive the $1? (Use Table E–1 to find the answer.)

Exercise E–6
Number of periods of an investment
(LO 1)

Tom Albertson expects to invest $1 at 15% and, at the end of the investment, receive $66.2118. How many years will elapse before Albertson receives the payment? (Use Table E–2 to find the answer.)

Exercise E–7
Number of periods of an investment
(LO 2)

Ed Teller expects to invest $1 for 35 years, after which he will receive $20.4140. What rate of interest will Teller earn? (Use Table E–2 to find the answer.)

Exercise E–8
Interest rate on an investment
(LO 2)

Helen Fanshawe expects an immediate investment of $9.3936 to return $1 annually for 13 years, with the first payment to be received in one year. What rate of interest will Fanshawe earn? (Use Table E–3 to find the answer.)

Exercise E–9
Interest rate on an investment
(LO 1)

Ken Priggin expects an investment of $7.6061 to return $1 annually for several years. If Priggin is to earn a return of 10%, how many annual payments must he receive? (Use Table E–3 to find the answer.)

Exercise E–10
Number of periods of an investment
(LO 1)

Steve Church expects to invest $1 annually for 40 years and have an accumulated value of $95.0255 on the date of the last investment. If this occurs, what rate of interest will Church earn? (Use Table E–4 to find the answer.)

Exercise E–11
Interest rate on an investment
(LO 2)

Bitsy Brennon expects to invest $1 annually in a fund that will earn 8%. How many annual investments must Brennon make to accumulate $45.7620 on the date of the last investment? (Use Table E–4 to find the answer.)

Exercise E–12
Number of periods of an investment
(LO 2)

Bill Lenehan financed a new automobile by paying $3,100 cash and agreeing to make 20 monthly payments of $450 each, the first payment to be made one month after the purchase. The loan was said to bear interest at an annual rate of 12%. What was the cost of the automobile?

Exercise E–13
Present value of an annuity
(LO 1)

Stephanie Powell deposited $4,900 in a savings account that earns interest at an annual rate of 8%, compounded quarterly. The $4,900 plus earned interest must remain in the account 10 years before it can be withdrawn. How much money will be in the account at the end of the 10 years?

Exercise E–14
Future value of an amount
(LO 2)

Sally Sayer plans to have $90 withheld from her monthly paycheck and deposited in a savings account that earns 12% annually, compounded monthly. If Sayer continues with her plan for 2½ years, how much will be accumulated in the account on the date of the last deposit?

Exercise E–15
Future value of an annuity
(LO 2)

Stellar Company plans to issue 12%, 15-year, $500,000 par value bonds payable that pay interest semiannually on June 30 and December 31. The bonds are dated December 31, 19X1, and are to be issued on that date. If the market rate of interest for the bonds is 10% on the date of issue, what will be the cash proceeds from the bond issue?

Exercise E–16
Present value of bonds
(LO 1)

Travis Company has decided to establish a fund that will be used 10 years hence to replace an aging productive facility. The company makes an initial contribution of $150,000 to the fund and plans to make quarterly contributions of $60,000 beginning in three months. The fund is expected to earn 12%, compounded quarterly. What will be the value of the fund 10 years hence?

Exercise E–17
Future value of an amount plus an annuity
(LO 2)

McCoy Company expects to earn 10% per year on an investment that will pay $756,400 six years hence. Use Table E–2 to calculate the present value of the investment.

Exercise E–18
Present value of an amount
(LO 1)

Comet Company invests $216,000 at 7% per year for nine years. Use Table E–1 to calculate the future value of the investment nine years hence.

Exercise E–19
Future value of an amount
(LO 2)

ANSWERS TO PROGRESS CHECKS

E–1 $70,000 × 0.6302 = $44,114

E–2   c $299,850/$150,000 = 1.9990
         Table E–2 shows this value for nine years at 8%.

E–3   c $10,000 × 5.2421 = $52,421

E–4 $45,000 × 6.3528 = $285,876

Financial Statements and Related Disclosures from Apple Computer Inc.'s 1993 Annual Report

Eleven-Year Financial History

	1993	1992	1991	1990
Results of Operations				
Net sales:				
Domestic	$ 4,387,674	$ 3,885,042	$ 3,484,533	$ 3,241,061
International	3,589,280	3,201,500	2,824,316	2,317,374
Total net sales	7,976,954	7,086,542	6,308,849	5,558,435
Costs and expenses:				
Cost of sales	5,248,834	3,991,337	3,314,118	2,606,223
Research and development (R&D)	664,564	602,135	583,046	478,019
Selling, general and administrative (SG&A)	1,632,362	1,687,262	1,740,293	1,728,508
Restructuring costs and other	320,856	—	224,043	33,673
	7,866,616	6,280,734	5,861,500	4,846,423
Operating income	110,338	805,808	447,349	712,012
Interest and other income, net	29,321	49,634	52,395	66,505
Income before income taxes	139,659	855,442	499,744	778,517
Provision for income taxes	53,070	325,069	189,903	303,622
Net income	$ 86,589	$ 530,373	$ 309,841	$ 474,895
Earnings per common and common equivalent share	$ 0.73	$ 4.33	$ 2.58	$ 3.77
Common and common equivalent shares used in the calculations of earnings per share	119,125	122,490	120,283	125,813
Financial Position				
Cash, cash equivalents, and short-term investments	$ 892,303	$ 1,435,500	$ 892,719	$ 997,091
Accounts receivable, net	$ 1,381,946	$ 1,087,185	$ 907,159	$ 761,868
Inventories	$ 1,506,638	$ 580,097	$ 671,655	$ 355,473
Net property, plant, and equipment	$ 659,546	$ 462,221	$ 447,978	$ 398,165
Total assets	$ 5,171,412	$ 4,223,693	$ 3,493,597	$ 2,975,707
Current liabilities	$ 2,515,202	$ 1,425,520	$ 1,217,051	$ 1,027,055
Deferred income taxes	$ 629,832	$ 610,803	$ 509,870	$ 501,832
Shareholders' equity	$ 2,026,378	$ 2,187,370	$ 1,766,676	$ 1,446,820
Cash dividends declared per common share	$ 0.48	$ 0.48	$ 0.48	$ 0.44
Other Data (Unaudited)				
Regular employees	11,963	12,166	12,386	12,307
Temporary employees and contractors	2,975	2,632	2,046	2,221
International net sales as a percentage of total net sales	45%	45%	45%	42%
Gross margin as a percentage of net sales	34%	44%	47%	53%
R&D as a percentage of net sales	8%	8%	9%	9%
SG&A as a percentage of net sales	20%	24%	28%	31%
Operating income as a percentage of net sales	1%	11%	7%	13%
Return on net sales	1%	7%	5%	9%
Return on average total assets	2%	14%	10%	17%
Return on average shareholders' equity	4%	27%	19%	32%
Price range per common share	$ 65–$24¼	$ 69⅞–$43¼	$ 72¾–$25	$ 49½–$28¼

The number of shares and per share amounts for fiscal years 1983 through 1986 have been adjusted to reflect the two-for-one stock split effected on May 15, 1987.

Net income for fiscal year 1989 includes a pretax gain of approximately $79 million ($48 million, or $0.37 per share, after taxes) from the Company's sale of its common stock of Adobe Systems Incorporated.

Certain prior year amounts have been reclassified to conform to the current year presentation.

(In thousands, except employee, percentage, and per share data)

	1989	1988	1987	1986	1985	1984	1983
	$ 3,401,462	$ 2,766,328	$ 1,940,369	$ 1,411,812	$ 1,490,396	$ 1,187,839	$ 764,416
	1,882,551	1,305,045	720,699	490,086	427,884	328,037	218,353
	5,284,013	4,071,373	2,661,068	1,901,898	1,918,280	1,515,876	982,769
	2,694,823	1,990,879	1,296,220	891,112	1,117,864	878,586	505,765
	420,083	272,512	191,554	127,758	72,526	71,136	60,040
	1,534,794	1,187,644	801,856	609,497	588,156	480,303	290,845
	—	—	—	—	36,966	—	—
	4,649,700	3,451,035	2,289,630	1,628,367	1,815,512	1,430,025	856,650
	634,313	620,338	371,438	273,531	102,768	85,851	126,119
	110,009	35,823	38,930	36,187	17,277	23,334	20,003
	744,322	656,161	410,368	309,718	120,045	109,185	146,122
	290,289	255,903	192,872	155,755	58,822	45,130	69,408
	$ 454,033	$ 400,258	$ 217,496	$ 153,963	$ 61,223	$ 64,055	$ 76,714
	$ 3.53	$ 3.08	$ 1.65	$ 1.20	$ 0.49	$ 0.53	$ 0.64
	128,669	129,900	131,615	128,630	123,790	121,774	119,734
	$ 808,950	$ 545,717	$ 565,094	$ 576,215	$ 337,013	$ 114,888	$ 143,284
	$ 792,824	$ 638,816	$ 405,637	$ 263,126	$ 220,157	$ 258,238	$ 136,420
	$ 475,377	$ 461,470	$ 225,753	$ 108,680	$ 166,951	$ 264,619	$ 142,457
	$ 334,227	$ 207,357	$ 130,434	$ 107,315	$ 90,446	$ 75,868	$ 67,050
	$ 2,743,899	$ 2,082,086	$ 1,477,931	$ 1,160,128	$ 936,177	$ 788,786	$ 556,579
	$ 895,243	$ 827,093	$ 478,678	$ 328,535	$ 295,425	$ 255,184	$ 130,094
	$ 362,910	$ 251,568	$ 162,765	$ 137,506	$ 90,265	$ 69,037	$ 48,584
	$ 1,485,746	$ 1,003,425	$ 836,488	$ 694,087	$ 550,487	$ 464,565	$ 377,901
	$ 0.40	$ 0.32	$ 0.12	—	—	—	—
	12,068	9,536	6,236	4,950	4,326	5,382	4,645
	2,449	1,300	992	636	325	—	—
	36%	32%	27%	26%	22%	22%	22%
	49%	51%	51%	53%	42%	42%	49%
	8%	7%	7%	7%	4%	5%	6%
	29%	29%	30%	32%	31%	32%	30%
	12%	15%	14%	14%	5%	6%	13%
	9%	10%	8%	8%	3%	4%	8%
	19%	22%	16%	15%	7%	10%	17%
	36%	44%	28%	25%	12%	15%	24%
	$ 49⅜–$33¾	$ 59¼–$28	$ 57½–$16¼	$ 19⁷⁄₁₆–$7½	$ 15⁵⁄₁₆–$7¼	$ 16⁷⁄₁₆–$8⅞	$ 31⁵⁄₁₆–$9¹⁄₁₆

Selected Quarterly Financial Information (Unaudited)

(Tabular amounts in thousands, except per share amounts)

	Fourth Quarter	Third Quarter	Second Quarter	First Quarter
1993				
Net sales	$ 2,140,789	$ 1,861,979	$ 1,973,894	$ 2,000,292
Gross margin	$ 550,428	$ 606,004	$ 760,763	$ 810,925
Net income (loss)	$ 2,664	$ (188,316)	$ 110,900	$ 161,341
Earnings (loss) per common and common equivalent share	$ 0.02	$ (1.63)	$ 0.92	$ 1.33
Cash dividends declared per common share	$ 0.12	$ 0.12	$ 0.12	$ 0.12
Price range per common share	$ 40⅛–$24¼	$ 58¾–$39⅝	$ 65–$52¾	$ 60⅝–$43⅜
1992				
Net sales	$ 1,767,734	$ 1,740,171	$ 1,716,025	$ 1,862,612
Gross margin	$ 755,068	$ 771,327	$ 755,529	$ 813,281
Net income	$ 97,612	$ 131,665	$ 135,078	$ 166,018
Earnings per common and common equivalent share	$ 0.81	$ 1.07	$ 1.09	$ 1.36
Cash dividends declared per common share	$ 0.12	$ 0.12	$ 0.12	$ 0.12
Price range per common share	$ 49½–$43¼	$ 62¾–$44¼	$ 69⅞–$56⅜	$ 55–$47¾

At September 24, 1993, there were 34,034 shareholders of record.

The Company began declaring quarterly cash dividends on its common stock in April 1987. The dividend policy is determined quarterly by the Board of Directors and is dependent on the Company's earnings, capital requirements, financial condition, and other factors.

The price range per common share represents the highest and lowest closing prices for the Company's common stock on the NASDAQ National Market System during each quarter.

Net loss for the third quarter of 1993 and net income for fiscal year 1993 include a restructuring charge of $321 million ($199 million, or $1.72 per share, after taxes).

Management's Discussion and Analysis of Financial Condition and Results of Operations

The following discussion should be read in conjunction with the consolidated financial statements and notes thereto. All information is based on the Company's fiscal calendar.

(Tabular information: Dollars in millions, except per share amounts)

Results of Operations	1993	Change	1992	Change	1991
Net sales	$ 7,977	13%	$ 7,087	12%	$ 6,309
Gross margin	$ 2,728	–12%	$ 3,095	3%	$ 2,995
Percentage of net sales	34.2%		43.7%		47.5%
Operating expenses (excluding restructuring costs and other)	$ 2,297	—	$ 2,289	–1%	$ 2,323
Percentage of net sales	28.8%		32.3%		36.8%
Restructuring costs and other	$ 321	—	—	—	$ 224
Percentage of net sales	4.0%		—		3.6%
Net income	$ 87	–84%	$ 530	71%	$ 310
Earnings per share	$ 0./3	–83%	$ 4.33	68%	$ 2.58

Net Sales

The net sales growth in 1993 over 1992 reflected strong unit sales of the Company's Apple Macintosh computers, including the Macintosh Color Classic,® the Macintosh LC III, and the Macintosh Centris™ line (which has recently been consolidated with the Macintosh Quadra line), all of which were introduced in 1993. Additions to the PowerBook line of notebook computers and the Performa line of Macintosh computers also contributed to net sales growth. This growth was partially offset by declining unit sales of certain of the Company's more established products and older product versions. Total Macintosh computer unit sales increased 32% over the prior year, compared with a 20% increase from 1991 to 1992. The average aggregate revenue per unit declined 15% in 1993 compared with 1992, primarily as a result of pricing actions undertaken by the Company in response to continuing industrywide pricing pressures. Going forward, the Company anticipates continued industrywide competitive pricing and promotional actions.

Growth in net sales in 1992 over 1991 reflected strong unit sales of the Macintosh Classic II, Macintosh LC II, PowerBook, and Macintosh Quadra computers, all of which were introduced in 1992. This growth was partially offset by declining unit sales of certain of the Company's more established products and older product versions. The average aggregate revenue per unit increased slightly in 1992 when compared with 1991, primarily as a result of a shift in product mix toward the Company's PowerBook and Macintosh Quadra computers, offset somewhat by pricing and promotional actions undertaken by the Company in 1992.

In 1993, domestic net sales increased 13% over the prior year, compared with an increase of 11% in 1992 over 1991. International net sales grew 12% from 1992 to 1993, representing a slight decrease in growth rate compared with 13% growth from 1991 to 1992. In 1992, growth in international net sales slowed to 13%, compared with 22% growth from 1990 to 1991. International net sales represented 45% of net sales in 1993, 1992, and 1991.

During the fourth quarter of 1993, the Company expanded its midrange and high-end computer offerings with the introduction of the Macintosh Centris 660AV (later renamed the Macintosh Quadra 660AV) and Macintosh Quadra 840AV, respectively, which combine communications and computing capabilities by incorporating telecommunications, video, and speech technologies. On July 30, 1993, the Company introduced its first personal digital assistant (PDA) product, the Newton MessagePad. The Company also introduced the AudioVision™ 14 Display, which integrates audio and video capabilities, and several new system software products.

In addition to the products introduced in the fourth quarter, on October 21, 1993, the Company introduced several products that extend its entry-level, midrange, and notebook computer offerings. The new products include five entry-level Macintosh computers, the Macintosh Performa 460 and 470 series, the Performa 550, the Macintosh LC 475, and the Macintosh Quadra 605; two midrange computers, the Macintosh Quadra 610 and 650; and two notebook computers, the PowerBook Duo 250 and 270c. The Company also introduced the LaserWriter Select™ 360 and the LaserWriter® Pro 810, two new printers that focus on the needs of small and large workgroups, respectively. It is anticipated that a significant portion of the Company's future revenues will come from these and future new products. However, there can be no assurance that these new products will receive favorable market acceptance, and the Company cannot determine the ultimate effect these products will have on its sales or results of operations.

Gross Margin

Gross margin as a percentage of net sales in 1993 continued to decline from 1992 and 1991 levels. The gross margin percentage declined to 34.2% in 1993 from 43.7% in 1992, and during the fourth quarter of 1993 was 25.7% of net sales, compared with 42.7% in the fourth quarter of 1992. The downward trend in gross margin as a percentage of net sales was primarily a result of pricing and promotional actions undertaken by the Company in response to industrywide competitive pricing pressures and higher levels of inventory for certain products. Inventory valuation reserves recorded against certain products also contributed to the decline in gross margin as a percentage of net sales. Inventory levels increased sequentially each quarter during 1993 in support of an expanded product line and distribution channels and anticipated higher sales volumes. These higher levels of inventory, in turn, reduced the Company's liquidity position and resulted in increased levels of short-term borrowings under the Company's commercial paper program and from certain banks. The Company has commenced a number of measures that it expects will result in improved management of inventory over the course of 1994. Although the Company believes that these measures will result in improved inventory management and liquidity during 1994, there can be no assurance that these measures will be successful or that further inventory reserves will not be necessary in future periods.

The Company's results of operations were minimally affected by changes in foreign currency exchange rates in 1993 compared with 1992. The Company's operating strategy and pricing take into account changes in exchange rates over time; however, the Company's results of operations can be significantly affected in the short term by fluctuations in foreign currency exchange rates.

The decline in gross margin as a percentage of net sales from 47.5% in 1991 to 43.7% in 1992 was primarily the result of industrywide competitive pressures and associated pricing and promotional actions, partially offset by a shift in product mix toward the Company's PowerBook and Macintosh Quadra products. The Company's results of operations were minimally affected by changes in foreign currency exchange rates in 1992 compared with 1991.

The Company anticipates that gross margins for its personal computers will remain under pressure and below historic levels due to a variety of factors, including continued pricing pressures, increased competition, and advances in technology. In response to these factors, the Company has implemented various pricing and promotional actions, and as a result, expects continued lower gross margins as a percentage of net sales in 1994 compared with 1993.

Operating Expenses	1993	Change	1992	Change	1991
Research and development	$ 665	10%	$ 602	3%	$ 583
Percentage of net sales	8.3%		8.5%		9.2%

Research and development expenditures increased in amount during 1993 and 1992 compared with 1992 and 1991, respectively, reflecting net additions to the Company's engineering staff and related costs as the Company continues to invest in the development of new products and technologies, and in the enhancement of existing products in the areas of hardware and peripherals, system software, and networking and communications. Research and development expenditures, as a percentage of net sales, have continued to decrease since 1991 as a result of revenue growth during 1992 and 1993, coupled with the Company's continuing efforts to focus its research and development project spending. The Company believes that continued investments in research and development are critical to its future growth and competitive position in the marketplace, and are directly related to continued, timely development of new and enhanced products. The Company anticipates that research and development expenditures in 1994 will decrease slightly in amount and as a percentage of net sales as the Company continues its efforts to manage operating expense growth relative to gross margin levels.

	1993	Change	1992	Change	1991
Selling, general and administrative	$ 1,632	–3%	$ 1,687	–3%	$ 1,740
Percentage of net sales	20.5%		23.8%		27.6%

Selling, general and administrative expenses decreased in amount and as a percentage of net sales in 1993 and 1992 compared with 1992 and 1991, respectively. These decreases reflect the Company's ongoing efforts to manage operating expense growth relative to gross margin levels.

General and administrative expenses decreased in 1993 compared with 1992, primarily because of reduced employee-related expenses resulting from the restructuring actions taken in the third quarter of 1993. This decrease in general and administrative expenses was offset slightly by an increase in sales and marketing expenses as a result of increases in product marketing and advertising programs related to new product introductions and efforts to increase product demand.

In 1992, selling expenses decreased in amount and as a percentage of net sales compared with 1991, primarily because of reduced sales programs and marketing expenditures, as well as lower employee-related costs. Revenue growth also contributed to the decrease in selling expenses as a percentage of net sales. General and administrative expenses also decreased in amount and as a percentage of net sales in 1992 compared with 1991,

primarily as a result of lower legal and employee-related costs. The decrease was offset slightly by an increase in bad debt expense resulting from generally weak worldwide economic conditions.

The Company will continue to face the challenge of managing growth in selling, general and administrative expenses relative to gross margin levels, particularly in light of the Company's expectation of continued pressure on gross margins as a percentage of net sales and continued weak economic conditions worldwide. The Company's objective is to reduce selling, general and administrative expenses as a percentage of net sales in 1994 compared with 1993.

	1993	Change	1992	Change	1991
Restructuring costs and other	$ 321	—	—	—	$ 224
Percentage of net sales	4.0%		—		3.6%

In the third quarter of 1993, the Company initiated a plan to restructure its operations worldwide in order to address the competitive conditions in the personal computer industry, including the increased market demand for lower-priced products. In connection with this plan, the Company recorded a $321 million charge to operating expenses ($199 million, or $1.72 per share, after taxes). The restructuring costs included $162 million of estimated employee-related expenses and $159 million of estimated facilities, equipment, and other expenses associated with the consolidation of operations and the relocation and termination of operations and employees.

The Company's 1993 restructuring plan consists of a series of actions, the majority of which have been initiated. The remaining actions are expected to be initiated during 1994. Spending associated with certain actions is expected to extend beyond the initiation of those actions. For example, lease payments under noncancelable leases generally extend beyond the closing of the facilities. A portion of the employee-related actions was implemented in the fourth quarter of 1993. Although plans are in place to carry out the remaining actions, some plans may be refined as

the Company continues to identify the best means of achieving reductions in its cost structure. The Company believes that the restructuring actions are necessary in light of competitive pressures on its gross margins as a percentage of net sales and in light of generally weak economic conditions worldwide. While no assurances can be given that the restructuring actions will be successful or that similar actions will not be required in the future, the Company has already realized some cost-reduction benefits in the fourth quarter of 1993, and expects to realize further benefits in the future.

In 1991, the Company recorded a $197.5 million charge to operating expenses under a plan to restructure its operations worldwide. The Company believed that the restructuring actions were necessary in light of its continued expectation of lower gross margins as a percentage of net sales and in light of generally weak economic conditions worldwide. Also in 1991, the Company recorded a reserve in the amount of $26.5 million in connection with certain trademark litigation filed against it by Apple Corps Ltd. and Apple Corps S.A. in 1989, which amount was paid in settlement of such litigation in 1992.

Interest and Other Income, Net	1993	Change	1992	Change	1991
Interest and other income, net	$ 29	–41%	$ 50	–5%	$ 52

Interest and other income, net, decreased in amount in 1993 compared with 1992 because of lower interest rates, lower cash balances, expenses associated with certain financing transactions, lower gains on the sale of certain of the Company's venture capital investments, an increase in the cost of hedging certain foreign currency exposures, and an increase in interest expense due to higher commercial paper borrowing levels. This decrease was partially offset by a payment received from the Internal Revenue

Service reflecting interest earned on an income tax refund, and gains realized on foreign exchange and interest rate hedges.

Interest and other income, net, decreased slightly in amount in 1992 compared with 1991 because of lower interest rates and an increase in the cost of hedging certain foreign currency exposures. This decrease was partially offset by a gain on the sale of certain of the Company's venture capital investments, gains realized on interest rate hedges, and larger interest-earning portfolio balances.

Provision for Income Taxes	1993	Change	1992	Change	1991
Provision for income taxes	$ 53	–84%	$ 325	71%	$ 190
Effective tax rate	38%		38%		38%

The Company's effective tax rate remained unchanged in 1993, 1992, and 1991. For additional information regarding income taxes, refer to pages 25 and 26 of the Notes to Consolidated Financial Statements.

Factors That May Affect Future Results

The Company's future operating results may be affected by a number of factors, including the Company's ability to increase market share in its personal computer business while expanding its new businesses and product offerings into other markets; broaden industry acceptance of the Newton PDA product, including effectively licensing Newton technology and marketing the related products and services; realize the anticipated cost-reduction benefits associated with its restructuring plan initiated in the third quarter of 1993; develop, manufacture, and sell its products profitably; reduce existing inventory levels; and manage future inventory levels effectively. The Company's future operating results may also be affected by uncertainties relative to global economic conditions; the strength of its distribution channels; industry factors; and the availability and cost of components.

During calendar year 1994, the Company plans to introduce several Macintosh computers based on a new PowerPC Reduced Instruction Set Computing (RISC) microprocessor. Accordingly, the Company's results of operations could be adversely affected if it is unable to successfully transition over time its line of Macintosh personal computers and servers from the Motorola 68000 series of microprocessors to the PowerPC RISC microprocessor. The success of this transition will depend on the Company's ability to continue the sales momentum of products based on Motorola 68000 processors through the introduction of the PowerPC RISC-based products, to successfully manage inventory levels between both product lines, to gain market acceptance of the new RISC-based products, and to coordinate the timely development and distribution of new versions of commonly used software products specifically designed for the PowerPC RISC-based products.

The personal computer industry is highly volatile and continues to be characterized by dynamic customer demand patterns, rapid technological advances, frequent introduction of new products and product enhancements, and industrywide competition resulting in aggressive pricing practices and downward pressure on gross margins. The Company's operating results could be adversely affected should the Company be unable to accurately anticipate customer demand; introduce new products on a timely basis; manage lead times required to obtain components in order to be more responsive to short-term shifts in customer demand patterns; offer customers the latest competitive technologies while effectively managing the impact on inventory levels and the potential for customer confusion created by product proliferation; effectively manage the impact on the Company of industrywide pricing pressures; or effectively implement and manage the competitive risk associated with certain of the Company's collaboration agreements with other companies, such as the agreements with International Business Machines Corporation (IBM). The Company's results of operations could also be adversely affected, and additional inventory valuation reserves could result, if anticipated sales unit growth projections for new and current product offerings are not realized.

A large portion of the Company's revenues in recent years has come from its international operations. As a result, the Company's operations and financial results could be significantly affected by international factors, such as changes in foreign currency exchange rates or weak economic conditions in foreign markets in which the Company distributes its products. The Company's operating strategy and pricing take into account changes in exchange rates over time; however, the Company's results of operations can be significantly affected in the short term by fluctuations in foreign currency exchange rates.

In July, August, and October 1993, the Company introduced the Newton MessagePad and several new Macintosh products that extend its notebook, low-end, midrange, and high-end offerings. In addition, the Company introduced several new or enhanced peripheral products. The success of these new products is dependent on a number of factors, including market acceptance, the Company's ability to manage the risks associated with product transitions, and the Company's ability to reduce existing inventory levels and manage future inventory levels in line with anticipated product demand and to manufacture the products in appropriate quantities to meet anticipated demand. Accordingly, the Company cannot determine the ultimate effect that these new products will have on its sales or results of operations.

The Company's products include certain components, such as Motorola microprocessors and monochrome active-matrix displays manufactured by Hosiden Corporation, that are currently available only from single sources. Any availability limitations, interruptions in supplies, or price increases of these and other components could adversely affect the Company's business and financial results.

The majority of the Company's research and development activities, its corporate headquarters, and other critical business operations are located near major earthquake faults. Operating results could be materially adversely affected in the event of a major earthquake.

A number of uncertainties also exist regarding the marketing and distribution of the Company's products. The Company's primary means of distribution is through third-party computer resellers and various education and consumer channels. Although the Company has in place certain policies to limit concentrations of credit risk, business and financial results could be adversely affected in the event that the generally weak financial condition of third-party computer resellers worsens. In addition, the Company is continuing its expansion into new distribution channels, such as mass-merchandise stores, consumer electronics outlets, and computer superstores, in response to changing industry practices and customer preferences. At this time, the Company cannot determine the ultimate effect of these or other future distribution expansion efforts on its future operating results.

Because of the foregoing factors, as well as other factors affecting the Company's operating results, past financial performance should not be considered to be a reliable indicator of future performance, and investors should not use historical trends to anticipate results or trends in future periods. In addition, the Company's participation in a highly dynamic industry often results in significant volatility of the Company's common stock price.

Liquidity and Capital Resources	1993	1992	1991
Cash, cash equivalents, and short-term investments	$ 892	$ 1,436	$ 893
Working capital	$ 1,823	$ 2,133	$ 1,647
Cash generated by (used for) operations	$ (662)	$ 921	$ 189
Cash used for investment activities, excluding short-term investments	$ 228	$ 264	$ 276
Cash generated by (used for) financing activities	$ 347	$ (114)	$ (18)

More cash was used for operations in 1993 compared with 1992, primarily because of a significant increase in inventory levels; decreases in net income, income taxes payable, and other current liabilities; and an increase in accounts receivable levels. Cash used for operations was offset slightly by increases in accrued restructuring costs and accounts payable.

Inventory increased substantially during 1993 as a result of higher levels of purchased parts, work in process, and finished goods inventory in support of an expanded product line and distribution channels and anticipated higher sales volumes. The Company expects that during the course of 1994, inventory levels will decline from fourth quarter 1993 levels, as the Company has identified measures intended to reduce inventory levels. These measures include promotional and pricing actions, increased emphasis on designing in commonality of parts among products, increased use of manufacturing-on-demand techniques based on product orders rather than forecasts, and greater rationalization of product offerings. Although the Company believes that these measures will result in improved inventory management and liquidity during 1994, there can be no assurance that these measures will be successful or that further inventory reserves will not be necessary in the future. The decrease in net income resulted primarily from a reduction in gross margins and the restructuring charge included in operating expenses for the third quarter. The reduction in earnings also contributed to the decrease in income taxes payable. Other current liabilities decreased as the Company continued to manage operating expense levels. The increase in accounts receivable corresponded with the higher sales levels achieved in 1993, coupled with slower collections resulting from economic pressures in the reseller industry, and the Company's expansion into consumer channels, where payment terms are generally longer. These uses of cash were offset slightly by increases in accrued restructuring costs as a result of the Company's plan to restructure its operations worldwide and increases in accounts payable, reflecting the higher level of inventory purchases.

In 1992, net cash generated by operations increased compared with 1991, primarily as a result of increased net income and lower inventory levels, offset somewhat by a reduction in accrued restructuring costs. Higher sales resulting from strong demand for new products and price reductions and other sales incentive programs, coupled with a decrease in operating expenses, contributed to the increase in net income. Inventory levels decreased as a result of higher sales levels and improved inventory management.

Improvement in cash flow from operations in 1994 will depend principally on the Company's ability to improve profit levels and reduce inventory levels.

Excluding short-term investments, net cash used for investments declined in 1993 compared with 1992 and 1991 levels. Net cash used for the purchase of property, plant, and equipment totaled $213 million in 1993, and was primarily made up of increases in land and buildings, manufacturing machinery and equipment, and leasehold improvements. The Company anticipates that capital expenditures in 1994 will be slightly below 1993 expenditures.

The Company leases the majority of its facilities and certain of its equipment under noncancelable operating leases. In 1993, rent expense under all operating leases was approximately $170 million. The Company's future lease commitments are discussed in the Notes to Consolidated Financial Statements.

On November 11, 1992, modifications were made to the terms of the Cupertino Gateway Partners partnership agreement. As a result of these modifications, the Company now consolidates its wholly owned subsidiary's 50.001% investment in the partnership. The Company previously accounted for this investment under the equity method. The Company recorded additional property, plant, and equipment of $139 million, relinquished related assets of $81 million, and assumed liabilities of $58 million as a result of this revised partnership agreement. This transaction has been excluded from the Company's Consolidated Statement of Cash Flows for 1993, because the change in accounting treatment did not involve a source or use of cash.

Net cash generated by financing activities increased in 1993 compared with 1992 and 1991, mainly because of a significant increase in short-term borrowings, which were used for working capital needs. Net cash generated by financing activities was partially offset by the repurchase of approximately 5 million shares of the Company's common stock in the open market under stock repurchase programs.

The Company's aggregate commercial paper borrowings at the end of 1993 were approximately $823 million, compared with $184 million and $149 million at the end of 1992 and 1991, respectively, which borrowings were incurred principally to finance increases in inventory levels in each period. As of October 29, 1993, the Company's commercial paper borrowings totaled approximately $936 million; its other short-term borrowings totaled approximately $80 million; and its cash, cash equivalents, and short-term investments totaled approximately $964 million. The Company expects that during 1994, its liquidity position will improve from recent levels, as the measures the Company has identified to reduce

inventory levels are implemented and take effect. Although the Company believes that these measures will result in improved inventory management and liquidity in 1994, there can be no assurance that these measures will be successful.

The Company expects that it will continue to incur short-term borrowings from time to time to finance U.S. working capital needs and capital expenditures, because a substantial portion of the Company's cash, cash equivalents, and short-term investments is held by foreign subsidiaries, generally in U.S. dollar–denominated holdings. Amounts held by foreign subsidiaries would be subject to U.S. income taxation upon repatriation to the United States; the Company's financial statements fully provide for any related tax liability on amounts that may be repatriated.

On May 5, 1993, the Company filed an omnibus shelf registration statement with the Securities and Exchange Commission for the registration of debt and other securities for an aggregate offering price of $500 million. The securities may be offered from time to time in amounts, at prices, and on terms to be determined in light of market conditions at the time of sale. The Company believes that the shelf registration provides financial flexibility to meet future funding requirements and to take advantage of attractive market conditions.

The Company believes that its balances of cash, cash equivalents, and short-term investments, together with funds generated from operations and short- and long-term borrowing capabilities, will be sufficient to meet its operating cash requirements in the foreseeable future.

Consolidated Statements of Income

(In thousands, except per share amounts)

Three fiscal years ended September 24, 1993	1993	1992	1991
Net sales	$ 7,976,954	$ 7,086,542	$ 6,308,849
Costs and expenses:			
Cost of sales	5,248,834	3,991,337	3,314,118
Research and development	664,564	602,135	583,046
Selling, general and administrative	1,632,362	1,687,262	1,740,293
Restructuring costs and other	320,856	—	224,043
	7,866,616	6,280,734	5,861,500
Operating income	110,338	805,808	447,349
Interest and other income, net	29,321	49,634	52,395
Income before income taxes	139,659	855,442	499,744
Provision for income taxes	53,070	325,069	189,903
Net income	$ 86,589	$ 530,373	$ 309,841
Earnings per common and common equivalent share	$ 0.73	$ 4.33	$ 2.58
Common and common equivalent shares used in the calculations of earnings per share	119,125	122,490	120,283

See accompanying notes.

Consolidated Balance Sheets

(Dollars in thousands)

September 24, 1993, and September 25, 1992	1993	1992
Assets:		
Current assets:		
Cash and cash equivalents	$ 676,413	$ 498,557
Short-term investments	215,890	936,943
Accounts receivable, net of allowance for doubtful accounts of $83,776 ($83,048 in 1992)	1,381,946	1,087,185
Inventories	1,506,638	580,097
Prepaid income taxes	268,085	199,139
Other current assets	289,383	256,473
Total current assets	4,338,355	3,558,394
Property, plant, and equipment:		
Land and buildings	404,688	255,808
Machinery and equipment	578,272	516,335
Office furniture and equipment	167,905	155,317
Leasehold improvements	261,792	208,180
	1,412,657	1,135,640
Accumulated depreciation and amortization	(753,111)	(673,419)
Net property, plant, and equipment	659,546	462,221
Other assets	173,511	203,078
	$ 5,171,412	$ 4,223,693
Liabilities and Shareholders' Equity:		
Current liabilities:		
Notes payable	$ 823,182	$ 184,461
Accounts payable	742,622	426,936
Accrued compensation and employee benefits	144,779	142,382
Income taxes payable	23,658	78,382
Accrued marketing and distribution	174,547	187,767
Accrued restructuring costs	307,932	105,038
Other current liabilities	298,482	300,554
Total current liabilities	2,515,202	1,425,520
Deferred income taxes	629,832	610,803
Commitments and contingencies	—	—
Shareholders' equity:		
Common stock, no par value; 320,000,000 shares authorized; 116,147,035 shares issued and outstanding in 1993 (118,478,825 shares in 1992)	203,613	282,310
Retained earnings	1,842,600	1,904,519
Accumulated translation adjustment	(19,835)	541
Total shareholders' equity	2,026,378	2,187,370
	$ 5,171,412	$ 4,223,693

See accompanying notes.

Consolidated Statements of Shareholders' Equity

(In thousands, except per share amounts)

	Common Stock		Retained Earnings	Accumulated Translation Adjustment	Notes Receivable from Shareholders	Total Shareholders' Equity
	Shares	Amount				
Balance at September 28, 1990	115,359	$ 136,555	$ 1,312,156	$ 4,142	$ (6,033)	$ 1,446,820
Common stock issued under stock option and purchase plans, including related tax benefits	7,377	253,523	—	—	(744)	252,779
Repurchase of common stock	(4,350)	(111,213)	(73,464)	—	—	(184,677)
Repayment of notes receivable from shareholders	—	—	—	—	4,941	4,941
Cash dividends of $0.48 per common share	—	—	(56,509)	—	—	(56,509)
Accumulated translation adjustment	—	—	—	(6,519)	—	(6,519)
Net income	—	—	309,841	—	—	309,841
Balance at September 27, 1991	118,386	278,865	1,492,024	(2,377)	(1,836)	1,766,676
Common stock issued under stock option and purchase plans, including related tax benefits	4,093	155,388	—	—	—	155,388
Repurchase of common stock	(4,000)	(151,943)	(60,682)	—	—	(212,625)
Repayment of notes receivable from shareholders	—	—	—	—	1,836	1,836
Cash dividends of $0.48 per common share	—	—	(57,196)	—	—	(57,196)
Accumulated translation adjustment	—	—	—	2,918	—	2,918
Net income	—	—	530,373	—	—	530,373
Balance at September 25, 1992	118,479	282,310	1,904,519	541	—	2,187,370
Common stock issued under stock option and purchase plans, including related tax benefits	2,693	101,842	—	—	—	101,842
Repurchase of common stock	(5,025)	(180,539)	(92,915)	—	—	(273,454)
Cash dividends of $0.48 per common share	—	—	(55,593)	—	—	(55,593)
Accumulated translation adjustment	—	—	—	(20,376)	—	(20,376)
Net income	—	—	86,589	—	—	86,589
Balance at September 24, 1993	116,147	$ 203,613	$ 1,842,600	$ (19,835)	$ —	$ 2,026,378

See accompanying notes.

Consolidated Statements of Cash Flows

(In thousands)

Three fiscal years ended September 24, 1993	1993	1992	1991
Cash and cash equivalents, beginning of the period	$ 498,557	$ 604,147	$ 374,682
Operations:			
Net income	86,589	530,373	309,841
Adjustments to reconcile net income to cash generated by (used for) operations:			
Depreciation and amortization	166,113	217,182	204,433
Net book value of property, plant, and equipment retirements	13,145	14,687	6,955
Changes in assets and liabilities:			
Accounts receivable	(294,761)	(180,026)	(145,291)
Inventories	(926,541)	91,558	(316,182)
Prepaid income taxes	(68,946)	23,841	(97,445)
Other current assets	(96,314)	(87,376)	(5,738)
Accounts payable	315,686	69,852	16,509
Income taxes payable	(54,724)	100,361	42,308
Accrued restructuring costs	202,894	(57,327)	162,365
Other current liabilities	(24,007)	96,524	3,570
Deferred income taxes	19,029	100,933	8,038
Cash generated by (used for) operations	(661,837)	920,582	189,363
Investments:			
Purchase of short-term investments	(1,431,998)	(2,121,341)	(610,696)
Proceeds from short-term investments	2,153,051	1,472,970	944,533
Purchase of property, plant, and equipment	(213,118)	(194,853)	(218,348)
Other	(15,169)	(69,410)	(57,165)
Cash generated by (used for) investment activities	492,766	(912,634)	58,324
Financing:			
Increase in short-term borrowings	638,721	35,895	25,936
Increases in common stock, net of related tax benefits and changes in notes receivable from shareholders	85,289	120,388	197,028
Repurchase of common stock	(273,454)	(212,625)	(184,677)
Cash dividends	(55,593)	(57,196)	(56,509)
Other	(48,036)	—	—
Cash generated by (used for) financing activities	346,927	(113,538)	(18,222)
Total cash generated (used)	177,856	(105,590)	229,465
Cash and cash equivalents, end of the period	$ 676,413	$ 498,557	$ 604,147
Supplemental cash flow disclosures:			
Cash paid during the year for:			
Interest	$ 11,748	$ 8,778	$ 9,755
Income taxes	$ 250,987	$ 98,330	$ 265,755
Schedule of noncash transactions:			
Tax benefit from stock options	$ 16,553	$ 36,836	$ 60,692

See accompanying notes.

Notes to Consolidated Financial Statements

Summary of Significant Accounting Policies

Basis of Presentation

The consolidated financial statements include the accounts of Apple Computer, Inc. and its wholly owned subsidiaries (the Company). Intercompany accounts and transactions have been eliminated. The Company's fiscal year-end is the last Friday in September.

Revenue Recognition

The Company recognizes revenue at the time products are shipped. Provision is made currently for estimated product returns and price protection that may occur under Company programs. Historically, actual amounts recorded for product returns and price protection have not varied significantly from estimated amounts.

Foreign Currency Translation

Gains and losses resulting from foreign currency translation are accumulated as a separate component of shareholders' equity until the foreign entity is sold or liquidated. Gains and losses resulting from foreign currency transactions are immaterial and are included in the statement of income.

Financial Instruments

The Company hedges certain portions of its exposure to foreign currency and interest rate fluctuations through a variety of strategies and instruments, including forward foreign exchange contracts, foreign currency options, and interest rate derivative instruments. Gains and losses associated with these financial instruments and the underlying exposures are generally recorded currently in income. Gains and losses are deferred and included as a component of the related transaction when the instrument hedges a firm commitment. Gains from purchased foreign currency options used to hedge certain probable future transactions are also deferred and included as a component of the related transaction, while any losses on sold options are recognized currently in income. The interest element of the foreign currency instruments is generally recognized over the life of the contract.

Cash, Cash Equivalents, and Short-Term Investments

All highly liquid investments with a maturity of 3 months or less at the date of purchase are considered to be cash equivalents; investments with maturities between 3 and 12 months are considered to be short-term investments. Short-term investments are carried at cost plus accrued interest, which approximates fair value. A substantial portion of the Company's cash, cash equivalents, and short-term investments is held by foreign subsidiaries and is generally in U.S. dollar–denominated holdings. Amounts held by foreign subsidiaries would be subject to U.S. income taxation upon repatriation to the United States; the Company's financial statements fully provide for any related tax liability on amounts that may be repatriated.

Income Taxes

U.S. income taxes have not been provided on a cumulative total of $194 million of undistributed earnings of certain of the Company's foreign subsidiaries. It is intended that these earnings will be indefinitely invested in operations outside the United States. Except for such indefinitely invested earnings, the Company provides federal and state income taxes currently on undistributed earnings of foreign subsidiaries. The Company has not elected early adoption of Financial Accounting Standard No. 109, Accounting for Income Taxes (FAS 109). FAS 109 becomes effective beginning with the Company's 1994 fiscal year and will not have a material effect on the Company's financial position or results of operations.

Earnings per Share

Earnings per share are computed using the weighted average number of common and dilutive common equivalent shares attributable to stock options outstanding during the period. Loss per share is computed using the weighted average number of common shares outstanding during the period.

Inventories

Inventories are stated at the lower of cost (first-in, first-out) or market.

Property, Plant, and Equipment

Property, plant, and equipment is stated at cost. Depreciation and amortization is computed by use of declining balance and straight-line methods over the estimated useful lives of the assets.

Reclassifications

Certain prior year amounts on the Consolidated Statements of Cash Flows and on the Industry Segment and Geographic Information and Income Taxes footnotes have been reclassified to conform to the current year presentation.

Inventories

Inventories consist of the following: (In thousands)

	1993	1992
Purchased parts	$ 504,201	$ 150,147
Work in process	284,440	94,790
Finished goods	717,997	335,160
	$ 1,506,638	$ 580,097

Notes Payable

As of September 24, 1993, notes payable represented unsecured commercial paper borrowings of approximately $823 million at varying interest rates. The carrying amount of the notes payable approximates their fair value due to their short maturities. The weighted average interest rate was approximately 3.3%, and the average days to maturity was 33 days. As of September 25, 1992, notes payable represented unsecured commercial paper borrowings of approximately $184 million at varying interest rates. The weighted average interest rate was approximately 3.5%, and the average days to maturity was 30 days. Interest expense in each of the 3 years ended September 24, 1993, was immaterial.

Restructuring of Operations

In the third quarter of 1993, the Company initiated a plan to restructure its operations worldwide in order to address the competitive conditions in the personal computer industry, including the increased market demand for lower-priced products. In connection with this plan, the Company recorded a $321 million charge to operating expenses ($199 million, or $1.72 per share, after taxes). The restructuring costs included $162 million of estimated employee-related expenses and $159 million of estimated facilities, equipment, and other expenses associated with the consolidation of operations and the relocation and termination of certain operations and employees.

The Company's 1993 restructuring plan consists of a series of actions, the majority of which have been initiated. The remaining actions are expected to be initiated during 1994. Spending associated with certain actions is expected to extend beyond the initiation of those actions. For example, lease payments under noncancelable leases generally extend beyond the closing of facilities. A portion of the employee-related actions was implemented in the fourth quarter of 1993. Although plans are in place to carry out the remaining actions, some plans may be refined as the Company continues to identify the best means of achieving reductions in its cost structure. The Company believes that the restructuring actions are necessary in light of competitive pressures on its gross margins as a percentage of net sales and in light of generally weak economic conditions worldwide. While no assurances can be given that the restructuring actions will be successful or that similar actions will not be required in the future, the Company has already realized some cost-reduction benefits in the fourth quarter of 1993, and expects to realize further benefits in the future.

In 1991, the Company recorded a $197.5 million charge to operating expenses under a plan to restructure its operations worldwide. The Company believed that the restructuring actions were necessary in light of its continued expectation of lower gross margins as a percentage of net sales and in light of generally weak economic conditions worldwide. Also in 1991, the Company recorded a reserve in the amount of $26.5 million in connection with certain trademark litigation filed against it by Apple Corps Ltd. and Apple Corps S.A. in 1989, which amount was paid in settlement of such litigation in 1992.

Commitments and Contingencies

Lease Commitments

The Company leases various facilities and equipment under noncancelable lease arrangements. The major facilities leases are for terms of 5 to 10 years and generally provide renewal options for terms of up to 5 additional years. Rent expense under all operating leases was approximately $170 million, $160 million, and $163 million in 1993, 1992, and 1991, respectively.

Future minimum lease payments under these noncancelable operating leases as of September 24, 1993, are as follows:

	(In thousands)
1994	$ 114,566
1995	95,238
1996	60,161
1997	43,089
1998	22,564
Later years	185,101
Total minimum lease payments	$ 520,719

Leases for facilities that were subject to the Company's restructuring actions initiated in the third quarter of 1991 and in the third quarter of 1993 are included in the preceding table. Future lease payments associated with these facilities were provided for in the Company's restructuring reserves recorded in 1993 and 1991, and therefore do not represent future operating expenses. Minimum lease payments may decline in the future, as the leases for facilities subject to restructuring actions are terminated or otherwise completed.

In July 1991, a subsidiary of the Company formed a partnership, Cupertino Gateway Partners, with a local real estate developer for the purpose of constructing a campus-type office facility to be leased to the Company by the partnership. The Company executed six noncancelable leases with the partnership to lease the buildings for terms of approximately 17 years. Modifications were made to the terms of the Cupertino Gateway Partners partnership agreement on November 11, 1992, and as a result of these modifications, the Company now consolidates its wholly owned subsidiary's 50.001% investment in the partnership. Because of the Company's consolidation of its investment, future minimum lease payments to the partnership of approximately $209 million have been excluded from the preceding table.

Off-Balance-Sheet Risk and Concentrations of Credit

Financial Instruments
At September 24, 1993, the Company had approximately $273 million ($538 million at September 25, 1992) in forward foreign exchange contracts in various currencies. Forward foreign exchange contracts not accounted for as hedges are carried at fair value. Deferred gains or losses on forward foreign exchange contracts accounted for as hedges were immaterial at September 24, 1993. The Company also enters into foreign currency options, both purchased and sold, generally to protect against currency exchange risks associated with certain firmly committed and certain other probable, but not firmly committed, transactions. The face value of the Company's foreign currency options with off-balance-sheet risk

of loss totaled approximately $2,691 million at September 24, 1993 ($577 million at September 25, 1992). While the notional amount of the foreign currency options discussed above reflects the volume of activity in those financial instruments at a single point in time, the notional amount at September 24, 1993, does not represent the Company's exposure to credit or market loss. Foreign currency options not accounted for as hedges are carried at fair value, with any gains and losses reflected in operating results. Deferred gains on foreign currency options accounted for as hedges were immaterial at September 24, 1993.

In addition, the Company has entered into interest rate risk management agreements (interest rate derivatives) with certain financial institutions. At September 24, 1993, the Company had outstanding interest rate derivatives with a total notional amount of approximately $179 million. Interest rate derivatives are carried at fair value. The agreements have maturities ranging from 3 months to 3 years and generally require the Company to pay a floating interest rate based on the 3-month or 6-month London InterBank Offered Rates and to receive interest at a fixed rate. Though the notional amounts of the Company's interest rate derivatives are an indication of the volume of these transactions, the amounts potentially subject to credit risk are generally limited to the amounts, if any, by which the present value of the counterparties' expected obligations exceed the present value of the expected obligations of the Company.

The value of any of these outstanding foreign exchange forward contracts, foreign exchange currency options, and interest rate derivative instruments as currently recognized in the consolidated balance sheet at September 24, 1993, may change in the future based on changes in foreign exchange and interest rate market conditions.

The estimates of fair values are based on the appropriate pricing models using current market information. However, in certain instances, judgment is required in estimating the fair values. The amounts ultimately realized upon settlement of these financial instruments will depend on actual market conditions during the remaining life of the instruments.

Concentrations of Credit Risk

The Company distributes its products principally through third-party computer resellers and various education and consumer channels. Concentrations of credit risk with respect to trade receivables are limited because of flooring arrangements for selected customers with third-party financing companies and because the Company's customer base consists of large numbers of geographically diverse customers dispersed across many industries. The counterparties to the agreements relating to the Company's investments and foreign currency and interest rate risk management financial instruments consist of a number of major international financial institutions. The Company does not believe that there is significant risk of nonperformance by these counterparties because the Company continually monitors its positions and the credit ratings of such counterparties, and limits the financial exposure and the amount of agreements and contracts it enters into with any one party. The Company generally does not require collateral from counterparties.

Income Taxes

The provision for income taxes consists of the following: (In thousands)

	1993	1992	1991
Federal:	$ 13,637	$ 108,512	$ 106,162
Current	(23,757)	100,355	22,131
Deferred	(10,120)	208,867	128,293
State:	3,144	26,935	26,866
Current	633	13,891	(9,591)
Deferred	3,777	40,826	17,275
Foreign:	39,512	65,144	40,614
Current	19,901	10,232	3,721
Deferred	59,413	75,376	44,335
Provision for income taxes	$ 53,070	$ 325,069	$ 189,903

The foreign provision for income taxes is based on foreign pretax earnings of approximately $416 million, $611 million, and $464 million in 1993, 1992, and 1991, respectively.

Deferred (prepaid) income taxes result from timing differences between years in the recognition of certain revenue and expense items for financial and tax reporting purposes. The sources of timing differences and the related tax effects are as follows:

                                                                                              (In thousands)

	1993	1992	1991
Income of foreign subsidiaries not taxable in current year	$ 53,150	$ 71,429	$ 103,912
Warranty, bad debt, and other expenses	(80,126)	35,494	(96,349)
Depreciation	(3,796)	(3,398)	(11,989)
Inventory valuation	(16,835)	(1,940)	(16,691)
State income taxes	2,607	(10,959)	4,585
Other individually immaterial items	41,777	33,852	32,793
Total deferred taxes	$ (3,223)	$ 124,478	$ 16,261

A reconciliation of the provision for income taxes, with the amount computed by applying the statutory federal income tax rate (34.75% in 1993, and 34.00% in both 1992 and 1991) to income before income taxes, is as follows:

		(In thousands)
	1993	1992	1991
Computed expected tax	$ 48,532	$ 290,850	$ 169,913
State taxes, net of federal benefit	2,465	26,945	11,401
Research and development tax credit	(8,000)	(7,000)	(13,000)
Indefinitely invested earnings of foreign subsidiaries	(21,083)	(31,280)	(13,940)
Other individually immaterial items	31,156	45,554	35,529
Provision for income taxes	$ 53,070	$ 325,069	$ 189,903
Effective tax rate	38%	38%	38%

The Company's federal income tax returns for 1981 through 1988 have been examined by the Internal Revenue Service (IRS). All contested issues for the years 1981 through 1983 have been resolved. During 1990, the IRS proposed tax deficiencies for the years 1984 through 1986, and the Company made prepayments thereon in 1991. During 1993, the IRS proposed tax deficiencies for the years 1987 and 1988, and the Company made prepayments thereon in May 1993. The Company is contesting these alleged deficiencies and is pursuing administrative and judicial remedies. Management believes that adequate provision has been made for any adjustments that may result from these examinations.

Preferred Stock

Five million shares of preferred stock have been authorized for issuance in one or more series. The Board of Directors is authorized to fix the number and designation of any such series and to determine the rights, preferences, privileges, and restrictions granted to or imposed on any such series.

Common Stock

Shareholder Rights Plan

In May 1989, the Company adopted a shareholder rights plan and distributed a dividend of one right to purchase one share of common stock (a Right) for each outstanding share of common stock of the Company. The Rights become exercisable in certain limited circumstances involving a potential business combination transaction of the Company and are initially exercisable at a price of $200 per share. Following certain other events after the Rights have become exercisable, each Right entitles its holder to purchase for $200 an amount of common stock of the Company, or, in certain circumstances, securities of the acquiror, having a then-current market value of two times the exercise price of the Right. The Rights are redeemable and may be amended at the Company's option before they become exercisable. Until a Right is exercised, the holder of a Right, as such, has no rights as a shareholder of the Company. The Rights expire on April 19, 1999.

Stock Option Plans

The Company has in effect a 1990 Stock Option Plan (the 1990 Plan) and a 1987 Executive Long Term Stock Option Plan (the 1987 Plan). The 1981 Stock Option Plan terminated in October 1990. Options granted before that date remain outstanding in accordance with their terms. Options may be granted under the 1990 Plan to employees, including officers and directors who are employees, at not less than the fair market value on the date of grant. These options generally become exercisable over varying periods, based on continued employment, and generally expire 10 years after the grant date. The 1990 Plan permits the granting of incentive stock options, nonstatutory stock options, and stock appreciation rights.

The 1987 Plan permits the granting of nonstatutory options to certain officers of the Company to purchase Apple common stock at prices not less than 75% of the fair market value on the date of grant. Options under the 1987 Plan are not exercisable for 18 months after the date of grant, and then become exercisable at varying rates over the subsequent 7 years, based on continued service to the Company.

On August 5, 1993, the Board of Directors adopted a resolution allowing employees below the level of vice president to exchange 1.5 options at their existing option price for 1.0 new options having an exercise price of $24.25 per share, the fair market value of the Company's common stock on September 14, 1993. Options received under this program are subject to 1 year of additional vesting such that the new vesting date for each vesting portion will be the later of September 15, 1994, or the original vesting date plus 1 year. Approximately 4.1 million options were exchanged under this program.

Summarized information regarding the Company's stock option plans as of September 24, 1993, which includes the grants made under the exchange program described in the preceding paragraph, is as follows:

(In thousands, except per share amounts)

	Number of Shares	Price per Share
Outstanding at September 25, 1992	14,462	$7.50–$68.00
Granted	5,728	
Exercised	(1,730)	$7.50–$57.75
Expired or canceled	(5,364)	
Outstanding at September 24, 1993	13,096	$7.50–$68.00
Exercisable	6,219	
Reserved for issuance	17,909	
Available for future grant	4,817	

Restricted Stock Plan

On April 1, 1993, the Company's Board of Directors approved a Restricted Stock Plan for officers of the Company (the RSP), which became effective July 1, 1993, subject to shareholder approval in January 1994. The RSP is designed to provide an incentive for officers to continue to own shares of the Company's common stock acquired upon exercise of options under any of the Company's Stock Option Plans, thus more closely aligning officers' financial interests with those of the shareholders. The RSP provides that officers who exercise stock options and continue to hold the exercised shares for at least 3 years will receive up to three Awards of shares of restricted stock. Each such Award is for one-third the number of shares held for the requisite retention period. Each restricted stock Award granted pursuant to the plan becomes fully vested 3 years after the grant date, provided that the officer maintains continuous employment with the Company and that other vesting requirements are met.

Employee Stock Purchase Plan

The Company has an employee stock purchase plan (the Purchase Plan) under which substantially all employees may purchase common stock through payroll deductions at a price equal to 85% of the lower of the fair market values as of the beginning or end of the offering period. Stock purchases under the Purchase Plan are limited to 10% of an employee's compensation. In January 1993, the Company's shareholders approved an amendment to the Purchase Plan proposed by the Board of Directors to increase the number of shares reserved for issuance by 2 million shares. As of September 24, 1993, approximately 2.1 million shares were reserved for future issuance under the Purchase Plan.

Stock Repurchase Programs

In November 1992, the Board of Directors authorized the purchase of up to 10 million shares of the Company's common stock in the open market. Approximately 3.4 million shares were repurchased under this authorization in 1993. In September 1990, the Board of Directors authorized the purchase of up to 10 million shares of the Company's common stock in the open market. During 1993, 1992, and 1991, the Company repurchased approximately 1.6 million, 4.0 million, and 4.4 million shares, respectively, in the open market under this repurchase program.

Savings Plan

The Company has an employee savings plan (the Savings Plan) that qualifies as a deferred salary arrangement under Section 401(k) of the Internal Revenue Code. Under the Savings Plan, participating U.S. employees may defer a portion of their pretax earnings, up to the Internal Revenue Service annual contribution limit ($8,994 for calendar year 1993). The Company matches 30% to 50% of each employee's contributions, depending on length of service, up to a maximum 6% of the employee's earnings. The Company's matching contributions to the Savings Plan were approximately $11.1 million in each of 1993 and 1992 and $10.6 million in 1991.

Litigation

Apple v. Microsoft Corporation and Hewlett-Packard Company

In March 1988, the Company filed suit in the U.S. District Court for the Northern District of California (the Court) against Microsoft Corporation (Microsoft) and Hewlett-Packard Company (HP), alleging that their Microsoft Windows 2.03 and HP NewWave computer programs infringe the Company's audiovisual copyrights protecting the Macintosh user interface. Microsoft and HP each filed separate answers setting forth affirmative defenses and counterclaims against the Company seeking declaratory relief and unspecified monetary damages. The Court entered final judgment for Microsoft and HP on August 24, 1993, dismissing the Company's action. The principal rulings leading to that action are presented below.

In 1989, the Court ruled that a 1985 license agreement relating to Windows Version 1.0 did not constitute a complete defense to the Company's claim because the visual displays of Windows 2.03 are fundamentally different from those of Windows Version 1.0, but the visual display elements of Windows Version 1.0 that are used in Windows 2.03 are licensed. The Court concluded that the visual displays in Windows 2.03 that are not licensed are those relating to the use of overlapping main application windows and the appearance and manipulation of icons.

On April 16, 1990, the Company filed a motion for partial summary judgment, asking the Court to hold that the Company's copyrights for the Lisa® and Macintosh computers are valid and to strike the defendants' defenses challenging the validity and scope of protection of those copyrights. Microsoft and HP each filed a motion for partial summary judgment, challenging the validity of the Company's copyrights and seeking to narrow the scope of protection. Each also continued to argue that additional visual displays relating to overlapping main application windows and the use and manipulation of icons should be deemed licensed.

On March 6, 1991, the Court issued a ruling acknowledging the originality of the Company's copyrighted works. By an order dated June 15, 1991, the Court granted the Company's request to supplement its complaint to add Windows 3.0 and NewWave 3.0 to the lawsuit, but denied its request to add a claim against Microsoft for breach of the 1985 license agreement, rescission, and unfair competition.

By stipulation the parties agreed to the voluntary dismissal of the following claims: Microsoft's counterclaims for tortious interference with contract, intentional interference with prospective business advantage, disparagement of property, slander of title, and unfair business practices; HP's counterclaims for intentional interference with prospective and existing business relations and unfair business practices; and the Company's claim for unfair competition.

By an order dated July 25, 1991, the Court (i) dismissed Microsoft's claim that the Company breached the 1985 license agreement; (ii) dismissed an HP counterclaim to the extent that it raised the issue of the originality of the Company's copyrights; (iii) stayed all litigation on HP's antitrust counterclaim; (iv) held that the originality of the Company's copyrights had already been established and that the Company was not obligated to prove the originality of each element or feature of its works; and (v) ordered all discovery of fact witnesses to be completed by January 31, 1992, and all discovery of expert witnesses to be completed by February 28, 1992.

By an order dated August 14, 1991, the Court granted defendants' motion for reconsideration on the issue of originality, holding that defendants may attempt to establish that individual elements in the Company's copyrighted works are not original. According to the Court's order, to meet their burden, defendants would be required to prove that the Company's expression of component features was directly copied from prior work.

On April 14, 1992, the Court issued a ruling on motions filed by the parties, which substantially narrowed the scope of the issues in the case and was not favorable to the Company. The Court held that most of the Windows and NewWave interface elements either were licensed by the Company to Microsoft or could not be protected under the copyright laws.

On August 7, 1992, the Court entered an order disposing of various motions that had been filed by the parties, including the Company's motion for reconsideration of the Court's April 14, 1992, order. In the August order, the Court (i) held that many of the similarities alleged by the Company were not entitled to copyright protection; (ii) ruled that, with respect to Windows, four of the similarities may be entitled to protection but only against a standard of virtually identical copying and, with respect to NewWave, a few additional similarities alleged by the Company were protectible; and (iii) declined to extend protection to the overall arrangement and organization of the Macintosh work.

By an order dated April 14, 1993, the Court held that certain issues of fact remained with respect to the question of whether there is substantial similarity between unlicensed, protected expression in the Apple works and either Windows 2.03 or Windows 3.0 or HP's NewWave products. The Court ruled that a standard of "virtual identity" would be applied to the works.

By an order dated May 18, 1993, the Court (i) denied Apple's Motion for Reconsideration of the Court's April 14, 1993, ruling directing the application of the "virtual identity" standard; (ii) denied Microsoft's motion for summary judgment on Apple's contributory infringement claim; (iii) denied Apple's motion seeking a ruling that HP did not have a sublicense under the 1985 agreement; (iv) granted defendants' motion striking all copyrighted works but the Lisa work; (v) denied HP's motion for summary judgment that it is not jointly and severally liable with Microsoft; and (vi) granted in part and denied in part defendants' motions for summary judgment seeking the dismissal of the remaining items of similarity between the Apple work and defendants' works. The Court ordered the case to proceed to trial on the principal issue of whether defendants' works "as a whole" are "virtually identical" to Apple's Lisa work.

Following the entry of this order, in the interest of justice and to facilitate a prompt review on appeal of all of the Court's rulings, the parties stipulated to the entry of a judgment in favor of defendants. Specifically, Apple agreed not to oppose defendants' motions for summary judgment based on the "virtually identical" standard between the Lisa work and defendants' works. In view of Apple's nonopposition, on August 24, 1993, the Court entered judgment for defendants. On September 20, 1993, Apple filed a Notice of Appeal.

On September 21, 1993, the Court denied defendants' motions for an award of full defense costs and attorneys' fees under 17 U.S.C. §505, but allowed defendants to renew their motions should the Supreme Court alter the standard for the award of attorneys' fees in copyright cases after review of a case presently pending before it. The Court also denied without prejudice Microsoft's motion for reconsideration of the Court's prior ruling dismissing its counterclaim for breach of contract.

The case is now pending before the U.S. Court of Appeal for the Ninth Circuit.

In re Apple Securities Litigation (1993)

In July 1993, six civil class action complaints relating to the drop in price of Apple stock were filed in U.S. District Court against the Company and certain of its officers and directors, alleging violations of federal securities laws for alleged material misrepresentations and omissions of fact concerning the Company's business. The six cases were subsequently consolidated into *Rovner et al. v. Sculley et al.* by virtue of Pretrial Order No. 1, entered by the Court on August 6, 1993. Pursuant to that order, the consolidated class action is known as *In re Apple Securities Litigation,* Civ. No. C-93-20521-RMW (EAI). These suits were filed on behalf of the named plaintiffs and all others who purchased the Company's common stock between October 15, 1992, and July 15, 1993. Plaintiffs seek an award of damages according to proof, with interest.

Subsequently, in August 1993, *Harris v. Sculley et al.* was filed on behalf of the named plaintiff and all others who purchased the Company's common stock between April 15, 1993, and July 15, 1993. It names as defendants the Company and certain of its officers and directors and is based on the same allegations as the class actions described above. The Harris suit is consolidated and subject to Pretrial Order No. 1, discussed above.

1993 Derivative Litigation

In August and September 1993, two derivative class action complaints relating to the drop in price of Apple stock were filed against the Company, as nominal defendant, and certain of its officers and directors. The suits, *Genduso v. Sculley et al.,* Civ. No. C-93-20581-RMW (EAI) (N.D. Cal. filed August 6, 1993), and *Selinger v. Sculley et al.,* Civ. No. C-93-3395-VRW (EAI) (N.D. Cal. filed September 13, 1993), both allege violations of California state law. On September 28, 1993, all parties entered into a stipulation that consolidated the derivative actions and stayed them in their entirety until the conclusion of the 1993 class action litigation.

Lemelson v. Apple

On September 25, 1992, Jerome Lemelson filed a complaint against the Company, Eastman Kodak Company, and Unisys Corporation in the U.S. District Court, District of Nevada, which complaint was amended on April 8, 1993, alleging infringement of two patents relating to information storage and retrieval systems. Unisys is being dismissed without prejudice from the action due to a conflict of interest pertaining to Lemelson's counsel. Mr. Lemelson seeks injunctive relief, damages in an unspecified amount, and an award of attorneys' fees and costs.

Grant v. Apple

On February 11, 1993, Richard B. Grant filed a complaint against the Company in the U.S. District Court for the Central District of California alleging infringement of a natural-language patent. Mr. Grant seeks damages in an unspecified amount and an award of attorneys' fees and costs.

The Company believes the suits cited above to be without merit and intends to vigorously defend against these actions. The Company believes the resolution of all these matters will not have a material adverse effect on its financial condition and results of operations as reported in the accompanying financial statements.

Industry Segment and Geographic Information

The Company operates in one principal industry segment: the design, manufacture, and sale of personal computing products. The Company's products are sold primarily to the business, education, home, and government markets.

Geographic financial information is as follows:

	1993	1992	1991
			(In thousands)
Net sales to unaffiliated customers:			
United States	$ 4,387,674	$ 3,885,042	$ 3,484,533
Europe	2,001,593	2,017,840	1,882,355
Pacific and Canada	1,587,687	1,183,660	941,961
Total net sales	$ 7,976,954	$ 7,086,542	$ 6,308,849
Transfers between geographic areas (eliminated in consolidation):			
United States	$ 420,323	$ 934,673	$ 774,059
Europe	262,554	246,745	147,713
Pacific and Canada	1,374,039	979,566	1,099,448
Total transfers	$ 2,056,916	$ 2,160,984	$ 2,021,220
Operating income:			
United States	$ (253,499)	$ 245,810	$ 9,036
Europe	79,440	301,865	222,893
Pacific and Canada	286,572	246,181	227,690
Eliminations	(2,175)	11,952	(12,235)
Interest and other income, net	29,321	49,634	52,360
Income before income taxes	$ 139,659	$ 855,442	$ 499,744
Identifiable assets:			
United States	$ 2,534,545	$ 1,536,705	$ 1,440,332
Europe	973,741	767,765	734,836
Pacific and Canada	799,189	456,472	461,555
Eliminations	(49,838)	(43,716)	(56,693)
Corporate assets	913,775	1,506,467	913,567
Total assets	$ 5,171,412	$ 4,223,693	$ 3,493,597

Net sales to unaffiliated customers is based on the location of the customers. Transfers between geographic areas are recorded at amounts generally above cost and in accordance with the rules and regulations of the respective governing tax authorities. Operating income consists of total net sales less operating expenses, and does not include either interest and other income, net, or income taxes. U.S. operating income is net of corporate expenses. Identifiable assets of geographic areas are those assets used in the Company's operations in each area. Corporate assets include cash and cash equivalents, joint-venture investments, and short-term investments.

Report of Ernst & Young, Independent Auditors

To the Shareholders and Board of Directors of Apple Computer, Inc.

We have audited the accompanying consolidated balance sheets of Apple Computer, Inc. as of September 24, 1993, and September 25, 1992, and the related consolidated statements of income, shareholders' equity, and cash flows for each of the three years in the period ended September 24, 1993. These financial statements are the responsibility of the Company's management. Our responsibility is to express an opinion on these financial statements based on our audits.

We conducted our audits in accordance with generally accepted auditing standards. Those standards require that we plan and perform the audit to obtain reasonable assurance about whether the financial statements are free of material misstatement. An audit includes examining, on a test basis, evidence supporting the amounts and disclosures in the financial statements. An audit also includes assessing the accounting principles used and significant estimates made by management, as well as evaluating the overall financial statement presentation. We believe that our audits provide a reasonable basis for our opinion.

In our opinion, the consolidated financial statements referred to above present fairly, in all material respects, the consolidated financial position of Apple Computer, Inc. at September 24, 1993, and September 25, 1992, and the consolidated results of its operations and its cash flows for each of the three years in the period ended September 24, 1993, in conformity with generally accepted accounting principles.

Ernst & Young
San Jose, California
October 11, 1993

Financial Statements (excluding footnotes) from the Annual Reports of Federal Express Corporation and Ben & Jerry's Homemade, Inc.

CONSOLIDATED BALANCE SHEET
ASSETS

(26)

	December 26, 1992	December 28, 1991
Current assets:		
Cash and cash equivalents	$ 7,356,133	$ 6,704,006
Accounts receivable, less allowance for doubtful accounts: $350,000 in 1992 and 1991	8,849,326	6,939,975
Income taxes receivable	306,193	
Inventories	17,089,857	8,999,666
Deferred income taxes	1,730,000	984,000
Prepaid expenses	208,996	107,325
Total current assets	35,540,505	23,734,972
Property, plant and equipment	39,312,513	28,496,080
Less accumulated depreciation	12,575,088	9,196,551
	26,737,425	19,299,529
Investments	25,200,000	
Other assets	728,885	21,598
	$ 88,206,815	$ 43,056,099

ASSETS ~ THINGS THE COMPANY OWNS.

~ CASH

~ ACCOUNTS RECEIVABLE · MONEY OWED TO THE COMPANY · MANUFACTURED PRODUCTS WAITING TO BE SOLD, ALSO INGREDIENTS, PACKAGING & SUPPLIES

~ INVENTORY · MANUFACTURED PRODUCTS WAITING TO BE SOLD, ALSO INGREDIENTS, PACKAGING & SUPPLIES

~ PROPERTY, PLANT & EQUIPMENT · BUILDINGS, MACHINERY, TRUCKS ETC. DEPRECIATION IS THE PART OF THE VALUE OF THESE ASSETS THAT HAS BEEN USED UP, BASED ON HOW LONG IT IS EXPECTED TO LAST.

~ PREPAID EXPENSES, DEFERRED INCOME TAXES, OTHER ASSETS · THESE ARE MISCELLANEOUS OTHER PURCHASED ASSETS THE COMPANY HAS THAT HAVE VALUE.

LIABILITIES AND STOCKHOLDERS' EQUITY

	December 26, 1992	December 28, 1991
Current liabilities:		
Accounts payable and accrued expenses	$16,858,919	$11,951,308
Income taxes payable		233,853
Current portion of long-term debt and obligations under capital lease	628,098	514,905
Total current liabilities	17,487,017	12,700,066
Long-term debt and obligations under captial lease	2,640,982	2,786,659
Deferred income taxes	1,319,000	1,300,000
Commitments and contingencies		
Stockholders' equity:		
$1.20 noncumulative Class A preferred stock - $1.00 par value, redeemable at $12.00 per share; 900 shares authorized, issued and outstanding, aggregate preference on voluntary or involuntary liquidation - $9,000	900	900
Class A common stock - $.033 par value; authorized 10,000,000 shares; issued 6,239,575 shares at December 26, 1992 and 5,033,917 shares at December 28, 1991	206,327	166,541
Class B common stock - $.033 par value; authorized 3,000,000 shares; issued 962,008 shares at December 26, 1992 and 986,888 shares at December 28, 1991	31,746	32,565
Additional paid-in capital	47,941,134	14,261,484
Retained earnings	19,984,461	13,309,121
Unearned compensation	(38,014)	(134,588)
Treasury stock, at cost: 66,453 Class A and 1,092 Class B shares at December 26, 1992 and 66,419 Class A and 1,075 Class B shares at December 28, 1991	(1,366,738)	(1,366,649)
Total stockholders' equity	66,759,816	26,269,374
	$88,206,815	$43,056,099

See accompanying notes.

LIABILITIES— WHAT THE COMPANY OWES.

- **CURRENT LIABILITIES**— BILLS, PAYROLL DUE, TAXES & OTHER OBLIGATIONS THAT HAVE TO BE PAID WITHIN A YEAR.
- **LONG TERM DEBT & OBLIGATIONS UNDER CAPITAL LEASES**— LOANS OR AGREEMENTS TO PAY FOR USE OF EQUIPMENT A YEAR OR MORE FROM NOW.
- **OTHER LIABILITIES**— MISCELLANEOUS OTHER FINANCIAL COMMITMENTS.

STOCKHOLDERS' EQUITY

THIS IS CALLED THE "BOOK VALUE" OF THE OWNERS' STAKE IN THE COMPANY. IT INCLUDES PROCEEDS THE COMPANY RECEIVED FROM THE INITIAL AND SUBSEQUENT SALES OF STOCK TO THE PUBLIC, PLUS ACCUMULATED PROFITS, CALLED RETAINED EARNINGS.

THIS BOOK VALUE IS NOT THE SAME AS THE VALUE OF STOCK ON THE PUBLIC STOCK MARKET WHICH IS CALLED THE "MARKET VALUE". THE STOCK MARKET DETERMINES IN ITS OWN WAYS WHETHER THE COMPANY IS WORTH MORE THAN THE BOOK VALUE OF WHAT IT OWNS MINUS WHAT IT OWES. FOR EXAMPLE, A COMPANY'S STOCK PRICE CHANGES REGULARLY WITHOUT REGARD TO THE VALUE OF THE ASSETS & LIABILITIES IT USES TO RUN ITS BUSINESS.

CONSOLIDATED STATEMENT OF INCOME

	December 26, 1992	Years Ended December 28, 1991	December 29, 1990
Net sales	$ 131,968,814	$ 96,997,339	$ 77,024,037
Cost of sales	94,389,391	68,500,402	54,202,387
Gross profit	37,579,423	28,496,937	22,821,650
Selling, general and administrative expenses	26,242,761	21,264,214	17,639,357
Operating income	11,336,662	7,232,723	5,182,293
Other income (expenses):			
Interest income	394,817	147,058	296,329
Interest expense	(181,577)	(736,248)	(868,736)
Other	(235,765)	(139,627)	(136,578)
	(22,525)	(728,817)	(708,985)
Income before income taxes	11,314,137	6,503,906	4,473,308
Income taxes	4,638,797	2,764,523	1,864,063
Net income	$ 6,675,340	$ 3,739,383	$ 2,609,245
Net income per common share	$ 1.07	$ 0.67	$ 0.50
Weighted average number of common shares outstanding	6,253,825	5,572,368	5,224,667

See accompanying notes.

28

STATEMENT OF INCOME

- NET SALES ~ THIS IS THE TOTAL SALES OF THE COMPANY MINUS THE VALUE OF PRODUCT DISCOUNTED OR RETURNED.

- COST OF SALES ~ WHAT IT COST TO MAKE & STORE THE PRODUCTS UNTIL THEY ARE SOLD. INCLUDES THE PACKAGING, LABOR COSTS, & THE COST TO RUN INGREDIENTS, & STORAGE MACHINERY.

- GROSS PROFIT ~ NET SALES MINUS COST OF SALES.

- SELLING & ADMINISTRATIVE EXPENSES ~ THESE ARE THE COSTS OF MARKETING & SELLING THE PRODUCT AFTER IT HAS BEEN MADE, PLUS ALL OF THE ADMINISTRATIVE COSTS TO RUN THE COMPANY.

- OPERATING INCOME ~ GROSS PROFIT MINUS SELLING, GENERAL & ADMINISTRATIVE EXPENSES (BEFORE TAXES) FROM HOW MUCH A COMPANY EARNS (BEFORE TAXES) FROM THE CORE BUSINESS IT IS IN.

- INCOME BEFORE TAXES, INCOME TAXES & NET INCOME ~ INCOME TAXES ARE THE AMOUNT OF FEDERAL & STATE TAXES PAID OR DUE BASED ON THE COMPANY'S BOOK INCOME. SUBTRACTING THOSE TAXES FROM INCOME BEFORE TAXES RESULTS IN NET INCOME OR THE "BOTTOM LINE." CONTINUED →
(REMEMBER, BEN&JERRY'S HAS TWO "BOTTOM LINES."

CONSOLIDATED STATEMENT OF CASH FLOWS

Years Ended	12/26/92	12/28/91	12/29/90
Cash flows from operating activities:			
Net income	$ 6,675,340	$ 3,739,383	$ 2,609,245
Adjustments to reconcile net income to net cash provided			
by operating activities:			
Depreciation and amortization	3,455,720	2,980,826	2,320,666
Provision for doubtful accounts receivable		100,000	88,000
Deferred income taxes	(727,000)	(294,000)	91,000
Amortization of unearned compensation	96,574	77,162	
(Gain) Loss on disposition of assets	(14,232)	13,250	3,666
Stock awards	57,000	302,601	
Changes in assets and liabilities:			
Accounts receivable	(1,909,351)	(1,995,530)	(1,462,567)
Income tax receivable/payable	(540,046)	(98,441)	390,413
Inventories	(8,090,191)	1,083,476	(6,086,592)
Prepaid expenses	(101,671)	10,601	72,363
Other assets	93,656		
Accounts payable and accrued expenses	4,907,611	4,399,156	3,198,786
Net cash provided by operating activities	3,903,410	10,318,484	1,224,980
Cash flows from investing activities:			
Additions to property, plant and equipment	(10,447,007)	(4,034,124)	(2,597,635)
Proceeds from sale of property, plant and equipment	105,084	70,000	42,500
Increase in investments	(25,200,000)		
Changes in other assets	(836,657)		
Net cash used for investing activities	(36,378,580)	(3,964,124)	(2,555,135)
Cash flows from financing activities:			
Borrowings on short-term debt		8,900,000	
Repayments of short-term debt		(8,900,000)	
Repayments of long-term debt and capital leases	(534,231)	(439,002)	(348,731)
Net proceeds from issuance of common stock	33,661,528	95,325	81,763
Payment of bond redemption costs		(102,867)	
Net cash provided by (used for) financing activities	33,127,297	446,544	(266,968)
Increase (decrease) in cash and cash equivalents	652,127	5,907,816	(1,597,123)
Cash and cash equivalents at beginning of year	6,704,006	796,190	2,393,313
Cash and cash equivalents at end of year	$ 7,356,133	$6,704,006	$ 796,190

See accompanying notes.

CONSOLiDATED STATEMENT of StockHoLDERS' EQUiTY

	Preferred Stock Par Value	Common Stock Class A Par Value	Common Stock Class B Par Value
Balance at December 30, 1989	$ 900	$131,909	$38,383
Net Income			
Common Stock forfeited under restricted stock plan (306 Class A shares and 150 Class B shares)			
Common Stock issued under stock purchase plan (12,462 shares)		411	
Conversion of Class B shares to Class A shares (78,048 shares)		2,576	(2,576)
Conversion of subordinated debentures to Class A shares (644 shares)		21	
Balance at December 29, 1990	900	134,917	35,807
Net Income			
Common stock issued under restricted stock plan (53,450 Class A shares)			
Amortization of unearned compensation			
Conversion of Class B shares to Class A shares (98,230 shares)		3,242	(3,242)
Conversion of subordinated debentures to Class A shares (847,804 shares)		27,976	
Common stock forfeited under restricted stock plan (40 Class A shares and 20 Class B shares)			
Common stock issued under stock purchase plan (12,292 Class A shares)		406	
Common stock contributed (89,624 Class A shares)			
Balance at December 28, 1991	900	166,541	32,565
Net Income			
Common stock issued through public offering (1,170,000 Class A shares)		38,610	
Common stock issued under stock purchase plan (8,778 Class A shares)		291	
Common stock issued under restricted stock plan (2,000 Class A shares)		66	
Common stock forfeited under restricted stock plan (34 Class A shares and 17 Class B shares)			
Conversion of Class B to Class A shares (24,880 shares)		819	(819)
Amortization of unearned compensation			
Balance at December 26, 1992	$ 900	$ 206,327	$ 31,746

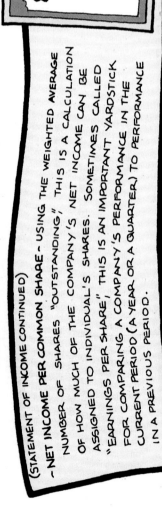

(STATEMENT OF INCOME CONTINUED)

~ NET INCOME PER COMMON SHARE ~ USING THE WEIGHTED AVERAGE NUMBER OF SHARES "OUTSTANDING". THIS IS A CALCULATION OF HOW MUCH OF THE COMPANY'S NET INCOME CAN BE ASSIGNED TO INDIVIDUAL'S SHARES. SOMETIMES CALLED "EARNINGS PER SHARE", THIS IS AN IMPORTANT YARDSTICK FOR COMPARING A COMPANY'S PERFORMANCE IN THE CURRENT PERIOD (A YEAR OR A QUARTER) TO PERFORMANCE IN A PREVIOUS PERIOD.

	Additional Paid-in Capital	Retained Earnings	Unearned Compensation	Treasury Stock Class A Cost	Treasury Stock Class B Cost
	$6,302,851	$6,960,493	$ 0	($24,729)	($4,413)
		2,609,245			
	82,149			(534)	(264)
	4,978				
	6,389,978	9,569,738	0	(25,263)	(4,677)
		3,739,383			
	(53,450)		(211,750)	567,907	
			77,162		
	5,925,527			(71)	(35)
	94,919				
	1,904,510			(1,904,510)	
	14,261,484	13,309,121	(134,588)	(1,361,937)	(4,712)
		6,675,340			
	33,467,490				
	155,226			(59)	(30)
	56,934		96,574		
	$47,941,134	$19,984,461	$ (38,014)	$ (1,361,996)	$ (4,742)

See accompanying notes.

WOW AGAIN. I'M BEGINNING TO THINK I CAN FIGURE THIS OUT!

HERE'S THE TEST. FLIP THROUGH THE FINANCIAL STATEMENTS IN THIS ANNUAL REPORT & TAKE A HARD LOOK AT THEM. READ THE MANAGEMENT'S DISCUSSION & ANALYSIS & THE FOOTNOTES. GO AHEAD - YOU CAN DO IT. THEN THINK OF THE QUESTIONS YOU WANT TO ASK. CALL OR WRITE TO OUR INVESTOR RELATIONS STAFF. SEE IF YOU CAN STUMP 'EM. I DARE YOU.

OOH! WHAT A CHALLENGE. SEE YOU AT THE ANNUAL MEETING!

TO BE CONTINUED·NEXT YEAR.

Consolidated Statements of Operations

FEDERAL EXPRESS CORPORATION AND SUBSIDIARIES

Years ended May 31 In thousands, except per share amounts	1993	1992	1991
REVENUES	$ 7,808,043	$ 7,550,060	$ 7,688,296
OPERATING EXPENSES:			
Salaries and employee benefits (Notes 8 and 9)	3,807,493	3,637,080	3,438,391
Rentals and landing fees (Note 4)	658,138	672,341	650,001
Depreciation and amortization	579,896	577,157	562,207
Fuel	495,384	508,386	663,327
Maintenance and repairs	404,639	404,311	449,394
Restructuring charges (Note 13)	(12,500)	254,000	121,000
Other	1,497,820	1,473,818	1,551,850
	7,430,870	7,527,093	7,436,170
OPERATING INCOME	377,173	22,967	252,126
OTHER INCOME (EXPENSE):			
Interest, net (Note 1)	(160,923)	(164,315)	(181,880)
Gain on disposition of aircraft and related equipment	4,633	2,832	11,375
Other, net	(17,307)	(8,312)	(8,679)
Payroll tax loss (Note 13)	—	—	(32,000)
	(173,597)	(169,795)	(211,184)
INCOME (LOSS) BEFORE INCOME TAXES AND CUMULATIVE EFFECT OF CHANGE IN ACCOUNTING PRINCIPLE	203,576	(146,828)	40,942
PROVISION (CREDIT) FOR INCOME TAXES (Note 7)	93,767	(33,046)	35,044
INCOME (LOSS) BEFORE CUMULATIVE EFFECT OF CHANGE IN ACCOUNTING PRINCIPLE	109,809	(113,782)	5,898
CUMULATIVE EFFECT OF CHANGE IN ACCOUNTING FOR POSTRETIREMENT BENEFITS, NET OF TAX BENEFIT OF $34,287 (Note 9)	(55,943)	—	—
NET INCOME (LOSS)	$ 53,866	$ (113,782)	$ 5,898
EARNINGS (LOSS) PER SHARE (Note 6):			
Before cumulative effect of change in accounting principle	$ 2.01	$ (2.11)	$ .11
Cumulative effect of change in accounting for postretirement benefits (Note 9)	(1.03)	—	—
	$ .98	$ (2.11)	$ .11
AVERAGE SHARES OUTSTANDING (Note 6)	54,719	53,961	53,350

The accompanying Notes to Consolidated Financial Statements are an integral part of these statements.

Consolidated Balance Sheets
FEDERAL EXPRESS CORPORATION AND SUBSIDIARIES

May 31 In thousands	1993	1992
ASSETS		
CURRENT ASSETS:		
Cash and cash equivalents	$ 155,456	$ 78,177
Receivables, less allowance for doubtful accounts of $31,308 and $32,074	922,727	899,773
Spare parts, supplies and fuel	164,087	158,062
Prepaid expenses and other	63,573	69,994
Deferred income taxes (Note 7)	133,875	—
Total current assets	1,439,718	1,206,006
PROPERTY AND EQUIPMENT, AT COST (Notes 3, 4 and 11):		
Flight equipment	2,843,253	2,540,350
Package handling and ground support equipment	1,413,793	1,352,659
Computer and electronic equipment	947,913	851,686
Other	1,501,250	1,433,212
	6,706,209	6,177,907
Less accumulated depreciation and amortization	3,229,941	2,766,610
Net property and equipment	3,476,268	3,411,297
OTHER ASSETS:		
Goodwill (Note 1)	432,215	487,780
Equipment deposits and other assets (Note 11)	444,863	358,103
Total other assets	877,078	845,883
	$ 5,793,064	$ 5,463,186

The accompanying Notes to Consolidated Financial Statements are an integral part of these balance sheets.

	1993	1992
LIABILITIES AND STOCKHOLDERS' INVESTMENT		
CURRENT LIABILITIES:		
Current portion of long-term debt (Note 3)	$ 133,797	$ 155,257
Accounts payable	554,111	430,130
Accrued expenses (Note 2)	761,357	799,468
Total current liabilities	1,449,265	1,384,855
LONG-TERM DEBT, LESS CURRENT PORTION (Note 3)	1,882,279	1,797,844
DEFERRED INCOME TAXES (Note 7)	72,479	123,715
OTHER LIABILITIES (Note 1)	717,660	577,050
COMMITMENTS AND CONTINGENCIES (Notes 11 and 12)		
COMMON STOCKHOLDERS' INVESTMENT (Note 6):		
Common stock, $.10 par value; 100,000 shares authorized, 54,743 and 54,100 shares issued	5,474	5,410
Additional paid-in capital	699,385	672,727
Retained earnings	969,515	906,555
	1,674,374	1,584,692
Less treasury stock and deferred compensation related to stock plans	(2,993)	(4,970)
Total common stockholders' investment	1,671,381	1,579,722
	$ 5,793,064	$ 5,463,186

Consolidated Statements of Cash Flows
FEDERAL EXPRESS CORPORATION AND SUBSIDIARIES

Years ended May 31 In thousands	1993	1992	1991
OPERATING ACTIVITIES			
Net income (loss)	$ 53,866	$ (113,782)	$ 5,898
Adjustments to reconcile income (loss) to net cash provided by operating activities:			
Depreciation and amortization	579,896	577,157	562,207
Provision for uncollectible accounts	33,552	31,670	59,721
Provision (credit) for deferred income taxes and other	19,910	(75,219)	36,935
(Gain) loss from disposals of property and equipment	(5,648)	1,810	(1,621)
Cumulative effect of accounting change	55,943	–	–
Changes in assets and liabilities, net of effects from purchases and dispositions of businesses:			
(Increase) decrease in receivables	(41,535)	(727)	20,431
(Increase) decrease in other current assets	(5,813)	61,749	(21,904)
Increase in accounts payable, accrued expenses and other liabilities	13,651	33,620	131,500
Other, net	21,259	4,543	(5,768)
Net cash provided by operating activities	725,081	520,821	787,399
INVESTING ACTIVITIES			
Purchases of property and equipment, including deposits on aircraft of $177,564 $212,291 and $92,587	(1,023,723)	(915,878)	(1,027,736)
Proceeds from disposition of property and equipment:			
Sale-leaseback transactions	216,444	400,433	275,347
Other	5,984	12,851	5,699
Purchase of businesses, net of cash acquired	–	–	(24,322)
Other, net	1,992	621	–
Net cash used in investing activities	(799,303)	(501,973)	(771,012)
FINANCING ACTIVITIES			
Proceeds from debt issuances	878,499	437,709	910,703
Principal payments on debt	(737,334)	(507,283)	(916,430)
Proceeds from stock issuances (includes treasury)	24,512	19,272	31,241
Purchases of treasury stock	(472)	(3,099)	(23,565)
Other, net	(13,704)	(4,962)	857
Net cash provided by (used in) financing activities	151,501	(58,363)	2,806
Net increase (decrease) in cash and cash equivalents	77,279	(39,515)	19,193
Cash and cash equivalents at beginning of period	78,177	117,692	98,499
Cash and cash equivalents at end of period	$ 155,456	$ 78,177	$ 117,692
SUPPLEMENTAL DISCLOSURE OF CASH FLOW INFORMATION			
Cash paid for:			
Interest (net of capitalized interest)	$ 162,648	$ 178,943	$ 190,054
Income taxes	188,943	89,729	36,500

Non-cash investing and financing activities:
In November 1992, approximately $73,000 of secured debt related to a portion of the purchase price of one MD-11 aircraft acquired by the Company was assumed by a third party in a sale-leaseback of the aircraft.

The accompanying Notes to Consolidated Financial Statements are an integral part of these statements.

Consolidated Statements of Changes in Common Stockholders' Investment

FEDERAL EXPRESS CORPORATION AND SUBSIDIARIES

In thousands, except common shares	Common Stock	Additional Paid-in Capital	Retained Earnings	Treasury Stock	Deferred Compen-sation
BALANCE AT MAY 31, 1990	$ 5,315	$ 639,676	$ 1,010,090	$ (21)	$ (5,873)
Purchase of treasury stock	–	–	–	(23,565)	–
Issuance of common and treasury stock under employee incentive plans (1,141,283 shares)	48	12,369	(4,483)	23,572	642
Amortization of deferred compensation	–	–	–	–	1,252
Foreign currency translation adjustment	–	–	3,700	–	–
Net income	–	–	5,898	–	–
BALANCE AT MAY 31, 1991	5,363	652,045	1,015,205	(14)	(3,979)
Purchase of treasury stock	–	–	–	(3,099)	–
Issuance of common and treasury stock under employee incentive plans (554,269 shares)	47	20,682	(287)	3,081	(2,792)
Amortization of deferred compensation	–	–	–	–	1,833
Foreign currency translation adjustment	–	–	5,419	–	–
Net loss	–	–	(113,782)	–	–
BALANCE AT MAY 31, 1992	5,410	672,727	906,555	(32)	(4,938)
Purchase of treasury stock	–	–	–	(472)	–
Issuance of common and treasury stock under employee incentive plans (655,938 shares)	64	26,658	(85)	468	(393)
Amortization of deferred compensation	–	–	–	–	2,374
Foreign currency translation adjustment	–	–	9,179	–	–
Net income	–	–	53,866	–	–
BALANCE AT MAY 31, 1993	$ 5,474	$ 699,385	$ 969,515	$ (36)	$ (2,957)

The accompanying Notes to Consolidated Financial Statements are an integral part of these statements.

PHOTO CREDITS

Chapter 9

Page 343	Courtesy of Mobil Oil Corporation
Page 345	©Nina Barnett Photography
Page 349	Courtesy of Ford Motor Company
Page 350	Courtesy of Ben & Jerry's
Page 351	©1993 Texaco Inc. Reprinted with permission from Texaco Inc.
Page 360	©Nicholas Communications, Inc.

Chapter 10

Page 373	©Nicholas Communications, Inc.
Page 374	Courtesy of Sony Corporation
Page 374	Courtesy of Wendy's International, Inc.
Page 377	Courtesy of Microsoft Corp.
Page 378	Courtesy of Boise Cascade Corporation
Page 380	©Nicholas Communications, Inc.
Page 386	Courtesy of America West Airlines
Page 387	©Nicholas Communications, Inc.
Page 389	Courtesy of Accessory Lady
Page 392	Courtesy of Rubbermaid Incorporated

Chapter 11

Page 407	THE FAR SIDE ©1985 FARWORKS, INC./Dist. By UNIVERSAL PRESS SYNDICATE. Reprinted with permission. All rights reserved.
Page 408	Courtesy of Aluminum Company of America
Page 409	Courtesy of the Exxon Corporation
Page 409	Courtesy of Corning Incorporated
Page 410	Courtesy of Blockbuster Entertainment
Page 411	Courtesy of The Walt Disney Company
Page 412	©Nicholas Communications, Inc.
Page 413	Courtesy of General Electric Company
Page 420	Courtesy of PepsiCo Inc.
Page 424	Courtesy of Reebok International Ltd.
Page 424	Courtesy of Nike, Inc.

Chapter 12

Page 441	Courtesy of Safeway Inc.
Page 443	©Fotopic: MGA/Photri
Page 443	Courtesy of Safeway Inc.
Page 447	Courtesy of Ford Motor Company
Page 447	Courtesy of The Clorox Company
Page 448	Courtesy of The Quaker Oats Company
Page 463	Courtesy of Federal Express Corporation

Chapter 13

Page 483	Courtesy of Mobil Oil Corporation
Page 485	©Nicholas Communications, Inc.
Page 488	Courtesy of American Greetings Corporation
Page 488	Courtesy of Federal Express Corporation
Page 489	Courtesy of Sara Lee Corporation
Page 496	Courtesy of Pitney Bowes

Chapter 14

Page 525	Courtesy of J. Walter Thompson U.S.A., Inc., on behalf of Sprint
Page 532	Photo courtesy of Hewlett-Packard Company
Page 535	Courtesy of William Wrigley Jr. Company
Page 537	Courtesy of International Business Machines Corporation
Page 539	©Nicholas Communications, Inc.
Page 539	©Nicholas Communications, Inc.
Page 541	Courtesy of Deere & Company
Page 542	Courtesy of Albertson's, Inc.
Page 543	Courtesy of J.C. Penney Company, Inc.
Page 546	©Richard Alcom/Courtesy of Colgate-Palmolive Company

Chapter 15

Page 569	Courtesy of L.A. Gear
Page 577	©Nicholas Communications, Inc.
Page 583	Courtesy of Chiquita Brand International
Page 591	©AdPhoto: MGA/Photri, Inc.
Page 591	Courtesy of Mattel, Inc.

Chapter 16

Page 607	©Photofest
Page 608	Courtesy of R.H. Macy & Company
Page 609	©The New York Times

Chapter 17

Page 647	Courtesy of Microsoft Corp.
Page 648	©Nicholas Communications, Inc.
Page 649	Courtesy of Microsoft Corp.
Page 649	Courtesy of Microsoft Corp.
Page 654	Courtesy of Microsoft Corp.

Chapter 18

Page 679	Courtesy of Olympic Homecare Products
Page 682	Courtesy of Chrysler Corporation
Page 683	©Nicholas Communications, Inc./Courtesy of Texas Instruments
Page 684	Courtesy of Olympic Homecare Products
Page 685	Photo supplied by the DuPont Company

Chapter 19

Page 721	Courtesy of Binney & Smith
Page 722	Courtesy of Nissan Motor Corporation
Page 723	Courtesy of Globe Metallurgical, Inc.
Page 723	Photo courtesy of The Document Company, Xerox
Page 724	Courtesy of Motorola
Page 725	Courtesy of Toyota Motor Sales U.S.A., Inc.
Page 726	©General Motors Corporation, used with permission
Page 727	Courtesy of Binney & Smith
Page 728	Courtesy of Binney & Smith

Chapter 20

Page 761	Courtesy of Boeing Commercial Airplane Group
Page 762	Courtesy of Dell Computer
Page 764	Property of AT&T Archives
Page 767	©Nicholas Communications, Inc.

Comprehensive List of Accounts Used in Exercises and Problems

Current Assets

101	Cash
102	Petty cash
103	Cash equivalents
104	Short-term investments
105	Short-term investments, fair value adjustment
106	Accounts receivable
107	Allowance for doubtful accounts
108	Legal fees receivable
109	Interest receivable
110	Rent receivable
111	Notes receivable
115	Subscriptions receivable, common stock
116	Subscriptions receivable, preferred stock
119	Merchandise inventory
120	_____ inventory
121	_____ inventory
124	Office supplies
125	Store supplies
126	_____ supplies
128	Prepaid insurance
129	Prepaid interest
131	Prepaid rent
132	Raw materials inventory
133	Goods in process inventory, _____
134	Goods in process inventory, _____
135	Finished goods inventory

Long-Term Investments

141	Investment in _____ stock
142	Investment in _____ bonds
143	Long-term investments, fair value adjustment
144	Investment in _____
145	Bond sinking fund

Plant Assets

151	Automobiles
152	Accumulated depreciation, automobiles
153	Trucks
154	Accumulated depreciation, trucks
155	Boats
156	Accumulated depreciation, boats
157	Professional library
158	Accumulated depreciation, professional library
159	Law library
160	Accumulated depreciation, law library
161	Furniture
162	Accumulated depreciation, furniture
163	Office equipment
164	Accumulated depreciation, office equipment
165	Store equipment
166	Accumulated depreciation, store equipment
167	_____ equipment
168	Accumulated depreciation, _____ equipment
169	Machinery
170	Accumulated depreciation, machinery
173	Building _____
174	Accumulated depreciation, building _____
175	Building _____
176	Accumulated depreciation, building _____
179	Land improvements _____
180	Accumulated depreciation, land improvements _____
181	Land improvements _____
182	Accumulated depreciation, land improvements _____
183	Land

Natural Resources

185   Mineral deposit
186   Accumulated depletion, mineral deposit

Intangible Assets

191   Patents
192   Leasehold
193   Franchise
194   Copyrights
195   Leasehold improvements
196   Organization costs

Current Liabilities

201   Accounts payable
202   Insurance payable
203   Interest payable
204   Legal fees payable
207   Office salaries payable
208   Rent payable
209   Salaries payable
210   Wages payable
211   Accrued payroll payable
213   Property taxes payable
214   Estimated warranty liability
215   Income taxes payable
216   Common dividend payable
217   Preferred dividend payable
218   State unemployment taxes payable
219   Employees' federal income taxes payable
221   Employees' medical insurance payable
222   Employees' retirement program payable
223   Employees' union dues payable
224   Federal unemployment taxes payable
225   FICA taxes payable
226   Estimated vacation pay liability

Unearned Revenues

230   Unearned consulting fees
231   Unearned legal fees
232   Unearned property management fees
233   Unearned _____ fees
234   Unearned _____
235   Unearned janitorial revenue
236   Unearned _____ revenue
238   Unearned rent _____

Notes Payable

240   Short-term notes payable
241   Discount on short-term notes payable
245   Notes payable
251   Long-term notes payable
252   Discount on notes payable

Long-Term Liabilities

253   Long-term lease liability
255   Bonds payable

256   Discount on bonds payable
257   Premium on bonds payable
258   Deferred income tax liability

Owners' Equity

301   _____, capital
302   _____, withdrawals
303   _____, capital
304   _____, withdrawals
305   _____, capital
306   _____, withdrawals

Corporate Contributed Capital

307   Common stock, $_____ par value
308   Common stock, no par
309   Common stock subscribed
310   Common stock dividend distributable
311   Contributed capital in excess of par value, common stock
312   Contributed capital in excess of stated value, no-par common stock
313   Contributed capital from the retirement of common stock
314   Contributed capital, treasury stock transactions
315   Preferred stock
316   Contributed capital in excess of par value, preferred stock
317   Preferred stock subscribed

Retained Earnings

318   Retained earnings
319   Cash dividends declared
320   Stock dividends declared

Other Owners' Equity

321   Treasury stock, common
322   Unrealized holding gain (loss)

Revenues

401   _____ fees earned
402   _____ fees earned
403   _____ services revenue
404   _____ services revenue
405   Commissions earned
406   Rent earned
407   Dividends earned
408   Earnings from investment in _____
409   Interest earned
410   Sinking fund earnings
413   Sales
414   Sales returns and allowances
415   Sales discounts

Cost of Goods Sold Items

502   Cost of goods sold
505   Purchases
506   Purchases returns and allowances
507   Purchases discounts
508   Transportation-in

Manufacturing Accounts

520   Raw materials purchases
521   Freight-in on raw materials

530	Factory payroll
531	Direct labor
540	Factory overhead
541	Indirect materials
542	Indirect labor
543	Factory insurance expired
544	Factory supervision
545	Factory supplies used
546	Factory utilities
547	Miscellaneous production costs
548	Property taxes on factory building
549	Property taxes on factory equipment
550	Rent on factory building
551	Repairs, factory equipment
552	Small tools written off
560	Depreciation of factory equipment
561	Depreciation of factory building

Standard Cost Variance Accounts
580	Direct material quantity variance
581	Direct material price variance
582	Direct labor quantity variance
583	Direct labor price variance
584	Factory overhead volume variance
585	Factory overhead controllable variance

Expenses

Depletion, Amortization, and Depreciation Expenses
601	Amortization expense, _____
602	Amortization expense, _____
603	Depletion expense, _____
604	Depreciation expense, boats
605	Depreciation expense, automobiles
606	Depreciation expense, building _____
607	Depreciation expense, building _____
608	Depreciation expense, land improvements _____
609	Depreciation expense, land improvements _____
610	Depreciation expense, law library
611	Depreciation expense, trucks
612	Depreciation expense, _____ equipment
613	Depreciation expense, _____ equipment
614	Depreciation expense, _____
615	Depreciation expense, _____

Employee Related Expenses
620	Office salaries expense
621	Sales salaries expense
622	Salaries expense
623	_____ wages expense
624	Employees' benefits expense
625	Payroll taxes expense

Financial Expenses
630	Cash over and short
631	Discounts lost

632	Factoring fee expense
633	Interest expense

Insurance Expenses
635	Insurance expense, delivery equipment
636	Insurance expense, office equipment
637	Insurance expense, _____

Rental Expenses
640	Rent expense
641	Rent expense, office space
642	Rent expense, selling space
643	Press rental expense
644	Truck rental expense
645	_____ rental expense

Supplies Expense
650	Office supplies expense
651	Store supplies expense
652	_____ supplies expense
653	_____ supplies expense

Miscellaneous Expenses
655	Advertising expense
656	Bad debts expense
657	Blueprinting expense
658	Boat expense
659	Collection expense
661	Concessions expense
662	Credit card expense
663	Delivery expense
664	Dumping expense
667	Equipment expense
668	Food and drinks expense
669	Gas, oil, and repairs expense
671	Gas and oil expense
672	General and administrative expense
673	Janitorial expense
674	Legal fees expense
676	Mileage expense
677	Miscellaneous expenses
678	Mower and tools expense
679	Operating expense
681	Permits expense
682	Postage expense
683	Property taxes expense
684	Repairs expense, _____
685	Repairs expense, _____
687	Selling expense
688	Telephone expense
689	Travel and entertainment expense
690	Utilities expense
691	Warranty expense
695	Income taxes expense

Gains and Losses
701	Gain on retirement of bonds
702	Gain on sale of machinery
703	Gain on sale of short-term investments
704	Gain on sale of trucks

705   Gain on _____
706   Foreign exchange gain or loss
801   Loss on disposal of machinery
802   Loss on exchange of equipment
803   Loss on exchange of _____
804   Loss on sale of notes
805   Loss on retirement of bonds
806   Loss on sale of investments

807   Loss on sale of machinery
808   Loss on sale of _____
809   Loss on _____

Clearing Accounts

901   Income summary
902   Manufacturing summary

INDEX